lw
6.3.08

CHILD ABUSE

Law and Policy Across Boundaries

Child Abuse

Law and Policy
Across Boundaries

LAURA HOYANO
AND
CAROLINE KEENAN

OXFORD
UNIVERSITY PRESS

OXFORD

UNIVERSITY PRESS

Great Clarendon Street, Oxford OX2 6DP

Oxford University Press is a department of the University of Oxford.
It furthers the University's objective of excellence in research, scholarship,
and education by publishing worldwide in

Oxford New York

Auckland Cape Town Dar es Salaam Hong Kong Karachi
Kuala Lumpur Madrid Melbourne Mexico City Nairobi
New Delhi Shanghai Taipei Toronto

With offices in

Argentina Austria Brazil Chile Czech Republic France Greece
Guatemala Hungary Italy Japan Poland Portugal Singapore
South Korea Switzerland Thailand Turkey Ukraine Vietnam

Oxford is a registered trade mark of Oxford University Press
in the UK and in certain other countries

Published in the United States
by Oxford University Press Inc., New York

© L. Hoyano and C. Keenan, 2007

British Library Cataloguing in Publication Data

Data available

Library of Congress Cataloging in Publication Data

Data available

Typeset by Newgen Imaging Systems (P) Ltd., Chennai, India
Printed in Great Britain
on acid-free paper by
Antony Rowe Ltd, Chippenham

ISBN 978–0–19–829946–2

1 3 5 7 9 10 8 6 4 2

To our families, with love and gratitude

Preface

This project was conceived on a train journey between the University of Bristol and the Home Office in 1999. We were members of a research team at Bristol University commissioned by the Home Office to conduct an empirical study of how the evidence in criminal prosecutions for child abuse was collected, evaluated by decision-makers and ultimately assessed by a trier of fact for those few cases which went to trial. Caroline's academic interests focused on family law and criminal law, and Laura's on evidence law and tort law. We realized that our respective territories of law did not speak to or otherwise deal with one another; instead they operated in their own closed systems of doctrine and procedure, yet professionals working in child protection were continually being exhorted to develop inter-agency working practices in order to protect children better.

From that conversation comes this book. It is probably fair to say that we did not have any conception as to how huge this project would become. In the course of the book's gestation, Caroline has given birth to three sons and has moved to the University of Durham and later to Queen's University, Belfast, while Laura moved to Wadham College, Oxford (where she remains happily ensconced) and took up criminal law in her spare time. Our editors at the Oxford University Press have been remarkably understanding as publication dates had to be repeatedly postponed.

Tracking developments in four sprawling and disparate areas of law in 75 jurisdictions has been like standing on the railway platform at Didcot Parkway watching 75 express trains continually whiz past at 100 mph. Constant research and rewriting has been necessary. No sooner had the chapter on hearsay been completed than the US Supreme Court reversed its own decision of 24 years previously, on the basis of which most American States have adopted statutes to receive hearsay evidence from children. The UK Government 2006 initiative *Every Child Matters*, implementing the recommendations of the Climbié Inquiry, resulted in a major collection of new child protection protocols being published in the two months before our deadline for submission. The Government published proposals to open up the family courts to public scrutiny in July 2006. But at some point the work had to come to an end. While we have endeavoured to state the law in criminal, family, tort, and evidence law in England and Wales up to July 2006, inevitably there will be some gaps. As for our comparator jurisdictions, primarily Scotland, Canada, United States, Australia and New Zealand, we have endeavoured to state the law correctly as of October 2005, but in many instances we were able to update particular sections.

While we have collaborated throughout the research and writing of this book, Caroline took primary responsibility for chapters 2 (Family Law), 3 (Liability in Criminal Law), and 5 (Investigating and Evaluating Allegations of Abuse), and Laura for Chapters 4 (Liability in Tort and Human Rights Law), 6 (Introduction to Adjudication of the Allegation), 7 (Access to Evidence), 8 (The Child Witness),

9 (Testing the Credibility of the Child Complainant), 10 (Testing the Credibility of the Alleged Abuser), and 11 (The Admissibility of Expert Evidence). We wrote chapter 1 (Introduction) and chapter 12 (Themes and Future Directions) together.

We are grateful to many people who kindly shared their expertise with us:

In Australia: Shannon Bellett, Coordinator of the Child Witness Service in the Court Service, Ministry of Justice in Perth, Western Australia; James Edelman, Fellow of Keble College, and Barrister, Western Australia; The Hon David Malcolm, former Chief Justice of Western Australia and Honorary Fellow of Wadham College, Oxford; Celia O'Grady, Ministry of Justice, Western Australia; The Hon. Justice Pidgeon, Chair of the Judges Committee, Supreme Court of Western Australia.

In Canada: HHJ Patricia Kvill, Family Court of Alberta; The Hon Jack Watson, Justice of Appeal, Court of Appeal of Alberta; Margaret Hall, University of British Columbia.

In the United Kingdom: Professor Andrew Ashworth, Fellow of All Souls College, Oxford; Dr Catherine Donnelly, *quondam* Fellow of Wadham College, Oxford; Elizabeth-Ann Gumbel QC; Sonia Harris-Short, University of Birmingham; Mary Hayes, Professor Emeritus, University of Sheffield; Neil Kibble, University of Aberystwyth; Martin Kirby-Sykes, Policy Directorate, Crown Prosecution Service; Lee Maitland, Solicitor; Sheilagh Morton (Crown Prosecution Service); John Riley, Barrister; Professor Paul Roberts, University of Nottingham; Richard Scorer, Solicitor; Leanne Smith, University of Cardiff; Professor Bob Sullivan, University of Durham; Catherine Williams, University of Sheffield; Warwick Maynard and Richard Pugh, Office of Criminal Justice Reform, Home Office.

In Northern Ireland: Dr Anne-Marie McAlinden, Professor Kieran McEvoy and Estelle Zinstagg, Queens University Belfast.

In New Zealand: Dr Claire Breen and Ruth Busch, University of Waikato; Professor Stephen Todd, University of Canterbury; the New Zealand Law Reform Commission; Dick Edwards of the New Zealand Law Society.

In South Africa: Dellene Clark of the South African Law Commission; Bronwyn Pithey, Senior State Advocate, National Directorate of Public Prosecutions.

In the United States: The National Center for Prosecution of Child Abuse, American Prosecutors' Research Institute, Virginia, USA.

We are greatly indebted to the late Allan Levy QC for his generosity in sharing his advice, knowledge, and enthusiasm at the earlier stages of this project. An indomitable advocate for children, he is much missed.

Mary Hayes, Allan Hoyano, Peter Keenan, Anne-Marie McAlinden, Robbie McDonald, HHJ Mary Jane Mowat, Joyce Plotnikoff, HHJ Peter Rook QC and Catherine Williams read and commented on various draft chapters for us. Allan Hoyano did much of the tedious proofreading of footnotes, the table of cases, and the bibliography, at unsociable hours.

We are very grateful to our indefatigable research assistants from Oxford and Queens University, whose enthusiasm for this huge project buoyed us up when ours was flagging: Sophie Weller, Andrew Legg, Tamsyn Allen, Nerisha Singh, Karen Golding, and Leanne Smith. Andy and his wife Hannah showed extraordinary dedication in the final hectic days before submission, dashing about Manila in the Philippines on motorcycle taxis in quest of open internet cafes at 2 am to send footnotes for Caroline's chapters.

We would like to thank our students at the University of Bristol, University of Durham, Queen's University Belfast and the University of Oxford for many fascinating discussions in which the ideas for this book have been refined. The postgraduate students in the Oxford BCL/MJur Evidence course have been invaluable sources of information about their respective jurisdictions around the world.

Caroline would like to thank Rory, Oscar, and Angus McDonald for their joyful presence. She would also like to thank all those who have made it possible for her to write this book while looking after three children under five, Tracey Gibson in particular. She is also enormously grateful for the friendship of Catriona Armit, Clare Bell, Claire Breen, Francesca Campion, George and Alyce Griffith, Alison McAtamney, Roger and Annabelle McDonald, Antonella Soro, and Lucy and Nicholas Wirz during this time. She would like to express her deep gratitude for the love, support (and the babysitting, proofreading and cooking) of her parents Janet and Peter Keenan, and her brother Philip. Finally she would like to thank her husband Robbie McDonald, for his invaluable presence and for making life good.

Laura thanks the Fellows of Wadham College, Oxford for their kindness in continuing to express interest in this book at Common Table over the past six years, and especially her Law colleague in Wadham, Jeffrey Hackney, who has shouldered administrative and pastoral burdens over the past six years to free her to write. Her students at Wadham, past and present, have been tactful and reassuringly optimistic when inquiring about 'The Book'. The Faculty of Law, Oxford has been very generous in providing research and technical support for this project. Mindy Chen-Wishart, Bevis Nathan, Michael Osborn, Andrew Souter, and David Walker will know why she owes much to them. Laura's family in Canada have been extraordinarily patient with the way this book has dominated her life. Laura simply could not have written this book without her husband Allan, who has been with her every word and punctuation mark of the way.

Laura Hoyano and Caroline Keenan
August 2006

Summary Contents

Contents

List of Diagrams

Table of Cases[1]

---

[1] Criminal cases are alphabetized according to the name of the defendant. Privy Council cases are listed both under the United Kingdom and Privy Council list, and under New Zealand where the appeal to the Privy Council emanated from there. European human rights decisions where the UK was the respondent are listed both under that heading and under the United Kingdom heading. We have endeavoured to make these citations as accessible as possible for readers from other jurisdictions, and so have not always followed domestic citation conventions. We have retained the standard abbreviations for the highest courts in each jurisdiction: Aus HC for the High Court of Australia, HL for House of Lords, PC for Privy Council, SCC for Supreme Court of Canada, and USSC for United States Supreme Court. As the New Zealand Supreme Court was founded only in 2004, we have not abbreviated it.

New Zealand

South Africa

United States

List of Abbreviations

Statutes
CJA 1988   Criminal Justice Act 1988
CYPA 1933   Children and Young Persons Act 1933
YJCEA 1999   Youth Justice and Criminal Evidence Act 1999

Organizations
ACPO   Association of Chief Police Officers (in England and
                                Wales)
CAIU   Police Child Abuse Intelligence Units (in England and
                                Wales)
CPS   Crown Prosecution Service of England and Wales
HMIC   Her Majesty's Inspectorate of Constabulary
LSCB   Local Safeguarding Children Board

Other
ICS   Integrated Children's System

Publications
Achieving Best Evidence   *Achieving Best Evidence in Criminal Proceedings:*
                                Guidance for Vulnerable or Intimidated Witnesses,
                                Including Children (Home Office, Lord Chancellor's
                                Department, Crown Prosecution Service, Department
                                Of Health, the National Assembly for Wales, 2001) 2
                                volumes.

Aus LRC, *Seen and Heard*   Australian Law Reform Commission and the Human
                                Rights and Equal Opportunity Commission *Seen and*
                                Heard: Priority for Children and the Legal Process
                                (Report 84 1997)

Badgley Report   *Sexual Offences against Children in Canada: Report of*
                                the Committee on Sexual Offences against Children and
                                Youths (Ottawa Ministry of Supply and Services 1984)

Birch and Powell,
Meeting the Challenges of   D Birch and R Powell *Meeting the Challenges of Pigot:*
Pigot   *Pre-trial Cross-Examination under s. 28 of the Youth*
                                Justice And Criminal Evidence Act 1999: a Briefing
                                Paper for the Home Office (February 2004)

Bristol Study   G Davis, L Hoyano, C Keenan, L Maitland and
                                R Morgan *An Assessment of the Admissibility and*
                                Sufficiency of Evidence in Child Abuse Prosecutions
                                (HMSO, London August 1999)

Burton et al
*Evidence from
Criminal Justice Agencies*

M Burton, R Evans and A Sanders *Are Special
Measures for Vulnerable and Intimidated Witnesses
Working? Evidence from the Criminal Justice Agencies*
(Home Office Online Report 01/06 London 2006)

Cleveland Report

Dame Elizabeth Butler-Sloss *Report of the Inquiry into
Child Abuse in Cleveland 1987* (Cm 412)

Cooper & Roberts
Analysis of *CPS Monitoring
Data*

D Cooper and P Roberts *Special Measures for
Vulnerable and Intimidated Witnesses: an Analysis of
Crown Prosecution Service, Monitoring Data* (Crown
Prosecution Service, London June 2005)

The Climbié Inquiry

Lord Laming (Chair) *The Victoria Climbié Inquiry*
(The Stationery Office, London 2003 Cm 5730).

Hamlyn et al
Surveys of VIWs

B Hamlyn, A Phelps, J Turtle and G Sattar *Are Special
Measures Working? Evidence from Surveys of Vulnerable
and Intimidated Witnesses* (Home Office Research,
Development and Statistics Directorate, London June
2004)

Law Com No 245, *Hearsay*

Law Commission of England & Wales *Evidence in
Criminal Proceedings: Hearsay and Related Topics* (Law
Com 245 Cm 3670 1997)

*Memorandum of Good
Practice*

Home Office and Department of Health
*Memorandum of Good Practice on Video-Recorded
Interviews with Child Witnesses for Criminal
Proceedings* (HMSO London 1992)

Myers, *Evidence in Child
Abuse Cases*

J Myers *Evidence in Child Abuse and Neglect Cases* (3rd
edn John Wiley & Sons, Inc, New York 1997)

NZLC Report No 55,
Evidence

New Zealand Law Commission *Evidence* (Report 55
August 1999)

NZLC PP No 26,
Evidence of Children

New Zealand Law Commission *The Evidence of
Children and Other Vulnerable Witnesses: a Discussion
Paper* (Preliminary Paper 26 October 1996)

Ontario LRC, *Child Witnesses*

Ontario Law Reform Commission *Report on Child
Witnesses* (1991)

Plotnikoff and Woolfson
In Their Own Words

J Plotnikoff and R Woolfson *In Their Own Words: the
Experiences of 50 Young Witnesses in Criminal
Proceedings* (NSPCC and Victim Support, London
2004)

Queensland LRC *Evidence of Children*	Queensland Law Reform Commission *The Receipt of Evidence by Queensland Courts: the Evidence of Children* (Report No 55 Dec 2000)
Pigot Report	HH Judge Thomas Pigot QC (Chair) *Report of the Advisory Group on Video-Recorded Evidence* (HMSO, London 1989)
Speaking Up for Justice	Home Office *Speaking Up for Justice: Report of the Interdepartmental Working Group on the Treatment of Vulnerable or Intimidated Witnesses in the Criminal Justice System* (June 1998)
Working Together to Safeguard Children 2006	H M Government *Working Together to Safeguard Children* A guide to inter-agency working to safeguard and promote the welfare of children (Stationery Office, London 2006)

PART I

THEMES AND QUESTIONS

'Children are our future' is a catchphrase often echoed in the media, in academic journals and in everyday conversations. But what does this mean? This question is particularly topical or salient . . . today given the recent (apparent) upsurge in child abuse and child deaths. These tragedies focus our attention on our government and non-government agencies and the efforts they put into the welfare aspects of children. The focus however does not end with a critical focus on the failures of these departments; it also spreads wider afield to the parental responsibilities that are obviously lacking in these prominent cases. Perhaps, it is even fair to say that we, the general public, the politicians and all concerned look immediately for the scapegoat, the persons, the body to point the finger at. There is then a public outcry for something to be done about the plight of these abused children in general terms. Generally we follow the pattern of all similar countries in this position, we ask for Inquiries or for Royal Commissions to provide an analysis, provide a scapegoat, to provide the solution to this problem. Meanwhile the media slowly burns itself out on that topic (unless there is another atrocity) and turns its front page to something else. So the catchphrase becomes less important as a real issue and relegated to the problem of a scapegoat. The Inquiries and Commissions continue and social and government agencies toil on, still unassisted, dreading the next atrocity. The knee-jerk reaction to these tragedies, and media frenzied attacks on the agencies providing support for children continue in the public backdrop. They are the ambulance at the bottom of the cliff picking up the wounded and dead from the most recent tragedy and waiting to pick up the next.[1]

[1] Judge M Brown *Care and protection is about Adult Behaviour: the Ministerial Review of the Department of Child, Youth and Family Services Report to the Minister of Social Services and Employment Hon Steve Maharey* (2000) 33.

1

Introduction

There is universal agreement that 'something must be done' about the problem of child abuse, but there is much less clarity about what behaviour qualifies as child abuse and what should be done about it. Policymakers often enact laws as a solution to problems which demand a strong societal response. The presence of more legislation on the statute book, or the creation of more rules which professionals must follow, is one socially acceptable sign that the problem has been recognized by the government of the day and an appropriate response has been made. Child abuse is the epitome of this phenomenon. Contemporary episodic panics about the extent and nature of maltreatment of children, as well as sundry research-led initiatives, have led to a patchwork of legislation, caselaw, procedures, circulars, guidance and inquiry report recommendations which investigators, other child protection professionals and the courts are expected to apply across the distinct areas of family law, criminal law, tort law and the law of evidence. Problems are caused by the plethora of guidance and procedures which professionals in a diverse range of disciplines are meant to read, digest and apply whilst performing an extraordinarily difficult and time-consuming job. While a great deal of the law is well thought out and constructive, its sheer weight and complexity makes applying it a daunting experience. To borrow the description of Sir William Utting, in relation to the guidance on children living away from home, the law is 'now so large that responsible managers have difficulty in comprehending it all and it is less a tool for practitioners than a subject for their research'.[2]

Legal responses to child abuse are not confined to one legal doctrine. The objective of family law is to prevent child abuse; of criminal law to punish it; and of tort law to compensate for the harm it inflicts. It is an irony that whilst professionals involved in child protection have been increasingly exhorted to work together across disciplines to protect children by coordinating their work, there has been minimal cross-fertilization between the areas of law within which they operate. The development and analysis of policy objectives and their implementation through statutes, procedural protocols and guidance, and ultimately caselaw, tend to be insular exercises. The starting premise for this book is that no one part of the law relating to child abuse can be considered or implemented in isolation. Accordingly this book presents a critical and comprehensive cross-boundary analysis of the investigation and adjudication of allegations of child abuse by the criminal, family and tort systems of law and of the rules of evidence operating in each of those legal systems. We seek to penetrate the rhetoric of coordination between agencies and legal systems with different objectives, ethos and legal and operational constraints.

We describe, compare and evaluate the templates used by these systems:

• to define the type and level of abuse recognized as warranting state intervention,
• to delineate what evidence is relevant to a decision-maker in respect of that allegation and the permissible modes of collecting it,
• to determine the sufficiency of that evidence necessary to trigger juridical or extra-curial action, and
• to establish the range of actions which are available where the allegation is proved to the requisite standard.

We also look across jurisdictional boundaries at the way in which several similar common law jurisdictions, notably the United States, Canada, Australia and New Zealand, have developed their own legal responses to particular—and universal—problems which child abuse raises. We do not attempt to describe all the law in each of these jurisdictions, but rather highlight initiatives and changes in the law which might (or might not) provide some solutions to the problems with which our own jurisdiction is struggling. In addition, our own analysis of the law in England and Wales has been greatly aided by the comparisons which we have been able to make between the law from one jurisdiction and another.

We aim in this book to bring together the law and procedures in key areas of the law concerning child abuse. However, this book is not intended to be a manual for professionals involved in cases where there are concerns about child abuse, for we firmly believe that there is no need for yet another manual. That said, we hope that they will find this book both interesting and useful. We aim to consider each type of law in the context of the other substantive law relating to child abuse and child protection in England and Wales, and in the context of analogous law from other jurisdictions.

---

[2] Sir William Utting *People Like Us—The Report of the Review of Safeguards for Children Living Away from Home* (HM Stationery Office, 1997) [17.1].

We are seeking to measure the match between black letter l
happens, as one indicator of the legitimacy of that law. Again,
as possible to consider the law realistically in terms of how it
context and constraints of practice. The best child protectior
and decision-making procedures will be futile if they canno
as lawyers, we are attempting to identify the reasons why cl
and other child protection professionals might not adhere
by the law.

While we have tried to include as much of the English law as possible there will
naturally be lacunae in our description. Our aim is to distil and compare the essence
of the legal approaches to this complex legal and social problem across juridical and
geographic boundaries. It is in this way that we seek to contribute to debate and to
practice. We identify below the overarching themes for our analysis.

A. Overarching Themes

1. Child abuse as a social and legal construction

The single unifying term 'child abuse' encompassing all child maltreatment emerged
in the late 1960s and early 1970s. In the 19th century no single term was used to
designate adult–child sexual contact. 'It could be called unlawful carnal knowledge,
incest, criminal assault, an outrage, an unnatural act, a slip.'[3] Similarly the child
protectors of the 1880s and onwards used several terms, predominantly 'child cruelty'
and 'child neglect', to define the types of evil which they were intent on preventing
and punishing.[4] Even when the term 'child abuse' began commonly to be used in the
1970s, it was used primarily to refer to the physical assault of children.[5] The term
became all-encompassing in the late 1980s when the problem of child sexual abuse
became more widely recognized. The, now common, use of the term 'child abuse' gives
the impression of a universal consensus about what acts and omissions are abusive;
however this is far from true.

Time[6], place[7], cultural norms and context[8] dictate which aspects of all the behaviour
towards children will be considered to be unacceptable.[9] The lack of a consistent,
universally accepted social definition of child abuse can make legal decisions particularly contentious, both in instances where the law breaks new ground in using legal
powers in circumstances which historically had not been considered to be abusive,

---

[3] C Smart 'A History of Ambivalence and Conflict in the Discursive Construction of the "Child Victim"
of Sexual Abuse' (1999) 8(3) *Social and Legal Studies* 391, 393.

[4] H Ferguson 'Cleveland in History: The Abused Child and Child Protection 1880–1914' in R Cooter
(ed) *In the Name of the Child—Health and Welfare 1880–1940* (Routledge, London 1992).

[5] 'The Battered Babies Scandal' *The Sunday Times* 11th November 1973; see N Parton *The Politics of
Child Abuse* (Macmillan, London 1985) 94–95.   [6] Smart (n 3).

[7] Lord Williams of Mostyn (Chair) *Childhood Matters: Report of the National Commission of Inquiry into
the Prevention of Child Abuse* (HMSO, London 1996) 1.

[8] S Creighton and N Russell *Voices from Childhood* (NSPCC, London 1995) 29.

[9] Department of Health *Messages from Research* (Studies in Child Protection HMSO, London 1995) 15.

as corporal punishment,[10] or conversely where the law has not kept in step, or is not viewed as having kept in step, with social views of what is abusive, such as sexual exploitation of relationships of trust.[11]

Not only do legal definitions have to reflect social expectations and definitions, they also have to comply with expected forensic legal norms. Thus in the context of family law, definitions of child maltreatment are ostensibly child-focused, inquiring into whether a particular state of affairs exists. However, since a finding that a child has been abused is a justification in family law for intervention by the state in the way in which a family is organized, the definition of what acts qualify is crucial. This is especially because family law acknowledges the state's interest in preserving the integrity of families. In terms of finding redress for injury, legal action is only justified when a claimant has suffered harm, and the harm was in some way brought about by a person (or organization) who owed him a duty of care. In criminal law the question becomes not only whether a person caused a defined harm, but also whether he did so intentionally, recklessly, or negligently. Often those working in fields other than the law, as well as families trying to cope with the system, may find these distinctions and differences in emphasis confusing and unclear. Many family members going through the family law process may feel themselves on trial and react accordingly, notwithstanding the claims that the family court system is non-adversarial.

For victims too the legal dictionaries of abuse can perplex. A sexual act of a child aged 13 with a man in his 50s is a criminal offence and also constitutes harm which may justify the family court's intervention depending on the circumstances, but the Criminal Injuries Compensation Board has ruled that it is not an act of violence, and hence not compensable, if the child is a prostitute.[12] Even though the child is deemed by the law to be incapable of consenting to the act, de facto consent bars compensation. The principles of one type of law rarely inform the development of another.

2. The protection of the family as a private sphere

While it is axiomatic that children should not suffer abuse, state involvement in the protection of children remains contentious. The boundary between what has been the 'state's business' and 'parents' choice' has been constantly re-negotiated across time and cultures.[13] The concept that parents naturally have their children's best interests at heart is challenged by the reality of child abuse and statistical evidence indicating that members of a child's family are the most likely abusers.[14] At the same time, it is also acknowledged in debate that 'good enough' parenting covers a range of behaviour which other people might consider potentially damaging to a child.

---

[10] See Chapter 3 section B.4.   [11] See Chapter 3 section E.1(d).

[12] See Chapter 4 section B.

[13] L Fox Harding *Perspectives in Child Care Policy* (2nd edn Longman, London 1997).

[14] P Cawson, C Wattam, S Brooker and G Kelly *Child Maltreatment in the United Kingdom; A Study of the Prevalence of Child Abuse and Neglect* (NSPCC, London 2000) Conclusions.

Moreover it is increasingly being recognized that state involvement can also damage children.[15]

Currently there is wide variation between the value that different jurisdictions place on supporting the child within her family and removing a child from home for her own protection. Underlying these variations are considerable differences in the priorities which are accorded the rights of the child and the rights of the parents. The United States has very little concept of children's rights in law,[16] a highly developed concept of parental ownership of children,[17] and at the same time, a draconian model of state intervention in family life involving the rapid termination of parental rights for those found by a court to have injured their child.[18] In contrast, the burgeoning jurisprudence from the European Court of Human Rights and from English courts under the Human Rights Act 1998,[19] and the children's rights movement in England, have led to a developing legal concept of children's rights in child protection matters. They have also led to a privileging of the child's birth family in law as the most likely promoter of the child's welfare in the future, unless evidence proves otherwise.

3. Child abuse and moral panics

The focus that the law adopts, and indeed the priorities of law-makers, are determined by the type of behaviour that is considered problematic at the time.[20] Fears about child abuse and child abusers may be placed into four main categories:

- child deaths at the hands of a parent, guardian or carer as a result of prolonged abuse within the family;
- sexual and physical abuse of children within an institutional setting such as a church or residential care centre;
- anxiety that paedophiles may be living unrecognized within the community, placing every child in peril;

and, allied to each of these three,

- concern about the mishandling of allegations of child abuse, such as the perpetuation of abuse due to the failure of investigators to respond competently to reports, or conversely the stigmatizing of innocent people as abusers due to the over-reaction of investigators.

---

[15] N Parton, D Thorpe and C Wattam *Child Protection—Risk and the Moral Order* (Macmilllan, Basingstoke 1997). [16] Discussed in Chapter 4 section F.5(c) and Chapter 2 section A.3.

[17] J Dwyer 'Parents' Religion and Children's Welfare: Debunking the Doctorine of Parents' Rights' (1994) 82 Calif L Rev 1371, 1378; K Hirosawa 'Are Parents Acting in the Best Interests of their Children when they make Medical Decisions Based on Their Religious Beliefs?' (2006) 44 Fam Ct Rev 316.

[18] C Ross 'The Tyranny of Time: Vulnerable Children, "Bad" Mothers and Statutory Deadlines in Parental Termination Proceedings' (2004) 11 Virginia J of Social Policy & L 176.

[19] Discussed in Chapter 4 section F.4(a) and (b) and Chapter 2 section E.

[20] S Cohen *Folk Devils and Moral Panics: The Creation of the Mods and Rockers* (Blackwell, Oxford 1972) 28.

Child deaths and sexual abuse within the family tend to make the headlines and thus enter public consciousness about child abuse when they are allied to concerns about the official response to the problem.[21] The 'panics' which these cases have created relate to the cruelty which parents can inflict upon their children and the ineffectiveness of the existing child protection mechanisms to prevent its occurrence.[22] Systemic problems have often been revealed within agencies involved in child protection linked to lack of skills, poor record-keeping, and a paucity of mechanisms for coordination and information-sharing between agencies which led to the replication of some work and still other avenues of inquiry and intervention being overlooked.[23]

The scandals emanating from systemic abuse in institutional settings have tended to be centred on situations where mismanagement, or denial that abuse could take place, created a culture in which those who wished to exploit children could do so with impunity, and where the abuse was condoned by inaction, wilful blindness or complicity by officials in the institution and public authorities. Numerous inquiry reports in every jurisdiction we examine have also attested to horrific and systematic abuse within children's residential care facilities and foster homes. The reports clearly concluded that children were abused because of serious failings in the public care system, including an inability to countenance the fact that children were being abused within the institution which was supposed to protect them from precisely that harm.[24]

---

[21] Dame Elizabeth Butler-Sloss *Report of the Inquiry into Child Abuse in Cleveland 1987* (Cm 412)196 [11.45]; The Right Hon Lord Clyde *Report into the Inquiry into the Removal of Children from Orkney in February, 1991* (HMSO, 1992) 260 [14.94–14.98]. For New Zealand see L Hood *A City Possessed: The Christchurch Civic Creche case* (Longacre Press, Dunedin 2001). For the USA L Wimberley 'The Perspective from Victims of Child Abuse Laws (VOCAL)' in J Myers (ed) *The Backlash: Child Protection Under Fire* (Sage Publications Thousand Oaks, California 1994) 58–59.

[22] H Hendrick *Child Welfare England 1872–1989* (Routledge, London 1994) 254.

[23] London Borough of Brent *A Child in Trust: The Report of the Panel of Inquiry into the Circumstances Surrounding the Death of Jasmine Beckford* (London Borough of Brent 1985) 121; London Borough of Lambeth *Whose Child?: The Report of the Public Inquiry into the Death of Tyra Henry* (London Borough of Lambeth 1987) chapter Four; L Blom Cooper (Chair) *A Child in Mind: Protection of Children in a Responsible Society Report of the Commission of Inquiry into the Circumstances Surrounding the Death of Kimberley Carlile* (London Borough of Greenwich 1987) 128; Lord Laming (Chair) *Victoria Climbié Inquiry* (Cm 5730, 2003) [1.16]; Newham Area Child Protection Committee *Ainlee [Walker] Born 24.06.1999 died 07.01.2000 Chapter 8 Review* (December 2002); Lauren Wright killed by her father and stepmother 6 May 2001: Norfolk Health Authority *Summary Report of the Independent Health Review of the Health Services Treatment of Lauren Wright* (March 2002). In other jurisdictions see for example the United States: the death of Rilya Wilson, discussed in C Keenan 'Lessons from America? Learning from Child Protection Policy in the USA' (2006) 18(1) Child and Family Law Quarterly 43, 62–64; Canada: the investigation into child deaths in British Columbia by Hon Ted Hughes OC, QC *BC Children and Youth Review: an independent review of BC's child protection system* (7 April 2006); New Zealand: Commissioner for Children *Final Report on the Investigation into the Death of James Whakaruru* (New Zealand Office of the Commissioner for Children, Wellington 2000).

[24] See amongst many other excellent reports, A Levy and B Khan *The Pindown Experience and the Protection of Children* (Staffordshire County Council Stafford 1991); G Williams and J McCreadie *Ty Mawr Community Home Inquiry* (Cwmbran Gwent County Council 1992); A Kirkwood *The Leicestershire Inquiry—The Report of the Inquiry into Aspects of the Management of Children's Homes in Leicestershire between 1973 and 1986* (Leicestershire County Council 1993); Sir Ronald Waterhouse (Chair) *Lost in Care: Report of the Tribunal of Inquiry into the Abuse of Children in Care in the Former County Council Areas of Gwynedd and Clwyd since 1974* (Stationery Office London 2000); Hon Stuart G Stratton, former Chief Justice of New Brunswick for the Nova Scotia Department of Justice *Report of an Independent Investigation in Respect*

For the first time public discussion has identified abusers of children as being not only those at the margins of society but those ensconced in positions of trust who have exploited the belief of others that they were decent members of society. When combined with a further moral panic about paedophiles living unrecognized within the community,[25] it has led to calls for more legal mechanisms in criminal and civil law by which the dangerous may be indelibly labelled and controlled. The communication of information to the public about those convicted or suspected of sexual assaults against children has become the key battleground in the debate about legal responses to sexual crimes against children, the premise of campaigners being that if the law can label the dangerous then the risk of abuse may be eradicated by avoiding them.[26]

The United States, Canada, Australia, and to a more limited extent New Zealand, have a long and tragic history of the use of child welfare provisions to effect the eradication of indigenous cultures.[27] Whilst more enlightened attitudes now prevail, the history of children removed forcibly from their families and cultures ostensibly for their own welfare still raises important questions about the operation of any threshold for the state's legal intervention in a multicultural society. It has led to a number of well-meaning attempts within child welfare legislation to recognize cultural diversity and not to penalize non-dominant cultures. The difficulty now is to strike the right balance between recognizing that child-rearing standards may be different in different societies, and applying a national and universally accepted standard of child welfare to prevent harm. For example, at present a cultural defence in relation to physical chastisement of children has been raised by minority groups in all the jurisdictions studied, that the level of violence used is acceptable within the minority culture, if not in the culture of the majority.[28] Some jurisdictions have adopted a model of

---

of Incidents and Allegations of Sexual and Other Physical Abuse at Five Nova Scotia Residential Institutions (1995), followed by The Hon Fred Kaufman CM, QC *Searching for Justice: an Independent Review of Nova Scotia's Response to Reports of Institutional Abuse* (Government of Nova Scotia 2002); Law Commission of Canada (DA Wolfe, PG Jaffe, JL Jetté and SE Poisson) *Child Abuse in Community Institutions and Organisations: Improving Public and Professional Understanding* (2002); Hon Mr Justice Sean Ryan, Chair, Commission to Inquire into Child Abuse (Ireland) *Identifying Institutions and Persons under the Commission to Inquire into Child Abuse Act 2000: a Position Paper*; Leneen Forde, Chairperson *Report of the Commission of Inquiry into Abuse of Children in Queensland Institutions* (1999).

[25] A Sampson *Acts of Abuse: Sexual Offenders and the Criminal Justice System* (Routledge, London 1994) 1; D West 'Sexual Molesters' in N Walker (ed), *Dangerous People* (Blackstone Press, London 1996) 52.

[26] T Thomas and B Hebenton 'Tracking Sex Offenders' (1996) 35(2) *Howard Journal* 97; R Ericson 'The Division of Expert Knowledge in Policing and Security' (1994) 45(2) *British Journal of Sociology* 149; *R v Chief Constable of the North Wales Police ex p Thorpe* [1999] QB 396 (CA); *R v Local Authority and Police Authority in the Midlands ex p LM* [2000] 1 FLR 612 (QB); *Re C (Disclosure: Sexual Abuse Findings)* [2002] 2 FLR 375 (Fam Div).

[27] M Bennett, C Blackstock and R de la Ronde *A Literature Review and Annotated Bibliography Focussing on Aspects of Aboriginal Child Welfare in Canada* (2nd edn First Nations Child and Family Caring Society of Canada 2005) 16; S Fournier and E Crey *Stolen from our Embrace: The Abduction of First Nations Children and the Restoration of Aboriginal Communities* (Douglas and McIntyre Ltd, Vancouver 1997); National Inquiry into the Separation of Aboriginal and Torres Strait Islander Children from their Families *Bringing them Home* (Commonwealth of Australia, Sydney 1997)108; L Graham 'The Past Never Vanishes: A Contextual Critique Of The Existing Indian Family Doctrine' 23 American Indian L Rev 1.

[28] T Taylor 'The Cultural Defense and its Irrelevancy in Child Protection Law' (1997) 17 B C Third World L Journal 331.

law-making that tries to reflect cultural differences: for example a cultural defence
to physical chastisement has been incorporated into three child protection statutes
in the United States.[29] Other jurisdictions such as England and Wales have tried to
develop a universal standard of child welfare.[30] Neither model has been very successful
in reconciling the competing arguments in relation to child-rearing standards.

4. A federation of agencies?

In practice, in each jurisdiction we examine, several different agencies have some
responsibility for the protection of children. Initially in England, when the problem
of child abuse was rediscovered the relationship of agencies was conceived as a federation.[31] Each would retain its own goals and working practices, and the law would
act as the glue between them, creating a shared model of inter-agency working.
To this end a series of inter-agency guidance has been published called *Working
Together* which aspires to create a shared pattern investigating an allegation for child
abuse.[32] An inter-agency body in each area has been expected to write local guidance on the demarcation of responsibility in child protection cases for particular
work, run joint training, and jointly investigate the deaths of children within the
local area.

However there have always been serious problems in this federation. Information about children has often not been routinely shared between agencies, as the
Victoria Climbié Inquiry showed so graphically.[33] Child protection has not always
been prioritized in individual agencies, and children's cases have fallen between the
cracks when all the professionals involved in their case have assumed that someone
else was responsible for protecting them. In practice those working on the ground
have had to reconcile competing goals between agencies in individual cases.[34] The
duty to cooperate has now been placed on a statutory basis.[35] The *Every Child Matters* initiative has lead to the creation of a shared database of all children who have
had contact with an agency in relation to their well-being[36] and to the launch of
Children's Trusts.[37] This has the potential to move child protection practice from a
federative model to a unitary one, as Children's Trusts are expected to bring together
practitioners trained by different agencies under a single umbrella to promote child
well-being.

---

[29] See below Chapter 2 section E.2.   [30] See below Chapter 2 section E.1(a).

[31] C Hallett and E Birchall *Coordination and Child Protection* (HMSO, Scotland 1992).

[32] H M Government *Working Together to Safeguard Children: A guide to inter-agency working to safeguard
and promote the welfare of children* (HM Stationery Office, London 2006).

[33] Lord Laming (Chair) *Victoria Climbié Inquiry* (Cm 5730, 2003) [1.16]. No fewer than 12 agencies
with child protection responsibilities knew about Victoria, but none took decisive steps to prevent her
death from torture and neglect.   [34] ibid.

[35] Children Act 2004 (England) s 10.

[36] ibid, s 11; HM Government *Information Sharing: Practitioners, Guide to Integrated Working to Improve
Outcomes for Children and Young People* (HM Stationery Office, London 2006).

[37] HM Government *Statutory Guidance on Making Arrangements to Safeguard and Promote the Welfare
of Children under s 11 Children Act 2004* (HM Stationery Office, London 2005).

It has been realized that 'to do something about child abuse' is not enough: the response must be 'appropriate and proportionate'. Law must also guide the conduct of those working in child protection and hold them, as well as the abusers, accountable for their actions, omissions, and decisions.[38] Family, criminal and tort law have historically developed independently in responding to child abuse cases, with minimal cross-fertilization. The question for the law now is the extent to which it can transcend the conflicting goals and ethos of these different systems of law and reflect the drive for a unified child protection policy and delivery of services. While it seems impossible that there will ever be a single child protection law, it should be possible that one system of law could reflect rather than ignore the responses of other legal systems to child abuse. We hope that this book can be the beginning of this process.

B. A Note on the Comparative Analysis of Other Jurisdictions

Our intention has not been to present a comprehensive view of the approach of other jurisdictions to all the issues we identify in this book. Instead, we have focused on specific aspects of the law elsewhere which are instructive, either as solutions which English law might wish to emulate or might wish to avoid; in a good number of instances the experience elsewhere supports the approach that English law currently takes to the problem. In this section we provide a brief introduction to the other common law legal systems which we consider, primarily to provide a jurisdictional context to their statutes and cases.

1. Canada

The Canadian constitutional system is based upon a Confederation of ten Provinces which are autonomous in their own areas of jurisdiction.[39] Powers not expressly devolved to the Provinces default to the Federal Parliament. There are also three Territories, all in the north of Canada and with First Nations populations in the majority, with some devolved powers from the national government exercised by legislative assemblies. The Province of Quebec has inherited a distinctive civil code tradition from France, and accordingly is not bound by common law decisions rendered by the Supreme Court of Canada.

Unlike Australia and the United States, in Canada jurisdiction over criminal law and the criminal rules of evidence is allocated to the Federal Parliament, with rulings of the Supreme Court of Canada binding on all lower courts, including those in Quebec. Canadian criminal law has been entirely codified in the Criminal Code of Canada since 1898, although the rules of criminal evidence have been only partially codified. There are two unusual features of Canadian criminal justice which are important for our analysis. The first is that the Crown has a general right of appeal from acquittals

---

[38] M Freeman *The Moral Status of Children—Essays on the Rights of the Child* (Martinus Nijhoff Publishers, The Hague 1997) 279–81.

[39] Allocated by the British North America Act 1867, now the Constitution Act 1981.

on any error of law, which is widely construed. The second is that all offences up to and including first-degree murder may be tried by trial judges sitting without a jury, at the accused's election.[40] One advantage for the defence of electing trial by a superior court judge sitting alone is that the detailed reasons for the verdict greatly expand the scope for an appeal. The defence may also wish to have a seasoned and case-hardened trier of fact in trials involving charges which are thought likely to stir the emotions of jurors. So many of the appellate child abuse cases we discuss were tried by trial judges sitting alone. Nevertheless the content of the rules of evidence is considered by the courts on the basis that cases will be heard by lay juries.

Since 1982, the Canadian Charter of Rights and Freedoms has radically changed substantive and procedural criminal law, as the courts have been given the power to strike down legislation and common law principles which contravene constitutional guarantees. The Charter of Rights largely parallels the guarantees of a fair trial under Articles 5 and 6 of the European Convention on Human Rights, and hence under the Human Rights Act 1998, as well as the right to security of the person (s 7). In the Canadian Charter, as in the European Convention, the guarantees are not absolute, unlike the American Constitution. The potential conflict between fundamental rights and freedoms is recognized and mediated through s 1, which envisages their reasonable limitation 'as prescribed by law', where this can be 'demonstrably justified in a free and democratic society'.[41]

Over the past decade the Supreme Court of Canada has reformed the rules of evidence, returning to first principles to evaluate their continuing validity in the modern criminal and civil trial setting. The Court has decided that if judges have created problems in the law, then the judiciary cannot abdicate responsibility to solve them.[42] The Court's determination to take a 'common sense approach'[43] to the evidential problems of child abuse prosecutions has broken the ground for reform on a much broader basis, such as the abolition of the exclusionary hearsay rule, with the express objective of admitting all relevant and probative evidence.[44] In contrast, Australian, New Zealand and English[45] courts have relied upon Parliament to reform the common law of evidence. For that reason, the evidence statutes in Canada are very far from comprehensive, but the jurisprudence is very instructive.

Marriage and divorce falls within federal jurisdiction; however other aspects of family law such as matrimonial property are governed by the Provinces under their constitutional jurisdiction for property and civil rights. Child protection statutes are enacted by the Provincial Legislatures. Tort law falls within provincial jurisdiction; however decisions from the Supreme Court of Canada, while strictly speaking not binding on Provinces other than the one from which the appeal originated, are considered to represent the common law across all other Provinces

---

[40] Criminal Code of Canada Part XIX. Juries are required for offences of treason, sedition and the like.
[41] Canadian Charter of Rights and Freedoms s 1.
[42] *Ares v Venner* [1970] SCR 608 (SCC); *R v Khan* [1990] 2 SCR 531 (SCC); *R v B(KG)* [1993] 1 SCR 740 (SCC).   [43] *R v B(KG)* (n 42) 54–55.
[44] *R v Khan* (n 42); *R v Smith* [1992] 2 SCR 915 (SCC); *R v B(KG)* (n 42).
[45] *Myers v DPP* [1965] AC 1001 (HL); *R v Kearley* [1992] 2 AC 228 (HL).

except Quebec, in the absence of any provincial statutes which make the decision distinguishable.

2. Australia

Australia is a federation of six States and one Territory; in addition the federal parliament has jurisdiction over the Australian Capital Territory. Unlike Canada, in Australia any jurisdiction which is not expressly allocated by the 1900 Constitution is deemed to belong to the States. The Australian Capital Territory has its own Legislative Assembly.

The States generally have jurisdiction over justice and criminal law prosecution, and all offences against children will be tried by the law of the State in which they were committed. All Australian States have much more comprehensive and detailed evidence statutes than Canadian jurisdictions. Although the Commonwealth of Australia has limited federal criminal law jurisdiction, it initiated the uniform Evidence Act 1995 which includes provisions relating to child witnesses. The federal model has now been adopted by New South Wales and Tasmania, although some specific provisions differ in the State versions. Western Australia is currently considering adopting it. The Commonwealth's Evidence Act 1995 has also been influential in the legislation of other Australian States.

There is a very clear demarcation in Australian family law between law-making which is the responsibility of the Commonwealth and law-making which is the responsibility of the individual States. The law of the Commonwealth determines all disputes between family members concerning where a child should live and with whom he should have contact, whereas the protection of the child by the State is the responsibility of the individual Australian States. There has been increasing concern that the wide variation in child protection legislation between States is directly hindering the child protection process and there have been some moves to create a single Commonwealth child protection statute.[46]

As in Canada, decisions of the High Court of Australia in areas of State jurisdiction technically are binding only on the State from which the appeal emanated, but are nonetheless for practical purposes considered as affecting the law on the point for all Australian jurisdictions. Australia is the only one of the jurisdictions we study which does not have a national human rights instrument.

3. New Zealand

New Zealand is a unitary state and so all the jurisdictional issues besetting Canadian, American and Australian courts are absent. Until 2004 the highest appellate court for New Zealand was the Privy Council in London, which could grant leave to appeal from decisions of the New Zealand Court of Appeal. The judges on the Privy Council

---

[46] Discussed in Chapter 2 section E.4.

are empanelled from the Law Lords. This system ended in 2004 with the creation of the new Supreme Court of New Zealand. As in Canada, in New Zealand criminal trials may be conducted by a trial judge sitting without a jury, but in New Zealand the accused must have the court's permission, and juries are required for any offence punishable by a term of life, or 14 years imprisonment or more.[47]

New Zealand has a Bill of Rights which has proved influential in the development of criminal, family and tort law. The rights apply only as against the three branches of government (the legislature, the executive, and the judiciary) or anybody in the performance of any public function, power or duty greeted by the law. Although the Bill of Rights has not been constitutionally entrenched, under s 4 the courts have power to rule that any provision of an enactment which is inconsistent with any provision of the Bill of Rights is 'impliedly repealed or revoked', is invalid or ineffective, or should not be applied by the courts. Modelled on the European Convention on Human Rights (ECHR) and the Canadian Charter, the rights guaranteed are subject to 'such reasonable limits prescribed by law as can be demonstrably justified in free and democratic society' (s 5). The rights guaranteed which are relevant for our discussion are very similar to those in the ECHR and the Canadian Charter of Rights: the rights to life (s 8) and freedom from torture or cruel, degrading or disproportionately severe treatment or punishment (s 9), and to a fair trial in criminal proceedings (s 24). Section 27 guarantees everyone the right to the observance of the principles of natural justice by any tribunal or other public authority which has the power to make a determination in respect of that person's rights, obligations, or interests protected or recognized by law, and so this would apply in child protection proceedings. Every person also has the right to bring civil proceedings against the Crown.

Finally, as discussed further in Chapter 4 section A.1(c), New Zealand is unique amongst the jurisdictions we study in its almost total replacement of the common law tort system with its no-fault compensation scheme for 'accidental' personal injury, which has been interpreted as also applying to intentional torts such as battery and assault committed by child abusers.

4. The United States

Criminal law is generally a matter of State jurisdiction in America, although there is limited Federal jurisdiction in respect of some offences, such as those committed across State boundaries or on Indian reservations or by members of the armed forces. Child abuse prosecutions usually fall within State jurisdiction, so there is a considerable variation across the 52 American jurisdictions in the procedural and substantive rules. Laws relating to child abuse, and in particular those applicable to child witnesses, must pass muster not only under the national Constitution, but also under the appropriate State Constitution. Thus some protective measures for child witnesses may be found to be constitutional in some States but not others, making generalization as to the American experience in protecting child witnesses difficult,

---

[47] Crimes Act 1961 (New Zealand) s 361B.

and even hazardous. Congress has also legislated in respect of child witnesses in the Federal Rules of Evidence, which provide a model for State legislatures.

Family law and tort law are also generally within State jurisdiction in the United States. However, 'constitutional tort' actions against State agencies for breach of a person's civil rights are tried in the Federal court system.[48] However, Congress has had a very significant influence upon the provision of family and child protection services in all States, by making federal funding contingent upon States enacting statutes with specific provisions detailed in the Child Abuse Prevention and Treatment and Adoption Reform Act,[49] and so there is a marked degree of uniformity across all States in this area. Similarly the Federal Rules of Evidence have proved very influential in State Codes.

5. Scotland

We consider Scottish law primarily in relation to vulnerable witnesses in criminal trials, which both have been influenced by and influence procedures for vulnerable witnesses in England. Even before devolution of powers by the Westminster Parliament to the Scottish Parliament in 1999, Scotland had its own substantive and procedural criminal law. Criminal trials are tried by juries of 15, and a strict majority of eight votes is sufficient for a final verdict. In addition to the usual verdicts of 'guilty' and 'not guilty', juries may return a verdict of 'not proven', which nonetheless does not have any penal consequences. Even the terminology used in the criminal justice system is distinctive—for example the prosecutor is called the procurator-fiscal, and barristers are called advocates. The system of pre-trial discovery, called precognition, permits the defence to interview all the prosecution witnesses.

These jurisdictions share with England and Wales a common legal heritage in the adversarial trial model and the creative development of the law through judicial decisions. They offer a rich terrain for exploration of the problems besetting all courts in the adjudication of child abuse allegations.

---

[48] Discussed in Chapter 4 section F.4.
[49] Child Abuse Prevention and Treatment and Adoption Reform Act 42 USCA ch 67 §5106a.

PART II

THE LEGAL FRAMEWORK FOR ADJUDICATING ALLEGATIONS

2

Family Law

The family law relating to child abuse is civil law governing both the relationships between family members and between family members and the state, about the care of children. Much of the behaviour within families is not proscribed by law. Indeed it is a basic principle of a liberal legal tradition that the family, as the fundamental building block of society, should be generally free of legal interference in governing its affairs.[1] However intervention is justified in law by both necessity and protection. Family law therefore has been created for the resolution of disputes, on occasions when the family cannot resolve the question themselves, and for the prevention of harm to family members. Family law allows the state to intervene in family life for the protection of children, including the compulsory removal of a child from home.

As in all other areas of the law relating to child abuse, the problematic area lies in the definition of boundaries. In family law the difficulty lies in the definition of the

---

[1] M Coady and C Coady 'There Ought to be A Law Against It: Reflections on Child Abuse, Morality and Law' in P Alston, S Parker and J Seymore (eds) *Children Rights and the Law* (OUP, Oxford 1991) 130.

point at which it is better for the child for the state to intervene compulsorily in her life than to offer the family services, or simply not to be involved at all. The question for lawyers is whether the existing law is adequate to guide the state's decisions on whether to intervene in the family to assist a child and whether the legal principles on which the state's decisions are made have solid foundations and are practicable.[2]

This chapter examines the current family law relating to child abuse. We begin with an analysis of the influences on the current English system and we examine the guiding principles of the Children Act 1989 which primarily dictate the family law response to child abuse in England and Wales. After this the chapter is divided into three sections: the first considers the powers which the state currently has to offer services to a child and his family under the Children Act 1989 Part III; the second section looks at the court orders which are available to enable the state to become involved in the care of a child without the consent of those who have parental responsibility for the child, and the third section considers the response of the law to allegations of child abuse in proceedings between family members about the care of the child. In each section we consider the law and its operation in other similar jurisdictions to determine whether the English system might be improved by changes which other common law jurisdictions have made; or indeed whether the English law has certain advantages over other jurisdictions in the way that it is framed. The depth in which each country's law is considered is linked to the context. We conclude that family legislation is polarized between a model premised on the central role of the child's biological family, supported by the state in the protection of the child in the future, and a model of permanency which advocates swift court-mandated intervention to remove children from abusive environments and place them with new adoptive families. The English legislation is currently rooted in the first tradition; but it is clear from the experience of the United States, Canada, and Australia how quickly the tide of support may turn and political support move towards the second model.

In the family law of each jurisdiction there are recurrent questions, the answers to which have determined the family law relating to child abuse. No jurisdiction has answered them in exactly the same way, and it is upon those differences that we focus in this chapter. The key questions are:

- What should be the overriding goal of family law which aims to protect children?
  — to enable children to live safely with their biological families?
  — to give children a home and family in which they can live permanently and safely, irrespective of whether they are biologically linked to this family?
- At what point should the state intervene in a child's family life?
  — to provide services for children in need?
  — to prevent harm?
  — when harm has occurred?
  — to prevent harm stemming from abuse?

---

[2] J Fortin 'The HRA's impact on litigation involving children and their families' (1999) 11(3) Child and Family LQ 237.

— when harm from abuse has occurred?
— to prevent significant or serious harm?
— when significant or serious harm has occurred?

• Should the court consider the acceptability of certain behaviour in a child's culture, for example physical chastisement, in determining whether a child is suffering harm or is likely to suffer harm?

This question has been considered in much greater detail in jurisdictions such as the United States, Canada, Australia and New Zealand where there is an acknowledged history of the use of child welfare laws to regulate and on occasion destroy cultural groups, but may also feature now in multicultural societies in relation to specific religious or cultural practices such as physical chastisement, faith healing, or female genital mutilation. The question is whether the determination that a child has suffered abuse might be simply the imposition of the cultural standards of the majority or the dominant social group, as being better than those of the minority.

• What should the role of the child's parents or guardians be in making decisions about the child's upbringing once the state has intervened to protect the child from harm?
— have the parents effectively given up their right to make decisions for the child?
— should the parents in fact be punished for their treatment of the child by the termination of their parental rights?
— should the parents remain involved in the child's life for the sake of the child, to ensure that the child does not herself feel abandoned?
— should the parents remain involved because the core aim of the family child protection process is the reunification of the family?

The final question which each jurisdiction has increasingly attempted to resolve as it has been hit by wave after wave of scandal about the inappropriate use of state power in cases of child protection has been:

• What is the most effective mechanism of 'guarding the guards' and ensuring that state care of children is itself both adequate and effective?
— is the law, particularly detailed guidance and procedure, the most effective mechanism for guiding state actors to behave appropriately in child protection cases?
— is the proliferation of guidance on how to respond to allegations of child abuse counterproductive in de-skilling professionals and making them prioritize bureaucratic tasks rather than those which would directly help a child in need?
— would a system which valued training above guidance as a mechanism for ensuring good standards in child protection staff produce better results?

Each of these questions has been asked in some form by legislators in all the jurisdictions which we have considered. It is in their answers to these questions that the differences between the systems lie.

A. Tracing the Influences on the Current Law

1. Scandals

Current family law relating to child abuse, like all other areas of the law, has been greatly influenced by past child protection scandals. As Nigel Parton has observed: 'Cleveland and the other child abuse inquiries . . . provided the central concerns and thereby constructed the agenda whereby the [Children Act 1989] was debated.'[3]

The scandals before the Children Act 1989 primarily concerned the misidentification of the point at which it was appropriate for the local authority to use statutory powers to intervene in an individual case. Briefly, scandals concerning physical abuse arose because of concerns that local authority social workers failed to use their statutory powers to protect children, known by them to be at risk, from harm and, on occasion, death. In the mid 1980s there had been further well-publicized deaths of children known to social workers and in some cases the subject of a court order.[4] Conversely scandals concerning sexual abuse centred on concerns that social workers had intervened too quickly and removed children from their homes without clear evidence justifying their removal. In addition, the Cleveland crisis demonstrated the real power that the state had to damage children by removing them from home when they could have been supported within it, by unnecessary court orders that left children's families defensive and uncooperative with the local authority, by lack of contact with their birth families and their lack of involvement in their care.[5] It was the conclusion of these scandals, most notably the Cleveland crisis, that those agencies attempting to protect children had also to be aware of the risk that children removed from home could suffer 'system abuse'.[6] The *Cleveland Report* stressed the importance of family life as a right of the child and the danger of undervaluing it, even in cases where state intervention is needed. Furthermore it upheld the importance of maintaining links between a child and her parent when the local authority is caring for the child.[7]

---

[3] N Parton *Governing the Family—Child Care, Child Protection and the State* (Macmillan, Houndmills 1991).
[4] London Borough of Lambeth *Whose Child?: The Report of the Public Inquiry into the Death of Tyra Henry* (London Borough of Lambeth 1987) and L Blom Cooper (Chair) *A Child in Mind: Protection of Children in a Responsible Society Report of the Commission of Inquiry into the Circumstances Surrounding the Death of Kimberley Carlile* (London Borough of Greenwich 1987).
[5] Dame Elizabeth Butler-Sloss *Report of the Inquiry into Child Abuse in Cleveland 1987* (HMSO, London Cm 412).
[6] Lord Williams of Mostyn (Chair) *Childhood Matters: the Report of the National Commission of Inquiry into the Prevention of Child Abuse* (HMSO, London 1996) 5.
[7] *Cleveland Report* (n 5) Final Conclusions [12–16].

In 1989 in introducing the Children Bill to the House of Commons at second reading David Mellor MP made clear the link between previous child abuse scandals and the aims and intentions of the Bill:

... [W]e have high ambitions for this Bill. We hope and believe that it will bring order, integration, relevance and a better balance to the law—a better balance not only between the rights and responsibilities of agencies, but most vitally between the need to protect children and the need to enable parents to challenge intervention in the upbringing of their children. Recent well-publicised cases, including the tragic case of Kimberley Carlile, Doreen Mason and the events in Cleveland in 1987, have graphically shown the consequences of getting that balance wrong. Of course of itself legislation cannot stop such tragedies, but we hope a clear legal framework will help to make more likely more clear eyed judgements by key people involved in child welfare, whether they are in social services departments, health authorities, the police, education or the courts.[8]

However although the crises were vital to the framing of legislation, they were not the sole reason for reform. Rather the inquiry report following the Cleveland crisis[9] was the final impetus for a reform of child law that had been contemplated for many years.[10]

2. Shifts in childcare policy

The findings of the Cleveland Report coincided with a shift in childcare policy, away from the prioritization of what Fox-Harding has described as 'state paternalism and child protection', to a policy which also aimed to support the child's birth family to enable the child to remain with them.[11] At the core of a policy based on 'state paternalism' is a perception that a child has a right to a certain standard of care. Biological parents are valued in this policy, but only if they can give a child what he needs. State paternalism values 'good rather than biological bonds'.[12] When no one is fulfilling the role of 'psychological' parent[13] a paternalistic policy would expect the state to step in to give the child what he needs. It envisages that when the state considers an objective standard of good childcare was not met it should have the power to transfer the care of children to those adults who could care for him better.

The earlier Children Act 1975 was written from the standpoint of state paternalism. It was the result of academic and political debate about the role of the state in safeguarding children brought together in the aftermath of the death of Maria Colwell.[14] Seven-year-old Maria had been killed by her stepfather. She had recently been returned to the care of her mother following a long and successful period when

---

[8] *Hansard* HC Standing Com B, 25 May 1989.

[9] *Cleveland Report* Butler-Sloss (n 5) Introduction.

[10] Lord Mackay 'The View Across the Tweed' (1988) Denning LJ 89, 93.

[11] L Fox-Harding *Perspectives in Child Care Policy* (2nd edn Longman, London 1997) Part Three.

[12] L Fox 'Two Value Positions in Recent Child Care Law and Practice' (1982) 12 (3) British Journal of Social Work 265, 272.

[13] J Goldstein, A Freud and A Solnit *Beyond the Best Interests of the Child* (Collier Macmillan, London 1973).

[14] Department of Health and Social Security *The Report of the Committee of Inquiry into the Care and Supervision Provided in Relation to Maria Colwell* (HMSO, London 1974).

she lived with her aunt, to whom she was very attached. Howells commented at the time that Maria's death forced society to confront the fact that 'the parent–child bond is not mystical, nor is it ever-present'.[15] Furthermore commentators criticized the lack of constructive long-term planning for children who were in care, were unlikely ever to go back to their families and could not benefit from a long wait in the vain hope that they would be returned. The Children Act 1975 expanded the power of local authority social workers to assume parental rights for children in their care,[16] and enlarged the number of grounds which allowed the courts to dispense with parents' consent to a child's adoption.[17] It was symptomatic of the change in childcare practice. Before the Act came into force there was already a move by social work teams to use the existing law to intervene in family life in a way that was 'authoritative, intrusive and insistent' to ensure that a child was physically protected from abuse.[18]

The tide had already turned away from a view of the state as the paternalistic defender of children and towards what Fox-Harding has called a policy of 'defence of the birth family and of parental rights', before the Cleveland crisis in 1987. Under such a policy, state intervention in family life may be justified as a support to families and to prevent family breakdown. The child's birth family is viewed as the optimum context for the child's development, even when the child receives a lower objective standard of care than other children. Poor quality childcare is considered to be often attributable to parental difficulties. These parental difficulties are in turn caused by circumstances outside their control such as poverty, which could be alleviated if parents were given more support. This 'defence of the birth family and of parental rights' in the Children Act 1989 harked back to the ethos of the legislation preceding the Children Act 1975—the Children Act 1948 and the Children and Young Persons' Act 1963.

As Fox-Harding has written 'the 1980s in England and Wales were genuinely a time of . . . greater tensions and conflicts in childcare policy, while the 1990s saw an attempt to resolve these conflicts under the Children Act 1989, against a background of accelerating family change'.[19] Pressure for reform of the law came from all quarters. Several inquiries had concluded that the existing law could not protect children from abuse, either by their families or by the state. Furthermore, research found that many children still drifted through local authority care with no settled home and no concrete measurable plans for their welfare, despite the legislative changes in the Acts of 1975 and 1980 which facilitated the acquisition of parental rights by local authorities.[20] 'Concerns . . . resulted in a wish for legislation and policy to proceed in two directions

---

[15] J Howells *Remember Maria* (Butterworths, London 1974) vii.

[16] The 'three-year ground' 'that throughout the three years preceding the passing of the resolution the child has been in the care of a local authority' Children Act 1975 (England) s 29 which became Care Act 1980 (England) s 3(d) and the 'same household ground' that 'a resolution under paragraph (b) is in force in relation to one parent of the child who is or is likely to become a member of the household comprising the child and his other parent'.　　　[17] Children Act 1975 (England) s 12.

[18] N Parton *The Politics of Child Abuse* (Macmillan, Houndsmills 1985) 114.

[19] Fox-Harding (n 11) 171.

[20] S Millham, R Bullock and M Haak *Lost in Care: The Problems of Maintaining Links between Children in Care and their Families* (Gower, Aldershot 1986).

at once, both towards better protection for the child and better protection for the parent.'[21]

The legislation was therefore the product of a desire to be 'all things to all men'. It glossed over any inherent rights and welfare conflicts within families, and between families and the state.

The underlying ethos of the family law response to child abuse has changed little in the years since the implementation of the Children Act 1989, in October 1991, although the 'buzz-words' have. It is important to note that while other jurisdictions, most notably the United States, prioritize a permanent safe home for a child, which may or may not be with a child's biological parents; the guiding ethos of English family law remains the search for a safe permanent home with the child's family where possible. We would argue that this remains true, despite the Prime Minister's enthusiastic endorsement of the need to find safe, permanent families for many children who were languishing in care,[22] which accompanied the adoption reforms at the beginning of this century.[23] The latest Government initiative for the protection of children *Every Child Matters: Change for Children*[24] has emphasized the centrality of the child's family in ensuring that her 'wellbeing' is 'safeguarded'[25] and the importance of state support for family life to help the family.[26] As the Green Paper *Care Matters: Transforming the Lives of Children and Young People in Care* set out in October 2006:

Few children want to come into care. Even those who have been through abuse or neglect usually continue to love their families and want to remain with them. We must have no hesitation about bringing children into care where safeguarding or other concerns mean that is the right thing to do. But children should be supported in their families unless it is against their interests for them to be. This means identifying problems early and responding quickly by offering sustained, multidisciplinary support.[27]

3. The European Convention on Human Rights and the United Nations Convention on the Rights of the Child

The European Convention on Human Rights (ECHR) should have been increasingly important in the development of family law in relation to child abuse, even before its incorporation into English law by the Human Rights Act 1998. Its overriding aim to prevent the violation of the rights of individuals by the state is particularly suited to defending unjustified state incursion in family life (Article 8). In addition Article 6 establishes an entitlement 'to a fair and public hearing within a reasonable time by an independent and impartial tribunal established by law' for everyone 'in

---

[21] Fox-Harding (n 11) 186.

[22] J Carvel 'Blair vows to increase number of adoptions' *The Guardian* 22 December 2000.

[23] Adoption and Children Act 2002.

[24] http://www.everychildmatters.gov.uk/ (accessed 10 October 2006).

[25] HM Government *Every Child Matters—Change for Children* (2004), 9. (http://www.every childmatters.gov.uk/_files/F9E3F941DC8D4580539EE4C743E9371D.pdf accessed 10 October 2006).

[26] http://www.everychildmatters.gov.uk/parents/ (accessed 10 October 2006).

[27] HM Government *Care Matters: Transforming the Lives of Children and Young People in Care* (2006) 20 <http://www.everychildmatters.gov.uk/_files/Green%20Paper.pdf> (accessed 11 October 2006).

the determination of his civil rights and obligations'. The right to remain together as a family is a civil right protected under this Article. Finally there is the prohibition on inhuman and degrading treatment and torture outlined in Article 3 which has become progressively more significant in the interpretation of the law in relation to child abuse.[28]

There is a line of jurisprudence from Strasbourg on the protection of children by public bodies. Initially it was predominantly parents who brought claims on the grounds that their rights under Articles 6 and 8 had been violated by intervention by the state in child protection. Thus it was held that a failure by a public body to provide opportunities for independent review of decision-making was a violation of parents' Article 6 rights.[29] Delay in decision-making in relation to a child may also be a violation of the parents' and the child's Article 6 rights.[30] Similarly the failure of the legislation preceding the Children Act 1989 to give a mechanism by which parents could challenge a denial of access by the local authority to their child in care was held to be a violation of Article 6.[31] Restrictions on parental contact with children in care were found to violate Article 8 if the restrictions imposed were not proportionate to the threat which the parent posed.[32]

The jurisprudence under the ECHR involving children's rights in relation to their families and the state is very much less developed. The Convention was drawn up for the protection of adult rights and any rights particular to children were not specifically considered as children are deemed to have the same rights as an adult.[33] The European Court of Human Rights (ECtHR) has not developed a clear approach to balancing the rights of children and parents in child protection cases. In practice, the interests of the child have often been conflated with those of the parents in determinations about state intervention in family life. As the judgment in *KA v Finland* states:

The mutual enjoyment by parent and child of each other's company constitutes a fundamental element of family life and domestic measures hindering such enjoyment amount to an interference with the right protected by Article 8. An interference with that right constitutes a violation of this provision unless it is 'in accordance with the law', pursues an aim, or aims, that are legitimate under paragraph 2 of Article 8 and can be regarded as 'necessary in a democratic society'. The fact that a child could be placed in a more beneficial environment for his or her upbringing will not on its own justify a compulsory measure of removal from the care of the biological parents; there must exist other circumstances pointing to the 'necessity' for such an interference with the parents' right under Article 8 of the Convention to enjoy a family life with their child.[34]

---

[28] *X and Y v Netherlands* (1986) 8 EHRR 235 (ECtHR) [27]; *A v UK* (1996) 23 EHRR 213 (ECtHR) [64].
[29] *O v UK* (1987) 10 EHRR 82.
[30] 'Human Rights Act 1998' (2000) XIII(9) Practitioners' Guide to Child Law Newsletter 109. *Zimmerman and Steiner v Switzerland* (1983) 6 EHRR 17 (ECommHR); *H v UK* (1988) 10 EHRR 95 (ECtHR); *Hendriks v Netherlands* (1983) 5 EHRR 233 (ECtHR) and *Hokkanen v Finland* [1996] 1 FLR 289 (ECtHR).
[31] *W v UK* (1987) 10 EHRR 29 (ECtHR); *R v UK* (1987) 10 EHRR 74 (ECtHR); *B v UK* (1987) 10 EHRR 87 (ECtHR). [32] *Erikkson v Sweden* (1990) 12 EHRR 183 (ECtHR).
[33] ECHR Art 1. [34] *KA v Finland* [2003] 1 FCR 2001 (ECtHR).

However the increasing influence of the UN Convention on the Rights of the Child has also had an effect upon the jurisprudence of the European Court.[35] It has clearly found that children's needs for protection from abuse can necessitate interference with their rights and the rights of their parents to enjoy family life and that even the most draconian of interference, emergency removal, may be justified on the basis of child protection, if it is unavoidable.[36] The ECtHR has interpreted the ECHR Articles 3 and 8 to recognize that children have a legitimate expectation of protection from abuse by state and non-state actors, including their parents and failures by child protection agencies to act to protect children have been found to violate their human rights. There has been further jurisprudence establishing that social workers must take measures after a child is compulsorily taken into care with a view to a child being reunited with his parents, unless it would harm the child's interests.[37] It has been argued that in so doing the ECtHR has moved close to the welfare principle which governs the Children Act 1989[38] and is discussed below.[39] However it should be noted that while child welfare is a consideration of 'crucial importance' in decision-making ECtHR judgments stop short of a statement that the welfare of the child should be the paramount consideration in any decision about the child. Any rights that a child may have should be balanced with those of their parents in relation to enjoyment of their rights under the ECHR.[40]

In truth the Convention principles relevant to child protection as interpreted by the ECtHR are in the process of development, as is family law's reaction to it in England and Wales. The incorporation of the ECHR into English law by the Human Rights Act 1998 was not greeted with enthusiasm by some members of the judiciary, who feared that it would lead to the Convention being 'routinely paraded in such cases as a makeweight ground of appeal', and discussion of Article 8 in some English family law cases can be perfunctory.[41] Harris-Short has concluded that 'a prevailing mistrust of rights among family lawyers and problematic public policy issues in the family law context have made a significant contribution to the emerging overall picture of judicial caution and restraint in the use of the Human Rights Act 1998 in family law cases'.[42] Exceptionally the courts have been comparatively innovative in some cases relating to the protection of children. Harris-Short found that the courts have taken the duties imposed by the ECHR extremely seriously in public law cases and in particular, 'are imposing increasingly high standards on local authorities in terms of

---

[35] Fortin (n 2), 254.   [36] *K and T v Finland* [2001] 2 FLR 707 (ECtHR) 755 [8].
[37] *Johnson v Norway* (1997) 23 EHRR 33, (ECtHR) [78]; *Olsson v Sweden (No 2)* (1994) 17 EHRR 134 (ECtHR).   [38] J Herring *Family Law* (Longman Pearson Education Ltd, Harlow 2001) 347.
[39] Discussed below, section B.1(a).
[40] S Harris-Short 'Putting The Child At The Heart Of Adoption?—*Re B (Adoption: Natural Parent)*' (2003) 14(3) Child and Family LQ 325.
[41] D Bonner, H Fenwick and S Harris-Short 'Judicial Approaches to The Human Rights Act' (2003) 52(3) Int Comp LQ 549. They give as an example *Re F (Minors) (Care Proceedings: Contact)* [2000] 2 FCR 481 (Fam Div), 527 (Wall J).
[42] S Harris-Short 'Family law and the Human Rights Act 1998: judicial restraint or revolution?' (2005) 17(3) Child and Family LQ 329.

their decision-making processes',[43] especially to acknowledge the due process rights of all private parties in the child protection process.[44] However the judiciary has hitherto shied away from using the ECHR to decide cases which touch on significant public policy questions including the enforcement of duties upon local authorities to provide services to the child which would have a significant economic impact.[45]

B. The Principles of Family Law Relating to Child Protection

This section describes the principles under which the child protection system as out-lined in family law should operate in England and Wales. It then contrasts that system with those in the other comparable jurisdictions. It concludes that the most influential factor on the substantive law in each jurisdiction remains the importance given to ensuring a permanent safe home for a child, rather than links between a child and his biological family.

The principles implicitly if not explicitly adopted by the Children Act 1989, that a child's welfare is linked to the support of the child's family and a partnership between the family and the state, place English law on one side of a dichotomy of child protection policy where it is allied with New Zealand law. On the other side lie child protection policies based on the permanency principle. The permanency principle values a child's right to a safe and stable home over a continuing relationship with her parents. It is the guiding principle of child protection legislation in the United States and is also beginning to take on increasing importance in the interpretation of Canadian legislation. It has increasingly been part of discussion of child protection in Australia, although attempts to alter the child protection legislation in New South Wales to incorporate the value of permanency explicitly, have failed.[46]

1. English law

The Children Act 1989 and its multifarious associated regulations principally dictate the family law response to child abuse in England and Wales. The Act was a 'root and branch' reform of the existing law relating to children between private individuals and between parents and guardians on the one hand and the state on the other. The Act privileges the child's family above other carers and the relationship between parent and child above all. It introduced the concept of continuing 'parental responsibility'[47] towards children, even when those children are cared for by others.

The drafting of the public provisions of the Children Act 1989 was dominated by a need to move away from an emphasis on a 'rescue approach to care' towards a 'preventative or respite approach which maintained family relationships where

---

[43] ibid.   [44] *Re L (Care Assessment: Fair Trial)* [2002] 2 FLR 730 (Fam Div).
[45] Discussed below, section D.1. (b).
[46] P Parkinson 'Child Protection, Permanency Planning and Children's Right to Family Life' (2003) 17 International Journal of Law Policy and the Family 147.   [47] Children Act 1989 (England) s 3.

possible'.[48] Thus the Act trusts the child's biological parents to be the primary mechanism for ensuring a child's well-being in the future, rather than the state. State intervention in a family's childcare arrangements is not justified under the Act on the grounds that a child could be brought up in a better way. Provided that the child is not suffering, or likely to suffer, harm in comparison to his peers, state involvement should be limited to the provision of *universal* services such as health visiting and education.

Even when the child is found to be suffering some harm any decision-maker in family law proceedings should weigh the harm which she is suffering against the harm which she could suffer if removed from everything which she knows and placed with alternative carers, particularly beleaguered state care.[49] It is only when the welfare of the child dictates it that a residence order may be granted to a private individual.[50] Furthermore it is only when the harm to the child is found to be significant that a care order may be granted. When a care order is granted a local authority will share parental responsibility with the parents.[51]

However unlike other jurisdictions, most notably in Canada, Australia, and New Zealand, the Children Act 1989 does not contain a statement of these and other guiding principles in the preamble. Instead the principles of the Children Act 1989 may be gleaned from the Act itself. Some of these principles have been stated specifically in the statute, but others have to be interpreted 'between the lines' of the statute as drafted.

(a) The welfare principle

The Children Act 1989 is constructed on the utilitarian principle of the goal of promotion of the welfare of the child. The Children Act 1989 s 1(1)(a) provides that when the court determines any question with respect to the upbringing of the child, the welfare of the child shall be the court's paramount consideration. The principle itself establishes that the interests of the child in crucial decision-making should take precedence over the interests of everyone else, including her parents. This does not mean that the wishes of the child will take precedence over the court's views of what is in her best interests, rather it is that the wishes and interests of the child's parents, other family members, or friends should not supersede those of the child.

In cases which concern alleged child abuse this 'paramountcy principle' applies to a decision to make a court order:

- giving a party parental responsibility for a child (parental responsibility orders, s 4, residence orders s 8 and care orders s 31(2));
- giving a party power to determine where a child shall live (residence orders s 8 and care orders s 31(2));

---

[48] R Hughes from the Department of Health quoted in M Adcock 'Significant Harm: Implications for the Exercise of Statutory Responsibilities' in M Adcock, R White and A Hollows (eds) *Significant Harm* (Significant Publications, Croydon 1991) 11; House of Commons *Second Report from the Social Services Committee (Session 1983–1984) Children in Care* (HMSO, London 1984) [16].

[49] *Re H (a Minor)(Custody)(Interim Care and Control)* [1991] FCR 736 (CA), 745C (Balcombe LJ).

[50] Children Act 1989 (England) s 1(1)(3) and (4) and s 8. [51] ibid s 31(2).

- appointing a supervisor to 'advise, assist and befriend' a child (supervision order s 31(2));
- determining contact between the child and another person (contact orders s 8 and contact arrangements when a care order is in place s 34);
- determining 'a specific question which has arisen or may arise in connection with any aspect of parental responsibility for a child' (specific issue order, s 8);
- preventing a parent from taking such steps in meeting his parental responsibility as are specified in the order without the consent of the court (prohibited steps order, s 8).

The paramountcy principle also applies to the discharge of a care order[52] and to any granting of leave to a local authority to withdraw their application for a care order.[53]

The welfare of the child need not be the courts' paramount consideration when making other court orders which will not affect the child's upbringing. In cases relating to child protection these would include court orders:

- to protect a child in an emergency (emergency protection order s 44 and s 44(a));
- to facilitate assessments of the child (child assessment order s 43 and under an interim care or supervision order s 38(6));
- to determine where a child will live temporarily (interim care order s 38 and s 38A).

Thus the welfare of the child should be paramount in the decision to make a care or supervision order following the satisfaction of the threshold test, but need not be the paramount consideration in an assessment of the sufficiency of the evidence that a child is suffering, or likely to suffer, significant harm (the threshold test) that necessarily precedes the making of either order, although it often is. In addition, the welfare of the child does not have to be the paramount consideration in decisions made by parties other than the court. The decisions of the local authority about whether to offer services to a child in need, for example, do not have to be driven by the welfare principle.[54] It is however used in a much wider context within child protection work, for example the police may use it as part of a decision to prosecute.[55]

The existence of the principle demonstrates clearly that family law is very different from other areas of the law under discussion in this book, criminal and tort, where the main aim is to establish blame. In one of the reported decisions arising out of the Cleveland crisis, Hollis J stated that it should be remembered that 'no person is on trial here, not the parents, nor anyone connected with the family or children'.[56] However the stakes remain high in all cases: a child may stand to lose some or all of the contact she has with one or both of her parents and her extended family; parents may have to share their parental responsibility with the local authority or another carer. There

---

[52] *Re T and E (Proceedings: Conflicting Interests)* [1995] 1 FLR 581 (Fam Div).
[53] *Southwark London Borough v B* [1993] 2 FLR 559 (CA).
[54] *Re M (a Minor) (Secure Accommodation Order)* [1995] 1 FLR 418 (CA).
[55] C Keenan and L Maitland ' "There Ought to Be a Law Against It": Police Evaluation of the Efficacy of Prosecution in a Case of Child Abuse' [1999] Child and Family LQ 397.
[56] *Cleveland CC v A; Cleveland CC v B* [1988] FCR 593 (Fam Div), 598.

ional concerns when a case is brought because of suspicions of child abuse.
g that a child has been abused, or is likely to be, carries blame and stigma,
ough its role is as a base for future decisions on the care of the child, and not
f her carers. The courts have recognized these concerns implicitly in framing
their judgments. Although these considerations do not dominate, they temper and in
some cases significantly influence judicial decision-making.

(b) A child/parent relationship is fundamental and lifelong

Secondly, the Children Act 1989 establishes that a parent's relationship with the
child is that of nurturer rather than owner. It is clear that a child is not seen as a
possession that a parent has a right to control. The Act talks instead of 'parental
responsibility' towards the child. Parental responsibility is defined as 'all the rights,
duties, powers, responsibilities and authority which a parent has in relation to a child
and his property'.[57] Parental responsibility is acquired automatically by those parents considered in law to have made an undertaking to exercise it. This means that
when a child's parents are married to each other, both parents will acquire parental
responsibility for her.[58] However when a child's parents are not married to each
other, only the child's mother acquires parental responsibility automatically,[59] and
the father must demonstrate his willingness to exercise parental responsibility in some
way.[60] The father will acquire parental responsibility if his name is placed on the
child's birth certificate at registration[61] or he may enter into an agreement with the
mother,[62] or he may acquire it by court order.[63] A parental responsibility order may
be granted by a court convinced that the father has shown sufficient commitment to
the child.[64]

The relationship between the parent and the child is expected to be lifelong. Parental
responsibility may normally only be extinguished by adoption or death.[65] In cases
when a child is found to be suffering from a low standard of health or development,
or is likely to do so, Children Act 1989 Part III creates a duty on the local authority to
support those children and their families, by offering a range of services.[66] Children
Act 1989 s 17 creates a duty on local authorities to promote the upbringing of children
within their family, so far as it is consistent with the need to safeguard and promote
their welfare.[67]

---

[57] Children Act 1989 (England) s 3(1).   [58] ibid s 2(1).   [59] ibid s 2(2)(a).
[60] ibid s 2(2)(b).

[61] ibid s 4 (1), as amended by the Adoption and Children Act 2002 (England) s 111. The provision is
not retrospective, although a child's birth may be re-registered under the Births and Deaths Registration
Act 1953 (England).   [62] Children Act (n 57) s 4(1)(b).

[63] ibid s 4(1)(a).

[64] *Re H (Minors) (Adoption: putative father's rights)(No 3)* [1991] 2 All ER 18 (CA) 189; *Re C (Minors)*
[1992] 2 All ER 86 (CA), 93.

[65] Although a father who has acquired parental responsibility via a parental responsibility agreement or
order may lose it on application to the court, Children Act 1989 (England) s 4(3) and (4).

[66] See also Children Act 1989 (England) sch 2. These provisions are discussed later in this chapter.
[67] ibid s 17(1).

Parental responsibility will not be extinguished by a judicial finding tha' has suffered significant harm as a result of abuse. It will continue to exist when a cɪ.. is looked after by the local authority, although if a care order is in place this 'parental responsibility' is shared with the local authority.[68] The Act sets up an expectation that a 'looked after'[69] child will have contact with her parents[70] and that her parents will be informed of what is happening and their views considered in decision making.[71]

(c) Partnership between parent and state

A fundamental goal of the Children Act 1989 was to establish a partnership between a child's family and the state in which the family feels able to ask for help and the local authority can give assistance which is relevant to the child and her family's needs. The aim is to respect the value of families and to strengthen them. As the then Lord Chancellor, Lord Mackay, explained before the Children Act 1989 came into force: 'the integrity and independence of the family is the basic building block of a free and democratic society and the need to defend it should be clearly perceivable in law'.[72] However this goal was not crystallized as a defined aim of the legislation. As Barton and Douglas have noted, the word 'partnership' does not appear in the Act, nor is the principle explained in any accompanying guidance, and it may be subject to a number of interpretations.[73]

The later *Every Child Matters* initiative does appear to be a promising attempt to move beyond rhetoric towards real attempts to encourage participation between parents and service providers. This is particularly in relation to the provision of services, such as *Sure Start* aimed at the prevention of impairment of children's health and development. The evaluations of the implementation of the *Sure Start* programme and Children's Trusts detail efforts to engage with parents who need services and ensure their contribution to the development of those services. This has included the use of informal 'fun days' to provide a first contact with service providers, parent forums to oversee and comment on the development of the programme and parental involvement in the monitoring of schemes although this latter involvement has hitherto been more limited.[74] Furthermore the aspiration of the Green Paper *Care Matters: Transforming the Lives of Children and Young People in Care* published in 2006 is to gear services towards an individual child's needs, and to ensure that services are delivered in a way that a child's family feel comfortable with.[75]

The equality of the partnership possible between large professional organisations and parents who have little experience of the system or who are suffering multiple

---

[68] ibid s 33(3).

[69] This is defined in Children Act 1989 (England) s22(1) as any child in the care of the local authority or provided with accommodation by them under Children Act 1989 (England) s 20.

[70] ibid s 34.   [71] ibid s 22 (4) and (5).

[72] Lord Mackay 'Perceptions of the Children Bill and Beyond' [1989] 139 NLJ 505, 507.

[73] C Barton and G Douglas *Law and Parenthood* (Butterworths, London 1995) 291.

[74] Institute for the Study of Children, Families and Social Issues, Birkbeck, University of London *Implementing Sure Start Programmes: an In-depth Study* (2005) <http://www.surestart.gov.uk/_doc/P0001450.pdf> (accessed 9 October 2006), 10 and Chapter 2.

[75] HM Government *Care Matters* (n 27) [2.6].

hardships, remains questionable. Legislative rhetoric is certainly not enough in this context to achieve the required goals. Legislation must also encourage practice which makes a child's family a meaningful part of the process. The difficulty then becomes the avoidance of the conflation of the child's interests with those of the child's parents in child protection cases.

(d) The state may only intervene once statutorily defined thresholds have been crossed

The architects of the 1989 Act were clear that a child should not be taken into the care of the state simply because of a general feeling that the state might be able to do better. They did not envisage that the business of the state is to remove children from parents considered feckless, so that they could be brought up by 'decent' people, as the Poor Laws had aimed.[76] The principle governing the Act was stated in a case preceding it, *Re KD*, where Lord Oliver stated that:

it matters not whether the parent is wise or foolish, rich or poor, educated or illiterate, provided the child's moral or physical health are not endangered. Public authorities cannot improve on nature.[77]

A court order which interferes, to a lesser or greater extent, with the way in which a child is brought up, may be granted under the Children Act 1989, when there is evidence that a child is suffering or likely to suffer *significant* harm. The standard to which that harm must be proved is dependent upon the severity of the order which may be granted. 'State intervention is a last resort . . . But when it is necessary our communal responsibility to protect children must outweigh everything.'[78]

(e) Delay in decision making is bad for the child and should be avoided

The principle that any court decision about a child's upbringing should be made as expeditiously as possible is enshrined in statute. The Children Act 1989 s 1(2) states that:

in any proceedings in which any question with respect to the upbringing of a child arises, the court shall have regard to the general principle that any delay in determining the question is likely to prejudice the welfare of the child.

This aim of the Children Act 1989 has never been realized. Delay is undoubtedly an enormous problem, existing across all levels of courts and across all areas of England and Wales. When the Children Act 1989 was implemented in October 1991, it was expected that cases would be completed within 12 weeks. By 2003, the National Society for the Prevention of Cruelty to Children (NSPCC) *Review of Legislation Relating to Family Proceedings* found that Manchester courts aimed for a

---

[76] See for example Poor Law Act 1899 (England) s 1 and the comment in S Cretney *Family Law* (4th edn Sweet & Maxwell, London 2000) 266. For a fuller history see R Dingwall, JM Eekelaar and T Murray 'Childhood as a Social Problem: A Survey of the History of Legal Regulation' (1984) 11(2) J of Law and Society 207.   [77] *Re KD* [1988] AC 806 (HL) 813.

[78] *Second Report from the Social Services Committee* (n 48) [16].

40-week hearing period, the High Court in London had an 11-month waiting list for hearings, and in one home county proceedings took up to 2 years, irrespective of the youth of the child at the time of the proceedings.[79] The Lord Chancellor's Department *Scoping Study on Delay in Children Act Cases* in 2002, concluded that the system, rather than the law, needed reform. To that end the now reconstituted Lord Chancellor's Department, the Department for Constitutional Affairs, contained some proposals for the reduction of delay in these cases in its new Family Justice Strategy 2003. These included the increased use of magistrates' Family Proceedings Courts. The Lord Chancellor's Select Committee Inquiry report into Children and Family Court Advisory and Support Service (CAFCASS) recommended further changes to enable CAFCASS to play its central role in cutting down delay in appointing guardians for children. This formed the background to *The Protocol for Judicial Case Management in Public Law Children Act Cases*. The authors of the protocol aimed to reduce delay by better planning and organization—setting out a timetable for cases to try to limit proceedings to 40 weeks, with set time limits for the 6 identifiable stages of the proceedings. The NSPCC review has also endorsed a long-felt need for a dedicated family law court with harmonized proceedings as an important step in the reduction of delay, particularly as the proposed solution of an increased role for the magistrates' court will be practically unsustainable.[80] The pressure on magistrates to meet targets for hearings in criminal proceedings can lead to a marginalization of family cases in the magistrates' courts and compound the delays within the system.[81]

The NSPCC *Review of Legislation Relating to Children in Family Proceedings* concluded that the problem of delay currently 'is effectively preventing the Act from being implemented in anything like the way originally envisaged'.[82] The current delays, in which an average care case takes a year to be decided, compound uncertainty and distress for children, damaging them yet further and making long-term stable solutions for them more difficult to achieve. There is enormous awareness of the problem of delay, with a number of reports being published within the last two years. It remains clear, however, from the number of different recommendations by different bodies, that the level of 'joined up' thinking at a policy level needed to alter this pernicious state of affairs on the ground has not yet been achieved.

(f) A court order is the last resort

The Children Act 1989 establishes a 'no order principle'. A court may only make an order under the Act if it is convinced that to do so 'would be better than making no order at all'.[83] The Act gives the local authority the power to offer services by consent

---

[79] B Essam (Chair) *Review of Legislation Relating to Children in Family Proceedings* (NSPCC, London 2003) 13.   [80] ibid, 14.

[81] 'Family Law—The Protocol For Judicial Case Management In Public Law Children Act Cases' (2003) 10(7) Mags CP 7.   [82] *Review of Legislation Relating to Children in Family Proceedings* (n 79).

[83] Children Act 1989 (England) s 1(5).

under Part III. Within this the local authority may 'look after' the child with the consent of the parents, obviating the need for an order.[84]

The decision on whether to make an order is usually made by a court well aware of the failings of the public childcare system. As Cretney has argued, the courts do not 'exaggerate the contribution which the law can make to child care [as] . . . recent inquiries have demonstrated only too vividly the failings of the public care service'.[85] If it is possible for the child to be cared for by his own family the courts will consider this possibility very seriously. Howard has bluntly stated the position that the courts may find themselves in—'if the choice is a bit of neglect, lack of stimulation and the occasional bruised eye . . . or the educational sterility of a children's home and the risk of "pindown" or sexual abuse, the choice is easily made'.[86]

However the court may still consider that it is in the child's best interests for an order to be made. This is because the local authority has very limited resources and court-ordered action, which is compulsory, will take precedence over action which the local authority can choose to take:

In crude terms a local authority may take the view that in such circumstances a care order will result in, say £5,000 of resources being put in; a supervision order will be worth £2,000; and 'no order' will mean that the case is unallocated and no resources put in.[87]

Whilst the local authority has the power to offer services under Children Act 1989 Part III, their limited s 17 budget means that the delivery of such services is far from automatic when no order is made.

2. Principles of child protection law in the United States

Permanency planning in childcare may mean several things: protection within the child's home, long-term foster placement with relatives, friends, or other carers, or termination of parental rights and adoption. In the United States adoption has been increasingly advocated as the best way to ensure permanence for children. The policy in the United States remains based on a language of rights; however the rights are framed differently from other jurisdictions. Current legislative thought in the United States is built around a perceived dichotomy of rights. The rights of a child to a permanent family and the rights of the parents to familial preservation are viewed as contrary and conflicting.[88] The consideration that children may also have a right to live with their own biological family has barely entered upon the American legislative radar.

The overall family law principles governing child protection work in the United States are contained in the Federal Adoption and Safe Families Act (ASFA) 1997. The ASFA supplanted previous Federal policy, embodied in the Adoption, Assistance and

---

[84] ibid s 20.   [85] Cretney (n 76) 268–269.
[86] H Howard 'Conspiracy to Cause Delay' (1998) 11(1) Public Child Law Bulletin 1.
[87] H Howard 'Care Plans and Cash Restraints' (1998) 12(5) Public Child Law Bulletin 1.
[88] Parkinson (n 46) 147, 148.

Child Welfare Act 1980 (AACWA).[89] The two Acts may be characterized using Fox-Harding's ideal types of childcare policy. While the AACWA was primarily geared towards 'defence of the birth family', creating mechanisms to encourage familial support and eventual reunification, the ASFA represented a sharp and decisive move towards 'state paternalism':[90]

The message conveyed by newspaper articles about ASFA and by the testimony during ASFA's hearings . . . is clear: the reunification with biological families is unsafe, risky, and dangerous and adoption is safer and better for children. Virtually every mention of biological families in the testimony was negative. When biological families were mentioned, usually it was a family that killed or severely injured their child. Most spoke of adoptive homes as loving, safe, and stable and rarely acknowledged the possibility that such homes could also be with the biological family. In other words, we can find permanence and safety only in the form of adoption. The family preservation mandate and reasonable efforts language remains a part of the law, but the rhetoric surrounding the passage of the ASFA contradicts this language.[91]

Thus the dominant current principle of Federal child protection policy which, as it carries Federal funding with it, is also the dominant principle of much of State policy in child protection, focuses upon clear identification of abuse and once this has been identified, upon planning for a child's permanent home, probably with adoptive parents. The critics of this view of child welfare in the United States have questioned whether this is not in fact social engineering by another route. Guggenheim[92] in his critique of the work of Bartholet[93](one of the advocates of 'permanency' within the United States), has argued:

The children who are currently removed from their biological families—and those who would likely be removed under Bartholet's expansive vision—are disproportionately poor and non-white. Most of the individuals who seek to adopt children are upper-class and white.

As Guggenheim has argued, the well-meaning nature of the principle should not blind critics to its effects. To compare the current American policy with the principle of 'good enough parenting' which has been supported in England and Wales, the danger of the US policy is that it *may* matter whether the parent is 'wise or foolish, rich or poor, educated or illiterate'[94] in child protection decisions under this policy.

3. Principles of child protection law in Canada

Each jurisdiction in Canada has a child welfare statute. Unlike England, each of these Acts starts with a statement of general principles to guide decision-making

---

[89] Adoption, Assistance and Child Welfare Act 1980 94 Stat 500 (1980).

[90] Fox-Harding (n 11).

[91] D Roberts 'Access to Justice: Poverty, Race, and New Directions in Child Welfare Policy' (1999) 1 Wash U J L & Pol 63, 74–75.

[92] M Guggenheim 'Somebody's Children: Sustaining the Family's Place in Child Welfare Policy' (2000) 113 Harv L Rev 1716, 1723.

[93] E Bartholet *Nobody's Children: Abuse and Neglect, Foster Drift, and the Adoption Alternative* (Beacon Press, Boston 1999).

[94] Taken from Lord Oliver's speech in *Re KD* [1988] AC 806 (HL) 813 (n 77).

under the statute. All of the statutes focus on a paramount need for children to be protected from abuse or ill-treatment. Like New Zealand, the guiding principles in each Canadian statute identify the child's biological family as the primary guardians of a child's well-being and define the role of the state to be the preservation and support of family autonomy where possible. The principles outlined in the Children Family and Community Service Act 1996 in British Columbia are typical. They state:

Guiding principles

2 This Act must be interpreted and administered so that the safety and well-being of children are the paramount considerations and in accordance with the following principles:

(a) children are entitled to be protected from abuse, neglect and harm or threat of harm;
(b) a family is the preferred environment for the care and upbringing of children and the responsibility for the protection of children rests primarily with the parents;
(c) if, with available support services, a family can provide a safe and nurturing environment for a child, support services should be provided;
(d) the child's views should be taken into account when decisions relating to a child are made;
(e) kinship ties and a child's attachment to the extended family should be preserved if possible;
(f) the cultural identity of aboriginal children should be preserved;
(g) decisions relating to children should be made and implemented in a timely manner.[95]

In the 1970s and 1980s child welfare practice reflected the principles of the legislation. Children would remain at home if they were assessed to be at low risk of abuse. There was increasing use of voluntary provisions and an enormous decrease in court orders. For example in Ontario, the number of children in care fell by 80 per cent from 1971 to 1988, despite a 160 per cent increase in the number of children receiving welfare services.[96]

However while the stated principles of the legislation still point clearly towards a policy of familial preservation and link this policy with the best interests of children, commentators have noted a distinct change in Canadian law and practice towards a more interventionist approach.[97] Again, the main impetus for change has been a number of tragic deaths of children, often where the children were known to the authorities but were not removed from parental care.[98] The interventionist approach in Canada, like the United States, has pitted a child's right to protection against familial rights to integrity and support. There has been increased impetus to intervene and remove children. Jurisdictions have made changes to their legislation to broaden the threshold for a judicial finding that a child is 'in need of care and protection' which

---

[95] Child, Family and Community Service Act 1996 (British Columbia) c 46.

[96] N Bala 'Reforming Ontario's Child and Family Services Act: Is the Pendulum Swinging Back Too Far?' (1999–2000) 17 Can Fam LQ 121, 132.

[97] D Blenner Hassett '*KLW* and Warrantless Child Apprehensions: Sanctioning Gross Intrusions into Private Spheres' (2004) 67 Sask L Rev 161.

[98] Judge T Gove (Commissioner) *Matthew's Story: The Inquiry into Child Protection in British Columbia* (Vancouver, British Columbia 1995) <http://www.qp.gov.bc.ca/gove/govevol1_01.htm> (accessed 1 July 2006).

in Canada places a child into care.[99] Ontario also amended its legislation to prioritize child safety over all other competing aims and principles of the Act, making the paramount purpose of the Child and Family Services Act to serve the 'best interests, protection and well-being of children'.[100] There have also been changes to the time children may spend in care before they are freed for adoption. This change in political emphasis has resulted in a large increase in the number of children in care in Canada. [101]

However, King and others[102] have detected a move away from a policy of permanence in some provinces, most notably British Columbia. British Columbia announced a 'new' policy of minimum intervention in families, and support for children within their biological families if possible, and supported this with legislative change. King and others attribute this change to the realization by policy makers of the level of 'moral and fiscal responsibility' needed to support the increasing number of children being taken into care.

4. Principles of child protection law in Australia

Under the Commonwealth constitution, neither the Commonwealth nor the States have exclusive power to legislate in family law matters relating to children. In practice, custody and guardianship arrangements between private individuals are determined by Commonwealth law[103] and Commonwealth courts, as all the States except Western Australia[104] have referred their judicial powers in relation to custody and guardianship to the courts.[105] Child protection by state bodies issues remain within the legislative power of the States.[106] While there are similarities between the statutes adopted by each State or Territory, it is difficult to discern a single 'Australian approach' to child protection law from which lessons may be learnt. Indeed this has been a major criticism of Australian child protection law which has been recently voiced by the Australian Senate. Many States adopt a list of principles on which child protection decisions should be made.[107] Some States adopt a paramountcy principle which is similar to

---

[99] C Farris-Manning and M Zandstra *Children in Care in Canada—A Summary of Current Issues and Trends with Recommendations for Future Research* (Child Welfare League of Canada, Ottawa 2004) 6.

[100] Child and Family Services Act 1990 (Ontario) s 1(1).

[101] Farris-Manning and Zandstra (n 99) 3.

[102] King and others *Child Protection in Ontario Past, Present and Future* (University of Western Ontario, London CA 2003).

[103] Family Law Act 1975 (Commonwealth of Australia), as amended by Family Law Reform Act 1995 (Commonwealth of Australia).

[104] Following the establishment of the Family Court of Western Australia, and the enactment of State laws that are, in relevant ways, identical to the provisions of the Family Law Act (Commonwealth of Australia), law in Western Australia as implemented is very similar to the Family Law Act 1975 (Commonwealth of Australia); R Chisholm 'The paramount consideration: Children's interests in Family Law' (2002) 16 Austr JFL 9, 13.

[105] Senate of Australia, Community Affairs References Committee *Protecting Vulnerable Children: A National Challenge; Second Report on Inquiry into Children in Institutional or Out-Of-Home Care* (March 2005) [2.6] [2.17]–[2.22].

[106] B Fehlberg and F Kelly 'Jurisdictional Overlaps Between the Family Division of the Children's Court of Victoria and the Family Court of Australia' (2000) AJFL LEXIS 13.

[107] Children and Young Persons Act 1989 (Victoria) does not.

England that the welfare of the child should be paramount in decision-making.[108] Some other States have adopted the principle that a child's safety should be the decision-makers' paramount concern.[109] Interestingly, some statutes have created the principle of 'least intrusive intervention' in articulating the principles on which child protection decisions should be made. It is useful to note that while this principle does appear in the Australian Capital Territory[110] and New South Wales[111] statutes as a general principle, in three other jurisdictions, South Australia,[112] Tasmania[113] and Victoria,[114] it is articulated as a number of specific considerations for decision-makers. These considerations, if used, should have the cumulative effect of reducing the disruption in a child's life from any intervention for their protection. An example of such a principle is contained in the Children, Young Persons and Their Families Act 1997 s 8(2)(b), from Tasmania:

Principles to be observed in dealing with children

(b) serious consideration must be given to the desirability of—
  (i) keeping the child within his or her family; and
  (ii) preserving and strengthening family relationships between the child and the child's guardians and other family members, whether or not the child is to reside within his or her family; and
  (iii) not withdrawing the child unnecessarily from the child's familiar environment, culture or neighbourhood; and
  (iv) not interrupting unnecessarily the child's education or employment; and
  (v) preserving and enhancing the child's sense of ethnic, religious or cultural identity, and making decisions and orders that are consistent with ethnic traditions or religious or cultural values; and
  (vi) preserving the child's name; and
  (vii) not subjecting the child to unnecessary, intrusive or repeated assessments; and
(c) the powers, wherever practicable and reasonable, must be exercised in a manner that takes into account the views of all persons concerned with the welfare of the child.[115]

The approach adopted by these five Australian jurisdictions of incorporating a 'least intervention principle' into their child protection statute, is a novel and potentially useful one. First, as expressed in the statute, it avoids an exclusive focus on the traditional fighting ground of child protection—whether children who have been found

[108] Children and Young People Act 1999 (Australian Capital Territory) s 12; Children, Young Persons and their Families Act 1997 (Tasmania) s 8(2)a; Child Protection Act 1999 (Queensland) s 5(1); Community Welfare Act 1983 (Northern Territory) s 9; Children and Community Services Act 2004 (Western Australia) s 7.
[109] Children and Young Persons (Care and Protection) Act 1998 (New South Wales) s 9(a), Children's Protection Act 1993 (Southern Australia) 4(a).
[110] Children and Young People Act 1999 (Australian Capital Territory) s 12(e).
[111] Children and Young Persons (Care and Protection) Act 1998 (New South Wales) s 9(d).
[112] Children's Protection Act 1993 (Southern Australia) s 4(2).
[113] Children, Young Persons and their Families Act 1997 (Tasmania).
[114] Children and Young Persons Act 1989 (Victoria) s 87(1).
[115] Children's Protection Act 1993 (Southern Australia) s 4(2) and Children and Young Persons Act 1989 (Victoria) 1989 s 87(1).

to have been harmed should remain living with their families, or whether the state should have a role in their care. Instead the principle focuses on the life of the child and the child's primary need for continuity and support to maintain his identity at such a difficult time. While the American principle of permanency acknowledges some of the dimensions of a child's need for continuity, the permanency principle has been translated into a territorial fight between the value of care by adoptive compared with birth parents. The second advantage of the principle of 'least intervention' is that it applies to the use of any of the powers under the Acts, not merely the decision about whether to make an order. While the 'no order' principle under Children Act 1989 s 1(5), discussed above, may be interpreted by some to mean that the least intrusive action is preferable in decision-making, it does only refer to the orders which may be made under the Children Act. The principle of 'least intervention' as articulated in the Australian statutes, is closer to the findings and recommendations of the *Cleveland Report*, than to the 'no order' principle of the Children Act 1989, particularly the Report's recognition that children in reporting abuse want the abuse to stop, not their whole life to change immediately and dramatically.[116]

5. Principles of child protection law in New Zealand

New Zealand undertook the same exercise of review and reform of child law at about the same time as England and Wales, but attempts at reform were limited to the relationship of children and their families with the state in public law proceedings, and private proceedings were not subjected to the same 'root and branch' reform and incorporation into a comprehensive statute.[117] The Children, Young Persons and their Families Act 1989 (CYP&F) incorporates all the law and principle in relation to the state's involvement in the protection of children and sets out the principles to be followed by the Youth Justice system.[118]

The CYP&F Act 1989 shares much of the ethos of its English counterpart; however it differs significantly in the way that legislators have attempted to realize the principles on which the Act is based. First, the principles of the CYP&F are clearly stated at the beginning of the statute in ss 4–6 and 13. This is very unlike the Children Act 1989, in which many of the guiding principles are implicit. For example, the principle of partnership between the state and parents under the Children Act 1989 is not explicitly stated at any point in the Act; rather it may be gathered from an interpretation of certain specific provisions and the guidance accompanying the Act. In contrast the CYP&F Act 1989 contains a 'principle of participation'.[119] Under the principle not only children's immediate family, but also their wider family, community and their tribe, if applicable, are expected to participate in decision-making.

---

[116] *Cleveland Report* (n 5) Introduction.
[117] CYP & F Act 1989 (New Zealand), which was described by the then Minister for Social Welfare, Hon M Cullen in his Second Reading Speech as 'the most far reaching changes to our children and young persons legislation since the Child Welfare Act 1925' (47 NZPD10246, 27 April 1989).
[118] CYP & F Act 1989 (New Zealand).   [119] ibid s 5(a).

The principle states:

Subject to section 6 of this Act (welfare and interests of the child are paramount), any Court which, or any person who, exercises any power conferred by or under this Act shall be guided by the principle that, 'wherever possible, a child's or young person's family, whanau[120], hapu[121], iwi[122] and family group should participate in the making of decisions affecting that child or young person, and accordingly that, wherever possible, regard should be had to the views of that family, whanau, hapu, iwi and family group.

The principle is qualified by the phrase, 'wherever possible'. This has been interpreted to mean that the principle might not be promoted in a particular case if it would be clearly against the welfare of the child to do so.[123] However the other principles of the CYP&F Act 1989 underscore the importance placed on the family to ensure the future well-being of children. Actions under the CYP&F Act 1989 should be guided by the principles that:

- 'wherever possible the relationship between a child and young person and his or her family, whanau, hapu, iwi and family group should be maintained and strengthened';[124]

- 'consideration must always be given to how a decision affecting a child or young person will affect the welfare of the child or young person and the stability of that child or young person's family';

- endeavours should be made to obtain the support of—the parents or guardians or other persons having the care of a child or young person and the child or young person himself or herself.

The second difference between the Children Act 1989 in England and the CYP&F Act 1989 in New Zealand lies in the level of legislative commitment towards realizing the ideals of state support for families in crisis and of familial involvement in child protection decision-making. Central to the New Zealand Act is a family-based decision making body, the family group conference. As discussed later in Part III in relation to investigation, the family group conference is made up of a child's wider family. The family hear evidence from professionals involved with the child and then have some private time to put forward proposals for the protection of the child in the future. Social workers and the police are statutorily obliged to give effect to the family's plan, unless the plan is clearly impractical or inconsistent with the terms of the Act.[125] Legislators have underscored the importance of a family group conference by making it a necessary precursor to any court order to protect the child.[126]

---

[120] The wider family group of a Maori child.
[121] The familial community to which a Maori child belongs.
[122] The tribe to which a Maori child belongs.
[123] *Re V* (1991) CYPF (Judge Inglis QC) Interim Judgment (Family Court Napier) cited in D Webb, J Adams, M Heneghan, B Atkin and J Caldwell *Family Law in New Zealand* (8th edn Butterworths, Wellington 1997) 915.   [124] CYP & F Act 1989 (New Zealand) s 5(b).
[125] ibid s 35.
[126] ibid s 18; P Marsh 'Partnership, Child Protection and Family Group Conferences—the New Zealand Children, Young Persons and their Families Act 1989' (1994) 6(3) J of Child Law 109.

C. The Structure of English Family Law Legislation Relating to Child Protection

The Children Act 1989 creates two mechanisms through which a local authority, as the agent of the state given statutory responsibility for the children living in its area, may be involved in safeguarding an abused child or a child at risk of abuse. The first is a voluntary system in which a local authority may offer services to a child and her family. The family may choose to accept or reject these services. The second is a system of orders which may be granted by the court giving a local authority specific powers and responsibilities in relation to the child. These may be granted without the consent of the parents. The voluntary provisions of the Act are contained primarily in Part III and Schedule II. The court orders may be found in Part IV and Part V.

It is important not to overlook or minimize the Children Act 1989 Part III simply because it creates a system of child protection decision-making which is not court-based. Part III should be the heart of the public law parts of the Children Act 1989. The underlying ethos of these sections is that the majority of problems encountered by a family which may potentially damage a child stem from difficulties that could be alleviated by services and support. Such difficulties comprehend poverty, unemployment and poor housing, as well as poor childcare skills. A court order under Part IV should be a last, rather than a first, resort when a child appears to be suffering harm. In fact the local authority has a statutory duty to try to prevent the problems with the child from reaching this stage.[127]

An allegation of child abuse may also be made in contested proceedings between two private parties, for example the child's parents. A court in these circumstances could make one or more of the four orders under the private law provisions of the Act. These orders are all described in s 8 of the Act and are often known as 'section 8 orders'. They are described below. Section 8 orders may also be made in care and supervision proceedings. It is immaterial whether they have been applied for and whether the criteria necessary for the granting of a care or supervision order exist.

There are two thresholds for intervention, each based on a finding of harm, or likely harm, to the child:

- intervention under Part III is justified when a child is 'in need', that is where a child's health and development has failed to reach a reasonable standard, or will do so in the future, or he is disabled; or
- intervention under Parts IV and V is justified when a child 'is suffering or likely to suffer significant harm'.

A finding that a child is 'in need' by a local authority simply allows the authority to offer services to the child's family under Part III, but it does not oblige his family to accept any court offer. It is only when the harm to the child is considered to be

---

[127] Children Act 1989 (England) Sch 2 s 7(i)(a).

substantial or likely to be so, that a court order may be made and the family is expected by law to accept services for the child, or in the case of a care order to share their parental rights and duties with the local authority.

In this context it is important to note that the boundaries of child protection work are changing following the launch of the *Every Child Matters* initiative and the accompanying guidance and legislation. This initiative has been described as a 'whole system approach to the needs of children'.[128] The Children Act 2004 and the accompanying guidance shift the threshold for state intervention in family life, to work 'safeguarding' the 'well being' of children, encouraging earlier and more wide-ranging state involvement.[129] The threshold for 'safeguarding' the 'well being' of children, appears to be the same as the threshold for Children Act 1989 Part III, but it is in fact more wide-ranging. The terms were first coined in the Children Act 1989 s 17 (the threshold provision for Part III services) in relation to decisions about the provision of services for children in need. However it was used in a wider context by Sir William Utting in his 1997 report *People Like Us*.[130] He defined safeguarding as a distinct activity involving 'taking proactive steps to keep children safe' that incorporates more conventional child protection responses. However the concept was not fully defined at the time of the review and it was acknowledged as such. The concept was utilized with renewed vigour following the damning inquiry into the death of Victoria Climbié.[131] The aim was to find a concept which would convince professionals that a child's problems did not belong to some other professional but were within their duties to act' and one that would ensure coordinated work.[132] Under the statutory guidance issued under Children Act 2004 s 11 which resulted from the Green Paper, 'safeguarding' a child's 'well being' is now defined as:

protecting children from maltreatment; preventing impairment of children's health or development;[133] and ensuring that children are growing up in circumstances consistent with the provision of safe and effective care; and undertaking that role so as to enable those children to have optimum life chances and to enter adulthood successfully.[134]

This widens the areas of a child's life which may legitimately be regarded as 'the state's business' in the protection of children and its effect on the use of the child protection provisions under the Children Act 1989 are discussed below.

From early in the implementation of the Children Act 1989 there has been considerable discussion about a perceived overuse of the Parts IV and V provisions of the Act. The argument has been made that the needs of many more children where

---

[128] HM Government *Care Matters* (n 27) [2.5].   [129] See Chapter 5 Section B.1.

[130] Sir William Utting *People Like Us—The Report of the Review of Safeguards of Children Living Away from Home* (HM Stationery Office, London 1997).

[131] Lord Laming (Chair) *Victoria Climbié Inquiry.* (Cm 5730, 2003).

[132] ibid [17.92] and [17.93]

[133] As defined in the Children Act 1989 s 31(9), health means 'physical or mental health' and development means 'physical, intellectual, emotional, social or behavioural development'.

[134] HM Government *Statutory Guidance on Making Arrangements to Safeguard and Promote the Welfare of Children under s 11 Children Act 2004* (HM Stationery Office, London 2005) [2.8].

there are abuse or neglect concerns would be responded to better if they were categorized as a child in need rather than a child at risk of significant harm. In 1995 the first large-scale studies funded by the Department of Health on the operation of the child protection provisions of the Children Act were published. They were also synthesized into *Child Protection: Messages from Research*,[135] which concluded that the child protection system needed to be rebalanced towards an increase in the use of Part III services. While the report acknowledged that there was a proportion of cases where the abuse was extreme and could not be reduced by family support alone, in the majority of cases at the lower end of the spectrum children should be defined as being 'in need' and for those needs to be assessed and responded to, rather than for the child to be defined as having been abused or at risk of abuse and for allegations of specific incidents of abuse to be investigated to determine whether they could be proved or not proved. The danger of the latter approach is an obvious one: all the money and resources on a child's case focus on the investigation of specific allegations of abuse, and if these are not found to be proved to a requisite standard the child may receive no help or support at all. *Messages from Research* received large-scale government support. The implication of this support was that all that was needed to make the refocus a reality was a change in front line attitudes and a refocus on inquiries into a child's needs rather than investigations into whether the child has suffered significant harm or is likely to do so. In response to *Messages from Research* and work completed by the Audit Commission the Department of Health produced a framework for the assessment of children's needs to encourage this refocus. However the very limited social services budgets coupled with an increasing societal need to protect children from the risk of abuse has ensured that there has not been a wholehearted political impetus towards this refocus which would ensure an increase in social services.

However the requirements to realize even the limited aspirations of Part III of the Act were actually much more fundamental. The majority of children 'in need' become so having been born into poverty and deprivation. There needed to be a shift away from the growing focus on the protection of children from specific incidents of abuse, back towards child welfare. In the next section we examine the current law and procedures in relation to the assessment of need and the provision of services under Part III. We argue that the successful implementation of Part III of the Act has been continually dogged by a lack of resources to provide the services suggested in the Act and that the law is complicit in this lack of provision, having been drafted and interpreted to ensure that local authorities are under no duty to provide services, even when the same authority has assessed that they are needed. We consider whether the *Every Child Matters* initiative, launched in 2003 but currently gaining momentum, may be the mechanism which places s 17 at the heart of the family law response to child welfare problems.

---

[135] Department of Health *Child Protection: Messages from Research* (Studies in Child Protection, HMSO, London 1995).

D. Offering Services to Children

1. Offering services to children in England and Wales

As described above, the Children Act 1989 Part III allows local authorities to offer services to children who are in need of them and to help them to continue to live with their families.

(a) Defining 'in need'

A child is defined by statute[136] as being 'in need' if—

(a) he is unlikely to achieve or maintain, or to have the opportunity of achieving or maintaining, a reasonable standard of health or development without the provision for him of services by a local authority under this Part [III];

(b) his health or development is likely to be significantly impaired, or further impaired, without the provision for him of such services; or

(c) he is disabled.[137]

The term 'health' is defined in the statute as 'physical or mental health' and 'development' as 'physical, intellectual, emotional, social or behavioural development'.[138] A child is defined as disabled under the Act if 'he is blind, deaf or dumb, suffers from mental disorder of any kind or is substantially or permanently handicapped by illness or congenital deformity or any other disability as may be prescribed'.[139]

An assessment should examine the needs of a child in accordance with his circumstances, age, sex, race, religion, culture, and language as well as the capacity of those caring for the child to meet those needs. It may be that the parenting which the child receives threatens her wellbeing.[140] Those conducting assessments are expected to be able to identify strengths in the care of the child by her family and to develop a cooperative working relationship with the child and her family. However the final focus of any assessment must be on the child's needs. For example it has been held that a local authority did not fulfil the requirements of Children Act 1989 s 17 when it considered a child's need for rehousing with that of his family, as this failed to acknowledge that a child may have different and separate needs from his immediate family.[141]

The local authority determines whether a child has suffered or is likely to suffer this level of harm and its decision is not subject to challenge.[142] However, the local authority's failure to take reasonable steps to assess the needs of a child who appears to be 'in need' is open to challenge and may result in a court order mandating an assessment.

---

[136] Children Act 1989 (England) s 17(1).   [137] ibid s 17(10).   [138] ibid s 17(11).

[139] ibid.

[140] Department of Health *The Children Act 1989 Guidance and Regulations Volume 2* (HMSO, London 1991) 6 [2.5].

[141] *R v Tower Hamlets London Borough Council, ex parte Bradford* [1998] 1 FCR 629 (QBD) (Kay J).

[142] *Re J (Specific Issue Order: Leave to Apply)* [1995] 1 FLR 669 (Fam Div).

In *R (on the application of AB and SB) v Nottinghamshire CC*[143] Richards J ordered
that the local authority conduct a full assessment of a child's needs in accordance with
the framework for the assessment of children in need.

From a national survey of local authorities across England the Department of Education and Skills estimated that 385,900 children were categorized by local authorities
as being 'in need' in a snapshot week in February 2005.[144] There was activity or
expenditure on behalf of 234,700 of these children in that week, of these the largest
proportion, (86,900 (37 per cent)) were children deemed to be 'in need' because of
concerns about child abuse or neglect. While there is concern from research on disabled children that some are not characterized as being 'in need' when they should
be,[145] it is fair to conclude that a substantial proportion of the work undertaken by
social workers in relation to children 'in need' relates to concerns about child abuse
and neglect.[146]

(b) Services which may be offered under Part III

The services which a local authority may offer are contained in the Children Act 1989
Part III and Schedule II. Services may not only be offered to the child who is 'in need',
but also to any other member of the child's family, 'if it is provided with a view to
safeguarding or promoting the child's welfare'.[147] The type of services which a local
authority may offer include

- day care for children in need who are under five and not yet attending school;[148]

- care and supervised activities outside school hours or during school holidays for
  children in need who do attend school;[149]

- assistance in kind, for example furniture or clothing,[150] a home help,[151] or transport to enable the family to take advantage of other services offered by the local
  authority.[152] In some circumstances the help provided by the local authority may
  include a cash payment;[153]

- advice, guidance and counselling for both the child and other members of her
  family, and family centres which the child or those caring for him may attend for
  this advice or to take part in 'occupational, social, cultural or recreational activities';

- the local authority should also offer to provide accommodation to a child in need
  if he has no one who has parental responsibility for him or he has been lost or
  abandoned. Accommodation should also be offered to a child in need whose carer

---

[143] [2001] EWHC (Admin) 235.

[144] Department for Education and Skills *Children in Need in England; Results of a Survey of Activity
and Expenditure as Reported by Local Authority Social Services' Children and Families Teams for a Survey week
in February 2005: Local Authority Tables and Further National Analysis* (National Statistics Volume Issue
Number vweb02–2006) [Table 5].

[145] J Morris *Still Missing? Vol 2 Disabled Children and the Children Act* (Who Cares? Trust, London
1998).

[146] Disabled children make up the second largest proportion of 'children in need' at 13 per cent
(29,700) (n 144).   [147] Children Act 1989 (England).

[148] ibid s 18(1).   [149] ibid s 18(5).   [150] ibid s 17(6).   [151] ibid Sch 2 s 8(c).
[152] ibid Sch 2 s 8(d).   [153] ibid s 17(6).

is prevented from looking after him, either permanently or temporarily, for whatever reason.[154]

Local authorities have interpreted the provisions of Children Act 1989 s 17 to include a power to provide help so that a child can continue to live with his parents in different accommodation. They have based this power upon the statutory expectation in s 17 that the local authority should act to promote the upbringing of children with their parents and a statutory duty on the local authority looking after a child to make arrangements for him to live with a parent, someone with parental responsibility or a relative, friend or other person connected with him (s 23(6)).[155] Local authorities have used the power in s 17(6) to give assistance in kind or in cash to a child in need, to include a down payment and the first month's rent to provide a child with accommodation with her family. This interpretation has been upheld by the Court of Appeal.[156] Assistance in kind in s 17(6) has also been interpreted to mean the provision of housing.[157] This interpretation was challenged successfully in the Court of Appeal by the local authority in *A v Lambeth London Borough Council*.[158] In response the government promised to amend the Children Act 1989 s 17(6) to make it clear that accommodation for the child and his family may be provided under the section. The section was amended by the Adoption and Children Act 2002 (England) s 117 to include accommodation.

It is not the legislation which places any real limitations on the range of services which may be offered to children considered to be 'in need'; it is resources. The framework of the Children Act 1989 was created without the resources to support such a system. As Wattam, Parton and Thorpe[159] have argued powerfully, s 17 attempts to address harm to children caused by large-scale social problems—poverty, long term unemployment and relationship problems. However the funding available lies on the minimal scale. While the powers under Part III are used extensively,[160] in many cases the local authority has not the money or other resources to be able to provide the level of help which an assessment has found the child needs:

Behind the legal questions . . . is the seemingly intractable problem of local authorities' lack of resources. Local authorities discharge a wide range of functions, from education to housing, upkeep of roads to disposal of waste. All these activities call for money, of which there is never enough to go round. Often there is also a shortage, sometimes acute, of other resources such as trained staff.[161]

In a number of cases the parents or guardians of children have applied to the court for a judicial review of the local authority's decision not to offer services, or more accurately a

---

[154] ibid s 20(1).   [155] *R v London Borough of Tower Hamlets ex p Byas* (1993) 25 HLR 105 (QBD).
[156] *R v Ealing Borough Council ex p C* (1999) 3 CCLR 122 (CA) (Judge LJ).
[157] *Foran v London Borough of Barnet* (QBD 20 October 1998).   [158] [2001] EWCA Civ 1624.
[159] C Wattam, N Parton and D Thorpe *Child Protection Risk and the Moral Order* (Macmillan, Basingstoke 1997) Conclusion.
[160] J Masson 'The Impact of the Adoption and Children Act 2000—Part 2—The Provision of Services for Children and Families' (2003) 33 Fam LJ 644.
[161] *R v London Borough of Barnet ex p G; R v London Borough of Lambeth ex p W; R v London Borough of Lambeth ex p A* [2004] 1 All ER 97(HL) [10].

failure to offer services, which the child has been assessed as needing. They have argued that the Children Act 1989 s 17 imposes a duty upon a local authority to provide the services that a child needs, once the local authority has completed an assessment and determined what those services are. It had been conceded without argument in several previous cases in the lower courts that an assessment of need crystallizes the general duty imposed by s 17 into a specific duty, which is then subject to challenge, if unfulfilled.[162] However this position has changed following the decisions in the Court of Appeal[163] and subsequently the House of Lords.[164]

The Court of Appeal held that s 17 creates what has become known as a 'target [statutory] duty'.[165] This term was first used by Woolf LJ in *R v Inner London Education Authority ex p Ali*.[166] The term means that the statute does not confer specific rights upon which an individual might rely; instead it creates a target duty which the body has a large measure of appreciation in determining how it may be achieved, within the confines of the legislation. The Court of Appeal upheld the dicta of Auld J in *R v London Borough of Barnet ex p B*,[167] where he acknowledged the importance of the resources available in these circumstances to local authority decision-making, and that as a result it was rare that a court could second-guess local authority decision-making as 'irrational':[168]

[I]t is essentially a matter for the local authority, not the court, to decide what consideration and what weight should be given to the circumstances of any individual child or children when his or their needs or interests may conflict with the appropriate provision overall. Secondly, the weight which a local authority should give to the general circumstances of children in need for whom it must provide day care, one way or another, when balancing them against its financial and budgetary constraints, must also be a matter for its judgment and experience. It is certainly a matter upon which the court would rarely be competent to intervene on the ground of irrationality.[169]

As Laws LJ acknowledged in the Court of Appeal,[170] the decision-making of the local authority remains open to limited challenge:

It is constrained by all our established public law precepts. It must not fetter its discretion; its particular decisions must satisfy the rule of reason, as the *Wednesbury* case enjoins; there may be

[162] *R v Tower Hamlets London Borough Council, ex p Bradford* (n 141); *R v Wigan Metropolitan Borough Council ex p Tammadge* (1998) 1 CCLR 581 (QBD); *Mayor and Burgesses of London Borough of Lambeth ex parte K* (2000) 3 CCLR 141 (QBD); *R v Ealing Borough Council ex p C* (n 156), 128A. See also *R v Northavon District Council ex p Smith* [1994] 2 AC 402 (HL) 410F–G (Lord Templeman).

[163] *A v Lambeth London Borough Council* [2001] EWCA 1624, [2001] 3 FCR 673.

[164] *R v LB Barnet* (n 161).   [165] *A v Lambeth London Borough Council* (n 163).

[166] (1990) 2 Admin LR 822.

[167] [1994] 1 FLR 592, [1994] 2 FCR 781 (CA). See also per Ward LJ, *G v London Borough of Barnet* [2001] 1 FCR 743 (QBD (Admin)) 'the duty is performed by providing a range and level of services appropriate to those children's needs. Given that there is a wide range of choice, it has to be inferred that there is power to do one or more of many things to meet the general duty.'

[168] *R v LB Barnet ex p B* (n 167).   [169] ibid, 612 C–F.

[170] *A v Lambeth London BC* [2001] EWCA Civ 1624, [2001] 3 FCR 673.

contexts in which issues of fair procedure would arise. But there is no specific duty enforceable at the suit of the individual.[171]

The three consolidated appeals *R v London Borough of Barnet ex p G; R v London Borough of Lambeth ex p W; R v London Borough of Lambeth ex p A* (*R v LB of Barnet*) then split the House of Lords. The majority determined that Children Act 1989 s 17 does not impose a duty on the local authority to offer services, even when the same authority has determined that a child needs those services. In Lord Nicholls' dissent from the views of the majority, he argued that:

if s 17(1) is apt to impose a duty on a local authority to take reasonable steps to assess the needs of an individual child in need, it is equally apt to impose the duty mentioned above to provide a range and level of services 'appropriate' to those needs[172] . . . Ordinarily cost, where relevant, will be a matter to be taken into account by a local authority when considering its response to an assessed need rather than at the stage of assessment.[173]

The majority concluded that the drafting of Part III of the Children Act 1989 could not sustain this conclusion:

An examination of the range of duties mentioned elsewhere in Pt III of the Act and Pt I of Sch 2 tends to support the view that s 17(1) is concerned with general principles and is not designed to confer absolute rights on individuals. These other duties appear to have been carefully framed so as to confer a discretion on the local services authority as to how it should meet the needs of each individual child in need.[174]

Lord Hope supported his argument by a description of the vagaries which characterize the duties imposed by the Children Act 1989 Part III and Schedule 2. The legislation uses the terms 'shall' and 'may' in stipulating the services which could be offered by a local authority. 'Shall' denotes services which the local authority is required to offer following a finding that a child is in need, while if a local authority 'may' provide a service, it is within their discretion to decide not to do so. However, whilst the legislation stipulates that the local authority shall provide services to a defined group, it does not state what those services should be. For example Schedule 2 s 6 states that the local authority 'shall' provide services designed to minimize the effect on disabled children of their disabilities, but does not stipulate the type of services that the local authority should contemplate. The discretion of the local authority is also preserved by the language used in addition to the exhortation that the local authority 'shall' provide the service. For example under s 20(1) the local authority is required to provide accommodation to a child in need who fulfils the additional qualifications. However it is only required to do so if it considers that the child appears to require it.[175] The discretion of the local authority is also preserved in the use of the term 'as

---

[171] ibid [43].   [172] *R v LB Barnet* (n 161) [33].   [173] ibid [35].
[174] ibid [80] (Lord Hope); see also *R v Kingston upon Thames RLBC ex p T* [1994] 1 FLR 798 (Fam Div).   [175] Children Act 1989 (England) s 20(1).

is appropriate'. For example the local authority shall only offer to provide day care to children under five who are not yet attending schools 'as is appropriate'.[176]

Lord Nicholls in his dissenting speech argued that if s 17 was interpreted to place an obligation on the local authority only to consider an assessment and decide whether to exercise its powers, this represented 'a lacuna in the law relating to "children in need". I cannot think that Parliament intended this should be so'.[177] It certainly is an enormous gap in the legislation, rendering an assessment of the needs of a child virtually worthless in individual cases because it can remain unenforceable. However, we disagree with Lord Nicholls that this result runs contrary to the intention of Parliament. Part III and Schedule 2 are both very carefully worded to avoid placing duties upon a local authority to act. In other words the law created a series of 'let out clauses' allowing local government to sidestep any potential duty to provide services for children. They appear to reflect aspirational legislative intent—a hope for a better future, combined with the knowledge that the financial position of local authorities was unlikely to improve to enable that hope to be fulfilled.

The judiciary could have used the ECHR at this point to interpret the law to require the provision of services.[178] Palmers has identified strong human rights arguments for an enforceable duty upon local authorities to meet the need for a child to be accommodated with her family, not least the argument put forward by counsel in the case that a decision to refuse accommodation once the child was assessed as needing it did not respect the family life of either the child or her parent. However, these were not considered in the judgment, even by Lord Nicholls who simply recorded that counsel had made the submission. As Harris-Short has argued, this judgment is a powerful example of the judiciary's unwillingness to engage with human rights arguments in child welfare cases if they touch upon policy decisions with wide-ranging socio-economic consequences which the judiciary view as the role of government.[179]

Could the *Every Child Matters* initiative change the historic lack of funding in Children Act 1989 s 17, and the low priority given to the provision in the past by the providers of children's services? Certainly the potential is there. *Every Child Matters* and Children Act s 17 share the same guiding ethos, the improvement in the well-being of children, rather than an exclusive focus upon the prevention of further damage to a child stemming from child abuse. The Children Act 2004, for which *Every Child Matters* was the Green Paper, made the coordination of work between professional bodies and the management of information to ensure an integrated professional response

---

[176] ibid s 18(1). See also Sch 2 [8] which details the provision of services to children who are living with their families and Sch 2 [9] which suggests that the local authority should provide family centres for the children in their area as they consider appropriate.   [177] *R v LB Barnet* (n 161) [33].

[178] E Palmer 'Courts, Resources and the HRA: Reading Section 17 of the Children Act 1989 compatibly with Article 8 ECHR' [2003] 3 EHRLR 308.

[179] Harris-Short 'Family Law and the Human Rights Act 1998' (n 42) 329.

to a child's needs a statutory requirement.[180] It also, importantly for the purposes of this discussion, raised the status of work with children, that was both preventative and holistic. Children Act 2004 s 11 created a statutory duty on a children's services agency, the police, all the health agencies and all agencies involved in youth justice to make arrangements to ensure that: '(a) their functions are discharged having regard to the need to safeguard and promote the welfare of children'. There has also been a large amount of promising rhetoric about a shift of policy focus 'away from managing short-term crises and towards an increasing emphasis on prevention and supporting children and young people in their families'[181] which should mean more money for the provision of services to families.

However the potential difficulty lies in the implementation of the government's plans. Much of this centres around the creation of Children's Trusts under Children Act 2004 s 10. The *Every Child Matters* initiative and the Children Act 2004 provided that inter-agency Children's Trusts should be established in each local area with the overarching aim of safeguarding children's well-being. These trusts can encompass social work, education and health, according to local requirements and should be able to respond to varying child need. In theory this should mean that s 17 requirements will rise in status and be more likely to be prioritized; however the involvement of yet more competing statutory priorities within one agency, particularly if one of the priorities is education, could actually reduce the budget allocated to s 17 alone.[182]

2. Offering services in the United States

All jurisdictions offer more services than they can deliver and it is difficult to assess the extent of the gap between the promise and delivery in each of the jurisdictions. This section is not therefore a catalogue of the failings of other jurisdictions, which look rather like our own. Instead we use the examples of each jurisdiction to make a simple point: each jurisdiction has in different ways advocated the use of services to reduce child need and therefore the likelihood that a child will be brought into the care of the state. However, these concepts have always been poorly developed at a legislative level and inadequately funded at a political one. The result of a failure to address what is essentially a core part of most child protection legislation, has led to an increase in the development of more draconian law to remove children from families when politicians become disillusioned with service provision as an answer to child protection concerns.

Federal legislation in the United States favoured a child protection system based on familial support ten years before the Children Act 1989. The Federal Adoption Assistance and Child Welfare Act 1980 (AACWA) freed Federal funding for schemes to help families to stay together, for example, respite childcare, counselling, parenting

---

[180] Children Act 2004 ss 10 and 12; the requirements of these sections are discussed in greater detail in Chapter 5 Section B1. (under the heading Coordination, Agreed Procedure and Shared Information).

[181] HM Government *Care Matters* (n 27) [2.5].

[182] We are grateful to Catherine Williams, University of Sheffield, for this point.

skills and financial aid.[183] If children needed to be removed from home for their own protection, further funding was available for schemes which would help families to function better so that the children could be returned to them. The origins of the AACWA lay in the attempt to remedy the growing problem of 'foster care drift',[184] using support to keep children out of foster care. The National Study of Social Services to Children and their Families in 1977 was particularly influential in highlighting the problem to Congress.[185] It found that foster care was not being used as it had been originally conceived, as short-term respite before children were either reintegrated with their families or adopted. Children were being removed from their homes too easily and then spending two and a half years on average in foster care.[186] The AACWA gave Federal funding for States that created new statutes and programmes which could give effect to its ethos. The AACWA created a standard for the State to make 'reasonable efforts (A) prior to the placement of a child in foster care, to prevent or eliminate the need for removal of the child from his home, and (B) to make it possible for the child to return to his home'.

Although the AACWA advocated family preservation and promised Federal funds so that this could be achieved, the funds never materialized, because of large-scale cuts in Federal spending for social programmes during the Reagan administration.[187]

While our society espouses family preservation as the goal, we have failed to provide the resources to really make it work . . . We are more generous by far in our talk about family preservation services than we are in the funding.[188]

Attempts were made to rectify some of the under-funding in the mid-1990s with a large increase in promised Federal funding; however it was by this time too late. The AACWA did not solve the pressing problems within the child protection system. Most fundamentally the number of children in foster care continued to rise, from 100,000 in 1980 when AACWA was passed, to 500,000 in 1997.[189] Legislators and commentators placed the blame on social workers and upon the Act itself. It was

---

[183] Adoption, Assistance and Child Welfare Act 1980 94 Stat 500 (1980) (US) 42 USCA (Supp. 1996) s 671(a)(15).

[184] *Del A v Roemer* 777 F Supp 1297 (Louisiana DC 1991), 1313 (defining drift as 'referring to children still in the foster care system after many years because permanent goals were not established, maintained and carried out') in K Hort 'Is Twenty-Two Months Beyond The Best Interest Of The Child? ASFA's Guidelines For The Termination of Parental Rights' 28 Fordham Urb LJ 1879, 1880; D Sanders 'Towards Creating a Policy of Permanence for America's Disposable Children: The Evolution of Federal Funding Statutes for Foster Care from 1961 to Present' (2003) 17 IJLPF 211, 212.

[185] S REP NO 336 96th Cong 2nd Sess 3 (1980), J Sheldon '50,000 Children are Waiting: Permanency, Planning and Termination of Parental Rights under the Adoption Assistance and Child Welfare Act of 1980' (1997) 17 B C Third World 211.

[186] The Supreme Court of the United States reached a very similar conclusion in *Smith v The Organization of Foster Families* 431 US 816, 97 Supreme Ct 2094 (1977).

[187] United States General Accounting Office 'Child Welfare: States' Progress in Implementing Family Preservation and Support Services' (Washington DC 1997) (GAO/HEHS–97–34) <http://www.gao.gov/archive/1997/he97034.pdf> (accessed 17 September 2004).   [188] Bartholet (n 93) 41.

[189] (1997) HR Rep 105–77, 8 in R Vernier 'Parental Rights And The Best Interests Of The Child: Implications Of The Adoption And Safe Families Act Of 1997 On Domestic Violence Victims' Rights' (2000) 8 AmUJ Gender SPL 517, 524; R Gordon 'Drifting Through Byzantium: The Promise and Failure of the Adoption and Safe Families Act of 1997' (1999) 83 Minn L R 637, 646–48.

concluded that children suffered injury or death or languished in foster care because of ill-considered attempts to reunite families under the 'reasonable efforts' requirement of the AACWA.[190] The blame for the enormous number of children still in foster care was placed, more fundamentally, upon 'cultural entrenchment' in the idea of preservation of the biological family at the expense of the child.[191]

The proposed system had lost credibility and many critics blamed the family support provisions for the deaths of some children at the hands of their parents, even in cases where it was later found there had been a clerical error not to remove the child, rather than a decision that the family needed support.[192] Advocates of the ideals of the AACWA have argued that it was also failed by its implementation, with services being offered to families using a 'cookie cutter' approach with all families entering the system in a particular state being offered the same services, irrespective of their actual need.[193] The rhetoric behind the Federal Adoption and Safe Families Act (ASFA) 1997[194] is that children deserve permanence and stability and that the adoptive rather than the biological family is more likely to provide them with that permanence.

The discrediting of policies of familial support within the United States has resonances for English policymakers. The money was never available in the United States for such a policy to succeed and when it did, inevitably, fail, disillusioned legislators created a much more authoritarian and arguably more expensive policy, which favoured childcare by adoptive families, or failing that the state, rather than familial support.

3. Offering services in Canada

As is consistent with the guiding ethos, the provision of services for the family is central to all Canadian child protection legislation. Some Acts contain an entitlement for families to be offered services within their declarations of principle. For example the Child and Family Services Act in Manitoba states: 'Families are entitled to receive preventive and supportive services directed to preserving the family unit'.[195]

Under the Ontario legislation the court, before removing the child from the parent, must be satisfied that less restrictive alternatives including residential services have been tried and failed, have been refused or would be inadequate to protect the child.[196] The Child, Family and Community Service Act in British Columbia allows the state to

---

[190] R Gelles *The Book of David: How Preserving Families Can Cost Lives* 143 Cong Rec H2012–06, H2022 (daily ed April 30 1997); (statement of Rep Harman) in Vernier (n 189), 523.

[191] 'Encouraging Adoption: Hearing Before the Sub-Committee on Ways and Means' (serial number 106–309) <http://www.liftingtheveil.org/106-39.pdf> (accessed 30 June 2005).

[192] Guggenheim (n 92) 1723.

[193] D Herring 'New Perspectives On Child Protection The Adoption And Safe Families Act—Hope And Its Subversion' (2000) 34(3) Fam LQ 329, 337.

[194] Adoption and Safe Families Act 1997 42 USCA 671–679 (West Supp 1998).

[195] Child and Family Services Act 1985 (Manitoba) Declaration of Principles.

[196] Child and Family Services Act 1990 (Ontario) s 57(3); see also Child, Youth and Family Enhancement Act (Alberta) 2000 (RSA chapter 12) s 6(3)a.

enter into several types of agreement with a child's family about the services which will be provided. These agreements may be made for up to six months, but are renewable. They are also enforceable against anyone over the age of 19 who makes an agreement with a director of children's services. The legislation also contains five principles in relation to the services provided:[197]

(a) families and children should be informed of the services available to them and encouraged to participate in decisions that affect them;

(b) aboriginal people should be involved in the planning and delivery of services to aboriginal families and their children;

(c) services should be planned and provided in ways that are sensitive to the needs and the cultural, racial and religious heritage of those receiving the services;

(d) services should be integrated, wherever possible and appropriate, with services provided by other ministries and community agencies; and

(e) the community should be involved, wherever possible and appropriate, in the planning and delivery of services, including preventive and support services to families and children.

Like the English legislation, the Canadian legislation explicitly makes the link between service provision and the aim of least disruption through state intervention in family life for the child's protection. Unlike the English legislation it explicitly sets out how the services should in principle operate. However, there remains a lack of clarity about how cases should be prioritized and what type of cases should be offered services first.

4. Offering services in Australia

Parkinson has identified a dichotomy of approaches to familial support across the different States of Australia.[198] In one, the legislation focuses on the notification and identification of child abuse rather than support of families, and the government role is to police families in order to protect children from abuse. In the opposing approach the family is not only seen as the source of the problem, but the law places great responsibility upon them to solve it. Since Parkinson identified these models within child protection legislation, the move has been towards an even greater advocacy of the latter model within legislation. For example, Parkinson's analysis of the Children (Care and Protection) Act 1987 (New South Wales) clearly demonstrates the Act's emphasis on state intervention rather than familial support to protect a child. However the subsequent Children and Young Person's Care and Protection Act 1998 (New South Wales) (CYPCPA) has clearly moved towards a stronger advocacy for familial support and familial responsibility in child protection cases. Thus one of the three guiding principles of the Act has become 'that appropriate assistance is rendered to parents and other persons responsible for children and young persons in the performance of their child-rearing responsibilities in order to promote a safe and nurturing environment'.[199]

---

[197] Child, Family and Community Service Act 1996 (British Columbia) s 3.

[198] P Parkinson 'Child Protection Law in Australia' in M Freeman (ed) *Overcoming Child Abuse: A Window on a World Problem* (Ashgate, Dartmouth 2000) 30.

[199] Children and Young Person's Care and Protection Act 1998 (New South Wales) Guiding Principles.

As is consistent with the second model of child protection legislation outlined by Parkinson, the CYPCPA places responsibility upon the family to seek solutions. The Act is phrased to import responsibility on the child or their parents to ask for services rather than upon the state to offer to provide services as the Children Act 1989 s 17 does. CYPCPA s 20 and s 21 provide that a child, young person or the parent of a child or young person, may 'seek assistance' from the Director-General of Social Services to obtain services that will enable the child or young person to remain in, or return to, the care of his or her family.[200] However it should be noted that in language resonant of the careful drafting of the service provision under Children Act 1989 Part III, CYPCPA s 22 describes a range of services which may be offered, but gives the Director-General complete discretion in determining whether services should be offered to the child and their family.

5. Offering services in New Zealand

New Zealand also conceives of familial support and services in terms of helping families to solve their own problems. The first objects and principles of the CYP&F Act 1989 are to

promote the well-being of children, young persons and their families and family groups by:
(a) establishing, promoting and assisting in the establishment and promotion of services and facilities within the community that will advance the well-being of children, young persons and their families and family groups
(b) assisting parents, families, whanau[201], hapu and iwi[202] and family groups to discharge their family responsibilities to prevent their children and young people from suffering harm, ill-treatment, abuse, neglect and deprivation.

Legislative support for the family to make decisions about their children is embedded in the Act, in particular in the central place given to child protection conferences in child protection decision-making,[203] which is discussed in detail below in Chapter 5 section H.1. However by 2003 a baseline survey[204] of the work being undertaken by the Children, Young Persons and their Families Services (CYFS), which is the equivalent of social services in England, found that the department was struggling to manage the weight of demand for services and consequently failing in its provision. Many of the problems of CYFS were attributed to the unrealistically broad aims of the CYP&F Act, which were criticized as placing: 'a wide range of obligations

---

[200] Under CYP&F Act 1989 (New Zealand) s 113, a parent, child or young person, or any other person may also ask the Director-General for assistance:

(a) if there is a serious or persistent conflict between the parents and the child or young person of such a nature that the safety, welfare or well-being of the child or young person is in jeopardy; or
(b) if the parents are unable to provide adequate supervision for the child or young person to such an extent that the safety, welfare or well-being of the child or young person is in jeopardy.

[201] Wider family circle, may include family friends as well as blood relatives.   [202] Tribe.

[203] CYP&F Act 1989 (New Zealand) ss 20–39.

[204] *Report of the Department of Child Youth and Family Services First Principles Baseline Review* (Ministry of Social Development, CYFS and the Treasury, Wellington 2003), 1.

on the Chief Executive of CYFS to provide broad-based support for families and may be contributing to this breadth of expectation [for CYFS to be] all things to all men'.[205]

The review concluded that the focus of CYFS should be on the safety and security of children and that it should abandon attempts to provide services to improve the child's general well-being. In streamlining and developing the system the CYPF should develop a tool for an assessment of need to target services to children and their families who needed them, which has of course been adopted in England.

6. Evaluation of the provision of services in jurisdictions

All the jurisdictions have set child welfare agencies impossible tasks within the legislation to offer services to children to change their lives and thus ensure that they are not in need of protection. The limitless reaches of this policy and the lack of funding given to achieve it have meant that the legislation has already been largely discredited in the United States. Yet the provision of services which families receive on a voluntary basis is vital, to support an overall principle within many jurisdictions, with the notable exception of the United States, that the welfare of the child is best supported within the child's family, unless the child would be significantly harmed as a result. As will be seen below, once a voluntary system has been bypassed and a child becomes the subject of a court order in relation to her care, it may be difficult in some jurisdictions to come back from a position which has pitted the child's family against the state and which has removed the child from the care of the family.

The provision of services has been at its most successful when it has been geared towards individual need, rather than a 'cookie cutter' approach which has become the norm in the United States. One advantage of the United States system has been that time limits have been placed on the offer of services by the legislation. If time limits had accompanied a system of services which was individually geared, it could have been useful in focusing professionals on their main aims in relation to a particular case. Otherwise it can be easy for a situation to drift with minimal involvement by social workers and few clear goals in relation to the child, particularly in this type of situation where there are few resources to achieve major changes in a child's life.

E. Granting a Court Order

Court orders are available in all jurisdictions to facilitate state involvement in family life. Such orders may be applied for in cases where the offer of services has not been taken up by the family, or where there has been no significant improvement in the child's situation, despite the provision of services. They may also be applied for where it is judged that there is no possibility that the child's family will ever be able to provide the child with the care which he needs. Although all the court hearings which we will be discussing in this section are ostensibly adversarial it would be wrong to consider that the child's family is 'on trial' when a court order in family law is discussed. While the

---

[205] ibid 24.

Diagram 1. The Threshold Test: s 31(2) Children Act 1989 as Interpreted by Caselaw

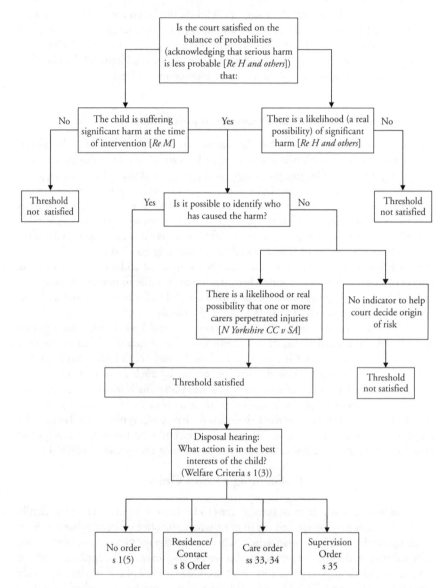

family undoubtedly may feel like they are defending allegations and fighting to retain their responsibilities in relation to their children, it is very important not to confuse the purpose of these hearings with those in criminal law. In criminal proceedings, discussed in Chapter 3, the purpose of the trial is to determine whether a person has committed a defined wrong, to the requisite standard of proof. In family law the focus remains upon the welfare of the child and the child's future. In some jurisdictions, including England and Wales, the purpose of the hearing is to determine whether a child has suffered significant harm. This may or may not include a finding as to who perpetrated that harm. There is then a second stage which examines what orders, if any, should be made to promote the child's welfare. Some States in Australia and the United States have legislation which requires the court to consider a child's safety as their single most important priority rather than the child's welfare, but the main principle is the same—the court should focus on the child's future rather than ensuring that blame is apportioned.

1. Care or supervision orders in England and Wales

The Children Act created two types of court orders, care and supervision orders, to facilitate longer-term involvement in the child's life by the local authority or probation service, when this involvement has not been accepted voluntarily by the child's family.

It remains the choice of the local authority or an authorized person[206] to make an application for a care or supervision order.[207] This position, established by Children Act 1989 s 31(1), was tested in the Court of Appeal in *Nottinghamshire CC v P*. In *Nottinghamshire CC v P* the Court found that the father had repeatedly sexually abused his daughter and that his other four children were seriously at risk from him. The mother was found not to have the capacity to protect the children. The local authority 'persistently and obstinately' refused to seek a care order and the Court of Appeal found that it had no powers under the Children Act 1989 which would allow them to direct the local authority to apply for a care or any other order.[208] The position may have been altered to some extent by the decision of the ECtHR in *Z v UK*. The finding in this case that the children's rights under ECHR Article 3 had been violated by the local authority's failure to apply for a care order in respect of them, despite evidence over a five-year period that the children were suffering 'appalling neglect', does mean that local authorities will have to consider whether their support for the family is an adequate response to the particular problems of the child or whether her rights will be violated if a care or supervision order are not applied for.

---

[206] At present the only authorized persons are members of the NSPCC (s 31(9) a). The statute does provide for other people and bodies to be authorized by the Secretary of State.

[207] Children Act 1989 (England) s 31(1).

[208] *Nottinghamshire County Council v P* [1993] 2 FLR 134 (CA)148; *R v E Sussex ex p W* [1998] 2 FLR 1082 (QBD).

(a) The threshold criteria

The test which must be satisfied before a care or supervision order is made is laid out in the Children Act 1989 s 31(2):

A care or supervision order may only be granted by a court satisfied—

(a) that the child is suffering, or is likely to suffer, *significant harm*; and
(b) that the harm, or likelihood of harm, is attributable to—
    (i) the care given to the child, or likely to be given to him if the order were not made, not being what it would be reasonable to expect a parent to give to him; or
    (ii) the child's being beyond parental control.[209]

This test is often referred to as the 'threshold criteria', to emphasize that the satisfaction of it will not automatically result in a care or supervision order being granted. The threshold criteria set the minimum circumstances in which either order may be made.[210] Once these criteria have been satisfied the court will go on to consider whether a care or supervision order is appropriate.

The term 'harm' is defined in the Children Act 1989 s 31(9) as the 'ill-treatment or the impairment of health or development including impairment suffered from seeing or hearing the ill-treatment of another'.[211] 'Development' is further defined as 'physical, intellectual, emotional, social or behavioural development'; 'health' as physical or mental health; and 'ill-treatment' as including sexual abuse and forms of ill-treatment which are not physical.[212]

(b) Creating the significant harm standard

The Review of Child Care Law which preceded the Children Act 1989 recommended the creation of a standard of 'significant harm' which would justify intervention by the state in families for the protection of children, on the principle that:

only a substantial deficit in that standard [sh]ould justify intervention. Minor short comings in health or minor deficits in physical, psychological or social development should not require compulsory intervention unless cumulatively they are having, or are likely to have, serious lasting effects upon the child.[213]

The term 'significant harm' was not clarified by the legislation. The Review of Child Care Law concluded that the judiciary were perfectly capable of determining whether the harm was significant in cases of parental abuse, because 'the courts are used to assessing degrees of harm, for example in the context of prosecution of assaults, and we consider that they could also do here'.[214] The Review did not acknowledge that although the quantification of assaults was the daily work of the courts, the

---

[209] Children Act 1989 (England) s 31(2).
[210] Lord Mackay of Clashfern 'Joseph Jackson Memorial Lecture' (1989) 139 NLJ 505, 506.
[211] Adoption and Children Act 2002 (England) s 120.
[212] Children Act 1989 (England) s 31(9).
[213] Department of Health *Children Act 1989 Guidance and Regulations Volume 1* (HMSO, London 1991) [3.2].
[214] Department of Health and Social Security *Review of Child Care Law* (HMSO, London 1985) [15.15].

jurisprudence in the measurement of the severity of those assaults against children was poorly developed.

As Chapter 3 discusses in the context of the criminal prosecution of assaults against children, the courts have not developed clear guidelines to determine when hurting a child moves across the nebulous dividing line from reasonable chastisement to assault. In addition, judges have historically been criticized for underestimating the significance of the harm that the child had suffered when sentencing for familial sexual assault.[215] However, these problems in measuring harm in child abuse cases in the criminal court were not recognized in the Children Act 1989. The Review of Child Care Law envisaged that the judiciary in the family courts might find the quantification of potential or present damage to a child's health and development more difficult.[216] Thus very limited guidance was introduced in the Act to aid this measurement. According to the Act 'whether the harm suffered by a child is significant turns on his health or development. His health or development shall be compared with that which could reasonably be expected of a similar child.'[217]

Most speculation raised by the use of the term 'significant' focused upon the problems of defining this 'similar child'. During the debates on the Children Bill, Lord Mackay differentiated between the 'physical attributes of a child' which the 'similar child' should also have and the background of the child which the 'similar child' should not.[218] Before the Act came into force, Freeman argued that this distinction 'obfuscates and overlooks the essential individuality of families and their problems'.[219] He contended that to ignore a child's circumstances in determining significant impairment to health or development was to prejudice those families who lived in poverty and make it more likely that the threshold test would be satisfied for their children. He stated that 'on this test a child from a deprived background is expected to achieve the intellectual growth and emotional maturity comparable with children who come from well-ordered, well-heeled, and stimulating environments'.[220] The published guidance was in fact more extensive than Lord Mackay's definition, stating that a judge could take account of 'environmental, social and cultural characteristics of the child'[221] in determining whether she had suffered significant harm in comparison to a similar child. However, it remained unclear how extensive the similarities should be.[222]

These questions have not really been resolved in the 15 years since the Act came into force. The term has not been refined by caselaw.[223] This may partly be because, although parents may question whether other parts of the threshold test are satisfied, they often concede that the harm is significant. Whatever the cause, the process by

---

[215] C Mitra 'Judicial Discourse in Father–Daughter Incest Appeal Cases' (1987) 15(2) *IJ of Sociology of Law* 121, 148.   [216] *Review of Child Care Law* (n 214) [15.15].

[217] Children Act 1989 (England) s 31(10).

[218] *Hansard* HL Official Series (5th series) (1988–9) volume 503 col 354.

[219] MDA Freeman 'Care after 1991' in D Freestone (ed) *Children and the Law* (Hull University Press, Hull 1990) 149.   [220] ibid 147.

[221] *Children Act 1989 Guidance and Regulations Volume 1* (n 213) [3.20].

[222] Freeman (n 219) 147.

[223] *Humberside County Council v B* [1993] 1 FLR 257 (CA) (Booth J).

which the courts determine the significance of the harm which a child has suffered remains generally opaque. It is difficult not to conclude from the reported cases that a judgment about the significance of harm in a particular case is made on intuition, using expert evidence and previous experience of other cases which satisfied the threshold test. Like many decisions in the criminal court relating to child abuse, a judgment on the significance of harm falls into the category of decisions made on the basis of 'I know it when I see it',[224] rather than on ostensible principles.

Used well, the standard of significant harm allows the court to examine evidence of any relevant factors in a child's life which may be causing or are likely to cause her significant harm, rather than solely the dramatic concerns of child abuse. In *Re H and others(Minors)(Threshold Criteria: Standard of Proof)* Lord Nicholls stated that the court was prepared to take into account an 'infinite' range of factors. These were, for example, 'the history of members of the family, the state of relationships within a family, proposed changes within the membership of a family, parental attitudes and omissions which might not reasonably have been expected, just as much as actual physical assaults'.[225] The House of Lords emphasized that factors 'minor or even trivial when considered in isolation', when considered together form part of a whole picture 'which may suffice to satisfy the court of the likelihood of future harm'.[226]

(c) 'Satisfied'

The more serious the order sought, the higher the standard of proof that the significant harm to the child exists or is likely to exist is required by the court. The order that interferes least with parental responsibility, the child assessment order,[227] requires only that the court is *satisfied* the applicant has *reasonable cause to suspect* that the child is suffering, or is likely to suffer, significant harm.[228] In contrast care and supervision orders which give the local authority the most powers over a child, may only be granted by a court *satisfied* that the child *is suffering or is likely to suffer significant harm.*

The usual standard of proof for evidence in civil cases is that the court must be satisfied on the balance of probabilities, whereas the criminal standard requires proof beyond reasonable doubt. There is however some precedent for the standard of proof to be raised to a point between the two standards. It has been established that the standard of proof in contempt of court applications is higher than the balance of probabilities. Lord Denning in the divorce case *Bater v Bater*[229] went further to suggest the creation of a floating standard of proof in civil cases commensurate with the gravity of the allegation and the seriousness of the consequences for a party to the proceedings. He stated that although civil cases 'may be proved by a preponderance of probability . . . there may be degrees of probability within that standard. The degree depends on the subject matter.'[230]

---

[224] C Cobley, T Sanders, and P Wheeler 'Prosecuting Cases of Suspected "Shaken Baby Syndrome"—A Review of Current Issues' [2003] Crim LR 93, 98.

[225] *Re H and others (Threshold criteria: Standard of proof)* [1996] 1 All ER 1 (HL), 21F (Lord Nicholls).

[226] ibid 21H (Lord Nicholls).   [227] Children Act 1989 (England) s 43.

[228] These short-term orders are discussed in detail in Chapter 5 sections F.2 and G.2.

[229] [1950] 2 All ER 458 (CA) 35.

[230] ibid. See also J Courts 'Standards of Proof in the Divorce Court' (1951) 14 MLR 411.

The consideration of whether there should be a higher standard of proof for allegations of child abuse in civil cases has been evident in judicial decision-making, ever since allegations of child abuse, particularly child sexual abuse, began to appear in wardship proceedings in the late 1980s. These cases focused primarily upon the social consequences for a person found to have abused a child in family proceedings. Judges asked, should a finding be made that a child had been abused by a named person solely on the balance of probabilities? Or were the consequences to the person named as an abuser so grave as to warrant a higher standard of proof? In *Re G (No 2) (a Minor)*[231] Sheldon J held that:

a higher degree of probability is required to satisfy the court that the father has been guilty of some sexual misconduct with his daughter than would be needed to justify the conclusion that the child has been the victim of some such behaviour of whatever nature and whoever may have been its perpetrator.

In *Re W (Minors) (Sexual Abuse: Standard of Proof)*[232] Balcombe LJ interpreted Sheldon J's statements to mean that a higher standard of proof was not only required to establish that a parent had committed abuse, but also to establish the identity of any perpetrator.

However in England and Wales, the appellate courts have inched away from explicit acknowledgements of the necessity of a higher standard to protect the interests of those against whom an allegation is made. In the leading case, *Re H and Others (Minors) (Threshold Criteria: Standard of Proof)*[233] Lord Nicholls, giving the majority judgment stated:

Where the matters in issue are facts the standard of proof required in non-criminal matters is the preponderance of probability, usually referred to as the balance of probability. This is the established general principle. There are exceptions . . ., but I can see no reason for thinking that family proceedings are, or should be an exception . . . Family proceedings often raise very serious issues, but so do other forms of civil proceedings.[234]

However it would be wrong to conclude that the seriousness of the allegation does not remain an important consideration in the satisfaction of the threshold criteria. Although the standard of proof remains 'on the balance of probabilities', the majority in the House of Lords in *Re H* concluded that the more serious the allegation, the more convincing the evidence that would be needed to tip the balance in respect of it.[235] Lord Nicholls in his leading opinion correlated the seriousness of an allegation with the probability that it would occur. Thus,

fraud is less likely than negligence. Deliberate physical injury is usually less likely than accidental physical injury. A step-father is usually less likely to have raped and had non-consensual oral sex with his under age step-daughter than to have lost his temper and slapped her.[236]

The courts maintain that this is not an addition to the balance of probabilities criteria, but is rather an acknowledgement of a reality that it is more difficult to persuade

---

[231] *Re G (No 2) (A Minor)* [1988] 1 FLR 314 (Fam Div) 321B.
[232] [1994] 1FLR 419 (CA) 429. [233] *Re H and others* (n 225). [234] ibid 9.
[235] ibid 7J. [236] ibid 16J (Lord Nicholls).

fact finders that serious allegations are well founded.[237] However seriousness was not defined as being seriousness to the child, but arguably the seriousness of the allegation against the parents. Serious was defined in terms of likelihood and deliberation. If an event was not likely, then it was more serious and if it was deliberate, then it was more serious. Neither of these issues are in any way related to a child's welfare. Neglect is seriously damaging to a child's welfare and development,[238] yet it is the most reported type of abuse[239] and therefore to the extent of our knowledge, the most likely. A child will be harmed by being starved whether this is a deliberate act of the child's parent or the parent's inability to understand nutrition. The current definition of a serious allegation warranting a higher standard of proof does not relate to the seriousness to the child of either the type of abuse, or the result of the case.[240]

The second concern raised by the decision in *Re H* is whether the standard is in reality a normal civil standard of proof, or whether it is a heightened or third standard. In *R (on the application of McCann) v Crown Court at Manchester; and Clingham v Kensington and Chelsea Royal London Borough Council* the House of Lords described the standard of proof used in *Re H* as a 'heightened civil standard'.[241] This case concerned the question whether applications for anti-social behaviour orders should be characterized as criminal or civil proceedings. Lord Justice Steyn in the Court of Appeal in *McCann* observed that a heightened civil standard was virtually indistinguishable from a criminal standard.[242] Even the House of Lords in *Re H* found that the result of their test was not 'materially different'[243] from the test adopted by the judge at first instance, which was 'a higher standard of proof albeit one falling short of the criminal standard'.[244] If the result of the test adopted is not materially different from the effect of a higher civil standard of proof, do the protestations of Lord Nicholls that the standard is in fact the ordinary civil standard, alter the reality of the situation? This question was considered by Butler-Sloss LJ in *Re U (A Child) (Serious Injury: Standard of Proof), Re B (A Child) (Serious Injury: Standard of Proof)*.[245] *Re U and B* examined the conclusions of *McCann* and two other cases, *B v Chief Constable of Avon and Somerset Constabulary*[246] and *Re ET (Serious*

---

[237] R Pattenden 'The Risk of Non-Persuasion in Civil Trials: The Case Against a Floating Standard of Proof' [1988] Civ JQ 220, 227.

[238] C Hobbs, C Hanks and J Wynne *Child Abuse and Neglect: A Clinician's Handbook* (Churchill Livingstone 1999) 10.

[239] Department for Education and Skills 'Statistics of education: referrals, assessments and children and young people on child protection registers: year ending 31 March 2005' (2006) <http://www.dfes.gov.uk/rsgateway/DB/VOL/v000632vol01-2006textvI.pdf> (accessed 6 October 2006).

[240] C Keenan 'The Impact of *Cannings* on Civil Child Protection Cases' (2005) 27 J Soc Wel & Fam L 173, 180–184.

[241] *R (on the application of McCann) v Crown Court at Manchester; Clingham v Kensington and Chelsea Royal London Borough Council* [2002] UKHL 39; [2002] 3 WLR 1313.   [242] ibid [37].

[243] *Re H and others* (n 225) 22J–23A (Lord Nicholls).

[244] *Re H and R (Child Sexual Abuse)* [1995] 1 FLR 643, 646.

[245] *Re U (A Child) (Serious Injury: Standard of Proof), Re B (A Child) (Serious Injury: Standard of Proof)* [2004] EWCA Civ 567; [2004] 2 FLR 263.   [246] [2001] 1 WLR 340.

Injuries: Standard of Proof).[247] In *B v CC of Avon and Somerset Constabulary* the Court of Appeal had concluded that the standard of proof in serious civil cases was for all practical purposes 'indistinguishable from the criminal standard'.[248] In *Re ET* Bodey J in the High Court found that the standards of proof differed between serious civil and criminal cases but that the 'result was much the same'.[249]

Butler-Sloss LJ in *Re U and B*[250] rejected the conclusions which these cases had reached. She found that in importing the criminal standard, the whole ethos of the court in civil child protection cases would necessarily change, and that the semi-inquisitorial nature of the proceedings would be lost:

We understand that in many applications for care orders counsel are now submitting that the correct approach to the standard of proof is to treat the distinction between criminal and civil standards as 'largely illusory'. In our judgment this approach is mistaken. The standard of proof to be applied in Children Act cases is the balance of probabilities and the approach to these difficult cases was laid down by Lord Nicholls in his speech in *Re H*. That test has not been varied nor adjusted by the dicta of Lord Bingham or Lord Steyn who were considering applications made under a different statute. There would appear to be no good reason to leap across a division, on the one hand, between crime and preventative measures taken to restrain defendants for the benefit of the community and, on the other hand, wholly different considerations of child protection and child welfare nor to apply the reasoning in *McCann* to public, or indeed to private, law cases concerning children. The strict rules of evidence applicable in a criminal trial which is adversarial in nature is to be contrasted with the partly inquisitorial approach of the court dealing with children cases in which the rules of evidence are considerably relaxed. In our judgment therefore Bodey J applied too high a standard of proof in the case of *Re ET* and the principles set out by Lord Nicholls should continue to be followed by the judiciary trying family cases and by magistrates sitting in the Family Proceedings Courts.[251]

Thus the protestations continue that the standard of proof for the threshold test of whether a child *is* suffering significant harm remains the balance of probabilities, bearing in mind the seriousness of the allegation. However, as we have argued, whatever 'box' the test is put into, it remains the same test, one that when an allegation of serious abuse is made, places a higher hurdle before the party wishing to prove it.

(d) Is likely *to suffer significant harm*

The threshold test may also be satisfied by evidence that a child is likely to suffer significant harm. The fact that the likely harm must be significant is vital to the courts' interpretation. In these circumstances the crucial question becomes a measurement of the type of risk involved as well as the weight of the evidence that it could occur. Lord Nicholls in *Re H* stated that 'what is in issue is the prospect or risk of the child suffering *significant* harm. When exposed to this risk the child may need protection

---

[247] [2003] 2 FLR 1205.
[248] (n 246) [31] (Lord Bingham CJ) (the decision whether to make a civil sexual offender order).
[249] (n 247).   [250] *Re U and Re B* (n 246).   [251] ibid [31].

just as much when the risk is considered to be less than 50/50 as when the risk is of a higher order'.[252]

Thus *likely* has been interpreted to mean 'a real possibility of harm' which cannot 'sensibly be ignored having regard to the nature and gravity of the feared harm in this particular case'.[253] As Hale LJ explained in *Re C and B (Children) (Care Order: Future Harm)*, this can mean that 'a comparatively small risk of really serious harm can justify action, while even the virtual certainty of slight harm might not'.[254]

In the guideline case of *Re H* the Law Lords were divided on the standard to which evidence of this risk of serious harm would have to be proved. In *Re H* the judge at first instance found that there was a real possibility that the allegations of sexual abuse made by the eldest girl were true, but not that they were true on the balance of probabilities. He therefore decided that he was not able to go on to consider the risk that the younger sisters would be abused, because there was no evidence which had been established on the balance of probabilities on which to base his decision. The minority in the House of Lords argued that his analysis was wrong. Lord Browne-Wilkinson contended that a number of concerning factors could be a sufficient basis for the court to make a prognosis that a child was likely to be abused, even though these factors could not be proved to exist on the balance of probabilities: 'the combined effect of a number of factors which suggest that a state of affairs, although not proved to exist may well exist is the normal basis for the assessment of future risk'.[255]

Lord Lloyd supported this view, arguing:

The finding of future risk must of course be based on evidence. It cannot be based on a hunch. If there is no evidence to support a finding of risk, the finding will be set aside. But if there is such evidence, then a finding may be made, even though the same evidence is insufficient to support a finding of past fact.[256]

This argument was rejected by the majority. Lord Nicholls concluded that 'an alleged but non-proven fact is not a fact' for the purpose of measuring the likelihood of significant harm, any more than it would be to measure whether a child was suffering significant harm at the time of the hearing.[257] Instead a risk of significant harm could only be found on the basis of facts which had each been found on the balance of probabilities to be true, bearing in mind the seriousness of each of the disputed facts. A finding of a risk of future harm cannot be made on the basis of judicial 'suspicions or lingering doubts'.[258] As Hayes has traced, this decision has had an enormous impact upon the operation of the threshold test in court, particularly in cases where the identity of a child's assailant is unclear.[259] It is this problem to which we will now turn as some of the problems with the threshold test as formulated

---

[252] *Re H and others* (n 225) 15 (Lord Nicholls).   [253] ibid 15J–16A (Lord Nicholls).
[254] *Re C and B (Children) (Care order: future harm)* [2001] 1 FLR 611, 619(28).
[255] *Re H and others* (n 225) 3J.   [256] ibid 10J–11A.   [257] ibid 20E.   [258] ibid 19A.
[259] M Hayes 'Case Commentary—*Re O and N*; *Re B*—Uncertain Evidence and Risk-Taking In Child Protection Cases' (2004) 16(1) Child and Family LQ 63.

in *Re H* in child abuse cases only become evident when considering the test in its entirety.

(e) Attributing the harm or likelihood of harm to the care of the child

In addition to a finding that a child is suffering or likely to suffer harm, the court must also find that this harm, or likelihood of harm is 'attributable to the care of the child not being what it would be reasonable to expect a parent to give him'.[260]

Although the test sounds like a fault-based test, in principle it should not be applied like one. Family law, unlike criminal law, is not a punitive system, but ostensibly works on the guiding principle of the improvement of the child's position. As Lord Nicholls stated in *Lancashire CC v A (A Child) (Care Orders: Significant Harm)* 'an absence of a reasonable standard of parental care need not imply that the parents are at fault. It may be, for instance, that for reasons beyond their control the parents are not able to provide a reasonable standard of care for the child.'[261] The point is that the child is suffering or likely to suffer significant harm because the care is not good enough, rather than necessarily his parents are blameworthy. However the use of the phrase 'attributable to' means that there must be some causal connection between the care which the child is receiving and the harm which the child is suffering, or is likely to suffer. It may not be the sole cause, but it must be a cause. For instance, if a parent entrusts a child to a third party without taking the precautionary steps a reasonable parent would take to check the suitability of the third party, and subsequently the third party injures or sexually abuses the child, the harm suffered by the child may be regarded as attributable to the inadequate care of the parent as well as the third party.[262] But for example when a child has suffered accidental injuries when being cared for by an entirely competent parent, it could not be found that a child has suffered harm *attributable* to the care given.[263] In cases where the injury was accidental it could be found that the child had suffered harm attributable to the care given if the parents lied about the way in which the child was injured or failed to call an ambulance in time and this delayed treatment.[264]

This part of the threshold test has become particularly problematic in cases where a child cared for by a number of people has been injured, but no one will accept responsibility, or apportion blame. These cases have become known in family law as 'the uncertain perpetrator' cases. The question which has concerned the courts is whether the identity of the perpetrator of the child's injuries must be established before the threshold test is satisfied. The root of this uncertainty is the finding in *Re H* that future risk of significant harm may only be found by a court on the basis of evidence established on the balance of probabilities, bearing in mind the seriousness of the allegation. Lawyers have argued in a number of cases since *Re H* that the

---

[260] Children Act 1989 (England) s 31(2).

[261] *Lancashire CC v A (A Child) (Care Orders: Significant Harm)* [2000] 2 AC 147 (HL) 151.

[262] ibid 151 (Lord Nicholls).

[263] *Re L (A Child) (Care Proceedings: Responsibility for Child's Injury)* [2006] EWCA Civ 49 [52]–[53] (Wall LJ). [264] ibid [55] (Wall LJ).

threshold test cannot be established if the court cannot determine who has harmed a child, as this would mean that the decision was made on the basis of mere suspicion, not proven fact.

In *Lancashire CC v A (A Child) (Care Orders: Significant Harm)*,[265] a child (A) aged seven months was shaken severely three times within a two-month period during which she was cared for both by her parents and by a childminder. The childminder also had a child of a very similar age. The local authority applied for care orders in respect of both children. The court at first instance considered whether it was required to identify which person injured the child before the threshold criteria could be satisfied. This problem was not directly considered by those drafting the Children Act 1989. However, as Lord Nicholls observed when the case reached the House of Lords, commentators on the Act, and indeed the then Lord Chancellor, Lord Mackay, interpreted the term 'attributable to the care of the child' to mean attributable to the care given by the *parent* to the child.[266] It had been ruled at first instance that the threshold test had not been satisfied. In doing so Gee J had relied on the construction of Children Act 1989 s 31(2) by Wall J in *Hackney London BC v G* that the court has to be satisfied by evidence that the significant harm suffered by the child is attributable to the care, or absence of care, given to the child by the *parent* against whom the order is sought.[267] This construction was rejected by the Court of Appeal[268] and the House of Lords. Lord Nicholls in the House of Lords stated:

I cannot believe Parliament intended that the attributable condition in s 31(2)b should operate in this way. Such an interpretation would mean that the child's future health, or even her life, would have to be hazarded on the chance that after all the non-parental carer rather than one of the parents inflicted the injuries. Self-evidently to proceed in such a way when a child is proved to have suffered serious injury on more than one occasion could be dangerously irresponsible.[269]

Instead, Lord Nicholls differentiated between two types of case:

- a 'typical case' in which the child has been cared for by 'a parent or parents or other primary carers'. In this case the authority must prove that the child has been harmed by poor care *given to her by her parents or primary carers.*

- a shared care arrangement 'where the care given by one or other of the carers is proved to have been deficient, with the child suffering harm in consequence, but the court is unable to identify which of the carers provided the deficient care'. In this case the phrase 'attributable to the care of the child' is apt to embrace the care given by *any of the carers* and it is not necessary to prove which of them caused the harm to the child.[270]

Lord Nicholls acknowledged that this 'interpretation of the attributable condition means that parents who may be wholly innocent, and whose care may not have fallen below that of a reasonable parent, will face the possibility of losing their child, with

---

[265] *Lancashire CC v A* (n 261).

[266] *Hansard* HL Official Series (5th series) (1988–9) volume 503 cols 349–350.

[267] *Hackney London BC v G* [1994] 2 FCR 216 (Fam Div), 222; sub nom *Re G (a minor) (care order: threshold conditions)* [1995] Fam 16, 20.

[268] *Lancashire County Council v A; Lancashire County Council v B* [2000] 2 WLR 346 (CA).

[269] *Lancashire CC v A* (n 261)152.   [270] ibid 153 (Lord Nicholls).

all the pain and distress that involves'.[271] However, unlike other interpretations of the threshold test the court was prepared to judge this to be a risk worth taking in the light of the level of threat involved.

However, as Hayes has demonstrated,[272] the earlier decision in *Re H* continued to cast a long shadow over the decisions in 'uncertain perpetrator' cases, most notably when the subsequent case of *Re O and N (Preliminary Hearing)* reached the Court of Appeal.[273] In this case L, then aged six months, was admitted to hospital with a fractured skull and several other fractures. The father confessed to punching L in the head, causing the skull fracture, but not to the other injuries, and pleaded guilty to charges of causing grievous bodily harm. The parents separated. The local authority applied for care orders in respect of L and her sibling K, who had been born after L had been injured. The Court of Appeal found that it could not be proved which parent had injured L. As a result Ward LJ held that:

the finding of the court is that the case against the mother cannot be elevated beyond suspicion that she may have harmed her baby. As I have indicated that does not establish that she did. On the facts of this case the fact of her harming the child in the past could be the only basis for asserting a risk of her harming the child in the future. The suspicions and doubts do not establish a risk of future harm by her. In my judgment, this case must proceed henceforth upon the clear basis and understanding by all concerned, lawyers, social workers and experts, that L was not harmed by her mother and there is no risk that either L or C is at risk of suffering physical harm from her.[274]

The decision of the Court of Appeal in *Re O and N* was reversed by the House of Lords.[275] The Law Lords found that the threshold test could be satisfied in relation to the risk of future harm to a child living with the injured child, even though the identity of the perpetrator could not be established. It approved the interpretation of the threshold test under *Lancashire CC v B* which construed the phrase 'care given to the child' as including the care given by any of the carers. What the House of Lords did not do was to find that when the perpetrator of an injury cannot be identified in a shared care arrangement, each of those within the arrangement may be considered by the court to be a risk to the child. It gave no guidance on this point. Lord Nicholls postponed any consideration of the risk which a particular carer may pose to the welfare stage of the process in which the court determines whether an order should be made. When the court has reached this stage the court should proceed on the basis that each of the possible perpetrators is 'just that: a possible perpetrator'.[276] The court should take this into account, but the 'importance to be attached to this possibility, as to every feature of the case, necessarily depends on the circumstances'.[277] The court

---

[271] ibid (HL) 153.
[272] Hayes (n 259) 63; J Hayes and M Hayes 'Child Protection in the Court of Appeal' [2002] Fam Law 817.   [273] *O and N (Care: Preliminary Hearing)* [2002] 2 FLR 1167 (CA).
[274] ibid [30].
[275] *In Re O and another (Minors) (Care: Preliminary Hearing); In Re B (A Minor)* [2004] 1 AC 523 (HL).   [276] ibid 541.
[277] ibid 542.

should also take into account any views expressed at the preliminary hearing about the likelihood that one or another of the carers was the perpetrator.

N Yorkshire CC v SA (A Child: Care Proceedings Non-Accidental Injury),[278] concerned an appeal from a first instance decision about the identity of the alleged perpetrators of a child's injury. Charles J at first instance had found that he could not exclude any of the four carers of an injured child because he could only exclude a carer if there was 'no possibility' that the carer had harmed the child. This interpretation was rejected by Dame Butler-Sloss P in the Court of Appeal:

Parliament has provided a two-limb threshold which requires to be satisfied before the court has the right to consider the welfare of the child. The first is met in this appeal since the child was injured and suffered significant harm. In relation to the second limb, the attributable condition, it seems to me that the two most likely outcomes in 'uncertain perpetrator' cases are as follows. The first is that there is sufficient evidence for the court positively to identify the perpetrator or perpetrators. Second, if there is not sufficient evidence to make such a finding, the court has to apply the test set out by Lord Nicholls as to whether there is a real possibility or likelihood that one or more of a number of people with access to the child might have caused the injury to the child. For this purpose, real possibility and likelihood can be treated as the same test. As Lord Nicholls pointed out in *Re O and N (Minors); Re B (Minors)* (above) the views and indications that the judge at the first part of a split trial may be able to set out may be of great assistance at the later stage of assessment and the provision of the protection package for the injured child. I would therefore formulate the test set out by Lord Nicholls as, 'Is there a likelihood or real possibility that A or B or C was the perpetrator or a perpetrator of the inflicted injuries?' There may perhaps also be the third possibility that there is no indicator to help the court decide from whom the risk to the child may come, in which eventuality it would be very difficult for the local authority and for the court to assess where the child might be at most risk.

These decisions move the assessment of risk to a child from a particular person into the disposal or welfare stage, where the court determines what, if any, orders to make, rather than the threshold stage. As Dame Butler-Sloss has highlighted, split hearings may be counter-productive in this context, particularly if the same judge does not hear both parts of the case. She advised that the nature of the case should be assessed at an early point, as the Protocol for Judicial Management in Public Law Children Act Cases advises for all cases,[279] and it should be determined whether it might be better to hear the whole case and if necessary, adjourn then for further assessments.[280]

Undoubtedly an inability to determine the identity of the person who has harmed a child causes significant problems in the assessment of whether any other children in the family are likely to suffer significant harm in the future. From the opinion of the Court of Appeal in *K (Children)*[281] it seems clear that in cases in which the court can conclude that one or other of the child's parents hurt or killed a child, it should also conclude that any other children of the family are likely to suffer significant harm, unless there are some particularly unusual circumstances in the case.

---

[278] *N Yorkshire CC v SA (a Child: Care Proceedings Non-Accidental Injury)* [2003] EWCA Civ 839.

[279] Dame Elizabeth Butler-Sloss 'The Protocol for Judicial Case Management in Public Law Children Act Cases' [2003] 2 FLR 719.

[280] *Re A (a Child) (Care Proceedings: Non-Accidental Injury)* [2003] EWCA Civ 839 (CA) [37].

[281] *K (Children)* [2005] EWCA Civ 1226 (Wall LJ).

On a theoretical and a practical level it might be argued whether these enormously difficult assessments have been made harder by the courts' interpretation of the threshold test, particularly the formulation of the standard of proof. The question at this point, as at all decision points in child protection, is which risk is the most important to guard against and which should take precedence? Is it the risk of future physical harm to the child? Or the risk of further psychological harm if the child is removed from home? Or the risk that the family will be broken up unnecessarily? Or finally that the parents or another adult will be found in a civil court to have seriously abused a child when they did not? The problem with the current standard of proof is that it only addresses the last risk. Unlike the other jurisdictions which we have considered below, it raises the standard of proof depending upon the type of abuse which is being considered, rather than the effect of such a finding. If the standard of proof was constructed to guard against any of the other risks outlined above it would not be constructed in relation to the type of abuse: because the type of abuse will not affect any of the other decisions; it would instead be linked to outcome. To value the parents' reputation above the risk of harm to the child or even the risk to family autonomy is fundamentally wrong in the interpretation of child protection legislation that purports to be based on the best interests of the child.

In England if the court is satisfied that the threshold criteria exist, it must consider whether it is appropriate to make a care or supervision order. At this welfare or disposal stage of the hearing the court may also choose to make a residence order. However in doing so the court must be satisfied that to make any order is better for the child than making no order at all.[282] Where there still is not sufficient information to make a care or supervision order the court may make an interim care or supervision order if it is satisfied that there are reasonable grounds for believing that the child is suffering or likely to suffer significant harm.

(f) Factors in the decision on whether to make an order

Decisions about whether to make a court order should be guided by the welfare, no-order and proportionality principles. The child's welfare should be the paramount consideration in a determination of which order, if any, the court should make. The Children Act 1989 contains guidance for decision-makers to aid interpretation in the form of a statutory checklist of factors relevant to a decision made on the basis of the child's welfare in s 1(3). These are:

(a) the ascertainable wishes and feelings of the child concerned (considered in the light of his age and understanding)
(b) his physical, emotional and educational needs;
(c) the likely effect on him of any change in his circumstances;
(d) his age, sex, background and any characteristics of his which the court considers relevant;
(e) any harm which he has suffered, or is at risk of suffering;

---

[282] Children Act 1989 (England) s 1(5).

(f) how capable is each of his parents, and any other person in relation to whom the court considers the question to be relevant, of meeting his needs;
(g) the range of powers available to the court under the Act in the proceedings in question.

The weakness of the welfare checklist is that like all other parts of the Children Act 1989 it does not create absolute rules about how these factors should be interpreted or create any hierarchy within the checklist. This lack of differentiation has been made on the grounds that each case should be decided individually, bearing in mind all the principles of the Children Act 1989. However, it leaves enormous scope for inconsistency and for decisions to be made essentially on the basis of individual prejudice about which factors should be the most important considerations in child abuse cases.

The choice of order and indeed the decision whether to make any order at all must be proportionate and thus linked to the harm which the child has suffered or is at risk of suffering. As it was held in *Re C and B (Care Order: Future Harm)*[283] orders must be made on 'the principle of proportionality'. The principle has to be that the local authority works to support, and eventually to reunite the family, unless the risks are so high that the child's welfare requires alternative family care'.[284] *Re C and B* demonstrates the principle in operation. The two elder children of a family were taken into care on the basis of the actual harm to the emotional and intellectual development of the oldest child and the risk of harm to the other child. Another child J was born. He was cared for well. However when he was ten months old he was removed from the home because of fears that he too would suffer the levels of emotional harm that his sisters had suffered. At the same time his younger sister, who had been born only days before, was also removed. Care orders were granted in respect of both children when C was thirteen months old and J was three months old. These care orders were dismissed on appeal on the ground that a care order was simply not proportionate to the risks posed to the children. Lady Justice Hale concluded that it could not possibly be 'a proportionate response to what was feared in this case, to remove the children for good, long before anything has been shown to have gone wrong'.[285]

This measurement of proportionality is made particularly difficult in cases of child abuse when the child's carers have made concessions and agreed that the threshold has been satisfied in respect of the children, but there have been no findings of fact about what happened. The court does have a common law discretion to choose to conduct such an inquiry; in weighing up whether or not to order an inquiry the court should consider

(a) the interests of the child (which are relevant but not paramount);
(b) the time that the investigation will take;
(c) the likely cost to public funds;
(d) the evidential result;
(e) the necessity or otherwise of the investigation;

---

[283] [2001] 1 FLR 611.　　　[284] ibid (31).　　　[285] ibid (29).

(f) the relevance of the potential result of the investigation to the future care plans for the child;

(g) the impact of any fact finding process upon the other parties;

(h) the prospects of a fair trial on the issue.[286]

Where parents have conceded that the threshold criteria have been made out, but not the facts, and where it may be possible to place the children with one or both carers, it is difficult to see how the second stage may take place effectively without an inquiry into which of them has perpetrated the harm, or might do so in the future.

(g) The effects of a care or supervision order

There is a significant difference in the powers that a care order or supervision order gives to the local authority and to the court. The effect of a care order is defined in Children Act 1989 ss 33 and 34. It gives the local authority parental responsibility for the child for the duration of the order. The local authority can decide where the child is going to live, and what schooling she will have. However this is a limited form of parental responsibility. The local authority does not have the right to release the child for adoption, nor to appoint a guardian for the child. These are exactly the same limitations that are placed upon any individual, other than the child's father who acquires parental responsibility as a result of a residence order in his favour under s 10(3).

Granting the local authority parental responsibility does not erase the parental responsibility of the parents of a child. In theory the parents of the child share parental responsibility with the local authority. However under s 33(3)(b) the local authority has the power to determine the extent to which a parent or guardian of a child may meet his parental responsibility (subject to the limitation under s 33(4) that they must be satisfied that it is necessary to do so to safeguard or promote the child's welfare).

The local authority's duties towards a child who is the subject of a care order are the same as those towards any child accommodated by them. Both accommodated children and children who are the subject of a care order are categorized in the Act as 'looked after' children. It is the duty of a local authority looking after a child 'to safeguard and promote his welfare', and 'to make such use of services available to children as appears to the authority reasonable in his case'.[287] The duties of the local authority towards 'looked after' children are discussed in greater detail below.[288] In the determination of whether to make a care order the local authority should put forward a plan of how they will discharge their duties in line with the separation of powers outlined in the Children Act 1989 which are discussed in section F.1 of this chapter. The court cannot alter the care plan: 'the only power of the court under Part IV is either to approve or refuse to approve the care plan put forward by the local authority. The court cannot dictate to the local authority what the care plan is to say'.[289]

---

[286] *A County Council v DP, RS, BS (By The Children's Guardian)* [2005] 2 FLR 1031 (Fam Div).
[287] Children Act 1989 (England) s 22(3).   [288] Discussed below, section E.1(i).
[289] *Re L (Care Proceedings: Human Rights Claims)* [2003] EWHC 665 (Fam Div) [11] (Munby J).

In these circumstances the court may find itself faced with the dilemma of choosing what it considers to be the lesser of two evils.[290]

The effect of a supervision order is defined in the Children Act 1989 s 35 and expanded upon in Parts I and II of Schedule 3. This places the child under the supervision of a designated local authority or probation officer whose duty is to 'advise assist and befriend the supervised child' and 'to take such steps as are necessary to give effect to the order'. A supervisor may require the child to live in a specified place for a period of time, participate in activities such as education, or to report to a specified person on certain days.[291] The supervision order may also require the supervised child to submit to a medical or psychiatric examination or treatment. However parental responsibility does not go to the local authority, but remains vested in those who had parental responsibility before the order was made.

The choice between a care order and supervision order will not usually be determined by whether the court considers that the child should live with her parent(s). In the majority of cases when a care order is in place the child will continue to live with her parent(s); conversely the child may be the subject of a supervision order and be accommodated voluntarily away from home. When a child is being 'looked after' by the local authority the authority is obliged under s 23(6) to consider whether the child could be placed with family or friends before placing the child with foster parents or in a children's home.

A care order places a positive duty upon the local authority to safeguard and promote the welfare of the child and to protect her from inadequate parenting. If the child's parent does something in caring or helping to care for the child to which the local authority objects, the local authority may enforce their will without returning to court because the local authority has parental responsibility for the child. Pursuant to a supervision order the court may make directions, which may be attached to the supervision order under Schedule 3, that the responsible person in relation to the child take all reasonable steps to ensure that the child complies with the directions of the supervisor. However these directions may only be made with the consent of the responsible person and, as Bracewell J recognized in *Re T (a Minor)(Care or Supervision Order)*,[292] the court cannot enforce any condition in the supervision order. The breach of conditions of a supervision order may be used as evidence in future proceedings, but the local authority cannot go to court to make the parents or the child do what the order tells them to do.

A supervision order is time-limited. It will usually be granted for one year, but may be extended for up to three years from the date at which the order is originally made,[293] whereas there is no time limit on a care order. Care orders may continue until they are discharged under s 39.

---

[290] *Re S and D (Children: Powers of Court)* [1995] 2 FLR 456 (CA) 463C and 464B (Balcombe LJ), *Re CH (Care or Interim Care Order)* [1998] 1 FLR 402 (CA) and *Re S (Minors) (Care Order: Implementation of Care Plan); Re W (Minors) (Care Order: Adequacy of Care Plan)* [2002] UKHL 10, [2002] 2 AC 291, [2002] 1 FLR 815.   [291] Children Act 1989 (England) Sch 3 [2].

[292] *Re T (a Minor) (Care or Supervision Order)* [1994] 1 FLR 103 (Civ Div).

[293] Children Act 1989 (England) Sch 3 [6].

The choice between a care or supervision order should be made by considering the case as a whole, including the gravity of the harm that the child has suffered and the particular risks of harm to the child. The court must then decide whether in the light of all these factors it is necessary for the local authority to be able to exercise the additional powers given by a supervision order. The court does not have to identify one particular aspect of the local authority's duties that it needs to exercise.[294]

(h) Interim care or supervision orders

The court may also in certain circumstances grant an interim care or supervision order rather than a full order. An interim order may be granted:

- when care or supervision proceedings have had to be adjourned; or
- when the court has been asked to make a care or supervision order but decides that it is in the child's best interests for a residence order to be made. In these circumstances the court must make an interim supervision order unless it is satisfied that the child's welfare will be satisfactorily safeguarded without the order;[295] or
- in private proceedings, when the court wishes to explore whether a care or supervision order may be appropriate in a child's case and thus directs the local authority to conduct an investigation into a child's circumstances under s 37(1).

An interim order has less serious consequences than a full care or supervision order and thus a lower standard of proof is required. An interim care or supervision order may be granted by a court satisfied that there are *reasonable grounds for believing* that the child is suffering or likely to suffer significant harm. The court does not need to be satisfied that the child is suffering or likely to suffer significant harm.

A court making an interim care order may also make an order under s 38A to exclude a 'relevant person' from the place in which the child lives for the duration of the order. This order may be made on the grounds that the court finds that there is reasonable cause to believe that if the relevant person is excluded the child 'will cease to suffer, or cease to be likely to suffer significant harm'.[296] The extent of these exclusion powers are the same as may be attached under an Emergency Protection Order,[297] which is discussed in greater detail in Chapter 5 F.2 (a). In making an interim order the court has to attempt to ensure that the making of any direction under an interim care order leaves both parties equal and does not prejudge the decision in the final hearing.

(i) Duties of the local authority when looking after children

The local authority has the same duties towards children placed in their care as a result of a court order as it does when those children are accommodated by the local authority for more than 24 hours with the consent of their parents.[298] All of these

---

[294] *Re S(J) (a Minor) (Care or Supervision Order)* [1993] 2 FLR 919 (Fam Div).
[295] Children Act 1989 (England) s 38(3).
[296] The court may alternatively accept an undertaking under s 38B (this is the same as under s 44B).
[297] Children Act 1989 (England) s 44(a).   [298] ibid s 20.

children are described by the Act as 'looked after' children. Section 22(3) stipulates that the local authority should:

(a) . . . safeguard and promote [their] welfare; and
(b) . . . make such use of services available to children cared for by their own parents as appears to the authority reasonable in his case.

A local authority should provide a child with a place to live[299] and should maintain a child, although it has the statutory power to ask for a financial contribution towards this from the child's parents or others, if such a request is reasonable.[300] There is a statutory duty to consult with a child and his family before making any decision if reasonably practicable to do so and it must then give 'due consideration' to those views.[301] In making any such decision the court should also give 'due consideration' to the child's religious persuasion, racial origin and cultural and linguistic background'.[302]

(j) Contact

The local authority also has a positive obligation to promote contact between a child and her parents, family and friends.[303] Section 34(1) requires the local authority to allow reasonable contact between the child and her parents, guardians, and those in whose favour a residence order had been previously made, or who had care of the child when the child was a ward of court. The court may also on the application of the local authority or the child allow contact between the child and a named person.[304] Similarly under s 34(3) the court may make an order on the appropriate level of contact between any of those mentioned in subs 1 or anyone else granted leave to apply, on the application of that party. The court may also deny contact with a specific party on the application of either the local authority, or the child.[305] This is the extent of the court's powers to control local authority powers in allowing contact. A court may not on the application of a third party forbid contact between a person and the child if the local authority and the child consent to it.[306]

A determination of whether to allow contact under s 34(2) or (3) or to refuse contact under s 34(4) should be made on the principle of the best interests of the child. Under the ECHR Article 8 a child in care has a right to see her parents, and her parents have a right to see her, when she is being 'looked after' by the local authority.[307] This right may be overridden but only if threatened harm necessitates such a breach. In *Re C (Care: Consultation with Parent not in Child's Best Interests)*[308] (which was actually a case about consultation with parents about children in care), the father had raped and indecently assaulted the child, and was currently serving 11 years' imprisonment for these offences. The child, who was the subject of a care order, did not wish the father to be informed or consulted at all in relation to her future, and had successfully applied for a discharge of his parental responsibility. However the local authority was

---

[299] ibid s 23(2) and s 33(1).   [300] ibid Sch 2 [21(2)].   [301] ibid s 22(4).
[302] ibid s 22(5)(a) and (b).   [303] ibid Sch (2) [15].   [304] ibid s 34 (2).
[305] ibid s 34(4).   [306] *Re W (Section 34(2) Orders)* [2000] 1 FLR 512 (Fam Div).
[307] *R v UK* [1988] 2 FLR 445 (ECtHR).
[308] *Re C (Care: Consultation with Parent not in Child's Best Interests)* (2006) 32 Family Law 246 (Fam Div) (Coleridge J).

obliged to consult and inform the parents about their plans for the child in care even after parental responsibility had been discharged. The court granted a declaration to the effect that the local authority was absolved, in these exceptional circumstances, from any obligation to consult the father. A similar balancing exercise should take place in cases concerning contact.

In the *Your Shout*[309] survey of children in care conducted by the NSPCC, many children and young people expressed great unhappiness at their loss of contact with their families following their entrance into care. Hundreds of young people told of their sadness and anxiety for their siblings from whom they had been separated. This led the NSPCC *Review of Legislation Relating to Children in Family Proceedings* to conclude that the requirements under Children Act 1989 s 34 needed urgent review.[310]

(k) Additional powers under a care order

A care order gives a local authority parental responsibility and the power to determine how a parent or guardian of a child may exercise his parental responsibility for the child.[311] In this way the granting of a care order gives the local authority much more power to make decisions than when the child is being accommodated under s 20. For example in *R v Tameside MBC ex parte J*[312] the local authority offered a foster placement to a 'looked after' child with severe disabilities, who was already being accommodated by them in a residential home for disabled children. This offer was made under Children Act 1989 s 20 which allows the local authority to offer accommodation to children in their area. Her parents did not wish to accept this offer, preferring that the child remained where she was. The court decided that although the local authority had the power under statute to make 'mundane' decisions about the day-to-day management of a child being looked after by them,[313] without a care order they did not have the power to make decisions which impinged upon the rights, responsibilities, and authority the parent has in relation to the child. Thus the parents have the right to question and indeed to veto any decision which involves their parental responsibility as defined by Children Act s 3.[314]

Similarly parents with parental authority have the right to remove an accommodated child from the place where they are being looked after by the local authority. Under Children Act 1989 s 20(8) 'any person who has parental responsibility for a child may at any time remove the child from accommodation provided by or on behalf of the local authority under this section'. This is subject to the proviso that the objecting parent must be able to offer alternative accommodation, but not subject to the proviso that this accommodation must be suitable.

All that the local authority can do at this point, if they do not agree with the parents, is to apply for the further powers that a court order would give them, if

---

[309] J Timms and J Thoburn *Your Shout! A Survey of the Views of 706 Children and Young People in Public Care* (NSPCC, London 2003).
[310] *Review of Legislation Relating to Children in Family Proceedings* (n 79) 19.
[311] Children Act 1989 (England) s 33(3)(a).   [312] *R v Tameside MBC ex p J* [2000] 1 FLR 942.
[313] ibid, 948F.   [314] See above B.1. (b).

the local authority concludes that to accede to the parents' wishes would 'make it impossible to implement a suitable plan' and this would lead to the child suffering significant harm.[315]

(l) Discharging a care or supervision order

A care order will last until the child reaches the age of 18, unless it is discharged under Children Act 1989 s 39(1). A supervision order may also be discharged or varied under this provision.

Under s 39(1) the child or anyone with parental responsibility for the child, including the local authority, may apply for the discharge of a care order, or the discharge or variation of a supervision order. An applicant for discharge of an order does not need to prove that the threshold conditions no longer exist.[316] An order can be discharged by the court following a finding that it is in the child's best interests to do so.[317] The court may at this point substitute a care order for a supervision order. The court should consider the welfare checklist under section 1(3), in particular 'any harm which the child is suffering or is at risk of suffering'.[318]

If the local authority is failing in its duty towards a child who is the subject of a care order, one option is to make an application for that order to be discharged. In *Re O (Care: Discharge of Care Order)*[319] the mother applied for the discharge of a care order after persistent local authority failure to offer the services which it had promised in the care plan followed by the local authority's decision to remove the children from her care when, unsurprisingly, the children showed little improvement. Judge Steel substituted supervision and residence orders for the original care order, in the hope that the work would be done by the local authority and that the mother would be more likely to cooperate once the parental responsibility of the local authority was removed.

2. Court orders in the United States

In the United States each State has a general standard which justifies intervention when a child has been or is at risk of being abused or neglected. All State legislation concentrates on abuse rather than more general standards of harm as the justification for state intervention. There are enormous variations between States in the level of specificity which may constitute abuse under the terms of the statute. For example the Alaska statute describes child abuse and neglect as:

the physical injury or neglect, mental injury, sexual abuse, sexual exploitation, or maltreatment of a child under the age of 18 by a person under circumstances that indicate that the child's health or welfare is harmed or threatened thereby. In this paragraph, 'mental injury' means

---

[315] Department of Health *The Children Act 1989 Guidance and Regulations Volume 2* (HMSO London 1991) [2.50].

[316] *Re S (Discharge of Care Order)* [1995] 2 FLR 639, 643D (Waite LJ); see also *Re T (Termination of Contact: Discharge of Order)* [1997] 1 FLR 517.   [317] Children Act 1989 (England) s 1(1).

[318] *Re S* (n 316) 643F (Waite LJ).

[319] *Re O (Care: Discharge of Care Order)* [1999] 2 FLR 119 (Fam Div).

an injury to the emotional well-being, or intellectual or psychological capacity of a child, as evidenced by an observable and substantial impairment in the child's ability to function.[320]

As may be seen here the requisite level of harm justifying intervention is lower. The abuse need only be shown to have caused or threatened harm, rather than the English threshold of significant harm for the threshold to be satisfied.

At the other end of the scale some statutes list all the types of abuse which the state may respond to and further define that abuse. In California the statute defines each type of child abuse which is not permitted under the statute, with the exception of physical abuse which is only defined as 'physical injury'. For example sexual assault is defined as including:

rape, statutory rape, rape in concert, incest, sodomy, lewd or lascivious acts upon a child, oral copulation, sexual penetration, or child molestation. Conduct described as 'sexual assault' includes, but is not limited to, all of the following:

- Any penetration, however slight, of the vagina or anal opening of one person by the penis of another person, whether or not there is the emission of semen.

- Any sexual contact between the genitals or anal opening of one person and the mouth or tongue of another person.

- Any intrusion by one person into the genitals or anal opening of another person, including the use of any object for this purpose, except that it does not include acts performed for a valid medical purpose.

- The intentional touching of the genitals or intimate parts (including the breasts, genital area, groin, inner thighs, and buttocks) or the clothing covering them, of a child, or of the perpetrator by a child, for purposes of sexual arousal or gratification, except that, it does not include acts which may reasonably be construed to be normal caretaker responsibilities; interactions with, or demonstrations of affection for, the child; or acts performed for a valid medical purpose;

- The intentional masturbation of the perpetrator's genitals in the presence of a child.[321]

There has been some debate amongst American academics about which of the many types of threshold standard is preferable.[322] Wald has argued in contrast that detailed statutory definitions can avoid arbitrary decisions by social workers based on particular prejudice, rather than careful consideration of the evidence in a particular case.[323] However Katz has argued that a wide and general definition allows a court to consider a child's individual circumstances and prevents a court from having to shoehorn complicated experiences into a particular definition of abuse[324]—an argument which would resonate with the drafters of the Children Act 1989 and is consistent with

---

[320] Alaska Statutes §47.290 (2005).   [321] Californian Penal Code 2006 §11165.1.

[322] T Taylor 'The Cultural Defense and its Irrelevancy in Child Protection Law' (1997) 17 B C Third World 331, 335–6.

[323] M Wald 'State Intervention on Behalf of "Neglected" Children: A Search for Realistic Standards' (1975) 27 *Stan J Child Sexual Abuse* 985, 988.

[324] S Katz 'When Parents Fail' (1971) 52, in Taylor 'The Cultural Defense and its Irrelevancy in Child Protection Law' (n 322), 335.

the findings of the Court of Appeal in *Re H and R*[325] and with the realities of child protection cases that reach the courts.

In the United States the religion and culture of a parent and child may be taken into account in a number of different ways in a determination of whether a child has been abused and therefore in a determination of whether the state may take further action to protect the child. The most common mechanism is through an exemption for parents from a finding of neglect if they refuse conventional medical treatment for their child because of their religious beliefs. A common version of this exemption is found in the Delaware Code:

No child who in good faith is under treatment solely by spiritual means through prayer in accordance with the tenets and practices of a recognized church or religious denomination by a duly accredited practitioner thereof shall for that reason alone be considered a neglected child for the purposes of this chapter.[326]

By 1993 44 States had incorporated a religious exemption clause into their definition of child abuse. Again there was a financial incentive for doing so. The Federal Child Abuse Prevention and Treatment Act of 1974 linked Federal funding for child abuse programmes to a number of specific changes in State law, including a religious beliefs exemption. The basis for these provisions appears to lie in a belief in parents' 'free exercise rights' in the First Amendment to the US Constitution, or at least a desire to ward off litigation based on the First Amendment.[327] It is important to note here that it is the parents' rather than the children's rights to exercise their religion which have been upheld in a series of cases in the lower courts and in *Jehovah's Witnesses v King County Hospital* in the Supreme Court of the United States:[328]

In most cases courts have been unwilling to allow either the State's determination or their own judgment of a child's best interests to supplant parental free exercise rights. Indeed, only when according decisive weight to parental free exercise rights would threaten the child with death or grievous bodily injury or would result in the child receiving a grossly inadequate education will the State prevail under the current legal regime.[329]

Such exemptions should fit uneasily in child protection laws predicated on decision-making in the best interests of the child. As Dwyer has argued, this exemption is based on an instrumentalist view of children, that they may be used by their parents to fulfil the parents' own religious goals and that the state should not interfere with that purpose, even when the child may be physically and emotionally harmed as a

---

[325] *Re H and R* (n 244) 653 (Sir Stephen Brown).

[326] Delaware Code Annotated title 16 [913] (Supp. 1998).

[327] Article 1 'the Congress shall make no law respecting an establishment of religion, or prohibiting the free exercise thereof' *Articles in Addition to, and Amendments of, The Constitution Of The United States Of America, Proposed by Congress, and Ratified by the Legislatures of the Several States, Pursuant to the Fifth Article of the Original Constitution* <http://www.law.emory.edu/FEDERAL/usconst.html> (accessed 10 October 2006).

[328] *Jehovah's Witnesses in the State of Washington et al v King County Hospital Unit No. 1 (Harborview) et al* 391 US 961 (1968) (US Supreme Ct).

[329] J Dwyer 'Parents' Religion and Children's Welfare: Debunking the Doctrine of Parents' Rights' (1994) 82 Calif L Rev 1371, 1378.

result.[330] It dramatically illustrates the very different underlying ethos of the family laws relating to children in the United States. While there is an acknowledgement of the child's need for protection, this generally relates to the protection of children from those outside the family group;[331] whereas the aim of much of the law relating to children within the family group has been to aid parents to resist state interference in the way that they choose to parent.[332]

Three States specifically address the cultural practices within a child's community in their definitions of child abuse. Unlike the religious exception, the cultural consideration appears to stem from attempts to gauge the actual harm to children, rather than the protection of parental rights to control over their child. All three statutory sections relate to the initial assessment of a report of child abuse. For example, the provision for American Samoa states, 'in all cases, those investigating reports of child abuse shall take into account accepted child rearing practices of the culture'.[333] The statutes attempt to incorporate the views of those within the cultural group (the *emic* perspective) and those of an outsider (the *etic* perspective). However it appears that the statute allows the *etic* perspective of what is damaging to a child to trump the *emic* perspective when such conflict occurs. For example the Minnesota statute states that:

persons who conduct assessments or investigations under this section shall take into account accepted child-rearing practices of the culture in which a child participates, which are not injurious to the child's health, welfare, and safety.[334]

Much of the law in relation to the court orders which may be granted in child protection cases in the United States varies so drastically between States that a general discussion such as this book can provide, can be unhelpful and at times positively misleading. However one general feature of child protection litigation across the United States which is very different from other jurisdictions is the existence of an order terminating parental rights which is part of the repertoire of child protection orders, rather than necessarily part of a hearing related to a child's adoption. In termination cases, 'victory by the State not only makes termination of parental rights possible; it entails a judicial determination that the parents are unfit to raise their own children'.[335]

Federal legislation creates a mechanism for court management of child welfare work with a child, rather than a series of court orders which give the welfare agencies the powers to make decisions in a child's case. The court management systems created

---

[330] ibid.

[331] S Ramsey 'The United States child protective system—a triangle of tensions' [2001] Child and Family LQ 25, 26.

[332] D Buss 'How the UN stole childhood: The Christian Right and the International Rights of the Child' in J Bridgeman and D Monk (eds) *Feminist Perspectives on Child Law* (Cavendish, London 2000), 271.

[333] American Samoa Code [45.2001(a)(2)] (AS Bar 2003).

[334] Minnesota Statute Annotated [626.556], Subd 2(c)(5), 2(d), 2(m). West Colorado's Code dictates that investigators must take into account 'accepted child-rearing practices of the culture in which the child participates including, but not limited to, accepted work-related practices of agricultural communities' in determining whether a particular act is abuse. Colorado Rev Stat Ann [19-1-103(1)(b)].

[335] *Santosky v Kramer* 455 US 745 (USSC 1982), 760 (Blackmun J).

following the AACWA should have five key stages.[336] Before court involvement there should be *a pre-trial conference*. At this conference the child's caseworker should present a detailed report of the child's position (usually known as a 'case service plan'). The case service plan should explain the needs of the child and those of the parents and what services the family needs to ensure reunification and the cessation of court involvement. The parents may admit some or all the allegations in the petition at the pre-trial conference; if so, the case should then go to court, for a consideration of what services the court will order on the basis of the 'case service plan' and the admissions of the parents. The court may then order a wide variety of services: in-home parenting support, parenting classes, anger-management counselling, treatment for addictions, individual or family counselling, or educational or employment assistance. The court will also consider whether the child should live at home while the services are received or should continue to live in foster care, or enter into it.

If the parents do not admit to the allegations in the petition at the pre-trial conference, the case should be set for *a temporary wardship or custody trial*. The purpose of this trial is to enable the court to decide whether to take 'jurisdiction over the children'. The parental rights are not extinguished at this stage. The purpose of the court taking 'jurisdiction' over the children is to order services which the parents are obliged to accept.

After the court takes 'jurisdiction over the child' there should be a number of *reviews* in court of the court-ordered case service plan and the progress of the services on offer. The AACWA permitted these reviews to be undertaken by an administrative body, but the majority of States implemented laws requiring that the reviews be undertaken by the court.[337] In these reviews the court should consider whether to maintain the services in place, add further services, or cease to offer some services. It should also consider whether to impose stricter guidelines to ensure that parents accept the services and fulfil the obligations expected by the court.

After the statutory time limit for engaging in services has been reached, a *permanency planning hearing* should be held. At this stage the court should review the initial allegations, testimony from any previous hearings, the care plan and whether all parties have 'substantially complied' with the terms of the court's orders. 'Substantive compliance' is a subjective question for the court. The court may at this point decide that its role should cease because the family have been successfully reunified or that the Child Protective Services should file a petition for the termination of parental rights. Parents may at this stage give up their parental rights freeing a child for adoption. If the parents do not voluntarily give up their rights the case will proceed to a *termination trial*. At this stage the court must determine whether it is in the best interests of the child for the parental rights to be terminated. It is not necessary for there to be particular adoptive parents available before parental rights are terminated.

---

[336] Federal Adoption, Assistance and Child Welfare Act 1980 42 U S C 672(a), A Philips 'Reasonable Efforts' (2004) 1(2) American Prosecutors Research Institute (Child Protection) Newsletter 1–2.
[337] Pub L No 96–272, 94 Stat 500 (1980) [671(a)(16)], Herring (n 193), 333.

As may be imagined from its emphasis upon adoption of children as often their best means to permanency, the ASFA 1997 has tried to limit the range of families who may be offered services by the court and to limit the time scale for court hearings. The ASFA created limitations on the 'reasonable efforts' requirement. First it tried to refocus all determinations about reasonable efforts in terms of child safety stating that: 'in determining reasonable efforts to be made with respect to a child, the child's health and safety shall be the paramount concern'.[338] Furthermore the ASFA removed the requirement on States to make 'reasonable efforts' to reunite children who had been subjected to 'aggravated circumstances'. 'Aggravated circumstances' should be defined in State law, but should include abandonment, torture, chronic abuse or sexual abuse at the hands of their parents.[339] In these cases parents would not be offered services by the court, but the case would be set for a trial for the termination of parental rights. It also introduces an expedited timetable for the termination of parental rights to a child in foster care.[340] Under the ASFA each State law should require that Child Protective Services file for the termination of parental rights after a child has spent 15 of the past 22 months in foster care (the '15/22 provision'). There are three exceptions to this provision: (1) if the child is living with a relative ('kinship placement'); (2) if the State agency has documented a compelling reason why filing for a termination order is not in the best interest of the child; and (3) if the State has failed to provide the family with the services necessary to safely reunite the child with her parents. Roberts amongst others has argued that the limitation of the 'reasonable efforts' provision will not affect many of the children in foster care, because the majority of children are received into foster care because of concerns about neglect, rather than other forms of abuse.[341]

The ASFA, like the AACWA, introduced financial incentives for each State to redraft their laws in order to give effect to the ethos of the statute. This has had the effect of creating large financial incentives for States to increase the number of children for whom parental rights are terminated and who are adopted out of the State's foster care system.[342] There has been a real fear amongst commentators that this will lead to more children in foster care who are 'nobody's children'; parental rights will have been terminated for them, but no places for adoption will have been found.[343]

In the United States the standard of proof which is required depends upon the gravity of the order which may be imposed. In a temporary wardship or custody trial, the court will usually conclude on the preponderance of the evidence whether a parent has abused a child. This is not universal and some States do require proof

---

[338] The Social Security Act (42 USC) s 471(a)(15) as amended by the Adoption and Safe Families Act 1997 s 101(a).   [339] ibid as amended by the Adoption and Safe Families Act 1997 s 101(d).

[340] ibid s 475(5)E as amended by Adoption and Safe Families Act 1997 s 103.

[341] P Wilhelm 'Permanency At What Cost? Five Years Of Imprudence Under The Adoption And Safe Families Act Of 1997' (2002) 16 ND J L Ethics & Pub P 617, 623; Guggenheim (n 92).

[342] The Federal legislation provides bonuses to States that increase their adoptions, giving them $4,000 for each child adopted above the previous year's number and $6,000 for each adoption of a child who is older or has some physical or emotional disability. 42 USC 673b(d)(1).

[343] C Ross 'The Tyranny of Time: Vulnerable Children, "Bad" Mothers, And Statutory Deadlines In Parental Termination Proceedings' (2004) 11 Virginia J Soc Policy & L 176.

by clear and convincing evidence at this stage.[344] The Supreme Court has held that once the court considers a petition to terminate parental rights, the grave effect of the order necessitates a requirement that the state must prove its allegations by clear and convincing evidence. Some States require proof 'beyond reasonable doubt' before making earlier temporary custody orders.[345] However, the Supreme Court in *Santosky v Kramer* has held that the higher standard need not be applied at a temporary custody hearing because the decision is not irrevocable and the placement of the children remains temporary.[346]

3. Court orders in Canada

The legislative threshold for granting an order varies across Canada. Some jurisdictions have favoured a standard that a child is 'in need of protection'[347] whereas others have used the term 'in need of intervention'.[348] However, legislation in each Province and Territory has attempted to clarify what each term means and the interpretation given to each of the terms is very similar.

There has been discussion of an 'enhanced civil' standard of proof in Canadian child protection cases over the past twenty years.[349] The origins of this discussion of an 'enhanced civil burden'[350] lie in the same English case, *Bater v Bater*[351] from which the heightened standard was originally derived in English caselaw, as discussed above. However, it is less clear whether the standard of proof has actually changed, or it remains the same but the judiciary are expressing a view on the necessity for strong evidence to justify orders with serious consequences.[352] McQuaid JA has argued that:[353]

the better view is that there are divergent opinions held by different courts in Canada on the issue of the burden of proof at the adjudication stage of a protection or wardship proceeding. Also I note, that while the Supreme Court of Canada has not directly addressed the issue

---

[344] For example General Statute (North Carolina) s 7B–805, Ohio Revised Code s 2151.35.

[345] *Santosky v Kramer* (n 335), 749.

[346] ibid 753–54, 759, *Wright v Arlington County Department of Social Services* (1990) 388 SE 2d 477 (Virginia Ct App), 478.   [347] Child Protection Act 2003 (Prince Edward Island) s 3.

[348] Child, Youth and Family Enhancement Act (Alberta) 2000 (RSA chapter 12) ss 1–2.

[349] *Children's Aid Society of the Niagara Region v MJ* [2004] OJ No 2872 (Ontario Superior Ct of Justice) [35] (Quinn J).

[350] *Children's Aid Society of the Niagara Region v DM and AK* [2002] OJ No 1461 (Ontario Superior Ct. of Justice) [37] (Quinn J).   [351] (n 229), 459.

[352] *W(N) v Prince Edward Island (Director of Child Welfare)* (1997) 156 Nfld & PEIR 241 (Prince Edward Island Supreme Ct) [18] (McQuaid JA); *Children's Aid Society of Winnipeg (City) v Bouvette* (1975) 24 RFL 350 (Manitoba CA) 352; *Children's Aid Society of Ottawa—Carleton (Regional Municipality) v L (DJ)* (1980) 15 RFL (2d) 102 (Ontario Prov Ct) 113; *Director of Child Welfare for Prince Edward Island v Victor* (1984) Nfld & PEIR 81, 139 APR 81 (Prince Edward Island CA); *Re G* (1984) 48 Nfld & PEIR 298 (Prince Edward Island CA) 304; *L(J) v Children's Aid Society of Halifax (City)* (1985) 44 RFL (2d) 437 (Nova Scotia CA), (sub nom *L and L v Children's Aid Society of Halifax and Attorney General of Nova Scotia)* 66 NSR (2d) 333, 152 APR 333 (Nova Scotia CA).

[353] *W(N) v Prince Edward Island* (n 352) [7] (McQuaid J A).

of the burden of proof in wardship matters, . . . courts have recognized the state had to present a strong case before a wardship order would be granted.

Initially this view was justified on the grounds that parental rights should not be disrupted without the strongest evidence and most careful consideration of the consequences of such action.[354] However even in these cases parental rights were not deemed to trump child welfare considerations. Latterly, parental rights have been deemed to be derived from children's rights to familial preservation in addition to the parents' own claims.[355] In *Catholic Children's Aid Society of Metropolitan Toronto v M (C)*[356] L'Heureux-Dubé J stated: '. . . the value of maintaining a family unit intact is evaluated in contemplation of what is best for the child, rather than for the parent. In order to respect the wording as well as the spirit of the Act, it is crucial that this child-centred focus not be lost'.[357]

The court orders which are available in Canada look rather like our own. Canadian jurisdictions have three basic court orders outside those reserved for the emergency protection of children.[358] These have different names depending on the jurisdiction, but they are an order allowing a child to remain with a care giver under the supervision of the agency, an order allowing the child to be placed in temporary custody of the agency for a given time period, usually no longer than a year. (The period depends very much on the age of the child, with shorter periods being allotted to children who are much younger.) The final order allows the agency to become the child's legal guardian until the child reaches the age of majority. The difference in Canadian legislation lies in the time limits. Like the legislation in the United States, the legislation in Canada is influenced by the search for permanence for children; thus there is much more of a sense within the legislation of a 'cutting of losses'. Once time limits have expired and children have not been reunited the legislation prompts a move to change the guardianship of the child and towards a new family for the children. However unlike the United States there are clear dicta that the courts will not make an order unless they have some clear idea of the fate awaiting a child. As King J found in *Children's Aid Society of Toronto v D(C)*:[359]

The children have been in care 18 months. The two boys are adolescents. The girl is nine. It is incumbent on the society in a case of this nature, where there is no plan for adoption, that the society set out clearly what the plan for each child is. And that this be done on the basis of reliable evidence. How can a court make a decision of such magnitude when it knows nothing of the affiants? How can a court make a decision of this magnitude when it knows nothing of the plans by the Society, whether they exist and whether they are practicable? It is insufficient for the Society to ask for Crown wardship with the prospect that these older children will drift

---

[354] 'Parental claims must not be lightly set aside' *King v Low* [1985] 1 SCR 87, 101.

[355] For a review of all the major cases see *Children's Aid Society of the Niagara Region v P-LR* (2005) Canlii 11791 (Ontario Superior Ct of Justice).

[356] *Catholic Children's Aid Society of Metropolitan Toronto v M (C)* [1994] 2 SCR 165 (SCC).

[357] ibid 191, cited with approval in *New Brunswick Minster of Health and Community Services v L(M)* (1998) 41 RFL (4th) 339 (Supreme Ct of Canada) [47].

[358] Child and Family Services Act 1990 (Ontario) s 57(1); Children Family and Community Service Act 1996 (British Columbia); Youth Protection Act 2004 (Quebec) Division IV and VI.

[359] *Children's Aid Society of Toronto v D(C)* (2004) ACWSJ LEXIS 4288.

in and out of treatment centres, group homes, foster houses, youth court, the whole panoply of state institutions.[360]

The Canadian judiciary at least appears to be attempting to guard against the fate that is befalling thousands of children in the United States.

4. Court orders in Australia

As discussed earlier, child protection legislation in Australia is a State rather than Commonwealth responsibility. Recent evidence to the Australian Senate has indicated that this has increasingly become a hindrance in operating a successful child protection system. The evidence described the system as 'fractured'[361] and in need of 'uniform child protection policies and legislation'.[362] The Senate Community Affairs References Committee noted these calls for a single piece of legislation to be enacted and that child protection, like private family law matters, become a Commonwealth rather than a State responsibility, without itself specifically recommending such a change.[363] At present each State retains its own child protection legislation.

Unlike the other jurisdictions which we have examined, there is no similar pattern of orders across Australia. Some of the States do adopt a model which is quite like the model of going into care which is the enduring feature within the English system. For example the Northern Territory has an order described as a 'care of child by minister' which gives the Minister the rights and powers of a parent to determine where the child should live and make other important decisions in a child's life.[364] This order, like the care order which may be granted under the Children Act 1989, is not time limited beyond the usual limitation of a child's majority. In other States the statute states clearly some of the options that are in reality available to the court in England. For example under the Queensland Child Protection Act 1999 s 61:

The Children's Court may make any of the following child protection orders it considers to be appropriate in the circumstances—
(a) an order directing a parent of the child to do or refrain from doing something directly related to the child's protection;
(b) an order directing a parent not to have contact, direct or indirect—
   (i) with the child; or
   (ii) with the child other than when a stated person or a person of a stated category is present;
(c) an order requiring the chief executive to supervise the child's protection in relation to the matters stated in the order;

---

[360] ibid [16] (King J).
[361] Senate of Australia *Protecting Vulnerable Children* (n 105) 65 [2135] Submission 61 (Mercy Community Services Inc).
[362] ibid 66 [2136] Submission 44 (Professor Chris Goddard).   [363] ibid 67–68.
[364] Community Welfare Act 1983 (Northern Territory) s 51.

(d) an order granting custody of the child to—[365]
  (i) a suitable person, other than a parent of the child, who is a member of the child's family; or
  (ii) the chief executive;
(e) an order granting short-term guardianship of the child to the chief executive;[366]
(f) an order granting long-term guardianship of the child to—
  (i) a suitable person, other than a parent of the child, who is a member of the child's family; or
  (ii) another suitable person, other than a member of the child's family, nominated by the chief executive; or
  (iii) the chief executive.

The difference between these provisions and those under England's Children Act 1989 is that where the child does live with another nominated person that person acquires rights at the time of the hearing and the state does not. Under the system as set out by the Children Act 1989, the state following a care order may place the child under the care of another person, but that person does not acquire rights by that process. The state and the child's parents have parental responsibility and the carer does not. The provisions set out in Queensland are better as they provide a level of certainty and clarity for those who are actually doing the difficult job of looking after children.

An interim care and protection order may be made if the court is satisfied that it would ensure the safety of the child.[367] In the Australian Capital Territory (ACT) the final care and protection orders are much more like domestic violence orders, particularly as the evidence which should be raised relates to the danger which a particular person has demonstrated towards a particular child. Under the Children and Young People Act 1999 (ACT) s 205A a final care and protection order may only be made if the children's court is satisfied that:

(b) . . . the person against whom the final protection order is proposed to be made—

  (i) has engaged in domestic violence in relation to the child or young person; or
  (ii) has engaged in personal violence towards the child or young person and may engage in personal violence towards the child or young person during the time the order is proposed to be made if the order is not made.

The wording of the section deliberately echoes the wording of the ACT's Domestic Violence and Protection Orders 2001 s 40.

Other States have adopted similar standards for intervention to those adopted by Canadian Provinces or New Zealand. For example, the Children and Young Persons Care and Protection Act 1998 in New South Wales allows a care order to be granted if either the parent is unable to care for the child, including the provision of adequate care, or there is evidence that the child is being abused or suffering or likely to suffer severe developmental or psychological impairment. It should be noted that the

---

[365] See also Children and Young People Act 1999 (Australian Capital Territory) s 207 (residence order).
[366] See also Community Welfare Act 1983 (Northern Territory) s 62 (no more than two months).
[367] Children and Young People Act 1999 (Australian Capital Territory) s 205.

statute specifically prevents the court from making orders simply on the grounds that the poverty of the child's parents prevents them from providing adequate care.[368] In Queensland a child protection order may only be made by a court which is satisfied that the protection sought to be achieved by the order is unlikely to be achieved by an order under this part on less intrusive terms.[369]

The burden of proof is also set out in some of the statutes. For example, under the Children and Young People Act 1999 (ACT) s 197 the burden is set at 'the balance of probabilities'.[370]

5. Court orders in New Zealand

The Children, Young People and their Families Act 1989 (CYP&FA) s 14 provides the single standard for investigations and any subsequent family court decision to protect a child—that a child or young person is 'in need of care or protection'. This standard is further defined considerably, unlike the English threshold of significant harm.

A child is defined as 'in need of care or protection' under CYP&FA s 14(1). This is very similar to definitions in Canadian legislation. 'Serious' is used throughout this section to indicate that the circumstances must be outside the normal range of familial disharmony. 'Serious' is also used to raise the threshold for intervention in family life in relation to cases of neglect and impairment.

The detail contained in CYP&FA s 14 and in the Canadian statutes, when compared with Children Act 1989 s 31(9), reflects the very different legislative styles of the two Acts. The architects of the New Zealand Act aimed to create a statutory guide for professionals, where much of the procedure which would guide their daily determinations was placed on a statutory footing and within the Act. The Children Act 1989, in contrast, is a statement of principle and much of the clarifying detail lies in the accompanying guidance. The problem in practice in implementing the Children Act 1989 has been that in the guidance clarity has often been sacrificed to detail and it is very difficult to find such a clear statement of what 'significant harm' can mean in practice. The benefit of the New Zealand legislation is that professionals can easily find the criteria for determining whether a particular child is in need of care and protection.

The New Zealand legislation and caselaw does not appear to have the failings of the law in the United States which can lead to an exclusive focus on proving that the child's parents were responsible for specific incidents of abuse, rather than a consideration of the overall situation of the child and whether this situation is harming or likely to harm the child. This may be because the legislation creates an overall standard of being 'in need of care and protection' which CYP&FA s 14 clarifies.

---

[368] Children and Young Persons (Care and Protection) Act 1998 (New South Wales) s 71; Community Welfare Act 1983 (Northern Territory) s 42.

[369] Child Protection Act 1999 (Queensland) s 59(1)e.

[370] See also Children and Young Persons (Care and Protection) Act 1998 (New South Wales) s 72 (1).

The standard of proof for a finding that a child is in need of care and protection is the ordinary civil standard of the balance of probabilities.[371] The courts in New Zealand have not accepted the cogent evidence test as outlined in the English case of *Re H*, instead holding that the evidence does not need to be more compelling if the accusation is more serious.[372] In cases in which the court must determine future harm to a child, the test is whether there is a 'real possibility of harm' (here following the House of Lords in *Re H*); this finding of future harm should again be based on facts established on the balance of probabilities.[373] For example in *Re C* it was found that a girl aged ten was likely to be sexually abused in the future on the basis that she was living with her mother and her mother's boyfriend. The boyfriend had been convicted of sexual assault against three young girls, he had not participated in treatment programmes whilst in prison, he had established a very close relationship with the girl over a very short period of time and the mother had no concerns about the protection of her daughter.[374]

Once the evidence is established to the requisite standard, the court should give clear reasons in reaching a conclusion on whether to make a declaration, under the CYP&FA s 75:

(1) The Court shall not make a declaration . . . that a child or young person is in need of care and protection unless it is satisfied that it is not practicable or appropriate to provide care or protection for the child or young person by any other means, including the implementation of any decision, recommendation, or plan made or formulated by a family group conference convened in relation to that child or young person.

The CYP&FA s 75 represents an expansion of the no-order principle found in Children Act 1989 s 1(5). Rather than the simple statement that a declaration need not be made unless it is necessary, it guides the court towards a consideration of the services which may be offered to a child and to her family as an alternative to making a court order.

This determination of which orders to make should be governed first and foremost by the welfare principle, CYP&FA s 6. The interpretation of this principle allows the court to consider the whole of the child's position in determining what action, if any, to take.

However, the existence or not of care and protection concerns is not the only embodiment of the interests and welfare of the child. While that question will generally be foremost in the consideration of the welfare and interests of the child, where the care and protection concerns on the one hand are dwarfed by a broader consideration of the welfare, interests and rights of the child, it may be that the more general consideration of interests and welfare prevail. Such a situation is rare. Where care and protection concerns are demonstrably focused

---

[371] *C and C v Chief Executive of the Department of Child, Youth and Family Services* [2003] NZFLR 643 (New Zealand High Ct) [26] (Durie J); *In the matter of the L children* [2001] NZFLR 681 (Auckland Fam Ct) [35] (Judge Inglis).

[372] *C and C v Chief Executive of the Department of Child, Youth and Family Services* (n 371).

[373] ibid [27]–[29] (Durie J).

[374] *Re C* [2004] NZFLR 49 (New Zealand Family Ct) [25] (Somerville J).

around immediate physical safety or irreparable emotional threat, then it is hard to imagine an application such as this succeeding.[375]

Once a court has made a declaration that a child is in need of care and protection under CYP&FA s 67, the court may do one or more of the following things.[376] The court may, without further order, discharge the child or young person, or any parent, guardian, or other person responsible for his or her care, or both, from the proceedings.[377] The court may also direct that, if called upon within two years, the child or young person, or any parent, guardian, or other person responsible for his or her care, or both, must come before the court so that further action can be taken.[378] On making a declaration the court may order one or more of the following persons to receive counselling: the child or young person; any parent, guardian, or other person responsible for his or her care; or any person in respect of whom a restraining order was sought or made in the proceedings.[379]

The court may also make one or more of a number of orders:

- a *services order* that certain persons be provided with services and assistance;[380]

- a *restraining order* that prevents a person named in the order from doing all or a number of things: living with a child; using, causing or threatening physical violence towards the child or molesting the child or young person, or any person with whom the child lives, by watching or besetting his or her place of residence, work, or education, or by following or waylaying him or her in any public place.[381] It is an offence to contravene a restraining order.[382] Unlike the English system of orders, which are discussed in Chapter 5.F, the restraining order is not time-limited, but ends when the child reaches 20 or marries.[383]

- the court may also order that *support* be given to a child or young person;[384]

- a *parenting order* giving a person or body the role of providing day-to-day care for a child;[385]

- a *guardianship order* appointing someone to be a guardian of the child or young person.[386] The powers given by a guardianship order are similar to the rights and duties of 'parental responsibility' under the Children Act 1989 s 3. However, unlike the English concept of parental responsibility, guardianship may be given separately to a State or other body. In England a state body can only acquire parental responsibility for the duration of a care order and may not acquire parental responsibility separately. A care order allows the local authority to determine how a person may exercise their rights of parental responsibility whereas a guardianship order suspends the guardianship of all others for the duration of the order. In New Zealand, guardianship, unless reversed, lasts until the child reaches the age of majority or marries.

---

[375] *Re HM (Care and Protection)* [2001] NZFLR 534.
[376] CYP&FA 1989 (New Zealand) s 83(1).　　　[377] ibid s 83(1)(a).　　　[378] ibid s 83(1)(b).
[379] ibid s 83(1)(c)(i)–(iii).　　　[380] ibid s 83(1)(d) and 86.　　　[381] ibid s 83(1)(e) and 87.
[382] ibid s 89.　　　[383] ibid s 90.　　　[384] ibid ss 83(1)(f) and 91.
[385] ibid s 83(1)(g) and 101, Care of Children Act 2004 (New Zealand) s 44.
[386] CYP&FA 1989 (New Zealand) s 83(1)(h) and 110.

Some of these orders are very similar to those which are available in England. The provisions of the support order under CYP&FA ss 91–100 are the equivalent of the requirements under a supervision order under the Children Act 1989 s 35(1) to 'advise assist and befriend a child', and the parenting orders in this context are similar to the provisions under the Children Act 1989 s 33. However both forms of order differ in some crucial respects. Unlike supervision orders, there are many more mechanisms to try to ensure that a support order is adhered to.[387] Unlike care orders, a parenting order in this context suspends the rights of all others to provide day-to-day care of the child.

The benefit of this system of orders is that the court can oblige an authority to offer services to a child which he needs, rather than the more limited range of options available under the Children Act 1989. However similar changes to the English law would not alter the basic problems in child protection practice. These orders come at the 'fire fighting' stage of the proceedings. The threshold that the child is 'in need of care and protection' has to be satisfied before they are made, which means that in most cases they are made once the damage has already been done. Damage may be further compounded by the process of taking the case to court with all its attendant delays and emotional stresses.

F. Monitoring State Care of a Child

1. Monitoring local authority care of a 'looked after' child in England and Wales

It has long been noted in relation to children cared for by the state that 'as a group, their deprivation remains and although they are "children of the public" they are not cherished by the state as a parent cherishes his own child'.[388] In essence these problems are created by the fact that the children now have a 'corporate parent'. The duties and responsibilities of parenthood are thus scattered between a number of different personnel whose identities may change. Studies of the position of children leaving the care of the local authority found that 'care was unable to compensate them from their damaging pre-care experiences and thus did not establish a successful pattern of schooling or a career path'.[389] The Annual Report of the Chief Inspector of Social Services 2001–2 found that only 69 per cent of the children continuously 'looked after' for at least a year had had all the necessary health checks, one in eight of them had been absent from school for at least 25 days in the year and only 37 per cent had achieved at least one GCSE grade A*–G.[390] To borrow the title of the Waterhouse

---

[387] ibid s 96, 100, 125, 127.

[388] S Jenkins 'Child Welfare as a Class System' in AL Schorr (ed) *Children and Decent People* (George Allen and Unwin, London 1975).

[389] N Biehal, J Clayden, M Stein and J Wade 'Moving On: Young People and Leaving Care Schemes' in Department of Health (ed) *Caring for Children Away from Home—Messages from Research* (John Wiley and Sons, Chichester 1999) 58.

[390] Social Services Inspectorate *Modern Social Services—A Commitment to Reform—The 11th Annual report of the Chief Inspector of Social Services 2001–2002* (Department of Health, London 2002) [2.64]; see also HM Government *Care Matters* (n 27) Chapter 1.

inquiry into abuse in children's homes in North Wales, many already vulnerable and damaged children have been 'lost in care'. As the courts and many other bodies have recognized, this can compound the losses that the child has already suffered in his or her life. In *Re F; F v Lambeth* the court held that, 'in consequence of Lambeth's long-term neglect both boys have suffered significant educational, emotional, psychological, social and behavioural harm'.[391] In recent years numerous inquiry reports have also testified to horrific and systematic abuse within local authority homes. The reports clearly concluded that the system was going wrong and that children were abused because of real failings in the public care system.[392]

These very public demonstrations of the failings of the public childcare system have had an impact on the current law in two ways. They have influenced the emphasis which the current law has placed on familial, rather than state care. Secondly it has led to the creation of a vast raft of legislation, circulars and guidance to set standards for care and to control the behaviour of those working in the system. Sir William Utting concluded in his review of the safeguards for children living away from home that the guidance relating to such children is 'now so large that responsible managers have difficulty in comprehending it all and it is less a tool for practitioners than a subject for their research'.[393] In addition to the Children Act 1989 the scandals have also resulted in the Protection of Children Act 1999 which placed the Department of Health's Consultancy Index listing individuals considered unsuitable to work with children on a statutory footing. The Care Standards Act 2000 created an independent national body to inspect all children's homes and other homes in which children are living away from their families and to monitor fostering and adoption agencies. Detailed Children Act Guidance and Regulations on residential care were issued with the Children Act.[394] They were followed by Quality Standards for Residential Care[395] to improve the inclusion of residential childcare in social work training. Guidance has also been issued on permissible forms of control in children's residential care.[396] Several other initiatives have also been launched to improve local authority care of children. *Quality Protects* was a government initiative to improve children's services through the creation

---

[391] *Re F; F v Lambeth* [2002] 1 FLR 217 [30].

[392] See amongst many other excellent reports, A Levy and B Khan *The Pindown Experience and the Protection of Children* (Staffordshire County Council, Stafford 1991); G Williams and J McCreadie *Ty Maur Community Home Inquiry* (Cwmbran Gwent County Council 1992); A Kirkwood *The Leicestershire Inquiry—The Report of the Inquiry into Aspects of the Management of Children's Homes in Leicestershire between 1973 and 1986* (Leicestershire County Council, Leicester 1993); R Waterhouse (Chair) *Lost in Care—Report of the Tribunal of Inquiry into the Abuse of Children in Care in the Former County Council Areas of Gwynedd and Clwyd since 1974* (Stationery Office, London 2000). See also D Berridge and I Brodie 'Residential Child Care in England and Wales—The Inquiries and After' in M Hill and M Algate (eds) *Child Welfare Services* (Jessica Kingsley, London 1996).   [393] *People Like Us* (n 130) [17.1].

[394] Department of Health *Children Act 1989 Guidance and Regulations Volume 4* (HMSO London 1991).

[395] Central Council for Education and Training in Social Work and the Department of Health Expert Group *Quality Standards for Residential Care* (Central Council for Education and Training in Social Work, London 1992).

[396] Department of Health *Guidance on Permissible Forms of Control in Children's Residential Care* (Department of Health, London 1993).

of a ministerial task force, designation of local councillors as guardians of 'looked after children's interests', the exchange of good practice information, and increased funding for children's services.[397] Despite these initiatives the potential remains for the local authority to fail in its duties towards children in its care, giving rise to the question whether the courts should have a role in supervising the local authority once a care order has been made, to ensure its compliance with the care plan. Latterly another initiative has been launched as part of the *Every Child Matters: Change for Children* programme.[398] Sadly the need for this initiative reflects the failure of the other programmes to improve the position of 'looked after' children, as it shares the same core aim of the previous initiatives, that is to improve on the very poor experience of 'looked after' children and the outcomes that they have on leaving care. However it is naturally hoped that the grand aims of the Green Paper *Care Matters* in relation to the care given to 'looked after' children will be realized.[399]

One of the aims of the Children Act was to reduce court control of the local authority's day-to-day care of a child. The court now has no power to control the local authority's use of a care order by placing conditions upon it or stipulating that a child be placed in a given setting.[400] This is significantly different from the position of the court before the Children Act 1989. The Family Law Reform Act 1969 s 7 gave the High Court the power to place a ward of court in the care or under the supervision of a local authority. The High Court also had inherent jurisdiction to make a child who was the subject of a care order, a ward of court. Once a child was made a ward of court, no important step could be made in her life without the permission of the court.[401] Certainly important decisions, such as where a child would live, or the contact that the child would have with her parents, was determined by reference to the court.[402]

The courts' inherent jurisdiction in wardship was severely curtailed first by the House of Lords in *A v Liverpool CC*[403] and then by the Children Act 1989. Lord Wilberforce in *A v Liverpool CC* held that it was the will of Parliament to deny the court any powers to review any discretionary decisions of the local authority made in the performance of its statutory role. This case concerned an attempt to use wardship to review a decision of a local authority.[404] In this case, a natural parent instituted wardship proceedings after a care order had been made, in an attempt to gain access to the child, possibly leading to care and control. This was at a time when a parent had no right to access (now named contact) after a care order had been made.

---

[397] *Quality Protects* website <http://www.dfes.gov.uk/qualityprotects/info/publications> (last accessed 4 October 2006).
[398] <http://www.everychildmatters.gov.uk/socialcare/lookedafterchildren> (accessed 4 October 2006).
[399] HM Government *Care Matters* (n 27).
[400] *Re B (Minors) (Termination of Contact: Paramount Consideration)* [1993] Fam 301 (CA); *Re T (A Minor) (Care Order: Conditions)* [1994] 2 FLR 423 (CA).
[401] Under the court's inherent jurisdiction, or Family Law Reform Act 1969 (England) s 7(2).
[402] *Re W and B and Re W* [2001] EWCA Civ 757 (18) (Thorpe LJ).
[403] (1981) 2 FLR 222 (HL).
[404] See also *Re W (a Minor) (Wardship: Jurisdiction)* [1985] AC 791.

The Children Act 1989 s 100 repealed the Family Law Reform Act 1969 s 7 and provided that no court could exercise its inherent jurisdiction to make a child who is the subject of a care order a ward of court. It also stipulated that a local authority could only make an application for the court to exercise its inherent jurisdiction with the leave of the court, and that the court could only grant that leave in very limited circumstances.[405] The effect of s 100 was effectively to draw a boundary between the decisions that were the province of the court and those which were not. The courts' role was to weigh the evidence and determine whether the threshold criteria were satisfied and whether a care order should be granted. However once that order was granted the responsibility for decision-making about the child passed to the local authority, in consultation with the child and her parents, if possible.[406] The statute does not allow the court a role in decision-making once a care order is in force, or in reviewing the local authority's performance in looking after a child under a care order.[407] There is one exception: the court has power to make an order with respect to the contact to be allowed between the child and a named person.[408] The court has also the power to discharge the order completely, but this is only on the application of a person with parental responsibility.[409] The Children Act 1989 instead established a programme to review each child's case by the local authority.[410] It also established a semi-independent complaints procedure that could consider amongst other things complaints about the exercise of a local authority's powers to look after a child.[411]

For the first six years after the Act came into force the higher courts accepted this division of decision-making. In the leading decision of *Re L (Sexual Abuse: Standard of Proof)*[412] Butler-Sloss LJ stated that 'at some point, if a care order is made by the court, it must hand over the future arrangements for the child to the local authority. That is not an abdication of responsibility by the court; it is acting in accordance with the intention of the legislation.'[413]

The higher courts endorsed a practice whereby the court attempted to gather as much information about the way in which the child would be looked after under an order before granting the order. The Court of Appeal in *Re T (A Minor) (Care Order: Conditions)* recognized the power of the court to refuse to make a care order, when the court did not agree with the care plan.[414] However once a care order was granted, the courts recognized the legislative policy of non-interference with the exercise of the local authority's discretion. The Court of Appeal also held that there was no judicial power to impose conditions upon care orders or to seek undertakings from the local authority before granting them.[415]

This was in the face of growing concern about the problems of drift in the management of children's cases in care and the failure of local authorities to adhere to the

---

[405] Children Act 1989 (England) s 100(3) and (4).   [406] ibid s 22(4).

[407] *Re L (Sexual Abuse: Standard of Proof)* [1996] 1 FLR 116, 124 (Butler-Sloss LJ).

[408] Children Act 1989 (England) s 34(2).   [409] ibid s 39(2).

[410] ibid s 26(1), and the accompanying regulations, The Review of Children's Cases Regulations 1991 SI 1991 No 895.   [411] Children Act 1989 (England) s 26(3).

[412] (n 407).   [413] ibid 124H.

[414] (n 400) 429; see also *Re J (Minors) (Care: Care Plan)* [1994] 1 FLR 253 (Fam Div).

[415] *Re C (Interim Care Order: Assessment)* [1996] 2 FLR 708 (CA) 711.

care plan agreed when a care order had been granted. The statute was clear, however, and there was no possibility apart from legislative change to engineer an alteration to allow the courts again to scrutinize the implementation of the care plan. However the implementation of the Human Rights Act 1998 gave the courts the opportunity to revisit the legislation and reinterpret it on the ground that it was not on its face compatible with the EHCR. In *Re W and B and Re W (Children)*[416] there had been a 'striking and fundamental' failure to implement the care plan after care orders were granted to the appropriate local authority in two separate cases. The Court of Appeal found that the denial of the power of judicial monitoring of the operation of care orders left the Children Act 1989 open to challenge under the Human Rights Act 1998 in certain instances. A public authority could act incompatibly with Convention rights in the case of a child in care 'by failing to take adequate steps to secure for a child, who has been deprived of a life with his family of birth; a new family who can become his new "family for life" to make up for what he has lost'. This could be 'readily inferred from the concept of positive obligations inherent in Article 8'.[417] The Court found that the state had a positive obligation to 'fill the gap' when depriving someone of her family life.

This cannot mean that all failures in implementing the care plan are a breach of this positive obligation towards the child. Only the fundamental failure to make good that which has been taken away could possibly qualify. Even that is limited by what is reasonable and appropriate. Local social services authorities have many demands upon their resources.[418]

The Court of Appeal suggested two ways in which the Children Act could be interpreted so that it would be compatible with Article 8. Thorpe LJ suggested that judges should, in limited and appropriate cases, be free to defer making a care order and make a series of interim care orders until there was a clear plan for the care of the child which the local authority was implementing.[419] Hale LJ thought this was an 'inconvenient and artificial' solution to the problem.[420] It was also inadequate, as on the face of the Children Act 1989 interim care orders leave the court with only slightly more power to control what happens during the period than a care order.

Thorpe LJ also made the more radical suggestion that a power in the court should be read into the Children Act 1989 'to require a report on progress. In effect, '. . . vital elements in the care plan would be "starred" and the court would require a report, either to the court or to the Child and Family Courts Advisory and Support Service who could then decide whether it was appropriate to return the case to court.'[421]

'Starred care plans' were rejected by the House of Lords on appeal in the same case (now renamed *Re S (Care Order) (Implementation of Care Plan)*). The House of Lords held that the division of responsibility between the courts and the local authority was a cardinal principle of the Act. To introduce starred milestones would be to amend the Act, rather than simply to interpret it so that it was consistent with the ECHR.[422]

---

[416] (n 402).   [417] ibid [55] (Hale LJ).   [418] ibid [60] (Hale LJ).
[419] ibid [29] (Thorpe LJ).   [420] ibid [60] (Hale LJ).   [421] ibid [30] (Thorpe LJ).
[422] Human Rights Act 1998 s 3 (England) requires primary legislation to be read and given effect in a way compatible with Convention rights. *Re S* [2002] UKHL 10, 2 AC 291 [36].

The House of Lords went further, attacking the reasoning on which the Court of Appeal had concluded that there had been a violation of Article 8 in this instance. Lord Nicholls concluded that it was not the Children Act which violated a child's right to family life under Article 8, but the very poor way in which it had been implemented in numerous cases of children in the care of the local authority. All that the Act did was to entrust the care of a child to the local authority once a care order had been made, and rely on the local authority to adhere to its provisions. This was not, he concluded, itself a violation of Article 8. The Law Lords found that failure to provide an adequate remedy for a violation of Article 8 was not in itself a violation of the right of family life guaranteed by Article 8 but was instead a violation of Article 13.[423] Article 13 is not a Convention right which may be enforced under the Human Rights Act 1998 s 1(1).[424] While this reasoning is not supported by other judgments in its interpretation of the requirements of Article 8 in relation to children in care, the case sounded the death knell for a wide interpretation of the Act which went against the specific language and intention of the Act in order to achieve compatibility with the ECHR.[425]

The judgment in *Re S* was proved out of step with other judgments which have interpretted Article 8 in this context. There have been further challenges to local authority decision-making about children in their care on the grounds that the local authority has violated a Convention right in its decision-making about the care of the child. As it may have been expected, the majority of the reported claims have been by parents who have argued that the local authority have violated their Article 8 right to family life by not considering or helping the rehabilitation of their children into their family. Some of these claims have been based on the interpretation of the local authority's obligations in *K & T v Finland*[426] where the ECtHR found that Article 8 did place a duty on the local authority to try to rehabilitate the family; where the local authority had altogether failed to consider rehabilitation in their plans for the child this could amount to a violation of the parents' and child's Article 8 rights to mutual enjoyment of family life, although this would have to be balanced with the overall best interests of the child in which there are considerations of child protection. In *Re V (Care Proceedings: Human Rights Claims)*[427] the Court of Appeal rejected the parents' claim under the Human Rights Act 1998 that the local authority's failure to fund therapy to help them to overcome their own abusive childhoods and to rehabilitate their family group was a violation of their Article 8 rights.

There is a very strong line of authority which interprets the Article 8 protection of family life as including the proper involvement of parents at every stage of the child protection process, including the implementation of a care order. As Munby J

[423] *Re S* (n 422) [113].

[424] (Lord McKay), J Munby 'Making Sure that the Child is Heard' [2004] Fam Law 34.

[425] G Phillipson '(Mis)-Reading Section 3 of the Human Rights Act' (2003) 119 LQR 183; C Gearty 'Revisiting Section 3 of the Human Rights Act' (2003) 119 LQR 551; A Kavanagh 'The Elusive Divide between Interpretation and Legislation under the Human Rights Act 1998' (2004) 24(2) OJ LS 259; R Masterman 'Taking The Strasbourg Jurisprudence Into Account: Developing A "Municipal Law Of Human Rights" Under The Human Rights Act' (2005) Int Comp LQ 907.   [426] (n 36).

[427] *Re V (Care Proceedings: Human Rights Claims)* [2004] EWCA Civ 54.

observed in *Re G (Care: Challenge to Local Authority's Decision)*, Article 8 requires that parents are properly involved in the decision-making process not merely before the care proceedings are launched, and during the period when the care proceedings are on foot, but also after the care proceedings have come to an end and whilst the local authority is implementing the care order.[428] In *Re M (Challenging Decisions by Local Authority)*, the Family Division quashed a decision made by the local authority following a care order because the parents had not been sufficiently involved in the decision-making process.[429] In *C v Bury Metropolitan Borough Council*[430] a mother unsuccessfully challenged a local authority decision to keep a child in their care at a residential school 350 miles away from where his mother was now living. Although the mother's application was not granted this was not because the court denied that she had procedural rights while her child was in the care of the local authority, but rather it decided that the decision to send the child to school was lawful, legitimate and proportionate and thus there had been no breach of Article 8. In *Re G (Care: Challenge to Local Authority's Decision)* when the parents had been looking after the children with a care order in place, Munby J heavily criticized the local authority's decision to remove the children from the parents' care with very little warning and no meaningful consultation with the parents:

In a case such as this, a local authority, before it can properly arrive at a decision to remove children from their parents, must tell the parents (preferably in writing) precisely what it is proposing to do. It must spell out (again in writing) the reasons why it is proposing to so do. It must spell out precisely (in writing) the factual matters it is relying on. It must give the parents a proper opportunity to answer (either orally and/or in writing as the parents wish) the allegations being made against them. And it must give the parents a proper opportunity (orally and/or in writing as they wish) to make representations as to why the local authority should not take the threatened steps. In short, the local authority must involve the parents properly in the decision-making process.[431]

There has been much more limited consideration of concerns put forward by children, it may be inferred (as the House of Lords recognized) largely because children have far fewer opportunities to engage advocates on their behalf.

There have also been further challenges by way of judicial review of local authority decision-making e.g. the successful case of *CD (A Child By Her Litigation Friend VD) v Isle of Anglesey County Council*[432] in which a 15-year-old girl with severe physical disabilities who was being looked after by the local authority successfully challenged the local authority's failure to consider her clearly expressed wishes and feelings in formulating a care plan. As Shargy has argued, the case 'represents a wake-up call to local authorities who fail to adequately consider the wishes and feelings of a child

---

[428] *Re G (Care: Challenge to Local Authority's Decision)* [2003] 2 FLR 42 (Fam Div) (Munby J).
[429] *Re M (Challenging Decisions by Local Authority)* [2001] 2 FLR 1300 (Fam Div).
[430] *C v Bury Metropolitan Borough Council* [2002] 2 FLR 868 (Fam Div).
[431] (n 428) (Munby J) [45].
[432] *CD (A Child By Her Litigation Friend VD) v Isle of Anglesey County Council* [2004] EWHC 1635 (Admin).

and its family environment'.[433] However her case was only made possible because the local authority employed a child advocate who aided the child and her mother (as her litigation friend) to challenge the decision.

2. Monitoring state care of a child in the United States

The most useful parallel in discussion about court monitoring of local authority care is the United States. For an observer most used to the system under the Children Act 1989, the most obvious difference in American law is the close involvement of the court from the point at which a case service plan is drawn up until a child returns home or is freed for adoption ('termination of parental rights').[434] This role is defined in both Federal and State law, originating in the Federal Adoption Assistance and Child Welfare Act 1980 (AACWA). The AACWA required that States establish court monitoring systems to check that the child protection services were making 'reasonable efforts' in each case to reunite families and foster care plans for children who did enter foster care, to avoid drift.

It appears that judicial monitoring of this process has never been the safeguard envisaged under the AACWA. There are several reasons for this failure to realize the hopes of the legislation that individual cases would be closely scrutinized. Some have argued that the first failing lies in the drafting of the legislation itself, which never clearly defined the terms 'reasonable' or 'efforts'.[435] Conversely it has also been argued that the aims of the provision were clear from its legislative history.[436] The second failing was to link Federal money to the completion of the court process of review and to a finding that the State has made reasonable efforts to reunite the family. States have encouraged or colluded with perfunctory judicial assessments of child protection work in individual cases. Some States created a pre-printed form with a 'tick box' for judges to indicate that they had considered whether the State and the parents were making 'reasonable efforts' for the family to be reunited. Such forms 'do not foster a hearing conducive to the individualised determinations that the . . . Act had contemplated'.[437] Indeed a review of determinations in Californian courts found that judicial conclusions that reasonable efforts had been made were unsupported by an in-depth review of the case files.[438] Massachusetts passed a law which went

---

[433] S Shargy '*CD (A Child By Her Litigation Friend VD) v Isle of Anglesey County Council*—Comment' (2004) 154 NLJ 1321.

[434] S Badeau and S Geserich *A Child's Journey Through the Child Welfare System* (Evidence to the Pew Commission on Children in Foster Care 2003).

[435] 'Improving the Well-Being of Abused and Neglected Children: Hearing Before the Senate Comm. on Labor and Human Resources' (104th Cong 16 1996) Statement of Richard Gelles, Director, University of Rhode Island's Family Violence Research Program <http://www.hhs.gov/asl/testify/t961120a.html> (accessed 28 September 2004).   [436] Herring (n 193), 337.

[437] W Crossley 'Defining Reasonable Efforts: Demystifying The State's Burden Under Federal Child Protection Legislation' (2003) 12 BU Pub Int LJ 259, 285.

[438] Office of Inspector General, Department of Health and Human Services, Audit of Title IV-E Foster Care Eligibility in California for the Period Oct 1 1988 through Sept 30 1991 (1994) in Crossley ibid 285.

even further, to establish a presumption that the court had made a reasonable efforts determination unless the court specifically documented otherwise. It is, however, surprising that the judiciary themselves have not upheld the standard and acted to scrutinize the actions of the child welfare agencies. In passing the AACWA, Congress expected the judges themselves to be the effective safeguards—upholding standards and enforcing the monitoring process.

The Committee is aware that the judicial determination requirement can become a mere pro forma exercise in paper shuffling to obtain Federal funding . . . While this could occur in some instances, the committee is unwilling to accept as a general proposition that the judiciaries of the States would so lightly treat a responsibility placed upon them by Federal statute for the protection of children.[439]

The reasons why individual judges have failed to perform their monitoring function are no doubt complicated. However there appear to be two reasons why the judiciary *en masse* has failed in this role, which may be of interest to a consideration of how the requirements of Article 8 ECHR may be best realized in England and Wales. The first reason is that the realities of the system never allowed time for a full case review.[440] Social workers carrying large case loads did not have the time to provide an in-depth case review or the services which the family needed. The attorneys and the judges handling the cases typically carry enormous case loads, with judges disposing of between forty to eighty cases in an eight-hour day in urban courts. 'Under such time-constrained, resource-poor conditions, the adversarial system breaks down almost completely. The case review process becomes a mere production line that achieves only paperwork conformity with federal law'.[441]

Secondly there has been no effective 'guarding of the guards' in some States. Federal monitoring of case reviews, as Raymond has argued, has amounted to 'little more than a pro-forma exercise of enforcement' because it does not require judges to give an explanation for the basis on which a finding of 'reasonable efforts' has been made.[442] All that is required to release Federal funding is that a court order states that 'reasonable efforts were made to prevent removal from the home', that 'it was not appropriate or in the best interests of the child to prevent removal from the home', or that the order conforms to State law which implements the provisions of the AACWA. Even more importantly for the judiciary, the US Supreme Court has rejected arguments that individuals can enforce 'reasonable efforts' requirements on a State. *Suter v Artist M*[443] in 1992 concerned a class action against the Illinois Department of Children and Family Services for failure to provide adequate services to children placed in State custody as a result of claims of abuse or neglect, specifically its non-compliance with

---

[439] S Rep No 96–336, 16 (1979), reprinted in 1980 US CCAN 1448, 1465.
[440] Gordon (n 189) 650–52.   [441] D Herring (n 193), 334.
[442] S Raymond 'Where Are the Reasonable Efforts to Enforce the Reasonable Efforts Requirement?: Monitoring State Compliance Under the Adoption Assistance and Child Welfare Act of 1980' (1999) 77 Tex L Rev 1235.   [443] *Suter v Artist M* 503 US 347 (USSC 1992).

the case plan requirements. The Supreme Court rejected this argument, holding that the AACWA's funding pre-requisite—that States would make 'reasonable efforts' to prevent the removal of children from their homes—did not create an enforceable right because its language was ambiguous. The Supreme Court concluded that in the absence of a stated intention that Congress wished to create an enforceable right, it was not inclined to infer that such a right existed.

In holding that the child plaintiffs did not have a Federally enforceable right to reasonable efforts, the Court claimed that 'the absence of a remedy under §1983 does not make the "reasonable effort" clause a dead letter, in fact the reasonable efforts clause has become a dead letter and the Court's preclusion of suits by private plaintiffs contributed significantly to the demise of this federal requirement.[444]

Suter v Artist M[445] effectively killed the challenges to the State child welfare agencies for their failure to make reasonable efforts to reunite families and with them much of the scrutiny of the appellate courts of judicial decision-making during the review process.[446] However it was unlikely that such a mechanism could succeed; given the weight of cases going through the courts at this time, it could only end up as a rubber-stamping mechanism.

There is undoubtedly a pressing need for more effective monitoring of children's cases once those children are the subject of a care order in England and Wales. It is clear that the system of review established by the Children Act 1989 does break down, and long-term planning for some children can be simply overlooked for years. This is a grave problem which the courts have acknowledged needs to be addressed.[447] However it is not clear that court monitoring of local authorities will be the most effective mechanism for achieving an overall improvement in the system of monitoring. Referral to the court is an expensive option and can extend the delays in a child's case.[448] Even if a court decision is made it may not improve the lot of all the children being 'looked after' by the local authority. It will focus attention on those cases which are the subject of court scrutiny and away from other cases which are just as needy. In *Re S (Care Order) (Implementation of Care Plan)* Lord Nicholls called for urgent parliamentary scrutiny of the problem.[449] In response the Adoption and Children Act 2002 s 118 amended the Children Act 1989 s 26 by requiring local authorities to appoint independent reviewing officers for each 'looked after' child (including those in care, placed for adoption and accommodated under a voluntary agreement). An IRO should participate in the review of children's cases, monitor the authority's function in respect of the review, and refer a child's case to the Children and Family Court Advisory and Support Service (CAFCASS) where appropriate.[450] The CAFCASS may then act for children who lack the means to affect a challenge and initiate civil or family proceedings. Harwin and Owen have argued that this can offer significant advantages in producing close monitoring of individual cases by those who understand social

---

[444] ibid 364.   [445] ibid.   [446] Crossley (n 437), 260.
[447] *Re F; F v Lambeth* (n 391) at [33] (Munby J); *Re S* (n 422) [112] (Lord Mackay).
[448] M Hayes 'The Proper Role of Courts in Child Care Cases' [1996] Child and Family LQ 201.
[449] *Re S* (n 422) [106].   [450] SI 2004/1419.

work.[451] It is to be hoped that this may be achieved given the current enormous failings in the operation of the CAFCASS.[452] What is important is that the process is monitored by those whose purpose is child-centred and who can ensure that children do not disappear within the care system and that their progress is monitored. Ensuring adherence to care plans is, after all, only a mechanism to achieve the main goal, which is the improvement in the welfare of children following a care order.[453]

G. Allegations of Child Abuse in Private Proceedings

Allegations about child abuse seem to be an increasing part of the work of the Family Court in disputed and protracted proceedings about the care of a child. There is no English study yet on the number of allegations of child abuse in private disputes concerning children. However, a national study of the Family Courts in Australia[454] has found that while allegations of abuse were only present in 5 per cent of the cases concerning children in the Family Court, they became half of the total cases at the midpoint of court proceedings because they were not as readily resolved as other children cases:

Thus, without public or professional awareness child abuse had become a core element of the load of the family court and the family court had become a significant part of the child protection system, almost as significant as the state children's court.[455]

The stealth with which the adjudication of child abuse matters has become a routine part of family court business is reflected in the law. Checklists have been developed for the courts to aid decision-making in all children cases which recognize that harm to the child should be a consideration in all court decisions. However it is currently a matter for debate across the jurisdictions which we have examined about how important a finding of abuse should be in the decision about where a child should live, or what contact she should have with family members. In New Zealand and in some parts of the United States there has been an explicit policy decision that there should be a presumption of no contact when a finding of abuse has occurred, whereas current English law favours a balancing exercise between the risks to the child in allowing or refusing contact with a parent. The concern for the law has become how to ensure that a child is protected by the court and sufficient weight is given to allegations of child abuse, while avoiding the pitfall that an allegation of child abuse becomes a 'trump card' in private proceedings, ensuring that one parent is denied contact with the child on very limited evidence.

---

[451] J Harwin and M Owen 'Research—The Implementation Of Care Plans And Its Relationship To Children's Welfare' (2003) 15(1) Child and Family LQ 71.　　[452] Masson (n 160), 647.

[453] Harwin and Owen (n 451).

[454] Brown and others *Child Abuse in the Family Court* (Australian Institute of Criminology, Canberra 1998).　　[455] ibid 2.

1. Orders under the Children Act 1989

The Children Act 1989 s 8 created four court orders in the determination of questions relating to the upbringing of a child between private parties, rather than between a child's family and the state. These are commonly referred to as 'section 8 orders':

- an order 'settling the arrangements to be made as to the person with whom the child is to live' (*residence order*);

- an order 'requiring the person with whom a child lives or is to live to allow the child to visit or stay with the person named in the order, or for that person and the child otherwise to have contact with each other' (*contact order*);

- an order that no step which could be taken by a parent in meeting his parental responsibility for a child and which is of a kind specified in the order shall be taken by any other person without the consent of the court' (*prohibited steps order*); and

- an order giving directions for the purpose of determining a specific question which has arisen, or which may arise, in connection with any aspect of parental responsibility for the child (*specific issue order*).

As each of these orders relates to the upbringing of the child, the courts should be guided by the welfare principle and the s 1(3) 'checklist'. As discussed above under the checklist the court must consider any harm that the child has suffered or is at risk of suffering. Allegations of child abuse are therefore relevant in making these orders, particularly a residence or a contact order. The question of the standard to which evidence of abuse should be proved has been considered by the appellate courts, albeit briefly and with no absolute firm conclusion. In *Re P (Sexual Abuse: Standard of Proof)*[456] Bedlam LJ and Wall J considered whether the same standard of proof adopted in *Re H*[457] in relation to the threshold test under Children Act 1989 s 31(2) should also be adopted in private proceedings in relation to the s 1(3)(e) criterion (the consideration of the harm that the child is suffering or is at risk of suffering). They found that the judge at first instance had erred in applying a standard of proof of 'real possibility' for events in the past. However the Court of Appeal reached no firm conclusion on whether the standard of proof laid out in *Re H* should be applied in interpreting the welfare checklist under s 1(3).[458]

However in *Re M and R (Minors) (Sexual Abuse: Expert Evidence)*[459] Butler-Sloss LJ definitively stated:

If there is a dispute as to whether the child has suffered or is at risk of suffering harm [under s1(3)(e)] the task of the judge, when considering whether to make any order, whether it be a care or supervision order under s 31 or a s 8 order (residence, contact and other orders with respect to children), must be to resolve that dispute. Unless this is done, it will remain in doubt whether or not the child has suffered harm or is at risk of suffering harm and thus it will remain in doubt whether or not there exist factors which Parliament expressly considered to be of

---

[456] *Re P (Sexual Abuse: Standard of Proof)* [1996] 2 FLR 333 (CA).
[457] *Re H and Others* (n 225).   [458] *Re P* (n 456) 337.
[459] [1996] 2 FLR 195 (CA).

particular importance to be taken into account. The question is how such a dispute is to be resolved. To our minds there can be only one answer to this question, namely the same answer as that given by the majority in *Re H*. The court must reach a conclusion based on facts, not on suspicion or mere doubts. If, as in the present case, the court concludes that the evidence is insufficient to prove sexual abuse in the past, and if the fact of sexual abuse in the past is the only basis for asserting a risk of sexual abuse in the future, then it follows that there is nothing (except suspicion or mere doubts) to show a risk of future sexual abuse.[460]

While the case concerned the interpretation of the welfare criteria in granting a care order, Butler-Sloss LJ's opinion is clearly directed at all decisions made using s 1(3)(e) of the welfare checklist. The statements in both *Re P (Sexual Abuse: Standard of Proof)* and *Re M and R (Sexual Abuse: Expert Evidence)* were cited with approval in *Re O and N; Re B* by Lord Nicholls.[461] While it is difficult to see how *Re P (Sexual Abuse: Standard of Proof)* may be regarded as adopting the standard as set out in *Re H*, Lord Nicholls clearly uses both cases as authority to support his inclination towards the use of the guidance in *Re H* in the interpretation of s 1(3).

The definition of what is abuse has been gradually widened by cases concerning section 8. In a consolidated appeal of four cases involving domestic violence,[462] the Court of Appeal held that violence towards a child's carer should be regarded as an abuse of the child and a significant failure in parenting by the assailant. The Adoption and Children Act 2002 s 120 has recognized the strength of this argument, amending the definition of harm in the Children Act 1989 s 31(9) to include impairment suffered from seeing or hearing the ill-treatment of another. However in 2004, the charity Women's Aid published a report into the homicides of children killed by their fathers following the breakdown of their parents' relationship.[463] While 18 of the 29 murdered children were not subject to any form of court proceedings, the report identified 5 cases (involving 11 children in all) in which a court order had been made to allow the father to have contact with his children. The report recommended that courts should be obliged to assess risk and prioritize the safety of all children in cases of domestic violence. As a result of this Wall LJ analysed the five cases and found that they did raise some questions about the courts' decisions, and in two cases (concerning three children in all) the court could have taken a more proactive stance in questioning whether the order should be made on the ground of the child's safety, notwithstanding that the parents had consented.[464] Most importantly in the context of our discussion, he found that there had been an assumption in some cases that because the violence

---

[460] ibid 203.   [461] [2003] UKHL 18, [2003] 1 FLR 1169 [45].

[462] *Re L (Contact: Domestic Violence), Re V (Contact: Domestic Violence); Re M (Contact: Domestic Violence) Re H (Contact: Domestic Violence)* [2000] 2 FLR 334.

[463] Hilary Saunders 'Twenty-nine Child Homicides: lessons still to be learnt on domestic violence and child protection' (Women's Aid Federation of England, London 2004) <http://www.womensaid.org.uk/page.asp?section=0001000100090005000500090004> (accessed 4 July 2006).

[464] Lord Justice Wall 'A Report to the President of the Family Division on the publication by the Women's Aid Federation of England entitled 'Twenty-nine child homicides: lessons still to be learnt on domestic violence and child protection' with particular reference to the five cases in which there was judicial involvement' (The Judiciary of England and Wales 2006) <http://www.judiciary.gov.uk/docs/report_childhomicides.pdf> (accessed 4 July 2006) [8.21].

had been perpetrated on the mother, it was necessarily safe to allow contact,[465] despite the clear guidance the Court of Appeal had provided.[466]

In making a decision about either a residence or contact order, the court will consider the effect upon the child if the parent with residence would be seriously psychologically harmed by the effect of a contact order. In the past the courts have considered that the feelings of the parent should not be relevant to an order because they were essentially an adult matter. However this position has been gradually altered. In *Re K (Contact: Mother's Anxiety)* the court acknowledged the very real damage that can be done to a child by the extreme and justified anxiety of the parent with residence about the effect on the child of contact with a violent or erratic parent. In this case the court concluded that despite the child's obvious pleasure in the contact that he had with his father, the overall damage which the child would sustain because of his mother's anxiety could not justify the granting of a contact order.[467]

The timing of the decision on whether a child has been abused has become an increasingly important factor in decisions about residence or contact where there is an allegation of abuse. Wall J in *Re M (Intractable Contact Dispute: Interim Care Orders)*[468] and Munby J in *Re D (Intractable Contact Dispute: Publicity)*[469] expressed their concern about a tendency by the courts to procrastinate when an allegation of abuse, or other harmful behaviour towards a child is made.

The court should grasp the nettle. Such allegations should be speedily investigated and resolved, not left to fester unresolved and a continuing source of friction and dispute. Court time must be found—and found without delay—for fact-finding hearings. Judges must resist the temptation to delay the evil day in the hope that perhaps the problem will go away. Judges must also resist the temptation to put contact 'on hold', or to direct that it is to be supervised, pending investigation of the allegations.[470]

Both judges suggested that a clear finding by the court on whether there is any substance to the allegations must be a priority in any case where such suggestions are raised. Furthermore the court's decision on the issue was final and any further argument by a parent in a further court hearing that the court 'got it wrong' and did not perceive the truth of the matter should be taken seriously, as a symptom of their intransigence in relation to the best interests of the children.[471]

A finding that the child has been abused should be placed in the balance with all other factors brought to the attention of the court in determining whether an order should be made. The 'harm that a child has suffered or is at risk of suffering' is only one of a number of factors which the court should consider as part of the welfare checklist. There are no statements of principle within the Children Act 1989 about how the court should balance these factors beyond the general statements that the

---

[465] ibid [8.22].   [466] *Re L,* (n 462).
[467] *Re K (Contact: Mother's Anxiety)* [1999] 2 FLR 703.
[468] [2003] EWHC 1024 (Fam Div).   [469] [2004] EWHC 727 (Fam Div).   [470] ibid.
[471] *Re M* (n 468) [12] (Wall J); *Re D* (n 469) [54] (Munby J)

welfare of the child is paramount[472] and that the court should not make an order unless it would be better for the child than no order at all.[473] To these considerations should be added the general judicial presumption in favour of contact.[474] In cases where there is a fear that a child may suffer harm by allowing contact the court should weigh whether the fundamental emotional need of every child to have an enduring relationship with both his parents (s 1(3)b) is outweighed by the depth of harm which in the light, *inter alia* of his wishes and feelings (s 1(3)a) this child would be at risk of suffering by virtue of a contact order.[475]

When it appears that the child will benefit from contact with a parent, even one who has in the past assaulted him physically or sexually, the court may be willing to consider making an order, usually for some form of contact.[476] The qualitative weighing of the relative harms is made on a case-by-case basis. Radford[477] has argued that it is unwise for the law to leave individual cases to the discretion of individual judges who may have very little understanding of the damage that certain types of abuse may cause, and might thus under-value the risk of harm in reaching their decision. Furthermore she contends that the law renders decision-making erratic, with one judge placing a great deal more weight than another upon evidence of abuse. Radford urges that English law lay down a statement of principle as in New Zealand which we discuss below, which includes a rebuttable presumption against contact in cases where violence has occurred. Her arguments echo the findings of the NSPCC *Review of Legislation Relating to Children in Family Proceedings* that 'the existing provisions do not allow the court to identify those children who may be at risk and whose interests may be in conflict with both or either parent'.[478] Against these arguments are those made particularly by fathers' rights lobby groups that the current operation of the process is biased and that too much weight is given by the courts to essentially unproven allegations of abuse. These allegations slow down the decision-making process and make it more likely that contact will not be resumed. A test based on the overall welfare of the child is in principle more likely to favour a non-resident parent than a rebuttable presumption against contact when an allegation is raised.[479]

At present it seems unlikely that a rebuttable presumption against contact with a person where there is an allegation of abuse will be introduced. Women's Aid did make a submission to the House of Lords that such a clause should at least be put

---

[472] Children Act 1989 (England) s 1(1).   [473] ibid s 1(5).

[474] *Re W (A Minor) (Contact)* [1994] 2 FLR 441 (CA) 447 (Sir Stephen Brown); *Re L (a Child) (Contact: Domestic Violence)* [2000] 2 FCR 404, 437 (Thorpe LJ refers to it as an assumption rather than a presumption born from a base of knowledge and experience).

[475] *Re M (Contact: Welfare Test)* [1995] 1 FLR 274 (CA).

[476] *Re H (Parental Responsibility)* [1998] 1 FLR 855 (CA), *Re P (Parental Responsibility)* [1998] 2 FLR 96 (CA), *Re R* (2003) EWCA Civ 455 [15].

[477] L Radford 'Peace at Home—Safety and Parental Contact Arrangements for children in the Context of Domestic Violence' in C Breen (ed) *Children's Needs, Rights and Welfare: Developing Strategies for the 21st Century* (Thompson Dunmore Press, Victoria 2004) 92.   [478] B Essam (n 79) 19.

[479] A Perry 'Safety First? Contact and Family Violence in New Zealand: an evaluation of the presumption against unsupervised contact' (2006) 18(1) Child and Family LQ 1, 20.

into contact activity directions introduced in the Adoption and Children Act 2006 s 1 and contact enforcement orders under the Adoption and Children Act s 4. These directions allow the court to require a person to facilitate contact between a child and another person and enforce a contact order against the intransigent custodial parent. However their submission was rejected. The Government instead favoured a risk assessment in each case where there were concerns about a child being at risk of harm. The Adoption and Children Act 2006 s 7 introduced an additional requirement into Children Act 1989. Section 16A requires that when an officer of CAFCASS or a Welsh family proceedings officer, carrying out any function in family proceedings is given cause to suspect that the child concerned is at risk of harm, he must—

(a) make a risk assessment in relation to the child, and
(b) provide the risk assessment to the court.

This new provision does not close the door to further reform, but it is consistent with a continuing emphasis in England on an analysis of circumstances in individual cases rather than the creation of any overarching presumption.

2. Making decisions in proceedings between family members in the United States

Some States have amended their statutes so that there is a rebuttable presumption against awarding custody to a parent who has perpetrated domestic violence in the checklist of factors to aid the court in determining the 'best interests of the child'. This standard can be placed at a high level and implicitly may refer to violence against the other parent, rather than abuse against the child themselves. For example in North Dakota a rebuttable presumption arises when the District Court finds 'credible evidence that domestic violence has occurred, and there exists one incident of domestic violence which resulted in serious bodily injury, or involved the use of a dangerous weapon, or there exists a pattern of domestic violence within a reasonable time proximate to the proceeding'.[480] The presumption prevents the abusive parent from obtaining custody of the child unless that parent proves 'by clear and convincing evidence that the best interests of the child require the abusive parent to take part in or have custody'.[481] Other statutes provide that domestic violence and abuse are factors to consider in the determination of the best interests of the child[482] and that the court should act to minimize future harm to the child. For example the Revised Statute of Missouri states:

If the court also finds that awarding custody to the abusive parent is in the best interests of the child, then the court shall enter written findings of fact and conclusions of law. Custody and visitation rights shall be ordered in a manner that best protects the child and the parent or other family or household member who is the victim of domestic violence from any further harm.[483]

---

[480] North Dakota Civil Code [14-09-06] (as amended) 2(1), *Dinius v Dinius* 1997 ND 115, P18, 564 NW 2d 300.   [481] North Dakota Civil Code [14-09-06] (as amended) 2(1)(j).
[482] Louisiana Revised Stat Ann 46:2136 (West 2004) (allowing for a court in Louisiana to issue a protective order to stop contact with children following abuse of a party or minor children).
[483] Missouri Revised Stat 452.375(2) (6).

In contrast to English law, the legislation establishes a hierarchy of welfare concerns in which direct or threatened harm to the child can take precedence over other considerations, bearing in mind the best interests principle (which may in certain cases determine that a child should remain with someone who has harmed her, or may do so in the future). Meier has detected some judicial resistance to this tiered approach to the determination of welfare issues in decisions about custody and access, particularly when the violence has been towards one of the child's parents, rather than the child.[484] This is largely due, White concludes, to a lack of education of the judiciary to domestic violence issues as they concern children, rather than adults. 'Most courts perceive the mother's allegations of domestic abuse as her opportunity to abuse the father because the father no longer wants a relationship with her.'[485]

Judicial resistance to the proper use of the legislation appears to reflect a wider scepticism about allegations of child abuse in private proceedings, usually between parents. The term *Parental Alienation Syndrome* was coined in 1985 by an American child psychiatrist, Gardener, to refer to the intense rejection of a parent by a child following a divorce.[486] It has been increasingly and controversially used to explain allegations of violence and child sexual abuse in disputed custody cases.[487] Gardener has written no fewer than seven books on the subject of the fabrication of child sexual abuse allegations in the context of custody trials.[488] Fear that parents would use an allegation of abuse in private proceedings to 'trump' all other considerations and gain custody of the child has led to a presumption that parents will lose custody of a child, if their contention that the child has been abused by the other parent turns out to be false. A party 'who wilfully alienates a child from the other parent may not be awarded custody based on that alienation'.[489] However it is a common theme in legislation from other jurisdictions that the court in private proceedings, unlike public proceedings, may very well not have the benefit of evidence gathered in a full investigation on which to reach a decision that the allegations of abuse are true or false. Furthermore, as investigation of child abuse is a specialized business, there may be very little evidence that the parties can adduce for the court. Instead the court must usually rely on its judgment about the relative merits of witnesses.

---

[484] J Meier 'Domestic Violence, Child Custody, And Child Protection: Understanding Judicial Resistance and Imagining the Solutions' (2003) 11 Am U J Gender Soc Pol'y & L 657, 701.

[485] P White 'You May Never See Your Child Again: Adjusting The Batterer's Visitation Rights To Protect Children From Future Abuse' (2005) 13 Am U J Gender Soc Pol'y & L 327, 335.

[486] R Gardener 'Recent trends in divorce and custody litigation' 29(2) *Academy Forum* 3–7; R Gardener *The parental alienation syndrome and the differentiation between fabricated and genuine sexual abuse* (Creative Therapeutics, Cresskill NJ 1987).

[487] J Dunne and M Hendrick 'The Parental Alienation Syndrome: An Analysis of Sixteen Selected Cases' (1994) 21 *J of Divorce & Remarriage* 21–38.

[488] *The Parental Alienation Syndrome* (n 486); *Sex Abuse Hysteria: Salem Witch Trials Revisited* (Creative Therapeutics, Cresskill NJ 1991); *The Parental Alienation Syndrome* (1992); *True and False Accusations of Child Sex Abuse* (Creative Therapeutics, Cresskill NJ 1992); *Protocols for the Sex-Abuse Evaluation* (Creative Therapeutics, Cresskill NJ 1995); *Psychotherapy With Sex-Abuse Victims: True, False, and Hysterical* (Creative Therapeutics, Cresskill NJ 1996); *Testifying in Court: A Guide for Mental Health Professionals* (1996); *Sex Abuse Trauma? or Trauma From Other Sources?* (2002).

[489] *Brown v Brown* 600 N W 2d 869; *Loll v Loll* 561 NW 2d 625.

3. Making decisions in proceedings between family members in Canada

In Canada concerns were raised in the late 1990s that false allegations of child abuse were routinely being made in private law proceedings to allow those making the allegations to deny access to the child.

Stories in the media of fathers being denied access to their children due to accusations of child abuse were reported to the Special Joint Committee on Child Custody and Access, which began hearings in 1998. Headlines such as "Divorce law 'Hell' for Dads; Urgent reform needed, MP says", "Senator fights to even the odds in child-custody battles", "Sex-abuse allegation a perfect ploy: Some mothers accuse dads to keep custody of kids", . . . may give the impression that the problem of false allegations of child abuse in the context of parental separation is very widespread.[490]

The Special Joint Committee on Child Custody and Access asked the Department of Justice to conduct a review of the number of cases in which there were allegations of child abuse and the problems that this created.[491] The Review found that:

it appears that a relatively small portion of all contested parental disputes raised abuse issues. [There were many allegations which were substantiated.] While some false allegations after separation may be the product of deliberate manipulation by one parent, the majority of unfounded allegations do not appear to be deliberate fabrications. Distrust or hostility between parents may result in misunderstandings that lead to false allegations, especially in cases where the children involved are young and the allegations are reported through a parent.[492]

However the Review acknowledged that there was little empirical work in Canada on which to found this conclusion and that it was based largely on American studies. Bala has subsequently argued that as awareness of child abuse has increased, so have the number of allegations made in the context of private law proceedings.[493]

Thus Canada shares the same problems as the other jurisdictions we study and any system established in custody and access cases has to be one which weighs the evidence carefully and without a particular bias built into it. At present the Canadian system favours dispute resolution, and if that fails the 'best interests' provision is the legal standard the court must use for determining what rights and responsibilities[494] separated parents should have for a child.[495] This is articulated at Federal level in the Divorce Act 1985 s 16(8)–(10) which states that:

(8) In making an order under this section, the court shall take into consideration *only* the best interests of the child of the marriage as determined by reference to the condition, means, needs and other circumstances of the child. [emphasis added]

---

[490] Department of Justice *Allegations of Child Abuse in the Context of Parental Separation: A Discussion Paper* (Department of Justice Canada 2001) [1.1].   [491] ibid.

[492] ibid [1.2].

[493] N Bala 'Introduction' in N Bala (ed) *Canadian Child Welfare Law: Children, Families and the State* (Thompson Educational Publishing 2004) 11.

[494] The responsibilities for and making major decisions about a child and the amount of contact time, Divorce Act (5) and (1)).   [495] Divorce Act (RSC c 3 as amended SC 1990 c 18) s16.

(9) In making an order under this section, the court shall not take into consideration the past conduct of any person *unless the conduct is relevant to the ability of that person to act as a parent of a child.* (emphasis added)

(10) In making an order under this section, the court shall give effect to the principle that a child of the marriage should have as much contact with each spouse as is consistent with the best interests of the child and, for that purpose, shall take into consideration the willingness of the person for whom custody is sought to facilitate such contact.

Some Provinces have further developed the test for best interests; of them McCleod and Daley have singled out Ontario's Children's Law Reform Act as the most comprehensive.[496] The test itself does not specifically address the question of the weight that should be given to evidence of any harm that the child has suffered or is likely to suffer. However it has been established in caselaw that in determining decisions on custody and access based on the child's best interests the court should consider any evidence of abuse to the child or to the child's parent.[497] Newfoundland also put legislation in place which specifically refers to violence as a factor to be considered in making a decision on the children's best interests.

4. Making decisions in proceedings between family members in Australia

In Australia disputes between family members and others concerning where a child should live and with whom he should have contact, are determined according to the law of the Australian Commonwealth,[498] and in the High Courts and Family Courts of Australia. The Commonwealth courts have directly engaged with the question of the importance of a finding that a child has been abused in the determination of where children may live or with whom they may have contact. The leading cases in this determination remain *M and M; B and B*.[499] In *M and M* the High Court of Australia found that:

The ultimate and paramount issue to be decided in proceedings for custody of, or access to, a child is whether the making of the order sought is in the interests of the welfare of the child . . . The Family Court's wide-ranging discretion to decide what is in the child's best interests cannot be qualified by requiring the court to try the case as if it were no more than a contest between the parents to be decided solely by reference to the acceptance or rejection of the allegation of sexual abuse on the balance of probabilities.[500]

The High Court concluded that when a court considers an allegation of sexual abuse in a custody or access dispute, it should only make a positive finding that a child has been abused if it is so satisfied on the balance of probabilities. If the court can reach

---

[496] J McLeod and T Daley McLeod *Child Custody Law and Practice* (Thompson Canada, Westlaw 2004) [5.1].

[497] *MacDonald v MacDonald* (1991) 288 APR 136 (NS Fam Ct); *M(PA) v M(AP)* (May 27 1991) Doc No. A890055 (BCSC).

[498] Primarily the Family Law Act 1975 (Cth Austr) as amended by the Family Law Reform Act 1995 (Cth Austr).

[499] (1988) 12 Fam LR 606 (Aust HC) and (1988) 12 Fam LR 612 (Aust HC) respectively, *Hamilton v The Queen* CCA SCt of W Aus, Library No 970082 4 March 1997 (Western Australia CCA), *Re David* (1997) 22 Fam LR 489 [9.15] (Aust HC). [500] (1988) 12 Fam LR 606, 610 (Mason CJ).

that conclusion on the evidence it would 'in all but the most extraordinary cases' have a decisive effect on decision-making in the case. The High Court found that in *M and M*, as in its view in many cases, it could not confidently make a positive finding that sexual abuse had taken place. However the court could also consider whether there was evidence of an unacceptable risk of sexual abuse of the child in the future in reaching a decision about the arrangements for custody and access. In *B and B*, which was decided on the same day and by the same panel of the High Court as in *M and M*, the Court approved the decision of the judge at first instance. He had concluded that in the light of the evidence which he had received he retained 'lingering and residual doubts' that the father had abused the daughter and that on the basis of this finding there was an unacceptable risk of sexual abuse which warranted the denial of access in the future.[501]

This approach was followed until amendments were made to the Family Law Act 1975 s 60 by the Family Reform Act 1995[502] which emphasized the right of children to have meaningful contact with both parents and with their siblings and extended family.[503] The law also changed the language of orders, opting for the terminology used in the Children Act 1989 of residence and contact. Research undertaken in 2000 suggested that the legal change had affected judicial decision-making in cases where it was suggested that a child had been abused or was at risk of abuse.

[E]ven though allegations of violence and abuse are now widespread in court matters, the rate of orders refusing contact at an interim hearing has declined dramatically since 1996, and contact is rarely suspended. This has occurred despite the fact that the allegations have not been tested and although the (possibly unsafe) interim arrangements may be in place for up to 2 years. In fact many judges who were interviewed were unaware of the new provisions dealing with violence, though all knew about the 'right of contact' principle.[504]

The new provisions dealing with violence to which Roades refers in the quotation were contained in a new statutory checklist of factors which the court should consider in private proceedings when there has been allegations of violence or abuse.[505]

(g) the need to protect the child from physical, or psychological harm caused, or that may be caused by:
  (i) being subjected or exposed to abuse, ill-treatment, violence or other behaviour; or
  (ii) being directly or indirectly exposed to abuse, ill-treatment, violence or other behaviour that is directed towards or may affect another person;
(i) any family violence involving the child, or a member of the child's family;
(j) any family violence order that applies to the child or to a member of the child's family.

These are three of twelve considerations for the court in the welfare checklist. As in England these considerations are not weighted in any way and it is for the court to consider in the circumstances the importance that child abuse should take in the court's decision. In 2002 the Family Law Council of Australia expressed concerns that family law judges did not have enough information on which to base these decisions

---

[501] (1988) 12 Fam LR 612, 616.
[502] Now Family Law Act 1975 (Commonwealth of Australia) s 60B.
[503] *Re David* (n 499) [9.15].
[504] H Roades 'Posing as Reform: The Case of the Family Law Reform Act' (2000) 14 Austr JFL 9, 17.
[505] Family Law Act 1975 (Commonwealth of Australia) s 68F, as amended by the Family Law Reform Act 1995 (Commonwealth of Australia).

and proposed that there should be an investigation service linked to the family courts to investigate allegations of abuse that were made in evidence in the case.[506] The courts had been able to request that the statutory agencies investigate particular cases, but the agencies did not always respond to these requests.

There has been increasing concern within the courts that parents are fabricating allegations of child abuse to gain a tactical advantage in custody hearings:

In Western Australia, it is not uncommon to hear court personnel describe 'false' allegations of child sexual abuse as 'rife' and 'on the increase'. Indeed three senior court officials, in a joint presentation to a 'Forum Relating to Men' (27–28 November, 1998, Perth) went so far as to state that the Family Court of Western Australia was being 'overrun by malicious allegations of sexual abuse by mothers against fathers'.[507]

Again there is little research to establish where the truth lies in these descriptions. However this concern appears to have an effect on judicial decision-making in cases. Where it has been concluded that parents have fabricated an allegation this has had on occasions a determinative effect on decision-making. In *B and B* day-to-day care was taken from the mother and given to the father on the grounds that she had fabricated allegations of abuse and in getting the child to believe them, had herself abused the child.[508]

5. Making decisions in proceedings between family members in New Zealand

New Zealand law contains the clearest provisions to guide a court in its determination of the weight to be given to evidence of child abuse in private proceedings, introducing a presumption against contact in child abuse cases. Under the Care of Children Act 2004, which replaced the Guardianship Act 1968, the court should follow certain principles and procedures where a case concerns an allegation of violence, defined under the Act as physical or sexual abuse. The Care of Children Act 2004 s 54 applies where it is alleged that a party to the proceedings has used violence against the child or against the other party to the proceedings.[509] In these cases the court must: 'as soon as practicable'

(a) consider whether to appoint a lawyer to act for the child;[510] and

(b) determine, on the basis of the evidence presented to it by or on behalf of the parties to the proceedings, whether the allegation of violence is proved.

The Care of Children Act 2004 s 54(3) introduces a statutory presumption that if the court is satisfied that a party to the proceedings has used violence against the child, or another child in the family or another party to the proceedings, then the

---

[506] Family Law Council *Family Law and Child Protection Final Report* (Commonwealth of Australia, Melbourne 2002) 10–11.

[507] S Jenkins *Are Children Protected In The Family Court? A Perspective From Western Australia* (Child Sexual Abuse: Justice Response or Alternative Resolution Conference convened by the Australian Institute of Criminology and held in Adelaide, 1–2 May 2003).

[508] *B and B: Family Law Reform Act 1995* (1997) 21 Fam LR 676 (Aust Fam Ct) 92–755.

[509] Care of Children Act 2005 (New Zealand) s 53(1)b.   [510] ibid s 6.

court should not allow the violent party to provide day-to-day care of the child or have contact with him (other than supervised contact). This presumption against contact may be rebutted by evidence that the child will be safe with the party alleged to be violent, and an order may be made under s 54(4) for the child to have contact with or day-to-day care from that party.[511] However this decision may only be made once the court has complied with s 55 which lists the considerations for the court in determining whether the child is safe. These are:

(a) the nature and seriousness of the violence used;
(b) how recently the violence occurred;
(c) the frequency of the violence;
(d) the likelihood of further violence occurring;
(e) the physical or emotional harm caused to the child by the violence;
(f) whether the other party to the proceedings
    (i) considers that the child will be safe while the violent party provides day-to-day care for, or has contact with, the child;
    (ii) consents to the violent party providing day-to-day care for or having contact (other than supervised contact) with, the child;
(g) any views the child expresses on the matter;
(h) any steps the violent party has taken to prevent further violence occurring; and
(i) all other matters the court considers relevant.

The presumption against contact and the statutory checklist is directly taken from the previous Guardianship Act 1968 s 16B (as amended). Radford in her analysis of the operation of s 16B under the previous law found that the courts tended to take a broad view of the range of harms that a child could suffer, including psychological abuse and intimidation; however, they remained reluctant to prevent contact unless the harm which the child had suffered was found to be of a high level.[512] However Perry[513] has recently found a willingness in the appellate courts to interpret the concept of safety in the Act widely to include emotional harm caused to the child by violence.[514] The Care of Children Act 2004 s 54(6) also allows the court to make 'any order under this Act as it thinks fit, in order to protect the safety of the child if the court is 'unable to determine, on the basis of the evidence presented to it, by, or on behalf of the parties to the proceedings, whether the allegation of violence is proved, but *is satisfied that there is a real risk to the child's safety*' [emphasis added]. This imports into legislation the type of test which the dissenting judges, Lord Browne-Wilkinson and Lord Lloyd, argued for in the decisive English case on the standard of proof in child protection cases *Re H*, which we have discussed in detail above.[515] The benefit of such a test is that it allows the court to reach a decision in an area of practice where decisive evidence is hard to come by. It is obviously open to the criticisms of the majority in *Re H* that decisions may be made on the basis of judicial suspicion without proof. However, in

---

[511] An order may also be made for supervised contact under Care of Children Act 2005 (New Zealand) s 54(5).   [512] Radford (n 477) 92.
[513] Perry (n 479) 7.   [514] *A v X* [2005] 1 NZLR 123 [60].
[515] *Re H and others* (n 225), 11–12.

choosing a test which balances out all the risks in this decision-making process, the law has clearly fallen on the side of protection of children from damage which abuse may cause to them.

The New Zealand legislation is clear in the weight that child abuse allegations should have in private proceedings. While other jurisdictions, including our own, would place a higher value on the balancing of welfare considerations and 'justice' for parents in deliberations and have not adopted the same principles that New Zealand has chosen, the value of a clear position on the circumstances in which a finding of child abuse would usually be decisive in private law deliberations is superior to the case-by-case basis on which such deliberations are undertaken under the Children Act (England) 1989. The weakness in the New Zealand legislation relates to investigations. Under the Care of Children Act 2005 s 54(2), the court is not required to make any inquiries on its own initiative in order to make a determination on the allegation. Child abuse in all its forms is often hidden and it may be very difficult for either party to produce sufficient evidence to satisfy the court without the resources and help of investigators. This problem in private proceedings concerning child abuse has already been recognized in Australia. However in New Zealand, while under s 54(6) the court may make an order on the basis that it is satisfied that there is a real risk of abuse without definitive evidence of abuse having occurred, it cannot be relied on as a routine mechanism in cases concerning child abuse. Instead it may be appropriate for the court to use its powers under ss 124 and 125 to order a report in cases concerning parenting orders.

Perry[516] has argued that, whatever the legal structure for decision making about allegations of abuse in private proceedings, there are a number of overarching problems in New Zealand. The most pressing of these relate to the question of supervised contact. It is not sustainable over a long period of time because the supervision is not conducive to the formation of a natural and relaxed relationship between parents and children. It can be useful where there are pressing concerns about a child's safety which will be able to be resolved. However there are insufficient places in contact centres to make supervised contact a realistic option. She also argues that the presumption has in fact exacerbated concerns that the system is biased towards those making allegations. She notes that in New Zealand many commentators are suggesting the need for a system of mediation which would routinely avoid court proceedings in these cases in an attempt to reduce the antagonism which these cases routinely present.

The American and Australian experience demonstrates that if child abuse is made a 'trump card' in determining private disputes about where children are going to live, more parents will fabricate abuse stories. This is the reason why other jurisdictions have adopted an equally weighted list of welfare considerations. However ignoring child abuse as a problem does not mean that the problem will go away. Courts will have to make decisions about the weight to be given to allegations of child abuse in private proceedings. It is suggested that in New Zealand the legislation at least gives the judiciary a clear framework on which to make these decisions rather than making

---

[516] Perry (n 479) 20.

decisions in a more ad hoc manner. It is also suggested that the Australian approach still tends to undervalue the very real problems that abuse can cause within families which is of direct relevance to child contact. Furthermore, the recent move by the Australian central government to introduce the widespread use of dispute resolution in cases concerning contact with children instead of involving the courts, looks likely to divert many of the cases concerning contact and child abuse away from judicial scrutiny. The Australian Government is proposing amendments to the Family Law Act 1975 to introduce requirements to attend dispute resolution before taking a parenting matter to court. Sixty-five Family Relationship Centres are due to be in place by the end of 2008.[517] While these amendments are not on the statute book at the time of writing, the current proposals are that cases concerning violence and abuse may be taken to dispute resolution if the parties wish it.[518]

Child abuse has become a significant feature of decision making in private proceedings in relation to children. However legislation governing private cases between family members typically does not provide as an arena in which risks to children from abuse can routinely be weighed.

While reform of child protection practice is critically important, the flurry of attention to this arena also highlights how little attention has been paid to the parallel problem of child welfare dispositions in private litigation concerning domestic violence. Children's safety and well-being are often just as much at stake in litigation for civil protection orders, custody and divorce awards, all of which frequently determine the terms of child visitation or custody for an adult batterer. Yet, far less policy or research attention has been directed to this arena.[519]

In fact more attention has been paid to weighing the damaging effect of domestic violence between adults with whom the child will have contact, than in direct abuse to the child. No decision about child welfare can be entirely about whether a child has been abused, but the legislation should not ignore the real difficulties of the courts in making decisions in cases where child abuse becomes an element of the dispute. While there are many counterproductive elements to rebuttable presumptions relating to contact in cases concerning abuse to the child, they do underline the importance of the threat of abuse or violence explicitly in decision making.[520]

H. Evaluation—Has Family Law Struck the Right Balance?

The principle that decisions should be made in the best interests of the child is central to all family law relating to child abuse. However, our analysis across jurisdictions highlights two contrasting means of realizing this principle, the protection of the child by supporting her in the family and the removal of a child from harm and their establishment in a permanent home.

[517] P Parkinson 'Keeping in contact: the role of Family Relationship Centres in Australia' (2006) 18(2) Child and Family LQ 157, 158.   [518] E Walsh 'Centres Forwards' (2006) 32 Fam Law 150.

[519] Meier (n 484), 661.

[520] R Bailey-Harris and J Dewar 'Variations on a Theme—Child Law Reform in Australia' 9 (2) Child and Family LQ 149.

In England, the biological family remains the foundation of the child's best interests. To return to Lord Oliver in *Re KD*: 'it matters not whether the parent is wise or foolish, rich or poor, educated or illiterate, provided the child's moral or physical health are not endangered. Public authorities cannot improve on nature'.[521]

The goal under this model is that the child should be supported within her own family and the family helped to look after the child adequately. The aim on the face of the law remains not to undermine family life. Only in cases where a child has suffered, or is likely to suffer, significant harm, does the law allow intervention in family life without the family's permission.

There is, however, a risk of losing focus on the interests of the child when they are only allied to, but not identical to, those of her family. Whilst it is important to recognize the threat to the parents' standing in proceedings concerning child abuse,[522] it is fundamentally wrong to allow this consideration to affect the standard of proof in family proceedings. By allowing the standard of proof to reflect the seriousness of the allegation[523] England and Wales are clearly out of step with jurisdictions that raise the standard based on the potential outcome of proceedings.

The primary goal of other jurisdictions, notably in the United States and Canada, is to establish a permanent home for a child, which may or may not be with the biological family. Here, the destruction of parental roles and their replacement with a better adoptive family is justified on the grounds that biological parents sacrificed their rights by their abusive behaviour. However, conflation of the objectives of family and criminal law often means that swift moves to terminate parental rights may stem more from a desire to punish the abuser than to uphold the interests of the child. The further problem with this model is that the grass of the alternative home is not necessarily greener. First, there is no vast pool from which to draw caring new parents to adopt children under difficult circumstances. Second, care by the state carries the risk that children will be neglected, poorly educated and, in the worst cases, abused further. So, while children await the slim chance of successful adoption, some form of positive familial relationship might have been rekindled from their former lives, had proper support been given. This has been articulated particularly well in the 'least intervention principle' of five Australian States,[524] where legislation has identified clear priorities for decision makers, including the retention of familiarity in the child's life.

Good family services cost a great deal and require a skilled and motivated workforce. In reality legislation tasks social workers with tackling severe deprivation, but often provides a trivial level of resources. The English judiciary is acutely aware of budgetary constraints and even in light of burgeoning jurisprudence relating to the child and family rights under the ECHR, the courts have been unwilling to require local authorities to provide the services that the legislation promises. However, the experience of

---

[521] *Re KD* (n 77).
[522] Discussed below in the context of defamation actions, Chapter 4 section F.6.
[523] *Re H and others* (n 225) 16J.   [524] Discussed above, section B.4.

the United States may be instructive; similar inconsistency between legislation and provision of support inevitably led to major failures of child protection. The operation of the law was denounced by legislators who then provided for draconian and court-focused child protection mechanisms governed by the permanency principle discussed above.

3

Liability in Criminal Law

There has not been any substantial parliamentary consideration of the way in which the criminal offences relating to child abuse are formulated until recent times when the abuse of children has come to be regarded as a pressing social concern. Since the turn of the century there has been a flurry of legislative activity. There has been a complete revision of the laws relating to sexual offences against children;[1] a reconsideration of the laws criminalizing the homicide of children, as part of the Law Commission proposals for a new Homicide Act for England and Wales.[2] The law relating to non-fatal assaults on a child has been substantially interpreted and

---

[1] Sexual Offences Act 2003 (England).
[2] Law Commission *A New Homicide Act for England and Wales? A Consultation Paper No 177* (Law Commission, London 2005). Law Commission *Murder, Manslaughter and Infanticide* No 304 (TSO, London 2006).

expanded by common law, although no new statute has been introduced which fundamentally alters the framework of non-fatal offences created 140 years ago.[3] While statutory change is not necessarily beneficial, as the new unwieldy Sexual Offences Act 2003 seems set to prove, it does reflect public, and thus political interest, and concern for the problem. This has not been reflected as a whole in relation to physical abuse and cruelty and neglect of children. The current 'moral panic' about sexual offending against children has left other offences against children in the shade.

This chapter examines the current criminal law relating to child abuse. We begin with an analysis of the influences on the current English system and consider the guiding principles of criminal law which seem to have affected the current criminal law in relation to child abuse. After this point the chapter divides into three further sections: the first section considers the current criminal law as it relates to the death of children; the second section examines non-fatal offences against children including cruelty and neglect; and the third section scrutinizes the law relating to sexual assaults on children. At each point we consider the law and its operation in other jurisdictions to determine whether the English system might be improved by changes that other common law jurisdictions have made; or indeed whether the English law has certain advantages over other jurisdictions in the way that it is framed. The depth in which each country's law is considered is linked to the context. In relation to the death or injury of a child, much of the law is very similar to our own and shares many of the same problems. However the United States, Canada and New Zealand have made real innovations in their adaptation of the law to the realities of child death and injury as a result of abuse. There has also been a significant period of reform in relation to sexual offences against children, and Canada, Australia and New Zealand in particular have made some substantial changes to the way in which sexual offences are framed. We conclude that the development of the criminal law in England in relation to child abuse has suffered considerably from an almost exclusive media and political interest on the damage that child victims of sexual abuse suffer. Thus the criminal law in relation to child deaths, injuries and neglect has been almost completely overlooked in proposals for reform that relate specifically to child abuse. In contrast there has been an over-proliferation of new sexual offences against children contained in the Sexual Offences Act 2003, that has the potential to render the law confusing and subject to legal challenge.

A. Tracing the Influences on the Current Law

1. The 'failure' of the criminal law in cases of child abuse

In discussing the background to the criminal law in England it is important to note at the outset that there has been much debate about whether the criminal law should be

---

[3] The Offences Against the Person Act 1861 (England).

routinely used as a response to child abuse. Criticism has been levelled at both a principled and a practical level. As the Criminal Bar Association has argued, the criminal law is retrospective and punitive; it focuses on whether the alleged abuser deserves punishment. The criminal law does not consider how the victim's best interests may be served in the future.[4] Much of the criticism of the use of the criminal law in these cases has been about its potential to compound the problems which the child abuse has created and act to the detriment of the child. To criminalize a parent, perhaps remove him from the home, or fine him or imprison him, may do little to improve the child's overall happiness. This argument has been accepted very recently by McLachlin CJ in the Canadian Supreme Court in relation to the abolition of the defence of reasonable physical correction, when she stated: 'The criminal law is the most powerful tool at Parliament's disposal. Yet it is a blunt instrument whose power can also be destructive of family and educational relationships.'[5] Many children can be silenced by threats that to speak out will result in such criminalization.[6] At a practical level there is increasing awareness that changes to the criminal law in relation to child abuse can have a serious impact upon the effectiveness of the civil family law in acting to protect the child in the future.

In the 1980s and early 1990s there was much debate in England about whether different types of response should be pursued, rather than criminalization. The question was best summed up by Wattam when she asked, '[s]hould we prosecute and be damned, or leave the legal system as it stands and ask a different question—what sort of help do children and families need?'[7]

However a lack of faith and interest in the role of the criminal law and justice system in responding to child abuse has waned, largely because, although the problems that the criminal process causes are readily acknowledged, criminal liability remains 'the strongest formal condemnation that society can inflict'.[8] Child abuse is taken very seriously within our society, and it would currently be unthinkable for the criminal law not to be part of the response. It is easy, however, to overstate the power of the criminal law as a force for constructive help in cases of child abuse. Current political rhetoric has equated criminal conviction and increasing sentence tariffs with protection of the vulnerable,[9] and this is largely unfounded. The criminal law may only protect in a limited number of cases where incarceration or registration may reduce the opportunity of a particular offender to commit a particular crime. The power of a criminal conviction in child abuse cases lies in its power to condemn behaviour, and through that, possibly to establish, or to maintain, standards of conduct. In this regard it may act as a mechanism for education within families of what is regarded

---

[4] Law Commission *Children: Their Non-Accidental Death or Serious Injury (Criminal Trials)* (HM Stationery Office, London 2004 LC 282) 21 [3.12].
[5] *Canadian Foundation for Children Youth and the Law v Canada (Attorney General)* 2004 SCC 4 (SCC).
[6] Childline <http://www.childline.org.uk/howcommonischildabuse.asp> (accessed 31 July 2006).
[7] C Wattam *'Kids on Film' Community Care* (7 October 1993) 21.
[8] A Ashworth *Principles of Criminal Law* (5th edn OUP, Oxford 2006) 1.
[9] A Ashworth 'Criminal Justice Act 2003: Part 2 Criminal Justice Reform—Principles, Human Rights and Public Protection' (2004) Crim LR 516, 523.

as appropriate:

The introduction of legal judgements cannot, in the end, prevent abusive attacks . . ., but [they] can help to make the justification . . . more difficult. Even the possibility of being in the wrong can endanger the normative consensus within families.[10]

This power of the criminal law has not, so far, been used particularly consistently or clearly in relation to child abuse, and the criminal law remains piecemeal in its development, another testament to the history of moral panic surrounding child abuse. Any educative function of the criminal law can only be successful if allied with real social education programmes.[11] This has been recognized and campaigned for by many of the major children's charities in England,[12] and to a limited extent by policy makers.[13] However, the major policy interest in the criminal law at present remains in its perceived power to mark out the dangerous indelibly, particularly those who have sexually assaulted children or may do so.

2. Fear of 'Paedophiles'

It is difficult to identify precisely when the public obsession with those who commit sexual offences against children began. By 1994, commentators recorded that 'public concern about sexual crime has become a panic . . . those who perpetrate such crimes are hated and despised more than any other type of offender'[14] and 'the danger to children from sexual offenders has become a matter of obsessive public concern'.[15] Such concern has been increased by an explosion of media coverage of sexual offending against children, which in turn has constructed and then reinforced an image of a person who sexually abuses children—'the paedophile'.[16] The word 'paedophile' literally means lover of children, but it has taken on, in the public's perception, certain accepted characteristics. First a 'paedophile' is seen as devious; he is considered to be someone who appears normal but who, beneath the surface, is leading another life involving the sexual subjugation of children.[17] This image has been supported by

---

[10] K Bussman *Evaluation of the German Prohibition on Violence Against Children* (European Society of Criminology, Toledo 2002) 14.

[11] J Durrant 'Legal Reform and Attitudes Toward Physical Punishment in Sweden' (2003) Int J of CR 147.

[12] G McDonald and A Winkley *What Works in Child Protection* (Barnardo's London 2000); NSPCC *Not Naughty but Normal: Protecting Your Baby and Toddler* (NSPCC, London 2003); NSPCC *Sexual Offences Act Media Briefing* (NSPCC, London 30 April 2004); Childline *Child Abuse* (Childline London Information Sheet 2); M MacLeod *Child Protection—Everybody's Business* (ChildLine/Community Care, London 1997).

[13] Home Office *Children and Families Safer from Sexual Crime* (Home Office Communications Directorate, London 2004).

[14] A Sampson *Acts of Abuse: Sexual Offenders and the Criminal Justice System* (Routledge, London 1994) 1.

[15] D West 'Sexual Molesters' in N Walker (ed) *Dangerous People* (Blackstone Press, London 1996) 52.

[16] T Thomas *Sex Crime: Sex Offending and Society* (Willan Publishing, Devon 2000).

[17] G Abel 'Self-Reported Sex Crimes of Non-Incarcerated Paraphiliacs' (1987) 2 J of Interpersonal Violence 3, 25.

revelations about the long-secret activities of those who have been later convicted of offences in the courts:

[A]busers may be good at their jobs, winning respect, admiration and fear . . . They are adept at avoiding detection . . . in which they are inadvertently assisted by the assumptions and values of our social institutions. They are very dangerous people.[18]

Secondly a 'paedophile' is perceived to be someone who is a stranger to the abused child. This has been an image which has been particularly enforced by press reporting. The Glasgow Media Group found particular reasons for this choice in their interviews with journalists on their coverage of sexual offending against children:

I think that people concentrate far more on the 'stranger danger' aspect of child sexual abuse because it is recognised that it is something that happens that people are not hideously embarrassed about talking to their children about it—advertisers . . . it is a subject that they're happy to talk about. People don't want to be associated with child abuse as incest . . . it's not a fun subject, it's likely to put readers off, may upset readers, it is easier and safer to concentrate on strangers.[19]

The image that the majority of sexual offenders against children are strangers to the child involved has never been borne out by any research on child abuse. Instead studies have consistently found the exact opposite, that the majority of children know their abuser and that the abuser may very well be part of the child's household or family.[20]

Thirdly, the perception of a 'paedophile' has been constructed so that the person is seen as a recidivist, someone who is more likely than other types of offender to repeat the crime and is less amenable to rehabilitation.[21] Research has not been conclusive on this point.[22] However it has been a fundamental theme of news coverage of sexual offending against children:

Once a paedophile always a paedophile . . . the safety of young children overwhelmingly outweighs the rights of a convicted paedophile . . . there have been too many cases in recent years of perverts obtaining jobs working with children.[23]

---

[18] Sir William Utting *People Like Us: The Report of the Review of the Safeguards For Children Living Away From Home* (HMSO, London 1997) [9.7]–[9.9].

[19] P Skidmore 'Telling Tales—Media Power, Ideology and the Reporting of Child Sexual Abuse in Britain' Paper given to European Group for the Study of Social Control and Deviance Annual Conference (September 1994).

[20] P Cawson, C Wattam, S Brooker, and G Kelly *Child Maltreatment in the United Kingdom* (NSPCC, London 2000).

[21] A McAlinden 'Sex Offender Registration: Some Observations on Megan's Law and the Sex Offenders Act 1997' (1999) 1(1) Crime Prevention and Community Safety 43.

[22] A McAlinden 'Managing Risk: From Regulation to the Reintegration of Sexual Offenders' (2006) 6 Criminology & Criminal Justice 197.

[23] Editorial 'Why We Did It' *Manchester Evening News* (30 August 1996) (justifying printing a picture of a convicted paedophile with his name on the front page of their newspaper) in Thomas (n 16) 22.

A 'paedophile' has become, in modern society, the worst type of offender:

The sexual offender is epitomised as a demented monster or fiend and in a form of 'criminal apartheid' is singled out above other dangerous criminals in society, the justification being that they constitute a serious risk to the community.[24]

This in turn has had an effect on who is considered to be a 'typical offender':

[t]he more concern is expressed about the threat of strangers, the less close relatives could be brought into the frame. The more child sexual abuse was depicted as a horrible pathology, the less could ordinary fathers be seen as depicting such deeds.[25]

This 'moral panic' in relation to sexual offending and in particular sexual offending against children has had an enormous impact upon the development of the criminal law's response to child abuse. This has been primarily because the criminal law has been considered as the main mechanism by which the risk posed by sexual offenders may be monitored and contained. Strategies have been formulated for increased incarceration of the worst sexual offenders and monitoring for all those convicted of an offence. The Criminal Justice Act 1991 formed a twin-track approach creating 'public protection' sentences for sexual and violent offenders. Following this the Powers of Criminal Courts (Sentencing) Act 2000 singled out sexual offenders for special consideration in terms of the nature and length of the sentence imposed, the release of the offender at the end of the custodial sentence and the period of supervision following the custodial sentence.[26] The Sex Offenders Act 1997 Part I created a mechanism for monitoring sexual offenders based on their convictions, which has been subsequently amended by the Criminal Justice and Court Services Act 2000. Convicted sexual offenders are required to place their name on a register of offenders kept by the police and to inform the police of any subsequent changes of address. The length of time that a person is required to keep their name on the register is linked to the seriousness of the offence for which the person has been convicted. The registered offender is also the subject of an inter-agency risk management plan.

The wide-scale changes to the sexual offences implemented in the Sexual Offences Act 2003, were rooted in the wave of public concern, particularly about sexual offending against children, and the subsequent attempts to manage the risk which these offenders pose. These strategies depend upon the conviction of those who have committed sexual offences against children and their conviction for an offence which reflects the nature of the acts that they committed. Neither of these requirements was in existence when the registration of sexual offenders was mooted in the mid-1990s. The Sexual Offences Act 2003 created numerous new offences. The drafters of the new law attempted to create offences which reflected the types of sexual predatory

---

[24] McAlinden 'Managing Risk (n 22), 203.

[25] C Smart *Feminism and the Power of Law* (Routledge, London 1989) 52; C Smart 'A History of Ambivalence and Conflict in the Discursive Construction of the "Child Victim" of Sexual Abuse' (1999) Social and Legal Studies 391.

[26] C Cobley 'The Legislative Framework' in A Matravers (ed) *Managing Sex Offenders in the Community: Managing and Reducing the Risks* (Willan Publishing, Devon 2003) 52–54.

behaviour in existence, in the hope that this would increase the number of convictions, and convictions for offences which reflected the nature of the sexually abusive behaviour, as part of an overall strategy of risk management.

3. The European Convention on Human Rights and the United Nations Convention on the Rights of the Child

An unforeseen consequence of the enormous social concern about sexual offences towards children has been a lack of public, and therefore legislative, discussion in relation to child injury and death resulting from physical abuse. As one witness to the NSPCC Commission in England on the prevention of child abuse explained, 'when some people use the expression "child abuse" they mean only sexual abuse. That of course is a horrific crime. Some would take the view that physical abuse is "nothing" when compared with it.'[27] The major impetus for legal reform in relation to the physical assault of children has come from certain charities and from the international community, most notably the European Court of Human Rights (ECtHR) and the United Nations Convention on the Rights of the Child (UNCRC), as interpreted by the UN Committee on the Rights of the Child. The UNCRC has had increasing influence upon the interpretation of the ECHR by the ECtHR in the rights that it confers on children which could affect criminal liability.[28] With the notable exception of the NSPCC campaign on the prosecution of the 'unidentified perpetrator' of abuse, international and charitable pressure has been concentrated on the single issue of the defence of reasonable chastisement of children. The demonstration by the UN Committee on the Rights of the Child of its increased disappointment in the UK government's refusal to abolish the defence[29] and the defeat in the ECtHR in *A v UK*[30] which ruled that the operation of the rule had meant that A was not protected from torture, placed further pressure on the government. It should however be noted that the UK Government has strenuously fought against reform of the law in this regard on the grounds of family privacy and parental discretion in relation to discipline and that the reform that has now been enacted following this pressure still does not conform to the UNCRC.

In its discussion of cases concerning child abuse the ECtHR has also created an important principle which, following the Human Rights Act 1998, is likely to influence the development of the criminal law in relation to child abuse. The ECtHR has held that 'children and other vulnerable individuals, in particular are entitled to state protection, in the form of effective deterrence against . . . serious breaches of personal integrity'.[31] A child's personal integrity is potentially breached by both physical and

[27] Lord Williams of Mostyn (Chair) *Childhood Matters: the Report of the National Commission of Inquiry into the Prevention of Child Abuse* (HMSO, London 1996).

[28] *Sahin v Germany* [2003] 2 FLR 619 (ECtHR) [39]–[41], [64].

[29] Concluding Observations of the Committee on the Rights of the Child: United Kingdom February 1995 [35] in 'Joint Committee on Human Rights United Kingdom Parliament Nineteenth Report Part 4 [152]'. <http://www.publications.parliament.uk/pa/jt200304/jtselect/jtrights/161/16107. htm> accessed 26 October 2004.   [30] (1998) 27 EHRR 611.

[31] ibid [22].

sexual assault. The (now defunct), European Commission of Human Rights found in *Stubbings v UK* that 'sexual abuse is unquestionably an abhorrent type of wrong doing, with debilitating effects on its victims. Children are entitled to state protection in the form of effective deterrents from such grave types of interference with essential aspects of their private lives.'[32] Not only does a state have a duty to provide deterrence in law, the deterrence has been expected to be found in criminal rather than civil law. In *X and Y v Netherlands*, for example, an application alleging a violation of Article 8 succeeded, on the grounds that no criminal remedy was available for a mentally handicapped child, who had been forced to have sex and been indecently touched by the adult son of the owner of the care home in which she lived, because she was unable to make a formal complaint herself. As no provision of the criminal law provided her with protection in these circumstances, it was held that she was a victim of a violation of Article 8 of the ECHR. The Court found that:

the protection afforded by the civil law in a case of wrongdoing of the kind inflicted on Miss Y is insufficient. This is a case where fundamental values and essential aspects of private life are at stake. Effective deterrence is indispensable in this area and it can be achieved only by criminal law provisions; indeed, it is by such provisions that the matter is normally regulated.[33]

Thus domestic criminal law will fail to be compatible with the ECHR if no criminal law remedy is available for a particular person, or group, for an assault which violates their right to protection either from torture or inhuman or degrading treatment or punishment under Article 3 or physical and sexual integrity derived from the right to respect for private and family life under Article 8. Article 8 has been interpreted by *X and Y v The Netherlands* to apply in cases concerning physical and sexual assault when a unanimous court found that the concept of private life includes 'the physical and moral integrity of the person, including his or her sexual life'.[34] In *MC v Bulgaria*[35] the ECtHR stated:

Positive obligations on the state are inherent, in the right to effective respect for private life under Article 8; ... Effective deterrence against grave acts such as rape, where fundamental values and essential aspects of private life are at stake, requires effective criminal law provisions. Children and other vulnerable individuals in particular, are entitled to effective protection.

A state will also be in violation of the Convention if it effectively removes the protection afforded to a child by the existence of a particular offence. In *A v UK* it was therefore held that the protection afforded to children was significantly reduced by the defence of reasonable chastisement, which ensured that the law failed to deter those who would assault children.[36]

---

[32] *Stubbings v UK* (1997) 23 EHRR 213 [64].
[33] *X and Y v Netherlands* (1986) 8 EHRR 235 [27].   [34] ibid [22].
[35] *MC v Bulgaria* (2003) 15 BHRC 627.
[36] (n 30) (Commission Opinion) [48].

B. Principles of Criminal Law

1. The harm principle

Criminal law imposes the harshest personal penalties of all types of law, including the deprivation of an individual's liberty against his will—as such the imposition of criminal liability has only been justified within criminal law on the basis of the prevention of harm to others.[37] The definition of what constitutes harm is naturally contentious and the battle has been fought particularly about when it may be justified to criminalize an act to 'save a person from himself' and prevent him from doing something which is regarded as harmful. In relation to child abuse the harm principle is played out in a number of ways, which may be regarded as a reflection of current attitudes to child abuse. First some hitting of children has not been regarded at a national level as harmful when it has been administered in the context of punishment by a caregiver and has therefore not been criminalized. Secondly, some failures to act to look after a child, commonly known as neglect, have been viewed in practice as not sufficiently harmful as to justify criminalization. In contrast, the harm which sexual assault towards children causes has been regarded as so great as to justify criminalizing preparatory acts, taken before the act has been attempted and thus before any identifiable harm been caused, in the crime of meeting a child following sexual grooming. The harm caused to a child by sexual contact also has been considered sufficiently great to justify the criminalization of all minors over the age of criminal responsibility who have sexual contact with another minor, on the assumption that some of those contacts will be non-consensual and abusive.[38]

2. Liability for acting rather than failing to act

The general principle in criminal law is that a person may only be punished for acts that he has committed rather than the consequences resulting from something that he has omitted to do. A person is not usually criminally liable if he ignores another's cries for help or fails to rescue someone from a dangerous situation. 'The conduct of the parabolical priest and Levite on the way to Jericho may have been indeed deplorable, but English law has not so far developed to the stage of treating it as criminal.'[39] The purported justification for such a rule has been that an omission to act cannot be regarded as bringing about or causing the harmful result, but rather it is a failure to prevent the harmful circumstances.

In English law the only exceptions to this rule are when a duty to act is imposed by statute, or a limited number of circumstances in which the defendant is regarded in common law as having assumed a duty. The Children and Young Person's Act 1933

---

[37] John Stuart Mill *On Liberty* (1859) [9].
[38] Sexual Offences Act 2003 (England) s 13.
[39] *R v Miller* [1983] 2 AC 161 (CA) 175 (Lord Diplock).

(CYPA) s 1(2) imposes a requirement on a person to supply any children who are legally dependent on him with adequate food, clothing, medical aid, and accommodation. Other adults who are not the parents of the child may be criminally liable for a failure to act at common law if they have assumed the care of the child. In *R v Charlotte Smith*,[40] Erle CJ held that, 'the law is undisputed that, if a person having the care or custody of another who is helpless, neglects to supply him with the necessities of life and thereby causes or accelerates his death is guilty of a criminal offence'. Thus in *R v Gibbons and Proctor*[41] the father's partner, who was not the mother of the child, was also found to have committed an offence when she failed to feed the child, because she had in the past provided the child with food. Where the person has begun to care for a child this assumption of responsibility would mean that were the adult to cease to care for the child his omission could constitute a criminal omission. This creation of a 'special relationship' by the assumption of responsibility could apply to step-parents or other adults who have begun to care for a child.

The statutory and common law exemptions in relation to children demonstrate a basic understanding in criminal law that committing an act which kills a child and failing to feed a child who has no other means of obtaining sustenance, are qualitatively different. However we shall argue below, in relation to the offences of child neglect and cruelty, that omissions to act in relation to children are unjustifiably regarded in English law as being less intentional and therefore less criminal than an act of commission.

3. The subjectivist principle

One reason perhaps for the distinction made between commission and omission in cases of child abuse lies in the inherent assumption that an act of commission is deliberate whereas an omission may be a simple mistake. The subjectivist principle, as outlined by the criminal law, dictates that criminal liability should only be imposed on people who have chosen to act in a certain way. This principle is the basis for three further principles.[42] The '*mens rea* principle' imposes liability for the commission or omission of certain criminal results only if the actor may be proved to have intended the result or to have knowingly run the risk that such a result would occur. The 'belief principle' imposes liability only for results that the actor believed would or could occur, rather than what any other person might believe would happen from his actions. Finally, the 'correspondence principle' requires that the defendant's intention or recklessness corresponds to the offence that he commits; thus that he either intends or is reckless in committing a particular type or level of criminal activity, rather than that a person is being generally reckless in his behaviour.

---

[40] A case in which a mistress was charged with the homicide of her servant when she neglected to give her sufficient food or habitable lodgings: *R v Charlotte Smith* (1865) 10 Cox 82.

[41] *R v Gibbons and Proctor* (1918) 13 Cr App R 134.

[42] A Ashworth *Principles of Criminal Law* (5th edn OUP, Oxford 2006).

The *mens rea* principle has been eloquently explained by Lord Bingham in *R v G*:

It is a salutary principle that conviction of serious crime should depend on proof not simply that the defendant caused (by act or omission) an injurious result to another but that his state of mind when so acting was culpable ... It is clearly blame-worthy to take an obvious and significant risk of causing injury to another. But it is not clearly blameworthy to do something involving an injury to another if (for reasons of self-induced intoxication) one genuinely does not perceive the risk. Such a person may fairly be accused of stupidity or lack of imagination, but neither of those failings should expose him to conviction of serious crime or the risk of punishment.[43]

These are ideals rather than the reality of the law as currently framed. Many offences are framed as strict liability offences including several of the offences relating to children in the Sexual Offences Act 2003,[44] and require no *mens rea*, merely evidence that a situation existed. For example the rape of a child under 13 is committed if a person 'intentionally penetrates the vagina, anus or mouth of another person with his penis' and the other person is under 13.[45] The actor need not intend to have sexual intercourse with a child, or intend to have sexual intercourse without consent, for the offence to be committed. Thus the principle that '*mens rea* is an essential ingredient of every offence unless some reason can be found for holding that that is not necessary'[46] can often mean that no *mens rea* is required if it is considered in the interests of justice to deny it. In the case of statutory rape it has been decided that it is in the interest of justice to punish those who have sexual intercourse with children and to ensure that the foolish actor, the risk taker and those exhibiting predatory behaviour are not excused their behaviour in law. In addition many offences now do not reflect the correspondence principle and very serious offences may be committed with the *mens rea* of a much less serious offence. In relation to a discussion of child abuse, the non-fatal offences against the person may all be satisfied by intention or recklessness to inflict some harm, irrespective of the level of harm actually caused and thus the seriousness of the offence, with the exception of the most serious of these crimes under Offences Against the Person Act 1861 (OAPA) s 18.

4. Legal certainty

However the principle that a person should only be punished for harms which they choose to commit runs deep within the criminal law and gives rise to a further principle, that of legal certainty. The principle essentially dictates that the criminal law should be articulated clearly so that a person may be punished when he has decided to commit an act knowing from the criminal law that such a harm was clearly punishable. The link between justice and legal certainty was articulated in the

---

[43] *R v G* [2003] UKHL 50 [32].   [44] See discussion in section E below.
[45] Sexual Offences Act 2003 (England) s 5(1).
[46] *Sweet v Parsley* [1969] 1 All ER 347 (HL) 349–350 (Lord Reid).

seventeenth century by Francis Bacon when he wrote:

Let there be no authority to shed blood; nor let sentence be pronounced in any court upon cases, except according to a known and certain law . . . Nor should a man be deprived of his life, who did not first know that he was risking it.[47]

This principle has also found form in ECHR Article 7 which states that, 'no one shall be held guilty of any criminal offence on account of any act or omission which did not constitute a criminal offence under national or international law at the time it was committed'.[48]

A criminal offence may be challenged on the grounds that it is so vague or unclearly framed that it failed to give a defendant 'fair warning' of the nature of the offence that he could commit by continuing with his actions. Such challenges might be undertaken in relation to several parts of the current range of offences relating to the homicide of children, particularly gross negligent manslaughter, and to some of the offences under the new Sexual Offences Act 2003, for example causing or inciting a child to engage in sexual activity s 8 and meeting a child following sexual grooming s 15.

5. Presumption of innocence

The criminal law is based upon the presumed innocence of the defendant until the evidence proves him guilty. This principle was articulated in 1935 in the case of *Woolmington* that 'throughout the web of the English Criminal Law one golden thread is always to be seen, that it is the duty of the prosecution to prove the prisoner's guilt'.[49] This principle is also enshrined in ECHR Article 6(2): 'Everyone charged with a criminal offence shall be presumed innocent until proved guilty according to law.' While the jurisprudence under Article 6(2) remains underdeveloped, an increasing body of caselaw has drawn attention to the imposition of reverse burdens of proof in statute as a potential area of incompatibility with the Convention. A reverse burden of proof requires the defendant to prove when the prosecution has established that a certain state of affairs existed, that he has one defence established in statute as particular to that offence. In *Lambert* the House of Lords has found that a requirement on the defendant to prove that crucial elements of the offence were not present contravened the presumption of innocence enshrined in Article 6(2).[50] Although there has been a retreat from this position, to an acceptance that some reverse burdens of proof may be justified on policy grounds, there remains confusion about the range of reverse burdens of proof which may be allowed under Article 6(2). There is considerable authority

---

[47] Aphorism 8 and Aphorism 39—A Treatise on Universal Justice quoted in *R v Misra and another* [2004] EWCA Crim 2375, [2004] All ER (D) 107 [32] (Judge LJ).

[48] 'In our judgment, the incorporation of the ECHR, while providing a salutary reminder, has not effected any significant extension of or change to the "certainty" principle as long understood at common law': *R v Misra* ibid [37] (Judge LJ).   [49] [1935] AC 462 (HL) 481 (Lord Sankey).

[50] *Lambert* [2001] 3 WLR 206 (HL); see A Simester and G Sullivan *Criminal Law—Theory and Doctrine* (2nd edn Hart Publishing, Oxford 2003) 63–70, A Simester and G Sullivan 'Burden of Proof' <http://www.hartpub.co.uk/updates/crimlaw/crimlaw_burden05.htm> (accessed 7 August 2006).

for an assumption that a reverse burden should not be imposed for an imprisonable offence,[51] yet this is by no means absolute and authority suggests that it may be better interpreted as a strong presumption against reverse burdens in custodial cases, which may still be justified 'for good reason'.[52]

The development of the criminal law in relation to child abuse has been characterized by 'the increasing conflict between the state's duties under Articles 2 and 3 of the ECHR to protect the rights of victims and the duty under Article 6 to secure fair trials for defendants'.[53] In each area the balance has been renegotiated. Whilst the drafters of the Sexual Offences Act 2003 have interpreted criminal law principles to justify some incursions into the rights of defendants, other groups have been more cautious. The Law Commission in its consideration on reforming the law in relation to the 'unidentified perpetrator' concluded that, 'it seems that an attempt to impose a legal burden of proof upon the defendant in [cases of serious child abuse] is very likely to be "read down" as imposing only an evidential burden, or declared to be incompatible'.[54] The child's right of protection from abuse is not an absolute 'trump card' in decisions about how the criminal law will be framed. The criminal law must also equally recognize the rights of anyone accused of a criminal offence to a fair trial, under ECHR Article 6 and also the defendant's rights under Article 8. Article 8 has been interpreted by commentators to require that the criminal law is not used arbitrarily or oppressively particularly when a person could be charged with alternative offences.[55] At present it appears that the courts have been very cautious in their use of the Human Rights Act 1998, particularly in their interpretation of the Sexual Offences Act 2003,[56] as discussed below. However such caution may not be exercised in future cases.

We now go on to consider the criminal offences which are most likely to be charged following the death, physical assault, ill-treatment or sexual abuse of a child. We start with the problems encountered in the prosecution of cases following a child's death. We look at the difficulties encountered in identifying who has committed an act or series of acts leading to the child's death. We examine the range of offences which may currently be charged under English law, comparing them particularly to the laws in the United States, Canada, Australia, and New Zealand. These jurisdictions, with the notable exception of Australia, have been much more willing than our own to infer either intention to kill or a common intention to assault a child from evidence of repeated assaults on the child in the past, or from failure to protect that child from assault. The law in relation to child deaths in Australia is in many ways more limited than our own, particularly as a result of the limited view of caretakers' duty to act to protect children from harm.

---

[51] *R v Johnstone* [2003] UKHL 28.
[52] *A-G's Ref (No 1 of 2004)* [2004] EWCA Crim 1025; *Sheldrake v DPP; A-G's Reference (No. 4 of 2002)* [2005] 1 AC 264 (HL).   [53] P Glazebrook 'Which of You Did It?' [2003] Crim LR 541.
[54] Law Commission, 'An Informal Consultation Paper of the Criminal Law Team of the Law Commission on Successfully Prosecuting Cases of Non-Accidental Death or Serious Injury of Children' in Law Commission *Children: Their Non-Accidental Death or Serious Injury (Criminal Trials)* (n 4).
[55] P Rook (ed) *Rook and Ward on Sexual Offences Law and Practice* (3rd edn Sweet & Maxwell, London 2004) [3.9].   [56] *G v R* [2006] EWCA Crim 821, [2006] All ER 197.

C. Homicide

The public perception of unlawful child death is that it is predominantly caused by the deliberate and intentional act of a stranger.[57] If this were true, the existing framework of the criminal law could be considered relatively unproblematic in the prosecution of non-accidental child deaths. As discussed below, the crime of murder aims to punish those whose purpose is to cause death, and a successful prosecution of those who have intentionally killed children is then primarily dependent upon the evidence gathered to satisfy the jury of this. However from current research and knowledge of unlawful child deaths it does not appear that many child deaths fall into this category. Instead the majority of deaths and serious injuries to children occur within a domestic setting and it is suspected that the majority of those deaths were caused by the child's caregivers. These cases raise particular problems in satisfying many of the criminal offences as currently constructed. It is often not possible to identify who inflicted the injuries, as the child was often cared for by more than one person during the relevant period. Unless one of those people confesses, and this of course does not mean that the person will be convicted, it can be impossible to construct a criminal case, because there remains no one person who may be identified as the alleged perpetrator.[58]

There appears to be a substantial number of cases which could fall into this category. A survey of police forces completed for the NSPCC 'Which of You Did it?' Working Group found that 492 children under the age of 10 (approximately three children a week over the three years studied) had been killed or seriously injured in circumstances in which one or more parent or carer could have been responsible for their injuries. The survey found that the majority of these cases were never prosecuted. Of these 492 children, the NSPCC received details of 366 cases which had either reached a conclusion in court, or which had been discontinued prior to court. Of these 366 cases, 225 were discontinued prior to reaching court, 21 defendants were acquitted and 21 dismissed. In 99 cases there was a successful prosecution; however it is not clear what crime the defendant was charged with.[59] Cobley et al[60] amongst others[61] have identified that suspects may be charged with lower offences which can be satisfied by proof of recklessness or in some cases of negligence. This may result in one of the cases being identified as a successful prosecution, but may not reflect the level of injury which the child has suffered. The successful prosecution of cases of child death may be further complicated by their domestic nature. In practice, as Cobley has identified, some cases

---

[57] 'NSPCC Steps UP Campaign on Child Abuse Killings' (Press Release 14 October 2002 citing MORI poll conducted for the NSPCC) <http://www.nspcc.org.uk/html/home/information resources/> (accessed 27 October 2004.)

[58] C Cobley, T Sanders and P Wheeler 'Prosecuting Cases of Suspected "Shaken Baby Syndrome"—A Review of Current Issues' [2003] Crim LR 93, 98.

[59] Judge I Plumstead *Papers for the NSPCC 'Which of You Did it?' Conference* (Cambridge 2 November 2002), [8], published in Law Commission *Children: Their Non-Accidental Death or Serious Injury (Criminal Trials)* (n 4) 17.   [60] Cobley, Sanders and Wheeler (n 58).

[61] *Bristol Study* 43.

may not be prosecuted successfully because they have fallen into the category of 'there but for the grace of God go I' (or in their position I might have done the same) cases.

Much of the current debate about child homicide has centred on whether the criminal law may be changed to increase the 'fit' between the circumstances in which children are killed and the homicide offences available. The Law Commission has reviewed all the law in this area and has made some proposals for change to expand the range of offences which may be charged in cases of death or serious injury to include more offences which may be satisfied by proof of negligence rather than intention or recklessness. The Law Commission completed a further review of the law of murder including the defences to it, a Consultation Document was issued in 2005[62] and final proposals were published in Autumn 2006.[63] In the next section we consider the range of offences which may be currently charged when a child has died and examine when they may be used. We then examine the proposals from the Law Commission to reform the law of murder and the defences to it made in Autumn 2006.

1. Murder

The criminal act which murder punishes is the unlawful killing of a person in the Queen's Peace. The phrase 'in the Queen's Peace' aims to exclude killing in times of war and has no relevance to our discussion. Similarly it is unlikely that the requirement that the killing be unlawful has particular relevance in the killing of a child, as lawful killing relates primarily to killing in self-defence. Foetuses and unborn children do not come within the scope of the offence of murder, as the law does not regard them as people. However a child who is injured by an assault while in the womb and then dies of his injuries, having been born alive, would be a person for the purposes of the offence.[64] The defendant's act must be a cause of the child's death, but it does not need to be the sole cause. In order to establish a causative link in law it must be shown first that the defendant's act was a factual cause of the child's death, that is that 'but for' the defendant's unlawful act the child's death would not have occurred.[65] Secondly it must be shown that the defendant's act was a 'substantial and operating cause' of the child's death. The act need not be the only cause, but it must contribute to the child's death to a significant extent and his act must continue to be a cause at the point at which the child died.[66]

A very limited number of people set out to kill a child, but provided that there is sufficient evidence that death was a purpose of their act the *mens rea* of murder would be satisfied. It would also be satisfied if the defendant intended to cause the

---

[62] Law Commission (n 2).   [63] ibid.   [64] *R v Senior* (1832) 1 Mood CC 346.
[65] *R v Dalloway* (1847) 2 Cox CC 273; *R v Dyson* [1908] 2 KB 959 (CA Crim).
[66] *R v Pagett* (1983) 76 Cr App R 279 (CA Crim); *R v Cheshire* [1991] 3 All ER 670 (CA Crim).

child grievous bodily harm (GBH). This latter definition of the *mens rea* for murder has drawn criticism, first on the ground that it offends the correspondence principle, that the *mens rea* should match the *actus reus* and secondly on the ground that an intention to cause GBH is too wide. Usually it could be argued that while an intention to cause GBH was tantamount to an intention to kill in previous times, because of the unlikelihood that medical treatment could save a patient, this argument is no longer sustainable bearing in mind the current high level of medical treatment. Critics of the current standard have argued that intention in murder should be limited to an intention to kill or to do a life-threatening act.[67] However this argument is less sustainable in relation to children, particularly young children who make up the majority of child homicide victims, who are weaker and more vulnerable than the general population. We would argue that in relation to children, intention to cause GBH or to wound is, in reality, an intention to do a life-threatening act and the arguments in favour of legal change here are not as pressing as they might be in other circumstances.

In cases of murder, juries are also allowed to use evidence of the defendant's knowledge that death or serious injury was a virtually certain consequence of his act to infer that the defendant had the requisite intention for murder. The leading case on inferred or oblique intention, *Woollin*,[68] concerned the death of an infant. The appellant lost his temper and threw his three-month-old child onto a hard surface. The child died from a fractured skull. The question for the court was whether the jury could infer that Mr Woollin intended to kill his child from his knowledge that the child's death or serious injury was a likely consequence of his actions. The appellate courts had accepted a lower test at an earlier point in time which allowed juries to infer intention from evidence that the defendant knew that death or serious injury was probable,[69] or highly probable.[70] However the House of Lords approved of the direction on inferring intention which had been set out by Lord Lane CJ in the case of *Nedrick,* 12 years before.[71] The court directed that if the jury was satisfied that 'at the material time the defendant recognised that death or serious harm would be virtually certain (barring some unforeseen intervention) to result from his voluntary act' then they could find that the defendant 'intended to kill or do serious bodily harm, even though he may not have had any desire to achieve that result'.[72] The House of Lords substituted a conviction for manslaughter, because although the jury had found that Mr Woollin appreciated that there was a substantial risk of death or serious injury to the child when he assaulted him, it was not clear that they had found that he knew that death or serious injury to the child was a virtual certainty.

In cases where a child has died as a result of deliberate physical assault, it may be difficult in a number of cases to infer that the attacker intended that the child would die or suffer serious injury as a result. There are a number of practical problems and

---

[67] J Herring *Criminal Law* (OUP, Oxford 2004) 278–297.
[68] *R v Woollin* [1999] AC 82 (HL).   [69] *Hyam v DPP* [1975] AC 55 (HL).
[70] *Walker and Hayles* (1990) 90 Cr App R 226 (CA Crim).
[71] *R v Nedrick* [1986] 1 WLR 1025 (HL).   [72] ibid, 1028.

some social expectations that can hinder a jury in making this inference:

> Motive is often unclear when a caretaker kills a child. Unlike a fight between adults that escalates to a killing, there may be little evidence as to why a caretaker would kill a child. Even when a motive exists, the reason for the killing may be so trivial as to be nearly incomprehensible to most people. Moreover, it is often difficult for the finder of fact to determine whether the fatal act resulted from a one-time response from frustration and anger, or if it was the result of hatred and genuine ill-will toward the child.[73]

When a child has died as a result of a sustained number of attacks it may be difficult to prove that in the last attack before the child's death, the assailant intended to kill the child or cause the child grievous bodily harm. It is an irony that the abuser of a child who has died after a prolonged series of attacks may argue that he did not intend the child's death as the child had survived many similar beatings in the past, and the assailant, in so much as he considered the injuries which the child would sustain from the beating, expected that the child would suffer a similar level of injury as the child had done on previous occasions.

As a result of the social construction of images of adults who look after children it may also be difficult for juries to infer that the purpose of any caregiver could ever actually be to kill a child. Even the words that we have available in English for those adults with whom the child lives or stays for a period of time—'looking after', 'caring for', 'minding'—imply a connection between the child and the adult in which the adult retains an overall interest in the child's welfare, whatever the adult actually does. It is enormously difficult to fit the death of a child, killed by repeated assaults, into the rules constructed by the law about purposive killing, because it is commonly assumed that the death of the child could not possibly have been the actor's purpose.

Midson has argued that those who kill a child as a result of a series of assaults should be charged with murder, rather than manslaughter. She contends forcefully that:

> a manslaughter conviction, and the resulting sentence is inconsistent with the conduct of the defendant in cases where the death of the child is the culmination of a period of physical abuse and neglect. In such cases, death is not only a risk, it is inevitable.[74]

Might a person be charged with murder in these circumstances as the law currently stands? In cases in which a child has been the victim of sustained physical abuse and dies as a result, it seems clear that in some cases a charge of murder can be sustained, on the grounds that there was, if not a clear intention to kill, a clear intention to inflict serious injury on the victim. The murderers of Victoria Climbié, who repeatedly beat her with a variety of instruments, fall into the category of those who certainly intended to inflict serious injuries upon a child victim, even if it was not their purpose to kill her.[75] However it may be more difficult to establish the requisite *mens rea* in cases where

[73] C Phipps 'Responding To Child Homicide: A Statutory Proposal' (1999) 89 J Crim L & Criminology 535, 538.

[74] B Midson 'Child Homicide in New Zealand: Charges, Convictions and Sentencing' in C Breen (ed) *Children's Needs, Rights and Welfare—Developing Strategies for the Whole Child in the 21st Century* (Thompson Dunmore Press, Victoria 2004) 135–136.

[75] Lord Laming (Chair) *Victoria Climbié Inquiry* (Cm 5730, 2003) [3.81]–[3.85].

the actor intended that the child would suffer some harm, but did not intend that the child would suffer serious harm as a result of the assault. In cases where a child has died as a result of a prolonged series of attacks upon him it may be difficult to infer that the defendant intended to kill the child. One argument that has been accepted in some American States, and is discussed below, is that evidence of prolonged abuse is actually evidence of a lack of intention to kill. The argument being that the perpetrator of the abuse thought that the child would survive the assault as she had done in relation to previous assaults. However, the converse implication has been accepted by some courts in Australia, namely that the assailant knew that the child victim was weak, because the assailant himself had weakened the child by previous assaults and thus he knew that further assaults would cause the child serious injury. This argument is also examined below. In relation to English law, evidence of that series of attacks on a weak and vulnerable victim is certainly evidence that a defendant must have appreciated that there was a substantial risk that a child would suffer serious injury in the future. However this interpretation of the test for inferring intention in murder which was used at first instance in *Woollin*, was subsequently clearly rejected by the House of Lords.[76] An imputation of intention in these circumstances falls outside the *Woollin* test, as it is an objective rather than subjective test of the defendant's intention at the time and secondly because it is essentially a test of the defendant's undoubted recklessness, rather than intention. Under the Law Commission's proposals for the reform of homicide,[77] there would be a reclassification of homicide into three rather than two categories: first degree murder, second degree murder or manslaughter.

'First degree murder' would encompass intentional killings, and killings with the intent to cause serious injury where the killer was aware that his or her conduct involved a serious risk of causing death. Under the proposed reforms, killings intended to cause serious injury, without the additional awareness of causing death, which would now be charged as second degree murder. The Law Commission has accepted the definition of intention currently established by common law: that is a person may be taken to intend an action when she acts to bring it about, or where the defendant thought that the result was a virtually certain consequence of her action. It therefore seems that very few child deaths could fall into the first category for first degree murder, for the reasons outlined above. However, might some child deaths be successfully prosecuted under the second category, on the grounds that the defendant intended to cause serious injury, and was aware that he was running a serious risk of the child's death? The Law Commission has definition awareness as *consciously adverting to a substantial or real chance of death*. Their definition would clearly comprehend a child death on the fact of *Woollin*, discussed above. But there could only be a successful prosection in cases where there had been a history of assaults which the child previously survived, when the Crown establishes that the defendant knew that there was a real chance that the child would die as a result of that final assault. This, as discussed above and further in this chapter, has been far from automatic in some of the jurisdictions we have examined.

[76] *R v Woollin* (n 68).
[77] Law Commission (n 2) 28–31, 53–59.

2. Manslaughter

The generic crime of manslaughter may currently be subdivided into two main categories, voluntary and involuntary manslaughter. Voluntary manslaughter is an intended killing, which would usually be categorized as murder, but is reduced to manslaughter because of a recognized defence. These defences all indicate that whilst the defendant did intend to kill, he lacked the requisite culpability for murder. The defences of provocation and diminished responsibility may be raised in the killing of children. Conversely involuntary manslaughter concerns instances in which the defendant did not intend to kill, but did knowingly commit a culpable act. Involuntary manslaughter occupies what Hogan has described as 'the shifting sands between the uncertain . . . definition of murder and the unsettled boundaries of excusable or accidental death.'[78] Instances of involuntary manslaughter may be further subdivided into gross negligent manslaughter, unlawful act, or constructive manslaughter. In all of these offences there remains a potentially good 'fit' between the nature of the child deaths as they occur and the crime as it is written.

(a) Voluntary manslaughter

(i) Provocation

The defence of provocation is currently laid down in the Homicide Act 1957 s 3.

Where on a charge of murder there is evidence on which the jury can find that the person charged was provoked (whether by things done or by things said or by both together) to lose his self-control, the question whether the provocation was enough to make a reasonable man do as he did shall be left to be determined by the jury; and in determining that question, the jury shall take into account everything both done and said according to the effect which, in their opinion, it would have on a reasonable man.

Some killings of children may be reduced under this provision from a charge of murder to manslaughter, if the prosecution does not prove that the defendant was not provoked. For a defence to succeed there must be evidence first that the defendant was provoked to lose his self-control. This is a subjective test and requires evidence of some conduct by the victim which caused a loss of self-control on the part of the defendant. A second, objective test must then be satisfied that the provocation was sufficient to make a reasonable man do as he did. This test has moved through a number of significant permutations and the present formulation could have notable repercussions in an extension in the use of provocation in cases concerning the killing of children. The interpretation of this second limb is discussed below.

The Law Commission has reviewed the defence of provocation, in response to many concerns about the existence of the defence and the framing of the defence in its current form.[79] These concerns are that it is morally unsustainable for the

---

[78] B Hogan 'The Killing Ground: 1964–73' [1974] Crim LR 387, 391 in M Allen (ed) *Elliott and Woods Cases and Materials on Criminal Law* (8th edn Sweet & Maxwell, London 2001).

[79] The Law Commission *Partial Defences to Murder Consultation Paper* (HM Stationery Office, London 2003 LC No 173); The Law Commission *Partial Defences to Murder Final Report* (HM Stationery Office, London 2004); Law Commission (n 2).

emotion of sudden anger to be elevated above other, arguably more noble, emotions of compassion or empathy in providing a partial defence, and that there is a clear gender bias in the framing of the defence. Provocation provides a partial defence for actions taken when a defendant suddenly becomes angry and kills, arguably a more male characteristic, whereas it does not provide a defence for those who react more slowly. This slower reaction has been accepted by the courts to be more characteristic of fearful women, and has been particularly discussed in relation to women who have suffered prolonged domestic violence.[80] The defence is also unpalatable in relation to the killing of children, particularly in allowing normal childhood behaviour to constitute provocation and in allowing evidence of the defendant's own lack of capacity to exercise self-control into the determination of whether the defendant's response to the provocation ought to give rise to liability only for manslaughter.

- 'that the person charged was provoked (whether by things done or by things said or by both together) to lose his self-control'

The common law has allowed a wide meaning of 'provocative' conduct, and provocation now has come to be interpreted as meaning 'caused'.[81] Thus any behaviour by the victim, however blameless, may constitute provocation. Normal childhood behaviour, such as crying, whining, or having tantrums, can be provocative behaviour if the behaviour and the defendant's reaction is found to be causatively linked. Thus in *Doughty*,[82] where the appellant killed his 17-day-old son by kneeling on a cushion put over the baby's face, the Court of Appeal found that the judge at first instance had erred in not allowing the defence of provocation to be put to the jury. This was because s 3 allowed the judge no choice in the light of evidence of a causative link between the baby's crying and the defendant's response. This result must be wrong in the specific context of a discussion of child abuse. The judge at first instance in *Doughty* rightly justified his decision not to allow the question of provocation to the jury, on the grounds that the term provocation was not originally designed to encompass ordinary, expected conduct by a victim:

It is notorious that every baby born cries, that every baby can at times be burdensome . . . I think that the episodes or events in the life of the baby of 17-days-old could not have been in the mind of Parliament when section 3 became the law. The words of section 3, I quote: 'Whether by things done or words said or by both together'—are not, in my judgment, apposite to embrace the perfectly ordinary, certain, and natural episodes or events in the life of a 17-day-old baby. Further, common law directions cannot be construed as including these natural and certain episodes that occur in the life of every baby of days old. Finally, I think civilised society dictates that the natural episodes occurring in the life of a baby only days old have to be endured and cannot be utilised as the foundation of subjective provocation to enable his killer to escape a conviction for murder.[83]

---

[80] A McColgan 'General Defences' in D Nicholson and L Bibbings (eds) *Feminist Perspectives on Criminal Law* (Cavendish Publishing, London 2000) 137–138.
[81] *DPP v Camplin* (1978) 67 Cr App R 14 (HL) 19 (Lord Diplock).
[82] *R v Doughty* (1986) 83 Cr App R 319 (CA Crim) 325.   [83] ibid.

The current law, which places none of the limitations suggested by the judge at first instance in *Doughty*, leads to an overriding impression that the victim was in some way to blame for his own death, in any case in which provocation may be raised. 'Provocation unduly makes the deceased the "defendant". It blames the victim for the defendant's inability to exercise self-control. In court the deceased cannot answer defence assertions.'[84] At present the English law contrasts unfavourably with the repeated findings of courts in the United States that childish behaviour such as crying[85] or bedwetting[86] cannot and should not[87] be considered in law to constitute a provocative act. It also should be contrasted with Canadian and Scottish law, and some Australian States which place limitations on the type of behaviour which may be considered in law as provocative conduct. Provocative conduct in Canada is limited to 'a wrongful act or insult'.[88] In Scotland provocation may be either violence or infidelity.[89] In New South Wales provocation must be something which has taken the defendant by surprise.[90] While New Zealand and other Australian territories have a common law definition of provocation[91] which has been influenced by the way that the common law has developed in England, the experience of these other jurisdictions demonstrates that even if the defence is not abolished the defence of provocation may be limited to exclude normal behaviour by victims.

The Law Commission has proposed that any reform of the defence of provocation should limit the range of behaviour which may be considered in law to be provocative 'to "gross provocation" (meaning words or conduct or a combination of words and conduct which caused the defendant to have a justifiable sense of being seriously wronged)'.[92] The requirement that the provocation be 'gross' means that the defence would be limited to situations in which the defendant had a legitimate ground to feel wronged. The term 'justifiable' imports an objective test into the jury's deliberations, and the Law Commission suggest that a jury would consider whether the defendant had sufficient reason to be provoked in these circumstances and whether the defendant's outlook should be condoned in civilized society.[93] Were such proposals to be accepted it should curtail the use of provocation as a defence to the killing of children.

- **whether the provocation was enough to make a reasonable man do as he did**

For a number of years there has been a hard-fought discussion in the courts as to whether the jury should be allowed to impute any of the characteristics of the

---

[84] The Law Commission *Partial Defences to Murder Consultation Paper* (n 79) 83 [4.169].

[85] *Isaac v State* 440 SE 2d 175 (Georgia Supreme Ct 1994) 178.

[86] *Patterson v State* 532 NE 2d 604 (Indiana Supreme Ct 1988) and *Robinson v State* 453 NE 2d 280 (Indiana Supreme Ct 1990).   [87] *State v Broseman* 947 SW 2d 520 (Missouri CA 1997) 527.

[88] Criminal Code 1985 (Canada) c 46 s 232(1).

[89] J Chalmers, C Gane and F Leverick *Appendix E* in The Law Commission *Partial Defences to Murder Consultation Paper* (n 79) 169.   [90] Crimes Act 1900 (New South Wales) s 23.

[91] The Law Commission *Partial Defences to Murder Consultation Paper* (n 79) 85–115.

[92] The Law Commission *Partial Defences to Murder Final Report* (n 79) 46–55.

[93] ibid 46–47.

defendant to the notional reasonable man in determining whether the provocation was enough to make him do as he did. Initially the courts did not allow evidence of the defendant's characteristics which might make him particularly susceptible to the provocation alleged, or might hinder his ability to exercise self-control. However *Camplin* liberalized the position considerably and allowed juries to consider any characteristics of the defendant which could affect the gravity of the provocation alleged and allowed them to consider the defendant's age and gender in determining what level of self-control could be considered ordinary. From *Camplin* a number of cases allowed the jury to consider permanent characteristics of the defendant, if they went to the 'sting' of the provocation, for example if a drug addict was taunted about his addiction. Discussion in cases concerning evidence raised of 'battered women's syndrome' also suggested that, if the defendant raised expert evidence demonstrating a specific personality syndrome, the jury could consider this syndrome in determining the standard of self-control which a 'reasonable person' might be expected to exercise in the circumstances. In *Smith (Morgan)* a split House of Lords held that any characteristic of the defendant may be considered in determining 'whether in all the circumstances people with his characteristics might have been able to exhibit more self-control than he did'.[94] The decision has been criticized on a number of levels. Most importantly in the context of child death, in cases where for example a depressed parent snaps and kills a child, the issue of whether that parent should have exhibited more self-control than he did in the light of the depression will now be a question for the jury. In this context 'the fears that the reasonable man may become cloned as the accused are real'.[95] It may be very difficult for a jury member to understand that the law does not require them to place themselves in the position of the defendant and then ask whether they would have behaved in the same way, but instead ask whether in the light of the defendant's characteristics the defendant should have exercised more self-control in the circumstances. If the question becomes in the minds of a jury member whether the reaction was 'understandable' in the circumstances, there is evidence throughout child abuse prosecutions that what Cobley *et al* have identified as the 'there but for the grace of God go I stance',[96] can increase the acceptance of excuses for physical injuries against children, and there is no reason to think that it would not also do so in the case of provocation.

The form that provocation now takes is far from any common understanding of provocation. 'The provocation excuse should be a concession to extra-ordinary external circumstances not to the extra-ordinary internal make-up of the accused . . . The defence of provocation is for those who are in a broad sense "mentally normal" but who snap under the weight of very grave provocation.'[97] Instead in many ways it has become a defence for those who cannot or do not wish to use the defence of diminished responsibility.[98]

---

[94] *Smith (Morgan)* [2001] 1 AC 146 (HL) 155E–F (Lord Slynn).
[95] S Edwards 'Current Developments' (2001) 23 J Social Welfare and Family Law 227, 228.
[96] Cobley, Sanders and Wheeler (n 58).
[97] A Ashworth 'The Doctrine of Provocation' (1976) 35 CLJ 292, 312.
[98] R Heaton 'Anything Goes' (2001) 10(2) Nottingham LJ 50, 55–56.

(ii) Diminished responsibility

The defence of diminished responsibility is also defined in statute. The Homicide Act 1957 s 2(1) provides:

Where a person kills or is a party to the killing of another, he shall not be convicted of murder if he was suffering from such abnormality of mind (whether arising from a condition of arrested or retarded development of mind or any inherent causes or induced by disease or injury) as substantially impaired his mental responsibility for his acts and omissions in doing or being a party to the killing.

The term 'abnormality of mind' can therefore be applied to uncontrollable urges, cognitive disorders and extreme emotional states. The definition of diminished responsibility has been criticized on a number of levels for its conceptual flaws.[99] However there are no particular criticisms of its use in relation to the killing of children. The defence does not appear to be used a great deal in child homicide cases. However it could be used in situations where a parent kills a child while suffering from delusions, or because of an uncontrollable urge.

(b) Involuntary manslaughter

(i) Unlawful or dangerous act (constructive) manslaughter

The crime of unlawful or dangerous act manslaughter punishes incidents when death results from another deliberate criminal act. Thus in a situation in which an actor intentionally or recklessly commits a criminal act and as a result a person dies the actor will also be liable for that death, even though he did not foresee that death. The criminal act must be something which an ordinary and reasonable man, 'would inevitably recognise it as an act which must subject the other person to at least the risk of some harm resulting there from albeit not serious harm.'[100] There is no need to prove that the defendant himself foresaw any harm, the test remains a purely objective one: whether a reasonable man would inevitably recognize it as an act which must subject the other person to at least some risk of harm.[101] In determining this question, any obvious physical frailties, such as age or disability of the victim may be taken into account,[102] but not those frailties which are not externally obvious, such as a heart condition.[103] Thus a person who set out to beat a child and as a result killed her, could be convicted of constructive manslaughter. However the offence may not currently be charged if the child's death was the result of a criminal omission to act. For example a child's death from malnutrition or dehydration, could not be punished by this offence. The rationale for this division is that the defendant should have taken an active and willing part in the commission of the crime which causes death. The principle was established in *Lowe*, which concerned the death of a child from dehydration and gross emaciation. In this case the Court of Appeal

---

[99] E Griew 'The Future of Diminished Responsibility' [1988] Crim LR 75, 81–82.

[100] *R v Church* [1966] 1 QB 59 (CA Crim) 70 (Edmund Davies LJ).

[101] *DPP v Newbury* [1977] AC 500 (HL).   [102] *R v Watson* [1989] 2 All ER 865 (HL).

[103] *R v Dawson* (1985) 81 Cr App R 150 (CA).

found that:

there is a clear distinction between an act of omission and commission likely to cause harm. Whatever may be the position of the latter, it does not prove that the same is true of the former. In other words if I strike a child in a manner likely to cause harm it is right that if the child dies, I may be charged with manslaughter. If however I omit to do something with the result that it suffers injury to health which results in its death, we think that manslaughter should not be an inevitable consequence, even if the omission is deliberate.

It seems strange that an omission which is wilful solely in the sense that it is not advertent and the consequences of which are not in fact foreseen by the person who is in fact neglectful, should if death results automatically give rise to a determinant sentence.[104]

In reality it is difficult in child abuse cases to infer a lack of deliberation into the fact that the child has been injured by an omission, rather than by an act of commission. As we argue strongly below, although acts of omission, such as neglect, are often regarded as the fault of circumstance, rather than deliberate cruelty, it is difficult on the facts of many of the cases to make that type of distinction. While some parents are clearly inadequate and have no intention to harm their children, some are not. It should be in the *mens rea* of the offence that this should be tested, not in the determination of the *actus reus*.

(ii) Criticisms of the offence

The existence of the offence of constructive manslaughter has been criticized by the Law Commission on the grounds that, 'it is wrong in principle for the law to hold a person responsible for causing a result that he did not intend or foresee, and which would not even have been *foreseeable* by a reasonable person observing his conduct'.[105] In the context of a child's death by abuse this criticism has less resonance when a person assaults a child, resulting in that child's death, as there is a level of foreseeability that the child could at least be seriously injured. However this is not a case where death is the inevitable result of an act, rather a person in beating or in another way subjecting a child to physical assault, is taking a clear risk that the child will die or suffer serious harm. The commission of the act of assault upon a child is a reckless act and could be labelled as such.

The Law Commission have recommended the creation of a new offence of reckless killing. In these circumstances the defendant could be found guilty of second degree murder—under the Law Commission's proposals for the reform of homicide laws, if he foresaw a serious risk of death being caused by his intention to cause injury or fear or risk of injury.[106] The Commission has proposed that recklessness which falls below this standard, where there was no awareness a risk of death, would fall into the less serious offence of gross negligent manslaughter.

The test for 'reckless killing' would not of course be satisfied by a defendant who raises evidence that he was not aware of the risk that he was taking with

---

[104] *Lowe* [1973] QB 702 (CA Crim) 709 (Phillimore LJ).
[105] Law Commission *Legislating the Criminal Code: Involuntary Manslaughter* (HM Stationery Office, London no 237) 23 [3.8].
[106] Law Commission 2005 (n 2) [3.21]–[3.28]; Law Commission 2006 (n 2) [2.95]–[2.111].

the child. Cobley *et al*'s research into the prosecution of injuries caused by shaking a baby, clearly demonstrates that some members of the judiciary themselves are sympathetic to argument that the defendant was unaware of the extreme risk in shaking babies and young infants that the child would be seriously injured. In halving the defendant's two-year sentence in *Scott*[107] Kay J explained in the Court of Appeal that:

it is necessary to go on and look at the particular acts that resulted in the injuries that this poor child suffered. They were not blows. They were not offences of throwing the child to the floor or against some object as this Court sometimes has to consider. They were simply shaking a child.

Cobley *et al*'s analysis of sentencing decisions in 'shaking' cases also demonstrates that the judiciary can place the shaking of a child or baby into a different category of involuntary acts performed as a result of frustration, rather than intention or even recklessness as to a child's injury. In *Hulbert*[108] the Court of Appeal distinguished shaking from voluntary abuse such as hitting, describing it as 'an involuntary expression of the exasperation that no parent has not at some time or another felt'.[109]

In the light of these comments it appears that while the death of a child from shaking would constitute constructive manslaughter, it is by no means certain that it would always constitute 'reckless killing' as framed by the Law Commission. This would of course depend upon the nature of the case and evidence that the defendant knew that the child had sustained injuries in the past, would be evidence that he knew the risk that he was running in shaking the child.

A child's death by abuse is an important loophole in the Law Commission's proposals on reckless killing, because it may evade the Commission's definition of knowledge of a serious risk of death, rather than knowledge of the risk of a serious injury. As discussed earlier it is almost impossible to prove in English law that someone who has repeatedly abused a child intended their death; because an abuser may say with perfect truthfulness that he imagined the child would survive, because the child had survived so many similar beatings in the past. It is difficult to see how this argument could not be used in this new offence. Yet children who die because of sustained and repeated abuse do not die because of a momentary aberration, but because of repetitive torture, which is arguably much worse. The law should recognize the inherent risks of torturing children in its construction of liability to ensure that the death that results is deemed to be second degree murder. As Australian law has proved, this can be done in child abuse cases by courts willing to infer knowledge of a risk of death from the defendant's knowledge of the child's state of health at the time of the fatal assault, despite a defendant's statement that he did not forsee a risk of death. However if this sadly proves impossible the Law Commission has proposed the retention of a form of constructive manslaughter. As discussed below in section C.8 the offence which now best fits an occasion on which a child is killed by abuse is 'cruelty contributing

---

[107] *R v Scott* (1995) 16 Cr App R 451 (CA Crim) 452.
[108] *Hulbert* (1998) EWCA Crim 2758 [13].   [109] ibid.

to death' under the Domestic Violence, Crimes and Victims Act 2004 s 5. This may be charged when a child has been killed by one or more people 'looking after' him and is based on the concept of constructive manslaughter, or the 'homicide by abuse' statutes of the US. However while this offence fills an important gap in relation to the prosecution of an 'unknown' perpetrator of child abuse leading to death, it cannot be seen as a replacememt for a charge of second degree murder or manslaughter in these cases.

(iii) Gross negligent manslaughter

A defendant may currently be charged with gross negligent manslaughter if he breaches a duty of care owed to the victim and, as a result of that breach, the victim dies. In order to find the defendant criminally liable for his act, the jury must determine that the breach was so gross as to be criminal:

> In explaining to juries the test which they should apply to determine whether the negligence in the particular case, amounted or did not amount to a crime, judges have used many epithets, such as 'culpable', 'gross', 'wicked', 'clear', 'complete'. But whatever epithet be used or not, in order to establish criminal liability the facts must be such that, in the opinion of the jury, the negligence of the accused went beyond a mere matter of compensation between subjects and showed such disregard for the life and safety of others as to amount to a crime against the state and conduct deserving of punishment.[110]

The existence of a duty of care between the defendant and the victim should be established on ordinary tort law principles.[111] The question of whether such a duty existed at the time of the child's death is a question of law to be decided by the judge in each case. The *mens rea* in gross negligent manslaughter is an objective one, namely that 'the circumstances must be such that a reasonably prudent person would have foreseen a serious and obvious risk not merely of injury, or even of serious injury, but of death'.[112]

The Law Commission has proposed that the crime of manslaughter through gross negligence would be satisfied if:[113]

(1) that person's conduct causes death;
(2) it would have been obvious to a reasonable person in the defendant's position that the conduct involved a risk of death;
(3) the defendant had the capacity to appreciate that his or her conduct involved a risk of causing death; and
(4) the conduct fell far below what could reasonably be expected in the circumstances.

---

[110] *R v Bateman* (1925) 19 Cr App R 8 (HL) 11–12 (Lord Hewart CJ).

[111] *R v Adomako* [1995] 1 AC 171 (HL) (Lord Mackay).

[112] *R v Singh (Gurphal)* [1999] Crim LR 582 (CA Crim); *R v Yaqoob* [2005] EWCA Crim 1269 [26]–[30].

[113] Law Commission (2006) (n 2) [3.60]. These proposals are similar, but not identical, to the proposals contained in Law Commission *Legislating the Criminal Code: Involuntary Manslaughter* (n 105) 53 [5.34].

The Commission envisaged that a person's reckless stupidity would be evidence that their conduct fell far below what could reasonably be expected in the circumstances.

A gross negligent manslaughter charge has been considered appropriate by courts in the past when a child has died as a result of an omission, such as a failure to feed or care for him or her. In this context it should be used where it was unlikely that the parent intended to kill the child by their behaviour, yet in the circumstances a reasonably prudent person would have foreseen the obvious and serious risk of death. However in circumstances in which the parent's neglect of the child stems from an inability to care, it may depend very much on the individual jury to determine whether the parent's negligence was so bad as to be criminal. As this is a jury decision there can be no clarification of this definition in caselaw, on which the decisions of both the prosecution and the defence may be based, as the process of determining whether the action was criminal, remains unrecorded.[114] In *Mitra*[115] the defence questioned whether the offence as currently described offended the right under ECHR Article 7 and the expectation at common law for certainty in offences, so that a defendant may be required to understand the nature of the offence before he decides to commit it. This argument was rejected by the Court of Appeal on the grounds that the law was clear and all the jury was required to do was to apply the law to the facts, rather than to create the law. However it remains doubtful how long this offence in its current form can survive challenge on this basis. It must be concerning to lawyers working in this area for the jurisprudence to remain so underdeveloped, when it relates to the most likely offence that a parent will be charged with.

3. Infanticide

Infanticide is formulated in legislation as an offence, although it operates as a defence reducing a crime of murder to manslaughter. It is only available to women who kill their own child when that child is under 12 months old, provided that 'at the time of the act or omission, the balance of her mind was disturbed by reason of her not having fully recovered from the effect of giving birth or by reason of the effect of lactation, consequent upon the birth of a child'.[116] The history of the provision lies in an attempt to give some leniency to women who through poverty and social isolation may have been driven to kill their child and who, without the defence, would have been convicted of murder and sentenced to death. Although the defence is couched in medical terms Wilczynski, amongst others, has argued that this was in order to allow the courts to feel comfortable in granting a lenient sentence, rather than because reformers believed that psychiatric rather than social conditions were entirely to blame for the child's death.[117] '[P]romoters of reform were as much, if not more, concerned with social conditions such as poverty, abandonment by the father, and social disgrace as with the effect on the woman's state of mind [as the result]

---

[114] Law Commission *Legislating the Criminal Code: Involuntary Manslaughter* (n 105).
[115] *Mitra* [2004] EWCA Crim 2375.   [116] Infanticide Act 1938 (England) s 1.
[117] A Wilcyzinski *Child Homicide* (OUP, Oxford 1997) 150.

of giving birth'.[118] The underlying ethos of the offence is obvious in its application, although the statute only allows the crime to be charged instead of murder, if there is evidence of a causal link between the defendant's disturbance of mind and the effect of giving birth or lactation. In fact research on the use of the defence has found that it is accepted readily when children under 12 months are killed by their mothers if there is evidence of any emotional disturbance.[119]

The existence of this offence has been criticized on a number of levels. First it has been argued that there is little medical evidence to support the existence of the offence as defined. While women certainly can suffer from post-partum psychosis and about five deaths a year are attributable to this illness,[120] it has been argued that it is not a separate form of psychosis, as the defence of infanticide presumes, but rather may be categorized with all other forms of psychosis and thus the category of killing while the defendant is suffering from diminished responsibility.[121] The time limit of a year has also been criticized as arbitrary.[122] Secondly it has been criticized by feminist scholars on the grounds that it is another example of the medicalization of female crimes and contributes to a reinforcement of stereotypical views of women as at the mercy of hormonal shifts, and of criminal women as 'not bad, but mad'.[123] It leads to an almost automatic assumption that women who kill children who are less than a year old are suffering from a mental abnormality.[124] Thirdly it has been criticized as disadvantageous to men who kill their children:

It is clear not only that mothers and fathers were treated differently by the criminal justice system but that mothers were dealt with more leniently. Mothers were less likely than fathers to be sentenced to imprisonment and were more likely to be given probation and psychiatric dispositions . . . It may be that women and men commit filicide for very different reasons and in very different circumstances. It is certainly perceived in this way: The very existence of the crime of infanticide is an example of this.[125]

In the words of Allen women who kill their children are 'rendered harmless'[126] by social perceptions and by the existence of defences like infanticide and male defendants may also suffer a disadvantage as a result. Finally and most importantly for a book relating to the protection of children, there is an argument that the existence of this defence devalues the lives of children.

---

[118] R Lansdowne 'Infanticide: Psychiatrists in the Plea Bargaining Process' (1990) 16 Mohash U L Rev 41, 45.

[119] R Mackay 'The Consequences of Killing Very Young Children' [1993] Crim LR 21.

[120] A Wilcyzinski and A Morris 'Parents Who Kill Their Children' [1993] Crim LR 31, 35.

[121] D Nicholson 'What the Law Giveth it also Taketh Away: Female Specific Defences to Criminal Liability' in D Nicholson and L Bibbings (eds) *Feminist Perspectives on Criminal Law* (Cavendish Publishing, London 2000) 165; this view has been contradicted in M O'Hara 'Post-partum "Blues", Depression, and Psychosis: A Review' (1987) 7 J Psychosomatic Obstetrics and Gynaecology 205, 217.

[122] Victorian Law Commission *Defences to Homicide: Final Report* (Victorian Law Commission, Melbourne 2004) [6.16].

[123] L Zedner *Women, Crime and Custody in Victorian England* (OUP, Oxford 1991).

[124] V Dobson and B Sales 'The Science of Infanticide and Mental Illness' (2000) 6 Psychol Pub Pol'y & L 1098, 1109. [125] Wilcyzinski and Morris (n 120).

[126] H Allen *Justice Unbalanced: Gender Psychiatry and Judicial Decisions* (Open University Press, Milton Keynes 1987) 27–28.

However, the offence/defence of infanticide undoubtedly possesses some pragmatic advantages for lawyers who are defending women who have killed their children, when the child was very young. The defence itself is wider than the defence of diminished responsibility and there is no requirement that the defendant's mental abnormality amount to a clinical disorder, for the defence to be used.[127] Furthermore, as the work of Wilczynski and Morris, amongst others, has shown, the existence of the defence of infanticide influences the sentencing of mothers who have killed children over the age of one, making it more likely that women will receive a non-custodial sentence for killing a child of whatever age. Some American commentators have looked at the legislation in England, Australia, New Zealand[128] and Canada, which are all very similar, and suggested that the offence has been retained in these jurisdictions because, while the medical basis for such a defence is undeniably weak, the resulting lenient sentences for women who kill very young children are generally accepted as appropriate.[129] This is the position favoured by the Law Commission which has merely proposed that the offence/defence should apply to both of the new categories of murder which it proposes.[130] However it is difficult to see that there is in reality any justification for the existence of such an offence in medicine or indeed in law, which already contains a number of mechanisms by which the frailties of an alleged perpetrator may be recognized and taken into account, irrespective of gender, or the age of a child.

4. Homicide law in the United States

The law on homicide in the United States is vast and there is considerable variation between States. The next section does not attempt to describe all of the law but rather to identify some areas in which State law has made innovations which could be considered in English law in relation to homicide.

(a) Inferring an intention to kill in cases of prolonged abuse

Some courts in the United States have been willing to allow juries to decide whether or not to infer an intention to murder from the evidence of the extent and range of the child's injuries in cases where a child has suffered prolonged abuse. In Nevada, courts have consistently upheld first degree murder convictions, which require proof of an intent to kill with premeditation and deliberation, when children have died as a result of chronic physical abuse. In *Hern v State*, the defendant beat the three-year-old son of his girlfriend to death. The court found that the 'nature and extent of the injuries, coupled with repeated blows, constitutes substantial evidence of wilfulness, premeditation, and deliberation'.[131] The court held that it should allow a jury to

---

[127] Simester and Sullivan *Criminal Law—Theory and Doctrine* (n 50) 582.
[128] The offence applies to children under ten in Crimes Act 1961 (New Zealand) s 178.
[129] C Fazio and J Comito 'Rethinking The Tough Sentencing of Teenage Neonaticide Offenders in the United States' (1999) 67 Fordham L Rev 3109, 3142.
[130] Law Commission (2006) (n 2) [8.6]–[8.43].
[131] *Hern v The State* 635 P 2d 278 (Nevada Supreme Ct 1981) 281.

draw reasonable inferences from evidence such as this.[132] However, as Phipps has documented, courts in other States have refused to allow an inference of intent from evidence of repeated abuse, on the grounds that they are evidence not of a specific intent to kill, but rather an indifference to life or recklessness in relation to death.[133] It may be, as the Arkansas Supreme Court recognised in *Midgett v State*, in a case of child abuse of long duration, that the jury could well infer that the perpetrator comes not to expect the death of the child, but rather the child will live so the abuse may be administered again and again.[134]

(b) Homicide by abuse

Another mechanism for recognizing that a person has undertaken an activity which can deserve a homicide charge is through the mechanism of a homicide by child abuse or by torture offence. Homicide by abuse is a form of unlawful act manslaughter and is triggered in jurisdictions in the United States when a death results from the commission of child abuse. This offence had been created in 23 jurisdictions in the United States by 2003[135] in response to the problem of proving intentional killing in cases where children have died as a result of repeated assaults in child abuse cases and the historical reduction of homicide charges to a lesser charge relating to neglect in child abuse cases.[136] The *mens rea* required for this offence is either the *mens rea* for a crime of child abuse, or that the circumstances evidence a depraved indifference to human life. This may sustain a charge of first degree murder. For example, Tennessee law allows a person to be convicted of murder when the death of a child results from a protracted pattern of abuse or the infliction of multiple acts of bodily injury.[137] Similarly in Oklahoma the normal requirement of intent to kill is satisfied by showing that the defendant committed child abuse in a wilful and malicious manner and the child's death resulted from this abuse.[138] This offence reflects a reality that many campaigners

---

[132] *United States v Woods* 484 F 2d 127 (US CA 4th Cir 1973) (eight-month-old suffocated by foster mother); *United States v Curry* (1990) 31 M J 359 (US Court of Military Appeals) (14-week-old shaken to death and 10-month-old asphyxiated by their father); *Curtis v State* 568 P 2d 583 (Nevada SC 1977) (two-year-old died of head trauma).

[133] *Midgett v State* 729 S W 2d 410 (Arkansas Supreme Ct 1987); *State v Carpenter* 570 A 2d 203 (Connecticut Supreme Ct 1990), 207 (murder conviction lowered to manslaughter—defined as 'evincing an extreme indifference to human life, he recklessly engages in conduct which creates a grave risk of death to another person'—because defendant's act of throwing child into a bathtub did not by itself prove a specific intent to kill required for second degree murder); *Massie v State* 553 P 2d 186 (Oklahoma CA 1976) 190 (court held evidence that four-year-old had numerous injuries and died of head injuries insufficient to support murder committed with a 'premeditated intent and design to effect the death' of the victim); *State v Brown* 836 SW 2d 530 (Tennessee Supreme Ct 1992) 537 (defendant's infliction of massive head injuries, multiple internal injuries, an untreated broken bone, bruises to his genitals and extremities, and numerous other injuries insufficient to support first degree murder because the evidence failed to prove premeditation and deliberation); *State v Bordis* 905 SW2d 214 (Tennessee CA 1995) 224 (court held failure to feed three-month-old child who died from malnutrition and dehydration did not in itself show an intent to kill as there were other 'reasonable interpretations of [defendant's] inaction', in Phipps (n 73), 554).

[134] *Midgett* ibid 413.

[135] APRI National Center for the Prosecution of Child Abuse *Investigation and Prosecution of Child Abuse* (3rd edn Sage Publications, Thousand Oaks 2004) 202.   [136] ibid 202–3.

[137] Tennessee Criminal Code (Annotated) [39–13–202].

[138] Oklahoma Statute Title 21 [701.7].

against child abuse have recognized, that the death of a child following a concerted campaign of abuse is neither an accident nor a mistake, but a consequence about which the perpetrator 'could not care less'. While this does not make the perpetrator's action murder in English law, the existence of an offence of homicide by abuse in some States reflects the nature of the assailant's behaviour and culpability in a way that English law currently does not.

(c) An infanticide offence or defence?

Conversely some commentators in the United States have looked towards England and advocated the enactment of a form of infanticide statute into their State law. They have argued that this is necessary to respond to occasions when a newborn infant is killed (neonaticide)[139] by his or her teenage mother. Others have argued that the law should be changed to address killings which are the result of post-partum psychosis explicitly and consistently.[140] At present, the United States remains the only one of the common law jurisdictions which we have considered, where a defence or offence of infanticide in State law does not exist. Instead infanticide falls into State homicide statutes which vary from State to State. Post-partum psychosis is not an independently recognized defence in any American jurisdiction; rather, it can form the basis for an insanity or diminished capacity defence. The legal standard for insanity and diminished capacity, where applicable, also varies.[141]

Critics of the present American State laws argue that they create great inconsistencies between different trials and sentences of mothers who kill. Brusca's analysis of the use of post-partum psychosis in defence argument found that one-half of the women were found not guilty by reason of insanity, one-quarter received light sentences, and one-quarter received long prison sentences.[142] Similarly Kelly found a wide disparity in the sentences which women received after the court accepted that they were suffering from a post-partum psychosis at the time of the killing. Kelly also concluded that, in some cases, women received longer sentences than they would have done had they not used the evidence of psychosis.[143] Similarly there is a wide variation in the sentences that those who kill their children within the first few hours of life receive:[144]

teen neonaticide offenders in the United States are subject to varying sentences, some of which can result in many years in prison, trials in adult court instead of juvenile court, and subjection to harsh criticism by the American public and media.[145]

---

[139] A term coined in P Resnick 'Child Murder by Parents: A Psychiatric Review of Fillicide' (1969) 126 Am J Psychiatry 325 and expanded in P Resnick 'Murder of the Newborn: A Psychiatric Review of Neonaticide' (1970) 126 Am J Psychiatry 1414.

[140] M Connell 'The Postpartum Psychosis Defense and Feminism: More or Less Justice for Women?' (2002) 53 Case W Res LR 143.

[141] C Kelly 'The Legacy of Too Little, Too Late: The Inconsistent Treatment of Postpartum Psychosis as a Defense to Infanticide' (2002) 19 J Contemp Health L & P 247, 248.

[142] A Brusca 'Postpartum Psychosis: A Way Out For Murderous Moms' (1990) 18 Hofstra L R 1133, 1166.   [143] Kelly (n 141) 247.

[144] S Farley 'Neonaticide: When the Bough Breaks and the Cradle Falls' (2004) 52 Buffalo LR 597, 607.

[145] Fazio and Comito (n 129).

Several writers have advocated the adoption of an infanticide statute in the United States. This would, they argue, mark out the killings which take place within the first year of the baby's life as different. Many commentators note the remarkably similar characteristics of the character and circumstance of those who kill their child within the first 24 hours of the child's life. They are young, socially isolated and usually have no support from the father of the child. Furthermore they:

tend to be exceedingly passive, and they respond to pregnancy with a combination of denial, wishful fantasy, and terror. In short, they are paralyzed and unable to settle on a course of action for responding to their pregnancies. Instead, when interviewed later, they report that they spent their pregnancies living day to day, focusing on the banal details of their lives, and hoping that the pregnancy would simply disappear, or that someone else would notice their condition and take charge of the situation.[146]

Other commentators, who have not advocated the creation of a specific statute, have instead advocated the acceptance of 'neonaticide syndrome' by the American courts. It has been suggested that this would allow expert testimony to explain the mother's state of mind at the time of the killing and would thus allow the court to determine whether that state of mind fell into any of the recognized mental abnormality defences for killing.[147]

5. Homicide law in Canada

Under Canadian Criminal Code s 222(5) a person commits culpable homicide when he causes the death of a human being:

(a) by means of an unlawful act,
(b) by criminal negligence,
(c) by causing that human being, by threats or fear of violence or by deception, to do anything that causes his death, or
(d) by wilfully frightening that human being, in the case of a child or sick person.

The degree, whether the offence may be considered to be first or second degree murder, is determined by the mental element. First degree murder is defined under Canadian Criminal Code s 231(2) as being 'planned and deliberate'. A death may also be categorized as first degree murder when it is not planned and deliberate, but 'death is caused by that person while committing or attempting to commit an offence'.[148] In this context the most relevant offences are sexual assault;[149] sexual assault with a weapon, threats to a third party or causing bodily harm;[150] aggravated sexual assault,[151] and kidnapping and forcible confinement.[152] There has been some discussion in the

---

[146] M Oberman 'Understanding Infanticide In Context: Mothers Who Kill, 1870–1930 and Today' J Crim L & Criminology 707, 710.

[147] J Macfarlane 'Neonaticide And The "Ethos Of Maternity": Traditional Criminal Law Defenses And The Novel Syndrome' (1998) Cardozo Women's L J 175, 180–181; B Bookwalter 'Throwing The Bath Water Out With The Baby: Wrongful Exclusion Of Expert Testimony On Neonaticide Syndrome' (1998) 78 BUL Rev 1185. [148] Criminal Code 1985 (Canada) s 231(5).

[149] ibid s 271. [150] ibid s 272. [151] ibid s 273. [152] ibid s 279.

Canadian courts in cases where it appears that a child was killed following a sexual assault on that child, on the spur of the moment in order to prevent detection, rather than part of a premeditated plan. It appears that if the child is killed once the sexual assault is complete, it would usually not be considered to be first degree murder; however it is finally a question for the jury to determine whether the sexual assault on the victim and the homicide of the victim 'formed part of a single transaction'.[153]

(a) Acts and omissions

In cases of child death, one of the clearest differences between Canadian law, particularly caselaw, and English and Australian law, is in the acceptance by the Canadian judiciary that there can be little qualitative difference between an act and omission in cases concerning the death of a child when the accused is a carer of the child and that in this context the distinction made between acts of commission and omission breaks down. The Canadian courts have accepted that not acting may not be qualitatively different from acting and that omissions may not always be regarded as 'advertent and the consequences ... not in fact foreseen'[154] as they have been in English law.

The premise that omission and commission are 'two sides of the same coin' is fundamental to the concept of criminal negligence[155] in Canadian law. It has been accepted in cases where the carer has failed to act to protect her child or to care for him. In *Canhoto*[156] a mother appealed her conviction for manslaughter following the death of her two-year-old daughter, Kira. Kira died from asphyxiation, having been forced to drink a quantity of water by her grandmother as part of an exorcism. Her grandmother had been attempting to make Kira vomit in order to remove evil spirits from her. During this time Kira was held down by a family friend, while her mother watched. One of the points raised by the mother's advocates on appeal was that the mother had not 'done' anything in relation to Kira's death. However the Ontario Court of Appeal (Doherty J A) concluded that the difference between commission and omission was often more semantic than real, particularly when a carer did not act in cases of child death and injury:

I . . . regard the attempt to distinguish between acts and omissions as a fruitless exercise in many situations. Human activity involves a course of conduct. It is artificial to dissect that conduct into its component parts and label one part action and another part omission. The scope of criminal liability should not depend on semantics. The facts of this case make the point. Counsel for the appellant, in describing the appellant's conduct, submits that she did not 'engage directly in dangerous risk creating activity'. He further submits that she did not 'voluntarily or willingly choose to embark on the dangerous activity'. I can accept that characterization. However, I think the appellant's conduct could equally be characterized as activity. She heard Kira screaming and chose to remain where she was rather than going to her assistance. In my view, it could be said,

---

[153] *R v Paré* 38 CCC (3d) 97 (SCC 1987) 105 (Wilson J); *R v Pengelly* 136 OAC 183 (Ontario CA 2000).   [154] *Lowe* (n 104).
[155] Criminal Code 1985 (Canada) c 46 s 219(1): 'Every one is criminally negligent who (a) in doing anything, or (b) in omitting to do anything that it is his duty to do' [emphasis added].
[156] *R v Canhoto* 140 CCC (3d) 321 (Ontario CA 1999).

without straining the meaning of the words that the appellant, by choosing to stay where she was, chose to embark on a dangerous activity which enhanced the risk to her daughter's life or safety.[157]

The Canadian courts have also not accepted that there is necessarily a distinction between commission and omission when a child relies upon a caregiver to look after him and the caregiver fails to do so. In *R v Younger*[158] the Court of Appeal of Manitoba upheld the conviction of the appellant for the second degree murder of his son Randy, who was then two and a half. Mr Younger had taken Randy from his cot in the middle of the night, when Randy was only wearing a T-shirt, and left Randy alone in an unheated vehicle in sub-zero temperatures while he made a series of abusive telephone calls from a public phone box. Randy died of hypothermia. On appeal the appellate court clearly found that the fact that Mr Younger's behaviour could be viewed as an omission, rather than an act of commission, was unimportant in determining whether Mr Younger was guilty of the *actus reus* in relation to Randy's death:

The fact that murder usually involves the direct application of force does not mean that you cannot have murder without it[159] . . . the *actus reus* required is an act or, perhaps, an omission which causes the death of another. The means by which the death is caused are irrelevant as long as the death is caused in some way by the offender.[160]

(b) Causation

The criminal law in Canada in relation to causation remains very similar to the English law. The offender's conduct need not be the sole cause of death as long as it was a significant contributing cause; a cause that is not trivial or insignificant.[161] A case in Ontario, which was, at the time of writing, in the process being appealed to the Canadian Supreme Court, has demonstrated how this very wide definition of causation may be used in abuse cases including those relating to homicide by abuse.

R v Trotta and Trotta[162] concerned the death of an eight-month-old boy Paulo. Initially the pathologist who examined Paulo following his death had concluded that he had been the victim of Sudden Infant Death Syndrome (SIDS) and that his death could not be explained. However a year later Paulo's brother Marco Jnr, then aged one month, was brought into hospital with a spiral fracture of the femur and recent bruising on his face, buttocks and neck. The nature of the fracture and bruising in the shape of a thumb on Marco Jnr's leg suggested that he had been held by the lower leg while the leg was twisted outward. His parents were very reluctant for any X-rays to be taken of his injuries and offered different and contradictory explanations of how the injuries occurred. The authorities opened an investigation in relation to Marco Jnr's injuries and, as a result of this, exhumed Paulo's body to investigate the causes of his death. The second autopsy found a number of old serious injuries including three skull fractures and a spiral fracture of the humerus. The second pathologist concluded

---

[157] ibid [35].   [158] *R v Younger* 186 CCC (3d) 454 (Manitoba CA 2004).   [159] ibid [14].
[160] ibid [16].
[161] *R v Smithers* 1 SCR 506 (Supreme Ct Canada 1984) and *R v Nette* 3 SCR 488 (Supreme Ct Canada 2001).   [162] *R v Trotta and Trotta* 23 CR 6th 261 (Ontario CA 2004).

that the cause of Paulo's death was 'undetermined'. In re-examination he was asked whether he could exclude any causes of death. He stated:

I don't have any evidence of natural disease to explain Pa[u]lo's death. If I accept the history that you gave me, that is that he was seemingly well at even 7 in the morning and dead at 7:30 or *in extremis* such that he ultimately died a little while afterwards, if that's true—and here once again you understand how frustrating this is because I don't know. There's a whole series of things I don't know whether they're true or not true. If that's true, then I have to regard Pa[u]lo's death as being non-accidental in nature unless an alternate credible explanation is given.[163]

The father was convicted of second degree murder, aggravated assault and assault causing bodily harm and the mother of criminal negligence causing death and failure to provide necessaries of life. The parents' lawyers appealed on a number of questions of law including the question of causation. They argued that the prosecution had failed to establish the cause of Paulo's death and therefore their convictions were unsafe. The Court Of Appeal of Ontario dismissed this argument:

The Crown is not required to establish a medical cause of death in a homicide case, although it almost inevitably does so. Nor is the Crown required to demonstrate that a specific act or event caused the death, although the Crown usually attempts to do so. The Crown must prove that the death was caused by an unlawful act and that the accused is legally responsible for that act.[164]

This case represents a very robust view of the question of causation in cases where there is a great deal of evidence that the child has been assaulted, but no clear evidence of the final cause of the child's death. However it is entirely within the realms of the law relating to causation that this imputation could be made. The danger remains that an absence of an innocent explanation could lead to the imputation of a nefarious one.

(c) Intention to cause death in cases of repeated abuse

In cases where children have died at the end of one of a series of assaults upon them, Canadian courts have been prepared to accept evidence of previous abuse as evidence of an intention to kill on the part of the defendant rather than the contrary. In *R v Barrett*[165] the Court of Appeal for British Columbia confirmed the conviction of the appellant for second degree murder in killing his partner's three-year-old son Tyler. Counsel for the appellant had raised the argument that as Mr Barrett had beaten Tyler in the past and Tyler had not died, this was evidence that Mr Barrett had not intended to kill Tyler on this particular occasion. In dismissing this argument both the trial judge and the appellate court accepted the argument that a history of abuse established the exact opposite proposition:

If anything, the fact that he had inflicted serious injuries to Tyler over the past several days leading up to Tyler's death would lend support to the Crown's submission that in deliberately inflicting further injuries to Tyler on this occasion Mr. Barrett could not but know that death

---

163 ibid [11].   164 ibid [30] (Doherty JA).
165 *R v Barrett* CanLII 6093 (British Columbia CA 1998).

would result. The trial judge alludes to the significance of Tyler's fragile state at the time of the fatal beating in para 35 of his reasons in which he is again dealing with Mr. Barrett's intent.[166]

While this evidence did not establish that the appellant had the requisite intention for first degree murder, it did establish that he had the intention for second degree murder, which requires that the defendant knew his actions were likely to cause the victim's death and was reckless as to whether death ensued or not. What is interesting about this judgment is that evidence that the defendant knew that he had abused a child in the past became part of the evidence that the defendant knew that the child had been made progressively frailer as a result of the abuse, and that the defendant therefore knew that it was more likely, rather than less likely, that the child would not survive the abuse on this occasion. This ratio subverts the presumption that has grown up in some States in the US that evidence of previous abuse undermines an argument that the defendant intended the death of a child, because the child had survived so many previous assaults.

6. Homicide law in Australia

Generally the laws relating to homicide across Australia are similar to the law in England and Wales. Homicide crimes are divided into murder and manslaughter; with manslaughter being further subdivided into voluntary manslaughter (where a defence of provocation or abnormality of the mind is accepted) and involuntary manslaughter (constructive manslaughter and negligent manslaughter).[167] The *mens rea* for murder is that, on a charge of murder, the Crown must prove that the fatal blow was inflicted with the intention of causing death or grievous bodily harm, or with the knowledge that it was probable that death or grievous bodily harm would result. In *The Queen v Crabbe*[168] the High Court found:

It should now be regarded as settled law in Australia, if no statutory provision affects the position, that a person who, without lawful justification or excuse, does an act knowing that it is probable that death or grievous bodily harm will result, is guilty of murder if death in fact results. It is not enough that he does the act knowing that it is possible but not likely that death or grievous bodily harm might result.[169]

There has recently been much debate within the courts about the nature of the requirement of *mens rea* in cases of negligent manslaughter. The Court of Criminal Appeal of New South Wales held in *Lavender* that the offence required proof of malicious intent.[170] This finding was reversed on appeal by the High Court of Australia.[171] Although the case of *Lavender* did not concern a case of child abuse[172] the principle

---

[166] ibid [42] (Madam Justice Prowse).
[167] *Wilson v The Queen* 174 CLR 313 (Australia HC 1992) 333.
[168] *The Queen v Crabbe* 156 CLR 464 (Australia HC 1984).   [169] ibid 469–470.
[170] *The Queen v Lavender* 41 MVR 492 (New South Wales CA 2004).
[171] *The Queen v Lavender* [2005] HCA 37 (Australia HC 2005).
[172] Although it did concern a case of child death.

which it reiterates is important in child abuse prosecutions. It is more difficult to prove in cases concerning child abuse that the defendant's actions were spurred on by malice, rather than simply not caring enough. A requirement of malice would have made many cases relating to death caused by familial child abuse very difficult to prosecute. The requirement in relation to manslaughter by criminal negligence in Australia remains:

In order to establish manslaughter by criminal negligence, it is sufficient if the prosecution shows that the act which caused the death was done by the accused consciously and voluntarily, without any intention of causing death or grievous bodily harm but in circumstances which involved such a great falling short of the standard of care which a reasonable man would have exercised and which involved such a high risk that death or grievous bodily harm would follow that the doing of the act merited criminal punishment.[173]

However the law across Australia remains problematic in relation to the prosecution of child deaths—most particularly because of the very limited view that there appears to be of the duties which parents and caretakers owe to their children, which could be the basis of a charge in criminal negligence. Under Australian Federal law an omission may only form the *actus reus* of an offence if State/Territorial law specifically proscribes it; there is no general expectation that omissions and commissions are 'two sides of the same coin'.[174] Thus each State determines the extent of liability for failing to act. In *R v Davies and Partridge*[175] which was decided in New South Wales, the trial judge put forward the view that parents did not owe their child a duty of care in relation to an omission, but only in relation to that behaviour which might be characterized as an act of commission. In this case an 18-month-old child had died after he had ingested a quantity of methadone. His parents were both heroin addicts, as were the couple with whom the parents shared a flat. The child had drunk the methadone, but it was unclear whether he had drunk it from a cup in which the parents had diluted the methadone with water, or in a bottle of milk which had been given to him. The judge found that the parents did not owe a duty to supervise their child and protect him from acts of third parties, in this case the people with whom they shared the flat, and that they would not owe a duty to protect him from any methadone solution which the other parties had left lying around: 'The failure, if there was one, was an omission, not an act . . . it would appear that there would be no duty owed by the parents to safeguard their child against the actions of others who may be negligent.'[176] He argued that the parents would owe their child a duty of care if the evidence pointed to the fact that the child had ingested methadone which they had prepared. This reasoning is based on the rule in Australian tort law that no general duty to exercise care in supervision for the protection of a child from harm exists in a parent.[177] 'Such a duty arises where a person, be he parent or stranger, has acted in relation to the child in such a way as to create

[173] *Nydam v R* [1977] VR 430 (Victoria Supreme Ct) 446.
[174] Criminal Code Act 1995 (Australia) s 4.3.
[175] *R v Davies and Partridge* [2005] NSWSC 324 (New South Wales Supreme Ct).
[176] ibid [123].
[177] *Posthuma v Campbell* (1984) 37 SASR 321 (S Australia Supreme Ct); *Robertson v Swincer* (1989) 52 SASR 356 (S Australia Supreme Ct); *Towart v Adler* (1986) 52 SASR 373 (S Australia Supreme Ct).

a foreseeable risk of injury to the child which apart from that action would not have existed'.[178]

This interpretation of the law as it relates to parental duties stands in stark contrast to the Canadian acceptance that it is very difficult to use the concept that commissions and omissions are qualitively different to determine culpability in cases concerning child abuse where the perpetrator has a duty to protect the child.

7. Homicide law in New Zealand

Homicide law in New Zealand as it relates to children may be found under the category of culpable homicide which encompasses murder, manslaughter, killing under provocation and infanticide. The *mens rea* of murder is set down in the Crimes Act 1961 s 167. The most interesting feature of s 167 in the context of the prosecution of child abuse is s 167(b) which states that:

Culpable homicide is murder
(b) If the offender means to cause to the person killed any bodily injury that is known to the offender to be likely to cause death, and is reckless whether death ensues or not.

Section 167(b) has been used in a number of cases concerning child death from abuse in New Zealand and indeed the leading case on the interpretation of s 167(b) concerned the death of a child as a result of abuse. In *R v Piri*[179] Cooke P stated that:

if the risk of the death of the victim was truly no more than negligible or remote in the offender's eyes, the stigma of murder should be withheld. To be distinguished from that, however, are cases where the risk is so appreciable that to indulge in the conduct is seen by society as the virtual equivalent of intentional killing. Every Judge who tries to formulate a test for the distinction in precise and simple terms, suitable for directing a jury, soon realises that no single formula is preferable or adequate. Expressions commonly used to indicate the degree of foresight of death required to be proved against the accused are *a real risk, a substantial risk, something that might well happen* (emphasis added).[180]

This interpretation was confirmed by the New Zealand Court of Appeal in *R v Meynell*[181] which again concerned the death of a child following a series of assaults. Thus instances of child death following assault which could not be categorized as murder under English law, because of the *Woollin*[182] requirement that the defendant knew that death or serious injury was a virtual certainty as a result of his act, may be classified as murder under New Zealand law. In cases relating to child death as a result of abuse this distinction between the two interpretations can be crucial.

Under New Zealand law, liability for manslaughter stems either from killing by an unlawful act or from an omission without lawful excuse to perform a legal duty.[183] One legal duty which is set out in statute is the duty on a parent, or a person in place of a parent, to provide necessaries of life to their children. The Crimes Act 1961 s 152

---

[178] *Robertson v Swincer* (1989) (n 177) 359 (King CJ); *Lorincz v Lonardo & Fischetto* [2000] SADC 97 (South Australia DC) (Judge Allan).   [179] *R v Piri* [1987] 1 NZLR 66 (NZ CA).
[180] ibid 79 (Cooke P).   [181] *R v Meynell* [2004] 1 NZLR 507 (NZ CA).
[182] *R v Woollin* (n 68).   [183] Midson (n 74) 133.

creates this legal duty and a criminal liability for those who omit 'without lawful excuse to do so, whether the child is helpless or not, if the death of the child is caused, or if his life is endangered or his health permanently injured, by such omission'. The *mens rea* for this type of manslaughter is criminal negligence, namely that 'the omission or neglect is a major departure from the standard of care expected of a reasonable person to whom that legal duty applies in those circumstances'.[184] In both of these types of manslaughter there is a good 'fit' between the nature of the crime in cases where a child dies as a result of child abuse and the offence. Midson has argued that this 'fit' is so good as to make prosecution of these cases for murder in New Zealand unlikely.[185] However as the *mens rea* of murder allows for an appreciation of significant risk, rather than virtual certainty of death, it may be that New Zealand law allows for the prosecution of more cases of child death as murder than English law currently does.

8. Establishing liability when the identity of the person who killed the child is not clear

The home is a secret place and few of the events that take place in it are witnessed by people other than the protagonists. The main witness, the child, may be dead, badly injured or too young to give clear evidence. In cases of physical abuse filing a charge against a specific perpetrator is particularly problematic when there was shared care at the time of the alleged assault.

Scenario 1: Child A is injured or killed when all those caring for her were present, all those present deny that anything untoward occurred and hold steadfast to their story that the injuries must have been accidental[186] or:

Scenario 2: Child B is injured or killed within a defined period of time in which she was cared for by one or other of a group of people. Each of the carers was alone with the child during this period.[187]

As explained at the beginning of this chapter, the purpose of criminal law is to blame those who have committed a defined wrong. However, in cases of shared care it may be impossible to identify which of the carers injured the child and thus who should be blamed. In cases such as this judicial attitudes have historically been quite clear. As Lord Goddard stated in 1955 in *Abbott*:

Very likely one or the other must have committed [the criminal act], but there was no evidence which one. Although it is unfortunate that a guilty party cannot be brought to justice, it is far more important that there should not be a miscarriage of justice and the law should be maintained rather than there should be failure in some particular case ... 'if two people are jointly indicted for the commission of a crime and the evidence does not point to one rather than the other, and there is no evidence that they were acting in concert, the jury ought to return a verdict of "Not Guilty" in the case of both because the prosecution have not proved the case'.[188]

---

[184] Crimes Act 1961 (New Zealand) s 150A.   [185] Midson (n 74) 133.
[186] *Marsh and Marsh v Hodgson* [1974] Crim LR 35 (DC).
[187] *R v Lane and Another* (n 187).
[188] *R v Abbott* (1955) 39 Cr App R 141 (CA), 148.

In the past the evidence against each defendant was considered separately and if each defendant's presence at the time of the assault was not established then the prosecution failed.[189] Thus if both carers denied liability and did not give incriminating evidence against the other then a prosecution was very difficult to sustain.

In response to campaigns by charities, and concerns expressed by judges, lawyers, and academics that in some cases carers were 'literally getting away with murder', the Law Commission reviewed the law[190] and put forward two proposals for reform of the offences relating to child death and serious injury: the first was an aggravated form of the Children and Young Person's Act (CYPA) 1933 s 1 and the second, a new offence of failure to protect a child. Their proposals were not without faults and the strengths and weaknesses are discussed below. However, subsequent legislative reform in the Domestic Violence, Crimes and Victims Act 2004 ss 5 and 7 only partially followed the Law Commission and, while some of the drafting changes may be regarded as improvements, they also made some errors, which the Law Commission had been careful to avoid. The next section contains an examination of both the law and the Law Commission proposals and compares them with the law in other jurisdictions.

(a) The Law Commission proposals

As part of its review of the law relating to child death and serious injury the Law Commission proposed two new offences. The first offence would have built on the existing law in relation to ill-treatment, cruelty and neglect. The CYPA s 1 created an offence which is still charged today and is discussed specifically in section D.1 (Ill treatment and Neglect) of this chapter. The CYPA s 1 states that:

(1) If any person who has attained the age of 16 years and has the responsibility for any child or young person under that age, wilfully assaults, ill-treats, neglects, abandons, or exposes him, or causes or procures him to be assaulted, ill-treated, neglected, abandoned, or exposed, in a manner likely to cause him unnecessary suffering or injury to health (including injury to or loss of sight, or hearing, or limb, or organ of the body, and any mental derangement), that person shall be guilty of a misdemeanour.

(i) Cruelty contributing to death

In a draft bill, published with their final report, the Law Commission formulated the proposed offence as:

1 Cruelty contributing to death
In the Children and Young Persons Act 1933 (c.12), after section 1 (cruelty to persons under sixteen), insert—
'1A Cruelty contributing to death
(1) A person is guilty of an offence if—
    (a) he commits an offence under section 1 against a child or young person ("C");
    (b) suffering or injury to health of a kind which was likely to be caused to C by the commission of that offence occurs; and
    (c) its occurrence results in, or contributes significantly to, C's death.

---

[189] *R v Lane and Another* (n 187).
[190] Law Commission *Children: Their Non-Accidental Death or Serious Injury (Criminal Trials)* (n 4).

(2) A person guilty of an offence under this section is liable on conviction on indictment to imprisonment for a term not exceeding 14 years or to a fine, or to both.'[191]

In building upon the offence of cruelty the Law Commission hoped to avoid the problem of the identification principle and the need to prove which person had caused the death of the child, by inflicting the fatal blow.[192] A person may be charged with an offence under CYPA 1933 s 1 when it is a third party who injures the child, but the defendant has placed the child in that situation, knowing that there was a risk that the child would be injured. For example in the case of *Creed*[193] the mother was found guilty under CYPA 1933 s 1; when it was found that her child had been killed by the mother's lover and that the mother had left her child in his care, knowing that the lover was violent and had injured the child on a number of previous occasions. It is important to note however that the offence must be wilful and that a person that left a child in danger which was obvious to others, but not to herself, would not be guilty of an offence under CYPA 1933 s 1.

(ii) Failure to protect

The Law Commission also recommended the creation of a second offence of failure to protect a child:

2 Failure to protect a child
(1) A person ('R') is guilty of an offence if—
   (a) at a time when subsection (3) applies, R is aware or ought to be aware that there is a real risk that an offence specified in Schedule 1 might be committed against a child ('C');
   (b) R fails to take such steps as it would be reasonable to expect R to take to prevent the commission of the offence;
   (c) an offence specified in Schedule 1[194] is committed against C; and
   (d) the offence is committed in circumstances of the kind that R anticipated or ought to have anticipated.

The phrase 'real risk' was borrowed from *Re H and Others (Minors) (Threshold Criteria: Standard of Proof)*,[195] the civil child protection case on the standard of proof for the

---

[191] ibid 45–6 [6.5].   [192] ibid 46 [6.7].
[193] *R v Creed* [2000] 1 Cr App R(S) 304 (CA Crim).
[194] 'The following are the specified offences for the purposes of section 2—
   (a) murder,
   (b) manslaughter,
   (c) an offence under section 18 or 20 of the Offences against the Person Act 1861 (c.100) (wounding and causing grievous bodily harm),
   (d) an offence under section 23 or 24 of that Act (administering poison),
   (e) an offence under section 47 of that Act (assault occasioning actual bodily harm),
   (f) an offence under section 1 of the Sexual Offences Act 1956 (c.69) (rape),
   (g) an offence under section 14 or 15 of that Act (indecent assault),
   (h) attempting to commit any such offence.'
Law Commission *Children: Their Non-Accidental Death or Serious Injury (Criminal Trials)* (n 4) 48–49 [6.11].
[195] *Re H and Others (Minors) (Threshold Criteria: Standard of Proof)* [1996] 1 All ER 1 (HL).

threshold for granting a care or supervision order, which is discussed in detail in Chapter 2. As described there it means 'a real possibility of harm' which cannot 'sensibly be ignored having regard to the nature and gravity of the feared harm in this particular case'.[196]

The Law Commission, cautious of creating a general mandatory duty to report suspicions of child abuse, which does not currently exist in English law,[197] proposed a limitation to this duty to those who are at least 16 years old; and had both a responsibility for the child and a connection with the child. The need for a connection between the child and the person who may be charged placed a further limit on the range of those who would be expected to protect the child to those who live in the same household as the child or are related to the child[198] or look after the child in a 'child care arrangement'. 'Child care arrangements' would be similarly limited to situations in which the potential reporter:

(a) looks after C (whether alone or with other children) under arrangements made with a person who lives in the same household as, or is related to, C; and
(b) does so wholly or mainly in C's home.[199]

The rationale of the Law Commission was that its primary aim was to address the specific problem of accountability of those who are complicit in violence within the domestic context and that it should confine its proposals to those people. In setting the boundaries of the offence the Law Commission was specifically aiming to avoid a proposal which would effectively create a mandatory duty to report suspicions or would be a mechanism for making those working in public authorities criminally liable for failure to protect children.[200] It is this principled limitation which Glazebrook has criticized, arguing that the limitations on liability which the Law Commission places on failure to protect are based on a 19th century concept that criminal liability for not acting should only be incurred in limited situations when a person has undertaken to act, or may be considered to have undertaken to act:

as the Commission repeatedly reminds us, 'society', or 'the state', has 'a special responsibility for the protection of children', which should be reflected in our criminal law, is not requiring every adult who is aware of a danger to the life, limb, or health of any child, to do what he reasonably can to protect that child from that harm the least that that law could and should do?[201]

---

[196] ibid 15J–16A (Lord Nicholls).   [197] See Chapter 5 section D.
[198] As defined by Family Law Act 1996 (England) s 63 (1) 'relative', in relation to a person, means—

    (a) the father, mother, stepfather, stepmother, son, daughter, stepson, stepdaughter, grandmother, grandfather, grandson or granddaughter of that person or of that person's spouse or former spouse, or
    (b) the brother, sister, uncle, aunt, niece or nephew (whether of the full blood or of the half blood or by affinity) of that person or of that person's spouse or former spouse, and includes, in relation to a person who is living or has lived with another person as husband and wife, any person who would fall within paragraph (a) or (b) if the parties were married to each other.

[199] It would not matter whether R looked after C for reward or on a regular or occasional basis.
[200] Law Commission *Children: Their Non-Accidental Death or Serious Injury (Criminal Trials)* (n 4) 50 [6.14].   [201] Glazebrook (n 53), 542.

Glazebrook suggests in effect a mandatory reporting law, arguing that while not everyone is in a position to save a child from harm directly, most are in the position to be able to report harm to agencies who have statutory powers to protect the child. Cobley has argued that while Glazebrook may indeed be right and that 'more radical reform may indeed follow', the offence is a significant step in the right direction.[202]

What the Law Commission did not adequately explain is why they chose to create a new offence in relation to failure to report, rather than to develop the law of cruelty and neglect, or to build on an already growing law on omissions liability.[203] It may be that the Law Commission was overly influenced by Williams' analysis of the current law. Williams has argued that English law limits a parent or person acting in the place of parent to 'protection from starvation, disease and ill-health generally' but not to the protection of his child from attack.[204] However Simester and Sullivan have disagreed with this analysis, arguing that the common law duties of a parent are much more wide-ranging and include a duty to effect an easy rescue.[205]

The reasoning of the Law Commission in proposing a new offence, rather than building on the offence already in existence under CYPA 1933 s 1, or on common law omissions liability, may have been that they wished to expand the range of those who might be expected to protect a child, beyond those on whom the law had imposed a duty to act. Under CYPA 1933 s 1 only those who have 'responsibility' for the child are liable. This is defined further in CYPA 1933 s 17 to mean a person who has parental responsibility for him, who has a liability to maintain the child or who has care of him. As defined above, the Law Commission proposed that those with a connection to the child, that is 'those who live in the same household as the child or are related to the child'[206] or look after the child in a 'child care arrangement' could be liable under the offence. The differences between the two are that the Law Commission included some people who might not be looking after the child at all, namely relatives and some of those living in the house with the child. It is not clear that these differences are so insurmountable as to justify the creation of another offence. It may be that some failures to act might not be seen as being cruel in themselves, but all failures to act are neglect.

---

[202] C Cobley 'Criminal Prosecutions When Children Die or Are Seriously Injured' (2003) Fam Law 899, 902.   [203] *Gibbons and Proctor* (n 41).

[204] G Williams 'Which of You Did It?' (1989) 52 MLR 170.

[205] Simester and Sullivan *Criminal Law* (n 50) 63–64, J Smith and B Hogan, would appear to concur with this view of the extent of parental duties, *Smith & Hogan Criminal Law* (10th edn Butterworths, London 2002) 151.

[206] As defined by Family Law Act 1996 (England) s 63 (1) 'relative', in relation to a person, means—

    (a) the father, mother, stepfather, stepmother, son, daughter, stepson, stepdaughter, grandmother, grandfather, grandson or granddaughter of that person or of that person's spouse or former spouse, or

    (b) the brother, sister, uncle, aunt, niece or nephew (whether of the full blood or of the half blood or by affinity) of that person or of that person's spouse or former spouse, and includes, in relation to a person who is living or has lived with another person as husband and wife, any person who would fall within paragraph (a) or (b) if the parties were married to each other.

(b) The Domestic Violence, Crimes and Victims Act 2004

The offence which has now been enacted in response to the campaigns and the Law Commission document is laid out in the Domestic Violence, Crimes and Victims Act 2004 s 5 (DVCV).

(1) A person ('D') is guilty of an offence if—
   (a) a child or vulnerable adult ('V') dies as a result of the unlawful act of a person

Rather than building on the CYPA 1933 s 1, as recommended by the Law Commission, the new offence owes much more to the homicide by abuse laws in the United States, which are themselves built on law relating to constructive manslaughter. 'Unlawful act' is defined under DVCV 2004 s 5(6) to include 'a course of conduct' and also to include omissions. In defining an act to include a 'course of conduct' the prosecution need not prove that a particular blow caused the death of a child, but need only prove that the child died as a result of ill-treatment or neglect. The recognition that in these circumstances an act does include an omission undermines the *ratio* in *Lowe*[207] that there should be a clear distinction between acts of omission and commission in constructive manslaughter and in cases of child death in particular. This must be welcomed. As criminal law in the United States and Canada has already recognized, there can be no qualitative difference between an act and a failure to act in cases in which a person is in a position of responsibility and the child relies upon them. The danger is that the creation of a new offence undermines the position and use of the offence under CYPA 1933 s 1. This offence should be at the heart of any criminal law which relates to child abuse and can encompass all the instances in which a child may be ill-treated or neglected, including instances of omission.

who—
   (i) was a member of the same household as V, and
   (ii) had frequent contact with him,
(b) D was such a person at the time of that act,

The range of people who might be charged with an offence was also altered from the Law Commission proposals. Rather than the Law Commission proposal that members of the child's household or a child's relative or someone who looked after the child in a childcare arrangement could be charged with the offence if they had responsibility for the child, the new law requires that the person was 'a member of the same household as V', and additionally 'had frequent contact with him'. This would exclude babysitters or other childminders, a parent or relative who did not live with the child and a lover or partner of the child's parent who also did not live in the household. In relation to the latter category s 5(4) states that 'a person is to be regarded as a "member" of a particular household, even if he does not live in that household, if he visits it so often and for such periods of time that it is reasonable to regard him as a member of it'. This wording is, as Hayes has argued, flexible enough to include a number of frequent visitors to the child's home. However, as Hayes also argues, 'it appears likely to be fortuitous whether

---

[207] *Lowe* (n 104).

relatives, ex-partners, boyfriends, girlfriends, baby-sitters, other friends, tenants and anyone else who visits the child's household will fall inside or outside the scope of section 5', because the definition does not appear to be based on a particular line of reasoning and the objective test within the definition will not save it from widely different interpretations.[208]

The Act creates an *actus reus* which is a combination of the two offences proposed by the Law Commission with some alterations. Thus once the relationship has been established it must be proved that:

> (c) at that time there was a significant risk of serious physical harm being caused to V by the unlawful act of such a person, and
> (d) either D was the person whose act caused V's death or—
>> (i) D was, or ought to have been, aware of the risk mentioned in paragraph (c),
>> (ii) D failed to take such steps as he could reasonably have been expected to take to protect V from the risk, and
>> (iii) the act occurred in circumstances of the kind that D foresaw or ought to have foreseen.
>
> (2) The prosecution does not have to prove whether it is the first alternative in subsection (1)(d) or the second (sub-paragraphs (i) to (iii)) that applies.

As the section indicates there is no separate 'failure to protect' offence as suggested by the Law Commission, as we have argued above there was no need for a separate offence as this can and should be prosecuted under CYPA 1933 s 1. Rather, under the new offence the prosecution must prove that D was the person whose act caused the death of the child or that he was the bystander who knew or ought to have known of the risk and failed to take such steps as he could reasonably have been expected to take to protect V from the risk. The construction of the offence is an attempt to avoid the perennial problem in these cases where all those who were part of a child's household remain silent about the circumstances in which a child met his or her death and it becomes impossible to determine whose act caused the child's death and who failed to protect the child. It certainly can sidestep many of the problems which have been associated with attempted prosecutions following child deaths. However the importation of an objective standard into the *mens rea* of the offence, while increasing the likelihood of convictions, remains problematic. Objective standards in relation to *mens rea* have been generally rejected in relation to other types of criminal offence. In *R v G*[209] the House of Lords re-established that the *mens rea* for criminal damage is either intention or subjective recklessness, rather than intention or objective recklessness as had been found in the case of *Caldwell* 20 years earlier. This subjective test was re-established for a number of reasons, the first one being fairness to the defendant:

it is a salutary principle that conviction of serious crime should depend on proof not simply that the defendant caused (by act or omission) an injurious result to another but that his state of mind when so acting was culpable. This, after all, is the meaning of the familiar rule *actus non*

---

[208] M Hayes 'Criminal Trials where the Child is the Victim: Extra Protection for Children or a Missed Opportunity?' (2005) 17 (3) Child and Family LQ 307, 317. [209] *R v G* [2004] 1 AC 1034 (HL).

facit reum nisi mens sit rea. The most obviously culpable state of mind is no doubt an intention to cause the injurious result, but knowing disregard of an appreciated and unacceptable risk of causing an injurious result or a deliberate closing of the mind to such risk would be readily accepted as culpable also. It is clearly blameworthy to take an obvious and significant risk of causing injury to another. But it is not clearly blameworthy to do something involving a risk of injury to another if (for reasons other than self-induced intoxication: *R v Majewski* [1977] AC 443) one genuinely does not perceive the risk. Such a person may fairly be accused of stupidity or lack of imagination, but neither of those failings should expose him to conviction of serious crime or the risk of punishment.[210]

There may be a similar argument that there are classes of people in child death cases that are also unable to perceive a risk to a child, even when they ought to have done. In the United States in particular, which is discussed below, academics have argued that women who have suffered repeated violence themselves may have been rendered unable to perceive the risk of violence to their children. It may also be argued that some people have very low parenting ability and again may be unable to perceive the substantial nature of the risk which the child was facing. Finally, some deeply held religious beliefs may prevent individuals from perceiving risks to a child which they would in other circumstances have done, for example in allowing an exorcism to take place to rid a child of evil spirits, as took place in the Canadian case of *Canhoto*,[211] which is discussed above. Some safeguards for weaker household members, particularly those who have been subjected to violence may lie in the requirement in s 5(1)d(ii) that the jury should be satisfied that the defendant 'failed to take such steps as he or she could *reasonably* have been expected to take to protect the child from the risk' [emphasis added]. Evidence of violence towards D, it could be argued, can affect the reasonableness of the steps which D could take in the circumstances. In justice this should be determined on a case-by-case basis as s 5(1)d suggests. In the New Zealand case of *Witika*[212] the NZ Court of Appeal held that while it may very well have been that the mother had suffered domestic violence at the hands of her partner, which might have made her afraid of him and thus unable to take her child to receive medical care for the injuries that the child had received, the evidence pointed to the fact that the mother had ample opportunity to ask for help as her partner was away from the house for long periods. The new section could operate in the same way and consider the steps that each defendant could have taken in the light of their own circumstances.

The justification for an objective standard in circumstances of child death is one that has been rehearsed in relation to the law on involuntary manslaughter in cases of child death. In the majority of cases when children die in their household as a result of child abuse it is not a dreadful accident, but the result of torture and ill-treatment either by physical assault or neglect. Those who have frequent contact with the child have several opportunities to save the child from his or her fate as a result, either by desisting from the abuse, or by ceasing to condone or ignore it. The fact that they did not do so, is in many cases because they did not care enough or they prioritized

---

[210] ibid [32] (Lord Bingham). [211] *Canhoto* (n 156).
[212] *R v Witika* [1993] 2 NZLR 424 (NZ CA).

their own concerns over child safety. The objective test in the crime of allowing or causing the death of a child encompasses those on whom the child relied and who should have considered the danger that the child was under, stresses that there is a standard that we should live up to in relation to childcare and that many child deaths are avoidable; on the facts of many of these cases, this is a conclusion on which it is difficult to disagree.

(c) Establishing liability in the United States

The efficacy of the creation of an offence of failure to protect a child from assault or death has been the subject of a great deal of debate in the United States where 24 States have enacted legislation specifically punishing such a failure. Generally under US law a person has no legal duty to aid another person in peril, even when that aid can be rendered without danger or inconvenience to himself. Four States in America have enacted statutes requiring that any person, including strangers, 'give reasonable assistance' to a person 'exposed to grave physical harm' if they can do so without 'danger or peril' to themselves or others.[213] The statutes limit liability to a conviction for a 'petty misdemeanour', which in this case would carry a potential sentence of up to six months imprisonment or a fine. The statutes do not create a general duty upon everyone to protect any person whom they perceive to be in danger. They have not proved to be very popular, as Levitt has noted: '[t]hirty years, four states—it hasn't been a groundswell of legislative activity'.[214]

However across the US legislation and common law have imposed a duty to act on those who have certain personal relationships. Failure to protect statutes and an interpretation at common law of the duties of care-takers have created an expectation of 'parental responsibility' for the child. In this context parental responsibility does not mean the same as in English family law where it encompasses all the 'rights, duties, powers, responsibilities and authority which, by law, a parent of a child has in relation to the child and his property'.[215] Instead it is based on omissions liability for failure to fulfil a duty:

[a] parent has a duty to protect their children and cannot stand passively by and refuse to do so when it is reasonably within their power to protect their children ... This is not to say that parents have the legal duty to place themselves in danger of death or great bodily harm in coming to the aid of their children. To require such, would require every parent to exhibit courage and heroism which, although commendable in the extreme, cannot realistically be expected or required of all people. But parents do have the duty to take every step reasonably possible under the circumstances of a given situation to prevent harm to their children.[216]

---

[213] Vermont Statute Annotated (1973) 519(a), *R v M(H)* (1999) 177 Sask R 189 (Saskatchewan CA) 604A.01(1); Rhode Island General Laws (1999) 11–56–1; Wisconsin Statute Annotated (West 1999) 940.34(2).

[214] N Levitt 'The Kindness of Strangers: Interdisciplinary Foundations of a Duty to Act' (2001) 40 Washburn L J 463, 466.   [215] Children Act 1989 (England) s 3(1).

[216] *State v Walden* (1982) 293 SE 2d 780 (North Carolina SC) 784 (Clarke J).

In some instances a parental omission to act has been used as the basis on which to charge the parent or caregiver with an offence, which may usually only be charged if there is evidence that the defendant had a specific intention to harm. Courts have been prepared to infer an intention to join in a 'common design' (what would be known under English law as a joint enterprise) of abusing the child:

It need not be shown that the defendant had a specific intent to kill or participated in a preconceived plan to commit murder. Where there is a common design to participate in an illegal act, such as aggravated battery to a child, and death occurs during the prosecution of the common objective, all participants are guilty of murder. Such a common design can be inferred from the circumstances surrounding the perpetration of the unlawful conduct such as: presence at the scene of the crime without disapproval or opposition; a continued close association with the perpetrator after the criminal act; a failure to report the incident to the authorities; and/or the subsequent concealing or destroying of evidence of the crime. . . . The defendant's acts need only have contributed to the death, and the defendant may be accountable even though he had no intent to and did not personally kill the victim.[217]

Much academic argument in the United States about the appropriateness of failure to protect statutes has surrounded the intersection between child abuse and domestic violence. In many cases the abuse of the child is part of a wider picture of violence and bullying within the home in which the passive, or non-protecting parent, is also a victim. The argument at an academic level has been that to punish the victims of domestic violence for failing to protect their children, as well as themselves, only has the effect of re-victimizing an already vulnerable person.[218] Those who have argued against the duty to protect statutes have contended that a failure to protect is not in fact a conscious, desired act by someone who can in reality protect their child:

The assumption underlying these cases—that a mother can always protect her children from a violent partner—is misplaced. A growing body of literature demonstrates the fallacy of this assumption. Experts have pointed to a mother's lack of financial resources, a well grounded fear of increased violence to herself and her children, potential criminal liability for leaving with the children, losing custody for leaving without the children, and being killed or seeing her children killed, as reasons why many mothers do not leave abusive relationships.[219]

Jacobs has asked whether we should really punish carers for not doing something which they are incapable of performing, pointing to a pattern of learned helplessness that women who are repeatedly beaten and bullied find themselves in.[220] Other critics

---

[217] *People v Novy* 597 N E 2d 273 (Illinois CA 5th d 1992) 295–96; also *Boone v State* 668 SW 2d 17 (Arkansas SC 1984); *R v Bell (No 1)* (1997) 115 CCC (3d) 107 (North West Territories CA); *LaBastida v State* 931 P 2d 1334 (Nevada SC 1996).

[218] M Trepiccione 'At The Crossroads Of Law And Social Science: Is Charging A Battered Mother With Failure To Protect Her Child An Acceptable Solution When Her Child Witnesses Domestic Violence?' (2001) 69 Fordham L Rev 1487, 1511.

[219] C Murphy 'Legal Images Of Motherhood: Conflicting Definitions From Welfare "Reform", Family, And Criminal Law' (1998) 83 Cornell LR 688, 721.

[220] M Jacobs 'Criminal Law: Requiring Battered Women Die: Murder Liability For Mothers Under Failure To Protect Statute' (1998) 88 J Crim L & Criminology 579, 638.

have argued that such provisions are gender-biased unfairly penalizing mothers, whom society automatically assumes have the primary caretaking responsibility.[221] However there remains a danger in generalizing in these situations; as discussed below in relation to the law in New Zealand, the situation varies between cases. The mother may have no or little financial relationship with the abusive partner. The relationship may be comparatively new and the mother may have been a single parent for some time before that. The law in relation to failure to protect does have the potential to take into account the circumstances in which any parent found themselves, because of its focus on what behaviour would be considered to be reasonable in the circumstances. While violence towards the mother is undoubtedly important in determining whether it was reasonable, it cannot be the basis for a blanket expectation in law that parents have no capacity to help their children in violent households.

(d) Establishing liability in Canada

Canadian law has in certain circumstances, inferred a common intention to kill between two people caring for a child when that child is killed and neither will identify the other as the killer. The basic rule in Canadian law is set out in *R v Schell & Paquette*[222]: the jury must be directed that in circumstances of multiple blows administered in a *single* beating, if they cannot decide which accused killed the child then both must be acquitted.

However, *R v Schell & Paquette (No. 1)* pointed out a basis upon which the impasse could be resolved, using the primary and secondary party routes presented under the Canadian Criminal Code s 21 and relying upon evidence of previous acts of abuse.[223] Under the Canadian Criminal Code s 21(2):

Where two or more persons form an intention in common to carry out an unlawful purpose and to assist each other therein and any one of them, in carrying out the common purpose, commits an offence, each of them who knew or ought to have known that the commission of the offence would be a probable consequence of carrying out the common purpose is a party to that offence.

In *R v Schell & Paquette (No. 1)* the Ontario Court of Appeal considered whether s 21(2) could apply in a case such as this where it was unclear which of two people had killed a child:

The accused Paquette was the mother of Diane and was under a legal duty to care for her. The evidence is not clear as to what duties Schell assumed toward the children; it is, therefore, not clear whether or not Schell had any responsibility toward Diane pursuant to s. 197 [am. 1974–75–76, c. 66, s. 8] of the Criminal Code. However, in the circumstances of this case Schell had at least a moral obligation to care for Diane. Against this background the evidence

---

[221] K Garcia 'Battered Women And Battered Children: Admissibility Of Evidence Of Battering And Its Effects To Determine The Mens Rea Of A Battered Woman Facing Criminal Charges For Failing To Protect A Child From Abuse' (2003) 24 J Juv L 101.

[222] *R v Schell & Paquette (No 1)* (1977) 33 CCC (2d) 422 (Ontario CA) and in *R v Schell & Paquette (No 2)* (1979) 47 CCC (2d) 193 (Ontario CA).

[223] Strictly speaking this is not tendered as similar fact evidence, but rather background evidence to explain an animus towards the victim through a course of conduct.

of separate and joint acts of abuse of Diane must be examined and construed. In my opinion *it would be open to a jury to find that both accused had formed a common intention to carry out an unlawful purpose (i.e., child abuse) and assist each other therein, and each knew, or ought to have known, that the unlawful infliction of bodily harm by the other was a probable consequence of carrying out that common purpose.*[224] [emphasis added]

Subsequent cases have stressed that mere passivity is unlikely to be sufficient to set up the 'common intention' requirement of s 21(2). In *R v Popen*[225] the court acknowledged that 'mere inactivity' could have the result of encouraging the legal act so as to set up secondary liability, but in such a case the second defendant would have to have a right and a duty to control the actions of the first defendant, and so be present at the commission of the illegal acts by the first defendant. Significantly, however, the court in *Popen* identified an alternative route, leading to primary rather than secondary liability: where the second defendant is criminally negligent in failing to protect her child from the first defendant's mistreatment when under a duty to do so, and such failure contributed to the child's death, then the second defendant is independently guilty of manslaughter, under s 197.[226] In *R v Roud*[227] the second defendant was present when the first defendant shot their son, and there was no dispute that he had done so. At issue was whether she was a secondary party to the shooting under s 21(1).[228] The second defendant claimed that she had been intimidated and beaten by the first defendant into tolerating and occasionally assisting in acts of cruelty against their children. The Ontario Court of Appeal held that the evidence of repeated violence committed by either or both parents against the three children, either alone *or* in the presence of one another, when viewed in the context of the parents' respective obligations to care for the children, was admissible to prove an intention in common to carry out the alleged unlawful purpose, ie the continued violent physical assaults on the children.[229]

The development of liability for both carers under the Canadian Criminal Code s 21 has been greatly helped by the decision of the Supreme Court of Canada in *R v Thatcher*[230] where the Crown presented to the jury alternative theories that the accused either murdered his ex-wife himself or hired a contract killer. The defence argued that the jury should have been directed that they must be unanimous[231] in finding that Thatcher was either the killer or the accomplice. Dickson CJC noted that s 21 was intended to abolish the (English) common law rule that accessories before the fact who were not present at commission of the offence had to be charged as accessories rather than as principals, and continued:

In sum, this Court has held that it is no longer necessary to specify in the charge the nature of an accused's participation in the offence: *Harder*. Moreover, if there is evidence before a jury that points to an accused either committing a crime personally or, alternatively, aiding and abetting another to commit the offence, provided the jury is satisfied beyond a reasonable

---

[224] *R v Schell & Paquette (No 1)* (n 222) 429.
[225] *R v Popen* (1981) 60 CCC (2d) 233 (Ontario CA).   [226] ibid [16].
[227] *R v Roud* [1981] OJ No 921 (Ontario CA).   [228] Criminal Code 1985 (Canada) c 46.
[229] *Roud* (n 227)   [230] *R v Thatcher* [1987] 1 SCR 652 (SCC).
[231] In Canada jury verdicts are required to be unanimous.

doubt that the accused did one or the other, it is 'a matter of indifference' which alternative actually occurred: *Chow Bew.* It follows, in my view, that s. 21 precludes a requirement of jury unanimity as to the particular nature of the accused's participation in the offence. Why should the juror be compelled to make a choice on a subject which is a matter of legal indifference.[232]

An unreported decision of the Ontario Court of Appeal illustrates how the case can be constructed by the prosecution so as to allow it to get to the jury: *R v AK and AV.*[233] The case reached the Court of Appeal on the basis of a ruling by an inquiry judge at a preliminary inquiry that there was sufficient evidence to require the parents to stand trial for the second degree murder of their three-month-old daughter. A subsequent *certiorari* application to the Superior Court to quash the committal was denied. The appeal to the Court of Appeal was based on the findings of the inquiry judge, first, that there was no direct or circumstantial evidence which could result in a reasonable inference that one accused was more likely than the other to have assaulted the child; and second, that there was no evidence as to which accused caused the injuries and no evidence of aiding or abetting or the formation of an intention in common to carry out the child abuse within the meaning of s 21.

However the inquiry judge had allowed the case to proceed on the basis that:

[The appellants] were the only two people who had custody and control of the child during the material times and by reasonable inference were virtually the only ones who had the opportunity to inflict the fatal injuries.

The judge also had regard to the evidence that the appellants were aware of their daughter's deteriorating health and condition and the previous significant injuries she had suffered, and also that they had a financial motive to kill her. From this evidence, he reasoned:

As a result of opportunity, motive, the number and location and timing of the wounds to the child, and the increasingly severe reaction to the abuse by [sic] the child which would have come to the attention of a reasonably attentive parent according to Dr Smith, there is sufficient evidence to support a reasonable inference that any perpetrator or party to the perpetration of these injuries meant to cause bodily harm to the child that he/she knew was likely to cause her death and was reckless as to whether death ensued. In other words if the Crown's evidence is believed it would be reasonable that a properly instructed jury could infer guilt in respect to second degree murder.[234]

Unfortunately the case never came to trial, a stay was granted on the charges against the couple because of the inordinate delay that there had been in bringing the case to trial,[235] this stay was confirmed, reluctantly, by the Ontario Court of Appeal.[236]

---

[232] *R v Thatcher* (n 230) [72]–[73].

[233] *R v AK and AV* May 27, 2002, docket: C3285, 3286 <http://www.canlii.org/on/cas/onca/2002/2002onca10466.html> (Ontario CA) (accessed 10 September 2005).

[234] Second degree murder under the Criminal Code 1985 (Canada) s 231, broadly speaking and in this context, is a killing which is not planned and deliberate.

[235] Canadian Charter of Rights 11: 'Any person charged with an offence has the right (b) to be tried within a reasonable time'.   [236] *R v AK1* (2005) CanLII 11389 (Ontario CA).

Some English judges in the past have been prepared to consider a limited number of cases in which a child had died, when more than one person was present, as an instance of a crime committed by joint enterprise (the English equivalent of the 'common purpose' provisions in Canadian Criminal code s 21).

In the English case of *Russell and Russell*[237] the 15-month-old child of heroin addicts died following the ingestion of a large quantity of methadone. The court found that this methadone had been deliberately given by one or other of the parents with the consent of the other, but could not identify which of the parents had administered the fatal dose. Both were convicted of manslaughter, as the court was convinced that there was only an intention to pacify the child rather than to kill or cause her severe injury. They were convicted following a direction from the trial judge that:

if one and only one administered the drug in fulfilment of what has been expressly or impliedly agreed with the other who was present and could see what was happening and could stop it happening and did not, in other words, if one acted in pursuance of a joint agreement, as sometimes it happened in the past when the dummy, the drugged dummy, was given to the child, then both could be found guilty although only one actually administered the drug, because where two persons undertake a joint enterprise, each is liable for the acts of the other if what is done is done in pursuance of that joint objective and within its scope. In other words, the responsibility would be joint.[238]

The Court of Appeal approved the use of evidence of past behaviour by the parents as evidence of their common intention in administering a fatal dose of methadone. At trial in *Russell and Russell* both parents gave evidence that they had in the past given the child methadone in order to pacify her. In *Marsh and another v Hodgson*[239] both parents were also found to be acting 'in concert' and both convicted of injuring the child under CYPA 1933 s 1. On this occasion the evidence relied on was circumstantial, rather than evidence of past behaviour. It was found that the child had been injured at some point during two days in which both parents agreed that they were jointly responsible for her care.

The problem in these cases, as in the determination that one party aided the other, is that much is inferred by presence at the time, rather than by any clear evidence of what happened and whether both parties were taking part in a jointly agreed crime. The use of the joint enterprise doctrine fits uneasily with the facts of this type of case. Although in the cases above the court was prepared to infer joint responsibility and agreement simply by the presence of those who have undertaken to care for a child or who are required by law to do so at the time the injuries are thought to have occurred. However when it is not clear that the parties were there throughout the period during which the child was injured and there is little evidence that there was a joint agreement to injure the child, the leading English case *Lane and Lane*[240] clearly states that this cannot in justice be considered a case of joint enterprise. There must be some evidence of an agreement between the parties or of assistance, by either omission

---

[237] *R v Russell and Russell* (1987) 85 Cr App R 388 (CA).   [238] ibid 390.
[239] *Marsh and Marsh v Hodgson* (n 186).
[240] *R v Lane and Another* (n 187).

or commission by the other, otherwise the law is simply establishing a reverse burden of proof and requiring those present to prove that their presence was innocent and they played no part in the assault.[241]

In considering the question of failure to protect, Canadian law does not separate out the action of failing to protect from the general liability for neglect. Canada has made a failure to protect part of a criminal liability for failure to provide the necessities of life,[242] which is the Canadian equivalent of neglect in CYPA 1933 (England) s 1. It was established in *Popen*[243] that the 'necessaries of life' may be interpreted to include necessary protection of a child from harm:

We are disposed to think that the words 'necessaries of life' in section 197 may be wide enough to include not only food, shelter, care, and medical attention necessary to sustain life, but also necessary protection of a child from harm. It is, however, not necessary to decide that question since, *in any event, a parent is under a legal duty at common law to take reasonable steps to protect his or her child from illegal violence used by the other parent or by a third person towards the child which the parent foresees or ought to foresee*. In our opinion such parent is criminally liable under the Code for failing to discharge that duty in circumstances which show *a wanton or reckless disregard for the child's safety, where the failure to discharge the legal duty has contributed to the death of the child or has resulted in bodily harm to the child.*[244] [emphasis added]

Liability for this offence is limited to 'a parent, foster parent, guardian or head of a family' in relation to a child under the age of 16.[245] Thus the step-father of children was not found to have a liability to provide for the wife's children.[246] The *mens rea* is not defined in the Canadian Criminal Code;[247] it has been held in *Naglik*[248] to be an objective test for the jury to determine whether there has been a marked departure from the conduct of a reasonably prudent parent, in circumstances where it was objectively foreseeable that the failure to provide the necessities of life would lead to a risk of danger to the life of the child or a risk of permanent endangerment to the health of the child. This is a purely objective standard. This standard was challenged in the Supreme Court of Canada in *Tutton*[249] in relation to the question of whether failure to provide the necessities of life constituted negligent manslaughter. However, although the question divided the Court, the objective standard was clearly endorsed for all allegations of criminal negligence, including cases where a parent had failed to provide the necessities of life.

(e) Establishing liability in Australia

There appears to be little published evidence that the difficulties in establishing who has killed a child in cases of domestic abuse, has become a topic of legal debate

---

[241] ibid 14 (Croom-Johnson LJ).

[242] Criminal Code 1985 (Canada) c 46 s 215(1) [am 1991 c 43 Sched s 2]. Criminal Code 1985 (Canada) s 197 (1). Everyone is under a legal duty (a) as a parent, foster parent, guardian, or head of a family, to provide necessaries of life for a child under the age of 16 years.

[243] *Popen* (n 225).   [244] ibid [18].   [245] Criminal Code 1985 (Canada) c 46 s 215(1)(a).

[246] *R v Charron* [1969] RL 125 (Quebec Trib).

[247] Criminal Code 1985 (Canada) c 46 s 215(2).

[248] *R v Naglik* 83 CCC (3d) 526 (SCC 1993).   [249] *Tutton* [1989] 1 SCR 1392 (SCC).

in Australia. This is not because the problem does not exist. In the recent case of *Macaskill*[250] the court did not convict either parent following the death of their daughter on the ground that it was impossible to identify which of the parents had been responsible for the numerous injuries preceding her death.

In some cases the court has been able to be sufficiently certain on the evidence as to the identity of the perpetrator of the child's fatal injuries. In *Foster*,[251] there was no direct evidence of who had struck the fatal blow killing the youngest of the mother's sons, Peter; although the mother and her lover were the only two people who had had the opportunity to inflict the injuries on the child. The Supreme Court in Southern Australia accepted evidence of propensity, that there was no evidence that the child or any of his siblings had suffered assaults before the mother began the relationship with Mr Foster. There was also evidence that Mr Foster did not like Peter and evidence that Peter had been injured in the past while the mother had left him in the care of Mr Foster. In these circumstances, with each of the parties blaming the other for Peter's death, the Supreme Court denied Mr Foster's appeal against conviction, although it did substitute a manslaughter, rather than murder, conviction on the grounds that there was not sufficient evidence of intent to cause death or GBH.[252] However each case is tried on its merits. In *Macaskill*,[253] also discussed above, the appellant's conviction was quashed and she was found not guilty on a retrial. Here there was evidence that both parents had been very short-tempered and stressed with their small baby, prior to her death. The father had a history of violence towards the mother and the mother had a history of an inability to cope with small children, which had resulted in her two older children being removed from her care. Thus, it was unclear on the evidence who had assaulted the child and neither parent was convicted.

In relation to liability for failure to protect a child from assault, Australia did produce a line of authority from as early as 1933 that a parent who stands by while her child is assaulted or killed or who fails to remove her child from the care of someone who she knows to be violent, could be considered to have aided the perpetrator of the assault on their child by creating the opportunity for the assault. In the 1933 case of *Russell*,[254] a man's conviction for complicity in the killing of his children was confirmed by the Supreme Court of Victoria. The man had been present when his wife had drowned their two children and then herself and had impassively done nothing. Cussen ACJ held that a person may be complicit in a crime if the evidence shows that he assents to it and that the principal knew this.[255] The court found that an absence of dissent could constitute assent. Mann J found that his effective agreement to his wife's conduct gave 'authority and approval to his wife's act'.[256] However, although the case of *Russell* has been cited as authority in cases relating to aiding and abetting across Australia,[257] we have found little evidence of its use in cases of child death to argue that a parent

---

[250] *R v Macaskill* [2003] SASC 61 (S Australia Supreme Ct).
[251] *Foster* [2001] SASC 20 (S Australia Supreme Ct).   [252] ibid.   [253] *Macaskill*, (n 250).
[254] *Russell* [1933] VLR 59 (Victoria Supreme Ct).   [255] ibid.   [256] ibid 76.
[257] *R v Tamme* [2004] VSCA 165 (Victoria Supreme Ct); *R v Guthrie & Watt* [2003] VSC 323 (Victoria Supreme Ct); *R v Rao* [1999] ACTSC 132 (Australian Capital Territory Supreme Ct); *Giorgianni v The Queen* (1985) 156 CLR 473 (Australia HC).

or carer created the opportunity for the child's death. This may be because of the apparent limited use of omissions liability in relation to parents and their children. A parent may be liable for failing to obtain medical treatment for her child. In this case she could be charged with negligent manslaughter in relation to her child. In *Taktak*[258] Carruthers J held that in such a case it was incumbent upon the Crown to prove the following elements beyond reasonable doubt:

(1) that the accused owed a duty of care in law to the person in question;

(2) that it was the omission of the accused to obtain medical treatment which was the proximate cause of that person's death; and

(3) that such omission by the accused was conscious and voluntary without any intention of causing death, but in circumstances which involved such a great falling short of the standard of care which a reasonable man would have exercised and which involved such a high risk that death would follow that the omission merited criminal punishment.

However there appears to be much more limited liability for an omission to act in other contexts. In *Rao*,[259] which actually was a case concerning the aiding and abetting of the murder of an adult, Crispin J in the Supreme Court for the Australian Capital Territory considered many of the potential routes to liability for aiding and abetting by evidence of omission. In this case the Crown submitted that the appellant had a duty to remove the deceased from danger that she had subconsciously created once she became aware or ought to have been aware of it. Crispin J regretted the limited development of such liability but held that the authority did not support such a proposition: 'As a matter of general morality I would wholeheartedly endorse the principle for which the Crown contends, but the authorities dealing with offences of manslaughter do not seem to have acknowledged such a principle.'[260]

Australia at present seems to be in a position in which the prosecution of those who have killed a child or who have failed to protect a child remains very difficult, unless the identity of the perpetrator is clear. Furthermore the very limited concept of liability in cases which may be categorized as an omission, has added to the problems in prosecuting cases where it is unclear who has harmed the child and who has sat by and let it happen. The concept that a carer of the child who failed to act actually aided the other in perpetrating the assault on the child which had been developed by *Russell*, appears now to be little used in the prosecution of child homicides in Australia.

(f) Establishing liability in New Zealand

However the train of legal thought which was started in Australia appears to have been further developed in New Zealand. In *R v Witika*[261] the New Zealand Court of Appeal upheld the conviction of both the mother of a little girl Delcelia and the mother's partner, for the manslaughter of Delcelia. In this case it was not clear which

---

[258] *R v Taktak* (1988) 14 NSWLR 226 (New South Wales) 250.
[259] *R v Rao* (n 257).   [260] ibid.   [261] *Witika* (n 212).

of the appellants had caused the death of Delcelia. The little girl had died following a series of brutal assaults against her over a number of months. Each appellant stated that the other had been responsible for the assaults. The Crown case was that the child was subjected to a course of brutal and increasing violence and that there had been a failure to secure necessary medical care, resulting ultimately in death. Even in closing submission the Crown acknowledged that it could not prove which of the appellants was responsible for the alleged acts of commission, but asked for verdicts of guilty against both appellants, either as principal offenders, or as parties to the offending through intentional encouragement. The argument put forward by the Crown was very similar to the argument which had been put forward in the Australian case of *Russell* that when there is a special relationship between a person and the victim, it would usually be expected that this person would intervene to protect the victim and a failure to do so can constitute encouragement of an offence. The Court of Appeal approved the summing-up given at pre-trial appeal by the court:

In those cases where there is by reason of a relationship, a positive duty to intervene then mere presence or simply passive acquiescence and deliberate failure to exercise that duty to take steps to avoid the commission of the offence, if accompanied by the intention to encourage or approve the offence may be enough if the person committing the offence takes such inaction as amounting to encouragement.

Now, if either the mother or the de facto father, because we are looking at each accused here, if either the mother or the de facto father each being a person having the custody and control of the child and being responsible for its care and safety and well-being, had knowledge of the propensity or the tendency of the other of them to commit any of the violent acts complained of and had knowledge of the risk that further such acts might be committed and if having the ability to do so she or he failed to take appropriate, reasonable steps to ensure that the other of them was deprived of the opportunity to continue those acts or to repeat them, intending by such failure to encourage those acts, then she or he is abetting those acts and is guilty as a party if the other party has been encouraged in that way. There has to be encouragement intentional and encouragement in fact.[262]

It seems unclear why the reasoning of the New Zealand Court of Appeal could not apply equally in English law. Under English law a person can assist the commission of an offence by an omission, provided that there is evidence that the defendant's presence or lack of action, encouraged or assisted the principal to commit the offence and that the defendant knew that his presence or failure to act was capable of encouraging or assisting the principal to act.[263] Simester and Sullivan have argued forcefully that a parent who fails to fulfil her legal duty to protect her children from ill-treatment under CYPA 1933 s 1 does not merely encourage the perpetrator to harm the child, but should be considered to have aided the perpetrator.[264] They argue that the parent in these circumstances is in a similar position to the policeman who has a duty to

---

[262] ibid.

[263] *R v Coney* (1882) 8 QBD 534; *R v Clarkson* [1971] 3 All ER 344 (CA); J Finn 'Culpable Non-Intervention: Reconsidering the Basis for Party Liability by Omission' (1994) 18 Crim LR 90.

[264] Simester and Sullivan *Criminal Law* (n 50) 195.

intervene and protect people from criminal violence. Williams has argued against this interpretation of the law on the grounds that failure to prevent an act of abuse should not automatically be deemed in law to be encouraging that abuse. He has sustained that a defendant should only be convicted of the offence of encouragement if he directly intended to encourage the offence, because it is only in these circumstances that he may be considered to be a party to the aggression.[265] However, whether a parent or those caring for a person intended to encourage the assault is only one element of the offence and, as Simester and Sullivan have argued, by supporting the perpetrator, for example by giving them the responsibility for physical discipline and allowing this 'discipline' to continue when it is clear that the child is being severely hurt, is evidence of a parent's intention to aid another in their assaults on the child. It is not clear why the English Law Commission did not consider that liability in certain cases could be constructed in the same way as the New Zealand case of *Witika*.[266]

As in Canada and Australia the courts in New Zealand have also been willing to admit evidence of similar assaults on the child in the past by one of the possible assailants as evidence which the jury may take into account in determining which of a group of people inflicted the fatal injury.[267]

There are also some possible avenues within the law which would allow prosecution for a lesser offence. The Crimes Act 1961 (NZ) s 152 creates a legal duty upon a parent, or a person in place of a parent, to provide necessaries of life to their children and a criminal liability for those who omit 'without lawful excuse to do so, whether the child is helpless or not, if the death of the child is caused, or if his life is endangered or his health permanently injured, by such omission'. Anyone found guilty of such an offence is liable to imprisonment for a term not exceeding seven years. This could be used, as the charge under CYPA 1933 s 1 has been used in cases in England in which it is clear that the parent or guardian delayed a request for medical treatment. However there does not appear to be caselaw that indicates that it has been used in cases where a parent has failed to protect a child or remove the child from a dangerous situation.

9. Evaluation: killing by carers—has the law gone far enough?

Commentary on all the offences relating to the homicide of children, recognizes the undoubted link between social position and hopelessness, and the killing of children. However the criminal law fails to recognize that children's deaths may also very well not be accidental. As Cobley, Sanders and Wheeler[268] have found in relation to the shaking of babies, judgments can very well overlook the fact that the child did not die, or was severely injured, as a result of one incident when the parent snapped from frustration and isolation, but the child had in fact sustained a number of injuries before the shaking incident. Judicial oversight is part of a much wider picture of legislative oversight, and a failure to recognize within society that in cases where children die as a result of a pattern of abuse, their death was not an unintended and

---

[265] Williams (n 204).   [266] *Witika* (n 212).   [267] *Meynell* (n 181).
[268] Cobley, Sanders and Wheeler (n 58).

unforeseen possibility. The difficulty remains that the child's death is often not seen to be inevitable by the abuser, because in cases of repeated physical abuse the child has survived many assaults before the one that killed her and the abuser can argue that on this occasion he believed that it would be no different. In some cases the facts belie this explanation and it has been accepted by some courts in the US that evidence of repeated blows and of serious past injuries is sufficient to determine that the killing was intentional. However while in the majority of cases the abuser did not intend to kill the child, he ran the risk that the child would die from the assault. However, under the new Law Commission proposals, if the risk taking was not conscious the perpetrator cannot be charged with second degree murder but should be charged with manslaughter on the grounds that he ran a risk that he knew or ought to have known about. In cases where a child is killed following abuse the most appropriate charge is now under Crime, Victims and Domestic Violence Act 2004 (Eng) s 5. However it is not part of the mainstream homicide offences. As the US, Canada and New Zealand have shown it is possible to use the homicide offences, but the court often has to infer a knowledge of a risk of death to the perpetrator. While this has been done in Crime, Victims and Domestic Violence Act 2004 (Eng) s 5 it seems unlikely that legislators will allow it into mainstream homicide offences.

Much of the development of law which would adequately reflect the reality of child homicide in a family setting has been held back by the notion that an omission to act is qualitatively different from an act of commission. Omissions have often been characterized as leading to unwanted and unforeseen events on the part of a parent who fails to act. However the Crime, Victims and Domestic Violence Act 2004 (Eng) reflects a growing recognition in the law that in cases where an adult is a child's only hope of protection, the failure of that adult to effect an easy rescue of the child from the violence the child is suffering, can be as culpable as the person who inflicts the blows which kill the child. This has been reflected in the law in Canada and New Zealand particularly in relation to the omissions of carers to protect children from fatal assault.

D. Non-Fatal Offences Against the Person

There are five main offences with which a person who injures a child may be charged: cruelty and neglect, common assault and battery, actual bodily harm, grievous bodily harm, and grievous bodily harm with intent. They form a ladder of offences rising in relation to the seriousness of the injury caused. Under English law these offences, with the exception of cruelty and neglect, were originally created by statute (Offences Against the Person Act 1861) but are almost entirely defined by common law. This has allowed the scope of the offences to be greatly expanded, for example to include a range of recognized psychiatric injuries as well as physical injuries.

Many of the general debates in relation to the definitions of these offences do not raise specific questions in relation to the prosecution of injuries inflicted on children. The main problem hampering the use of these offences in relation to younger children is the difficulty of identifying the perpetrator of the child's injuries when the child has been looked after by more than one person during a given period. The problem of identification dies away when the child becomes older and able to speak of what has happened, but is replaced by the problems created by the existence of the defence of reasonable chastisement. This defence has made assaults on children very difficult to prosecute when they have taken place within a family context, when the child may have been perceived to have done something wrong. In the next section we consider the range of offences which are available, the current difficulties which hamper their use and proposed changes and potential improvements.

1. Ill-treatment and neglect

Although often regarded as the lowest of the offences and a 'catch-all' when other offences cannot be proved, the offence of ill-treatment and neglect of a child should be considered to be one of the worst offences which may be committed against a child. While it is acknowledged that some behaviour which could be the *actus reus* of this offence may not be done deliberately, this should not blind us to the nature of much of the behaviour under this offence. This offence is charged in cases where day in and day out children are subjected to physical and mental torture, breaking their spirit and damaging their fundamental trust in others. As Hobbs, Hanks, and Wynne have noted 'it is important to keep in mind that the greatest loss of human potential in childhood arises from neglect.'[269] Although not regarded as an offence which is committed with a great deal of deliberation, in fact the difference between offenders under this offence and other types of offence can be that the offender sees the child every day, sees the damage that her lack of care is inflicting upon them and persistently continues to inflict damage upon them. Stone has argued that it is the very long-term nature of the abuse, and the fact that in some cases the neglect is not intended, that makes it difficult for practitioners and lawyers to perceive neglect in the same terms as sexual or physical assault.[270]

The offence is enshrined in Children and Young Person's Act 1933 s 1[271] which states that:

(1) If any person who has attained the age of 16 years and has the responsibility for any child or young person under that age, wilfully assaults, ill-treats, neglects, abandons, or exposes him, or causes or procures him to be assaulted, ill-treated, neglected, abandoned, or exposed, in a manner likely to cause him unnecessary suffering or injury to health (including injury to or loss of sight, or hearing, or limb, or organ of the body, and any mental derangement), that person shall be guilty of a misdemeanour.

Ill-treatment may include an assault or battery, but may also be shown by evidence of psychological injury and bullying.[272] Ill-treatment may also include a series of assaults which would not of themselves be sufficient to constitute a criminal assault;

---

[269] C Hobbs, C Hanks and J Wynne *Child Abuse and Neglect: a Clinician's Handbook* (Churchill, Livingstone 1999) 10.

[270] B Stone *Child Neglect: Practitioners' Perspectives* (NSPCC Policy Practice Research Series, London 1998) 5–6.   [271] As amended by Children Act 1989 (England) Sch 13(5).

[272] *Attorney-General's Reference (No 80 of 2004)* [2004] EWCA Crim 2061.

for example, repeatedly giving a child food and then pulling it away from the child, would constitute ill-treatment of a child although it might not constitute a battery.

The statute recognizes that an omission to provide a child with the necessities of life, 'adequate food, clothing, medical aid or lodging for him' can constitute neglect.[273] The *actus reus* of this offence must be judged on an objective basis, thus the question to be asked is whether the food, clothing, medical aid or home provided for the child was adequate according to ordinary standards, not whether the defendant thought it was.[274] Although this offence is often also used as a charging alternative to other non-fatal offences, and on occasion fatal offences,[275] it is also used in relation to child abuse, when it is difficult to prove who has injured a child, but it is clear that the child needed medical attention before he received it.[276]

As the statute suggests, carers may be convicted of an offence under CYPA 1933 s 1 whether or not they are the principal instigator of the behaviour. The case of *Creed*[277] clearly recognizes that a parent or someone *in loco parentis* may commit the *actus reus* of the offence when she leaves her child with someone whom she knows is likely to hurt that child. In *Creed* the mother left her child, L, in the sole care of her partner Sate, while she was at work. The mother knew that Sate had hurt L on previous occasions. Finally Sate threw the child down the stairs and she died later from internal injuries. This case is interesting because the court went beyond the mother's delay in calling for medical assistance, a well used mechanism to sustain a charge under CYPA 1933 s 1. The judge at first instance, found that the mother's act of entrusting the care of L to her partner breached CYPA 1933 s 1. In sentencing Creed, he found that Creed knew that there was a risk of violence before her daughter was assaulted and that following the violence against her daughter Creed persisted in leaving her daughter with Sate, knowing that she was being subjected to violence. Similarly Creed's failure to act 'to release [her] daughter from the hellish cruelty and risk she was exposed to' was also found to be an offence under CYPA 1933 s 1.

There has been some debate within the courts as to whether CYPA 1933 s 1 actually in effect creates five separate distinct offences and whether in charging under this section the prosecution must be clear what type of behaviour they are alleging and the basis on which the jury makes a finding under CYPA 1933 s 1 is therefore clear. The Court of Appeal in *Hayles*[278] found that where the indictment charges one type of behaviour, in that case ill-treatment and the defendant's conduct could fall into behaviour which that term describes, the defendant may be properly convicted under CYPA s 1, even though the behaviour might be more properly described as another type of conduct, in this case neglect.[279] This was followed in *Beard*,[280] although the Court of Appeal was clearly concerned about the impact of the earlier decision, particularly in creating a risk that juries would convict on an uncertain basis and that this would in turn present difficult problems in sentencing.[281] The matter was

---

[273] Children and Young Persons Act 1933 (England) s 1(2).
[274] *Sheppard* [1981] AC 394 (HL) 400. [275] *R v B* [2001] EWCA Crim 1463.
[276] Cobley, Sanders and Wheeler (n 58). [277] *Creed* (n 193).
[278] *R v Hayles* [1969] 1 QB 364 (CA Crim). [279] ibid.
[280] *R v Beard* (1980) 85 Cr App R 395, 401–2. [281] ibid.

clarified to some extent in *Young*[282] which has stated that the section creates one offence which may be proved in a number of different ways. However, the Court of Appeal continued that it might well be wrong for the jury to be given the impression that they could convict under CYPA 1933 s 1 if some were satisfied that there had been neglect, but others were not satisfied as to neglect, but were satisfied that there had been assault or ill-treatment. In *Young*, the nature of the Crown's case against the appellant had been in relation to one aspect of the offence under CYPA 1933 s 1, namely neglect alone, thus there had been no danger of the jury not being unanimous on the factual basis of the conviction. It has been proposed that when there is a good reason to suggest alternatives, it would be more appropriate to have more than one count charged to enable both the jury and the judge to be clear about exactly which events are the subject of the charge.[283]

The use of the term 'wilfully' within the statute imports a requirement of *mens rea*, for all five possible types of behaviour with which the offence is concerned. In the leading case of *Sheppard*[284] the majority in the House of Lords interpreted 'wilfully' to mean either intentionally or subjectively reckless:

The primary meaning of 'wilful' is 'deliberate'. So a parent who knows that his child needs medical care and deliberately, that is by conscious decision, refrains from calling a doctor, is guilty under the subsection. As a matter of general principle, recklessness is to be equated with deliberation. A parent who fails to provide medical care which his child needs because he does not care whether it is needed or not is reckless of his child's welfare. He too is guilty of an offence. But a parent who has genuinely failed to appreciate that his child needs medical care, through personal inadequacy or stupidity or both, is not guilty.[285]

The term 'wilfully' may also limit the liability of the very poor parent, because it denotes a level of deliberation. Certainly it is evidence of wilfulness if the parent has the means to provide the child with the necessary care but does not do so.[286] It is also evidence if 'having been unable otherwise to provide such food, clothing, medical aid or lodging, he has failed to take steps to procure it to be provided under the enactments applicable in that behalf'.[287] However carers who fail to provide the necessities of life and who do apply for benefits to enable them to provide them, would not under CYPA 1933 s 1(2) be considered wilfully neglectful.

In this respect the criminal law differs significantly from family law in the same context. In family law the lack of intention by a child's carer is not crucial to the case. As the focus of family law is on the future progress of the child victim, the crucial aspect is the fact that the child suffered significant harm. The threshold test could be satisfied even if the parent or carer's action was not deliberate but stemmed from inadequacy on their part, because the aim of the law is to guard the child from further harm, not to blame the actor.

---

[282] *R v Young* (1992) 97 Cr App R 280 (CA).
[283] *Archbold* (Sweet & Maxwell, London 2002) [19–294].
[284] *Sheppard* (n 274) 418 (Lord Keith).   [285] ibid.
[286] *R v Ryland* (1867) LR 1 CCR 99, 31 JP 790.   [287] CYPA 1933 (England) s 1(2).

2. Offences against the person

The least serious offences under the Offences Against the Person Act 1861 are assault and battery. The criminal act of assault is committed when D causes V to fear immediate personal violence. The act of simply shaking a fist at someone, or of moving towards him in a threatening manner, could constitute an assault. Conversely if the complainant knows that the threat is empty and that he cannot possibly be hurt the act cannot be an assault. The rule of law has historically been that the violence apprehended must be immediate and that threats of violence at some point in the future will not constitute an assault. However this aspect of the rule has been considerably loosened in more recent assault cases. In these cases the courts grappled with whether forms of harassment could constitute an assault. In *Constanza*[288] the defendant sent threatening letters to the complainant, and in *Ireland*,[289] the defendant subjected the three complainants to a series of silent phone calls. In neither case could the threat of violence be immediately implemented. In *Constanza* the Court of Appeal concluded that the prosecution need only prove that the complainant feared 'violence at some time not excluding the immediate future'.[290] In *Ireland* the question of whether the complainant was in fear of an immediate attack was found to be a question of fact for the jury. Lord Stein further suggested that a trial judge could advise a jury that if they found that the victim had been put in fear they should consider what, 'if not the possibility of imminent personal violence was V terrified about?'

A person commits a battery when she applies unlawful force to the body of another, but does not leave any lasting injury or mark. A battery of a child could include pushing, pinching, poking and some instances of shaking. It was also concluded in *DPP v K* that a person may also commit a battery if he omits to act to rectify a dangerous situation that he has created. Thus in *DPP v K*[291] in which the defendant put acid into the hot air dryer at his school toilets and the next person to use the machine was burned by the acid, Parker LJ found that the accused had committed battery on the next user just as if he had himself switched on the machine. However this judgment contradicted the earlier precedent of *Fagan v MPC* that held that a battery could only be committed by a positive act accompanied by the requisite *mens rea*.[292] Hirst argued that as a result of this *DPP v K* must be regarded as having been decided erroneously and that *Fagan v MPC* represents a proper interpretation of the law.[293] However *DPP v K* has been preferred in subsequent cases and it appears therefore that an argument that a parent or caregiver's omission to rectify a dangerous situation which he or she has created could arguably be a battery leads to the injury to the child being seen as a result of the battery. For example in *DPP v Santa-Bermudez*[294] V, a police officer, was injured during a search by a hypodermic needle which D was carrying in his pocket and which D omitted to remove or to warn her of, despite her

---

[288] *R v Constanza* [1997] 2 Cr App R 492 (CA).   [289] *R v Ireland* [1998] AC 147 (HL).
[290] *Constanza* (n 288) 494.   [291] *DPP v K* [1990] 1 All ER 331 (CA Crim).
[292] *Fagan v MPC* [1969] 1 QB 439 (DC).
[293] M Hirst 'Assault, Battery and Indirect Violence' [1999] Crim LR 557.
[294] *DPP v Santa Bermudez* [2003] EWHC 2908; [2004] Crim LR 471 (QBD Admin Ct).

direct question about whether he was carrying any more needles.[295] It might therefore be argued that caregivers could be liable for any failure to rectify obviously dangerous situations which they have created within the home, for example leaving needles or non-prescription drugs in places where children could find them.

Actual bodily harm can be charged when the victim suffers a battery or an assault which results in an injury to the victim.[296] This 'hurt or injury does not have to be permanent but must be more than transient or trifling'. A range of injuries may be encompassed within the term of actual bodily harm, including bruising, grazes, tenderness lasting for a few days,[297] temporary loss of consciousness[298] as well as psychiatric injury, which is discussed later.

The most serious injuries punishable under the OAPA 1861 are grievous bodily harm and wounding. Wounding has been interpreted to necessitate the breaking of both layers of skin, although the slightest cut would suffice.[299] The term 'grievous' bodily harm has been interpreted to mean really 'serious' harm.[300] This would include breaking bones, the loss of consciousness for a period including the induction of fits resulting from shaking and the transmission of serious diseases.[301] GBH and wounding may be charged under two different offences (s 20 and s 18 OAPA) and the choice of which offence to charge depends upon the intention of the defendant at the time of the offence.

With the exception of OAPA 1861 s 18 all the offences above may be satisfied with the same *mens rea*. The leading cases *R v Savage*; *R v Parmenter*[302] held that the defendant need not have foreseen the level of harm which he caused; it is sufficient in proving that the defendant had the requisite *mens rea* to find that either the defendant intended to cause harm, or that he understood the risk that harm would result, but went on to take that risk. *Parmenter* was a case of alleged child abuse in which a father handled his three-month-old child roughly, but argued that he did not intend to cause him the very serious harm which resulted. Parmenter claimed that he had no experience of handling very young children and that he had not appreciated that his behaviour towards his son (which it was accepted by a paediatrician would have been acceptable handling of a three-or four-year-old child) would injure him.

Lord Ackner in the House of Lords in *R v Savage; DPP v Parmenter* found that s 20 only required foresight of some physical harm: 'It is enough that he [that is the defendant] should have foreseen that some physical harm to some person, albeit of a minor character, might result.'[303]

---

[295] ibid.   [296] *Miller* [1954] 2 QB 282 (Winchester Assizes).

[297] *R v Reigate Justices ex p Counsell* [1984] 148 JP 193 (QBD).

[298] *T v DPP* [2003] EW HC 2408 (QBD).

[299] *Moriaty v Brooks* (1834) 6 C & P 684; *C v Eisenhower* (1984) 78 Cr App R 48 (DC).

[300] *DPP v Smith* [1961] AC 290 (HL).

[301] *R v Wilson* [1984] AC 242 (HL); *Ireland* (n 289); Simester and Sullivan *Criminal Law* (n 50) 391–393.

[302] Savage threw a pint of beer over Miss Beal. Unfortunately the glass hit a table and shattered. A piece of the glass cut Miss Beale's wrist.

[303] *R v Savage; DPP v Parmenter* [1991] 4 All ER 699 (HL) 752F (Lord Ackner).

It is important to note that Lord Ackner's use of the word 'should' does not import an objective test of recklessness into the offence. The test remains a subjective question of whether the defendant foresaw some injury resulting from his act, albeit slight. Thus the appeal of *Parmenter* against conviction was allowed on the grounds that he did not foresee any resulting injury. As a result of *R v Savage; R v Parmenter*, the *mens rea* of all the offences discussed above with the exception of the most serious offence of OAPA s 18, may be satisfied by this test. For offences under OAPA s 18 it must be proved that V was wounded or suffered grievous bodily harm caused by D, and that D intended to cause V grievous bodily harm or to wound him.

3. Psychiatric injury

It has now been acknowledged in English law that a child may be significantly harmed by witnessing domestic violence. As discussed in Chapter 1, the meaning of harm in Children Act 1989 s 31(9) was amended by the Children and Adoption Act 2002 s 120 to include 'impairment suffered from seeing or hearing the ill-treatment of another'. While there has not been the same level of discussion within the criminal law about whether a person who is violent towards a child's caregiver and as a result causes the child psychiatric harm may be charged with injuring the child, it seems clear that in the light of the precedent which has built up in this area he may be so charged.

There is now a long line of cases which clearly establish that psychiatric injury may be considered a non-fatal offence against the person. In *Chan-Fook*,[304] which concerned an incident in which the victim was punched and locked in a room, the Court of Appeal held that 'actual bodily harm' may include injury to any part of the body, including internal organs, the nervous system and the brain. Fundamentally it found that it is capable of including psychiatric injury. Psychiatric injury would not include 'mere emotion such as fear, distress or panic', nor does it include states of mind that are not themselves evidence of some identifiable clinical condition'.[305] In *Ireland*, the complainants, who were subjected to repeated silent telephone calls, suffered a range of psychological symptoms. These included 'palpitations, difficulty in breathing and cold sweats of an intensity which made it difficult for her to leave her home or to answer the telephone'; anxiety, inability to sleep, tearfulness, headaches, tingling in her fingers, dizziness and 'a constant feeling of being on edge'.[306] It is important to note that these symptoms were not self-certified but were testified to by a psychiatrist. In *Morris*, evidence of similar symptoms of anxiety, fear and sleeplessness was given by a general practitioner but was found to be insufficient to establish that the victim had suffered actual bodily harm.[307]

It may be possible to charge actual bodily harm or grievous bodily harm in a case where a child who was a witness to violence within the home suffered psychological damage as a result, provided that there is a clear causal connection, between the

---

[304] *R v Chan Fook* [1994] 1 WLR 689 (CA).   [305] ibid 698 (Hobhouse LJ).
[306] *R v Ireland* [1998] AC 147 (HL).   [307] *R v Morris* [1998] 1 Cr App R 386 (CA).

violence and the injury the child sustained. From *Haystead v Chief Constable of Derbyshire*[308] it seems clear that the child need not be the direct victim of the assault for a charge to be brought. In *Haystead* the appellant punched his former girlfriend in the face. The girlfriend was holding her 12-month-old child at the time. She dropped the child and the child hit his head on the floor. The Queen's Bench sitting as an appellate court concluded that for a charge of battery to be sustained it was not necessary for the child to have been directly assaulted by the appellant, provided that it could be shown that the battery which the child sustained was a direct consequence of his act.

Here the movement of Miss Wright whereby she lost hold of the child was entirely and immediately the result of the appellant's action in punching her. There is no difference in logic or good sense between the facts of this case and one where the defendant might have used a weapon to fell the child to the floor, save only that this is a case of reckless and not intentional battery.[309]

It does not appear necessary that the child thought that he or she would be hurt immediately for the reqirements of the offence to be satisfied. It also does not appear necessary for the defendant to have foreseen that the child would suffer harm. Actual bodily harm is a constructive offence which means that provided it may be shown that D committed an assault and battery, and provided that it may further be shown that this assault or battery occasioned the actual bodily harm in question, it is not necessary to prove that D intended or foresaw the harm which was in fact caused. To draw an analogy from constructive manslaughter, in *A-G's Ref No 3 of 1994*,[310] it was not necessary to prove that the appellant in this case intended or was reckless or grossly negligent about the death of the baby. Provided that it could be proved that he intended or was reckless in stabbing his pregnant girlfriend and that the stabbing caused the baby's death, the charge of constructive manslaughter was made out. Similarly it appears that a defendant may be charged with actual bodily harm if a child's psychiatric injury was caused by an intentional or reckless battery by the defendant to someone else.

In relation to circumstances in which a child suffers even more serious psychiatric harm, a defendant may be charged with inflicting grievous bodily harm contrary to OAPA 1861 s 20. Although the defendant must foresee some harm for this offence to be charged, he does not need to foresee either the level of harm that he causes or that the child herself would be harmed. If D attacks a child's carer intending to cause or foreseeing that he might cause some physical harm to that carer and in so doing he inflicts psychiatric injury on the child, that would be sufficient. The intention or foresight that he might hurt X provides the 'malice' the offence requires.

So, in cases of domestic violence involving physical violence to X and causally connected psychiatric injury to V it should be possible to establish liability for offences against V without showing that V apprehended force or that D foresaw that she

---

[308] *Haystead v Chief Constable of Derbyshire* [2000] 3 All ER 890 (QBD).
[309] ibid [32] (Laws LJ).   [310] *A-G's Ref No 3 of 1994* [1998] AC 245 (HL).

would. Further it would not be necessary to prove that D foresaw the causing of any form of injury to V provided he intended to cause or foresaw that he might cause harm to somebody else. The difficulty, as ever in psychiatric harm, remains in identifying a clear causative link between the violence witnessed and the damage caused. However it may be easier to establish this link in the case of little children who are, it is usually presumed, unlikely to demonstrate psychiatric illness without a clear trauma.

4. Reasonable parental chastisement

It is an established principle of English law that a parent, or someone in the position of parent, may hit a child for the purposes of disciplining the child for wrongdoing. This exception for parents and caregivers was enshrined in statute by the CYPA 1933. This defence allows a parent, or those in the position of parent, to counter accusations of assault by arguing that the force applied was not unlawful, but was in fact the 'reasonable chastisement of a child'. The onus is on the prosecution to prove in cases where the defence is available that the defendant did more than inflict 'merely moderate and reasonable physical chastisement on the child'.[311] The Court of Appeal in *R v APM* described the requirement on the prosecution alternatively as, 'to prove that any blow struck was not struck by way of chastisement or that, if it was struck by way of chastisement, it was unnecessary or unreasonable in extent'.[312] As the unreasonableness of the chastisement is essentially a question of fact for the jury there remains little precedent on this matter and most of it is confined to statements of what is not reasonable chastisement, rather than what would be. Thus *B v Harris*[313] found that hitting a child with a belt leaving marks on legs was not excessive. However in *Smith*[314] it was held that the act of hitting a child with a belt leaving bruising went beyond moderate and reasonable chastisement. The very old case of *R v Hopley* has remained the primary statement of what type of chastisement would be considered to be unreasonable:

If it be administered for the gratification of passion or of rage, or if it be immoderate or excessive in its nature or degree, or if it be protracted beyond the child's powers of endurance, or with an instrument unfitted for the purpose and calculated to produce danger to life and limb, in all such cases the punishment is excessive and the violence unlawful.[315]

The Government has come under increasing pressure to clarify, if not abolish, the defence. In the seminal case of *A v UK*[316] the ECtHR held that the United Kingdom had failed in its obligations under ECHR Article 3 because it had not ensured that the criminal law prohibited treatment amounting to torture. The facts of the case were that A had been hit by his stepfather with a variety of instruments including a garden cane

---

[311] *R v Smith* (1985) CLR 42 (CA) (May LJ).

[312] *R v APM* (2000) Westlaw Transcript 1841688 (CA).

[313] *B v Harris* [1990] S LT 208 (Scottish Court of Session Inner House Ist Div).

[314] (n 311) in C Lyon *Loving Smack or Lawful Assault? A Contradiction in Human Rights and Law* (IPPR, London 2000) 9.   [315] *R v Hopley* (1860) 2 F & F 202.

[316] *A v UK* (n 30).

leaving bruising and linear scarring. At the trial of the stepfather the jury found that these injuries had been incurred in the course of 'reasonable chastisement' and did not convict the stepfather of any offence. The court found that the failure of the United Kingdom lay in its lack of definition of the term 'reasonable chastisement' which had to be construed by the jury and thus was capable of a number of different interpretations. The court held that the 'imprecise nature of the expression of reasonable chastisement as contained in these legal provisions may pave the way for it to be interpreted in a subjective and arbitrary manner'.[317]

Thus the argument which was sustained by the ECtHR was for clarification, not necessarily for abolition. The Government's response was robust. A statement by the then Home Office Minister, Paul Boateng, following the decision in *A v UK* stated that the line between punishment and assault was easily drawn. He claimed that 'the overwhelming majority of parents know the difference between a smacking and a beating'[318] and that the law in allowing these common standards to be used in its interpretation was sufficiently clear. Furthermore he recognized that parents had a right to 'exert discipline by smacking their children when they misbehave'.[319] However in response to the defeat in *A v UK* the Government did issue a consultation paper on possible reform.[320] Throughout the document the Government remained committed to clarification rather than abolition and the consultation paper stated that: 'we do not consider that the right way forward is to make unlawful all smacking and other forms of physical rebuke and this paper explicitly rules out this possibility'.[321] Thus the consultation document put forward suggestions for changes to the law to define more clearly what would and would not constitute reasonable parental chastisement. There has been considerable scepticism amongst children's rights academics and the anti-smacking lobby about whether it is possible to delineate clearly the line between reasonable and unreasonable hitting of children. Although there was a high level of consensus in the responses to the consultation on the level of injury that should not be considered to be reasonable chastisement, nevertheless the Government at this point decided not to change the law. Their justification for inaction was the incorporation of the ECHR into English law following the Human Rights Act 1998. They argued that any court was now obliged to consider the ECHR and the rulings of the ECtHR on this matter, and thus the law had, by default, now been clarified:

Given such recorded consensus on the outer limits of permissible punishment and the agreed need to protect children from harm, it is extraordinary that the government's professed commitment to 'improving safeguards for children' resulted in a decision to leave English law unchanged.[322]

---

[317] ibid [20].

[318] R Ford 'Minister Defends Parents' Right to Smack Children' *The Guardian* 8 November 1997.

[319] Department of Health *Government to clarify law on parental discipline (Press Release)* (Department of Health, London 7 November 1997).

[320] Home Office *Protecting Children, Supporting Parents: A Consultation Document on the Physical Punishment of Children* (Home Office, London 1999).   [321] ibid [1.5].

[322] R Smith ' "Hands-Off Parenting?"—Towards A Reform of The Defence Of Reasonable Chastisement In The UK' (2004) 16(3) Child & Fam L Q 261, 266.

However pressure from charitable and other pressure groups[323] and the international community continued to build. Their argument was not that the law needed clarification, but that it needed abolition because it represented unequal protection for children as opposed to adults in relation to physical assault.

The Government's refusal to reform lasted until s 58 was added to the Children Act 2004 which curtailed the use of the defence to occasions when a parent or carer might be charged with an offence of assault or battery. Thus the defence is no longer available to a charge of grievous bodily harm or wounding under OAPA 1861 s 18 and s 20, actual bodily harm OAPA s 47 and cruelty CYPA 1933 s 1. This reform recognizes that cruelty to a child can never be beneficial to a child and 'for their own good'. However it would be wrong to consider that the law is now entirely clarified. There remains an enormous range of behaviour which may not on some occasions cause injury sufficient to constitute actual bodily harm, but is damaging to a child. It remains up to a jury to determine whether each set of circumstances constitutes grounds for reasonable chastisement. The Office of Law Reform in Northern Ireland concluded this type of reform lacks clarity and simplicity; it is uncertain how it would be applied and does not send out a clear message about what is or is not acceptable behaviour.[324] As Freeman has concluded, such reform leaves many questions unanswered for prosecutors and the jury to determine, 'What is a "loving" smack? Or a "safe" smack? Is it lawful to smack babies? Or disabled children? Are you to be allowed to hit a child's head, or face, or "box" his ears?'[325]

More fundamentally the law retains the concept that hitting children can be not only acceptable, but right. In response to the changed law the Director of the NSPCC stated:

Bad legal reform is worse than no legal reform and that is what these proposals amount to. Violence towards children is still legally acceptable—as long as you are careful not to leave a mark. The law needs to send out a clear message that it is just as wrong to hit a child as it is to hit an adult.[326]

The Committee on the Rights of the Child specifically rejected the UK Government proposals to limit rather than abolish the defence, on the same basis.[327]

The Committee is of the opinion that governmental proposals to limit rather than remove the 'reasonable chastisement' defence do not comply with the principles and provisions of the Convention ... Moreover, they suggest that some forms of corporal punishment are acceptable and therefore undermine educational measures to promote positive and non-violent discipline.[328]

---

[323] Children are Unbeatable Alliance <http://www.childrenareunbeatable.org.uk>; EPOCH Worldwide Global Initiative to End all Corporal Punishment <http://www.endcorporalpunishment.org> (accessed 10 December 2005).

[324] Office of Law Reform *Physical punishment in the home: thinking about the issues, looking at the evidence* (OLR, Belfast 2001) 41–43.

[325] M Freeman 'Children are Unbeatable' (1999) 11 Children and Society 130, 139.

[326] M Marsh (Latest Developments) <http://www.childrenareunbeatable.org.uk/> (accessed 4 December 2004).

[327] Concluding Observations of the Committee on the Rights of the Child (n 29) [35].

[328] ibid.

5. Allowing physical chastisement in the United States

As has been noted before, the US law in relation to child protection is often influenced by considerations of parental rights, particularly the right of a parent to control and bring up his child as he sees fit, which several cases[329] have found is enshrined in the due process clause of the Constitution.[330] In *Troxel v Granville* Justice O'Connor giving the majority decision in the US Supreme Court observed:

The Fourteenth Amendment's Due Process Clause has a substantive component that 'provides heightened protection against government interference with certain fundamental rights and liberty interests',[331] including parents' fundamental right to make decisions concerning the care, custody, and control of their children.[332]

The right to chastise physically and not be punished in criminal law for it appears to be fundamental to this conception of the place of the law in relation to child protection across the United States; although according to Pollard's analysis,[333] the Supreme Court has never ruled on the issue of whether parents have a right to use corporal punishment on their children as part of the parent's right to rear. However the 'due process' clause has been widely held to encompass a right to chastise reasonably by the lower courts.[334]

All 50 States allow a defence in relation to non-fatal offences against the person that the force was administered for the purposes of parental discipline. In cases where there is a possible defence in relation to parental discipline the defence must show three things: the appropriate person administered the discipline or force, for a proper purpose, with a reasonable amount of force.[335] As the defence is very similar to the defence as it is framed in England and Wales, it is unsurprising that the same problem arises with the lack of clarity in the meaning of reasonableness in this context: 'the extent to which many courts disagree in individual cases on whether a parent's conduct was unlawful demonstrates the lack of guidance such a general statement provides courts.'[336]

---

[329] *Santosky v Kramer* 455 US 745 (US SC 1982) 753; *Stanley v Illinois* 405 US 645 (US SC 1972) 651.

[330] Amendment to the Constitution Article XIV: 'No State shall make or enforce any law which shall abridge the privileges or immunities of citizens of the United States; nor shall any State deprive any person of life, liberty, or property, without due process of law; nor deny to any person within its jurisdiction the equal protection of the laws.' <http://www.law.emory.edu/FEDERAL/usconst.html> (accessed 10 October 2006).   [331] *Washington v Glucksberg* 521 US 702 (USSC) 720.

[332] *Troxel v Granville* 530 US 57 (USSC 2000) 65.

[333] DA Pollard 'Banning Corporal Punishment: A Constitutional Analysis' (2002) 52 Am U L R 447, 454.   [334] *Emery v Emery* 289 P 2d 218 (California SC 1955).

[335] B Townsend 'Defending the "Indefensible": A Primer to Defending Allegations of Child Abuse' (1998) 45 Air Force Law Rev 261, 271; see also: 'the general authority states that a parent physically punishing his or her children is not unlawful as long as he or she is acting in good faith, with parental affection, within the bounds of moderation, and without cruelty or mercilessness': S Davidson 'When is Parental Discipline Child Abuse?—The Vagueness of Child Abuse Laws' (1995) 34 U of Louisville J of Fam L 403, 411; *People v Whitehurst* 12 Cal Rptr 2d 33 (California Ct App 1992) 34, *United States v Brown* 26 MJ 148 (Court of Military Appeals 1988) 150; *United States v Robertson* 36 MJ 190 (Court of Military Appeals 1992) 191.   [336] Davidson (n 335) 411.

6. 'Justifiable force' in Canada

Justifiable force for the purposes of correction of a child is allowed under the Canadian Criminal Code s 43:

Every school teacher, parent or person standing in the place of a parent is justified in using force by way of correction toward a pupil or child, as the case may be, who is under his care, if the force does not exceed what is reasonable under the circumstances.

Section 43 was recently challenged in the Canadian Supreme Court by the Canadian Foundation for Children, Youth and the Law[337] on the grounds that the section was unconstitutional. Primarily the Foundation argued that s 43 violated ss 7 (security of the person), 12 (cruel and unusual punishment or treatment), and 15(1) (equality) of the *Canadian Charter of Rights and Freedoms*.[338] However the arguments of the Foundation were rejected by a majority of six to three.

The argument that s 43 allows behaviour which constitutes cruel and unusual punishment contrary to the prohibition in s 12 of the Canadian Charter was given particularly short shrift by the majority in the Supreme Court. Their argument was that as the Canadian Parliament only allowed the defence where the hitting was 'reasonable' there must therefore be instances where the punishment is not cruel and unusual and, furthermore, the requirement of reasonableness means that the defence does not extend to instances where the punishment was cruel and unusual. Corporal punishment 'cannot be at once both reasonable and an outrage to standards of decency'.[339] This argument is undermined by the outcome of the operation of the defence in all the jurisdictions which we have examined where juries have found a range of behaviour to be deemed 'reasonable punishment' which, if it had been committed against an adult, would undoubtedly have been considered a fairly serious assault. In relation to Canada itself, the dissenting judgment of Madam Justice Arbour lists a number of instances of behaviour which were found by a jury to have been reasonable punishment, such as binding children with tape, or hitting children with a horse harness, belt, or ruler leaving welts, which could equally well have been found to be 'cruel and unusual punishment'.

The Foundation also argued that s 43 offended the principle of vagueness. Arbour MJ (dissenting) agreed:

A vague law violates the principles of fundamental justice as it offends two values that are fundamental to the legal system. First, vague laws do not provide 'fair warning' to individuals as to the legality of their actions, making it more difficult to comply with the law. Second, vague

---

[337] *Candian Foundation for Children, Youth and the Law v Canada (Attorney General)* 2004 SCC 4, [2004] 1 SCR 76 (SCC).

[338] Part 1 of the Constitution Act 1982 (Canada) being Schedule B to the Canada Act 1982 (UK) c11.

[339] *Candian Foundation for Children, Youth and the Law v Canada* (n 337) [49].

laws increase the amount of discretion given to law enforcement officials in their application of the law, which may lead to arbitrary enforcement.[340]

However in the same way that the Court of Appeal in *R v H* in England drew on the judgment in the ECtHR in *A v UK* to demonstrate that the parameters of what constituted reasonable chastisement were actually clear and well-defined, the majority verdict of the Canadian Supreme Court constructed a list of elements of behaviour which constituted 'reasonable chastisement' which the Chief Justice argued was based in law and from expert evidence.[341] These were:

(i) the force used must be 'transitory and trifling' in nature
(ii) only children between the ages of three and twelve may be punished using hitting or other force
(iii) the use of force by way of correction must not be degrading, inhuman or harmful
(iv) force may not be administered by the use of objects
(v) blows or slaps to the head are not permitted
(vi) teachers may only use force to remove a child from the classroom or to ensure that the child complies with instructions and not solely as a punishment
(vii) the force used must be for the correction of the child and not for the gratification of rage, an abusive personality or stemming from the frustration of a parent.

The equality argument that as adults are protected from assault the criminal law should do the same for children, was also rejected by the majority in the Supreme Court. The Canadian Charter of Rights s 15 statement that 'every individual is equal before and under the law' was used by the Foundation in their argument that Criminal Code s 43 discriminated against children by denying them equal protection under the law. The Supreme Court's reasoning in rejecting this argument echoes much of the reasoning in other common law jurisdictions, including our own, that criminalizing all assaults on children jeopardizes family integrity and therefore the child's happy family unit:

The reality is that without s 43, Canada's broad assault law would criminalise force falling short of what we think of as corporal punishment, like placing a child in a chair for a five-minute 'time-out'. The decision not to criminalise such conduct is not grounded in devaluation of the child, but in a concern that to do so risks ruining lives and breaking up families—a burden that would in large part be borne by children and outweigh any benefit derived from applying the criminal process.[342]

The Foundation's argument that such problems could be solved by prosecutorial discretion, was dismissed on the grounds that it was simply replacing one set of allegedly unclear considerations for another. As discussed later in relation to the English law surrounding sexual contact between children, prosecutorial discretion is essentially legislative 'buck-passing' of decision-making. As in the case of sexual contact between minors the legislative justification is that each case is different and must be responded to on an individual basis. However it is also used in instances where there is little moral

---

[340] ibid [177].   [341] ibid [40].   [342] ibid [62] (McLachlin CJ).

consensus within society and as such the result is dependent upon which prosecutor reviews the case.

7. 'Reasonable chastisement' in Australia

Corporal punishment in the home is regulated at State rather than Commonwealth level, and is lawful throughout Australia under law in each State allowing 'reasonable chastisement' or similar defences.[343] Reform to these laws has been minimal. New South Wales enacted an amendment to the law which prohibited the use of the defence in certain circumstances: if the force is applied to a child's head or neck, or 'the force is applied to any part of the body in such a way as to cause, or threaten to cause, harm to the child which lasts more than a short period'.[344]

8. 'Reasonable force' in New Zealand

The current law in New Zealand is just as nebulous as it is in England and Wales. The Crimes Act 1961 s 59 allows parents to use 'reasonable force' to chastise their children. Section 59 states that:

(1) Every parent of a child and subject to subsection (3) of this section,[345] every person in the place of parent of a child is justified in using force by way of correction towards the child, if the force used is reasonable in the circumstances.

(2) The reasonableness of the force used is a question of fact.

Campaigners against the New Zealand law have used very similar arguments to those used in other common law jurisdictions: that the law actually allows and condones serious violence against children; that it is unpredictable and very similar cases can produce very different results and that it is inconsistent with civil child protection law. In relation to the latter point in the unreported case of *Sharma v the Police* the High Court held that the existence of a protection order protecting a child from an abusive parent does not preclude that parent from raising a defence in s 59 to assaulting his or her child.[346]

At present it appears that their concerns may have been listened to in some quarters and a private member's bill which would repeal s 59, but offer no replacement, the

---

[343] Child Welfare Ordinance 1957 (Australian Capital Territory) s 124; Criminal Code Act (Northern Territory) s 27; Criminal Code Act 1899 (Queensland) s 280; Criminal Law Consolidation Act 1935 (South Australia) s 39 and subsequent amendments; Criminal Code Act 1924 (Tasmania) s 50; Criminal Code Act 1913 (Western Australia) s 257; Victoria under common law rule <http://www.endcorporalpunishment.org/pages/progress/reports/australia.html> (accessed 13 September 2005).

[344] Crimes Act 1900 (New South Wales) s 61AA(2) (as amended by the Crimes Amendment (Child Protection—Physical Maltreatment) Act 2001 (New South Wales)).

[345] '(3) Nothing in subsection (1) of this section justifies the use of force towards a child in contravention of section 139A Education Act 1989.'

[346] *Sharma v the Police* A 168/02 07/02/03 (NZ HC) Fisher J at J Hancock *Case Summaries: Parental Corporal Punishment of Children in New Zealand: Report for UN Committee on the Rights of the Child* (Action for the Child, Aotearoa 2003) 2.

Crimes (Abolition of Force as a Justification for Child Discipline) Amendment Bill passed its first reading and went to the Justice and Electoral Committee in September 2005,[347] but at the time of writing did not make it to the statute books. It is not yet recorded whether it ran out of time.

E. Sexual Offences Against Children

1. Sexual offences in English Law: the Sexual Offences Act 2003

The law governing sexual offences was completely reformed in 2003, by the Sexual Offences Act 2003. There were several ostensible reasons for reform. First there was a need for coherence and clarity in the law dealing with sexual offences. A Home Office review entitled *Setting the Boundaries*, on whose proposals the new law was eventually based, described the former law as 'a patchwork quilt of provisions ancient and modern that works because people make it do so, not because of its coherence and structure'.[348] Secondly reform was driven by a need to create a greater 'fit' between the nature of sexual assault in all its forms, as society now understood it to be, and the essential elements of the offence as it was written on the statute book. The resulting changes were intended to 'plug existing gaps and seek to protect society from rape and sexual assault'.[349] The new law was to be gender-neutral—the previous Sexual Offences Act 1956 had generally presumed victims of sexual assault to be female and perpetrators male, which was no longer a prevalent view of sexual offending and contravened the non-discrimination requirements of the ECHR.[350] *Setting the Boundaries* also proposed to change the law to reflect the 'looser structure of modern families', making laws in relation to families based on the social rather than biological relationship. The need to create a greater 'fit' between the nature of sexual assault and the elements of the offences would be completed by the establishing of new offences that proscribed activities that had only recently been exposed: 'the risks to children of sexual abuse, particularly from people they know, are now better understood than ever before'.[351] Unfortunately and rather surprisingly the Act is not retrospective and any offences committed before the Act came into force on 1 April 2004 should be charged under the old Sexual Offences Act 1956. This appears a particularly surprising decision in the context of child sexual abuse when it can take years for a complainant to develop enough courage to make a complaint.

In viewing the reform of the Sexual Offences Act as being a mechanism to protect 'the public, particularly children and the vulnerable',[352] the Government was linking

---

[347] <http://publications.clerk.parliament.govt.nz.clients.intergen.net.nz/BillsBeforeSelectCommittees.aspx> (accessed 13 September 2005).

[348] Home Office *Setting the Boundaries—Reforming the Law on Sexual Offences* (Home Office, London 2000) iii [0.2].

[349] Home Office *Protecting the Public: Strengthening Protection Against Sexual Offenders and Reforming the Law on Sexual Offences* (HM Stationery Office, London 2002) 9.

[350] Home Office *Setting the Boundaries* (n 348) iii [0.3] (terms of reference).

[351] ibid 33 [3.1.1].

[352] D Blunkett (Home Secretary) *Hansard* HC 19 November 2002 col 506.

the sexual offences with the registration of sexual offenders, which was also extended in the Sexual Offences Act 2003. As discussed above in section A.2 sex offender registration had been promoted and developed in the mid 1990s as a mechanism for monitoring those considered to be dangerous to society and to prevent further offending. It had become clear in the late 1990s that evidential reform had not led to a hoped increase in the number of convictions for sexual offences. Part of the rationale for the new Act was to improve the conviction rate for those perpetrating sexual offences.

The Sexual Offences Act 2003 created 24 offences relating specifically to sexual activity with a child and a further 11 which may be charged in relation to a sexual offence with a child. The acknowledged rationale for the creation of such a wide number of offences was the avoidance of loopholes, so that those accused of offences could not slip through them and to ensure that the offence reflected the nature of what the offender had done.[353] However in creating this very complicated statute the legislators ran the risk that the jurisprudence on parts of the Act would remain undeveloped and that prosecutors would not be routinely familiar with the range of offences and would only charge within a narrow band.

(a) Offences against children under 13

Sexual Offences Act 2003 ss 5–8 relate to offences against children under the age of 13. The first of these, rape of a child under 13, is committed if a person 'intentionally penetrates the vagina, anus or mouth of another person with his penis' and the other person is under 13.[354] There is then a further offence of 'assault of a child under 13 by penetration' which is committed if a person intentionally penetrates the vagina or anus of another person with a part of his body or anything else', where 'the penetration is sexual' and 'the other person is under 13'.[355] The merit of these offences is that they create a crime of statutory rape. Consent has been the great battleground in sexual offences in the past. The requirement on the prosecution to prove an absence of consent to sexual activity has often meant that the complainant can feel on trial. This is particularly troubling in cases concerning children and has the potential to undermine the purposes of the Act—as those who care about the child may very well attempt to shield her from potentially combative and confusing questioning on whether the child understood what was happening and agreed to it.

Under the Sexual Offences Act 1956 there was no fixed age below which a child could be considered incapable of forming a valid consent. Instead the issue was decided on a case-by-case basis. As Scarman LJ stated in *R v Lang*[356] 'the critical question is . . . whether she understood her situation and was capable of making up her mind'. The prosecution had to demonstrate in cases where the girl is under 16 that her 'understanding and knowledge were such that *she was not in a position to decide whether to consent or resist*'. Temkin criticized this formulation for its lack of clarity and for its

---

[353] Home Office *Children and Families Safer from Sexual Crime* (n 13) 2.
[354] Sexual Offences Act 2003 (England) s 5(1).　　　[355] Sexual Offences Act 2003 (England) s 6.
[356] *R v Lang* (1975) 62 Cr App R 50 (CA).

misunderstanding of the nature of children's comprehension, arguing that many children understand what the physical act of sex is without understanding its emotional consequences.[357] The Home Office Sexual Offences Review[358] proposed instead that there should be a cut-off point below which children should be considered incapable in law of consenting to sexual acts and there could be no question about a child's consent during the trial:

Very young children will not know or understand sufficiently to give free and informed agreement to sex. If they do seem to 'agree', this may be because of persuasion, inducement or ignorance of what it meant. Indeed for small children the imbalance of power with an adult or older child is so strong that they will do as they are told—which can then be interpreted (and presented in court) as 'consent'. For these young children there should be no question of true consent—with the meaning of free agreement—being possible. There is neither the knowledge nor understanding of consequences which we suggest as the test for capacity to consent . . . [The Review considered the possibility of developing a test for capacity to consent but concluded that while it would be possible to devise.] . . . this would lead to uncertainty in the operation of the law and the capacity of each child would need to be tested in court. Having special provision for younger children would remove arguments about capacity to consent and the test of the victim's/complainant's capacity in court. We thought that would provide improved protection, especially in recognising the particular needs of pre-pubertal victims.[359]

There is no requirement to prove lack of consent in the new offences of statutory rape and assault by penetration which should be charged in cases concerning children under the age of 13. In these cases the offences which relate to adult rape (Sexual Offences Act 2003 s 1) and assault by penetration (Sexual Offences Act 2003 s 2) should not be charged as this undermines the purpose of the creation of the offences in ss 5 and 6. However it does appear that the sections which require consent are being charged when they should not be. For example in *R v H*[360] a 14-year-old boy was convicted of rape under Sexual Offences Act 2003 s 1 when he forced at knife point a little boy of 6, to suck his penis, on a number of occasions. While the behaviour clearly falls within the provision of s 1[361] it should have been charged under s 5 which does not require the prosecution to prove that the child did not consent. It is difficult to know how widespread this charging practice, is as this observation is based on reported cases rather than an empirical study. However it is important to observe that this use of s 1 rather than s 5 is contrary to one of the explicit aims of the legislation.

Two further offences have been created which are aimed specifically at sexual activity in relation to a child under the age of 13: sexual assault of a child under 13 and a

---

[357] J Temkin *Literature Review into Rape and Sexual Assault* in Home Office *Setting the Boundaries* (n 348) 94.   [358] Home Office *Setting the Boundaries* (n 348).
[359] ibid [3.5.9].   [360] *R v H* [2006] EWCA Crim 853.
[361] Sexual Offences Act 2003 (England) s 1
    'Rape
    (1) A person (A) commits an offence if—
        (a) he intentionally penetrates the vagina, anus or mouth of another person (B) with his penis,
        (b) B does not consent to the penetration, and
        (c) A does not reasonably believe that B consents.'

further offence of 'causing or inciting a child under 13 to engage in sexual activity'. A sexual assault of a child under the age of 13 would be committed when a person 'intentionally touches another person, the touching is sexual, and the other person is under 13'.[362] 'Touching' has been defined in Sexual Offences Act 2003:

Section 79. Part 1: general interpretation . . . (8) Touching includes touching—(a) with any part of the body, (b) with anything else, (c) through anything, and in particular includes touching amounting to penetration.

This definition therefore includes the touching of clothing, even in circumstances where the body is not touched through the clothing.[363]

The previous Sexual Offences Act 1956 had used the term 'indecent' to divide those assaults which did or did not have a sexual connotation. The Home Office Sexual Offences Review considered the term 'indecent' as both unnecessarily broad and unclear, recommending its replacement with the term 'sexual'. This is defined in Sexual Offences Act 2003 s 78 as an objective test for the jury if a reasonable person would consider that:

(a) whatever its circumstances or any person's purpose in relation to it, it is because of its nature sexual, or
(b) because of its nature it may be sexual and because of its circumstances or the purpose of any person in relation to it (or both) it is sexual.[364]

This definition borrows much from the previous definition of the term 'indecent' as outlined by the House of Lords in *Court*.[365] In *Court* the House of Lords identified three types of act which could potentially be indecent:

- An assault that is inherently indecent or rendered indecent by its accompanying circumstances, for example the removal of a person's clothing against their will. In this case the *mens rea* of the defendant was irrelevant.

- An assault that is incapable of being considered indecent by an ordinary observer, for example the removal of a shoe, in which case the intention of the defendant was also irrelevant as the act was not inherently indecent.[366]

- An assault that an ordinary observer could consider indecent, for example the spanking of a complainant.[367]

In this final category the intention of the defendant could be important in determining whether or not the act was in fact indecent. The revised definition in Sexual Offences Act 2003 s 78 excludes the second type of act from its definition of the offence, but retains the two other categories of behaviour outlined in *Court*, substituting the requirement of indecency with a requirement that the behaviour be 'sexual'.

---

[362] Sexual Offences Act 2003 (England).

[363] 'We have no doubt that it was not Parliament's intention by the use of that language to make it impossible to regard as a sexual assault touching which took place by touching what the victim was wearing at the time': *R v H (Karl Anthony)* [2005] 2 All ER 859 (CA Crim) [26] (Lord Woolf CJ).

[364] Sexual Offences Act 2003 (England) s 78.   [365] *R v Court* [1989] AC 28 (HL).

[366] *R v George* [1956] Crim LR 52 (Assizes).   [367] *Court* (n 365).

As Bainham and Brookes-Gordon have argued 'sexual' is not simply an updated word for 'indecent'. The use of 'indecent' is a pejorative term indicative not only of legal, but of moral wrong doing, whereas 'sexual' is not. This could lead to a jury accepting conduct as 'sexual' which they would not have accepted as indecent.[368]

Temkin and Ashworth, in their analysis of the Sexual Offences Act 2003 before it came into force, suggested that the majority of cases would fall into the first category of sexual assaults, those which, whatever their nature or circumstances, would be regarded as 'sexual' (Sexual Offences Act 2003 s 78a), rather than those acts which are dependent on circumstances or purpose to be defined as sexual (Sexual Offences Act 2003 s 78b).[369] However the Court of Appeal has described their prediction as 'probably optimistic' in the light of the emerging caselaw;[370] and in *R v H (Karl Anthony)*[371] it set out further guidance on the interpretation of 'sexual' in the context of s 78b. In this case the adult complainant had been approached by the appellant who had asked her 'Do you fancy a shag?', before grabbing her tracksuit bottoms in the area of her right hand pocket and attempting to place his hand over her mouth. She had then managed to break free before he had touched her mouth and she had escaped. The appellant was convicted of sexual assault. On appeal he argued that, *inter alia*, the judge was in error in declining to stop the case, on the basis that there was no evidence of a sexual assault that could properly be left to the jury. The Court of Appeal found that the judge had been in error in considering the criteria in s 78b as a whole and as one question rather than as two. Instead the Court suggested that the model direction to the jury should be:

First, would they, as 12 reasonable people (as the section requires), consider that because of its nature the touching that took place in the particular case before them could be sexual? If the answer to that question was 'No', the jury would find the defendant not guilty. If 'Yes', they would have to go on to ask themselves (again as 12 reasonable people) whether in view of the circumstances and/or the purpose of any person in relation to the touching (or both), the touching was in fact sexual. If they were satisfied that it was, then they would find the defendant guilty. If they were not satisfied, they would find the defendant not guilty.[372]

Ormerod, in his commentary on this case rightly suggests that there are dangers in leaving the determination of whether an assault is 'sexual' to the jury.[373] First it is not conducive to the development of consistent jurisprudence in an area of law which so badly needs it. Secondly it will be very difficult for a jury to keep the two questions under s 78(b) separate. The judge at first instance in this case could not. In fact such a conflation may be regarded as inevitable as nearly any act can potentially be 'sexual', and it must be the second question which is determinative.

---

[368] A Bainham and B Brookes-Gordon 'Reforming the Law on Sexual Offences' in B Brookes-Gordon, L Gelsthorpe, M Johnson and A Bainham (eds) *Sexuality Repositioned: Diversity and the Law* (Hart Publishing, Oxford 2004).

[369] J Temkin and A Ashworth 'The Sexual Offences Act 2003: (1) Rape, Sexual Assaults and the Problems of Consent' [2004] Crim LR 328, 331.

[370] *R v H (Karl Anthony)* (n 363) [4] (Lord Woolf CJ).   [371] ibid.

[372] ibid [13] (Lord Woolf CJ).

[373] D Ormerod 'Sexual Assault: Whether Touching of Complainant's Clothing Without Bringing Pressure Against Complainant's Body "Touching" for Purposes Of Sexual Assault' [2005] Crim LR 735.

Finally a person may be charged under Sexual Offences Act 2003 s 8 with 'causing or inciting a child under 13 to engage in sexual activity' if he intentionally causes or incites another person (B) to engage in an activity, the activity is sexual, and B is under 13. The term 'sexual activity' is further limited in relation to this offence in Sexual Offences Act 2003 s 8(2) to mean:

(a) penetration of B's anus or vagina,
(b) penetration of B's mouth with a person's penis,
(c) penetration of a person's anus or vagina with a part of B's body or by B with anything else, or
(d) penetration of a person's mouth with B's penis.

The aim of this offence was to punish behaviour in which a child is forced into sexual behaviour as part of a process of degradation and repression. An example of this would be a child being forced or encouraged to have sex with his mother or a sibling by his father.[374] Under the old law this could have been charged as an indecent assault, which required evidence that an assault or battery had been committed. In *Sergeant,* a case under the old law, the defendant was convicted of indecent assault after he threatened a young man with a knife and forced him to masturbate into a condom.[375] Section 8 creates a second offence, that of intentionally inciting a person under 13 to engage in sexual activity. Thus the law can also be used to convict those who encourage a child to engage in sexual activity, but the child does not, for whatever reason go through with it. In *R v Walker*[376] a man who rang a telephone box situated near a group of children and who asked the 11-year-old girl who answered it to 'show her fanny' was successfully prosecuted under Sexual Offences Act 2003 s 8. The Court of Appeal held that the essence of the offence of incitement was the intentional or deliberate encouragement of a person under 13 to engage in such activity. Whilst the offence requires that the defendant know what he was doing he does not have to incite sexual activity, and the prosecution did not have to prove that the defendant intended that the incited activity should take place.

The intention in all these offences was to create crimes of statutory rape and sexual activity for which the consent of the child was immaterial. As Spencer has argued the names of the offences are unhelpful in this regard as the terms rape and assault have always been used in the criminal law to denote actions which the victim does not consent to. In criminal law consent would usually be a defence to both a rape (in relation to both adults and children) and an assault,[377] rendering both these activities lawful. It was intended by these provisions to create crimes of strict liability, so that the belief or supposition by a defendant that a child was in fact over the age of 13

---

[374] Home Office *Protecting the Public* (n 349) 44 [3.64].
[375] *R v Sergeant* [1997] Crim LR 50 (CA Crim).   [376] *R v Walker* [2006] All ER 08 (CA Crim).
[377] Consent to an assault would not always be a defence in relation to children. It would probably be a defence if the child was engaged in 'horseplay' or 'manly pursuits': *R v Brown* [1994] 1 AC 212 (HL). A child may give consent to some other assaults, depending upon their age and understanding, for example medical procedures. Although linked together in many people's minds, the law relating to reasonable chastisement has no connection with consent, as the child does not consent to the 'chastisement'.

could not be raised by the defence. To this end the drafters of the Bill did not include any specific requirement in relation to a defendant's *mens rea* and did not include any defences. In doing so they ran the risk that a requirement for *mens rea* would be read into the offence by the judiciary.[378] This was surprising because during the period in which the Sexual Offences Act 2003 was being drafted there were two cases under the old law which had concluded that the strict liability element of laws prohibiting sexual activity with minors could not be sustained. In *B v DPP*[379] a boy was charged with an offence under the previous law of inciting a child under the age of 14 to commit an act of gross indecency.[380] In his defence he argued that he had believed the victim to be over the age of 14. The House of Lords held that the Indecency with Children Act 1960 s 1(1), neither specifically excluded the general requirement of *mens rea* nor did so by implication. Furthermore they held that belief in the child's age was a specific element of the offence and that the necessary mental element regarding the age ingredient was an absence of a genuine belief by the accused that the victim was 14 years of age or above. This was a matter for the prosecution to prove to the satisfaction of the jury. Similarly in *R v K* the House of Lords interpreted Sexual Offences Act 1956 s 14(2) which related to indecent assault, to which no child under the age of 16 could give consent in law,[381] to require the prosecution to prove an absence of a genuine belief on the part of the defendant as to the age of the victim. However despite these two very important judgments the Sexual Offences Act 2003 was silent on the defendant's state of mind. It may be argued that strict liability on the question of the child's age is to be inferred from the silence in these sections when compared to the offences created in relation to child victims between the ages of 13 and 18 which require the prosecution to prove that the defendant does not reasonably believe that the child is over the stipulated age. Spencer argued when the Act came into force that in the light of the very serious nature of the offences and the severe penalties available and the construction of the offences in relation to older victims, the courts might be unwilling to impose an offence of strict liability.[382] His argument was considered by the Court of Appeal in *G v R*.[383]

Whilst the Court of Appeal agreed that Sexual Offences Act 2003 s 5 could be interpreted to require *mens rea* the Court did not agree with the argument made by counsel for the appellant that Sexual Offences Act 2003 s 5 was inconsistent with Article 6(2) (the right to a fair trial) and Article 8 (the right to family life) and should be 'read down' to require the *mens rea* of the defendant to be considered in order to achieve compatibility. Instead the Court of Appeal relied on jurisprudence from the ECtHR, particularly the case of *Salabiaku v France*[384] that Article 6(2) does not preclude the creation of strict liability offences. In fact the court went as far as to argue that Article 6(2) refers to the procedural elements of a trial, rather than

---

[378] J Spencer 'The Sexual Offences Act: The Child and Family Offences' [2004] Crim LR 347, 353.
[379] [2000] 2 AC 428 (HL).   [380] Indecency with Children Act 1960 (England) s 1(1).
[381] [2002] 1 AC 462 (HL).   [382] Spencer (n 378), 353.   [383] *G v R* (n 56).
[384] *Salabiaku v France* [1998] 13 EHRR 379.

the substantive elements of the offence on which a person is tried and thus cannot preclude the imposition of strict liability in relation to an offence.[385] This reflects a cautious approach by the Court of Appeal to a law which in its previous incarnation under the Sexual Offences Act 1956 had been held to have the potential to create a reverse burden of proof and by doing so limit a defendant's opportunities for a fair trial. However it reflects the fact that Parliament had the opportunity to consider the judgments in *B v DPP* and *R v K* in formulating the Sexual Offences Act 2003 and it was obviously the intention of Parliament to create a strict liability offence. However as children under 13 are obviously very young the implication is that anyone who did have sexual contact with them did have a criminal intent in some form and on some level knew that they were engaging in sexual activity with a child. The creation of a strict liability offence is an attempt to prevent defendants from raising spurious arguments that they were unaware of the child's age and it is consistent with the underlying ethos of the Act that those engaging in sexual activity should be careful to ensure that the other person truly consented.

(b) Sexual offences against children under the age of 16

Sexual Offences Act 2003 ss 9–15 contain offences relating to children under the age of 16. In Sexual Offences Act 2003 s 9 a person aged 18 or over (A) commits an offence if (a) he intentionally touches another person (B), and (b) the touching is sexual. The offence is further limited to sexual touching, if the touching involved 'penetration of B's anus or vagina with a part of A's body or anything else', 'penetration of B's mouth with A's penis', 'penetration of A's anus or vagina with a part of B's body', 'penetration of A's mouth with B's penis'.

Section 10 creates a crime of causing or inciting a child to engage in sexual activity; this is exactly the same offence as Sexual Offences Act 2003 s 8, differing only in the age limit for the offence which is 16, rather than 13 under s 8. These offences can be charged when the child has ostensibly agreed to the activity. Were it to be that the sexual activity was non-consensual it could also be charged as rape,[386] assault by penetration,[387] and sexual assault.[388] These offences are all offences proved by evidence of lack of consent by the victim and may be charged when the victim is 13 or over and does not consent to the activity.

Sexual Offences Act 2003 ss 11 and 12 created offences of engaging in sexual activity in the presence of a child and causing a child to watch a sexual act respectively. Section 11 aims to punish a person (A)[389] who intentionally engages in a sexual activity, and for the purpose of obtaining sexual gratification, he engages in it—

(i) when another person (B) is present or is in a place from which A can be observed, and
(ii) knowing or believing that B is aware, or intending that B should be aware, that he is engaging in it[.]

---

[385] *G v R* (n 56) [37]–[42].   [386] Sexual Offences Act 2003 (England) s 1.   [387] ibid s 2.
[388] ibid s 3.   [389] Over the age of 18.

Section 12 aims to punish a person who causes a child to watch a third person engaging in an activity, or to look at an image of any person engaging in a sexual activity, for the purposes of the person's own sexual gratification. However the decision in *Abdullahi*[390] could be important in closing a potential loophole in the law. Before *Abdullahi* commentators had speculated that it could be difficult to charge someone who showed a child sexualized images as part of a process of 'grooming' (see below) that child for sexual contact with the adult in the future, but did not feel sexual gratification at the time and had not gone as far as to arrange the commission of the offence. Gillespie[391] and Ost[392] have both argued that s 12 implies that the sexual gratification must be immediate when showing the child such an image. However the Court of Appeal in *Abdullahi*[393] held that the elements of the offence do not have to apply contemporaneously. Thus in *Abdullahi* the Court of Appeal held that there was nothing in s 12 which required that the sexual gratification had to be immediate, or could not extend to a longer plan in obtaining further gratification in the event of the obtaining a sexual act with the child. It remained a matter for the jury to decide whether the facts of the case satisfied the section and the offence had been made out. If the jury is satisfied that the defendant did show the child sexualized images in order to achieve sexual gratification, it does not, it appears, matter that the sexual gratification occurred at a later time.

The court rejected an argument made by the defence that such an interpretation leads to an overlap between s 12 and s 14 of the Sexual Offences Act 2003. Section 14, as will be discussed below, relates to 'arranging or facilitating the commission of a child sexual offence'. The court held that s 12 could be charged in cases such as these where the child was shown pornographic images to 'get him in the mood'. The drafters of the Sexual Offences Act 2003 by choosing to create such a multitude of slightly different offences always ran the risk of overlap and confusion between offences. It may very well be that some offences are routinely charged and some rarely. This is what happened under the previous Sexual Offences Act 1956. There are problems in this approach as it means that prosecutors become unfamiliar with offences and do not charge defendants with them in circumstances where the offence is best suited to the circumstances.

These offences may apply to behaviour towards a child under the age of 16. They were originally conceived as offences where the child victim was aged between 13 and 16. However initially they were poorly drafted . The original draft stated that the defendant might not be convicted of an offence relating to a child victim under the age of 16 if he could be convicted of an offence in relation to a child victim under the age of 13. This gave a defendant prosecuted for one of the under-16 offences, a potential defence of proving that the child was under the age of 13.[394] This enormous loophole was only rectified at the last moment by the House of Lords and the offences

---

[390] *R v Abdullahi* [2006] All ER (D) 334 (CA).
[391] A Gillespie 'Indecent Images, Grooming and the Law' [2006] Crim LR 412.
[392] S Ost 'Getting to Grips with Sexual Grooming? The New Offence under the Sexual Offences Act 2003' (2004) 26 JSWFL 147.   [393] *Abdullahi* (n 390).
[394] Spencer (n 378), 353.

were redrafted so that they overlap with the offences in relation to a child under the age of 13. The offences in ss 9–12 may all be committed negligently when a child is 'under the age of 16 and a defendant does not reasonably believe that B is 16 or over' or with strict liability if B is under 13. This reform has the potential to undermine the aim of the Home Office to create strict liability offences in relation to children under the age of 13. There are now virtually identical crimes in ss 5–6 and s 9. However s 9 may clearly be a strict liability offence in relation to the child's age when the child is under the age of 13. Section 9 carries a penalty of up to 14 years' imprisonment. In contrast ss 5 and 6 carry up to life imprisonment.

The defendant must be 18 years or over to be charged under ss 9–12; however s 13 extends liability to a child aged between 10 and 18 who 'does anything which would be an offence under any of sections 9 to 12 if he were aged 18'. An offence committed by this age group is triable either way and is subject on summary conviction to imprisonment for a term not exceeding six months or a fine; or on conviction on indictment, to imprisonment for a term not exceeding five years. This provision has been extensively criticized for criminalizing all sexual activity between minors. The Government maintained its stance that there was no other mechanism for ensuring that young people were protected from coercive sexual activity by their peers. During the debates on the Sexual Offences Bill 2003, the Home Secretary offered a magnum of champagne to the Member of Parliament who could find a form of words which would solve the problem. This was rather disingenous. In fact many countries have tried to reflect consensual relationships between children by lowering the age of consent for these relationships.[395] The Canadian Criminal Code s 150 sets the age of consent at 14 and then creates a series of exceptions where the accused is between 12 and 16, is less than 2 years older than the complainant, and where there is no position of trust. This provision is discussed in more detail below in relation to the Canadian offences. The English Government was not prepared to lower the age of consent on any basis and has in fact raised the age of consent to 18 for offences relating to abuse of trust and family relationships. Instead the Government proposed guidelines to prosecutors telling them not to prosecute consensual sexual relationships. This was an unfortunate solution and has the potential to contribute to a 'culture of fear and confusion' for young people about sexual activity.[396] While it is clear that most sexual offenders start offending before their 18th birthday, it is wrong to create a law that potentially criminalizes everyone in the hope of also marking out the dangerous. The problem is then that the criminal law acts in exactly the opposite way to what was intended, and those who have coerced and abused children in sexual relationships while they were under the age of 18 benefit from an assumption that they have been convicted for having a relationship that was in fact consensual.

The possible benefit of the debate surrounding the new law is that it has contributed to the development of guidelines on prosecution. Guidelines do make the

---

[395] Home Office *Setting the Boundaries* (n 348) 41 [3.5.4].

[396] D Jack (Head of Policy, Brook Advisory Service) *Sexual Offences Bill will create Culture of Fear and Confusion* (Brook Advisory Service Press Release 17 September 2003).

process of determining which sexual relationships will be investigated and prosecuted more apparent and perhaps more rigorous. *Working Together to Safeguard Children* now contains a checklist of considerations in cases where under-age sexual activity is taking place to help investigators to determine whether there should be a strategy discussion to include the level of maturity and understanding of the child, the child's background, and whether the misuse of substances places a child at risk of harm so that he cannot make informed choices about any activity.[397] There are also some examples of local inter-agency procedures on the investigation and prosecution of cases concerning under-age sexual activity.[398] However this means that policy does vary from area to area and there is a potential for inconsistency. It would have been more appropriate to lower the age of consent and prosecute relationships where there was a disparity in age or an abuse of trust or other evidence of a lack of true consent to sexual activity, as the Canadian legislation has done.

(c) Meeting a child following sexual grooming

The final two offences which may be described as general sexual offences relating to children are contained in Sexual Offences Act 2003 ss 14 and 15. Section 14 creates an offence of 'arranging or facilitating the commission of a child sexual offence' and s 15 meeting with a child with the intention of committing a sexual offence, having previously communicated with the child. Both offences are intended to criminalize behaviour which would not otherwise be considered in criminal law to be even an attempted offence because the offender was merely preparing for the commission of an offence and had not embarked upon the crime itself.

The offence of meeting a child following sexual grooming in s 15 was created in response to some high-profile cases in which children were sexually assaulted when they arranged to meet men that they had corresponded with on the internet and following the recommendations of a Government taskforce on child protection on the internet.[399] The White Paper *Protecting the Public* which preceded the Act described the 'mischief' which the offence was to address in these terms:

The Internet has opened up new possibilities for children both for learning and leisure and to chat electronically with others. It has revolutionised how we communicate. We need though to ensure that we tackle those who want to use it to take advantage of the innocence of children. Grooming children for sexual abuse is not new. Sex offenders have always found ways of gaining the trust and confidence of children and some have seen the possibilities of misusing the Internet to befriend children for their own purposes. There have been a number of cases in which sex offenders have deceived children in chatrooms into believing that they are also children or teenagers and share similar interests and have then arranged meetings with them. To tackle

---

[397] Department of Health *Working Together to Safeguard Children* (2006) [5.27]   [398] ibid.
[399] P Goggins MP, Sexual Offences Bill House of Commons Standing Committee B 16th September 2003 Col 196.

grooming both on and off-line, we will be introducing a new offence of sexual grooming with a maximum penalty of five years imprisonment.[400]

The psychological term 'grooming' has crept into discussions about sexual offending against children. Essentially it denotes a process by which someone wishing to have sexual contact with a child befriends that child and gains their trust over a period of time. It was created as a mechanism to understand a particular process in psychological terms, although psychologists themselves disagree about the precise definition of the term. Leberg has identified three types of 'grooming' behaviour:

1. *physical*—innocent normal and appropriate behaviours, such as wrestling, tickling and cuddling, that sooner or later become more sexualized;

2. *psychological*—use of verbal statements, or other communication, that the perpetrator uses to reduce the child's resistance and decrease the likelihood that he or she will reveal the molestation;

3. *social environment*—manipulating others to foster situations where molestation can take place or to provide allies should allegations be made.[401]

However this process is very difficult to criminalize. It is only in retrospect once an offence is committed that this process becomes important; before that no harm might have been committed at all. The criminal law purpose is to punish defined harm or an attempt to commit harm when the attempt in itself has become more than just a hope in the mind of the offender. Usually grooming would only be important in denoting the level of *mens rea* which the defendant had in committing the offence.[402]

Although labelled as an offence to protect children from being 'groomed', and considered during the passage of the Bill to be such,[403] the offence actually relates to a meeting with a child with the intention of committing a sexual offence. The offence itself states:

(1) A person aged 18 or over (A) commits an offence if—
    (a) having met or communicated[404] with another person (B) on at least two earlier occasions, he—
        (i) intentionally meets B, or
        (ii) travels with the intention of meeting B in any part of the world,

---

[400] Home Office *Protecting the Public* (n 349) [54].

[401] E Leberg *Understanding Child Molesters: Taking charge* (Sage Publications, Thousand Oaks CA 1997); L McFarlane and P Bocji 'Cyberstalking: Defining the Invasion of Cyberspace' (2003) 72 Forensic Update 18, 20.   [402] We are grateful to Leanne Smith, University of Cardiff for this point.

[403] Sexual Offences Bill, House of Commons Standing Committee B 16th September 2003 Col 196.

[404] Sexual Offences Act 2003 (England) s 15(2) 'In subsection (1)—
    (a) the reference to A having met or communicated with B is a reference to A having met B in any part of the world or having communicated with B by any means from, to or in any part of the world[.]'

(b) at the time, he intends to do anything to or in respect of B, during or after the meeting and in any part of the world, which if done will involve the commission by A of a relevant offence,[405]

(c) B is under 16, and

(d) A does not reasonably believe that B is 16 or over.

The difficulties which this offence throws up encapsulate many of the problems with an Act which was written at a time of high tension and fear of sexual offending against children. It reflects the construction of sexual offenders against children as being predatory strangers searching the world for vulnerable children, who because they cannot be punished for their thoughts, society is powerless to stop. Thus the Act tries to criminalize behaviour which has not resulted in injury but which might. In this case it criminalizes behaviour which usually could not in law constitute an attempt to commit a crime. The human rights pressure group Liberty in its response to the Sexual Offences Bill argued that the offence aims to prosecute people 'not for anything they've done but for things that someone thinks that they might do— because someone is second-guessing their thoughts.'[406] It remains very difficult to see how intention on the part of a defendant to this offence would be proved: in some cases, a jury may be faced with a problem of inferring intent from seemingly innocuous communication with a child. Liberty suggested an amendment to the Act to require that the communication be sexual in nature, or involve a deception of the child concerned. However this limitation was rejected in committee.[407] Furthermore there does remain the potential for this offence to be used as a tool to repress and criminalize entirely innocent friendships between children and adults. At the committee stage of the Sexual Offences Bill Sandra Gidley MP posited a scenario in which a lonely old gentleman chats to children on their way to school and in an atmosphere of suspicion someone brings a complaint against him. This would be entirely possible under s 15 and it would be for the jury to interpret his intention. The dangers inherent in this section may be limited if the offence is charged in part because of other information known about the defendant, rather than an isolated event. In this case it may be a useful addition to the offences which the CPS have hitherto been able to charge. In *Tomlinson*[408] the appellant was convicted after he had met a nine-year-old girl on three occasions over a nine-week period. On each occasion she was with other young children. On the first occasion he had spoken to her while he was mending his car in the street and had shown her how to use a screwdriver. On the next occasion he had spoken to her while he was in his car and had given her some puzzles and riddles to work out.

---

[405] Sexual Offences Act 2003 (England) s 15(2) (b): 'relevant offence' means—

    (i) an offence under this Part,

    (ii) an offence within any of paragraphs 61 to 92 of Schedule 3, or

    (iii) anything done outside England and Wales and Northern Ireland which is not an offence within sub-paragraph (i) or (ii) but would be an offence within sub-paragraph (i) if done in England and Wales.

[406] Liberty, *Sexual Offences Bill: Liberty Response* (Press Release 29th January 2003).

[407] Sexual Offences Bill, House of Commons Standing Committee B 16th September 2003 Col 195.

[408] *R v Tomlinson* [2005] EWCA Crim 2681.

On the final occasion he had asked the girl to sit in the passenger seat of the car, asked her to be his 'little girlfriend' and had dropped two sweets down the front of her top. The girl was upset by this incident and when she got out of the car asked a neighbour to write down the number plate of the car. The appellant was prosecuted under s 15, after a criminal records check revealed a long list of serious sexual offences against children.

Section 14 creates a further criminal offence for behaviour which would usually under criminal law be deemed preparatory to the commission of an offence and not criminal in itself. Under s 14 a person commits an offence if:

(a) he intentionally arranges or facilitates something that he intends to do, intends another person to do, or believes that another person will do, in any part of the world, and

(b) doing it will involve the commission of an offence under any of sections 9 to 13.[409]

The provision contains various exemptions for people who act to protect the child from sexually transmitted infection, protecting the physical safety of the child, preventing the child from becoming pregnant, or promoting the child's emotional well-being by the giving of advice, not for the purpose of obtaining sexual gratification or for the purpose of causing or encouraging the activity constituting the offence within subsection (1)(b) or the child's participation in it.

(d) Abuse of trust

The Sexual Offences Act 2003 also created four offences in relation to sexual activity by people who are in a position of trust. The behaviour which they punish is the same as is covered in the offences under ss 9–12. Thus s 16 concerns sexual activity with a child when in a position of trust, s 17 concerns causing or inciting a child to engage in sexual activity when in a position of trust, s 18 concerns sexual activity in the presence of a child when in a position of trust, and s 19 concerns causing a child to watch a sexual act when in a position of trust. The age limit was raised for the purposes of these sections to 18, rather than 16 as in the offences ss 9–12. A position of trust is defined in s 21 and s 22 to include those looking after children 'detained in an institution by virtue of a court order or under an enactment', 'accommodated or cared for in an institution' including a hospital or care home, in an educational institution, or if a person is appointed a child's guardian, or is engaged in the provision of services for a 'looked after child', or regularly has unsupervised contact with an 'accommodated child', or is a personal adviser to a child subject to a care, supervision, or education supervision order, or in any way supervises or assists a child following their detention in prison. The sections are enormously detailed and specific and the categories above represent the main categories of the abuse of trust provisions. It is a defence to prove that the relationship predated the position of trust, provided that the sexual activity did not take place when the child was under the age of 16,[410] or that the defendant and a victim over the age of 16 were validly married at the time.[411]

---

[409] Sexual Offences Act 2003 (England) s 14(3).   [410] ibid s 24.   [411] ibid s 23.

It is to be questioned whether these offences needed to exist at all. They represent a further example of the 'overkill' with which sexual offending against children was dealt with in the Act. In the light of the comparative work undertaken by the Home Office Sexual Offences Review team to examine the sexual offences in other jurisdictions, it is surprising that the team did not appear to consider the legislative framework adopted by Canada, which is discussed below. Here rather than creating further offences, the Canadian Criminal Code establishes a few offences for which there are aggravating factors. In the light of the replication in these offences and the problems under the previous Sexual Offences Act 1956, in which only a few offences were ever used in relation to children, it seems surprising that reformers decided to create four new separate offences to deal with abuse of positions of trust, rather than to make abuse of trust an aggravating factor to the basic offence. It is also worth noting that New Zealand and parts of Australia have also adopted a similar framework to Canada in the creation of aggravating factors in relation to core offences, rather than a raft of very similar offences which each encompass an aggravating factor.

(e) Familial sexual offences

The Sexual Offences Act 2003 created two further offences specifically penalizing sexual behaviour towards children by family members. Section 25 relates to sexual activity with a child family member and s 26 to inciting a child family member to engage in sexual activity. Again the offences are very similar to those discussed above. The differences lie in the age limit for these offences which is 18, rather than 16 as in ss 9–12 and in the activity proscribed in s 26, which is more limited than in ss 10 and 17 as it only concerns sexual activity incited by the defendant on himself and not in relation to third parties. Unlike the other offences above the defendant does not have to be 18 or over to commit the offence; rather the mode of trial sentencing differs depending upon the age of the defendant and the nature of the offence; these differences are set out in a series of provisions which Spencer has kindly called 'convoluted'.[412] A defendant over the age of 18 at the time of the offence is liable to up to 14 years' imprisonment. If he has committed a crime of penetration his offence is indictable only. However if he has committed another offence this is triable either way and he may be sentenced to up to 14 years on indictment, or 6 months on summary trial. However a defendant who was under 18 at the time of the offence may be tried either way and sentenced to up to five years on indictment or six months on summary trial.

These offences were a replacement and restructuring of the crime of incest. Under the previous Sexual Offences Act 1956 s 10 it was 'an offence for a man to have sexual intercourse with a woman whom he knows to be his grand-daughter, daughter, sister or mother'. This was rightly criticized for ignoring the reality of sexual exploitation within families.[413] The law was limited to male perpetrators and female victims, and then only to blood relatives and only punished sexual intercourse rather than all sexual

---

[412] Spencer (n 378) 355.
[413] A Ashworth *Principles of Criminal Law* (2nd edn OUP, Oxford 1995) 353; J Temkin *Rape and the Legal Process* (Sweet & Maxwell, London 1987) 29; Card 'Sexual Relations with Minors' [1975] Crim LR 370; V Bailey and S McCabe 'Reforming the Law of Incest' [1979] Crim LR 749, 761.

behaviour.[414] The new law attempts to expand the range of people considered to be family members for the purpose of this provision and thus to reflect more closely the current nature of family life. Thus the Act describes family in terms of three groups,[415] those who are deemed in the act to be a family member irrespective of whether the child has lived with them.[416] The second group contains those who live or have lived in the same household as the child and are or have been involved in caring for the child, including step-family members (whether or not these have been established by marriage), those who share a common foster-parent or cousins. The third group contains anyone who lives with the victim in the same household and has been involved in caring for them.

These offences should be at the heart of the Act as it relates to children. The majority of sexual offending against children takes place in the child's home or is committed by someone with whom the child has a particular relationship because they are part of the child's family. The destruction of the trust that a child has in the ones closest to them should undoubtedly be recognized as one of the most serious aggravating factors in a sexual offence against a child. What is interesting therefore is that offences relating to incidents in which strangers to the child gain their trust take such a prominent part of the Act. This is not simply in the number of offences which essentially relate to 'stranger assaults', but in the ordering of the Act in which offences relating to planning sexual assaults against children and abuse of trust are dealt with in great detail before the provisions relating to the child's family.

2. Sexual offences in the United States

Legislation in the United States has been characterized by highly punitive legislative regimes in relation to sexual offending against children. The United States was also the first jurisdiction to develop the registration of sexual offenders on the basis of their criminal record. Unlike the United Kingdom, the register is usually available to the public in the United States.[417] There have been further developments to mark out those who sexually assault children and some States require offenders not only to register but to mark themselves out obviously to the community as a sex offender by the wearing of t-shirts or the placing of signs outside their homes.[418] The sexual offender legislation, perhaps even more than in the United Kingdom operates on the premise that sexual offenders are strangers to the child and that they are highly mobile and thus strangers to the community.

Whilst it is not possible to discuss the range of sexual offences which are in existence across the States, all the States do have a common element in their legislation, a

---

[414] J Temkin 'Do We Need the Crime of Incest?' (1991) *Current Legal Problems* 185, 191.

[415] Sexual Offences Act 2003 (England) s 27.

[416] Parent, grandparent, brother, sister, half-brother, half-sister, aunt or uncle, (including relationships created by adoption) or foster parent.

[417] A Kabat 'Scarlet Letter Sex Offender Databases And Community Notification: Sacrificing Personal Privacy for a Symbol's Sake' (1998) 35 Am Crim L Rev 333.

[418] D Feldman 'The "Scarlet Letter Laws" of the 1990s: A Response to Critics' (1997) 60 Albany L Rev 1081.

presumption that children below a certain age are incapable of consenting to sexual contact.[419] Most States retain a version of statutory rape where a child below a certain age is presumed not to be able to engage in sexual activity. Under these statutes the State does not have to prove lack of consent, and challenges to the presumption of lack of consent have been universally unsuccessful.[420] Some States, for example Oregon, have retained a defence of consent where the actor is less than three years older than the victim at the time of the alleged offence.[421] Marriage is a more widespread defence, and one which is also allowed under the abuse of trust provisions under Sexual Offences Act 2003 s 23 and sexual activity with a family member s 25 and s 26. Connerton[422] has questioned the validity of marriage as a defence in any circumstances. Her argument is that if behaviour is considered so abusive as to incur a strict liability penalty because of a child's age then surely there should not be a defence that allows the activity to continue. It may be argued further that policy should not encourage children to marry people whom the criminal law would normally regard as abusers. The reason for the defence in English law is that the abuse of trust and familial relationships provisions raise the age of consent to 18 for these offences and this is in conflict with the legal age at which people may marry, of 16. In these circumstances where abuse of a relationship has led to consent in circumstances where children would not otherwise have done so, would not it be more appropriate to consider the definition of consent to include a consideration of breach of trust violation, as has been done in Canada,[423] rather than essentially to use marriage to condone what is set out to be wrong in criminal law?

3. Sexual offences in Canada

There are three offences in Canadian law which relate specifically to the sexual assault on children. The crimes of sexual interference[424] and invitation to sexual touching[425] refer to victims under the age of 14 and the crime of sexual exploitation[426] to victims over the age of 14 but under the age of 18.[427] The crime of sexual interference may be charged when a person 'for a sexual purpose, touches, directly or indirectly, with a

---

[419] C Phipps 'Children, Adults, Sex and the Criminal Law' (1997) 22 Seaton Hall J 1.

[420] C Carpenter 'On Statutory Rape, Strict Liability and the Public Welfare Offense Model' (2003) 53 Am U LR 313, 335.   [421] Oregon Revised Statute 163.345 (2003).

[422] K Connerton 'The Resurgence Of The Marital Rape Exemption: The Victimization Of Teens By Their Statutory Rapists' (1997) 61 Albany L Rev 237.

[423] No consent is obtained, for the purposes of sections 271, 272 and 273, where

    (a) the agreement is expressed by the words or conduct of a person other than the complainant;

    (b) the complainant is incapable of consenting to the activity;

    (c) the accused induces the complainant to engage in the activity by abusing a position of trust, power or authority;

    (d) the complainant expresses, by words or conduct, a lack of agreement to engage in the activity; or

    (e) the complainant, having consented to engage in sexual activity, expresses, by words or conduct, a lack of agreement to continue to engage in the activity.

    Criminal Code 1985 (Canada) c 19 (3rd Supp) s 273.1(2).

[424] ibid s 151.   [425] ibid s 152.

[426] ibid s 153 (1).   [427] ibid s 153 (2).

part of the body or with an object, any part of the body of a person under the age of fourteen years'. An invitation to sexual touching concerns behaviour when a person 'for a sexual purpose, invites, counsels or incites a person under the age of fourteen years to touch, directly or indirectly, with a part of the body or with an object, the body of any person, including the body of the person who so invites, counsels or incites and the body of the person under the age of fourteen years'. The offence of sexual exploitation concerns a circumstance when:

Every person who is in a position of trust or authority towards a young person or is a person with whom the young person is in a relationship of dependency or who is in a relationship with a young person that is exploitative of the young person[428] and who

(a) for a sexual purpose, touches, directly or indirectly, with a part of the body or with an object, any part of the body of the young person, or

(b) for a sexual purpose, invites, counsels or incites a young person to touch, directly or indirectly, with a part of the body or with an object, the body of any person, including the body of the person who so invites, counsels or incites and the body of the young person.

Many of the key elements of the offence are purposively left undefined. 'Sexual purpose' has been interpreted to take into account a *motive of sexual gratification* in determining whether conduct is sexual, depending upon the circumstances of the case.[429] Interestingly, in the light of the extensive list of relationships which constitute a position of trust included in the English law, 'position of trust', 'authority', and 'relationship of dependency' are all left undefined.

In declining to include in s 153(1) of the Criminal Code, a list of the cases in which a person must refrain from sexual contact with the young person, Parliament intended to direct the analysis to the nature of the relationship between the young person and the accused rather than to their status in relation to each other. Rather than the concept as defined in equity, the word 'trust' as used in s 153(1) of the *Criminal Code* must instead be interpreted in accordance with its primary meaning of confidence or reliance.[430]

The term 'authority' must not be restricted to cases in which the relationship of authority stems from a role of the accused, but must extend to any relationship in which the accused actually exercises such a power.[431]

Section 153 was recently amended to include anyone 'who is in a relationship with a young person that is exploitative of the young person'. It is suggested from the accompanying notes to the Bill that a judge may infer that a young person is being exploited in a relationship from the nature and circumstances of the relationship. Factors that a judge may consider include the age of the young person, the age difference between the parties, the evolution of their relationship, and the degree of control or influence exercised over the young person.[432]

---

[428] As amended by An Act To Amend The Criminal Code (Protection Of Children And Other Vulnerable Persons) And The Evidence Act 2005 (Canada) c 2 s 4.

[429] *R v Chase* [1987] 2 SCR 293 (SCC) (Macintyre J).

[430] *R v Audet* [1996] 2 SCR 171 (SCC) 194 [35] (La Forest J).   [431] ibid [34].

[432] <http://www.parl.gc.ca/common/Bills_ls.asp?Parl=38&Ses=1&ls=C2#byoungpersons> (accessed September 2005).

The statute does create one defence of consent based on age. When the complainant is either 12 or 13 and the accused is:

(i) 12 years of age, but less than 16,
(ii) is less than two years older than the complainant, and
(iii) is not in a position of trust or dependency to the complainant

in these circumstances then consent may be a defence.[433] Furthermore a person aged 12 or 13 cannot be tried for an offence under s 151, or s 152, or s 173(2) unless the person is in a position of trust or authority towards the complainant or is a person with whom the complainant is in a relationship of dependency. These types of reform could have been mechanisms by which the blanket criminalization of sexual contact between adolescents which is imposed in Sexual Offences Act 2003 s13, could have been avoided. However given the Government's refusal to consider any 'watering down' of the age of consent, and the unwillingness to perceive youth as being intrinsically less likely to commit such an offence, such reform proved impossible.

In Canada sexual assault against children may also be charged with one of the three sexual offences which may be charged irrespective of the age of the complainant: sexual assault, sexual assault involving bodily harm, weapons or third parties, or aggravated sexual assault in which in committing the sexual assault the assailant 'wounds, maims, disfigures or endangers the life of the complainant'.[434] The simplicity of the drafting of these provisions is very attractive when compared with the cumbersome Sexual Offences Act 2003. However their substance is unhelpful in the context of the prosecution of child abuse. The aggravating factor in Canadian law is the degree of violence used, rather than the type and level of sexual touching. In particular there is no difference in law between penetration and any other form of sexual touching.[435] The purpose of Canadian law reform was to 'shift attention away from rape as a sexual offence and towards the right of every person to be free from physical assault'.[436] However this type of definition is particularly problematic in the prosecution of sexual offences against children, which are largely perpetrated without the need of violent forms of coercion.

The defence of consent is not available for an offence under s 271, s 272, or s 273 if the complainant is under 14 years of age (s 150.1) except in certain circumstances. It is not a defence to a charge under s 271, s 272, or s 273 that the accused believed the complainant was 14 years old or more, unless the accused took all reasonable steps to ascertain the age of the complainant.[437] The onus is on the prosecution to prove that the defendant did not take all reasonable steps.[438] The term 'reasonable steps' has been

---

[433] Criminal Code 1985 (Canada) s 150.1(2).
[434] ibid c 46 s 273 (1995 c 39 s 146).
[435] There is a separate offence of anal intercourse: ibid c 46 s 159.
[436] Canadian Law Reform Commission *Sexual Offences Working Paper No 22* (Law Reform Commission Canada, Ottawa 1978) 21.   [437] Criminal Code 1985 (Canada) c 19 (3rd Supp) s 150.1(4).
[438] *R v Hayes and Morris* (1991) 12 WCB (2d) 282 (Alberta QB); *R v P(LT)* (1997) 113 CCC (3d) 42 (British Columbia CA) 86.

defined in case law. In *R v K (RA)* the court held that 'reasonableness of steps' did not require that the accused directly ask the complainant's age, but it did require that all the circumstances in each case should be examined—for example, the accused's and complainant's common association with group of older persons, relatively narrow age differential, complainant's behaviour, appearance and lack of curfew.[439]

4. Sexual offences in Australia

All States in Australia have undertaken some reform of their sexual offences legislation in recent years, although the reform has tended to be piecemeal, with the addition of some new offences, rather than complete reform. New South Wales reformed all its sexual offences in 2003 and the reformed offences may now be found in Crimes Act 1900 ss 61H to 80AA. Australian statutes are particularly interesting in their creation of an offence of 'the persistent abuse of a child'. This is a common provision across most of the States in Australia.[440] The section creates a separate offence committed by a person 'on 3 or more separate occasions occurring on separate days during any period' who 'engages in conduct in relation to a particular *child* that constitutes a *sexual offence*'. The penalty for the offence is potentially very high as a person convicted of this offence is liable to imprisonment for 25 years. What is more important is the creation of an offence which recognizes persistent abuse as being particularly serious. It is another way in which sexual abuse, rather than a single sexual assault, may be recognized as having particular aggravating characteristics outside those recognized by abuse of trust offences. In New South Wales, abuse of authority is an aggravating factor for offences, but it is not an offence in its own right as in the Sexual Offences Act 2003 (England).[441]

Another interesting and potentially useful piece of drafting in relation to offences against children lies in Queensland's Criminal Code Act 1899 (as amended) s 210. This created the offence of indecent treatment of children under 16 and covers a range of behaviour towards a child including taking photographs of that child or exposing the child to any indecent object. In the section the drafters use the term 'deals with' to describe behaviour which, if done without consent, would constitute an offence under the Code. Thus the offence of indecent treatment could be charged in relation to anyone who 'unlawfully or indecently deals with a child under the age of 16 years' and 'unlawfully permits himself or herself to be indecently dealt with by a child under the age of 16 years'.

In relation to sexual behaviour between children, the ACT Crimes Act 1900 s 55 and the Victorian Crimes Act 1958 s 45 allow a defence of consent to sexual intercourse

---

[439] *R v K (RA)* (1996) 106 CCC (3d) 93 (New Brunswick CA).

[440] There are almost identical provisions in Australian Capital Territory (Crimes Act 1900 s 56); Crimes Act 1990 (New South Wales) s 66 EA; Criminal Code Act (Northern Territory) s 131A; Criminal Code Act 1924 (Tasmania) s 125A; Crimes Act 1958 (Victoria) s 43A; Criminal Code Act 1913 (Western Australia) s 321A.

[441] Crimes Act 1900 (New South Wales) ss 66A–C. See also Crimes Act 1900 (Australian Capital Territory) s 56, Criminal Code Act 1983 (Northern Territory) s 131A, Criminal Code Act 1924 (Tasmania) s 125A, Crimes Act 1958 (Victoria) s 43A, Criminal Code 1913 (Western Australia) s 321A.

where the child is over ten and the perpetrator is no more than two years older than him or her. The Tasmanian Criminal Code 1924 ss 124 and125B allows a defence of consent for those who are of a similar age to the child in cases where it can be shown:

(a) that person was of or above the age of 15 years and the accused person was not more than 5 years older than that person; or

(b) that person was of or above the age of 12 years and the accused person was not more than 3 years older than that person.

While there may be some debate about the starting point of ten for a defence of consent, it may be argued that these types of provision guide prosecutorial discretion and reflect the reality of some sexual relationships between children and the ability of some children to consent. It does mean that the concept of consent must be robustly defined to reflect current knowledge of the vulnerability of children, to further predatory behaviour particularly those who have been victims of abuse before.

5. Sexual offences in New Zealand

The majority of sexual offences in New Zealand were reformed by the Crimes Amendment Act No 2 2005 to the Crimes Act 1961. The Crimes Act 1961, as discussed earlier, has become the criminal code of New Zealand. The reforms abolished many of the old criminal offences against children, which had shared many of the problems of the old English law, namely a focus upon sexual behaviour against girls, and a limited view of the nature of abusive relationships within families, so that only sexual relationships with blood relatives were included in the sexual offences.

The core offence under New Zealand law is now sexual violation. Sexual violation defined under Crimes Act 1961 s128 as the act of a person who:

(a) rapes another person; or

(b) has unlawful sexual connection with another person.

Sexual connection is further defined as:

connection effected by the introduction into the genitalia or anus of one person, otherwise than for genuine medical purposes, of—

'(i) a part of the body of another person; or

(ii) an object held or manipulated by another person; or

    (b) connection between the mouth or tongue of one person and a part of another person's genitalia or anus; or

    (c) the continuation of connection of a kind described in paragraph (a) or paragraph (b)]'.

The reforms do not create an offence which may be labelled as 'statutory rape'. Instead the reform created an offence which prohibits sexual connection with a child under the age of 12, to which the child's consent and any presumption that the child was over the age of 12 renders no defence to the perpetrator. If the child victim complains of rape, it is to be assumed on the face of the statute that the alleged perpetrator could also be charged with sexual violation under Crimes Act 1961 s 128. Crimes Act 1961 s 128A creates a non-exclusive list of situations in which a person who allows sexual activity may not in law be considered to have consented. This includes situations which could be interpreted to include a child victim, but which are not specifically tailored to a child's position. Thus while one may imagine scenarios where a child submits because 'threats or force are applied'; or where the child is mistaken about the 'nature and quality of the act'; and also instances in of a child may rightly be considered to be affected by 'an intellectual, mental, or physical condition or impairment of such a nature and degree that he or she cannot consent or refuse to consent to the activity'; none of these categories provide an exact fit with the problems of a child's presumed acquiescence to sexual intercourse. There is a further offence prohibiting sexual contact with a child who is over the age of 12, but under the age of 16: in these circumstances the child's consent may be a defence, but 'only if before the time of the act concerned, he or she had taken reasonable steps to find out whether the young person concerned was of or over the age of 16 years; and (b) at the time of the act concerned, he or she believed on reasonable grounds that the young person was of or over the age of 16 years'. This is very similar to the Canadian provisions.

The Crimes Act 1961 is silent on the position of children who have sexual contact with another child, beyond the stipulation that there is no presumption in law that a person is incapable of sexual contact because of their age. It is to be assumed that much is left to prosecutorial discretion to determine which child will be prosecuted, and thus on the face of the legislation it is very similar to English law.

The reformed Act retains the crime of incest, but adds on a further crime of sexual contact with a dependent family member. This crime expands the range of people whose sexual relationship with a child or adult should be prohibited on the grounds that the person is in a position of 'power and authority' over the other. This includes some biological and non-biological familial relationships, some wider tribal relationships and relationships in which the person has 'a responsibility for, or significant role in, [the complainant]'s care or upbringing' at the time of the alleged offence. It would therefore include those people who would be covered by the abuse of trust offences in England, for example foster-parents and those working in schools or care homes. However it neatly avoids the repetitious and convoluted abuse of trust and familial sexual offences sections in the Sexual Offences Act 2003.

F. Evaluation—An Adequate 'Fit' Between Current Conceptions of Child Abuse and the Criminal Law?

The moral panic in relation to paedophiles has had enormous repercussions in the way that the criminal law in relation to child abuse is now framed in England. First, there has been considerable impetus to reform the outdated sexual offences to ensure that the crimes on the statute book reflected the nature of the crimes as they were now understood. This was an attempt to ensure that more sexual assaults were prosecuted and furthermore that those convicted of them could be properly labelled and thus monitored. These reforms have now been enacted in the Sexual Offences Act 2003.

There were very many offences on the statute book in relation to sexual offending under the previous law which appeared never to be charged in relation to assaults against children. Instead most sexual offenders against children were charged with the 'catch all' offence of indecent assault. This was partly because of some problems in determining the exact nature of the assault on the child. Had the child's description been clearer it might have been possible to charge the defendant with rape or unlawful sexual intercourse. Indecent assault was also charged because no other offence fitted, for example because the complainant was a boy and there was a very limited range of offences that could be charged in relation to boys. The Sexual Offences Act 2003 aimed to redress this position and to reflect the nature of the behaviour fully in the offence. However this aim has resulted in a proliferation of offences thus repeating the mistake of the previous legislation.[442]

The Act remains very much a product of its time in which fear of stranger assault by predatory paedophiles on children predominated. Thus the Sexual Offences Act 2003 attempted to criminalize acts preparatory to attempting to commit a sexual act. It also criminalized all sexual contact between minors.

The Act offends in a fundamental way, a number of key precepts of the criminal law including the principles of minimum criminalisation, maximum certainty and fair-warning. The Act represents . . . a dangerous departure from the usual requirements of subjective mental culpability for serious offences and brings about an unwanted proliferation of criminal liability where no identifiable harm has yet occurred.[443]

It is only in time that it will become clear whether this well-meaning but convoluted piece of legislation will be simplified by practice. Our suspicion is that the Sexual Offences Act 2003 will be treated in some respects like the previous Sexual Offences Act 1956 and only a few of the offences will be routinely charged.

In contrast the law in relation to child homicide and injury within the home is equally outdated and has major flaws which positively hinder prosecutions. However the much lower level of public concern and media energy expended upon the physical assault and death of children within the home has meant that the law has remained almost entirely untouched. The main difficulties in the current law concerning homicide relate to the *mens rea* of the offences. Even when a child dies as a result of sustained and repeated physical abuse and neglect it is often difficult to satisfy the legal requirements for murder, or intention to kill, or to cause grievous bodily harm. While the Law Commission has put forward proposals for the reform of all fatal and non-fatal offences, it has not specifically considered the particular problems of prosecuting those responsible for child injury or death within the home. This is with the notable exception of the problem of prosecuting injuries to a child when it is not clear who of a group of carers is to blame. Thus proposals for reform of homicide appear likely to place the majority of child deaths from physical abuse or neglect into the category of manslaughter rather than second degree murder. Child deaths in the home as a result of abuse are rarely accidental, there is often a high degree of culpability. This should

---

[442] Spencer (n 378).
[443] Bainham and Brookes-Gordon (n 368).

be reflected in the criminal law. Any reform of the law must fundamentally consider the current law on omissions. English law is based on the principle that child deaths resulting from a failure to act are essentially accidental, whereas in fact in these cases the offender has seen the child every day, seen the damage that their lack of care is inflicting upon him, and has persistently continued to inflict damage upon him, by a failure to act. The culpability of this behaviour has notably been recognized in Canada where acts and omissions are often treated in the same way in these cases.

There has very recently been reform of the law relating to the defence of reasonable parental chastisement in relation to assaults on children, due in large part to pressure from the ECtHR, the UN Committee on the Rights of the Child as well as many children's charities and action groups. However these reforms are partial and some assaults are still justified on the grounds that they have the potential to improve a child and teach a child right from wrong.

There simply does not appear to be the focus on attempts to prosecute the neglect, physical assault and even homicide of children in the home that there is in relation to sexual assault on children. The lack of moral panic in relation to child deaths and injuries within the home and the contrasting enormous concern about 'paedophilia' appears to be at least in part responsible for this disparity and the consequent lack of 'fit' between the law in relation to fatal and non-fatal offences against the person and the problems of physical abuse and neglect as we now know them to be.

4

Liability in Tort and Human Rights Law

A. Tracing the Influences on the Current Law

In the Family Law and Criminal Law chapters we have discussed the legal bases upon which the state can intervene either to protect the child's well-being or to punish wrongdoing. The focus of the family courts is on the prevention of significant harm to the child in the future. In reaching this decision the child's welfare should be paramount under the Children Act 1989 s 1. However, it remains a hazard that the needs and rights of the family are conflated with those of the child, particularly following the introduction of ECHR Article 8 into English law, as the child also has a Convention interest in the preservation of family life and the status quo. In criminal law the focus is on the conviction and punishment of the guilty abuser. Only in tort law is the focus exclusively on vindicating the child's legal rights to be kept safe from harm, by holding directly accountable to the child those people and agencies who have contravened those rights. Here, the child[1] rather than the state initiates, and to a certain extent directs, the court's involvement.

1. The objectives of suing in tort

The overriding objective of tort law is often said to be the Aristotelian concept of corrective justice: that no one should gain through inflicting on another loss by acting intentionally or negligently.[2] However undermined that concept has become by a

---

[1] Nominally the victim will be the claimant, but if he is still a minor the action is brought by the child's 'next friend' or 'litigation friend', being an adult who undertakes responsibility for any costs awarded to the defendant, and usually also gives instructions to the child's lawyers.

[2] E Weinrib 'Understanding Tort Law' (1989) 23 Val L Rev 485; J Gordley 'Tort Law in the Aristotelian Tradition' in DG Owen (ed) *Philosophical Foundations of Tort Law* (Clarendon Press, Oxford 1995).

judiciary increasingly enticed by distributive justice to constrain the reach of tort,[3] it has been rightly pointed out[4] that tort actions by child abuse victims exemplify the traditional justifications for tort law: the individual accountability of a wrongdoer to the person on whom he has inflicted harm, vindication of legal entitlements, retribution, and deterrence of the wrongdoer and others. The motivations of individual litigants in deciding to sue their abusers, and those who had the opportunity and power but failed to protect them from abuse, are complex, but usually they are influenced by some of the following five objectives.

(a) To supplement or supplant criminal prosecution[5]

In some cases the claimant sees the civil claim as supplementing a criminal prosecution. For entirely justifiable reasons, the defendant's interests are the focus of the criminal trial, and so the complainant may feel that the verdict does not reflect a vindication of his right not to be harmed. One of the earliest cases in England of a tort claim following a criminal prosecution was *D v Meah, W v Meah*,[6] where two of the five victims of a rapist successfully sued him for battery.[7] In other cases the criminal proceedings may have ended in an acquittal verdict,[8] or the complainant may have been unhappy with the sentence imposed.[9]

Claimants may intend tort proceedings to supplant criminal prosecution. A complainant may decide not to undergo the rigours of a criminal trial before a jury. In defended civil proceedings the trial still is likely to be a contest of credibility between the claimant and the alleged abuser, but the question will be reframed as to whose story is the most credible and hence probable,[10] whereas in criminal proceedings the question will be whether the prosecution has proved that the complainant's story is

---

[3] First invoked by Lord Hoffmann in *White v Chief Constable of the South Yorkshire Police* [1999] 2 AC 455 (HL) 504, 510–511; for further analysis see LC Hoyano 'Misconceptions about "Wrongful Conception"' (2002) 65 MLR 883, 888–899, 901, 904–906.

[4] B Feldthusen 'The Civil Action for Sexual Battery: Therapeutic Jurisprudence?' (1993) 25 Ottawa L Rev 203, 212.

[5] For discussion of the implications of tort actions for criminal offences, see J Stapleton 'Civil Prosecutions Part 1: Double Jeopardy and Abuse of Process' (1999) 7 Torts LJ 244 and J Stapleton 'Civil Prosecutions Part 2: Civil Claims for Killing and Rape' (2000) 8 Torts LJ 15.

[6] *D v Meah, W v Meah* [1986] 1 All ER 935 (QB (Woolf J)).

[7] Their objective was to gain access to damages the rapist had been awarded against the negligent driver who was responsible for the brain damage which had caused his radical personality change, creating a propensity to assault women. Meah, controversially, was awarded damages against the driver for loss of his liberty as he was sentenced to life imprisonment [*Meah v McCreamer (No 1)* [1985] 1 All ER 367 (QB (Woolf J))]. He was not awarded reimbursement of the damages he had to pay to his victims, this claim being considered as going too far down the road of foreseeability and public policy; nevertheless the rape victims were able to tap the damage award to the rapist to satisfy their judgments against him [*Meah v McCreamer (No 2)* [1996] 1 All ER 943 (QB (Woolf J)) 951].

[8] eg *C(M) v M(F)* (1990) 74 DLR (4th) 129 (Ontario Gen Div) (defendant was acquitted of sexual assault (to which he had pleaded consent), buggery and forcible confinement, and was convicted of ordinary assault; defended civil action in battery succeeded). If the case has been tried in summary proceedings in England or Wales, criminal proceedings will be a bar to further civil proceedings; however, child abuse is most likely to be charged under indictment where there is no statutory impediment to a civil action [Offences against the Person Act 1861, ss 42–46].

[9] eg *Lyth v Dagg* (1988) 46 CCLT 25 (British Columbia Supreme Ct) [18]–[19] (claimant enticed into a homosexual relationship with his teacher sued because he and his mother were unhappy with the suspended sentence and 300 hours of community work imposed when the defendant pleaded guilty to gross indecency).   [10] *C(M) v M(F)* (n 8) [1].

true beyond all reasonable doubt. The claimant also may be able to take advantage of more lenient rules for the admissibility of evidence, such as hearsay and evidence of abuse against other alleged victims. Precision with dates and the specific circumstances of the abuse will not be required to establish culpability, provided that the pleadings and the disclosure of evidence process permit the defendant to meet the allegations.

Alternatively, an action in battery offers the opportunity to a disappointed complainant to launch a collateral attack on decisions by the criminal prosecuting authorities not to take further action on the case.[11] *Halford v Brookes*[12] is the first and the strongest example in English law of tort law forcing the Crown Prosecution Service (CPS) to think again. In 1978 the claimant's daughter Lynn Siddons, aged 16, was repeatedly stabbed and strangled whilst she was on a walk with a 15-year-old neighbour, Fitzroy Brookes. Fitzroy had confessed in the presence of his stepfather and stood trial for murder, where he was acquitted. The boy's defence was that his stepfather Michael Brookes had killed her, and he had been forced by her stepfather to participate but he had only inflicted superficial wounds. After that trial the CPS concluded that there was insufficient evidence to prosecute the stepfather, notwithstanding a sustained campaign in the press and elsewhere. In tort proceedings for battery against both Brookes, brought some 13 years after Lynn's death,[13] her mother's avowed purpose was to target and expose Michael Brookes whom she believed to be the primary author of her daughter's death.[14] The trial judge, clearly uncomfortable at trying a murder case without a jury and under the civil rules of procedure, decided to apply the criminal standard of proof beyond reasonable doubt.[15] Rougier J held that the stepfather was solely responsible for Lynn's death. Faced with that reasoned judicial conclusion, the CPS no longer had any basis for refusing to proceed with the prosecution. Ultimately, after an interlocutory appeal to the House of Lords on the issue of legal professional privilege in 1995,[16] Michael Brookes was convicted of murder, some 18 years after Lynn Siddons was killed.

(b) To 'empower' victims: tort law as therapy

Civil litigation may have a therapeutic purpose:[17] 'empowering' victims by vindicating their autonomy interests, and enabling them to reclaim, in a protected environment,

---

[11] eg *Harder v Brown* (1989) 50 CCLT 85 (British Columbia Supreme Ct). Another prominent contemporary example is the class action in tort being brought against members of the 'Real IRA' by the victims of the Omagh bombing, where the Northern Ireland authorities have decided that as yet there is insufficient evidence to prosecute them.   [12] *Halford v Brookes* [1992] PIQR 175 (HC).

[13] An application to strike out the proceedings as the six-year limitation period had expired was dismissed by the Court of Appeal in *Halford v Brookes (No 1)* [1991] 3 All ER 559 (CA) 567, 576 exercising their discretion under s 14 of the Limitation Act 1980, as the crucial event was of such terrifying and dramatic nature that the lapse of time would not seriously impede a verdict, which would depend upon who was giving a truthful account of an incident they could never forget. The decision must be taken as being overruled by *Stubbings v Webb* [1993] AC 498(HL), discussed below, section 2.

[14] *Halford v Brookes* (n 12) 176.

[15] ibid 176, 178. This ruling in effect appeal-proofed the judgment on the trial judge's findings of fact.

[16] *R v Derby Magistrates' Court ex p B* [1996] AC 487 (HL), discussed below in relation to access to evidence, Chapter 7 section A.

[17] N Des Rosiers, B Feldthusen, and O Hankivsky 'Legal Compensation for Sexual Violence: Therapeutic Consequences and Consequences for the Judicial System' (1998) 4 Psychology, Public Policy and

the power that they had lost to the aggressors.[18] Although the parties may well differ in their ability to access resources in the litigation, the nature of the pleadings and the courtroom put them in a position of formal equality,[19] unlike criminal proceedings where the court's focus is on ensuring a fair trial for the accused perpetrator rather than protecting and promoting the interests of the victim.

There is a danger however that the notion of the trial as a healing process advocated by some[20] may be incompatible with the fundamental principles of the adversarial civil trial which aspire to equal treatment of the participants. Moreover, civil trials also have undeniable disadvantages. Litigation has heavy costs, both monetary and human,[21] where extraordinarily painful events must be relived through testimony, particularly in intrafamilial tort actions. The claimant has to portray herself as a victim whose life has been blighted by the abuse,[22] which can undercut the objective of vindicating personal autonomy. Every personal victory in coping with the consequences of the abuse, particularly if it is long-term, can be reinterpreted as trivializing the tort itself. To counter this, expert witnesses may take the predominant role in the trial, describing the claimant's experiences and reactions in order to fit them within psychiatric diagnoses such as post-traumatic stress disorder, so as to justify a compensatory award.[23]

(c) To make the abuser and the system within which he operated accountable to victims

The importance which victims place on being given a forum in which to tell their story should not be underestimated. The Irish experiment with a child abuse commission set up in 1999 by the Government to make awards to victims who had been physically and sexually maltreated in industrial schools run by religious orders in the 1960s has proved controversial, with Tom Sweeney going on a highly publicized hunger strike when his compensation was cut from €113,000 to €67,000 because he wanted to be able to tell his story in a full hearing.[24]

Tort law offers a system of direct and individual accountability, making the abuser and the system within which he operated publicly and directly accountable to victims. Claimants receive a public and official acknowledgement of what has been done to them. The trial has compiled a record of what happened to the claimant, as accurate as the constraints of the availability of admissible evidence permit. Individual guilt can be

---

Law 433; Feldthusen (n 4); B Feldthusen 'The Canadian Experiment with the Civil Action for Sexual Battery' in N Mulaney (ed) *Torts in the Nineties* (LBC Information Services, Sydney 1997).

[18] Des Rosiers, Feldthusen, and Hankivsky ibid 433, 439, 444.

[19] Feldthusen (n 4) 214–215.

[20] Des Rosiers, Feldthusen, and Hankivsky (n 17) 433, 446–448 propose changes to the adversarial trial to further its therapeutic purpose, such as judges being encouraged to show sadness and empathy when the plaintiff is testifying, to take a broader view of their power to control cross-examination 'to preserve the possibility of the healing aspect of the process', to write to all parties before giving judgment, and to describe the plaintiff's story in her own words in the reasons for judgment so that her 'voice' is not silenced, even if she wins the case. Judicial impartiality seems to have been overlooked in these proposals.

[21] N Bala 'Tort Remedies and the Family Law Practitioner' (1998) 16 CFLQ 423, 423–24.

[22] Des Rosiers, Feldthusen, and Hankivsky, (n 17) 433, 443.   [23] ibid 433, 444–445.

[24] A Chrisafis 'Hunger Striker Bears Witness to Ireland's Dirty Secret' *The Guardian* 4 May 2004 p 10.

established, thereby preventing unwarranted collective blame,[25] which is particularly important where other branches of the institution concerned continue to provide conscientious and high-quality care of children.

Does, and should, tort law have a punitive role in this area? Should exemplary damages, intended to punish the wrongdoing of the tortfeasor rather than to reflect any loss inflicted on the claimant, be available where criminal proceedings have been or might be initiated? This is a vexed question for all common law jurisdictions, because the torts of assault and battery directly correspond to the criminal offences, raising the spectre of double jeopardy and double punishment.[26] A civil judgment for exemplary (or punitive) damages may be viewed as implying that the criminal court's sentence was inadequate to punish the defendant properly in the circumstances.

The issue of punitive damages has been sharpest in New Zealand because of its no-fault compensation system for 'accidental' personal injury, which has been interpreted as applying to intentional torts such as battery and assault.[27] Whether an incident is considered an 'accident' is considered from the perspective of the victim, and hence can include intentional actions of third parties, but probably would not encompass neglect.[28] The legislation bars common law tort actions for compensatory damages for personal injury (including abuse) which occurred after 1 April 1974, in exchange for the victims' entitlement to capped statutory pecuniary benefits from the Accident Compensation Corporation.[29] A revision of the scheme in 1998 deemed the limitation period for mental injury to run from the date of the first treatment, which apparently was intended to sweep many historic abuse claimants within the statutory benefits regime.[30] However, the Court of Appeal in a technical interpretation of the legislation considered that the deeming provision related to claims administration only, and hence was not intended to deprive people retrospectively of existing common law rights before the legislation came into force.[31] It has been suggested that historic abuse victims might well have been better off with the certainty of statutory benefits than with their common law rights[32] which might be stale.

The Accident Rehabilitation and Compensation Insurance Act 1992 placed the system on an insurance footing, removing the NZ $10,000 lump sum for pain and suffering, substituting a weekly allowance of NZ $ 40 for a permanent disability greater than 10 per cent, and limiting the amount of counselling available. These reforms severely affected victims of child abuse, particularly the removal of any monetary payment with symbolic significance.[33] As a consequence, a tort action acquired greater attraction. The leading New Zealand appellate cases ascertaining whether child

---

[25] M Gannage for the Law Commission of Canada *An International Perspective: a Review and Analysis of Approaches to Addressing Past Institutional or Systemic Abuse in Selected Countries [Argentina, South Africa and Australia]* (1998) 13.   [26] Des Rosiers, Feldthusen, and Hankivsky (n 17) 433, 449.
[27] *G v Auckland Hospital Board* [1976] 1 NZLR 638 (New Zealand Supreme Ct).
[28] G McLay 'Antipodean Perspectives on Child Welfare Tort Claims against Public Authorities' in D Fairgrieve and S Green (eds) *Child Abuse Tort Claims against Public Bodies: a Comparative Law View* (Ashgate, Aldershot 2004) 120.   [29] Accident Compensation Act 1972 (New Zealand).
[30] Now in the Injury Prevention, Rehabilitation, and Compensation Act 2001 (New Zealand) s 36(1).
[31] *S v Attorney-General* [2003] NZCA 149 (New Zealand CA) [26]; *W v Attorney-General* [2003] NZCA 150 (New Zealand CA).   [32] McLay (n 28) 123.
[33] R Tobin 'Civil Actions for Sexual Abuse in New Zealand' (1997) 5 Tort L Rev 190, 190–193.

protection authorities could owe a common law duty of care to the child or to the suspected parent have involved claims of historic abuse,[34] or have proceeded on the basis that the issue of coverage for different heads of damage under the accident compensation scheme should be sorted out at trial.[35]

In 1982 in *Donselaar*[36] the Court of Appeal had held that a claim for exemplary damages respecting a battery or assault was not barred by the compensation regime, Cooke J (as he then was) reasoned that it was necessary to maintain a punitive remedy for commonplace types of trespass or assault 'if accompanied by insult or contumely' which touch the lives of ordinary people.[37] He concluded that the law of damages should be consciously moulded to meet social needs, and the only feasible way of doing so without intruding on the no-fault compensation scheme was to allow damages for 'purely punitive purposes' which would have to take over part of the role of compensatory damages.[38] This judgment encouraged victims of historic child abuse to sue. In *Bottrill v A*, the Privy Council ruled that exemplary damages falling outside the statutory scheme could be awarded where there was intentional wrongdoing with an additional element of flagrancy or cynicism or oppression; exceptionally, negligence might qualify where the defendant departed flagrantly from ordinary or professional precepts of prudence or standards of care, even in the absence of conscious recklessness.[39]

However, in 1998 in *Daniels v Thompson*[40] the Court of Appeal greatly diminished the availability of tort actions for child abuse victims, ruling that exemplary damages are barred where the defendant has already been convicted and punished. If the defendant has been acquitted, then the action should be struck out as an abuse of process. Where a criminal prosecution has been commenced or is likely, the civil proceedings for exemplary damages should be stayed to prevent an abuse of process. The majority expressly resiled from the suggestion of Cooke J in *Donselaar* that the advent of the accident compensation regime meant that some element of compensation should be attached to exemplary damages, holding that it was not appropriate for the court to circumvent the policy of removing civil liability for personal injury by altering the role of exemplary damages.[41] This approach removes the element of chance in making exemplary damages—in effect, the entire personal injury tort action in New Zealand—dependent on the sequencing of criminal and civil proceedings, but its consequence is to strip from the victims any sense of having achieved vindication and accountability.

Ironically, one motivating force behind the New Zealand Court of Appeal's ruling was that criminal courts are increasingly aware of the need to protect the interests

---

[34] *S v Attorney-General* n 31; *W v Attorney-General* (n 31).
[35] *Attorney General v Prince and Gardner* [1998] 1 NZLR 262 (New Zealand CA) 292; presumably the child's claim which was permitted by the Privy Council to proceed to trial in *B v Attorney General of New Zealand* [2003] UKPC 61, [2003] 4 All ER 833 would have been determined on the same basis.
[36] *Donselaar v Donselaar* [1982] 1 NZLR 97 (New Zealand CA).   [37] ibid 106.
[38] ibid 107.
[39] *Bottrill v A* [2001] 3 NZLR 662 (PC on appeal from New Zealand CA); S Todd 'Twenty Years of Professional Negligence in New Zealand' (2005) 21(4) PN 257, 261–262.
[40] *Daniels v Thompson* [1998] 3 NZLR 22 (New Zealand CA) (Thomas J dissenting) 47, 48, 51, 52.
[41] ibid 29.

of victims of crime, and restorative justice and victim impact statements mean that the aims of exemplary damages are likely to be taken into account in the sentencing process.[42] Other jurisdictions espouse the same aspirations for their criminal justice system, but have been more equivocal about the availability of exemplary damages where criminal proceedings have been or might be initiated.[43]

In the UK, the issue has not really arisen yet in the context of child abuse actions, as until 2002 under the doctrine in *Rookes v Barnard*[44] exemplary damages were regarded as being restricted to cases of oppressive, arbitrary or unconstitutional action by public servants, or cynical profiteering. The previous common law had set its face against exemplary damages where the defendant had received a criminal sentence for the same conduct.[45] The Law Commission has recommended that exemplary damages (renamed punitive damages) be retained and be available for any tort or equitable wrong where the defendant had deliberately and outrageously disregarded the claimant's rights, but considered that they 'usually' must not be available where the defendant has been convicted before the date of the civil judgment.[46]

On one view, any compensation awarded the victim punishes the wrongdoer because he is out of pocket. The problem posed by exemplary or punitive damages is whether the award becomes one of vengeance where the defendant has already been convicted and has (it must be assumed) already been ordered to compensate the victim adequately for the losses inflicted, leaving no principled basis upon which the amount of the exemplary damages can be calculated. Conversely, it is strongly arguable that the damage award in the civil case should not be determined by the sequence of civil and criminal proceedings. Given that aggravated damages are available to reflect the increased damage to the claimant because of the nature of the tort inflicted, it is submitted that tort law as a general principle should not have an overt and distinct punitive role beyond the stigma of the public adverse judgment and the burden of the compensatory damage award to the victim. Where however the defendant has profited monetarily from the abuse, such as from selling child pornography, then punitive damages to strip that profit would seem appropriate, unless the defendant

---

[42]　ibid 32–34.

[43]　The Supreme Court of Canada in 1992 had reiterated a long-held view that a criminal conviction would operate as a bar to exemplary damages [*Norberg v Wynrib* [1992] 2 SCR 226 (SCC) 267–268 (*obiter*)] but more recent cases have suggested that a criminal prosecution is not a bar but merely a matter to be taken into consideration in quantifying damages: eg *Glendale v Drozdazik* (1993) 77 BCR (2d) 106 (British Columbia CA) 115; *Queen (Litigation Guardian of) v Hodgins* (1991) 36 RFL (3d) 159 (Ontario Gen Div). In Australia the matter still appears open. In the United States the authorities conflict, but the majority of States appear to allow exemplary damages regardless of whether the defendant may be criminally prosecuted for the same conduct; some allow a criminal penalty already imposed to be taken into account in mitigation of any exemplary damages award ['Damages' 25 *Corpus Juris Secundum* ¶122, discussed in *Daniels v Thompson* (n 40) 53–59].

[44]　*Rookes v Barnard* [1964] AC 1129 (HL), overruled in *Kuddus v Chief Constable of Leicestershire* [2002] 2 AC 122 (HL). Australia, New Zealand, and Canada had already rejected the restrictions in *Rookes v Barnard*: *Uren v John Fairfax & Sons Pty Ltd* (1966) 117 CLR 647 (Aus HC) 122–123; *Donselaar v Donselaar* (n 36); *Vorvis v Insurance Corporation of British Columbia* [1989] 1 SCR 1085 (SCC) 1104–1106.

[45]　*Archer v Brown* [1985] 1 QB 401 (QB (Peter Pain J)).

[46]　Law Commission of England & Wales *Aggravated, Exemplary and Restitutionary Damages* (LC 247 1997) 65–69, Recommendation 1.3 and Draft Bill Clause 4(1).

has been fined by a criminal court in an amount approximating the amount of the profit.

(d) To expose the wider context of the alleged abuse to external scrutiny

Litigants can deploy a tort action to prise open closed institutions, such as children's residential care facilities, schools and churches, social services, and the police, to external scrutiny. Cleverly framed pleadings can effectively set up a judicial examination of the wider context of the alleged abuse, the reasons why previous complaints were not acted upon, or why investigations or protective measures were foiled or inadequate. Tort provides the weapon to the individual litigant to investigate what really happened, to fulfil what is sometimes described as tort's 'ombudsman function'.[47] The mother of the 13th murder victim of the Yorkshire Ripper did not want compensation from the police; rather she wanted to know why the police had not collated evidence in their possession to identify the perpetrator, and so made an earlier arrest before he reached her daughter.[48] Ahmet Osman and his mother wanted to know why eight previous complaints to the police about a teacher stalking his young pupil were not acted upon, leaving him at large to murder the boy's father and the deputy headteacher of his school, and to seriously wound the boy.[49]

Public inquiries into how institutions have failed children, if they are not required by statute,[50] often are ordered only after sustained pressure by the victims and their families and supporters which can drain their will and resources,[51] and too often are ineffective in causing significant changes in the system.[52] Tort law puts that power into the hands of the individual litigant, by compelling the defendant institutions to produce all relevant evidence and witnesses in their control to answer the allegations.

Tort litigants often have a corollary prophylactic aspiration of ensuring that systems for child protection are made more effective. It must be conceded that individual

---

[47] A Linden 'Reconsidering Tort Law As Ombudsman' in F Steel and S Rodgers-Magnet (eds) *Issues in Tort Law* (Carswell, Toronto 1983).

[48] *Hill v Chief Constable of West Yorkshire* [1989] 1 AC 53 (HL) 64.

[49] *Osman v UK* (2000) 29 EHRR 245, [1999] 1 FLR 193 (ECtHR) 153; LC Hoyano 'Policing Flawed Police Investigations: Unravelling the Blanket' (1999) 62 MLR 912, 933–934.

[50] Under HM Government *Working Together to Safeguard Children: a Guide to Inter-Agency Working to Safeguard and Promote the Welfare of Children* (2006) [3.38–3.39], [3.70] and chapters 7 and 8, the Local Safeguarding Children Boards have the power to investigate unexpected deaths or serious injuries suffered by children from birth up to age 18 in their areas; reviews by a Child Death Overview Panel will become compulsory from 1 April 2008.

[51] eg Human Rights and Equal Opportunities Commission, *Bringing Them Home: Report of the National Inquiry into the Separation of Aboriginal and Torres Strait Islander Children and Their Families* (1997); Sir William Utting, *People Like Us: The Report of the Review of the Safeguards for Children Living Away From Home* (HMSO, 1997); Sir Ronald Waterhouse *Lost in Care: Report of the North Wales Child Abuse Tribunal of Inquiry* (HM Stationery Office, London 2000).

[52] Allan Levy QC 'Inquiries into Child Abuse: How Valuable are They?' Fifth Australasian Conference on Child Abuse and Neglect, Melbourne 18 October 1995, noted that the end result of many public inquiries has been 'something of a view of what happened to the child and who was to blame but not *why* it happened' (emphasis in the original).

lawsuits may have limited impact, but they can reveal patterns creating an impetus for systemic change. If they become numerous they may force a system to respond (as the multitude of claims against clergy in North America, Ireland, the UK, and Australia have demonstrated).

The tragic plight of First Nations children wrenched from their families under a misguided policy of assimilation with an alien culture has been documented in Canada[53] and Australia.[54] The courts have difficulty considering past policy wrongs in the context of a tort action on the basis of historical studies, the validity of which can be difficult to evaluate. In Canada as in Australia and New Zealand, it has been argued in negligence cases that the system of residential schools for aboriginal children robbed them of their communities, culture, and support and placed them in environments of abuse.[55] As the Chief Justice of Canada has noted, '[c]ompensation for the impact of attending residential schools is fraught with controversy and difficulty'.[56]

Notwithstanding these difficulties, tort litigation has successfully compelled governments and churches to reflect on their involvement or complicity in the maltreatment of aboriginal children, their families, and their societies. Tort actions provided part of the pressure on the Government of Australia to investigate the plight of the 'Stolen Generations' of aboriginal children.[57] In Canada, after a deluge of criminal prosecutions and tort actions[58] brought by former residents, usually children from First Nations, the Federal Government commissioned a series of in-depth studies from the Law Commission of Canada on the causes of and solutions for systemic child abuse in Canadian institutions.[59]

Other jurisdictions have been watching the soul-searching of Canadian authorities in belatedly confronting the legacy of their treatment of aboriginal children and their

---

[53] Royal Commission on Aboriginal Peoples, Canada *Report of the Royal Commission on Aboriginal Peoples: Vol 1: Looking Forward, Looking Back* (1996); Law Commission of Canada *Restoring Dignity: Responding to Child Abuse in Canadian Institutions* (2000); Law Commission of Canada (Rhonda Claes and Deborah Clifton) *Needs and Expectations for Redress of Victims of Abuse at Native Residential Schools* (Research Paper 1998).

[54] Human Rights and Equal Opportunity Commission of Australia *Bringing Them Home* (n 51).

[55] *Blackwater v Plint* 2005 SCC 58, [2005] 3 SCR 3 [61].   [56] ibid [86].

[57] A Buti 'Unfinished Business: the Australian Stolen Generations' (2000) 7 Murdoch U Electronic J of Law [16], describing the creation of a 'Stolen Generations Litigation Unit' within the Northern Australian Aboriginal Legal Service; Human Rights and Equal Opportunity Commission of Australia *Bringing Them Home* (n 51).

[58] For example, as of 2002 there were more than 4,000 claimants in 1,479 Indian Residential School actions in Alberta alone: *Re Residential Indian Schools* 2002 ABQB 667, 222 DLR (4th) 124 (Alberta QB) [2].

[59] Law Commission of Canada *Restoring Dignity* (n 53); GM Shea for the Law Commission of Canada *Institutional Child Abuse in Canada: Civil Cases* (October 1999); GM Shea for the Law Commission of Canada *Institutional Child Abuse in Canada: Criminal Cases* (October 1999); A Bowlus, K McKenna, T Day, and D Wright for the Law Commission Canada *The Economic Costs and Consequences of Child Abuse in Canada* (March 2003); S Alter for the Law Commission of Canada *Apologising for Serious Wrongdoing: Social, Psychological and Legal Considerations* (May 1999); M Gannage for the Law Commission of Canada *An International Perspective* (n 25).

efforts in making reparation and effecting reconciliation and social reconstruction.[60] Progress in dealing with the claims of aboriginal Canadians was so slow that in May 2005 the Federal Government appointed a retired Justice of the Supreme Court of Canada, Justice Iacobucci, to mediate the negotiations for compensation packages, and to consider the creation of a national truth and reconciliation forum.[61] This initiative resulted in the announcement on 23 November 2005 of an agreement in principle, subject to court approval, providing compensation to all of the estimated 86,000 Indian, Inuit and Inuvialuit Canadians who attended Church-run schools across Canada, at a cost of Cdn$1.9 billion.[62] The agreement in principle provides for a symbolic 'Common Experience Payment'[63] payable to all former residents in Indian residential schools, and a truth and reconciliation process. Acceptance of this payment will release the Canadian Government and the Churches of liability for the children's experiences in Indian residential schools, except for claims of sexual abuse and more serious physical abuse, which will be adjudicated through a mandatory alternate dispute resolution process. The Churches have agreed to waive any limitations or latches defences. It is strongly arguable that the Canadian Government and the churches would never have come to the negotiating table were it not for the estimated 12,000 claimants suing them for the abuse they suffered in the residential school system.

(e) To obtain individuated compensation

It is trite that the desire for compensation drives tort as a system of law. For that reason readers might challenge our listing of compensation as the fifth rather than the first objective. However, for victims of child abuse—or their families if a child has died—their objectives take on a very different complexion from those of other victims of torts. Frequently abusers do not even defend the actions against them, and if they do, they may be judgment-proof, in that they do not have the assets to satisfy the claimants' claims for costs, much less for the damages awarded them, especially if they are serving custodial sentences.

Nevertheless, the need for compensation must not be overlooked. A victim of physical abuse may well have long-lasting physical and psychological injuries, and may need ongoing medical care and an award to compensate for blighted prospects of employment. Victims of sustained sexual abuse often carry invisible scars into their adult life: psychological damage such as depression, self-harming, suicidal behaviour, eating disorders, sleep disturbances, sexual dysfunction, and inability to form and

---

[60] P O'Connor 'Squaring the Circle: How Canada is Dealing with the Legacy of Its Indian Residential Schools Experiment' [2000] Australian J of Human Rights 9.

[61] 'Former Supreme Court Judge to Mediate Residential School Talks', Canadian Broadcasting Corporation website 30 May 2005 <http//www.cbc.ca/news/background/aboriginals/timeline-residentialschools.html>.

[62] *Agreement in Principle between Canada, The Assembly of First Nations, The General Synod of the Anglican Church of Canada, the Presbyterian Church in Canada, the United Church of Canada and Roman Catholic Entities* 20 November 2005 <http://www.irsr-rqpi.gc.ca/english/pdf/AIP_English.pdf>.

[63] All children placed in an Indian residential school are eligible to receive a lump sum of Cdn$10,000, plus Cdn$3,000 for each year spent in a school beyond the first year.

sustain intimate relationships. Their loss of self-worth makes them vulnerable to promiscuity, prostitution, substance abuse, and revictimization.[64] Moreover, childhood sexual abuse creates heavy economic costs as well. A study for the Law Commission of Canada[65] demonstrated that in six areas of costs, ie judicial,[66] social services,[67] education,[68] health,[69] employment[70] and personal,[71] the total cost of child abuse in Canada in 1998 was computed at Cdn\$15,705,910,047—a figure which the authors considered represented the minimum estimate of the cost to society.[72] Whilst Governments and others responsible for abuse, such as an established church, may offer reparation, such offers are often only feasible without a trial or a hearing if a general award is granted representing the assumed harm to each victim. Only tort law automatically offers compensation that is specifically calculated according to the harm done and the consequential needs of each victim.

The objective of compensation also explains why tort litigants are not content with the statutory routes for making complaints of maladministration against child protection agencies, which Lord Browne-Wilkinson in *X v Bedfordshire* thought were adequate replacements for a duty of care actionable in negligence.[73] Complaint procedures to the Local Authority Ombudsman about the conduct of a child abuse investigation, or under the Children Act 1989 for children who are provided accommodation by a local authority or voluntary organization,[74] should be regarded as supplementing rather than supplanting a tort action for compensation.[75]

Each of these objectives of tort litigants mirrors the obligations of states under international law, and in particular under the United Nations Convention on the Rights of the Child (UNCRC) to which all members of the United Nations have

---

[64] *KM v HM* [1992] 3 SCR 3 (SCC) 28.

[65] Bowlus, McKenna, Day, and Wright (n 59). The economic model adopted is explained at 5–8.

[66] Comprising policing, court trials, legal aid, criminal injuries compensation and penal costs of incarceration, parole and statutory release.

[67] Comprising foster care, and provincially and privately funded social welfare and child protection programmes.

[68] Comprising increased demand for special education services relating to behavioural problems and learning disabilities among child abuse victims.

[69] Including costs paid by both governments and individuals and comprising the immediate effects of abuse of a child, persistent medical problems as a result of an abuse of history, and long-term medical costs experienced by adult survivors of abuse.

[70] Measuring lost income from (1) the more marginal labour force activity characteristic of the abused population, reflecting lower educational attainment, problems in holding a job, and low self-esteem because of childhood maltreatment, (2) lost earnings as a result of incarceration related to child abuse for both perpetrators and victims, and (3) reduced tax revenues as a result of lower productivity and consequently lower GDP.

[71] Comprising costs for victims and their families including transportation, relocation, legal costs, drugs, therapies, alcohol abuse, self defence systems, or any good or service produced as a direct or indirect result of child abuse.   [72] Bowlus, McKenna, Day, and Wright (n 59) 91–93.

[73] *X v Bedfordshire County Council* [1995] 2 AC 633 (HL) 751.

[74] The Children Act 1989 Representations Procedure (England) Regulations 2006 SI 2006 No 1738 (in force 1 September 2006) Regulation 9.

[75] As Lord Slynn pointed out in *Barrett v Enfield London Borough Council* [2001] 2 AC 550 (HL) 568.

subscribed (with the regrettable exceptions of the United States and Somalia). Article 39 of the UNCRC states:

State Parties shall take all appropriate measures to promote physical and psychological recovery and social reintegration of a child victim of: any form of neglect, exploitation, or abuse; torture or any other form of cruel, inhuman or degrading treatment or punishment; or armed conflicts. Such recovery and reintegration shall take place in an environment which fosters the health, self-respect and dignity of the child.

Article 8 of the Universal Declaration of Human Rights (1948) establishes the principle that everyone has the right to an effective remedy by competent national tribunals for acts violating the fundamental rights guaranteed by the national constitution or by law. Tort law has a role to play in ensuring that the victim or those responsible for that victim can instigate court proceedings to provide the necessary compensation to ensure that the victim has access to such treatment programmes.

Our analysis will focus upon the following themes:

- the extent to which the current law of tort fulfils these objectives for childhood victims of physical and sexual abuse and neglect, and whether the tort rules need to be changed or other avenues of redress be pursued;
- the oscillating views of common law courts about tort law as the instrument and as the nemesis of public policy;
- varying views as to whether an institution's liability to children for whom they are in some way responsible should be formulated as strict or fault liability;
- the influence upon the development of tort law of fears about the negative implications of imposing tort liability upon child protection authorities in respect of their investigative functions; and
- the infiltration of tort law by human rights principles which establish the child as a rights-holder vis-à-vis the state and its subsidiary bodies, as well as vis-à-vis private persons and entities.

2. Some points on procedural issues

First, a few points about the structure and scope of the discussion of tort liability in Chapter 4. Tort law is volatile and rapidly developing, especially so in relation to claims arising out of physical and sexual abuse. In tort law perhaps more than any other legal area adjudicating claims of child abuse, there has been cross-pollination of principles and arguments amongst the common law jurisdictions. To illustrate this, we will usually weave the views of the different jurisdictions into the substance of our discussion, rather than first outlining the English position and then comparing it with those of other jurisdictions, as we have done elsewhere in this book.

In 1998, as part of the comprehensive reform of the rules governing civil litigation in England and Wales, the term for the party commencing the civil action, 'plaintiff', was replaced by 'claimant'. Thus far no other Commonwealth jurisdiction has followed this lead. This poses a problem for any writer in tort law. We have decided to use the term 'claimant' throughout our analysis of the caselaw from all jurisdictions, leaving 'plaintiff' only where it appears in a quotation from a case or statute.

Courts in England and Wales considering the burden on the claimant to prove child abuse have adopted the standard formulated by the House of Lords in care proceedings in *R v H (Minors) (Sexual Abuse: Standard of Proof)*, that the inherent probability or improbability of an event is itself a matter to be taken into account when weighing the probabilities and deciding whether, on balance, the event occurred, and that in general the more serious the allegation, the less likely it is that it occurred.[76]

There are many other more important procedural issues arising from civil actions for child abuse. A detailed discussion of these issues is beyond the scope of this Part, which is focusing on the construction of liability rules for child abuse in tort law, but we will mention them briefly. We will not address remedies, and specifically the quantification of damage in a tort claim, and the problems of establishing causation of that damage (for example, the requirement that the claimant prove that but for the abuse, the psychological damage leading to loss of educational and employment opportunities, subsequent criminal behaviour etc, would not have occurred). Nor will we discuss in detail compensation available from criminal injury compensation bodies in the different jurisdictions. We do not discuss the evidential problems of pursuing or defending an action which are peculiar to cases of 'historic abuse', where claimants allege that they were abused, often in an institutional setting, many years earlier. We also will not be discussing liability insurance coverage issues, and in particular whether the insurer's covenant to defend an insured (usually the abuser's employer or through another institutional connection) extends to the panoply of actions in which child abuse claims might be pleaded, except where such cases give rise to issues pertaining to the rules of liability in tort law as opposed to insurance law.

We will however pause briefly to consider the universal problem of limitation periods, which usually takes up at least a major chapter in books on child abuse tort actions,[77] because of its distorting effects upon the civil liability rules in all the jurisdictions we are considering. The vast majority of compensation claims are still brought as historic abuse cases, when the alleged victim is an adult. The cause of action in tort nonetheless arises at the instant the tort is committed, raising some very difficult questions. Firstly, the period within which a claimant can sue will be prescribed by statute, usually in the range of two to six years from the date the cause of action was complete. Where the claimant is a child or suffering from a disability such as mental incompetence or unsoundness of mind, common law jurisdictions usually extend the limitation period until some prescribed time after the child reaches her majority or has overcome that disability so as to be aware of her legal rights to sue.[78] Sometimes

---

[76] *Re H (Minors: Sexual Abuse: Standard of Proof)* [1996] AC 563 (HL), applied in *Various Claimants v Flintshire CC (formerly Clwyd CC) [North Wales Children's Homes Litigation]* Case No HQ9901416, [2000] WL 33793637 (QBD) [17]; *AR [Various Claimants] v Bryn Alyn* 26 June 2001, No HQ/99/01473, [2003] EWCA Civ 85 (QBD Connell J) [10].

[77] Limitation periods can be the greatest procedural obstacle to pursuing a tort claim in all the jurisdictions we are considering: E-A Gumbel QC, M Johnson and R Scorer *Child Abuse Compensation Claims* (The Law Society, London 2002) 131 5.1.1; EK Grace and SM Vella *Civil Liability for Sexual Abuse and Violence in Canada* (Butterworths, Toronto and Vancouver 2000) 111–131.

[78] eg Limitation Act 1980 (UK) s 28.

the statute also has a prescribed 'long-stop' period which extinguishes the cause of action. The rationales for limiting the period within which a defendant can be sued include providing an incentive to prospective claimants to act with diligence and dispatch, giving potential defendants legal certainty and finality (sometimes described as 'repose'), and preventing the potential injustice if courts were required to pass judgment on events which took place in the distant past on the basis of evidence which might have become unreliable and incomplete.[79]

All common law jurisdictions have found that historic claims of child abuse, often brought decades after the incidents in issue, test limitation statutes to destruction.[80] As Sedley LJ has observed, limitations issues are inevitable in child abuse tort cases, 'because it is in the nature of abuse of children by adults that it creates shame, fear and confusion, and these in turn produce silence. Silence is known to be one of the most pernicious fruits of abuse. It means that allegations commonly surface, if they do, only many years after the abuse has ceased.'[81]

Stratagems to prolong or evade the prima facie applicable limitation period have been developed by creative counsel for claimants, engendering much caselaw, mostly of a highly technical nature, in all of the jurisdictions we are considering. One approach is to sue in equity, since claims in equity can usually escape the rigours of limitation of actions statutes. Canadian[82] and New Zealand[83] courts, in a blatantly instrumentalist use of equity, have 'discovered' a fiduciary relationship between the alleged abuser and the victim, or between the institution in whose care the child was placed, and the child.[84] Thus far British courts have been resistant to extending fiduciary duties from a child's property to a child's person.

Another stratagem is to argue that a claimant cannot be expected to sue until she is reasonably capable of discovering the wrongful nature of the defendant's acts, and the nexus between those acts and her psychological injuries. This argument builds upon statutory postponement of the limitation period until the claimant is mentally competent to make the decision to sue. The Supreme Court of Canada went so far down this route as to set up a rebuttable evidential presumption that the cause of action crystallizes only at the time when the victim receives psychotherapy.[85]

---

[79] *Stubbings v UK* (1997) 23 EHRR 213 (ECtHR) [49]; J Mosher 'Challenging Limitation Periods: Civil Claims by Adult Survivors of Incest' (1994) 44 U Toronto LJ 169, 181–200.

[80] A useful compendium of provisions and reform proposals in common law jurisdictions may be found in Irish Law Reform Commission *Consultation Paper on the Law of Limitation of Actions Arising from Non-Sexual Abuse of Children* (LRC CP 16–2000, [2000] IELRC 2).

[81] *Ablett v Devon County Council and the Home Office* A3/2000/3187, A2/2000/3281, 4 December 2000 (CA) [4].

[82] *KM v HM* (n 64). Pleadings of concurrent liability can cause problems where civil juries are permitted, as they can judge only the tort claims, and not the claims in equity which must be separately adjudicated by the trial judge: *J(LA) v J(H)* (1993) 102 DLR (4th) 177 (Ont Gen Div).

[83] *T v H* [1995] 3 NZLR 37 (New Zealand CA); *S v G* [1995] 3 NZLR 681 (New Zealand CA); *H v R* [1996] 1 NZLR 299 (New Zealand HC).

[84] For detailed analysis, see Hoyano 'The Flight to the Fiduciary Haven' in P Birks (ed) *Privacy and Loyalty* (Clarendon Press, Oxford 1997) 226–247; R Flannigan 'Fiduciary Regulation of Sexual Exploitation' (2000) 79 Can Bar Rev 308.

[85] *KM v HM* (n 64) 292–305, Sopinka J dissenting on this issue.

In England, the situation is much more complicated. The Limitation Act 1980 provides for extension of the limitation period in case of 'disability' (s 28), which is defined as unsound mind or a child under the age of 18 years (s 38(2)). The difficulty for English and Welsh child abuse litigants is that s 14, providing that the limitation period starts to run from the date on which the claimant has acquired the specified knowledge,[86] apples only to claims for personal injury caused by negligence, nuisance or breach of duty (under s 11), or death (under s 12), for which the limitation period is three years. For all other torts, s 2 prescribes the limitation period of six years from the date when the cause of action accrued. What is more, the court's discretion to allow a time-barred action where it is equitable to do so under s 14 applies only to personal injury claims under s 11.

In *Stubbings v Webb* the Court of Appeal applied the 'discoverability' approach to claims of battery arising from incest beginning 28 years earlier when the claimant was aged two to fourteen.[87] In sensitive discussions of the psychological impact of abuse upon the victim,[88] Bingham LJ and Browne-Wilkinson LJ (as they then were) pulled intentional torts such as trespass to the person within s 11 on the basis that they constitute a breach of the duty not to infringe the child's legal right not to be interfered with. Therefore the claimant had to sue within three years of acquiring the knowledge that her personal injury was attributable to the defendants' acts alleged to constitute a 'breach of duty'.[89] However, this interpretation of the Limitation Act 1980 was firmly rejected by the House of Lords,[90] Lord Griffiths remarking that he had 'the greatest difficulty in accepting that a woman who knows that she has been raped does not know that she has suffered a significant injury'.[91] The ECtHR held that the interpretation of the legislation by the House of Lords fell within a Member State's margin of appreciation.[92] However, the European Court warned that

[t]here has been a developing awareness in recent years of the range of problems caused by child abuse and its psychological effects on victims, and it is possible that the rules on limitation of actions applying in Member States of the Council of Europe may have to be amended to make special provision for this group of claimants in the near future.[93]

---

[86] The gist of the prescribed actual or imputed knowledge under s 14 is that the injury in question was significant, attributable to the act or omission which is alleged to constitute negligence, nuisance or a breach of duty, and the identity of the defendant.   [87] *Stubbings v Webb* [1991] 3 All ER 949 (CA).
[88] ibid 954–956 (Bingham LJ), 959–960 (Browne-Wilkinson LJ).   [89] ibid 953–954.
[90] *Stubbings v Webb* [1993] AC 498 (HL) 325, 329. Lord Griffiths held that the famous case of *Letang v Cooper* [1965] 1 QB 232 (CA), where Lord Denning MR held in *obiter* that 'breach of duty' covered breach of any duty under the law of tort, including trespass to the person, interpreted the Limitation Act 1963, and so was not applicable to the Limitation Act 1980.
[91] ibid 506. It should be noted that the claimant alleged that the sexual and physical abuse started when she was aged 2 and continued until she was 14. Cases applying *Stubbings v Webb* to intentional torts committed in an institutional setting include *AR v Bryn Alyn* (n 76), [2003] QB 1441 (CA), leave to appeal to HL dismissed [2004] 1 WLR 1394, and *C v Middlesbrough Council* [2004] EWCA Civ 1746.
[92] *Stubbings v UK* (n 79).
[93] ibid 234. As of the date of writing, the Council of Europe has not taken action on civil claims for child abuse.

The Law Commission, responding to the Court of Appeal's invitation in 1995 to consider the anomalies in this area,[94] rejected arguments for a special limitation period, or indeed for no limitation period at all, for litigating child sexual abuse actions.[95] Instead, it recommended that the limitation periods be generally consistent for all civil claims including tort, with child abuse being encompassed by the personal injury provisions.[96] That period should run not from the date the cause of action accrues, but rather from the date the claimant had actual or constructive knowledge of the facts which give rise to the cause of action; the identity of the defendant; and that any injury, loss, damage, or benefit was significant. Where the litigant was a child at the time of the alleged events, the limitation period would be treated as ending three years from the date on which the child attains the age of 18 (regardless of the limitation period prescribed for a particular claim) or the end of the period when the limitation period would otherwise end, whichever is the later.[97] However, the court would have a wider discretionary power in cases of personal injury to rule that a limitation of action defence should not apply.[98] These recommendations have not been implemented to date. In February 2006 the Court of Appeal gave leave to appeal to the House of Lords in three cases involving sexual assault tort actions against the abusers, in the express hope that the Law Lords will reconsider *Stubbings v Webb* given Parliament's inaction.[99] Added impetus may be added by the ruling of the Australian High Court in July 2006 interpreting Victorian limitation of actions legislation (which was deliberately drafted on the English model) as encompassing trespass to the person in 'breach of duty'; the High Court rejected *Stubbings v Webb*, as 'statutes of limitation are more concerned with practical justice than with jurisprudential analysis' and that 'no legislative purpose is served by putting the perpetrators of intentional torts in a better position than the perpetrators of unintentional torts'.[100]

Reliance on psychological findings to postpone the tolling of the limitation bell has given rise to a fierce debate in the United States, and to a lesser extent in Britain and Canada, about whether memories of abuse can be repressed, and then 'discovered' in the course of psychotherapy, labelled according to its partisans as 'repressed/recovered memory syndrome' and 'false/fabricated memory syndrome'.[101]

---

[94] *Seymour v Williams* [1995] PIQR P470 (CA) [100].

[95] Law Commission of England & Wales *Limitation of Actions* (Law Com 270, 9 July 2001) [4.23]–[4.29].

[96] ibid [4.29]. In 2005 the Association of Child Abuse Lawyers started a campaign for implementation of that recommendation.   [97] Draft Limitation Bill (Law Com No 270) s 28.

[98] ibid s 12.

[99] *A v Hoare; H v Suffolk County Council; X and Y v London Borough of Wandsworth* [2006] EWCA Civ 395 [39]–[41].   [100] *Stingel v Clark* [2006] HCA 37 (Aus HC) [8], [17].

[101] There is an enormous corpus of scientific and polemical works on repressed memory. For a taste, see MA Conway (ed) *Recovered Memories and False Memories* (OUP, Oxford 1997); EF Loftus 'The Reality of Repressed Memories' (1993) 48 American Psychologist 518; SJ Ceci and M Bruck *Jeopardy in the Courtroom: a Scientific Analysis of Children's Testimony* (American Psychological Association, Washington DC 1995) chapters 13 and 14; A Memon and M Young 'Desperately Seeking Evidence: the Recovered Memory Debate' (1997) 2(2) Legal & Criminal Logical Psychology 131; DH Gleaves, SM Smith, LD Butler, and D Spiegel 'False and Recovered Memories in the Laboratory and Clinic: a Review of Experimental and Clinical Evidence' (2004) VII N1 Clinical Psychology: Science and Practice; E Loftus and K Ketcham *The Myth of Repressed Memory* (St Martin's Press, New York 1994); M Pendergrast *Victims of Memory: Incest Accusations*

There has been a flurry of legislation in American States postponing the tolling of the limitation period for alleged victims of child sexual abuse until the psychological effects and causal connection with the abuse are recognized by the claimant. In our view, it is difficult to justify privileging child abuse litigants by giving them a special (or no) limitation period when other 'deserving' claimants such as victims of physical abuse and neglect, or long-hidden industrial disease, might not benefit in the same way.

So, the current position in England is that a cause of action based on an intentional tort such as rape or indecent assault is limited by s 2 of the Limitation Act 1980 to six years from the date of the assault, or three years from the claimant's 18th birthday, regardless of the victim's knowledge that what had occurred is actionable. Therefore the claimant, usually by the age of 21, has to have overcome the complex psychological consequences of the abuse to the extent of appreciating who was responsible, and have received the necessary medical and legal advice to commence an action. There is no judicial discretion to remove the time bar. The irony is that a claim in negligence, or for another type of breach of duty against someone who has not directly abused the claimant but failed to prevent it, will benefit from the postponement of the limitation period until the claimant has the necessary knowledge, whereas the claim against the actual abuser is time-barred.[102] The Irish Law Reform Commission aptly describes this situation as 'anomalous and absurd',[103] and the English Court of Appeal has said that it is 'illogical and surprising'.[104] It is submitted that the recommendations of the Law Commission should be implemented forthwith.[105]

We turn now to analysing the wide range of tort actions which may be available to a victim of sexual or physical abuse or neglect. We shall discover that while tort can be a very powerful and effective weapon, the liability rules (as well as the procedural

---

and Shattered Lives (HarperCollins, London 1996). In the British context, see S Brandon, J Boakes, D Glaser and R Green 'Recovered Memories of Child Sexual Abuse: Implications for Clinical Practice' (1998) 172 British J of Psychiatry 296 (reporting on the recommendations of the Royal College of Psychiatrists' Working Group on Reported Recovered Memories of Child Sexual Abuse); British Psychological Society *Recovered Memories: the Report of the Working Party of the British Psychological Society* (1995); GH Gudjonsson 'Accusations by Adults of Child Sexual Abuse: a Survey of the Members of the British False Memory Society (BFMS)' (1997) 11(1) Applied Cognitive Psychology 3 with a response by EF Loftus 'Repressed Memory Accusations: Devastated Families and Devastated Patients' (1997) 11(1) Applied Cognitive Psychology 25.

[102] Noted in *S v W (Child Abuse: Damages)* [1995] 1 FLR 862 (CA). See also JR Allinson 'Limitation of Actions in Child Abuse Cases' [April 1996] J of Personal Injury Litigation 19.

[103] Irish Law Reform Commission *Consultation Paper on the Law of Limitation* (n 80) [2.013].

[104] *S v W* (n 102) [867] (Sir Ralph Gibson), reiterated in *AR v Bryn Alyn* (n 91) [100] *per curiam*: 'early statutory implementation . . . would obviate much arid and highly wasteful litigation turning on a distinction of no apparent principle or other merit'.

[105] The impetus for reform may be provided by public outrage when the tort claim of a victim of attempted rape was struck out under *Stubbings* after the perpetrator won £7,000,000 from the National Lottery whilst serving a sentence for that offence [*A v Iorworth Hoare* [2005] EWHC 2161 (QB); appeal dismissed but leave to appeal to HL granted by CA: *A v Hoare etc* (n 99)].

rules) can make the road to a verdict in all of our jurisdictions both convoluted and scattered with potholes.

B. The Tort Liability of the Abuser

1. Liability in battery for physical and sexual abuse

Battery, one form of trespass to the person,[106] is a powerful tort, predicated on the absolute right of the individual to control what is done with and to his or her own body. As an affirmation of the personal autonomy and bodily integrity which this choice implies, it can be a crucial bulwark against the exploitation of a position of dominance over others, such as adults and children, police officers and citizens, health professionals and patients, and the wrongful exercise of statutory authority.[107] It should be noted however that parents and others standing *in loco parentis* have the right at common law to use physical force to chastise a child, and so tort law parallels criminal law in establishing a reasonable chastisement defence which immunizes liability for what would be a battery against an adult.[108] Subject to this qualification, battery is actionable '*per se*', that is, without any proof of actual damage (such as physical or psychiatric harm) to complete the cause of action. It is therefore the pre-eminent tort against sexual and physical abusers, including homicide, and Commonwealth courts have rightly resisted attempts to displace it with new nominate torts such as incest[109] or sexual battery.[110]

Given the long history of the tort at common law, and its relative simplicity, it is surprising that its parameters are still a matter for debate. The issues which continue to be litigated in all the jurisdictions we are considering are:

- whether the claimant must prove a fault element in relation to the defendant's state of mind to set up a prima facie case for battery, or whether it suffices to prove direct interference with the claimant's person;

- if he must, whether that fault element is defined as:
  — the defendant's intention to cause the physical contact, or
  — in addition, the defendant's intention that such contact be harmful or offensive to the claimant;

---

[106] The other two forms of trespass against the person are assault (the apprehension of infliction of a battery), and false imprisonment. Assault and battery are therefore tort analogues of the common law criminal offences.

[107] Thus in *Muir v Alberta* (1996) 132 DLR (4th) 695 (Alberta QB), the Alberta Government was found liable for the wrongful sterilization of a child in 1959, under the purported authority of eugenics legislation, when she was incorrectly classified as a 'moron' and wrongfully detained at a government-operated training school for 'mental defectives'.

[108] *Cleary v Booth* [1893] 1 QB 465 (QB) 468. For the early cases delineating what is and is not actionable in punishing a child see WE McCurdy 'Torts Between Persons in Domestic Relation' (1930) 43 Harvard L Rev 1030, 1059–1062.　　　　　[109] *KM v HM* (n 64) 24 (La Forest J).

[110] *T v H* (n 83).

- whether negligence in causing the physical contact is relevant as part of the claimant's case or as a defence;

- whether the issue of consent is a positive element of the tort, such that the claimant must prove he did not consent to the touching, or whether it is a defence, the burden of proof of which lies upon the defendant; and

- whether identifiable harm must result from the contact.

These issues are all relevant to child abuse.

(a) Does battery require proof of fault?

The issue about characterization of the tort of battery has arisen in Canadian[111] and American[112] courts in the context of insurance coverage, and specifically the insurer's covenant to defend an action in tort, where the insurance policy typically excludes 'bodily injury or property damage caused intentionally' by the insured. It has also arisen in the United States in connection with limitation periods, which typically are shorter for battery than for negligence.[113]

In Canada, trespass to the person does not require proof that the interference was intentional, provided that there is a direct connection between the defendant's act and the harm.[114] Because of this direct connection, it is viewed as just to allocate to the defendant the burden of proving that his act was neither intentional nor negligent, and therefore that he was not at fault.[115] As in criminal law, reasonable corporal punishment to enforce discipline pursuant to a legal authority over a child can serve as justification for physical contact.[116] 'Force' in the context of an allegation of sexual battery simply refers to physical contact of a sexual nature, and is neutral in the sense of not necessarily denoting a lack of consent.[117] In the specific context of sexual battery, in a case alleging a series of sexual assaults against a girl between the ages of 14 and

---

[111] *Scalera v Non-Marine Underwriters, Lloyd's of London* 2000 SCC 24, [2000] 1 SCR 551; *Sansalone v Wawanesa Mutual Insurance Co* 2000 SCC 25, [2000] 1 SCR 627.

[112] O Reynolds 'Tortious Battery: Is "I Didn't Mean any Harm" Relevant?' (1984) 37 Oklahoma L Rev 717, 726, 731. In the specific context of child sexual abuse: *CNA Insurance Co v McGinnis* 666 SW 2d 689 (Arkansas Supreme Ct 1984) 690; *BB v Continental Insurance Co* 8 F 3d 1288 (US CA 8th Cir 1993); *JC Penney Casualty Insurance Co v MK* 804 P 2d 689 (California SC 1991); *Horace Mann Insurance Co v Leeber* 376 SE 2d 581 (West Virginia Supreme CA 1988); *State Farm Fire & Casualty Co v DTS* 867 SW 2d 642 (Missouri CA 1993); *American States Insurance Co v Borbor* 826 F 2d 888 (US CA 9th Cir 1987); *Troelstrup v District Court* 712 P 2d 1010 (Colorado Supreme Ct (en banc) 1986); *Rodriguez v Williams* 729 P 2d 627 (Washington Supreme Ct (en banc) 1986); *Linebaugh v Berdish* 376 NW 2d 400 (Michigan CA 1985); *Horace Mann Insurance Co v Independent School District No 656* 355 NW 2d 413 (Minnesota Supreme Ct 1984).	[113] O Reynolds ibid 729.

[114] R Sullivan 'Trespass to the Person in Canada: a Defence of the Traditional Approach' (1987) 19 Ottawa L Rev 533, 540.

[115] *Cook v Lewis* [1951] SCR 830 (SCC) 839; *Scalera* (n 111) [12]–[13].

[116] *Murdoch v Richards* [1954] 1 DLR 766 (Nova Scotia Supreme Ct); *Moore v Slater* (1979) 101 DLR (3d) 176 (British Columbia Supreme Ct).	[117] *Scalera* (n 111) [1].

18, a narrow majority of the Supreme Court of Canada in *Scalera v Non-Marine Underwriters, Lloyds of London* held:

The tort of battery is aimed at protecting the personal autonomy of the individual. Its purpose is to recognise the right of each person to control his or her body and who touches it, and to permit damages where this right is violated. The compensation stems from violation of the right to autonomy, not fault. When a person interferes with the body of another, a *prima facie* case of violation of the plaintiff's autonomy is made out. The law may then fairly call upon the person thus implicated to explain, if he can. If he can show that he acted with consent, the *prima facie* violation is negated and the plaintiff's claim will fail. But it is not up to the plaintiff to prove that, in addition to directly interfering with her body, the defendant was also at fault.[118]

This stance means that there is no obligation on liability insurers to defend 'sexual battery' litigation, because if the sexual act was not consensual, the defendant is presumed by Canadian tort law to have intended to injure the claimant, and intentional torts are expressly excluded from coverage; conversely, if the act was consensual, then the tort of battery was not committed.[119] This conclusion also leads to the unfortunate consequence that the defendant is likely to be judgment-proof, particularly if he has been convicted and is serving a custodial sentence.

The view that trespass imposes liability upon proof of direct contact without proof of fault represented the traditional common law approach to battery,[120] albeit not always couched in rights-based terminology. However, since 1959 English law has developed in a different direction. In *Fowler v Lanning*[121] and later in *Letang v Cooper*,[122] it was held that trespass is a fault-based tort, and that fault is expressed in the intentional application of force, however trivial.[123] Unintentional contact is consigned to the tort of negligence. New Zealand courts have also adopted this classification of battery as an intentional tort.[124] Windeyer J of the Australian High Court, sitting as a trial judge in *McHale v Watson*,[125] declined to follow *Fowler v Lanning*, placing the onus of negativing intention or negligence on the defendant, but this has since been doubted.[126] American law generally also adopts the fault-based approach requiring a claimant to prove intentional action.[127]

Thus Canadian law is generally out of step with the rest of the common law world in imposing liability in trespass without proof of any fault (in the sense of an intentional

---

[118] ibid [15].

[119] ibid [37]–[39] (the majority and minority agreeing on this conclusion); *State Farm Fire and Casualty Co v Williams* 355 NW 2d 421 (Minnesota 1984) 424 reached the same conclusion.

[120] Sullivan (n 114) 540.

[121] *Fowler v Lanning* [1959] 1 QB 426 (QB), 440 (Diplock J (as he then was)).

[122] (n 90) 239 (Lord Denning MR).

[123] S Deakin, A Johnston, and B Markesinis *Markesinis & Deakin's Tort Law* (5th edn OUP, Oxford 2003) 414–415. [124] *Beales v Hayward* [1960] NZLR 131 (New Zealand Supreme Ct).

[125] *McHale v Watson* (1964) 111 CLR 384 (Aus HC (Windeyer J sitting as trial judge), appeal dismissed by the Full Court on another ground (1966) 115 CLR 199, 388–389.

[126] *Hackshaw v Shaw* (1984) 155 CLR 614 (Aus HC) [6], *obiter*.

[127] *Second Restatement of Tort* Div 1 Ch 2 Topic 1 §13 Battery: Harmful Contact.

or negligent act). The Supreme Court in *Scalera* defended this position on the basis that violation of another person's right to protection from invasions of his personal integrity can be considered a form of fault.[128] Moreover, cases of direct interference with the person tend to produce high 'demoralization costs':

> Victims and those who identify with them tend to feel resentment and insecurity if the wrong is not compensated. The close causal relationship between the defendant's conduct and the violation of the plaintiff's bodily integrity, the identification of the loss with the plaintiff's personality and freedom, the infliction of the loss in isolated (as opposed to systemic) circumstances, and the perception of the defendant's conduct as anti-social, all support the legal position that once the direct interference with the plaintiff's person is shown, the defendant may fairly be called upon to explain his behaviour if indeed it was innocent.[129]

These arguments have a particular resonance in the context of sexual abuse. One reason why jurisdictions other than Canada require the claimant to prove fault in some form is the perceived need to confine the tort to harmful or offensive contact, and so immunize casual and trivial physical contact which we all might reasonably be expected to tolerate, such as jostling in the street. In English law, the House of Lords has created a general exception 'embracing all physical contact which is generally acceptable in the ordinary conduct of everyday life'.[130] McLachlin J in *Scalera* was able to reconcile this exception with her position that battery does not require proof of fault or lack of consents on the basis that sexual contact is not a casual, accidental or inevitable consequence of general human activity and interaction, but rather involves singling out another person's body in a deliberate, targeted act.[131]

In those jurisdictions which require the claimant to prove some form of intention, the target may be simply the defendant's intention to cause the physical contact, or additionally, the defendant's intention or awareness (actual or constructive)[132] that the contact will be harmful or offensive to the recipient. The predominant view in England,[133] and in Canada before *Scalera*,[134] is that it suffices for the claimant to prove intentional touching which has the consequence of being offensive to the person touched. This is necessary because otherwise battery could not operate in the field of medical law, where the intent of the medical professional in providing treatment will almost invariably be to benefit the patient who has not consented to it.

---

[128] *Scalera* (n 111) [10].   [129] ibid [14].

[130] *In Re F* [1990] 2 AC 1 (HL) 73 (Lord Goff); *Wainwright v Home Office* [2003] UKHL 53, [2004] 2 AC 406 [9]; see also *Collins v Wilcock* [1984] 1 WLR 1172 (CA); *Wilson v Pringle* [1986] 2 All ER 440 (CA).   [131] *Scalera* (n 111) [21]–[22].

[132] Iacobucci J in dissent in *Scalera* asserted that in sexual battery consent, in so far as it is concerned with whether something is harmful or offensive, is an objective standard, the issue being whether the defendant should have known there was no valid consent, from which intention to harm can be inferred: *Scalera* (n 111) [108], [118], [119].   [133] *Wilson v Pringle* (n 130).

[134] See the academic and case authorities cited by the minority in *Scalera* (n 111) [96]–[98].

The *Second Restatement of Tort*[135] distils the predominant American approach to battery as follows:

An actor is subject to liability to another for battery if

(a) he acts intending to cause a harmful or offensive contact with the person of the other or a third person, or an imminent apprehension of such a contact, and

(b) a harmful contact with the person of the other directly or indirectly results.

However, even this summary is subject to considerable qualification and some disagreement; it has been pointed out that it is equivocal in that the requirement that the actor intend 'to cause a harmful or offensive contact' could mean intent to cause contact that in fact turns out to be harmful or offensive to the recipient, or it could also mean intent to harm or offend.[136] The preponderance of American authority holds that intent to harm or offend is not necessary to the tort of battery[137] but also finds that sexual assault is intentional.[138]

(b) The issue of consent

(i) Allocation of the burden of proof

There are two facets to the issue of consent: does the claimant have to prove that she did not consent to establish a prima facie case; and does she also have to prove that the defendant knew or should have known that she did not consent? The Canadian Supreme Court has pointed out that such rules, particularly if they are created specially for sexual battery, would run the risk of inappropriately shifting the focus of the trial from the defendant's behaviour to the claimant's character,[139] as notoriously happened in criminal cases before so-called 'rape shield' legislation.[140]

In Canada and Australia, the onus is on the defendant to prove consent by the claimant or, the obvious fall-back, his actual or constructive belief in consent as a discrete defence.[141] The rationale for the latter rule is that the claimant should not have to prove an issue of fact which lies first and foremost within the defendant's sphere of knowledge.[142] There is no special rule for battery involving sexual contact.[143]

It should be noted however that in *Scalera* Iacobucci J mounted a vigorous dissent on this point, arguing that consent should be an issue for the claimant because, unlike more traditional batteries, sexual activity by itself is not inherently harmful. Therefore, since the claimant has to prove that the touching was harmful or

---

[135] *Second Restatement of Tort* (n 127).   [136] Reynolds (n 112) 717.   [137] ibid 717, 718.
[138] And hence not covered by accident insurance (see cases cited in n 112).
[139] *Scalera* (n 111) [27]–[34], adopting the argument of Feldthusen (n 17) 282.
[140] Discussed below Chapter 9 section D.3.
[141] *Cook v Lewis* (n 115) 839; *Reibl v Hughes* [1980] 2 SCR 880 (SCC) [10]; *Norberg v Wynrib* (n 43) 246 (La Forest J) (*obiter*); *Department of Health & Community Services (NT) v JWB and SMB ('Marion's Case')* (1992) 175 CLR 218 (Aus HC) 311–312 (McHugh J).
[142] *Scalera* (n 111) [31].   [143] ibid [27]–[34].

offensive to her, that must be on the basis of her lack of consent.[144] While this is a defensible position, unfortunately His Lordship then muddied the waters by contending that the claimant must prove (a) the defendant intended to do the action, and (b) the reasonable person would have perceived that action as being non-consensual, and so harmful or offensive.[145] This is unpleasantly reminiscent of the mirage of the 'reasonable complainant' which has so long plagued the criminal courts.

Compared to other common law jurisdictions, there is a paucity of authority on sexual battery in England, but the current authorities on 'traditional' batteries hold that the claimant bears the burden of proving lack of consent.[146] New Zealand courts have taken a similar position on the basis that demonstrating lack of consent is necessary to establish the defendant's hostile intent and so must be proved by the claimant.[147]

(ii) Vitiation of consent

We have seen that consent has been removed by the Sexual Offences Act 2003 as a defence to all sexual offences against children under 16.[148] Since in English tort law absence of consent remains intrinsic to the civil tort of battery, however the burden of proof may be allocated, it should not be readily assumed that consent also has become irrelevant where the claimant is an adolescent at the relevant time. Therefore we must consider what can vitiate apparent consent. In *Freeman v Home Office (No 2)*[149] and in *Makanjuola v Commissioner of Police for the Metropolis*[150] the English courts have accepted that apparent consent is not necessarily conclusive, where the circumstances suggest that it has not been given fully and freely.

In *Norberg v Wynrib*,[151] where a physician fed his patient's addiction to prescription drugs in exchange for her sexual services, the majority of the Canadian Supreme Court found that the notion of consent must be modified to appreciate the reality of a power/dependency relationship between the parties.[152] Consent is vitiated where inequality of power is combined with exploitation of that power. Therefore the doctor was liable in battery. In contrast, the two women on the Court, Justices McLachlin and L'Heureux-Dubé, considered that the tort of battery is incapable of being cognizant of inequality between the parties, and that Ms Norberg gave actual and valid consent to the sexual acts. Instead, they resorted to constructing a fiduciary relationship between

---

[144] ibid [53], [104]–[105], [107].   [145] ibid [107], [118].

[146] *Freeman v Home Office (No 2)* [1984] 1 QB 524 (HC and CA) 537–539 (Cowan J). Sir John Donaldson in the Court of Appeal is less clear, but describes consent as 'a complete defence', implying that the onus is on the defendant: ibid 556–557.   [147] *H v R* (n 83) 305; *T v H* (n 83) 687.

[148] Discussed above Chapter 3 section E.

[149] (n 146) 556, 557 (CA), approving the trial judge's statement at 542–543 (in the context of a prisoner consenting to medical treatment).

[150] *Makanjuola v Commissioner of Police for the Metropolis The Times*, 31 July 1989 (QB) (claimant submitted to sexual assault by an immigration officer who threatened to have her deported for a minor breach of her visa conditions).   [151] *Norberg v Wynrib* (n 43).

[152] ibid [26]–[41] (La Forest J, Gonthier and Cory JJ concurring).

physician and patient, a radical departure from the previous confines of the fiduciary principle to protection of property and analogous interests. While the fiduciary analysis is very powerful, it is submitted that Their Ladyships should not have dismissed the possibility of concurrent liability for the tort of battery and breach of fiduciary duty.[153]

The distorting effects of the fiduciary analysis in *Norberg v Wynrib* are apparent when battery is considered in the context of sexual relations with adolescents. In *Taylor v MacGillivray*,[154] a girl aged 16 entered into a sexual relationship with a physician who was purporting to give her psychotherapy for abuse she had suffered in early childhood. He induced her to live with him and his wife as their foster daughter and as his employee in his medical office. The trial judge found that she was suffering from chronic severe emotional and physical health problems which made her emotionally immature, and that there was an actual inequality of power between her and the defendant in their multiple-layered relationship of psychotherapist, foster father and employer. Nevertheless, he concluded that she had consented freely and voluntarily to the sexual relationship, and therefore the action in battery failed. Liability was ultimately hung on the peg of his fiduciary duty as a physician, following the minority in *Norberg v Wynrib*. It is submitted that the evidence clearly satisfied the liability test for battery propounded by the majority in *Norberg*, as an inequality of relationship patently existed which was exploited by the defendant, such as to vitiate the girl's apparent consent.

In practical terms, in child abuse cases the issue of actual consent being vitiated by a relationship of inequality will rise only with adolescents, particularly those with previous sexual experience. In another Canadian example, *M(M) v K(K)*, it was held that there could be no valid consent between a 41-year-old man and his foster daughter aged 15, notwithstanding that she had initiated the sexual contact.[155] In *Lyth v Dagg*,[156] a homosexual relationship between a 15-year-old pupil and his teacher was deemed to be non-consensual because the claimant's will was overborne by the dominating influence of his teacher and his desire to please him; any apparent consent by the adolescent claimant was 'entirely spurious'. However, when the sexual relationship continued after the claimant had turned 16, since he had not availed himself of abundant opportunities to put an end to it, there was an inescapable inference of consent, and damages were limited to the previous incident. In contrast, in *Harder v Brown* where a very vulnerable girl was treated as 'a slave' by her own family, and a 62-year-old man confined to a wheelchair was her only source of affection, his abuse of her starting at age ten was clearly non-consensual, and the court was not prepared to accept that her apparent acquiescence in later years amounted to what the law recognised as consent.[157]

---

[153] For more detailed analysis, see Hoyano 'The Flight to the Fiduciary Haven' (n 84) 226–238.
[154] *Taylor v MacGillivray* (1993) 110 DLR (4th) 64 (Ontario Gen Div).
[155] *M(M) v K(K)* (1989) 61 DLR (4th) 382 (British Columbia CA).   [156] *Lyth v Dagg* (n 9).
[157] *Harder v Brown* (n 11) [29]–[34].

The notion of exploitation of a power/dependency relationship as vitiating consent has yet to be firmly implanted in English civil law. The issue has been litigated as a matter of interpretation in relation to claims for compensation by child prostitutes under the Criminal Injuries Compensation Scheme,[158] which requires as a precondition for compensation for physical or mental injury[159] that the applicant be the victim of 'a crime of violence'. In a series of applications for judicial review from decisions of the Criminal Injuries Compensation Appeals Panel, the issue was whether it should be open to that tribunal to take into account the factual consent of the applicant to the acts causing his injury, even though that factual consent would in law not be effective to prevent the acts from being criminal.

In the first case, the applicant Brown was an inmate of an 'approved school', a youth correctional facility, where sexual activity between the boys was commonplace. The panel found that he had willingly offered himself to the other boys in the school as a rent boy, and concluded that his factual consent precluded him from being a victim of a crime of violence. Collins J in the court of Queen's Bench ruled that this was an error as a matter of public policy because consent could not make the difference where the act itself was violence towards a child.[160]

The matter went to the Court of Appeal in a conjoined appeal with Carl August,[161] who was already emotionally disturbed when he was taken into care at age eight and who probably had been sexually abused in early childhood. He subsequently became a 'rent boy', and applied for compensation under the Scheme for an act of buggery in return for money when he was 13 or 14, on a 53-year-old man (who was subsequently convicted). Over the next four months this sexual activity continued until August reported the man to Social Services (who took no action) and then to the police. The Appeals Panel had rejected his application on the same basis as they did Brown. A psychiatric report filed in the court proceedings stated that August was a damaged and vulnerable child with a serious mental health problem, that predatory paedophiles target such boys, and that given the age of the perpetrator the boy could not be regarded as being able to make an 'informed choice' in the matter.[162] Buxton LJ reasoned that under the Sexual Offences Act 1956, it was misconceived to argue that a child could not give a valid consent in law to buggery.[163] Buxton LJ held that in each case the panel had to decide whether the events that actually occurred were (a) a crime, and (b) a crime of violence.[164] This

---

[158] Given statutory footing by the Criminal Injuries Compensation Act 1995, although it had already been in operation for many years.

[159] Para 19(c) of the Scheme specifically excluded compensation for mental injury arising out of sexual activity which was consensual in fact, albeit not in law.

[160] *R v Criminal Injuries Compensation Appeals Panel ex p Andrew Stuart Brown* unreported, 30 June 2000 (QB) [29].

[161] *R v Criminal Injuries Compensation Appeals Panel ex p August and ex p Brown* [2001] 2 All ER 874 (CA).

[162] Included in the statement of facts before the ECtHR: *August v UK* (2003) 36 EHRR CD115 (ECtHR).

[163] *ex p August and Brown* (n 161). Pill LJ forcefully disagreed on this point [111]. Fortunately, this loophole was closed by the Sexual Offences Act 2003 ss 5–13.

[164] ibid [24].

meant that the panel had not been irrational in Brown's case to hold that the consensual acts were not crimes of violence. The Court of Appeal rejected the argument of Allan Levy QC that current public policy requires that such a child, especially one with the horrific background of Carl August, be treated as a victim and not as a consenting participant, holding that the scheme could not award compensation for general failings on the part of society.[165] August's application to the House of Lords for leave to appeal was denied, as was his application to the ECtHR under Articles 6 to 8 of the ECHR. The European Court rejected August's complaint that he was being penalized because of his background of sexual abuse and damage and that considerations of voluntariness should not be taken into account where children are concerned.[166]

The only crack in the barrier excluding child prostitutes from access to the Criminal Injuries Compensation Scheme was the gloss by Sir Anthony Evans in *August* and *Brown* that 'non-consent' implicit in the definition of a 'crime of violence' means the absence of 'real' consent, freely and voluntarily given.[167] In *JE*,[168] the applicant for judicial review claimed compensation for sexual acts committed against him by a much older cellmate, who was probably a paedophile, whilst he was on remand in prison. JE had had no sexual experience prior to these encounters. The Appeals Panel had found that although he was mentally handicapped and suggestible to the extent that he could not consent in law to the sexual acts,[169] he had actually consented in fact, because he was twice the active participant in anal intercourse and did not complain to the prison authorities.[170] The Court of Appeal allowed the appeal, suggesting that a crime could be one of violence so long as there is no 'real consent', and that submission to the act did not meet that test. In each case the tribunal should ask itself whether the applicant, notwithstanding the appearance of consent, could still be properly regarded as a victim.[171] An important factor for our present analysis was the emphasis placed by Lord Woolf CJ on the tribunal looking for an imbalance in the relationship between the parties which put the vulnerable party at a significant disadvantage.[172]

Subsequent decisions have shown however that children who are deemed to be victims by the criminal law on the basis of assumed vulnerability will not necessarily be treated as such for the purposes of criminal injuries compensation. Silber J found that a 12-year-old girl, CD, who had been plied with alcohol prior to unlawful sexual intercourse with a man aged 21, was not 'vulnerable', relying upon her sexual banter with the man, her inconsistent statements to others about whether she had enjoyed it, and a sexual encounter a few months earlier with a boy aged 13.[173] In contrast, in the companion appeal, *JM*, Silber J. found the requisite vulnerability where a girl

---

[165] ibid [32], [43], [50].   [166] *August v UK* (n 162) [3].

[167] *ex p August and Brown* (n 161).

[168] *R v Criminal Injuries Compensation Appeals Panel ex p JE* [2002] EWCA Civ 1050 (permission for leave to appeal).   [169] Under the Sexual Offences Act 1956 ss 15(3), 45.

[170] *ex p JE* (n 168) (permission for leave to appeal).

[171] *R v Criminal Injuries Compensation Appeals Panel ex p JE* [2003] EWCA Civ 234 [28].

[172] ibid [32]–[33].

[173] *R v Criminal Injuries Compensation Appeal Panel ex p CD and ex p JM* [2004] EWHC 1674 (Admin) 1674 [33]–[39].

aged 12 to 14, already conditioned to being sexually abused by adults, was sexually exploited by the much older son of her foster mother.[174]

The European Court seemed to be strongly influenced in *August v UK* by the fact that the statutory compensation scheme provided ex gratia payments to victims of violent criminal offences, and therefore the criteria for such compensation lay within the Contracting State's margin of appreciation.[175] It may be that a different view would be taken under the ECHR in relation to a child's claim for tort compensation against the abuser for battery, where sexual contact is proved but the older party alleges factual consent.

Bruce Feldthusen has rightly warned that the traditional view of consent in relation to battery, which holds that the claimant's knowledge of the nature of the act will excuse the tort, is deeply inappropriate to prolonged patterns of sexual wrongdoing and especially incest. He points out that teenagers, and often even very young victims after the first attack, are capable of appreciating the nature of the sexual contact.[176] Courts have recognized that children who have previously been victims of sexual abuse may submit to others in the belief that it is their desert in life;[177] their previous sexual experience enhances their vulnerability rather than equipping them with the means to fend off unwanted contact.

Therefore consent needs to be reconceptualized for the tort of battery in a sexual context, whether it is configured as a discrete defence or its absence as a necessary element of the tort. A civil court should never accept a defendant's protestation that he did not regard his sexual contact with a child before puberty as being harmful, or that he relied upon apparent consent. It is submitted that in relation to adolescents, consent should be regarded as necessarily vitiated where the child is under the legal age of consent to sexual contact (16), coupled with evidence of exploitation of an obvious and significant imbalance of power in the relationship, in keeping with the reasoning in *JE*. The second requirement should avoid problems which can arise from adolescents' sexual experimentation with one another. Such analysis would project into tort law Parliament's policy decisions in the Sexual Offences Act 2003 that a child under 13 is conclusively deemed to be incapable of consent, and creating offences based upon sexual grooming and abuse of a position of trust with a child.[178]

(c) Negligent battery?

Physical injuries can result from negligence, and sexual contact may occur where the defendant claims he did not realize that the touching would be interpreted by the claimant or others as sexual in nature, or claims that he did not realize that the claimant (for example, an adolescent) would find the touching offensive. Occasionally, it is

---

[174] ibid [69]–[75].   [175] *August v UK* (n 162) [2].

[176] Feldthusen 'The Canadian Experiment with the Civil Action for Sexual Battery' (n 17) 282.

[177] *ex p CD and ex p JM* (n 173) [74]–[75].

[178] Sexual Offences Act 2003 ss 5–9, 15–22 discussed in Chapter 3 section E.1. The statutory definition of 'positions of trust' in s 21 includes situations where a child is accommodated in a community home, voluntary home or children's home, a home provided under s 82(5) of the Children Act 1989, or is under age 18 and is receiving education at an educational institution.

suggested that it should suffice if the claimant can prove that the defendant should have known that she did not consent, in effect a plea of negligence.[179] This argument is particularly attractive to jurisdictions which require the claimant to prove fault beyond intentional conduct. In *Fowler v Lanning*, Diplock J (as he then was) would have permitted a category of negligent trespass to the person in a case of unintentional shooting.[180] However, such suggestions seem to have fallen on infertile ground. Ruth Sullivan has perceptively pointed out that under the negligent fault theory, the existence and scope of the claimant's right to security is controlled by the existence and scope of the defendant's freedom to act; the claimant's right begins where the defendant's freedom ends, and the latter is defined first.[181] While trespass to the person recognizes the individual's right to control of, and access to, her person by acknowledging 'the person within the physical shell', negligence is inadequate because the claimant's right to physical security is sacrificed to the goals of the defendant where these have been reasonably pursued.[182] It is submitted that there is no place for negligent battery, at least in relation to sexual contact, and that a robust view of trespass to the person should continue to be applied.

(d) Actionable harm

It is obvious that the contact must be harmful or subjectively offensive to the claimant to constitute battery.[183] Beyond this, all jurisdictions accept that there need be no proof of actual physical or mental harm to complete the cause of action. However, where physical abuse is concerned there must be proof of harm going beyond that which might be viewed as reasonable chastisement.

In *T v H*[184] Cooke P (as he then was), dissenting, advocated the creation of a new and distinct tort of sexual battery which would have required proof of actual damage before the cause of action was complete. While the motivation, to circumvent limitation problems in cases of historic abuse, was commendable, it is submitted that the proposal would seriously undermine the premise of the torts clustering under trespass to the person: the right of victims to vindicate their right to personal autonomy and bodily integrity without having to prove additional actionable damage.

(e) Liability for unforeseen consequences

Whilst battery does not require any proof of specific harm, any harm that does ensue is recoverable in its entirety, with no limiting devices of foresight or remoteness of

---

[179] See the cases discussed by Reynolds (n 112) 726–730.

[180] *Fowler v Lanning* (n 121) 439–441.   [181] Sullivan (n 114) 546.

[182] ibid 533, 571. Diplock J (as he then was) made the same point in *Fowler v Lanning* (n 121) 432.

[183] *Scalera* (n 111) [18] (McLachlin J). The minority in *Scalera* considered that this can be inferred from lack of consent: [105], [110], [113] (Iacobucci J).

[184] *T v H* (n 83). For a contrary view to our criticism, see Tobin (n 33) 196–198.

damage applying.[185] This means that it is no answer for an abuser to say that a victim's emotional distress or psychiatric harm, substance abuse, or eventual loss of educational and employment opportunities were unforeseeable when the physical or sexual assault was inflicted. In the case of prolonged sexual abuse of a child, it is thought inconceivable that the defendant could be oblivious to the probability of psychological harm.[186] The real problem for the claimant will be establishing a sufficient causal link between the abuse and the psychiatric illness or loss of employment prospects. Similarly, it is no answer to physical battery that the nature or extent of the child's injuries was unforeseeable, for example if a child is deliberately pushed and suffers a brain injury by striking his head. In a case in Colorado, a five-week-old infant sued two children aged three and four for assault and battery by causing her to fall on the floor, crushing her skull (the real targets of the tort action were the mothers of all three children, sued for negligence in leaving the children unsupervised). It was held that Colorado law required proof that the children appreciated the offensiveness and wrongfulness of the tortious act, but not that the resulting harm was intended or even foreseen.[187]

2. Liability for intentional infliction of mental suffering

An underdeveloped cause of action is liability for intentional infliction of mental suffering. It originated in the famous 1897 case of *Wilkinson v Downton*,[188] where the claimant successfully sued for mental suffering intentionally caused by a malicious lie. It has been applied rarely by English courts.[189] The House of Lords has indicated that *Wilkinson v Downton* does not provide a remedy for distress falling short of a recognized psychiatric injury, keeping the cause of action in line with negligence, and so usually there would not seem to be much advantage to pleading it separately.[190] However, a recent case has shown how *Wilkinson v Downton* can have independent utility in child abuse cases involving voyeurism, where a monk employed at an abbey school watched and video-recorded boys in the school showers, and required the claimant to expose his own genitals whilst he was unwell in the school infirmary; in such cases there has been no actionable battery, and the child may not fear that he is about to be touched and hence there is no actionable assault.[191]

An issue which remains undecided in English law is the form of intention required by the *Wilkinson v Downton* tort:[192] must the claimant prove that the defendant's acts were calculated to cause psychiatric harm, or that he was reckless as to the infliction of

---

[185] *Allan v New Mount Sinai Hospital* (1980) 109 DLR (3d) 634 (Ontario HC) 643 (Linden J); Deakin, Johnston and Markesinis (n 123) 295.

[186] *Wilkieson-Valiente v Wilkieson* [1996] ILR ¶1-3351 (Ontario Ct (Gen Div)).

[187] *Horton v Reaves* 526 P 2d 304 (Colorado Supreme Ct 1974) 155. Both mothers were found not to be liable.   [188] *Wilkinson v Downton* [1897] 2 QB 57 (QBD).

[189] In *Janvier v Sweeney* [1919] 2 KB 316 (CA) (blackmail); *Khorasandjian v Bush* [1993] QB 727 (CA) (telephone harassment campaign).

[190] *Wainwright v Home Office* (n 30) (Lord Hoffmann).

[191] *C v D and SBA* [2006] EWHC 166, [2006] All ER (D) 329 (QB) [87]–[101].

[192] ibid [99]–[100].

such harm? Or may such intention may be imputed if such harm was likely to result from the conduct? In *obiter dicta* Lord Hoffmann has suggested that the defendant must have acted in a way that he knew to be unjustifiable, and either intended to cause harm or at least acted without caring whether he caused harm or not.[193] It is submitted that recklessness as to the infliction of psychiatric harm should suffice in the context of non-contact sexual abuse.

The tort of intentional infliction of mental suffering has enjoyed some success in Canada[194] and the United States,[195] where it is usually pleaded in relation to sexual harassment or bullying. The American tort requires (a) an extreme, outrageous or flagrant act or statement, or a combination of the two, (b) which was calculated to produce harm, or there was reckless disregard as to the probability of causing harm and (c) in fact caused harm in the form of emotional distress.[196] A course of conduct over an extended period will qualify as well as a single event.[197] The tort has been successfully pleaded as a corollary to battery and negligent failure to protect a child[198]—in effect, emotional abuse—but there do not appear to be any child abuse cases in Canada where it has succeeded where all other causes of action against the abuser had not been pleaded or had failed on their merits. *Wilkinson v Downton* is also regarded as being good law in Australia[199] and New Zealand[200] but apparently has not yet been applied in the child abuse context.

3. Liability in negligence for neglect

Unlike assault and battery, there is no direct tort analogue for the criminal offence of wilful neglect. Thus if parents were charged with wilful neglect for leaving children unattended at home while they went on holiday, the children could only sue for negligence. This is problematic since negligence requires proof of harm of a type recognized by negligence law before it is actionable. For psychological harm, a diagnosis of a condition recognized by psychiatry, such as post-traumatic stress disorder, is required.[201]

A parent's legal obligation to take reasonable steps to protect a child from known or reasonably foreseeable harm[202] is readily meshed with the statutory duty to provide a child with the necessaries of life[203] to set up a duty of care actionable in negligence.

---

[193] *Wainwright v Home Office* (n 30) [45].   [194] Grace and Vella (n 77) 11–12.

[195] Second Restatement of Tort (n 127) §46(1); Bala (n 21) s 7.

[196] *MH v State* 385 NW 2d 533 (Iowa Supreme Ct 1986) 539.   [197] Grace and Vella (n 77) 12.

[198] eg *Y(AD) v Y(MY)* [1994] 5 WWR 623 (British Columbia Supreme Ct); *K(G) v K(D)* (1999) 122 OAC 36 (Ontario CA).

[199] *Bunyan v Jordan* (1937) 57 CLR 1 (Aus HC); *Northern Territory v Mengel* (1995) 185 CLR 307 (Aus HC); *Carrier v Bonham* [2000] QDC 226 (Queensland DC) [30]–[33].

[200] *Attorney-General v Gilbert* [2002] NZCA 55 (New Zealand CA) [97].

[201] *McLoughlin v O'Brian* [1983] 1 AC 410 (HL) 433; *Alcock v Chief Constable of South Yorkshire* [1992] 1 AC 310 (HL) 317.

[202] *Y(AD) v Y(MY)* (n 198). We discuss the liability of the passive parent or carer in section D.

[203] Children and Young Person's Act 1933 s 1(2).

4. Evaluation: making tort law fit the reality of child abuse?

It is submitted that the tort of battery should be aligned with criminal sexual offences against children, so that consent cannot be a live issue where the person touched is below age 13. For children between ages 13 and 15, we have argued earlier that consent should be considered as vitiated where the defendant has exploited a position of power in relation to the child to make the sexual contact. We contend that child prostitutes are victims of torts when subjected to sexual acts by persons who set out to exploit their vulnerability for their own ends.

For physical abuse to constitute tortious battery, it is submitted that the defence of reasonable chastisement should be abolished in tort law, as it should be in criminal law.[204] Clearly there must be a sphere of permitted physical contact by a parent or carer, but that must stop short of violence. For sexual abuse without physical contact, such as voyeurism, then reckless disregard to the infliction of psychiatric harm should set up tort liability for infliction of psychiatric injury. Liability for emotional abuse is more tricky, because it raises the spectre of tort actions for poor parenting. However we have argued that the criminal law needs to take cognizance of the intentional nature of emotional abuse and neglect, and its corrosive effects on the child,[205] and so also should tort law.

C. The Principles Relating to the Civil Liability of Third Parties who Fail to Protect a Child

1. Tort liability for omissions

> If a child is neglected, it is not only his father who omits to look after him; everyone else omits to look after him also.[206]

In the remaining sections discussing liability in tort we will assess the extent to which this controversial proposition is true in law, whatever moral purchase it holds on the conscience of society. The fundamental dilemma is to determine in what circumstances tort law does, and should, convert a general duty to *abstain* from inflicting harm on another to a positive duty to act to *protect* another from foreseeable harm. More specifically, in what circumstances does, and should, tort law impose liability on a third party who is in a position to protect a child from negligent or intentional harmful acts of another, but who fails so to act?

At the heart of the issue of liability for omissions lies two crucial facts:

- the risk of harm was not originally *created* by the third party;[207] and
- the harm itself was not *directly* inflicted by the third party.[208]

---

[204] Discussed above, Chapter 3 section D.4.   [205] Discussed above, Chapter 3 section D.1.

[206] Glanville Williams *Criminal Law: the General Part* (2nd edn Stevens, London 1961) 4.

[207] The basis of the American general 'no-duty' rule' [*Draft Third Restatement of Tort* chapter 3 §7, chapter 7 §37].

[208] For a penetrating discussion of the problems of omissions and tort liability, see *Stovin v Wise* [1996] AC 923 (HL) 929–937 (Lord Nicholls).

The trite response offered by orthodox tort theory prevalent in all common law jurisdictions is that there can be no liability for omissions unless there was a pre-existing duty to act. But this is question-begging:

- When will tort law impose a duty to act where the *opportunity* exists to act, in the absence of an explicit statutory duty so to act?
- What is the relevance for tort liability where there is an explicit statutory *duty* to act?
- Where public authorities are concerned, when will tort law convert a statutory *power* to act into a common law *obligation* to act?

As Honoré has put it, 'not-doing when one has a duty to act and not-doing when one has a right to act are not symmetrical notions'.[209] In other words, the power to act and the duty to act are not two sides of the same coin. Lord Nicholls famously observed that 'compulsory altruism needs more justification than an obligation not to create dangers to others when acting for one's own purposes'.[210] However, at best his proposition applies only to true bystanders, however callous, who have had no previous relationship with the person in peril. The questions we must address in searching for a special justification for imposing liability for failure to protect a child at risk include:

- *Should the duty be set up by the nature of the* outcome? In other words, is foreseeable harm to a child a sufficient justification to impose a duty to protect that child? Theorists about the role of economic factors in tort law argue that action should be required only where the foreseeable harm to C outweighs the cost to D of acting. This may be relevant in considering the limited resources of a child protection agency, such as the scarcity of foster parents or emergency accommodation, or finances to obtain expert medical opinions as to the cause of suspicious injuries.
- *Can the duty be premised upon a distinction between vulnerability and dependency?*[211] All children are vulnerable to abuse from some source, whether identified or unknown, but it would not be feasible for the law to consider that general vulnerability as sufficient justification to impose an affirmative duty to act upon all adults in society who come into contact with them. *Dependency*, on the other hand, implies some specific relationship between the child and the adult whereby it is reasonable for the adult to protect the child. Note however that dependency does not necessarily mean that the adult in fact has the *power* to protect the child, as we shall discuss in the next chapter in relation to the tort liability of the non-abusing carer. However, child protection agencies do have the power, and the issue is when tort law will impose a duty to exercise that power.

---

[209] T Honoré 'Are Omissions Less Culpable?' in P Cane and J Stapleton (eds) *Essays for Patrick Atiyah* (Clarendon Press, Oxford 1991) 42.   [210] *Stovin v Wise* (n 208) 930.

[211] See the helpful distinction drawn by Honoré between background duties owed to all, which are imposed by ordinary social norms and are usually formulated as a duty to refrain from positive acts which cause harm, and distinct duties owed to specific persons varying according to the individual circumstances and past dealings between them, such as the duty owed by parents to their children. Honoré (n 209) 33.

- *Must the existence of the duty* precede *the emergence of the specific risk?* This has been the position of some courts in holding that a duty of care by social services to a child arises only when and if the child was taken into care, but that there is no earlier tort duty to rescue the child from a specific risk to his safety.[212]

The difficulties do not stop at the construction of a duty to act. There are two conundrums created by the conceptual framework of liability for omissions. Firstly, the *definitional problem*: the categorization of something as a 'pure omission' may depend on how broadly the court identifies the parameters of the relevant course of events proved by the evidence.[213] Like a camera with a zoom lens, if the court chooses to focus on the specific failure to intervene in an event which directly causes the child harm, it is easy to describe the defendant's position as a pure omission which cannot set up a duty to act, and hence liability. If however the camera operator pulls back to take a panoramic view of the entire course of events, it might be seen that the defendant had set it in motion, or at least had intervened at some stage. Therefore, a court may choose to identify a specific failure to take the child into emergency care on a particular date as being a pure omission which does not attract liability, or conversely may view the matter from a broader perspective starting with the initial concerns communicated to social services about the child's welfare, and the decisions taken in respect of those concerns.[214]

Secondly, the *causation and identification of harm problem*: how can the claimant satisfy his burden of proof of showing that but for the defendant's failure to act, he would not have been harmed? The outcome depends at least in part on which particular point in the chronology is identified as pivotal.[215] Also, the terminology chosen by the court sets the stage and to a certain degree predicts the answer. If the issue was formulated as merely the failure to confer a benefit,[216] here to protect the child, then the failure to act has not had a causal impact on the child's fate. However, can a failure to intervene make things worse for the child? Can it be said that the defendant's inaction diverted the child's fate from the course that it otherwise would have followed? Did the failure to intervene constitute a positive intervention in the child's world so as to bring about change?[217] We will be examining this conundrum in sharper focus when we discuss the tort liability of public authorities, and in particular child protection agencies. For the moment, it suffices to say that tort law recognizes that a failure to intervene can have positive causal consequences where:

---

[212] eg *Barrett v Enfield London Borough Council* (n 75); *DeShaney v Winnebago County Department of Social Services* 489 US 189 (USSC 1988).   [213] *Stovin v Wise* (n 210) 930.

[214] See the discussion of *X v Bedfordshire County Council* (n 73) and of its American analogue, *DeShaney v Winnebago County Department of Social Services* (n 212), below at sections F.1(b), 2.(a)(v), F.4.

[215] FV Harper and PM Kime 'The Duty to Control the Conduct of Another' (1934) 43 Yale LJ 886.

[216] As Lord Hoffmann has characterized negligence claims against public authorities: *Gorringe v Calderdale Metropolitan Borough Council* [2004] UKHL 15, [2004] 1 WLR 1057 [32]; Lord Hoffmann 'Human Rights and the House of Lords' (1999) 62 MLR 159, 163.

[217] Honoré 'Are Omissions Less Culpable?' (n 209) 41.

- there is a 'special',[218] usually pre-existing, relationship[219] which gives the claimant a right to protection by the defendant; or

- the defendant has specifically undertaken to act, whether expressly or impliedly, such as by intervening previously in the situation or by making promises to the child to deal with it;[220] or

- the defendant is subject to a general undertaking or direction to act in the circumstances, for example by the conferral of statutory powers; this might or might not be coupled with:

- reliance by the claimant, or reliance by others who might have intervened had they not expected the defendant to act, such as
  — general reliance by the community on the child protection agency doing its job, or
  — specific reliance by teachers, neighbours or health visitors who thought that the agency would act upon their reports of suspected abuse;[221]

- reliance by the perpetrator on the third party's inaction, in the belief that he could continue the abuse with impunity.[222]

In all of these situations, the reasoning in the caselaw traces the causal link backwards from what actually happened to the claimant to the existence of a duty to act to prevent that outcome occurring. The important point relating to causation, however, is that the traditional distinction between misfeasance and nonfeasance fades into insignificance,[223] because there is a special justification for imposing a distinct and specific obligation to act in the circumstances—even if concepts such as 'special relationship' or 'assumption of responsibility' are not self-defining.[224] We turn now to a brief analysis of the structure of negligence to ascertain how that special justification may be found.

2. The structure of liability in negligence

Since the mid 20th century, negligence has become the default tort for English litigants, habitually pleaded as a fallback even where other torts seem more obviously to fit the claimant's case.[225] Unlike criminal law, or the intentional torts such as battery and

---

[218] eg *Second Restatement of Tort* (n 127) §315; *DeShaney v Winnebago County* (n 212) 199–200 (Rehnquist CJ); *Williams v Natural Life Health Foods Ltd* [1998] 1 WLR 830 (HL) 834–835.

[219] Claire McIvor describes this as 'the infamous, undefined "special relationship" ': C McIvor *Third Party Liability in Tort* (Hart Publishing, Oxford 2006) 13.

[220] eg as in *Nicini v Morra* 212 F 3d 798 (US CA 3rd Cir 2000); *Sabia v State* 669 A 2d 1187 (Vermont Supreme Ct 1985), discussed below section F.2(a)(v).

[221] *DeShaney v Winnebago County* (n 212) 208–210 (Brennan J, dissenting).

[222] As in *Sabia v State* (n 220).

[223] JM Adler 'Relying upon the Reasonableness of Strangers: Some Observations about the Current State of Common Law Affirmative Duties to Aid or Protect Others' [1991] Wisconsin L Rev 867.

[224] TA Eaton and ML Wells 'Governmental Inaction as a Constitutional Tort: *DeShaney* and Its Aftermath' (1991) 66 Washington L Rev 107, 147.

[225] eg *Spring v Guardian Assurance* [1995] 2 AC 296 (HL) (negligent mis-statement pleaded as a fallback from defamation).

assault, negligence liability is based upon an *objective* rather than a subjective assessment of fault; it deploys the language of '*should have* foreseen/known/done/refrained from doing'. Diagram 2 sets out the steps required to establish liability in negligence in English law. All common law jurisdictions follow this template, with relatively minor variations.

(a) The initial premise

As the template illustrates, the threshold issue is whether a duty of care was owed by the defendant to the claimant in the circumstances. In recent years there have been major swings in the Law Lords' pendulum as to the starting premise. In the landmark case of *X v Bedfordshire* in 1994, where the issue was whether social workers owe a duty of care to children whose well-being is said to be at risk, Sir Thomas Bingham MR wrote that 'the public policy consideration which has first claim on the loyalty of the law is that wrongs should be remedied and that very potent counterconsiderations are required to override that policy . . .'[226] However, in 1996 Lord Hoffmann cautioned in *Stovin v Wise* that '[t]he trend of authorities has been to discourage the assumption that anyone who suffers loss is *prima facie* entitled to compensation from the person . . . whose act or omission can be said to have caused it. The default position is that he is not.'[227] Lord Hoffmann has also argued that tort's aspiration to provide 'a comprehensive system of corrective justice, giving legal sanction to a moral obligation on the part of anyone who has caused injury to another without justification to offer . . . compensation' has been abandoned in favour of 'a cautious pragmatism'.[228] However, we shall see that in recent cases, in particular those dealing with tort liability for failing to prevent child abuse, Lord Bingham's approach appears once again to be in the ascendancy.

American tort law starts from the premise that an actor owes a duty of care where his conduct creates a risk of physical harm. Determinations of no duty or modifications of the duty of reasonable care are exceptional and are based on special problems of principle or policy in a particular class of cases.[229] The actor need not be the agent inflicting the physical harm, provided that that person's conduct is a factual cause of the risk of physical harm. Therefore, in principle, someone who carelessly exposes a child to the risk of physical harm by a third party owes a duty of care to the child.

(b) The test for duty of care

In English law, the formulation of the duty of care question has attracted much striving on the part of the judiciary to arrive at an all-purpose litmus test. The current answer for English and Welsh courts is the 'three-stage test' propounded by *Caparo*:[230]

1. Was it foreseeable that C might suffer damage if D did not take reasonable precautions?

---

[226] *X v Bedfordshire* (n 73) 749 (Lord Browne-Wilkinson) quoting Sir Thomas Bingham MR in the Court of Appeal below, 663, but disagreeing as to the potency of those counter-considerations in the case of the abused children at Bar.   [227] *Stovin v Wise* (n 210) 949.

[228] *White v Chief Constable of the South Yorkshire Police* (n 3) 502.

[229] *Restatement (Third) of Torts* (Proposed Final Draft April 2005) §7.

[230] *Caparo v Dickman* [1990] 2 AC 605 (HL) 616–618.

2. If so, was there a sufficient relationship of proximity between C and D?
3. If so, is it fair, just and reasonable in all the circumstances to impose a duty of care?

The *Caparo* test replaced the two-stage test for duty of care developed in 1978 in *Anns v Merton*:[231]

1. As between D and C, was there a sufficient relationship of proximity or neigh-bourhood such that, in the reasonable contemplation of D, carelessness on his part may be likely to cause damage to C?

   If so, a prima facie duty of care arises.

2. If so, are there any considerations which ought to negate, or reduce or limit the scope of
   (a) the duty of care, or
   (b) the class of person to whom it is owed, or
   (c) the damages to which breach may give rise?

Whilst the three elements of foreseeability, proximity, and policy considerations are present in both tests, the burden of persuasion on the more nebulous issues of policy is reallocated from the defendant (under *Anns*) to the claimant (under *Caparo*). *Anns* also directs the court to a more nuanced approach to moulding the scope of the duty to accommodate policy considerations. Nevertheless, as Lord Nicholls noted in *Stovin v Wise*, the difference between the two tests is 'perhaps more a difference of presentation and emphasis than substance'.[232] Not wholly content with this reformu-lation, Lord Bridge cautioned that it must be applied to novel situations according to an 'incremental approach' of reasoning by analogy to precedent.[233]

Yet a third basis for constructing a duty of care re-emerged in the mid 1990s which is of particular relevance to our discussion: 'assumption of responsibility' in the context of a 'special relationship'. Initial scepticism about the value of assumption of responsibility as a test to determine the circumstances in which the law will impose liability or its scope, expressed in *Caparo* itself,[234] was brushed aside in a series of cases from the House of Lords,[235] and it was directly applied to impose and withhold duties of care in relation to pure economic loss. Yet Lord Slynn in 2000 conceded that 'the phrase "assumption of responsibility" means simply that the law recognises that there is a duty of care. It is not so much that responsibility is assumed as that it is recognised or imposed by the law.'[236]

As Brooke LJ has somewhat wryly noted, since 1984 successive decisions of the House of Lords have made the law of negligence much more complicated.[237] Thus the lower courts in England in analysing novel cases are constrained to acknowledge three

---

[231] *Anns v Merton London Borough Council* [1978] AC 728 (HL) 751–752.
[232] *Stovin v Wise* (n 210) 931.   [233] *Caparo* (n 230) 618.
[234] *Smith v Eric S Bush* [1990] 1 AC 831 (HL) 862 (Lord Griffiths); *Caparo* ibid 628 (Lord Roskill).
[235] *Spring v Guardian Assurance* (n 225); *White v Jones* [1995] 2 AC 207 (HL); *McFarlane v Tayside Health Authority* [2000] 2 AC 59 (HL).
[236] *Phelps v London Borough of Hillingdon Anderton* [2001] 2 AC 619 (HL) 654.
[237] *Parkinson v St James and Seacroft University Hospital NHS Trust* [2001] EWCA Civ 530, [2002] QB 266 [16].

Diagram 2. The Negligence Template in English Law

Step #1   **Did D owe C a duty of care?**

• The 'three stage' *Caparo* test in vogue since 1990:

— Was it **reasonably foreseeable** to D, before embarking on his activity or course of conduct, that if he was careless he might cause harm, of a type recognized by negligence law,* to someone in the position of C? (aka 'the foreseeability test')

— If so: was there a sufficient **proximity** of relationship between D and C? (aka 'the neighbour test')

— If so: is it **fair, just, and reasonable** in all the circumstances to impose a duty of care upon D to take reasonable care to avoid harming C? (aka 'the public policy test')

• Other fashionable supplementary duty of care concepts:

— assumption of responsibility

— distributive justice

Step #2   If so: what **standard of care** did that duty impose on D in embarking on the activity which foreseeably might harm C?

• What reasonable precautions could be expected of D, having regard to:

— the likelihood the risk will occur, and

— the seriousness of the harm should the risk eventuate, and

— the cost of precautions to reduce or eliminate the risk?

Step #3   If so: did D's conduct (or failure to act) fall below that standard, such that **D has breached D's duty of care?**

Step #4   If so: **did D's breach of duty** cause **harm** to C's person/property/financial interests? (aka '**cause in fact**')

• Would C have suffered loss 'but for' the fault of D?

— alternative causes

— cumulative causes

— supervening causes

Step #5 If so: is D responsible in law to C for causing that *type* of harm? (aka 'cause in law' or **'proximate cause'**)

- Formulations:
  - —— Is this type of harm compensable in the law of negligence?*
  - —— Was the risk of this type of harm reasonably foreseeable to a person in D's position as a probable (or possible) consequence of D's breach of duty?
  - —— Was this harm **too remote** a consequence of D's conduct?
  - —— Was there a break in the chain of causation, by an unforeseeable intervention by a natural force or a third party? (aka *novus actus interveniens*)
  - —— Did this harm fall within the scope of the risk created by D's breach of duty?

Step #6 If so: are there any **defences** which would **eliminate** D's liability?

- illegality (aka *ex turpi causa non oritur actio*)
- voluntary assumption of risk, or consent by C (aka *volenti non fit injuria*)
- exclusion of D's liability [subject to Unfair Contract Terms Act 1977 s 2(1) invalidating exclusions of business liability for personal injury or death caused by negligence]

Step #7 If not: are there any **defences** which would **reduce** D's liability?

- contributory negligence by C
- apportionment amongst two or more tortfeasors, ie can D obtain partial or full indemnity for D's own liability from others also at fault?

Step #8 If so: **how much monetary compensation** is D liable to pay to C:

- Has C failed to take reasonable steps to mitigate C's loss?
- Did C already suffer from a pre-existing condition which could **reduce** the quantum of D's liability? (aka the 'take the victim as you find him' rule)
- Did C have a pre-existing susceptibility to greater harm which could **extend** the quantum of D's liability? (aka the 'thin skull rule')

* The issue of the compensability of a particular type of harm may be adjudicated at Step # 1 or Step # 5.

parallel paths to a duty of care: the three-stage test; incrementalism; and assumption of responsibility. The Court of Appeal has observed, perhaps resignedly, that the fact that all these approaches have been used and approved by the House of Lords in recent years suggests that 'if the facts are properly analysed and the policy considerations correctly evaluated the several approaches will yield the same result.'[238]

While it is strongly arguable that assumption of responsibility expresses a conclusion, not a path to that conclusion, we shall see that the concept has had a major influence in unravelling the immunity blanket for public authorities, especially for those working in the field of child protection. There are several routes to a conclusion of assumption of responsibility which are of direct relevance to our discussion:

- indirectly through undertaking to confer a benefit on a third party which D can reasonably foresee will also benefit C, such as providing medical services to an expectant mother;

- indirectly through embarking on a risk-creating activity, such as operating a nursery;

- directly through undertaking to confer a positive benefit on C, such as placing a child with a foster family or in a children's home; and

- directly through being ordered by statute to confer a positive benefit on C, such as a requirement imposed on a child protection agency to investigate suspected child abuse, or mandatory reporting of suspicions of child abuse.

It has to be said that other Commonwealth courts have not agonized as much over the formulation of the test for duty of care. In *Canadian National Railway Co v Norsk Pacific Steamship Co*[239] the Supreme Court of Canada explicitly declined to abandon the two-stage test of duty of care in *Anns*, finding it worked perfectly well in providing a principled discipline to the ascertainment of a duty of care in novel cases. The Australian High Court has declined to adopt either *Anns* or *Caparo*, although the issue is one of continuing debate amongst the current members of the Court.[240] The High Court takes the pragmatic position that the quest for a unifying test across all categories of negligence is futile.[241] The New Zealand Court of Appeal uses a modified form of *Anns*, considering the relationship between the parties at the proximity stage, including the degree of analogy with precedents, and wider policy considerations at the second stage in balancing the claimant's moral claim to compensation for avoidable harm with the defendant's moral claim to be protected from undue restrictions on

---

[238] *Bank of Credit and Commerce International (Overseas) Ltd v Price Waterhouse (No 2)* [1998] PNLR 564 (CA) 583–587 (Sir Brian Neill).

[239] *Canadian National Railway Co v Norsk Pacific Steamship Co* [1992] 1 SCR 1021 (SCC).

[240] *Sullivan v Moody* [2001] HCA 59, 207 CLR 562 (Aus HC). Kirby J conceded that he had lost the battle to adopt *Caparo* in *Graham Barclays Oysters Pty Ltd v Ryan* (2002) 211 CLR 540 (Aus HC) [236]–[238], but continued to protest against that conclusion in *Cattanach v Melchior* [2003] HCA 38 (Aus HC) [120]–[122].

[241] *Perre v Apand Pty Ltd* [1999] HCA 36 (Aus CA) [70]–[83] (McHugh J).

freedom of action and from an undue burden of legal responsibility.[242] American courts seem comfortable in considering the duty of care question without a formula.

3. The structure of liability for breach of statutory duty

English law recognizes a distinct tort of breach of statutory duty, although it has a limited reach. The tort is based upon a marriage of statute law and common law whereby the statute imposes a duty on a designated person, office holder or agency, and the common law confers a right on an individual claimant to have that obligation performed for his personal benefit.[243] Because of the constitutional doctrine that Parliament can speak impliedly as well as explicitly, the threshold question is whether the statute discloses an intention by Parliament that a breach of statutory duty be actionable by a citizen. If the court finds this express or implied intention, using imprecise canons of interpretation, then the tort will only be actionable where:[244]

- the claimant is within the category of persons the statute was intended to protect;
- the claimant suffered loss as a result of the breach of statutory duty;
- that damage was of the type which the legislation was intended to prevent, and
- the damage was also of a type recognized by the common law as compensable.

The advantage to the claimant of clearing all these hurdles is that liability is strict, and so proof of carelessness by the duty-holder is not required, unless the statutory duty itself is formulated in such a way as to import a fault standard (such as a duty to provide 'reasonable' services to a family). It is not therefore a claim in negligence, and the reason why the defendant did not perform the obligation is irrelevant.[245]

The notoriously murky, complex, capricious and arbitrary quest[246] for that elusive parliamentary intention has prompted the Supreme Court of Canada to abandon breach of statutory duty as a separate nominate tort, holding that the statutory obligation merely serves to provide evidence of the standard of care, and hence of breach, in the tort of negligence.[247] American law has also assimilated breach of statutory duty into the tort of negligence, although there is a divergence in the jurisprudence between holding that the breach constitutes negligence per se, or merely serves as evidence of the breach,[248] as in Canada. New Zealand courts also apparently do not see much value in an independent tort of statutory duty,[249] and the Australian courts have applied a public–private law dichotomy narrowly to protect public authorities providing services.[250]

---

[242] *Rolls-Royce New Zealand Ltd v Carter Holt Harvey Ltd* [2005] 1 NZLR 324 (New Zealand CA); Todd (n 39) 265–268.

[243] *London Passenger Transport Board v Upson* [1949] AC 155 (HL) 168.

[244] *Cutler v Wandsworth Stadium* [1949] AC 398 (HL). [245] *X v Bedfordshire* (n 73) 731.

[246] See the English textbook writers quoted in *Canada v Saskatchewan Wheat Pool* [1983] 1 SCR 205 (SCC) [20]. [247] ibid [29]–[38].

[248] Discussed in ibid [26]–[28].

[249] McLay 'Antipodean Perspectives (n 28) 119–120, citing *Attorney General v Carter* [2003] 2 NZLR 160 (New Zealand CA).

[250] S Kneebone *Tort Liability of Public Authorities* (LBC Information Services, Sydney 1998) 146–167.

California has allowed an action for breach of statutory duty where the defendant has failed to comply with a statute requiring that suspicions of child abuse be reported to child welfare authorities,[251] but this has not generally been followed in other American States.[252] We shall see that in the United States, Australia and New Zealand, statutes requiring prompt investigation of reported suspicions of child abuse have been the foundation for constructing a duty of care in negligence owed by such individuals to the child at risk, rather than as a basis for an actionable breach of statutory duty.[253] The English courts have generally regarded statutory regulatory or social welfare systems as being established for the public at large, not as setting up a private right of action for damages for breach of statutory duty. The tort has not figured in the context of child protection since it was rejected in relation to the investigatory powers of social services in *X v Bedfordshire*.[254]

4. The structure of secondary liability

The species of tort liability which we have been considering thus far are all primary or direct forms of liability. Defendants may also or alternatively be made liable not for their own breach, but for the breach of another for whom they are responsible.

(a) Vicarious liability

The most common situation where vicarious or indirect liability may be imposed is where the defendant is the employer of the tortfeasor, although the principle may also appy to volunteers with charitable organizations. We will describe the employer as the secondary defendant, because the usual practice is to sue both the tortfeasor and the employer in the same action, so as to obtain evidence from both of them. For vicarious liability (also known as the *respondeat superior* doctrine), legal responsibility is imposed on a secondary defendant, although it is itself free from blame. This is to be contrasted with primary liability, where the employer is directly at fault, be it in relation to the negligent hiring of the tortfeasor, negligent training or negligent supervision.

---

[251] *Landeros v Flood* 551 P 2d 389 (California Supreme Ct 1976) (civil liability being restricted to intentional breaches of the statute).

[252] *Perry v SN* 973 SW 2d 301 (Texas Supreme Ct 1998); *Arbaugh v Board of Education, County of Pendleton* 591 SE 2d 235 (West Virginia Supreme CA 2003); *Fischer v Metcalf* 543 So 2d 785 (Florida Dist CA 3rd Dist 1989).

[253] *Brodie v Summit County Children's Services Board* 554 NE 2d 1301 (Ohio Supreme Ct 1990); *Sabia v State* 669 A 2d 1187 (Vermont Supreme Ct 1985); *Gonzalez v Avalos* 866 SW 2d 346 (Texas App El Paso 1993); *Mammo v State* 675 P 2d 1347 (Arizona Ct App 1984).

[254] *X v Bedfordshire* (n 73) 731–732, 747–748. See also *Bluett v Suffolk County Council* [2004] EWCA Civ 1707 [22]–[25]; *T (A Minor) v Surrey County Council* [1994] 4 All ER 577 (QB) 596–601 (breach of statutory duty to cancel registration of a childminder under the Nurseries and Child-Minders Regulation Act 1948, after a baby in her care suffered a serious brain injury, was not actionable as a tort or in negligence at the instance of another baby injured in the same way from violent shaking three months later; however the local authority was vicariously liable for negligent mis-statement by their childminding adviser to the mother, that he knew of no reason why a baby should not safely be left with that childminder).

Vicarious liability sets up strict liability of the employer if the following criteria are satisfied:

- the tortfeasor is in an employment relationship with the secondary defendant;
- the tortfeasor committed the tort in the course of his employment with the secondary defendant (a temporal test); and
- the tort was within the scope of that employment (a legal test based primarily but not exclusively on the contract between those parties).

We shall see that the third criterion, the scope of employment, is particularly difficult to apply in the case of intentional torts such as child abuse.

(b) Non-delegable duty

The concept of 'non-delegable duty' is a hybrid of primary and secondary liability. This is an obscure and ill-defined tool to circumvent the bar on vicarious liability where the court finds there was no employment relationship between the tortfeasor and the secondary defendant. Usually it has been applied where the tortfeasor has been found to be an independent contractor vis-à-vis the secondary defendant, although this is not necessary.

The legal issue here is whether the delegator has successfully delegated away from himself legal responsibility for the due performance of a task. A duty will be designated as delegable where it can be satisfied by employing an independent contractor to perform a function on the defendant's behalf; in this circumstance the duty of care *devolves to* the independent contractor. A duty will be categorized as non-delegable where any negligence, be it by an employee or independent contractor, is a breach of the duty *by the delegator;* in short, the delegator has committed a personal wrong, albeit through the act or omission of another party. The simplest example of a non-delegable duty is the work of a repairer or other independent contractor retained by an employer to fix building premises under the Occupiers' Liability Act 1957.[255] The owner will be insulated from any liability for defective work only if it has exercised reasonable care in deciding to delegate the job, and in selecting the contractor and supervising and inspecting the work. If the owner has done so, then only the contractor must answer to a visitor injured by the defect. The distinction all depends on what aspect of the duty is being targeted: if the duty is to ensure that reasonable care is taken by the delegate, then it is non-delegable. The key here is that whilst the delegator can delegate *performance* of the task—and indeed may have to do so where the delegator is a corporate entity—the delegator cannot delegate away from itself legal *responsibility* for the competent performance of that task.

It will be immediately apparent that these descriptions are circular, and provide no assistance in ascertaining when a duty will be considered as delegable or non-delegable. The courts have developed a list of miscellaneous situations which they have categorized as non-delegable duties, usually for covert policy reasons such as the availability of insurance. The list remains open; by way of illustration it includes

---

[255] Occupiers' Liability Act 1957 (England) s 2(4)(b).

the statutory duty of an NHS hospital to provide reasonable care to its patients using consultants as independent contractors, hazardous activities on or adjoining a highway, and the duty of an employer to provide a safe working environment for its employees. Mason J of the Australian High Court sought to discover a guiding principle for the designation, concluding that a non-delegable duty arises where there is a 'special duty on persons in certain situations to take particular care for the safety or property of others',[256] but it is immediately obvious that this also expresses a conclusion rather than a test. We shall see in Section E that Canadian, American and Australian child abuse litigants have been creative in trying to extend the list of non-delegable duties in relation to institutions with children in their care, particularly in relation to schools.

A question that is even more vexed is to identify the nature of the liability for breach of a non-delegable duty. Is it strict or fault liability? What do the cases mean in saying that a non-delegable duty is a duty not only to take care, but to *ensure* that care is taken?[257] Here there are two views in Commonwealth courts. The strict liability theory, espoused by the Supreme Court of Canada,[258] is an analogue to strict vicarious liability for employees' torts. The strict liability chain is constructed as follows:

- the delegator has a duty to take reasonable care;
- the delegator assigns performance of that task to the delegate, giving rise to an additional duty to *ensure* that the delegate takes reasonable care in performing the task;
- the delegate breaches his duty to take reasonable care in performing the delegated task;
- therefore the delegator must not have taken reasonable care, as the fault of the delegate will be attributed to the delegator because the delegator did not ensure that the delegate took reasonable care;
- therefore, separate and independent proof of fault by the delegator is not required, and it is no answer for the delegator to say 'I was not negligent', provided that the delegate committed the tort.[259]

The alternative view, adopted by a majority of the Australian High Court, is that non-delegable duty is fault liability, and therefore the delegator must take *reasonable care* to ensure that reasonable care is taken by the independent contractor; there is no automatic attribution of fault back to the delegator.[260]

It is submitted that policy grounds favour strict liability for two reasons. Firstly, if the delegator has the choice of delegating a task to its own employee or to an independent contractor, there should be no incentive to choose an independent contractor to insulate the delegator from vicarious liability. Secondly, strict liability will provide an incentive for the delegator to require the independent contractor to take out insurance

[256] *Kondis v State Transport Authority* (1984) 154 CLR 672 (Aus HC) 687.
[257] *Lewis (Guardian ad litem of) v British Columbia* [1997] 3 SCR 1145 (SCC) [54]; *Kondis* ibid.
[258] *Lewis* ibid [50]; *EDG v Hammer* 2003 SCC 52, [2003] 2 SCR 459 [16].
[259] *Lewis* (n 257) [50].   [260] *Lepore v New South Wales* [2003] HCA 4; 212 CLR 511 (Aus HC).

to indemnify the delegator from liability to third parties; the tort victim should not have to rely upon the solvency of the delegate.

Thus far the English courts have not taken a position on this controversy. As we shall see, the Australian High Court has preferred to deal with the problem of an employer's liability for an employee's intentional torts such as sexual abuse through the device of non-delegable duty, rejecting the Canadian and English choice of the vicarious liability route for the same situation. So it is likely that the Australian conception of non-delegable duty as fault liability will not be adopted by the English courts, nor, we submit, should it be.

5. Liability in equity: the Canadian experiment with fiduciary duty

Finally, a few words about constructing civil liability on the basis of breach of fiduciary duty. Canadian courts have resorted to constructing a fiduciary relationship between a child and an agency or institution responsible in some way for the well-being of that child, usually in order to circumvent limitation periods and other procedural barriers. Thus far this innovation has been taken up only in New Zealand, and there only in a very limited context,[261] and so we do not discuss it at length in this book. Suffice it to say that the following elements must be established in Canadian law before an institution or public authority is found to be in a fiduciary relationship with a child:

- the fiduciary has scope for the exercise of some discretion or power;
- the fiduciary can unilaterally exercise that power or discretion so as to affect the beneficiary's legal or practical interest; and
- the beneficiary is peculiarly vulnerable to, or at the mercy of, the fiduciary holding the discretion or power.[262]

In the context of child protection, in Canada a claim for breach of fiduciary duty generally has not succeeded where a plea of negligence has failed on the merits. While there is much to be said for the fiduciary analysis, in our view the common law torts should not abdicate their role to protect the vulnerable.[263]

At the beginning of this discussion we posited the dilemma of when tort law should impose a duty to act. Whatever the enormous difficulties this question poses in cases

---

[261] *T v H* (n 83); *S v G* (n 87); *H v R* (n 83).   [262] *Frame v Smith* [1987] 2 SCR 99 (SCC).

[263] For detailed analysis see Hoyano 'The Flight to the Fiduciary Haven' (n 84). In the context of the claims of child abuse and cultural genocide by the 'Stolen Generations' of the indigenous people of Australia, see J Stapleton 'The Golden Thread at the Heart of Tort Law: the Protection of the Vulnerable' (2003) 24 Australian Bar Rev 135, 142–145. Fiduciary arguments invoked by the 'Stolen Generations' have fallen on stony ground: *Williams v The Minister, Aboriginal Land Rights Act 1983* [2000] NSWCA 255 (New South Wales), dismissing appeal from the New South Wales Supreme Ct (1999) Aus Torts Rep 81–526, leave to appeal denied by Aus HC S246/2000 (22 June 2001), but see *SD v Director General of Community Welfare Services (Victoria)* [2001] NSWSC 441 (New South Wales Supreme Ct) [42] holding that it was arguable that a fiduciary duty existed between social services and children at risk whilst in the custody of their father.

of true 'compulsory altruism', when it comes to child protection, there is increasing judicial activism in the arena of tort. Here there are no qualms about saving another from his own folly where proximity between the parties must be particularly strong to set up a cause of action in negligence.[264] There can be no question as to the vulnerability of a child to abuse; the real question is whether the defendant knew or should have known about the peril, and was best placed to act to protect a child from the imminent harm.

D. The Tort Liability of the Passive Parent or Carer

Children do not live alone. When they are repeatedly sexually or physically abused, it is common that another person either knows of the abuse and decides to do nothing about it, or is aware of signs that abuse is taking place but either wilfully or subconsciously decides to ignore it.[265] While the typical case concerns a parent, grandparent, step-parent or other carer in the child's home, this configuration of tortious passivity can also attach to a teacher who becomes aware of a colleague's abusive activities, to staff in a nursery or daycare centre or in a sports club, or even to a neighbour with a special connection to the person posing a risk to the child.

The issues with which courts have to grapple in considering the liability of an individual who has failed to intervene to protect a child include the following.

Duty of care:

- Are parents insulated from negligence liability by parental or intrafamilial tort immunity or by other public policy considerations?

- If not, do parents owe a special duty of care to their children by virtue of the parental relationship to protect them from abuse?

- Alternatively, are parents subject to the same restrictive liability rules as people who are strangers vis-à-vis the child and who are in a position to appreciate the risk posed by a third party?

---

[264] As in the case of the local authority which approved plans by the negligent architect hired by the claimant developer [*Peabody v Parkinson* [1985] AC 210 (HL)] and the civil aviation authority which inspected the claimant's defective aircraft [*Philcox v Civil Aviation Authority* (1995) 92 (27) LSG 33 (CA)].

[265] eg G Davis, L Hoyano, C Keenan, L Maitland and R Morgan *An Assessment of the Admissibility and Sufficiency of Evidence in Child Abuse Prosecutions* (HMSO, London August 1999) case 55B; when the victim aged eight told her brother of her father's first sexual assault, her father berated her in the presence of her mother who did not support her, causing her to conclude that there was no option but to remain silent. The escalating sexual abuse continued until she was 15 years old, when her father pleaded guilty to specimen counts of indecent assault and to an unrelated charge of manslaughter. See also J LaFontaine *Child Sexual Abuse* (Polity Press, Cambridge 1990) 192–194; J Neeb and S Harper *Civil Action for Childhood Sexual Abuse* (Butterworths Canada Ltd, Toronto 1994) 307; BA Micheels 'Is Justice Served? The Development of Tort Liability against the Passive Parent in Incest Cases' (1997) 41 St Louis U LJ 809, 823–824.

Standard of care:

- Does complete passivity (a 'pure omission' to take any steps to protect the child) suffice for breach of duty, or must the claimant prove that the defendant positively intervened, for example to deflect inquiries by outside agencies?

- What is the level of culpable knowledge which the claimant must prove the defendant possessed at the relevant time:
  - actual knowledge of the abuse; or
  - wilful blindness to the abuse; or
  - actual awareness of facts which reasonably could give rise to suspicion of abuse; or
  - constructive or imputed knowledge of facts which reasonably could give rise to suspicion of abuse?

- In ascertaining what steps a reasonable carer would have taken to protect the child, to what extent should the court take into account the actual circumstances of the passive defendant, such as victimization by domestic abuse?

Causation of harm:

- Must the claimant prove that the abuse continued as a result of the defendant's failure to act?
- If so, must the claimant prove that the subsequent abuse after the defendant's failure to act caused at least some of the harm for which the claimant seeks compensation?

English courts have yet to grapple directly with the tort liability of a private individual who was in a position to act to protect a child from harm at the hands of a third party but failed to do so. Increasingly these issues are being litigated in other common law jurisdictions, making a comparative analysis of their approaches all the more valuable.

A preliminary point: many of the reported cases address these issues in a procedural context, in interlocutory applications to determine whether an insurer is bound by a covenant to defend the action against its insured, or whether the defendant sued (usually the alleged perpetrator) can add the non-abuser as a third party, so as to seek contribution from that party if the claimant wins the case. Apart from the United States, actual rulings on liability are comparatively few.

1. A duty of care to protect from harm by a third party

(a) A parental immunity doctrine?

A common anxiety with common law courts has been that if they recognize a general duty of care to protect children from foreseeable harm they will be opening the 'floodgates' of litigation by disgruntled children against their parents. The concern is that if parents could be sued by their children, this would undermine parental authority and discipline, and threaten to substitute judicial discretion for parental discretion.[266] Thus the same concerns about the state intervening in the family which we have discussed in the context of child welfare statutes such as the Children Act 1989 have been transferred into the realm of tort law.

The American courts have gone the farthest in developing a home-grown[267] distinct common law doctrine imposing an absolute bar on tort actions by children against their parents, in a trilogy of cases a century ago, all involving child sexual and physical abuse or neglect.[268] Whilst those cases involved intentional torts, the immunity was applied to negligence actions as well.[269] The doctrine was adopted by the courts in 44 States.[270] The consequence was that children were protected from harm at the hands of their parents or those standing *in loco parentis* only by the criminal law and family law.

The justifications invoked by American courts for the immunity included:[271]

- protection of the family unit and family harmony;
- a policy of non-interference with parental care, discipline and control of children;
- prevention of fraud or collusion within the family, particularly where insurance is available for the claim;
- prevention of family resources being depleted in favour of the claimant at the expense of other family members;
- prevention of inheritance of the compensation by the parent tortfeasor if the child dies;
- an analogy to the interspousal immunity doctrine.

The first two justifications have been perhaps the most robustly defended but are the most obviously flawed, since it is the abusive conduct of the parent which has destroyed family tranquillity, not the assertion of legal rights by the child. Even the most libertarian view acknowledges that there must be limits to proper parental control. As the Supreme Court of Washington observed, immunizing an incestuous

---

[266] R Bagshaw 'Children Through Tort' in J Fionda (ed) *Legal Concepts of Childhood* (Hart, Oxford 2001) 135–137.

[267] Micheels (n 265). It appears that there was no tort immunity between parents and children in the early English common law, according to *Hurst v Capitell* 539 So 2d 264 (Alabama Supreme Ct 1989) 265 and McCurdy (n 108) 1059–1063. For analysis of the modern American doctrine see CE Johnson 'A Cry for Help: an Argument for Abrogation of the Parent–Child Tort Immunity Doctrine in Child Abuse and Incest Cases' (1993) 21 Florida State U L Rev 617; AL Nilsen 'Speaking out against Passive Parent Child Abuse: The Time Has Come to Hold Parents Liable for Failing to Protect Their Children' (2000) 37 Houston L Rev 261.

[268] *Hewellette v George* 9 So 885 (Mississippi Supreme Ct 1891) (action for false imprisonment—committal to a mental institution—against mother); *McKelvey v McKelvey* 77 SW 664 (Tennesee Supreme Ct 1903) (overruled by *Broadwell v Holmes* 871 SW 2d 471 (Tennessee Supreme Ct 1994)) (action against father and stepmother for cruel and inhuman treatment); *Roller v Roller* 79 P 788 (Washington Supreme Ct 1905) (action against father for rape) (overruled in part by *Borst v Borst* 251 P 2d 149 (Washington Supreme Ct 1952)).   [269] *Gibson v Gibson* 479 P 2d 648 (California Supreme Ct 1971) 650.

[270] Johnson 'A Cry for Help' (n 267) 267–270 and appendix. Six States and the District of Columbia have never adopted the doctrine: Hawaii, Montana, North Dakota, South Dakota, Utah, and Vermont.

[271] McCurdy (n 108) 1072; Johnson 'A Cry for Help' ibid 627–628; Nilsen 'Speaking out against Passive Parent Child Abuse' (n 267) 270–279.

rapist from tort liability takes the doctrine of the sacredness of the family unit 'to the most absurd degree yet'.[272] Moreover, in cases of domestic abuse the family might already have been split up, especially if the abuser was in prison. Rather oddly, many State courts ceased to apply the doctrine once the child had been 'emancipated', that is, had reached the age of majority, as the first two justifications were no longer relevant.[273] This kept the door open for claims of historic abuse but did nothing to vindicate the child's interests during her minority, when the need for compensation might be the greatest, for example to pay for medical and psychological treatment.

Some American courts have also recognized that the other justifications are as tenuous,[274] and that the blanket immunity conferred on parents is simply not sustainable, the obvious example being if a child is injured in an automobile accident where the negligent driver happens to be his parent. Consequently most of the jurisdictions which have recognized a form of parental immunity have felt compelled by the existence of liability insurance for the claim[275] to create unwieldy exceptions to make 'ordinary negligence' actionable.

More problematic than the motor vehicle accident cases have been cases where the alleged negligence arises directly from the parent–child relationship, such as negligent supervision. Some State courts have abrogated parental immunity in relation to all negligence cases, but with two exceptions, where the alleged negligent act (1) involves an exercise of parental authority over the child, or (2) involves an exercise of 'ordinary parental discretion' with respect to the provision of food, clothing, housing, medical care and the like.[276] Cases of alleged physical ill-treatment and neglect can readily be slipped into the first exception protecting parental discipline.

The Alabama Supreme Court has created a special exception for sexual abuse, reasoning that '[t]o leave children who are victims of such wrongful, intentional, heinous acts without a right to redress those wrongs in a civil action is unconscionable, especially where the harm to the family fabric has already occurred through that abuse'. However, to preserve 'the unqualified right of parents to reasonably discipline their children' the court deemed it appropriate to raise the standard of proof of sexually abusive conduct from a mere 'substantial evidence' standard to a 'clear and convincing' standard.[277] Quite how sexual contact with the child can be justified as discipline remains a mystery. Some other States have followed this lead, allowing children or their representatives to sue during their minority for injuries resulting from their

---

[272] *Merrick v Sutterlin* 610 P 2d 891 (Washington Supreme Ct 1980), criticizing *Roller v Roller* (n 268).

[273] *Hewellette v George* (n 268) 887.

[274] eg *Kirchner v Crystal* 474 NE 2d 275 (Ohio Supreme Ct 1984) 276 found the rationales 'outdated, highly questionable and unpersuasive'.

[275] eg *Streenz v Streenz* 487 P 2d 282 (Arizona Supreme Ct 1970) 284; *Sorensen v Sorensen* 339 NE 2d 907 (Massachusetts Supreme Judicial Ct 1975) 914.

[276] *Goller v White* 122 NW 2d 193 (Wisconsin Supreme Ct 1963) 197–198. Seven States followed Wisconsin's lead in this approach: Johnson 'A Cry for Help' (n 267) 635.

[277] *Hurst v Capitell* (n 267) 266.

parents' wilful or intentional misconduct, and in particular sexual abuse,[278] physical abuse,[279] and wrongful death.[280]

These exceptions however do not serve to catch actions framed in negligence relating to a parent's failure to intervene in an abusive situation, which necessarily entail a challenge to parental care, and so judicial intrusion into the family.[281] Such actions can be assured of getting to trial only in the 15 or so States which have no form of parental immunity.[282] In States with partial parental immunity, the courts must be persuaded that the claim falls outside ordinary parental discretion. In *Frideres v Schiltz*, the Iowa Supreme Court held that parental immunity does not protect non-intervening parents who allow abuse to continue.[283] The Michigan Court of Appeal has also held that a claim against the passive carer is one of child neglect, which is not barred by parental immunity, unlike negligent supervision which is caught by the doctrine.[284]

Other courts have been willing to countenance negligence pleas against the non-perpetrating parent on the basis that parental immunity is no longer viable in relation to any case involving sexual abuse.[285] However, in Connecticut this rule is limited to actions against a mother for failing to protect a child from sexual assaults by the father but not by a third party, because this falls into the immune category of negligent supervision of the child.[286] The Missouri Court of Appeal has found a compromise which surely must be unsatisfactory to all parties: parental immunity against the non-offending parent must be determined on an ad hoc basis through an evidentiary hearing to assess the impact which the child's action would have on the harmony of the family unit.[287] This must place any liability insurer in the odd position of having to argue that this family is harmonious and hence immune from judicial intrusion when at least one family member obviously takes a contrary view.

The *Second Restatement of Tort* has sought to move the law forward by stating that a parent or child is not immune from tort liability to the other solely by reason of that relationship, but with the caveat that repudiation of general tort immunity does not establish liability for an act or omission which the parent–child relationship would otherwise make privileged or is not tortious.[288] The *Draft Third Restatement of Tort* does not include the parent–child relationship in its list of recognized special relationships giving rise to an affirmative duty to protect, although it recognizes a family relationship as being a likely candidate for addition.[289]

---

[278] eg *Herzfeld v Herzfeld* 781 So 2d 1070 (Florida Supreme Ct 2001) 1077–1078.

[279] *Barnes v Barnes* 603 NE 2d 1337 (Indiana Supreme Ct 1992); *Dunlap v Dunlap* 150 A 352 (New Hampshire Supreme Ct 1930).   [280] *Newman v Cole* 872 So 2d 138 (Alabama Supreme Ct 2003).

[281] *Robinson v Robinson* 914 SW 2d 292 (Arkansas Supreme Ct 1996) [3]; *McGee v McGee* 936 SW 2d 360 (Tex App 1996) 367.

[282] eg the doctrine was judicially abolished in California: *Gibson v Gibson* (n 269).

[283] *Frideres v Schiltz* 540 NW 2d 261 (Iowa Supreme Ct 1995) 270.

[284] *Spikes v Banks* 586 NW 2d 106 (Michigan CA 1998) 111 [10]–[12] (foster child aged 15 made pregnant by foster parents' nephew).

[285] *Hurst v Capitell* (n 267); *Coburn v Ordnur* 14 Conn L Rptr 9 (Connecticut Superior Ct 1995); *Gladwell v Gladwell* 14 Conn L Rptr 71 (Connecticut Superior Ct 1995).

[286] *Doe v Colletto* 24 Conn L Rptr 387 (Connecticut Superior Ct 1999).

[287] *Swartz v Swartz* 87 SW 2d 644 (Missouri Ct App WD 1994).

[288] *Second Restatement of Tort* (n 127) §895G (current to April 2005).

[289] *Draft Third Restatement of Tort* chapter 7 §41, Comment *o*.

English,[290] Scottish,[291] Canadian,[292] New Zealand,[293] and Australian[294] courts have never recognized a tort immunity between parent and child.[295] They generally have preferred to reflect public policy concerns about importing into family relationships the conflicts inherent in legal proceedings by setting the standard of care to take account of the circumstances of typical parents, and the rough-and-tumble of home life.[296] Some still claim that negligent supervision must remain non-justiciable on the basis that it is impossible for a court to set a standard of 'reasonable parenting'[297] (although the advent of judicial parenting orders in England and Wales must cast doubt even on this argument).

(b) A duty to take positive action?

Assuming that parental immunity does not bar tort litigation (whether as a matter of law, as in the Commonwealth, or in a particular case, as in some American States), the question then arises as to when liability will be imposed upon a parent or someone standing *in loco parentis* for failing to take positive action to protect his child. Here the line dividing courts is drawn between those holding that a general legal duty to take reasonable care to protect that child from foreseeable dangers arises *automatically* from the parent–child relationship, and those holding that a parent acquires a duty to protect the child only when he has accepted immediate care and charge of that child *on the specific occasion* in question. Put another way, the question is whether the situation of parental responsibility is the same as that of a stranger, so that the adult must have taken positive steps to assume specific responsibility for the child before the tortious event. Either analysis creates difficult problems of adjudication where both parents are involved in the care of the child.[298] If a parent is equated with a stranger,

---

[290] *Ash v Ash* (1696) Comb 357, 90 ER 526 (KB) (assault, battery and false imprisonment); *Carmarthenshire County Council v Lewis* [1955] AC 549 (HL) 561, 563, 566 (child injured in road accident); *Surtees v Kingston-upon-Thames Borough Council* [1991] 2 FLR 559 (CA) 570 (Stocker LJ) (negligence alleged to have caused burns to two-year-old); *Barrett v Enfield LBC* (n 75) 573 Lord Slynn (*obiter*). [291] *Young v Rankin* [1934] SC 499 (Sessions Court of Scotland).
[292] *Fidelity and Casualty Co v Marchand* [1924] 4 DLR 157 (SCC) (Duff and Migneault JJ); *Teno v Arnold* (1974) 55 DLR (3d) 57 Ontario Supreme Ct, affd 67 DLR (3d) 9 (Ontario CA), revd on liability while accepting the principle of a parent-child duty of care [1978] 2 SCR 287 (SCC). An immunity for parenting decisions was specifically rejected in *B(D) v C(M)* 2000 SKQB 64, [2000] 7 WWR 186 (Saskatchewan QB [26], affd 2001 SKCA 9, [2001] 5 WWR 617 [22]–[23] (Saskatchewan CA)) and in *H(DL) v F(GA)* (1987) 43 CCLT 110 (Ontario Supreme Ct). The Yukon Territory has enacted a ban on negligence actions between children and their parents unless the defendants are insured: Children's Act (Yukon) s 179. [293] *McCallion v Dodd* [1966] NZLR 710 (New Zealand CA) 722, 724, 727–728.
[294] *Rogers v Rawlings* [1969] Qd R 262 (Queensland Supreme Ct); *Hahn v Conley* (1971) 126 CLR 276 (Aus HC) 283–284.
[295] See the discussion in LCH Hoyano 'The "Prudent Parent": the Elusive Standard of Care' (1984) 18 U of British Columbia L Rev 1, 6.
[296] *Carmarthenshire County Council v Lewis* (n 290) 566 (Lord Reid); *Surtees v Kingston-upon-Thames Borough Council* (n 290) 583–584 (Sir Nicholas Browne-Wilkinson VC).
[297] Bagshaw (n 266) 135–136.
[298] See for example the divided opinions in *McCallion v Dodd* (n 293), where a family was walking together on a roadside at night with their backs to approaching traffic, with each parent holding a child, when a driver killed the mother and seriously injured the boy she was holding by the hand. Turner J held that the father had effectively divested himself of the immediate physical charge and custody of the little boy, and so owed no duty of care (726), whilst McCarthy J held that the father and mother jointly shared responsibility for both children, and hence a duty of care, at the time

negligence law might require that the defendant parent have taken steps to place the child in the care of the abuser on the occasion when a specific act of abuse occurs. If the duty arises by virtue of the parental relationship, then it would suffice to establish breach if the parent brought the abuser into contact with the child, when she knew or (arguably) should have known[299] that he posed a risk to the child, or could not be trusted to look after the child safely.

In New Zealand, the prevailing view before the introduction of the no-fault accident compensation scheme was that a parental relationship did not automatically give rise to a duty of care.[300] The High Court of Australia in the difficult case of *Hahn v Conley* also appears to have held that the law does not impose a general duty on parents to take reasonable care to protect the child against foreseeable danger simply because of the blood relationship.[301] Instead Barwick CJ attempted to draw a distinction between action and inaction, holding that a parent or someone standing *in loco parentis* will not owe a duty of care to take positive acts to protect the child from harm by others but, like everyone else, will owe a duty to protect the child from her (the parent's) own actions which have created a risk of harm.[302] It has been argued that *Hahn v Conley* creates an immunity only for those standing *in loco parentis*, and so does not protect other custodians who still must take positive steps to protect children under their care from harm.[303] This seemingly paradoxical position has been defended on public policy grounds similar to those invoked for the American doctrine of parental immunity, in particular anxiety about intruding into the domestic sphere and fettering parental judgment and discretion.[304]

Canadian law has taken the opposite approach: it is well established that parents by virtue of that relationship owe a general duty of care to their children to protect them from foreseeable hazards, including the risk of harm from a third party.[305] This duty continues even when the children are under the supervision of others.[306] Since 1993 this duty has been readily extended to protecting a child from sexual[307] and physical and emotional abuse and neglect[308] at the hands of a third party. Pleading breach of fiduciary obligations has also served to rope in the passive parent for failing to protect

of the accident because they were walking together (730), North P concurring in this conclusion (723–724).

[299] This being subject to the issue set out at the beginning of this chapter as to what constitutes carelessness, in relation to the non-abusing parent's knowledge respecting the risk posed by the abuser.

[300] *McCallion v Dodd* (n 293) 724–726 (Turner J), 729 (McCarty J). North P advocating the opposite view (721–722). [301] *Hahn v Conley* (n 294) 283, 284 (Barwick CJ).

[302] ibid 283–285 (Barwick CJ).

[303] S Yeo 'Am I My Child's Keeper? Parental Liability in Negligence' (1998) 12 Australian J of Family Law 150, 152–155.

[304] *Posthuma v Campbell* (1984) 37 SASR 321 (South Australia Supreme Ct); *Robertson v Swincer* (1989) 52 SASR 356 (South Australia Supreme Ct); *Towart v Adler* (1986) 52 SASR 373 (South Australia Supreme Ct); Yeo ibid, 158. [305] *Teno v Arnold* (n 292); *J(LA) v J(H)* (n 82).

[306] *B(D) v C(M)* (n 292).

[307] *J(LA) v J(H)* (n 82), reasoning by analogy from the parental duty of care to intervene to protect the child in criminal law [*R v Popen* (1981) 60 CCC (2d) 233 (Ontario CA) 241 discussed above; *B(D) v C(M)* ibid. [308] *Y(AD) v Y(MY)* (n 198).

the child from harm, although usually this is pleaded concurrently with negligence and the courts tend to reach the same conclusion on liability and damages in both causes of action.[309]

The starting premise of American tort law is that an actor whose conduct has not created a risk of physical harm to another owes no duty of care to the other.[310] The traditional approach to liability for non-intervention is a 'no-duty' rule, propounded in §315 of the *Second Restatement of Tort*:

There is no duty to control the conduct of a third person as to prevent him from causing harm to another person unless:

(a) a special relationship exists between the actor and the third person which imposes a duty upon the actor to control the third person's conduct, or
(b) a special relationship exists between the actor and the other which gives the other a right to protection.

The term 'special relationship' has no independent significance, merely signifying that American courts recognize an affirmative duty arising out of the relationship where otherwise it would not exist because the actor had not created the risk.[311] The *Second Restatement of Tort* states that 'the fact that the actor realizes or should realize that action on his part is necessary for another's aid or protection does not of itself impose upon him a duty to take such action'.[312] The authors of the *Draft Third Restatement* criticize this formulation as failing to clarify that the 'no-duty' rule is conditioned on the actor having played no role in *facilitating* the third party's conduct, thereby increasing the risk of harm; in these circumstances an affirmative duty to protect arises.[313] So once the barrier of parental immunity has been overcome, American negligence law follows a middle road between an automatic parent–child duty and a situation-specific duty by taking a wider historical perspective of the conduct of the passive party to see if she has taken positive action earlier to facilitate the abuse, for example by bringing the abuser into the household.

Some American courts have constructed the requisite special relationship on the foundations of statutory obligations imposed on carers by family and criminal statutes, which assist in prescribing the scope of the common law duty.[314] In *Phillips v Deihm*,[315] for example, a grandmother was held to owe a duty of care to protect a boy from being raped by his grandfather because under Michigan criminal

---

[309] *KLB v British Columbia* 2003 SCC 51, [2003] 2 SCR 403 [49] (*obiter*); *J(LA) v J(H)* (n 82) 182–187; *M(M) v F(R)* [1999] 2 WWR 446 (British Columbia CA) 715–720.
[310] *Draft Third Restatement of Tort* chapter 7 §37.
[311] ibid chapter 7 §41 Comment *h*.   [312] *Second Restatement of Tort* (n 127) §314.
[313] *Draft Third Restatement of Tort* chapter 7 §37 Comments *a* and *e*.
[314] *Draft Third Restatement of Tort* chapter 7 §39; *CC and MS v RTH* 714 A 2d 924 (New Jersey Supreme Ct 1998) 933–934; *Hite v Brown* 654 NE 2d 452 (Ohio CA 1995) 455–457.
[315] *Phillips v Deihm* 541 NW 2d 566 (Michigan CA 1995) [9]–[16], applying Michigan Compiled Law §722.622(i).

law she was a person responsible for the child's health and welfare, and so had a statutory duty to intervene to eliminate any unreasonable risk when she was able to do so and knew or should have known of the risk. The statutes in all American States requiring reporting of suspected child abuse have also been used to set up a duty to the child of affirmative action in tort on the part of someone with a family relationship with the abuser.[316]

A special relationship may be constructed by American courts by reliance not just on statutory obligations, but also on the specific facts, by virtue either of the defendant's particular responsibility for the child, or the defendant's relationship with the abuser. Where intrafamilial violence or incest is concerned, it does not matter which of these two routes is followed. However, where the defendant is outside the family unit and plays a different role, for example as an adult neighbour inviting the child to visit the defendant's home, the difference in routes takes on significance, as any special relationship will be predicated upon her actual or imputed knowledge of any risk this may create for the child's safety. Yet a third possible route to a duty of care is the 'affirmative act' doctrine, whereby a person has a duty not to place another in the way of foreseeable criminal activity.[317] In several cases the perpetrator's spouse was held to have breached a duty of care to child visitors where she had reason to suspect that her husband posed a risk to children but she did nothing to prevent him having unsupervised access to them, and indeed may have been instrumental in enticing the children to visit their home.[318] We shall return to the issue of foreseeability of risk to a child in our discussion below of breach of the duty of care.

English courts have not yet directly confronted the issue of affirmative duties on carers to protect children from abuse; thus far the courts have only had to contend with situations where the parent's duty is the same as that of any stranger, to take reasonable care to avert risks she has created.[319] It is usually assumed that the problem of liability for omissions can be circumvented by finding a pre-existing relationship between the parties giving rise to a duty to act, one of several commonly cited exceptions being that of parental responsibility for a child.[320] In *S v W (Child Abuse: Damages)*,[321] the

---

[316] *CC and MS v RTH* (n 314); *Hite v Brown* (n 314) 459; Child Abuse Prevention and Treatment Act, 42 USCA ch 67 §5106a(b)(2)(A)(vii) as amended 25 June 2003. See discussion below Chapter 5 section D.3.

[317] *Doe v Franklin* 930 SW 2d 921 (Texas Ct App 1996) 927–928.

[318] *CC and MS v RTH* (n 314) (two adolescent sisters molested by their neighbour whom they visited daily to help care for and ride his horses); *Pamela L v Farmer* 112 Cal App 3d 206 (California CA 1980) (wife invited children to use their swimming pool and left them with her husband whom she knew to be a paedophile); *Doe v Franklin* ibid (grandmother invited child victim to stay overnight, and left her alone with her grandfather even after being told by the child of the sexual assaults). Compare *TA v Allen* 669 A 2d 360 (Pennsylvania Superior Ct 1995, appeal denied 676 A 2d 1201 Pennsylvania Supreme Ct 1996) (step-grandmother not liable for sexual abuse of children by their grandfather as they were his guests, not hers, so no special relationship; minority would have held her liable for breach of her duty to warn, as she knew of his paedophilic practices and was wilfully blind to the abuse occurring in her home).

[319] *Surtees v Kingston-upon-Thames* (n 290); *S v Walsall Metropolitan Borough Council* [1986] 1 FLR 397 (CA).

[320] A duty on the part of a parent to protect a child from physical harm was assumed in *Carmarthenshire County Council v Lewis* (n 290) 561 by Lord Goddard, when it was applied by analogy to a schoolteacher.

[321] *S v W (Child Abuse: Damages)* (n 102).

claimant sued her mother for breach of her duty of care in failing to protect her from the ongoing sexual abuse of her father, who had pleaded guilty to multiple charges of incest, and in particular for failing to remove her daughter from the home or to report the father's activities to the police or social services. The specific issue on an interlocutory appeal to the Court of Appeal was the limitation period applicable to the action in negligence against the mother. The defendant did not seek to have the pleading struck out on the ground that she did not owe a duty to protect her daughter from the abuse.

In *Barrett v Enfield LBC*, a case involving alleged negligence in managing a child in care, Lord Woolf MR in the Court of Appeal noted in an *obiter dictum* that 'parents are daily making decisions with regard to their children's future and it seems to me that it would be wholly inappropriate that those decisions, even if they could be shown to be wrong, should be ones which give rise to a liability for damages'. The Master of the Rolls observed that the point was not argued in *S v W (Child Abuse: Damages).*[322] In the House of Lords, which reversed the Court of Appeal decision, Lord Hutton agreed with this observation. However, Lord Hutton's *obiter dictum* that a child should not be permitted to sue his parents for their decisions in respect of his upbringing[323] was not specifically referred to or endorsed by the other Law Lords on the panel. Lord Slynn observed that it was clear that parents may owe an actionable duty of care in some (undefined) circumstances to their child, and that courts should 'be slow' to hold that a child can sue his parents for negligent decisions in his upbringing.[324]

In any event, these judicial ruminations do not address the critical issue discussed here, of whether a parent is under a legal obligation to take positive steps to protect the child against foreseeable harm from a third party, and specifically from physical and sexual abuse or neglect. The excuse that 'this was a decision relating to my child's upbringing' is simply implausible when applied to these circumstances. It reverts to a view of the child not as a person vested independently with rights, but as an object of concern within the family, a view which surely must be outmoded now. As Freeman eloquently argues, children are individuals whose physical, sexual, and psychological integrity is as important, if not more important, than that of the adult population.[325] Simply stating that tort law treats a parent as a stranger vis-à-vis his child exposes the fallacy.

It is submitted that English courts should adopt the simple solution, that by virtue of the parental relationship a general duty of care arises to take positive steps to protect a child from foreseeable harm. The first two requirements of the *Caparo* three-stage test for a duty of care, foreseeability of harm if the parent does not take reasonable steps to protect the child from foreseeable risks, and proximity of relationship, are clearly satisfied. It is fair, just and reasonable to impose a general duty of care to protect the

---

[322] *Barrett v Enfield London Borough Council* [1998] QB 367 (CA) 377.
[323] *Barrett v Enfield* [2001] (n 75) 587.
[324] ibid 569, citing *Carmarthenshire County Council v Lewis* (n 290) and 573.
[325] M Freeman 'The End of the Century of the Child?' (2000) 53 *Current Legal Problems* 505, 541.

child from hazards which might arise in the future, in so far as it is within the capacity of any parent to do so in the circumstances. Judicial concerns that this would mean that a parent on the other side of the country from the child could be found liable if he is injured[326] are unfounded, since before liability can be found the defendant must be proved to have been in a position to take action which would have averted the harm. This is an issue not of the existence of a duty of care but of whether it was breached in the specific circumstances in which the harm occurred.

The difficulty with the Australian notion of an intermittent duty of care dependent on the circumstances is that it becomes an evidentially difficult issue of fact in every case as to when the duty has materialized and evaporated. Prospective tortfeasors, at least in theory, should be able to predict when they come under a duty of care to another. An automatic legal duty arising out of the relationship itself would be perfectly aligned with the moral duty attributed by society to every parent of a child.

The notoriously difficult distinction between pure omissions and positive acts adopted by the Australian High Court in *Hahn v Conley* for cases of parental negligence is unsustainable. The argument that the parent must have created the risk for a moral duty to be converted to a legal duty can easily be tested to destruction: would anyone seriously argue that the parent has no legal duty to help a child who is choking on something she has picked up, or to race after her when she suddenly runs towards danger? The callous parent surely cannot be equated with a callous passer-by. If one accepts that argument, then why should this legal duty be removed where the child is at risk of physical or sexual harm at the hands of a third party? Moreover, the omission/commission distinction is a recipe for litigation, since, as we discussed in the preceding Section C on the principles of third party liability, the characterization of the events depends on how widely the court is prepared to view the facts. Because of the ongoing interaction between a parent and her child, it is virtually inevitable that the causal chain can be traced back to an act of the parent, however remote that link may be.

On a more practical front, the duty of care debate has been distorted by more practical concerns that holding the passive parent liable will ultimately reduce the level of compensation to the child, because that parent is often brought into the action by the abuser or his insurer.[327] McBride and Bagshaw go so far as to contend that the negligent third party parent would have to dip into the child's award to satisfy the primary defendant's claim for contribution.[328] There are (at least) four difficulties with this contention.

---

[326] As suggested by Turner J in *McCallion v Dodd* (n 293) 725; in an apparent attempt to circumvent this difficulty, North P inserted a caveat to his formulation of the general duty of care: 'at least when the parent is present' (721).

[327] Yeo (n 303) 157; C McIvor 'Expelling the Myth of the Parental Duty to Rescue' (2000) 12 Child and Family LQ 229, 234.

[328] NJ McBride and R Bagshaw *Tort Law* (2nd edn Pearson Longman, Harlow 2005) 183.

Firstly, where the abuser and the passive parent are members of the same household, they both are likely to be covered by homeowner liability insurance.[329] As a matter of practicality, it may be only if the child or the perpetrator brings the non-abusing parent into the action that insurance coverage may be triggered, because liability insurance usually excludes liability for intentional torts and criminal acts by the insured,[330] whereas a properly drafted plea in negligence[331] is likely to be covered.[332] This may be the only avenue for the victim to receive substantive compensation to cover the cost of counselling and other financial losses caused by the abuse.[333]

Secondly, tort law has always set its face against taking insurance into account in ascertaining whether a duty of care applies and has been breached in a particular situation, at least where some form of physical harm or personal injury has been suffered. Insurance-driven arguments that as a matter of principle a duty of care should be held never to apply to parental omissions to act are not only contrary to public policy[334] but also illogical, as insurance coverage typically reflects the liability rules of tort law.

Thirdly, whilst it is true that the passive parent is often brought into the action through third party procedures invoked by the abuser or his insurer, or by a party said to be responsible for the abuser, it is also true that the child often directly sues that parent. It is wrong that the existence of a duty of care to that defendant's child should be determined by the court based on assumptions about the existence and provisions of the family's liability insurance.

Finally, it is not possible for the passive parent to have access to the child's tort damages to satisfy his own liability to the abuser or his insurer. The abuser and the passive parent are tortfeasors contributing to the same harm, and so the child

---

[329] Additional coverage problems may arise if the definition of 'insured' in the homeowner's liability policy includes the child, as one insured person may not sue another insured person if there is no cross-liability clause: *P Samuel & Co v Dumas* [1924] AC 431 (HL) 1467; *Scott v Wawanesa Mutual Insurance Co* [1989] 1 SCR 1445 (SCC), rightly criticized by Neeb and Harper *Civil Action for Childhood Sexual Abuse* (n 265) 308–311.

[330] As in *Scalera* (n 111) [59]–[69]; *Sansalone v Wawanesa Mutual Insurance Co* (n 111). Intention to harm is usually inferred by the court even if the litigant has attempted to circumvent the exclusion clause by pleading a form of negligence by the abuser: DS Florig 'Insurance Coverage for Sexual Abuse or Molestation' (1995) 30 Tort Trial and Insurance Practice LJ 699, 699–707. For a contrary argument that paedophiles typically do not intend harm, and that the intentional injury exclusion should not apply, see Neeb and Harper (n 265) 300–303. However, insurance coverage for the intentional acts of the perpetrator is rightly seen as contrary to the insurance doctrine of reasonable expectations in relation to the risks covered: R Bell 'Sexual Abuse and Institutions: Insurance Issues' (1996) 6 Canadian Insurance LR 53, 54–55.

[331] Pleas in negligence of failure to warn, to take the proper measures to safeguard visitors to the home, and to seek assistance, are most likely to trigger coverage for the non-offending insured under a homeowner's policy: Neeb and Harper (n 265) 308.

[332] Unless the policy denies coverage for bodily injury caused by failure 'of any person insured' to act, in which case the insurer would not be obliged to defend and indemnify the non-intervening parent: *G(P) v James* (2001) Canadian Insurance Law Reporter ¶I-3927 (Ontario).

[333] It should be noted however that if the wording of the policy is such as to include the children of the homeowner in the same household as insureds, it may be impossible for the child as an 'innocent insured' to sue another insured: Neeb and Harper (n 265) 308–311.

[334] *McCallion v Dodd* (n 293) 721 (North P).

is entitled to recover all of the award from one or the other defendant, leaving the paying defendant to pursue his co-defendant for indemnity in accordance with the Court's apportionment of responsibility.[335] The Civil Procedure Rules[336] provide that the court must approve any settlement involving a child, and that the court must give directions as to the investment or payment into court of any award in favour of a child. The court may also appoint the Official Solicitor as guardian of the child's estate, where the child has recovered money subject to a court order, or the child has received an award from the Criminal Injuries Compensation Board or Authority.

Therefore, concerns that making the negligence of passive parents actionable will ultimately reduce the *child victims'* compensation are ill-founded.[337] It is true that the parent's *own* financial resources will be diverted from the family to satisfy the contribution claim from the other defendant. This is not, however, justification for withholding a parental duty of care from any and every child.

2. Breach of the duty to protect

It is crucial to appreciate that a potential tortfeasor is not the guarantor of the safety of the person to whom he owes a duty. Even failure to report child abuse as required by American statutes does not attract automatic liability to compensate the child.[338] If a parent or carer acts reasonably in the measures he takes to protect the child, then he is not liable if the child is nonetheless harmed. So, for example, if he contacted child protection authorities but the child was further injured before the authorities intervened, he *may* have done all that tort law expects of him, depending on the circumstances (for example, if he had no opportunity to remove the child in the interim).

(a) The level of culpable knowledge of the risk

The language of negligence law is objective: what reasonable precautions would a reasonable person in the defendant's position take to avert reasonably foreseeable harm to someone in the claimant's position? But the question thus framed is deceptively simple. As stated at the outset of this discussion, there are at least four levels of awareness of the risk which a court might choose, either to set up the special relationship, or to establish breach of a duty to protect arising from that duty. In descending order of culpable knowledge, and difficulty of proof, they are:

(1) actual knowledge of the abuse;
(2) wilful blindness to the abuse;
(3) actual awareness of facts which reasonably could give rise to suspicion of abuse; or

---

[335] Civil Liability (Contribution) Act 1978 (England) ss 1(1), 2(1).
[336] Civil Procedure Rules and Practice Directions (England), Part 21 Children and Patients Rules 21.10, 20.11 and 21.12.   [337] McBride and Bagshaw (n 328) 183.
[338] *Perry v SN* (n 252) 302, 304.

(4) 'constructive' or imputed knowledge of facts which reasonably could give rise to suspicion of abuse.

Physical injuries are visible or detectable, and may be explained away by the batterer as accidental, whilst sexual abuse is usually clandestine and furtive. Actual knowledge, or deliberate avoidance of knowledge, of ongoing abuse can be very difficult for a claimant to prove; since the defendant inevitably will deny such guilty knowledge, it will be largely a matter of inference from the surrounding circumstances. If proof of actual knowledge of the abuse is not required, the issue arises as to what circumstances are relevant in determining whether a particular defendant *should* have appreciated the risk.

While some Canadian[339] and American[340] courts appear to espouse the most rigorously objective test on the bottom rung of the ladder, in the cases before them they have been able to find concrete grounds in the evidence for attributing knowledge, wilful blindness or suspicion to the passive defendant, so the strength of the objective test of imputed knowledge was not directly tested. However an opposing line of authority has developed in Canada requiring the claimant to prove that the defendant actually knew of or suspected abuse, the top rung of the ladder.[341]

The predominant preference amongst American judges seems to be for the third rung, actual knowledge of facts which reasonably would provide grounds for suspicion. The New Jersey Supreme Court in *CC and MS v RTH* set out a catalogue of factors which should alert a wife that her husband might sexually abuse a child, such as the pattern of any previous sexual offences including the age, gender and type of victim targeted, the husband's therapeutic history and regimen, and any unusual and age-inappropriate behaviour by the children concerned. The New Jersey Court claimed that this 'particularised foreseeability' made the usual objective negligence standard of reasonable foreseeability conform to the empirical evidence and common experience that a wife often may actually know, or have special reason to know, that her husband was likely to abuse an identifiable victim. The Court considered the standard to be realistic and fair in accommodating concerns about the inherent difficulties in predicting such furtive behaviour; it ensures that the wife would not be subject to a broad duty which could expose her to liability to every child whom her husband might threaten or harm.[342] This quasi-subjective approach makes it easier to identify the reasonable precautions the defendant could have taken to avoid exposing the child

---

[339] *J(LA) v J(H)* (n 82) 179–181, 184–185; *Y(AD) v Y(MY)* (n 198) [83]–[88].

[340] *National Union Fire Insurance Co v Lynette C* 279 Cal Rptr 394 (California Ct App 1991) 395; *Phillips v Deihm* (n 315); *Gladwell v Gladwell* (n 285).

[341] *M(M) v F(R)* (n 309); *B(M) v British Columbia* [2000] BCSC 735 (British Columbia Supreme Ct); *H(C) v British Columbia* [2003] BCSC 1055 (British Columbia Supreme Ct).

[342] *CC and MS v RTH* (n 314) 930–931, citing United States Department of Justice *Child Victimizers: Violent Offenders and Their Victims* (March 1996) 5.

to the risk, such as declining to look after the child, warning a caregiver or notifying the child protection authorities.[343]

California seems to perch uneasily on the ladder between the second and third rungs. In *Chaney v Kennedy*,[344] the claimant alleged that a close family friend had sexually assaulted her from the age of 10 to 18 in his home. She also sued his wife, claiming that she had negligently failed to recognize signs that her husband was abusing the claimant (excessive attention and gifts given to her). The Court of Appeal held that it was insufficient for the misconduct to be *conceivable*; it must have been *foreseeable*, in the sense that there must have been facts from which it could be inferred that the wife *must* have known about the misconduct. If she had no knowledge of her husband's deviant propensities, then the danger he posed could not have been reasonably foreseeable:

Although the wife's knowledge may be proven by circumstantial evidence, such inference must reflect the wife's actual knowledge and not merely constructive knowledge or notice. '[A]ctual knowledge can be inferred from the circumstances only if, in the light of the evidence, such inference is not based on speculation or conjecture. Only where the circumstances are such that the defendant 'must have known' and not 'should have known' will an inference of actual knowledge be permitted'.[345]

California's requirement that the wife must be shown to have actual, not just constructive, prior knowledge of her husband's propensities to trigger the obligation to protect children with whom he came into contact was reinforced in *Samantha H v Fields*.[346] Another Circuit of the Court of Appeal held that it was immaterial that the non-abusing defendant might have increased the risk of abuse by actively inviting children to visit their home, as this provided no basis for an inference of actual knowledge. California's approach thus is little short of requiring wilful blindness to the abuse (the second rung). This contrasts with the position on the third rung of many other American courts, requiring only that the passive defendant be proved to have actual knowledge of facts which objectively could give rise to suspicion—facts which could be far less culpable than proven propensity to paedophilia.

(b) A subjectivized standard of care?

Traditionally in child–parent negligence actions English and Canadian law has adhered to a standard of the 'prudent parent' rather than the 'reasonable parent'. It is doubtful whether this makes any difference in the result, at least where that standard is applied to parents.[347] Some American courts have incorporated both in the standard of care, asking: what would an ordinarily reasonable and prudent parent have understood and done in similar circumstances? It is thought that this standard permits

---

[343] *Doe v Franklin* (n 317) 929 (grandmother's burden of protection was slight, as she could have refused to provide childcare or ensured child was not left alone with her grandfather).

[344] *Chaney v Kennedy* 39 Cal App 4th 152 (California CA 2nd District 1995).

[345] ibid 157, omitting references (*obiter dicta* as the negligence claim was time-barred).

[346] *Samantha H v Fields* 2003 WL 193471 (California CA 3rd District).

[347] It does however make a difference where the 'prudent parent' standard is applied to professionals dealing with children, such as school staff: Hoyano 'The "Prudent Parent" ' (n 295) 1.

parents to invoke their ordinary discretion to exercise reasonable authority and impose discipline.[348]

The orthodox objective test of negligence for the standard of care takes into account the specific *circumstances* of the risk of harm, including how it had arisen, the level of the risk and the level of the harm should it eventuate, in concluding what the reasonable parent would have done to deal with the situation. So it might be reasonable for a parent to decide to leave his child with an unregistered childminder if he had no basis for suspecting that the child might be harmed in that environment.

But is it relevant that he cannot afford a licensed nursery or a registered childminder? To what extent does and should the standard of care take into account the specific *characteristics* of the parent or carer? Several American courts have responded to arguments that women typically do not have the power or the opportunity to monitor and control the behaviour of their abusive partners, by applying a flexible standard of care, considering the specific protective measures which they could have taken such as ensuring that the children were not left alone with the potential perpetrator or warning other carers.[349] This of course is easier to achieve where the children at risk are outside the defendant's immediate family.

In some Canadian cases considering a parent's breach of fiduciary duty, the courts have taken into account the limited means and education of the parent in considering the options she had available to her to protect her child.[350] The British Columbia Court of Appeal in *M(M) v F(R)*[351] justified this approach:

[I]n relation to the question whether a defendant should have become aware of a danger of another person committing a criminal assault in a necessarily clandestine manner, the subjective characteristics of the defendant must be taken into account. In such a case, the question must be whether a reasonable person, having the background and capacity for understanding of this defendant, would have appreciated the risk.[352]

So the foster mother was held not to be liable for failing to stop her natural son from abusing the claimant from the age of four, notwithstanding complaints about his conduct towards three other girls and her discovery of a pornographic photograph of the claimant in his room. Her age, limited education and experience of the world, strict religious beliefs, and aversion to discussing sexual matters meant that she had limited ability to recognize indications of paedophilia. She had however

---

[348] eg *Gibson v Gibson* (n 269) 652–653; *Hite v Brown* (n 314) 456.

[349] *CC and MS v RTH* (n 314) 934–937; *Doe v Franklin* (n 317) 928–929; *TA v Allen* (n 318) 364–365 (dissent).

[350] eg *J(LA) v J(H)* (n 82) 185 (holding that the mother's limited resources nonetheless did not prevent her from contacting child protection agencies and relatives in the area for help); *T(L) v T(RW)* (1997) 36 BCLR (3d) 165 (British Columbia Supreme Ct) [35]–[39] (mother migrated from Germany about 30 years earlier, had seven children with her 'domineering and bullying' husband and was 'of limited education and imagination', making her powerless to respond to the abuse her daughter disclosed to her).

[351] *M(M) v F(R)* (n 309).   [352] ibid [120].

instructed her son to dispose of the photograph, suggesting she was not as naive as the defence claimed. A vigorous dissent argued for an objective test with a normative element: what level of awareness and perceptivity ought a foster parent to have?[353]

It is submitted that the latter approach is correct. It is not justifiable to dilute negligence liability, which classically is objective, merely because—especially because—the protection of children is in issue. It should simply not be good enough for a carer such as a foster parent to argue that she was not the primary caregiver, and so was not responsible for protecting the child.[354] There is also a danger that the court will use patronizing stereotypes such as the young and single (and hence inadequate) mother to excuse her failure to intervene to protect her child.[355]

Moreover, the conduct of a child tortfeasor is judged against an objective standard of the reasonable child with the knowledge and understanding expected of a child of that age. This standard disregards the child's other specific characteristics such as being 'abnormally slow-witted, quick-tempered, absent-minded or inexperienced'.[356] The conduct of a parent or carer towards a child in his care should be judged against a no less rigorous standard.

We acknowledge that there is some precedent in the English tort of nuisance for taking into consideration the individual capacities and resources of defendants and their subjective awareness in considering whether they should be liable for failing to protect claimants from hazards the defendants had not created.[357] However, the analogy is neither direct nor persuasive, because it is virtually inevitable that the non-intervening parent or carer historically did something to expose the child to that risk, such as her choice of partner.

We are strongly of the view that a parent or carer should be tested by reference to what a reasonable parent or carer in the same circumstances could and would have done to protect the child. Provided those circumstances offered opportunities to obtain protection for the child, then the defendant's inaction should be judged accordingly. We have taken the same stance in respect of criminal liability for failure to protect a child.[358] The avenue for reporting suspected child abuse anonymously to such organizations as Childline and the NSPCC makes the burden of taking at least some steps light.[359]

---

[353] ibid [52] (Donald JA).

[354] Such an argument was accepted to exonerate a 'withdrawn and uninvolved' foster mother when her husband abused their foster daughter in *B(M) v British Columbia* (n 341) [115].

[355] MK Kearney 'Breaking the Silence: Tort Liability for Failing to Protect Children from Abuse' (1994) 42 Buffalo L Rev 405, 442.

[356] *Mullin v Richards* [1998] 1 All ER 920 (CA) 924, adopting *McHale v Watson* (1966) 115 CLR 199 (Aus HC) 213–214.

[357] eg the liability of an occupier for a nuisance created by a trespasser [*Sedleigh-Denfield v O'Callaghan* [1940] AC 880 (HL)] or by a natural hazard [*Goldman v Hargrave* [1967] 1 AC 645 (HL)].

[358] Discussed above Chapter 3 section B.2.

[359] MA Franklin and M Ploeger 'Of Rescue and Report: Should Tort Law Impose a Duty to Help Endangered Persons or Abused Children?' (1999–2000) 40 Santa Clara L Rev 991, 1023.

3. Non-interference as causing harm to the child

We have noted above in Section C the difficult issue of how an omission can cause harm. All of the jurisdictions we are considering view the causation question at two levels:

- whether on the evidence the defendant in fact caused the harm (the 'cause-in-fact' issue); and

- if so, whether the defendant should be held responsible for that harm (variously described as the 'cause-in-law' or the 'proximate cause' issue, or the 'remoteness of damage' or the 'scope of consequences' liability rule).

On the first question, in English law the claimant need only prove that the defendant's breach of duty materially or substantially contributed to the harm; it need not have been the sole or even the predominant cause.[360] So it does not matter that another party directly inflicted the abuse.[361] Nor is the claimant required to rule out all other potentially causative acts or omissions by other parties where the opportunity to stop the abuse might have been missed.

Recently, and very controversially, the House of Lords endorsed a cause-in-fact test of 'substantial contribution to the risk of harm' in medical cases where the burden on the claimant of proving cause-in-fact is intrinsically impossible to discharge, due to the limits of human knowledge.[362] Notwithstanding the obvious logical fallacy, some American courts have deployed a substantial risk test to prove factual causation by passive parents, perhaps surprisingly in the criminal context.[363]

The choice of the standard of care—what the parent should have done in the circumstances—can also serve to set up the causation question. If the standard of care requires that suspicions be reported to child protection authorities, which the defendant failed to do, if it can be established that the abuse continued[364] or worsened[365] thereafter (as some authors suggest is the typical pattern of battering),[366] then the defendant's omission may be found to have had harmful consequences for the child's welfare.[367] The causal link might also be established by evidence that the perpetrator believed that the defendant's passivity indicated acquiescence in her behaviour, and

---

[360] *Bonnington Castings Ltd v Wardlow* [1956] 1 AC 613 (HL) 621. American law takes much the same approach with its 'substantial factor' test: *Anderson v Minneapolis St Paul and Sault Ste Marie Rwy Co* 179 NW 45 (Minnesota Supreme Ct 1920); Kearney (n 355) 450–451.

[361] *Wisconsin v Williquette* 385 NW 2d 145 (Wisconsin Supreme Ct 1986) 150.

[362] *McGhee v National Coal Board* [1973] 1 WLR 1 (HL); *Fairchild v Glenhaven Funeral Services Ltd* [2002] UKHL 22, [2003] 1 AC 32.

[363] *Wisconsin v Williquette* (n 361) 150; *State v Fabritz* 348 A 2d 275 (Maryland CA 1975; *certiorari* denied *sub nom Hopkins v Fabritz* (1979) 443 US 915 (USSC)).

[364] *J(LA) v J(H)* (n 82) 185.   [365] *Landeros v Flood* (n 251) 395.

[366] SA Collier 'Note, Reporting Child Abuse: When Moral Obligations Fail' (1983) 15 Pacific LJ 189, 191.   [367] *CC and MS v RTH* (n 314) 935.

perhaps even that such conduct was broadly appropriate as the child deserved that treatment,[368] for example, as part of an exorcism ritual.

Most importantly, a parent's or carer's failure to intervene may increase the child's sense of helplessness, and so deter him from seeking help elsewhere, whilst aggravating the resultant harm.[369] Serious psychological harm to the child can result from the sense of having been abandoned by the passive parent or carer. That harm can be translated into legal terminology as neglect[370] or negligent or intentional infliction of emotional distress.[371]

One form in which the 'cause-in-law' issue may arise in this context is what is known as *novus actus interveniens*. At common law an intentional or grossly negligent act by a third party may be viewed as 'breaking' the chain of causation between the defendant's tort and the ultimate harm.[372] However, this argument cannot be invoked where it was the tortfeasor's duty to protect the claimant from exposure to the risk of that harm.[373] Therefore it is very unlikely that a court in the jurisdictions we are considering would permit the non-intervening parent to disclaim responsibility for the physical or emotional harm inflicted by the perpetrator once it is established that it was his duty to take steps to protect the child from that risk.

4. Evaluation: victimizing victims?

To recap, we have argued that English courts should answer the questions we set out at the beginning of this discussion as follows.

Duty of care

- A general duty of care should rise by virtue of the parental or carer relationship to take positive steps to protect a child from foreseeable physical or emotional harm.

Standard of care and breach

- Given the automatic nature of this duty and the likelihood that the passive parent had exposed the child to the risk, failure to take any steps to protect the child should suffice for establishing breach of that duty. It should not be necessary for the claimant to prove that the defendant otherwise actively engaged in the situation.
- In setting the standard of care, the claimant should be required to prove that the defendant had constructive or imputed knowledge of facts which reasonably could give rise to suspicion of abuse (the lowest rung on the culpable knowledge ladder).
- The inaction of a parent or carer should be tested by reference to what a reasonable person in the same circumstances could and would have done to protect the child.

---

[368] Collier (n 365) 191.   [369] Micheels (n 265) 823–824.
[370] *Phillips v Deihm* (n 315) 572; *Spikes v Banks* (n 284) 111.   [371] *Spikes v Banks* ibid 453.
[372] *Smith v Littlewoods* [1987] AC 241 (HL).
[373] *Reeves v Commissioner of Police of the Metropolis* [2000] 1 AC 360 (HL); *Landeros v Flood* (n 251).

Causation of harm

- It should suffice for the claimant to prove that he suffered serious psychological harm attributable to the defendant's unwillingness to intervene. In short, passivity engenders emotional abuse and neglect.

Feminist critics of the judgments holding the passive parent liable in tort to the abused child have argued that this construction of tort liability overlooks the plight of women within the family. Some appear to take the position that women should never have responsibility because they are always powerless. Vella and Grace argue that '[u]ntil we are prepared to provide women with the means by which they can escape lives of abuse and poverty, the law should not be used to punish individual mothers for their inability to protect their children'.[374] Thus a negative stereotype of the powerless woman would dictate a comprehensive legal rule that, whatever the circumstances, a mother or a female carer never owes a duty to protect a child. In the case which Vella and Grace were criticizing, *J(LA) v J(H)*, the trial judge observed:[375]

Some may think it harsh to hold a mother to a standard by which she must, in certain circumstances, choose to take action which is destructive to her family unit. However, where serious sexual abuse of the child within a family unit must be weighed against the destruction of that unit, there can be no doubt how the balance must tip. The consequences of serious child abuse are so clear, both for the immediate development of the victim as well as in terms of the sins of parents being repeated in subsequent generations, that the risks inherent in the fracturing of a family unit in order to separate a child from abuse are infinitely preferable to the risk of the consequences, both immediate and long-term, of leaving an abusive situation to continue to its natural conclusion.

If in a specific case a woman was in such a plight that she had no reasonable opportunity to protect the child, then she would satisfy the standard of care of a reasonable parent. It is unfair to criticize a court for not taking that context into account where the evidence was not tendered;[376] that is the price of an adversarial system. Certainly the court cannot assume that she was acting or failed to act under 'social, economic, political and psychological constraints that affect women generally',[377] because this is not evidence.

It must be remembered that very often the only other adult in the child's world cast in a protective role is that parent. The plight of the child is not mitigated or excused by the situation in which that parent has placed herself through her chosen relationships. As Jean La Fontaine has argued, women may be physically powerless relative to men and economically at a disadvantage, but this does not mean that they lack the capacity to protect their children; when a child is abused there has been a failure of responsibility on the part of adults.[378] Child protection agencies such as the NSPCC provide the means for child welfare concerns to be reported anonymously. As

---

[374] EKP Grace and S Vella 'Vesting Mothers with Power They Do Not Have: the Non-Offending Parent in Civil Sexual Assault Cases: *J.(L.A.) v J.(H) and J.(J.)*' (1994) 7 Canadian J of Women and the Law 184, 195; see also 186, 188–190.   [375] *J(LA) v J(H)* (n 82) 186.
[376] As do Grace and Vella (n 374) 184, 190.   [377] To cite the criticism of Grace and Vella ibid.
[378] La Fontaine (n 265) 194, 221.

the New Zealand Court of Appeal said in a criminal case of omission to seek medical attention for a physically abused child, if an abuser is not present 24 hours per day there are windows of opportunity for the non-abusing parent to seek assistance and so bring the child's ill-treatment to an end.[379]

The situation we are addressing here should not be characterized as a 'pure' omission, because the parent has, at least historically, contributed to creating the risk by allowing the abuser the opportunity to commit the abuse. The distinction between 'act' and 'omission', always thin, becomes meaningless in these circumstances. The critical issue is one of fact: what did the non-intervener know, or should have known? The signs of sexual abuse can be difficult to identify and interpret, as its markers can be covert and subtle. The court must be wary of expert evidence interpreting those signs in hindsight. Physical abuse and ill-treatment and neglect on the other hand usually leave injuries or induce a malaise in the child, and so are easier to detect. We must not forget the evidence before the Victoria Climbié Inquiry that maltreatment is the biggest single cause of morbidity in children.[380] It must be exceptionally rare that such maltreatment has been inflicted without another adult knowing about or suspecting it.

Adult excuses mean nothing to a child—nor should they. A child's fundamental right to proactive protection should not be the first fatality in the crossfire of adults blaming one another after she has died or suffered irreparable harm.

E. Abuse in an Institutional Setting: The Tort Liability of a Party with a Legal Connection with the Abuser

'If the scourge of sexual predation is to be stamped out, or at least controlled, there must be a powerful motivation acting upon those who control institutions engaged in the care, protection and nurturing of children.'[381]

1. The dynamics of abuse in an institutional setting

By 'institutional abuse' we mean abuse inflicted on a child away from home, where the child has been placed, whether for a few hours or for a much longer period, in the care of an organization. Analyses of institutional child abuse such as government-appointed inquiries usually focus on 'total institutions', being residential care or educational or penal correction facilities in which almost every aspect of the child's life is controlled by the institution and by the same single authority.[382] However, there is a growing understanding that abuse can occur in other

---

[379] *R v Witika* [1993] 2 NZLR 424 (New Zealand CA) 436.

[380] Lord Laming *The Victoria Climbié Inquiry* (CM 5730) (January 2003) [11.41].

[381] *GJ v Griffiths* [1995] BCJ No 2370 (British Columbia Supreme Ct) [69] (Wilkinson J), cited with approval by McLachlin J in *Bazley v Curry* [1999] 2 SCR 534 (SCC) [32].

[382] As defined by Law Commission of Canada (DA Wolfe, PG Jaffe, JL Jetté and SE Poisson) *Child Abuse in Community Institutions and Organisations: Improving Public and Professional Understanding* (2002) 4.

types of institution and community service organization to which paedophiles are attracted because as adults they are put in a position of power and authority over children and youth, and have a 'legitimate cover' for their activities.[383] Over the past two decades every jurisdiction in our study has experienced high-profile 'scandals' where children are alleged to have been systematically abused in spiritual, cultural, sporting, recreational, educational, and special needs organizations. For simplicity's sake, we will include such 'organizational abuse' in our references to 'institutional abuse'.

Because of the number of victims and perpetrators involved in allegations of institutional abuse, such cases tend to attract wide publicity. This in turn has engendered heated public debate as to the veracity of such claims, particularly where the allegations relate to incidents long past and institutions long since closed. Supporters of those accused argue that there is a high risk of fabrication, as adults who had contact with those institutions might be enticed to make the allegations by the prospect of compensation, whether from criminal injuries compensation bodies or from the civil courts in tort claims. These suspicions are not necessarily ill-founded.[384] Moreover, it can be exceptionally difficult for those accused to defend themselves. Similar hazards, albeit of a lesser scale, exist in cases of contemporaneous allegations, as the nursery 'scandals' in all of the jurisdictions we study attest.[385]

The practical importance of the fact that the abuse occurred in an institutional setting for our present discussion lies in the availability of other parties, usually more solvent than the abuser, against whom compensation claims can be made. However, it is also conceptually relevant to liability as well; recognition that the foreseeability of the risk of abuse need not be specifically associated with a particular employee, but rather is a generalized risk arising from the institutional culture, makes it easier to set up direct or vicarious[386] liability.[387]

---

[383] ibid; The Hon Justice JRT Wood *Royal Commission into the New South Wales Police Service: The Paedophile Inquiry* (1997) 1059.

[384] *The Conduct of Investigations into Past Cases of Abuse in Children's Homes: the Government Reply to the Fourth Report from the Home Affairs Select Committee Session* 2001–2002 HC 836 Cm 5799, April 2003; The Hon Fred Kaufman CM, QC *Searching for Justice: an Independent Review of Nova Scotia's Response to Reports of Institutional Abuse* (Government of Nova Scotia 2002).

[385] England: *Lillie and Reed v Newcastle City Council, Barker and others* [2002] EWHC 1600 (QB); Australia: Justice Wood *The Paedophile Inquiry* (n 383) Vol IV Ch 7.B: The Kindergarten Cases; Canada: The satanic abuse nursery scandal in Martensville, Saskatchewan: Canadian Broadcasting Corporation <http://www.cbc.ca/fifth/martin/scandal.html>; <http://www.cbc.ca/fifth/martin/timeline.html>; New Zealand: L Hood *A City Possessed: the Christchurch Civic Crèche Case—Child Abuse, Gender Politics and the Law* (Longacre Press, Dunedin 2001) (critiquing the case against Peter Ellis); United States: Ceci and Bruck (n 101) (critiquing the McMartin and Little Rascals nursery cases).

[386] But see *EB v Oblates of Mary Immaculate* 2005 SCC 60, [2005] 3 SCR 45 [4], [36] suggesting that organizational characteristics of an institution which set up a generalized risk of abuse justify direct rather than vicarious liability (discussed below Section 5).

[387] M Hall 'After Waterhouse: Vicarious Liability and the Tort of Institutional Abuse' (2000) 22(2) Journal of Social Welfare and Family Law 159, 168.

The features characteristic of an abusive institutional culture are:[388]

- the institution was highly valued and trusted by society, and served important functions such as educational, religious, or healthcare roles, or community-based personal development activities;

- the institution may have been isolated from the wider community and external and unbiased scrutiny was absent or inadequate;[389]

- the abuser had been put in a position of power and authority over the children in the institution;

- the child victim typically was vulnerable due to previous abuse, family problems, criminal behaviour, abstraction from the child's cultural environment, or special developmental needs or disabilities, and so was an obvious target for sexually predatory or physically abusive staff;

- the child had been instructed to obey all adults in the institution, which often was enforced by a strict disciplinary regime;

- those within or dealing with the institution were ignorant of or misunderstood the risks of abuse, resulting in a pattern of denial and repression of any allegations (particularly in religious organizations,[390] and especially where celibacy was mandatory);[391]

- there were no clear protocols, guidelines and lines of communication with the police concerning the management of complaints, both from children and from concerned staff members;

- the failure to take complaints of abuse seriously sent a message to the children that they had no reliable authority to whom they could appeal for protection, which enabled the abusive behaviour to continue unchecked and unpunished;

---

[388] This list is a compilation of findings from a series of reports: Sir Ronald Waterhouse *Lost in Care* (n 51) Chapter 55; Justice Wood *The Paedophile Inquiry* (n 383) Vol V Chapters 11–13; *Report of the Royal Commission on Aboriginal Peoples (Canada)* (n 53) vol 1); Law Commission of Canada (DA Wolfe, PG Jaffe, JL Jetté and SE Poisson) *Child Abuse in Community Institutions and Organisations* (n 382); Leneen Forde, Chairperson *Report of the Commission of Inquiry into Abuse of Children in Queensland Institutions* (1999); Law Commission of Canada *Restoring Dignity* (n 53) 14–16, 24–39; Senate of Australia, Community Affairs References Committee *Forgotten Australians: a Report on Australians Who Experienced Institutional or Out-of-Home Care as Children* (August 2004) Chapters 4–5; Senate of Australia, Community Affairs References Committee *Protecting Vulnerable Children: a National Challenge; Second Report on Inquiry into Children in Institutional or Out-Of-Home Care* (March 2005); Human Rights and Equal Opportunity Commission of Australia *Bringing Them Home* (n 51), chapter 5. Hall (n 387) 161 describes such findings as identifying 'institutional abuse syndrome'.

[389] Children's homes were described by the Chair of Clwyd's social services committee as 'a gulag archipelago, stretching across Britain—wonderful places for paedophiles but, for the children who suffered, places of unending nightmares' (quoted in *The Guardian* 12 June 1996).

[390] Uniting Church in Australia *Procedures For Use When Complaints of Sexual Abuse are Made against Ministers* (1994) 4; Australian Catholic Bishops Conference *Pastoral Statement on Child Protection and Child Sexual Abuse* (1993).

[391] A Roman Catholic priest testified before the Royal Commission into the New South Wales Police Service that it was a widely held belief that the vow of celibacy is confined to heterosexual relations involving penetration, and so was not breached by acts of indecency or sexual encounters with males, although this was seen as a 'moral wrong' (Justice Wood *The Paedophile Inquiry* (n 383) 1000).

- superiors felt confusions of loyalty to the institution and accused staff member on the one hand, and to the child and the wider community on the other;

- in the case of religious institutions, senior clergy treated the abuse as a moral failure rather than as a criminal offence, and so saw the appropriate response as helping rather than punishing the offender;

- decision-makers did not understand that paedophile activity is strongly compulsive and recidivist in nature, so that moving a perpetrator to another geographic region is not a solution;[392]

- the institution failed to see the child as a victim, and so to offer support such as therapy;[393]

- investigating and prosecuting authorities might not have evaluated the complaint impartially, instead helping the institution to close ranks;

- superiors were concerned to avoid or limit legal liability to protect the institution through a strategy to create as many obstacles as possible to tort litigation, such as reliance upon technical defences and delaying tactics.

The forms of abuse in an institutional setting encompass physical, sexual and emotional abuse as well as neglect. Some analysts also identify 'programme abuse' and 'system abuse', the former occurring when programmes operate below acceptable standards or rely upon harsh or unacceptable methods to control behaviour, and the latter relating to shortcomings of agencies responsible for the care and well-being of children.[394]

Victims of institutional maltreatment commonly display:

- disruption of the child's normal developmental progress, resulting in visible signs of emotional and behavioural problems;

- loss of trust of those in their immediate environment, and a sense of dislocation and fear of intimacy;

- shame, guilt and humiliation, resulting in a sense of isolation from society in general;

- fear of or disrespect for authority, exacerbated where the victim has had to deal with betrayal by the institution as well as by the abuser, and with disbelief and shunning by his community for breaking 'the comfortable silence';[395]

- deliberate and persistent avoidance of situations reminiscent of the trauma, such as churches and schools, and a general emotional numbing, or lack of reactivity to a wide range of situations; and

---

[392] Sometimes called 'passing the trash': Ontario Ministry of the Attorney General *Protecting Our Students: a Review to Identify and Prevent Sexual Misconduct in Ontario Schools* (2000).

[393] As in *FSM v Clarke and the Anglican Church of Canada* [1999] 11 WWR 301 (British Columbia Supreme Ct) [33], [157].

[394] Law Commission of Canada (Wolfe, Jaffe, Jetté and Poisson) *Child Abuse in Community Institutions and Organisations* (n 382) 3; Forde, *Report of the Commission of Inquiry into Abuse of Children in Queensland Institutions* (n 388) Executive Summary iv–v.　　　　[395] Wolfe, Jaffe, Jetté and Poisson, ibid 18.

- intrusive symptoms including flashbacks (vivid intrusive memories which are often described as having 'cinematic' quality), recurrent nightmares and panic and anxiety attacks.[396]

Substance abuse, education and employment difficulties, homelessness, sexual dysfunction, interpersonal problems, and criminal behaviour may follow the child victim into adulthood, and so form part of a claim for pecuniary loss in a tort action.

Institutions are usually sued for negligence in failing to prevent the abuse, and in the alternative for vicarious liability for the torts committed by the abuser. Both avenues of liability present difficulties for victims of child abuse. It can be extraordinarily difficult to establish fault liability, particularly in the case of historic abuse claims. The orthodox definition of vicarious liability—that the abuser must have been employed by the institution and must have committed the tort in the course of his employment—raises the obvious objection that the abuser was employed to protect the child from harm, not to inflict harm. The resulting stalemate has provided an impetus for the highest courts in Canada and England to rewrite the rules of vicarious liability. The American response has been to modify the rules of direct liability in negligence, setting up a duty to control an employee when he is acting outside the scope of his employment but on the employer's premises.[397] The Australian response has been somewhat similar, developing the concept of non-delegable duty.

Diagram 3 depicts the American routes to liability in tort and in equity which might be incurred by institutions, including child protection agencies, which fail to prevent a child from being abused. Diagram 4 does the same for Canadian tort law.

2. Primary liability in negligence

Direct claims of negligence against institutions where abuse occurred are usually framed along the following lines:

- negligence in employing and continuing to employ staff members whom the institution knew or should have known were paedophiles;
- negligence in failing to take reasonable steps to prevent or stop physical and sexual assaults;
- negligence in failing to exercise reasonable supervision and direction over its employees;
- negligence in failing to investigate abuse following reports by the victims.

---

[396] ibid iii, 5–9; *North Wales Children's Homes Litigation* (n 76) [5]–[9].
[397] *Second Restatement of Tort* (n 127) § 317.

Diagram 3. The American Routes to the Liability of Third Parties in Common Law Tort

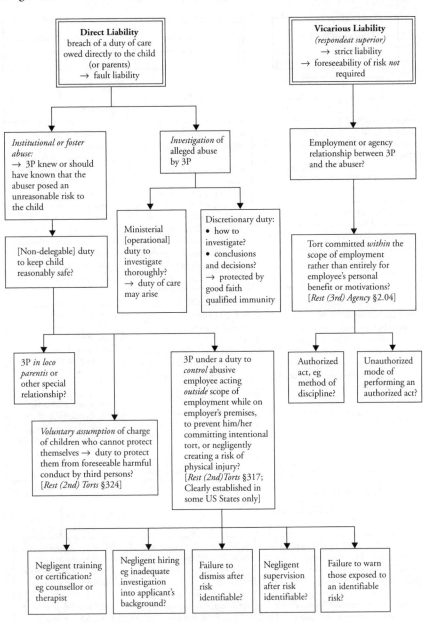

3P = Third Party

Diagram 4. The Canadian Routes to the Liability of Third Parties in Tort and Equity

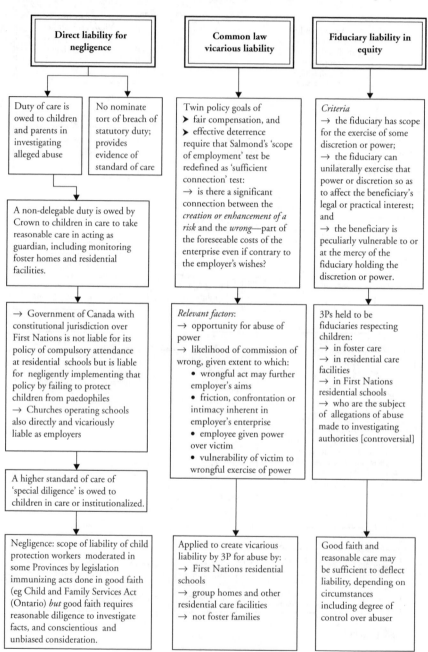

Direct liability for negligence	Common law vicarious liability	Fiduciary liability in equity

Direct liability for negligence

Duty of care is owed to children and parents in investigating alleged abuse

No nominate tort of breach of statutory duty; provides evidence of standard of care

A non-delegable duty is owed by Crown to children in care to take reasonable care in acting as guardian, including monitoring foster homes and residential facilities.

→ Government of Canada with constitutional jurisdiction over First Nations is not liable for its policy of compulsory attendance at residential schools but is liable for negligently implementing that policy by failing to protect children from paedophiles
→ Churches operating schools also directly and vicariously liable as employers

A higher standard of care of 'special diligence' is owed to children in care or institutionalized.

Negligence: scope of liability of child protection workers moderated in some Provinces by legislation immunizing acts done in good faith (eg Child and Family Services Act (Ontario) *but* good faith requires reasonable diligence to investigate facts, and conscientious and unbiased consideration.

Common law vicarious liability

Twin policy goals of
➤ fair compensation, and
➤ effective deterrence
require that Salmond's 'scope of employment' test be redefined as 'sufficient connection' test:
→ is there a significant connection between the *creation or enhancement of a risk* and the *wrong*—part of the foreseeable costs of the enterprise even if contrary to the employer's wishes?

Relevant factors:
→ opportunity for abuse of power
→ likelihood of commission of wrong, given extent to which:
  • wrongful act may further employer's aims
  • friction, confrontation or intimacy inherent in employer's enterprise
  • employee given power over victim
  • vulnerability of victim to wrongful exercise of power

Applied to create vicarious liability by 3P for abuse by:
→ First Nations residential schools
→ group homes and other residential care facilities
→ not foster families

Fiduciary liability in equity

Criteria
→ the fiduciary has scope for the exercise of some discretion or power;
→ the fiduciary can unilaterally exercise that power or discretion so as to affect the beneficiary's legal or practical interest; and
→ the beneficiary is peculiarly vulnerable to or at the mercy of the fiduciary holding the discretion or power.

3Ps held to be fiduciaries respecting children:
→ in foster care
→ in residential care facilities
→ in First Nations residential schools
→ who are the subject of allegations of abuse made to investigating authorities [controversial]

Good faith and reasonable care may be sufficient to deflect liability, depending on circumstances including degree of control over abuser

3P = Third Party

Thus direct claims in negligence usually plead procedural failings of the system within the institution. Many direct negligence claims arising from institutional abuse originate in actions and omissions dating from several decades before the trial. The difficulty for the claimants in establishing liability is proving that the risk of sexual assault of children in the care of such institutions—often established for laudable charitable purposes—was reasonably foreseeable *at that time*. By contemporary standards, the possibility of sexual abuse by carers may have been 'almost unthinkable'.[398] However, in the tort cases arising from maltreatment in children's residential care facilities in North Wales, Justice Scott Baker pointed out that while sexual abuse per se might not have been foreseeable by local authorities in the period from 1977 to 1990, the existence of an abusive *culture* was foreseeable if there was inadequate inspection and supervision.[399]

(a) Negligence in hiring the abuser

Direct claims against institutions for negligence have been characterized by Margaret Hall as based on the 'honeypot' conceptualization of institutional abuse: the abuser as a predatory and pre-inclined infiltrator of an otherwise healthy system.[400] Pre-employment screening then becomes the remedy.

Establishing that an institution owes a duty of care to the children in its temporary or long-term care in appointing staff to be involved in that care is generally unproblematic in Commonwealth jurisdictions.[401] In American law there is a developing line of authority that an employer owes a duty of care to screen applicants for posts which present them with unusual or special opportunities to commit intentional torts, a form of primary liability known as 'negligent hiring'.[402] This has been applied to the screening of prospective employees who will have access to children in performing their jobs, particularly where they will have supervisory or disciplinary authority over them, and may themselves be unsupervised.[403] It has also been extended to the screening

---

[398] *Blackwater v Plint* (n 55) [13]–[16]; *Beach v Jean* 746 A 2d 228 (Connecticut Superior Ct 1999); *DW v Starr and Attorney General of Canada* 1999 SKQB 187, (1999) 187 Sask R 21 (Saskatchewan QB) [8]–[16].

[399] *North Wales Children's Homes Litigation* (n 76) [15]–[16].

[400] Hall (n 387) 160, 162; MI Hall 'Institutional Tort Feasors: Systemic Negligence in the Class Action' (2006) 14 Tort LJ 135; see also J Wangmann 'Liability for Institutional Child Sexual Assault: Where Does *Lepore* Leave Australia?' (2004) 28 Melbourne U LRev 169, 195.

[401] *North Wales Children's Homes Litigation* (n 76); *AR v Bryn Alyn* (n 91).

[402] *Smith v Orkin Exterminating Co.* 540 So 2d 363 (Louisiana App Ct 1st Cir 1989) 366–377; *DRR v English Enterprises* 356 NW 2d 580 (Iowa CA 1984); *Haddock v City of New York* 553 NE 2d 987 (New York CA 1990); *Kansas State Bank & Trust Co v Specialized Transp Services Inc* 819 P 2d 587 (Kansas Supreme Ct 1991).

[403] *Williams v Butler* 577 So 2d 1113 (Louisiana Ct App 1st Cir 1991); *Marquay v Eno* 662 A 2d 272 (New Hampshire Supreme Ct 1995); MA Shields 'Liability of Church or Religious Organization for Negligent Hiring, Retention or Supervision of Priest, Minister, or Other Clergy Based on Sexual Misconduct' (2005) 101 American LR 5th 1.

of volunteers.[404] Since 1994, Federal and State law have mandated criminal background checks for childcare and youth service workers.[405]

A rather peculiar series of cases in some American States holds that questions of hiring, ordaining, supervising and retaining clergy would necessarily involve the courts in the interpretation of religious doctrine, policy and administration. This would have the effect of inhibiting the exercise of religion contrary to the First Amendment; therefore such claims in negligence are considered not justiciable.[406] Other courts have refused to immunize churches from direct negligence liability; the Illinois Appellate Court caustically observed that 'the First Amendment's freedom of religion clause has lofty goals; the protection of sexual abusers of children . . . is not one of them'.[407]

But if a duty of care is generally accepted in Commonwealth jurisdictions, the real difficulty has lain in establishing breach of that duty. In setting the standard of care, the courts have generally resisted the temptation to impose standards retroactively which are higher than those considered to be best practice at the time the tort was committed.[408] Even a decision to employ male counsellors at a reform school for troubled young girls to deal with security problems has been held not to be negligent, albeit 'perplexing', by the standards of the time.[409]

---

[404] *Big Brother/Big Sister, Inc v Terrell* 359 SE 2d 241 (Texas App Ct 1987). For a contrary case involving the Boy Scouts of America see *Broderick v King's Way Assembly of God Church* 808 P 2d 1211 (Alaska Supreme Ct 1991), criticized by MC Lear 'Just Perfect for Pedophiles? Charitable Organisations That Work with Children and Their Duty to Screen Volunteers' (1997) 76 Texas L Rev 143.

[405] National Child Protection Act 42 USC §5119–5119c (1994) superseded by the Child Abuse Prevention and Treatment and Reform Act 42 USCA ch 67 §5106(a) (2003). Every American State has developed procedures for maintaining records of child abuse and neglect. Most States maintain some sort of central registry, which is a centralized computerized database of child abuse and neglect investigation records. As of August 2005, approximately 42 States, the District of Columbia, and the US Territories of American Samoa, Guam, and Puerto Rico have statutorily created central registries [National Clearinghouse on Child Abuse and Neglect Information *Gateways to Information: Protecting Children and Strengthening Families: Central Registries/Reporting Records: Establishment and Maintenance* (2003)].

[406] *Gibson v Brewer* 952 SW 2d 239 (Missouri Supreme Ct 1997) 246–248. The court did however draw the line at *intentional* failure to supervise clergy known to be paedophiles (248, 249). See also *Isely v Capuchin Province* 880 F Supp 1138 (US Dist Ct of Michigan 1995) 1150–1151; *Avon v Gourley* 47 F Supp 2d 1246 (Dist Ct Colorado 1998), affd on other grounds 185 F 3d 873 (US CA 10th Cir 1999); *JM v Minnesota District Council of Assemblies of God* 658 NW 2d 589 (Minnesota Ct App 2003); *Heroux v Carpentier* 1998 WL 388298 (Rhode Island Superior Ct 1998).

[407] *Parks v Kownacki* 711 NE 2d 1208 (Illinois App Ct 1999) 1216; see also *Roman Catholic Diocese of Jackson v Morrison* 905 So 2d 1213 (Mississippi Supreme Ct 2005) 1226 holding that there is 'nothing remotely religious or ecclesiastical' about the sexual molestation of children; *Bivin v Wright* 656 NE 2d 1121 (Illinois App Ct 1995) 1124 noting that sexual misconduct was not rooted in the church's religious beliefs—query if it was?; *Gagné v O'Donoghue* 1996 WL 1185145 (Massachusetts Superior Ct 1996).

[408] eg *H(TEG) v K(P)* [2001] ABQB 43, [2001] 6 WWR 546 (Alberta QB) [25]–[26] (employers of staff working with children could not have been expected to do more than check references in the early 1980)s; *SGH v Gorsline and The Calgary School Board* 2004 ABCA 186, (2004) 29 Alta LR 203 (Alberta CA) [30]–[31] (teaching professionals in 1978 had no awareness of child sexual abuse at school and so the education authority was not negligent in failing to put in place policies and programs to protect students); *Isely v Capuchin Province* (n 406) 1146–1147 warning of the dangers of 'bootstrapping of past incidents into contemporary mores'.

[409] *R(GB) v Hollett and Nova Scotia* (1995) 143 NSR (2d) 38 (Nova Scotia Supreme Ct), varied as to damages (1996) 154 NSR (2d) 161 (Nova Scotia CA)) [18]–[20].

When procedures have been in place they sometimes have not been followed, even in recent times. The Waterhouse inquiry into systemic sexual and physical abuse of children in care in North Wales reported that there were many breaches of approved practice in the appointment of residential care staff over the period investigated from 1974 to 1996. Several staff were recruited informally without references or any adequate investigation of their past records. In some cases 'manifestly unsuitable residential care staff' were appointed to vacant senior posts in community homes without any adequate assessment of their suitability for those posts. Checks of the records of potential employees and foster parents held by the police, the Department of Health, and the Department of Education were not routinely made before appointments were confirmed, or were unnecessarily limited in scope, or, where negative, were not followed through by the Social Services Department itself.[410] Following the Waterhouse report, the local authorities admitted liability for a plethora of claims by former residents of the homes examined by the tribunal. Similarly, the Government-appointed inquiry into the treatment of children in Queensland institutions in Australia found that in 1999 police checks were being relied upon to 'clear' staff to be employed in residential facilities for children, but there was very little evidence of comprehensive reference and qualifications checks or intensive interview procedures; because of the difficulty of attracting qualified staff, agencies were reluctant to make it more difficult to recruit them.[411]

In addition to establishing breach of the standard of care, the claimant must prove a causal link between that breach and the resulting abuse. For historic claims of abuse in particular, the problem is one of evidence: the claimant must establish that an appropriate vetting system would have disclosed that the applicant posed a risk to children and so he would not have been offered the post (or been permitted to act as a volunteer). That information might not be available because the applicant had not previously offended, or had not previously been identified as a possible offender, or had never been convicted of a criminal offence relating to children.[412] Another reason might be that the register or other sources then reasonably available to the prospective employer did not disclose that specific information. It was on this basis that the direct negligence claims against the employer of the abuser failed in the landmark Canadian and English cases of *Bazley v Curry*[413] and *Lister v Hesley Hall*,[414] which we discuss below in Section 3 in relation to vicarious liability.

---

[410] *Lost in Care* (n 51) chapter 55, Findings (25)–(27).

[411] Forde *Report of the Commission of Inquiry into Abuse of Children in Queensland Institutions* (n 388) Executive Summary viii.

[412] As in the case of D1, a convicted paedophile and former Scout leader: Justice Wood *The Paedophile Inquiry* (n 383) 1063; *R(GB) v Hollett and Nova Scotia* (n 409) [18]–[20]; *K(W) v Pornbacher and Roman Catholic Bishop of Nelson* [1998] 3 WWR 149 (British Columbia Supreme Ct) [38]–[39]. In *DW v Starr and Attorney General of Canada* (n 398) [17] the employer was exonerated because the employee's paedophilia had not been discovered when social services vetted him as a prospective adoptive parent.

[413] *Bazley v Curry* (n 381).

[414] *Lister v Hesley Hall Ltd* [2001] UKHL 22, [2002] 1 AC 215 [7]–[8].

(b) Negligence in failing adequately to train and supervise the abuser

Difficulties in proving breach of the duty to screen applicants for a post, and in proving that but for that breach the child would not have been victimized, have caused
many litigants to plead in the alternative negligent failure to train and supervise the
abuser after he had been employed. The distinction then between a claim for negligent hiring and a claim for negligent supervision or retention depends upon the time
at which the employer is fixed with actual or imputed knowledge of the employee's
unfitness.[415] This theory of liability reflects the 'crucible' theory of institutional abuse,
in which the combination of isolation, power imbalance, and hierarchy is conducive
to the development of internal cultures in which abuse becomes normalized, creating
abusers among susceptible adult staff and vulnerable child residents.[416] The institution's negligence then pertains to permitting (through structural or wilful blindness)
an environment conducive to abuse to arise and be perpetuated.

Training is most likely to be an effective precaution—and so the lack of it easier
to constitute a breach of duty—where emotional or physical abuse of children is
concerned. The Waterhouse inquiry found that training opportunities and practice
guidance for residential care staff in North Wales were grossly inadequate and no
instructions were given to them in proper measures of physical restraint.[417]

Where failure to stop sexual abuse is at issue, its clandestine nature makes it harder
for employers to prevent, short of surveillance which could offend the privacy rights
of the children as well as of other staff. It has been argued that constant behind-the-
scenes surveillance may not be required by the institution's duty to children in its care;
it might be reasonable instead to have regular monitoring and evaluation of employee
conduct, staff training on the dynamics of child abuse to sensitize co-workers to the
dynamics of abuse,[418] inspections without warning, prohibiting staff from being alone
with a child, and encouragement of complaints by children and their parents.[419] It is
difficult to see how this would deter a determined paedophile, particularly where a
supervisor is also an abuser.[420]

In American law, claims for negligent supervision of an employee have been built
upon the *Second Restatement of Tort)* §317. This sets up a direct duty on the part
of employers to exercise reasonable care to control the conduct of an employee so
as to prevent him from intentionally or negligently harming others, even where the
employee is acting outside the scope of his employment so that vicarious liability will
not attach. The duty arises where the employee is on the employer's premises or is
using the employer's equipment, the employer has reason to know of the employee's
propensity and hence the necessity of controlling him, and the employer has the ability
to exercise that control. This has been applied to set up an independent cause of action

---

[415] *Malicki v Doe* 814 So 2d 347 (Florida Supreme Ct) 362 fn 15; *FSM v Clarke and the Anglican
Church of Canada* (n 393) [174]–[183].   [416] Hall 'Institutional Tort Feasors' (n 400).

[417] *Lost in Care* (n 51) chapter 55, Finding (28).

[418] J Lynch 'A Matter of Trust: Institutional Employer Liability for Acts of Child Abuse by Employees'
(1992) 33 Wm & Mary L Rev 1295, 1337.

[419] *Lepore v New South Wales* (n 260) [164] (McHugh J).

[420] As in *FSM v Clarke and the Anglican Church of Canada* (n 393) [22]–[40], [182].

for negligent supervision of abusers where the employer or church authorities knew or should have known of their sexual proclivities.[421]

The United States has witnessed a plethora of claims against American churches alleging that they turned a blind eye to the risk of abuse by their clergy. As with ordaining and hiring clergy, here again American courts encounter difficulty with the constitutional guarantee of freedom of religion when the liability of church authorities for failing to supervise a priest is at issue.[422] The majority of State and Federal courts have held that religious freedom is not put at risk where the church allegedly knew or should have known of the priest's predilection, for example because of past complaints of abuse. The reasoning is that this does not entail state interference with religious doctrine or practice, but rather can be adjudicated according to neutral secular rules.[423] Other courts however have considered that state enforcement of a church's duty to oversee its employees would violate the free exercise of religion clause.[424] Some courts draw a distinction between the negligent failure to supervise a cleric, which is not actionable, and an intentional failure, which is.[425] As yet there is no authoritative ruling on the issue from the United States Supreme Court.

Constitutional concerns about the free exercise of religion have not troubled Canadian courts, which have held bishops directly liable for their failure adequately to supervise paedophile priests in their dioceses.[426] In *John Doe v Bennett*,[427] over a period of almost two decades Father Kevin Bennett, a Roman Catholic priest in the Diocese of St. George's in Newfoundland, sexually assaulted boys in his parishes. Two successive bishops failed to take steps to stop the abuse. In 1979 a victim revealed the abuse to the archbishop of the neighbouring diocese, St. John's, who was also

---

[421] SJ Buck 'Church, Liability for Clergy Sexual Abuse: Have Time and Events Overthrown *Swanson v Roman Catholic Bishop of Portland*?' (2005) 57 Maine L Rev 259; *Jones v Father Trane and Roman Catholic Diocese of Syracuse* 591 NYS 2d 927 (New York Supreme Ct 1992).

[422] Shields (n 403); *Nelson v Gillette* 571 NW 2d 332 (North Dakota Supreme Ct 1997) 240–341.

[423] *Doe v Hartz* 52 F Supp 2d 1027 (USDC Iowa 1999); *Kenneth R v Roman Catholic Diocese of Brooklyn* 654 NYS 2d 791 (New York SCAD 1997) 164–165; *Malicki v Doe* (n 415); *Konkle v Henson* 672 NE 2d 450 (Indiana Ct App 1996) 456; *Gagné v O'Donoghue* (n 407); *Leary v Geoghan* 2000 WL 1473579 (Massachusetts Superior Ct 2000) (holding that while training for the priesthood and ordination is not justiciable, subsequent supervision of a priest is justiciable as 'although the freedom to believe is absolute, the freedom to act cannot be').

[424] *Swanson v Roman Catholic Bishop of Portland* 692 A 2d 441 (Maine Law Ct 1997).

[425] *Gibson v Brewer* (n 406).

[426] e.g. *TM v Poirier* [1994] OJ No. 1046 (Ontario Gen Div) (bishop had negligently allowed a priest to terminate prematurely his residential therapeutic treatment for his sexual proclivities and to return to the diocese to resume counselling young men with drug, alcohol or sexual problems); *K(W) v Pornbacher and Roman Catholic Bishop of Nelson* (n 412) [45]–[46] (bishop, aware of sexual misconduct allegations against some priests, failed to take steps to prevent other clergy in his diocese, including the claimant's priest, from sexually abusing children) (overruled on the issue of an episcopal corporation being a responsible and suitable entity by *John Doe v Bennett and Roman Catholic Episcopal Corporation of St George's* 2004 SCC 17, [2004] 1 SCR 436); *S v Glendinning and Roman Catholic Episcopal Corporation of London Ontario* 2004 CanLII 5011 (Ontario Supreme Ct) [203]–[217] (seminary should have become suspicious of priest through young boys' frequent overnight visits in his room and unsupervised camping trips); *FSM v Clarke* (n 393) [181]–[184] (bishop did nothing after being informed that a lay child careworker in a residential school had abused boys in his dormitory).

[427] *John Doe v Bennett and Roman Catholic Episcopal Corporation of St George's* (2002) 218 DLR (4th) 276 (Newfoundland CA), revd on other grounds 2004 SCC 17, [2004] 1 SCR 436.

Metropolitan of the broader ecclesiastical province. He referred the complaint to Bennett's Bishop but again nothing was done. The 36 claimants sued Bennett as well as the episcopal corporations through which the Bishops held their dioceses' assets. The Supreme Court of Canada upheld the Newfoundland courts' decisions that the Bishops were personally liable for their failure to deal with Bennett beyond transferring him from one parish to another, notwithstanding widespread knowledge of his activities amongst the priests of the diocese; the episcopal corporations were held vicariously liable for the negligence of the Bishops.[428]

In England and Wales there is as yet little jurisprudence on inadequate supervision creating the opportunity for child abuse. Claims against churches for failure to supervise clergy, or for exporting problematic clergy to other dioceses rather than confronting the problem, are just beginning to come through the legal system. In one case the Roman Catholic Archbishop of Birmingham admitted liability to the son of a very devout family for failing to prevent ten years of sexual abuse by Father Clonan, who was never prosecuted. When the abuse was revealed, the repercussions for the family were so great that they had to move from England to Northern Ireland. The victim suffered very severe mental illness as a consequence, and was awarded £635,000, the largest component being damages for loss of future income.[429] This is believed to be the largest reported award of damages in a child abuse compensation claim in the UK.[430]

Other actions in England and Wales involve complaints of mismanagement based upon the poor supervision systems of government authorities. The Home Office and local authorities have been sued for allegedly failing to supervise staff in youth correctional facilities, so as to protect the residents from physical and sexual abuse.[431] In the litigation arising out of systemic physical and sexual abuse in the North Wales Children's Homes,[432] Justice Scott Baker found that vicarious liability was foreclosed by the then current perception of the law,[433] but found a route to primary liability through the breach of the local authority's direct duty *in loco parentis* to the children to take all reasonable steps to provide a safe home for them.[434] He formulated the test for breach as being whether the perpetrator in question would have committed the assault if supervised to the relevant standard. He accepted the local authority's arguments that the relevant standard of supervision had to be judged against the contemporary state of awareness of the risk of abuse, and that 20 years earlier that risk was perceived as low. However, Scott Baker J ruled that it was not appropriate to

---

[428] ibid [16].   [429] *A v The Archbishop of Birmingham* [2005] EWHC 1361 (QB) [116].

[430] R Scorer 'Paying for the Sins of the Fathers' 8 July 2005 New LJ 1029.

[431] e.g. more than 70 actions for damages for physical and sexual abuse brought by former inmates of Forde Park Approved School, where three staff members were convicted of sexual offences: *Ablett v Devon County Council and The Home Office* (n 81).   [432] *North Wales Children's Homes Litigation* (n 76).

[433] Based on *ST [Trotman] v North Yorkshire County Council* [1999] IRLR 98 (CA).

[434] This duty was also found to exist and to have been breached by Connell J in *KR v Bryn Alyn* 26 June 2001, No HQ/99/01473, 2001 WL 753345 (QBD), and in *FSM v Clarke* (n 393) [169]–[171].

sever sexual abuse completely from physical abuse, because '[t]he fact is if these homes were not properly supervised there was an increased risk of abuse full stop, and the defendants ought to have appreciated this'.[435] The local authority's mismanagement of the children's homes created the conditions in which physical and sexual abuse could occur, and rendered it likely that the children would be abused by staff.[436] Such supervision would have made it a much greater risk for the senior management to embark upon such abuse and probably would have resulted in it being discovered.[437]

Where the abuser is himself in a supervisory position, the pleading of negligent supervision becomes contorted. This is illustrated by the strategy adopted at trial by claimant's counsel in *Lister v Hesley Hall* to circumvent the problem that the sexual abuse itself was viewed as being obviously outside the scope of the abuser's employment. Hesley Hall Ltd operated an independent school to which children with emotional and behavioural difficulties were sent by local authorities. Grain was appointed as warden, responsible for the day-to-day running of the boarding annex for boys, including maintaining discipline; the intention was to establish a home-like atmosphere. Unbeknownst to his employers, the warden systematically sexually abused the children. The claimants' argument for Hesley Hall's direct liability was formulated as follows:

- the defendant owed a duty of care to the pupils to take all reasonable steps to safeguard them in their physical, moral and educational development while at school;

- in carrying out its duty of care the defendant corporation had to appoint a hierarchy of responsible agents, one of whom was Grain;

- Grain had a duty to report any harm or risk of harm to a boy in his care, so that the defendant could take further remedial or preventative steps to fulfil its own duty of care;

- failure by Grain to report any harm would amount to a failure to carry out his own duty to each boy;

- a report of abuse would have resulted in the defendant dismissing the source of the abuse, in this case Grain himself, and a report of the incident to the police;

- the defendant therefore was vicariously liable for Grain's failure to *report* his *own* torts, rather than for his torts themselves.[438]

The trial judge imposed vicarious liability on this basis. The Court of Appeal reversed the trial judge's judgment, holding that sexual abuse of children by persons responsible for their welfare was by its nature a secret act, and it was unrealistic to attempt to

---

[435] *North Wales Children's Homes Litigation* (n 76) [15].
[436] ibid [16], quoting *Lost in Care* (n 51) [29.86], [30.43].   [437] ibid [256].
[438] As summarized by Lord Steyn in *Lister v Hesley Hall Ltd* (n 414) [8].

distinguish the actual act from the fact that the abuser kept that act secret from his employers, or failed to inform them of the risk that he would repeat it. The fact that Grain did not report that he was abusing the children was integral to that abuse, and that conduct was also wholly outside the course of his employment.[439]

It is submitted that the more logical last step to this chain of reasoning would be that Hesley Hall had directly breached its *own* duty of care for negligent supervision, in this case of the supervisor himself. The House of Lords found it unnecessary to deal with this line of argument, but did not rule it out,[440] although Lord Millett described it as indulging in sophistry and unrealistic.[441] The issue is still being litigated in a case which is bound for the House of Lords on a limitation of actions point; the Court of Appeal had shown a strong inclination to adopt the argument were they not constrained by authority.[442]

Under American law, for an employer to be held liable for negligent supervision of its employee, the employer must have had constructive or actual notice that the employee was unfit to work. In Florida it was held that notwithstanding that an abusive pastor was a director and president of the defendant religious corporation, his knowledge of his own past sexual misconduct could not be imputed to the corporation because he had committed the sexual abuse outside the scope of his employment.[443] It is submitted that it is not logical to block primary liability on the basis of a theory of secondary liability in this way.

(c) Negligence in dealing with complaints of abuse

We have seen that it can be difficult to establish negligence in hiring, training or supervising the abuser, particularly when the employer followed the usual practices for the time. Failure to terminate the abuser's employment upon receipt of complaints is much more clearly negligent, but this avails the claimant only if (a) the previous complaints were sufficiently clear as to put the institution on notice of the abuse,[444] and (b) the claimant was abused after those complaints had been made.[445]

As *Doe v Bennett*[446] discussed earlier illustrates, pleas of negligence in dealing with complaints of abuse are often bound together with complaints about negligent supervision of the abuser.[447] The breach of duty may be based upon the employer's failure to

---

[439] *Lister v Hesley Hall Ltd* 13 October 1999 *The Times* LR (CA).

[440] *Lister v Hesley Hall Ltd* (n 414) [12].   [441] ibid [84].

[442] *A v Hoare; H v Suffolk County Council; X and Y v London Borough of Wandsworth* (n 99) [113]–[115], the binding precedent being *Stubbings v Webb* (n 90), discussed above, section A.

[443] *Iglesia Cristiana La Casa Del Senor, Inc v LM* 783 So 2d 353 (Florida Dist CA 3d District 2001) 358.

[444] The ambiguity of complaints of children in an Indian residential school from the 1940s to the 1960s was held not to have put the church and federal government authorities on notice of the abuse, and so absolved them of direct liability, in *Blackwater v Plint* (n 55) [11]–[15].

[445] As in *R(GB) v Hollett and Nova Scotia* (n 409) [23]–[30], but not in *SGH v Gorsline and The Calgary School Board* (n 408) [36]–[37].   [446] *John Doe v Bennett* (n 427).

[447] e.g. *Kenneth R v Roman Catholic Diocese of Brooklyn* (n 423).

take further action such as investigating, dismissing or reassigning the employee,[448] or negligently implementing measures to protect children from abuse once the employer has notice of the risk.[449] Where a national body assumes investigatory and disciplinary jurisdiction over abuse allegations against a particular institution under its umbrella, it may attract tort liability.[450] Evidence that a religious body with authority over a paedophile cleric has failed to deal with previous complaints, and to control his activities, is probative of negligence, as may also be failure to report incidents of sexual abuse to the appropriate authorities.[451]

As we discuss in Chapter 5, the Federal Child Abuse Prevention and Treatment Act obliges all American States to adopt reporting statutes and to grant tort immunity to reporters in order to be eligible for Federal funding.[452] American courts have generally been reluctant to set up a private right of action arising from failure to comply with a mandatory reporting statute, since the institution or individual will be subject to criminal or civil statutory penalties.[453]

The doctrinal and evidential difficulties[454] of establishing a direct claim against an institution for negligence in employing or supervising an abusive employee have

---

[448] *Waters v Commissioner of Police for the Metropolis* [2000] 1 WLR 1607 (HL) 1607 (arguable duty of care on an employer to investigate complaints that an employee was sexually assaulted by another employee); *Jones v Father Trane and Roman Catholic Diocese of Syracuse* (n 421); *Rosado v Bridgeport Roman Catholic Diocesan Corp* 716A 2d 967 (Connecticut Superior Ct 1998); *Evan F v Hughson United Methodist Church* 8 Cal App 4th 828 (California CA 3rd Dist 1992); *Doe v Hartz* (n 423); *Gagné v O'Donoghue* (n 407); *Doe v Redeemer Lutheran Church* 531 NW 2d 897 (Minnesota CA 1995); *Kenneth R v Roman Catholic Diocese of Brooklyn* (n 423).

[449] Shields 'Liability of Church Negligent Hiring' (n 403) § 2[a]; *Moses v Diocese of Colorado* 863 P 2d 310 (Colorado 1993) (failure to act on psychological reports about a priest); *Hutchison v Luddy* 763 A 2d 826 (Pennsylvania Superior Ct 2000, appeal denied 788 A 2d 377 (Pennsylvania Supreme Ct 2001)) (diocese allegedly had prior knowledge of a priest's propensity for paedophilic behaviour before hiring him); *Mark K v Roman Catholic Archbishop* 67 Cal App 4th 603 (California CA 2nd Dist 1998) (failure to warn of a priest's known propensity for engaging in sexual conduct with boys); *FSM v Clarke* (n 393) [22]–[40], [182]–[183] (failure of residential school principal to take investigative action beyond dismissing abusive dormitory supervisor, to cover up his own paedophilia; the Anglican Church was also found liable for breach of fiduciary duty on the same basis [196]–[197]).

[450] *Olson v Magnuson and the Redeemer Covenant Church of Brooklyn Park* 457 NW 2d 394 (Minnesota CA 1990) 397; *Winkler v Rocky Mountain Conference of United Methodist Church* 923 P 2d 152 (Colorado CA 1995).

[451] *Hutchison v Luddy* (n 449); Shields 'Liability of Church for Negligent Hiring' (n 403) § 2[b].

[452] USCA § 5106a(6) (1988), amended and reauthorized on June 25, 2003 by the Keeping Children and Families Safe Act of 2003 (PL 108–36); National Clearinghouse on Child Abuse and Neglect Information *Gateways to Information* (n 405), discussed below Chapter 5 section D.3.

[453] *Isely v Capuchin Province* (n 406) 1148; *Borne v Northwest Allen County School Corp.* 532 NE 2d 1196 (Indiana Superior Ct 1989, app denied 558 NE 2d 828); *Doe "A" v Special School District of St Louis County* 901 F 2d 642 USCA (US CA 8th Cir 1990); *Fischer v Metcalf* (n 252). However, the violation of the reporting statute may give rise to liability on the theory of negligent hiring or retention where the claimant can show that reporting would have prevented subsequent abuse: *Marquay v Eno* (n 403) [23].

[454] eg *C v Middlesbrough Council* [2004] EWCA Civ 1746; [2005] 1 FCR 76 (claim for alleged negligence in failing to have a social worker assigned to a child placed in a local authority residential special needs school failed due to lack of expert evidence as to proper social work practice; school authorities had conducted a reasonable investigation of concerns about a teacher which nonetheless failed to uncover his abuse).

caused litigants in Canada and England to turn to vicarious or indirect liability, which is not premised upon proof of fault.

3. Vicarious liability for the intentional tort of the abuser

(a) The conventional approach

As noted earlier, the fundamental difficulty in imposing vicarious liability on employers for the intentional torts of their employees lies in establishing that the torts were committed in the course of the tortfeasors' employment. The traditional test for this requirement is commonly described as the 'Salmond test':

A master is not responsible for wrongful acts done by his servant unless it is done in the course of his employment. It is deemed to be so done if it is either (1) a wrongful act authorised by the master, or (2) a wrongful and unauthorised mode of doing some act authorised by the master.[455]

This formulation of the test would seem to exclude unauthorized intentional torts from vicarious liability in most cases, where the employee is likely to be classified as, in the stock phrase, 'on a frolic of his own'[456]—and never more so than in the case of criminal abuse of children by those employed to protect them. Courts inclined to rule in favour of the victims had to set up the characterization of the authorized act in such a way as to admit the abuse as the improper mode of performing that act. For example, a Roman Catholic priest who abused a child parishioner in the rectory was held to be exercising the authority vested in him by the Church over the spiritual care of children, the sexual abuse being an unauthorized mode of exercising that authority.[457]

Many courts refused point-blank to engage in such result-oriented manipulation of 'modes' in this way.[458] In *Trotman v North Yorkshire County Council* the English Court of Appeal rejected the argument that the deputy headmaster of a special needs school was acting within a perverted form of his duty to the Council, his employer, when he

---

[455] RFV Heuston and R Buckley *Salmond and Heuston on the Law of Torts* (21st edn Sweet & Maxwell, London 1996) 443. This formulation was judicially approved as early as 1927: *Poland v Parr (John) & Sons* [1927] 1 KB 236 (CA) 240.

[456] An oft-quoted phrase originating in *Joel v Morrison* (1834) 6 C&P 501 per Parke J; *Williams v A & W Hemphill Ltd* 1966 SC (HL) 31, 46. [457] *K(W) v Pornbacher* (n 412).

[458] eg cases involving sexual abuse by a priest: *McDonald v Mombourquette* (1996) 152 NSR (2d) 109 (Nova Scotia CA), leave to appeal refused [1997] 2 SCR xi (SCC); *Mount Zion State Bank & Trust v Central Illinois Annual Conference of United Methodist Church* 556 NE 2d 1270 (Illinois App Ct 1990); sexual abuse by teachers: *John R v Oakland Unified School District* 769 P 2d 948 (California Supreme Ct 1989); *Randi F v High Ridge YMCA* 524 NE 2d 966 (Illinois App Ct); sexual assault of a patient by a nurse: *J-PB v Jacob* (1998) 166 DLR (4th) 125 (New Brunswick CA); *Lisa M v Henry Mayo Newhall Memorial Hospital* 907 P 2d 358 (California Supreme Ct 1995).

sexually assaulted a mentally handicapped and epileptic child on a school trip to Spain. The tort was a negation of the duty of the Council to look after children for whom it was responsible, and was 'an independent act of self-indulgence or self-gratification'.[459] As the California Supreme Court put it in another case involving sexual assaults by a teacher on a pupil, 'a more personal escapade less related to an employer's interests is difficult to imagine'.[460] Some American courts have held that there can never be vicarious liability by a Roman Catholic diocese for the sexual wrongs of priests who violate their oath of celibacy.[461]

(b) Rewriting the rules of vicarious liability: the Canadian policy-based approach

The battle over 'unauthorized' modes' of doing authorized acts was arguably waged over false ground,[462] because Salmond put a gloss on his test later in the same paragraph: an employer is liable for unauthorized acts provided they are *so connected* with acts which he has authorized that they may rightly be regarded as modes—although improper modes—of doing them. An employer is thus responsible not merely for what he authorizes his employee to do, but also for the way in which he does it.[463] Once the significance of this elaboration was appreciated, it provided the wedge to crack open vicarious liability for intentional torts on a principled basis. As elsewhere in the law of tort and evidence, the reform was initiated in cases involving child abuse. The first court to deploy the 'sufficient connection' concept in this context was the Supreme Court of Canada, in the companion cases of *Bazley v Curry* and *Jacobi v Griffiths* decided in 1999.[464]

In *Bazley v Curry*, The Children's Foundation, a non-profit organization, operated two residential care facilities for the treatment of emotionally troubled children. As a substitute parent it practised 'total intervention' in all aspects of the lives of these children. The Foundation's employees were to do everything a parent would do, from general supervision to intimate duties such as bathing and tucking in at bedtime. The Foundation employed Curry after making checks and being told he was a suitable employee. It immediately dismissed Curry after investigating a complaint about him. Curry was subsequently convicted of 19 counts of sexual abuse, including two against Patrick Bazley. The Foundation argued that the assaults were acts independent of his employment, whereas the victim contended that they were a mode of performing authorized tasks (intimate care). The Supreme Court of Canada concluded that the Salmond test provides no criterion to make the distinctions sought

---

[459] *ST [Trotman] v North Yorkshire County Council* (n 435) [18], [26], overruled by *Lister v Hesley Hall Ltd* (n 414). See also *North Wales Children's Homes Litigation* (n 76) [16].

[460] *John R v Oakland Unified School District* (n 498) 953.

[461] eg *Richelle L v Roman Catholic Archbishop* 106 Cal App 4th 257 (California App Ct 2003).

[462] See the remarks by Lord Steyn in *Lister v Hesley Hall Ltd* (n 414) [15], [20], Lord Millett [70].

[463] Adopted in *Canadian Pacific Railway Co v Lockhart* [1942] AC 591 (PC) 599; *Salmond and Heuston on the Law of Torts* (n 455) 437.

[464] *Bazley v Curry* (n 381); *Jacobi v Griffiths* [1999] 2 SCR 570 (SCC).

by the parties,[465] and that the judicial manoeuvring it invites makes the outcome frequently unpredictable.[466]

Instead, the Supreme Court decided to embark on a fresh examination of the vicarious liability doctrine. It developed a two-stage analysis for Canadian courts, which should determine, first, whether there are any precedents which unambiguously determine a solution; and if not, whether vicarious liability should be imposed in light of the broader policy rationales behind strict liability.[467]

The numerous policy rationales for vicarious liability conventionally recited by tort lawyers were distilled into two:[468]

- *fair and effective compensation* for the wrong:
  — *fair* in the sense that the employer has introduced into the community a risk-creating enterprise, and so should bear the cost of the risk materializing, regardless of the employer's reasonable efforts to avoid the risk;[469] and

  — *effective* in that vicarious liability leads to the internalization and distribution of the loss, to minimize the dislocative effect of the tort within society; and
- *deterrence* of future harm, in that strict liability creates greater motivation to prevent future harm through more efficient organization and supervision than prospective negligence liability with its inherent evidential difficulties[470] can afford.

The key to the vicarious liability doctrine is found in the economic concept of 'enterprise risk'. In using it, Canadian courts are to be guided by the following principles:

(1) They should openly confront the question of whether liability should lie against the employer, rather than obscuring the decision beneath semantic discussions of 'scope of employment' and 'mode of conduct'.

(2) The fundamental question is whether the wrongful act is *sufficiently related* to conduct authorized by the employer to justify the imposition of vicarious liability. Vicarious liability is generally appropriate where there is a significant connection between the *creation or enhancement of a risk* and the wrong that accrues therefrom, even if unrelated to the employer's desires. Where this is so, vicarious liability will serve the policy considerations of provision of an adequate and just remedy and deterrence. Incidental connections to the employment enterprise, like time and place (without more), will not suffice. Once engaged in a particular business, it is fair that an employer be made to pay the generally foreseeable costs of that

---

[465] *Bazley v Curry* ibid [11].   [466] ibid [7], [24]; *EB v Oblates of Mary Immaculate* (n 386) [25].
[467] ibid [15].   [468] ibid [29]–[34].

[469] This was found to be the unifying principle behind the English and Canadian cases falling into the categories of (1) furtherance of the employer's aims (2) the employer's creation of a situation of friction, and (3) the dishonest employee [ibid [17]–[22]].

[470] The Supreme Court might also have added that primary liability in negligence sets the standard of care at a level where the cost of reasonable precautions is less than the harm should the risk eventuate, and so creates less of an incentive than does strict liability.

business. In contrast, to impose liability for costs unrelated to the risk would effectively make the employer an involuntary insurer.

(3) In determining the sufficiency of the connection between *the employer's creation or enhancement of the risk* and the wrong complained of, subsidiary factors may be considered. These may vary with the nature of the case. When related to intentional torts, the relevant factors may include, but are not limited to, the following:

(a) the opportunity that the enterprise afforded the employee to abuse his or her power;

(b) the extent to which the wrongful act might have furthered the employer's aims (and hence be more likely to have been committed by the employee);

(c) the extent to which the wrongful act was related to friction, confrontation or intimacy inherent in the employer's enterprise;

(d) the extent of power conferred on the employee in relation to the victim;

(e) the vulnerability of potential victims to wrongful exercise of the employee's power.[471]

Thus the 'sufficient connection' test was first clearly and fully isolated. How is it to be applied to sexual misconduct? At first blush, it would seem that providing an employee of paedophilic tendencies with access to a child would suffice, since in so doing the employer has clearly increased the risk of abuse. However, McLachlin J (as she then was) stressed that the test must be applied in a more nuanced way than this implies:

In summary, the test for vicarious liability for an employee's sexual abuse of a client should focus on whether the employer's enterprise and empowerment of the employee materially increased the risk of the sexual assault and hence the harm. The test must not be applied mechanically, but with a sensitive view to the policy considerations that justify the imposition of vicarious liability—fair and efficient compensation for wrong and deterrence. This requires trial judges to investigate the employee's specific duties and determine whether they gave rise to special opportunities for wrongdoing. Because of the peculiar exercises of power and trust that pervade cases such as child abuse, special attention should be paid to the existence of a power or dependency relationship, which on its own often creates a considerable risk of wrongdoing.[472]

The power/vulnerability analysis is tied directly to the enterprise risk: '. . . the more an enterprise requires the exercise of power or authority for its successful operation, the more materially likely it is that an abuse of that power relationship can be fairly ascribed to the employer'.[473]

How does the 'enterprise risk' premise for the vicarious liability doctrine apply to children's charities, such as the defendants in *Bazley v Curry* and *Jacobi v Griffiths*? There are two reasons why it may appear to have little explanatory value in this specific context: the charity is not seeking to profit financially by introducing the risk of tortious conduct into the community; and the 'enterprise' is often one on which society depends for the care of its most needy citizens such as troubled children.

---

[471] *Bazley v Curry* (n 381) (emphasis in the original text).   [472] ibid [46].   [473] ibid [44].

Moreover, the consequence of imposing vicarious liability may be to over-deter or even prevent such beneficial activities, to the ultimate disadvantage of society.

The Supreme Court rejected a plea for an exemption for non-profit organizations based upon such arguments.[474] From the child victim's perspective, it would be fair to place the loss on the institution that introduced the risk and had a better opportunity to control it. He should not have to bear the cost of the harm done to him so that others could benefit from the good work done by charities (an argument McLachlin J said 'smacks of crass and unsubstantiated utilitarianism'). Vicarious liability, she held, should motivate charitable organizations entrusted with the care of children to take not only such precautions as the law of negligence requires, but all possible cautions to ensure that those children are not sexually abused.[475]

These ripostes are perhaps a trifle glib, but it is difficult to argue convincingly that Patrick Bazley should not have succeeded under the criteria for liability in the 'sufficient connection' test. The charity fostered a special quasi-parental relationship of intimacy and respect and provided the abuser with special opportunities of private control and intimacy to exploit that relationship.[476] It is submitted that vicarious liability should not depend on whether the institution which creates such a high risk relationship with a child was originally established for profit or non-profit motives.

The Canadian Supreme Court's call for transparent discussion and application of policy considerations in unprecedented cases may be brave as well as intellectually sound, but it does give rise to the risk that liability under such an open-textured analysis could be as unpredictable as it was under the traditional Salmond test.

This concern was borne out by the decision in *Jacobi v Griffiths*[477] handed down on the same day as *Bazley v Curry*. Here the Court split four to three on whether the defendant Boys' and Girls' Club was vicariously liable for sexual assaults perpetrated by the Club's employed programme director on two siblings attending it. The Club offered group recreational activities for children to be enjoyed in public facilities and in the presence of volunteers and other members. All but one of the assaults were committed away from its premises, and out of hours. It was common ground that the claimants were vulnerable to a sexual predator such as Griffiths because of their unsettled home life. Justice Binnie for the majority held that the case for vicarious liability was not made out, because while the Club had encouraged the programme director to form a rapport with the children, it had not stood in a relationship of power or authority over them, nor did it confer any such authority on the abuser.[478] His relationship with the children, as the Club had envisaged it, had no element of intimacy comparable to the situation in *Bazley*. The opportunity that the Club afforded Griffiths to abuse whatever power he may have had was slight, since the sexual abuse only became possible when he managed to subvert the public nature of the Club's activities through a series of independent initiatives for his personal gratification.[479] In a vigorous dissent, McLachlin J contended that the Club positively encouraged Griffiths to form a mentoring and intimate relationship with the children, many

---

[474] ibid [47]–[54].   [475] ibid [50].   [476] ibid [58].
[477] *Jacobi v Griffiths* (n 464).   [478] ibid [41]–[43].   [479] ibid [80].

of whom were troubled and vulnerable, which enabled him to exercise a 'god-like' authority over his victims.[480]

The sharp judicial disagreement in *Jacobi v Griffiths* over the application to the evidence of *Bazley*'s five subsidiary factors to measure the sufficiency of the connection between the perpetrator's job and the abuse is disquieting. Of equal concern is the narrow split on the court about how the policy rationales should be applied to a non-profit children's charity.

First, the majority stated that since sexual abuse is antithetical to the ethos of churches and other 'high-minded' organizations, this is relevant in assessing the measure of risks that may *fairly* be regarded as *typical* of the enterprise in question.[481] Although this may seem to hearken back to the traditional approach to the 'scope of employment' question in cases involving intentional torts, it does not similarly result in the *automatic* ejection of the tort from the scope of employment on the basis that the conduct was not in furtherance of the employer's aims. Nonetheless it does seem to raise the benchmark of the inherent risk test considerably when the institution's *raison d'être* is to nurture children.

Second, while repeating that there is no exemption from the ordinary rules of vicarious liability for non-profit organizations, the majority observed that the enterprise risk rationale may yield different results when applied to them as opposed to commercial organizations. Not only do they not have deep pockets, but they have no efficient mechanism to internalize the cost of strict liability, so the compensation policy rationale has little or no application to them.[482] The deterrence rationale also has to be assessed with some sensitivity to context. According to the majority, the sexual abuse of children by caregivers is rarely foreseen and is always surreptitious, so 'conventional incentives and disincentives used by enterprises simply do not work to deter compulsive sexual misconduct' where the prospect of criminal conviction has obviously failed to do so.[483] This would seem to preclude vicarious liability of children's charities altogether, but the majority insisted that fairness to them would be entirely compatible with vicarious liability where a strong connection was established between the enterprise risk and the sexual assault. But non-profit organizations were entitled to insist that the strong connection test be applied with 'appropriate firmness' given the weakness of the policy justifications.[484]

Thus the benchmark for claimants suing children's charities seems to be raised not only for the degree of the inherent risk created by the enterprise, but also for the strength of the connection between it and the abuse. It is submitted that the majority in *Jacobi v Griffiths* is correct in the result, but that the reasoning is not entirely consistent with the unanimous judgment of the same panel of judges in *Bazley v Curry*.

---

[480] ibid [16]–[17], refuted by the majority [82]–[84].

[481] ibid [54], quoting and adding emphasis to *Bazley v Curry* (n 381) [39]. McLachlin J for the minority held that the Club created and sustained the risk that materialized: *Jacobi v Griffiths* [22].

[482] ibid [71].

[483] ibid [72]–[73], quoting *Ciarochi v Boy Scouts of America, Inc.* Ketchikan Registry IKE-89-42 CI, August 6, 1990 (Alaska Supreme Ct) 22. The minority contended that the rationales of risk distribution and deterrence supported vicarious liability: [22], [25]. [484] ibid [78].

Bazley and *Jacobi* rewrote the rules of vicarious liability to create a clear but potentially unstable framework against which to analyse an institution's legal responsibility for child abuse. We shall see that this uncertainty has shaped the House of Lords' response.

(c) Rewriting the rules of vicarious liability: the English response

In *Lister v Hesley Hall Ltd*, discussed earlier in relation to direct liability for negligent supervision,[485] the House of Lords was asked to adopt the Canadian approach in *Bazley v Curry* to vicarious liability for intentional torts. All five Law Lords held that Hesley Hall was vicariously liable for the sexual assaults by its warden, overruling *Trotman v North Yorkshire CC.*[486] Four of them approved the sufficient connection test in *Bazley v Curry.*[487] However, they were not entirely *ad idem* on how it should be applied in English courts.

Lord Steyn, with whom Lord Hutton concurred, described the conventional approach based on the abbreviated Salmond test as preoccupied with conceptualistic reasoning and divorced from reality.[488] He did not consider it necessary to express views on the policy considerations in *Bazley* and *Jacobi*, decisions which he described as 'luminous and illuminating'; instead he preferred to employ 'the traditional methodology of English law' to hold that the warden's torts were 'so closely connected' with his employment that it would be 'fair and just' to hold the employers vicariously liable.[489]

Lord Clyde also considered that the sufficient connection test in the Canadian cases reflects orthodox English (and Scottish) law.[490] He expressed scepticism as to whether principle or policy could provide substantial guidance in any particular case to determine whether an employer should be vicariously liable for a particular wrong,[491] an implicit rejection of the Canadian open-textured and policy-reflective approach. Lord Clyde preferred instead to go directly to the sufficient connection test, which he described as asking whether, taking a broad approach, the wrongful acts could be seen as ways of carrying out the work which the employer had authorized.[492] The factors relevant to evaluating the sufficiency of the connection include:

- the purpose and the nature of the act, without concentrating too closely on the particular act complained of;
- the context and circumstances in which the act occurred;
- the time and place which are relevant but not conclusive; and
- a greater connection than merely providing the opportunity to commit the act provided by access.[493]

---

[485] *Lister v Hesley Hall Ltd* (n 414) discussed above section E.2(b).
[486] *ST [Trotman] v North Yorkshire County Council* (n 433), discussed above section E.2(b).
[487] *Lister v Hesley Hall Ltd* (n 414) [27] per Lord Steyn; [48] per Lord Clyde, [70] per Lord Millett.
[488] ibid [16].   [489] ibid [27]–[28].   [490] ibid [48].   [491] ibid [35].
[492] ibid [37].   [493] ibid [42]–[45].

Lord Clyde's solution does not present a departure from the standard abbreviated formulation of the Salmond test with all its flaws; at best the enumerated factors repeat the obvious.

Only Lord Millett acknowledged (albeit indirectly) the role of policy, in embracing the Supreme Court's inherent risk principle: if experience shows that the employer's objectives cannot be achieved without a serious risk of the employee committing this kind of wrong, the employer ought to be liable.[494] He also signed up to the test of close connection between the employee's duties and his wrongdoing, but signalled the importance of avoiding the constraints of verbal formulae.[495] Like the Supreme Court of Canada, Lord Millett concluded that the tortfeasor must have done more than make the most of an opportunity presented by his employment; he must be proved to have exploited the position in which the employer has placed him to achieve its business purposes—here, the care and welfare of boys entrusted to the warden's care by the school.[496]

Lord Hobhouse espoused a different approach which grounded liability in the employer's assumption of a relationship with the claimant and its choice to entrust the performance of the specific duties arising from that relationship to its employee.[497] This explanation looks much more like non-delegable duty than vicarious liability. However, Lord Hobhouse then seemed to step away from that model by asserting that the correct approach to the 'scope of employment' question is to ask what was the employee's duty to the claimant which he breached, and what was the employee's contractual duty towards his employer.[498] The direct duty between employer and claimant seems to have vanished from the analytical template. Lord Hobhouse was alone in rejecting *Bazley v Curry*, remarking that 'legal rules have to have a greater degree of clarity and definition than is provided by simply explaining the reasons for the existence of the rule and the social need for it, instructive though that may be'.[499] Lord Hobhouse's two questions seem to offer an attractive solution: on the facts of *Lister*, the employee's duty to the child and his duty to his employer were synonymous: to protect the child. However, the level of generalization or specificity in which the duties are defined for the purposes of the comparison is prone to result-oriented manipulation, just as the traditional Salmond test is.

It is clear that the Law Lords were wary of allowing the lower courts to engage in explicit explorations of policy which could produce unpredictable results. Their response was to propound a simple fact-based test shorn of its justifications: vicarious liability is to be imposed if there is a sufficient connection between the tort and the tortfeasor's employment duties. However, Lord Steyn's invocation of fairness and justice in gauging the sufficiency of the connection, and Lord Clyde's espousal of 'a broad approach' to the acts authorized by the employer, make the English version of the sufficient connection test as vague and as susceptible to surreptitious manipulation as the old 'unauthorised mode' test.

In *Dubai Aluminium v Salaam* Lord Nicholls, who was not on the *Lister* court, seemed to acknowledge this hazard. He explicitly embraced the enterprise risk theory

---

[494] ibid [65].   [495] ibid [69]–[70].   [496] ibid [79], [82].   [497] ibid [54].
[498] ibid [60].   [499] ibid [60].

as the legal policy underlying the vicarious liability doctrine, and found that policy best expressed in the close connection test.[500] He expressed concern that the close connection test affords no guidance on the type or degree of connection required to impose vicarious liability, but accepted that this imprecision is inevitable. He concluded that any decision necessarily involves the court making a value judgment, expressed in a conclusion of law in each case.[501] In the same case, Lord Millett reiterated his adherence to the enterprise risk theory, and invited overt consideration of the underlying rationale of vicarious liability in considering the closeness of the connection between the employee's wrongdoing and the class of acts he was employed to perform.[502] Thus the enterprise risk principle as the legal policy underpinning vicarious liability, and its inescapable role in the court's conclusion in a particular case, seems now to have claimed the support of a majority amongst the Law Lords.

(d) Rewriting the rules of vicarious liability: the Canadian shift towards rules

As discussed earlier, *Bazley* and *Jacobi* did not leave the doctrine of vicarious liability free from doubt. It was unclear how the enterprise risk concept relates to the sufficiency of connection test, and at what stage the policy considerations of fair and effective compensation and deterrence are to be considered. It was also unclear whether non-profit organizations merit separate and special treatment. These issues were clarified in a series of five rulings from the Canadian Supreme Court, all of them relating to child sexual abuse.

Where there are no applicable precedents, the sufficient connection template has now been reduced to two primary questions, the burden of persuasion being on the claimant:

(1) *Is the relationship between the tortfeasor and the organization or person against whom liability is sought sufficiently close as to make vicarious liability appropriate?*

It will not be appropriate where the tortfeasor is so remote from the organization that the tort cannot reasonably be regarded as a materialization of the organization's *own* risks, so that compensation would be unfair and would have no deterrent effect because the organization could not take any measures to prevent such conduct.[503]

(2) *If so, is the tort sufficiently connected to the tortfeasor's assigned tasks that the tort can be regarded as a materialization of the risks created by the enterprise?*[504]

Here the five factors from *Bazley* (opportunity; furtherance of the employer's aims; friction, confrontation or intimacy inherent in the enterprise; power over the victim conferred on the employee; and vulnerability of potential victims) remain relevant guidance. At the heart of the inquiry lies the question of power and control by the employer: both that *exercised over* the employee and that *granted to* the employee over the victim. Where this power and control can be

---

[500] *Dubai Aluminium Co Ltd v Salaam* [2002] UKHL 48, [2003] 2 AC 366 [21]–[23], Lords Slynn and Hutton concurring. [501] ibid [24]–[26].
[502] ibid [107], [124], Lord Hutton concurring. [503] *KLB v British Columbia* (n 309) [20].
[504] ibid [19]; *John Doe v Bennett* (n 427) [20].

identified, the imposition of vicarious liability will meet the goals of fair and effective compensation and deterrence of future harm.[505]

In relation to the first question, the Supreme Court has not restricted vicarious liability to its traditional ambit of employment and agency relationships. In *Blackwater v Plint*, the court found that both the Federal Crown and the United Church of Canada were vicariously liable for the sexual abuse of students in an Indian residential school operated by them, on the basis that both entities had a sufficient degree of control over the school's operation and management, acting in partnership. The Supreme Court did not find any impediment to finding two unrelated parties vicariously liable for the torts.[506] The English Court of Appeal has recently also accepted that dual vicarious liability is possible, but has insisted that liability must be apportioned equally between the two parties for the purposes of contribution,[507] whereas the Canadian Supreme Court allocated responsibility on the basis of the degree of control of each defendant over the operations of the school.

The Canadian template is now more akin to the orthodox rule-based common law methodology preferred by the Law Lords in *Lister*. In effect the policy rationales of fair and effective compensation and deterrence now serve as a cross-check on the result reached by application of the 'sufficient connection' rules. The 'enterprise risk' principle is firmly embedded in the connective link between the wrong and the tortfeasor's responsibilities and job-created power.

A clearer map of vicarious liability for child sexual abuse has emerged from a sequence of decisions of the Supreme Court of Canada, applying the sharpened 'close connection' test.

- Two episcopal corporations were vicariously liable for a Roman Catholic priest's sexual assault of 36 boys in his parishes. The relationship between priest and bishop is akin to an employment relationship, as the priest takes a vow of obedience to the bishop who exercises extensive control over him. The bishop conferred an enormous degree of power on the priest relative to his victims, particularly in isolated and devout parishes. The bishop provided the abuser priest with the opportunity to abuse that power. His wrongful acts were strongly related to the psychological intimacy inherent in his role as priest. A strong and direct connection was established between the conduct of the diocesan enterprise and the abuse.[508]

- Schools will not be vicariously liable for sexual abuse of pupils by their janitors, because they have merely created the opportunity for the abuse, without conferring job-created power over the victim or another link between the janitor's employment and the abuse.[509]

---

[505] *John Doe v Bennett* ibid [20]–[21].   [506] *Blackwater v Plint* (n 55) [18]–[38].
[507] *Viasystems (Tyneside) Ltd v Thermal Transfer (Northern Ltd)* [2005] EWCA Civ 1151, [2005] 4 All ER 1181 [85].   [508] *John Doe v Bennett* (n 427) [27]–[32].
[509] *EDG v Hammer* (n 258) [9], *Jacobi v Griffiths* (n 464) [45].

- A religious order operating a residential school for First Nations children was not vicariously liable for sexual abuse perpetrated by a resident lay employee who worked as a baker, boat driver and odd-job man. The conduct in the course of which the abuse occurred had nothing to do with furthering the employer's aims. He was not required or permitted to be with the children unsupervised. Intimacy between the employee and the students was prohibited. The school did not confer any power on the employee in relation to the victim; rather, the vulnerability of the students resulted from the nature of the institution and its operations (which was more properly the subject of a direct liability claim).[510]

- Vicarious liability should not be extended to the relationship between government and foster parents for their maltreatment of the children in their care. The independence of foster families is essential to the government's goal of providing family care. Imposing vicarious liability in the face of such independence would be of little use, as exacting supervision or stricter monitoring in the foster home would not be effective deterrence measures. Moreover, vicarious liability could do harm in deterring a government from placing children in foster homes, in favour of less efficacious institutional settings.[511]

By October of 2005 a sufficient corpus of appellate precedent developing the *Bazley* approach had been built up that Binnie J felt it appropriate to instruct lower courts to seek guidance in analogous cases rather than resorting over-hastily to the second stage of the *Bazley* analysis.[512]

As mentioned earlier, *Jacobi v Griffiths* had created some confusion as to the application of the enterprise risk principle to non-profit employers, and whether the majority's dicta indirectly revived the doctrine of charitable immunity.[513] In *Doe v Bennett*, Chief Justice McLachlin for a unanimous court confirmed that while non-profit status may sometimes negatively impact on the policy rationales underlying vicarious liability, it would be entirely fair and consistent to impose it provided there was a *strong* connection between the enterprise risk and the sexual assault, which was lacking in *Jacobi*.[514] In *Blackwater v Plint*, the Chief Justice explicitly rejected the doctrine of charitable immunity, and explained how vicarious liability can motivate non-profit organizations to take precautions to screen their employees and protect children from sexual abuse, since by placing the children in their employees' care they enhance the risk of abuse.[515]

---

[510] *EB v Oblates of Mary Immaculate* (n 386) [37], [41], [47–52] (Abella J dissenting).

[511] *KLB v British Columbia* (n 309) [23]–[25]; *MB v British Columbia* 2003 SCC 53, [2003] 2 SCR 477 [16].

[512] *EB v Oblates of Mary Immaculate* (n 386) [47].

[513] Such that the Newfoundland Court of Appeal had concluded that non-profit employers should not be held vicariously liable for a sexual assaults by their employees: *John Doe v Bennett and Roman Catholic Episcopal Corporation of St George's* 218 DLR (4th) 276 (Newfoundland CA), revd on other grounds 2004 SCC 17, [2004] 1 SCR 436, as did the British Columbia Court of Appeal in *Blackwater v Plint* (2003) 235 DLR (4th) 60.   [514] *John Doe v Bennett* (n 427) [24].

[515] *Blackwater v Plint* (n 55) [39]–[44]. See also *Doe v O'Dell and Roman Catholic Episcopal Corporation for the Diocese of Sault Sainte Marie* [2003] OJ No 3546 (Ontario Superior Ct) [255]–[257] (imposing vicarious liability on a diocese could serve a deterrent function through greater supervision of priests,

(e) Adhering to the orthodox rules of vicarious liability: the Australian response

In Australia, apart from New South Wales, the vicarious liability of a public authority is subject to a special public law rule. The much criticized 'independent discretion function immunity' *Enever* doctrine holds that the Federal Crown cannot be made liable for decisions by public officers on whom a statutory discretion has been specifically conferred; this has been applied to immunize the Crown from vicarious liability for the acts of appointed officials.[516] However it has also been held that the public employee does not have the necessary independent discretion if the employee is subject to the control of the relevant minister.[517] The *Enever* doctrine has immunized the Federal Crown from liability for the removal of aboriginal children from their parents, in the 'stolen generation' cases.[518]

In a trio of cases involving sexual abuse of pupils by schoolteachers, *Lepore v New South Wales, Samin v Queensland* and *Rich v Queensland*,[519] the Australian High Court had the opportunity to consider *Bazley, Lister* and *Dubai Aluminium*. In the New South Wales case, a teacher (on the pretext of corporal punishment) had repeatedly physically assaulted a boy, the assaults having sexual overtones. In the Queensland cases, two girls in a remote country school were raped and indecently assaulted by the only teacher in the school. In all three cases the abusers had been convicted of criminal offences. The prospect of success against the school authorities under the vicarious liability doctrine, as conventionally conceived in Australian law, was considered foreclosed by the claimants' counsel, so the cases were argued in the courts below entirely on the basis of non-delegable duty. The Australian High Court gave leave to hear vicarious liability arguments after the *Lister* decision was rendered.

All three cases were remitted for a new trial of the issue of vicarious liability. It is difficult to extract a single principle from the six highly complex judgments, especially as they were complicated by arguments as to whether non-delegable duty is fault or strict liability, which we will consider later in Section E.4 of this chapter.

Gleeson CJ noted that the 'enterprise risk' theory of vicarious liability has been influential in North America, but as a test for determining whether conduct is in the course of employment (as distinct from an explanation of the willingness of the law to impose vicarious liability) it has not been taken up in Australia or, he thought, the UK. However all of these common law jurisdictions saw the sufficiency of the connection

psychological testing of candidates for the priesthood, and possible proactive responses to child sexual abuse in the church).

[516] *Enever v The King* (1906) 3 CLR 969 (Aus HC), approved *Attorney-General (NSW) v Perpetual Trustee Co Ltd* [1995] AC 457 (PC); Kneebone (n 250) 302–312. The doctrine has been repealed in New South Wales [Law Reform (Vicarious Liability) Act 1983 (NSW) ss 5(1), 8] and partially abolished in the Commonwealth, Queensland and the Northern Territory, but for police officers only [Australian Federal Police Act 1979 (Commonwealth of Australia) s 64B(1); Police Service Administration Act 1990 (Queensland), s 10.5; Police Administration Act 1979 (Northern Territory) s 163]. The Australian Law Reform Commission has recommended its abolition: Australian Law Reform Commission *The Judicial Power of the Commonwealth: a Review of the Judiciary Act 1903 and Related Legislation, Part 25 Liability of the Commonwealth at Common Law and in Equity* (ALRC Report 92 2001) Recommendation 25–1.

[517] *Cubillo v Commonwealth (No 2)* [2000] FCA 1084, 103 FCR 1 (Aus Fed Ct 2000) [1117].
[518] ibid [1116]–[1133].   [519] Reported collectively as *Lepore v New South Wales* (n 260).

between the employment and wrongdoing as central, and he predicted that in most cases the answer would be the same. Gleeson CJ concluded that in Australia as in England and Canada, the possibility of a school authority's vicarious liability for sexual abuse could not be dismissed merely by pointing out that it constituted serious misconduct on the part of a teacher.[520] While the risk of sexual abuse could not be regarded as an incident of most schools, he accepted that there could be circumstances where teachers had responsibilities which involved a relationship of such power and intimacy with the pupils that sexual abuse could properly be regarded as sufficiently connected to that employment. The relevant factors in gauging the degree of power and intimacy in the teacher–student relationship are: the age of students; their particular vulnerability if any; the tasks allocated to teachers; the number of adults concurrently responsible for student care; and the nature and circumstances of the sexual misconduct. Gleeson CJ held in the *Lepore* case that as the teacher was responsible for the maintenance of discipline, whether excessive or inappropriate chastisement resulted from a sadistic tendency of the teacher or a desire for sexual gratification, it was conduct in the course of employment for which the school authority was vicariously liable.[521] Chief Justice Gleeson's list of factors has been criticized as overlooking the lengthy grooming process antecedent to sexual abuse, and as failing to appreciate that child sexual abuse is fundamentally about an abuse of power and trust rather than about intimate opportunities.[522]

Kirby J also was attracted to the reasoning in *Bazley* and *Lister*, and concluded that the common law of Australia 'marches in step' with those courts in dealing with child abuse in an institutional setting.[523] He accepted that policy considerations must be decisive in developing the law's response to a new problem in society, and found the Canadian 'enterprise risk' rationale persuasive.[524] He favoured adoption of the Canadian and English broader 'connection' analysis, notwithstanding that this must involve the court in value judgments and policy choices from which, he bluntly admonished his colleagues, formulation of specific rules cannot ultimately escape.[525] In his view, as a matter of legal principle it is impossible and undesirable to turn the clock of vicarious liability backwards—an apparent reference to Justice Callanan who would have extradited deliberate criminal conduct from vicarious liability altogether.[526] Kirby J asserted that there is no reason why the common law of Australia should be less protective of the legal entitlements of child victims of sexual assault on the part of teachers and carers than is the common law of England and Canada.[527]

Gaudron J developed *de novo* a rather odd estoppel argument as being the only principled basis on which vicarious liability could be imposed from the deliberate criminal acts of another. In her view, the employer would be estopped from asserting that the tortfeasor was not acting as its employee, provided there was a close connection between what was done and what the person was engaged to do.[528]

---

[520] *Lepore v New South Wales* (n 260) [65], [67], [72], [74].   [521] ibid [78].
[522] Wangmann (n 400) 193.   [523] *Lepore v New South Wales* (n 260) [277].
[524] ibid [300], [303], [331].   [525] ibid [320], [322]   [526] ibid [345].
[527] ibid [331]–[332].   [528] ibid [130]–[131].

The joint judgment by Gummow and Hayne JJ criticized the Canadian and English 'sufficiency of connection' analysis as not providing any bright line test for vicarious liability, instead just restating the 'course of employment' problem. In their view the Canadian inquiry about the creation and enhancement of risk becomes a general and abstract inquiry about the opportunity for wrongdoing created by the enterprise, distracting attention from the underlying task of identifying what the employee was engaged to do. They criticized the focus on power and authority creating or enhancing the risk of abuse as leading 'inexorably to a conclusion' that a school will always be vicariously liable for a teacher's assaults.[529] They thought that the risk analysis ignores three critical facts, that the conduct was intentional, was contrary to the core of the employee's responsibilities, and the perpetrator was not deterred by the criminal law.[530] The correct approach, according to Gummow and Hayne JJ, is to hold that an employer will be vicariously liable for the intentional tort of an employee only if the conduct was done in the intended or ostensible pursuit of the employer's business.[531] This narrow conception of vicarious liability would cast outside any deliberate sexual assault on a pupil, as it is a predatory abuse of the teacher's authority in deliberate breach of a core element of the employment contract.[532]

To summarize, of the six Justices on the High Court of Australia to consider vicarious liability,[533] only Gleeson CJ and Kirby J were influenced by the Canadian and English approaches to the conundrum of intentional torts by employees, and accepted the viability in principle of vicarious liability claims arising from child sexual abuse. Gummow, Hayne, and Callanan JJ refused to contemplate an employer being vicariously liable for an employee's intentional sexual misconduct toward a child. Gaudron J could see little point in imposing vicarious liability when, in her view, direct liability through non-delegable duty would provide greater protection to those who were young or especially vulnerable.[534] The net result is that in Australian law there remains no clearly defined route for victims of child sexual abuse to hold to account the institutions under whose auspices the abuse occurred, to the dissatisfaction of many commentators.[535]

---

[529] Decisions in the lower Canadian courts on the contrary show that the vicarious liability determination is invariably based upon a detailed analysis of the evidence, without any assumptions of liability based on category of employment [eg *SGH v Gorsline and The Calgary School Board* (n 408) [21]–[27] (school board not vicariously liable for sexual abuse by physical education teacher because its educational services did not significantly contribute to the risk of sexual abuse, as teacher's duties did not require intimate contact with students); *HL v Starr and Attorney General of Canada* 2002 SKCA 131 (Saskatchewan CA) [142]–[170] (employer liable for abuse by school administrator of boys in his after-school boxing club) appeal allowed in part on the quantum of damages 2005 SCC 25.

[530] *Lepore v New South Wales* (n 260) [212]–[218].   [531] ibid [239].

[532] ibid [241].

[533] McHugh J considered the issues to be determined by non-delegable duty, as a 'simpler and stricter test of liability' than vicarious liability: ibid [166].   [534] ibid [127].

[535] See DJ Stewart and AE Knott 'Australian School Authorities' Liability (without Fault) for Sexual Abuse of Students by Employees' (2003) 170 Education LJ 4; P Vines '*New South Wales v Lepore*; *Samin v Queensland*; *Rich v Queensland*: Schools' Responsibility for Teachers' Sexual Assault: Non-Delegable Duty and Vicarious Liability' [2003] 27 Melbourne U LRev 612; Wangmann (n 400); NJ McBride 'Vicarious Liability in England and Australia' [2003] Cambridge LJ 255. The New Zealand Court of Appeal concluded that *Lepore* was 'of limited utility': *S v Attorney-General* (n 31) [63].

(f) New Zealand law: avoidance of institutional care

We need not tarry long in New Zealand, since the accident compensation schemes cover any abuse occurring after 1 April 1974. The Child Welfare Act 1925 s 19 directed that children committed to the care of the state should not, save in exceptional cases, be permanently maintained in institutions, but instead should be cared for by any suitable person approved by the Superintendent of Child Welfare.[536] The New Zealand Court of Appeal has held that for foster placements prior to 1974, the Superintendent is vicariously liable for any physical or sexual abuse perpetrated by foster families, on an agency rationale which precludes vicarious liability for abuse by other members of the foster family.[537] This ruling necessarily has very limited application.

(g) American law: a diversity of approaches

Finally, a brief word about American law. Some American courts take an approach similar to the Canadian 'sufficiently close connection' test for vicarious liability for sexual assaults. The court must find a causal connection between the employee's work and the commission of the tort which goes beyond the usual 'but for' test of factual causation (in effect, as in England and Canada, creation of the opportunity to commit the tort does not suffice). The risk of the tort occurring must be an inherent part of the employment environment, and so be a foreseeable risk arising from the employer's business.[538] The question becomes whether the employment relationship was instrumental in enabling the abuser to commit the assault by exploiting his employment-related power, authority or access.[539] However, California's highest appellate court has vacillated over adopting a vicarious liability theory based on a job-created foreseeable risk arising from conferral of official authority by the employer on the abuser.[540] Many State courts seem to adhere to an approach reminiscent of the Salmond test which absolves the employers of child sex abusers of vicarious liability.[541]

4. Non-delegable duty

Non-delegable duty differs from primary negligence in that it does not necessarily entail the direct attribution of fault to the institution or organisation, and so is a hybrid of primary and secondary liability. This device is usually invoked in English courts where the vicarious liability doctrine does not apply because of the remoteness of the relationship between the secondary defendant and the tortfeasor, usually

---

[536] *S v Attorney-General* (n 31) [51].   [537] ibid [68]–[74].

[538] *Lisa M v Henry Mayo Newhall Memorial Hospital* (n 458) 361, 362, 364.

[539] See the cases cited by Lear (n 404) fn 54, 55.

[540] Compare *John R v Oakland Unified School District* (n 458) 954–957 with *Mary M v City of Los Angeles* 814 P 2d 1341 (California Supreme Ct).

[541] See the American cases discussed by M Hall 'Responsibility without Fault: *Bazley v Curry*' (2000) 79 Canadian Bar Rev 474, 476–477, on which defence counsel relied in *Bazley*.

an independent contractor. However, the argument is occasionally raised where the tortfeasor was the defendant's employer.[542]

In Canadian law (which does not recognize an independent tort of breach of statutory duty), the availability of the non-delegable duty analysis for tort claimants is constrained by the requirement that any applicable statute use imperative rather than permissive language in conferring power over the child. The Supreme Court of Canada on three occasions has considered, and rejected, non-delegable duty arguments in the context of child abuse. In *EDG v Hammer*, the British Columbia School Act imposed only specific duties on school boards pertaining to student health and safety, and hence did not permit the inference that they were generally and ultimately responsible for the health and safety of children on school premises so as to make them liable for abuse at the hands of a school employee.[543] In *Blackwater v Plint* the non-delegable duty argument on behalf of First Nations children abused in residential schools was thwarted because the provisions of the Indian Act authorizing the federal Minister of Indian Affairs to enter into agreements for their education with, *inter alia*, religious or charitable organizations, were permissive only, and did not create a mandatory duty to ensure their health and safety.[544] Similarly, the British Columbia government did not owe a non-delegable duty to children in the care of foster parents, because the Protection of Children Act did not impose a specific duty to ensure that no harm came to children in care through the abuse or negligence of foster parents. However, the government did owe a non-delegable duty to protect children who were in the system until they had been placed with foster families.[545]

Some Commonwealth commentators,[546] as well as some Justices of the Australian High Court in *Lepore v New South Wales*,[547] consider that *Bazley v Curry* and *Lister v Hesley Hall* are really cases about non-delegable duty, but the Supreme Court of Canada and the House of Lords had failed to recognize this. As the preceding paragraph shows, the Supreme Court of Canada has not been oblivious to non-delegable duty arguments, which have frequently been advanced in child abuse cases as alternative arguments to vicarious liability. Moreover, the Supreme Court has interpreted an appropriately worded statutory duty as creating

---

[542] In *G(ED) v Hammer*, two members of the British Columbia Court of Appeal dismissed the non-delegable duty argument on the basis that it applied only to independent contractors, because its purpose is to supplement vicarious liability: (2001) 197 DLR (4th) 454 per Mackenzie JA and McEachern CJBC, affd without commenting on this issue *EDG v Hammer* (n 258).

[543] *EDG v Hammer* ibid [15]–[21].

[544] *Blackwater v Plint* (n 55) [45]–[55], interpreting the Indian Act Statutes of Canada 1951, c 29, ss 113–115, 117.

[545] *KLB v British Columbia* (n 309) [30]–[37]; *MB v British Columbia* (n 511) [17]–[18].

[546] McBride and Bagshaw *Tort Law* (n 328) 652; Vines (n 535) 621.

[547] *Lepore v New South Wales* (n 260) [123]–[125] (Gaudron J) [148], [166]; McHugh J Gummow and Hayne JJ considered that the analyses of Lord Millett as well as Lord Hobhouse had 'strong echoes of non-delegable duties' [207]–[208].

non-delegable obligations actionable in tort, so it is not averse to this form of liability.[548]

As we discussed earlier, difficulties with the non-delegable duty analysis arise from the ambiguity as to the scope of the doctrine and its content.[549] There is no consensus as to the principle which will identify when it arises, nor as to the fundamental question as to the nature of that liability. In *Lepore* the Australian High Court ruled that non-delegable duty is not absolute liability so as to make the duty-holder the insurer of the child's safety.[550] Gleeson CJ pointed out that if non-delegable duty did create absolute liability, then vicarious liability as analysed by the highest courts in Canada and England would be unduly restricted, as an employer would be liable for intentional and criminal conduct of an employee in circumstances extending well beyond the scope of his employment.[551]

By a majority the High Court of Australia held that non-delegable duty sets up fault rather than strict liability, so it cannot result in liability for intentional criminal wrongdoing where there was no fault on the part of the school authority or its other staff.[552] Gummow and Hayne JJ on the other hand held that non-delegable duty is strict liability, in that the duty is breached if reasonable care is not taken by the delegate, regardless of whether the delegator has itself acted carefully. They joined the majority in the conclusion that non-delegable duty should be confined to institutional responsibility for negligence,[553] but on the basis that otherwise there would be no room for the orthodox doctrine of vicarious liability to operate in relation to intentional wrongdoing—notwithstanding that, as shown previously, they had so narrowly circumscribed vicarious liability to render it virtually useless for institutional child sexual abuse.[554] As a consequence of *Lepore*, non-delegable duty would seem to have a minimal role to play in Australian child abuse litigation, unless a negligence plea against the institution itself is plausible.

Moreover, the conception of non-delegable duty as fault liability creates severe problems of proof when it is applied to child abuse in an institutional setting, as we discussed earlier in Section E.2 of this chapter in relation to direct liability in negligence. Justice Gaudron argued that a material increase of a risk of abuse in a childcare setting necessarily means that it is a foreseeable risk.[555] A common theme in our discussion of institutional abuse has been that while the risk of child abuse is, objectively speaking, inherent to some degree in virtually every organization exerting some power or authority over children, this has not been appreciated until very recently, and courts have frequently ruled that those in a supervisory role could not have been expected to foresee such risks in historic abuse cases.

---

[548] *Lewis (Guardian ad litem of) v British Columbia* (n 257).

[549] Discussed above, section C.4(b).

[550] Overruling the New South Wales Court of Appeal on this point: *Lepore v New South Wales* 2001) 52 NSWLR 420 (New South Wales CA). [551] *Lepore v New South Wales* (n 260) [32].

[552] *Cathey v Bernard* 467 So 2d 9 (Louisiana Ct App 1st Cir 1985).

[553] McHugh J dissented on this point: *Lepore v New South Wales* (n 260) [136]. He also correctly pointed out that one can sue in negligence even if the act is intentional: [162].

[554] ibid [257], [261], [265]–[269], [241]. [555] ibid [123].

Those who object to the vicarious liability analysis in *Lister* and *Bazley* seem to approve of the results in the institutional child abuse cases, and contend that the same result would be reached through the non-delegable duty route.[556] If this is so, does this doctrinal dispute actually matter? Yes, it can make a difference. The consequence of the Australian formulation of non-delegable duty as fault liability would be to establish institutional liability toward child victims in very few cases predating the last two decades or so of the 20th century. It is submitted that non-delegable duty is a concept too immature to grapple effectively with the immediate problem of child abuse in an institutional setting. It should in any event not apply where the wrongdoer is the employee of the secondary defendant, as the appropriate pigeonhole for the claim is vicarious liability.[557]

5. Abuse in an institutional setting: fixing blame

In the words of one victim of institutional abuse, 'when very right people do very wrong things, it's hard for a child to know the difference'.[558] It is the moral rectitude automatically imputed by society to people working or volunteering within institutions which have the laudable objective of protecting and enhancing opportunities for children, which creates the opportunity for a perpetrator. Characterizing the abuse as being antithetical to that moral stance generates a response that abusers are aberrations in a system, who must be dealt with in a disconnected way which minimizes institutional responsibility.[559] Within the institution, there is often a conspiracy of silence and concealment. Even the well-meaning superior may feel conflicted over the interests of the complainant, the alleged perpetrator, and the institution.

While the public is coming to accept the reality of intrafamilial child abuse, it has proven much more difficult to come to grips with the complicity of trusted institutions, especially religious ones. As Justice Binnie of the Supreme Court of Canada has noted, it is 'difficult to imagine greater "job-conferred power" than that vouchsafed to a priest who not only has power in this world but claims stewardship of the child's immortal soul'.[560] For government departments and the public alike, the availability of religious and other charitable institutions to which children in need of care outside their families can be sent has assuaged consciences, but also has provided a perverse incentive not to scrutinize their operation too closely.[561] A complaint is greeted with scepticism which can endure notwithstanding judicial findings of criminal guilt or civil liability. Victims are told that they were better off in the institutions and should not complain; that the times were different in 'those days' and standards of discipline

---

[556] ibid [123]–[125] (Gaudron J) [166] (McHugh J); J Neyers 'A Theory of Vicarious Liability' (2005) 43 Alberta L Rev 1, 32–35; McBride and Bagshaw *Tort Law* (n 328) 652.

[557] *Lepore v New South Wales* (n 260) [295] (Kirby J).

[558] Quoted in Wolfe, Jaffe, Jetté and Poisson *Child Abuse in Community Institutions and Organisations* (n 382) 18. [559] Hall 'After Waterhouse' (n 387) 160–163; Wangmann (n 400) 195–196.

[560] *EB v Oblates of Mary Immaculate* (n 386) [42].

[561] *Report of the Commission of Inquiry into Abuse of Children in Queensland Institutions* (n 388) Executive Summary v.

were different; and that they should just get on with their lives.[562] Often lost in the cacophony of extreme responses is the essential fact that it is the trust fostered and then betrayed by a revered institution, followed by its denial of responsibility for what it regards as a (mere) aberration, which has deepened and prolonged the damage inflicted by the abuse. The public discussion often very quickly turns to false allegations of abuse or the financial plight of institutions, rather than the long-term impact on the victim:

> Much of the general public's current understanding of child abuse that occurs in institutions and organisations is derived from high-profile media reports of investigations, arrests, and court outcomes. An unfortunate consequence is that the public often is presented with a biased or incomplete picture of the circumstances surrounding institutional abuse. For example, media accounts of large monetary settlements for victims or group of victims of institutional and organisational child abuse are commonly reported. However, to someone with little understanding of the long-term effects of such abuse, these sums of money may seem only to foster a 'victim mentality' in which one's life is put on hold in hopes of obtaining financial gain. Offending institutions, which declare that such settlements are causing them undue financial hardship that threatens their important role, or a future existence, in the community, worsens this prejudice. The result can be a backlash toward survivors, who may be seen as being responsible for the troubles experienced by the institutions, rather than the institutions or perpetrators being held accountable.[563]

For example, the announcements by Roman Catholic and Anglican dioceses in Newfoundland and Ontario that they will have to declare bankruptcy as a result of the payouts they are making to victims have received widespread publicity. Cardinals and Archbishops in the United States, Australia, Canada, England, and Ireland have discovered that their handling of sex abuse claims against clergy has jeopardized their positions in the Catholic Church. To those who lament the cost of vicarious liability for such institutions, Margaret Hall provides a salutary reminder that the social costs of abuse have already been incurred for victims and those who deal with them, including social services and the criminal justice system. Vicarious liability provides a mechanism for making the real costs of abuse visible and for transferring that loss to the institution which created the risk of the tort in the first place.[564]

The value of making the 'enterprise' risk principle a necessary step in the 'sufficient connection' test for vicarious liability is that it explains both *why* and *when* strict liability is to be imposed.[565] It incorporates the institutional dimensions of the abuse, looking beyond the individual perpetrator to link the risk of the tort inherent in the enterprise to the employer's decision to confer power over the victim on the tortfeasor; provided the tort is committed within the scope of that risk (as opposed to within the scope of his employment), there is a sufficient connection to

---

[562] *Forgotten Australians* (n 388) [5.49]–[5.55].

[563] *Child Abuse in Community Institutions and Organisations* (n 382) (2002) 18.

[564] Hall 'Responsibility without Fault (n 54) 488.

[565] We are indebted to Laura Hoyano's students Teniola Onabanjo and Benjamin Kent of Merton College for this point.

warrant vicarious liability. In contrast, Lord Steyn's formulation of the sufficient connection test, that the tort be so closely connected with the tortfeasor's employment that it would be 'fair and just' to hold the employers liable, holds little explanatory value.[566]

Non-delegable duty has pretensions to explain why and when liability is to be imposed, but is deeply problematic in both doctrine and application. It is submitted that the Supreme Court of Canada and the House of Lords are on the right track here. In effect they have recognized that institutional child abuse is a societal problem which cannot be effectively tackled by fault-based liability.[567]

Even in the new era of 'close connection' vicarious liability, institutional negligence may have a part to play. Direct fault-based liability extends the evidential inquiry far into the inner workings of an institution, to investigate who authorized the activities which led to the abuse, and who knew or should have known about the risk the abuser posed for the child. Vicarious liability, on the other hand, greatly simplifies the issues for the trier of fact, as it establishes liability in the absence of any evidence that the employer knew of the abuse or had grounds to suspect it. However, it does not perform the forensic ombudsman function that an action for negligence can, to ascertain why the abuse was allowed to happen unchecked, and so the need of victims for accountability may not be entirely satisfied.

In 2001 the Supreme Court of Canada certified a class action for former pupils of a provincial residential school for sight- and hearing-impaired children whom the British Columbia Ombudsman and a special counsel had found were subjected to sexual, physical and emotional abuse by staff and peers between 1950 and 1992. The class action would determine the issue of systemic negligence and issues of injury and causation would be then tried in individual proceedings.[568] It did not matter that the standard of care might have varied over time, as this just meant that the trial court might have to provide a nuanced answer to that common question through subclasses of claimants.[569] The Chief Justice of Canada concluded that the communications barriers faced by these claimants, who were extraordinarily vulnerable both at the time of the assaults and during the litigation, favoured a common process to explain the significance of those barriers and to marshal the expertise required to assist individual witnesses in communicating their testimony effectively.[570] The same argument might be made of children abused in institutional care: a class action could buffer to some extent their vulnerability from the financial and emotional strains and hazards of litigation, and provide them with mutual support to see the case through. Canadian courts have gone on to certify other class actions by abused children in a wide range of contexts, such as sea cadets aged 12 to 17 who were abused while on a training

---

[566] P Giliker 'Rough Justice in an Unjust World' (2002) 65 MLR 269, 277–278.

[567] Grace and Vella (n 77) 56.

[568] *Rumley v British Columbia* 2000 SCC 69, [2001] 3 SCR 184 [27]–[28]. The claimants sued for compensatory and punitive damages, rejecting a compensation programme set up by the provincial government, the Jericho Individual Compensation Program, which compensated only for pain and suffering from sexual abuse, and was capped at CDN$60,000 [17]. [569] ibid [31]–[32].

[570] ibid [39].

course.[571] Class actions may be the most effective and efficient way for the tort system to investigate the existence and causes of an abusive institutional environment.

It should not be assumed that institutional fault liability will necessarily also result in vicarious liability. In *EB v Order of Oblates*, Justice Binnie of the Supreme Court of Canada noted that evidence that the *operational* characteristics of an institution created generalized risks of abuse to every child from every employee, regardless of the particulars of his job, goes to direct rather than vicarious liability for the abuser's misconduct. Vicarious liability requires the features of the institutionally-created relationship of power and dependency between the victim and the particular wrong-doing employee, and the contribution of the employer's enterprise which enabled the wrongdoer to do as he did in the particular case.[572]

The prospect of vicarious liability can have the salutary effect of forcing institutions to be more innovative in considering how to protect children against the risk of abuse. In *Bazley v Curry*, McLachlin J noted that 'beyond the narrow band of employer conduct that attracts direct liability in negligence lies a vast area where imaginative and efficient administration and supervision can reduce the risk that the employer has introduced into the community'.[573] In imposing vicarious liability, the courts must be mindful that deterrence is to be confined to situations where it can be effective, as otherwise there is a danger that the general community will be over-deterred from activities which are socially useful and are to be promoted rather than penalized.[574] In the United States it has been argued that the imposition of vicarious liability for abuse committed by a volunteer over-deters beneficial activities, and that the alternative of imposing fault liability for negligent failure to screen volunteers better calibrates the liability to the charity's ability to control risk, with the incidental benefit of making it more insurable.[575] While there is merit to this argument, it is submitted that the laudable objectives of a non-profit organization, even if it functions through community volunteers, should not serve as an excuse where the abuse is strongly connected to the relationship of trust and dependency fostered by the organization.

It is important to acknowledge that the institutions which have been in the line of fire in all of the jurisdictions we study, especially religious bodies, have now developed

---

[571] *WW v Canada (Attorney General)* [2003] BCJ No 442 (British Columbia CA) (on 7 April 2006, 35 former sea cadets were awarded CDN$8 million against the Canadian government in the class action, and CDN$1.8 million was set aside for claimants who had not yet come forward; *White v Attorney General of Canada* 2006 BCSC 561 (British Columbia Supreme Ct) [8]); *Griffith v Winter and British Columbia* 2003 BCCA 367, 15 BCLR (4th) 390 (British Columbia CA) (class action on the part of children in care sexually abused by Winter, a foster carer); *MCC v Canada (Attorney General)* [2004] OJ No 4924 (Ontario CA) (class action by Mohawk children at a residential school); *Vennell v Barnardo's* [2004] OJ No 4171 (Ontario SJC) (class action on the part of child migrants brought to Canada from England in the late 19th and early 20th centuries); Hall 'Institutional Tort Feasors (n 400).

[572] *EB v Oblates of Mary Immaculate* (n 386) [4], [21], [36].

[573] *Bazley v Curry* (n 381) [32]–[33].

[574] As Binnie J warned in *EB v Oblates of Mary Immaculate* (n 386) [55]; see also *John R v Oakland Unified School District* (n 458) 956.   [575] Lear (n 404) 166–172.

clear protocols for the management of abuse claims. The institutional abuse claims typically adjudicated in the courts date back to an earlier and less sensitive era—but that era is not too distant, with many abuse claims originating in the late 1980s and even the mid-1990s[576] displaying at least some of these features. Organizations and institutions have come to recognize that safeguards built into their systems protect not only children but also the organizations themselves and their staff. It is submitted that this response would not have happened, or at least would not have been as effective, had those organizations not faced substantial tort liability for their shortcomings and omissions.

F. The Tort and Human Rights Liability of Child Protection Agencies

A social worker was asked by a health visitor to visit a four-year-old girl and her 21-year-old mother because of concerns about her care. A case conference after the visit decided to place the child on the child protection register on grounds of emotional abuse. The child's doctors were concerned that her recurrent urinary infections might be caused by sexual abuse. A psychiatrist video-interviewed the child in the presence of a social worker but in the absence of the mother. They concluded that the child had been sexually abused and that her mother's partner was the abuser. In fact the child did not identify the partner as the abuser but a cousin with the same first name who had previously lived at the mother's address. The child said that the abuser had left her home and that it was not her mother's partner. The local authority already had on file a history of the family which confirmed that what the child said was correct. After the child's interview the mother obtained confirmation from the child that the partner had not abused her. The mother tried to tell the social worker of this denial, but he and the psychiatrist took this as an attempt to persuade the child to retract the allegation that they understood her to have made. They concluded that the mother would be unable to protect the child against further abuse by her boyfriend and that she would put pressure on the child to retract her allegation against him, and so it was necessary to remove the child from her mother's care. The mother was not asked if she was willing to require her partner to leave her home. The mother excluded all men including her partner from her home, but nevertheless the child was taken into care for almost a year, the mother having only limited access rights. During this year the mother became pregnant again, the father being her partner. The local authority obtained a wardship order as soon as the baby was born on the basis of the previous history involving the baby's sister. In the course of the wardship proceedings the mother saw the interview transcript for the first time and it became evident that there was no evidence in the interview to suggest that

---

[576] eg the criminal convictions in 2005 of monks at Ampleforth Abbey School in North Yorkshire were for assaults dating from 1966 to 1995: 'Silence and Secrecy at School Where Child Sex Abuse Went on for Decades' *The Guardian* 18 November 2005; 'Catholic School Faces a Series of Lawsuits over Sexual Abuse' *The Guardian* 19 November 2005.

her partner was the abuser. The wardship orders for both children were set aside. These are the facts of *M v Newham London Borough Council*.[577]

Five siblings were repeatedly reported to Bedfordshire County Council social services as being at risk of sexual and other abuse. Starting in 1987 these reports came from the children's grandmother and other relatives, neighbours, the police, the family's general practitioner, the headteacher of the school which the two older children attended, the NSPCC,[578] a social worker and a health visitor. It was reported that the children were locked out of the house for long periods with the oldest (aged five in 1987) supervising the younger children, that the children appeared hungry and were seen taking food out of school waste bins, and that they lived in squalid conditions with faeces smeared on the wall and beds soaked with urine. The County Council repeatedly refused to put the children on the Child Protection Register. Both parents at various times asked that the children be taken into care, but social services took no action beyond eventually providing short-term respite care in 1991. The children's physical condition started to improve whilst with respite carers. Eventually the mother told the County Council that if it did not remove the children from her care she would batter them. In 1992 the County Council finally decided to place the children on the Child Protection Register, and later decided to seek care orders. Over these five years the children suffered ill-treatment and illness, their proper development was neglected, and their physical and psychological health was significantly impaired. These are the facts of *X v Bedfordshire*.[579]

The House of Lords ruled in 1994 that the children in these two cases could not sue the local authorities in negligence or for breach of statutory duty. In 2005 the Law Lords accepted that this ruling no longer represented good law in England and Wales.[580]

These are the scenarios which haunt all those involved in decision-making in child protection cases, who may feel that they are either 'damned if they do or damned if they don't' use their statutory powers to intervene. Analogues for these cases may be cited in each of our comparator jurisdictions. In this chapter we will be exploring a territory scarred by many legal battles: the tort liability of those involved in child protection work in a professional capacity, be they social workers, police officers in child protection units, or medical professionals. Here we will be investigating the themes and issues introduced in our initial discussion of the principles of tort liability of third parties. To recap, we will be considering how such agencies might incur liability by failing to exercise their statutory powers appropriately to protect a child: should the special justification be based upon the foreseeability of risk to a particular child, or dependency arising from a special relationship between the child and the agency, or the agency's decision to take legal steps in the exercise of those powers?[581] For the purposes of our initial discussion about blanket immunity from tort liability, we will

[577] *M v Newham London Borough Council*, reported with *X v Bedfordshire County Council* [1995] 2 AC 633 (HL) 651–653.
[578] The National Society for Prevention of Cruelty to Children, the leading English charity involved in child protection.   [579] *X v Bedfordshire County Council* (n 577) 653–655.
[580] *JD v East Berkshire Community NHS Trust et al* [2005] UKHL 23, [2005] 2 AC 373 [30] (Lord Bingham), [82] (Lord Nicholls), [106] (Lord Rodger), [124] (Lord Brown).
[581] See above, section C of this Chapter.

refer compendiously to all potential defendants who have some involvement in child protection work as 'child protection agencies', including the police and medical professionals. However, once we have moved on to the liability of investigators to the child in section F.2, we will divide the analysis into the potential liability of social services, police child protection officers, and health professionals and health authorities.

1. The evolution of civil liability of public authorities to compensate members of the public

All common law jurisdictions have had doctrinal difficulty in defining how the private law of torts should affect public authorities. The situation is particularly complex where the legislature has conferred on the public body merely a power to act: under what circumstances can private law impose a *duty* where that body has exercised or failed to exercise its statutory powers? In English law public authorities have never enjoyed blanket immunity from the ordinary operation of tort liability.[582] That said, many English judgments in the past 25 years can leave the impression that it is tort law which is the interloper, encroaching on and destabilizing public law by making public authorities accountable in court at the instance of an aggrieved citizen. However, the recent remarkable expansion of judicial review as a public law mechanism to challenge the legality of a public authority's use of its powers is an important indicator of judicial activism. Like their counterparts in other common law jurisdictions, the English courts have also come to recognize that it is both impossible and undesirable to exclude the operation of tort law from many sectors of governmental activity.

Conversely, courts are justifiably concerned that they do not become a political forum, being asked by litigants to second-guess policy decisions about the expenditure of taxpayers' money. Another concern is that public bodies may have been only peripherally involved in the chain of causation leading to the infliction of harm, but their 'deep pockets' makes them attractive defendants. Perhaps the most potent consideration in relation to child protection and other agencies has been a concern that potential tort liability will have a detrimental impact on the performance of their public functions, particularly where they have an investigatory role. We will analyse the validity of these concerns in detail later, but first we need to consider how the fact that the defendant is a public authority affects the duty of care analysis in respect of child protection agencies.

In an attempt to reflect these public interest considerations, the English courts have constructed a complex set of obstacles for claimants which bewilders tort lawyers from other jurisdictions, especially civil law jurisdictions which do not share the same concerns about opening the floodgates of litigants wishing to sue public authorities.[583] Diagram 5 maps the different legal routes which English and Welsh litigants who wish to hold child protection agencies to account might follow.

---

[582] *Mersey Docks and Harbour Board Trustees v Gilts* (1866) LR 1 HL 93 (HL).
[583] D Fairgrieve, M Andenas, and J Bell *Tort Liability of Public Authorities in Comparative Perspective* (British Institute of International and Comparative Law, London 2002) Part III; B Markesinis, Jean-Bernard Auby, C Waltjen, and S Deakin *Tortious Liability of Statutory Bodies: a Comparative and Economic Analysis of Five English Cases* (Hart Publishing, Oxford 1999).

Diagram 5. Tort Liability of Public Authorities in English Law

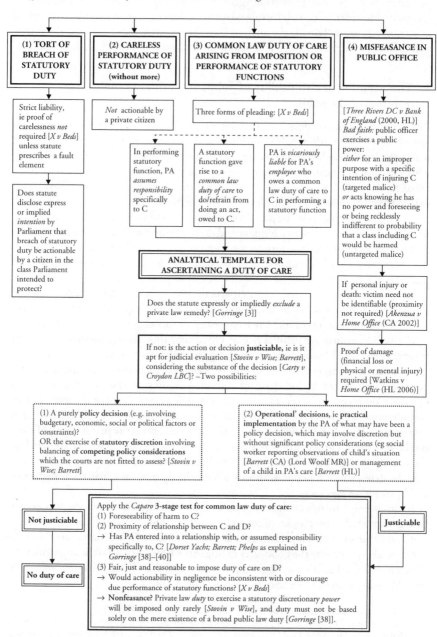

PA = Public Authority

There has been no attempt to apply the first route, namely the tort of breach of statutory duty, to child protection matters since *X v Bedfordshire*. Lord Browne-Wilkinson observed that it would require 'exceptionally clear statutory language' to show a parliamentary intention that those responsible for striking a balance between protecting a child from feared immediate harm and disrupting the relationship between the child and her parents should be liable in damages if, on subsequent investigation with the benefit of hindsight, it was shown that they had reached an erroneous conclusion and therefore failed to discharge their statutory duties.[584]

The tort of misfeasance in public office (the fourth route on Diagram 5) has only recently been revived and clearly defined by the House of Lords, in *Three Rivers District Council v Bank of England*.[585] This requires the claimant to prove that a public officer acted in bad faith and either exercised his power specifically intending to injure the claimant, or acted in the knowledge of, or with reckless indifference to, the illegality of his act, knowing or being recklessly indifferent to the probability of causing harm to the claimant.[586] It would require extraordinary circumstances to hold an employee of a child protection agency liable for misfeasance in public office. In *JD v East Berkshire*,[587] Lord Nicholls noted that health professionals would be acting in bad faith for the purpose of the tort of misfeasance in public office if they acted recklessly, without caring whether an allegation of child abuse is well-founded or not. His Lordship implied that this could set up liability to the suspected parents.

In *X v Bedfordshire* Lord Browne-Wilkinson concluded that the second route on the template, namely the careless performance of the statutory duty, does not in itself give rise to any cause of action, in the absence of either a statutory right of action or common law duty of care. In short, the mere assertion of the careless exercise of statutory power or duty is not sufficient.[588]

This pattern leaves the tort of common law negligence as the predominant route for those affected by decisions, actions and omissions by child protection agencies. Since *X* was decided, and partly as a specific consequence of that case, human rights concepts have leavened English tort law as disappointed English litigants have sought recourse through the European Convention on Human Rights (ECHR) for the failure of the state to protect them from abuse. As we shall see, the decisions of the European Court of Human Rights (EctHR) have been enormously influential in compelling English courts to strip tort immunity from child protection agencies.

(a) Justiciability: threshold or fall-back?

The primary mechanism by which the application of negligence is constrained is the determination of whether the alleged action or inaction by a public authority is a matter upon which the courts can or should adjudicate in the context of a private law

---

[584] *X v Bedfordshire County Council* (n 577) 747–748.
[585] *Three Rivers District Council v Governor and Company of the Bank of England (No 3)* [2003] 2 AC 1 (HL)
[586] ibid 191–193; *Akenzua v Home Office* [2002] EWCA Civ 1470, [2003] 1 WLR 741.
[587] *JD v East Berkshire Community NHS Trust et al* (HL) (n 580) [74]–[77].
[588] *X v Bedfordshire County Council* (n 577) 732–735.

action. This 'interface of public and private law obligations'[589] is often described in England as the justiciability issue, although we shall find that the same considerations are reflected in other parts of the negligence template both in England and elsewhere. In all of these cases the concern has been with whether tort law can construct a duty arising from the exercise or non-exercise of a discretionary power conferred by statute on a public official or authority.

Here we must retrace our steps to the seminal case of *Anns v London Borough of Merton*,[590] where Lord Wilberforce identified a spectrum of decision-making by public bodies, with policy decisions at one extreme and operational decisions at the other. Decisions involving significant areas of policy, such as the budgetary allocation of scarce resources to a list of priorities or the allocation of risk, are labelled as 'discretionary' because the decisions are for the authority or body to make, not the courts, and hence are not justiciable. At the opposite end of the spectrum is the practical execution of policy decisions, labelled 'operational', which is justiciable, and in respect of which a duty of care *might* arise. Lord Wilberforce acknowledged that this is really a distinction of degree, as many operational powers or duties carry a measure of discretion, but it can 'safely be said that the more "operational" a power or duty may be, the easier it is to superimpose on it a common law duty of care'.[591] Crucially, merely categorizing the decision as being more operational- than policy-oriented in nature, and hence justiciable, does not mean that a duty of care necessarily will be found to exist.[592]

Perhaps inevitably a judge's assignment of a decision to a particular point on the policy/operational spectrum will appear to be a matter of impression, and so the courts attempted to imbue this assessment with more concrete, and hence more predictable, notions which borrowed from public law concepts and which address whether the decision in question fell within or outside the ambit of the discretion conferred by Parliament. In *Anns* Lord Wilberforce himself stated that a claimant would have to prove that the action taken was *not* within the limits of a discretion bona fide exercised before he could begin to rely on a common law duty of care.[593] One way of concluding that the decision exceeded statutory discretion had been flagged up in the earlier seminal case of *Home Office v Dorset Yacht*, where Lord Reid stated that while every error of judgment by a public official or body in exercising a discretion could not be justiciable, 'there must come a stage where the discretion is exercised so carelessly or unreasonably that there has been no real exercise of the discretion which Parliament conferred'.[594]

This was reinforced in respect of an omission to exercise a discretionary power in 1996 in *Stovin v Wise* where Lord Hoffmann (long averse to imposing negligence

---

[589]   *Stovin v Wise* (n 208) 928 (Lord Nicholls).
[590]   *Anns v Merton London Borough Council* (n 231).   [591]   ibid 754.
[592]   *Rowling v Takaro Properties Ltd* [1988] AC 473 (PC) 501 (Lord Keith).
[593]   *Anns v Merton* (n 231) 1068.
[594]   *Home Office v Dorset Yacht Co Ltd* [1970] AC 1004 (HL) 1067.

liability on public authorities)[595] stated that:

... the minimum preconditions for basing a duty of care upon the existence of the statutory power, if it can be done at all, are that it would in the circumstances have been irrational not to have exercised the power, so that there was in effect a public law duty to act, and secondly that there are exceptional grounds for holding that the policy of the statute requires compensation be paid to persons who suffer loss because the power was not exercised.[596]

In 2004 in *Gorringe v Calderdale MBC* Lord Hoffmann restated this view even more strongly: he found it difficult to imagine a case in which a common law duty could be founded simply upon a failure (however irrational) to provide some benefit which a public authority has a power (or a public law duty) to provide.[597] This would seem to suggest that all child protection decisions are immune from tort liability, but we shall see that this is not so.[598]

In *X v Bedfordshire* Lord Browne-Wilkinson asserted that it is neither helpful or necessary to introduce public law concepts as to the validity of a decision into the question of liability at common law for negligence.[599] However he then proceeded, unhelpfully, to discuss at length the implications of a decision being found to be *intra vires* or *ultra vires* the statutory discretion for making it actionable in negligence, summarizing the case law to that point as holding:

Where Parliament has conferred a statutory discretion on a public authority, it is for that authority, not for the courts, to exercise the discretion: nothing which the authority does within the ambit of the discretion can be actionable at common law. If the decision complained of falls outside the statutory discretion, it *can* (but not necessarily will) give rise to common law liability. However, if the factors relevant to the exercise of the discretion include matters of policy, the court cannot adjudicate on such policy matters and therefore cannot reach the conclusion that the decision was outside the ambit of the statutory discretion. Therefore a common law duty of care in relation to the taking of decisions involving policy matters cannot exist.[600]

Unfortunately the introduction of the *intra vires/ultra vires* and irrationality tests familiar to administrative law encumbered negligence with public law concepts without clearly and consistently defining their applicability and function. *X v Bedfordshire* had constructed a two-level analysis:

The justiciability question:

- A legitimate decision about general policy, including the allocation of resources, would not be justiciable.
- An operational decision would not be actionable if it fell within the ambit of reasonable discretion, but otherwise might be.

---

[595] See Lord Hoffmann (n 216) 163.   [596] *Stovin v Wise* (n 208) 953.
[597] *Gorringe v Calderdale Metropolitan Borough Council* (n 216) [32]; see also [23], [38].
[598] As illustrated by *Barrett v Enfield London Borough Council* (n 75); *J D v East Berkshire Community NHS Trust et al* (HL) (n 580) discussed below in section F.I.(b).
[599] *X v Bedfordshire County Council* (n 577) 736.   [600] ibid 738.

The duty of care question:

- If an operational decision was outside the ambit of reasonable discretion, then a duty of care might arise after the three-stage test in *Caparo*[601] was applied and satisfied.

- The question whether there was a common law duty and, if so, its scope would be profoundly influenced by the statutory framework within which the decisions and acts complained of were done.

- A common law duty of care would never be imposed on a statutory duty if the observance of a tort duty would be inconsistent with or have a tendency to discourage the due performance by the local authority of its statutory duties.[602]

When this template was applied in *X v Bedfordshire* to the decision of social workers whether to apply for a care order, it resulted in a decision that the issue was justiciable, since it did not necessarily involve any question of the allocation of resources or the determination of general policy.[603] However, for reasons we consider below, a common law duty of care on the part of social workers making a risk assessment was found to be incompatible with the statutory provisions, leading to the conclusion under the third stage of the *Caparo* test that it was not fair, just, and reasonable to impose a duty of care.[604]

There is a beguiling logic to the argument that a public authority should not be liable in damages for a valid decision it took within its statutory jurisdiction conferred by Parliament. The argument is seductive but fallacious, because a decision may be *intra vires* (in the sense that it falls short of irrationality,) but nonetheless careless. It was not until the decisions in *Barrett* and *Phelps* in 2001[605] that the House of Lords moved away from the public law invalidity of the decision or action in question as a precondition to consideration of negligence liability, whilst leaving the justiciability hurdle intact. In *Phelps*, Lord Slynn emphasized the primacy of the common law principles of negligence. He indicated that the courts will decide that the decision or action is non-justiciable only where it concerns the weighing of competing public interests, or where the decision has been dictated by considerations on which Parliament could not have intended that the courts would substitute their views for the views of ministers or public officials.[606] Therefore a perfectly valid decision under administrative law can still be the subject of evaluation on negligence principles.[607] However, in the case of a failure to exercise statutory powers, the courts remain reluctant to impose a duty to

---

[601] Described above, section C.2(b).   [602] *X v Bedfordshire County Council* (n 577) 739.
[603] ibid 748–749.   [604] ibid 749–751.
[605] *Barrett v Enfield London Borough Council* (n 75) 586 (Lord Hutton, Lords Nolan and Steyn concurring); *Phelps v London Borough of Hillingdon Anderton* (n 236) (Lord Slynn).
[606] *Phelps v London Borough of Hillingdon Anderton* (n 236) 635.
[607] For a more detailed analysis of the implications of *Barrett* see P Craig and D Fairgrieve '*Barrett*, Negligence and Discretionary Powers' [1999] Public Law 626; S Bailey and M Bowman 'Public Authority Negligence Revisited' (2000) 59(1) Cambridge LJ 85.

act unless it is shown to have been irrational for the authorities not to have exercised those powers.[608]

The 2004 case of *Gorringe v Calderdale MBC* provides the final tile to slot into our template of English law: the first step in considering negligence against the background of the statutory duty or power is to consider whether the statute excludes a private law remedy.[609] The House of Lords reiterated that public bodies' discretionary judgments which the courts consider they are able to assess should not preclude the possibility of negligence liability; rather, the presence of such discretion will be relevant in concluding whether there has been a breach of any duty of care found to exist.[610] That said, the Law Lords made it clear that a common law duty of care must not be imposed on a public body simply because the statutory duty or power existed; in the absence of a claim under the tort of breach of statutory duty, a common law duty of care will arise only where the public authority has done acts, entered into relationships, or undertaken responsibilities that would give rise to negligence liability under ordinary principles.[611] Accordingly, the negligence liability of public authorities has finally been liberated from the public law strictures which have inhibited its rational development for over a decade.

In Diagram 5 the factors governing the ruling as to justiciability seem to re-emerge in the application of the public policy considerations invoked under the third stage of the *Caparo* test for a common law duty of care. It has been suggested that, as exemplified in *X v Bedfordshire*, this amounts in effect to double jeopardy:[612] the difficulty and delicacy of social workers' decisions whether to seek a care order are considered at two levels in the template.

This is so, but it does not necessarily mean that the second decision is redundant. Practically speaking, counsel may well raise the same considerations at both stages. However, the focus at the justiciability stage is the legislative framework in which the decision was made: what did the legislators contemplate would be taken into consideration by the decision-maker? If this was a matter of establishing policies, budgetary priorities, the allocation of risk etc, then this will not be justiciable. If on the other hand it was merely the implementation of a policy decision already taken, then it will be justiciable. *Barrett* and *Phelps* made it clear that the mere fact that the decision is discretionary does not preclude it from being potentially actionable in negligence.

When a decision or action has been found to be justiciable, the question then arises whether it is actionable in negligence. At the third stage of the *Caparo* test, similar arguments may be raised as at the justiciability stage, but many more can also be

---

[608] *Stovin v Wise* (n 208) 953; D Fairgrieve 'Pushing Back the Boundaries of Public Authorities Liability' in Fairgrieve, Andenas and Bell (eds) *Tort Liability of Public Authorities in Comparative Perspective* (n 583) 487.　　　　　　　　　　　　　　　　　[609] *Gorringe v Calderdale* (n 216), [3] (Lord Steyn).

[610] ibid [5], approving P Craig *Administrative Law* (5th edn Sweet & Maxwell, London 2003) 898. See also *Carty v Croydon London Borough Council* [2005] EWCA Civ 19, [2005] 1 WLR 2312 [26] advocating that attention be focused on the substance of the decision rather than on the elusive question of whether it involved exercise of discretion.　　　　　　　　[611] *Gorringe v Calderdale* (n 216) [38]–[40].

[612] R Bailey-Harris and M Harris 'The Immunity of Local Authorities in Child Protection Functions— Is the Door Now Ajar?' (1998) 10(3) Child and Family LQ 227, 242.

canvassed. For example, would imposing a duty of care encourage or deter a public authority in monitoring its employees more carefully? Could it result in detrimental 'defensive practice'? Or might imposing a duty of care be useful to decision-makers and actors in setting a benchmark for competence, so that they would then know what they had to do to immunize themselves from negligence liability? Loss-spreading issues may also arise: who can best bear the loss, the claimant or the taxpayer?

Moreover, it is arguable that the structure of analysis can make a difference as to whether a court can strike out a claim before trial on the basis that it discloses no reasonable grounds for bringing or defending the claim.[613] At the justiciability stage the courts are not looking at what actually happened but merely the *nature* of the administrative decision or action, as a matter of principle. At that stage of the analysis an intensive investigation of the facts (ie what went wrong) which a trial would permit would not be necessary. If a decision is found not to be justiciable, then the courts will not feel constrained in striking out the action. However if the justiciability threshold is passed, then in novel cases the court must consider all three stages of the *Caparo* test, and can strike out the claim on the basis of stage three only if it is satisfied that no further investigation of facts would assist the court in evaluating those policy considerations.[614]

We turn now to see how the issue of justiciability is handled in our comparator jurisdictions. In Canada the *Anns* two-stage test for duty of care[615] has been interpreted as encompassing the justiciability issue. This is located in the second stage where, after the prima facie duty of care has been set up at stage one by a finding of foreseeability of harm and proximity of relationship, the court must consider whether there are any policy considerations which might negate or limit the scope of the duty of care. At the second stage, the court must review the applicable legislation to see if it imposes any obligation upon the public authority to do the tasks which would be the subject matter of the duty of care, or alternatively if it provides an exemption from liability for failure to do them. It must also be determined whether the public authority is exempted from liability on the ground that the matter constitutes a policy decision.[616] The Supreme Court of Canada has acknowledged the continuing judicial struggle to differentiate between 'policy' and 'operational' decisions and acts. It has warned that, whilst the Crown must be free to govern and make true policy decisions without becoming subject to tort liability as a result, characterization of every government decision as one of 'policy' would in effect restore complete Crown immunity from tort liability.[617]

The Australian High Court has also set out some helpful guidelines in determining how to distinguish between policy and operational decisions on the *Anns* spectrum which are particularly germane to the tort liability of child protection agencies:

The distinction between policy and operational factors is not easy to formulate, but the dividing line between them will be observed if we recognise that a public authority is under no duty

---

[613] Civil Procedure Rule 3.4(2)(a).

[614] *Kent v Griffiths and London Ambulance Service* [2000] 2 All ER 474 (CA) [38] (Lord Woolf MR); *Barrett v Enfield London Borough Council* (n 75) 557 (Lord Browne-Wilkinson), 573–74 (Lord Slynn).

[615] Described above, section C.2(b).

[616] *Just v British Columbia* [1989] 2 SCR 1228 (SCC) [16]–[20].   [617] ibid [16].

of care in relation to decisions which involve or are dictated by financial, economic, social or political factors or constraints. Thus budgetary allocations and the constraints which they entail in terms of allocation of resources cannot be made the subject of a duty of care. But it may be otherwise when the courts are called upon to apply a standard of care to action or inaction which is merely the product of administrative direction, expert or professional opinion, technical standards or general standards of reasonableness.[618]

American courts have also been conscious of the policy trap. Becker J of the US District Court has highlighted the need for the judiciary to confine itself to the adjudication of facts based on discernible objective standards of law, remarking that:

> ... those objective standards are notably lacking where the question is not negligence but social wisdom, not due care but political practicability, not reasonableness but economic expediency. Tort law simply furnishes an inadequate crucible for testing the merits of social, political or economic decisions.[619]

American common law in most States draws a distinction similar to the policy/operational continuum in *Anns*, between the State's discretionary functions and its 'ministerial' or operational functions. Discretionary functions which involve planning and the formulation of public policy do not subject the State to tort liability. A ministerial function, which is the approximate analogue of an operational decision under *Anns*, is not immunized. Therefore, if a government agency negligently performs a purely ministerial function, it may be held responsible in tort or for an actionable breach of civil rights, for injuries which flow from that negligence.[620]

    Thus in most common law jurisdictions issues of justiciability are still adjudicated as a threshold question, but increasingly similar concerns appear again in another guise under the final policy stage of the test for duty of care. We now turn to the tort analysis which ensues once the court determines that the decision or action or omission is justiciable.

(b) Common law negligence: converting a statutory discretion to act into a duty to act

(i) The negligence liability of investigatory agencies: weaving blanket immunity

In 1988, the House of Lords in *Hill v Chief Constable of West Yorkshire*[621] struck out a claim by the mother of the 21st victim of the 'Yorkshire Ripper' which alleged that the West Yorkshire police had negligently failed to collate information they possessed pointing to Peter Sutcliffe as a likely suspect, and so did not arrest him before he could kill again. The claimant failed to clear the 'proximity' hurdle to establishing a duty of care on the basis that Ms Hill was 'one of a vast number of the female general public' at risk from Sutcliffe, but 'at no special distinctive risk'.[622] Lord Keith however was concerned to block future claims against the police in respect of their

---

[618] *Sutherland Shire Council v Heyman* (1985) 60 ALR 1 (Aus HC) (Mason J) 35–34; approved in *Just v British Columbia* ibid [19].

[619] *Blessing v United States* 447 F Supp 1160 (US DC Pennsylvania 1978) 1170, approved in *Just v British Columbia* ibid [17].   [620] Discussed further below, section F.1(b)(ii).

[621] *Hill v Chief Constable of West Yorkshire* (n 48). See also *Calveley v Chief Constable of Merseyside* [1989] 1 AC 1228 (HL).   [622] *Hill v Chief Constable of West Yorkshire* ibid 62.

investigatory functions, and so enumerated the public policy grounds against the existence of potential liability in principle. Whilst his Lordship acknowledged the salutary effect of potential tort liability on the standards with which many activities are conducted, he considered that this could not be said of police activities, because it could not be doubted that the police apply their best endeavours to the performance of their public duty in investigating and suppressing crime.[623] The imposition of liability, it was claimed, could lead to the investigative operations of the police being carried out in a 'detrimentally defensive frame of mind'. The floodgates spectre was raised, as well as the harmful diversion of police resources from suppressing crime to defending policy and discretionary decisions in the 'elaborate post-mortems' of closed investigations which litigation would entail, to no good purpose.[624] *Hill* thus recast negligence law from its previous judicially acknowledged role as an instrument of public policy governing public authorities[625] to becoming its antagonist.

Six years later in *X v Bedfordshire*, the House of Lords spread this blanket immunity over local authorities 'in performance of their statutory duties to protect children'.[626] Whilst the cases before the House of Lords involved decisions by local authorities as to whether to intervene to protect the child claimants, the Law Lords apparently intended the immunity to envelop all statutory child protection functions under the Children Act 1989.[627]

Lord Browne-Wilkinson, speaking for a unanimous panel of Law Lords, listed six policy reasons for this immunity, which have been widely cited in subsequent cases in England and in the Commonwealth, and which will govern our analysis in this chapter.

First, ... a common law duty of care would cut across the whole statutory system set up for the protection of children at risk. As a result of the ministerial directions contained in 'Working Together'[628] the protection of such children is not the exclusive territory of the local authority's social services. The system is inter-disciplinary, involving the participation of the police, educational bodies, doctors and others. At all stages the system involves joint discussions, joint recommendations and joint decisions ... To introduce into such a system a common law duty of care enforceable against only one of the participant bodies would be manifestly unfair. To impose such liability on all the participant bodies would lead to almost impossible problems of disentangling as between the respective bodies the liability, both primary and by way of contribution, of each for reaching a decision found to be negligent.[629]

This reasoning is flawed. Whilst government guidance indicates that the investigation should be conducted on an interdisciplinary basis, and all those involved are expected to confer at an inter-agency strategy discussion about the way forward, the ultimate statutory responsibility for the decision as to whether to apply to the court for protective measures in relation to the child, is allocated to the local authority alone under the Children Act 1989.

---

[623] ibid 63.   [624] ibid 63.

[625] *Home Office v Dorset Yacht Co Ltd* (n 594) 1032 (Lord Reid), 1048 (Viscount Dilhorne), 1056 (Lord Pearson), 1058, 1065 (Lord Diplock).   [626] *X v Bedfordshire County Council* (n 577) 749.

[627] ibid 751.

[628] Referring to the government guidance for inter-agency joint investigations of allegations of child abuse, described below in Chapter 5 section B.2.

[629] *X v Bedfordshire County Council* (n 1) 749–750.

Lord Browne-Wilkinson's second policy consideration was that the task of the local authority in dealing with children at risk is 'extraordinarily delicate', as social services must have regard not only to the physical well-being of the child but also to the advantages of not disrupting the child's family environment under s 17 of the Children Act 1989, and so 'must tread a delicate and difficult line between taking action too soon and not taking it soon enough'.[630] This is true, but other professionals who do not enjoy immunity also have to make difficult judgement calls balancing competing objectives, and in any event the Children Act 1989 makes it clear that the child's welfare is paramount.

Lord Browne-Wilkinson then raised the spectre of 'defensive practice' as the third consideration:

Next, if a liability in damages were to be imposed, it might well be that local authorities would adopt a more cautious and defensive approach to their duties. For example, as the Cleveland Report makes clear, on occasions the speedy decision to remove the child is sometimes vital. If the authority is to be made liable in damages for a negligent decision to remove a child (such negligence lying in the failure properly first to investigate the allegations) there would be a substantial temptation to postpone making such a decision until further inquiries have been made in the hope of getting more concrete facts. Not only would the child in fact being abused be prejudiced by such delay: the increased workload inherent in making such investigations would reduce the time available to deal with other cases and other children.[631]

As a fourth consideration, Lord Browne-Wilkinson warned that as the relationship between a social worker and the child's parents is frequently one of conflict, there was a very high risk of vexatious and costly litigation diverting both money and human resources from their statutory purposes.[632]

The fifth policy reason sustaining the case for tort immunity was that the statutory complaints procedures allowed grievances about maladministration to be investigated. The fact that those procedures do not provide any compensation to the children or families affected by social services' negligent decisions was not noted.[633]

Finally, there were no close analogies in the established categories of negligence for this claim. The Law Lords cautioned that, by analogy to *Hill*, the courts should proceed with great care before holding liable in negligence those who have been charged by Parliament with the task of protecting vulnerable members of society from the wrongdoings of others.[634]

The Law Lords' resort to blanket immunity in *Hill* and *X v Bedfordshire* betrayed a new-found scepticism about the utility of negligence law in setting standards of professional competence and in enabling individuals affected by public bodies' decisions to subject them to external and independent judicial scrutiny. The legitimacy of these policy reasons was extensively tested in subsequent cases in England and Wales and elsewhere in the Commonwealth.

---

[630] ibid 750, quoting Dame Elizabeth Butler-Sloss *Report of the Inquiry into Child Abuse in Cleveland 1987* (Cm 412) 244.   [631] *X v Bedfordshire County Council* (n 577) 750.

[632] ibid 750–751.

[633] As Lord Bingham pointed out in *JD v East Berkshire Community NHS Trust et al* (HL) (n 580) [35].

[634] *X v Bedfordshire County Council* (n 577) 751.

(ii) The negligence liability of investigatory agencies: unravelling blanket immunity

The seemingly adamant stance of the House of Lords against any role for negligence law in the sphere of criminal or family justice prompted the lower courts to refuse even to countenance the possibility of an actionable duty of care arising from the conduct of an investigation.[635] Until 1998 the only exception was *Swinney v Chief Constable of Northumbria Police*[636] where a police officer breached an express undertaking to an informer to keep her involvement in an murder investigation confidential; the Court of Appeal viewed the undertaking as arguably giving rise to a special relationship to take reasonable care to honour the promise.

The first serious challenge to blanket immunity came in 1998 from the ECtHR in *Osman v UK*. Ahmet Osman aged 14 and his mother attempted to sue the police for negligence in investigating repeated complaints about an obsessed and aggressive schoolteacher who was stalking him and his family, and who eventually shot and seriously injured Ahmet and killed his father. The Metropolitan Police applied to strike out the pleadings. The Court of Appeal accepted that the claimants had an arguable case that the numerous complaints established very close proximity amounting to a special relationship between them and the investigating officers, but interpreted the *obiter dicta* in *Hill* as clearly establishing blanket immunity even in a case where the potential victim and the source of the threat were identified, and hence sufficiently proximate.[637]

When the House of Lords denied leave to appeal, the Osman family complained to the European Court of Human Rights (ECtHR) that the ruling of the Court of Appeal deprived them of the right of access to the civil courts contrary to Article 6(1) of the ECHR.[638] By a 12 to 3 majority, the ECtHR upheld the complaint.[639] The UK Government had argued that *Hill* did not automatically doom to failure any civil action against the police, and relied on *Swinney* to show that in principle a domestic court was free to make a considered assessment as to whether a particular case was suitable for the application of the blanket immunity rule.[640] The ECtHR used that concession to point out that the Court of Appeal had proceeded in *Osman v Ferguson* on the basis that the rule provided 'a watertight defence to the police and that it was impossible to prise open an immunity which the police enjoy from civil suit in respect of their acts and omissions in the investigation and suppression of crime'.[641] Whilst acknowledging the force of the public policy concerns expressed in *Hill*, the majority held that it must remain open to a domestic court to have regard to the presence of other public interest considerations which pull in the opposite direction from the blanket immunity rule, under the *Caparo* three-stage test.[642] In effect, the Court of Appeal had slammed the courtroom door on the Osman family,

---

[635] *Alexandrou v Oxford* [1993] 4 All ER 382 (CA); *Ancell v McDermott* [1993] 4 All ER 355 (CA); *Osman v Ferguson* [1993] 4 All ER 344 (CA); *Calveley v Chief Constable of Merseyside* (n 621).

[636] *Swinney v Chief Constable of Northumbria Police* [1996] 3 All ER 449 (CA).

[637] *Osman v Ferguson* (n 635). See section A.1(d).

[638] We discuss the Osmans' claim in negligence below in section F.2(c)(i), and under Articles 2 and 8 of the ECHR below in section F.4(a).

[639] *Osman v UK* (2000) 29 EHRR 245, [1999] 1 FLR 193 (ECtHR). For a more detailed analysis of the facts and the reasoning, see Hoyano 'Policing Flawed Police Investigations (n 49).

[640] ibid [138], [144].   [641] ibid [150].   [642] ibid [149]–[152].

without permitting them to point to the factors which arguably distinguished their case from *Hill*: the alleged failure to protect the life of a child resulting in the most serious harm; a catalogue of acts and omissions by the police which amounted to 'grave negligence as opposed to minor acts of incompetence'; and the family's claim (derived from *Swinney*) that the police had assumed responsibility to them for their safety when dealing with them regarding their litany of complaints.[643]

Osman v UK received a largely hostile reception from English judges and academic tort lawyers. Lord Hoffmann wrote that the decision 'fills me with apprehension',[644] and Lord Browne-Wilkinson confessed to finding the decision of the Strasbourg court 'extremely difficult to understand', leaving English tort law in a 'very unsatisfactory state of affairs', where it would be virtually impossible to strike out unmeritorious claims.[645] Lord Woolf MR, who had comprehensively reformed the Civil Procedure Rules to make litigation more efficient, took a more temperate view, remarking that 'in so far as *Osman*'s case underlined the dangers of a blanket approach so much the better', because there is a danger that statements in judgments about determining a duty of care are applied more widely and rigidly than originally intended; they are 'tools not rules'. Lord Woolf pointed out that where the legal position was clear and there was no real prospect of success, cases still could be struck out at an early stage without contravening Article 6.[646] What followed was a series of judgments from the House of Lords and Court of Appeal which purported not to apply *Osman*,[647] but nonetheless had the consequence of completely unravelling the blanket immunizing police and child protection investigations.

The first significant step in the retreat from *X v Bedfordshire* and *Hill* was taken in *Barrett v London Borough of Enfield*,[648] where the House of Lords held that a local authority arguably owes a common law duty of care to a child placed in its care by court order to take reasonable care in exercising its statutory responsibilities in relation to the child's upbringing. Lord Slynn in the leading speech did not even refer to *Osman*; Lord Hutton expressly stated that it was unnecessary to discuss *Osman*'s implications, and Lord Browne-Wilkinson in his concurring speech felt that it was pointless to strike out Barrett's claim because he would likely then have recourse to Strasbourg.[649] On the substantive issue, the Law Lords unanimously held that whilst the decision to take a child into care was non-justiciable under *X v Bedfordshire*, once the care order was granted, some careless decisions or omissions of the local authority in respect of that child, such as foster placements or adoption, might be actionable as operational decisions. The policy considerations in *X v Bedfordshire* were not as powerful because interdisciplinary decision-making no longer featured in the child's care; the local authority's statutory powers did not necessarily involve the kind of discretion involved in taking the child from his family; and the public law remedies

---

[643] ibid [151].   [644] Lord Hoffmann 'Human Rights and the House of Lords' (n 216) 164.

[645] *Barrett v Enfield London Borough Council* (n 75) 558. Stuart-Smith LJ concurred in this criticism in *Palmer v Tees Health Authority* [1999] All ER (D) 722 (CA) [14].

[646] *Kent v Griffiths and London Ambulance Service* (n 614) [37]–[38].

[647] At least for so long as the English courts were able to ignore jurisprudence from the ECtHR, before the Human Rights Act 1999 s 2(1) came into force on 2 October 2000.

[648] *Barrett v Enfield London Borough Council* (n 75).   [649] ibid 560.

available in *X* were not likely to be as efficacious as a court's recognition that a duty of care may be owed at common law. Most significantly, Lord Slynn refuted the 'defensive practice' argument which had proved so powerful in *X*, stating that this 'should normally be a factor of little if any weight', and rejecting the general proposition that the imposition of a duty of care does not contribute to the maintenance of high professional standards.[650]

In *Phelps v Hillingdon LBC*, involving the liability of educational psychologists and other educators for professional negligence in assessing children's special education needs, the Law Lords took the opportunity again to evince their renewed faith in the objectives of negligence law. Recognizing liability for educational malpractice 'may have the healthy effect of securing that high standards are sought and secured', and those standards would not be set unreasonably high. The fears of the education authorities about 'the spectre of a rash of "gold digging" actions brought on behalf of underachieving children by discontented parents' were unjustified, and in any event did not mean that valid claims should necessarily be excluded.[651]

Lord Browne-Wilkinson's foreboding in *Barrett* that *Osman* meant that no negligence action could be struck out on the basis that it did not disclose a cause of action proved groundless. In *Palmer v Tees Health Authority*, the Court of Appeal struck out an action by the mother of a four-year-old girl raped and killed by a known paedophile who had recently been released from a psychiatric hospital. There was insufficient proximity of relationship between the hospital and the victim and so recourse to stage three of the *Caparo* duty of care test or to blanket immunity was unnecessary.[652]

The House of Lords revisited blanket immunity for social services in 2000 in *W v Essex County Council*, considering it arguable that social workers owed a duty of care to foster parents to avoid inflicting psychiatric injury on them by ignoring their express instructions not to place a foster child known or suspected of being a sexual abuser in their family. The fostered boy sexually abused all four of their children within a month of the placement.[653] Significantly, the local authority did not contest beyond the Court of Appeal that it owed a duty of care to the claimants' children who had been sexually abused.

In two decisions in 2001 the Court of Appeal moved well beyond the territory delineated by these House of Lords cases. The Court of Appeal dealt with the converse situation to *Barrett* in *S v Gloucestershire County Council*, holding (contrary to caselaw

---

[650] ibid 568–569, citing with approval Evans LJ, dissenting in the Court of Appeal [*Barrett v Enfield London Borough Council* (n 322) 380], and Lord Bingham MR, dissenting in the Court of Appeal in *X v Bedfordshire* [*X v Bedfordshire County Council* (n 73) 662].

[651] *Phelps v London Borough of Hillingdon Anderton* (n 236) 667, 672 (Lord Nicholls), 653 (Lord Slynn).

[652] *Palmer v Tees Health Authority* (n 645). The Court of Appeal confirmed that the power to strike out pleadings which disclosed no cause of action survived *Osman* in *S v Gloucestershire County Council; L v Tower Hamlets London Borough Council* [2000] 3 All ER 346 (CA) 934–937.

[653] *W v Essex County Council* [2001] 2 AC 592 (HL), discussed further below, section 4.F.3(a)(i). See also *A and B v Essex County Council* [2002] EWHC 2707, [2003] FLR 615 (QB) (social services owes a duty of care to prospective adoptive parents).

relying upon *X v Bedfordshire*)[654] that children in care who had been abused by their foster carers could sue the local authority for primary negligence in selecting the carers and in supervising their subsequent care. May LJ expressly recognized that social workers were now akin to other professionals in that they no longer enjoyed blanket immunity, and that it would be incorrect to say that child abuse cases against local authorities were bound to fail as a class.[655] In *L & P v Reading Borough Council* the Court of Appeal held that arguably both the police and social services investigating alleged child abuse owed a duty of care to the child in conducting her interview, and also to the parent suspected of abuse when using that evidence in family court proceedings after it was decided not to lay criminal charges. [656]

This then was the state of English law when the claims of the children in *X v Bedfordshire* (renamed *Z v UK*[657]) and in the companion decision of *M v Newham London Borough Council* (renamed *TP and KM v UK*[658]) which we described at the beginning of this section reached the ECtHR. The European Commission had unanimously applied *Osman* to conclude that the children's rights of access to the civil courts under Article 6(1) had been breached.[659] The strategy of the UK Government in the *Z v UK* case was to admit breaches of Article 3, because state officials had failed to protect the children from torture or inhuman or degrading treatment or punishment, and a breach of Article 13 because the victims did not have access to an adequate range of remedies against the state,[660] hoping that these concessions would make it easier for the ECtHR to retreat from *Osman*. It is implicit in the judgment that the ECtHR was conscious of the furore which its decision in *Osman* had caused with the English judiciary. The ECtHR noted that *X v Bedfordshire* had been litigated with vigour up to the House of Lords, and their decision could not be characterized as either an exclusionary rule or an immunity which had deprived the claimants of access to the court.[661] Instead, the Law Lords, after weighing in the balance the competing considerations of public policy, decided not to extend liability in negligence into a new category.[662] Crucially, the ECtHR noted that the decision in *X v Bedfordshire* had not arbitrarily removed the courts' jurisdiction to determine a whole range of civil claims against local authorities, because of the line of authority developed after *Osman*:

It may be noted that in subsequent cases the domestic courts have further defined this area of law concerning the liability of local authorities in child care matters, holding that a duty of care may arise in other factual situations, where, for example, a child has suffered harm once in local authority care or a foster family has suffered harm as a result of the placement in their

---

[654] *H v Norfolk County Council* [1997] 1 FLR 384 (CA).

[655] *S v Gloucestershire County Council; L v Tower Hamlets London Borough Council* (n 652) 932–933.

[656] *L & P v Reading Borough Council and Chief Constable of Thames Valley Police* [2001] EWCA Civ 346 [2001] 1 WLR 1575 (CA), discussed further below, section F.3(b)(i).

[657] *Z and others v UK* (2002) 34 EHRR 3, [2001] 2 FLR 612 (ECtHR).

[658] *TP and KM v United Kingdom* (Application no. 28945/95) (2001) 34 EHRR 42 (ECtHR).

[659] *Z v UK* (Application no. 29392/95) (1999) 28 EHRR CD 65 (EComHR). Because the British judge on the ECtHR, Justice Nicholas Braza, had sat on the European Commission of Human Rights panel, Arden LJ from the English Court of Appeal sat as an ad hoc judge when the cases were heard in the ECtHR.   [660] *Z and others v UK* (n 657) [103], [109]–[110].

[661] ibid [94]–[95].   [662] ibid [97].

home by the local authority of an adolescent with a history of abusing younger children (see *W and Others v. Essex County Council* and *Barrett v. Enfield LBC* . . .).

The Court considers that its reasoning in the *Osman* judgment was based on an understanding of the law of negligence . . . which has to be reviewed in the light of the *clarifications subsequently made by the domestic courts and notably the House of Lords*. The Court is satisfied that the law of negligence as developed in the domestic courts since the case of *Caparo* . . . and as recently analysed in the case of *Barrett v. Enfield LBC* includes the fair, just and reasonable criterion as an intrinsic element of the duty of care and that the ruling of law concerning that element in this case does not disclose the operation of an immunity. In the present case, the Court is led to the conclusion that the inability of the applicants to sue the local authority flowed not from an immunity but from the applicable principles governing the substantive right of action in domestic law.[663] [emphasis added]

The ECtHR's decision that there was no breach of Article 6 can be read as a diplomatic climbdown, reciprocating that made by the English courts post-*Osman*. The 'clarifications' provided by *Barrett* and *W v Essex* stripping away the blanket immunity of social workers enabled the ECtHR to step away from *Osman*. However, the ECtHR's tactful language should not be read as reversing its view about what *X v Bedfordshire* actually purported to do; in the later case of *E v UK* the ECtHR noted that *X* 'gave the impression that the highest judicial authority had ruled out the possibility of suing local authorities in the exercise of their child protection functions on grounds of policy', and so four children who complained of a Scottish local authority's failure to protect them from their stepfather's abuse could not be faulted for failing to sue social services before resorting to Strasbourg.[664]

Although *Z v UK* seemed to bless the partial tort immunity of social services regarding their decisions whether to intervene to protect a child, the process of unravelling even those remaining shreds of the blanket continued. In 1998 in *Attorney General v Prince*, the New Zealand Court of Appeal had robustly rejected *X v Bedfordshire*, holding that a child and his birth mother could sue the Crown for negligence in relation to a child welfare officer's reports which led to the child's adoption by unsatisfactory parents.[665] The New Zealand court confronted the spectres of 'defensive practice', wasted resources, and the delicacy of decision-making which had haunted the House of Lords in *X* with this riposte:

But like lawyers and doctors, social workers are professionals. At that triggering step (and at other steps) they should be expected to have shouldered willingly a standard of reasonable skill and care that their private sector counterparts were expected to discharge. And in the absence of any data as to potential claims based on the roles and responsibilities of the department and social workers . . . it would be unwise to give any particular weight to the resource implications of allowing for a common law duty of care.[666]

A subsequent claim by a father and two daughters against a social worker, clinical psychologist, and the Attorney General of New Zealand, for negligent investigation of

---

[663] ibid [99], [100].

[664] *E v UK* (2003) 36 EHRR 31, [2003] 1 FLR 348 (ECtHR) [114]–[115]. The ECtHR noted that *X v Bedfordshire* was applicable in Scottish as well as English law.

[665] *Attorney General v Prince and Gardner* (n 35).　　　[666] ibid 284–285.

suspected abuse by their father, went to the Privy Council, which was then the highest appellate court for New Zealand.[667] The Law Lords did not treat *X v Bedfordshire* as an obstacle to allowing the children's claim (but not the father's) to proceed.[668]

After these prolonged death throes, *X v Bedfordshire* finally gave up the ghost in 2005. In three conjoined appeals, *JD v East Berkshire Community Health NHS Trust, K v Dewsbury Healthcare NHS Trust,* and *K v Oldham NHS Trust,* physicians had misdiagnosed children as being victims of abuse when they were in fact suffering from serious medical illnesses; as a consequence social services intervened in the lives of the families and proper medical treatment was delayed. In all three cases it was the parents who had sought medical advice for their children. The children and their parents sued the NHS health authorities for negligence, and in the *Oldham* case the child also sued social services. The Court of Appeal held that claims under the ECHR and the Human Rights Act 1998 (HRA 1998) required the courts to enter into a factual inquiry in which the policy reasons in *X* (to the extent that those reasons had not already been discredited by subsequent House of Lords decisions) would largely cease to apply.[669] If the risk of legal proceedings could 'inhibit individuals from boldly taking what they believed to be the right course of action' in the delicate situation of suspected child abuse, this would happen regardless of whether the litigation was founded on the HRA 1998 or on the common law duty of care.[670] Lord Phillips MR concluded:

In so far as the position of a child is concerned, we have reached the firm conclusion that the decision in *X v Bedfordshire* . . . cannot survive the 1998 Act. Where child abuse is suspected the interests of the child are paramount: see s 1 of the Children Act 1989. Given the obligation of the local authority to respect a child's convention rights, the recognition of a duty of care to the child on the part of those involved should not have a significantly adverse effect on the manner in which they perform their duties. In the context of suspected child abuse, breach of a duty of care in negligence will frequently also amount to a violation of arts 3 or 8. The difference, of course, is that those asserting that wrongful acts or omissions occurred before October 2000 will have no claim under the 1998 Act.[671] This cannot, however, constitute a valid reason of policy for preserving a limitation of the common law duty of care which is not otherwise justified. On the contrary, the absence of an alternative remedy for children who were victims of abuse before October 2000 militates in favour of the recognition of a common law duty of care once the public policy reasons against this have lost their force.

It follows that *it will no longer be legitimate to rule that, as a matter of law, no common law duty of care is owed to a child in relation to the investigation of suspected child abuse* and the initiation and pursuit of care proceedings. It is possible that there will be factual situations where it is not fair, just or reasonable to impose a duty of care, but each case will fall to be determined on its individual facts.[672] [emphasis added]

---

[667] The Supreme Court of New Zealand became New Zealand's highest Court of Appeal, replacing the Judicial Committee of the Privy Council, as of 1 January 2004: Supreme Court Act 2003 (NZ) s 2.

[668] *B v Attorney General of New Zealand* (n 35).

[669] *JD v East Berkshire Community NHS Trust et al* [2003] EWCA Civ 1151, [2003] 4 All ER 796 (CA) [81].   [670] ibid [82].

[671] The HRA 1998, which came into force in October 2000, has been interpreted as not having retrospective effect: *R v DPP ex p Kebilene* [2000] 2 AC 326 (HL).

[672] *JD v East Berkshire Community NHS Trust* (CA) (n 669) [83]–[84].

The Court of Appeal therefore allowed the claims of the children[673] to proceed. The parents' claims were struck out because their interests could potentially conflict with those of their children.[674] These conclusions were confirmed on appeal, where the Law Lords in the majority and minority accepted that *X v Bedfordshire* was no longer good law;[675] indeed, the perceived obsolescence of *X* was such that the defendant health authorities did not seek to rely on it to defend the children's claims.[676] The *dicta* suggest that all agencies involved in child protection were now brought within the reach of negligence law.

Finally, in *Brooks v Metropolitan Police*,[677] delivered on the same day as *JD v East Berkshire*, the House of Lords held that the ethical and professional obligation of the police to treat victims and witnesses appropriately in the course of an investigation should not be translated into a legal duty of care. Their Lordships feared detrimental effects for law enforcement.[678] Nonetheless, all of the Law Lords signalled that in the appropriate case, which they suggested would be exceptional, they would not endorse the full breadth of *Hill.*[679]

This narrative has shown a discrepancy between what the English courts said and how they in fact responded to the criticisms of blanket immunity advanced in *Osman*. The Law Lords handled *Osman* adroitly and shrewdly: in *Barrett*, where Lords Hutton and Slynn declined to base their stripping of immunity from social services upon *Osman*, and in *W v Essex*, where no reference was made at all to *Osman*, the House instead relying upon *Barrett*. This enabled the precedents against blanket immunity to be established without being imperilled by reliance upon a much criticized judgment of the ECtHR.

Thus human rights law revitalized tort law by forcing it to discard wholly untested assumptions about the deleterious consequences of imposing a duty of care on public investigatory agencies. A decade ago, the law of negligence seemed to have become ossified and unresponsive to the needs of some of the most vulnerable members of society, children. With the demise of *X v Bedfordshire*, negligence law has been recognized as playing an appropriate role in monitoring the quality of social services provided by public authorities. The assimilation of child welfare work to that of other professionals was long overdue. As Lord Bingham said in *JD v East Berkshire*:

> The second policy ground relied on [in *X v Bedfordshire*] was . . . that the task of a local authority and its servants in dealing with children at risk is extraordinarily delicate. There is a difficult line to tread between taking action too soon and not taking it soon enough. The truth of this may be readily accepted. It is however a standard function for any professional to assess what may be a fraught and difficult situation. That is not generally treated as a reason for not requiring

---

[673] In *RK v Oldham*, the child's claim was dismissed at first instance, because she was an infant during the period of separation from her parents, and so suffered no recognizable psychiatric injury [*RK v Oldham NHS Trust* [2003] Lloyds Rep Med 1 (QB) [21]; only the parents appealed.

[674] *JD v East Berkshire Community NHS Trust* (CA) (n 669) [86].

[675] *JD v East Berkshire Community NHS Trust et al* (HL) (n 580) [30] (Lord Bingham), [82] (Lord Nicholls), [106] (Lord Rodger), [124] (Lord Brown).   [676] ibid [21].

[677] *Brooks v Metropolitan Police* [2005] UKHL 24, [2005] 1 WLR 1495.

[678] ibid [4] (Lord Bingham), [5] (Lord Nicholls), [30] (Lord Steyn).

[679] ibid [3] (Lord Bingham), [6] (Lord Nicholls), [28], [34] (Lord Steyn).

the exercise of reasonable skill and care in the task. The professional is not required to be right, but only to be reasonably skilful and careful.[680]

Lord Bingham's criticism of the 'defensive practice' objection was similarly tart: 'to describe awareness of a legal duty as having an "insidious effect" on the mind of a potential defendant is to undermine the foundation of the law of professional negligence'; instead, it should be 'a badge of professional status'.[681]

We turn now to consider the extent to which other jurisdictions have immunized the activities of child protection agencies from tort liability.

(iii) The negligence liability of investigatory agencies in New Zealand

We have already seen that New Zealand rejected *X v Bedfordshire* and that negligence claims against child protection agencies have been actionable in New Zealand since 1998, subject to the statutory accident compensation scheme described earlier.[682]

(iv) The negligence liability of investigatory agencies in Australia

We have noted that in Australia, apart from New South Wales, the much-criticized 'independent discretion function immunity' *Enever* doctrine holds that the Crown cannot be made liable for decisions by public officers on whom an independent statutory discretion has been specifically conferred, where that officer is not subject to the control of the relevant minister.[683] Apart from this, Australian courts have accepted the imposition of a common law duty of care upon a statutory discretion, provided that:

- the imposition of a common law duty is consistent with and complementary to the performance by the public body of its statutory functions;
- the duty can be seen to arise specifically in relation to a known claimant rather than generally in relation to the public at large;
- the defendant is in a position of control and is under a statutory obligation, or at least has specific power to protect the claimant from danger;
- the claimant is in a position of special vulnerability or dependence on the defendant and cannot reasonably be expected to safeguard herself from danger; and
- on a policy overview there is no good reason for giving the defendant an immunity from liability.[684]

The view Australian courts have taken of blanket immunity is that if the legislature has not totally precluded the imposition of a common law duty of care (and only South

---

[680] *JD v East Berkshire Community NHS Trust et al* (HL) (n 580) [32].   [681] ibid [40].

[682] Section A.1(c).

[683] *Enever v The King* (n 516); *Cubillo v Commonwealth (No 2)* [2000] (n 517) [1117], discussed above section F.1(b).

[684] *Crimmins v Stevedoring Industry Finance Committee* (1999) 200 CLR 1 (Aus HC) [91], citing with approval S Todd 'Liability in Tort of Public Bodies' in N Mullany and A Linden (eds) *Torts Tomorrow—a Tribute to John Fleming* (LBC Information Services, North Ryde 1998) 55.

Australia and Tasmania have done so by immunizing good faith acts or omissions of child protection authorities)[685] then the statute will be interpreted as conferring immunity only to the extent that harmful consequences of the authorized acts cannot be avoided by reasonable skill and care.[686] Where the public authority has created or increased the risk of foreseeable damage in exercise of its statutory powers, as where a child protection agency has already taken steps regarding a child,[687] a duty of care will ordinarily be attracted.[688] Australian courts appear to be more willing than their English counterparts to make public authorities liable in negligence for omissions, while accepting that any issues of justiciability will be determined on the familiar policy/operational continuum.[689] The degree and nature of control exercised by the public authority over the risk of harm that eventuated, the degree of vulnerability of those dependent upon the proper exercise by the authority of its powers, and the consistency of the asserted duty of care with the terms, scope and purpose of the relevant statute are of fundamental importance.[690] To date the High Court of Australia has considered *X v Bedfordshire* only once and in that case was not required to consider its applicability to Australian law nor to express a view as to the merits of blanket immunity.[691]

(v) The negligence liability of investigatory agencies in Canada

In all Canadian federal, provincial and territorial jurisdictions the common law immunity of the Crown from tort liability has been abrogated by statute. The Crown's liability is imposed through vicarious liability for torts committed by public servants, except in British Columbia and Quebec where statutes have imposed direct liability for torts on the provincial Crown.[692] The common law has immunized neither social services nor the police[693] in their investigatory functions, and, as we shall discuss

---

[685] Children, Young Persons and Their Families Act 1997 (Tasmania) s 111; Children's Protection Act 1993 (South Australia) s 62.

[686] *Benning v Wong* (1969) 122 CLR 249 (Aus HC) 256 (Barwick CJ); *Sutherland Shire Council v Heyman* (n 618) 484 (Brennan J).

[687] *SB v New South Wales* [2004] VSC 514 (Victoria Supreme Ct) [139], [291].

[688] *Sutherland Shire Council v Heyman* (n 618) 479 (Brennan J), 460 (Mason J); *Pyrenees Shire Council v Day* [1997–98] 192 CLR 330 (Aus HC) [177] (Gummow J). For further analysis see Hon John Doyle and J Redwood 'The Common Law Liability of Public Authorities: the Interface between Public and Private Law' [1999] Tort L Rev 30.

[689] *Graham Barclays Oysters Pty Ltd v Ryan* (n 240) [5] (Gleeson CJ), [81] (McHugh J); *Cubillo v Commonwealth (No 2)* (n 517) [1207]–[1208].

[690] *Graham Barclays Oysters Pty Ltd v Ryan* (2002) ibid [149]–[150] (Gummow and Hayne JJ).

[691] *Sullivan v Moody* (n 240) [30]–[32], [39], [50].

[692] Grace and Vella (n 77) 101–110.

[693] *Hill v Chief Constable of West Yorkshire* was rejected in *Jane Doe v Board of Commissioners of Police for Metropolitan Toronto* (1990) 72 DLR (4th) 580 (Ontario Gen Div, leave to further appeal to Ontario CA refused (1991) 1 OR (3d) 487), discussed in Hoyano 'Policing Flawed Police Investigations' (n 219). It was also rejected in *Hill v Hamilton-Wentworth Regional Police Services Board* (2005) 259 DLR (4th) 4676 (Ontario CA, leave to appeal granted by SCC 27 April 2006) [54]–[71] (also rejecting *Brooks v Metropolitan Police* (n 677), MacPherson JA commenting that the ' "chilling effect" scenario painted fairly vividly in *Hill* and *Brooks* is . . . both speculative and counter-intuitive' [63]).

further below, duties of care have been held to be owed both to the victim[694] and to the suspect.[695] As one appellate judge said in rejecting the policy reasoning in *Hill v Chief Constable of West Yorkshire*, Canadian courts are not so protective of the police.[696] Instead, legislators in most Canadian provinces and territories have conferred qualified immunity from tort liability on social workers and agencies in performing their duties to protect children in good faith.[697] Actions which do not plead bad faith will be struck out in interlocutory proceedings.[698] We address the content of the concept of good faith immunity at the end of this section.

(vi) The negligence liability of investigatory agencies in the United States

In American law the situation governing tort immunity for child protection workers and agencies is more complex. Diagram 4 depicts the routes to common law tort liability.[699] Where sovereign immunity from tort liability has been expressly[700] revoked wholly or in part (and Georgia for example has not in relation to its State-wide foster care system)[701] then an action may lie in a common law or constitutional tort.[702] We will consider constitutional torts separately when discussing breach of a child's human rights by a child protection agency;[703] suffice it to say for now that the federal Government has not waived sovereign immunity for constitutional violations, although individual public employees may be sued.[704]

Constructing a duty to act in American law It is important to bear in mind that there is considerable overlap between common law tort liability and constitutional tort

---

[694] *Jane Doe v Board of Commissioners of Police for Metropolitan Toronto* ibid; *J(A) v D(W)* [1999] 11 WWR 82 (Man QB); *Odhavji Estate v Woodhouse* [2003] SCC 69, [2003] 3 SCR 263 (SCC) [57].

[695] *B(D), B(R) and B(M) v Children's Aid Society of Durham Region* (1996) 136 DLR (4th) 297 (Ontario CA); *AAD, TD and KGD v Tanner, Winnipeg Child and Family Services Agency et al* 2004 MBQB 213 (Manitoba QB) [181]; *Beckstead v Ottawa (City) Chief of Police* (1997) 37 OR (3d) 62 (Ontario CA); *Hill v Hamilton-Wentworth Regional Police Services Board* (n 693); *André v Quebec (Procureur général)* [2003] RJQ 720 (Quebec CA, leave to appeal to to SCC denied); *Jauvin v Quebec (Procureur général)* [2004] RRA 37 (Quebec CA, leave to appeal to SCC denied) [42]–[47].

[696] *BM [Bonnie Mooney], MM and KM v Attorney General (British Columbia) and Attorney General (Canada)* 2004 BCCA 402, [2004] 10 WWR 286 (British Columbia CA, leave to appeal to SCC refused 3 March 2005 No 30546) [47] (Donald JA, dissenting on another ground).

[697] Child, Family and Community Service Act (British Columbia) s 101; Protection against Family Violence Act (Alberta); Family Law Act (Alberta) s 44(6); Child and Family Services Authorities Act (Alberta) s 19; Child and Family Services Act (Saskatchewan); The Child and Family Services Act (Manitoba) ss 8.11, 18(1), 85; Child and Family Services Act (Ontario) s 15(6); Child Protection Act (Prince Edward Island); Child, Youth and Family Services Act (Newfoundland); Child and Family Services Act (Nunavut) s 69.

[698] *ANDB v Ferguson* [1999] MJ No 170 (Manitoba QB).   [699] See above, section E.2.

[700] Statutory provisions alleged to waive sovereign immunity will be strictly construed: *Smith v United States* 507 US 197 (USSC 1993) 203.

[701] CA Kubitschek 'Social Worker Malpractice for Failure to Protect Foster Children' 41 Am Jur Trials 1 §36.

[702] The Federal Tort Claims Act 28 USC §1346, §§2671 ff is the exclusive basis for tort claims against the United States government: HM Goldberg 'Tort Liability for Federal Government Actions in United States: an Overview' in Fairgrieve, Andenas and Bell (eds) *Tort Liability of Public Authorities* (n 583).

[703] See below, section F.5.

[704] Goldberg (n 702) 528; *Bivens v Six Unknown Federal Narcotics Agents* 403 US 388 (USSC 1971).

liability in American law, and the two causes of action are usually pleaded together against a State child protection agency in the same case.[705]

The starting position is that there is no common law duty to act imposed on public authorities or on individuals. Many statutes impose a duty on public officials to perform certain acts. Generally, however, most States[706] regard such officials as enjoying an immunity in their personal capacity from a private cause of action under the 'public duty' doctrine. This holds that public officials are generally not liable to individuals for their negligence in discharging their duties, as the duty is owed to the public at large rather than to any one individual:[707] 'a duty owed to all is owed to none'.[708] There are three primary exceptions (not always distinct) which State law may carve out from the no-duty rule whereby an affirmative duty is imposed to protect the claimant from the risk of harm created by a third party: a *special duty* owed to a child rather than to the public only; a *special relationship* established between a child and the public official; and the *state-created danger* theory.

Turning first to the *special duty exception*, the South Carolina Court of Appeals developed a test comprised of six elements to determine when it may arise:

- an essential purpose of the statute is to protect against a particular kind of harm;
- the statute, either directly or indirectly, imposes on a specific public officer a duty to guard against or not cause that harm;
- the class of persons which the statute intends to protect is identifiable before the fact;
- the claimant is a person within the protected class;
- the public officer knows or has reason to know the likelihood of harm to members of the class if he fails to do his duty; and
- the officer is given sufficient authority to act in the circumstances or he undertakes to act in the exercise of his office.[709]

Recent cases involving child protection agencies have emphasized the need for a flexible approach rather than a bright line test.[710] Maryland and Vermont have judicially

---

[705] See below, section F.5(a)(ii).

[706] Some States have considered that the public duty doctrine impermissibly reinstates sovereign immunity, and have treated public bodies and officials on the same basis as private tort litigants, eg *Adams v State* 555 P 2d 235 (Alaska Supreme Ct 1976); *Martínez v Lakewood* 655 P 2d 1388 (Colorado App Ct 1982); *Faulkner v The McCarty Corp* 853 So 2d 24 (Louisiana CA 4th Cir 2003); *Coffey v Milwaukee* 247 NW 2d 132 (Wisconsin Supreme Ct 1976).

[707] *Jensen v Anderson County Dept. of Social Services* 403 SE 2d 615 (South Carolina Supreme Ct 1991).

[708] *Massee v Thompson* 90 P 3d 394 (Montana Supreme Ct 2004) 403.

[709] *Rayfield v South Carolina Dept of Corrections* 374 SE 2d 910 (S Carolina CA,1988) *certiorari* denied 379 SE 2d 133 (1989)); SL Abbott 'Liability of the State and Its Employees for the Negligent Investigation of Child Abuse Reports' (1993) 10 Alaska L Rev 401, 405.

[710] *Horridge v St Mary's County Department of Social Services* 854 A 2d 1232 (Maryland CA 2004) 1244; *Radke v County of Freeborn* 694 NW 2d 788 (Minnesota SC 2005) 794.

developed guidelines for a special duty which set out the additional factors:

- the governmental unit had actual knowledge of the dangerous condition;
- persons reasonably relied on the governmental unit's specific representations and actions, which caused them to forego alternative ways of protecting themselves; and
- the governmental unit used due care to avoid increasing the risk of harm.[711]

Exceptions to the public duty rule may be found to apply where child protection legislation imposes a *special duty* on a child protection agency and its social workers to investigate and intervene when suspected abuse respecting a specified child has been reported.[712] This may also establish a *special relationship* between the agency and the child.[713]

An alternative concept of State liability rests upon the *state-created danger theory.* This theory ispredicated upon the State's affirmative acts which work to the claimants' detriment in terms of exposure to danger, rather than upon a special relationship between the State and the victim.[714] We shall see that this exception becomes very important where the child protection agency has returned a child to a dangerous family situation, or placed a child with foster carers who go on to abuse her.

Absolute and qualified immunity in American law As we discussed earlier,[715] the duties of public officials are in general classified as 'ministerial' and 'discretionary'; another distinction is drawn between 'ministerial' and 'quasi-judicial' duties. Notwithstanding the existence of an exception to the general absence of a duty to act, tort liability for public officials generally will not arise if the negligence occurs during the performance of a quasi-judicial duty, which attracts absolute immunity from tort liability, or a discretionary duty, which is subject to qualified immunity. Ministerial acts are not protected by any form of immunity from tort liability. Therefore the initial classification of the public official's duty is highly significant.[716]

The classification of a child protection official's public duties is determined by the nature of the act performed. A duty is *ministerial*, and so actionable in tort, when it involves no element of judgement or choice, requiring merely execution of a specific duty arising from fixed and designated facts or conditions such as a specific mandatory directive.[717] It is thus roughly analogous to the 'operational' concept in English law under *Anns.*[718] *Quasi-judicial* duties which are entirely non-actionable encompass

---

[711] *Cracraft v City of St Louis Park* 279 NW 2d 801 (Minnesota CA 1979) 806–807; *Sabia v State* (n 253).   [712] Discussed further below, section F.2(a)(i).

[713] *Jensen v Anderson County Dept of Social Services* (n 707); *Radke v County of Freeborn* (n 710).

[714] *DR v Middle Bucks Area Vocational Technical School,* 972 F 2d 1364 (US CA 3rd Cir (en banc) 1992); KM Blum '*DeShaney*: Custody, Creation of Danger, and Culpability' (1994) 27 Loyola of Los Angeles L Rev 435.   [715] Section F.1(b).

[716] For a description of the discrepant approaches of State courts to immunity for child protection functions, see LH Martin, 'Caseworker Liability for the Negligent Handling of Child Abuse Reports' (1991) 60 U of Cincinnati L Rev 191.

[717] *Berkovitz v United States* 486 US 531 (USSC 1988) 544; *Gaubert v United States* 499 US 315 (USSC 1991) 322.   [718] *Anns v Merton* (n 231), discussed above section F.1(a).

the witness immunity doctrine in English law[719] which protects witnesses from civil liability for their testimony in court and for their pre-trial witness statements, but in American law also can extend well beyond that territory. *Discretionary* functions which benefit from qualified immunity refer to governmental acts or omissions which (1) involve an element of judgement or choice and (2) are susceptible to policy analysis, but are not confined to the planning level.[720] Again to draw an analogy with the taxonomy of actions against public authorities mapped by Lord Browne-Wilkinson in *X v Bedfordshire*, the discretionary function immunity would not bar tort claims based upon a breach of statutory duty, but would exclude claims based upon the careless exercise of the statutory power if the conduct involved an element of judgement that was susceptible to policy analysis.[721] However, discretionary duties are given only qualified immunity, and so may give rise to tort liability if they are conducted in bad faith.

This classification of functions has been applied inconsistently and therefore unpredictably to the duties of American child protection agencies.[722] However, a general pattern may be discerned. The dividing line between absolute and qualified immunity may be determined by whether the harm depends on the judicial decision. If there would be no injury but for the judge's rulings in relation to the child and family, then the prosecutor or witness who induces the judge to act has absolute immunity.[723] Therefore by analogy to public prosecutors, judges and witnesses, child protection officers are protected by absolute immunity for their actions in relation to preparing for, initiating and prosecuting child protection proceedings, including the formulation and presentation of recommendations to the court, because no harm could be caused until the court makes an order.[724] This is so even if it is alleged that the social worker acted out of improper motives and misled the court in an *ex parte* (without notice) application, because 'immunity that applies only when the defendant did no wrong is no immunity at all'.[725] Absolute immunity has also been held to apply to the highest executive officer of a child protection agency where the negligence claims relate to inadequate training and supervision of staff in the reporting and investigation of alleged child abuse, and so fall within his statutory duties.[726]

---

[719] *Darker v Chief Constable of West Midlands* [2001] 1 AC 435 (HL).

[720] *Gaubert v United States* (n 717) 325.

[721] HM Goldberg 'Liability for Government Actions: a Comparative Study of English and American Law' in Duncan Fairgrieve and Sarah Green (eds) *Child Abuse Tort Claims against Public Bodies: a Comparative Law View* (Ashgate, Aldershot 2004) 100.

[722] Martin (n 716) 212–218.

[723] *Millspaugh v County Department of Public Welfare of Wabash County* 937 F 2d 1172 (US CA 7th Cir 1991) 1175.

[724] ibid 1176; *Ernst v Child & Youth Service of Chester County* (n 724) 495–496; *Vosburg v Department of Social Services* 884 F 2d 133 (US CA 4th Cir 1989) 135; *Salyer v Patrick* 874 F 2d 374 (US CA 6th Cir 1989) 378; *Myers v Contra Costa County Department of Social Services* 812 F 2d 1154 (US CA 6th Cir 1989) 495–496.

[725] *Millspaugh v County Department of Public Welfare of Wabash County* (n 723) 1175–1176. This is very unlikely to be the case in English law: compare *L (a Minor) and P (Father) v Reading Borough Council and Chief Constable of Thames Valley Police* [2001] EWCA 346, [2001] 1 WLR 1575 (CA) discussed below, section F.2.(b)(i) and (ii).

[726] *LaShay v Department of Social and Rehabilitation Services* 625 A 2d 224 (Vermont Supreme Ct 1993) 227.

However, most American appellate courts have been careful to stipulate that the 'quasi-judicial immunity' attaching to preparation for court proceedings does not extend to the investigation of suspected child abuse outside that context.[727] Discretionary decisions taken in the course of an investigation are protected only by good faith qualified immunity,[728] whilst ministerial functions are actionable in tort without qualification. The duty to conduct a 'thorough' investigation before a decision is taken to close a file is characterized as a ministerial duty mandated by statute.[729] The manner in which the investigation is conducted is one of discretion, unless the investigation is so incomplete that it could not be found to be 'thorough'.[730]

Many American States have preferred not to rely upon the classification of functions through caselaw, enacting legislation expressly conferring absolute or qualified immunity from tort liability on public officials and employees. Qualified immunity is usually predicated upon a benchmark of good faith, so that the claimant must prove significantly more culpable conduct than mere negligence to strip away the immunity, such as gross negligence, deliberate indifference[731] or recklessness.[732] One might think that this would require that the case go through a full trial to enable all the evidence of culpable omissions by the State agency to be evaluated by the trier of fact,[733] but summary judgment after pre-trial disclosure (or 'discovery') does occur, even where the inferences to be drawn from material facts are in dispute.[734] A robust approach to summary judgment on the ground of qualified immunity has been supported by the US Supreme Court, which observed that qualified immunity 'is an immunity from suit rather than a mere defence to liability.'[735] Because qualified immunity is intended

---

[727] *Miller v City of Philadelphia* 174 F 3d 368 (US CA 3d Cir 1999) 375–376; *Ernst v Child & Youth Service of Chester County* (n 724) 497 n 7. However recently a Pennsylvania court has expanded the quasi-judicial category to encompass removing a child as the beginning of child protection proceedings: *Bowser v Blair County Children and Youth Services* 346 F Supp 2d 788 (US DC Pennsylvania 2004) 791–794.

[728] *Snell v Tunnell* 920 F 2d 673 (US CA 10th Cir 1990) (pre-adjudication investigative activities by child welfare workers); *Achterhof v Selvaggio* 886 F 2d 826 (US CA 6th Cir 1989) (opening and investigating child abuse case and placing parent's name on central registry of abusers); *Austin v Borel* 830 F 2d 1356 (US CA 5th Cir 1987) (filing of a complaint which allowed the agency to obtain custody but did not initiate an adjudicative proceeding).

[729] *Brodie v Summit County Children's Services Board* (n 253) 1308; *Horridge v St Mary's County Department of Social Services* (n 710) 1242–1245; *Turner v District of Columbia* 532 A 2d 662 (District of Columbia CA 1987) 688. There are some cases to the contrary: Abbott (n 709) 414–416.

[730] *Jensen v Anderson County Dept of Social Services* (n 707) 620; *Department of Health & Rehabilitative Services v Yamuni* 498 So 2d 441 (Florida 3rd District CA 1986) 260.

[731] As under the New Jersey Tort Claims Act NJSA s 59: 3–3, interpreted *Nicini v Morra* (n 220).

[732] As in Vermont: *Sabia v State* (n 253); *Sabia v Neville* (n 220).

[733] See *Yvonne L by and through Lewis New Mexico Dept of Human Services* 959 F 2d 83 (US CA 10th Cir 1992); see also *Armstrong v Squadrito* 152 F 3d 564 (US CA 7th Cir 1998) 577 respecting the inappropriateness of summary judgment for constitutional tort claims under §1983 where the degree of culpability is in issue.

[734] *Nicini v Morra* (n 220) 814, 816, where the court split 2:1 on whether the issue of deliberate indifference should go to trial.

[735] *Mitchell v Forsyth* 472 US 511 (USSC 1985) 526.

to balance redress of the wronged with the freedom which public officials must have to perform their obligations without fear of retaliation, that freedom is viewed as threatened not just by ultimate liability but by the distraction and expense of defending the claim.[736] The courts are especially concerned about the 'chilling effect' which the prospect of having to defend a claim would have on officials charged with the difficult task of investigating child abuse.[737] So in a summary judgment application the court should measure the public employee's conduct against a standard of objective reasonableness, to weed out insubstantial claims.[738] Only if the unlawfulness of the impugned actions reasonably should have been apparent to the official should the case be allowed to proceed to trial.[739]

English lawyers despondent at the complexity of the English template for the tort liability of public authorities may take comfort in knowing that their American counterparts have to deal with an even more complicated framework which generates seemingly endless litigious points and can yield inconsistent results across States. Qualified immunity for child protection staff is increasingly being seen as the straightforward and the right solution.[740]

We turn now from the threshold issue of immunity of child protection agencies from actions in negligence to consider the situations which may give rise to liability. As this is clearly a burgeoning area in all of our comparator tort jurisdictions, we will confine our discussion to a few representative cases to give an indication of where English tort law might go in the coming years, now that it has been unshackled from *X v Bedfordshire*.

2. Liability of child protection investigators to the child

(a) Failure to investigate an abuse allegation

Failure to investigate reports of suspected child abuse raises all the issues and difficulties attendant upon liability for omissions which we canvassed earlier.[741] The conundrum is whether a party with the capacity, opportunity and power to act should be required to take steps to avert a risk which that party did not create. The definitional problem of categorizing something as a 'pure' omission is particularly acute here, because it is rare that the child protection agency merely receives the complaint and does nothing whatsoever. Therefore the distinction between nonfeasance and malfeasance in responding to a complaint can be arbitrarily drawn on the facts of a particular case. As we discussed, it is much easier to set up a duty of care where there has been some decision—even not to follow up the complaint—than where there has been nothing

---

[736] *Levinsky v Diamond* 559 A 2d 1073 (Vermont CA 1989) 1087; *Murray v White* 587 A 2d 975 (Vermont CA 1991).　　　　　　　　　　　　[737] *Murray v White* 7 ibid 981.

[738] *Harlow v Fitzgerald* 457 US 800 (USSC 1982); *Murray v White* ibid.

[739] *Murray v White* ibid 981.

[740] CB Sailor 'Qualified Immunity for Child Abuse Investigators: Balancing the Concerns of Protecting Our Children from Abuse and the Integrity of the Family' (1991) 29 J of Family L 659; Martin (n 716).

[741] See above, section C.1.

at all. Even where a decision has been taken, however, the difficulties of proving causation of harm can be intractable. The issue will be whether the inaction of the agency in any way altered the risk to which the child *ex hypothesi* was exposed before the involvement of the agency.

(i) Breach of a statutory duty to investigate

We saw earlier that English law recognizes a nominate and distinct common law tort of breach of statutory duty.[742] Whilst the strict liability nature of the tort makes it attractive to litigants, it is very difficult to establish that the tort is available to an aggrieved citizen, who must show that Parliament intended the statutory duty to be actionable by someone in the class of persons the legislation was intended to protect. In *X v Bedfordshire*, Lord Browne-Wilkinson was emphatic in rejecting any possibility of the tort operating in the sphere of child protection:

My starting point is that the [child welfare] Acts in question are all concerned to establish an administrative system designed to promote the social welfare of the community. The welfare sector involved is one of peculiar sensitivity, involving very difficult decisions how to strike the balance between protecting the child from immediate feared harm and disrupting the relationship between the child and its parents. Decisions often have to be taken on the basis of inadequate and disputed facts. In my judgment in such a context it would require exceptionally clear statutory language to show a parliamentary intention that those responsible for carrying out these difficult functions should be liable in damages if, on subsequent investigation with the benefit of hindsight, it was shown that they had reached an erroneous conclusion and therefore failed to discharge their statutory duties.[743]

While the legislation was introduced primarily for the protection of children at risk, the Children Act 1989 and its predecessors use language which is dependent upon the subjective judgment of the local authority, and so it was considered impossible to treat such duties as being more than public law duties.[744] This conclusion has doomed all other attempts in English courts to plead breach of statutory duty in connection with child protection powers,[745] and it is very unlikely that this particular conclusion in *X* has been superseded in the way that the ruling on duty of care has been. Therefore any liability for failure to investigate reports of child abuse must be brought in negligence.

In the United States courts have often dismissed actions based on failure to remove a child from an abusive parent asserted on grounds of breach of statutory duties.[746] *Department of Health & Rehabilitative Services v Yamuni*,[747] is an example of a decision where the State of Florida was successfully sued for breach of its duties to investigate and act on reported child abuse, which was pleaded concurrently with negligence; the

---

[742] See above sections, C.3 and F.1(a).   [743] *X v Bedfordshire County Council* (n 73) 747.
[744] ibid.   [745] *Barrett v Enfield London Borough Council* (n 75) 562.
[746] eg *Rittscher v State* 352 NW 2d 247 (Iowa Supreme Ct 1984); *MH, DH and PT v State* 385 NW 2d 533 (Iowa Supreme Ct 1986) 536–537, applying the four-stage test for ascertaining whether a statute sets up a private law tort for breach of statutory duty in *Cort v Ash* 422 US 66 (USSC 1975); MR Flaherty 'Tort Liability of Public Authority for Failure to Remove Parentally Abused or Neglected Children from Parents' Custody' 60 AmericanLR 4th 942 §2 [a], §5.
[747] *Department of Health & Rehabilitative Services v Yamuni* (n 730) 442–443.

Court of Appeal construed the statute as intending the protection of a limited class, children, from a particularized harm of abuse and neglect.

In Commonwealth jurisdictions statutory duties to investigate imposed upon child protection agencies are considered primarily to be relevant as establishing a special and proximate relationship between the agency and the child possibly at risk; this serves to set up a duty of care in negligence as well as setting the standard of care. So the tort of breach of statutory duty has tended to be sidelined in this context.[748]

X v Bedfordshire was a paradigmatic case of failure to investigate repeated complaints about the welfare of children who obviously were being physically and emotionally abused and neglected. We turn now to consider how other jurisdictions have dealt with this fact pattern in the tort of negligence.

(ii) Liability for negligent failure to investigate in New Zealand law

We have seen that New Zealand's approach to the tort liability of child protection agencies had a powerful influence on the fate of *X v Bedfordshire* in English law. In *Attorney General v Prince and Gardner*[749] a child and his birth mother (Gardner) sued the Department of Social Welfare for negligence in managing the child's adoption into a neglectful and emotionally abusive adoptive family in 1969, and for failure to investigate a complaint from a third party when he was 14 about his welfare and care by his adoptive parents. When Prince sued, he was serving a prison sentence which he attributed to his childhood deprivation. The New Zealand Court of Appeal refused to recognize a duty of care in relation to the adoption proceedings as it was inconsistent with the policy and scheme of the Adoption Act, and it was the family court, not social services, which determined that the statutory criteria were satisfied.[750]

The New Zealand Court of Appeal (by a majority of four judges to one) did however recognize that social workers owe a duty of care to a child to investigate a complaint. The relevant legislation imposed a duty on the Director-General to arrange for prompt inquiry where he knew or had reason to suspect that any child or young person was suffering or was likely to suffer from ill-treatment or from inadequate care or control, and to take positive action to provide reasonable assistance to that child and his parent or guardian to overcome deficiencies in the child's care.[751] Interestingly, the statute provided that any social worker furnishing a report to the court about the child's circumstances was not under any civil or criminal liability in respect of that report 'unless he has acted in bad faith or without reasonable care'.[752] Richardson P for the majority held that there is proximity of relationship derived from the professional relationship between a social worker and a client child, and that when a social worker exercises statutory powers she assumes responsibility for that child. The duty to consider a complaint of neglect is specific to that particular child; it is not a generalized duty to the community at large, nor is it a discretionary power. Doing nothing is

---

[748] eg *TC v New South Wales* [1999] NSW SC 31 (New South Wales Supreme Ct) [11]. B Atkin and G McLay 'Suing Child Welfare Agencies—a Comparative View from New Zealand' 13 Child and Family LQ 287.   [749] *Attorney General v Prince and Gardner* (n 35).

[750] ibid 275–277.   [751] Children and Young Persons Act 1974 (New Zealand) s 5.

[752] ibid s 41(8). The New Zealand Court of Appeal did not however base its judgment recognizing the duty of care on that wording.

not an option. It was reasonable to conclude that 'given the community expectations reflected in the statute', the child claimant was to be regarded as 'implicitly relying' on the department and its officers to consider complaints that he was in need. In such a case the officer must have known that failure to give adequate consideration to the complaint and to take any appropriate action might *increase* the risk of harm (although Richardson P did not specify how this causative link might come about).[753]

The majority also concluded that the policy considerations against negligence liability enumerated in *X v Bedfordshire* were inapplicable in the New Zealand context. The Director-General had a positive duty to take proactive steps to prevent children from suffering harm. Imposing a duty of care at this 'early triggering step' would not cut across the entire statutory scheme, and would not involve other agencies. The concerns in *X* about the delicacy of the social worker's task and judgements showed the difficulties of establishing that an assessment made by a social worker fell outside the bounds sanctioned by professional opinion, but could not absolve the Department and social workers from the responsibility of considering and responding to a specific complaint with professional skill and care, like other professionals. Therefore in New Zealand liability may arise where the person charged with the responsibility of investigating complaints either unreasonably fails to carry out the duty to consider the matter, or reaches a conclusion so unreasonable as to show failure to do his duty.[754]

(iii) Liability for negligent failure to investigate in Australian law

There seems to be only one reported appellate decision in Australia regarding negligent nonfeasance by social workers, although a number of others are working their way through the judicial process. In *TC v New South Wales*,[755] the claimant alleged that the New South Wales Department of Youth and Community Services (YACS) had failed to act on several warnings by his father that he was being physically and emotionally abused by his mother, who had a history of psychotic mental illness. An allegation of sexual abuse was made considerably later. Since TC's birth, his parents had been estranged and locked in a bitter battle over custody. For different periods the mother and her son lived in a refuge. The father made repeated complaints about his welfare to YACS and to the family court over a six-year period.

The applicable New South Wales legislation established a statutory scheme of notification of the Director of Child Welfare of suspected abuse or neglect, whereupon the Director was required to 'promptly cause an investigation to be made', and then to take appropriate action if he was satisfied that the child might have been assaulted, ill-treated or exposed. Section 158 of the statute also conferred immunity from tort liability only where the Minister or the officer or employee had acted in good faith and with reasonable care.[756] The parallels with the New Zealand legislation considered in *Prince* are clear. Unlike most of the other cases we are considering, the judgment under appeal was after a full trial.[757] Studdert J at trial rejected the Crown's submissions

---

[753] *Attorney General v Prince and Gardner* (n 35) 282–284.   [754] ibid 284–285.

[755] *TC v South Wales* [1999] NSWSC 99, appeal allowed in part [2001] NSWCA 380 (New South Wales CA).   [756] Child Welfare Act 1939 (New South Wales), as amended in 1977, ss 148B, 158.

[757] Indeed two trials as the issue of liability was tried separately from causation (the latter being reported at [2000] NSWSC 292).

that s 158 meant that there was potential liability only after it had intervened and removed the child from his former environment, and distinguished *X v Bedfordshire* on the basis that the English legislation had no parallels to the mandatory investigation provisions.[758] He held that the child protection agency owed a duty of care to the child: it was reasonably foreseeable that any failure to respond appropriately to a notification could result in harm to the child concerned; the statutory scheme created the necessary proximity; and it was fair, just, and reasonable to impose a duty of care given the mandatory investigation requirement which recognized the need to protect vulnerable children at risk of abuse or neglect.[759]

The measure of the duty was to exercise reasonable care in conducting the mandatory investigation in response to the notification; the irrationality standard for exercising a discretionary power posited in *X v Bedfordshire* was rejected.[760] Of the 13 child welfare officials and lawyers involved in TC's case, 11 were found by the trial judge to have acted with reasonable care in responding to the father's concerns. The remaining two were found to be negligent only for their failure to investigate one report that the mother had left the child alone in the refuge, tied to his cot, almost 12 months earlier, and a six-month delay in dealing with a later allegation of sexual abuse against the mother.[761] In both instances the social workers had not followed their own practice guidelines. The Court of Appeal upheld the finding of negligence relating to the delay, but reversed the finding relating to the cot-tying incident, concluding that YACS' proper concern was the current welfare of the child. 'YACS was not a detective agency set up to hunt down and prosecute past misconduct. True, the past could be an indicator of the present, but there were matters of degree.'[762] Simply to point to something that might have been done was not enough to establish that failure to do it would constitute a breach of duty.[763] Both the trial judge and the Court of Appeal ultimately dismissed TC's claim because he had failed to establish a causal link between the established breaches and his severe psychiatric disorder (which was assumed for the purpose of the causation hearing to have flowed from acts of sexual abuse which did not involve the mother, but might also have been genetic).[764] *TC* thus signalled a balanced approach to the issue of breach of duty by social workers, and a reluctance to hold them responsible for all adverse events later in the child's life.

(iv) Liability for negligent failure to investigate in Canadian law

Canadian courts have found little difficulty in holding that child protection agencies owe a duty of care to children about whom an allegation of abuse has been made.[765]

---

[758] *TC v New South Wales* (n 748) [162]–[164].   [759] ibid [169]–[185].

[760] ibid [186]–[191].

[761] ibid [228]–[265], [505]–[544]. Sexual abuse was found to have occurred, but by an unknown third party.   [762] *TC v New South Wales* (n 755) [142].

[763] ibid [141].   [764] *Derrick v Cheung* [2001] HCA 48 (Aus HC) [12].

[765] eg *B(D), B(R) and B(M) v Children's Aid Society of Durham Region* (n 695).

In *J(A) v Cairnie and the Government of Manitoba*[766] the claimant when aged 14 on several occasions told a government social worker, Cairnie, that she was being sexually and physically abused by her stepfather. Cairnie did not believe her, called her a liar, and took no steps to remove her from the abusive situation. Her parents retaliated violently for her disclosure to the social worker. Her stepfather refused to continue with the family psychiatric counselling sessions in which he had confessed to the sexual abuse. The abuse resumed and escalated to weekly rapes and other violent assaults. Nine months later another social worker reviewed the claimant's file and immediately intervened to take her into care and placed her in a foster home. Twenty years later the stepfather was convicted of indecent assault. There was contemporary evidence that Cairnie's work colleagues, superiors, and other professionals involved in child protection had serious concerns about her performance; she insisted on working independently and was drinking heavily at the time, but she was married to a senior official in the social services office and no action was taken to remove her from her duties. Here again, the applicable child welfare legislation required the agency immediately to investigate any information it received which caused it to suspect that a child was in need of protection, but unlike some other Canadian provinces did not immunize social workers who acted in good faith.[767] The trial judge declined to read into the legislation a good faith exemption for the exercise of discretionary powers or to construct one at common law. The decision of the social worker about whether to remove a child from her family is operational rather than policy in nature, and so a duty of care can arise when the social worker is required to make an evaluation as to whether a child is in need of protection.[768] By the professional standards prevailing at that time, the social worker had been given enough information (particularly the evidence of previous admitted sexual abuse) to have tilted the balance in favour of taking some positive steps to investigate further in such a way as to protect the child in the interim. This was not merely an error in judgment.[769] The Government of Manitoba was vicariously liable for the social worker's negligence, but (perhaps surprisingly) was not found directly negligent for continuing to employ her or supervise her more closely when there were concerns about her effectiveness.[770]

(v) Liability for negligent failure to investigate in American law

Some American courts, like their counterparts in New Zealand, Australia and Canada, have constructed a tort duty to inquire into an allegation on the back of imperative statutory language, as all States have legislation requiring prompt investigation.[771] However American courts have generally been reluctant to enforce child protection

---

[766] *J(A) v Cairnie and the Government of Manitoba* [1999] 11 WWR 82 (Manitoba QB) (appeal allowed on a limitation of action issue: *J(A) v Cairnie and the Government of Manitoba* 2001 MBCA 59, 198 DLR (4th) 659 (Manitoba CA)).

[767] Child and Family Services Act (Manitoba) SM 1985–86 c 8, s 18.4(1).

[768] *J(A) v Cairnie and the Government of Manitoba* (n 766) [140]–[148].

[769] ibid [154]–[156].   [770] ibid [166].

[771] Derived from the Federal Child Abuse Prevention and Treatment and Adoption Reform Act 42 USCA ch 67 §5106a s (b)(2)(A)(iv).

agencies' statutory duties through negligence actions, especially where parental abuse or neglect is involved.[772]

The American analogue to *X v Bedfordshire* in both reasoning and notoriety is *DeShaney v Winnebago County Department of Social Services*.[773] The Family Court had awarded custody of one-year-old Joshua to his father. Social services initially ignored concerns about his well-being expressed by his mother in 1982. Eventually the child was taken into temporary custody in January 1983, after he was hospitalized for multiple injuries. However, social services concluded that there was insufficient evidence of child abuse and decided to return the child to his father's custody. A case worker decided there was no need for further action when he was hospitalized again for suspicious injuries. The caseworker in the course of nearly 20 visits to the home 'dutifully recorded'[774] further incidents and injuries she noticed, along with her continuing suspicions that someone in the DeShaney household was physically abusing Joshua, but she did nothing more. In November 1983 staff at the hospital emergency ward notified social services that Joshua had been treated once more for injuries that they believed to be caused by violence. On the case worker's next two visits to the DeShaney home, she was told that Joshua was too ill to see her. Still social services took no action. In March 1984, the father beat four-year-old Joshua so ferociously that he fell into a life-threatening coma. Joshua suffered brain damage so severe that he was permanently placed in an institution for the profoundly mentally handicapped. The social worker later said 'I just knew the phone would ring some day and Joshua would be dead'.[775]

DeShaney was a paradigmatic case for the two critical issues about liability for omissions which we identified earlier. Was the case properly defined as a 'pure omission'? And what harm could it be said had been caused by the inaction of social services?[776] A majority of six to three Judges on the US Supreme Court held that social services did not incur liability for a breach of Joshua's civil rights. We consider the issue of the constitutional tort further below,[777] but the following passage is key to the analysis of liability under common law and constitutional torts alike:

While the State may have been aware of the dangers that Joshua faced in the free world, it played no part in their creation, nor did it do anything to render him any more vulnerable to them. That the State once took temporary custody of Joshua does not alter the analysis, for when it returned him to his father's custody, it placed him in no worse position than that in which he would have been had it not acted at all; the State does not become the permanent guarantor of or of an individual's safety by having once offered him shelter.[778]

The minority[779] vigorously contested this analysis. Justice Brennan pointed out that the majority's conclusion was dictated by its construction of the facts as setting up a

[772] Flaherty (n 746) §2[a].

[773] *DeShaney v Winnebago County Department of Social Services* (n 212).   [774] ibid 192.

[775] ibid. As the case did not proceed to trial, it is unknown why the caseworker did not take further action [812 F 2d 298 (USCA 7th Cir 1987) 329–330].   [776] See above, section C.1.

[777] See below, section F.5.   [778] *DeShaney v Winnebago* (n 212) 201.

[779] Justices Brennan, Blackmun and Marshall.

'pure omission', whereas the minority approached the case from the opposite direction, focusing on the action which the State of Wisconsin had taken. Through its
child protection programme which gave the Department of Social Services exclusive
control of decision-making in responding to an allegation of child abuse, the State had
actively intervened in Joshua's life by taking him into temporary custody. By virtue
of this intervention it acquired 'ever more certain knowledge that Joshua was in grave
danger'.[780] In response to the majority's insistence that it was Joshua's father, not the
State, who caused his injuries, Justice Brennan pointed out that since social services
had complete control over how they responded to abuse allegations, a private citizen
or the hospital or employees of other agencies felt that they had done their job by
notifying social services of their concerns; 'conceivably, then, children like Joshua are
made worse off by the existence of this program when the persons and entities charged
with carrying it out fail to do their jobs'.[781] Justice Brennan pinpointed his dissent as
arising from the majority's 'failure to see that inaction can be every bit as abusive of
power as action, that oppression can result when a State undertakes a vital duty and
then ignores it'.[782] The *DeShaney* case caused much academic commentary, most of
it highly critical.[783]

The majority in *DeShaney* did signal that ordinary tort law might set up an affirmative duty to act on the basis of a special relationship: 'it may well be that, by voluntarily
undertaking to protect Joshua against a danger it concededly played no part in creating,
the State acquired a duty under state tort law to provide him with adequate protection
against that danger'.[784] This remedy was of little use to Joshua as the State of Wisconsin
had legislated a very low ceiling for its own liability for tort damages.[785] However,
that *obiter dictum* has kept conventional tort doctrine at the forefront of child abuse
litigation, and has provided a route for some State courts to evade the strictures of
DeShaney.

In *Brodie v Summit County Children Services Board*,[786] a case reminiscent of Victoria
Climbié's plight,[787] a court ordered the child protection agency to provide protective
services to a ten-year-old child who was subjected to starvation, torture and imprisonment by her father and stepmother. The case worker asked the mother and the
child's guardian to stop visiting the child because it disrupted her adjustment to living
with her father. The agency ignored other reports from the school and the police of

---

[780] *DeShaney v Winnebago* (n 212) 208–210.

[781] ibid 209–210. In *Jensen v Anderson County Dept of Social Services* (n 707) FN 3, the child protection
agency had actively discouraged relatives of the child from further action by warning that unfounded
reports of abuse might be subject to criminal action, and that they should not interfere with the relationship
between the mother and her child, whom she subsequently killed. Obviously most cases will fall far short
of this.   [782] *DeShaney v Winnebago* (n 212) 212.

[783] Kearney (n 355); Eaton and Wells (n 224); CA Crosby-Currie and ND Reppucci 'The Missing
Child in Child Protection: the Constitutional Context of Child Maltreatment from *Meyer* to *DeShaney*'
(1999) 21 Law & Policy 129; DA Bjorkland 'Crossing *DeShaney*: Can the Gap be Closed between Child
Abuse in the Home and the State's Duty to Protect?' (1990) 75 Iowa L Rev 791; A Sinden 'In Search of
Affirmative Duties toward Children under a Post-*DeShaney* Constitution' (1990) 139 U of Pennsylvania
L Rev 227; Blum (n 714).   [784] *DeShaney v Winnebago* (n 212) 201–202.

[785] Wisconsin's common law tort liability for Joshua DeShaney's injuries was limited to US$50,000:
Eaton and Wells (n 224) 134.   [786] *Brodie v Summit County Children's Services Board* (n 253).

[787] Discussed above, Chapter 5 section A.1.

continuing abuse. There was no further contact with the agency until the child was admitted to hospital in a comatose condition six months after the last complaint. The Ohio Supreme Court held that *DeShaney* did not bar an action for what the court characterized as negligent misfeasance rather than nonfeasance. The Ohio legislature expressly intended child welfare agencies to take responsibility for investigating and proceeding with appropriate action to prevent further child abuse or neglect in specific individual cases. Therefore qualified immunity for discretionary public functions exercised in good faith was not an available defence for the agency's negligent failure to perform mandatory ministerial acts such as launching an investigation within 24 hours.[788]

In *Sabia v State*,[789] sisters who were sexually molested by their stepfather throughout their early childhood and adolescence sued the Department of Social and Rehabilitation Services for negligence and intentional infliction of emotional distress. Employees of the Department had been repeatedly informed of the abuse over the years by several reliable sources as well as by the sisters themselves, but social workers failed to assist them. The Vermont Supreme Court held that a 'very special relationship' was established between a specifically identified abused child and the agency required by statute to protect her; social policy considerations warranted imposition of liability on the agency which knew the child was in danger and on which the child depended, not only to provide compensation but also to encourage the agency to perform its duty diligently in future.[790] The Court alternatively constructed a duty of care on a promise to the girls that action would be taken within days; this was used to establish a causal link to the harm, as the breach of that undertaking disheartened and deterred the girls from seeking help elsewhere, and sent a message to the perpetrator that he could act with impunity.[791]

In other cases where children have been killed after a non-custodial parent's reports of physical abuse to police and social services were ignored, liability has been imposed on the back of mandatory speedy investigation statutes construed as being enacted for the protection of threatened individuals rather than a duty owed to the general public.[792] The argument that this interpretation would render social services the guarantor of a particular child's safety has been firmly rejected.[793] The decision to classify a child

---

[788] *Brodie v Summit County Children's Services Board* (n 253). The same conclusion was reached in another brain damage case, *Gammons v North Carolina Department of Human Resources* 459 SE 2d 295 (North Carolina Supreme Ct 1995).   [789] *Sabia v State* (n 253).

[790] ibid 1195–1196.

[791] ibid 1194–1195. A similar ruling was made respecting a parallel claim against the social workers: *Sabia v Neville* 687 A 2d 469 (Vermont Supreme Ct 1996).

[792] *Mammo v State* (n 253); *Gonzalez v Avalos* (n 253); *Horridge v St Mary's County Department of Social Services* (n 710); *Jensen v Anderson County Department of Social Services* (n 707) 617–618; *Coleman v Cooper* 366 SE 2d 2 (North Carolina CA 1988) (social worker liable for failure to investigate allegations of physical abuse but police were not liable for failing to protect the two children from being murdered by their father as they had made no promises of protection to the children or the mother).

[793] *Horridge v St Mary's County Department of Social Services* ibid 1241.

inappropriately in a lower priority category was considered to be a ministerial function to which good faith immunity did not apply.[794]

A few State courts have recognized a private right of action against the State arising from the Federal Child Abuse Prevention and Treatment Act which sets out a statutory scheme which must be enacted by State legislatures to qualify for Federal grants.[795] Statutory requirements to conduct a prompt and *thorough* investigation of each reported incident of abuse, including seeing the child within 24 hours, attempting to have an on-site interview with the child's carer, and deciding on the safety of the child, were recently interpreted by the Maryland Court of Appeals as setting up a duty of care actionable under the State Tort Claims Act (even though inquiries into previous complaints had led to a decision to take no further action).[796] In *Jensen v Anderson County Department of Social Services*[797] the South Carolina Supreme Court interpreted a similarly worded provision the same way. Whilst a decision to classify a report of child abuse as 'unfounded' ordinarily would be discretionary as it involved the application of judgement to particular facts, if the file was closed because the investigation was incomplete and there were not enough facts upon which to make an informed decision, this breached the ministerial duty to conduct a thorough investigation and hence was actionable without proof of bad faith.[798] Therefore a social worker who decided not to pursue concerns about unexplained bruising of a three-year-old who said he was afraid of his mother's boyfriend, beyond speaking to the teacher who had contacted social services, could be sued in negligence when the man subsequently beat the child to death.

However, the preceding paragraphs do not represent a uniform picture of American States' common law tort liability. Some State courts have refused to set up a private right of action on the foundation of the Federal Child Abuse Prevention and Treatment Act,[799] or their own child abuse statutes.[800] They have shown themselves willing to classify anything beyond the most minimal initial action on receipt of a complaint as being discretionary and so presumptively non-actionable: to whom to speak, what type of information to seek, the possible use of various types of experts, determinations of witness credibility and recommendations to the appropriate authorities all call for discretion by the investigator and so are not actionable in the absence of bad faith.[801]

---

[794] *Gonzalez v Avalos* (n 253).

[795] *Marisol A by Forbes v Giuliani* 929 F Supp 662 (US DC New York 1996) motion denied 104 F 3d 524 (US CA 2nd Cir 1997) *certiorari* denied 520 US 1211 (USSC 1997); *Jordan v City of Philadelphia* 66 F Supp 2d 638 (US DC Pennsylvania 1999); *Turner v District of Columbia* (n 729).

[796] *Horridge v St Mary's County Department of Social Services* (n 710).

[797] *Jensen v Anderson County Department of Social Services* (n 707).   [798] ibid 619–620.

[799] *Tony L by and through Simpson v Childers* 71 F 3d 1182 (Kentucky CA 1995) *certiorari* denied 517 US 1212 (USSC 1996); *Jordan v City of Philadelphia* (n 795).

[800] *MH, DH and PT v State* (n 746) 536–537.

[801] eg *Purdy v Fleming* 655 NW 2d 424 (South Dakota Supreme Ct 2002).

To recap: only English law, as propounded in *X v Bedfordshire*, considers that a duty to investigate is owed to the public at large and not to the child at risk.[802] New Zealand, Canadian and some American courts have been prepared to construct a common law duty of care on the back of mandatory investigation requirements in child welfare legislation; in Australia the authority is as yet scant. A duty sounding in negligence is seen as an appropriate way to enforce the statutory duty to launch an investigation promptly. Most of these jurisdictions have constrained the scope of potential liability by protecting discretionary decisions made in good faith in the course of an investigation.

(b) Negligent investigation of an abuse allegation by social services

Misfeasance in the conduct of an investigation does not pose quite the same conceptual difficulties as does failing to investigate at all because the investigators have decided to take some action to protect the child, but here the issues of fact become more difficult to adjudicate. These are the delicate and difficult decisions described by Lord Browne-Wilkinson in *X v Bedfordshire* and by so many other courts. The decisions of social workers which might be the target of a negligence action could be to keep the child in the abusive environment on an assessment that the child was not at risk, or to return the child to that environment having previously decided to remove her. Or the impugned decision might be to remove the child from her family when the allegations were in fact unfounded. In relation to the police, the complaint of negligence might turn on the way that they collected the evidence and made decisions whether to prosecute. In relation to health professionals, the alleged negligence is likely to turn on a medical assessment as to whether the child has been sexually or physically abused or neglected.

(i) Liability of social services for negligent investigation in New Zealand law

We start with New Zealand law, because it was a New Zealand appeal which first signalled that the Law Lords were prepared to reconsider the blanket immunity spread over social workers in *X v Bedfordshire*. We have seen that in 1998 in *Prince* the New Zealand Court of Appeal held that social workers owe a duty of care to a child to investigate complaints.[803] The question whether this duty extended to an alleged failure to investigate *properly* arose the following year in *B v Attorney General of New Zealand*. B, a widower, had two daughters aged seven (D1) and five (D2). The younger child told a school friend that she had been sexually abused by her father. On the same day an investigation was launched by the sexual abuse team, the children were interviewed by a psychologist and social worker, and a court order was obtained placing them in foster care. The father was only then told what had happened by the police, who interviewed but did not charge him. The father after a nine-week trial ultimately obtained joint custody with his parents, who lived in England. The family was split up for three years. The father and the children sued the psychologist and the Department of Social Welfare for negligence in the way the interview and

---

[802] *X v Bedfordshire County Council* (n 73) 747.
[803] *Attorney General v Prince and Gardner* (n 35).

the investigation was conducted. They alleged that the psychologist failed to note or evaluate important factual errors such as D2's detailed description of an attic in her house when the psychologist knew the home was a single-storey building, and ignored the elder sister's denials that either of them had been abused. They also failed to follow up the younger child's statements early in the investigation to the medical examiner that she sometimes told lies, and to her father's friend that the allegations were untrue and that she had lied because she was allowed to tell lies at school.

The Court of Appeal struck out their claim on the basis that the common law duty recognized in *Prince* applied only to the 'triggering step' of arranging a 'prompt inquiry', and not to assembling relevant information before deciding whether to exercise statutory powers, as the statutory scheme would cut across a common law duty of care.[804] This created the seemingly anomalous result that social workers could be liable for nonfeasance but not for misfeasance.[805] The Privy Council on further appeal viewed the Court of Appeal's decision as emasculating the scope of the common law duty of care recognized in *Prince*'s case,[806] a surprisingly undeferential conclusion given that *Prince* had rejected *X v Bedfordshire* on the basis of the distinctive New Zealand culture of community expectations regarding civil servants responsible for child protection. Lord Nicholls for a unanimous committee held that the statutory obligation to arrange for a 'prompt inquiry' comprehended the duty to arrange and conduct an adequate inquiry: 'a duty to set an inquiry . . . in motion, but no duty to take reasonable steps to see that the inquiry duly proceeded, would be a poor sort of statutory duty'.[807] The legislation required an ongoing investigation and there was no reason why the common law duty of care should have a less extensive temporal scope. Lord Nicholls was careful to distinguish the investigatory obligation from decisions and assessments of what should be done in light of the evidence revealed by the investigation.[808] Therefore the psychologist and the individual social worker as well as the Department of Social Welfare owed a duty to both of the children to conduct a competent investigation, but not to the father as the alleged perpetrator of the abuse, as that would 'travel far outside the rationale' in *Prince*.[809]

(ii) Liability of social services for negligent investigation in English law

It seems that local authorities were resigned to the inevitability of a court holding that they owed a duty of care to children to conduct competent investigations for several years before the House of Lords gave a definitive ruling in *JD v East Berkshire*. In the 2001 decision of the Court of Appeal in *L (a Minor) and P (Father) v Reading Borough Council and Chief Constable of Thames Valley Police*,[810] which is more fully discussed in the next section concerning the liability of police investigators, the local authority

---

[804] *B v Attorney General of New Zealand* [1999] 2 NZLR 296 (New Zealand CA), affirming [1997] NZFLR 550 [26]–[28].   [805] Atkin and McLay (n 748).

[806] *B v Attorney General of New Zealand* [2003] UKPC 61, [2003] 4 All ER 833 (PC) [24], (n 35).

[807] ibid [25].   [808] ibid [27].   [809] ibid [30].

[810] *L (a Minor) and P (Father) v Reading Borough Council and Chief Constable of Thames Valley Police* (n 725).

did not apply to have struck out claims in negligence, conspiracy and misfeasance from a child and her father. The claimants pleaded that a social worker had engaged in 'outrageous and oppressive questioning' in the course of an interview of the child (then aged three) which was jointly conducted with a police child protection officer, and that notwithstanding that the interview did not disclose any sexual abuse whatsoever, the social worker informed a child protection case conference and later the family court that the child had given a detailed description of fellatio.[811]

Of the trio of cases against health professionals which were appealed to the House of Lords in *JD v East Berkshire*, in only one was the local authority also sued in negligence by the child and suspected parent. The court at first instance struck out the claim against the local authority on the basis that it was not fair, just, and reasonable to impose a duty of care on the investigation.[812] The local authority chose not to appeal further from the decision of the Court of Appeal to reinstate the child's claim against the local authority which, as we saw earlier, spelled the end to blanket immunity for investigators in child protection cases.[813] Thus far there have been no cases testing Lord Phillips' proviso that it is possible that there will be factual situations where it is not fair, just or reasonable to impose a duty of care, but each case will fall to be determined on its individual facts.[814]

It is difficult to conceive of facts which could block imposition of a duty of care to a child who is the subject of an investigation under the Children Act 1989.

That the duty of care does not automatically trigger liability is illustrated by *H v Bury Metropolitan Borough Council* in 2006.[815] The claimant when aged five months suffered rib fractures while in his parents' care. A family court made an interim order giving the Council parental responsibility, and directed that a full risk assessment be carried out. The child and his family resided in a family resource centre for 12 weeks for this assessment. Eight months after the injury, the court renewed the interim care order and the child was placed in foster care. It was then discovered that the child had brittle bone disease, and four months later the family was reunited. The local authority admitted that it owed the child a duty of care to 'carry out its reasonable plans of child protection in a professional manner' but disputed that any actionable damage had been caused to him.[816] The child had been diagnosed with a reactive attachment disorder, post-traumatic stress disorder and possibly autistic syndrome disorder, although the aetiology was in doubt. The parents separated as a consequence of their ordeal. The Court of Appeal upheld the trial judge's ruling that it was impossible to identify what psychological harm the child had suffered by his removal from his parents' care for four months, and that whatever harm he had suffered was transient and did not give rise to a claim in damages.[817]

---

[811] ibid 1580–1581.
[812] *MAK and RAK v Dewsbury Healthcare NHS Trust and Kirklees Metropolitan Council* [2003] Lloyds LR 13 (Leeds Cty Ct) [20].
[813] *JD v East Berkshire Community NHS Trust; MAK v Dewsbury Health Care NHS Trust; RK v Oldham NHS Trust* [2003] EWCA Civ 1151, [2003] 4 All ER 796 [81]–[84], discussed above section F.1(b)(ii).
[814] ibid [84].
[815] *H v Bury Metropolitan Borough Council* [2006] EWCA Civ 1, [2006] 1 WLR 917.
[816] ibid [33].   [817] ibid [82], [87].

(iii) Liability of social services for negligent investigation in Canadian law

A duty of care sounding in tort to conduct competent child protection investigations has been established in Canada since at least 1994, and indeed provincial child protection authorities seldom contest the issue, instead denying that they have breached the standard of care.[818] The duty is owed to the child and sometimes also to the suspected parent or carer.[819]

B v Children's Aid Society of Durham Region is instructive in how liability may be incurred and good faith refuted. In Ontario the Children's Aid Society for each region had statutory responsibility for child protection. A respected Anglican minister and his two adopted daughters, aged 4 years and 18 months at the time events began, sued the Children's Aid Society for negligence in investigating allegations of sexual abuse made by his estranged wife. She had left the matrimonial home with the children, accompanied by a convicted child rapist who had been living in their home on his release from prison. The complaint was that the father took too long in changing the baby's nappy and applying cream to her vaginal area to combat an infection. Two doctors examined the child and found no evidence of sexual abuse but in accordance with the statutory reporting requirements contacted the Children's Aid Society. The caseworker immediately formed the view that the father was guilty of sexual abuse after she interviewed the mother and the older daughter. Protracted proceedings culminated in a 51-day hearing, when the judge dismissed the child protection application, absolved the father of all allegations of sexual abuse and awarded him sole custody of the children with no access by the mother. In the professional negligence action, the caseworker's conduct was found to be tainted by bias and to fall well below the standard of care expected of a professional social worker (as established by expert evidence) in the following respects:

- She failed to follow up with the doctors and to conduct a full and complete interview with them; had she done so they would have said there was no physical evidence of sexual abuse.

- She failed to interview the father and refused to meet with him to hear his side of the story.

- She failed to follow up with the police and she did not have the mother and children interviewed by a police officer experienced in child abuse.

- She failed to properly record her interviews with the mother and the older daughter, and to make timely and accurate notes.

- She failed to consider the source of the allegations and the motivation behind them (the context being a bitter custody dispute, and the mother's reluctance to allow

---

[818] *CH v British Columbia* 2004 BCCA 385, 242 DLR (4th) 470 (British Columbia CA) [4]; *LC and LS v British Columbia* 2005 BCSC 1668, 49 BCLR (4th) 164 (British Columbia Supreme Ct) [97].

[819] *B(D), B(R) and B(M) v Children's Aid Society of Durham Region* (n 695) 304; *G(A) v British Columbia (Superintendent of Family & Child Services)* (1989) 61 DLR (4th) 136 (British Columbia CA) [34]; *LC and LS v British Columbia* ibid [130], declining to apply *JD v East Berkshire Community NHS Trust et al* (HL) (n 580) 373.

the father any access because she had moved from the area and was required by court order to bring them to him).

- Due to lack of training and experience she was unable to keep an open mind and conduct a fair and balanced investigation.
- She was willing to allow the mother to act as a co-investigator, telling the mother what questions to ask the children at home.[820]

The statutory defence of good faith was held not to immunize the finding of professional negligence, notwithstanding that the caseworker was conscientious and hard-working, and thought she was acting in the best interests of the children, for the following reasons:[821]

- The caseworker knowingly filed a false and misleading affidavit in support of the application for an emergency interim protection order, even though the geographic distance meant that the father could not pose an immediate risk to the children.
- She ensured by design that the father would not be notified of the interim protection proceeding, the trial judge describing her conduct as 'a declaration of all-out war'.[822]
- She closed her mind to any other avenues of investigation such as contacting the doctors and the police.
- She ignored evidence that should have raised serious concerns about the mother's inappropriate and possibly sexualized conduct toward the children, and her motivation for implicating the father.
- She viewed the father's conduct toward the children with hostility, cynicism and suspicion; notwithstanding that he drove 1,200 miles for one hour of supervised access per week she considered that his avowals of love for his children were artificial.
- She turned a deaf ear to the father's protestations of innocence and ignored information from him which should have led to further investigation.
- She prepared a report for a colleague that portrayed the father as demonic and the mother as a sympathetic victim of abuse.

The Society on the 16th day of the hearing concluded that the father was not a risk to the children, and offered to settle on the condition that the father would bear his own substantial legal costs, which he refused to do. The Society continued to run the court case for a further 35 days on the basis that the children were in need of protection from their father, conduct which the trial judge described as 'utterly unconscionable and indefensible'.

The children were awarded a low level of damages for the emotional distress and disruption to their lives, and the father received substantial damages for his stress-induced depression, his out-of-pocket costs, and also punitive damages of CDN$10,000. The Ontario Court of Appeal affirmed the trial judge's finding of both negligence and lack of good faith on the part of the Society in the execution of its statutory duty, holding

---

[820] *B(D), B(R) and B(M) v Children's Aid Society of Durham Region* ibid 301.   [821] ibid 303.
[822] *B(D), B(R) and B(M) v Children's Aid Society of Durham Region* [1994] OJ No 643 (Ontario Gen Div) [97].

that the findings of fact revealed an investigation tainted by bias and lack of good faith, culminating in a course of conduct akin to malicious prosecution.[823]

Thus the standard of care imposed on the social worker was set realistically low and should have been readily satisfied: to conduct a balanced, fair and thorough investigation so as to ensure that allegations are reasonably substantiated, by seeking relevant information from available sources and being careful not to be biased in favour of one parent.[824] Of the handful of other actions for negligent investigation against Canadian child protection agencies which have reached trial,[825] few have succeeded, compared to the plethora of negligence cases involving foster care placements.[826]

In contrast to Canada, there have been many negligence actions brought in American courts against child protection agencies for failure to comply with their statutory duty to investigate complaints promptly,[827] but because these are almost invariably coupled with claims of infringement of constitutional rights to due process, they are best analysed in that context below.[828]

(c) Negligent investigation of an abuse allegation by police child protection officers

The negligence liability of police investigators can be conceptualized in two ways: as a failure to protect the child from harm at the hands of a third party, and as a failure to control that third party. In this latter sense the liability of child protection officers is distinct from other investigators of child abuse allegations, because they have the power to arrest and lay criminal charges against the suspected perpetrator.

(i) Liability of police for negligent investigation in English law

We have seen that the House of Lords has signalled its willingness to reconsider the immunity for the police in the conduct of criminal investigations conferred by *Hill v Chief Constable of West Yorkshire*.[829] As discussed, the impetus was provided by the ruling of the ECtHR in *Osman v UK* that the UK had breached Article 6 of the ECHR when the Court of Appeal had struck out an action alleging that the police failed to protect a child's safety after they had received repeated reports that he was being stalked by a mentally imbalanced and violent teacher.[830] The negligence pleaded lay in part in failing to execute an arrest warrant beyond simply checking to see if the teacher was at home during school hours. Thus Ahmet Osman's claim

---

[823] *B(D), B(R) and B(M) v Children's Aid Society* (n 695) 303, 304.

[824] According to the expert testimony adduced at trial from a social worker experienced in child abuse investigations *B(D), B(R) and B(M) v Children's Aid Society of Durham Region* (n 822) [51]–[77].

[825] *KJ and MT* [1999] BCJ No 2909 (British Columbia Supreme Ct) (social worker's unprofessional conduct in entering into personal relationship with father in a custody dispute with the mother caused no compensable harm to the child or the mother); *G(A) v British Columbia (Superintendent of Family & Child Services)* (n 819) (good faith immunized errors of judgement in taking seven siblings into care); *LC and LS v British Columbia* (n 818) [145]–[147] (social workers acted within their discretion and in good faith in taking interim custody of a seven-week-old infant with a severe skull fracture in light of the conflicting medical evidence). [826] Discussed below, section F.3.

[827] Child Abuse Prevention and Treatment and Adoption Reform Act 42 USCA ch 67 §5106a s (b)(2)(A)(iv). [828] Discussed below, section F.5.

[829] *Hill v Chief Constable of West Yorkshire* (n 48); *Brooks v Metropolitan Police* (n 677), discussed above, section F.1(b). [830] *Osman v Ferguson* (n 635) *Osman v UK* (n 639).

turned on their failure to protect him and his family by controlling the source of the risk. The police's alleged specific duty to control the suspected perpetrator arose due to the family's eight previous complaints about criminal damage and other acts in a campaign of escalating aggressive harassment committed by the teacher, and the assurances they and the school authorities claimed to have received from the police about their safety.[831] Yet no measures had been put in place to protect the child and his family when the teacher invaded their house and seriously wounded the child and shot dead his father, and then drove to the home of the deputy headteacher whom he shot and wounded and whose son he also killed. These facts indicate how extreme the circumstances in *Osman* were. Sadly however it is not unusual for a child to be at risk from a violent and irrational adult, and for the police to be aware of this from previous incidents of threats or domestic violence in the household. Such a case does show however the difficulties in locating investigatory decisions on the policy/operational continuum; the decision to issue the arrest warrant might be considered to be non-justiciable discretion, but the later failure to make any further attempt to execute it might be considered an operational omission to implement that decision, and hence justiciable.

The tide against absolute immunity for police investigations had already turned in 2001 when the Court of Appeal declined to strike out a negligence action by a child and her father against the Thames Valley Police and social services based upon their investigation of a complaint of very serious sexual abuse made by her mother.[832] A social worker and a police officer interviewed the three-year-old over two days. The first interview was not video-recorded nor were any contemporaneous notes made. The second was video-recorded and was conducted in a manner that was strongly criticized by HHJ Kenny in the family court:

These statements were grossly misleading. I am appalled that two professional persons engaged in child protection work should have been so unscrupulous in seeking to prove that sexual abuse had occurred, rather than to establish the facts. They show a degree of prurience and an appetite for a witch hunt that are really shocking. It also shows a complete disregard of the child's interests and the importance of her not having her relationship with her father ruined, and her childhood overshadowed by unfounded suspicions and accusations.[833]

The claimants alleged that the interview was conducted improperly and was grossly unfair to the child and her father, pestering the child until she became upset whilst eliciting no evidence of improper conduct by her father (she said her mother also played the game interpreted as sexual by the interviewers). Yet the interviewers concluded that the complaint by her mother was well founded and that she was at risk of further abuse, and social services proceeded with the care application. The police

---

[831] For a more detailed analysis of the facts pleaded in *Osman*, see Hoyano 'Policing Flawed Police Investigations' (n 219), 913–915.

[832] *L (a Minor) and P (Father) v Reading Borough Council and Chief Constable of Thames Valley Police* (n 725). We have already noted that social services did not apply to strike out the action against them: section F.2(b)(ii).

[833] Quoted in *J and another v Reading Borough Council and Thames Valley Police* [2002] EWHC 2905 (QBD) [13].

did not proceed with a prosecution. It subsequently transpired that the mother suffered from Munchausen's syndrome by proxy and that her allegations of abuse were fabricated.

The Court of Appeal refused the Chief Constable's application to strike out the statements of claim of the child and her father pleading negligence, conspiracy and misfeasance in public office. Otton LJ held that there was an arguable case that police and social services interviewers form a special relationship with a child whom they interview, to investigate not merely past events, but also to protect her from future harm. This takes the relationship outside the usual situation in interviewing a potential victim of crime, as the police are not solely performing a function for the benefit of the public. They assume responsibility to prevent the investigation itself from harming her, as there is a real risk of interference with family life.[834]

However there was no proximity of relationship formed with the father as a suspect in a potential crime in the course of his police interview. This changed when, notwithstanding there was no evidence to support criminal proceedings, the investigating officer concluded that the child had been abused and was at risk of further harm from her father, and reported this to her superior with a view to triggering the unfounded family proceedings. It was arguable that from then on there was a legal assumption of responsibility and a special relationship formed between the police officer and the social worker on the one hand and the father on the other, and that a duty of care arose to take reasonable steps not to damage the father by their subsequent conduct.[835] The balancing of policy and public interest considerations at the third stage of the *Caparo* duty of care test could best be done at trial.

The claims of both child and parent in the bad faith torts of misfeasance in a public office and conspiracy to injure were also allowed to proceed to trial. Whilst any malice was not targeted at the child, she was caught in the crossfire and was foreseeably harmed by the allegedly reckless conduct and conspiracy directed at the father; it was a matter for evidence at trial as to whether the police officer and social worker consciously decided dishonestly to misrepresent the content of the child's interview.[836] The Court of Appeal also held that the doctrine of witness immunity did not apply to things done by the police during the investigative process which could not fairly be said to form part of their participation in the judicial process as witnesses, and in particular could not extend to cover the fabrication of evidence arguably designed to defeat the ends of justice by causing family proceedings to be initiated which were based on groundless allegations of abuse.[837]

The investigatory immunity conferred by *Hill* may soon be put to the test. On 26 July 2006 the Independent Police Complaints Commission issued a report critical of the handling by the South Wales police of the abduction by Craig Sweeney, a convicted paedophile, of a three-year-old girl from her home. Despite the police immediately being told the perpetrator's identity and address and a description of

---

[834] *L (a Minor) and P (Father) v Reading Borough Council and Chief Constable of Thames Valley Police* (n 725) 1583. [835] ibid 1583–1584.

[836] ibid 1588–1590.

[837] ibid 1591–1594, applying *Darker v Chief Constable of West Midlands* (n 719).

the vehicle, Sweeney was not apprehended until three hours later when he crashed his car (in which the child was a passenger) in Wiltshire, whilst being pursued by police (who were not aware of the abduction). Sweeney had already seriously sexually assaulted the child in his home in Wales. The delayed and ineffective response was partly attributed to the failure of the police force to access and collate the information in its possession about the incident and about Sweeney, in particular data (which had not been updated) on the Violent and Sex Offender Register. The failure is thus reminiscent of *Hill*. The Commission concluded that had proper procedures been followed, Sweeney's vehicle would been identified within 15 minutes of the reported abduction. The Commission found insufficient evidence to substantiate the allegation that this would have prevented the sexual assault at his house. However, the Commission did find that prompt and appropriate police action might have spared the child from a further terrifying ordeal when Sweeney was able to leave his home and cross the Severn Bridge into England.[838] Upon release of the report, the child's parents announced that they intend to sue the police force in negligence.

(ii) Liability of police for negligent investigation in Canadian law

As indicated earlier,[839] Quebec and Ontario courts have recognized a tort of negligent police investigation for the past decade, rejecting *Hill v Constable of West Yorkshire*.[840] The courts in other Canadian provinces have been more reluctant to recognize negligent criminal investigation as a cause of action, concerned that it might supplant the bad faith torts such as malicious prosecution and conspiracy with their higher thresholds for liability.[841] The Supreme Court of Canada has granted leave to appeal on a case which will settle this point definitively for Canadian common law jurisdictions.[842] The test of liability, whether the police had reasonable and probable grounds to investigate and lay charges or take other actions, was readily satisfied in the one child abuse case thus far in which the police have been sued for a negligent investigation of sexual and physical abuse; while the adolescent later admitted to fabricating the allegations, as a consequence of which both she and her youngest sister were taken into foster care, there had been corroborative evidence which lent plausibility to her statements, and the police had kept her credibility under constant review.[843]

---

[838] Independent Police Complaints Commission *Independent Investigation into the Police Response to the Report of the Abduction of Child A from Her Home in Rumney on 2 January 2006* (26 July 2006) 6, 27, 37–43.   [839] Discussed above, section F.1(b)(v).
[840] *Hill v Chief Constable of West Yorkshire* (n 48).
[841] *AAD, TD and KGD v Tanner, Winnipeg Child and Family Services Agency* (n 695) [136]–[148]; *Dix v Canada (Attorney General)* 2000 ABQB 580, [2003] 1 WWR 436 (Alberta QB) [558]–[559]; *Kleysen v Canada (Attorney General)* [2001] MJ No 350 (Manitoba QB) [5].
[842] *Hill v Hamilton-Wentworth Regional Police Services Board* (n 693) (leave to appeal granted by SCC 27 April 2006) [54]–[71].
[843] *AAD, TD and KGD v Tanner, Winnipeg Child and Family Services Agency* (n 695) [182]–[187].

The Canadian analogue of *Osman* is *Bonnie Mooney v Attorney General (Canada)*.[844] Mooney had been the repeated victim of domestic violence at the hands of her former partner, who had an extensive criminal record of violence. She made a complaint to the local detachment of the Royal Canadian Mounted Police (RCMP) that he had just chased her through the town in a vehicle, in breach of the terms of his probation for a previous brutal assault on her which had been witnessed by her 12-year-old daughter. The RCMP Constable made only a very perfunctory investigation, in breach of the protocol for giving domestic violence cases immediate priority and a thorough investigation, especially where the offender has breached court orders to protect the victim. Seven weeks later the man invaded her home with a shotgun, killed a neighbour and shot and wounded the 12-year-old daughter; Mooney and her six-year-old daughter were able to escape before he set the house on fire and killed himself. An internal investigation of their complaint found that the constable had acted unprofessionally in failing to conduct an adequate investigation of the breach of probation. The British Columbia Court of Appeal by a majority upheld the ruling of the trial judge that the children and their mother could not establish that the police's negligent investigation of her previous complaint had any factual causal connection with the murderous rampage several weeks later, rejecting English authority that a material increase in risk in some circumstances may be sufficient to bridge an evidential gap in causation.[845]

(iii) Liability of police for negligent investigation in Australian law

Australian appellate courts have yet to determine definitively whether to follow *Hill* in immunizing the police from liability for negligence in relation to their statutory powers to arrest and control criminal wrongdoers. In the Tasmanian analogue of *Osman* a child sued the police for their handling of a complaint by his mother about a serious assault and threats to kill committed by his father. Police officers did not obtain an arrest warrant, contrary to their domestic violence policy, but instead accompanied the mother to the family home to collect the father's firearms. They noted that one was missing, but then allowed the mother to remain alone inside the house, which enabled the father to shoot her dead through a window, and then to kill himself. The Tasmanian Supreme Court refused to strike out the child's claim in relation to the mother's death under the Fatal Accidents Act, preferring to follow Canadian and New Zealand authorities which declined to adopt the *Hill* doctrine of police immunity.[846] It was also arguable that the child was owed a duty of care by the police to protect him from the risk of consequent psychological injury from being told of the killings, as

---

[844] *BM [Bonnie Mooney], MM and KM v Attorney General (British Columbia) and Attorney General (Canada)* (n 696).

[845] ibid [140]–[144] (Hall JA), [167]–[168] (Smith JA), distinguishing *Fairchild v Glenhaven Funeral Services Ltd* (n 362). For criticism of the causation analysis see MI Hall 'Duty, Causation and Third-Party Perpetrators: the Bonnie Mooney Case' (2005) 50 McGill LJ 597.

[846] *Batchelor v Tasmania* [2005] TASSC 11 (Tasmania Supreme Ct) [22]–[26]. The child's claim under the Fatal Accidents Act in respect of his father's death was struck out on the basis that police officers do not have a duty of care to prevent suicides by exercising their arrest powers [32].

in Tasmanian law such claims are actionable without the victim having to have been present at the traumatic event.[847]

Thus far the issue of the liability of the police for negligently investigating an allegation of child abuse does not appear to have been litigated in Australia. There is a case in South Australia relating to a duty to control an offender, where *Hill* and *Osman v Ferguson* were held not to apply. The claimant aged eight (and seven other boys) was repeatedly raped by a paedophile who was supposed to be under the close supervision of the parole board following his release from prison for abduction and sexual offences against boys. The South Australia Supreme Court held that the parole board did not owe any duty of care to members of the public at large as to the manner in which it exercised its powers to release and supervise convicted persons. However, a duty of care did arise to the claimant when the parole board became aware that the paedophile had blatantly breached his parole conditions not to have unsupervised contact with children under 14, and that boys were staying overnight in his flat, but accepted his lies that another adult was present without further inquiry or surveillance.[848]

To recap, most Commonwealth jurisdictions acknowledge at least the possibility that the police may incur tort liability for the manner in which they conduct investigations, where a known person was at risk from an identified perpetrator but they have failed to protect her. The trickiest task is proving causation. This will be less problematic where there is close proximity in time and space between the complaint to the police and the subsequent commission of the crime against the claimant.

English law has already addressed the alternative scenario, where the police have subjected a child who was not a victim to a form of interviewing and a process which is positively harmful to her. The children taken into care in the Rochdale 'satanic ritual abuse' scandal are now suing the police and social services for subjecting them to abusive investigative techniques and wrongfully wresting them from their homes and families,[849] suggesting that *L and P v Reading Borough Council* may not remain an isolated and exceptional case.

(d) Negligent investigation of an abuse allegation by health professionals and health authorities

Medical professionals often play a crucial role in the instigation and verification of concerns about child abuse. Potential negligence liability to a child may arise from a misdiagnosis leading to an erroneous opinion that a child has or has not been the victim of abuse. In jurisdictions with mandatory reporting legislation, civil liability may also be constructed on the basis of nonfeasance. It might also take a different form where it is alleged that the patient is the abuser, and the competence of the physician in treating the patient or in assessing the risk he posed for children will be in issue. It

---

[847] ibid [34]. This is contrary to the general position of English law on the negligent infliction of psychiatric injury: *Alcock v Chief Constable of South Yorkshire* (n 201), but in the specific context of a parent being told his children had been abused see *W v Essex County Council* (n 653), discussed below, section F.3(a)(i).

[848] *Swan v South Australia* (1994) 62 SASR 532 (South Australia Supreme Ct) 548–549, 551–552.

[849] *Rochdale BC v A and Others* [1991] 2 FLR 192 (Fam Div, Douglas Brown J); *BBC News* 9 January 2006.

is also possible that the physician may incur liability for failing to warn the authorities or a person known to be at specific risk from a dangerous patient.[850] We will consider each form of potential liability, and then discuss the immunities for reporters and witnesses which provide a large measure of protection to health professionals involved in child abuse cases.

(i) Misdiagnosis of abuse or neglect

It is a fundamental premise of the doctor–patient relationship that the doctor owes a duty of care to the patient to provide a reasonably competent diagnosis and treatment. So it is odd that it should ever have been questioned in the English courts that a child patient could sue a physician or health authority for clinical negligence in making an erroneous diagnosis as to whether she had or had not been sexually or physically abused. It was only because of the blanket immunity provided to social services in *X v Bedfordshire* and to the police in *Hill* that the possibility arose of a similar immunity for health professionals instigating or otherwise involved in a child abuse investigation. In the *Newham* case, where the child had been wrongly taken into care on the basis of a misidentification of her abuser, the House of Lords held that the psychiatrist who interviewed the child had been retained to advise the local authority, and so did not assume any general professional duty to the child, since she was not asked to treat her.[851] The objection to this reasoning is that the psychiatrist was being asked to make a professional diagnosis as to whether the child had been sexually abused, a medical conclusion from which treatment might or might not follow.

In the three conjoined appeals in *JD v East Berkshire*, it was alleged that medical negligence triggered the child abuse investigations. In each case the parents had voluntarily sought medical advice in relation to their child's physical symptoms. In *JD v East Berkshire NHS Trust* the child's very serious multiple allergies were not treated because a consultant paediatrician had concluded that the mother had Munchausen's syndrome by proxy and so she had fabricated the allergic attacks; the boy was placed on the 'at-risk' register for several months. In *RK v Dewsbury Healthcare NHS Trust* a girl aged nine suffered from progressive pigmented purpuric dermatitis which caused purple patches to erupt on the skin, but she was diagnosed as having been sexually and physically abused; her father was excluded from their house for several weeks. In *MK v Oldham NHS Trust* a two-month-old baby with a spiral fracture to the femur suffered from brittle bone disease which was not discovered until she had another fracture eight months later whilst in foster care. Lord Brown remarked that if the allegations were well founded in these three cases, the doctors appeared to have displayed 'an egregious over-confidence in their own opinions and a marked reluctance to test them'.[852] In all three cases the parents sued the health authorities for psychiatric injury arising from the erroneous diagnoses, whereas only in the Dewsbury case was the affected child joined as a claimant in the action. Judge Grenville at first instance allowed the child's claim against the health authority to proceed on the basis that the diagnosis predated

---

[850] *Tarasoff v Regents of the University of California* 551 P 2d 334 (California Supreme Ct 1976).
[851] *M v Newham Borough Council*, reported with *X v Bedfordshire County Council* (n 73) 752–753.
[852] *JD v East Berkshire Community NHS Trust et al* (HL) (n 580) [122].

the involvement of social services, at which point public policy precluded a finding of a duty of care.[853] The Court of Appeal, as we discussed earlier,[854] held that public policy immunity no longer prevented a duty of care owed by professionals involved in child protection to the affected child from arising.[855] In the House of Lords, Lord Bingham concluded that 'it could not now be plausibly argued that the common law duty of care may not be owed by a publicly-employed healthcare professional to a child with whom the professional is dealing', the other Law Lords concurring on this point.[856]

(ii) Failure to report suspected abuse to the authorities

In issue here is a doctor's obligation where she suspects that her patient may be the victim or the perpetrator of abuse but fails to act on that suspicion. There is no statutory obligation imposed on English and Welsh health and childcare professionals to report suspicions of child abuse. In contrast, all American States, all Canadian Provinces and most Australian States have enacted legislation requiring health professionals, amongst others, to report suspicions of abuse to the child welfare authorities, with criminal and sometimes also disciplinary sanctions for non-compliance, but breaches are rarely penalized.[857] The issue then arises as to whether an action in negligence or for breach of statutory duty can be built on the back of non-compliance with such statutes.

Dealing first with liability respecting the patient as victim, child abuse reporting statutes in some American States expressly create a private cause of action by a child who can prove that the failure to report was a proximate cause of further injury to him.[858] In California the mandatory reporting legislation has been construed as setting up potential liability in the tort of breach of statutory duty and negligence, provided that the physician actually formed the view that the child's injuries were intentionally inflicted.[859] Most American courts have not adopted the same interpretation; some have regarded the reporting requirement as setting up the standard of care and also breach—as either prima facie or conclusive[860] proof of negligence—but the claimant

---

[853] *MAK and RAK v Dewsbury Healthcare NHS Trust* (n 812) [29].

[854] Above, section F.2(b)(ii).

[855] *JD v East Berkshire Community NHS Trust* (CA) (n 669) [108]–[109].

[856] *JD v East Berkshire Community NHS Trust et al* (HL) (n 580) [30] (Lord Bingham), [106], [110] (Lord Rodger), [124] (Lord Brown).

[857] The merits of mandatory reporting systems are discussed below, Chapter 5 section D. For a Canadian perspective on the difficulties such systems create, see M Bailey 'The Failure of Physicians to Report Child Abuse' (1982) 40 U of Toronto Faculty L Rev 49.

[858] Including Arkansas, Colorado, Iowa, Michigan, Montana, New York, and Rhode Island, as noted in *Arbaugh v Board of Education, County of Pendleton* (n 252) 239 n 3; TL Gowen and RJ Kohlman 'Professional Liability for Failure to Report Child Abuse' 38 Am Jur Trials 1 (updated to June 2006) §26.

[859] *Landeros v Flood* (n 251) 415 (a severely beaten baby was returned by a hospital to her mother and stepfather, who resumed physically abusing her, inflicting very serious injuries).

[860] Known as the 'negligence per se doctrine'. *Landeros v Flood* ibid 396–397 found liability under this doctrine in the alternative to breach of statutory duty; Gowen and Kohlman (n 858) §25.

still has to establish a common law duty of care to 'rescue' the child from the abuser, which many courts have refused to do.[861]

In Canada there has been only one reported case of a physician being sued for breaching his statutory duty to report suspected abuse to the child welfare authorities. In *Brown v University of Alberta Hospital*[862] a ten-week-old baby was admitted to hospital with bilateral subdural haematoma. The neuro-radiologist was aware that this injury was consistent with shaken baby syndrome and contradicted the parents' explanation that she had fallen off the sofa, but failed to warn the treating paediatrician that the injuries were likely to be non-accidental. A few days later the baby was again admitted to hospital with fresh injuries resulting in severe and permanent brain damage. The court in the tort action found that both sets of injuries had been deliberately inflicted by the father. The neuro-radiologist was found to have breached a duty of care to the baby and to her mother to warn the paediatrician and the child welfare authorities, on the basis of 'common sense, hospital policy and precise legislation [sic] mandate'.[863]

Where the patient is the alleged perpetrator, the medical professional is still bound by the statutory reporting provisions.[864] However, in America attempts by representatives of abused or murdered children to sue parties under reporting obligations for failure to report previous offences by the same perpetrator against another unrelated child have generally failed.[865]

A common law duty to warn may provide an alternative route to liability in the absence of an applicable reporting statute, on the basis that the professional has a special relationship with the abuser. In the controversial case of *Tarasoff v Regents of the University of California*[866] the California Supreme Court held that when a psychotherapist determines, or pursuant to the standards of his profession should determine, that his patient presents a serious threat of violence directed at an identified person, he incurs a legal obligation to use reasonable care to protect the intended victim against such danger by warning her.[867] 'The protective privilege ends where the public peril begins'.[868] The Court further held that the decision whether to warn was not a discretionary act which could shelter behind the immunity provisions of the California Government Code. The *Tarasoff* doctrine has subsequently been restricted in its application to cases of specific threats against specific individuals.

---

[861] *Cuyler v US* 362 F 3d 949 (US CA 7th Cir 2004); *Perry v SN* (n 252); *Fischer v Metcalf* (n 252); *Arbaugh v Board of Education, County of Pendleton* (n 252); *Cechman v Travis and Hospital Authority of Gwinnett County* 414 SE 2d 282 (Georgia CA 1991) 257–258; *Marquay v Eno* (n 403); *Doe v Marion* 605 SE 2d 556 (New Hampshire CA 2004).

[862] *Brown v University of Alberta Hospital* (1997) 145 DLR (4th) 63 (Alberta QB).

[863] ibid [195]–[203].

[864] *State ex rel Juvenile Department of Multnomah County v Spencer* 108 P 3d 1189 (Oregon CA 2005).

[865] *Cuyler v US* (n 861) (doctor who failed to report physical abuse of a baby by a childminder could not be sued by the estate of another baby killed by the childminder 28 days later); *Arbaugh v Board of Education, County of Pendleton* (n 252); *Marcelletti v Bathani* 500 NW 2d 124 (Michigan CA 1993), appeal denied 505 NW 2d 582 (Michigan Supreme Ct 1993); *Doe v Marion* (n 861).

[866] *Tarasoff v Regents of the University of California* (n 850).

[867] ibid 340.   [868] ibid 347.

Thus a psychiatrist treating a physician for his paedophilia was not obliged to warn all foreseeable child patients with whom he might come into contact,[869] and County officials who released a juvenile from custody knowing that he had dangerous and violent propensities toward young children did not have a duty to warn the parents of such children in his neighbourhood.[870] Justice Cory of the Supreme Court of Canada in considering these decisions has suggested that it will not always be necessary in Canadian law to identify a specific individual as the victim; rather it may be sufficient to engage the duty to warn if the class of victims, such as little girls under five living in a specific area, is clearly identified.[871]

The concept of a duty to warn in English law was broached in *Palmer v Tees Health Authority*.[872] Rosie Palmer, aged four, was abducted, sexually assaulted and murdered by Armstrong, a man living on her street in Hartlepool. For more than two years preceding this attack Armstrong had been treated as an inpatient and outpatient by the health authority's general hospital for a personality disorder or psychopathic personality arising from an extremely disturbed childhood. Whilst in the hospital he told medical staff that he had sexual feelings towards children and that a child would be murdered after his discharge. The child's estate and her mother sued the health authority for negligence in failing to carry out any adequate assessment and diagnosis of Armstrong's mental condition, to provide any adequate treatment and to make an evaluation of the risk which Armstrong posed to others. The Court of Appeal struck out both claims. Stuart-Smith LJ held that there was insufficient proximity of relationship between Rosie and the health authority. He suggested that it would be (at least) necessary for the potential victim to be identifiable to establish proximity, as the most effective way of providing protection would be to warn the victim, her parents or social services so that some protective measures could be taken. He reserved his position as to whether assumption of responsibility by a physician to treat the patient might suffice for proximity if the victim was a child in the household of the abuser.[873] The idea of a duty to warn sounding in negligence may re-emerge in the wake of the current controversy over whether England should adopt its own version of the American 'Megan's Law' requiring that a community be notified of a paedophile residing in the vicinity.

Reporting statutes and common law duties to warn raise issues of trust and confidentiality between the patient posing a risk to children and his physician and the health service. Reporting statutes usually abrogate any professional obligation of confidentiality to the perpetrator,[874] and equivalent exceptions may also be developed at common law. The Supreme Court of Canada has ruled that a psychiatrist was not bound by doctor–patient confidentiality nor by legal professional privilege to withhold information from the prosecution and the police that an accused whom he was assessing on behalf of the defence was highly dangerous, and would

---

[869] *Doe v Marion* (n 861) 561.

[870] *Thompson v County of Alameda* 614 P 2d 728 (California Supreme Ct 1980).

[871] *Smith v Jones and Southam, Inc* [1999] 1 SCR 455 (SCC) [68] (Cory J, *obiter*).

[872] *Palmer v Tees Health Authority* (n 645).   [873] ibid [31]–[32].

[874] eg *People v Gearhart* 560 NYS 2d 247 (New York Cty Ct 1990) (physician could testify as to incriminating statements made by defendant in criminal proceedings for child abuse).

more likely than not commit future offences unless he received treatment. Public safety outweighs solicitor–client privilege where (1) there is a clear risk to an identifiable person or group of persons; (2) there is a risk of serious bodily harm or death; and (3) the danger is imminent.[875] While English appellate courts have not yet had to consider whether there is a public safety exception to litigation privilege or legal advice privilege, the House of Lords has held that legal professional privilege is absolute and cannot be abrogated where the innocence of another person is at stake in criminal proceedings,[876] so it is possible that they might differ from the Canadian Supreme Court on this issue.[877] However, if a medical professional retained for the purposes of family court proceedings forms the view that a child might be at risk from a particular person, then the principle of the paramountcy of the child's best interests would prevail over any legal professional privilege.[878]

(iii) Immunity from civil liability for reporters of suspected abuse

In American, Canadian and Australian mandatory reporting statutes, the obligation is often coupled with immunity from civil and criminal liability for having made the report. Usually this immunity is conditional upon the report having been made in good faith, but in California the immunity is absolute for mandatory (but not discretionary) reporters, and so applies even when the suspicion was not reasonable,[879] and arguably even where a false report is maliciously filed.[880] Many American courts regard this form of good faith immunity as subjective and so to be determined by the trier of fact,[881] in contrast to the qualified immunity which shields government officials performing discretionary functions where an objective test is applied to determine whether they should have known that their conduct violated statutory or constitutional law.[882] Some reporting statutes require (or are construed as requiring) proof of reasonable cause for making the report, which is interpreted as requiring objective good faith.[883]

---

[875] *Smith v Jones* (n 871), discussed below, Chapter 7 section C.3(c).

[876] *R v Derby Magistrates' Court ex p B* (n 16).

[877] There is however earlier Court of Appeal authority to the contrary: *W v Egdell* [1990] 1 All ER 835 (CA) (psychiatrist retained by solicitor for a serial killer was not liable for breach of confidence in forwarding his report that he was still dangerous to the mental institution in which he was detained, notwithstanding that the solicitor had refused consent).

[878] *Re L (A Minor) (Police Investigation: Privilege)* [1997] AC 16 (HL), discussed below Chapter 7 section A.2.   [879] *Stecks v Young* 38 Cal App 4th 365 (California CA 4th Dist 1995).

[880] Gowen and Kohlman (n 858) §30.

[881] *Wojcik v Town of North Smithfield* 874 F Supp 508 (Rhode Island Dist Ct 1995).

[882] *Harlow v Fitzgerald* (n 738) 818; *Anderson v Creighton* 483 US 635 (USSC 1987) 646, discussed further below, section F.5(a)(i).

[883] eg *Blaney v O'Heron* 568 SE 2d 774 (Georgia CA 2002); *Warner v Mitts* 536 NW 2d 564 (Michigan CA 1995); *FA by PA v WJF* 656 A 2d 43 (New Jersey Superior Ct App Div 1995). The California reporting statute of 1980 replaced the 'actual knowledge' standard of *Landeros v Flood* (n 251) with a 'reasonable suspicion' standard: 'it is objectively reasonable for a person to entertain such a suspicion, based upon facts that could cause a reasonable person in a like position, drawing when appropriate on his or her training and experience, to suspect child abuse' [Child Abuse and Neglect Reporting Act (California) Cal Penal Code §111666(a) §111666(a)].

In many States good faith in making the report is a rebuttable presumption.[884] The immunity covers not just the report of suspicions but also subsequent cooperation in the child abuse investigation,[885] but courts differ as to whether it insulates clinical negligence preceding the report.[886]

It has been argued that mandatory reporting provisions are seldom enforced through the prescribed penalties,[887] and so tort actions are better able to perform the educational function of setting the standard of care required of reporters such as physicians in relation to child abuse diagnosis, with the added benefit of providing compensation to the victims.[888] Good faith immunity can undercut this standard-setting objective, because it shields errors of judgment and honest mistakes. Nevertheless, good faith immunity is undoubtedly the best way to protect children at risk. Some diagnoses such as Munchausen's syndrome by proxy can be singularly difficult to make: the physician risks providing the child with inappropriate treatment due to falsified information, whilst risking alienating a wrongly accused or suspected parent with genuine concerns about her child.[889] It is submitted that even the most difficult of diagnoses should not be automatically insulated from civil liability, as a physician who has leapt to such a conclusion without conducting any of the investigations necessary to rule out a differential diagnosis would not be acting in good faith.

(iv) Witness immunity

Another form of immunity insulating professionals involved in judicial proceedings relating to child abuse is witness immunity (or 'quasi-judicial immunity' in American terminology), which is unqualified by any requirements of good faith. It does not however insulate a witness who has fabricated evidence from civil liability.[890] In the *Newham* case Lord Browne-Wilkinson had held that witness immunity applied to protect investigations by a local authority considering whether to bring child protection proceedings pursuant to its statutory duty. The psychiatrist who interviewed the child in that case was insulated from liability for misidentifying the abuser because she must have known that if abuse was disclosed, her findings would be the evidence upon which the local authority commenced care proceedings.[891] However, the House of Lords subsequently examined witness immunity in greater depth in *Darker v Chief*

---

[884] *Howe v Andereck* 882 So 2d 240 (Mississippi CA 2004) (describing a 'bubble of immunity' which is burst by evidence of bad faith); *Dobson v Harris* 530 SE 2d 829 (North Carolina Supreme Ct 2000); *Heinrich v Conemaugh Valley Memorial Hospital* 648 A 2d 53 (Pennsylvania Superior Ct 1994).

[885] *Warner v Mitts* (n 883).

[886] *Webb v Neuroeducation Inc* 88 p 3d 417 (Washington CA 2004) holds that good faith immunity does not apply to pre-report medical services; for the contrary view see *Robbins v Hamburger Home for Girls* 32 Cal App 4th 671 (California CA 1995); *DLC v Walsh* 908 SW 2d 791 (Missouri CA 1995).

[887] Discussed further in Chapter 5 section D, and in W Renke 'The Mandatory Reporting of Child Abuse under the Child Welfare Act' (1999) 7 Health LJ 91.   [888] Bailey (n 857), 66.

[889] CM Perman 'Diagnosing the Truth: Determining Physician Liability in Cases Involving Munchausen Syndrome by Proxy' (1990) 54 J of Urban and Contemporary Law 267, 275–276.

[890] *Darker v Chief Constable of West Midlands* (n 719).

[891] *M v Newham London Borough Council*, reported with *X v Bedfordshire County Council* (n 73) 755.

Constable West Midlands Police and drew a distinction between carrying out an investigation and preparing evidence to be given as a witness at a trial. The purpose of the immunity is to protect witnesses against claims made against them for something said or done in the course of giving or preparing to give evidence in the judicial process. It cannot be used to shield the police from civil liability for things done while they are acting as law enforcers or as investigators.[892]

On the basis of this rereading of witness immunity, the Court of Appeal in *JD v East Berkshire* suggested that while it might not be easy in some child abuse cases to draw the line between investigation and preparation of evidence, the activities of the social workers[893] in the *Newham* case described at the beginning of this chapter probably fell into the category of investigations. For this reason Lord Phillips MR concluded that neither the social workers nor the doctors were insulated by witness immunity from negligence liability to the misdiagnosed child in the case of *RK v Dewsbury Healthcare NHS Trust*, and this conclusion was not seriously disputed on appeal to the House of Lords.[894]

In reflecting on these cases alleging investigatory negligence on the part of social services, police child protection officers, and health professionals, it is important to remember that the courts can and do constrain the scope of liability by setting the standard of care at a realistic level to take account of the difficulties of decision-making in the context of an ongoing investigation for child protection, as they have done for decades for other areas of professional malpractice where judgment calls are required in difficult circumstances. Whilst cases against social workers alleging incompetence have been uncommon in the Commonwealth, the reasonableness of social work practice has frequently been questioned in public inquiries such as that into the murder of Victoria Climbié; so it is possible to set an appropriate standard of competence, and it should not be necessary to have a child die to set that standard in hindsight.[895] To reiterate Lord Bingham's pithy observation in *JD v East Berkshire*, being under a legal duty to provide competent services is the badge of a profession.[896]

In the cases we have examined, the breaches of duty were generally related to a failure to adhere to established procedures, rather than the courts imposing what they considered to be best practice. That standard of care will be measured against the expected practices at the time the decisions were made, not by comparison with the accepted standards prevailing at the time of trial.[897]

We turn now to consider the potential negligence liability of social services in dealing with these damaged children once they have been removed from their home environment.

---

[892] *Darker v Chief Constable of West Midlands* (n 719) 448 (Lord Hope).

[893] And, presumably, the psychiatrist.

[894] *JD v East Berkshire Community NHS Trust* (CA) (n 669) [116]; *JD v East Berkshire Community NHS Trust et al* (HL) (n 580) [136] (Lord Brown).

[895] PA Swain 'Social Workers and Professional Competence—A Last Goodbye to the Clapham Omnibus?' (1995) 4 Torts LJ 24.

[896] *JD v East Berkshire Community NHS Trust et al* (HL) (n 580) [40].

[897] *J(A) v Cairnie and the Government of Manitoba* (n 766) [150], [153]–[156].

3. Liability of social services for failure to protect the interests of a child in care

(a) Negligent placement or monitoring of a child with a foster family

One might think that it is inconceivable that someone who is vetted by social services and appears to be motivated by a social conscience to help abused children in the care of the state would in turn abuse them. But it does happen. As Chief Justice McLachlin of the Supreme Court of Canada has observed:

It is reasonably foreseeable that some people, if left in charge of children in difficult or over-crowded circumstances, will use excessive physical and verbal discipline. It is also reasonably foreseeable that some people will take advantage of the complete dependence of children in their care, and will sexually abuse them. To lessen the likelihood that either form of abuse will occur, the government must set up adequate procedures to screen prospective foster parents. And it must monitor homes so that any abuse that does occur can be promptly detected.[898]

Here we will discuss placements in foster families. Tort liability for placement in abusive institutions has been discussed earlier.[899] In the jurisdictions discussed in this book, courts have overcome their early reluctance to hold that public authorities are liable for negligent mistakes they make in the placement and monitoring of children in the care of the state. In this context it is conceptually easier to impose tort liability on a child protection agency for the offences and torts committed by a third party because it has assumed legal and practical responsibility for the child who is entirely dependent on it for his future care and development, and it has selected and (supposedly) trained and supervised the carer who inflicts the abuse or neglect. These positive acts set up a special relationship between the agency and the child, making it less likely that the role of the agency in allowing the abuse to occur will be characterized as a 'pure omission'. That said, a recurring concern is that the local authority and foster parents stand in the position of a parent in making difficult and delicate decisions with regard to the child's future, and judges are loath to contemplate tort actions for poor parenting.[900]

(i) Negligent placement or monitoring of a child in care in English law

Whilst a local authority's tort duty to take due care in selecting and monitoring foster placements now seems quite obvious, it was not until 2000 that this was accepted in English law. In 1986 the Court of Appeal had held that foster parents were not agents of the local authority in fulfilling its statutory duties to look after a child, and so it was not vicariously liable for their negligence which resulted in physical injury to the child.[901] In 1997 in *H v Norfolk County Council* the Court of Appeal dealt with the issue of direct liability of a local authority for abuse inflicted by foster carers, and concluded that the policy considerations in *X v Bedfordshire* justifying blanket immunity for local authorities in their investigatory duties applied with equal force

---

[898] *KLB v British Columbia* (n 309) [14]–[15].   [899] *Discussed above, section E.*
[900] *Barrett v Enfield London Borough Council* (n 322) 377–378 (Lord Woolf MR).
[901] *S v Walsall Metropolitan Borough Council* (n 319) 402.

to the local authority's responsibilities for a child in care.[902] Both the judge at first instance and Simon Brown LJ accepted arguments that if a duty of care were imposed, local authorities might be reluctant to take children into care.[903]

This stance changed completely after the House of Lords in 1999 in *Barrett v Enfield London Borough Council*[904] held, that whilst the decision to take a child into care pursuant to a statutory power was not justiciable under *X*, it did not follow that decisions taken after a child was in care could not give rise to a duty of care. Although there might well be cooperation between different social welfare bodies concerning a child, the responsibility remained that of the local authority and its social and other professional staff. Since the child was already removed from his natural parent, the duties of social services were not so delicate, although questions could arise as to whether the child should remain with particular foster parents.[905] The 'defensive practice' argument was firmly rejected as being a factor 'of little, if any weight', as the imposition of a duty of care was efficacious in contributing to the maintenance of high standards in helping children in care, more so than the administrative remedies cited in *X*.[906] Moreover, the bar on a child suing his parents for negligent decisions in his upbringing did not apply to a local authority which had to take decisions which a parent never had to take (such as putting up a child for adoption) and which had trained staff to advise on such decisions.[907]

Although the Law Lords in *Barrett* were careful not to express a view as to the correctness of *H v Norfolk County Council*,[908] when the opportunity arose in *S v Gloucester County Council* the following year the Court of Appeal disapproved of its previous decision.[909] In conjoined appeals, the claimants alleged that the local authorities had been negligent in failing to operate a competent system of investigation, vetting, and monitoring of foster parents, and so they suffered sexual abuse at the hands of their foster fathers with resulting physical and long-term psychological damage. The local authorities had persuaded the lower courts that cases which could be labelled as 'child abuse cases' were bound to fail as a class, and so the claims were struck out. The Court of Appeal rejected this concept of class immunity. Lord Justice May considered that after *Barrett* a local authority in an ordinary case will be unlikely to establish a defence which relies on a blanket immunity. The decisions of social workers in relation to a child in care are justiciable, and are capable of being held to be negligent by analogy with the decisions of other professional people.[910] Such cases must be considered individually, and usually a detailed factual enquiry through a trial would be necessary.[911] In considering whether a discretionary decision of a local authority in child welfare matters was negligent, the court would not substitute its own view unless the decision was 'plainly wrong', and not a mere error of judgement.[912] That said, in striking-out

---

[902] *H v Norfolk County Council* (n 654).   [903] ibid 386–387.

[904] *Barrett v Enfield London Borough Council* (n 75).

[905] ibid 589 (Lord Hutton).   [906] ibid 568 (Lord Slynn), echoed by Lord Hutton, 589.

[907] ibid 588 (Lord Hutton).   [908] ibid 590 (Lord Hutton).

[909] *S v Gloucestershire County Council; L v Tower Hamlets London Borough Council* [2000] 3 All ER 346 (CA).   [910] ibid 375, 369.

[911] ibid 369–370.   [912] ibid 369, 377.

proceedings defendant local authorities could not dissect part of a composite case to locate discretionary decisions which might attract immunity.[913]

This does not mean that all cases against local authorities have to go to trial, however. In one of the cases before the Court of Appeal, *L v Tower Hamlets LBC*, the evidence showed that the social workers had taken great care in approving the foster carers and had monitored the children on a monthly basis; there was no prospect of success at trial in showing failures to comply with the standard of care reasonably to be expected of social workers 20 years earlier, so that claim had been properly struck out.[914]

(ii) Negligent placement or monitoring of a child in care in Canadian law

We have seen that in *KLB v British Columbia*[915] the Supreme Court of Canada ruled out both vicarious liability and breach of non-delegable duty on the part of provincial governments for intentional torts committed by foster parents.[916] A major reason for the Court's conclusion was that social workers are already directly liable for negligent breaches of standard practices in the instructing, training, and periodic monitoring of foster parents, and in developing good communication with the foster children whom they have placed.[917] A statutory requirement that child welfare authorities arrange a foster home placement 'as will best meet the needs of the child' has been interpreted as imposing a high standard of care, that of 'a prudent parent solicitous for the welfare of his or her child'. Whilst the government is not a guarantor against all harm, it is held responsible for harm sustained by children in foster care when, judged by the standards of the day, it was reasonably foreseeable that the government's conduct would expose these children to harm including physical, emotional and sexual abuse.[918] The Supreme Court noted that in the 1960s and 1970s the standards were lower than those of 2003, but still required proper assessment of the proposed foster parents and whether they could meet the children's needs, discussion with the foster parents of the acceptable limits of discipline, and frequent supervisory visits, especially where there were previously documented problems with a foster home.[919] Failure to supervise a child's placement with a biological parent or other family member may also attract negligence liability, as may a decision to withdraw from child protection proceedings.[920]

We have previously noted the extension by Canadian courts of the fiduciary concept beyond the protection of property interests to the protection of children,[921] to supplement rather than duplicate the common law causes of action.[922] It is accepted in Canadian law that a fiduciary relationship arises between a child welfare authority and children in foster care, just as parents owe a fiduciary duty to children in their care which encompasses a duty not to injure the child through physical or sexual abuse.[923]

---

[913] ibid 375.   [914] ibid 375–378.   [915] *KLB v British Columbia* (n 309).
[916] Discussed above, sections E.3(d) and 4.   [917] *KLB v British Columbia* (n 309) [26].
[918] ibid [14]–[15].   [919] ibid [16].   [920] *CH v British Columbia* (n 818) [55]–[59].
[921] Discussed above, section C.5; Hoyano 'The Flight to the Fiduciary Haven' (n 84).
[922] *KLB v British Columbia* (n 309) [48].   [923] *KM v HM* (n 64).

Children in care are seen as doubly vulnerable, first as children, and second because of their difficult pasts and the trauma of being removed from their birth families. The authority's actions as their legal guardian in making and monitoring placement decisions may affect their lives and well-being in fundamental ways.[924]

However, the content of this fiduciary duty was narrowly defined by the Supreme Court of Canada in *KLB v British Columbia*.[925] McLachlin CJC reasoned that a fiduciary obligation to promote the best interests of foster children cannot be implied as a public law duty, because child welfare statutes evince a clear intent that children be nurtured in a private home environment, which precludes close day-to-day supervision of foster parents.[926] Rather, the fiduciary concept must be understood as a private law duty arising simply from the relationship of discretionary power and trust between the authority and the foster children. The obligation cannot be formulated as a duty to act in the best interests of the child because this is too vague a standard to be workable or justiciable. Instead, the fiduciary duty is the same as that owed by parents: not to put their own or others' interests ahead of the child's, nor to commit acts which harm the children in a way that amounts to betrayal of trust or disloyalty.[927] Whilst this ruling confirms the liability in equity of the foster parent who abuses, or who turns her face from abuse inflicted by another, it would seem generally to preclude the liability of a governmental agency for breach of its fiduciary duty to a child in foster care. It is conceivable however that such liability might arise if a social worker deliberately ignores a child's complaints of abuse by foster carers, and in any event that situation would seem to set up direct liability in negligence.

(iii) Negligent placement or monitoring of a child in care in New Zealand law
New Zealand's accident compensation statutes have operated generally to bar claims in negligence for placement of children with abusive foster families occurring after 1 April 1974.[928] For foster placements occurring before that date, the New Zealand Court of Appeal has held that foster parents were agents of the Superintendent of Child Welfare, who had a specific statutory duty to place children in need of protection in suitable private homes rather than in institutions, and in so doing created or increased the risk of child abuse. Consequently, unlike in Canada, the government was held vicariously liable for sexual and physical abuse perpetrated by foster parents, as the burden of compensation should be borne by and distributed amongst the community.[929] The agency rationale was seen as forestalling vicarious liability for abuse perpetrated by other members of the foster family,[930] yet it is difficult to see why this must be so,

---

[924] *KLB v British Columbia* (n 309) [38], decided with *MB v British Columbia* (n 511).

[925] For criticism, arguing that this conclusion breaches the children's Canadian Charter s 7 right to security of the person, see S Grover 'Nowhere to Turn: the Supreme Court of Canada's Denial of a Constitutionally-Based Governmental Fiduciary Duty to Children in Foster Care' (2004) 12 International J of Children's Rights 105.   [926] *KLB v British Columbia* (n 309) [39]–[40].

[927] ibid [40]–[49].   [928] *S v Attorney-General* (n 31) [25].

[929] ibid [68]–[71]. This decision relied upon authority from the British Columbia Court of Appeal which was later reversed by the Supreme Court of Canada in *KLB v British Columbia* (n 309).

[930] *S v Attorney-General* (n 31) [73].

given that the foster parents were arguably negligent in permitting the abuse to occur or continue unchecked.

The Superintendent of Child Welfare was also found directly liable for negligence in 1970 in placing two Maori sisters with a woman with a history of attempted suicide and with three children of her own as well as five foster children, including two with learning difficulties. Her husband immediately began sexually assaulting the two girls, but a senior social worker refused to listen to their complaints and did not undertake any investigation as to whether there was abuse of other children who had been in their care.[931]

The New Zealand Court of Appeal has been content to accept that the Superintendent of Child Welfare was a fiduciary respecting a child placed in foster care, but, like the Supreme Court of Canada, could not see that there had been any breach of a duty properly characterized as fiduciary, which would be distinct from the duty of care in negligence.[932] Claims based upon failure to recognize or nurture Maori foster children's ethnic and cultural background have failed on the basis that the child welfare authorities could be excused for attitudes in 1970 which would not now be tolerated.[933]

(iv) Negligent placement or monitoring of a child in care in Australian law

The Australian High Court has not had the opportunity to rule on the issue of a duty of care on the part of the state owed to children taken into its care. The issues seem to have been primarily litigated in the State courts in the context of the forced removal of aboriginal children from their homes and placement in institutions or with non-aboriginal foster families; this has created complications as to the constitutional responsibility of the Commonwealth of Australia for these decisions.[934] The Federal Court of Appeal has accepted that once an aboriginal child came into the care of the Director of Native Welfare, then the Director (but not the Commonwealth of Australia) 'positively' assumed responsibility for their safety and well-being and hence owed a duty of care.[935] However the trials of 'stolen generation' cases have been severely hampered by evidential gaps as to what occurred as long as 50 years earlier, and the courts seem reluctant to find that a public officer actually knew or should have known about a carer's sexual and physical assaults or his predilection to such conduct, even where there is contemporary documentary evidence of some awareness of such misconduct.[936]

---

[931] *W v Attorney General* (n 31) [13]–[19].

[932] *S v Attorney-General* (n 31) [76]–[80]; *W v Attorney General* ibid [44].

[933] *W v Attorney General* ibid [11], [43]–[44].

[934] As opposed to the responsibility of named public office holders vested with discretionary powers, under the *Enever* doctrine: discussed above, section E.3(e).

[935] *Cubillo v Commonwealth (No 2)* [2001] FCA 1213 (Aus Fed CA), affirming *Cubillo v Commonwealth (No 2)* [2000] FCA 1084, 103 FCR 1 (Aus Fed Ct 2000) [1222].

[936] *Cubillo v Commonwealth (No 2)* (n 517) [1255]; (n 935) [380]–[386] affirmed on the ground that the issue had not been litigated on that basis at trial. In *Johnson v Department of Community Services* [1999] NSWSC 641 (New South Wales Supreme Ct) [100] the court appeared to assume that an actionable duty would arise only if the social worker became aware of a child's mistreatment and still failed to act.

Cases concerning children who were taken into care by Australian States for the usual child protection reasons are rather more straightforward than those involving aboriginal communities for which the Federal Crown is responsible. The applicability of limitation periods remains a significant constraint on such cases.[937] In one of the very few cases to go to trial, *SB v New South Wales*[938] the claimant had been in care since the age of three. When she was 16 she was discovered to have been sexually abused by her foster parent from the age of four. The child welfare authorities then placed her with her natural father, who had a criminal record and with whom she had previously had virtually no contact. Psychiatric counselling for the abuse by her foster father was recommended to social workers before she was placed with her father but was never provided. There was no real attempt to monitor her thereafter. Her father withdrew her from school and isolated her from contact with others, and over a period of ten years sexually abused her. Two children were born as a result of the incest, one whilst the claimant was still a ward of the State. Both her foster father and natural father were convicted of sexually abusing her. At trial Redlich J noted the erosion of *X v Bedfordshire* in England, and that successive Australian decisions had found it arguable that a common law duty exists where a child protection authority negligently exercises or failed to exercise its powers. Redlich J held that a duty of care based on the special relationship between the State and its ward would encourage the maintenance of higher standards in pursuing the statute's paramount objective of the welfare of the child.[939] The State had breached that duty by failing to exercise with reasonable care its power of restoration to her natural father, exposing her to further significant risk of harm. For the duration of her wardship the State failed to take reasonable care to monitor her welfare. The State of New South Wales therefore was liable to compensate her for her multiple serious psychiatric disorders.[940]

(v) Negligent placement or monitoring of a child in care in American law

For litigants to set up common law tort liability for failure of government agencies to protect children in care from abusive foster parents, they must supplant the American constitutional idea that the state does not owe its citizens a general duty of protection. There are four legal theories on which a duty of care has been based:[941]

- a common law duty to exercise due care in supervising foster children because one who acts must act with reasonable care;

    or

- a common law duty to protect foster children because of a special relationship between the governmental custodian and its ward, constructed on the basis of taking custody of the child as:
    — the state obligated itself to protect the child;

---

[937] eg *Hopkins v Queensland* [2004] QDC 21 (Queensland Dist Ct) (application for extension of limitation period denied). [938] *SB v New South Wales* (n 687).
[939] ibid [291]–[294], [300]–[306]. [940] ibid [305]–[307].
[941] Kubitschek (n 701) §§24–25, §28.

— the state effectively prevented anyone else from rescuing the child; and

— the State took on a duty to supervise those who come into contact with the child on a daily basis, to ensure that they are not threats to the child's safety;

or

- in placing and supervising foster children, government agencies perform a ministerial rather than a discretionary function and so are held to a 'reasonable person' standard of care;

or

- State statutes requiring agencies to select and supervise foster parents give foster children a cause of action in tort where the agencies failed to select or supervise them properly.

Since 1970, several States have held social workers liable under State tort law for failing to protect abused foster children in their placement and to monitor their well-being and progress. However, it is far more common for such claims to be brought under the constitutional cause of action provided by §1983, which we discuss later.[942]

In Virginia, as in New Zealand but unlike in Canada, the government has been held vicariously liable for the acts of the person with whom the child was placed, on the rationale that the child welfare agency under State law had legal custody and therefore the responsibility to provide for the physical, mental, moral, and emotional well-being of the child. However, as is common in American tort law, the court's reasoning conflated vicarious liability with the concept of non-delegable duty and hence direct negligence.[943] Elsewhere liability has been based upon breach of the government's duty of care owed directly to the child in foster care.[944] However, negligence liability requires proof of fault, and it can be difficult to prove that social services knew or should have known that someone in the foster family posed a risk to children,[945] in the absence of any criminal record or cause for suspicion discoverable by a reasonable background check.[946] Compliance with government guidelines for foster care will generally protect social workers.[947]

Here again in American law we encounter the issue of whether the governmental agency or its employees are protected by absolute or qualified immunity for discretionary acts. In *Elton v County of Orange*[948] it was held that decisions with respect to the care, supervision, or placement of a dependent child did not achieve the level of

---

[942] In section F.5, below.

[943] *Vonner v State* 273 So 2d 252 (Louisiana Supreme Ct 1973) [4]–[7].

[944] See SA Soehnel 'Governmental Tort Liability for Social Service Agency's Negligence in Placement, or Supervision after Placement, of Children' 90 ALR 3d 1214 (updated 2006).

[945] As in *Beltran v Washington Department of Social and Health Services* 989 P 2d 604 (Washington CA), where it was held that the foster mother did not know and did not have any reason to know of her son's dangerous proclivities, and hence social services could not have known either.

[946] As in *Babcock v State* 809 P 2d 143 (Washington Supreme Ct 1991) where the foster parent had a criminal record for sexual offences which had not been checked by social services.

[947] eg *County of Los Angeles v Superior Court* 102 Cal App 4th 67 (California CA 2nd Dist 2002); *Koepf v York County* 251 NW 2d 866 (Nebraska Supreme Ct 1977); *Beltran v Washington* (n 946).

[948] *Elton v County of Orange* 3 Cal App 1053 (California CA 4th Dist 1970).

basic policy decisions so as to attract immunity. Interestingly, the California Court of Appeal commented in *obiter* that the decision whether to take a child into care would be immune as a basic policy decision, on reasoning reminiscent of *X v Bedfordshire*.[949] The issue as to whether qualified immunity protects a caseworker or her employer who negligently places a child with an abuser or who disregards warnings about the risk of abuse will often preclude summary judgment.[950] However, there is also a substantial body of case law where immunity was successfully invoked to render foster placement decisions and supervisory failures non-actionable.[951]

To recap, all of the jurisdictions we are examining concur with the House of Lords in *Barrett v Enfield LBC* that, whatever the case may be for negligence immunity in conducting investigations of alleged abuse, once the child is taken into the state's care a duty of care arises to take reasonable steps to choose an appropriate placement which will meet the child's needs, and to continue to monitor the child's well-being in that placement.

(b) Negligent placement of a dangerous child with a foster family

Severely mistreated children have often lost any ability to trust, and this lack of trust is perpetuated as a child drifts through the system, abandoned by one caregiver after another.[952] So physically and sexually abused children may continue the cycle of abuse in residential care facilities and foster homes where they have been placed, perpetuating a tragic situation for all. In these cases the abused victim becomes the perpetrator, and so our focus here will be on the safety of other children in the foster home.

(i) Negligent placement of a dangerous child with a foster family in English law

The leading pertinent case is *W v Essex County Council*.[953] When the claimant foster parents had been approved as specialist adolescent foster carers by the Council, they had stipulated to the social worker that they would not accept any child who was known or suspected of being a sexual abuser. Despite that stipulation the same social worker placed with the family a 15-year-old boy who had admitted, and been cautioned by the police, for an indecent assault on his own sister, and who was under investigation for an alleged rape. These facts were on the Council's files and were known to the social worker, but she did not give this information to the foster parents. Within one month the boy had systematically committed serious sexual offences against all four of the claimants' children, aged 8 to 12 years. The children sued the Council in negligence for damages for their personal and psychiatric injury, to

---

[949] ibid 1058. To the same effect are *Little v Utah State Division of Family Services* 667 P 2d 49 (Utah Supreme Ct 1983) 51–52; *Koepf v York County* (n 947) 867–868.

[950] *LaShay v Department of Social and Rehabilitation Services* (n 726); *Babcock v State* (n 946).

[951] eg *Becerra v County of Santa Cruz* 68 Cal App 4th 1450 (California CA 2nd Dist 1998); *Jackson v Department of Human Resources* 497 SE 2d 58 (Georgia CA 1998); *County of Los Angeles v Superior Court* (n 948).

[952] HHJ Patricia Kvill 'Concluding Thoughts from the Bench: The Failed Promises' in Nicholas Bala, Michael Kim Zapf, R James Williams, Robin Vogl and JP Hornick (eds) *Canadian Child Welfare Law: Children, Families and the State* (2nd edn Thompson Educational Publishing, Inc, Toronto 2004) 422, 424.

[953] *W v Essex County Council* [1998] 3 All ER 111 (CA), appeal allowed [2001] 2 AC 592 (HL).

which the parents added a claim for their own psychiatric injury on learning of the abuse, pleading their case in the additional causes of action of negligent misstatement, breach of contract and misfeasance in public office. The Council and social worker applied to strike out all of the actions against them by the children and their parents.

The majority of the Court of Appeal (deciding the case before the Law Lords rendered their decision in *Barrett*) held that it was arguable that the policy considerations in *X v Bedfordshire* did not apply where the local authority did not have any immediate caring responsibilities under the child welfare system for the children whose safety was under consideration. Therefore the abused children's claims could proceed to trial.[954] Stuart-Smith LJ dissented on the basis that the policy considerations in *X* applied to foster placements as well. In his view it was likely that there would be conflicts of interest between an adolescent foster child and the foster parents in which the social worker might have to intervene; his primary concern must be the welfare of the foster child, and imposition of a duty of care to the foster family as well would place the social worker in an impossible position. Stuart-Smith LJ concluded that the giving of information or advice to foster parents was all part and parcel of the local authority's performance of its statutory powers and duties immunized by *X*.[955] All of the judges on the Court of Appeal panel agreed that the claims for the parents' post-traumatic stress disorder should be struck out on the basis that they did not comply with the strict criteria for liability for the negligent infliction of psychiatric harm on secondary victims, established by the House of Lords in a series of decisions.[956]

When *W v Essex* reached the House of Lords, the defendants no longer contested that the abused children's claims should proceed.[957] In a remarkable—and oddly ambivalent—deviation from their recent decisions which had painfully constructed a set of rigid rules for recovery of damages for psychiatric injury, the Law Lords unanimously allowed the parents' claims for their own psychiatric injury to go to trial, on the basis that they might be classified as either primary or secondary victims.[958] It was arguable that the parents were primary victims (even though they had not been at risk of physical harm themselves as the law previously had required)[959] because their post-traumatic stress disorder was caused by their shock and sense of guilt at having introduced the abuser into their family and not having detected earlier what was happening. The parents might alternatively be classified as secondary victims: although they had not been present at the shocking events (the abuse), they could be considered as being present at their immediate aftermath, notwithstanding that this criterion previously had been limited to an inelastic few hours,[960] but here was stretched to four weeks. It was suggested that the shocking event itself might be when

---

[954] *W v Essex County Council* [1998] 3 All ER 111 (CA) 132–136 (Judge LJ), 141–142 (Mantell LJ).

[955] ibid [124]–[125] (Stuart-Smith LJ dissenting).

[956] *McLoughlin v O'Brian* (n 201); *Alcock v Chief Constable of South Yorkshire* (n 201); *Page v Smith* [1996] AC 155 (HL); *Frost v Chief Constable of South Yorkshire* [1999] 2 AC 455 (HL).

[957] *W v Essex County Council* (n 653) 597. The claims for breach of contract and misfeasance in public office were also dismissed by the Court of Appeal and not pursued further.   [958] ibid 599–601.

[959] *Page v Smith* (n 956).

[960] *McLoughlin v O'Brian* (n 201); *Alcock v Chief Constable of South Yorkshire* (n 201).

the parents were told of the abuse, contrary to their previous ruling that notification of bad news was not actionable, which they did not cite.[961] All these definitional issues were left to the trial judge, but the case was settled before trial.

(ii) Negligent placement of a dangerous child with a foster family in Canadian law

The Canadian analogue for *W v Essex, D(B) and D(SV) v British Columbia* may provide some comfort for local authorities in England.[962] The claimant was a foster mother experienced in dealing with emotionally disturbed children, many of whom had been sexually or physically abused. She had three children of her own, the youngest being a three-year-old girl. A 13-year-old girl, F, was placed in the home by her social worker, who told the claimant that she had come from a highly dysfunctional family and had suffered extensive physical, emotional and sexual abuse from an early age for which she was receiving on-going therapy. The social worker knew that the previous foster parent had reported that F could be short-tempered and rough with younger children in the household, but did not pass this information on to the new foster mother. Within ten days the mother noticed adverse changes in the behaviour of her three-year-old daughter, who five months later disclosed that she had been sexually and physically abused and terrorized by F. Counsel for the Superintendent of Family and Child Services and the social worker accepted that they owed a duty of care to the foster mother and her daughter. The trial judge had found that a social worker must take into account the concern of protecting children in the family when placing a foster child, and that here he negligently failed to do so and acted in bad faith because he had not honestly considered the effect of her behavioural problems on younger children in the home.[963] The British Columbia Court of Appeal reversed the findings of liability to the mother and the abused child on the basis of the statutory immunity for decisions made in good faith:

> The theme running through the important cases in this area is the difficulty facing those who work with disturbed children. Decisions have to be made about care when the outcome is unpredictable. It is too easy to say when things turn out badly that it was the fault of the person who made the judgment. Social workers should not be so afraid of making a mistake that they cannot do their job properly. The statutory immunity is intended to protect workers in the field so their judgments will be focused on child welfare and not their exposure to liability.[964]

> It was a matter of judgement for the social worker whether the home was a suitable placement, having due regard for the safety of other children or household, as was the judgement about the extent of disclosure of F's background.[965]

(iii) Negligent placement of a dangerous child with a foster family in American law

It is perhaps inevitable that there are American cases falling on either side of the liability line on this issue. In some cases the state immunity doctrine has operated

---

[961] *McLoughlin v O'Brian* ibid.
[962] *D(B) and D(SV) v British Columbia* [1997] 4 WWR 484 (British Columbia CA).
[963] *D(B) and D(SV) v British Columbia* [1996] 1 WWR 581 (British Columbia Supreme Ct) [24]–[30].
[964] *D(B) and D(SV) v British Columbia* (n 962) [40]–[41].   [965] ibid 500.

to defeat claims,[966] but in other jurisdictions where the doctrine is not as powerful social workers have been found liable for negligent non-disclosure to foster families. In a case with facts almost identical to those in *W v Essex*, the Supreme Court of Nebraska held that the Department of Social Services negligently failed to abide by its own procedures which required investigation of the foster child's background and, where appropriate, a psychological evaluation. Had these procedures been followed, social workers would have discovered the 15-year-old boy's violent behaviour toward his own mother, information which should have been disclosed to his foster parents. They were also negligent in persuading the foster parents to withdraw their request to remove the boy after he had been detected in suspicious circumstances with one of the children. The four children sexually abused throughout the 11-month placement recovered damages for psychiatric injury, as did their parents, notwithstanding that, as in *W v Essex*, they did not observe the abuse of their children.[967]

In a similar case the Alaskan Supreme Court was careful to stress that the social worker's standard of care is to take reasonable steps to investigate a child's background in the totality of the circumstances, and to disclose the information necessary to give foster parents an informed basis for their decisions as to whether to accept the child and how much supervision the child might need. The case-specific analysis should balance factors such as how recent, reliable and accessible any undisclosed information was, the nature and degree of risk stemming from non-disclosure, the child's legitimate interests in privacy, the state's compelling need in ensuring prompt and appropriate placement for children in need of protection, the limited resources of child welfare agencies, and compliance with internal policies.[968]

Thus American and Canadian courts are enjoined to be realistic about the difficulties faced by social workers in placing children, and by foster families in accepting and helping them. These cases were not quite as strong on the facts as *W v Essex* where the foster parents had stipulated that they would not take a child who had himself been an abuser, but nonetheless in these cases a duty of disclosure in the interests of the foster family was clearly established. It is submitted that the starting point for local authorities should be that wide disclosure of a foster child's background and any risks he poses for persons he encounters will be in the best interests of that child, as the foster parents will better be able to help him settle into a normal family life. If prospective foster carers are concerned that the local authorities may withhold pertinent information, they may decide not to open their home to abused children at all. Given the wide range of children's services practitioners who will have access to the comprehensive database of all British children under the Integrated Children's System to be fully operational by 1 January 2007, as recommended by the Climbié Inquiry, it becomes even more indefensible not to allow foster parents access to that information unless there is a considered and compelling reason not to do so. If however the social

---

[966] eg *Huff v Williams* 743 A 2d 1252 (Maine Supreme Judicial Ct 1999); *MDR v New Mexico Human Resources Department* 836 P 2d 106 (New Mexico CA 1992).

[967] *Haselhorst v State* 485 NW 2d 180 (Nebraska Supreme Ct 1992). The court split four to three on the recoverability of damages for the parents' psychiatric injury.

[968] *PG and RG v State* 4 P 3d 326 (Alaska Supreme Ct 2000) 332. See also *Hobbs v North Carolina Department of Human Resources* 520 SE 2d 595 (North Carolina CA 1999).

worker records her reasons why full disclosure of specific information was not made in a particular case, and the social worker genuinely believes that her professional responsibilities and the local authority's protocols require non-disclosure, then it is likely that the court will take a pragmatic view and conclude that she discharged her duty of care to the foster family.

(c) Negligent management of a child in care

We are dealing here with the plight of children who have become 'lost in care', to borrow Sir Ronald Waterhouse's phrase,[969] but who have escaped the additional misfortune of being physically or sexually abused. It might seem that the experience of such children falls outside the remit of this book about child abuse, but we think it relevant because of the growing concern about the problems of drift in the management of children in care. The family courts can now do nothing when local authorities fail to adhere to the care plan agreed when a care order has been granted,[970] since the House of Lords disapproved of the Court of Appeal's brief experiment with 'starred care' plans whereby the court took jurisdiction to monitor the essential milestones of the care plan.[971]

Can a child in care sue his 'corporate parent' for negligence for failing to discharge its parental duties and responsibilities toward him? In 1999 in *Barrett v Enfield LBC*,[972] the House of Lords said yes. We have already discussed the great significance of this case in the unravelling of blanket immunity for child protection agencies.[973] It is important to consider the facts pleaded as setting up negligence liability. Barrett had been taken into care in 1973 as an infant after he had been admitted to hospital suffering from injuries inflicted by his mother. The following year his three-month-old sister was taken into care and for a time they lived with the same foster carer. When he left care at age 18 he had been in nine different placements with foster carers and various institutions for disturbed children, had no family or other attachment whatsoever, had developed a psychiatric illness causing him to self-harm and had been involved in criminal activities. His marriage failed, he was chronically unemployed and he had an alcohol problem. Barrett pleaded that Enfield LBC owed him a common law duty of care to act *in loco parentis* and to provide him with the standard of care which could be expected of a reasonable parent, including a duty to provide a home and education, to take reasonable steps to protect him from physical, emotional, psychiatric, or psychological injury and to promote his development. This legal duty was to be discharged by providing competent social workers with responsibility to monitor his welfare. He claimed that this duty was breached by placing him in unsuitable foster and institutional accommodation, by not considering him for adoption nor for a placement on a long-term basis with his sister or with other relatives, by not helping

---

[969] Sir Ronald Waterhouse Chair, *Lost in Care: Report of the North Wales Child Abuse Tribunal of Inquiry* (n 51).   [970] Discussed above Chapter 2 section F.1.
[971] *Re W and B (Children) and Re W (Children)* [2001] EWCA Civ 757, reversed by *In Re S (Minors) (Care Order: Implementation of Care Plan)* [2002] UKHL 10, [2002] 2 AC 291.
[972] *Barrett v Enfield London Borough Council* (n 75).   [973] Above, section F.1(b)(ii).

him in his meetings with his mother after 11 years of separation resulting in her refusal to see him again, and by failing to obtain proper psychiatric treatment for him.[974]

The court of first instance and the Court of Appeal had struck out his claims as disclosing no reasonable cause of action, pursuant to *X v Bedfordshire*. The House of Lords unanimously held that it was arguable that the local authority owed a duty of care to him, for reasons which we have already canvassed.[975] Lord Slynn noted that Barrett's allegations were largely directed at the way in which the powers of the local authority had been *exercised*, which arguably was both justiciable and set up negligence liability. They involved decisions which parents never or rarely have to take, such as adoption and placement with an appropriate foster parent or institution. So it was irrelevant that the same claims against natural parents might not be actionable. Whilst other averments such as whether it was right to arrange adoption might not be justiciable, the question of whether adoption was ever considered, or if not why not, might properly be a matter for investigation in a claim of negligence. Lord Slynn cautioned that each allegation should not be considered separately to ascertain if it was justiciable; rather the claim was one of on-going failure of duty and should be seen as a whole.[976] This solution adroitly avoided the evidential intricacies of linking each actionable allegation to causation of identified harm, which the Court of Appeal had concluded were insurmountable.[977] Lord Slynn pointed out that causation is largely a question of fact and that expert evidence before the court showed that it should be possible to establish whether the negligent management of his care had been a significant causal determinant of his psychological difficulties. Therefore the case should go to trial so that the court could apply the operational–policy distinction to concrete facts.[978] In the event the case was settled without a trial.

Barrett's case sadly was not unique or even unusual, and the House of Lords had been warned in oral argument that hundreds of claims against local authorities were awaiting the judgment.[979] Other jurisdictions have their analogues for *Barrett*.[980] One suspects that in past decades a child in care was at greater risk of unconscious neglect than from sexual or physical abuse. Whilst the attention of the media has been captured by the cases of systemic sexual and physical abuse in children's residential

---

[974] *Barrett v Enfield London Borough Council* (n 75) 561–562.   [975] Above, section F.3(a)(i).

[976] *Barrett v Enfield London Borough Council* (n 75) 573 (Lord Slynn).

[977] *Barrett v Enfield London Borough Council* (n 322) 378 (Lord Woolf MR), 379 (Evans LJ).

[978] *Barrett v Enfield London Borough Council* (n 75) 574–575.

[979] For a review of the practical issues in suing local authorities remaining after *Barrett*, see E-A Gumbel QC 'Child Abuse Compensation Claims: a Practitioner's Perspective' in D Fairgrieve and S Green (eds) *Child Abuse Tort Claims against Public Bodies: A Comparative Law View* (Ashgate, London 2004) 45–58; Gumbel, Johnson and Scorer (n 77) chapters 4–8.

[980] eg *JH v British Columbia* [1998] BCJ No 2926 (British Columbia Supreme Ct) [45], [100]–[115] (the common law duty of care owed by the Superintendent of Child Welfare to the plaintiff required the exercise of 'special diligence' in providing suitable facilities, to which the statutory defence of good faith did not apply, and was breached by some of his multiple placements over 17 years as a ward); *BJM v Florida Department of Health and Rehabilitative Services* 67 So 2d 512 (Florida Dist CA 1993) (sovereign immunity bars a child's negligence claim for improper placement which did not provide psychiatric treatment recommended by the juvenile court).

care facilities in Leicestershire, North and South Wales, and elsewhere, there is a large pool of forgotten children whose life chances, already impaired by their adverse experiences with their families, were further damaged by drifting through the care system in inappropriate foster placements and care homes without clear direction from social services as to how to promote their well-being. As we discussed earlier,[981] whilst the problem of children disappearing into the care system is now acknowledged, it remains doubtful that the very limited resources of local authorities and the much-criticized Children and Family Court Advisory and Support Services (CAFCASS) will be able to provide the immediate and long-term planning and monitoring for each child in care required by the Children Act 1989 s 26 and foster placement regulations. Awareness of these problems must influence those with the heavy responsibility of deciding whether a child would be better off remaining with her family, however deficient that environment might be, or taken into care with the attendant uncertainties and risks.

It is ironic that, Parliament having decided that family courts should no longer have jurisdiction to monitor and supervise the essential milestones of the local authority's care plan for a child, the civil courts through *Barrett* have seized on the jurisdiction conferred by negligence law to examine the local authority's care of a child—but only *post hoc*, after much irremediable damage has been done. The spectre of tort liability may provide additional incentive to policymakers to provide local authorities with greater resources to look after children in care in a proactive way, so that the tort courts in future will be seldom called upon to establish professional standards in the provision of services to children in care.

4. Failure of a child protection agency to protect a child's human rights

The eminent children's rights advocate Allan Levy QC delivered a lecture in Cambridge in 2001 provocatively entitled 'Do Children Have Human Rights?'[982] He pointed out that it is easy to cite a raft of international instruments ascribing 'rights' to children but it is more difficult to identify which ones are more than aspirational statements of ideals and are realistically enforceable by and for children. For example, the Universal Declaration of Human Rights, 1948 proclaims that childhood is entitled to special care and assistance.[983] The International Covenant on Civil and Political Rights, 1966 imposes obligations on the part of the child's family, society and the state to give children such measures of protection as are required by their status as minors.[984] It is unclear whether these instruments are intended to make children positive rights-holders, rather than merely imposing vague duties on those dealing with them as 'objects of concern'.[985]

The United Nations Convention on the Rights of the Child is more specific in imposing positive obligations on States Parties to protect children. Article 19(1)

---

[981] See above Chapter 2 section F.

[982] The Henry Sidgwick Memorial Lecture delivered by Allan Levy QC at Newnham College Cambridge in February 2001, published as Allan Levy QC 'Do Children Have Human Rights?' [2002] Fam Law 204.

[983] Universal Declaration of Human Rights, 1948 Arts 2, 25.

[984] United Nations International Covenant on Civil and Political Rights, 1966 Art 24.

[985] In the memorable phrase of Dame Elizabeth Butler-Sloss in *Report of the Inquiry into Child Abuse in Cleveland 1987* (Cm 412).

requires that:

States Parties shall take all appropriate legislative, administrative, social and educational measures to protect the child from all forms of physical or mental violence, injury or abuse, neglect
or negligent treatment, maltreatment or exploitation, including sexual abuse, while in the care
of parent(s), legal guardian(s) or any other person who has the care of the child.[986]

Article 9 requires States Parties to ensure that a child is not separated from his parents
against his will except when competent authorities subject to judicial review determine
in accordance with applicable law and procedures that such separation is necessary for
the best interests of the child, for example in the case of parental abuse or neglect. All
interested parties must be given an opportunity to participate in the proceedings and
make their views known.[987] A child who is temporarily or permanently deprived of
a family home environment is entitled to special protection and assistance provided
by the state under Article 20. Moreover Article 16 gives the child the right to the
protection of the law against arbitrary or unlawful interference with her privacy,
family or home.

A much more powerful instrument for conferring enforceable rights upon children
in the UK has been the European Convention on Human Rights (ECHR)—
notwithstanding that children are expressly mentioned only in Articles 5 and 6, in the
contexts of apprehending a child for educational supervision or to bring him before
a competent legal authority, and juvenile misconduct. We have already discussed the
impact of the ECHR on family law, particularly procedurally.[988] We have also seen
how the ECHR has been the catalyst in prising open the tort immunity of English
child protection agencies, beginning with *Osman v UK*.[989] We turn now to considering
how human rights law can be called in aid to hold public authorities accountable to
children for the way in which they have exercised or failed to exercise their statutory
powers and duties in relation to the investigation of alleged child abuse. This is a
very broad canvas, and so we will focus on the key cases which have had an impact
on British child protection agencies. We consider first judgments from the European
Court of Human Rights (ECtHR), then from British courts under the HRA 1998
since it came into effect on 1 October 2000, and then analyse the development of
constitutional tort liability to children in the United States.

(a) Breach of the European Convention on Human Rights

The Convention rights most likely to be applicable to the investigation of child
protection cases include:

- *Article 2*: 'Everyone's right to life shall be protected by law';
- *Article 3*: 'No one shall be subjected to torture or to inhuman or degrading treatment
  or punishment';

---

[986] See also Article 34 dealing with all forms of sexual exploitation and abuse, and Article 39 requiring
States Parties to take all appropriate measures to promote physical and psychological recovery and social
reintegration of the child victim of any form of neglect, exploitation or abuse.

[987] This is reinforced by Article 12(2) requiring that the child be provided the opportunity to be heard
in any judicial and administrative proceedings affecting the child, either directly or through a representative
or an appropriate body in accordance with national legal procedures.

[988] See above, Chapter 2 section A.3.

[989] *Osman v UK* (n 639), discussed above section F.1(b)(ii).

- *Article 5*: 'Everyone has a right to liberty and security of person';
- *Article 6*: In the determination of his civil rights and obligations or of any criminal charge against him, everyone is entitled to a fair and public hearing within a reasonable time by an independent and impartial tribunal established by law'; and
- *Article 8*: '(1) Everyone has a right to respect for his private and family life, his home and his correspondence. (2) There shall be no interference by public authorities with the exercise of this right except as is in accordance with the law and is necessary in a democratic society . . . for the prevention of disorder or crime, for the protection of health or morals, or for the protection of the rights and freedoms of others.' The ECtHR applies the following template to Article 8 cases.

— Does the subject matter fall within the scope of Article 8?
— If so, has there been interference by a public authority?
— If so, was it in accordance with the law, ie is the law clear and accessible to everyone?
— If so, did it pursue one of the legitimate aims set out in Article 8(2)?
— If so, was it necessary in a democratic society, ie did the interference correspond to a 'pressing social need' and was it 'proportionate' to that need?

(i) Positive rights to protection

Whilst instruments protecting civil liberties are often expressed as being the negative right to be free of interference from the state, the American Constitution being the paradigm, the ECtHR since 1979 has interpreted some Convention rights as imposing positive obligations on the state to take steps to secure their enjoyment by its citizens.[990] The boldness of this move has been tempered by the Strasbourg Court's deference to a wide margin of appreciation on the part of Contracting States to determine the steps to be taken, with due regard to the needs and resources of the community and individuals.[991]

Thus Article 8 has been interpreted as requiring the state to take positive steps to regulate the ordering of private relationships,[992] and to ensure a person's physical safety and integrity[993] including her sexual life.[994] So the Article 8 rights of a 16-year-old girl sexually assaulted in an institution for the mentally handicapped had been infringed by Dutch criminal law which required that she personally file a complaint before it could be investigated and prosecuted; it was no answer that her father could take civil proceedings on her behalf for compensation.[995]

Since 1995 the ECtHR has also planted positive obligations in the territories covered by Articles 2 and 3. The state's duty under Article 2 is not only to refrain from the intentional and unlawful taking of life, but also to take appropriate steps to safeguard the lives of those within its jurisdiction.[996] Similarly Article 3 requires the state to

---

[990] J Wright *Tort Law & Human Rights* (OUP, Oxford 2001), chapter 5; RA Mowbray *The Development of Positive Obligations under the European Convention on Human Rights by the European Court of Human Rights* (Hart Publishing, Oxford 2004). [991] *Johnston v Ireland* Series A no 112 (1986) (ECtHR). [992] *Marckx v Belgium* Series A no 31 (1979) (ECtHR) (civil rights and legal status of illegitimate children); *Airey v Ireland* Series A no 32 (1979) (ECtHR) [32] (right to legal aid to seek a judicial separation on marriage breakdown). [993] *Osman v UK* (n 639) [125]–[126]. [994] *X and Y v The Netherlands* (1986) 8 EHRR 235 (ECtHR) [23]. [995] ibid [27]–[30]. [996] *McCann v UK* (1995) 21 EHRR 97 (ECtHR); *LCB v UK* (1998) 27 EHRR 212 (ECtHR).

provide adequate protection against the infliction of inhuman or degrading treatment by private individuals. Compliance with Articles 2 and 3 requires the state to put in place effective criminal law provisions to deter the commission of offences against the person, backed up by law enforcement machinery for the prevention, suppression and punishment of breaches.[997] The Convention requires thorough, prompt and effective investigation and prosecution, attaching weight to the particular vulnerability of young persons and the special psychological factors involved in cases concerning sexual abuse of minors.[998]

Having a system of criminal law and enforcement in place does not suffice for compliance with the Convention; the state is also specifically obliged to protect potential victims at risk from the actual or threatened criminal acts of third parties. The landmark decision for this development was *Osman v UK*.[999] We have already discussed this case in relation to the highly controversial finding that the blanket immunity from tort liability which the police enjoyed after *Hill* in respect of their investigatory functions breached Article 6, by operating to deprive the Osman family of their right to access to the civil courts. We have explained that the case had a great but transitory impact in inducing English appellate courts to revisit their sceptical views of the effect of negligence liability on the performance of public authorities' discretionary functions. Of perhaps more enduring significance was the ECtHR's interpretation of Article 2.

In *Osman*, the UK government conceded that Article 2 may in certain circumstances imply a positive obligation on a state to take preventive measures to protect an individual whose life is at risk from the criminal acts of someone, but the scope of the obligation was in dispute. The ECtHR was conscious of the need not to impose an impossible or disproportionate burden on the authorities, given the difficulties involved in policing modern societies and the unpredictability of human conduct in the operational choices which must be made in terms of priorities and resources. It ruled that the positive obligation will be violated where the authorities knew, or ought to have known at the time, of the existence of a real and immediate risk to the life of an identified individual or individuals from the criminal acts of a third party and they failed to take measures within the scope of their powers which, judged reasonably, might have been expected to avoid that risk.[1000]

The same work of defining a positive obligation was done for Article 3 by *Z v UK*,[1001] the complainants being the children in *X v Bedfordshire* who had not been taken into care until five years of severe ill-treatment had elapsed. The ECtHR had already held that Article 3 requires Contracting States to ensure that children within their jurisdiction are not subjected to severe ill-treatment administered by private individuals, in its landmark judgment on the defence of reasonable chastisement in

---

[997] *Kılıç v Turkey* [2000] ECHR 22492/93 (ECtHR) [62].
[998] *MC v Bulgaria* (2003) 40 EHRR 20 (ECtHR) [183]–[184].
[999] *Osman v UK* (n 639) discussed above sections F.1(b)(ii) and F.2(c)(i).   [1000] ibid [115].
[1001] *Z and Others v UK* (n 657).

A v UK.[1002] In *Z v UK* this interpretation was extended to the investigation of alleged child abuse.[1003]

(ii) The standard required for a finding of breach of a positive obligation

As with common law negligence, the ECtHR's determination of the content of the state's protective duty sets up the proof required for breach. The rights to life and to protection against inhuman and degrading treatment are regarded as fundamental and absolute values in a democratic society,[1004] and no derogation from Articles 2 and 3 is permitted by a Contracting State. This may be because of the extreme nature of the conduct which all states must themselves refrain from inflicting, and must proscribe and enforce through the criminal law. When the state fails to fulfil its positive obligation to protect a person from the criminal acts of a third party, then breach must be pegged at a realistic level which will secure those rights to everyone within the state's jurisdiction under Article 1, whilst not imposing standards of perfection upon public authorities.

In *Osman* the UK government contended that a breach of Article 2 should be established only if the failure to perceive the risk to life in the circumstances known at the time, or to take preventive measures to avoid that risk, was tantamount to 'gross negligence or wilful disregard of the duty to protect life'. The ECtHR rejected this standard as being too rigid, and incompatible with the obligations of Contracting States to secure the practical and effective protection of the rights and freedoms in the ECHR. Instead, it will be sufficient for an applicant to show 'that the authorities did not do all that could be reasonably expected of them to avoid a real and immediate risk to life of which they have or ought to have knowledge'.[1005]

This objective test does not appear to differ materially from the standard of care imposed by common law negligence, although when tort law recognizes a duty to protect from the acts of third parties, it pitches the the level and severity of the foreseeable risk to be averted at a much lower level than does the Article 2 standard. This is revealed by the way in which the ECtHR applied its newly minted test for Article 2 to the facts in *Osman* (bearing in mind that the case had never gone to trial). It will be recalled that the risk to the child and his family was posed by an obsessed teacher at his school. The ECtHR reasoned that since a psychiatrist who interviewed the teacher three times had concluded that he did not display signs of mental illness or a propensity to violence, it would be unreasonable to expect the police to have considered the actions reported by the school as those of a mentally disturbed and highly dangerous individual. At no decisive stage could it be said that the police knew or ought to have known that the lives of the Osman family were at real and immediate risk. Given that the police must discharge their duties in a manner which is compatible with the rights and freedoms of individuals, they could not be criticized for attaching weight to the presumption of innocence or for failing to use their powers of arrest or search, given their reasonably held view that they lacked the required standard of

---

[1002] *A v UK* (1998) FLR 959, 27 EHRR 611 (ECtHR).
[1003] *Z and others v UK* (n 697) [73].   [1004] ibid [73].   [1005] *Osman v UK* (n 639) [116].

suspicion to use those powers, and that any action taken would not have produced concrete results.[1006] A similar analysis warranted a dismissal of the application under Article 8.[1007] Yet the failure of the police to retain or even make any records of their many meetings with the Osman family, and their sole attempt to execute the arrest warrant, pointed to a desultory investigation which a court might well find to be negligent according to the ordinary tort standard.

In *Z v UK* the government did not contest that the severity of the treatment suffered by the children at the hands of their parents reached the threshold of inhuman and degrading treatment prohibited by Article 3, and that it had failed to provide them with effective protection.[1008] The benchmark for compliance set by the ECtHR required the UK government to take 'reasonable steps to prevent ill-treatment of which the authorities had or ought to have had knowledge'.[1009] From October 1987 when the local authority learned of the children's treatment until April 1992 when they were taken into emergency care at the insistence of their mother, the children had been subjected to horrific experiences. The ECtHR concluded that, whilst acknowledging the difficult and sensitive decisions facing social services and the important countervailing principle of respecting and preserving family life, there was no doubt that the system failed to protect these children from serious long-term neglect and abuse.[1010]

In the *Newham* case which had accompanied *X v Bedfordshire* through the English courts, now renamed *TP and KM v UK*,[1011] the ECtHR reiterated its acknowledgement of the difficult decisions which must be taken in a child protection investigation. Here the claim was brought under Article 8, as a breach of the mother's and daughter's right to respect for their family life by taking her into care upon a negligent factual assumption about the identity of her abuser. It was accepted that this had been done in accordance with the law and had the legitimate aim of protecting the child's health and rights. In determining whether the local authority's actions under the Children Act 1989 were proportionate to their legitimate aim, the ECtHR stressed that in child protection matters generally national authorities enjoy a wide margin of appreciation, particularly when assessing the necessity of taking a child into care, not least because they have the benefit of direct contact with all the persons concerned. However, a stricter scrutiny is required of any further limitations such as restrictions on parental rights of access which might entail the danger that the family relations between the parents and a young child would be effectively curtailed.[1012] In *TP and KM* the child's disclosure of sexual abuse in the videotaped interview justified the initial measure of taking her into emergency protection through a place of safety order. However thereafter it is essential that a parent be informed of the nature and extent of the child's allegations of abuse, both to persuade the authorities of her capability to protect and care for the child, and to enable her to understand and come to terms with traumatic events affecting the family as a whole. Here the local authority's decision not to disclose

---

[1006] ibid [117]–[122].   [1007] ibid [128]–[130].

[1008] Such concessions being made as part of its strategy to close the gateway to Article 6 opened by *Osman*.   [1009] *Z and others v UK* (n 657) [72]–[73].

[1010] ibid [74].   [1011] *TP and KM v United Kingdom* (n 658).   [1012] ibid [70]–[71].

the video interview deprived the mother of involvement in the decision-making process concerning her daughter's care, and so this procedural default constituted a breach of Article 8.

These three landmark decisions enforcing a child's human right to be kept safe from abuse demonstrate a flexibility and sensitivity to the dilemmas faced by child protection agencies as an investigation progresses. From a practical perspective, egregious neglect of duty seems to be the 'breach benchmark' set by *Osman* and *Z v UK* under Articles 2 and 3. In contrast common law negligence seems to require child protection investigators to comply with higher standards of care, established through expert evidence as to what would be reasonable professional practice in the circumstances of that investigation.[1013] So the cryptic remark of Lord Phillips MR in *JD v East Berkshire* that the common law duty of care to the child will not replicate Articles 3 and 8 (although the area of factual inquiry is likely to be the same) because liability for breach of the Convention duty 'can arise in circumstances where the tort of negligence is not made out' is a bit puzzling.[1014] It is difficult to conceive of a situation where inaction or inadequate action by a local authority which knows or should know that a child is being subjected to inhuman and degrading treatment breaches that child's human rights, but does not attract liability in negligence to that child.

(iii) Remedies for breaches of human rights

Article 13 requires Contracting States to provide an effective remedy before a national authority for violation of Convention rights, notwithstanding that the violation may have been committed by persons acting in an official capacity. Thus a private individual's invasion of the applicant's civil rights under Articles 2, 3, 5, or 8 becomes a breach by the state if it does not provide an effective means of enforcing those rights at the national level. 'Effective' here means effective in practice as well as in law.[1015] As we discussed earlier,[1016] this provided the leverage to the ECtHR to hold in *Z v UK* that the UK government had not provided an appropriate forum to inquire into the substance of the children's complaints of violation of their rights under Article 3 to protect them from inhuman and degrading treatment—in effect, because of blanket immunity from tort liability.

This stance was reinforced in the later decision of *E v UK* from Scotland.[1017] Four girls had been sexually and physically abused by their stepfather over a long period of time. In 1977 he had been convicted of indecently assaulting two of them, but in breach of his probation order continued to have close contact with the family. In 1989 after three of the four children reported the continuing abuse to police, he was convicted and they were awarded compensation by the Criminal Injuries Compensation Board. A civil action for damages was abandoned on the advice of counsel following the decision of the House of Lords in *X v Bedfordshire*. The children were thwarted in their efforts to have an investigation undertaken into the allegations of negligence and maladministration on the part of the local authority as the ombudsman had declined

---

[1013] As in *B(D), B(R) and B(M) v Children's Aid Society of Durham Region* (n 822).
[1014] *JD v East Berkshire Community NHS Trust* (CA) (n 669) [85].   [1015] *E v UK* (n 664) [109].
[1016] In section F.1(b)(ii)   [1017] *E v UK* (n 664).

jurisdiction, so they brought complaints to the ECtHR under Articles 3, 8, and 13. The government's own expert in social work found the girls were failed by breaches of well-established contemporary practices by the local authority.[1018] The ECtHR found a breach of Article 3 in that social services should have been aware that the children remained at potential risk of further abuse by their stepfather. The government's submission that in 1977 social services lacked today's knowledge of the prevalence and persistence of sexual victimization within a family was 'not significant', because here they knew of the convictions for sexual abuse and so came under an obligation to monitor the offender's conduct in the aftermath.[1019]

The government argued that the children could not show that, had social services monitored the family after the first set of convictions, they would necessarily have either uncovered the abuse or prevented it. If accepted, this challenge to causation would have seriously inhibited the power of the ECHR to enforce children's rights to the state's protection from abuse. Fortunately the ECtHR rejected the 'but for' test familiar to tort lawyers, holding that a failure to take reasonably available measures which could have had 'a real prospect of altering the outcome or mitigating the harm' is sufficient to engage the responsibility of the state under Article 3.[1020]

The ECtHR held that neither the Criminal Injuries Compensation Board nor the local authority ombudsman sufficed to fulfil the UK's obligation under Article 13 to provide a practical and effective remedy at the national level to deal with the substance of an arguable complaint. While Article 13 may not always require the authority to undertake responsibility for investigating allegations, a mechanism must be available for establishing any liability of state officials or bodies for acts or omissions breaching the victim's rights under the Convention. Moreover compensation for the non-pecuniary damage flowing from the breach should in principle be available as part of the range of redress. The consequence of *X v Bedfordshire* had been to leave the impression that the highest judicial authority had ruled out the possibility of suing local authorities in the exercise of their child protection functions, and the applicants could not be faulted for not challenging this.[1021] Therefore the unavailability of a cause of action in tort to trigger external scrutiny of the acts and omissions of the child protection agency constituted a breach of Article 13.

(b) Liability under the Human Rights Act 1998

We turn now to the implications of the HRA which 'brought human rights home' to the UK by making breaches of the ECHR directly actionable in British courts, which are empowered to award compensation. Under s 7 only a victim of an unlawful act (in the sense of being actually affected by the violation alleged)[1022] will have standing to bring an action. There is no bar to bringing an action under the HRA concurrently with one in common law negligence.[1023] The HRA provides remedies

---

[1018] ibid [50]–[54].   [1019] ibid [96]–[98].   [1020] ibid [99].   [1021] ibid [109]–[115].
[1022] *Klass v Germany* (1978) 2 EHRR 214 (ECtHR) [33].
[1023] Indeed in child abuse cases it is advisable to plead both causes of action, since under the HRA s 7 there is a one-year limitation period running from the date of the alleged violation, although the court has discretionary jurisdiction to extend the limitation period under s 7(5).

only against a public authority, not against private entities or persons. However, s 6(1) provides that it is unlawful for a public authority to act in a way that is incompatible with a Convention right, and 'public authority' is defined by s 6(3) as including a court or tribunal and any person who exercises functions of a public nature. Thus the HRA affords the ECHR an indirect measure of horizontal effect, in that a court arguably would be acting unlawfully were it to enforce a common law rule which was incompatible with a Convention right of one of the parties before it. This provides a conduit between the Convention and the common law.

Significantly, Article 13 is not amongst the Articles of the ECHR made action-able under domestic law through Schedule 1 to the HRA. This is because s 8 allows the British court to grant such relief or remedy within its powers as it con-siders just and appropriate, and so provides a range of remedies which is broader and potentially more powerful than that permitted by Article 41. Thus while the ECtHR can only award non-pecuniary damages,[1024] legal fees and expenses, an English court can now order a party to take positive steps to redress the infringe-ment. For example, the domestic court could order disclosure to a person of social services records pertaining to the reasons he was taken into care and his foster place-ments, as the ECtHR could only award symbolic compensation for the breach of Article 8.[1025]

The HRA s 8 replicates ECHR Article 41 in providing that damages can be awarded where they are necessary 'to afford just satisfaction' to the injured party. It is important to note that this concept is in part symbolic, and so is not equivalent to compensatory damages awarded by tort law which have the (necessarily unattainable) objective of placing the victim in the position he would have been in had the tort not occurred. Thus Ahmet Osman who had been shot by his stalker and whose father had been killed in the same incident was awarded only £10,000 for breach of his right of access to the civil courts to obtain a ruling on the merits of his claim for damages against the police.[1026] The grossly abused children in *Z v UK* received significantly more compensation in their human rights claim for their pecuniary losses including psy-chotherapy expenses and loss of future earnings.[1027] However, the ECtHR paid some heed to the UK government's submission that it should not rely upon English caselaw and scales of assessment for personal injury damages, holding that such awards are 'a relevant but not decisive consideration' in determining the quantum of compensation to achieve just satisfaction for violation of Convention rights.[1028] It is submitted that that tort law offers a much more nuanced approach to the quantification of claims which are in essence for personal injury, including the availability of court-imposed

---

[1024] Although the scope of non-pecuniary damages is far wider than under English tort law, extending to trauma, anxiety, distress and feeling of injustice [J Wright 'Child Abuse Claims against Public Authorities under the Human Rights Act 1998' in D Fairgrieve and S Green (eds) *Child Abuse Tort Claims against Public Bodies: A Comparative Law View* (Ashgate, London 2004) 33].

[1025] As the ECtHR could not order in *Gaskin v UK (access to personal files)* [1989] ECHR 10454/83 (ECtHR); *MG v UK (access to social services records)* Application no 39393/98, (2002) 13 BHRC 179 (ECtHR). [1026] *Osman v UK* (n 639) [163].

[1027] The damages totalling £320,000 apparently were the highest ever awarded by the ECtHR under Article 41: Wright *Tort Law & Human Rights* (n 990) xxiv. [1028] *Z v UK* (n 659) [115]–[121].

'structured judgments' for periodic payments which can provide the most appropriate compensation for victims of long-term abuse.[1029]

The normative force of the HRA on tort law is exemplified by *JD v East Berkshire*: the Court of Appeal pronounced the death sentence for *X v Bedfordshire* on the basis that it could not survive the HRA. Lord Phillips MR reasoned that since local authorities are under an obligation to respect a child's Convention rights, the same factual inquiry would be made regardless of whether the claim was brought in negligence or under the HRA.[1030] 'In so far as the risk of legal proceedings might inhibit individuals from boldly taking what they believe to be the right course of action in the delicate situation of the case where child abuse is suspected, that factor will henceforth be present whether the litigation is founded on the HRA or the common law duty of care'.[1031] The fact that the HRA could apply to claims only after 2 October 2000 provided the necessary leverage to change the common law to provide a remedy for children who were victims of abuse before that date.[1032]

We turn now to consider another possible model for protection of children's fundamental rights, offered by the American Constitution.

5. Constitutional tort liability of child protection agencies in American law

In American cases seeking compensation for the action or inaction of child protection agencies, a constitutional tort is frequently pleaded alongside common law negligence liability. The alternative plea may be motivated by concerns about sovereign immunity,[1033] and some States impose a low statutory ceiling on common law tort recovery against governmental agencies.[1034] So in the discussion below some overlap with our previous discussion of common law tort liability under State law will be unavoidable.

The proactive stance of the ECtHR and the English courts in interpreting the ECHR and the HRA as vesting children with positive entitlements to the state's protection from abuse stands in stark contrast to the starting premise of American courts, as exemplified by *DeShaney*, that the American Constitution is a set of a negative liberties protecting the people from the intrusion of the state, not ensuring that the state protects them from one another. It does not create a set of positive rights to state action.[1035] However, many American courts have been adroit in circumventing the harsh result in *DeShaney*,[1036] exploiting the opening left by an *obiter dictum* in the majority judgment that 'in certain limited circumstances the Constitution

---

[1029] Pursuant to the Courts Act 2003 (England) s 100.

[1030] *JD v East Berkshire Community NHS Trust* (CA) (n 669) [79]–[81], [85].   [1031] ibid [82].

[1032] ibid [83].

[1033] BM Douthett 'The Death of Constitutional Duty: the Court Reacts to the Expansion of Section 1983 Liability in *DeShaney v Winnebago County Department of Social Services*' (1991) 52 Ohio State LJ 643, 650. It should be noted that under American law government employees in constitutional cases are not protected by vicarious liability on the part of the public authority. It has been suggested that this is why American courts adhere so strongly to qualified immunity for such officials: Goldberg 'Liability for Government Actions (n 721) 111.   [1034] Eaton and Wells (n 224) 134.

[1035] *DeShaney v Winnebago* (n 212) 194–196; Bjorkland (n 783).

[1036] *DeShaney v Winnebago* ibid discussed above, section F.2(a)(v).

imposes upon the State affirmative duties of care and protection with respect to particular individuals'.[1037] The decisions of Federal courts across America are not easy to reconcile.

(a) A violation of a constitutional right

The constitutional right usually invoked in child abuse cases is the Due Process Clause of the 14th Amendment, which provides that 'no State shall . . . deprive any person of life, liberty, or property, without due process of law, nor deny to any person within its jurisdiction the equal protection of the laws'. There are two forms of due process: substantive and procedural. The former 'protects individual liberty against certain government actions regardless of the fairness of the procedures used to implement them.'[1038] Substantive due process rights are so fundamental that they cannot be abrogated by the State, and are usually found in the Bill of Rights but may also arise from other sources of Federal law; they include the right to physical safety.[1039] Procedural due process claims involve explicit interests and expectations created specifically by State law, and which can be taken away by the State if procedural safeguards are provided, such as the right to a court hearing before or after the deprivation.[1040]

As a general proposition, the failure of a State or local government entity to protect an individual against violence by private actors does not constitute a violation of substantive due process. The Due Process Clause therefore does not confer an affirmative right to governmental aid, even where such aid may be necessary to secure the life, liberty or property interests of which the government itself could not deprive the individual.[1041] The tragic case of Joshua DeShaney confirmed that mere knowledge by State child abuse authorities of a child's danger, and expressions of willingness to protect him against that danger (as evidenced by monthly visits to Joshua's home by a case worker), do not establish a special relationship giving rise to an affirmative constitutional duty to protect him.[1042]

However, the majority in *DeShaney* accepted that positive duties of protection can arise under the substantive Due Process Clause where:

- the State has created a danger or has taken a positive act which made an individual more vulnerable to a danger;[1043] or

- the State has taken an affirmative act to restrain the individual's freedom to act on his own behalf through placing him in an institution or in an environment governed

---

[1037] ibid 198.

[1038] *Collins v City of Harker Heights, Texas* 503 US 115 (USSC 1992) (quoting *Daniels v Williams* 474 US 327 (USSC 1986) 331).   [1039] *Youngberg v Romeo* 457 US 307 (USSC 1982) 315.

[1040] *Taylor v Ledbetter* 818 F 2d 791 (US CA 11th Cir 1987) *certiorari* denied 489 US 1065 (USSC 1989) 798; Crosby-Currie and Reppucci (n 783), 152–153.

[1041] *DeShaney v Winnebago* (n 212) 196.

[1042] ibid 19 described above, section F.2(a)(v). The 3rd and 4th Circuits had previously held that a special relationship did arise between a child protection agency and a child, from actual knowledge and previous involvement with the family: *Bailey v County of York* 768 F 2d 503 (US CA 3rd Cir 1985); *Jensen v Conrad* 747 F 2d 185 (US CA 4th Cir 1984) *certiorari* denied 470 US 1052 (USSC 1985). This constitutional concept of special relationship had been borrowed from common law tort doctrine: Sinden (n 783), 234.

[1043] *DeShaney v Winnebago* ibid 201. These are sometimes called the 'snake pit' cases: *Bowers v DeVito* 686 F 2d 616 (US CA 7th Cir 1982) 618.

by the State or its agents, and so has become responsible for his reasonable safety and general well-being.[1044]

Obviously these are not discrete routes; placing a child in institutional care can satisfy the State custody requirement whilst also exposing the child to new dangers, and the same can also be true for foster care.

(i) Creating a 'constitutional tort'

The mechanism making a breach of due process actionable in a claim for compensation is §1983 of the Civil Rights Act.[1045] This allows an action for damages in the federal courts where a government official has violated a person's constitutional or federal statutory rights.[1046] It addresses a misuse of power possessed by virtue of State law, and made possible only because the wrongdoer is clothed with the authority of State law.[1047] §1983 explicitly includes within its scope both those who violate constitutional rights and those who allow constitutional rights to be violated, and so provides compensation for misfeasance and nonfeasance so long as they violate Federal law. That said, the positive constitutional right to protection must have been triggered by previous State involvement, using one of the two routes left open by *DeShaney*, before nonfeasance becomes actionable.

§ 1983 creates no new substantive constitutional rights but rather provides a channel for a tort-like claim against a public official. However, the US Supreme Court has repeatedly emphasized that §1983 does not convert every tort committed by a State actor into a constitutional violation,[1048] nor can the Due Process Clause be so stretched that it becomes 'a font of tort law to be superimposed upon whatever systems may already be administered by the States'.[1049] Nevertheless all §1983 cases are to be read against the background of tort liability,[1050] and, at least until *DeShaney*, the lower appellate courts borrowed from tort concepts such as a special relationship to set up liability for State inaction.

The first step in evaluating a §1983 claim is to identify the exact contours of the underlying right said to have been violated and to determine whether the claimant has alleged a deprivation of a constitutional right at all.[1051] If the right or interest can be brought within the Due Process Clause, then the court must determine if

---

[1044] ibid 201; *Youngberg v Romeo* (n 1039) (State must provide protection to involuntarily committed patients in a mental health facility); *Estelle v Gamble* 49 US 97 (USSC 1976) (State must provide adequate medical care to incarcerated prisoners). This is often described as the 'special-relationship doctrine' [*Uhlrig v Harder* 64 F 3d 567 (US CA 10th Cir 1995) 572] although the Supreme Court did not use this terminology.

[1045] Originally framed under the Ku Klux Klan Act of 1871, now codified as 42 USC §1983, which provides: 'Every person who, under color of any statute, ordinance, regulation, custom, or usage, of any State or Territory, subjects, or causes to be subjected, any citizen of the United States or other person within the jurisdiction thereof to the deprivation of any rights, privileges, or immunities secured by the Constitution and laws, shall be liable to the party injured in an action at law, suit in equity, or other proper proceeding for redress.' The section was not invoked until 1961 [*Munro v Pape* 365 US 167 (USSC 1961)], and has since become a widely pleaded supplement to common law torts actionable under State law.

[1046] *Kneipp v Tedder* 95 F 3d 1199 (US CA 3rd Cir 1996) 1204.

[1047] *US v Classic* 313 US 299 (USSC 1941) 326.　　　[1048] *DeShaney v Winnebago* (n 212) 202.

[1049] *Daniels v Williams* (n 1038) 332.　　　[1050] *Munro v Pape* (n 1045) 187.

[1051] *County of Sacramento v Lewis* 523 US 833 (USSC 1998) 841 n 5.

the requisite threshold for breach has been established.[1052] It is well settled that mere negligence cannot trigger substantive due process protection.[1053] The problem lies in the placement of the higher benchmark. In *Youngberg v Romeo*, the US Supreme Court held in the context of medical care for involuntarily committed patients in State mental institutions that a decision made by a professional is presumptively valid; liability under §1983 will be imposed only when the decision is such a substantial departure from accepted professional judgement, practice or standards as to demonstrate that the person responsible actually did not base the decision on such a judgement.[1054]

After much disagreement in the lower courts, the standard of culpability was supposedly settled by the US Supreme Court in 1998 in *County of Sacramento v Lewis*: the touchstone of due process is protection of the individual against arbitrary action of government.[1055] The action will not be arbitrary if the constitutional right had not been clearly established at that time, because then the State actor could not have been expected to know that he was violating the person's constitutional rights.[1056] Where the challenge is to executive action 'only the most egregious official conduct' can be said to be 'arbitrary in the constitutional sense'.[1057] Substantive due process liability attaches only to action that is 'so ill-conceived or malicious' that it 'shocks the conscience,' the exact degree of wrongfulness depending on the circumstances of a particular case.[1058] The Court in *Lewis* adopted the term 'deliberate indifference' as useful in denoting the requisite level of culpability in most circumstances.[1059] But it also noted that in some contexts conduct in the middle range of culpability between negligence and intentional conduct can be shocking in the constitutional sense; it cautioned that rules of due process are not subject to mechanical application but may vary from one environment to another.[1060]

Since *Lewis* the lower courts have been debating whether the professional judgement standard in the Supreme Court's earlier decision in *Youngberg* should continue to apply to decisions by child protection workers.[1061] *Youngberg* had rejected the 'deliberate indifference' standard approved in *Lewis* on the basis that it is inappropriate for the vulnerable persons involuntarily committed to institutions. In the final analysis it should make little practical difference, because a decision by a social worker deviating so far from accepted professional standards as to constitute an abdication of the duty to act professionally[1062] surely must qualify as arbitrary under *Lewis v Sacramento*.

§1983 has been invoked where the State did not intervene to protect a child, and also where it did intervene, and so neatly encapsulates the familiar dilemma of

---

[1052] *Daniels v Williams* (n 1038).   [1053] ibid.   [1054] *Youngberg v Romeo* (n 1039) 323.

[1055] *County of Sacramento v Lewis* (n 1051) 845 (citing *Wolff v McDonnell* 418 US 539 (USSC 1974) 558.   [1056] *Yvonne L v New Mexico Department of Human Services* (n 733).

[1057] *County of Sacramento v Lewis* (n 1051) 846 (citing *Collins v City of Harker Heights, Texas* (n 1038) 129.   [1058] *County of Sacramento v Lewis* ibid 846.

[1059] The Supreme Court however recognized that a middle level of culpability might still 'shock the conscience' in the constitutional sense, depending on the circumstances: ibid 850.   [1060] ibid 850–851.

[1061] See the extended analysis in *TM v Carson* 93 F Supp 2d 1179 (US DC Wyoming 2000) 1187–1191.

[1062] *Yvonne L v New Mexico Department of Human Services* (n 733) 890, 893–894; *Whitley v New Mexico Children, Youth and Families Department* 184 F Supp 2d 1146 (US DC New Mexico 2001) 1155–1156; *Nicini v Morra* (n 220) 810–811.

child protection agencies.[1063] However, this dilemma is cast in terms of competing constitutional rights: the liberty interest of the child to be free from harm, and the liberty interest of the parent to be free from governmental interference with the integrity of the family unit, both being protected by the Due Process Clause.[1064] It has been powerfully argued that this is a false antithesis, and that the juridical basis for parental constitutional rights is the trust of society that this is the best way to secure the best interests of the child.[1065] There is some judicial support for this view. As a Rhode Island court trenchantly observed, any constitutional protection for familial integrity does not include a right to be free from child abuse investigations; fairly conducted investigations brought for any reason do not violate or even implicate any constitutional rights of the investigated family.[1066] However, whilst the family's constitutional interest in privacy and integrity may have to yield to the perceived necessity for temporary emergency removal of the child, their collective interests as a family may come to prevail where a social services in bad faith persists in keeping the child in foster care after it is apparent that the allegations are groundless.[1067]

§1983 is most obviously applicable where the State has placed a child with foster carers.[1068] Given the robustness of the constitutional objections in *DeShaney*, it is very difficult to construct a constitutional tort from failure to investigate an abuse allegation,[1069] or to do so diligently and competently.[1070] More than 25 years after *DeShaney*, the pattern of liability across the federal court system remains unclear. The following discussion aims only to give some indication of the difficulties of applying Federal constitutional concepts to State-operated child protection systems in a principled way.

(ii) Circumventing *DeShaney*: a state-created or state-enhanced danger to a child as a substantive due process right

The majority in *DeShaney* held that in returning Joshua to his father's custody whilst continuing to supervise through monthly visits, the State placed him in no worse position than that in which he would have been had it not acted at all; the minority condemned this conclusion as permitting a State 'to displace private sources of protection and then, at the critical moment, to shrug its shoulders and turn away from the harm that it has promised to try to prevent'.[1071] The majority's reasoning also can

---

[1063] Recognized by the majority in *Estelle v Gamble* (n 1044) 203.

[1064] *DeShaney v Winnebago* (n 212) 203; *Stanley v Illinois* 405 US 645 (USSC 1972) 651.

[1065] Crosby-Currie and Reppucci (n 783).

[1066] *Wojcik v Town of North Smithfield* (n 881) 519.

[1067] *Morris v Dearborne* 69 F Supp 2d 868 (US DC 1999) 883–884.

[1068] DL Skoler 'A Constitutional Right to Safe Foster Care?—Time for the Supreme Court to Pay Its IOU' (1991) 18 Pepperdine L Rev 353; M Miller 'Revisiting Poor Joshua: State-Created Danger Theory in the Foster Care Context' (2000) 11 Hastings Women's LJ 243.

[1069] eg *Sapp v Cunningham* 847 F Supp 893 (US DC Wyoming 1994).

[1070] eg *Pierce v Delta County Department of Social Services* 119 F Supp 2d 1139 (US DC Colorado 2000) (two-year-old child killed after numerous reports to social services of suspicious injuries which were only cursorily investigated).   [1071] *DeShaney v Winnebago* (n 212) 201, 212.

be criticized on the basis that it provides an incentive for social workers to leave the child in an abusive home.[1072]

Several courts have followed *DeShaney* in holding that a decision to return a child to the custody of a parent or carer from whom it had earlier rescued her did not increase the risk of abuse so as to come within the State-created danger exception,[1073] nor did allowing a child in the legal custody of the State to remain with the abusive parent.[1074] This was also the case where a parent voluntarily placed her child with private carers whom the child protection service had reason to know to be abusive.[1075] Where however the State intervenes to transfer custody of a child from one parent to another, then a §1983 action may become available on the theory that the State has created a new danger of abuse.[1076] This was also the case where a child in the permanent custody of the State was returned to her father, notwithstanding that social services knew that he consorted with a convicted paedophile, and there had been concerns reported about her safety during previous unsupervised visits.[1077] The problem is that there can be a continuum of a child protection agency's involvement between mere supervision of a family, which under *DeShaney* does not set up an affirmative duty to protect, and foster care with a third party approved by the State, which can do so.[1078]

In respect of third party foster care, the State-created danger exception has been regarded as applying only where social services knew or had reason to suspect that a foster parent or other custodian was a child abuser, at the time of the placement or at some point during the period of foster care whilst the State remained the child's guardian. Negligence does not suffice.[1079] However, it has not yet been definitively settled in the child protection setting whether 'deliberate indifference' under *Lewis v Sacramento* requires actual rather than putative ('should have known') knowledge of the risk that the placement may not be safe.[1080] Moreover, the right to be safe in a foster placement has been treated by some courts only as a prima facie right; if because of resource constraints social services cannot find another safe placement for a child, they cannot be held liable in damages for a risky placement when they had no choice.[1081] Shuttling a young child amongst numerous foster homes is not a basis for

---

[1072] Bjorkland (n 783), 814; Eaton and Wells (n 224), 131; *White v Chambliss* 112 F 3d 731 (US CA 4th Cir 1987) 736.

[1073] *SS v McMullan* 225 F 3d 960 (US CA 8th Cir 2000); *Powell v Department of Human Resources of the State of Georgia* 918 F Supp 1575 (US DC Georgia 1996); *Terry B v Gilkey* 229 F 3d 680 (US CA 8th Cir 2000).   [1074] *AS v Tellus* 22 F Supp 2d 1217 (US DC Kansas 1998).

[1075] *Sayles v Pennsylvania Department of Public Welfare, County of Monroe* 24 F Supp 2d 393 (US DC Pennsylvania 1997); *Sapp v Cunningham* (n 1069).

[1076] *Currier v Doran* 23 F Supp 2d 1277 (US DC New Mexico 1998) (three-year-old transferred from mother's custody to father's custody who killed him by scalding).

[1077] *SS v McMullan* (n 1073). See also *Tazioly v City of Philadelphia* WL 633747 (US DC Pennsylvania 1998) (child of a cocaine addict mother was returned to her from State custody because social services was under great pressure to discharge children from the foster care system, and then ignored repeated reports of serious injuries and neglect; liability was established under the State-created danger theory).

[1078] Sinden (n 783) 258–260.

[1079] *Lewis v Anderson* 308 F 3d 768 (US CA 7th Cir 2002) 773–774; Skoler (n 1068) 371.

[1080] *Nicini v Morra* (n 220) 811.

[1081] *KH v Morgan* 914 F 2d 846 (USSC 7th Cir 1990) 853–854 relying upon *Youngberg v Romeo* (n 1039) 323; *Bailey v Pacheco* 108 F Supp 2d 1214 (US DC New Mexico 2000).

liability under §1983, even though it was predictable that it would damage her mental health, unless the right to be protected from such administrative incompetence was clearly established by caselaw at the time.[1082]

(iii) Circumventing *DeShaney*: affirmative duty arising from taking control of a child as a substantive due process right

It has been persuasively argued that it is incongruous to apply an exception predicated upon State custody of an adult in a prison or institution, which prevents him from protecting himself, to children who are inherently unable to care for themselves and so are dependent on adults and ultimately the State for protection, regardless of their custody status.[1083] Whatever the strength of that objection, it is generally easier to set up an affirmative duty to protect where a State child protection agency has removed a child from her family and placed her in a State-approved foster home or institution where she is abused or neglected.[1084]

Where children are in foster care, they are generally held to have a substantive due process right to a safe environment, and to be protected from harm at the hands of State-regulated foster parents, or by others in the foster home.[1085] The rationale is that an involuntary foster placement is analogous to incarceration or institutionalization: 'without the investigation, supervision, and constant contact required by statute, the child placed in a foster home is at the mercy of the foster parents.'[1086] The Court of Appeals Fourth Circuit stands against this authority, holding that children placed in foster care have no Federal constitutional right to State protection because a foster parent is a private actor not controlled by the State, and so the child is not in the State's 'custody'.[1087]

Difficulties can still arise on the margins where the parent initially consented to foster care, or the State placed the child with other family members.[1088] Child protection agencies provide a continuum of services with a wide grey area in which distinctions between the State and private spheres become ambiguous or arbitrary.[1089] In *Nicini v Morra*,[1090] at issue was a voluntary placement which had not been initially arranged

---

[1082] *KH v Morgan* ibid 849–850, 853–854 (from the age of 17 months child had eight sets of foster parents in four years).   [1083] Bjorkland (n 783), 814.

[1084] As indeed indeed the majority in *DeShaney* noted without expressing a view as to the validity of the analogy: *DeShaney v Winnebago* (n 212) 201 fn 9. The analogy had set up State liability for abuse perpetrated in a foster home in *Doe v New York City Department of Social Services* 649 F 2d 134 (US CA 2nd Cir 1981) *certiorari* denied 464 US 864 (USSC 1983) and in *Taylor v Ledbetter* (n 1040).

[1085] *Lintz v Skipski* 25 F 3d 304 (US CA 6th Cir 1994) 305; *Norfleet v Arkansas Department of Human Services* 99 F 2d 289 (USSC 8th Cir 1993) 293; *Yvonne L v New Mexico Department of Human Services* (n 733) 891–893; *KH v Morgan* (n 1081), 848–849; *Morris v Dearborne* (n 1067); *Ray v Foltz* 370 F 3d 1079 (US CA 11th Cir 2004); *Meador v Cabinet for Human Resources* 902 F 2d 474 (US CA 6th Cir 1990) *certiorari* denied 498 US 867 (USSC 1990).   [1086] *Taylor v Ledbetter* (n 1040) 796–797.

[1087] *White v Chambliss* (n 1072) 737–738; *Milburn v Anne Arundel County Department of Social Services* 871 F 2d 474 (US CA 4th Cir 1989) 476–477.

[1088] Sinden (n 783), 247–254. However in *Hebein v Young* 37 F Supp 2d 1035 (USDC Illinois 1998) the substantive due process right was triggered by placing a child with her grandfather whose history of domestic violence would have been discovered through any reasonable investigation prior to or immediately following the placement.   [1089] Crosby-Currie and Reppucci (n 783), 148.

[1090] *Nicini v Morra* (n 220).

by social services, but they acquiesced in the arrangement once the child came into their custody, so as to attract the special relationship doctrine. The child alleged that the case worker, acting under colour of State law, deprived him of 'the right to be free from the infliction of unnecessary pain or abuse . . . and the fundamental right to physical safety' by violating his right 'to be free from deprivation of liberty by reason of a foster care placement preceded by an investigation so lacking in thoroughness and precision that it can be said to shock the conscience', as the trial court described it. The US Court of Appeal's Third Circuit upheld the claimant's assertion of a principle that a State's role in placing children in foster homes gives rise to a constitutional right of protection to the child. To import Canadian terminology,[1091] a power/dependency relationship arises by virtue of the State-sponsored foster placement, in that the child is rendered dependent upon the State to meet the child's basic needs.[1092]

Liability in a §1983 action for abuse in a foster home is still difficult to establish, as most authorities hold that the child will have in addition to show that the child protection agency personnel actually knew of the abuse or deliberately failed to learn what was occurring in the foster home, in order to establish deliberate indifference.[1093]

(iv) Circumventing *DeShaney*: reliance on a procedural due process right

We have seen that *Deshaney* has been generally limited to situations where the State is not involved in the harm, either as the child's custodian or as an actor,[1094] but this generates far too much uncertainty and litigation on the margins of substantive due process cases. An alternative constitutional route to relief under §1983 is based on the premise that if the State law sets up an entitlement to State services and so creates an expectation of performance upon which the individual relies, then a protectable liberty or property interest arises which cannot be withheld without procedural due process.[1095] The procedural due process argument may be raised by children or by their parents who claim that their removal was unwarranted. The courts have generally been assiduous to protect emergency measures thought necessary to avert imminent harm to a child, provided that the parents had an opportunity to contest their removal in short order.[1096]

The argument was raised in *DeShaney* that Joshua was entitled to receive protective services under State child protection law, but it had not been advanced in the courts below and so the Supreme Court refused to consider it.[1097] The advantage of this approach is that it is focused very sharply upon child protection services and places the best interests of the child in the forefront of consideration, which otherwise risk becoming invisible in the technical arguments over substantive due process.[1098] It is not necessary to find a special relationship, nor is nonfeasance an impediment

---

[1091] *Bazley v Curry* (n 381).
[1092] *DR v Middle Bucks Vocational Technical School* (n 714); see also *Horton v Flenory* 889 F 2d 454 (US CA 3rd Cir 1989) 457.
[1093] *Ray v Foltz* (n 1085) 1083–1084; *Lewis v Anderson* (n 1079). For a contrary view holding that the professional judgment standard does not require actual knowledge or suspicion, see *TM v Carson* (n 1061) 1193–1194.   [1094] *Horton v Flenory* (n 1092) 457.
[1095] *Board of Regents of State Colleges v Roth* 408 US 564 (USSC 1972) 571–572, 577–578.
[1096] *White v Chambliss* (n 1072).   [1097] *DeShaney v Winnebago* (n 212) 195 fn 2.
[1098] Crosby-Currie and Reppucci (n 783), 152–156.

due to the entitlement to a State action.[1099] Thus in *Taylor v Ledbetter* (decided before *DeShaney*) where a two-year-old child placed in a foster home was beaten so badly she was rendered permanently comatose, it was held that the Georgia child care statutory scheme provided more than just procedural guidelines to be followed in arriving at decisions as to the child's needs; it mandated officials to take affirmative actions to ensure the well-being and promote the welfare of children in foster care, and their failure to do so gave rise to a procedural due process claim for deprivation of her liberty interest.[1100]

Thus the §1983 procedural due process action can provide additional protection for existing statutory rights, triggering an obligation to compensate for their breach.[1101] However the specific language of the statute is crucial to the creation of entitlements, and if a statute directs the child protection agency to investigate reported child abuse, but not then to act to secure a particular or guaranteed outcome, there may be no grounds for a §1983 action if protection was not competently rendered.[1102] For example, the District of Columbia Circuit Court held that the codification of procedures for investigating child abuse, including mandatory reporting procedures, did not create an entitlement to protective services because the District had not assumed a constitutional obligation to protect children from abuse.[1103] *Taylor v Ledbetter* has not been applied outside the Eleventh Circuit.

The availability of a procedural due process claim for negligent child protection services is likely to have been substantially undermined by the 2005 decision of the US Supreme Court in *Town of Castle Rock v Gonzales*.[1104] The claimant had obtained a restraining order from a State court against her violent estranged husband. Enforcement of domestic restraining orders was mandated by a Colorado statute directing that 'every reasonable means' be used to enforce a restraining order, including arrest or seeking a warrant, and the restraining order itself was in specific terms and used mandatory language. Nevertheless the police refused to enforce the order or to take other action when the claimant repeatedly reported that her husband had abducted their three daughters aged three, seven and nine. The father murdered the children, and then died in a shoot-out with police. The US Court of Appeal Tenth Circuit held that Mrs Gonzales had a property interest in the enforcement of the restraining order, which set up a claim under §1983 for breach of procedural due process, but the individual police officers were protected by good-faith immunity.[1105] The US Supreme Court by a majority of seven justices to two reversed this decision. The majority held that the procedural component of the Due Process Clause does not protect everything that might be described as a 'benefit'; the person must have a legitimate claim of entitlement to it under State law, which will not be the case if government officials may grant

---

[1099] *Taylor v Ledbetter* (n 1040) 799–800.　　　　[1100] ibid.

[1101] Skoler (n 1068) 372–375.

[1102] *Tony L by and through Simpson v Childers* (n 799) 1186; *Pierce v Delta County Department of Social Services* (n 1070) 1152–1153; *Doe by Nelson v Milwaukee County* 903 F 2d 499 (US CA 7th Cir 1990) 501–504.

[1103] *Doe by Fein v District of Columbia* 93 F 3d 861 (District of Columbia Circuit 1996) 868.

[1104] *Town of Castle Rock v Gonzales* 125 S Ct 2796 (USSC 2005).

[1105] *Gonzales v City of Castle Rock* 366 F 3d 1093 (US CA 10th Cir 2004).

or deny it in their discretion. Notwithstanding the wording of the restraining order, there was a well-established tradition of police discretion coexisting with apparently mandatory arrest statutes[1106] (which was what, according to the minority, the statute had been enacted to overcome).[1107] The contours of the duty to enforce the order were indeterminate as several options were open to the police, and in any event any entitlement did not amount to a property interest in police enforcement.[1108] The majority concluded that *Gonzales* together with *DeShaney* meant that the benefit a third party might receive from having someone else arrested for a crime generally does not trigger protection under the Due Process Clause, either in its procedural or in its substantive manifestations. The majority in reiterating that the 14th Amendment should not be treated as a font of tort law pointed out that this did not mean that States are powerless to provide victims with personally enforceable remedies under State law.[1109]

It would seem that a child protection statute would have to be framed in extremely narrow and stringent terms, leaving no room whatsoever for discretion by social workers, before a refusal of child protection services to a child could constitute a breach of her procedural due process rights. Even a mandatory requirement for prompt investigation of a child abuse allegation might still leave the agency some latitude as to what steps should be taken, when and how. The loophole left by *DeShaney* has not been closed altogether, but it appears to have been narrowed to such an extent that very few claimants will be able to pass through it. Children and their families will be thrown back on substantive due process claims under §1983, with all the difficulties of establishing that the child protection agency has exposed the child to a new or enhanced risk. The foster family abuse cases might continue to be actionable under §1983 on the basis that the State has taken over control of the child, but the firm stance of the Supreme Court, as currently constituted, that the American Constitution does not confer affirmative rights is likely to deter the lower federal courts from being as proactive, not to say creative, as the Tenth Circuit Court of Appeal was in *Gonzales*.

Although the Federal Child Abuse Prevention and Treatment and Adoption Reform Act has had an admirable impact on securing a consistent baseline of child protection services in all 50 states, the ability of children and families to enforce those provisions through common law and constitutional tort actions varies enormously, depending on the eagerness of the courts in their jurisdiction to follow or to distinguish *DeShaney*. Notwithstanding the storm of criticism which *DeShaney* continues to generate,[1110] in 2005 the US Supreme Court reinforced and extended rather than reconsidered it.

There is clearly a jurisprudential gulf between the approach of the ECtHR and English courts in applying the European Convention as a source of positive rights and protections for all private individuals, and the American view that their Constitution is a charter of negative liberties which protects only against State action, and which can be invoked by victims of violence at the hands of others only in extraordinarily narrow

---

[1106] *Town of Castle Rock v Gonzales* (n 1104) 2798–2799.   [1107] ibid 2814–2815.
[1108] ibid 2808–2009.   [1109] ibid 2810.
[1110] eg Douthett (n 1034), 650 ('*DeShaney* calls into question the legitimacy and logic of a nation governed by a bureaucracy which has no constitutional duties toward its citizens unless they are in captivity.')

yet ambiguous circumstances. More than 25 years after *DeShaney*, a high volume of litigation in the United States continues to be generated to ascertain whether children have rights to protection from the State. The American position that the State owes no obligation to a child under human rights law to intervene to stop abuse of which it is aware is alien to English and other European jurists. It is inconsistent with Article 19 of the UN Convention on the Rights of the Child (which, it will be remembered, the United States has not ratified). We conclude that the American experience with the constitutional rights of children has little to offer except by way of negative example to English courts considering child protection issues under the Human Rights Act 1998.

6. Liability of child protection investigators to the suspect

It is beyond the scope of this book to provide a detailed analysis of the potential liability of child protection agencies to the person suspected of abuse. We provide only a very brief overview here to provide an additional context for our concluding evaluation of the utility of tort law in improving effective child protection services to families.

(a) Liability in negligence

In England,[1111] New Zealand,[1112] and Australia,[1113] child protection investigators including social workers, police and health professionals may not be sued in negligence by those who become the targets of an investigation. In these jurisdictions it is thought that child abuse investigators would be placed in an inevitable conflict of interest if they were to owe a duty of care both to the alleged victim and the alleged perpetrator in relation to the same investigation. In contrast many Canadian[1114] and American[1115] courts have been less troubled by this contention. They have concluded that there is no inherent conflict where the selfsame duty to take reasonable care to conduct a thorough and competent investigation which tests, explores, checks and verifies the evidence is owed concurrently to the child and the suspect. There is the greatest likelihood of a commonality of interest in the conduct of a balanced inquiry where

---

[1111] *JD v East Berkshire Community NHS Trust et al* (HL) (n 580).

[1112] *B v Attorney General of New Zealand* (n 804).

[1113] *Sullivan v Moody* (n 240) approving *Hillman v Black* (1996) 67 SASR 490 (South Australia Supreme Ct).

[1114] eg *B(D), B(R) and B(M) v Children's Aid Society of Durham Region* (n 695); *LC and LS v British Columbia* (n 818); *AAD, TD and KGD v Tanner, Winnipeg Child and Family Services Agency et al* (n 695); *André v Québec (Procureur général)* (n 695). See also the peculiar case of *Young v Bella, Rowe and Memorial University of Newfoundland* 2006 SCC 3, [2006] 1 SCR 108 (SCC) holding that professors in a university School of Social Work breached a duty of care to a student by reporting her to the Child Protection Service as a suspected abuser, based entirely on speculation and conjecture due to a missing footnote in a term paper.

[1115] eg *Murray v White* (n 736); *Wilkinson v Balsam* 885 F Supp 651 (US DC Vermont 1995); *Caryl S v Child & Adolescent Treatment Services, Inc* 614 NYS 2d 661 (New York Supreme Ct); *Althous v Cohen and University of Pittsburgh Western Psychiatric Institute and Clinic* 710 A 2d 1147 (Pennsylvania Superior Ct 1998).

the child is alleged to have been abused by another member of the family. It is note-worthy that in the great majority of reported cases, the suspected parents have sued as co-claimants with the child, on the basis that all of the family had suffered from the incompetence of the investigators.[1116]

In this context it is important not to overlook that persons accused of child abuse are protected under the ECHR by Article 6 (the right to a fair trial) and Article 8 (the right to family life and privacy, where intrafamilial abuse is alleged). Jane Wright has argued that the decision in *JD v East Berkshire*, holding that the HRA requires the fashioning of a duty of care on the part of child protection authorities to the child but not to the parents, is illogical because the ECtHR has on many occasions found that proceedings in relation to the care of a child have violated a parent's rights—at least where the child's interests would not conflict with those rights.[1117]

The second objection to a concurrent duty of care is based upon the spectre of 'defensive practice'. In *JD v East Berkshire* there was a clear split amongst the majority on the issue of defensive practice. Lord Brown was concerned about the 'insidious effect' that awareness of the proposed duty would have upon the mind and conduct of the doctor—'suddenly tending to the suppression of doubts and instincts which in the child's interests should rather be encouraged'.[1118] Lord Nicholls rather disdainfully dismissed the possibility that health professionals would be consciously swayed by the consideration that they might owe a duty to the parents, as they are 'surely made of sterner stuff', as did Lord Bingham.[1119]

It is apparent that the potential for conflict depends upon the level of generality at which the duty of care is pegged. If the duty is simply to conduct a reasonable and thorough investigation, as a competent and prudent professional would do, then in principle there is no conflict between the obligations owed to the suspect and to the victim. Where however it is the decisions based upon the evidence discovered which are in issue, then the potential for conflict becomes more real. Although in principle the duties could hold the same content—to make objective, rational and prudent decisions in the best interests of the child—in practical terms the decision-maker may feel placed in a dilemma between immediate intervention to protect the child and postponement of action until further evidence is gathered or less radical measures have been assayed.

In the jurisdictions which do recognize a duty of care to the child and to the alleged perpetrator, statutory immunity for investigations conducted in good faith is seen as an effective bulwark against 'defensive practice' and obviously unmeritorious lawsuits.[1120]

[1116] A notable exception is *D(B) v Children's Aid Society of Halton (Region)* (2006) 264 DLR (4th) 135 (Ontario CA, leave to appeal granted by SCC 10 August 2006): a 14-year-old child with apparent delusions that she had been abused by her parents had been made a ward of the court and sent to a secure mental health treatment centre for her own protection; the CA held that the parents had an arguable case that the treatment centre and its social worker were negligent in failing to attempt to reintegrate the child into her family.   [1117] Wright (n 1025) 39 (discussing the Court of Appeal's decision).

[1118] *JD v East Berkshire Community NHS Trust et al* (HL) (n 580) [137].

[1119] ibid [86] (Lord Nicholls) [33] (Lord Bingham).

[1120] eg *AAD, TD and KGD v Tanner, Winnipeg Child and Family Services Agency et al* (n 695).

(b) Liability in the bad faith torts

In *JD v East Berkshire*, Lord Nicholls noted that health professionals (and impliedly other child protection professionals) must not act in bad faith, which he defined as acting 'recklessly without caring whether an allegation of abuse is well founded or not'.[1121] If bad faith is present, then the professional could be liable to the parents in the torts of malicious falsehood, misfeasance in public office, or the malicious misuse of criminal or civil proceedings.[1122] Thus parents are given the same protection as is afforded generally by tort to persons suspected of committing crimes, and so the majority of the Law Lords considered that it was not necessary to extend that liability to good faith careless acts.[1123] Therefore a narrow area of potential liability by child abuse investigators to the suspect remains.

The bad faith torts most likely to be raised in relation to a botched child abuse investigation are malicious prosecution, misfeasance in public office,[1124] and conspiracy.

To succeed in an action of malicious prosecution the claimant must show:[1125]

- that the defendant procured the prosecution, having been actively instrumental in setting the law in motion;
- that the prosecution ended in the claimant's favour;
- that there was no reasonable and probable cause for the prosecution;
- that the defendant was actuated by malice; and
- the claimant suffered damage as a consequence.

Malice may be interpreted as requiring more than recklessness or gross negligence; the claimant must adduce evidence of a wilful and intentional effort on the Crown's part to abuse or distort its proper role in the criminal justice system.[1126] A simple lapse of judgement on the part of the prosecutor will not suffice. Malice will be established if the prosecutor decided to go after the accused to secure a conviction at all costs, and conducted the case with not only 'tunnel vision' but 'tainted tunnel vision', such that there is a flagrant disregard for the rights of the accused fuelled by motives that were improper.[1127]

In Canada, there have been several successful actions for malicious prosecution by accused who have been cleared of child abuse charges in high-profile prosecutions. Susan Nelles successfully sued the Attorney General of Ontario and Crown prosecutors in relation to charges that she had murdered four babies in intensive care at the Toronto Hospital for Sick Children where she was a paediatric nurse. She was discharged on all counts at the conclusion of a highly publicized preliminary inquiry where the judge

---

[1121] *JD v East Berkshire Community NHS Trust et al* (n 580) [74].   [1122] ibid [74]–[78].
[1123] ibid [90].
[1124] Discussed above, section F.1. Sally Clark, a solicitor whose convictions for the alleged murders of her two baby sons were quashed in 2003, has sued the forensic pathologist who withheld critical evidence from his post-mortem report [*The Guardian* 19 Sept 2005] (discussed below Chapter 11 section B).
[1125] *Martin v Watson* [1996] AC 74 (HL).
[1126] *Proulx v Quebec (Attorney General)* 2001 SCC 66, [2001] 3 SCR 9 [35].   [1127] ibid.

found that there was no case to answer. In *Kvello v Miazga*[1128] 16 individuals were arrested and charged with over 70 counts of sexual assault against 8 foster children, which were stayed after a year and a half. The charges were laid almost exclusively on the evidence of three siblings in foster care who had come from a deeply dysfunctional home, and who were known to be persistent and manipulative liars. Their evidence was ultimately found to be almost entirely incredible and they recanted all of their allegations against the ten claimants. Two of the child complainants testified on behalf of the claimants at the subsequent civil trial. In their successful action for malicious prosecution against two Crown prosecutors, the senior investigating officer, and a child therapist who had interviewed the children, the trial judge described the case as 'a prime example of what happens when gullible child care workers, police officers and prosecutors ignore time-tested legal principles and throw commonsense to the wind'.[1129] The malicious prosecution case was subsequently settled for more than CDN\$10 million. Two of the child complainants were paid CDN\$560,000 for the sexual abuse which they suffered at the hands of their brother whilst in foster care during the investigation; their complaints about this abuse had been ignored by social workers and police because they were fixated on proving the allegations against the foster parents. In 2004 the Saskatchewan Government also paid out almost CDN\$1 million in compensation to a couple who ran a day-care centre in Martensville who were the targets of bizarre satanic abuse and human sacrifice allegations which proved groundless.[1130]

(c) Liability in defamation

In *JD v East Berkshire*, the health authorities argued that it was unnecessary to impose a duty of care on child protection agencies vis-à-vis wrongly accused parents and carers, because their interests are adequately protected by their right to claim in defamation in appropriate cases, and to complain to professional bodies about individual doctors and under statutory complaints procedures.[1131] This argument found favour with Lord Rodger and Lord Brown.[1132] However, whilst in English law liability in defamation is strict, in that having taken reasonable care in making the statement is not a defence,[1133] the protection afforded by defamation is small because initial or subsequent reports of suspected child abuse would inevitably attract the defence of qualified privilege, which could be defeated only by proof of malice.

Moreover, defamation actions against those who have reported suspicions of child abuse to the authorities have generally been forestalled in English law by *D v NSPCC*[1134] in which the House of Lords imposed public interest immunity on disclosure of the names of reporters. Similar requirements of confidentiality for all recipients of information relating to the investigation appear in Australian child protection

---

[1128] *Kvello and Klassen et al v Miazga, Hansen et al* 2003 SKQB 559, 234 DLR (4th) 612 (Saskatchewan QB).   [1129] ibid [161].

[1130] 'Settlement Reached in Martensville Sex-Abuse Case' 15 Nov 2004 Canadian Broadcasting Corporation <http://www.cbc.ca/story/canada/national/2004/11/15/sask_martensville041115.html>

[1131] *JD v East Berkshire Community NHS Trust et al* (HL) (n 580) 379.

[1132] ibid [77] (Lord Nicholls), [134] (Lord Brown).

[1133] *Horrocks v Lowe* [1975] AC 135 (HL) 149–150.   [1134] *D v NSPCC* [1978] AC 171 (HL).

statutes.[1135] In practical terms confidentiality reduces the chances of a defamation action against providers of that information almost to nil if the accused person cannot otherwise discover the name of the informant. Most Australian States which have mandatory or permissive statutory reporting provisions have also conferred on reporters immunity from liability in civil or criminal law, or from professional disciplinary proceedings,[1136] although in Queensland, South Australia, and Tasmania this is qualified immunity applying only to good faith reports.[1137] This is also the case in some Canadian jurisdictions.[1138] All American jurisdictions have enacted provisions conferring immunity from civil and criminal proceedings under State and local laws and regulations for individuals making good faith reports of suspected or known instances of child abuse or neglect.[1139]

Lilllie and Reed v Newcastle City Council provides an extraordinary example of how malice can defeat qualified privilege.[1140] The claimants were staff members at a local authority-run child nursery who were charged with having systematically sexually abused very young children in their care. After the criminal trial collapsed when the video interview of the prosecution's strongest child witness was ruled inadmissible,[1141] the Newcastle County Council ordered an inquiry by a review team to evaluate the management of the nursery by the Council.[1142] The report unequivocally concluded that Lillie and Reed had in fact sexually, physically and emotionally abused a large number of young children at the nursery, and that Lillie was involved in a paedophile ring and had procured young children to be raped and abused by others while being filmed. The report received extensive media coverage both locally and nationally. In the subsequent defamation action, the authors of the report and the Council pleaded qualified privilege, as they had a duty in the public interest to investigate the allegations and to communicate the report to the public at large, who had been very exercised by the nursery scandal. A highly experienced defamation trial judge, Mr Justice Eady, held in a massive judgment that the allegations in the report were untrue, and that the review team's qualified privilege defence was forfeited by their malice. They had clearly exceeded their originally expressed terms of reference, which had not entitled them to make public pronouncements of guilt against individuals who had

---

[1135] eg Child Protection Act 1999 (Queensland) ss 186–188, 246; Children, Young Persons and Their Families Act 1997 (Tasmania) ss 16, 103; Children and Young Persons Act 1989 (Victoria) s 43.

[1136] Family Law Act 1975 (Australian Capital Territory) s 67ZB.

[1137] Qualified immunity for good faith reports is conferred by the Child Protection Act 1999 (Queensland) s 246F, Children's Protection Act 1993 (South Australia) s 12, Children, Young Persons and Their Families Act 1997 (Tasmania) s 15   [1138] Child and Family Services Act (Nunavut) s 8(3).

[1139] The flurry of State enactments resulted from the Child Abuse Prevention and Treatment and Adoption Reform Act making it a condition of Federal funding for child protection services [42 USCA ch 67 §5106a Grants to States for child abuse and neglect prevention and treatment programs b(vii)]. Note that clause b(viii) requires a representative of the child protective services agency, at the first contact with the suspected individual, to inform him or her of the allegations in a manner that is consistent with laws protecting the rights of the informant.

[1140] *Lillie and Reed v Newcastle City Council, Barker and others* (n 385).

[1141] Discussed below Chapter 8 section A.1(a).

[1142] Richard Barker (Chair) Newcastle upon Tyne City Council *Abuse in Early Years: Report of the Independent Inquiry into Shieldfield Nursery and Related Events* (1998).

been acquitted of serious criminal offences.[1143] They approached their task with a closed mind, and failed to analyse the evidence in a dispassionate way, misrepresenting and even grossly distorting it. The review team 'chose to withhold questions that needed asking; they declined to challenge in any way the police interviews of these children',[1144] which Justice Eady had found to be tainted by oppressive and leading questioning.[1145] The authors were malicious because they had included in their report a number of fundamental claims which they must have known to be untrue and which could not be explained on the basis of incompetence or mere carelessness.[1146] The City Council was at fault for sanctioning an inquiry into the commission of acts tantamount to criminal offences but without proper safeguards for the accused, but nonetheless had not lost its qualified privilege shield as malice on its part had not been proved.[1147]

In the malicious prosecution and defamation cases which have been successful, the claimants have been able to demonstrate fundamentally flawed investigative techniques which themselves became abusive of the children involved. Credulous social workers and police officers had failed to probe, verify and evaluate the credibility of the allegations in a balanced inquiry; instead their tactics contaminated the evidence irreparably. But it was bad faith rather than professional negligence which made them tortfeasors. The trial judges in *Kvello* and in *Lillie and Reed* were excoriating in their critique of the interviewing techniques used on the children. It has been rightly observed[1148] that being labelled a child abuser is one of the most loathsome labels in society, with grave physical, emotional, professional and personal ramifications. Even when such accusations are proved false there is lasting social stigma and damage to personal relationships. Because the criminal charges collapsed or convictions were quashed, the tort actions provided the only means by which those wrongly accused could expose the criminal investigations as travesties and so vindicate their reputations.

7. Evaluation: is tort law the enemy or the instrument of effective child protection?

Negligence liability on the part of social services towards children in care is now firmly ensconced in English law, as in the other jurisdictions we have considered. Child protection agencies are most likely to feel the sharp edge of evolving tort law in relation to their investigatory functions, and so it is to this contentious territory that we return.

(a) Liability for failing to act

Here, the conceptual difficulties of imposing liability for 'pure' omissions can be exaggerated. Where a public authority has a specific statutory responsibility, then

---

[1143] *Lillie and Reed v Newcastle City Council, Barker and others* (n 385) [798].
[1144] ibid [814], [820], [898–899], [1188].
[1145] Discussed further below Chapter 5 section G.2(a).
[1146] *Lillie and Reed v Newcastle City Council, Barker and others* (n 385) [1234].
[1147] ibid [1236]–[1240].
[1148] *Hungerford v Jones* 422 A 2d 478 (New Hampshire Supreme Ct 1998) 480.

the usual objections to liability for failure to rescue someone in peril derived from the Good Samaritan hypothesis—the 'why pick on me' argument, the definitions of the circumstances triggering the obligation and of what should be done and to what standard of competence—dwindle into insignificance. However questionable those reasons may be when applied to a private individual, they are not necessarily transferable to public bodies with specific discretionary powers to act.[1149] We identified a conundrum in section C of this chapter regarding the principles relating to the liability of third parties who fail to protect a child: that the risk of harm was not originally created by the third party, and the harm itself was not directly inflicted by the third party. Whilst the conundrum doubtless will continue to haunt tort theory and liability of public authorities for other functions, it should pose no great difficulty in the specific context of child protection agencies whose *raison d'être* is to protect children from abuse.

The causation chasm which typifies cases of 'pure' omissions is capable of being bridged in such cases, if it is foreseeable that other people and bodies who have contact with the child are likely to relax their vigilance once they know that social services, the experts in child welfare, has been notified of their concerns. This hypothesis could be difficult to prove on the facts, but not impossible; the neighbours, family members, health visitors, doctors and teachers who reported the extreme neglect of the children in *X v Bedfordshire* could reasonably conclude that social services had investigated and found their concerns unwarranted, and so relaxed their vigilance. The problem of proving such causation is arguably due to the child protection agencies having pre-empted the field.[1150] Some American courts brush aside the causation problem by holding that an agency cannot claim that abuse following notification was a supervening event which broke the chain of causation because it was that very danger which the agency was required to take steps to avert,[1151] an argument for which there is some authority in English law.[1152]

Moreover, the ECHR and the HRA 1998 conceptualize human rights as vesting in the individual rights of positive protection, rather than negative rights to non-interference on the part of the state. Inaction is not presumptively excusable or non-actionable. In this new context, then, the arguments about nonfeasance on the part of child protection agencies which found receptive judicial audiences in *X v Bedfordshire* and *DeShaney* have been exposed as hollow and indeed incongruous.

(b) The human rights alternative

Is human rights rather than tort law the best legal response for children ignored or harmed by incompetent investigations by child protection agencies? Certainly the absence of retrospectivity of the HRA means that the ECHR is likely to continue to have an independent influence on the development of children's rights in tort law, a factor of which English judges are clearly conscious.[1153] There remains considerable

---

[1149] Craig (n 610) 903.   [1150] Eaton and Wells (n 224) 156–157.
[1151] *Horridge v St Mary's County Department of Social Services* (n 710).
[1152] *Reeves v Commissioner of Police of the Metropolis* (n 373).
[1153] *JD v East Berkshire Community NHS Trust et al* (HL) (n 580) [3] (Lord Bingham).

scope for using the HRA and the ECHR to provide substance to children's rights to flourish in a safe and protective environment. For example, it has been suggested that Article 3 might provide a ground for challenging the frequent movement of children between care placements,[1154] and Article 8 might be used more generally to buttress the positive obligations on the part of local authorities to children in care under the Children Act 1989.

The ECHR and the HRA will continue to be a powerful force, even if only in the background, because recourse to them will always be available if a substantive Convention right has been infringed and there is no compensatory remedy available through domestic legal mechanisms. In such cases the absence of a tort remedy is likely to constitute an infringement of both ECHR Article 13(1) and the HRA s 8. Whilst *Z v UK* signals that the remedies under Article 13 are likely to be fashioned along the negligence model (although they were not in *Osman* itself) it is unclear whether this will be the case under the HRA. The possibility of a human rights 'just satisfaction' claim may well encourage English courts to continue to develop tort law instead.

Lord Nicholls suggested in *JD v East Berkshire* that courts adjudicating on human rights claims can make value judgments based on more flexible notions than the common law standard of reasonableness, and so be free from the legal rigidity of a duty of care; His Lordship warned against transplanting this approach wholesale into the domestic law of negligence.[1155] This point might be regarded as implicitly licensing civil courts to extradite all difficult issues involving public authorities into the territory of human rights. Fortunately however the retreat of the ECtHR from *Osman* in *Z v UK* has not resulted in a concomitant retreat by the English courts to blanket tort immunity for public authorities, as some had feared.[1156] It is submitted that a negligence tort action is a far more refined instrument to yield nuanced principles for determining the parameters and quantum of liability than the HRA can afford. The concept of a standard of care set by negligence law is not as rigid as Lord Nicholls suggests, but it draws a much sharper line as to what good professional practice requires in particular circumstances than can the Articles of the European Convention. Moreover, Articles 2 and 3 set very high thresholds of misconduct for breach: a child must show a real and immediate risk to his life, or torture or inhuman and degrading treatment, of which the state agency has actual or constructive knowledge,[1157] to be able to claim compensation from the state. As Lord Bingham concluded his dissenting opinion in *JD v East Berkshire*:

[T]he question does arise whether the law of tort should evolve, analogically and incrementally, so as to fashion appropriate remedies to contemporary problems or whether it should remain

---

[1154] Allan Levy QC 'The Human Rights Act 1998: the Implications for Children' (2000) 6 Child Care in Practice 288, 294.

[1155] *JD v East Berkshire Community NHS Trust et al* (HL) (n 580) [93]–[94].

[1156] Wright (n 791) xxxiv.

[1157] While this requirement has only been imposed by the ECtHR for Article 2 claims under *Osman v UK*, it is likely that it also would apply to Article 3 [McIvor *Third Party Liability in Tort* (n 219) 97–98].

essentially static, making only such changes as are forced upon it, leaving difficult and, in human terms, very important problems to be swept up by the Convention. I prefer evolution.[1158]

And so do we.

(c) Negligence liability and public policy: efficacious or pernicious?

In the decade between the decisions of the House of Lords in *X v Bedfordshire* and *JD v East Berkshire*, we have witnessed a growing judicial acceptance that tort law has a beneficial role to play in the delivery of competent public services. As the Australian public lawyer Susan Kneebone has observed:

> In the context of public authorities we need an approach which encourages administrative efficiency on the assumption that liability is in the general public or collective interest. We need to recognise that tort law can both deter a public authority and require it to provide a service. The premises of such an approach are that tort liability does not impose unattainable standards of conduct upon a public authority or unduly increase the economic burden on the public. It must be accepted that over a period of time the distribution of costs amongst the public will be balanced by the benefit in terms of awareness of responsibilities on the part of public authorities and increased efficiency. It must be recognised that in many situations, the public authority is in the best situation to avoid the loss.[1159]

(i) 'Defensive practice' versus standard-setting for public services

'Defensive practice' is an enigmatic term. The ethos of negligence law could be said to be to encourage 'defensive practice': its function is to set standards of competent conduct whereby those who comply with those standards can be confident that they will not have committed a tort even if harm has resulted from their act or omission. In the 1990s however 'defensive practice' became a pejorative label without defined content, used to furnish excuses for failing to comply with accepted professional norms. In his dissenting opinion in *JD v East Berkshire*, Lord Bingham noted somewhat quizzically that 'to describe awareness of the legal duty as having an "insidious effect" on the mind of a potential defendant is to undermine the foundation of the law of professional negligence'.[1160] The apprehension expressed by the label is that the professional under the legal duty to act competently will be paralysed by indecision, always looking for additional evidence to justify a particular course of action when this is not in the best interests of the person to whom the duty is owed. But as Stephen Bailey has argued, it is remarkable that a duty which is entirely reasonable as to its formal content should be denied because of the risk that imposing it would cause professionals to act unprofessionally, other than in accordance with accepted practice.[1161] Certainly 'defensive practice' has not served as a reason to foreclose negligence actions for other professionals whose responsibilities also involve difficult and oft-times delicate decisions involving competing factors and interests, such as health professionals and lawyers.

[1158] *JD v East Berkshire Community NHS Trust et al* (HL) (n 580) [50].
[1159] Kneebone (n 250) 46.
[1160] *JD v East Berkshire Community NHS Trust et al* (HL) (n 580) [33].
[1161] S Bailey 'Public Authority Liability in Negligence: the Continued Search for Coherence' (2006) 26 *Legal Studies* 155, 181.

Regardless of the merits of the debate about 'defensive practice', it is extremely important for child protection professionals to appreciate that the standard of care is not a counsel of perfection. As Lord Bingham noted in *JD v East Berkshire*, the professional is not required to be right, but only to be reasonably skilful and careful.[1162] All that negligence law requires of professionals is that they adhere to accepted and reasonable standards of investigation of the pertinent evidence, and of decision-making based on a reasonable evaluation of that evidence. In *TC v New South Wales*,[1163] Mason P quoted from a High Court of Australia judgment considering liability for negligent omissions:

Few occurrences in human affairs, in retrospect, can be said to have been, in absolute terms, inevitable. Different conduct on the part of those involved in them almost always would have produced a different result. But the possibility of a different result is not the issue and does not represent the proper test for negligence. That test remains whether the plaintiff has proved that the defendant, who owed a duty of care, has not acted in accordance with reasonable care.[1164]

A study of the Canadian experience of social services working with potential liability noted that Canadian courts and legislators have taken a 'social work friendly approach to accountability by not only respecting the expertise that underlies discretionary decision making in general but also undertaking a contextual analysis that appreciates the dynamics of child protection practice'.[1165] The authors concluded that 'defensive practice' is an entirely unnecessary strategy to deal with potential liability:

Consequently social workers in child welfare, who exercise reasonable caution and engage in good clinical social work practice, good record-keeping and effective communication and verification of information, can continue to strive to offer the high-quality services to children and their families as they have always done without any serious fear of recrimination.[1166]

(ii) Direct accountability versus opening the floodgates

It must be remembered that the cases successfully sued in tort discussed in this chapter have generally been those at the outer boundaries, involving wide deviations from normal professional practice and indeed egregious neglect of duty. The tort action empowers an individual to prise open a closed institution and subject it to external scrutiny to discover what went wrong, in proceedings which she initiates and in which she can be a full and active participant. This form of direct accountability is particularly critical for a child who has been in care, and who needs to reconstruct what happened in her early formative years, to understand why it happened and to come to terms with its implications. Complaints procedures or applications to the Criminal Injuries Compensation Board cannot replicate this process of discovery; and in any event administrative procedures provide no compensation, and the CICB inadequate compensation, to help the victim contend with the ongoing consequences of the abuse.

With regard to fears that investigators will be subject to a flood of claims, the experience in Canada over the past 25 years or so suggests that it is unlikely there will be a

---

[1162] *JD v East Berkshire Community NHS Trust et al* (HL) (n 580) [32].

[1163] *TC v New South Wales* [2001] NSW CA 380 (New South Wales CA) [143].

[1164] *Derrick v Cheung* (n 764) [13].

[1165] K Kanani, C Regehr and M Bernstein 'Liability Considerations in Child Welfare: Lessons from Canada' (2002) 26 *Child Abuse & Neglect* 1039.　　　　[1166] ibid 1040–1041.

massive further expansion of liability for public authorities for negligent investigations beyond the tort liability they already face.[1167] It must also be remembered that there are formidable barriers to a successful tort action against a child protection agency. The claimant must prove that a duty of care arose to protect a particular child, which is unlikely to be recognized absent specific and highly plausible information that this child was at risk. The claimant must also prove, normally through expert evidence, that the agency's employee did not comply with the standards of investigation or monitoring applicable to professionals at the time of the alleged breach;[1168] it will be very exceptional for the standards themselves to be found wanting. As Lord Bingham contended in *JD v East Berkshire*, if breach rather than duty becomes the touchstone of recovery against child protection professionals, the claimant should have to prove a very clear departure from ordinary standards of skill and care, as is the case in France and Germany.[1169]

Causation flowing from inaction can be extraordinarily difficult to establish, given that it is the deliberate act of the abuser which directly inflicts the harm.[1170] As several courts have pointed out, factual causation in sexual abuse and neglect cases can be exceptionally problematic: the child must prove on the balance of probabilities that had a reasonably competent investigation been carried out, a different decision would have been reached which would have averted the harm which the child suffered thereafter.[1171] It has been argued that the causation question where a public body has failed to act to protect an identified victim from foreseeable harm at the hands of an identified third party perpetrator is not whether its inaction has *increased* the risk of harm, but rather whether it has failed to *reduce* the risk in a material way,[1172] an apposite analysis for a defective investigation which fails to stop ongoing child abuse.

Once factual causation of further harm is established, it should be easier for a child claimant to show that the harm was not too remote, ie that it fell within the scope of consequences for which the child protection agency should be liable.[1173] To illustrate, as one of the characteristics of battered child syndrome is recurring abuse, it may be possible through expert evidence to show that further battering was foreseeable where a physician failed to report the child's injuries to child welfare authorities.[1174] It is submitted that this should also be the case for the agency which fails to investigate reported concerns about sexual abuse properly or at all. Moreover, because the risk of further abuse defines the harm which the party with reporting or investigatory powers is under a duty to avert, the argument that the intervening and deliberate act of the

---

[1167] ibid 1040.

[1168] *S v Gloucestershire County Council; L v Tower Hamlets London Borough Council* (n 652) 376; *M(M) v K(K)* (n 155) 404–405; *KLB v British Columbia* (n 309) [16].

[1169] *JD v East Berkshire Community NHS Trust et al* (HL) (n 580) [49].

[1170] As illustrated by *BM [Bonnie Mooney], MM and KM v Attorney General (British Columbia) and Attorney General (Canada)* (n 696).

[1171] *Attorney General v Prince and Gardner* (n 35) 292 (Tipping J).

[1172] *BM [Bonnie Mooney], MM and KM v Attorney General (British Columbia) and Attorney General* (n 696) [10]–[12], [66] (Donald JA, dissenting).

[1173] Or, in American parlance, was the proximate cause of the further harm.

[1174] *Landeros v Flood* (n 251); Bailey (n 857), 63.

abuser broke the chain of causation between the negligence and the further harm should not available to a defendant.[1175]

Further difficulties will likely arise in the proof of damages, as the claimant must show that, but for the negligent investigation, he would not have sustained the psychological harm which impaired him emotionally and financially in dealing with the adult world. As *TC v New South Wales*[1176] shows, it is likely to be extremely difficult to disentangle post-investigation psychological damage from that which had already occurred due to the past acts of abuse, as there is no way of comparing the child's psychological status 'before and after'. The long line of cases wending their way through the courts assessing damages for the children who were physically and sexually abused in children's residential care facilities in Leicestershire, Flintshire and Bryn Alyn demonstrates how complex and tortuous the process can be.[1177]

(iii) Investing in child protection versus diversion of scarce resources

The work of social workers, residential care workers, and police child protection officers is extremely stressful, and can lead employers to be liable for stress-related illnesses if they are not adequately supported.[1178] Judges tend to be sensitive to the dilemmas involved in child protection work, and appellate judges hear particularly difficult child protection cases as part of their caseload.[1179] Whilst sympathetic to the constraints and prioritization imposed on social workers by an inexorably heavy workload,[1180] some judges have recognized that sympathy is not enough to rectify the plight of child and social worker alike:

I recognize and appreciate the particular difficulties and pressures that [the social worker] may have been under during the time of this investigation. Shortages in social service resources are reaching legendary levels with the obvious concomitant stress on field workers. However, conducting an investigation into alleged abuse of children requires the utmost professionalism and skilled judgment. That professionalism and informed judgment should not be compromised by placing dedicated social workers in situations where the demands exceed the available time and resources.[1181]

Making local authorities directly accountable to children whom they have failed to protect without good reason is one way, albeit indirect, of addressing the chronic scarce resources problem. Whether local authorities choose to obtain liability insurance or to self-insure, they will have to confront the financial implications of their potential

---

[1175] *Reeves v Commissioner of Police of the Metropolis* (n 373).

[1176] *TC v New South Wales* (n 755); *A(M) and A(T) v Attorney General of Canada* 2003 SKCA 002 (Saskatchewan CA) (damages must take into account children's previous abuse by third parties before they were abused by a childcare worker in a residential school for First Nations children).

[1177] An overview of the claims is provided by Gumbel, Johnson and Scorer (n 77) chapter 4.

[1178] *Walker v Northumberland County Council* [1995] 1 All ER 737 (QBD) (social worker); *Rowntree v Commissioner of Police for the Metropolis* 2001 WL 1346941 (QBD 18 July 2001) (police child protection officer).

[1179] eg *Re H (Minors: Sexual Abuse: Standard of Proof)* (n 76) 592 (Lord Nicholls).

[1180] *MM v KK* (n 155) [12].

[1181] *W(D) v White, the Durham Region Police Services Board, The Children's Aid Society of the Durham Region et al* [1998] OJ No 2927 (Ontario Gen Div) [35].

liability for child protection services. Of course, that liability has been a reality since *Barrett*[1182] was decided in 2001 and historic institutional abuse claims entered the court system.

Two investments with guaranteed dividends would be better education and ongoing training of professionals involved in child protection, and better management of case loads. In Canada, for decades social workers have been required to hold a minimum of an undergraduate degree in social work or another degree with a postgraduate qualification in social work. As three analysts of Canadian social services have written, social workers' increased exposure to liability is an indicator of their increased professional status, visibility and sphere of responsibility: 'the profession has arrived'.[1183] In the ten Provinces the profession is regulated by self-governing statutory bodies,[1184] with the Canadian Association of Social Workers providing a national umbrella to monitor credentials and standards. Only in 2003 was professional qualifying training in England changed to require a degree approved by the General Social Care Council. It is a fairly safe prediction that as the educational requirements rise, so too will the prestige of the profession, bringing, one may hope, a concomitant improvement in the calibre of services to children and their families.

It may be contended that public inquiries can act as engines of change more quickly and more efficiently than can individual tort actions, which only serve to divert scarce resources to defending past mistakes in a specific case. The *Every Child Matters* initiative of central government in 2006 was a direct and commendably prompt response to the *Climbié Report*. But if Victoria Climbié had survived her ordeal, would anyone seriously contend that she should not be entitled to compensation for the failure of four social services departments, two child protection teams of the Metropolitan Police Service, a specialist centre managed by the NSPCC, three housing authorities, and two hospitals to notice her suffering? As Lord Laming concluded:

The final irony was that Haringey Social Services formally closed Victoria's case on the very day she died. The extent of the failure to protect Victoria was lamentable. Tragically, it required nothing more than basic good practice being put into operation. This never happened.[1185]

(iv) Constraining fears of liability: good faith qualified immunity

We have seen that jurisdictions which recognize that child protection agencies owe a duty of care to children about whom abuse is suspected generally immunize discretionary actions and decisions taken in good faith as a counterbalance.

In New South Wales, immunity is conferred only if the Minister or State officer acted 'in good faith and with reasonable care', which would seem not to fetter

---

[1182] *Barrett v Enfield London Borough Council* (n 75).

[1183] Kanani, Regehr and Bernstein (n 1165) 1039.

[1184] eg Board of Registration for Social Workers (British Columbia) regulated by the Social Workers Act 1969; Ontario College of Social Workers and Social Service Workers, regulated by the Social Work and Social Service Work Act 1998; the Alberta College of Social Workers, regulated by the Health Professions Act 2003 (Alberta).   [1185] Lord Laming (Chair) *Victoria Climbié Inquiry* (Cm 5730, 2003) [1.16].

negligence actions at all.[1186] The New Brunswick legislation is unique in Canada in restricting the immunity to the exercise of statutory authority, power, duty or function exercised in good faith and without negligence, which essentially precludes liability only for the intentional torts.[1187] Most other statutes simply refer to good faith without qualification, and so insulate public servants from all but the 'bad faith' torts.

'Good faith' immunity has been variously defined by the courts. In *JD v East Berkshire* Lord Nicholls suggested that professionals would be acting in bad faith if they acted 'recklessly', that is 'without caring whether an allegation of abuse is well founded or not'.[1188] The US Supreme Court has held that qualified immunity provides 'ample protection to all but the plainly incompetent or those who knowingly violate the law'.[1189] In South Dakota there must be some evidence that the defendants acted with an improper purpose in their failure to take further investigatory steps, which is 'far more extreme' than a failure to observe reasonable standards—indeed, it has been described as being a case of 'pure heart and empty head'.[1190] So if social workers in South Dakota act with honest intentions and a desire to protect the best interests of the children, they are likely to be immune from suit.[1191] New South Wales interprets 'good faith' similarly: the act must not be done for a malicious or ulterior purpose, and there must be a genuine and honest attempt to perform the function correctly.[1192] In Ohio it is displaced by evidence of 'wilful, reckless or wanton disregard of rights established under law',[1193] and so the issue of competence seems not to figure in the defence. Yet the US Court of Appeals Second Circuit has held that qualified immunity protects objectively reasonable decisions of social workers, which seems to equate good faith with the usual negligence standard.[1194]

In Ontario, acting with conspicuous bias against and unfairness towards one parent, and so refusing to conduct a balanced investigation, will prevent reliance upon the statutory good faith defence even though the social worker genuinely believes she is acting in the best interests of the child.[1195] In British Columbia, good faith has been judicially defined as a duty by the social worker to consider honestly the facts he knew or *ought* to have known before he made his decision, and which would justify that decision.[1196] Good faith may be rebutted by evidence that child protection investigators acted in abuse or excess of power; mere errors of judgement and acting

---

[1186] Child Welfare Act (New South Wales) 1939 s 158(1), considered in *SB v New South Wales* (n 687) [123]–[131]; see also Family Services Act 1980 (New Brunswick) s 3(3), discussed above section F.1(b)(v).

[1187] Family Services Act 1980 (New Brunswick) s 3(3).

[1188] *JD v East Berkshire Community NHS Trust et al* (HL) (n 580) [74].

[1189] *Robison v Via* 821 F 2d 913 (US CA 2nd Cir 1987) 341.

[1190] *Purdy v Fleming* (n 801) 433.

[1191] *Cotton v Stange* 582 NW 2d 25 (South Dakota Supreme Ct 1998).

[1192] *SB v New South Wales* (n 687) [125].

[1193] *Brodie v Summit County Children's Services Board* (n 253) 1307.

[1194] *Robison v Via* (n 1189) 920.

[1195] *B(D), B(R) and B(M) v Children's Aid Society of Durham Region* (n 695) [81], [101]–[103]; affirmed *B(D), B(R) and B(M) v Children's Aid Society of Durham Region* (1996) 136 DLR (4th) 297 (Ontario CA) 300–304.

[1196] *CH v British Columbia* (n 818) [27], citing *Chaput v Romain* [1955] SCR 834 (SCC) 859.

unreasonably in exercising their discretion will not suffice.[1197] Significantly, errors of judgement will not be made in good faith where the social worker has not sufficiently informed herself of the information necessary to make an honest decision: then a finding of absence of good faith is not about the social worker being wrong, but about her not properly turning her mind to a question about the child's safety she has a duty to answer.[1198] These courts are at pains to emphasize the difficulties of decision-making which cases of suspected child abuse raise for investigators, and the importance of ensuring that they focus on the child's welfare rather than on their potential liability.[1199]

One Ontario court set out the following factors which might raise concerns as to whether a child protection agency lacked good faith:[1200]

- refusal to take account of information that should inform the agency's decision-making in the case to be faithful to its statutory duties;
- rigid reliance on a parent's history as a basis for current protective intervention without any meaningful attempt to ascertain whether that pattern continues in the present;
- a tenacious hold to a theory about the child's need for protection in the face of the facts which common sense and objectivity would require be revisited;
- selective and biased representation of facts in court that may mislead a judge as to the nature and extent of the present risk to the child;
- malice towards a parent or other party;
- arbitrary alignment with one parent to the prejudice of another, ignoring information which would cause a reasonable person to question the reliability of the parent with whom the alliance has been formed;[1201] or
- defiance of the court's orders or directions in the case, such as filing a notice of appeal as a delaying measure.

In the final analysis, negligence liability to the child who is the subject of a protection investigation is here to stay in England. It is submitted that the way forward, to give child protection professionals the necessary latitude and confidence to take the difficult

---

[1197] *G(A) v Superintendent of Family and Child Service for British Columbia* (n 819) 148, 150; *D(B) and D(VS) v British Columbia* (n 962) [48]; *MM v KK* (n 155) [12]–[29] (social workers' failure to discover that foster mother had left the home and that foster father was abusing child, and failure to develop and monitor a life plan for her, not negligent and in any event protected by good faith).

[1198] *CH v British Columbia* (n 818) [40]–[49]; *Delaronde v British Columbia* 2000 BCSC 700 (British Columbia Supreme Ct) [56]–[59] (Ministry could not rely upon good faith defence when it filed court affidavits saying that claimant should be placed with foster family with expertise in dealing with drug-addicted infants and opposing aunts' custody application, but then a social worker, not knowing of her special needs, placed her with a single foster mother with no expertise and two other children to care for, who inflicted severe brain injury and quadriplegia on claimant).

[1199] *D(B) and D(VS) v British Columbia* (n 962) [30], [48]; *G(A) v British Columbia (Superintendent of Family & Child Services)* (n 819); *LC and LS v British Columbia* (n 818) [112]–[118], [132].

[1200] *Catholic Children's Aid Society of Toronto v V(S)* 2000 CanLII 5844 (30 June 2000) (Ontario CJ, leave to appeal dismissed 16 October 2000 (Ontario Supreme Ct)) [24].

[1201] As in *B(D), B(R) and B(M) v Children's Aid Society of Durham Region* (n 695) discussed above, section F.2(b)(iii).

decisions, is an amendment to the Children Act 1989 to confer qualified immunity from liability in negligence upon all those charged with investigatory responsibilities in connection with child protection. Given the diverse definitions which courts have attributed to good faith immunity, it might be wise to define the term in the legislation, or to accompany it with guidance, our preferred form being the judicial guidance in British Columbia.

PART III

THE INQUIRY PROCESS

5

Investigating and Evaluating Allegations of Abuse

All child protection guidance must be examined with an understanding of the intense difficulty of child protection work at both theoretical and practical levels. Practice is plagued by the seemingly insoluble problem of defining the role of the state in protecting children living in families. On a practical level, child protection services are stretched in all the jurisdictions we have examined.[1] Furthermore, the intensely stressful nature of the job, particularly when little money is available to respond to pressing needs, has often led to high turnover of staff. This lack of money and of trained staff often leads to the practice of crisis management, despite paper policies advocating more consistent familial support. The best child protection procedures will be inadequate to protect children if they are not or cannot be acted upon.[2]

In this chapter we consider the current guidance for professionals in responding to suspicions of child abuse. We begin with an analysis of the influences on the current English system and we consider the guiding themes of the current law and procedures. The structure of the chapter then echoes the investigation process. We examine the law relating to the decision to report a suspicion of child abuse, followed by the assessment of the type of response that investigators may make. We then go on to consider the law, procedure and practice as it relates to the protection of children in an emergency. Following from this, we consider the process of evidence gathering for both civil and criminal proceedings and the law by which it is governed. Finally we consider the decision-making fora following an investigation and the method by which a decision is made whether to place a child's name on the child protection register, apply for a care or supervision order in the Family Court or mount a prosecution. At each stage we will consider the law and its operation in other similar jurisdictions to deepen our analysis of the choices that those framing the system in England and Wales have made. We conclude that while adherence to the law may potentially prevent children 'disappearing' into the child protection system without consideration of whether such

---

[1] N Parton, D Thorpe and C Wattam *Child Protection, Risk and the Moral Order* (Macmillan, Basingstoke 1997) 18–44; E Fishwick 'Child Protection Inadequate in Australia' (1993) 2 HRD 1; Judge M Brown, *Care and protection is about adult behaviour: the ministerial review of the Department of Child, Youth and Family Services Report to the Minister of Social Services and Employment Hon Steve Maharey* (2000) 104; L Burnside and D Bond 'Making a Difference Mentoring Programmes in Child Welfare Agencies' (2002) 1(1) *Envision: the Manitoba Journal of Child Welfare* 50; M Freeman 'Child Protection in the 21st Century: Privatization of Child Protective Services: Getting the Lion Back in the Cage?' (2003) 41 Fam Ct Rev 449.

[2] Commissioner for Children *Final Report on the Investigation into the Death of James Whakaruru* (New Zealand Office of the Commissioner for Children, Wellington 2000) 2.

drastic action is justified, the law has also contributed to some of the problems which have dogged child protection practice in all jurisdictions. In particular the continual reinvention of guidance to limit discretion and attempt to ensure that past problems do not recur has led to a lack of clarity in the law in each jurisdiction and confusion and defensiveness among those operating it.

In each jurisdiction a number of recurrent questions have emerged which have determined the contours of its law governing investigations. No jurisdiction has answered them in exactly the same way. The key questions are:

- **By what means may the law encourage professionals and the general public to report cases of child abuse?**
  — Should the law require people to report allegations of abuse by means of a mandatory reporting law? Should this law be supported by criminal sanction?
  — Would guidance detailing the common signs of child abuse be more effective?
- **How prescriptive should guidance on investigating child abuse be, when it is aimed at professionals?**
- **What behaviour and what level of injury to the child should trigger a response by the state?**
  — What if any sanctions should be in place for investigators who fail to respond to clear indications that abuse has occurred?
- **How may the state's response be best executed?**
  — How can information be shared, action coordinated and inaction avoided, both within big organizations and between them?
  — How may procedure be made effective in ensuring the efficacy of the state's involvement with a child and her family?
- **How can the immediate protection of children be effected?**
  — Are court orders a necessary evil or an unnecessarily bureaucratic mechanism to protect children?
- **What constitutes 'good' evidence of child abuse?**
  — How does this evidence differ from that in cases concerning adults?
  — How can this evidence best be gathered?
  — How may the rights and interests of the suspect be protected?

It is to the answers to these questions that we now turn.

A. Tracing the Influences on the Current English Guidance

Parton has argued powerfully that the manner in which the state responds to child abuse is not self-evident, but rather the result of political choice.[3] Social and economic pressures and the professional culture at the time in which procedures are written dominate their content. In England and Wales procedures and guidance for the investigation of child abuse have been driven by two primary influences. The first of these was the scandals of the last four decades, in which the state's handling of a

---

[3] N Parton *The Politics of Child Abuse* (Macmillan, London 1985).

child's case was considered to have gone badly wrong. The second, counterbalancing, influence which emerged in the mid 1990s to become equally influential was a desire to limit the number of investigations that were taking place. The latter was driven by both ideological and economic considerations.

1. Scandals

Scandals in relation to individual cases may be divided into three types: the deaths of children whom the local authority had undertaken or been given some duty to protect; investigations into suspected cases of child sexual abuse; and the abuse of children looked after by the local authority. These cases generated enormous media, political and public concern. However, while the concern that was generated may generically be referred to as relating to child abuse, each type of scandal focused on different aspects of the problem.

(a) Child deaths

The death of Maria Colwell in 1972 was crucial in establishing child abuse as a major social problem for policy-makers in England and in introducing fundamental changes in policy and practice.[4] Much of the criticism which her death aroused was levelled at the failure of services responsible for childcare to mount an organized, coordinated response to a report of child maltreatment. In Maria Colwell's case 31 separate reports expressing concern for her well-being had been received by social services before her death.[5] Such a lack of response has been a recurring finding of inquiry reports into the deaths of children for the subsequent 30 years. The causes included the absence of mechanisms by which information could be efficiently circulated between agencies,[6] the replication of work and the lack of a sense of common purpose and responsibility for child protection. For example, many inquiries noted the unwillingness of professionals other than social workers or the police to take on what they regarded as child protection roles, for example reporting suspicions of child maltreatment, when social services was already involved with a child.[7] The inquiry into the death of Kimberly Carlile described the social worker in charge, who had attempted to encourage collaboration, as 'like a puppeteer, where none of the parts responded to the strings that he was pulling. An arm was perfectly prepared to be an arm, but was not going to be part of a body'.[8] The report into the death of Victoria Climbié in 2002 found a similar number of instances in which agencies failed to intervene and protect her in

---

[4] ibid 68.

[5] Department of Health and Social Security *The Report of the Committee of Inquiry into the Care and Supervision Provided in Relation to Maria Colwell* (HMSO, London 1974).

[6] London Borough of Brent *A Child in Trust: The Report of the Panel of Inquiry into the Circumstances Surrounding the Death of Jasmine Beckford* (London Borough of Brent, London 1985) 121; London Borough of Lambeth *Whose Child?: The Report of the Public Inquiry into the Death of Tyra Henry* (London Borough of Lambeth, London 1987) Chapter 4.

[7] L Blom Cooper (Chair) *A Child in Mind: Protection of Children in a Responsible Society Report of the Commission of Inquiry into the Circumstances Surrounding the Death of Kimberley Carlile* (London Borough of Greenwich 1987) 128.   [8] ibid 142.

the face of clear indications of abuse.[9] Victoria was tortured to death by her aunt and the aunt's boyfriend, despite the fact that she had been known to a number of agencies involved in child protection. The inquiry into her death revealed organizational failures in communication between agencies, coordination in their work, and knowledge of the procedures, and an absence of clear lines of authority amongst the professionals involved. It also identified organizational malaise in which notes were not kept and concerns not followed up. Finally there were failures at an individual level: no person or organization took responsibility for ensuring that Victoria was safe; all assumed that someone else would do it:

> Victoria was not hidden away. It is deeply disturbing that during the days and months following her initial contact with Ealing Housing Department's Homeless Persons' Unit, Victoria was known to no less than two further housing authorities, four social services departments, two child protection teams of the Metropolitan Police Service (MPS), a specialist centre managed by the NSPCC, and she was admitted to two different hospitals because of suspected deliberate harm. The dreadful reality was that these services knew little or nothing more about Victoria at the end of the process than they did when she was first referred to Ealing Social Services by the Homeless Persons' Unit in April 1999. The final irony was that Haringey Social Services formally closed Victoria's case on the very day she died. The extent of the failure to protect Victoria was lamentable. Tragically, it required nothing more than basic good practice being put into operation. This never happened.[10]

While there are differences between the two inquiries, what is clear is that although Maria and Victoria were 'a generation apart' the problems of coordination that the inquiries into their deaths identified were remarkably similar.[11] The problem which the *Climbié Inquiry* identified, that of a lack of a coordinated response by agencies and a failure to prioritize the protection of children, has had the greatest impact of all its findings, and contributed directly[12] to the *Every Child Matters* initiative which is discussed below.[13]

(b) Investigations into child sexual abuse

The public inquiries into the handling of child sexual abuse investigations shared some of the conclusions of the inquiries into child deaths. Both types of inquiry found failures in coordination of activity and in information management. However in some notorious cases the target of inquiry critique was not the lack of social services intervention to protect children from abuse, but rather the excess of it.[14] Concern arose from the scandals surrounding investigations into the alleged sexual abuse of children in Cleveland, Rochdale and Orkney that over-zealous investigation could also cause

---

[9] Lord Laming (Chair) *Victoria Climbié Inquiry* (Cm 5730, 2003).   [10] ibid [1.16].

[11] N Parton 'From Maria Colwell to Victoria Climbié: Reflections on Public Inquiries into Child Abuse a Generation Apart' (2004) 13 *Child Abuse Review* 80, 83.

[12] Department of Health, Home Office, Department of Education and Skills *Keeping Children Safe: the Government's Response to the Victoria Climbié Inquiry and the Joint Inspectors' Report Safeguarding Children* (Department of Health, London 2003).   [13] See below section B.1.

[14] N Parton *Governing the Family—Child Care, Child Protection and the State* (Macmillan, Basingstoke 1991) 81.

children damage. Concern solidified around the conduct of interviews with children, which placed a great deal of pressure on them to state that they had been sexually assaulted, and which failed to acknowledge any contra-indications.[15] The inquiries also highlighted the dangers of repeating medical examinations and interviews with children for the parallel investigations of the police and social services, as well as by experts engaged by their parents.[16]

(c) Abuse and mismanagement in an institutional setting

The crises surrounding allegations of systematic abuse and mismanagement of children's homes reiterated many of the concerns that had already been raised in relation to child deaths and the investigation of child sexual abuse. Inquiries followed the discovery of the extent and nature of child abuse in children's homes. They highlighted systemic failures to respond to reports of abuse. Complaints made by adults who had previously lived or worked in the homes[17] were overlooked or dismissed for years before they were taken seriously.[18] In some cases this was because the person to whom the informant complained was also involved in perpetrating abuse and indeed in some cases even went on to abuse the child complainants. In many cases the problems stemmed from poor management. At a local government level, managers had been incompetent or disinterested in the workings of children's homes. Managers ignored allegations of abuse or did not treat the allegation as demonstrating a serious problem.[19] Children's homes were isolated places with little opportunity for children to complain about their care and few mechanisms through which staff could raise concerns about their colleagues.[20]

As Fox-Harding has written, 'it is impossible to overlook the impact of individual cases which achieve scandal status and difficult to overestimate their importance in English policy'.[21] With each tragedy the government of the day has been placed under enormous public pressure to respond clearly and decisively, to ensure that the tragedy does not occur again. The symbolic power of law-making has been harnessed to reassure the public that their concerns have been addressed. There has been a proliferation of law, procedure, guidance, inquiry reports, and circulars as each scandal has emerged.

---

[15] Dame Elizabeth Butler-Sloss *Report of the Inquiry into Child Abuse in Cleveland 1987* (Cm 412) [12.42]; The Right Hon Lord Clyde *Report into the Inquiry into the Removal of Children from Orkney in February, 1991* (HMSO, 1992) [14.86–14.93].   [16] *Cleveland*, [11.45]; *Orkney*, [14.94–14.98].

[17] A Kirkwood *The Leicestershire Inquiry—The Report of the Inquiry into Aspects of the Management of Children's Homes in Leicestershire between 1973 and 1986* (Leicestershire County Council 1993).

[18] Sir Ronald Waterhouse, Chair *Lost in Care: Report of the Tribunal of Inquiry into the Abuse of Children in Care in the Former County Council Areas of Gwynedd and Clwyd since 1974* (HM Stationery Office, London 2000) [34.17].

[19] G Williams and J McCreadie *Ty Maur Community Home Inquiry* (Gwent County Council, Cwmbran 1992) 13.

[20] *Lost in Care* (n 18) [33.120–33.122] [41.31–41.54] [45.14–45.16] [45.17–45.19] [45.20–45.23].

[21] L Fox-Harding *Perspectives in Child Care Policy* (Longman, London 1991) 218.

2. The influence of research and inspectorate reports

Research conducted for the Department of Health and synthesized into the document *Messages from Research*[22] was a crucial influence on the first version of *Working Together to Safeguard Children 1999*. The research found that work with a child and her family was overwhelmingly focused on investigating suspected incidents of abuse and providing services, or taking court action, only after there was evidence that abuse had occurred. In one of the Department of Health studies, Cleaver and Freeman concluded this was particularly unhelpful, as most families subject to investigation needed some help and support from an outside agency, even when no abuse had been proved.[23] In another Department of Health study, Farmer and Owen argued that not only was it short-sighted to see the problems of the child outside a broader familial context, it was also counter-productive to long-term child protection needs. They concluded that children could experience 'unresolved feelings of loss or guilt' when little attention was paid to maintaining family links once they were removed from home for their own protection. This in turn could incline them to seek to return home swiftly to a potentially abusive environment.[24] Secondly children's and their parents' other needs were not felt to deserve attention if not immediately and ostensibly linked to a child's need for protection. Consequently social workers could leave a parent to deal with very difficult situations, for example, cases where a child's behaviour was severely disturbed or where the abuser had left home and the family had no income.[25] This might mean that children received little or no treatment to enable them to recover from the harm they had suffered. It could also mean that the parent could turn again to the support of an abusive partner.

Messages from Research concluded that in the past many investigations in England and Wales had been started inappropriately by social workers to gain access to services for children, rather than because a threshold for investigation had been crossed. The most quoted piece of information from *Messages from Research* was that 75 per cent of the children initially involved in a process of investigation were filtered out before the stage of the child protection conference, and that only 15 per cent of the original reports resulted in the child's name being placed on the child protection register.[26] This statistic raised the question whether the outcome for the majority of the children would have been better if social workers had considered them as a child 'in need',[27] rather than as a case needing investigation. The overall findings of the research fitted well with the inclinations of policy makers, who aimed to reduce expenditure on investigations and to refocus practice on the provision of services for children 'in need' and their families.[28] The Department of Health published two key documents to

---

[22] Department of Health *Child Protection: Messages from Research* (HMSO, London 1995).

[23] H Cleaver and P Freeman *Parental Perspectives in Cases of Suspected Child Abuse* (HMSO, London 1995) 134.

[24] E Farmer and M Owen *Child Protection Practice: Private Risks and Public Remedies* (HMSO, London 1995) 205.   [25] ibid 283–284.

[26] J Gibbons, S Conroy and C Bell *Operating the Child Protection System* (HMSO, London 1995) 115.

[27] Children Act 1989 (England) s 17, discussed at Offering Services in England and Wales Chapter 2, section 1.D.1.

[28] C Davies 'Developing Interests in Child Care Outcome Measurement: A Central Government Perspective' (1998) 12 *Children and Society* 155.

govern a professional response to a concern about child abuse which were significantly influenced by *Messages from Research*. The first document was *A Framework for the Assessment of Children in Need and their Families*[29]—a guide for social workers in their assessment of whether a child was in need, the nature of the child's needs and what services the child and her family could potentially be offered. The second was a revised version of existing inter-agency guidance on the investigation of abuse (*Working Together*), which was renamed *Working Together to Safeguard Children*.[30] The influence of *Messages from Research* is heavily in evidence in these two documents and particularly in their emphasis on finding the appropriate response to an allegation of child abuse, which might not necessarily be an investigation.

However although this influence remains, particularly because the *Framework for the Assessment of Children in Need* was not revised following the *Every Child Matters* initiative and the Children Act 2004, it is no longer absolutely dominant. The revised *Working Together to Safeguard Children 2006* is heavily influenced by the *Climbié Inquiry*, but it is also influenced by Inspectorate reports on practice,[31] particularly, the two reports by the Joint Chief Inspectors[32] *Review of Children's Safeguards* in 2002[33] and in 2005.[34] The *Review of Children's Safeguards* judged those safeguards from standards which were inclusive and multi-disciplinary. It examined safeguards for children living at home and away from home including children in the justice and asylum system. It stressed the importance of focusing on the child and making their well-being a priority. However the reports are both very realistic, examining the problems in information sharing and lack of resources on the ground in work surrounding the safeguarding of a child. These reports have undoubtedly been influential in the new guidance. The Inspectorate reports do focus upon improving the processing of information; however they also acknowledge the reality of poor resourcing.[35] What the reports do not do is to identify how to resource the system better which, as the judiciary has also identified,[36] is essentially a policy matter. *Working Together to Safeguard Children 2006* uses the technique of record-keeping to ensure clarity in decision-making and to ensure that children are not overlooked. However it does so by adding further layers of administration. The system may only succeed with very different levels of resourcing than those described in the Joint Chief Inspectors' Reports amongst others.

---

[29] Department of Health *Framework for the Assessment of Children in Need and their Families* (HM Stationery Office, London 2000).

[30] Department of Health, Home Office and the Department of Education and Employment *Working Together to Safeguard Children* (HM Stationery Office, London, 1999).

[31] HM Government *Working Together to Safeguard Children: a Guide to Inter-Agency Working to Safeguard and Promote the Welfare of Children* (2006) [1.6]–[1.9].

[32] Chief Inspector, Commission for Social Care Inspection, Her Majesty's Chief Inspector of Schools, Her Majesty's Chief Inspector of Court Administration, Her Majesty's Chief Inspector of Probation, Sir Ronnie Flanagan GBE MA, Her Majesty's Chief Inspector of Constabulary, Her Majesty's Chief Inspector of Prisons, Chief Executive, Healthcare Commission, Her Majesty's Chief Inspector of the Crown Prosecution Service.

[33] It can now be found in Joint Chief Inspectors *Safeguarding Children: The Second Joint Chief Inspectors Report on Arrangements to Safeguard Children* (HM Stationery Office, London 2005) Appendix A.

[34] ibid Appendix A.   [35] ibid Appendix A [2.12].

[36] Chapter 2 section 4 s 17 Fam L Department for Education and Skills.

B. Dominant Themes of the Guidance for Investigators

1. Coordination, agreed procedure, and shared information

As we have identified above, inquiry reports have consistently emphasized the need to coordinate child protection activity. This is not surprising. The focus upon partnership between professionals through coordinated agency activity has been 'a continuing refrain in social welfare and is intended to solve a range of policy problems—essentially to produce more efficient, comprehensive and holistic services'.[37] Thus the terms of reference for many of the public inquiries included an examination of 'the care and supervision provided by local authorities and other agencies . . . and the coordination between them'.[38] However, as outlined above,[39] the findings of these inquiries were highly influential in identifying areas of concern to be overcome in any policies written by central government.

There have been a number of different legal initiatives to bring agencies together and ensure cooperation in child protection cases. Until recently, inter-agency procedures have been regarded as the core mechanism to ensure cooperation. The national procedures for responding to a child protection concern and investigating any suspicions of child abuse contained in *Working Together* are now in their fifth incarnation, including an initial draft version.[40]

Working Together has also established a standard pattern for investigations. Social services (now renamed local authority child social care) and the police (Child Abuse Intelligence Unit (CAIU)) are designated as the key investigative agencies. Both agencies are expected under the guidance to work together following an initial complaint in gathering and sharing information. All other agencies involved with the child should share whatever knowledge they have about the child and his circumstances with investigators. They should also take part in key decision-making: the strategy discussion following a report of abuse[41] and the child protection conference following the completion of the initial investigation.[42]

The coordination of work in child protection has never been easy and it has persisted in being problematic, despite the creation of the procedures. There are several sources of the problems. The most fundamental is the difficulty in encouraging professions

---

[37] C Hallett and E Birchall *Co-ordination and Child Protection* (HMSO, Scotland 1992) 2; L Challis (ed) *Joint Approaches to Social Policy—Rationality and Practice* (Cambridge University Press, Cambridge 1988) 24.

[38] *The Report of the Committee of Inquiry into the Care and Supervision Provided in Relation to Maria Colwell* (n 5) 86.   [39] Above section A.1.

[40] DHSS and the Welsh Office *Working Together—Draft* (HMSO London 1986); Department of Health and Social Security *Working Together: A Guide to Arrangements for Inter-agency Cooperation for the Protection of Children from Abuse* (HMSO, London 1988); Home Office, Department of Health, Department of Education and Science and the Welsh Office *Working Together—Under the Children Act* 1989 (HMSO, London 1991); *Working Together to Safeguard Children 1999* (n 30); *Working Together to Safeguard Children 2006* (n 31).   [41] *Working Together to Safeguard Children 1999* (n 30) [5.28–5.33].

[42] ibid [5.53–5.57] [5.90–5.96].

with very different rules and working ethos to work together. Of course it is true that all the professions wish to protect children, but they have different priorities and mechanisms for achieving this goal. Area Child Protection Committees (ACPC) were created to be the glue that held the agencies together. Containing representatives from each key agency, the ACPC was charged with writing local procedures, organizing inter-agency training and reviewing child deaths in the area. However, as the Joint Chief Inspectors' Review of Children's Safeguards 2002[43] found, the agencies were not always sufficiently committed to, or willing to fund, the work of their ACPC. Many ACPCs lacked authority in governing the behaviour of individual agencies, particularly if the agency representative on the committee was low-ranking.[44]

The Climbié Report concluded that the procedures had hitherto placed too much reliance on achieving coordination through some shared procedures and some joint training. Lord Laming, in his speech introducing the Report stated forcefully that:

[m]ore exhortation that services should work better together manifestly is not enough. Actual change is required if the safety and welfare of children is not to depend to an unacceptable degree on the personal working relationships of individual professionals.[45]

The conclusions of the Climbié Report that coordination of work would not come without major organizational change was one of the influences on a widespread reform of children's services. It cannot be stressed strongly enough however that these reforms go far beyond the narrow question of investigating an allegation of abuse. The Government concluded from the Climbié Report that 'child protection cannot be separated from policies to improve children's lives as a whole'.[46] Instead the Green Paper *Every Child Matters: Change for Children*[47] set out five government aims for every child: being healthy; staying safe; enjoyment and achievement; making a positive contribution; and achieving economic well-being.

It also identified four ways that these aims could be achieved: support for parents through both universal and targeted services; early intervention and effective protection of children; accountability and integration; and workforce reform.[48] Three of these ways of achieving reform led directly to reforms which could impact upon the coordination of work in child protection cases. The Government has committed itself to legislation and funding to break down barriers between organizations through the creation of directors of children's services, overseeing children's trusts (which bring together children's educational and social services). It also agreed to create a replacement for the Area Child Protection Committees. The Government agreed to remove legal and practical barriers to information sharing between agencies, developing a

---

[43] (n 33).   [44] HMIC *Child Protection—Thematic Report* (Home Office, London 1999) [3.82].
[45] Lord Laming 'Speech by Lord Laming' (8 June 2004) <http://www.victoria-climbie-inquiry.org.uk/keydocuments/lordstate.htm> (accessed 30 June 2006).
[46] Chief Secretary to the Treasury *Every Child Matters* (The Stationery Office London Green Paper 2003 Cm 5680) [4].   [47] ibid.
[48] ibid [12]–[21].

common assessment framework, introducing the concept of a lead professional for a child's case who will be in overall responsibility for that child. Finally, the Green Paper suggested that professionals should be encouraged to work in multi-agency teams based in schools and children's centres to provide rapid multi-disciplinary response to concerns about children.

Some of these proposals were enacted in the Children Act 2004. On the grounds that mere procedures had hitherto failed to ensure that agencies worked together, the Government used a more coercive mechanism: the Children Act 2004 s 10 places the promotion of cooperation on a statutory footing. The Act requires each children's services authority to make arrangements to 'promote cooperation between the authority, the authority's relevant partners and such other persons or bodies that the authority considers appropriate, being persons or bodies of any nature who exercise functions or are engaged in activities in relation to children in the authority's area'[49] to improve the well-being of children. This is an addition to the cooperation provisions under the Children Act 1989 s 27, which allows a local authority in exercising its functions under Part III of the Act (local authority support for children and their families to request help from education, housing and health authorities and authorized persons).[50] It should be noted that the requirement to coordinate work under the Children Act 2004 s 10 and indeed the Children Act 1989 s 27 has been conceived as being much wider than child protection. Under the Children Act 2004 s 10 children's 'well-being' includes s (2)(b) protection from harm and neglect; but it also includes s (2)(a) physical and mental health and emotional well-being; s (2)(c) education, training and recreation; s (2)(d) the contribution made by them to society and s (2)(e) their social and economic well-being.

With the Children Act 2004 s10, came further guidance on cooperating coordinated work in children's services, following the creation of Children's Trusts. Under the *Every Child Matters* initiative local areas are encouraged to bid for funds to create Children's Trusts which can incorporate all the services involved in safeguarding children. By 2008 every area is expected to have a Children's Trust, which it is hoped will develop according to local needs. Certainly the review of the operation of the first 35 Children's Trusts indicates that some have had a specific focus, for example children with disability, whereas others have been more wide-ranging.[51]

The old Area Child Protection Committees have been replaced by the creation of a Local Safeguarding Children Board in each Children's Services Authority area of England. It is unclear at this stage how the Boards will be markedly different from the old Area Child Protection Committees. Certainly the membership of the Boards remains the same. The Boards should contain representatives of all agencies involved in safeguarding children, as the ACPCs did before them. The only difference on the face of the Act or indeed the regulations accompanying it[52] is that the Local Safeguarding

---

[49] Children Act 2004 (England) s 10.

[50] This does not therefore include the functions exercised under Children Act 1989 (England) Part V which include the powers to investigate.

[51] University of East Anglia and National Children's Bureau *Realising Children's Trust Arrangements: National Evaluation of Children's Trusts—Phase 1 Report* (2005) Chapter 5.

[52] The Local Safeguarding Children Boards Regulations (2006) SI 2006/90.

Children Board is now placed on a statutory level.[53] There is a further exhortation in the Children Act 2004 s 13(7) that 'the authority establishing it must cooperate with each of their board partners; and (b) each board partner must cooperate with the authority'. The hope is that as so many funding decisions hang on whether an agency is required by statute to undertake a particular action, the policy decision to place the Local Safeguarding Children Boards on a statutory footing will mean that they are properly funded and thus able to do their job.

Working Together to Safeguard Children 2006 has also been rewritten to take account of these changes and to guide professionals through yet another new statutory working environment. Although priority has been given to coordinated procedure in responding to concerns about children, *Working Together to Safeguard Children* and the *Framework for the Assessment of Children in Need* remain two separate documents, the first being an inter-agency guide and the second aimed at social work with a child. This has the potential to continue the fragmentation of the process. The guidance claims that this will be overcome by the use of a *Common Assessment Framework* at the very initial stages of dealing with any child, to assess his 'needs and strengths',[54] and on the use of central recording in children's cases for each stage in the key tasks of assessment, planning, intervention and review.

It is on new mechanisms for information sharing that much of the hope for the system is now placed. Countless inquiries have found that if only information had been held properly and shared it would have been much more likely that a child would have been protected. The *Climbié Inquiry* concluded:[55]

Effective action designed to safeguard the well-being of children and families depends upon sharing relevant information on an inter-agency basis. The following contribution to one seminar was compelling in this respect:

'Whenever we do a Part 8 case review [into a child's death] . . . we have this huge chronology of information made available to the Panel and it is very frustrating to read that . . . a long way before that happened, a pattern of things [was] emerging, but knowing that at the time . . . separate agencies held those bits of information. So GPs will be seeing things, accident and emergency will be seeing things, the police may be dealing with other aspects of what is going on in that child's life, and nobody is bringing it together.'

There were similar findings from the 2004 *Bichard Inquiry*[56] into the handling of information on the previous allegations of sexual assault and rape against the murderer of Holly Wells and Jessica Chapman. As a result of this Children Act 2004 s 12 created a national data handling system. The Integrated Children's System is a national mechanism for recording information on a centralized computer about a child in the key tasks of assessment, planning, intervention and review. Each child will have a unique identifying number into which all the information about the child will be input in the same form. This system replaces the localized and often paper-based systems which had been so problematic. It remains to be seen whether it can handle the level of information which it will need in practice, and there remain concerns

---

[53] Children Act 2004 (England) ss 13–16.
[54] HM Government *Common Assessment Framework for Children and Young People: Practitioners' Guide* (2006) [1.1].   [55] *Victoria Climbié Inquiry* (n 9) [1.45].
[56] Sir Michael Bichard, Chair *Bichard Inquiry Report* (HC 653 June 2004).

about children's privacy and database security; as well as the ability of computer based programmes to change the large amount of information without the problems which have hitherto dogged similar projects in other parts of government.[57]

2. Partnership between parents and investigators

The *Cleveland Report*[58] was fundamental to the development of procedures that acknowledged parental interests during an investigation into an allegation of child abuse. In Cleveland 168 children were diagnosed as having been sexually abused on ambiguous physical signs alone; they were all removed from their homes by social services. As the furore surrounding the events in Cleveland developed the press stressed the draconian nature of social workers' powers to intervene in families.[59] This was underlined in the House of Commons, when the local MP Tim Devlin asked:

Is the Minister aware that children are being collected from their beds at two o'clock in the morning by social workers? Does not my Honourable Friend see a clear parallel with the activities of another body which carried the initials SS?[60]

The crisis in Cleveland came to public attention as a result of parental complaints,[61] and the views of the parents involved were well represented at the public Inquiry and in the House of Commons.[62] The parents' submissions to the Inquiry emphasized they had little or no contact with their children for the duration of the investigation.[63] Parents also complained that they had had no input into decisions about how their children were treated whilst in the care of the local authority and that they knew very little about what had happened to their children, for example, how many times their children had been interviewed.[64] A pressure group, the Family Rights Group, in their evidence to the Cleveland Inquiry, asked that the rights accorded to parents during investigations should be extended:

Parents and other family members unhappy with a service in such a crucial area should not have to wait on the goodwill of those who provide the service, but should be able to challenge decisions made by them. By comparison with the safeguards in criminal law for those threatened with loss of liberty, the opportunities for challenge in this area are very limited.[65]

Procedure and guidance published in the decades following the Cleveland Inquiry have consistently advocated a partnership between parents and other family members and the state in protecting children. The purpose of the 1995 guidance *The Challenge*

---

[57] J Dowd 'Delays to NHS computer system could cost taxpayers £40bn' *The Observer* 1 October 2006; S Ranger 'Government holds back £13.3m over CSA computer problems: Significant problems remain with new system' *Silicon* 30 March 2005 <http://management.silicon.com/government/0,39024677,39129061,00.htm> (accessed 12 October 2006).

[58] *Cleveland* (n 15) [4.39].   [59] B Campbell *Unofficial Secrets* (Virago Press, London 1988) 3.

[60] *Hansard* HC col 257 (29 June 1987).   [61] *Cleveland* (n 15) [2.1].

[62] K Gieve 'Where Do Families Stand After the Cleveland Inquiry?' in P Riches (ed) *Responses to Cleveland—Improving Services for Child Sexual Abuse* (National Children's Bureau, London 1989) 34–35.

[63] *Cleveland* (n 15) [4.15].   [64] ibid [2.45].   [65] Gieve (n 62) 34–35.

of Partnership in Child Protection: Practice Guide was to promote this partnership and the involvement of children.[66] This was followed by the very positive statements included in *Working Together to Safeguard Children 1999*. This guidance reiterated the 15 essential principles for professionals to work in partnership with families,[67] initially published in the *Challenge of Partnership*.[68] These include treating all family members 'with dignity and respect' and regard for the 'impact and implications' of any power wielded by professionals in their relationship with parents.[69] However the partnership envisaged by *Working Together to Safeguard Children 1999* was very much one in which parents 'could contribute'[70] to decisions that were made about their children and family, rather than being the leaders of the process, as for example the New Zealand legislation has at least in theory tried to do.[71]

As Lindley and Richards, amongst others,[72] observed at the time:

despite the positive spin which pervades the guidance on the importance of involving parents, it remains the case that parents whose children are the subject of compulsory intervention by the state are inevitably unequal partners in the process.[73] . . . When the state intervenes in family life on a compulsory basis . . . equality is not achievable, because ultimately, such intervention may involve the local authority overriding the parents wishes.[74]

This fundamental power imbalance can undermine any concept of partnership. It is only with a reversal of some of the power for decision-making that the partnership rhetoric has any meaning. An attempt at this has been made in the latest *Working Together to Safeguard Children 2006*. For the first time it acknowledges the place of parents as the primary decision makers in their children's lives even when an investigation is taking place:

A wide range of services and professionals provide support to families in bringing up children. In the great majority of cases, it should be the decision of parents when to ask for help and advice on their children's care and upbringing. However, professionals do also need to engage parents early when to do so may prevent problems or difficulties becoming worse. Only in exceptional cases should there be compulsory intervention in family life: for example, where this is necessary to safeguard a child from significant harm. Such intervention should—provided this is consistent with the safety and welfare of the child—support families in making their own plans for the welfare and protection of their children.[75]

---

[66] Department of Health *The Challenge of Partnership in Child Protection: Practice Guide* (Social Services Inspectorate HMSO, London 1995).

[67] *Working Together to Safeguard Children 1999* (n 30) 76 [7.5].

[68] *The Challenge of Partnership in Child Protection: Practice Guide* (n 66) 14 [2.20].

[69] The requirements for improving partnership at each stage of the process are discussed throughout this chapter. [70] *Working Together to Safeguard Children 1999* (n 30) 75 [7.2].

[71] Discussed below section H. 2 in relation to Family Group Conferences.

[72] B Corby, M Millar and L Young 'Parental Participation in Child Protection Work: Rethinking the Rhetoric' (1996) 26 British Journal of Social Work 475; M Bell 'Working in Partnership in Child Protection: The Conflicts' (1999) 29 British Journal of Social Work 437; J Thoburn, A Lewis and D Shemmings *Partnership and Paternalism? Family Involvement in the Child Protection Process* (HMSO, London 1995).

[73] B Lindley and M Richards '*Working Together* 2000—How Will Parents Fare Under the New Child Protection Process?' [2000] Child and Family LQ 213. [74] ibid 222.

[75] *Working Together to Safeguard Children 2006*, (n 31) [1.5]

It seems likely that this change of stance has been influenced by the very strong jurisprudence on parental involvement in child protection cases following the Human Rights Act 1998 came into force. As Munby J stated in *Re G (Care: Challenge to Local Authority's Decision)*, Article 8 requires that parents are properly involved in the decision-making process not merely before and during the care proceedings, but also when they have come to an end and whilst the local authority is implementing the care order.

3. The involvement of children

The *Cleveland Report* was also influential in its emphasis upon the position of the child in the inquiry process. The phrase from the *Cleveland Report* that a child should be regarded 'as a person and not an object of concern'[76] has often been repeated. The *Cleveland Report* has been influential in creating mechanisms to enable children to share confidences with investigators and for investigators to support children in expressing their views. There has never been an expectation that children would be in the same position as their parents in the investigation process. The Children Act 1989 was conceived as 'a bilateral partnership between parents and the local authority rather than a trilateral one including the children themselves'.[77] As Fortin has argued, the law has not developed any clear concept of the child as being capable of self-determination in the process of investigation and while much work has been undertaken to enable children to speak of what happened to them, there is much less expectation that children will contribute to decision-making at the end of the investigation.[78]

In theory child protection work that follows the guidance that is part of the *Every Child Matters* initiative should be much more child-focused than it has been in the past. In fact 8 of the 11 principles outlined in *Working Together to Safeguard Children 2006* for the investigation of allegations of child abuse could be defined as child-focused. 'Any intervention' should be: 'child centred'; 'rooted in child development', 'focused on outcomes for children', 'Holistic in approach' (ie having an understanding of a child within the context of the child's family (parents or caregivers and the wider family) and of the educational setting, community and culture in which he is growing up);'ensuring equality of opportunity for all children'; 'involving the child and her family'; 'building on strengths as well as identifying difficulties'; and ongoing, rather than a single event. However it is the operation that is the key factor in this process. Procedures can set the tone for an investigation, but an investigation will only be child-centred if the professionals implementing those procedures work in a way that places the child's interests and welfare first during an investigation For example, of the 211 social work days spent on Victoria Climbié, only 30 minutes were spent talking

---

[76] *Cleveland* (n 15) Part 3 Recommendations.
[77] A Bainham 'The Children Act 1989: The State and the Family' (1990) 20 Family Law 231.
[78] J Fortin *Children's Rights and the Developing Law* (1st edn Butterworths, London 1998) 388.

to her, amounting to four occasions. Professionals spoke English, a language which was not her own (French) and on only two of those occasions was she seen by herself.[79]

C. The Procedures

Initially the guidance contained in *Working Together* was conceived as being essentially a national resource to advise and guide local policy-makers who would develop their own procedures; however it has always been issued under the Local Authority Social Services Act 1970 s 7, which requires local authorities to act under the general guidance of the Secretary of State in exercising their social services functions. The whole of Part I of *Working Together to Safeguard Children* 2006 is statutory guidance, whereas Part II is non-statutory practice guidance.[80] Part I 'should be complied with by local authorities carrying out their social services functions unless local circumstances indicate exceptional reasons which justify a variation.'[81] Part I encompasses: the principles under which child protection work following *Working Together* should operate; the roles and responsibilities of all those agencies and professionals involved in child protection (Chapter 2); the operation of Local Safeguarding Boards (Chapter 3); training (Chapter 4); managing individual cases (Chapter 5); additional guidance on specialist investigations, including prostitution and induced and fabricated illness (Chapter 6); child deaths (Chapter 7); and reviewing and investigating individual cases, Serious Case Reviews (Chapter 8). Chapters 3, 4, 7 and 8 are issued under the Children Act 2004 s 16, which says that Children's Services Authorities (county level and unitary local authorities) and each of the statutory partners must, in exercising their functions relating to a Local Safeguarding Children Board, have regard to any guidance given to them for the purpose by the Secretary of State. This again means that they must take the guidance into account and only depart from it with good reason.

The Local Safeguarding Children Boards should create additional local standards which expand upon *Working Together*, for example:

- setting out thresholds for referrals to children's social care of children who may be in need, and processes for robust multi-agency assessment of children in need;

- agreeing inter-agency procedures for s 47 enquiries and developing local protocols on key issues of concern such as children abused through prostitution or children living with domestic violence.[82]

When a local agency decides that it is necessary to deviate from the guidance, it does not have the 'freedom to take a substantially different course' in its own guidelines.[83]

---

[79] L Goldthorpe 'Every Child Matters: A Legal Perspective' (2004) 13 *Child Abuse Review* 115, 127.
[80] *Working Together to Safeguard Children 2006* (n 31) xxv.   [81] ibid xxv.
[82] ibid [3.18].   [83] *R v London Borough of Islington ex p Rixon* [1997] ELR 66, 71D (Sedley J).

Thus the court in *R v Cornwall County Council ex p LH*[84] found that the council had acted unlawfully in creating a policy to refuse to provide a child's parents with a copy of the minutes of the child protection conference that they had attended, despite clear guidance in the relevant *Working Together* that parents should always be provided with them.

D. Reporting Child Abuse

The first stage of an inquiry process begins when a suspicion of child abuse is reported to investigators. A professional may be alerted to the possibility that a child has been maltreated or is at risk of maltreatment through several main channels of information. Cleaver and Freeman found that suspicions of child abuse came to the attention of investigators through one of three means. In just over half (51 per cent) of the cases studied, a child or another family member spoke to a professional; in 39 per cent of cases child abuse was identified by professionals who were already working with a family. In the remaining 10 percent of cases professional suspicion was raised by an unrelated event, such as a home visit or an arrest.[85]

This figure however relates only to the cases of suspected child abuses that were reported to investigators. It is clear that not all cases are reported. In the past the majority of cases of child abuse were never reported. Abuse often remained secret because children were not equipped to recognize what was happening to them and their family, or professionals had no knowledge of the signs and symptoms of abuse. While as a society we have become more knowledgeable and more open about child abuse as a problem, it is clear that many cases of child abuse still are never reported to investigators. Cases may not come to light because the child does not tell others.[86] In sexual abuse cases there is often no evidence of what has happened other than the word of the child, so no disclosure means no discovery. Cases may also not come to light because a professional who suspects or is told about abuse decides not to report it. In the countries we have studied the most common reasons given by professionals for not reporting suspicions in the past has been a desire to protect the relationship between the child and the person to whom they have spoken, and to respect the child's desire for confidentiality.[87] There is also some question about whether investigation would actually prove counter-productive, producing little protection for the child and damaging the relationship between the child and the child's family irreparably.

In the next section we consider the reasons why cases are not reported and examine the efforts of policy makers to encourage the reporting of child abuse. In policy terms much of the debate centres around whether there should be a mandatory reporting

[84] *R v Cornwall County Council ex p LH* [2000] 1 FLR 236.

[85] Cleaver and Freeman (n 23), 32.

[86] C Wattam and C Woodward 'And Do I Abuse My Children? No!—Learning About Prevention From People Who Have Experienced Child Abuse' in *Childhood Matters: The Report of the National Commission of Inquiry into the Prevention of Child Abuse* (Vol 2 Background Papers HMSO, London 1996).

[87] *Cleveland* (n 15) [12.69].

requirement enshrined in legislation, to override any concerns about reporting. While England and New Zealand have resisted the creation of such a requirement, the United States, Canada and many States in Australia have concluded that a 'stick' rather than a 'carrot' approach should be adopted to ensure that cases are reported.

1. Reporting child abuse in England and Wales

(a) Education

In England and Wales the primary focus of the guidance has been upon the development of professional understanding of the signs and symptoms of child abuse to enable professional recognition, rather than upon the expansion of knowledge amongst the general population.[88] Many inquiry reports have identified weaknesses in professional knowledge of the signs and symptoms of abuse. Monro's study of 45 inquiry reports into child abuse cases, published between 1973 and 1994, found that 25 (55 per cent) of the reports criticized social workers for a failure to recognize the significance of the information which they were being told in determining the severity of the risks which the child was facing.[89] This does not seem to have changed, at least in some areas, and the finding was replicated in the Laming Report on the death of Victoria Climbié.[90] Inquiry reports, particularly the *Cleveland Report*, also identified weaknesses in professional understanding of the evidential requirements of the court.[91] The guidance *What to Do if You're Worried a Child is being Abused*[92] and *Working Together to Safeguard Children*, is primarily aimed at professionals who may be involved in the detection and investigation of child abuse.[93] The guidance describes the behaviour that may constitute child abuse and the results stemming from it.[94] However it is necessarily brief and could not constitute training on the subject; this should be provided by employers, or at least if not delivering the training themselves the employers should satisfy themselves that employees meet the standard of knowledge of the signs and symptoms of abuse to enable them to work effectively in this field.[95] Current inquiry reports indicate that levels of training on the identification of abuse remain variable. Her Majesty's Inspectorate of Constabulary (HMIC)'s Inspection of the Investigation and Prevention of Child Abuse 2005[96] established that, while just under half of all

---

[88] 'The Department for Education and Skills has no current plans to run any public information campaigns. Our principal role is in increasing awareness of child abuse among people who work with children. We work closely on this with the NSPCC, ChildLine and a wide range of other voluntary organisations.' M Eagle 'Reply to Parliamentary Question from Department for Education and Skills' (31 October 2005 column 806W–807W) <http://www.publications.parliament.uk> (3 July 2006).

[89] E Munro 'Improving Social Workers' Knowledge Base in Child Protection Work' (1998) 28 *British Journal of Social Work* 89. [90] *Keeping Children Safe* (n 12).

[91] *Cleveland* (n 15) [4.155].

[92] Department of Health, Home Office, Department for Education and Skills, Department for Culture, Media and Sport, Office of the Deputy Prime Minister and the Lord Chancellor's Department *What to do if You Suspect That a Child is Being Abused* (Children's Services Guidance, London 2003).

[93] *Working Together to Safeguard Children 2006* (n 31) [1.14]–[1.16]. [94] ibid [1.22]–[1.33].

[95] ibid [4.5].

[96] Her Majesty's Inspectorate of Constabulary *Keeping Safe, Staying Safe: Report of the Thematic Inspection of the Investigation and Prevention of Child Abuse* (HM Inspectorate of Constabulary 2005) [3.39].

forces (46 per cent) had included a specific child protection element within detective training courses, only 8 per cent provided specialist officers with specialist training in the investigation of child abuse.

(b) Professional identification of child maltreatment

There is no mandatory reporting law in England and Wales. The 'Review of Child Care Law'[97] which preceded the Children Act 1989 concluded that 'the shadow of near automatic reporting' would raise 'barriers between clients and their professional advisors and even between professionals concerned in the same case' which could actually hinder the process of child protection.[98] It also concluded that such a requirement could also weaken the individual professional's sense of personal responsibility.[99] The Review focused instead on how to heighten any sense of duty to report suspected child abuse, which would outweigh any other consideration, to ensure that cases were reported. It was felt that this sense of duty already existed amongst many professions. Many of those working with children were public servants and 'imbued by their training, tradition and the character of their work with a strong emphasis upon the welfare of children and their families'.[100]

The expectation that professionals will report their suspicions is contained in national guidance for all professions and in guidance issued by individual professional bodies. The national guidance, *What to do if you suspect that a child is being abused*[101] states that all practitioners with 'concerns about a child's welfare' should:

(a) discuss those concerns with their manager and other designated practitioners;

(b) following this discussion, if the practitioner still 'has concerns, and considers the child and their parents would benefit from further services, she should refer the child and her parents on, to another agency including another part of their own';

(c) before doing so the referrer should discuss the referral with the child and her parents, unless such a discussion would place the child at risk of significant harm;

(d) once a referral is made the referrer should agree what the child and her parents should be told and by whom; and

(e) follow up any verbal referral in writing within 48 hours.[102]

However such exhortations gloss over the two main problems for practitioners in making a referral. The first consideration is the nature of the concern that should be referred, particularly whether suspicions of harm or need which might fall short of 'significant harm' should be referred. The second problem is the extent to which the child or parent's confidences should be kept; this has on occasions been allied to the first. Both of these problems were most clearly identified and discussed in a

---

[97] Department of Health and Social Security *Review of Child Care Law* (HMSO, London 1985).

[98] ibid 80–81 [12.4]. (The House of Lords had already decided in *D v NSPCC* [1977] 2 WLR 201 for the same reasons that the NSPCC could not be compelled to reveal the name of someone who had given them information.)   [99] ibid 80 [12.4].

[100] ibid 80 [12.3].   [101] *What to do if You Suspect That a Child is Being Abused* (n 92).

[102] ibid [11.1–11.4].

document written by the Royal College of Paediatrics and Child Health (RCPCH), *Responsibilities of Doctors in Child Protection Cases with Regard to Confidentiality*[103] and by the *Climbié Inquiry.*

(i) The nature of the concern that should be referred

National guidance does not clearly indicate the level of harm which should be referred. Instead individual professions and individual local bodies, schools and churches have been expected to write their own policies for reporting concerns and suspicions of child abuse. There is therefore, unsurprisingly, a degree of variation in the guidance on the threshold for reporting a suspicion to an investigating authority. The guidance issued by the RCPCH states that a fear that a child is at risk of death or serious injury should override doctor–patient confidentiality, as should a situation where the doctor has information which 'would help prevent, detect or prosecute a serious crime'. When a child or parent does not consent to the disclosure of information a doctor is obliged to act where the child is 'in danger'. Sharing information remains a matter for the doctor to determine in each case (bearing in mind the fact that a whole view may only be gathered once information has been shared): 'when deciding upon sharing information, it is important to ask yourself whether such disclosure is a *proportionate response* to the need to protect the welfare of a child to whom the confidential information relates' (emphasis added).[104]

In contrast the model child protection policy published by the Churches Child Protection Advisory Service does not differentiate between the level of harm which a child may suffer and states that any concern about abuse should be referred to local authority child social care.[105] This is a model policy and it is expected that each church would accept it and adapt it as appropriate. This might mean that the standard for reporting might vary between churches. Some churches have not yet adopted a child protection policy. The picture is again very unclear in education where the Department for Education and Skills have encouraged each school to write its own child protection policy, within the guidance issued by the department.[106]

The police are in a rather different position from some of these other agencies. They will be involved in an investigation if the information that they have indicates that it is likely that a crime has taken place or may have taken place. Where there is evidence that a child is 'in need' rather than likely to suffer significant harm it is not expected that the police would be involved in the child's case further. HMIC[107] found that there were very wide-ranging disparities in the cases which the police thought should be referred to local authority child social care and those which they thought suitable for joint investigation or for the police alone.

---

[103] RCPCH *Responsibilities of Doctors in Child Protection Cases with Regard to Confidentiality* (RCPCH, London 2004). [104] ibid [4.15].
[105] Churches Child Protection Advisory Service *Guidance to Churches* (CCPAS 2003).
[106] NUT *Education the Law and You* (2003), *Protecting Children from Abuse: The Role of the Education Service* Circular 10/95 [4(i)]. [107] *Keeping Safe, Staying Safe* (n 96).

[E]xamples were found of physical assaults which clearly went beyond 'over-chastisement' and instances of allegations of sexual abuse which were being passed to social services for an initial assessment without any police involvement. In practice, a number of these assessments were, in fact, initial criminal investigations with social services interviewing suspects as well as victims, arranging medical examinations and making value judgements about evidence.

HMIC recommended that agreement and understanding be reached with social services departments on operational definitions and criteria for investigation, including clarity on cases that should be undertaken as joint investigations.[108] The problem of reporting has not only raised the question of the severity of the suspected abuse before a referral can be made, but has also been marked by confusion about whether a concerning fact may be referred, if it does not give an entire picture of a child's situation. The *Climbié Inquiry* was told repeatedly that concerns were not reported because they fell short of a clear concern which would trigger an investigation under Children Act 1989 s 47. This process was described by the RCPCH as making 'the mistake of trying to assemble the whole of the jigsaw before seeking help for the child'.[109] It is entirely consistent with the Children Act 1989 and its interpretation in caselaw for practitioners to share information with colleagues, even when they do not have a complete picture of the child's circumstances.[110] However this is obviously a matter that remains unclear for many practitioners.

(ii) Confidentiality

The question is further complicated by questions of confidentiality. Witnesses told the *Climbié Inquiry* that unless there was a clear allegation '*no dialogue* (Lord Laming's emphasis) could take place between the protective agencies until the child's carer had been informed and their permission given'.[111] As Lord Laming identified, such an interpretation runs contrary to the spirit of the Children Act 1989. However as the RCPCH noted this confusion may be the result of considerable ambivalence within *Working Together 1999*, which was the forerunner of *Working Together 2006*:

> Para 5.11 and 5.6 of *Working Together* state that parental permission should be sought before discussing the child with another agency, unless doing so may place the child at risk of significant harm. Para 2.27 of the same document, however, reflects the findings of virtually all 36 enquiries into child deaths between Maria Colwell and Victoria Climbié, namely that research and experience dictate that keeping children safe requires professionals and others to share information at an earlier stage. Importantly the paragraph adds: '*Often it is only when information from a number of sources has been shared and is then put together that it becomes clear that a child is at risk of or is suffering significant harm.*' (Para. 3.55).[112]

The guidance was unclear about how the ideal of partnership with parents during an investigation might be translated into a reality at the reporting stage and how this might affect questions of confidentiality. Obviously parents have an interest in

---

[108] ibid 15.   [109] RCPCH (n 103) [4.42].

[110] See the threshold test for action by the state in family life, 'significant harm' (Children Act 1989 (England) ss 31(2) and (9)), discussed above, Chapter 2 section E.1.

[111] *Keeping Children Safe* (n 12) [17.103].   [112] RCPCH (n 103) [3.55].

knowing that the report exists, and any concept of partnership is illusory if they do not have this basic knowledge. Yet if partnership is primarily for the benefit of a child, rather than the parents as the guidance suggested, parental permission to share knowledge or suspicions at this very early stage should not have been required. This is the conclusion reached by Lord Laming and the RCPCH.

The complicated drafting of the Data Protection Act 1998 muddies the water further. In principle the rules under the Data Protection Act 1998 do not allow a child or adult's need for confidentiality to trump an expectation that suspicions of child abuse will be reported. Information held in health, education, social services and housing records are all subject to the provisions of the Data Protection Act 1998, as is any information which is processed using a computer or other processor, or is kept in a filing system where information about a particular individual is accessible. The Data Protection Act 1998 applies to 'sensitive personal data', including information about a person's physical or mental health or condition, or sexual life, the commission or alleged commission by him of any offence, or about any criminal proceedings.[113] The Act sets up an expectation that information held on a person (a 'data subject') will only be shared with a third party with the consent of the individual concerned. However this may be overridden where disclosure is necessary for the data subject's 'vital interests'.[114] Consent is not required where the data subject cannot give consent.[115] Refusal of consent may be overridden, or consent is not required at all, for the release of personal data to a third party in relation to:

- information necessary to protect the vital interests of another person in a case where consent has been unreasonably withheld (Sch 3 s 2(b));
- the prevention or detection of crime, or the apprehension or prosecution of offenders (s 29(1)(a) and (b));
- information as to the physical or mental health or condition of the data subject, or information held by a school about its pupils (s 30(1) and 30(2)(a));
- personal data where the disclosure is required by or under any rule of law or order of the court, or for the purpose of any legal proceedings or for the purpose of obtaining legal advice or is otherwise necessary for the purpose of establishing, exercising or defending legal rights (s 35).

Thus although the Data Protection Act 1998 allows breaches in confidentiality, it could be interpreted on a brief reading that it only allows disclosure when a criminal act is suspected. This is not correct. A person would be allowed to disclose a suspicion of child abuse or of mistreatment, even if it was not suspicion of a criminal offence, because it could become part of civil child protection proceedings under the Children Act 1989. The claim in a press conference of the Chief Constable of Humberside Police respecting the murders of Jessica Chapman and Holly Wells, that his force could not disclose information about previous police investigations of Ian Huntley

---

[113] Data Protection Act 1998 s 2(e), (f), (g) and (h).   [114] ibid Sch 2 s 4.
[115] ibid Sch 3 s 2(3)(a)(i).

for sexual offences to another police force due to the Data Protection Act 1998, was clearly incorrect.

In response to high levels of professional confusion the Government published *Information Sharing: Practitioners' Guide*[116] under the auspices of the *Every Child Matters* initiative. This contains non-statutory guidance on the sharing of information by professionals about a child. It contains six core principles for information sharing:[117]

- Children, young people and families should have an explanation at the outset, openly and honestly, about what and how information will, or could be shared and why, and their agreement should be sought.

- Exceptionally this practice should be overstepped if to do so would put that child, young person or other persons at increased risk of significant harm, or if it would undermine the prevention, detection or prosecution of a serious crime, including where seeking consent might lead to interference with any potential investigation.

- The safety and welfare of a child or young person should always be considered when making decisions on whether to share information about them. Where there is concern that the child may be suffering or is at risk of suffering significant harm, the child's safety and welfare must be the overriding consideration.

- The wishes of children, young people or families who do not consent to share confidential information should where possible be respected. However information may still be shared if in your judgement on the facts of the case, there is sufficient need to override that lack of consent.

- Professionals should seek advice when in doubt, especially when doubts relate to a concern about possible significant harm to a child or to others.

- The information which is shared should be checked for accuracy and to ensure that it is up to date, necessary for the purpose, shared only with those people who need to see it, and shared securely.

Could this guidance and the accompanying guidance on the specific legal issues[118] on sharing information avoid some of the pitfalls identified by the *Climbié Inquiry* and the RCPCH? The answer is a qualified yes. They provide very clear advice which complies with Article 8 ECHR, and the equitable duty of confidentiality which permits the disclosure of confidential information if it is in the public interest;[119] where there is evidence that a child is at risk of significant harm, the public interest requirement certainly would be satisfied. The problem identified by the *Climbié Inquiry* was the belief by professionals that their individual concern did not amount to concern about a risk of significant harm. The guidance in *Information Sharing* suggests that in these cases a professional should discuss their concerns with another colleague and make a decision about whether the information should be shared. The problem remains

---

[116] HM Government *Information Sharing: Practitioners' Guide. Integrated Working to Improve Outcomes for Children and Young People* (HM Stationery Office, London 2006).   [117] ibid 6–7.
[118] ibid.   [119] For further discussion see Chapter 7 sections A and C.

that in many cases the effect is cumulative and it is only when the information is all brought together that evidence of significant harm is clearly there. In such circumstances caution should indicate that mere suspicions should be shared rather than the opposite; however it is likely to be only the confident practitioner who will interpret the guidance in this way.

2. Reporting child abuse in New Zealand

New Zealand is the other common law jurisdiction that we have studied which like England and Wales has chosen not to create a mandatory reporting law. However there continues to be much public debate about whether there should be such a law.[120] It was decided not to include a requirement to report in the Children, Young Persons, and their Families Act 1989 despite some recommendations to do so.[121] It was concluded that most of the resources for child protection would be exhausted by responding to an increased number of reported suspicions of child abuse, many of which would not show a demonstrable need for action.[122] It was argued that overseas experience of mandatory reporting showed an over-reporting of 'grey area' cases. It was also concluded that families would be afraid to ask for help, or to take their child to the doctor lest their act resulted in a report to the Child, Youth and Family Service (CYFS). The Maori members of the committee said that they would have difficulty reporting Maori families to an investigatory body dominated by *Pakeha* (white settler) principles.

Instead the strategy underlying the section that was eventually passed[123] relied upon education programmes targeted at community and professional groups, and upon national and local protocols for the reporting of child abuse cases aimed at governmental and non-governmental organizations, professional and occupational groups.[124] However a review of child protection in 2000 found that national and local protocols were not widely known or disseminated. As in England, protocols were continually being reinvented. At the time of the report 23 national protocols for the voluntary reporting of child abuse were in existence.[125]

A further disadvantage for New Zealand of the current system of voluntary reporting has been that a misunderstanding of the terms of the Privacy Act has lead to non-reporting because of professional fears that they would face legal action for breaching confidentiality. A survey of general practitioners in New Zealand found that doctors who did not report said that they would need first to complete further examinations or question the child or her caregivers further and they felt that this would run the risk of either ensuring that the child was not returned to their clinic, or that they

---

[120]   *Care and protection is About Adult Behaviour* (n 1) 65.

[121]   Judge K Mason *Report of the Ministerial Review Team to the Minister of Social Welfare Hon Jenny Shipley* (Auckland 1992).

[122]   B Dalley *Family Matters—Child Welfare in Twentieth Century New Zealand* (Auckland University Press, Auckland 1998).   [123]   CYPFA 1989 (New Zealand) s 7(2)(ba).

[124]   Department of the Child, Youth and Family Services *The Child, Youth and Family Care and Protection Handbook* (NZCYPS, Wellington 1996 and 1997).   [125]   *Care and Protection* (n 1) 67.

would incur legal action by being held to be in breach of the Privacy Act.[126] This is despite the existence of a provision under Children, Young Persons, and their Families Act CYPFA 1989 s 16 specifically protecting people who report suspicions of child abuse from any '*civil, criminal or disciplinary proceedings . . . unless the information was disclosed or supplied in bad faith*'.

It appears therefore that New Zealand shares many of the English problems of lack of clarity of the thresholds for reporting and uncertainty about the relationship between confidentiality and the expectation to report.

3. Reporting child abuse in the United States

In contrast by 1967 the United States had established a national mandatory reporting system for professionals implemented through State statutes.[127] The mandatory reporting laws 'were the most rapidly adopted pieces of legislation in the history of the United States'.[128] They were driven by a desire to do something positive to ensure that child abuse was not ignored as it had been in the past, with the additional incentive of Federal funding for prevention programmes if the law was introduced.[129] Doctors were the primary focus of early statutes,[130] but this was soon expanded to include other professionals who have frequent or daily contact with children. Some States also place a requirement on any citizen to report suspected child abuse or neglect.[131] Lawyers remain a rather special category of reporters. The attorney–client privilege still applies in 23 States.

The reporting requirements are typically cumbersome because they list all those professionals who are expected to report their suspicions. For example Section 26–14–3 (a) of the Alabama Code states that:

All hospitals, clinics, sanitariums, doctors, physicians, surgeons, medical examiners, coroners, dentists, osteopaths, optometrists, chiropractors, podiatrists, nurses, school teachers and officials, peace officers, law enforcement officials, pharmacists, social workers, day care workers or employees, mental health professionals, or any other person called upon to render aid or medical assistance to any child, when the child is known or suspected to be a victim of child abuse or neglect, shall be required to report, or cause a report to be made of the same, orally, either by telephone or direct communication immediately, followed by a written report, to a duly constituted authority.

Anyone who could not be categorized by this provision may make a report provided that they have 'reasonable cause to suspect' that a child is being abused or neglected.

---

[126] G Maxwell, L Barthauer and R Julian *The Role of Primary Health Care Providers in Identifying and Referring Child Victims of Family Violence* (New Zealand Office for the Commissioner for Children, Wellington 2000).

[127] H Davison 'A Model Child Protection Legal Reform Instrument: The Convention on the Rights of the Child and its Consistency with United States Law' (1998) 5 *Geo J Fighting Poverty* 185.

[128] J Myers *Legal Issues in Child Abuse and Neglect* (Sage Publications, Newbury Park 1992) 100.

[129] D Besharov 'The Legal Aspects of Reporting Known and Suspected Child Abuse and Neglect' (1977) 23 Vill L Rev 458, 460.   [130] ibid 466.

[131] R Mosteller 'Child Abuse Reporting Laws and Attorney–Client Confidences: the Reality and the Spectre of Client as Informant' (1992) 42 Duke LJ 203, 211–215.

As Renke has argued, listing professionals to whom the statute applies appears unnecessary and potentially counterproductive. The purpose of a mandatory reporting statute is to impress upon all those who come into contact with children whom they suspect are being abused of the need to report, rather than to counter under-reporting by a particular group of professionals.[132]

The sanctions are typically small fines, with the threat of imprisonment for non-payment of those fines. However they appear to be rather erratically enforced. Jones notes that in Kentucky, while there have been a few prosecutions of non-reporters of child abuse, enforcement of the reporting statute is patchy at best and prosecutions have uncertain results.[133] Besharov has concluded that the mandatory reporting laws are working well by raising awareness of the problem and the need to pass on information to investigators.[134] He uses the vast national increase in reports of child abuse, from 669,000 in 1976 to 2.5 million by the beginning of the 1990s to support his view, whilst acknowledging that there remain practical problems in the implementation of the statutes.[135]

Some of the problems encountered in the United States are the same as those encountered in England. Under-reporting remains a problem, despite the statutory requirements to report[136] and the reasons given for this failure to report would be familiar to practitioners in England. Professionals in the US have described their lack of confidence in the validity of their suspicions and their uncertainty about signs and symptoms of child abuse.[137] Other reasons for failure to report have been that the professional believes that it is not in the child's best interests,[138] that the child's treatment will be disrupted,[139] that he will lose work time because of potential legal proceedings[140] and that there will be legal repercussions resulting from the breach in confidentiality.[141]

Conversely there has been some concern that the mandatory reporting laws have led to over-reporting of acts which are on the borderline between abusive and non-abusive behaviour, swamping the authorities with cases that they do not have the resources to investigate and children for whom they do have not the resources to provide services. Sagatun and Edwards attribute over-reporting in the US again to the

---

[132] W Renke 'The Mandatory Reporting of Child Abuse Under the Child Welfare Act' (1999) 7 Health LJ 91, 111.

[133] J Jones 'Kentucky Tort Liability For Failure To Report Family Violence' (1999) 26 N Ky L Rev 43, 45.

[134] D Besharov 'Child Abuse and Neglect Reporting and Investigation: Policy Guidelines for Decision Making' in M Robin (ed) *Assessing Child Maltreatment Reports: The Problem of False Allegations* (Haworth Press, New York 1991).

[135] D Besharov 'Gaining Control Over Child Abuse Reports: Public Agencies Must Address Both Under and Over Reporting' [1990] *Public Welfare* 34.

[136] M Frias-Armenta and B Sales 'Discretion in the Enforcement of Child Protection Laws in Mexico' 34 Cal W L Rev 203, 211.

[137] A Reiniger and others 'Mandated Training of Professionals: A Means for Improving Reporting of Suspected Child Abuse' (1995) 24 *Child Abuse & Neglect* 63.

[138] W Crenshaw and others 'Mental Health Providers and Child Sexual Abuse: A Multivariate analysis of the Decision to Report' (1993) 2 *J Child Sexual Abuse* 19.

[139] G Zellman 'Child Abuse Reporting and Failure to Report Among Mandated Reporters: Prevalence, Incidence and Reasons' (1990) 5 *Interpersonal Violence* 3.   [140] Reiniger and others (n 137) 63.

[141] ibid.

lack of knowledge amongst professionals and the public about what would constitute physical and sexual abuse within the terms of reference for investigators.[142]

4. Reporting child abuse in Australia

Australian States, with the exception of Western Australia, have a mandatory reporting law. Western Australia obliges professionals contracted to work with the family court to report suspicion or belief that a child has been harmed.[143] The State has recently considered the possibility of introducing a mandatory reporting law, but has rejected it on the ground that the majority of the mandatory reporting laws in existence across Australia are 'in chaos'.[144] Some voluntary protocols are in existence in Western Australia in relation to the reporting of specific sexually transmitted infections in children.[145] The Western Australian Report identified recurring the problem of inconsistency in the thresholds for reporting. A professional is required to report:

- If she *suspects* on reasonable grounds that the child is being abused (South Australia);[146]

- If she *forms the belief* on reasonable grounds that a child has suffered or is likely to suffer significant harm as a result of physical or sexual assault and the child's parents have not or are not likely to protect the child from harm of that type (Victoria);[147]

- *All* suspicions of risk (Tasmania);[148]

- If a child is at risk of harm and the professional has concerns about the safety, well-being, and welfare of the child (New South Wales);[149]

- If a child has suffered or is suffering sexual abuse or non-accidental physical injury (Australian Capital Territory);[150]

- If harm is suspected to children in residential care, schools and daycare (Queensland);[151]

---

[142] I Sagatun and L Edwards *Child Abuse and the Legal System* (Nelson-Hall Publishers, Chicago 1995) 38.

[143] Child Welfare Act 1947 (Western Australia) and Community Services Act 1972 (Western Australia).

[144] Harries and others *Mandatory Reporting of Child Abuse Evidence and Options Report by the Discipline of Social Work and Social Policy for the Western Australia Child Protection Council* (University of Western Australia 2002) 56.

[145] Australian Institute of Health and Welfare Child Protection Australia 2003–4 (2005) Appendix 4 'Mandatory Reporting Requirements'.

[146] Family and Community Services Act 1972 (South Australia) and Children's Protection Act 1993 (South Australia).   [147] Children and Young Person's Act 1989 (Victoria) s 64 (IC).

[148] Children Young Persons and their Families Act 1997 (Tasmania).

[149] Children and Young Persons (Care and Protection) Act 1998 (New South Wales) s 24.

[150] Children and Young People Act 1999 (Australian Capital Territory) s 159.

[151] Medical practitioners are required to report under the Health Act 1937; the Commissioner for Children and Young People is required to report under the Commission for Children and Young People Act 2000 (Queensland); Family Court personnel, including court counsellors, mediators, welfare officers and registrars are required to report under the Family Law Act 1975 (Queensland); under the Child Protection Act 1999 (Queensland), an authorized officer of the Department or a person employed in a licensed care service must report harm caused to a child in residential care; under the Juvenile Justice Act

- Any form of abuse in which there is a substantial risk of suffering (Northern Territory).[152]

There is evidence of under-reporting following the introduction of the mandatory regimes, with only 7 per cent of professionals admitting to any increase in their reporting behaviour as a result.[153] More recent research has found that doctors' non-reporting rates in Queensland have improved from 43 per cent in 1998, to 26 per cent in 2006, but that referrals by doctors still only made up between 1 and 3 per cent of the referrals to child protection workers. Doctors were still determining not to refer cases on the basis of their hope that the child's carers would reform, and were not influenced to change their minds by the existence of legislation requiring them to report.[154] However there is also evidence that Southern Australia and New South Wales have been overwhelmed by reports and are considering reforming their reporting requirements.[155] This seems to reflect a fairly similar pattern to the other jurisdictions we have examined that while mandatory reporting statutes have raised the profile of child abuse amongst the general population and, it appears, increased the level of reporting, it has not demonstrably altered the conduct of professionals who come across child abuse in their daily work.

5. Reporting child abuse in Canada

There is a mandatory requirement to report child abuse in all Canadian jurisdictions, except the Yukon Territory which has a discretionary provision to report.[156] All the statutes place their requirement to report upon 'all persons', rather than professional bodies alone. The majority of the statutes, with the exceptions of Newfoundland, the Northwest Territories and Nova Scotia, protect legal professional privilege and exempt lawyers from a duty to report information received in confidence from clients. Each statute is worded slightly differently, but most are framed around a threshold for reporting of 'belief or reasonable grounds for belief that a child is in need of protective

---

1992 (Queensland) a detention centre employee of the Department must report harm, or suspected harm, caused to a child in a detention centre; and licensees of childcare services must report under the Child Care Act 2002 (Queensland) where abuse or allegations relate to the childcare service.

[152] Community Welfare Act 1983 (Northern Territory).

[153] P Lamond 'The Impact of Mandatory Reporting Legislation on Reporting Behaviour' (1989) 13 *Child Abuse & Neglect* 471, 477.

[154] R Schweitzer, L Buckley, P Harnett and N J Loxton 'Predictors of failure by medical practitioners to report suspected child abuse in Queensland, Australia' (2006) 30 Australian Health Review 298.

[155] Harries and others (n 144) 13.

[156] Child Welfare Act 1984 (Alberta) ss 3, 4, 91(4); Child, Family and Community Service Act 1996 (British Columbia) ss 14, 15; Child and Family Services Act 1985 (Manitoba) ss 18, 18.1–18.4; Family Services Act 1980 (New Brunswick) s 30; Child Youth and Family Services Act 1998 (Newfoundland) s 15; Child and Family Services Act 1997 (Northwest Territories) s 8(1); Children and Family Services Act 1990 (Nova Scotia) c 5 ss 22(2)(a), (c), (e), (f), (h)–(j), 23, 24, 25; Child and Family Services Act 1984 (Ontario) s 68; Child Protection Act 2000 (Prince Edward Island) ss 1(a), 22, 59(b); Youth Protection Act (Quebec) s 39; Children's Act 1986 (Yukon) s 115.

services'.[157] A person may be fined if they fail to report their belief. However, like the United States there has been a very low level of prosecutions for a failure to report given the known low rate of reporting in Canada:

This offence, and its kindred offence in other Canadian child welfare statutes, creates a paradox. On the one hand, we feel so strongly about the protection of children that we impose an obligation to report abuse on an extremely broad group of people, and we back up that obligation with a penalty. On the other hand, there are no reported cases of prosecutions [in Alberta] and few for the like offence across the rest of Canada. One might observe that we feel strongly enough to write laws, but not strongly enough to enforce them. Less charitably, one might observe that we do not really care about the reporting of child abuse, but only wish to create the appearance of caring.[158]

6. Evaluation: do mandatory reporting provisions help?

Mandatory reporting laws appear to fit into one of the patterns in legislating for child protection—that of the grand and headline-grabbing declaration of intent, with the aims of demonstrating that societal concern is being attended to, but the substance of the declaration would be extremely expensive to enforce properly. It is therefore not really used. However it can have the useful side-effect of placing the blame if things go wrong upon professionals involved with a child in an individual case and away from policy makers.

All jurisdictions share some of the same problems whether or not they have a mandatory reporting law on their statute book. Confusion over the threshold for reporting, and concerns about confidentiality, prevent those who have suspicions that a child is being abused from reporting some concerns. These real problems are inadequately dealt with by law. Jurisdictions in which there is a mandatory reporting statute appear to have used it to make a symbolic point, rather than to change behaviour. According to Walter, 'the appeal of such legislation is that it communicates a high degree of concern with, and the appearance of, doing something about child maltreatment at very little cost'.[159] Mandatory reporting statutes have become a very good example of a 'taking child abuse seriously' law. In making this ostensibly cheap and easy point legislators have created additional problems for those dealing with child abuse 'on the ground' of over-reporting of cases by members of the public with concerns about a child. These reports often fall into the category of cases where the child and her family may require help but where a formal investigation into an allegation of child abuse is not required. Mandatory reporting laws

---

[157] With the exceptions of British Columbia, 'any person who has reasonable grounds to believe that a child has been, or is likely to be, physically harmed, sexually abused or sexually exploited by a parent or other person, or is in need of protection' Child, Family and Community Service Act 1996 (British Columbia) ss 14, 15, and New Brunswick, 'a person suspects that a child has been abandoned, deserted, physically or emotionally neglected, physically or sexually ill-treated or otherwise abused' Family Services Act 1980 (New Brunswick) s 30. [158] Renke (n 132) 140.

[159] B Walter *In Need of Protection: Children and Youth in Alberta* (Children's Advocate, Edmonton 1993) 43.

do seem to lead to situations in which social work departments are swamped with reports, which can lead to an increase in inappropriate or inadequate responses in individual cases.[160]

This does appear to be a situation where an absolute obligation does not solve the problem. Professionals may regard the concerns in individual cases as nuanced and blanket standards inappropriate. Professionals' behaviour might be altered by rigorous prosecution or an action in negligence, although clearly it would be better to concentrate on convincing professionals that a child's position would be significantly improved if they did report their concerns, rather than to use the fear of legal repercussions to force a certain type of behaviour. In relation to the public, clear standards which are freely available to guide everyone as to when suspicions should be reported are more appropriate. Child welfare agencies' use of websites in particular have set the standard for dissemination of useful information for those not working in the field who wish to report a suspicion of child abuse.[161]

E. Responding to a Report

Once a report has been made, investigators must determine how to respond to it. In England and Wales the mode of response by social services, the NSPCC and the police to any report indicating potential child abuse has been laid down in successive editions of *Working Together*. The process as set out in the latest guidance, *Working Together to Safeguard Children 2006* starts when concerns about a child are referred to the local authority children's social care team. From this point social workers are expected to assess the referral quickly and work toward an appropriate response.[162]

The influence of *Messages from Research* and *Every Child Matters* is clear throughout this section of the guidance. It points to an initial assessment of any referral focusing on the needs of a child, rather than upon evidence-gathering, prior to a decision on whether action may be taken through the civil and criminal courts. It aims to direct professional thought towards an examination of the whole picture of a child's life, not merely a particular allegation. Any assessment of a child's life should now be undertaken using the Common Assessment Framework[163] for all work with children which is part of the Children's Integrated System for information sharing discussed above. In considering their response to an allegation *Working Together* suggests that the local authority child social care team determine which long-term

---

[160] In New South Wales the first independent review by the ombudsman found that 55% of the cases reported had been 'mishandled': M Rayner 'The State of Children's Rights in Australia' in B Franklin (ed) *The New Handbook of Children's Rights—Comparative Policy and Practice* (Routledge, London 2002) 345, 347.
[161] See for example Western Australia <http://www.community.wa.gov.au/> (last accessed 3 October 2006), Child Welfare League of America <http://www.cwla.org/programs/childprotection/childprotectionpubs.htm>, CYFS New Zealand <http://www.cyf.govt.nz/suspectabuse.htm> (accessed 3 October 2006).   [162] *Working Together to Safeguard Children 2006* (n 31) [5.32].
[163] *Common Assessment Framework* (n 54) [1.1].

Diagram 6. The Investigation Process

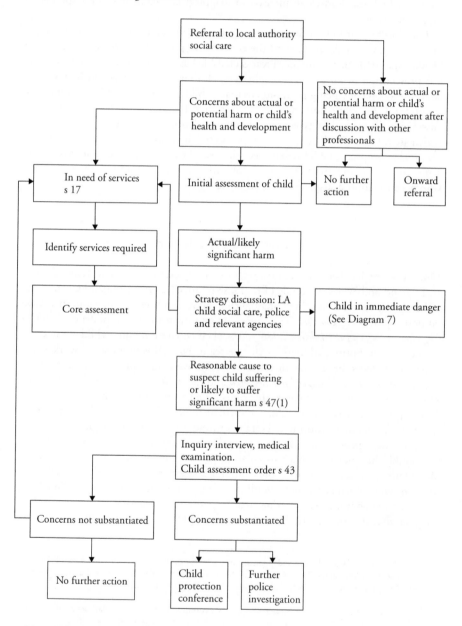

LA = Local Authority

outcomes they hope to achieve in each child's case and how the child's needs might be provided.[164]

The initial judgement of the nature of the referral is expected to be made quickly. Having clarified the nature of the concerns with the referrer, the local authority child social care team should decide the next steps for action within 24 hours of the complaint.[165] They are expected to make this decision on the basis of discussion with other professionals or services 'as necessary' and having consulted any existing records. Should the situation appear acute, social workers may decide to take emergency protective action, as discussed below. Similarly, where it appears that a criminal offence has been committed, social workers should inform the police Child Abuse Intelligence Unit, and both agencies should work together on an investigation. Conversely local authority child social care may at this point decide that there is no justification for further inquiries. They may decide to do nothing further, or to provide a specific service to the child and their family, or to ask another agency to do so. Following from the *Climbié Inquiry*, *Working Together to Safeguard Children 2006* places an additional duty on referrers to oversee this process to a limited extent, in the hope that the referral to the local authority child social care team does not fall through the cracks and disappear. Professionals should confirm their oral referral in writing within 48 hours and if they do not receive a written acknowledgement of that referral within three days they should contact the department again.[166]

Social workers may also decide to gather more information about the child's needs, known in *Working Together* as the 'initial assessment'.[167] This should assess three areas of need: the child's developmental needs, parenting capacity, family and environmental facts.[168] For the purposes of this assessment social workers should see and speak to the child and appropriate family members as well as gathering information from records and from professionals and others who are in contact with the child and her family. In line with the concept of partnership and involvement, discussions with the child and her parents should also be important in the decision about what to do next, unless such a discussion would place the child at risk of significant harm.[169] From this initial assessment social workers should determine what course to follow, whether this be to take no further action, to complete an in-depth assessment of the child's needs ('core assessment'), to offer services under the Children Act 1989 s 17, or to start an investigation under the Children Act 1989 s 47. Further discussion of the assessment of need and the provision of services in each jurisdiction may be found in Chapter 2 section D.1.

---

[164] *Working Together to Safeguard Children 2006* (n 31) [5.38].   [165] ibid [5.33].
[166] ibid [5.32].   [167] ibid [5.37]–[5.45].
[168] *R (on the application of AB and SB) v Nottinghamshire County Council* [2001] EWHC Admin 235; *R v Guilfoyle (No 2)* [2001] 2 Cr App R 57.
[169] *Working Together to Safeguard Children 2006* (n 31) [5.39].

1. Starting an investigation in England and Wales

(a) Children Act 1989 s 47 inquiry

Under the Children Act 1989 s 47(1), an inquiry may commence if a local authority

(a) are informed that a child who lives, or is found in their area—
    (i) is the subject of an emergency protection order; or
    (ii) is in police protection; or
(b) have *reasonable cause to suspect* that a child who lives, or is found, in their area is suffering, or is likely to suffer, significant harm.

This was an important expansion of the previous legislation, under which an investigation could be triggered only when the local authority received information suggesting that there were grounds for bringing care proceedings. The grounds for beginning an inquiry—reasonable *suspicion*—are low and may be contrasted with the grounds for emergency orders and use of police powers under the Children Act 1989 ('reasonable cause to *believe*')[170] and the grounds for granting a care or supervision order (*satisfaction* on the balance of probabilities that a child *is* suffering or is *likely* to suffer significant harm).[171] The Children Act 1989 s 47 places the onus on the representatives of the local authority to make the decision about whether an investigation should take place. However each incarnation of *Working Together* including *Working Together to Safeguard Children 2006* states that the decision should be made during an inter-agency strategy discussion. This meeting should be convened following the initial assessment and should include representatives of the local authority children's social care team, the police, and relevant agencies including the referring agency. The meeting is intended to be a forum for sharing information and decision-making. Those attending the strategy discussion should not only decide whether an investigation led by the local authority children's social care team should begin, but also determine if and when a criminal investigation should commence and whether any emergency protection measures should be put in place.[172] In practice HMIC[173] found that the strategy meeting was often delayed until an initial assessment had been made and at that point it could be decided that there was no need for police involvement. If this occurs the investigation becomes a single agency investigation by the local authority children's social care team and not a joint investigation. HMIC stressed the danger of leaving the decision about whether there was a potential criminal case to answer to social workers. First HMIC found examples of physical assaults which went beyond 'over-chastisement' and allegations of sexual abuse which were passed to the local authority children's social care team without any police involvement. This meant that evidence was overlooked and witnesses to a potential crime were interviewed by social workers on their own, rather than as part of a joint investigation with the police.

---

[170] Children Act 1989 (England) ss 43–46.   [171] ibid s 31(2).
[172] *Working Together to Safeguard Children 2006* (n 31) [5.54]–[5.59].
[173] *Keeping Safe, Staying Safe* (n 96) [5.36]–[5.40].

The law does not establish an absolute duty to investigate when a determination is made that the threshold has been crossed. Instead the statute gives the local authority the duty to make or cause to be made 'such inquiries as they consider necessary to enable them to decide whether they should take any action to safeguard and promote the child's welfare'.[174] Section 47 allows the authority to gather the necessary information on which to decide whether the authority has reasonable cause to suspect that a child is likely to suffer significant harm.[175] Investigators may therefore decide that no further inquiries are necessary before reaching this decision, especially if that is to take no further action.

However a failure to investigate allegations of abuse when it is subsequently found that a child was being abused may be found to be a violation of a child's rights under the ECHR Article 3, and may also give rise to tort liability.[176] In *E v UK* the ECtHR ruled that 'a failure to take reasonably available measures which could have had a real prospect of altering the outcome or mitigating the harm is sufficient to engage the responsibility of the State' to protect a child from torture or inhuman or degrading treatment.[177] The ECtHR noted that one of the measures which social workers could have undertaken was an investigation into the children's circumstances. It found that 'the social services failed to take steps which would have enabled them to discover the exact extent of the problem and, potentially, to prevent further abuse taking place'.[178] In this case social workers failed to investigate indications of a clear and obvious risk to the children following their stepfather's conviction for the sexual assault of two of them. The parties did not ask the Court to consider whether social workers should have investigated before this point.

(b) Other mechanisms for starting an inquiry by a local authority

The Court of Appeal in *Gogay v Hertfordshire CC*[179] suggested that a s 47 inquiry should usually be commenced when a child is living at home or has been removed in an emergency. However Hale LJ concluded that s 47 'is not obviously apt to deal with cases of children who are already subject to orders made under the Children Act 1989'. In this situation Hale LJ suggested the local authority might pursue inquiries under s 22(3), which gives them a duty to safeguard and protect the welfare of any child which they look after. This would include, the court suggested, an inquiry to determine whether the child is at risk of harm from within the agency. 'Any authority or agency looking after vulnerable people . . . must be under a duty to take reasonable care to safeguard them from harm. That duty must include making reasonable enquiries when there is information to suggest that they may be at risk of harm from within the agency.'[180]

A local authority may also commence an investigation when ordered to by the court. Under the Children Act 1989 s 37 the court may direct, 'the appropriate authority

---

[174] Children Act 1989 (England) s 47(1)(b).
[175] *R v Swindon BC, Wiltshire CC ex p S* [2001] EWHC Admin 334 [2001] FLR 776 [34].
[176] Discussed above Chapter 4 section F.2(a).   [177] *E v UK* (2003) 36 EHRR 31 [99].
[178] ibid [97].   [179] *Gogay v Hertfordshire County Council* [2001] 1 FLR 280 (CA).
[180] ibid 288.

to undertake an investigation of the child's circumstances' 'in any family proceedings in which a question arises with respect to the welfare of a child', where 'it appears to the court that it may be appropriate for a care or supervision order to be made with respect to him'. No guidance was given about the circumstances in which it would be appropriate to order such an investigation. Concern has been expressed in the past that some orders have been made inappropriately. One particular concern when the Act first came into force was that it was being used as a way of generating a report from a local authority to give the court general welfare advice, or an 'interim report' on the child's welfare,[181] or of appointing a *guardian ad litem* in private law proceedings.[182] It has been decided however that the court cannot control the way in which a case is investigated following a s 37 order by giving the local authority strict instructions or by using the Official Solicitor to oversee the investigation and ensure that it is undertaken in the way that the judge hoped.[183]

2. Gathering information

Once the local authority determines that the threshold has been crossed, s 47 does not establish a duty to investigate, but rather a duty to make inquiries. As Eekelaar suggests it is not clear from the statute that an inquiry is formatively very different from an investigation and we will use the terms interchangeably.[184]

The purpose of the inquiry is to gather information which will enable the local authority 'to decide whether they should take any action to safeguard or promote the child's welfare'.[185] The Court of Appeal in *Gogay v Hertfordshire CC*[186] has interpreted the term 'action' primarily to denote orders under the Act. Certainly the Children Act 1989 s 47(3) requires that:

Inquiries shall be directed towards establishing—
(a) whether the authority should make any application to the court,
(b) whether an application should be made for an emergency protection order for a child already in police protection.

However given the ethos of the Children Act[187] and the fact that s 47 also states that enquiries should also be directed towards establishing whether:

(a) the authority should . . . exercise any of their other powers under the Act or,
(b) a child who is the subject of an emergency protection order, but is not at present accommodated by the authority should be accommodated;

it is likely that the Act intends that the local authority child social care should gather information to help them to decide what to do next, not merely to satisfy the evidential

---

[181] A Wells 'Section 37 Directions: Are They Working?' (1994) 6(4) Journal of Child Law 181—186.
[182] Children Act Advisory Committee *Annual Report 1992/93* (Department of Health, London 1993) 35.   [183] *Re M (a Minor) (Official Solicitor: Role)* [1998] 2 FLR 815.
[184] J Eekelaar 'Investigation under the Children Act 1989' [1990] Fam Law 486.
[185] Children Act 1989 (England) s 47(1)(b).   [186] *Gogay v Hertfordshire County Council* (n 179).
[187] Its focus on voluntary agreement rather than coercive measures.

requirements of a court order.[188] This decision on what to do next may include a decision that a child is suffering or is likely to suffer significant harm. It may also 'frequently . . . embrace a view that the harm is coming or is likely to come from a particular individual . . . It may be a necessary step in their process of making decisions about what action to take'.[189] This was the conclusion which was reached by the Court of Appeal in *R v Hertfordshire CC ex parte A*[190] and *R v Swindon Borough Council, Wiltshire Borough Council ex p S.*[191] Both of these cases concerned men who had been tried for sexual assaults on children and had been acquitted, but where the local authority had concluded from their investigation that the men were perpetrators of abuse. The Court of Appeal endorsed the actions of the local authority as part of the necessary decision-making at this point in the investigation.

3. Starting an investigation in the United States

In the United States social workers (child protective services) bear the primary responsibility for investigating a report of abuse. The police should also be involved in an investigation following a report of serious injury, sexual abuse or the death of a child.[192]

Many State laws imposed a mandatory duty to investigate allegations of child abuse to determine whether there is any basis for the report, when introducing mandatory reporting laws in the 1960s and 1970s.[193] Each of these laws is slightly different, but each focuses on the need to make an immediate evaluation of the report and a clear plan of action.[194] Adherence to this type of provision has been erratic, as numerous tort claims on behalf of the child for failure to investigate or respond in any way to reports have demonstrated.[195] 'In reality, CPS workers perform "triage" generally allocating available resources to investigate the serious allegations and using their discretion to dismiss vague or trivial sounding reports.'[196] Statutory time limits between report and investigation have not necessarily guaranteed a timely and effective investigation in the United States. It has been common practice in some areas to close a file on the grounds that the time limit for a response had expired, irrespective of whether any kind of investigation had been undertaken.[197]

Child protective services in the United States have been commonly perceived to be in crisis. With some notable exceptions, the investigation of child abuse has been

---

[188] *Working Together to Safeguard Children 1999* (n 30) [5.22].
[189] *R v Hertfordshire County Council ex p A* [2001] EWCA Civ 2113, [2001] FLR 666.
[190] ibid.
[191] *R v Swindon Borough Council, Wiltshire Borough Council ex p S* (n 175)
[192] C Trost 'Chilling Child Abuse Reporting: Rethinking the CAPTA Amendments' (1998) Vanderbilt LR 183, 201.
[193] H Clark *The Law of Domestic Relations in the United States* (West Publishing 1988), 355.
[194] See for example General Statute Annotated 1986 (Connecticut) s 17a–101g, Revised Statute 1986 (Colorado) s 19–3–308, *Mammo v State* 675 P 2d 1347 (Arizona Ct App 1984) s 328.
[195] Discussed above Chapter 4 section F.2a(v).   [196] Trost (n 192) 183, 201.
[197] L Oren 'The State's Failure to Protect Children and Substantive Due Process: *Deshaney* In Context' (1990) 68 NCL Rev 659, 679.

beleaguered by 'a chronic disease of frequently overworked, understaffed, inadequately trained, and even uncaring child protectors'.[198] The implementation of provisions exhorting investigation has only been successful in cases where social workers have been sufficiently trained to respond adequately to each individual report and have had the time to do it. Caseloads are reputedly very high, more than double that recommended by some courts.[199] Coordination of service response has been very poor within and between agencies.[200] Various solutions to the perceived widespread malaise have been suggested. In Illinois and Alabama there has been enormous investment in the training of social workers, and encouragement and generous leave to allow social workers to undertake the training.[201]

4. Starting an investigation in Canada

The Canadian legislative framework differs from the United States. While Manitoba,[202] Nova Scotia,[203] Quebec,[204] Saskatchewan,[205] and the Yukon[206] require child protection workers to investigate all reports that a child is in need of protective services, the other Provinces allow child protection workers discretion in assessing an allegation and determining how to respond to it.[207]

There are several joint Province-wide protocols for the investigation of child abuse.[208] A child protection worker and a police officer should discuss any referral and determine whether it should be a joint investigation or whether the report should be assessed or investigated by only one of the agencies. The police would only investigate reports where a crime may have taken place.

Provincial governments can now recognize a self-governing First Nations or Aboriginal group as a provider of child services. The Provincial Government can agree with them that they have authority over some or all aspects of child welfare for the children who are part of their group. Such agreements have been entered into in

---

[198] Freeman 'Child Protection in the 21st Century' (n 1) CA Crosby-Currie and ND Reppucci 'The Missing Child in Child Protection: the Constitutional Context of Child Maltreatment from *Meyer* to *DeShaney*' (1999) 21 Law & Policy 129.

[199] W Crossley 'Defining Reasonable Efforts: Demystifying The State's Burden Under Federal Child Protection Legislation' (2003) 12 BU Pub Int LJ 259.

[200] L Baca, P Jendrucko, and D Scott' "Silent Screams"—One Law Enforcement Agency's Response to Improving the Management of Child Abuse Reporting and Investigations' (2002) 22 J Juv L 29, 31.

[201] Freeman 'Child Protection in the 21st Century' (2003) (n 1) 451.

[202] Child and Family Services Act 1985 (Manitoba) s 18.14.

[203] The Child and Family Services Act (amended 2002) (Nova Scotia) s 8.2(2).

[204] Youth Protection Act (amended 2004) (Quebec) s 49.

[205] Child and Family Services Act 1989–90 (Saskatchewan) s 13.

[206] Children's Act 1986 (Yukon) s 119(1).   [207] Child Protection Act s11(1).

[208] Child and Family Services *Child Welfare in Canada 2000—the Role of Provincial and Territorial Authorities in the Provision of Child Protection Services: Practice Standards in Child Protection* (2000) British Columbia 163–4 or the Yukon 184–5.

British Columbia, Manitoba, Ontario, and Alberta.[209] The First Nations group would usually be expected to abide by the overall principles of the child protection legislation in the Province, but can legislate for and deliver child welfare services which are culturally appropriate to their group.[210] These legislative changes have been an attempt to remedy enormous past wrongs in which child welfare legislation was used to achieve 'cultural cleansing'. However critics have argued the legislation now adopted still sets the agenda and does not give First Nations groups sufficient autonomy in child welfare:

First Nation authority has not been recognized in practice by the federal or provincial/territorial governments in Canada ... A great deal is needed to heal the colonial wounds of culture-loss, paternalistic and racist treatment and official policies of assimilation through forced education and abduction of children ... Such healing must be accompanied by self-government.[211]

5. Starting an investigation in New Zealand

The CYPFA 1989 s 17 gives social workers and the police the power to investigate a report of ill-treatment or neglect of a child, but does not require an investigation to take place following every report. The position in practice appears similar to England. Staffing levels and particularly the very high turnover of staff in social work investigatory teams has led to slow response times or no response for some reports.[212] 'The greatest risk to the quality and speed of the assessment process currently is the volume of notifications'.[213]

The Act also gives the minister the power to approve an Iwi (tribal) body or any other cultural group to provide child welfare services.[214] The minister retains the right of inspection over the work of any approved Iwi social services.[215] The progress towards the creation of Maori Social Service organizations has been described as 'funereal'. Whilst some Iwis have successfully established their own social work teams these remain in the minority. 'What might have been a watershed for a vibrant pluralist society is currently a pathetic meandering trickle polluted with the detritus of failed opportunities'.[216] Judge Brown attributes this failure to the desire to delegate responsibility for child welfare services, but not the control of those services, a position which resonates with the Canadian experience.

---

[209] M Bennett, C Blackstock and R de la Ronde *A Literature Review and Annotated Bibliography Focussing on Aspects of Aboriginal Child Welfare in Canada* (2nd edn First Nations Child and Family Caring Society of Canada 2005), 47–55.

[210] A good example of such is the Child and Family Services Act 1990 (Ontario) ss 208–213.

[211] Bennett *et al* (n 209) 47.

[212] Department of Child Youth and Family Services *Annual Report 2003* (CYFS, Wellington 2004) 1.

[213] *Care and protection is About Adult Behaviour* (n 1) 60.

[214] CYPFA 1989 (New Zealand) s 396.

[215] ibid s 401.   [216] *Care and Protection is About Adult Behaviour* (n 1) 77.

Diagram 7. Protecting the child immediately

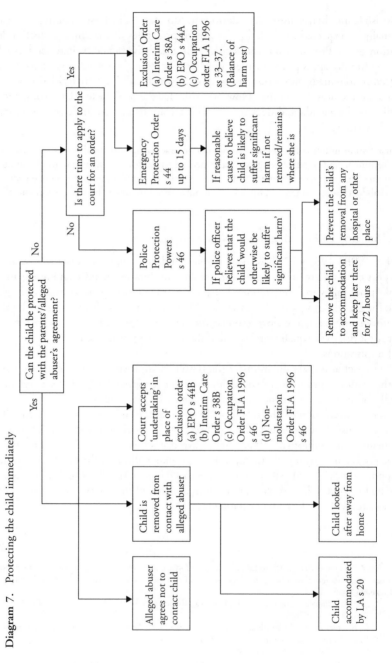

References are to the Children Act 1989 unless otherwise stated.

6. Starting an investigation in Australia

Tasmania and the Australian Capital Territory give investigators complete discretion under the statute to evaluate a report and determine whether to investigate. In the Australian Capital Territory the Children and Young People Act 1999 s 161 states that:

(1) On receiving a report under section 158 or 159, the chief executive may, after consideration of the report, act in relation to it.

(3) Nothing in this Act requires the chief executive to act in relation to a report made to him or her.[217]

Southern Australia gives investigators some discretion in responding to a report upon which a chief executive does not have to act, if 'the Minister or the Chief Executive Officer is satisfied—

(a) that the information or observations on which the notifier formed his or her suspicion were not sufficient to constitute reasonable grounds for the suspicion; or

that, while there are reasonable grounds for such a suspicion, proper arrangements exist for the care and protection of the child and the matter of the apparent abuse or neglect has been or is being adequately dealt with.[218]

All the other Territories have a mandatory duty to investigate a report of child abuse or maltreatment expeditiously. For example the Community Welfare Act 1983 s 16(1) (Northern Territory) states that:

Where the Minister receives a report under section 13 or 14 that a child has suffered or is suffering maltreatment,[219] he shall, as soon as practicable, cause the circumstances of the child to be further investigated or investigated, as the case may be, and shall take such other action under this Act as he thinks fit.[220]

Child protection services across Australia have adopted case streaming mechanisms, irrespective of the mandatory or voluntary investigation provisions within their statutes. There has been an adoption of central intake systems in some States. These central systems employ specialist social workers to assess an initial referral and determine the level of response required. Australia, like Canada, has drawn heavily on risk assessment models in forming their assessment practice. The impetus in changing practice over the past ten years has been to encourage familial and community support, addressing familial ills holistically and to tailor state response to individual cases.[221]

The Australians, like the Canadians and New Zealanders, have acknowledged, in a way that the United States has not, the misuse of child welfare legislation to remove Aboriginal children from their homes. Nevertheless Aboriginal children remain over-represented in the child protection system.[222] The emphasis in practice on risk assessment and on mechanisms for familial support may be attributed in part to the need to break from the past and only investigate when the circumstances require.

---

[217] CYPFA 1997 (Tasmania) s 18.   [218] Children's Protection Act 1993 (South Australia) s 14.

[219] As defined by Community Welfare Act 1983 (Northern Territory) s 4(3).

[220] A very similar provision exists in Child Protection Act 1999 (Queensland) s 14 and Children and Young Person's Act 1989 (Victoria) s 66.

[221] A Torrinson *Current Issues in Child Protection Policy and Practice* (National Child Protection Clearing House Australian Institute of Family Studies 2004) 15–47.

[222] D Thorpe *Evaluating Child Protection* (OUP, Buckingham 1994) 161.

It does not appear that the legislation has been the main influence on the decision to investigate a case of child abuse. Certainly it is difficult to tell from an analysis of the commentary on the operation of the child protection system in the United States whether the mandatory requirement to investigate has galvanized investigators to respond to reports. In fact it may in some cases have had the entirely counterproductive effect of encouraging social workers to close files before investigating to ensure that they meet time limit targets. The law can set a standard of when to intervene, but exhortation can only work if there are witnesses to the existence of the law. By this we mean, if there is simply no social worker to respond to a referral nothing will be done, and if there is no political will or interest in the operation of the child protection system at a higher level, any failures at the grass roots to implement the law will never be noticed.

F. Protecting the Child Immediately

The first question for professionals responding to a report of suspected child abuse should be whether the child is in need of immediate protection. All the jurisdictions which we have examined have created laws to allow state bodies to remove children from their home or prevent children from returning to their parents in situations where it is deemed that a child needs to be protected in an emergency. These powers conflict considerably with parental autonomy and rights to family life and with any child's wish to remain living with his parents. Human rights instruments, and at a more basic level society's view that the family should be free from state interference, have created the principle that the state may only intervene if the benefit of such intervention would outweigh the negative impact of state power. The most draconian of the potential powers given to the state, of removing a child without warning from the home, has only been justified in law on the basis of a child's need for emergency protection.

Standards vary considerably amongst jurisdictions' legislation, procedures and practice in interpreting what circumstances constitute an emergency when it is suspected that a child may be the victim of abuse or is likely to be.

In England the decision whether to intervene immediately to protect a child has been increasingly perceived by the courts as a balancing act.[223] On one side is the damage done to the child by the removal of that child from everything she knows; on the other is the risk of maltreatment should she remain in her current situation.[224] In addition inquiry reports, most notably the *Cleveland Report*, have focused on the needs of a child for certainty and security and questioned whether it might not be better to remove an alleged abuser from the home for a child's immediate protection, rather than effectively punishing the child by taking him or her away from home.[225] This echoes the principles articulated by the ECtHR, including the expectation that states would make a careful assessment of the impact of the proposed care measure

---

[223] *Re H* [1991] FCR 737, 745 (Balcombe LJ); *Re A (Minors)* [1992] 1 All ER 153 [1991] 1 WLR 1026; *Re C and B (Children) (Care Order: Future Harm)* [2000] 2 FCR 614 (CA).
[224] *Working Together—Under the Children Act 1989* (n 40) 27 [5.11.3].
[225] *Cleveland* (n 15) 7 [21] and 213 [13.4].

on the parents and the child, as well as of the possible alternatives to taking the child into public care . . . prior to implementation of such a[n emergency] measure.[226]

The guidance in *Working Together to Safeguard Children* places limits on the use of emergency powers to instances 'where there is a risk to the life of a child or a likelihood of serious immediate harm'; in these cases the 'agency with statutory child protection powers *should act quickly to secure the immediate safety of the child*' (original emphasis).[227]

In each case the judgement of what constitutes an emergency rests first with those applying the law in daily child protection practice. The courts at first instance will often accept the judgment of those social workers actually dealing with the case. Nevertheless, the existence of a court order in a particular child's case is an important safeguard, because it imposes time limits on the period a child may be removed from home before his case is reconsidered. Many jurisdictions allow children to be removed without a court order when it is absolutely imperative that a child is removed for his own protection. However, when used inappropriately, these powers can mean that the child's case is lost in the system and is allowed to drift for a long period of time aimlessly and with little recourse for the child's family, or indeed the child himself, to alter the situation. This may be in instances where the child's circumstances do not on the face of the law, justify emergency protection.[228] These problems have been discussed in particular in relation to the United States recently where the problem of inappropriate use of emergency powers appears particularly acute; however many of the same concerns which have been voiced in relation to the US system have also been noted in our own.

1. Separation without a court order in England and Wales

A child may be protected without court order by ensuring separation between the child and the alleged abuser. This may be achieved in three different ways.

(a) Removing the alleged abuser

Investigators may ask a non-abusing adult with whom the child is living to ensure that the alleged abuser leaves the home or they may ask that the alleged abuser to leave voluntarily.[229] Some provision is made for voluntary separation in the Children Act 1989, which allows a local authority to assist a person living with a child to obtain alternative accommodation when that person is causing a child to suffer or is likely to cause the child to suffer ill-treatment.[230]

The weakness of this strategy is that it relies primarily on the strength of character of the other adult or adults with whom the child lives. Such strength should not always be assumed or relied upon.[231] One aspect of child abuse is that the abuser may

---

[226] *K and T v Finland (No 2)* [2001] 2 FLR 707 (ECtHR) [147]; *Kutzner v Germany* [2002] ECHR 46544/99[67], and *P, C and S v UK* [2002] 2 FLR 631 (ECtHR).

[227] *Working Together to Safeguard Children 2006* (n 31) [5.49].

[228] eg *Re X (Emergency Protection Orders)* [2006] EWHC 510 (Fam Div) [19], [20], [85].

[229] *Re FS (Child Abuse: Evidence)* [1996] 2 FLR 158.

[230] Children Act 1989 (England) Sch 2 s 5.

[231] For the criminal liability of the passive parent or other carer see Chapter 3 section C. For the tort liability of the passive parent or other carer, see above Chapter 4 section D. (For orders in family law in relation to the care of a child see above, Chapter 2 section E.1.)

be a dominant personality ruling both the children and his partner. While the non-abusing adult may agree initially, he or she may be persuaded by the alleged abuser to view the situation differently with the passage of time. She may weaken and allow the alleged abuser to visit or remain in the home. Investigators have reported that they may use the threat of court action to remove the children to 'strengthen the resolve' of hesitant parents.[232] This practice is not contained in the guidance and it is not clear how prevalent it is, although research would suggest that it is fairly common.[233] It is clear that this strategy does raise a further problem, namely the rights of the alleged abuser in the process, particularly if such a separation rather than the investigation itself, leads to a conclusion that abuse has been found.

(b) Undertakings

Under the Children Act 1989 and the Family Law Act 1996 the court may accept an undertaking by the alleged abuser rather than making an order. Undertakings were commonly used before the Family Law Act 1996 came into force.[234] They are a promise to the court, in the terms of the order that would have been made. An undertaking may be accepted by the court in place of an exclusion order that is attached to an emergency protection order or interim care order under the Children Act 1989.[235] It may also be accepted when the court has a power to make an order to regulate the occupation of the family home, or prohibit the molestation of a child under the Family Law Act 1996.[236] However under the Family Law Act 1996 an undertaking should not be accepted in cases where, if an order were made, the court would usually attach a power of arrest.[237] These circumstances are where 'it appears to the court that the respondent has used or threatened violence against the applicant or 'relevant child'.[238]

There will always be a question of enforceability in these difficult cases. An undertaking is enforceable as if it were an order of the court, but the court may not attach a power of arrest to an undertaking. As Lowe and Douglas have noted, 'the applicant (in this case a child or non-abusing parent) who agrees to an undertaking rather than proceeding with her application therefore runs the risk of facing difficulty if she needs practical enforcement measures to be taken in the future.'[239]

(c) Placing the child outside the home

Another strategy is to ask that the child be placed voluntarily away from home. This may be more disorienting and distressing for the child than remaining at home,

---

[232] *Re Y and another (Children) (Care Proceedings; Split Hearing)* [2003] EWCA Civ 669, [2003] 2 FLR 273; C Keenan *The Development and Implementation of Procedures for the Investigation of Allegations of Child Sexual Abuse* (University of Sheffield, PhD thesis, 1995); Fortin (n 78) 375.

[233] J Masson, M Winn-Oakley and K Pick *Emergency Protection Orders—Court Orders for Child Protection Crises* (Warwick University 2004) 59–60.

[234] District Judge Gerlis 'The Family Homes and Domestic Violence Bill—Undermining the Undertaking' [1994] Fam Law 700.   [235] Children Act 1989 (England) s 38B, 44B.

[236] Family Law Act 1996 (England) s 46. The powers of the court to make orders are discussed below, under Court Orders in England and Wales.   [237] ibid s 46.

[238] Children Act 1989 (England) s 47(2), (3). The court may only choose not to attach a power of arrest when it is satisfied that the parties will be adequately protected without it.

[239] N Lowe and G Douglas *Bromley's Family Law* (Butterworths, London 1999) 210.

particularly when the child is accommodated by the local authority[240] rather than going to stay with trusted friends or family members.

(d) Using police protection powers

Where the parents do not consent to the alleged abuser or the child leaving home, the child may be removed by a police officer without a court order. The Children Act 1989 s 46 gives a police officer the power:

(a) to 'remove a child to suitable accommodation and keep him there' or
(b) to prevent a child's 'removal from any hospital or other place in which he is being accommodated' by reasonable steps.

It may not be used to facilitate the discovery of child maltreatment, because police have no power to search premises under this order.[241] Under the Children Act 1989 a police officer is only justified in exercising this considerable power in circumstances where he *believes* that the child 'would otherwise be likely to suffer significant harm.'

An extensive study by Masson, Winn-Oakley and McGovern of the use of police protection powers estimated that approximately 6,000 children were taken into police protection each year outside the area covered by the London Metropolitan Police.[242] They found that in practice police forces varied widely in the extent to which they used their protection powers. For example, cases of children deemed to be 'at risk' of abuse varied from 70 per cent of the cases in one force area to 16 per cent in another. Social workers asked the police to use their protection powers in an emergency, but also out-of-office hours.[243] At these times protection was unlikely to be achieved using a court order because social work emergency teams usually only operated a very limited service and legal advice from local authority solicitors was not available. In the Masson study, police protection was used at the request of social workers for a variety of reasons, to prevent children from being removed from hospital at birth or because they had non-accidental injuries, to prevent the removal of children from voluntary accommodation,[244] when social workers found children alone, when social workers had been refused access to the child's home or where it was feared that the parent would abscond with the child.[245] The police used their powers when, in the course of other work, they came across children whom they concluded needed protection. Children were taken into police protection on a police officer's initiative when found at home or in vehicles, either alone or with a carer who was unconscious. The police could also take children into their protection following their parents' arrest or if they were found in a dangerous situation by police attending their home to serve their parent with a warrant.[246]

---

[240] Children Act 1989 (England) s 20.

[241] R White, P Carr and N Lowe *The Children Act in Practice* (Butterworths, London 1995) [7.58].

[242] J Masson, M Winn-Oakley and C McGovern *Working in the Dark— Executive Summary* (University of Warwick) 1.

[243] J Hunt, A McLeod and C Thomas *The Last Resort—Child Protection, the Courts and the 1989 Children Act* (HM Stationery Office, London 1999) 57.

[244] Children may be accommodated without a court order by the local authority with the consent of a person with parental responsibility under the Children Act 1989 (England) s 20; see above section F.1.

[245] Masson, Winn-Oakley and Pick (n 233) 67–68.   [246] ibid 67–68.

It is possible that there will be an increase in the use of police protection or emergency protection orders discussed in the next section to prevent a child's removal from hospital following the *Climbié Report* which recommended that:

no child known to social services who is an inpatient [be] allowed to be taken home until it has been established by social services that the home environment is safe, the concerns of the medical staff have been fully addressed, and there is a social work plan in place for the ongoing promotion and safeguarding of that child's welfare.[247]

Some questions have been raised about the use of the threshold in police protection powers. HMIC have raised concerns about the wide variation in their use.[248] First, that powers were not being used in situations in which they could have been because of a lack of clarity amongst uniformed officers about the extent and nature of the powers. Conversely there remained a lack of understanding amongst officers about the meaning of *significant harm*. Masson found that if in doubt police officers tended to err on the side of caution and remove the child in case a child was not removed and was later harmed.[249] HMIC found that many police officers lacked training in the powers which could lead them to accede to a social worker's request for police protection when actually a court order was much more appropriate.[250]

Police protection can last for up to 72 hours, although Masson *et al* found that it was uncommon for it to last so long. In their study 25 per cent of the children, for whom the length of time in police protection was recorded, spent less than two hours in police protection and a further 70 per cent spent less than six hours.[251] The local authority is under a duty under Children Act 1989 s 21(2) to provide accommodation for the child for the duration of the order. However Masson's study found that two-thirds of children were initially taken to a police station, often because of difficulties in contacting social workers and then social workers locating a placement. Once a placement was found just over half of the children were accommodated by the local authority, a fifth were accommodated by relatives and friends and a fifth of the children returned home.[252] There was informal use of police protection, in which the police handed the child into the temporary care of relatives without formally using the police powers. Masson *et al* concluded that, while a placement with a relative may be the most suitable and least disruptive, it was not always clear that the necessary checks had been carried out. Only when children are in local authority placements do carers receive fostering allowances and ongoing social services support. They found it was possible that children could be taken to relatives under police protection and remain there for some time without the level of social services involvement envisaged in the Children Act 1989.[253]

As Masson *et al* have shown so clearly, there remains very little knowledge of the national use of police protection. There are no national figures and no consistent monitoring at a local level of their use at the request of local authorities. On one level

---

[247] *Victoria Climbié Inquiry* (n 9) [6.594].   [248] *Keeping Safe, Staying Safe* (n 96) chapter 4.
[249] Masson, Winn-Oakley and McGovern (n 242) 3.   [250] *Keeping Safe, Staying Safe* (n 96) [4.11].
[251] Masson, Winn-Oakley and McGovern (n 242) 2.   [252] ibid 3.
[253] ibid 2.

this need for better monitoring could be reduced to a simple requirement to fill in more paperwork, but this is not a response to a central problem of lack of clarity and inconsistent use of the threshold for police powers. Police powers may be regarded as less draconian because there is no court order involved and they last for a very limited amount of time, but apart from the disorientating affect that any abrupt removal from home can have, police protection can be the beginning of a child's entrance into the care system or to an ad hoc care arrangement with family or friends without a court order. As such the exact threshold on which they are made should be considered. This is not to say that police protection should not exist; the power can be the only immediate response to actual danger for a child, and an application for a court order for the child's protection requires a considerable amount of paperwork and organization. HMIC recommended that the guidance in the national police protection form should include prompts to ensure that details of where the child is initially and subsequently taken are recorded and information of all reviews and the reasons for police protection ending are specifically documented.[254]

2. Court orders in England and Wales

(a) The emergency protection order

The Children Act 1989 s 44 also created a court order to allow the removal of children from their present home or to ensure that children remain at home and are not removed from there by others. This order, known as the Emergency Protection Order (EPO)[255] replaced the problematic Place of Safety Order (POSO), which had controversially been used extensively in the investigations in Cleveland. Some of the changes may be considered as routine legislative housekeeping. For example, the mechanism by which an emergency order might be granted was simplified.[256] Other changes were driven by consideration of parental and child interests in ensuring minimal disruption by preventing unjustified orders of lengthy duration. The *Review of Child Care Law*[257] in 1985 cited research by Packman[258] and by the Dartington Research Group,[259] which found high usage of Place of Safety Orders and that their use was not confined to emergencies.

---

[254] *Keeping Safe, Staying Safe* (n 96) 4.26 and Appendix E.

[255] Children Act 1989 (England) s 44.

[256] Until the EPO there were a number of orders for the protection of children that could be made under different Acts, all of which had very similar effects. Thus although POSOs were usually made under s 28 (1) Children and Young Persons Act 1969 (England), a child could be kept in a place of safety awaiting care proceedings (ss 2(4) and 2(5) Children and Young Persons Act 1969 (England)) and pending an application to vary or discharge a supervision order (s 16(3) Children and Young Persons Act 1969 (England)). Similar orders were also available generally under s 40 Children and Young Persons Act 1933 (England) and in special circumstances under Foster Children Act 1980 (England) s 12 and Adoption Act 1976 (England) s 34. *Review of Child Care Law* (n 97) Discussion Paper 6 [2].

[257] ibid Discussion Paper 6 [43].

[258] J Packman *Decision Making on Admissions of Children to Local Authority Care* (unpublished) cited in the *Review of Child Care Law* ibid Discussion Paper 6, 6.

[259] Dartington Research Unit *Place of Safety Orders* (University of Bristol, Dartington Research Unit Bristol 1984).

The EPO simplified the grounds on which an order may be granted by a court. The criterion for an order is that the court is satisfied that—

(a) there is reasonable cause to believe that the child is likely to suffer significant harm if—
   (i) he is not removed to accommodation provided by or on behalf of the applicant; or
   (ii) he does not remain in the place in which he is then being accommodated.[260]

Legislators aimed to limit the applications for the new order and to ensure that they were only used when the circumstances truly indicated an emergency by the creation of a high threshold for intervention of 'reasonable cause to believe that the child is likely to suffer significant harm'. There are also two alternative criteria for applications for an EPO for investigators, (either the local authority or an 'authorised person')[261] where their inquiries have been frustrated by a refusal of access to a child[262] or by a denial of information about his whereabouts.[263] These provisions are discussed in greater detail below.[264]

A further major criticism of the POSO was its long duration (a maximum of 28 days).[265] This was a particular hardship when the parents were not allowed to appeal the order.[266] In contrast the EPO may be granted initially for a period up to eight days, although the period may be extended for one further period, not exceeding seven days, upon application to the court. A parent or anyone with parental responsibility or with whom the child was living immediately before the order was made may appeal an order, after it has been in place for 72 hours.[267] The child also has standing to appeal, although the exercise of this right rarely will be feasible. Furthermore the Children Act 1989 s 44(5) provides that the local authority may exercise its parental responsibility only in such manner 'as is reasonably required to safeguard or promote the welfare of the child'. Thus even when an order is granted the local authority should consider first whether it is actually necessary to remove the child from home for his own protection and if it decides that it is initially necessary that decision should be reviewed daily.[268]

Anyone may apply under Children Act 1989 s 44(1) for an EPO when they have reasonable cause to believe that a child is likely to suffer significant harm if an order is not granted. Such an order may be granted *ex parte* by the Family Proceedings courts.[269] For the term of the order any applicant acquires parental responsibility (s 44(4)(c)). Only those who have acquired parental responsibility by virtue of an

---

[260] Children Act 1989 (England) s 44(1).

[261] At present the NSPCC alone is authorized under the Children Act 1989 (England).

[262] Children Act 1989 (England) s 44(1)(b), (c).   [263] Children Act 1989 (England) s 47(6).

[264] See the discussion on facilitating interviews, medical and other examinations below, G.1.

[265] Department of Health and Social Security, Home Office, Lord Chancellor's Department, Department of Education and Science, Welsh Office and Scottish Office *The Law on Child Care and Family Services* (HMSO, London 1987) [10].   [266] *A Child in Trust* (n 6) 256.

[267] Children Act 1989 (England) s 45(8), (9).

[268] *Working Together to Safeguard Children 2006* (n 31) [5.53].

[269] Family Proceedings Courts (Children Act 1989) Rules 1991 SI 1991/1395 (England) r 4(4).

emergency protection order or who are also entitled to apply for a care order may apply for an extension.

Caselaw in both England and in the ECtHR clearly establishes the execution of an EPO that removes a child from her parents, particularly one which has been granted *ex parte* (without notice) and without warning, as the most serious and potentially draconian child protection order. In England these orders are typically granted by a panel of three lay magistrates. The leading case remains *X Council v B (Emergency Protection Orders)*[270] in which Munby J outlined the factors which magistrates should consider and the procedural safeguards which must be adopted to ensure that orders are not made routinely or on insufficient evidence. This judgment brings together the caselaw from both England and the ECtHR, and the guidance within it has been cited with approval by McFarlane J in the later case of *Re X (Emergency Protection Orders)*.[271]

What is clear is that a child's removal from home without warning is regarded by the higher courts as an 'extremely harsh measure'[272] which may only be justified in an absolute and extreme emergency.[273] The circumstances of each case should be weighed by both the social workers applying for the order and the Family Proceedings Court to determine whether first emergency protection is really necessary to ensure a child's immediate safety[274] and whether there are other less draconian alternatives, and secondly, even if an order is granted, whether it is really necessary to use it, or whether the protection may be achieved by voluntary means.[275] In other words the question for investigators and for the courts is whether the order is 'unavoidable'.[276] McFarlane J has underscored that the words 'genuine emergency' and 'only what is necessary to provide immediate short-term protection' in the guidance accompanying the Children Act[277] cannot be stressed enough.[278] Applicants and the courts should consider how the protection of the child may be achieved with the least intervention possible, for example by using a child assessment order to facilitate interviews or medical examination of a child.[279]

Again and again the courts return to the importance of clear evidence rather than speculation and hearsay as the key safeguard in ensuring that EPOs are only granted when absolutely necessary. 'The evidence in support of the application for an EPO must be full, detailed, precise and compelling. Unparticularised generalities will not suffice. The sources of hearsay evidence must be identified. Expressions of opinion

---

[270] [2004] EWHC 2015 (Fam Div) [2005] 1 FLR 341 (Munby J).

[271] (n 228) [64] (McFarlane J).

[272] *Re M (Care Proceedings: Judicial Review)* [2003] 2 FLR 171 (Fam Div) [44] (Munby J).

[273] *Re C and B* (n 223) 617(19) (Hale LJ); *Re X* (n 228) (Fam Div) [25]–[29] (McFarlane J).

[274] *X Council v B* (n 270) [54].

[275] *P, C and S v UK* [2002] 2 FLR 631 (ECtHR) [127–130] [132–133].

[276] *K and T v Finland* (n 226) 755 [8] (Judge Bonello).

[277] Children Act 1989 (England) Guidance and Regulations Volume 1, 51.

[278] *Re X: Emergency Protection Order* (n 228).

[279] This under-used order under Children Act 1989 (England) s 43 is discussed later in this chapter in facilitating an investigation: section G.1.

must be supported by detailed evidence and properly articulated reasoning.'[280] The problem revealed in the reported cases has been that lay magistrates in the Family Proceedings Courts can accept the word of a social worker without more detailed evidence and give very limited reasons. In *Re X (Emergency Protection Orders)* the only record of the Justices' reasons was in the clerk's note which read: 'Having heard from Ms K, Team Manager, Child Protection Register Scheme, that the child would suffer imminent harm unless an EPO is made'.[281] The caselaw on EPOs emphasizing the protection which can be afforded by proper records and documentation clearly fits into the wider jurisprudence on investigation in general and with the latest government initiatives on record-keeping, which have been discussed earlier in this chapter.[282]

Research in 1999 by Hunt, Macleod and Thomas concluded that 'for the most part post-Children Act practice has been characterised by more strenuous *attempts* to avoid compulsory intervention on an emergency basis' (their emphasis).[283] Social workers tried to operate under a model of best practice in which a child would ideally be protected by voluntary agreements with parents, which might include the child remaining at home with agreements from the parents about their behaviour, or relatives looking after the child. When an order was considered it was much more likely that legal advice would be taken, and lawyers tended to be cautious in applying to the court for an order. The criteria on which an EPO was granted were also perceived to be much tighter than had previously existed under the POSO, and the scrutiny of the evidence by the courts to be much more stringent.

However more recent research by Masson, Winn-Oakley and Pick, as well as the limited caselaw on the operation of EPOs, has raised several questions about the use of emergency protection orders which resonate with concerns expressed in other jurisdictions, most notably the United States, discussed below. Masson *et al* raised several concerns about the use of EPOs.[284] EPOs were predominantly used in the case of families who had already had some dealings with social services. They were not generally used because the incident or circumstances in which social workers found the children was significantly different from previous incidents in which social services had been involved, but the incident constituted the 'last straw' or at this point parents failed to cooperate with the social worker, or were perceived to be doing so.[285] Of course some of these cases do represent an emergency in the child's care; as several social workers explained to the researchers, it is sometimes simply inhumane to leave a child to suffer extreme neglect while awaiting an interim care order. However some of these chronic situations may be more suited to an interim care order, where parents receive warning of what will happen and can instruct solicitors, with legal aid if required. Furthermore it seems clear that EPOs were used at crisis point for unallocated cases, or cases which had been allowed to drift when less drastic measures could have been used at an earlier stage.[286] Masson *et al* also concluded that there were a number of occasions in which meaningful notice of the proceedings could have been

---

[280] *X Council v B* (n 270) [54] (Munby J).   [281] *Re X: Emergency Protection Orders* (n 228).
[282] See above, section C.   [283] Hunt, McLeod and Thomas (n 243) 48.
[284] Masson, Winn-Oakley and Pick (n 233) 72.   [285] *Re X: Emergency Protection orders* (n 228).
[286] Masson, Winn-Oakley and Pick (n 233) 72.

given to parents and to those representing the interests of the child. In almost half the cases studied the child was already in police protection when the EPO was initiated and so notice to the parents would not have jeopardized the child's safety. In cases of the removal of children at birth Masson and others concluded that cases of removal of children from their parents at birth were sufficiently numerous to necessitate a new addendum to *Working Together to Safeguard Children* to ensure that all aspects of the case were considered, as this marks the beginning of a process which usually ends in their adoption. Although the problems identified by this research do not appear to be on the same scale as in the US which we discussed below, the extent of the trends which this research has identified remains unclear in the absence of any national monitoring of the use of EPOs by local authorities.

(b) Orders for the removal of the alleged abuser instead of the child

An EPO may be a solution for the immediate physical protection of a child, but it is far from ideal for many children. They are deprived of home and familiar people and surroundings at an enormously difficult time for them. Another solution discussed earlier is for the alleged abuser to leave the familial home for the duration of the investigation. If the alleged abuser does not consent to go, he may now be excluded. The ousting of the abuser may be achieved by three statutory mechanisms. An exclusion requirement may be included in an EPO or interim care order. A person may also be excluded from the child's home by means of an 'occupation order' granted under the Family Law Act 1996. A 'non-molestation order' may also be applied for or granted by the court under the Family Law Act 1996 to prevent the alleged abuser from contacting the family under the terms of the Act.

(i) The development of exclusion orders

An exclusion requirement for alleged abusers was not included in the original Children Act 1989, because of the ongoing consultation process by the Law Commission at the time on the possible form that such an order could take.[287] However the Law Commission's final report in 1992 did recommend that such an exclusion provision be attached. Adults' long-term property rights were, however, allowed to trump the child's right to protection. The Law Commission proposed legislative change to enable an alleged abuser to be ousted for a short time, as 'in the short term the needs of the child can take precedence over other considerations'. However 'in the longer term considerations of property rights and the balance of hardship between adults must play a part'.[288]

Powers to exclude an alleged abuser were introduced by the Family Law Act 1996, which reformed much of the law relating to domestic violence and the familial home. In the interim period several cases had illustrated a need for an order facilitating the exclusion of a suspected abuser. In *Nottinghamshire CC v P* the judge at first instance found that the father had seriously sexually abused his eldest daughter and that he

---

[287] *Hansard* HC Deb vol 158 cols 1314–1319 (27 October 1989).

[288] Law Commission of England and Wales *Domestic Violence and Occupation of the Family Home* (Law Com No 207 1992) 53–55 [6.15–6.22].

posed a significant threat to his two younger daughters then aged 16 and 13 who continued to live at home. He also found that the mother was totally incapable of protecting her children and was in the power of the father. The Court of Appeal wished to exclude the father from the home, but could find no mechanism by which this could be achieved. The local authority argued that this could be done by means of a prohibited steps order.[289] However this was rejected by the Court of Appeal on the grounds that a prohibited steps order would effectively create a residence order in favour of the local authority. The Children Act 1989 prohibits a local authority from applying for a residence order and specifically stipulates that no residence order may be made in favour of a local authority.[290] In *Re S*[291] Connell J rejected the local authority's contention that the Children Act 1989 s 34(4) could be used to prevent contact between parent and child and by that effect an ouster.[292] However he did grant the local authority's application using the courts' inherent jurisdiction as reformulated and constrained by s 100 of the Children Act 1989.[293]

The Family Law Act 1996 rewrote the complicated legal provisions for the exclusion of individuals from the family home in cases of domestic violence. It created 'occupation orders' enabling the court to declare or regulate the right to occupy the family home. These are discussed below. It also altered the law to allow an exclusion order to be attached to an emergency protection order or an interim care order.

(ii) The content of exclusion orders

An exclusion order gives the courts the power

- to require the relevant person to leave the dwelling house in which he is living with the child;
- to prohibit the relevant person from entering the dwelling house in which the child lives; and
- to exclude a person from a defined area in which the child's home is situated.

The court may also append a power of arrest to the order.[294] An exclusion order may be attached to an interim care order, provided that:

- there is reasonable cause to believe that 'if a person ... is excluded from a dwelling house in which the child lives the child will cease to suffer, or cease to be likely to suffer significant harm';[295]

---

[289] This is an order issued under the Children Act 1989 (England) s 8 which states that 'no step which could be taken by a parent in meeting his parental responsibility for a child and which is of a kind specified in the order, shall be taken by any person without the permission of the court'.

[290] Children Act 1989 (England) s 9(2).   [291] *Re S* [1994] 1 FLR 623 (Fam Div).

[292] Children Act 1989 (England) s 34(4) allows the court to make an order authorizing a local authority to refuse contact between a child in its care and a named person, who would usually be allowed reasonable contact, by virtue of s 34(1).   [293] *Re S* (n 291) 631E.

[294] Children Act 1989 (England) s 38A(5), s 44A(5) as amended by the Family Law Act 1996 (England).

[295] Children Act 1989 (England) s 38A(1), s 44A(1) as amended by Family Law Act 1996 (England) s 52 and Sch 6.

- there is 'another person living in the dwelling house (whether the parent of the child or some other person)—who is able and willing to give the child the care which it would be reasonable to expect a parent to give him', and

- the other person living in the dwelling house 'consents to the exclusion requirement'.

An exclusion order may also be attached to an EPO if the above conditions are satisfied and additionally that one of the following conditions are satisfied:

- the child will not be likely to suffer significant harm, even though the child is not removed to accommodation, or
- the enquiries will cease to be frustrated.

This procedure remains a very short-term solution. The exclusion order may last for as long as the order to which it is attached or the court may choose to limit it to a period that is less than that of the order.[296]

(iii) Occupation orders

The Family Law Act 1996 also created 'occupation orders' to declare or regulate the right to occupy the family home. An occupation order may give an applicant:

1. the right not to be evicted from a dwelling house or any part of it by the respondent and prohibit the respondent from evicting or excluding the applicant during that period;[297]

2. the right to enter into and occupy the dwelling house for the period specified in the order; and require the respondent to permit the exercise of that right.[298]

A child may apply for an occupation order with the leave of the court. Such leave may be granted by a court satisfied that the child has sufficient understanding and legal advice to make the application. In cases when the child is considered not to have sufficient understanding to make his own application, the non-abusing parent may apply for an occupation order with the stated aim of preventing harm to the child. The parent does not need to be the victim of domestic violence herself to make the application. An order may only be made in respect of a 'relevant child' which is defined as a child who is living with, or might reasonably be expected to live with either party to the proceedings, or a child in relation to whom an order under the Adoption Act 1976 or the Children Act 1989 is in question in the proceedings. However the court may also deem a child to be a 'relevant child' for the purposes of the proceedings if it considers that his interests are relevant in the decision whether to make an order.[299]

The Family Law Act 1996 privileges the married over those who are not and those who have property interests over those who do not. It therefore creates a system of 'entitled' and 'non-entitled' applicants under the Act. While much of the detail of this

---

[296] Children Act 1989 (England) s 38A(4), s 44A(4).

[297] Family Law Act 1996 (England) s 35(3)—former spouses and s 36(3)—cohabitants and former cohabitants.

[298] Family Law Act 1996 (England) s 35(4)—former spouses and s 36(4)—cohabitants and former cohabitants. [299] Family Law Act 1996 (England) s 62(2).

system is irrelevant to those interested in the protection to be afforded to a 'relevant child', it is important to understand the terms by which adults qualify for entitled and non-entitled status. The status of the adult will affect the duration of the order that may be granted to protect the child and the extent of the powers contained in that order. It is consistent with the stance of the preceding Law Commission report that interference with property rights may only be justified on a short-term basis in the interests of child protection. However it is wrong in principle that the length of an order granted solely in the interests of child protection will depend upon the property interests of the adult applicant.

The mechanism of decision-making within the Act reflects the Law Commission's view that the decision should be made after balancing the competing interests. In making an order the court has to have regard to a number of considerations. This is collectively known as the 'balance of harm test'. These factors vary according to the nature of the relationship between the adult applicant and respondent, and each adult's interest in the home. However the courts continue to be extremely cautious in granting such an order:

> The gravity of an order requiring the respondent to vacate a family home [was recognized under the previous law] . . . The order remains Draconian, particularly in the perception of the respondent. It remains an order that overrides proprietary rights and . . . is only justified in exceptional circumstances.[300]

One consideration of the court should be 'the likely effect of any order, or of any decision by the courts not to exercise its powers under subsection 3, on the health, safety or well-being of any of the parties and of any relevant child'. This must be balanced against considerations of the housing needs and financial resources of each party, the conduct of each party towards the other and the length of time since the parties lived together.[301] However the court must grant such an occupation order if it appears that a 'relevant child' is likely to suffer significant harm, attributable to the conduct of the respondent, if the order is not made. The court must not however make an order if it appears to the court that the relevant child is likely to suffer greater harm as a consequence of the order being made.[302]

The obvious weakness of both the exclusion order attached to an EPO or interim care order and the occupation order is that they require a high level of cooperation by another adult, with whom the child is living. The argument may be made that if a non-abusing parent agrees to an order to evict an alleged abuser, the same effect may be achieved by them, without the necessity of recourse to an order. The advantage of an order however can be that it can give the parent more power. She can blame the court's will, rather than her own for her partner's exclusion from the home. However

---

[300] *Chalmers v Johns* [1999] 1 FLR 392, 397 (Thorpe LJ).

[301] In cases where the applicant and respondent have been cohabitants, the court must also consider the nature of the party's relationship, the length of time which they lived together as husband and wife and any children who are children of both parties, or for whom both parties have had parental responsibility.

[302] Family Law Act 1996 (England) s 33(7) (occupation orders for an entitled applicant), s 35(8) (occupation orders when the applicant is a former spouse with no existing right to occupy), s 36(8) (occupation order when the applicant is a cohabitant or former cohabitant with no existing right to occupy), s 37(4), with s 33(6), (7) (when neither spouse is entitled to occupy the home) and s 38.

once an order is made the non-abusing parent is left in a very difficult situation, with little support. The only help that may be offered by the court is to attach a power of arrest to an order that it has made. It has the power to do so in cases where it appears that the respondent has used or threatened violence to the applicant or a relevant child.[303] In cases when no power of arrest has been attached the applicant may return to court a warrant, which may be where there are reasonable grounds for believing that the respondent has failed to comply with the order. The application must be substantiated on oath.[304]

3. Emergency protection in the United States

State law authorizes the police or child protection workers to take custody of a child without court action in an emergency. The standard of proof is comparatively low—a reasonable cause to believe or reasonable grounds to believe—and in this respect the powers are similar to the police protection powers under the Children Act 1989 s 46. However the type of harm which justifies removal is more limited. For example the Pennsylvania statute allows a law officer or duly authorized officer of the court to take a child 'into custody' 'if there are reasonable grounds to believe that the child is suffering from illness or injury or is in imminent danger from his surroundings, and that his removal is necessary'.[305] This power should only be exercised if there is an imminent danger to a child's life or health.[306] A child may also be removed by an emergency order granted *ex parte* (without notice), in proceedings similar to those for granting a search warrant.[307] However emergency removal should be effected only in exceptional circumstances; the State should usually give the child and their family notice of proceedings to remove a child and there has to be a hearing during which the evidence for that removal may be considered.[308] Underlying these rules is the US Supreme Court interpretation of the guarantee of procedural and substantive due process in the 14th Amendment to the American Constitution. In a series of cases[309] the Supreme Court has held that the 14th Amendment

---

[303] Family Law Act 1996 (England) s 47(2).

[304] Family Law Act 1996 (England) ss 47(8) and (9).

[305] 42 Pennsylvania Consolidated Statute §6324(3) (West 1982 & Supp 1998) cited in KC Pearson 'Cooperate Or We'll Take Your Child: The Parents' Fictional Voluntary Separation Decision and a Proposal For Change' (1998) 65 Tenn L Rev 835, 846.

[306] *Tenenbaum v Williams* 193 F 3d 581, 594 (US CA 2nd Cir 1999) (child must be 'immediately threatened with harm'); *Hollingsworth v Hill* 110 F 3d 733, 739 (US CA 10th Cir 1997) (immediate threat to a child's safety); *Jordan v Jackson* 15 F 3d 333, 343 (US CA 4th Cir 1994) (imminent harm to a child).

[307] P Chill 'Burden of Proof Begone: The Pernicious Effect of Emergency Removal in Child Protective Proceedings' (2004) 42 Fam Ct Rev 540 cites Massachusetts General Statute c 119, §24 (2003); New York Family Court Act §1022 (McKinney 2003).

[308] *LaChance v Erickson* 522 US 262, 266 (US SC 1998) (right to notice and meaningful opportunity to be heard are 'core of due process'). See also *Cleveland Bd of Educ v Loudermil* 470 US 532, 542 (US SC 1985) (pre-deprivation hearing is 'root requirement' of due process).

[309] *Troxel v Granville* 530 US 57, 65 (US SC 2000); *Santosky v Kramer* 455 US 745, 753 (US SC 1982); *Parham v JR* 442 US 584, 602 (US SC 1979); *Quilloin v Walcott* 434 US 246, 255 (US SC 1978); *Wis v Yoder* 406 US 205, 232 (US SC 1972); *Stanley v Illinois* 405 US 645, 651 (US SC 1972); *Prince v Mass* 321 US 158 (1944); *Pierce v Soc'y* 268 US 510, 534–35 (US SC 1925); *Meyer v Neb* 262 US 390, 399 (US SC 1923).

provides a fundamental right to 'family integrity': a right of parents and children to be free of unwarranted governmental interference in matters of child rearing. Furthermore this has been interpreted to mean that parents and children will not be separated by the state without due process of law except in an emergency. Officials may remove a child from the custody of her parents without prior authorization by the court only if the information they possess at the time of the seizure is such as provides reasonable cause to believe the child is in imminent danger of serious bodily injury and that the scope of the intrusion is reasonably necessary to avert that specific injury.[310]

When a child is removed without a court order or by an order issued *ex parte* the State is usually required to bring the matter back before the court without delay.[311] There is no consistent name for these post-removal hearings. They may be called 'emergency hearings', 'shelter care hearings', 'preliminary protective hearings', and 'temporary custody hearings' throughout the various statutes.[312] Failure to observe due process standards in taking children into custody without a hearing may result in a finding that the process was unconstitutional.[313]

However, while the rhetoric of the law may point towards considered and planned removal of children in the majority of cases, all the evidence points to the exact opposite happening in practice. Chill has concluded that:

in practice, however, children are seldom removed on anything but an emergency basis—either unilaterally, without a court order, or on the basis of some form of *ex parte* judicial authorization. The number of emergency removals, moreover, has increased steadily for the past two decades, to the point where removals now occur at nearly double the rate of 20 years ago.[314]

It appears that poverty is the clearest predictor in judgments that a child needs emergency protection,[315] with the ethnicity of the child and the adults with whom she is living an important and allied factor.[316] Children are often removed at night, with little planning for them once they have been removed. While such behaviour has been criticized by the court,[317] the pressure on investigators, not least by the government, to protect children from abuse at any cost has meant that the practice continues. Chill attributes the extensive use of emergency powers to a growth in defensive practice

---

[310] *Doggett v Perez* 348 F Supp. 2d 1198 (US DC Washington 2004); *Stanley v Illinois* (n 309), 651.

[311] *Jordan v Jackson* (n 306), 343; *Duchesne v Sugarman* 566 F 2d 817, 826 (US CA 2nd Cir 1977).

[312] SA Dobbin, SI Gatowski and M Springate 'Child Abuse and Neglect: A Summary of State Statutes' (1997) 48 Juv & Fam Ct J 43, 45.

[313] *Sims v State Department of Social Welfare of Texas* 438 F Supp 1179 (Texas DC 1977) reversed by *Moore v Sims* 442 US 415, 99 S Ct 2371, 60 L Ed 2d 994 (US SC 1979) *Pamela B v Ment* 709 A 2d 1089, 1100 (Connecticut SCT 1998) ('We have been properly forewarned of the well recognized harm to children caused by delayed hearings . . . It is thus imperative that parents be given a prompt and meaningful opportunity to challenge an order of temporary custody.')   [314] Chill (n 307) 541.

[315] M Guggenheim 'Somebody's Children: Sustaining the Family's Place in Child Welfare Policy' (2000) 113 Harv L Rev 1716, 1735.

[316] D Roberts 'Access to Justice: Poverty, Race, and New Directions In Child Welfare Policy' (1999) 1 Wash U J L & Pol 63, 64.

[317] *Nicholson v Williams* 203 F Supp 2d 153 (US DC New York 2002) (quoting expert testimony that removal in such circumstances may be 'tantamount to pouring salt on an open wound').

amongst investigators, rather than an increase in the seriousness of the cases which are reported:

Defensive social work has flourished in the past 20 years, fuelled by the news media's appetite for sensational child maltreatment stories as well as by laws that purposely magnify the public visibility of child maltreatment fatalities and near fatalities. This has led to a series of removal stampedes or 'foster care panics', in which thousands of children have been swept up by child welfare authorities in the aftermath of high-profile child fatalities.[318]

A further concern which is not evident on the face of the child protection statutes is the use of voluntary separations. This in principle is better than an unplanned emergency removal of the children. Instead, as in England, the alleged abuser would be asked to leave the home, during the course of an investigation, so that the children may remain. This separation may be labelled as a voluntary act, although, again as in England, the alleged abuser may be threatened with the removal of the child if they do not comply.[319] However as Pearson has powerfully argued, this voluntary separation can have fundamental repercussions under American law, for the possibility of reuniting the family.[320] First of all, a voluntary separation places the case outside the constitutional safeguards set down in statute and by caselaw. There is no hearing to determine the strength of the evidence, no lawyers need be appointed and, most fundamentally, no time limits are set. The case can drift on for months or even years with no clear plan for treatment of the child, the gathering of evidence, or family rehabilitation. The decision in *Croft v Westmoreland County* has now established that there should be an 'articulable, reasonable suspicion' that the child is in imminent danger before initiating any emergency separation or even an 'agreement'.[321] However as this standard has not been adhered to in the use of emergency child protection powers, it remains doubtful whether it will act as a sufficient safeguard in these cases.

4. Emergency protection in Canada

The legislation in Canada follows a similar pattern to England and the United States. The statutes and caselaw use the term 'apprehend' to mean the removal of the child from the home. Each Province allows a child welfare worker to remove a child from their home without a court order (a 'warrantless apprehension') and also provides a mechanism for a child to be removed from home by court order.[322] Canadian law also allows for an officer to enter premises without a warrant, by force if necessary, to search for and remove a child.[323] The statutes do place limits on the length of time

---

[318] Chill (n 307) 542.
[319] eg *Croft v Westmoreland County Children and Youth Services* 103 F 3d 1123 (US CA 3rd Cir 1997).
[320] Pearson (n 305).   [321] *Croft v Westmoreland* (n 319), 1125 (nt 1).
[322] M Bernstein, H Bernstein and LM Kirwin *Child Protection Law in Canada* (Thompson Canada Ltd) chapter 6.
[323] With the exception of Alberta, where the statute does not specifically refer to entering premises: Child Welfare Act 1984 (Alberta) C-8.1, ss 17,18.

that any Province may keep a child away from home without a court order. This varies from Province to Province, but does not exceed ten days.

There are significant points of difference from English and American law. First, each statute contains a statement of principle that the child should be protected in the least disruptive manner for the child and for the child's family life.[324] There is therefore a statutory presumption that emergency removal of children is the last resort. In support of this presumption, there are several innovative provisions in statutes and guidance to remove the alleged offender from the home. In New Brunswick child protection procedures dictate that if possible an alleged abuser should be removed from the home instead of a child during an investigation. An alleged abuser might be asked to leave voluntarily, or a 'no contact order' may be made as a condition for release on bail for a criminal charge before the hearing takes place, or a 'protective intervention order' may be granted.[325]

There is also provision for a warrant to remove an adult as an interim measure pending the granting of a protective intervention order. In New Brunswick a protective intervention order may be granted on the grounds that a person is 'a source of danger to a child's security or development'. It may last for up to 12 months and then be extended for further periods of 12 months on application.[326] A person subject to the order may be directed by the court to support his dependents or in other ways to fulfil his responsibilities for them during the period of the order. A very similar provision exists in Alberta,[327] Manitoba,[328] Newfoundland,[329] Nova Scotia,[330] Ontario,[331] Prince Edward Island,[332] and the Yukon.[333] These may be granted for up to six months and extended for further six-month periods, with the exception of Ontario where the statute does not allow for a further extension.[334] In Manitoba there is also a provision to allow a homemaker to live in the home of a child temporarily if that child has no one to care for him, for a period of up to seven days until someone can be found. If no one could be found at that point a child protection assessment would take place.[335]

However a decision by the Supreme Court of Canada has undermined the statutory principle of least disruption in child protection cases. The Supreme Court of Canada has held that s 7 of the Canadian Charter of Rights and Freedoms which

---

[324] See for example Child and Family Services Act 1985 (Manitoba) Principles 3 and 4; Youth Protection Act 2004 (Quebec) s 4; Child Protection Act 2003 (Prince Edward Island) Preamble; Child and Family Services Act 1989–90 (Saskatchewan) s 3.   [325] Family Services Act 1980 (New Brunswick) s 58.
[326] ibid s 58(4).   [327] Child Welfare Act 2000 (Alberta) s 30.
[328] Child and Family Services Act 1985 (Manitoba) s 20(1) (an order not to contact a child).
[329] Child Youth and Family Services Act 1998 (Newfoundland) s 21 (a child who needs to be protected from contact with someone order).
[330] Children and Family Services Act 1990 (Nova Scotia) s 30.
[331] Child and Family Services Act 1990 (Ontario) (a restraining order).
[332] Child Protection Act 2003 (Prince Edward Island) s 44 (a restraining order).
[333] Children's Act 2002 (Yukon) s 36 (a restraining order).
[334] Child and Family Services Act 1990 (Ontario) s 80(3).
[335] Child and Family Services Act 1985 (Manitoba) s 13.

guarantees security of the person does not require that a 'warrantless apprehension' of a child be made only in an emergency. The Court found that provincial statutes which allow removal without a warrant 'if the child is at risk of serious harm' are constitutional, provided that when read as a whole, the statute provides such a removal as the last resort.[336] The majority in the Supreme Court reasoned that there were 'evidential difficulties' in proving that a child was in need of emergency protection[337] and that the state needed to act to prevent abuse as well as to protect children from it.[338]

The reasoning of the court has been strongly criticized by Blenner Hassett. She has argued that the fear of 'getting it wrong' and failing to protect a child has again justified erosion in the principles of the legislation. She continued:

> The decision in *K.L.W.* sets child protection law on a path back to the 1960s and 1970s, a time before the *Charter,* when the state interventionist school of thought permeated provincial child welfare statutes and authorized the state to enter homes and intrude into family life, without regard to due process and procedural protections of the rights of children or the rights of parents . . . The rule of law, and the law's time-honoured attributes of certainty and predictability, have been jettisoned in favour of a dangerous and unpredictable rule of an unfettered state. *K.L.W.* endorses the harmful theory that the ends justify the means.[339]

This judgment may be another indication that the tide is turning in child protection practice in Canada towards the removal of children, however small the risk that those children will be physically harmed. It again places the rights of children to protection and those of adults to familial preservation as being diametrically opposed, a view of child protection which the legislation had, until that point, moved away from.

5. Emergency protection in Australia

In Australia a child may be 'apprehended' from his home in the majority of States without a warrant if he is found to be in need of emergency protection.[340] The threshold for action is set at different points, from 'an assessment of reasonable likelihood of risk'[341] to a 'belief that [the] child is in need of immediate care and protection'[342]

---

[336] *Winnipeg Child and Family Services (Central Area) v KLW* [2000] SCCD LEXIS 82, 2000 SCC 48, 191 DLR (4th) (SCC) 1.

[337] *Gareau v British Columbia (Superintendent of Family and Child Services)* (1986) 5 BCLR (2d) 352 (SC) aff'd (1989) 38 BCLR (2d) 215 (British Columbia CA).

[338] *Winnipeg Child and Family Services* (n 336) 1, citing *Young v Young* (1993) 108 DLR (4th) 193 (SCC); *P (D) v S (C)* (1993) 108 DLR (4th) 287 (SCC).

[339] D Blenner Hassett 'KLW and Warrantless Child Apprehensions: Sanctioning Gross Intrusions into Private Spheres' (2004) 67 Sask L Rev 161, 164.

[340] Children and Young People Act 1999 (Australian Capital Territory) ss 222–223; Child Protection Act 1999 (Queensland) ss 14–20; Children's Protection Act 1993 (South Australia) ss 16–17; CYPFA 1997 (Tasmania) s 20–21; Children and Young Person's Act 1989 (Victoria) s 69; Child Welfare Act 1947 (Western Australia). [341] CYPFA 1997 (Tasmania) s 20–21.

[342] Children and Young People Act 1999 (Australian Capital Territory) s 222–223.

or only when a child is 'in serious danger'.[343] In New South Wales a child may not be removed from all parental control without a court order in any circumstances.[344] A consistent problem in the application of these laws in the past has been their over-use in Aboriginal families. 'The more coercive and intrusive the child protection operation becomes, so the overrepresentation of Aboriginal children increases.'[345]

In recent years there has been a clear focus amongst legislators in some States to limit the removal of all children from home for their own protection to cases where it is judged absolutely necessary. In Victoria and New South Wales[346] the principle of the statutes and the guidance accompanying them has been that child abuse should be taken seriously and that children should be protected from danger, but that the removal of a child from home should be the last rather than first resort. In deciding what work to undertake social workers must work to the principle that the least intrusive intervention be used.[347] Prior to any decision to remove a child, the state must first decide whether the provision of other services will be sufficient to adequately reduce the identified risk to the child and preserve the family unit. Social workers should work with families to ensure that children are protected; this should include a clear risk assessment of the child's position in determining what action should be taken.[348] For example it is a statutory principle of intervention under the Children and Young Persons (Care and Protection) Act 1998 (New South Wales) s 36 that the immediate protection of the child should be given paramount consideration, but that removal of the child from his usual carer should only be undertaken when it is necessary to protect the child from serious harm. This measure also requires police officers to consider whether it is possible to remove the alleged abuser on an apprehended violence order under the Crimes Act when the child needs to be protected immediately and this cannot be achieved by voluntary means.[349]

6. Emergency protection in New Zealand

Under the CYPFA 1989 s 39 the court may issue a warrant authorizing a police officer to search for and seize a child or young person who has suffered or is likely to suffer ill treatment, abuse or serious neglect, deprivation or harm. Section 40 contains

---

[343] Children's Protection Act 1993 (South Australia) s 16–17.

[344] Children and Young Persons (Care and Protection) Act 1998 (New South Wales) ss 35–43.

[345] Thorpe (n 222) 161.

[346] Western Australia adopted similar principles when its Children and Community Services Act 2004 ss 8, 9 came into force.

[347] Children and Young Persons (Care and Protection) Act 1998 (New South Wales) ss 8, 9 and 63.

[348] See for example Community Care Division *An Integrated Strategy for Child Protection and Placement Services* (Community Care Division, Department of Human Services Victoria, Australia 2002) [3.1] <http://www.office-for-children.vic.gov.au/children/ccdnav.nsf/>; more recently the *Every Child: Every Chance* initiative launched in the White Paper State Government of Victoria; *Protection Children: The Next Steps* (Office for Children, Melbourne Victoria Australia 2005) <http://www.office-for-children.vic.gov.au/children/ccfnav.nsf.> (accessed 5 October 2006).

[349] Children and Young Persons (Care and Protection) Act 1998 (New South Wales) s 43. P Parkinson *Children and Young Persons (Care and Protection) Act 1998 (An Overview)* (Faculty of Law University of Sydney 2000) 9.

analogous provisions where there is a reasonable belief that a child or young person is in need of care and protection.[350] Section 42 allows entry, search and removal without warrant but only in emergency situations. The jurisprudence from the New Zealand courts has consistently emphasized that the powers given in these sections are intrusive and for use only in an emergency.[351]

The execution of a place of safety warrant is of course a serious step, to be undertaken only if the invasion of the parent's rights—and for that matter the rights of the child—is necessary for the child's protection. So the threshold test of suspicion—not knowledge—on reasonable grounds of any matter specified in s 39(1) must necessarily be based on a responsible assessment of the situation as it appears at the time.[352] In particular the Court of Appeal has emphasized the very narrow circumstances in which the power to search without a warrant may be used, holding that the circumstances must be 'most pressing and exceptional'.[353] Furthermore decisions must be made on reasonable grounds; 'wild statements and threats' made by a stressed parent in the heat of the moment would not justify its use.[354]

7. Evaluation: is the need to protect children from unnecessary change valued sufficiently in emergency protection law?

Clearly the effect of removal from home upon a child can be enormous:

For these young people the experience of abuse and of being rejected by their families became closely interwoven. Some felt that placement away from home was a punishment for telling about the abuse, or others that they had not been believed or had been held to blame for what had happened. For all of them it was hard to feel that telling had been the right thing when it had had such dire consequences ... The distress experienced by the children who were excluded from the family after disclosing abuse was evident from the suicide attempts made by two of them and the high scores on the depression inventory for all of them ... The depression scores reduced dramatically for those who later returned home.[355]

This has been insufficiently recognized in some jurisdictions which have interpreted the debate as being largely between the interests of the parents and the state. To generalize, the ethos of child protection in the United States is currently that the end justifies the means. Whilst children will be upset by removal from home it is much better that this is achieved and the child is safe. This is no longer the position in Australia and has never been the position in New Zealand, which have adopted the least disruption principle. This principle of least disruption is also present in many parts of Canadian child protection legislation, if not entirely accepted by the Supreme Court of Canada. Legislators in Canada and New South Wales have been

---

[350] New Zealand Law Commission Preliminary Paper *Entry, Search and Seizure* (a discussion paper) preliminary paper 50 Appendix A.
[351] D Webb, B Atkin, J Caldwell, J Adams, M Heneghan, D Clarkson, D Partridge and P Treadwell *Butterworths Family Law in New Zealand* (12th edn Butterworths, Wellington 2006) 958–963.
[352] *Re M* [1990] NZFLR 575; 1990 NZFLR LEXIS 112 (Fam Ct Palmerston North) 113.
[353] *R v K* [1995] NZFLR 341, (New Zealand CA) 342.   [354] ibid 343.
[355] Farmer and Owen (n 24) 205.

particularly innovative in including a statutory presumption in child protection law that a child should remain with their primary caregiver if this is possible, coupled with an expectation that social workers should support families in order that this may be achieved. Some of the innovations in legislation may be linked to the history of removal of aboriginal children in Australia and Canada. Whilst this has undoubtedly also happened in the United States there appears to have been much less shame on the part of successive governments about it, and less general public recognition of the unjustified misery it created. In contrast:

for Australians, our concerns about the removal of children are acute. We live with the suffering and damage done to generations of Aboriginal children raised separate to their kin; of non-Aboriginal children institutionalised because of parental poverty and children removed from parents with disabilities ... For us, the dangers of an excessive, or inappropriate, use of an emergency power to remove children have been demonstrated.[356]

Whilst there are some statements to this effect in English law we do not have the clear statement of principle that Australian law contains, although we may be moving towards it in the decisions about the removal of babies at birth. The clearest articulation of this principle in English law lies in *Re H (Minors) (Wardship: Sexual Abuse)* where Balcombe LJ stated:

Although society is rightly astute to protect children from sexual abuse, society may cause other, and possibly greater harm to the children it seeks to protect. To take children away from the only home they may have known, from parents however inadequate, to whom they are attached, and to put them into the care of foster parents (however loving and skilled) or into a residential home, clearly carries a risk of harming those children.[357]

G. Gathering Evidence from the Child

A decision that a child should be separated from the alleged abuser may be made at any stage of the process; at the same time further information will be gathered to try and determine what has happened and whether the child will need to be protected in the future. The most important source of information is the child himself.

1. Facilitating an assessment

Children may demonstrate signs of abuse in their language and description of events, their behaviour and on their bodies. A variety of assessments of the child and interviews for the purposes of gathering evidence may take place.

It is a fundamental element of the Children Act 1989 that those with parental responsibility under s 2 should be asked to consent to the examination of their

---

[356] R Best 'Emergency removal of children for their care and protection' (2003) AJFL LEXIS 14 [3], see for Canada S Fournier and E Crey *Stolen from our Embrace: the Abduction of First Nations Children and the Restoration of Aboriginal Communities* (Douglas and McIntyre, Vancouver 1997).

[357] *Re H (Minors) (Wardship: Sexual Abuse)* [1992] 1 WLR 243, [1991] FCR 736, 745C.

minor child if she is not considered to be of sufficient understanding to consent herself. However *Working Together* and *Achieving Best Evidence*[358] (the guidance on interviewing children for criminal proceedings discussed later) suggest that a child could be interviewed without parental consent or even knowledge and without one of the court orders discussed below. This appears to be justified either on the grounds of an overriding need for justice: 'relevant circumstances would include the possibility that a child would be threatened or otherwise coerced into silence; a strong likelihood that evidence would be destroyed' or the wishes of the child not to involve the parent at this stage.[359] While these paragraphs are rather 'throw away', and are not part of a discussion on the legal framework for facilitating interviews, they constitute the core guidance for investigators and do clearly suggest that in these circumstances investigators may go ahead and an interview may be conducted. For example a child could be taken out of school to be interviewed, or an accommodated child also be interviewed without consent. It is not suggested that investigators take a child for medical or other examinations without a parent's consent, presumably because in the absence of an emergency a physical examination would then constitute a battery in tort law and possibly also criminal law.

(a) Child assessment orders

The need for parental permission may be circumvented by court order. The Children Act 1989 s 44(6) allows the court to make directions with regard to medical, psychiatric or other assessments of a child when making an EPO. The court may also order that the local authority conduct any assessment when making an interim care or supervision order.[360] Conversely, the court may order that the local authority does not conduct a specific assessment. This is a power 'manifestly directed to the type of conduct by social services revealed by the Cleveland Inquiry, ie repeated interviews and assessments which are detrimental to the child'.[361] Much more controversially, the Children Act 1989 created the Child Assessment Order (CAO) the sole purpose of which is to facilitate an assessment of a child despite parental objection. The order was controversial because of residual doubt as to its necessity.

The CAO was introduced into the Children Bill during its passage through Parliament. Such an order had been initially suggested by the report into the death of Kimberley Carlile. Before Kimberley's death social workers had tried in vain to gain access to her, which her stepfather had refused. In these circumstances they could not apply for a court order without some evidence of maltreatment, yet they could not get any evidence because their access to Kimberley was being frustrated. The *Carlile Report* recommended that a court order be created in addition to any EPO which would require parents to produce a child for the sole purpose of ensuring that that child could be examined. The *Carlile Report* envisaged that such an order would result

---

[358] Home Office *et al Achieving Best Evidence in Criminal Proceedings: Guidance for Vulnerable or Intimidated Witnesses, Including Children* (2001) [3.7.4].
[359] *Working Together to Safeguard Children 1999* (n 30) [5.37].
[360] Children Act 1989 (England) s 38(6); *Re C (Interim Care Order)* [1997] 1 FLR 1, 7H.
[361] *Re C* ibid (HL) 8B (Lord Browne-Wilkinson).

in much less familial disruption as the child would not need to be accommodated away from home, and thus the impact upon the exercise of parental rights would be much less than any emergency order.[362]

The CAO was one of the most fiercely debated parts of the Children Bill.[363] It was initially excluded from the Bill on the recommendation of the *Cleveland Report*, which concluded that the presence of an additional order could only confuse social workers. This view continued to be advocated by the Association of Directors of Social Services (ADSS) during the passage of the Bill. ADSS argued that the new EPO could suffice in all situations, as it could be granted on the grounds of suspicion and the failure of the child's parents to agree to an examination. In their view the child should not be removed from home until the examination had been conducted and the suspicions confirmed. The dissenters from this view within both Houses of Parliament and outside it, particularly the NSPCC, argued that Justices might refuse to grant EPOs in situations where access to the child had been denied, on the basis that sufficient ground for emergency action had not been demonstrated.

The results of the debate were twofold. First an additional ground for an EPO was created, allowing an order to be made when access to a child is being frustrated during an inquiry and investigators have reasonable cause to believe that access to the child is required as a matter of urgency.[364] Section 43 then created a second court order solely to facilitate examinations of the child which the child's parents would not allow, when the situation was not considered to be an emergency. The guidance accompanying the Children Act 1989 envisaged the use of child assessment orders as being particularly suitable for cases where there was a suspicion of sexual abuse, as 'the harm to the child can be long term and it does not necessarily require emergency action'.[365] As the degree of intrusion on the family should be much less, a CAO may be granted on a lower standard of proof than an EPO, that of proof of reasonable cause to suspect.

Despite the time and effort expended by legislators and pressure groups in formulating a provision to accommodate a perceived need, the CAO appears to be rarely used, although there is limited information to substantiate this as the published judicial statistics do not include information on the number of CAOs granted.[366] What information is available is out of date. Dickens' research into the lack of use of the CAO was completed just after the Children Act 1989 came into force and was published in 1993.[367] In his study of an inner London borough, the order was only applied for on two occasions, and in both it was later decided to withdraw the application. Dickens attributed the lack of use of the order to several factors, all of which had been raised

---

[362] *A Child in Mind* (n 7) 154.   [363] Parton *Governing the Family* (n 14) 176–192.
[364] Children Act 1989 (England) ss 47(6), 44(1)(b)(c).
[365] Department of Health *The Children Act 1989 Guidance and Regulations Volume 1—Court Orders* (HMSO London 1991) 46 [4.9].
[366] Lord Chancellor's Department *Judicial Statistics 1999* (HM Stationery Office, London 2000) 53.
[367] J Dickens 'Assessment and Control of Social Work: An Analysis of Reasons for the Non-Use of the Child Assessment Order' (1993) 2 J SWL 88–100; R Lavery 'The child assessment order—a reassessment' [1996] CFLQ 41.

in the debate on the Children Bill, by those who opposed the additional order. The time limit of seven days was felt to be insufficient to facilitate a proper assessment of the child, a factor previously identified by the then Lord Chancellor during debate.[368] As the ADSS had foretold, social workers were unsure about the provisions of the order and therefore did not use it. Dickens also found that social workers were much more confident about being able to obtain parental consent to examinations when the situation was not an emergency, whereas if it was necessary to apply for a court order, then it was unlikely that cooperation between investigators and parents would be achieved.

The most recent version of *Working Together to Safeguard Children 2006* does draw the attention of investigators to the possible use of a child assessment order. It suggests that a child assessment order be used when the parents do not agree to an assessment and emergency protection order is not needed.[369] It may be that child assessment orders are used more often during investigations if the very strong jurisprudence, discussed above in section F.2 on limiting the use of emergency protection orders, can be communicated effectively to investigators.

(b) Refusing to be examined

All of the court orders which facilitate examination against the wishes of parents under the Children Act 1989 allow a child to refuse to be examined.[370] However this is subject to the proviso that they are considered by the court to have sufficient understanding to make an informed decision. The measurement of capacity to consent to medical treatment was famously decided in the case of *Gillick v West Norfolk and Wisbech Area Health Authority*.[371] The case concerned the capacity of a child to consent to contraceptive advice and treatment, but the principles which it established have been extrapolated to any form of medical treatment or assistance. The judgment of the majority of the House of Lords contained many elements, but at its heart was the conclusion that as the child grew in understanding, so she should be accorded the right to consent to medical treatment. The judgment did not stipulate an age beyond which a child could be considered to have sufficient understanding to consent to treatment. Instead Lord Scarman held that, 'as a matter of law the parental right to determine whether or not their minor child below the age of 16 will have medical treatment terminates if and when the child achieves sufficient understanding and intelligence to enable him to understand fully what is proposed. It will be a matter of fact whether a child seeking advice has sufficient understanding of what is involved to give a consent valid in law'.[372]

---

[368] *Hansard* HC Deb cols 433–434 (19 January 1989) in Parton *Governing the Family* (n 14) 181.
[369] *Working Together to Safeguard Children 2006* (n 31) [5.68].
[370] Children Act 1989 (England) ss 38(6); 43(8) and 44(7).
[371] *Gillick v West Norfolk and Wisbech Area Health Authority* [1986] AC 112 (HL).
[372] ibid 423J.

The Children Act 1989 gives a child the right to refuse to be examined rather than the right to consent. This is not a semantic difference. Caselaw following *Gillick* established that doctors may override the wishes of a child and seek parental consent when a child refuses treatment.[373] However it was a 'clearly stated intention of Parliament in the Children Act 1989 to provide that children would have the right to say "no" to such examination and assessment being conducted against their wishes'.[374] A child's statutory right to refuse an assessment has not been questioned in the courts. It has been held that no conclusions may be drawn from a child's refusal to be examined.[375]

As we have discussed there are many fine words in the guidance about consulting with children when there is a protection concern. However what resonates most strongly at this point is the request from the *Cleveland Report* that in these situations, 'children are people and not just objects of concern' and that they should be treated as such. It is unclear how much has changed in practice over the 16 years since the report. In the case of Victoria Climbié, she was never spoken to by a professional throughout the many contacts which she had with health, social services professionals and the police until her death. Admittedly this contact would have had to have been made through an interpreter, as Victoria spoke French. However this was never arranged.

2. Interviewing a child

A child's description of abuse is one of the most important pieces of evidence that can be offered to the court that sexual abuse has taken place, since sexual abuse is rarely witnessed and physical signs (compatible with though not proof of, abuse) are found in some 50 per cent of children by the time they come to be examined.[376] A child's evidence will be less important when there are clear physical signs of injury, and where the identity of the person causing the injury is not in dispute. Thus it may be decided not to interview a child in some cases of alleged physical assault or neglect where the child is very young or very inarticulate, but these cases can still proceed to prosecution because of the weight of physical evidence. In contrast it is highly unlikely that a prosecution of an allegation of sexual abuse would be continued if the child said nothing indicative of sexual abuse in interview.

There can be no doubt that conducting a forensic interview of a young child witness as part of an investigation into alleged wrongdoing is an extraordinarily difficult task. The interviewer will be constrained by the linguistic, cognitive, motivational and emotional characteristics of the child. She must contend with the general linguistic problem of obtaining detailed information from a child who is likely to be unaccustomed to providing elaborate verbal narratives about his experiences. Inevitably there are cognitive problems where a child is asked to recall events which happened long

---

[373] *Re W* [1992] 2 All ER 627 (CA) and *Re R (a Minor) (Wardship: Medical Treatment)* [1991] 4 All ER 177 (CA).

[374] C Lyon 'What Happened to the Child's "Right" to Refuse?—*South Glamorgan CC v W and B*' (1994) 6(2) JCL 84.

[375] *Re E (a Minor) (Child Abuse: Evidence)* [1987] 1 FLR 269 (Fam Div) 275H–276A (Ewbank J).

[376] D Glaser 'Evaluating the Evidence of a Child—The Video-Taped Interview and Beyond' (1989) 19 Fam Law 487.

before the interview. Moreover, reporting information about stressful, embarrassing, and painfully intense events may be very difficult.[377]

There are now two sets of guidance for interviewers of children in cases where child abuse is suspected and the interview with the child may be used in evidence. The guidance contained in the *Cleveland Report* remains the key guidance for interviewers who wish to gather evidence admissible in civil proceedings under the Children Act 1989.[378] *Achieving Best Evidence in Criminal Proceedings*[379] is the guidance on video-taped interviews which conform to the evidential requirements of a criminal trial and may replace the child's evidence-in-chief in a criminal trial. However, it would be wrong to think that the guidance in *Achieving Best Evidence* is only followed in the relatively small number of cases which are heard in the criminal courts. Interviews with children take place at the beginning of the process of investigation, particularly when sexual abuse is suspected. At that time it is unclear whether there will be suffi-cient evidence to mount a criminal trial and the child's interview can often take the form of an *Achieving Best Evidence* interview 'just in case'. The interview may then subsequently be used as evidence in civil proceedings.

(a) Legal concerns about questioning techniques

The law in this area has been primarily driven by a desire to preserve the evidence that a child may give and to avoid the contamination of that evidence by interviewers. The testimony of children has long been regarded as particularly open to distortion by questioning. Spencer and Flin have traced the origins of this legal view to cultural and legal mythology about the effect of immaturity in lowering ability to resist sug-gestion.[380] This scepticism was supported by very early psychological evaluations of children's capacity to testify, which argued that 'children are the most dangerous of witnesses and ... their testimony should be excluded from court record wherever possible'.[381]

A much more nuanced view has emerged from a plethora of empirical studies conducted over the past two decades. However, there is a sharp division amongst experimental psychologists as to the strength of the conclusions to be drawn from this body of research,[382] not least because ethical constraints mean that it is not possible to

---

[377] SJ Ceci and M Bruck *Jeopardy In The Courtroom: a Scientific Analysis of Children's Testimony* (American Psychological Association, Washington DC 1995) 76.

[378] *Cleveland* (n 15) See above in relation to care orders Chapter 2 section E.1.

[379] *Achieving Best Evidence in Criminal Proceedings* (n 358). For the Scottish equivalent, designed to complement *Achieving Best Evidence*, see Scottish Executive *Guidance on Interviewing Child Witnesses in Scotland* (2003) [19].

[380] J Spencer and R Flin *The Evidence of Children: the Law and the Psychology* (2nd edn Blackstone Press, London 1993) 285–288.

[381] A Baginsky in 1910 paraphrased by G Whipple 'The Psychology of Testimony' (1911) 8 *Psychology Bulletin* 307, 308; J Varendonck 'Les témoignages d'enfants dans un procès retentissant' (1911) 11 *Archives de Psychologie* 129 (in a classic experiment a group of seven-year-olds were asked about the colour of their teacher's beard; 84% indicated a colour when in fact he did not have a beard at all); G Goodman 'Children's Testimony in Historical Perspective' (1984) 40 *J of Social Issues* 9.

[382] eg JE Myers 'New Era of Skepticism regarding Children's Credibility: Suggestibility of Child Witnesses—the Social Science Amicus Brief in *The State of New Jersey v Margaret Kelly Michaels*' (1905) 1

expose the children in the research sample to traumatic events similar to abuse,[383] nor to replicate other aspects of a formal investigation.[384] Gail Goodman argues that whilst there are age differences in suggestibility, children are much less likely to assent falsely to questions related to physical or sexual abuse,[385] but this contention is extremely difficult to verify.

Although research in experimental psychology suggests that we cannot expect very young children to provide the coherent, detailed and chronological account of the events which is often demanded in a court of law, they can provide valuable and reliable information.[386] The difficulty for persons questioning child witnesses is to extract the information whilst minimizing the risk of introducing inaccuracies in a child's report.

(i) Suggestibility

The main legal concern about interviews conducted with children has been that the questioning mechanism itself could irreparably damage the quality of a child's testimony. As Swinton-Thomas J suggested in *Re N (Minors) (Child Abuse: Evidence)*,

> . . . it is inevitable that a court will be slow to act upon conclusions which are based to a very large extent on answers given by a small child in reply to direct or leading questions which certainly strongly suggest that they require particular answers from the child.[387]

The courts' concern about suggestion in interviews increased when child interviews conducted by non-lawyers became admissible evidence in court proceedings, particularly when such interviewers did not share the same priorities and concerns as criminal investigators. Before 1991 when the law changed to allow videotaped interviews with children to replace their evidence in chief, many commentators expressed concern about the competence of interviewers who were not legally trained to take over the role of barristers in questioning children.[388] This was supported by the findings of civil courts following the *Cleveland Report* that interviewers had failed to observe the guidance contained within it, approaching interviews with a clear belief that abuse had taken place and so asking children leading questions.[389]

Psychology, Public Policy, and Law 387 and TD Lyon 'The New Wave in Children's Suggestibility Research: a Critique' (1999) 84 Cornell LR 1005 attacking the research findings in Ceci and Bruck (n 377).

[383] G Goodman 'Child Sexual and Physical Abuse: Children's Testimony' in SJ Ceci, M Toglia and DF Ross (eds) *Children's Eyewitness Memory* (Springer-Verlag, New York 1987) 6–8.

[384] Lyon (n 382), 1026–1030.   [385] G Goodman (n 383); TD Lyon ibid.

[386] Although adult stereotypes of children's capabilities as witnesses may also affect juries' evaluation of their testimony: CE Luus and GL Wells 'The Perceived Credibility of Child Witnesses' in H Dent and R Flin (eds) *Children As Witnesses* (John Wiley & Sons, Chichester 1992).

[387] *Re N (Minors) (Child Abuse: Evidence)* [1987] 1 FLR 280 (Fam Div, Swinton Thomas J), 283F.

[388] J Morton 'Videotaping Children's Evidence—A Reply' (1987) 137 NLJ 216.

[389] *Re E (a Minor) (Child Abuse: Evidence)* [1991] 1 FLR 420 (Fam Div) 433F; *Rochdale BC v A and Others* [1991] 2 FLR 192 (Fam Div, Douglas Brown J), 210; *Re M (Minors) (Sexual Abuse: Evidence)* [1993] 1 FLR 822.

In every jurisdiction considered in this book, there have been acknowledged or alleged high-profile miscarriages of justice, usually involving multiple young complainants and defendants and often concerning alleged ritual abuse, because investigators were too credulous and relied upon contaminated evidence resulting from seriously flawed interviewing techniques.[390] As Ceci and Bruck concluded in their detailed study of American nursery cases:

> our argument is that the accuracy of a child's report decreases when the child is interviewed in highly leading and suggestive ways by interviewers who were uninterested in testing alternative hypotheses; such interviews may tarnish the evidence to such a degree that markers of the truth may be buried forever. Presently, there is no scientifically acceptable test or procedure that allows one to determine whether allegations that emerge under such circumstances are accurate or merely a product of the suggested interviewing procedures. When children have been subjected to relentlessly suggestive interviews over long periods of time, there is no 'Pinocchio Test'.[391]

In the context of testimony, suggestibility refers to the process of making a witness believe that events occurred which did not. The idea that children are infinitely and invariably suggestible has been definitively refuted; the real issue is the extent to which they are more suggestible by post-event influences than adults.[392] Here there is a welter of studies yielding variable results; statistical comparisons are difficult because of different definitions of what constitutes leading questions and suggestive interviewing.[393] There appears to be some consensus amongst experimental psychologists that while both adult and child witnesses have been shown to be suggestible through leading questions (a question which 'assumes an answer or assumes facts which are likely to be in dispute'[394]), children aged six and under are particularly susceptible.[395] This

[390] The United Kingdom: *Rochdale BC v A and Others* ibid *Cleveland* (n 15). *Orkney* (n 15) *Lillie and Reed v Newcastle City Council, Barker and others* [2002] EWHC 1600 (QB). The United States: *State v Kelly* 456 SE 2d 861 (North Carolina Ct App, 1995); LS McGough 'For the Record: Videotaping Investigative Interviews' (1995) 1 Psychology, Public Policy and Law 370; Ceci and Bruck (n 377). New Zealand: New Zealand Minister of Justice 'Comments on the Investigation and Interviewing of children in the Ellis Case' in Sir Thomas Eichelbaum, *The Peter Ellis Case Report of the Ministerial Inquiry* (2001). Canada: *Kvello and Klassen et al v Miazga, Hansen et al* [2003] SK QB 559, 234 DLR (4th) 612 (Saskatchewan QB) [69]–[84], [98]–[114]. Australia: The Hon Justice JRT Wood *Royal Commission into the New South Wales Police Service: The Paedophile Inquiry* (August 1997) Vol IV ch 7 Part B 'The Kindergarten Cases' (including the notorious 'Mr Bubbles' case at the Seabeach Kindergarten).

[391] ie their noses do not grow longer when they are inaccurate (Ceci and Bruck) (n 377) 84–85.

[392] J Myers, K Saywitz and G Goodman 'Psychological Research on Children As Witnesses: Implications for Forensic Interviewing and Courtroom Testimony' (1996) 28 Pac LJ 3, 28.

[393] Lyon 'The New Wave in Children's Suggestibility Research' (n 382) 1033–1042; A Warren and L McGough 'Research on Children's Suggestibility: Implications for the Investigative Interview' in B Bottoms and G Goodman (eds) *International Perspectives on Child Abuse and Children's Testimony* (Sage, London 1996).

[394] *Achieving Best Evidence* (n 358) [2.121]; *Guidance on Interviewing Child Witnesses in Scotland* (n 379) [95]–[96].

[395] G Davies and H Westcott *Interviewing Child Witnesses under the Memorandum of Good Practice: a Research Review* (Police Research Series Paper 115 Police Policing and Reducing Crime Unit, Home Office Research, Development and Statistics Directorate, London 1999) 10; SJ Ceci, DF Ross and MP Toglia

may be because young children are more sensitive to contextual cues from an adult in responding to an unfamiliar situation,[396] or because of their relatively impoverished semantic knowledge base for many different types of events and experiences.[397] Repeated interviews with four- to six-year-olds in which leading questions were used to imply the same misleading account of events led to free recall as well as prompted recall being affected, with convincing but false corroborating detail being offered by the child.[398]

However, critics of such research findings emphasize that their relevance is tempered by the reality of sexual abuse and abuse investigations. Lyon points out that there is little empirical evidence to support the view that highly suggestive interviewing techniques are the *norm* in abuse investigations. Moreover, such research neglects the characteristics of child sexual abuse which make false allegations less likely, such as embarrassment, fear of or loyalty towards the abuser, which if anything serve to increase the likelihood of false denials. Lyon maintains that the apparently value-free scientific treatment of the suggestibility issue obscures value judgments regarding the trade-off between false allegations and false denials of sexual abuse.[399] Lyon also contends that if leading questions can create false allegations, counter-suggestions through leading questions in cross-examination can equally undermine them.[400]

We must also not forget the flipside of suggestibility, that true allegations may be undermined by admissions obtained through leading questions in cross-examination of a child complainant.

Psychological research studies have consistently reported that free recall or free narrative is a more accurate means of securing information in an interview than cued recall or recognition (for example, multiple choice questioning) for both children and adults.[401] The amount of information provided during free narrative increases with age, reaching adult levels by about 12 years. Moreover, the information freely recalled by children tends to be as accurate as adult accounts, although children younger than 12 tend to provide less information spontaneously.[402] The omission of details is much more common than the invention of false ones. Children between the ages of three and six seem to forget more rapidly than older people, but while their free recall is typically more incomplete, it is no less accurate. Nevertheless, it seems that eight- to

---

'Age Differences in Suggestibility: Narrowing the Uncertainties' in SJ Ceci, DF Ross and MP Toglia (eds) *Children's Eyewitness Memory* (Springer-Verlag, New York 1987) 89–91.

[396] MA King and JC Yuille 'Suggestibility and the Child Witness' in SJ Ceci et al *Children's Eyewitness Memory* 30–31.

[397] Ceci and Bruck (n 377) 255.

[398] M Leichtman and SJ Ceci, 'The Effects of Stereotypes and Stands on Preschoolers' Reports' (2005) 31 *Developmental Psychology* 568.

[399] Lyon 'The New Wave in Children's Suggestibility Research' (n 382), 1046–1084.

[400] ibid 1042–1046.

[401] C Cole and E Loftus, 'The Memory of Children' in SJ Ceci, et al *Children's Eyewitness Memory* (n 395) 183; Davies and Westcott (n 395) 8.   [402] Cole and Loftus (n 401) 183.

nine-year-old children are most likely to add extraneous, often implausible, information, while adults seem to be the most susceptible to errors of inference.[403] Conversely,
while questioning increases the amount of information provided, prompted recall is
less accurate than free recall. Open-ended questions are answered more accurately
than specific questions, which in turn are answered more accurately than leading
questions.[404]

Thus courts have rightly placed great weight on spontaneous statements made in
response to open questions. For example in the early case of *Re W (a Minor) (Child
Abuse: Evidence)*[405] the court was very impressed by statements a little girl had made to
non-leading questions. 'When she was asked to demonstrate the lying dolls, she was
asked the question in the neutral form, "What is happening now?", and answered, "I
can feel a little bit of wet on my bottom".' Conversely a failure to elicit any spontaneous
statement indicative of abuse has been the basis of a judicial decision that abuse could
not be proved.[406] Many American courts are prepared to receive expert evidence on
the effects of suggestive questioning in investigative interviews on the reliability of
the child's recollection of events, in considering not only the admissibility of those
interviews but also whether a child's *viva voce* testimony in court should be barred as
unreliable.[407]

Thus strategies to guard against the suggestibility of young child witnesses are
(rightly) a consistent theme in investigative interviewing protocols,[408] and indeed
appears in the Scottish guidance for advocates.[409]

(ii) Interviewer bias

Therapeutic interviews, designed to enable a child to speak about abuse for the purpose
of diagnosis and treatment, are often conducted on the assumption that the child
has been abused, thus seriously impairing the evidential value of any disclosures.[410]

[403] ibid 183, 205.   [404] Davies and Westcott (n 395) 9.

[405] *Re W (a Minor) (Child Abuse: Evidence)* [1987] 1 FLR 297, (Fam Div) 303F–H.

[406] *C v C (Child Abuse: Evidence)* [1987] 1 FLR 321, 327E–F 'It is quite clear to me that there was no
spontaneous complaint at all during this interview', *Cechman v Travis and Hospital Authority of Gwinnett
County* 414 SE 2d 282 (Georgia CA 1991), 453; *Re A and B (Minors) (No 1) (Investigation of Alleged Abuse)*
[1995] 3 FCR 389.

[407] eg 1379; *People v Michael M* 618 NYS 2d 171 (New York Supreme Ct 1994) 810, which prompted
widespread concern that all children's evidence would be regarded as compromised: JE Myers 'Taint Hearings for Child Witnesses? A Step in the Wrong Direction' (1994) 46 Baylor L Rev 873. In a nationwide
survey 86% of American prosecution offices reported that the defence always or frequently challenged the
testimony of children on the basis of suggestibility, and 87% alleged coaching GS Goodman J Buckley
JA Quas and C Shapiro 'Innovations for Child Witnesses: a National Survey' (1999) 5 *Psychology, Public
Policy, and Law* 255, 275.

[408] *Achieving Best Evidence* (n 358) (2001) [2.126]–[2.130]; *Guidance on Interviewing Child Witnesses
in Scotland* (n 379) [95]–[99], [115]; Council of Europe *Recommendation No. R(97)13 of the Committee
of Ministers to Member States concerning Intimidation of Witnesses and the Rights of the Defence* (adopted 10
Sept 1997) Explanatory Memorandum [113]–[114].

[409] *Guidance on the Questioning of Children in Court* ibid [17].

[410] *Guidance on Interviewing Child Witnesses in Scotland* (n 379) [15], [30], [44].

Investigative interviewers may fall into the trap of a preconceived notion of what has happened to the child, so that the interview becomes a single-minded attempt to gather only confirmatory evidence, and to avoid all avenues which might produce a negative or inconsistent evidence.[411]

This is most likely to occur with interviewers investigating what they think is a multi-victim case, as they are more likely to confront children with allegations of other children,[412] and to provide assurance that the suspect is a bad person.[413] Interviews may be designed 'to match the trauma which the child has suffered through the abuse by placing equal pressure on the child to talk about what had occurred'.[414] Questions may be used which are leading, or hypothetical, in order to show a small child that she will be believed if she talks about abuse. This type of technique would not usually produce evidence which is admissible in court. Eady J concluded that the following interview by a police officer of a three-year-old child at the Shieldfield Nursery in Newcastle had no value as evidence that the child had been abused and was in fact a 'grotesque' example of poor interviewing.

Q: What clothes did he [Chris] have on?
A: Don't know.
. . .
Q: Have you seen Chris's willy?
A: No.
Q: Have you seen anybody's?
A: No.
. . .
Q: Can you tell us what they look like?
A: It looks like a bum.
Q: Like a bum?
A: No, fairy.
Q: Like a fairy? And have you seen Chris's?
A: [Non-committal].
Q: And where have you seen Chris's?
A: Don't know.

Despite the child's negative response the officer persists:

Q: And when you saw it, what did it look like when you saw Chris's willy?
A: [No response].
Q: What did Chris's willy look like?
A: [No response].[415]

---

[411]   Ceci and Bruck (n 377) 79–81, 121–125.
[412]   As in the *Bristol Study, Appendix* Case 27B.
[413]   Lyon 'The New Wave in Children's Suggestibility Research' (n 382) 1031.
[414]   G Douglas and C Willmore 'Diagnostic Interviews as Evidence in Cases of Child Sexual Abuse' (1987) 17 Fam Law 151.
[415]   *Lillie and Reed v Newcastle City Council* (n 390) [943].

(iii) Multiple interviews

Any deficits in a child's memory or cognitive ability are likely to be amplified by the structural dynamics operating in an interview situation, where the child may respond to subtle verbal and non-verbal cues about the adult's goals for the discussion, and may strive to answer the questions to provide the information that she thinks the interviewer wishes to hear.[416] The risk of this occurring will be exacerbated where the child is subjected to several interviews. Judicial suspicion of evidence gathered from a series of long interviews with a child is allied to their concerns about suggestive questioning. In *H v H and C (Kent County Council Intervening) (Child Abuse: Evidence)*[417] it was observed that:

> frequent, repetitive interviews with young, suggestible children, reminding them of what they previously said, would be likely to have decreasing evidential value . . . Where allegations are made spontaneously in early interviews, they are more likely to be believed than those which occur later in so-called therapeutic interviews where the child has been encouraged to vent its aggression against the father or the alleged abuser.[418]

The only alternative legal view was put forward in the *Orkney Report*. The Inquiry found that a limitation of one or two interviews at the most was 'unduly restrictive and . . . could be contrary to the child's needs. One interview so conducted as to pressurize the child could be more harmful than several conducted impeccably.'[419] The *Orkney Report* suggested that the limit should be four, although more could be added if necessary if all the agencies agreed and understood the effect that it could have on the evidential value of any information gathered.[420] This suggestion was never taken up and the proposal outlined in the *Cleveland Report* of one interview of 'not too long' duration, with one further interview if necessary, has become commonly accepted by lawyers as appropriate.[421] Whilst the guidance for interviewing in criminal cases, *Achieving Best Evidence in Criminal Proceedings*, does not encourage further interviews, it does conceive of a number of occasions, in addition to those which had been envisaged by the now superseded *Memorandum of Good Practice* discussed below, when a second interview might take place.[422]

---

[416] King and Yuille (n 396); Ceci and Bruck (n 377) 125.

[417] *H v H and C (Kent County Council Intervening) (Child Abuse: Evidence); K v K (Haringey London Borough Council Intervening) (Child Abuse: Evidence)* [1989] 3 WLR 933 (CA), 949A.

[418] ibid 933, 949B. This was repeated again in *Cechman v Travis and Hospital Authority of Gwinnett County* (n 406), 425 where it was held that, 'where a child has been interviewed more than once, second and subsequent interviews are likely to be of diminishing, if not negligible value'.

[419] *Orkney* (n 15) 315 [17.75].

[420] The important element was that the number of interviews would be planned in advance and that no child would be interviewed more than twice in any week. ibid 314 [17.73].

[421] *Cleveland* (n 15) [12.34]; *Re S (Minors)* CA (Civ D) (20 January 2000 unreported Lexis transcript) (Ward LJ).

[422] Where children indicate to a third party that they have significant new information which was not disclosed at the initial interview, but they now wish to share with the interview team; where the initial interview opens up new lines of enquiry or wider allegations which cannot be satisfactorily explored within the time available; where in the preparation of his or her defence, an accused raises matters not covered in the initial interview and where significant new information emerges from other witnesses or sources. Again

Not only may multiple interviews be abusive, but there is also a sound basis for concern about their impact on the evidential value of the child's statements. As interviews are repeated, and the time between the original event and subsequent interviews lengthens, more intrusions are likely to infiltrate the child's memory traces and reporting becomes more inaccurate. However, the contaminating effect is diminished if the initial interview is neutral and reinforces the accurate memory, which can lead to greater resistance to suggestive questioning. Another hazard is that young children will be anxious to please the questioners, and if questions are repeated they may change the answers on the mistaken assumption that the first answer was incorrect.[423]

(iv) Use of props

Again lawyers have been wary of some uses of demonstrative materials in gathering information from children. There is a danger that irrelevant cues will have a suggestive function and mislead young children into making errors in their reports.[424] The main controversy has been around the use of anatomically correct dolls in interviewing children about sexual abuse.[425] This was particularly an issue when play was used as a diagnostic device, rather than as a means to help children to explain what they mean.[426] This concern is reflected in the judgment of Ewbank J in *Re G (Minors) (Child Abuse: Evidence)* quoting with approbation the evidence of a consult ant psychiatrist in the case.

Dr McCarthy now takes the view that it is about as valuable as producing in a fire raising case, concerning a child, model houses, a model fire engine, a can of petrol and a box of matches. He says that you could not draw any conclusion from a child who started a fire under those circumstances and by that token ought not to draw any conclusions from anything the child does with sexually explicit dolls.[427]

The current guidance in *Achieving Best Evidence* supports the use of conventional play materials such as drawing and ordinary dolls in helping a child to explain what they mean, but urges caution in their use with very young children who may not be able to associate the toys with the real-life objects that they are meant to represent. Caution is also advised in the use of anatomically correct dolls with all age groups.[428]

---

an interviewer should decide whether to re-interview a child in consultation with the CPS and the reasons for the interview should be recorded: *Achieving Best Evidence* (n 358) [12.1.1].

[423] Ceci and Bruck (n 377) 121–122.   [424] Myers Saywitz and Goodman (n 392) 29–30.
[425] Ceci and Bruck (n 377) chapter 12.
[426] Myers, Saywitz and Goodman (n 392) 30–32; J Spencer and Flin (n 380) 352–353.
[427] *Re G (Minors) (Child Abuse: Evidence)* [1987] 1 FLR 310 (Fam Div), 316–317.
[428] *Achieving Best Evidence* (n 358) [14.1]; *Guidance on Interviewing Child Witnesses in Scotland* (n 379) [111]–[114].

(v) Protection from system abuse

The view that the observation of evidential constraints in interviews also prevents damaging questioning was offered tentatively at first,[429] but it has become a consistent theme, particularly in the caselaw on interviewing children.[430] It has been repeatedly stated that observance of rules which are expected to guard the evidential validity of what a child had said will also protect the child from the potentially damaging effect of interviews reputed to be therapeutic. As Wall J observed in *B v B (Child Abuse: Contact)*:[431]

> Where the interviewer approaches the case with the belief that abuse has occurred it is dangerously easy for the interviews with the child, as happened here, to degenerate into a cross-examination of the child in which the interviewer puts, in leading form, and in an increasingly pressurised way, what he or she believes has happened. It cannot be said too often that such an approach is wholly unacceptable. It not only renders the interview valueless as evidence but is abusive of the child, particularly where, as here, I find that the child has not been abused in the manner which emerged particularly in the final interview.

(b) The development of guidance for interviews to be used as evidence in civil family proceedings

The *Cleveland Report* in 1988 published 12 key points that should be observed in the conduct of interviews with children in civil proceedings. The guidance stated that interviews should be conducted by those who were trained in interviewing children and who had demonstrated some aptitude for the task. The child should be interviewed in 'suitable and sympathetic surroundings'. Interviews must be approached by the interviewer with an open mind and to this end the interviews should not be referred to as 'disclosure interviews' as this 'precluded the notion that sexual abuse had not occurred.'

Questioning during the interview should be open-ended and should encourage the child to recall abuse without prompting and encouragement. Interviewers should consider therapeutic 'facilitative' techniques, such as those pioneered by Great Ormond Street which matched the pressure to keep quiet with a pressure to disclose, as potentially problematic should the interview result in court proceedings. It should be set at the child's pace, rather than the interviewer's. A child should usually be interviewed once, or twice at the most for the purposes of gathering evidence. Furthermore the interview should not be 'too long'. The interview should be recorded carefully, by video-recording or by other means. Interviewers must accept that 'at the end of the

---

[429] *Re G (Minors) (Child Abuse: Evidence)* (n 427), 316H (Ewbank J). See also *C v C (Child Abuse: Evidence)* (n 406), 330E (Hollis J) 'It seems possible—and I emphasise again it is only possible—that it has damaged M herself . . . Dr Connell made, I thought a remark which is worth repeating, when he said "I would not want a child of mine to be put through . . . this type of interview". I should think not.'

[430] *H v H and C* (n 417) 949A; *Cechman v Travis and Hospital Authority of Gwinnett County* (n 406), 433E (where the interviews were described as a 'professional disgrace'), *Rochdale BC v A and Others* (n 389) (Douglas Brown J), 210.   [431] [1994] 2 FLR 713 (Fam Div), 729.

interview the child may have given no information to support the suspicion of the sexual abuse and the position will remain unclear'.[432]

Whilst the Cleveland guidelines have remained the key guidance to be observed when interviewing children to gather evidence in a civil case, many more interviews conducted according to the guidance for applicable to criminal proceedings are now being used as evidence in civil proceedings. Although *Achieving Best Evidence* was not primarily designed to produce evidence acceptable in a civil court and the guidance which it contains 'may not have to be strictly adhered to' in public or private family law cases 'its underlying principles are equally applicable to care and family law cases':[433]

Spontaneous information provided by a child is obviously more valuable than information fed to the child by leading questions or prompting. The questioning of young children is a difficult and skilled art. Some children have to be helped to give evidence, but the greater the help provided by facilitating the answers the less reliable the answers will be. If it is necessary to prompt in the investigative stage, it must be done so far as possible in a non-leading form so as not to indicate to the child the possible answer. It may be difficult to obtain the information which the young child has to impart within a single session, which also must not go on for too long. It may be necessary to interview the child again. But the more often the child is asked questions about the same subject the less one can trust the answers given. To remind a child of earlier answers and, for instance, to show the child earlier drawings to nudge the child's recollection has its own dangers as to the reliability of the answers then given. Efficient video and/or audio recording of the question and answer sessions is most desirable and should always be put in place if it is available. There will always be cases (and some are reported), where these general guidelines are not followed and the evidence is none the less accepted but those cases are unusual.[434]

It seems unlikely that the civil courts will accept as evidence interviews where the evidential requirements have been abandoned altogether in favour of facilitative interviewing, which could include leading questions.[435] However as Butler-Sloss suggested in *Re D (Minors) (Sexual Abuse: Evidence)*[436] there may be occasions in which 'the revelations ... were so significant that the basic criticisms of the procedures used were overcome' in a civil case.[437]

(c) The development of guidance for interviews to be used as evidence in a criminal trial

The *Report of the Advisory Group on Video Evidence* (the *Pigot Report*) which preceded the reforms of the Criminal Justice Act 1991, recommended the creation of a 'code of conduct of video-recorded interviews' to guide those interviewing children, where

---

    [432] *Cleveland* (n 15) 207–208 [12.34].

    [433] *Re D (Minors) (Sexual Abuse: Evidence)* [1998] 2 FCR 419 (CA) [27] (Butler-Sloss LJ).

    [434] ibid.

    [435] *Re B (Sexual Abuse: Expert's Report)* [2000] 1 FLR 871 [14] (Thorpe LJ) 'flaws as profound as this are simply incapable of rectification'.	[436] *Re D* (n 433) [27].

    [437] *Re X (a Minor) (Child Abuse Evidence)* [1989] 1 FLR 30 (Fam Div), 37D and *Re M (Minors) (Sexual Abuse: Evidence)* (n 389) 831C (Butler-Sloss LJ).

the interview was likely to become the child's evidence in chief.[438] The Advisory Group hoped that this would create 'a climate in which video-recorded interviews will be recognised by the courts as a safe and acceptable source of evidence'.[439] The guidance produced on interviewing child witnesses was intended to both guide and control interviewers, preventing them from interviewing in a way that would produce unacceptable evidence.

The first draft of guidance on interviewing was published in 1992 as the *Memorandum of Good Practice*,[440] following the Criminal Justice Act 1991 which allowed a child's evidence in chief in a criminal trial to be pre-recorded on video. A second version, *Achieving Best Evidence in Criminal Proceedings*[441] was published in 2001, following the enactment of the Youth Justice and Criminal Evidence Act 1999, which envisaged that all the evidence from a child and other vulnerable witnesses could be pre-recorded in certain circumstances and shown at a criminal trial.[442] Both sets of guidance were written by psychologists and lawyers and were an attempt to marry psychological studies about how to interview children with the rules of evidence.

There was initially a mixed response to the first guidance on interviewing contained in the *Memorandum*. Guidance on how to interview children and gather forensically acceptable evidence was welcomed, especially by social workers who had been publicly criticized in a number of well-publicized cases for their failure to observe legal rules. Eileen Vizard, a child psychologist at Great Ormond Street Hospital, welcomed the *Memorandum* because it

... does introduce for the first time a research based and methodological approach to interviewing children. This is much to be welcomed after the ludicrously adversarial criticisms of professional interviewing skills prevalent in civil courts in the mid and late 1980's, which did little to offer constructive alternatives to practitioners.[443]

However the underlying ethos and some specific parts of the guidance were criticized by some as poorly thought-out. 'It is based on the premise that children will spontaneously narrate their experience of sexual abuse, if this has indeed occurred, to sensitive interviewers. There is little empirical evidence to support this.'[444] The guidance as a whole was described by McEwan as 'neither fish nor fowl', 'an uneasy mixture of legal technicality, sympathy for the child and advice drawn from professionals'.[445]

---

[438] HH Judge Thomas Pigot QC (chair) *Report of the Advisory Group as Video-Recorded Evidence* (HMSO, London 1989) 36 [4.8].   [439] ibid.

[440] Home Office and Department of Health *Memorandum of Good Practice on Video Recorded Interviews with Child Witnesses for Criminal Proceedings* (HMSO, London 1992).

[441] *Achieving Best Evidence* (n 358) (2001).

[442] Examined in detail below, Chapter 8 section B.2.

[443] E Vizard Letter to the Editor *The Independent* (London 23 October 1993).

[444] G Smith 'Good Practice or Yet Another Hurdle: Video Recording Children's Statements' (1993) 5(1) J CL 21.

[445] J McEwan 'Where the Prosecution Witness is a Child: The Memorandum of Good Practice' (1993) 5 J CL 16, 19.

From its publication there were calls for reform.[446] Interviewers found the guidance too rigid and too far away from their experience of therapeutic interviews.[447] Many found that there was inadequate guidance on good practice and interviewers had to guess what it should be.[448] Davies *et al* found that officers were concerned that the courts were treating the *Memorandum* as an inflexible code and were dismissing cases where there was even the slightest deviation from it.[449] The *Bristol Study* found that interviewers' interpretation of the guidance was consequently very rigid.[450] Having been sensitized by years of judicial criticism of interviews and by public scandals about the handling of abuse cases, interviewers tended to stick to what they thought the guidance said even in instances where it appeared to lead to nonsensical results. As Myers, Goodman and Saywicz have described the interviewer's dilemma:

If they limit themselves to open-ended questions, some abused children will not disclose their abuse. On the other hand, as interviewers proceed along the continuum to focused, specific, and leading questions, interviewers run increased risks of obtaining incorrect information and are being criticised for 'improper' interviewing. There is no escaping the risk–benefit calculation inherent in asking suggestive questions.[451]

This could lead for example to the unnecessary abandonment of interviews or any prospect of prosecution once a leading question had been asked.[452]

By the time the *Memorandum* was rewritten, the principles of the guidance were more accepted, although many police officers continued to criticize the substance of the guidance.[453]

(d) Content of the interview

In an effort to protect the integrity of the evidence gathered, the interview is expected to take place as 'soon after an allegation or referral emerges as is practicable'.[454] However the guidance in *Achieving Best Evidence* advocates a more measured approach than that envisaged by the *Memorandum of Good Practice*. The *Memorandum* declared that 'delay is bad for the child and bad for justice'.[455] In contrast *Achieving Best Evidence* warns that 'rushing to conduct an interview, without properly considering the child's needs and consulting them as far as possible, and without proper planning, can undo the benefits of obtaining an early account from the child'.[456] This type of guidance does appear to reflect a more confident approach to the interviewing of children which allows interviewers to use their skill and most importantly common sense in dealing with children in these very difficult circumstances.

---

[446] B Hughes, H Parker and B Gallagher *Policing Child Sexual Abuse: The View from Police Practitioners* (Home Office Police Research Group, London 1996), 47.

[447] J Holton and L Bonnerjea *The Child The Court and the Video: A Study of the Memorandum of Good Practice on Video Interviewing of Child Witnesses* (Social Services Inspectorate, London 1994).

[448] Davies and Westcott (n 398) 3.   [449] ibid 38.

[450] *Bristol Study*, 20–23.   [451] Myers, Saywitz and Goodman (n 392) 35.

[452] *Bristol Study* 82; *Guidance on Interviewing Child Witnesses in Scotland* (n 379) [99].

[453] Davies and Westcott (n 395) 3.   [454] *Achieving Best Evidence* (n 358) [2.57].

[455] *Memorandum of Good Practice* (n 440) [1.19].   [456] *Achieving Best Evidence* (n 358) [2.57].

There will usually be two interviewers. The first interviewer leads the interview whilst the second interviewer 'should be alive to gaps in a child's account, interviewer errors and confusion in the communication between interviewer and child'. Usually one of the interviewers will be a police officer and the other a social worker, but it is permissible for another person who has developed a rapport with the child and under-stands the evidential requirements to be the interviewer. An 'appropriately accredited' interpreter should also be present at the interview if the child's first language is not English or they use sign language. An intermediary may also be used 'if the child is very young, traumatised, or has an idiosyncratic system of communication'.[457] However at the time of writing this provision has not yet been implemented, although it seems clear that it will be. A very young or distressed child may also be allowed a supporter during the interview, provided that that supporter does not contribute or influence the interview.[458]

Achieving Best Evidence follows the 'phased approach' to interviewing recommended in the *Pigot Report* and adopted in the *Memorandum of Good Practice*. This was in turn based on the 'step-wise' approach created by Professor John Yuille of the University of British Columbia. It starts with a 'rapport-building stage', the purpose of which is 'to build up trust and mutual understanding with the child and help them to relax as far as possible in the novel environment' and to set up the ground rules for an interview.[459]

The interview should then proceed into the second, 'free narrative phase'. The purpose of this phase is to gather 'as full and comprehensive account from the child of an alleged incident, in the child's own words' as possible.[460] This narrative should not be interrupted by questioning from the interviewer, but should be reserved for the next stage of the interview.[461] This is because of the risk that a question could prematurely interrupt the flow of the child's account.[462]

The substantive part of the interview may finish at this point, if the child has said nothing that indicates that anything untoward has occurred or a satisfactory and verifiable explanation of events has emerged. The interviewers should then proceed to the closure phase.

However if the child has given some information about the alleged events, the interviewer can proceed to the third 'questioning phase'. Questions should be as open-ended as possible, moving towards specific questions on a particular area of the child's story which can then be used to clarify details and to probe inconsistencies.

The interviewer is strongly warned against using leading questions.[463] Where the interviewer believes that leading questions are tactically necessary, he is encouraged to revert to a neutral mode of questioning as and when the child volunteers information.

---

[457] ibid [2.39].   [458] *Achieving Best Evidence* (n 358) [2.42].
[459] ibid [2.100].   [460] ibid [2.101].   [461] ibid [2.101].
[462] ibid [2.101].
[463] Or as the Scottish guidelines put it, *mis*leading questions: *Guidance on Interviewing Child Witnesses in Scotland* (n 379) [97]–[98].

The interview does not have to contain each questioning stage. The interviewer may close the interview at any time if the child says nothing relevant to the allegation.

When the interviewer is ready to bring the interview to a close there should be a distinct closure phase of the interview. This phase should have two separate purposes. The first is a 'mopping up' exercise. He should go over the relevant information in the child's language. He should then thank the child for her time and effort and answer any questions that she might have.

The guidance is advisory only and does not constitute a legally enforceable code of conduct. *Achieving Best Evidence* does contain a warning that 'interviewers and other practitioners should bear in mind that significant departures from the guidance provided in this document may have to be justified in the courts'.[464] Interviews which fail to adhere to the guidance and are relied upon as evidence in a criminal case have to be considered on a case-by-case basis.

It will not necessarily be a question that can be determined by considering the nature and extent of the breaches that have occurred. It will depend on the extent to which passages in the evidence affected by the breaches are supported by other passages in respect of which no complaint can be made. It can depend also on the other evidence in the case and the extent to which this corroborates the evidence given in the video interviews.[465]

(e) Interview protocols in the United States

A great deal of effort has been expended to improve interviewing skills and practice.[466] However there is no standard protocol for interviewing children across the United States, while practice within some States remains variable.[467] There does not appear to be consensus on limiting the number of times that a child is interviewed. It has been estimated that on average a child will be interviewed 12 times before a criminal court case, including in some cases rehearsal of their testimony by prosecution attorneys.[468] Furthermore there are no universally enacting statutes authorizing and regulating child witness videotaping.[469] At least 39 States now explicitly allow at least some use of videotaped interviews of child victims, although no State as yet requires them to be used, or provides significant incentives for videotaping forensic interviews.[470] Lack of consistency may be attributed to defensive practice amongst prosecutors, who are afraid of defence and judicial criticism of the questioning of the child witness.

---

[464] *Achieving Best Evidence* (n 358) 1.

[465] *G v DPP* [1997] 2 All ER 755 (QBD), 759 (Phillips LJ); *Re D and Others* (CA 3 November 1995), 53 (Swinton Thomas LJ).

[466] JE Myers 'A Decade of International Legal Reform regarding Child Abuse Investigation and Litigation: Steps toward a Child Witness Code' (1996) 28 Pacific LJ 169, 176.

[467] L McGough 'Children as Victims and Witnesses in the Criminal Trial Process: Good Enough for Government Work: The Constitutional Duty to Preserve Forensic Interviews of Child Victims' (2002) 65 Law & Contemp Prob 179, 182.

[468] ME Lamb, KK Sternberg and PW Esplin 'Conducting Investigative Interviews of Alleged Sexual Abuse Victims' (1998) 22 *Child Abuse & Neglect* 813, 818–819.

[469] McGough 'Children as Victims and Witnesses (n 467) 190.		[470] ibid 182.

Some commentators have traced this reluctance back to the notorious cases in the 1990s, such as *McMartin*[471] and *Michaels*[472] in which the interviewing of children was rightly heavily criticized.[473] There are also significant constitutional concerns about the admissibility of videotaped interviews which are technically hearsay and so may breach the right of an accused to confront his accuser, which we discuss in detail later.[474]

The pragmatic response in some States has been to rehearse child witnesses for oral testimony in court and to discourage the videotaping of investigative interviews. Prosecutors have then relied upon hearsay statements of what the child said during interview given by investigators during their testimony to support the child's story.[475]

The more commonly-expressed prosecutorial fear is that a videotaped record fuels the effectiveness of cross-examination, and that overreaching, overzealous defense counsel will misuse any discrepancies in the child's account or flaws in the interviewer's elicitation of the narrative to undermine or even destroy the child's credibility.[476]

Such practice must hinder the development of clear protocols and reduce the consistency of initial interviews with children during an investigation. It must remain almost impossible to encourage consistent good practice if the process of interviewing a child at the initial stages of an investigation remains largely hidden.

The courts could encourage consistent practice in interviewing, but have not yet done so. For example the New Jersey Supreme Court in *State v Michaels* established a pre-trial 'taint hearing', to determine whether improper interviewing so far undermined the reliability of children's memories that their out-of-court statements or trial testimony should be excluded.[477] This is primarily a negative and case-limited process. An alternative mechanism, albeit unwieldy, for encouraging consistency was dismissed by the Ninth Circuit Court of Appeal, when it rejected claims that defendants have a constitutional due process right to have child witnesses in a child sexual abuse investigation interviewed in a particular manner.[478]

(f) Interview protocols in other jurisdictions

Although there is less information available about the interviewing process in other jurisdictions it appears that the same lesson may be learnt from the experiences of interviewing in New Zealand, Canada, and Australia. It is the videotaping of interviews

---

[471] Jury trial, no published opinion—discussed in *The People of the Territory Of Guam, Plaintiff-Appellee, v Thomas V. Mcgravey* (1994) 14 F 3d 1344 (US CA 9th Cir 1994), 1361.

[472] *State v Michaels* 642 A 2d 1372 (New Jersey Supreme Ct 1993), 1380.

[473] Myers 'New Era of Skepticism (n 382).

[474] See below Chapter 8 section B.3(b)(iii) and Chapter 9 section B.8.

[475] T Campbell 'Psychology and the Law: Interviewing Children: Taking Notes or Relying on Memory is Not Good Enough' (2002) 81 Michigan Bar Jnl 32, 33.

[476] McGough 'Children as Victims and Witnesses (n 467) 189.

[477] *State v Michaels* (n 472), 1380.

[478] *Devereaux v Abbey* (2001) 263 F 3d 1070, (USCA 9th Cir) 1080.

which increases the consistency of interviewing practices and reduces the number of times that a child may be interviewed.

Thus in New Zealand where videotaping of child interviews is very common and has been so since the late 1980s, there is a standard form for interviews, backed up by regulations which state what matters should be recorded.[479] Consistency appears to have been achieved because the interview may very well be seen by others. Interviews can be used as evidence in both civil and criminal proceedings.

In contrast, in Canada cognitive interviewing[480] is frequently used to gather evidence from children during investigations[481] and interviewers have often adopted the 'step-wise' approach to interviewing which has been the basis of *Achieving Best Evidence*.[482] This remains the closest to a standard form of interview for Canada. The need for clearer and more detailed interviewing protocols and better training for interviewers has been recognized.[483]

In 1996 the Australian Law Reform Commission found that there were no specific State laws concerning initial interviews with children, nor were there any specific guidelines for the conduct or length of the interview.[484] There were no formal court guidelines in the jurisdictions for training police officers or social workers or concerning the procedures for the interview. There have been acknowledged problems with repeated interviewing by a number of different agencies.[485] There have also been some concerns about coercive interviewing at the initial stages of the investigation. Any lack of consistency may again be linked to the fact that interviews may well not form the child's evidence in court. These interviews may be reported on by police witnesses but not seen. Like the United States, the lack of visibility of the interview means that there is little opportunity and impetus for interviewers to standardize practice.

---

[479] Evidence (Videotaping of Child Complainants) Regulations 1990 SR 1990/164.

[480] 'This consists of a package of mnemonic techniques (eg mental reinstatement of context; changing order of recall, etc) designed to assist witnesses to search their memory more exhaustively through multiple attempts at recall within a single interview session. The cognitive interview has been adapted for use with children, though it is not advised for children below a developmental age of 7, nor for incidents where there is a strong element of personal trauma': *Achieving Best Evidence* (n 358) [14.2.3].

[481] JP Schuman, N Bala and K Lee 'Developmentally Appropriate Questions for Child Witnesses' (1999) 25 Queen's LJ 251, 280, N Bala 'Child Witnesses in the Canadian Criminal Courts' (1999) 5 *Psychology Public Policy & Law* 323, 352.

[482] Secretariat to the Federal/Provincial/Territorial Working Group on Child and Family Services Information *Child Welfare in Canada—The Role of Provincial and Territorial Authorities in the Provision of Child Protection Services* (CFS information, Quebec 2002) <http://www.hrdc-drhc.gc.ca/socpol/cfs/cfs.shtml> (accessed 3 August 2004).

[483] N Bala 'Response to the Department of Justice Consultation Paper on Child Witnesses and the Criminal Justice System' (2000) <http://www.qsilver.queensu.ca/law/witness/witness.htm> (accessed 10 August 2004).

[484] Australian Law Reform Commission *Speaking For Ourselves: Children and the Legal Process* (1996 Commonwealth of Australia) [10.8–9] <http://www.austlii.edu.au/au/other/alrc/publications/issues/18/ALRCIP18Ch10.html# ALRCIP18Ch10InvestigationInterviewingchildren> (accessed 10 August 2004).

[485] Justice J Wood 'Child Witnesses—Best Practice For Courts' A paper presented at The Australian Institute of Judicial Administration: District Court of New South Wales, Parramatta, Friday 30 July 2004'.<http://www.aija.org.au/child/papers.htm> (accessed 6 October 2006).

(g) Evaluation—an example of procedure improving practice

The standard protocol for interviewing in England and Wales contains weaknesses. As we discuss in Chapter 8,[486] it remains questionable whether it produces evidence which is clear and easy for a jury to follow. It is not necessarily therapeutic in helping children to recover from abuse that they may have suffered. Nevertheless the admission of videotaped interviews as evidence in the civil and criminal courts has had an enormous impact on interviewing practice. In jurisdictions which do not routinely use videotaped interviews children may be repeatedly interviewed before a court case and the manner in which those interviews are conducted remains invisible to the court system. Videotaped evidence may save a child from some of the ordeal of giving evidence in court and, it appears, of being repeatedly interviewed, perhaps badly, before getting there.

3. Medical examination

(a) Guidance on medical examination in England and Wales

The nature of the current guidance on medical examinations has been primarily dictated from the findings of two inquiries, the *Cleveland Report* and the *Climbié Inquiry*. However unlike social workers or the police, doctors have been expected to develop the substance of their own protocols at either a national or local level. Guidance has been confined to statements of principle which the medical profession has had discretion on how to apply.

Much of the initial guidance stemming from the *Cleveland Report* and the subsequent civil child protection cases focused on the forensic requirements of the court. The most important of these requirements was the need to keep clear, accurate comprehensive and contemporaneous notes'.[487] In many of the court cases arising out of Cleveland, medical evidence was rejected for procedural reasons, often because there were incomplete or non-existent notes of examinations.[488] In taking a history of the child's complaint a doctor should be alive to the possibility of an evidential interview with the child and so should not question a child closely about the detail of his complaint. Just as interviewers were advised in the *Cleveland Report* to be 'alert to any indications of an innocent, as well as a sinister, interpretation' of the child's words,[489] doctors are advised to be open-minded in approaching an examination of a child.[490] However the *Cleveland Report* or the subsequent wardship cases did not suggest guidelines to be followed by the medical examiner. This was in sharp contrast to judicial

---

[486] In Chapter 8 section B.3(a).

[487] British Medical Association *Doctors' Responsibilities in Child Protection Cases: Guidance from the Ethics Department* (BMA, London 2004) 1.

[488] I Weyland 'The Response of Civil Courts to Allegations of Child Sexual Abuse' (1989) 19 Fam Law 240, 243.   [489] *Re M* [1987] 1 FLR 293 (Fam Div) 295B–D (Latey J).

[490] 'Dr Wyatt's only concern was to look for sexual abuse and he was not interested in investigating any other cause for his findings and any other condition from which the child was suffering' [1988] FCR 615 at 623B (Judge Cohen).

willingness to offer such suggestions about the conduct of investigative interviews. A model of diagnosis was suggested by Dr Zeitlin[491] which was very similar to the guidance given to interviewers by Latey J in *Re M*.[492]

The guidance stemming from the *Climbié Report* echoed some of the same concerns as the *Cleveland Report*. Again in Victoria's case the medical diagnosis of her injuries had a crucial impact upon social work decision-making. Injuries were misdiagnosed as signs of scabies and not indicative of abuse.[493] The doctors' conclusion that it was 'not a child protection issue' had an important impact upon how her case was handled by Brent social services.[494] As Parton has identified:

not only does the report demonstrate numerous examples where 'erroneous' medical diagnosis and communications had a tragic impact on the way that the case was handled by other professionals, but it also clearly argues that medical diagnosis and opinion must not be treated at face value and uncritically. Social workers, police officers and other doctors were all found culpable in this respect. The contribution of medical expertise cannot be seen as providing easy answers or be treated unproblematically.[495]

During the *Climbié Inquiry* it became clear that there had been major failures in the information management in relation to Victoria's case. A failure to write detailed notes of all the findings from the physical examinations of Victoria and a failure to note down observations about the child's behaviour and appearance had led to a minimization of the concerns about physical abuse. Lord Laming concluded that there was:

. . . a generalised failure at both hospitals to appreciate the importance of efficient information management as an integral part of Victoria's care. They also show a failure to recognise that competence in information management is no less critical in cases of deliberate harm to a child, than competence in diagnosis or competence in treatment.[496]

Victoria fell through the cracks in both the hospitals she attended. Examinations and further checks were put off, but not completed, and then assumed to be complete but not checked. Lord Laming concluded that 'Victoria's case clearly demonstrates the need for doctors and nurses to document information, actions and referrals consistently and unambiguously, to share that information, and to ensure subsequently that what has been agreed is carried through'.[497]

In response to the findings of the *Climbié Inquiry* the British Medical Association have issued guidance on *Doctors' Responsibilities in Child Protection Cases*. This is the most recent in the guidance issued by the professional medical bodies on medical

[491] H Zeitlin 'Investigation of the Sexually Abused Child' (1987) *The Lancet* 842.   [492] (n 489).
[493] *Victoria Climbié Inquiry* (n 9) [9.41–43].   [494] ibid [5.147].
[495] Parton 'From Maria Colwell to Victoria Climbié' (n 11) 87.
[496] *Victoria Climbié Inquiry* (n 9) [11.6].   [497] ibid [11.37].

issues in child protection[498] and is intended to augment the guidance issued by the Department of Health, *What to do if you're worried that a child is being abused.* The Royal College of Physicians was also asked by the Department of Health to make recommendations for training.[499] Much of the guidance issued by the professional bodies echoes the recommendations of the *Climbié Report*; for example the BMA's guidance recommends that 'any child admitted to hospital about whom there are concerns about deliberate harm must receive a thorough, carefully documented examination within 24 hours of their admission, except when doing so would compromise the child's care or the child's physical and emotional well-being'.[500]

This guidance attempts to avoid future problems in relation to the management of information in relation to medical examinations. However the problems which the *Cleveland* and *Climbié Reports* both identify concerning an uncritical acceptance of medical diagnosis in relation to child abuse are more insoluble. Diagnoses may only be questioned from a position of knowledge and understanding. Such confident discussion cannot be required by procedures. In fact procedures may have the unwonted effect of reducing the range of professional discretion and thus social workers' confidence in questioning other professionals' conclusions.[501]

(b) The development of guidance in other jurisdictions

Canada is the only jurisdiction which we have studied where the majority of Provinces and Territories have a mandatory medical examination as part of the investigation process.[502] The criteria for such an examination differ between jurisdictions. For example in the Yukon a medical examination should take place 'immediately' in cases of alleged child sexual abuse and serious physical abuse and 'as soon as possible' in cases of 'less serious physical abuse' and neglect.[503] The purpose of this examination appears to be evidence-gathering rather than treatment as 'less serious' physical abuse and neglect both might need as much, if not more, medical treatment as sexual assault. This may be contrasted with Child and Family Services Act 1997 s 7(3) j, 31 and 32 in the Northwest Territories which provides for a child to be medically examined if she 'requires medical treatment to cure prevent or alleviate serious physical harm or serious suffering and the child's parent does not provide, or refuses or is unavailable or unable to consent to the provision of the treatment'.[504] Thisprovision stretches further than a case of child abuse, to refusals for medical

---

[498] Royal College of Physicians *Physical Signs of Sexual Abuse in Children* (RCP, London 1991); Royal College of Physicians *Physical Signs of Sexual Abuse in Children* (RCP, London 1997).

[499] *Keeping Children Safe* (n 12) 11.

[500] *Doctors' Responsibilities in Child Protection Cases* (n 48) 5; *Victoria Climbié Inquiry* (n 9) recommendation [10.41].

[501] D Howe 'Child Abuse and the Bureaucratisation of social work' (1992) 40(3) *Sociological Review* 491. [502] With the exception of Newfoundland and Labrador.

[503] *Child Welfare in Canada* (n 482); (Manitoba,107; Saskatchewan, 125; Alberta, 144; British Columbia, 164).

[504] There is a similar provision in New Brunswick, *Child Welfare in Canada* ibid 53.

treatment in any case when the child is suffering. The requirements in Nova Scotia lie somewhere in between these two types: a medical examination should be conducted within 24 hours of a suspicion of physical abuse, but in cases of sexual abuse a medical examination should be conducted depending on the 'unique circumstances of each case'.[505]

At present a mandatory medical examination would not improve the particular problems evidenced in England, unless it had the knock-on effect of improving knowledge about the signs and symptoms of child abuse amongst all child protection professionals. The particular problems highlighted in the *Cleveland* and *Climbié Reports* were not linked to an avoidance of medical examinations, but were rather linked to limited knowledge of how child abuse should be diagnosed and a failure to treat the children involved as people who could be consulted on what had happened to them.

H. Further Phases of the Child Protection Process

Once information has been gathered the next stage of the child protection process may begin following a determination that there are ongoing child protection concerns. An inter-agency decision-making forum, the child protection conference is the place to bring all the information together on the child's health, development and functioning with information on the child's carers' abilities to promote these aspects, make decisions about the likelihood that a child will suffer significant harm in the future and decide what action is needed to 'safeguard the child and promote his welfare'.[506] If at the end of an investigation there is no evidence that a child has suffered significant harm, or is unlikely to do so, there will be no child protection conference. Similarly if the investigation finds that a child has been abused, but it is very unlikely that he or she will be again in the present circumstances (for example because the alleged abuser is in prison) there will be no child protection conference.

1. The child protection conference

(a) Organization of the conference

A child protection conference is a multi-agency meeting of the professionals most involved in a case together with the child's family and the child, where appropriate.[507] This should include a child's social worker, teacher, health visitor, doctor, and the police, but also can include other professionals with whom the child and her family have had contact. The purpose of this meeting is to bring together all those who have knowledge of the child's circumstances and to share information and skills in determining what should happen next. The existence of this meeting is symbolic of the ethos of *Working Together*, that no one agency has a monopoly of understanding

---

[505] ibid 37.   [506] *Working Together to Safeguard Children 2006* (n 31) [5.80].
[507] ibid [5.80].

and knowledge of child protection and of a child's individual case. The lesson from past scandals is that child protection decision-making is not and should not be simply placed on the shoulders of social workers. However the reality has often been very different. In the past there have been problems in ensuring that enough different types of professional attend. This led the authors of *Working Together to Safeguard Children 2006* to include a requirement that Local Safeguarding Children Boards' guidance define a quorum for attendance of a representative of the local authority children's social care team and at least two other professional groups or agencies, who have had direct contact with the child. It is difficult to see that this requirement will fundamentally improve the problem besetting conferences from their inception that child protection is only one of the duties of the other professionals involved with a child, and doctors or teachers often find it difficult to cancel their other work to attend conferences.[508]

An initial conference should be called when the agencies most involved in the inquiry 'judge that a child may continue to suffer, or be at risk of suffering significant harm'.[509] The purpose of the meeting is:

- to bring together and analyse in an inter-agency setting the information which has been obtained about the child's developmental needs, and the parents' or carers' capacity to respond to these needs to ensure the child's safety and promote the child's health and development within the context of their wider family and environment;
- to consider the evidence presented to the conference, make judgements about the likelihood of a child suffering significant harm in future and decide whether the child is at continuing risk of significant harm; and
- to decide what future action is required to safeguard and promote the welfare of the child, how that action will be taken forward, and with what intended outcomes.[510]

The main decision which the conference must reach is whether the child is at continuing risk of significant harm and so should be the subject of a child protection plan to reduce this risk through inter-agency help and intervention.[511] Guidance on the circumstances in which a plan should be written and carried out should be written in a local protocol by the Local Safeguarding Children Boards.[512] The conference should establish who will be the key worker charged with developing the detailed and inter-agency plan; who will be the core group of professionals involved in realizing the plan; what involvement the family should have in the process and the information that should be made available to them. The conference should identify what major work should be done, a timetable for that work and a contingency plan if the work is not achieved.[513] Where it is considered that the child is not at risk of significant harm

---

[508] Keenan *Procedures for the Investigation of Allegations of Child Sexual Abuse* (n 212), chapter 12.
[509] *Working Together to Safeguard Children 2006* (n 31) [5.79].   [510] ibid [5.80].
[511] ibid [5.102].   [512] ibid [5.105].   [513] ibid [5.105]–[5.118].

but he is in need of services the conference together with the family should consider the child's needs and what further help would assist the family in responding to them. If the child's needs are complex a child in need plan should be drawn up in line with the *Framework for the Assessment of Children in Need and their Families*.[514]

Following the initial conference if a decision is made to draw up a child protection plan for a child, a review conference should then be held within three months of the initial conference and then at six-month intervals thereafter until the child's name is removed from the register. The purposes of each of these review conferences are:

- to review 'the safety, health and development of the child against intended outcomes set out in the child protection plan',
- to ensure that the child continues to be protected; and
- 'to consider whether the child protection plan should continue in place or should be changed'.[515]

(b) Parental and child involvement

Whilst the rhetoric of the child protection conference may be about partnership between all the different agencies and the child's family, it has been acknowledged by *Working Together to Safeguard Children* that family and professionals meet to plan the child's future on a far from equal basis. Not only do the professionals have a familiarity with the process, each other, and each agency's respective roles, the local authority has the additional power of recourse to an application for a care order should they consider alternative solutions inappropriate. *Working Together* suggests strategies for the redress of this balance. It advocates that the family and the child are informed of the purpose of the conference, who will attend and the way in which the conference will operate.[516] It advises that their participation be planned carefully to avoid incidents where one family member or professional feels intimidated.[517]

A family member or child may also ask an advocate, friend or supporter to be with them.[518] Brandon *et al* found that in many cases parents did not bring a supporter, but when they did the supporter was greatly valued.[519] *Working Together* does not specifically address the question of whether the advocate accompanying the family member or child can be a solicitor. However the role of solicitors was considered in the case of *R v Cornwall CC ex p LH*.[520] Cornwall County Council as a matter of policy did not allow solicitors to represent family members at child protection conferences; it merely allowed them to attend for the purposes of reading out a prepared statement. Scott Baker J in the Family Division found these rules to be unlawful and contrary to the then statutory guidance *Working Together under the Children Act 1989*. He held that as a general rule solicitors ought to be allowed to attend and to participate, unless or until they undermined the purpose of the conference by making it unnecessarily

---

[514] *Framework for the Assessment of Children in Need* (n 29) [4.33]–[4.36].
[515] *Working Together to Safeguard Children 2006* (n 31) [5.102].   [516] ibid [5.84].
[517] ibid [5.84].   [518] ibid [5.84].
[519] M Brandon and others, *Safeguarding Children with the Children Act 1989* (HM Stationery Office, London 1999) 40.   [520] *R v Cornwall County Council ex p LH* (n 84).

confrontational.[521] In these circumstances the conference chair could determine that they should be excluded.

Although there have now been two versions of *Working Together to Safeguard Children* published since the events in this case took place, in neither does the guidance clarify the role of solicitors or other advocates for the parents. It merely suggests that social workers should inform parents about local advice and advocacy agencies and explain their entitlement to bring an 'advocate, friend, or supporter'.[522] Advocacy schemes for parents and carers of children have grown up in some areas of the country, although research by Lindley and Richards has found that the provision of advocacy remains variable, as does the reaction of local authorities to the presence of advocates in child protection conferences.

[I]t is still quite rare for advocates to become involved in such cases, with the result that, not surprisingly, there is some evidence of caution amongst professionals about their involvement, especially when they are not familiar with the advocate's work and/or when the advocate is being, or is perceived as being, confrontational.[523]

Lindley and Richards also found that many advocates had to develop their skills in providing advocacy in a child protection context 'on the hoof'. In response to this research, the Department of Health has funded a national protocol developed by Lindley and Richards to aid in the development of advocacy skills for child protection conferences in particular.

Some advocacy schemes are also available for children who wish to attend the conference or who have an advocate to attend in their stead to express their views. These schemes remain limited, with the children's charity Barnardo's as one of the few services that routinely offers advocacy to all young people over ten years of age in certain areas of the country. This scheme has been very well received by children using the service and a study by a team from the University of the West of England is due to be published soon.[524]

These welcome developments do not radically alter the nature of the child protection conference. It remains a professional decision-making body which determines the next course of action to which parents and children are invited guests.

2. Family group conferences

One alternative which has been adopted in certain parts of England is the family group conference. Pioneered in New Zealand, the family group conference has become the cornerstone of the child protection system in that jurisdiction, and holds a key place in the CYPFA 1989. Advocates of the family group conferencing system have argued that whilst the English and New Zealand systems share the same partnership rhetoric,

---

[521] ibid, 244C. [522] *Working Together to Safeguard Children 2006* (n 31) [5.84]

[523] B Lindley and M Richards *Protocol on Advice and Advocacy for Parents* (Centre for Family Research Cambridge 2002), 2.

[524] http://www.barnados.org.uk/whatwedo/working_with_children_and_young_people/advocacy.htm (accessed 6 October 2006).

only the New Zealand system makes real steps towards realizing parental and familial involvement in child protection decision-making.[525] The very different aims of the family group conference may be attributed in part to attempts to reflect Maori culture of wider familial involvement in decision-making.[526]

A family group conference should be convened[527] by a Care and Protection Coordinator if an investigation concludes that a child is in need of 'care and protection'.[528] The conference has been designed to be a meeting of the child, parents, *whanau*[529] or family group which professionals are invited to attend. Family Group is defined in CYPFA 1989 s 2 to include a child's extended family, adults to whom the child or young person has a significant psychological attachment; or who are in the child's or young person's *whanau* or other culturally recognized group. This includes cases when the child has more than one family. However a child's family group extends to neighbours and friends of the family.[530] Some professionals are entitled to attend the meeting: the Care and Protection Coordinator,[531] a social worker or police officer,[532] and an examining doctor, but they are meant to be witnesses who give information and advice to the conference, rather than the controllers of the conference. This difference is also reflected in the location of the conference, which may be held in homes or community centres as well as in social services offices. The conference should begin with an information session.

The convener of the conference, the Child Protection Coordinator, should at this point explain why the conference is being held, what the issues are that need to be resolved and what resources are available to help to resolve the problem. This should be in clear and uncomplicated language and in the first language of the family. Family members can also question professionals who have come to give evidence at this point. At the end of the information session the professionals should withdraw and the family should discuss in private about the future care and protection of the child. At the final stage of the conference the family reports back to all those attending the conference on its decisions and the conference as a whole should make a finding of whether or not there is a child protection problem and whether the proposed plan will keep the child safe.[533] According to research completed during the first year of implementation, conferences reach agreement in 90 per cent of cases.[534]

---

[525] P Marsh 'Partnership, Child Protection and Family Group Conferences—the New Zealand 'Children, Young Persons and their Families Act 1989' (1994) 6(3) JCL 109.

[526] Te-Ata-Tu *Report of the Ministerial Advisory Committee on a Maori Perspective for the Department of Social Welfare* (Wellington 1986).   [527] CYPFA 1989 (New Zealand) ss 18–20.

[528] As defined by CYPFA 1989 (New Zealand) s 14.

[529] A child's extended family, a group which is core to New Zealand's Maori Community.

[530] *CMP v D-GSW* [1997] NZFLR 1 (New Zealand High Court Auckland) 32.

[531] Who is appointed by the Director-General of Social Services (s 423 CYPF A 1989 (New Zealand)) and is authorized under the Act to convene Family Group Conferences (s 424(b) CYPFA 1989 (New Zealand)).

[532] When the conference has been convened on the basis of a social work or police inquiry report under s 18(1). CYPFA 1989 (New Zealand) s 22(1)(c).   [533] CYPFA 1989 (New Zealand) s 28.

[534] P Marsh and G Crow *Family Group Conferences in Child Welfare* (Blackwell Science 1998) 94.

If the recommendations and plans are agreed then social workers and the police 'shall give effect to that decision recommendation or plan', unless it is clearly impractical or clearly inconsistent with the principles set out in the Act.[535] The Coordinator does retain the power to refer the case to the family court if she feels that the child needs protection which cannot be achieved through the plan which the family has put forward and the family will not alter their position.[536]

Advocates of family group conferences account for some of the success of the conference system to the fact that it is mandated by the legislation.

Unless the Family Group Conference is a legally mandated process, it is susceptible to the changing views of changing policy makers and has the potential to become a weak shadow of its intended self. Issues of privacy and confidentiality become huge barriers, big enough to sabotage a social worker's best efforts, unless the legislation deals with entitlements and empowers the involvement of the family group. If extended family are not to be involved or even consulted in matters concerning their child or young person, the required protective monitoring networks, which need to be built around the child, cannot be put in place.[537]

The question remains however about the place of the child as opposed to the child's family in the process. As Hayes notes:

[T]he legal framework within which the family group conference is conducted exposes the child to a form of decision-making which may not have his or her best interests at heart … decision-making is placed in the hands of the family group in circumstances where it is possible that some of the decision-makers are the very same people who are endangering the child.[538]

As Hayes has explained, the legislators had such confidence in the ability of family members, who might not, after all, have been able to protect the child in the past, to put this behind them and consider the interests of the child in the future that a child's legal representative or advocate is also excluded by legislation from any decision-making by the family. This confidence must be misplaced. While it must be important to include the family, as without them many of the potential mechanisms for protecting the child are excluded, any system has to be based on the principle that the child's interests and well-being are at its core, not the family's interests.

Family group conferences are important to the English system because they clearly show that there are other, less professionalized ways of making decisions in child protection which can include the child's family, and they have already been used in parts of England and Wales. However they cannot be embraced wholeheartedly as the saviour for the problems in the English child protection conference, without adaptation to place the child and the child's views much more centrally within the process. Empirical evidence showing that the agreed plan is often not implemented[539] following family group conferences supports the view that proposals drawn up by

---

[535] CYPFA 1989 (New Zealand) ss 34, 35. [536] CYPFA 1989 (New Zealand) s 31.
[537] M Doolan 'The Family Group Conference Ten Years On' <http://www.iirp.org/library/vt/vt_doolan.html> (accessed 10 August 2004).
[538] M Hayes 'Protecting Children in England and New Zealand' (1999) 7 Canterbury LR 297, 306.
[539] Marsh and Crow (n 534) 96.

family members without the constant input of those whose primary role is to represent the child may simply fail in reality and hence not protect the child.

3. Child protection mediation

A third alternative is to embrace a form of mediation in child protection decision-making. Thirty States in the United States currently use some form of alternative dispute resolution to resolve child protection cases, rather than going to court.[540] These include family group conferencing,[541] facilitated family group meetings and mediation.[542] Mediation may occur at any interval in a child protection case. Some programmes mediate at the initial hearing or at any point until a final adoption or the child returns home. Other programs focus at a particular point in the court process such as at emergency hearings, adjudication, or termination of parental rights. The mother who is usually assumed to be the main carer, her attorney, an attorney for child services, the caseworker, and the child's representative, who may or may not be an attorney, are usually present. Fathers and their attorneys, other relatives, foster parents, and court-appointed special advocate volunteers may also attend. Children may participate depending on their age and maturity level.[543] During the mediation, the legal and social work professionals assigned to the case, together with the parents, develop a case plan or determine where a child will live, the contact arrangements she will have with her family and resolve disputes between parents and the state. In some States such as California, mediation is used a great deal and has a high success rate in reaching a resolution of cases that all parties are happy with. The requirement to consider mediation in child protection cases has now been incorporated into the California Welfare and Institution Code.[544]

Some Provinces and Territories in Canada have also incorporated a power to mediate[545] or hold a group conference into statute. The Child Family and Community Services Act 1996 in British Columbia gives a director as the designate of the Minister the power to offer to refer the child's parents or other family members to a conference, once an investigation has concluded that a child is in need of protection.[546] If the family and the director are unable to resolve the questions about the child's safety or agree a plan of care the parties may enter into mediation or alternative forms of dispute

---

[540] 'Child Dependency Report Office of the Executive Secretary of the Supreme Court of Virginia' (November 2002). <http://www.courts.state.va.us/publications/child_dependency_mediation_report.pdf> (2 July 2004).

[541] As discussed above in relation to New Zealand section H.2.

[542] S Brooks 'A Family Systems Paradigm For Legal Decision Making Affecting Child Custody' (1996) 6 Cornell L Rev 1, 22.

[543] K Brown Olson 'Child Protection In The 21st Century: Lessons Learned from a Child Protection Mediation Program: If at First You Succeed and then You Don't' (2003) 41 Fam Ct Rev 480.

[544] California Welfare & Institution Code §350(a)(2).

[545] See Child Youth and Family Services Act 1998 (Newfoundland) 1998 s 13; Child and Family Services Act 1989–90 (Saskatchewan) s 15; Children's Act 1986 (Yukon) s 42; Child and Family Services Act (Northwest Territories) 1990 s 21(1) which allow the appointment of a mediator.

[546] Child Family and Community Services Act (British Columbia) 1996 c 26 s 20.

resolution.[547] There is also a power to delay any court proceedings for a period of up to three months so that any of these alternative mechanisms to resolve residual concerns about the child's safety may be tried.[548] The Northwest Territories and Nunavut have a slight variation to this model—a 'plan of care committee', which may be convened when there are concerns that a child is in need of protection.[549] The core members of this committee are the child's parents, the child (if she is aged 12 or over and wishes to attend), a member of the child's community (who is a member of that community's child and family services committee) and a child protection worker. The committee is responsible for drawing up a plan of care and may co-opt other family members or professionals on to the committee to do so.[550] It may also request services for the child and her family in order to fulfil the plan of care.[551]

To sum up, child protection decisions at this stage cannot simply be placed in the hands of professionals if they are to acknowledge sufficiently the important place of the child's family in her future protection. Many child protection plans are premised on the willingness of a member of the child's family to look after her or at least to play some role in her life. While it must be acknowledged that children's families should be intrinsic to decision-making at this stage and must not be placed in a position where they are effectively intimidated into silence by the professionals and their decision-making structures, it cannot be forgotten that the process is primarily about the child. In a desire to acknowledge families in child protection, New Zealand legislation appears to have lost the focus on the child. In contrast the best practice of advocacy in England and mediation in the United States and Canada, appears to have facilitated greater participation by both children and their families.

4. The decision to apply for a civil order to protect the child

The Children Act 1989 does not place the local authority under a duty to take steps to protect a child following an inquiry. There are clear judicial statements that in cases where children are found to be at risk of suffering significant harm within the meaning of the Children Act 1989 s 31, a clear duty arises on the part of local authorities to take steps to protect them. In such circumstances, a local authority is required to assume responsibility and to intervene in the family arrangements in order to protect the child or children. In Eekelaar's commentary on the Children Act 1989 before its implementation, he expressed surprise there was no provision equivalent to that of Children and Young Persons Act 1969 s 2(2). This section had placed the local authority under a duty to bring court proceedings in cases when it judged that a child was suffering or likely to suffer significant harm but the parents refused local authority offers of services and support, unless it determined that this was neither in

---

[547] Child Family and Community Services Act (British Columbia) 1996 c 26 s 21.
[548] ibid c 26 s 23.
[549] If an investigation concludes that a child is not in need of protection the plan of care committee should be disbanded: Child and Family Services Act 1997 (Northwest Territories) c 13 s 13(2).
[550] Child, Family and Community Service Act 1996 (British Columbia) s 14(3.1).
[551] ibid s 14(6).

the interests of the child nor the public. No amount of judicial guidance can force the local authority into taking action which it has decided against. This is illustrated by *Nottinghamshire CC v P*[552] where the court at first instance did everything within its power by judicial statement and by a direction to the local authority to conduct an investigation of the child's circumstances. This was in the vain hope that the local authority, required by the Children Act 1989 s 37(2) to consider 'whether they should apply for a care or supervision order with respect to the child' would in fact decide to apply for a supervision order.

I. Further Phases of a Criminal Investigation

The initial stages of an investigation are completed by both the police and social services, working together to establish whether there is any evidence that a child has been abused. However, once some evidence has been established, the very different purposes of the two organizations begin to emerge. The child's parent, with whom social services may wish to work to establish whether he may able to care for the child in the future, may also be a person whom the police wish to interview as a potential suspect of a criminal offence. It is at this point that the ideals of *Working Together* are almost impossible to achieve. Social workers wish the parent to admit any abuse as they would consider that this is the beginning of the process of working with the child's family to protect the child in the future. Admission by the parents may mean that social workers decide not to apply for a care order. However an admission to the police almost certainly means that they will mount a prosecution. Offences relating to child abuse are notoriously difficult to prove. Usually child abuse takes place in the secrecy of the home. Most victims and suspects live together therefore forensic evidence is difficult to find. As it is usually a 'family matter' the loyalty of family members means that witnesses are very difficult to find. Child victims themselves are usually inarticulate and scared. Thus a confession by a suspect is vital to building a criminal case. What this means is that the fact of police involvement will often hamper social work goals in getting carers to admit what has happened so that work may be undertaken to try and ensure that it does not happen again. This is the point where currently those working in child protection cannot currently 'work together' if the goals of their individual professions are to be achieved. In Chapter 7 we consider the extraordinarily difficult issues of disclosure to the police of evidence obtained at a child protection conference.[553]

1. Interview with the suspect

The basic standards for interrogation of suspects are set down in the Police and Criminal Evidence Act 1984 Code C. An empirical study by Hughes, Parker and Gallagher of the police experience of investigating sexual abuse found that interviews with those

---

[552] [1993] 2 FLR 134 (CA), 143 (Stephen Brown P).   [553] See Chapter 7 section C.1(a).

suspected of child abuse presented particular problems that standard interviewing training did not address, and that training in interviewing of suspects should be 'an immediate priority'.[554] However the problem remains that the techniques of interviewing a child abuse suspect are little discussed, at least publicly. Although the very important review by HMIC[555] was wide-ranging in its consideration of the role of the police in the investigation of alleged child abuse, it did not specifically consider the current standards of suspect interviewing nor did it suggest further reforms in skills and training. Whilst there are specialist interviewers of children in child abuse cases, the usual practice has been that the same officers from the Child Abuse and Investigation Protection Unit (CAIU) did not conduct the interview of the suspect. Instead this task would be handed over to a detective who routinely conducts interviews with suspects. However this could mean that a CID detective did not build up a reservoir of experience about child abuse cases on which he could draw. He might only interview a few people accused of a crime related to child abuse in his professional career. This fragmentation of work may explain why training in interviewing those suspected of committing crimes against children had not been systematically developed.

This may change if the recommendation of the *Climbié Inquiry* that more officers in CAIU are trained in criminal investigation is carried through to its natural conclusion in practice.[556] In its 2005 report HMIC indicated that many forces had increased the number of members of the CAIUs who had been trained as detectives.[557] One of the problems hitherto has been that those working in child protection have not had the skills in interviewing suspects which would allow them to complete the entire investigation. If the majority of officers in CAIUs become detectives this would allow them to build up a reservoir of knowledge about the investigation of an entire case which could be of vital importance in creating specialist child abuse suspect interviewers. Now that many officers are conducting whole investigations the standard of suspect interviews may improve. Hitherto there was a poor picture of suspect interviews revealed in the *Bristol Study* of the admissibility and sufficiency of evidence in child abuse cases[558] and Cobley, Sanders and Wheeler's study of alleged shaken baby cases.[559] The origins of these problems were because police interviewers were trained to obtain the suspect's account of the time period during which the alleged assault occurred, and then to identify inconsistencies within this account, or discrepancies between the suspect's account and that of the child. Cases of abuse usually involve people who know each other, and who share family routines. Their accounts tend to be very similar except, usually, regarding the alleged incident. Interviews can follow a familiar pattern. The interviewer will put a particular allegation that the complainant had made. The suspect will then deny it. The vast majority of suspects have little reason to offer any account of the events related by the child, beyond their own feelings of

---

[554] Hughes, Parker and Gallagher (n 446), 26–27.   [555] *Keeping Safe, Staying Safe* (n 96).
[556] *Victoria Climbié Inquiry* (n 9) Recommendation 103.   [557] *Keeping Safe, Staying Safe* (n 96).
[558] *Bristol Study*, 25–26.
[559] C Cobley, T Sanders and P Wheeler 'Prosecuting Cases of Suspected "Shaken Baby Syndrome"—A Review of Current Issues' [2003] Crim LR 93.

guilt and repentance if they have indeed sexually abused a child. Unlike the cases involving a physical assault, there is usually little or no medical evidence.

In cases of physical abuse suspects in the cases in the *Bristol Study* did try to explain why the children for whom they were caring had signs of injury.[560] In some cases this included an admission that some of the child's injuries could not have been caused accidentally, or that he had noticed the child's injuries but had failed to take her for medical treatment. Any apparently innocent explanation could open up further lines of inquiry aimed at confirming or undermining the story. A study of the prosecution of alleged 'shaken baby' cases by Cobley, Sanders and Wheeler, found that very few suspects were prepared to admit that they had shaken the child; and unlike the suspects in the *Bristol Study* 'the most common response when interviewed was to deny any knowledge of how the injury was caused or to blame an accident'.[561] In some cases alternative explanations were offered; such as blaming a partner, a sibling, or birth complications, none of which seemed likely to open up successful lines of enquiry.

There appears to be very little incentive for confession of child abuse. Cobley has argued that this could be altered in cases in which the abuser is a family member if the goals of the child protection and criminal justice system were to be considered together and there is a reconsideration of the place of the confession in the prosecution of child abuse.[562] She argues that in the same way as there is an incentive in child protection for carers to admit if they have abused a child because it means that there may not be an application for a court order, consideration should be given to rewarding confession in prosecution. This could be achieved either by using it as a basis to decide that the case should not be prosecuted on the ground that the risk of further abuse is now reduced or that prosecution would hinder family rehabilitation. Alternatively it could be used to guide the type of sentence imposed to favour family therapy and rehabilitation, rather than straight incarceration. What Cobley's argument demonstrates is that the question of confession must be considered across the types of systems dealing with child abuse and the notorious problems of encouraging confession to child abuse be approached constructively and at all levels. It is important that a child's rights to protection are not bargained away in order to ensure a confession and that any bargain made is with the interests of the child at its centre.

2. The search for corroboration

The police investigation should also search for evidence which may corroborate or refute a child's story. This again should be a specialized process. Although child abuse is often described as a secret crime, witnesses may be useful in providing evidence of opportunity to commit the alleged acts. In cases of physical assault or neglect, witnesses might have seen some of the behaviour which forms the basis for the charge, or know about hostility between the adult and the child which could be admissible as

[560] *Bristol Study*, 25–26.   [561] Cobley *et al* (n 560) 98–99.
[562] C Cobley, "Working Together?"—Admissions of Abuse in Child Protection Proceedings and Criminal Prosecutions' (2004) 16.2 Child and Family LQ 175, 177.

background evidence.[563] In some cases a number of children might have made very similar allegations against the suspect. Medical evidence can be important, particularly in cases of physical assault. It would be unusual for a case of physical assault to proceed without medical evidence of non-accidental injury. Specialist guidance available to officers investigating incidents where it is suspected that a baby sustained injury from shaking emphasizes the importance of visiting the scene of the suspected crime, preserving forensic evidence, and video-recording a reconstruction of events wherever possible.[564] However as discussed above in section E evidence can be lost if a case is filtered out at the stage of an initial assessment and social workers become the sole investigators. HMIC identified cases in which potential witnesses were not identified and interviewed, inconsistencies in the suspect's story were not probed and evidence of injuries were minimized.[565]

3. The evaluation of the evidence collected

The police will conduct an initial evaluation of the evidence collected to determine whether there is sufficient evidence to lay a charge against a person suspected of abusing a child. They may determine at this point that there is no evidence on which to proceed. The police may filter out cases of physical assault which might be considered by a jury to be a case of reasonable chastisement at this point, or even earlier. This does seem to be the fault of a lack of clarity in the criminal law in relation to the hitting of children. As discussed above in Chapter 3 section D.4 the question of whether an assault is reasonable chastisement remains a jury matter so there is no precedent on what constitutes chastisement in this context. Research undertaken before the Children Act 2004 s 58 reforms demonstrated a pattern of police officers being over-cautious in the assault cases which they were referring to the CPS, because of the existence of the defence of reasonable chastisement, and the social context of the defence which accepted a certain level of violence towards children for the purpose of punishment.[566] Alternatively if the police consider that the case may be prosecuted they must refer the case and file on to a crown prosecutor who will make a final decision on whether to prosecute the case. The CPS applies a two-stage sequential test in the decision to prosecute set out in the Code for Crown Prosecutors:

(a) The *evidential test*: is there enough evidence to provide a realistic prospect of conviction for each defendant on each charge?

If this test is satisfied prosecutors should then consider:

(b) The *public interest* test: do the factors in favour of prosecution outweigh those against prosecution?[567]

---

[563] See Chapter 10 section B.4(a)(i).

[564] P Wheeler and M McDonagh *A Report into the Police Investigation of Shaken Baby Murders and Assaults in the UK* (Home Office, London 2002).   [565] *Keeping Safe, Staying Safe* (n 96), [5.42].

[566] C Keenan and L Maitland 'There ought to be a law against it' [1999] Child and Family LQ 397.

[567] CPS *Code for Crown Prosecutors* (2004) <http://www.cps.gov.uk/victims_witnesses/code.html>.

The process by which the CPS operate this two-stage test remains largely opaque. The CPS Policy Directorate's publication of CPS Policy on *Prosecuting Criminal Cases involving Children and Young People as Victims and Witnesses*[568] in 2006, has done nothing to dispel the secrecy with which a decision on the sufficiency of evidence or the public interest in prosecuting is made. With regard to the question of what evidence of an offence against a child is 'good evidence' the Policy states:

> We will work with the police to build strong cases by collecting good evidence, but we will stop cases where the evidence is not strong enough for the court to find the defendant guilty. We cannot prosecute if there is not enough evidence that can be used in a trial.[569]

In relation to the question of how the public interest test is interpreted by Crown Prosecutors, there is a clear implication that it should usually be considered in the public interest to prosecute serious cases of child abuse:

> We think carefully about the effect on children and their families when we make these decisions. The younger a child is the more careful we will be. There may be several children involved. What is best for one of them may not be best for all of them. There will often be adults involved as well and we have to think how our decisions will affect them. If a crime against a child is serious, and the evidence is strong enough, we will nearly always prosecute. We will always think about the effect on that child of going to court, and make sure there is good support before, during and after the trial.[570]

This claim is belied by numerous recent empirical studies.[571]

(a) Application of the sufficiency of evidence test

The *Bristol Study* found that the most crucial piece of evidence in a sexual abuse case was the child's account.[572] In judging the evidential strength of this account the police and CPS looked for clarity, detail and consistency. An assessment of the child's demeanour in giving her account included a consideration of whether the child's manner of describing the abuse was in keeping with society's image of how an abused child 'should' behave in an interview. Some evidence supporting the child's account was felt to be necessary before a case of sexual abuse could be prosecuted. However, the strength of the additional evidence required was dependent on the clarity and consistency of the child's account. Where a child's testimony was considered to be exceptionally clear and detailed, evidence of opportunity might be considered sufficient. When the child's account was vague or inconsistent, a case would only be prosecuted where there was other strong evidence supporting the child's account, such as clear medical signs or testimony from other children who were making similar allegations. Cases of alleged sexual abuse were examined to see whether there was

---

[568] CPS Policy Directorate *CPS Policy on Prosecuting Criminal Cases involving Children and Young People as Victims and Witnesses* (CPS Policy Directorate, London 2006).   [569] ibid 7.
[570] ibid, 8.   [571] Chapter 8 section B.4.   [572] *Bristol Study* 32–35.

anything in the child's past which could be used to suggest that she was an untruthful or otherwise unreliable witness.[573]

In contrast, the child's account had little weight in a decision to prosecute physical abuse. Cases were most likely to be prosecuted which had medical evidence of a serious assault on a young child and where the suspect had previously been suspected of an assault on a child. Conversely, cases of physical assault were less likely to be prosecuted when the complainant was older and had behaved badly in the prelude to the assault. In these cases it was considered that the suspect could raise the defence of 'reasonable parental chastisement'. Cases were also less likely to be prosecuted when social services were working with the suspect to modify his behaviour.[574] When the injured child was younger, while there was not a question that the jury might ask whether the child deserved a beating or shaking, prosecutors were aware of the 'there but for the grace of God go I' factor in decision-making. All parents understand that young children can put carers under extreme stress and pressure. Prosecutors did consider whether the jury might decide that this case was evidence of parents under extreme stress on one occasion rather than systematic abuse.[575]

(b) Application of the public interest test

The Code for Crown Prosecutors provides a number of factors which a prosecutor should consider in evaluating whether a case satisfies the public interest test. Some of these can be particularly relevant in child abuse cases: the defendant was in a position of authority or trust; there is evidence that the offence was pre-meditated; the victim was vulnerable; there was a marked difference in the ages of the defendant and the victim; the offence had an element of corruption; and the offence was committed in the presence of or in close proximity to other children. Factors to be weighed against prosecution which may be relevant in child abuse cases include, the level of the penalty which the defendant might receive, and whether the victim's mental or physical health would suffer as a result of the prosecution.[576]

There has been little research undertaken on use of the public interest test by crown prosecutors in evaluating child abuse cases. The *Bristol Study* found that prosecutors could vary widely in their interpretation of the public interest test in a child abuse case.

It is in the public interest that we're not just doing it for political reasons; there are political pressures, but we are dealing with real people, not just with thieves; not even adults, we're dealing with children. I do believe in the public interest test in this field . . . It is very difficult to [define the public interest] in this context, but for example, if it's one against one, no corroboration and a six-year-old child, are you going to put that child into the witness box? Is it in the public interest? There has to be something in it . . . If the complainant ends up getting humiliated in court and there's no conviction anyway . . . what do the public get out of it? They have to get something out of it . . . We're not just here to gratify a desire to prosecute perverts.[577]

---

[573] *Bristol Study* 32–41.   [574] ibid 41–44.   [575] Cobley *et al* (n 559), 101.

[576] *CPS Policy on Prosecuting Criminal Cases Involving Children and Young People* (n 568) 8–13.

[577] *Bristol Study* 31.

In contrast, some lawyers operated a presumption that it was in the public interest to prosecute all cases of child sexual abuse, evidence permitting. 'It is our duty to send more cases, not less ... to educate the court about what they can reasonably expect from a child'.[578]

Their attitudes reflected a clear division between pragmatism and principle which underscores much of the child abuse investigation.

J. Evaluation: Legal Procedures to Guide the Inquiry Process: A Help or a Hindrance for Investigators?

The substance of the law governing the investigation of child abuse has been largely driven by scandal and the need to prevent particular crises and tragedies from happening in the future. There is a great temptation to attempt to ensure that past problems do not recur by subjecting certain aspects of the investigation process to further regulation by statute or procedure.

Child protection practice does appear to benefit from legislation with clearly articulated principles, particularly when those principles are consistently repeated in the accompanying procedures. There are examples of clear child-focused legislative principles to guide investigative work in Australia and Canada. The law may also contribute to best practice by ensuring that child protection work is scrutinized. For example, the advent of video-recording of children's testimony has made the practice of interviewing children visible to other investigators and to the courts. In jurisdictions where investigative interviews with children are not consistently video-recorded, notably the United States, practice remains inconsistent and needlessly traumatic for the child witness. The courts can also act to support children and their families and ensure that children are not removed from their homes without scrutiny of the evidence and a consideration of the range of options available. In jurisdictions such as the United States where the courts are routinely excluded from this decision and where the legislative principles are unclear, children and their families may be permanently separated on the basis of weak and ultimately unjustifiable grounds.

The law has also contributed to some of the problems which have beset child protection practice. There has been a constant addition of new layers of legislation and procedures to guide investigators in the hope of forestalling the recurrence of past mistakes. This continual reinvention breeds its own problems. Investigators can be overwhelmed by the sheer amount of information which they are expected to digest. The guidance is so dense that it is difficult to understand and remember easily from the first or even the third reading. This is also an apt description of the guidance directly concerning the investigation of allegations of child abuse. In addition the *post hoc* critical scrutiny of practice by the courts and public inquiries has understandably led to a defensive attitude amongst investigators. This defensiveness in turn has affected

---

[578] *Bristol Study* 31.

the implementation of procedures, particularly fostering rigidity in the interpretation of guidance.[579]

It seems that law which aims to coerce professionals into particular behaviour has not been very successful. For example all jurisdictions share some of the same problems whether or not they have a mandatory reporting law on their statute book. Confusion over the threshold for reporting and concerns about confidentiality prevent those who have suspicions that a child is being abused from reporting some concerns. Experience elsewhere indicates that mandatory reporting laws can lead to situations in which social service departments are swamped with reports, which can lead to an increase in inappropriate or inadequate responses in individual cases.[580] This does appear to be a situation where an absolute obligation does not solve the problem; professionals may regard the concerns in individual cases as nuanced and blanket standards inappropriate. Professional behaviour might be altered by rigorous prosecution or an action in negligence, but clearly it would be better to concentrate on convincing professionals that a child's position would be significantly improved if they did report their concerns, rather than again to use the creation of fear of legal repercussions to compel a certain type of behaviour. In relation to the public, clear standards which are freely available to guide everyone on when suspicions should be reported are more appropriate. Child welfare agencies' use of websites in particular have set the standard on appropriate and useful dissemination of information, for those not working in the field who wish to report a suspicion of child abuse.

[579] C Keenan 'The Use of Folk Law in Child Protection Practice' (2002) 32 Fam Law 838.
[580] In New South Wales the first independent review by the ombudsman found that 55% of the cases reported had been 'mishandled': M Rayner 'The State of Children's Rights in Australia' in B Franklin (ed) *The New Handbook of Children's Rights—Comparative Policy and Practice* (Routledge, London 2002) 345, 347.

PART IV

ADJUDICATION OF THE
ALLEGATION

6

Introduction: Themes and Influences

Until the last decade, English law accepted without question that the evidence of all children, and all complainants of sexual assault regardless of age, must be regarded with deep scepticism. The perception has been that children are prone to fantasy, that they are suggestible, and that their evidence is inaccurate,[1] even though these sweeping assumptions have been challenged by empirical psychological studies of children's reliability as witnesses. The equally unfounded assumption that females are prone to fabricate allegations of sexual assault has imposed a double burden of suspicion on female children who disclose sexual abuse. As recently as 1993 English trial judges were reprimanded by the appellate courts for expressing scepticism to juries about the conventional direction that false allegations about sexual offences are easy to make and very difficult to challenge.[2] These fallacies underpinned the common law rules of evidence, which were often codified by statute. Although legislative reforms since 1988 have sought to expel these stereotypical views from the law, the legacy of the old rules lingers in some corners of legal doctrine, and influences the practices of those in the criminal justice system responsible for prosecuting and adjudicating allegations of child abuse.

Not only was the reliability of such witnesses suspect; the competence of jurors to give evidence its appropriate weight was also doubted by 19th and 20th century

---

[1] For a classic exposition and advocacy of this view, see J Heydon *Evidence: Cases and Materials* (2nd edn Butterworths, London 1984) 84 (now Heydon J of the High Court of Australia).

[2] *R v Chambers* (The Times 6 May 1993) (CA) (complaints of indecent assault of three sisters under 13 at bathtime); *R v Izard* (1992) 156 JPN 826; The Times (22 June 1992) (CA) (reversible error to direct jury that false allegations are made 'very occasionally'. While such directions were necessary accompaniments to the mandatory corroboration warning, trial judges still frequently give the caution to juries.

judges. Whilst lauding the institution of the jury as trier of fact,[3] at the same time they erected over the adversarial trial system an extraordinarily intricate superstructure of legal rules to intercept information which, it was thought, might derail the jurors' reasoning from the 'correct' mode, and to instruct juries on how to use the evidence which did reach them.

In recent years however there has been a growing appreciation that modern jurors are both better educated and more experienced in evaluating the reliability of the information with which they are bombarded on a daily basis. This has stimulated both judicial and political reformers to attack rules labelled as 'arcane' and 'ossified', and 'founded on a lack of faith in the capacity of the trier of fact properly to evaluate evidence'.[4] The Government's 2002 White Paper setting out its reform project for the criminal justice system in England and Wales adopted as its premise that evidence relevant to the search for truth is wrongly excluded by legal rules which are 'difficult to understand and complex to apply in practice', and that magistrates, judges and juries should be trusted to give 'appropriate' evidence 'the weight it deserves' when they exercise their judgment.[5] With a comprehensive Evidence Code promised[6] but still on the far horizon, it is likely that those participating in the child protection system will still have to contend with the current *mélange* of common law and statutory rules, many of them controversial, and some archaic, for some time to come.

Part IV explores the complexities of the matrix of legal rules of evidence which currently are most germane to the investigation and adjudication of allegations of child abuse, and analyses both the underlying reasoning and judicial interpretation of the statutory rules and the extant common law doctrines.[7] We will compare the adversarial model of the criminal trial with the hybrid inquisitorial/adversarial model adopted in civil child protection proceedings. We will identify discrepancies in the procedures and admissible evidence in cases which may proceed in tandem in the criminal and family courts.

In this exploration, it is crucial to bear in mind that child abuse cases are unique in that it is not just seasoned judges and lawyers who must navigate the shoals of the law of evidence; so too must the investigators, because of their anomalous role in not just collecting evidence but also adducing the testimony-in-chief of child witnesses. A criminal prosecution or a civil case may stand or fall on non-lawyers' understanding of legal rules with which even experienced lawyers can feel a degree of discomfort.

---

[3] Sir Patrick Devlin *Trial by Jury* (Stevens & Sons, London 1956) 164.

[4] *R v Smith* [1992] 2 SCR 915 (SCC) [31] [40].

[5] Home Office *Justice for All* (CM 5563 HMSO, London July 2002) [4.52]–[4.53].

[6] ibid [4.51]. The Home Office proposes to place on a statutory footing a Criminal Procedure Rules Committee chaired by the member of the higher judiciary to oversee the development of a criminal evidence code and a criminal procedure code, but no timescale was given for implementation in the White Paper.

[7] This is not intended to be a comprehensive discussion of the law of Evidence; the reader is referred to the leading modern texts: C Tapper *Cross & Tapper on Evidence* (10th edn Butterworths London 2004); A Keane *The Modern Law of Evidence* (6th edn LexisNexis UK, London 2005); P Roberts and A Zuckerman *Criminal Evidence* (OUP, Oxford 2004); I Dennis *The Law of Evidence* (3rd edn Sweet & Maxwell, London 2007).

A. Systems with Different Objectives?

The divergent procedures and evidential rules of the family and criminal courts are often justified on the basis that they have different objectives: in the family courts the paramount consideration is the best interests of the child, whereas in the criminal courts the wider public interest in a fair trial and justified verdict is the overarching principle. However, this assertion can be facile. Crown Prosecutors are instructed to consider the best interests of the child in relation not only to the decision to prosecute but also in relation to the conduct of the trial.[8] The family courts must comply with the Human Rights Act 1998, and so must consider the rights of the parents or carers to a fair trial, and to privacy and to a family life, guaranteed by Articles 8 and 6 of the European Convention on Human Rights (ECHR).

B. Inquisitorial versus Adversarial Inquiries?

It is frequently said that the primary procedural difference between the two systems is that fact-finding in the family court is the result of an inquisitorial inquiry,[9] whereas in the criminal court it is adduced and tested in an adversarial forum. However, the process of fact-finding in child protection proceedings involves adversarial cross-examination of each party's witnesses, and all parties have the right to be heard and to present evidence.[10] It is fallacious to assert that any type of judicial proceeding is either wholly adversarial or wholly inquisitorial.[11] The process whereby the local authority has to establish the existence of the threshold criteria to justify public intervention in the life of the family has been described as largely adversarial, with the proceedings adopting an inquisitorial nature only at the next stage, where the issue is what would best promote the welfare of the child.[12] The label matters, because as we shall see it has consequences for such issues as whether litigation privilege may be invoked in that phase of the proceedings.[13]

In both court systems the critical threshold for invoking the courts' powers is evidence of physical or sexual abuse or neglect of the child, by an identified perpetrator. True, the family courts' inquiry looks specifically to the future,[14] and so must be predictive: is the child likely to suffer significant harm, and is that likelihood of

---

[8] Crown Prosecution Service *Children and Young People: CPS Policy on Prosecuting Criminal Cases Involving Children and Young People As Victims and Witnesses* (27 June 2006).

[9] *Re L (A Minor) (Police Investigation: Privilege)* [1997] AC 16 (HL) 26 (Lord Jauncey).

[10] *Re B (Minors) (Disclosure of Medical Reports)* [1993] 2 FCR 241 (Fam Div).

[11] Even criminal proceedings, since the Criminal Procedure and Investigations Act 1996 has imposed a duty of disclosure on the defence.

[12] *Re R (Care: Disclosure: Nature of Proceedings)* [2002] 1 FLR 755 (Fam Div Charles J) 772, citing *Re M (A Minor) (Care Orders: Threshold Conditions)* [1994] AC 424 (HL) and *Re H (Minors: Sexual Abuse: Standard of Proof)* [1996] AC 563 (HL).

[13] *S County Council v B* [2000] 2 FLR 161 (Fam Div Charles J) 185.

[14] *Re M (A Minor) (Disclosure of Material)* [1990] 2 FLR 36 (CA) 42 (Butler-Sloss LJ).

harm attributable to her care?[15] However this prediction must be based upon factual evidence about the child and her past and current environment.

As Lord Nicholls has pointed out, attaching the 'bewitching label of inquisitorial' to child protection cases can all too easily divert attention from the crucial question as to what fairness demands in the context of that type of proceedings.[16] Child protection proceedings have been described as difficult to characterize because they are 'a unique amalgam of elements—criminal, civil, family, administrative'.[17] This ambiguity makes it singularly difficult to develop evidence and procedural rules which accommodate the competing tensions in child protection proceedings.[18] There is a temptation to dispense with the rules of evidence in family law proceedings on the assumption that they impede rather than further the search for truth. However, it has rightly been pointed out that the involvement of the state in child protection raises many of the same concerns as criminal law, in particular its heightened concern for accuracy in fact-finding and its special concern for the proper treatment of those parents suspected of abuse.[19] The English Court of Appeal has recently stressed the need for Family Court Judges to probe the evidence of abuse and to provide detailed reasons for their decisions as to the best interests of the child.[20] In all of the common law systems we study in this book, the deceptively straightforward 'best interests of the child' protective principle masks tension between anxiety about wrongful interference in familial relationships and fear of the implications of non-interference.

C. Free Proof versus Filtered Proof?

Notwithstanding the judiciary's avowals of renewed faith in the common sense and practical experience of modern jurors in criminal trials, a strong suspicion lingers that they are still susceptible to stereotypical views, especially where the trial amounts to a credibility contest between the accused and the complainant. This apprehension is in tension with the desire to give the trier of fact the full factual context in order to evaluate the competing claims of the prosecution and defence about what has happened to the child. The English courts' response, since they cannot know how jurors will actually deliberate on the cases, is still to intervene by intercepting evidence which enhances the risk of fallacious use,[21] whereas the Canadian courts have developed ever more complex prophylactic jury directions instructing them about the 'true' value of the evidence.

---

[15] Children Act 1989 s 31.

[16] *Re L (A Minor) (Police Investigation: Privilege)* (n 9) 31–32 (dissenting).

[17] D Thompson 'Taking Children *and* Facts Seriously: Evidence Law in Child Protection Proceedings— Part 1' (1988) 7 Can J Fam L 11 12, cited with approval in *New Brunswick (Minister of Health and Community Services) v G(J)* [1999] 3 SCR 46 (SCC) [78] (Lamer CJC). [18] ibid 13.

[19] D Thompson 'Are There *Any* Rules of Evidence in Family Law?' (2003) 21 Can Fam LQ 245.

[20] *Re D (Children)* [2005] EWCA Civ 825; *L v K* [2005] EWCA Civ 918.

[21] Since jurors might well indulge in stereotypical thinking anyway, without the spur of actual evidence.

In contrast, family lawyers have been heard to claim that the rules of evidence do not apply in proceedings under the Children Act 1989, and that it is a system of free proof.[22] However, evidence does not *acquire* greater probative value merely because the court's inquiry is directed towards a different objective. Secondhand hearsay is intrinsically weak evidence regardless of the juridical context. The powers of the family court judge can be just as devastating for a child and his family if exercised upon a flawed evidential foundation as a conviction may be.

One justification for the lowering of evidential barriers under the Children Act 1989 is that the trier of fact will be a seasoned judge, whereas in the criminal courts the verdict will be rendered by lay jurors who must be shielded from evidence which throws more heat than light upon the issues they must determine. However, it must not be forgotten that lay magistrates sitting in the Family Proceedings Court have their role in child protection proceedings as well.

D. Visible Justice versus Invisible Justice?

The importance of justice being seen to be done has long been an article of faith with common law courts.[23] The principle of open justice in public courts is enshrined in the ECHR Article 6(1), the premise being that the public character of proceedings protects litigants against the administration of justice in secret with no public scrutiny, and is one of the means whereby confidence in the courts can be maintained.[24]

In the criminal courts there is a strong presumption that all proceedings will be open to the public, although the trial judge has jurisdiction to order as a Special Measures Direction that the evidence of a witness be given in a closed court if the proceedings relate to the Sexual Offences Act 2003, or there are reasonable grounds to believe that a person other than the accused has sought or will seek to intimidate a witness.[25] It is important to note that the Special Measures Direction must permit one nominated representative of the media to remain in the courtroom,[26] so that public scrutiny of the criminal trial is not precluded by the witness being permitted to testify in private. In cases involving persons under 18, it is standard practice for the trial court to issue publication bans relating to any information which might

---

[22] The same concern that relevant evidence may be inadmissible in child protection proceedings if the 'technical rules of evidence' apply features in Canadian family law statutes: D Thompson 'The Cheshire Cat, or Just His Smile? Evidence Law in Child Protection' (2003) 21 Canadian Fam LQ 319.

[23] *Scott v Scott* [1913] AC 417 (HL) 437 (Viscount Haldane LC), 477 (Lord Shaw of Dunfermline); *Clibbery v Allan* [2002] EWCA Civ 45, [2002] 1 FLR 565 (CA) [16], quoting *Select Extracts from the Works of Jeremy Bentham* (1843) 115: 'Publicity is the very soul of justice . . . it keeps the judge himself while trying under trial . . . .'

[24] *Sutter v Switzerland* (1984) 6 EHRR 272 (ECtHR) [26]; *B v UK; P v UK* [2001] 2 FLR 261 (ECtHR) [36].   [25] Youth Justice and Criminal Evidence Act 1999 (Eng) s 25.

[26] ibid s 25(3).

lead to the identification of children involved in the process as defendants, victims or witnesses.[27]

In stark contrast, the default position in the family courts is that hearings under the Children Act 1989 take place in Judge's chambers, that is, in private.[28] The Administration of Justice Act 1960 section 12(1) prohibited disclosure[29] of information relating to proceedings under the Children Act 1989 in courts sitting in private, with unauthorized disclosure constituting contempt of court. This prohibition was interpreted as applying to the oral and documentary evidence, proofs of witnesses, interviews, reports, advocates' submissions, accounts of what has gone on in front of the judge,[30] and any observations about the gist of the evidence, even where the parties have been anonymized.[31] Even the experts who participated in the case could not see the reasons for judgment analysing their evidence, and so were deprived of an important source of feedback.[32] Furthermore, the Family Proceedings Rule 4.23(1) stipulated that none of the evidence in child protection proceedings could be disclosed to anyone without leave of the court. This means that parties had to seek the court's permission to discuss any aspect of the evidence, for example with an expert whom they have retained. Furthermore they could not refer to the evidence if they discuss their concerns about the outcome of a case, for example with a journalist.

The necessity of such a regime of secrecy is not self-evident. In Scotland,[33] New Zealand,[34] Australia[35] and several Canadian Provinces[36] the default position is that family court proceedings are open to the media, and in some jurisdictions also to the public. Nevertheless, the European Court of Human Rights (ECtHR) by a majority has concluded that the presumptive closed-court regime for all cases

---

[27] ibid Chapter IV ss 44–45.

[28] Family Proceedings Rules 1991(SI 1991/1247) Rule 4.16(7) (High Court or County Court), and Rule 16(7) (Magistrates Court); Magistrates Court Act 1980 (England) s 69. This was also the position at common law: *Scott v Scott* (n 23) 483.

[29] The technical term in s 12 is 'publication', which has been interpreted as having the same meaning as the law of defamation, that is, that it includes private communications to individuals: *Re B (A Child) (Disclosure)* [2004] EWHC 411 (Fam), [2004] 2 FLR 142 (Fam Div Munby J) [67]–[73].

[30] ibid [66], [81]; *Re W (Disclosure to Police)* [1998] 2 FLR 135 (CA).

[31] *X v Dempster* [1999] 1 FLR 894 (Fam Div Wilson J) 901, 903. Like other common law jurisdictions, it is a criminal offence for anyone to publish any material which could identify a child involved in family court proceedings unless the court has decided that the welfare of the child requires disclosure: Children Act 1989 (England) s 97(2).

[32] Sir James Munby 'Access to and Reporting of Family Proceedings' [2005] Fam Law 1, 8.

[33] According to *B v UK; P v UK* (n 24) [33]; *Pelling v Bruce-Williams* [2004] EWCA Civ 845, [2004] Fam 155 [56]–[57].

[34] Care of Children Act 2004 (New Zealand) s 137(1) (media are permitted to attend as well as limited members of the public with a legitimate interest in the proceedings).

[35] The public and the media may attend in both Federal Court and State Court: Family Court Act 1997 (Commonwealth of Australia) ss 97(1) and 212(1).

[36] The public are allowed to attend in several provinces: eg Provincial Court Act (British Columbia) s 3(1); Code of Civil Procedure (Quebec) art 13; whilst in other provinces the media but not the public may attend: eg Family Court Act (Nova Scotia) s 10(3); Child and Family Services Act 1990 (Ontario) s 45(4). Reporting restrictions apply in all the Provinces. The UK government's discussion paper commented that the concept of public and press attendance in family cases 'appears to be so entrenched in Canadian culture that it is beyond question' [Department of Constitutional Affairs *Confidence and confidentiality: Improving transparency and privacy in family courts* (Cm 6886 July 2006) 29].

involving child protection[37] is consistent with the fair trial guarantee of the ECHR Article 6, due to the express exceptions for cases involving juveniles or the protection of the private life of the parties (separately guaranteed by Article 8), but subject to the caveat that the issue must remain in the court's control.[38] The Court considered that it was not necessary to address arguments under the freedom of expression guarantee in Article 10.

This ruling has not quelled the arguments for greater openness in the family courts, mounted most forcefully, but by no means exclusively, by campaigners for fathers' rights. The Court of Appeal has acknowledged that the extent to which family proceedings are conducted in private hearings has been much criticized, and that there are powerful arguments for more openness, as many of the issues litigated in the family justice system require public debate in the media with participation by aggrieved parents.[39] In one case a mother and her solicitor were found in contempt of court for giving an anonymized copy of the judgment in a causation hearing and other documents to her Member of Parliament, the Solicitor-General, the Minister of State for Children, and the BBC and other journalists, to publicize what they considered to be a miscarriage of justice.[40] She would have been entitled to do so had the evidence been adduced in any parallel criminal proceedings.[41] It is important to note however that the same judge did authorize the mother to be interviewed by the media if she wished, and permitted her to put into the public domain various facts to enable her to participate in the public debate over the reliability of expert evidence, and to disclose certain papers to the General Medical Council hearing her complaint against two of the expert witnesses. As Munby J stated in making the order, 'we [family court judges] must have the humility to recognise—and to acknowledge—that public debate, and the jealous vigilance of an informed media, have an important role to play in exposing past miscarriages of justice and in preventing possible future miscarriages of justice'.[42]

---

[37]   Children Act 1989 (England) s 97, Family Proceedings Rules 1991(SI 1991/1247) Rule 4.16(7).

[38]   *B v UK; P v UK* (n 24), an application following the rejection of a father's application for public hearing in child custody proceedings in *Re P-B (a Minor) (Child Cases: Hearings in Open Court)* [1997] 1 All ER 58 (CA). Undaunted, the father (who appeared without counsel in each case and was a supporter of Families Need Fathers) continued his argument for public hearing in the English courts: *P v BW (Children Cases: Hearings in Public)* [2003] EWHC 1541 (Fam), [2004] 1 FLR 171 (Fam Div Bennett J), affd *Pelling v Bruce-Williams* (n 33).

[39]   *Re G (Celebrities: Publicity)* [1999] 1 FLR 409 (CA) 417; *Re W (Wardship: Discharge: Publicity)* [1995] 2 FLR 466 (CA) 474; *Harris v Harris; Attorney-General v Harris* [2001] 2 FLR 895 (Fam Div Munby J) [360]–[389]; *Pelling v Bruce-Williams* ibid [35]–[36].

[40]   *Re B (A Child) (Disclosure)* (n 29) (Munby J). The court's strongest criticism of the solicitor was for misleading the court in making an application for leave to disclose the documents when she had already done so. The judgment in the care proceedings was reported as *Re B (Threshold Criteria: Fabricated Illness)* [2003] EWHC 20 (Fam), [2004] 2 FLR 200 (Fam Div Bracewell J), appeal dismissed *Re U (Serious Injury: Standard of Proof); Re B* [2004] EWCA Civ 567, [2004] 2 FLR 263; the mother's application to re-open the appeal under CPR 52.17 was refused: *Re Uddin (A Child)* [2005] EWCA Civ 52. The solicitor was subsequently suspended from practice for three months by the Law Society of England and Wales.

[41]   As pointed out extrajudicially by Sir James Munby (n 32) 5.

[42]   *Re B (A Child) (Disclosure)* (n 29) (Munby J) [101].

In the wake of the Munchausen's syndrome by proxy controversy concerning sudden infant deaths, the disparity in terms of permitted public scrutiny between the criminal and civil courts became starkly evident, as parents whose children had been taken into care and in some cases adopted on the basis of expert evidence from the same sources discredited in criminal proceedings, could not discuss their cases in public.[43] In the wake of the *Cannings* case the President of the Family Division said in administrative directions to family court judges that 'in view of the current climate and the increasing complaints of "secrecy" in the family justice system, a broader approach to making judgments public may be desirable'.[44] Nevertheless in another controversial case in 2005, two children were taken into care on the basis that the parents, whilst committed, had limited parenting ability; the case received widespread and inaccurate attention in the media, but the Court of Appeal refused the parents' request to publish the care order to correct the publicity (whilst recommending that family court judges routinely prepare anonymized summaries of the reasons for care and adoption orders to improve accurate reporting).[45] The Court of Appeal has emphasized that judges have inherent discretion to relax the normal restrictions on attendance in court if requested by a party. Thorpe LJ acknowledged that there is such an inherited convention of privacy that the judicial mind is almost never directed to that discretion, and in the rare cases where an application is made, the court may be prejudiced by that tradition or by an unconscious preference for the atmosphere created by a hearing in chambers.[46] The court was opened to the media in an application for contact where paternity was disputed at the request of the applicant, the then Home Secretary David Blunkett.

In 2004 the Solicitor General launched a major consultation exercise with a view to permitting disclosure of information to parties with a legitimate interest in receiving it, but excluding the media.[47] The Government did not wait for the results before making the most urgent changes. On 12 April 2005 s 62 of the Children Act 2004 came into force, which means that it is no longer a criminal offence for a party to family proceedings involving children to disclose orders to other individuals and bodies, so long as disclosure is not made to the general public or any section of the general public, or to the media. Moreover, it will no longer be contempt of court to communicate specified information relating to family proceedings involving children and held in private without a court order, where the Rules so authorize.[48] Significantly,

---

[43] As in the criminal prosecution of Angela Cannings, Sally Clark and Trupti Patel, discussed below, Chapter 11 section B.

[44] Administrative directions issued on 28 January 2004, cited in *Re B (A Child) (Disclosure)* (n 29) (Munby J) [14], [104].   [45] *Re H (Children) (Freeing Orders: Publicity)* [2005] EWCA Civ 1325.

[46] *Pelling v Bruce-Williams* (n 33) [54]–[55].

[47] Department of Constitutional Affairs *Disclosure of Information in Family Proceedings Cases Involving Children* (CP 37/04 December, 2004).

[48] The list is still very restrictive, but includes legal representatives, experts, spouses, co-habitees and close family members, an elected representative or peer, mediators, Children's Commissioner, health care professionals providing medical care or counselling; researchers on approved projects: Family Proceedings Rules 1991 Rule 10.20A as amended; see Department of Constitutional Affairs *Disclosure of Information in Family Proceedings Cases Involving Children: a Response to the Public Consultation* (Cm 66 23 July 2005) Annex C <http://www.official-documents.co.uk/document/cm66/6623/6623.pdf>.

the list now includes a police officer conducting a related criminal investigation and a member of the Crown Prosecution Service (CPS). A Government response to the public consultation was published in July 2005 which decided to relax many of the restrictions which previously had prevented families and individuals from seeking advice and support, and had inhibited research into the functioning of the family court system. That these decisions went well beyond what some interest groups wanted, but still not as far as the House of Commons Constitutional Affairs Select Committee had recommended, shows the degree of controversy in this area.[49]

Yet the human needs of the persons whose lives are rummaged through in the family courts must be acknowledged. As Munby J has observed,

Lawyers and others who spend their professional lives dabbling in the stuff of other people's misery may not always appreciate as much as they should the embarrassment and worse— sometimes, understandably, the shame, humiliation and anger—that someone in [a party's] position must feel as strangers pick over and dissect the most intimate aspects of private and family life. Recognition of that reality of course underlies the restrictions which the Family Division traditionally imposes on the public dissemination of information relating to proceedings in chambers, more particularly when those proceedings concern children.[50]

Some English family court judges have defended the practice of closed courts as being essential to the proper administration of justice, enabling witnesses to express themselves candidly on highly personal issues without fear of public curiosity or comment, to enable the court to gain a full and accurate picture of the case.[51] It must not be forgotten that the 'curtain of privacy' imposed by the family court is for the protection of the child.[52] It is beyond question that children should not be identifiable in any publication relating to the case, and it must also be recognized that the privacy interests of a parent and a child often may conflict. The paramount consideration in children's cases in the family courts is their best interests; the parents' own interests under the ECHR Articles 6, 8 and 10 will usually be satisfied by a private hearing.

That said, the closure of the family courts to public scrutiny is excessive, particularly where an allegation of child abuse may be subject to adjudication in a parallel criminal trial which is open to the media and the public, and where a child affected by the proceedings has no absolute right to anonymity.[53] As Munby J has pointed out extrajudicially, care orders and freeing orders are amongst the most drastic that any judge in any jurisdiction is ever empowered to make, making the arguments in favour of openness, public scrutiny, and public accountability particularly compelling; moreover, it becomes all too easy to attack the family justice system when the system

---

[49] Department of Constitutional Affairs ibid.

[50] *Re B (Disclosure to Other Parties)* [2001] 2 FLR 1017 (Fam Div Munby J) [14].

[51] *P v BW (Children Cases: Hearings in Public)* (n 38) (Bennett J), affd *Pelling v Bruce-Williams* (n 33). For a summary and analysis of the competing interests and arguments, see Sir James Munby (n 32) 2–4.

[52] *Re Manda (Wardship: Disclosure of Evidence)* [1993] 1FLR 205 (CA) 215.

[53] *In Re S (a Child) (Identification: Restrictions on Publication)* [2004] UKHL 47, [2005] 1 AC 593.

itself prevents anyone correcting the misrepresentations being fed to the media.[54] The Government's proposals published in July 2006 to enhance transparency of the family courts to the media and the public are to be welcomed.[55]

E. System Abuse?

A final theme we will be exploring in Part IV is the widespread perception that the criminal justice system is unnecessarily harsh to the victims (and the alleged victims) of crime, and especially so in relation to women and children. Statutory reform since 1988 has been directed at dispelling this image. The reform agenda of successive Labour Home Secretaries has been overtly aimed at 'rebalancing the criminal justice system in favour of the victim', the premise being that the current model favours the accused too much. It is submitted that this 'seesaw' image is seriously misleading. Fairness to the alleged victim does not necessarily derogate from fairness to the accused. If the overall objective of the trial is to ensure and protect the integrity of the ultimate verdict, then enabling all witnesses to give the best evidence of which they are capable does not give rise to inevitable conflict.

   In the specific area of child witnesses, reform to a considerable degree has been driven by a 'headlines' view of their experiences in court. Journalists and police officers like to highlight abusive cross-examination of child witnesses. Yet it is rare now for counsel to subject a child witness to a destructive attack, if only because it is simply not good advocacy as it will serve only to engender sympathy for the witness. Nevertheless these rare examples acquire a disproportionate importance in the folklore of police child protection units, social services and the CPS.

---

[54] Sir James Munby (n 32) 6, 7.   [55] *Confidence and confidentiality* (n 36).

7

Access to Evidence

The disclosure of evidence is one of the most important intersections between child protection proceedings and criminal court proceedings, since the same information is highly relevant to the facts in issue in both types of proceedings. It was once thought that where the facts of the case might give rise to a criminal prosecution, that should be concluded before any family court proceedings took place.[1] However this practice changed due to the anti-delay principle expressed in the Children Act 1989 s 1(2).[2] Even in the case of a pending murder charge respecting a child's sibling, the advisability of adjourning the care proceedings must be decided on a case-by-case basis, to ensure that the children are not left in limbo:

The detriment to the family of having to face criminal proceedings and care proceedings and to have a trial run, as they might see it, in the care court, is not of itself a reason for delaying the care proceedings. There will be cases where it is right, in the interests of the children, that the care proceedings are delayed for the outcome of the criminal proceedings. It is a relevant but not a determining factor in considering the welfare of children that they should have parents whose case is properly tried and who have not been put at risk in their criminal trial for some particular reason that may come out in the care proceedings. But the issue of delay is all-important.[3]

The Government in July 2005 reiterated its position that there should be full cooperation and sharing of information between the police, the CPS and local authorities conducting child protection proceedings without the need to seek the express permission of the court,[4] but there is considerable evidence that often this is still not the case.[5]

A criminal conviction for abuse or child homicide will usually be treated in care proceedings as conclusive of the issue of harm or risk of harm at the hands of the convicted party, even where the family court judge might entertain doubts about the

---

[1] *R v SL* [2006] EWCA Crim 1902 [72].

[2] *R v Exeter Juvenile Court ex p H and H; R v Waltham Forest Juvenile Court ex p B* [1988] 2 FLR 214 (President of Family Division) 222.

[3] *Re TB (Care Proceedings: Criminal Trial)* [1995] 2 FLR 801 (CA) 804, 805, doubting *Re S (Care Order: Criminal Proceedings)* [1995] 1 FLR 151 (CA) which had held that only in exceptional circumstances should a care case precede a murder trial.

[4] Department of Constitutional Affairs *Disclosure of Information in Family Proceedings Cases Involving Children: Response to the Public Consultation* (Cm 6623 July 2005) [5.5]–[5.6].

[5] As in *R v SL* (n 1) [75], where the CPS became aware of the care proceedings only at 'a very late stage'.

conclusion.[6] However the opposite is not the case, and the decision and findings in the care proceedings are not admissible in a criminal trial.[7] Where the anti-delay principle has expedited the care proceedings, this gives rise to the possibility that a defendant could be found guilty in criminal proceedings when the family court judge had previously found the evidence that he had harmed the child did not satisfy the civil standard of proof. This occurred in 2006 in *R v LS*,[8] where the accused was charged with the murder of his infant son. The family court in care proceedings relating to the baby's brother had held that it was not satisfied on the balance of probability which of the two parents had inflicted the injuries. The child's mother testified for the prosecution. The accused argued that the criminal trial should have been stayed as an abuse of process, on the basis that inconsistent verdicts on the same issue had been rendered by two courts. The Court of Appeal said this would be 'an astonishing result of litigation in care proceedings to which the prosecution was a stranger' and which were ultimately concerned with the future care and welfare of the sibling and not criminal responsibility for the infant's death.[9]

The Court of Appeal seemed perturbed at what had transpired in that case and directed that wherever possible linked criminal and care directions hearings should take place as the cases progress, to avoid such procedural and evidential difficulties.[10] It is essential that there be close liaison between the local social services authority and the CPS. In this way consistent rulings could be made on disclosure of evidence, requests for third party disclosure in the criminal proceedings and any issues of public interest immunity, and any requests for leave to interview children in care for the purposes of the criminal proceedings.[11] However a Practice Statement to this effect has been in place since 1993 in the Greater London area,[12] and the number of cases involving disclosure and admissibility of evidence in parallel proceedings shows that it is not always adhered to. Moreover, requiring care proceedings to proceed in tandem with criminal prosecutions threatens to impede their already slow progress[13] even further, not least because two sets of counsel will be involved.

Because of the Children Act 1989's anti-delay principle, often it is the child protection case which has outstripped the criminal prosecution, and so there may be evidence already adduced or prepared in the child protection case to which the prosecution or the defence wishes to have access. Since the evidence typically originates in the care proceedings, we will examine first the issues surrounding access to that evidence in the family court, and then the transfer of that evidence to the criminal court.

---

[6] *R v David D; Phillip J* [1996] 1 Cr App R 455 (CA).
[7] *Hollington v F Hewthorne & Co Limited* [1943] KB 587 (CA) applied in *R v SL* (n 1) [58].
[8] *R v SL* ibid. This also occurred in *R v D and Others* (CA 3 November 1995) discussed below Chapter 10 section C. [9] *R v SL* ibid [58].
[10] A Practice Statement in Respect of Linked Criminal and Care Directions Hearing has been issued for the Southeastern Circuit in November 2003: S Bradley 'Child Law Update' [2005] NLJ 591.
[11] *R v SL* (n 1) [73]–[74]. [12] ibid [73]. [13] Discussed above Chapter 2 section B.1(e).

There are four arguments which may be available to a party resisting disclosure in the English courts:

- lack of relevance or materiality to the issues being litigated;[14]

- *public interest immunity*, usually asserted by a party exercising powers conferred by the public law,[15] whereupon the court must carry out a balancing exercise to weigh the public interest in preserving confidentiality of the information against the public interest that the administration of justice not be frustrated by the withholding of relevant evidence;[16]

- *confidentiality*, which in recent years has tended to elide with public interest immunity where a public authority created or received the information,[17] but which also may be asserted by a third party such as a medical professional or therapist;

- *legal professional privilege*, being advice given by a lawyer to her client (*advice privilege*), or communications by a lawyer or her client with third parties in connection with anticipated or ongoing litigation (*litigation privilege*); this differs from public interest immunity in that the subject matter of the communication may still be tendered in evidence if discovered from a separate source, whereas public interest immunity attaches to the content of the evidence.[18]

A. Disclosure of Evidence in Child Protection Proceedings

The culture of interagency investigations fostered by numerous government directives[19] has led to some pooling of information. However, occasionally the police or CPS may have concerns that disclosure in the family court proceedings could jeopardize a pending prosecution. In such instances the court will approach the matter in two stages: first, disclosure to the local authority, and subsequently, disclosure to the parents, at which stage public interest immunity might apply.[20] For example, in *Nottinghamshire County Council v H*, where parents of young children ignored the warnings of social workers and persisted in leaving them in the care of a known drug abuser, even after one of them died from ingested drugs, the local authority sought disclosure of the parents' witness statements in a prosecution against the drug addict. Limited disclosure was ordered where necessary to enable the local authority and

---

[14] We shall see that the legal definition of materiality is not self-evident: see the discussion of *R v Derby Magistrates' Court ex p B* [1996] AC 487 (HL) below, section C.1(b) (iii).

[15] *D v NSPCC* [1978] AC 171 (HL) held that the categories of public interest immunity materials are never closed, and that anyone, even a non-party or the court, may raise public interest immunity at any stage in the proceedings.

[16] The basic principles were developed in *Conway v Rimmer* [1968] AC 910 (HL) and *Air Canada v Secretary of State for Trade* [1983] 2 AC 394 (HL). See the discussion below section B.1(c) of *R v H, R v C* [2004] UKHL 3, [2004] 1 All ER 1269 which may have supplanted the balancing test.

[17] *D v NSPCC* (n 15).

[18] C Tapper 'Evidential Privilege in Cases Involving Children' (1997) 9 Child and Family LQ 1.

[19] eg *Home Office Circular 84/1991*; HM Government *Working Together to Safeguard Children: a Guide to Inter-Agency Working to Safeguard and Promote the Welfare of Children* (2006).

[20] *Nottinghamshire County Council v H* [1995] 1 FLR 115 (Fam Div).

the family court to make a more informed decision about the future of the surviving children.

While evidence collected for the purpose of criminal proceedings such as video interviews with the child,[21] parents' witness statements, and expert reports is routinely admitted in child protection proceedings, the converse has not been the norm. While the local authority is bound by statutory obligations of confidentiality, the police do not operate under the same statutory constraints, making full reciprocity of information sharing at times difficult.[22] A protocol between the CPS and local authorities was published in October 2003 with a view to breaking through these barriers to enhance police access,[23] which we will discuss later.[24]

1. Disclosure by the local authority to the family

It is wrong to regard cases of alleged parental child abuse as setting up an automatic confrontation between the conflicting claims of child welfare represented by the local authority on the one hand, and natural justice championed by the parents on the other.[25] All of the parties to family court proceedings are required to give 'full and frank disclosure' in all matters concerning children. This is necessary to fulfil the parties' obligation to 'use their best endeavours' to confine the issues and the evidence adduced to what is reasonably considered to be essential for the proper presentation of their case, to reduce or eliminate issues for expert evidence, and to agree which are the issues in advance of the hearing.[26]

All children have an interest, as part and parcel of their general welfare, not only in having their own voices heard and their own needs sensitively considered, but also in ensuring that their parents are given every proper opportunity to have the evidence fairly tested and to prepare themselves in advance to meet the grave allegations against them.[27] The common law position is consistent with caselaw under ECHR Articles 6 (the right to a fair trial) and 8 (the right to family life).[28] Therefore a 'high duty' is imposed upon local authorities to disclose all relevant information which might assist parents in rebutting allegations against them, or which might modify or cast doubt upon the case advanced against them.[29]

In the usual type of disputed case, disclosure should be made by the local authority of original material recording factual information in relation to the children and their parents or other relevant persons, especially transcripts and records regarding matters in issue. The notes from which affidavits were prepared should be disclosed

---

[21] *Re R (Child Abuse: Video Evidence)* [1995] 1 FLR 451 (Fam Div) 452–453.

[22] *Re M (Care Proceedings: Disclosure: Human Rights)* [2001] 2 FLR 1316 (Fam Div) 1328.

[23] CPS *A Protocol between the Crown Prosecution Service Police and Local Authorities in the Exchange of Information in the Investigation and Prosecution of Child Abuse Cases* (October 2003).

[24] See below section C.1(a).

[25] *R v Hampshire County Council ex p K and Another* [1990] 1 FLR 330 (QB) 335–336.

[26] *Practice Direction* [1995] 1 FLR 456 (Sir Stephen Brown, President of the Family Division) [4].

[27] *R v Hampshire County Council* (n 25) 336; *Re B (Disclosure to Other Parties)* [2001] 2 FLR 1017 (Fam Div Munby J) [68].   [28] eg *Feldbrugge v Netherlands* (1986) 8 EHRR 425.

[29] *Re C (Expert Evidence: Disclosure: Practice)* [1995] 1 FLR 204 (Fam Div) 209–210.

to allow the court and the other parties to evaluate the assertions in the sworn evidence.[30] However, documents or notes recording opinions or advice, for example in a case conference, need not be disclosed unless expressly permitted by the local authority, due to the 'chilling effect' disclosure might have on the frank exchange of views.[31]

This duty is qualified only by the inherent jurisdiction of the family courts to avert harm to a child by disclosure, and by the principle of public interest immunity. The caselaw before the Human Rights Act 1998 (HRA) took the position that in any case concerning the welfare of a child, the trial judge had discretionary jurisdiction to direct that such material not be disclosed to a party to custody or care proceedings.[32] It was necessary for the court to satisfy itself that the probable consequence of disclosure would be to cause such 'real harm' to the child as to outweigh the normal requirements for a fair trial of full disclosure. That jurisdiction was to be exercised only in exceptional circumstances and then only for the shortest period possible consonant with preserving the child's welfare.[33]

This discretion has survived the HRA.[34] Although Article 6 confers on a litigant prima facie entitlement to disclosure of all materials which might be taken into account by the court when reaching a decision adverse to him, Article 8 allows a limited qualification so that the rights of other parties are respected. However, the interests of all participants may now be engaged by Article 8, and not just those of the child.[35] Non-disclosure must be limited to what the situation imperatively demands and is justified only when the party seeking to withhold disclosure has convincingly and compellingly demonstrated that this is strictly necessary.[36]

It is nonetheless probable that the HRA will have further enhanced the parents' entitlement to access to any evidence on which the judge may base her decision. In *McMichael v UK*, the European Court of Human Rights (ECtHR) held that, notwithstanding the special characteristics of adjudication in the family courts, as a matter of general principle the right to a fair—adversarial—trial means the opportunity to respond to the evidence and submissions of the other party. Non-disclosure of such vital documents as social services reports is capable of affecting the ability of parents to influence the outcome of the case, and hence could breach the fair trial guarantee in Article 6(1).[37]

In 1970 the Court of Appeal held that public interest immunity automatically attached to social services records, on the basis that immunity was necessary to

---

[30] *Re A and others (Minors) (Child Abuse: Guidelines)* [1992] 1 FLR 439 (Fam Div) 445.
[31] ibid 446–447.   [32] *Re M (Minors) (Disclosure of Evidence)* [1994] 1 FLR 760 (CA).
[33] *Official Solicitor v K (Infants)* [1965] AC 201 (HL) 201, 219–220, 222, 235, 242) *Re B (a Minor) (Disclosure of Evidence)* [1993] 1 FLR 191 (CA) 197–199; *Re C (Disclosure)* [1996] 1 FLR 797 (Fam Div) 803; D Burrows *Evidence in Family Proceedings* (Family Law, Bristol 1999) 107–112.
[34] *Re B (Disclosure to Other Parties)* (n 27) (Munby J) [66]–[68].
[35] As Lord Mustill had concluded in *Re D (Minors) (Adoption Reports: Confidentiality)* [1996] AC 593 (HL).   [36] *Re B* (n 27) [89].
[37] *McMichael v UK* (1995) 20 EHRR 205 (ECtHR) [80].

ensure the candour of child protection workers.[38] This position was accepted by the House of Lords in 1978 as correct and extended to the names of callers to the NSPCC helpline reporting suspicions of abuse, on the basis that protecting their identity from the person about whom the allegation was made was necessary for the effective functioning of an organization authorized by Parliament to bring legal proceedings for the welfare of children.[39] The Court of Appeal subsequently assumed that public interest immunity also applied to case conference reports.[40]

Nevertheless Butler-Sloss LJ revisited the case for class immunity for such records in 1990,[41] in light of the subsequent development of a more flexible approach to public interest immunity, and statutory provisions entitling the *guardian ad litem* to full access to all relevant social work records and conference notes.[42] Her Ladyship considered that social work and case conference records are in a special category of immunity justified by the particular circumstances of the welfare of the children. Disclosure of documents chronicling the continuing discussions and concerns of the local authority might be very damaging to the child's welfare in the potential souring of relations between the social workers and the family when they are likely to be locked into a continuing relationship over the child or other children in the family.[43] But the Court of Appeal confirmed that there is now no absolute rule against disclosure. The wider interests of the child may require consideration of the parents' position and the narrower concerns of the case put forward by the local authority for the protection of the child, as well as the more general public interest in the due administration of justice.[44] Recently family court judges have been reproving local authorities for their general reluctance to disclose documents in proceedings involving children and their frequent reliance on incorrect claims to confidentiality or public interest immunity as justification.[45]

Thus it is for the court, not the local authority, to decide whether public interest immunity applies to a particular record. Public bodies can no longer claim immunity for entire classes of records.[46] The local authority is expected to notify the other parties of the existence of the information, and should prepare a précis of the information which would be disclosed if ordered.[47] As with the prophylactic harm principle, the party claiming public interest immunity must build a convincing and compelling case to support its claim that the apprehended, and specifically identified, harm to the public interest in the protection of children outweighs the public interest in a fair trial.[48]

---

[38] *Re D (Infants)* [1970] 1 WLR 599 (CA) 601 (Lord Denning MR), 601 (Harman LJ).
[39] *D v NSPCC* (n 15) 220 (Lord Diplock), 227 (Lord Hailsham), 245 (Lord Edmund Davies).
[40] *Re S and W (Minors) (Confidential Reports)* (1982) 4 FLR 290 (CA).
[41] *Re M (A Minor) (Disclosure of Material)* [1990] 2 FLR 36 (CA).   [42] Children Act 1989 s 42.
[43] ibid 42.   [44] *Re S and W* (n 40) 42–43.
[45] *Re R (Care: Disclosure: Nature of Proceedings)* [2002] 1 FLR 755 (Fam Div Charles J); *Re J (Care Proceedings: Disclosure)* [2003] EWHC 976, [2003] 2 FLR 522 (Fam Div Wall J); *Re W (Children) (Care Proceedings: Disclosure)* [2003] EWHC 1624, [2003] 2 FLR 1023 (Fam Div Wall J).
[46] *R v Chief Constable of the West Midlands police ex p Wiley* [1995] AC 274 (HL).
[47] *Re C (Expert Evidence: Disclosure: Practice)* (n 29) 210.
[48] *Re D (Minors)* (n 35) 615; *Re B* (n 27); *Re R* (n 45) 777–778.

2. Disclosure by the family to the local authority or other investigators

The full disclosure rule in care proceedings trumps even the usual legal litigation privilege which attaches to expert reports commissioned by parties such as the parents, notwithstanding that privilege is both a procedural and substantive right.[49] This stands in stark contrast to criminal and other more adversarial civil proceedings where litigation privilege is absolute and cannot be abrogated by a court order, even where the privileged material might assist the defence of a person charged with murder.[50]

The withdrawal of litigation privilege from child protection proceedings was confirmed by a bare majority of the House of Lords in *Re L (A Minor)(Police Investigation: Privilege)*[51] in 1997. A two-year-old child of heroin addicts was admitted to hospital unconscious as a result of methadone poisoning. The mother claimed that the child had accidentally drunk the methadone from a beaker left carelessly in the kitchen. She obtained the family court's permission to disclose the court papers to a consultant chemical pathologist to obtain his opinion as to whether the child's medical condition when admitted to hospital was consistent with the mother's account. The court order required that the report be filed with the court and made available to the other parties. The report concluded that there was no evidence of habituation to methadone by the child, but expressed doubts about the mother's account of the time when the accidental ingestion had taken place. The police sought disclosure of the report to assist them in determining whether charges should be laid against the mother.

All three levels of court considering the police application decided that the mother's entitlement to litigation privilege[52] had to yield to the paramountcy of the child's welfare in the care proceedings. Lord Jauncey drew a sharp distinction between litigation privilege and legal advice privilege, and reasoned that since litigation privilege is essentially a creature of adversarial proceedings, it does not even arise in care proceedings, which he characterized as essentially non-adversarial and investigative.[53] This however overlooks other authority holding that the threshold question in care proceedings as to whether the child is at risk of harm is adjudicated in an adversarial context as between the local authority and the child's carers.[54] An appeal by the mother to the ECtHR failed on the basis that all parties were subject to the same rules of disclosure of expert reports they commissioned.[55]

---

[49] *Three Rivers District Council v Governor and Company of the Bank of England (No 5)* [2004] UKHL 48, [2005] 1 AC 610 [26] (Lord Scott).   [50] *R v Derby Magistrates' Court ex p B* (n 14).

[51] *Re L (A Minor) (Police Investigation: Privilege)* [1997] AC 16 (HL) (Lords Mustill and Nicholls dissenting).

[52] The mother was held to have waived her privilege against self-incrimination by filing the report in accordance with the initial court order: *Re L* ibid 28–29, application on this ground dismissed *L v UK* [2000] 2 FLR 322 (ECtHR) 331–332.   [53] *Re L* (n 51) 26–27.

[54] *Re R* (n 45) 772, citing *Re M (A Minor) (Care Orders: Threshold Conditions)* [1994] AC 424 (HL) and *Re H (Minors: Sexual Abuse: Standard of Proof)* [1996] AC 563 (HL).

[55] *L v UK* [2000] 2 FLR 322 (ECtHR) 330.

In a vigorous dissent, Lord Nicholls pointed out that there is no property in a witness, and that it was open to another party to the care proceedings to subpoena the expert to give evidence as to his findings and opinion without overriding legal professional privilege; all that would be protected from disclosure by the privilege would be the content of communications with the party or the solicitor who retained him.[56]

Significantly, *Re L* has been extended from criminal investigations and proceedings to other civil cases such as tort claims.[57] To summarize: any document which is not subject to litigation privilege because it was created in the purportedly non-adversarial context of child protection proceedings will not be privileged in any other type of adversarial legal proceedings, notwithstanding that it normally would be so protected.

It is submitted that the stance of the minority in *Re L* is correct.[58] The consequence of *Re L* is that any communication between the instructing solicitor and the expert is automatically disclosable, which must hinder the free and frank exchange which legal professional privilege is intended to protect.[59] This may serve to deter families from retaining experts to advise them in care proceedings whilst a criminal investigation is ongoing since privilege will never attach to the information, which means that less information will be before the family court. Notwithstanding the failure of the mother's appeal to the ECtHR, it is possible that the HRA 1998 will require reconsideration of the majority's sweeping assertion that the notion of a fair trial between opposing parties assumes far less importance in care proceedings than in other more adversarial cases.[60]

A further fact variation: can an accused be required to disclose to the family court the identity of medical experts whom he has instructed in *criminal* proceedings arising out of the same incident, so that other parties such as the *guardian ad litem* may seek to subpoena their evidence? This, it seems, is a step too far. In *S County Council v B*[61] it was held that, notwithstanding the paramountcy of the child's welfare, a party to Children Act 1989 proceedings retains absolute litigation privilege in relation to direct or indirect communications with experts instructed *solely* for the purpose of the criminal trial. Nor can a witness or potential witness volunteer material covered by legal professional privilege. *Re L* was distinguished on the basis that the report in question there was founded entirely on the hospital case notes—evidence available to all parties—and so did not involve any communication with the mother, nor was it prepared in connection with other, adversarial, proceedings.[62]

The net result is that legal advice privilege remains sacrosanct in child protection proceedings, but not so litigation privilege. As Charles J noted in *S County Council v B*, these privileges can overlap, since each may entail communication by the client with his lawyer or with his expert to prepare his position in connection with the litigation.[63] What remains unclear is whether caselaw before *Re L* placing a wide responsibility on

---

[56] *Re L* (n 51) 34.   [57] *Vernon v Bosley (No 2)* [1997] 1 All ER 614 (CA) 629.
[58] For a contrary view see Tapper (n 18).   [59] *Re L* (n 51) 36 (Lord Nicholls).
[60] ibid 27 (Lord Jauncey).   [61] *S County Council v B* [2000] 2 FLR 161 (Fam Div Charles J).
[62] ibid 176–177.   [63] ibid 174.

all the parties to disclose all relevant reports and overriding professional confidence remains good law,[64] so that solicitors have a duty to advise the other parties of the existence of documents such as medical reports.[65] We see here again the asymmetry between child protection and criminal proceedings: in a criminal trial the accused cannot be required to relinquish either form of legal professional privilege, whereas in the family court he can be required to disclose reports from third parties which he may not have intended to use in evidence at all. Therefore the timing of the parallel proceedings can be critical.

B. Prosecution and Defence Disclosure of Evidence in Criminal Proceedings

1. Prosecution disclosure

The 'golden rule' is that fairness under ECHR Article 6 requires full disclosure to the defence of any unused material held by the prosecution which serves to weaken its case or strengthen that of the defendant.[66] That said, the ECtHR has held that the entitlement to disclosure of relevant evidence is not an absolute right. In some cases it may be necessary to withhold certain evidence from the defence so as to preserve the fundamental rights of another individual (such as a child) or to safeguard an important public interest. However, only such measures restricting the rights of the defence which are strictly necessary are permissible under Article 6(1).[67]

(a) Staged disclosure under the CPIA 1996 and the CJA 2003

The scope of prosecution disclosure demanded by the 'golden rule' has been controversial in England for the past 20 years, after several high-profile miscarriages of justice were shown to have resulted from prosecution non-disclosure of vital evidence. The common law rules developed by the Court of Appeal in response to these cases[68] were criticized by the police and CPS as being both too expansive and too expensive. They were replaced by Part II of the Criminal Procedure and Investigations Act 1996 (CPIA 1996), supplemented by a very detailed Code of Practice. This legislation set up a regime of staged disclosure, which has been modified somewhat by the Criminal Justice Act 2003 (CJA 2003).

Briefly, at the first stage called primary disclosure, the prosecutor must first disclose any material which in the prosecutor's opinion might undermine the case for

---

[64] *Essex County Council v R (Legal Professional Privilege)* [1996] 2 All ER 78 (CA).

[65] *Clarke, Hall and Morrison's Law Relating to Children and Young Persons* (10th edn Butterworths, London 1985, updated to July 2004) [1387]–[1390].

[66] *Edwards and Lewis v UK* (2003) 15 BHRC 189 (ECtHR); *Rowe v UK* (2000) 8 BHRC 325 (ECtHR); *R v H, R v C* (n 16) [14].

[67] *Fitt v UK* (2000) 30 EHRR 480 (ECtHR) [44]–[45]; *Brown v Stott (Procurator Fiscal, Dunfermline) and Another* [2003] 1 AC 681 (HL) 695.

[68] In particular in *R v Ward* [1993] 1 WLR 619 (CA); *R v Keane* [1994] WLR 746 (CA).

the prosecution against the accused.[69] A more objective test was introduced by the CJA 2003, whereby the prosecutor is required to disclose any material which might reasonably be considered capable of undermining the prosecution case.[70] Primary disclosure is not limited to material in the possession of the prosecution, but also encompasses material which the prosecutor has inspected under the Code of Practice. This has particular significance for documents in the possession of a third party, such as social services files and medical records,[71] to which we will return below.

To be entitled to any further disclosure, the defence must file a defence statement setting out in general terms the nature of the accused's defence, indicating the matters regarding which he takes issue with the prosecution, and the reasons therefor,[72] which must go beyond a mere denial of guilt.[73] The prosecutor thereupon is required to provide secondary disclosure of any material which might be 'reasonably expected to assist' the accused's case as disclosed.[74] The CJA 2003 has placed the prosecution under a stronger obligation of continuing disclosure of evidence which is reasonably considered to be capable of undermining the prosecution case or assisting the defence,[75] and the defence may apply to the court for any undisclosed material it thinks meets either test.[76] Unused material which is neutral or which damages the defendant's case need not be disclosed by the prosecution.[77]

(b) Treatment of 'sensitive material'

The police disclosure officer must provide to the prosecutor a schedule of any material which he believes it is not in the public interest to disclose, and the reason for that belief. One stipulated category of potentially sensitive material is information supplied to an investigator during a criminal investigation which relates to a child or young person and which has been generated by a local authority social services department, an Area Child Protection Committee (soon to be replaced by Local Safeguarding Children's Boards), or another party contacted by an investigator.[78] The prosecutor will then decide whether that information should not be disclosed to the defence, in which case the defence may then apply for a court order for disclosure.[79] The court, on the prosecutor's application, may then order that it is not in the public interest to disclose material.[80]

(c) Prosecution claims to public interest immunity

In *Keane*[81] Lord Taylor CJ set out the principles applicable to prosecution claims of public interest immunity. Where the prosecution wishes to withhold from the defence documents or information which are possibly relevant to a live issue or raise a new issue, or hold out a real prospect of providing a lead on evidence going to such issues,

---

[69] CPIA 1996 s 3(1).   [70] CJA 2003 s 32.

[71] P Rook and R Ward *Rook & Ward on Sexual Offences Law and Practice* (3rd edn Sweet & Maxwell, London 2004) 604.   [72] CPIA s 5(6).

[73] *Disclosure: a Protocol for the Control and Management of Unused Material in the Crown Court* 20 February 2006 (Her Majesty's Courts Service) [34].   [74] CPIA 1996 s 7.

[75] CJA 2003 s 37, inserting s 7A into CPIA 1996; *Disclosure: a Protocol* (n 73) [1], [16], [30], [31].

[76] CJA 2003 s 38 amending CPIA 1996 s 8.   [77] *R v H, R v C* (n 16) [17].

[78] Disclosure: Criminal Procedure and Investigations Act 1996: Code of Practice under Part II [6.12].

[79] CPIA 1996 s 8.   [80] CPIA 1996 s 8(5).   [81] *R v Keane* (n 76) 751–753.

Diagram 8. Public Interest Immunity Template: *R v H* (2004, HL)

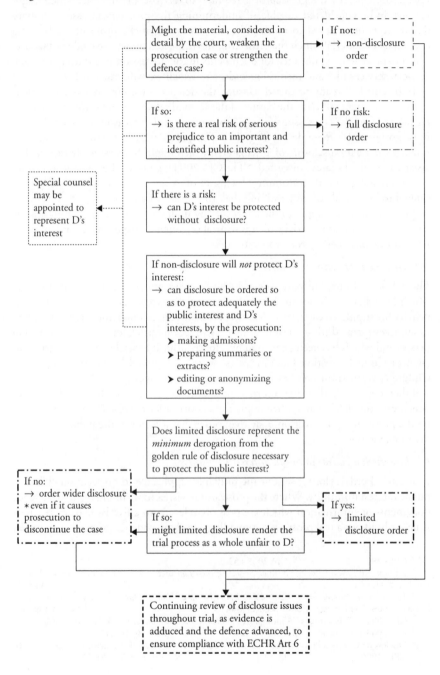

the material must be placed before the court. The judge should carry out a balancing exercise, having regard both to the weight of the public interest in non-disclosure and to the importance of the documents to the issues of potential interest to the defence. 'If the disputed material may prove the defendant's innocence or avoid a miscarriage of justice, then the balance comes down resoundingly in favour of disclosing it.'[82] Thus the public interest in the fair administration of justice always outweighs that of preserving the secrecy of sensitive material when its non-disclosure may lead to a miscarriage of justice. This common law test is reflected in the CPIA 1996.[83]

In 2004 the House of Lords set out a template to govern the court's consideration of a public interest immunity claim, which is depicted in Diagram 8. Of paramount importance is the test for public interest immunity: disclosure must give rise to 'a real risk of serious prejudice' to an identified important public interest, notwithstanding that it would assist the defence. Any non-disclosure of relevant material must be measured against an absolute minimum derogation from the 'golden rule'. If the consequence is to render the trial as a whole unfair to the accused, then the court must order wider disclosure, even if the consequence is that the prosecution collapses to avoid disclosure.[84] It would appear that the *Keane* test of 'balancing of interests' has been supplanted by the requirement that the court decide whether non-disclosure would compromise the overall fairness of the trial.[85] This shift may require reconsideration of previous caselaw invoking public interest immunity to withhold third party records from defendants charged with child abuse.

2. Defence disclosure

This topic can be dealt with briefly as there are no particularly complex issues peculiar to child abuse prosecutions. Now that consent has been removed as a defence to sexual offences against children, the usual position of the defence will be that the incident did not occur at all (ie a denial of the *actus reus*). This will usually also be the case for child homicide. For cases of physical abuse, the defence may be 'reasonable chastisement'.

As explained earlier, the defence position must be disclosed under the CPIA 1996 following primary disclosure by the prosecution, in order to trigger the right to secondary disclosure by the prosecution. The CJA 2003 now requires that the defence also disclose points of law to be taken and the authority to be relied upon.[86] The CJA 2003 also has significantly expanded the scope of disclosure of defence evidence to include the names, addresses and dates of birth of all defence witnesses, and not just of alibi witnesses as heretofore.[87] Furthermore, the defence is required to disclose details relating to all experts from whom opinions have been sought for possible use

---

[82] ibid 751–752.
[83] CPIA 1996 ss 3(6), 7(5), 8(5), 14–16; Sir Robin Auld *Review of the Criminal Courts of England and Wales* (September 2001) 476. [84] *R v H, R v C* (n 16) [36].
[85] M Caplan QC and S Parkinson 'Testing the PII Template' [2004] New LJ 238, 239.
[86] CJA 2003 s 6A. [87] CJA 2003 s 6C.

by the defence at trial, and not just the substance of any expert evidence which it proposes to adduce, as was previously the case;[88] apparently the aim is to prevent 'expert-shopping'.[89] If the defence fails to file its statement, the court or jury is entitled to draw adverse inferences against the accused.[90] There is no concomitant penalty if the prosecution breaches its disclosure obligations.

C. Disclosure of Evidence in the Possession of Third Parties

The most problematic issue in child abuse prosecutions concerning access to evidence is the disclosure to the prosecution and to the defence of confidential records concerning a child held by a third party such as social services, a local education authority, a therapist, or a treating physician or hospital. These records may contain valuable information which can assist investigators and prosecutors in evaluating the child's intellectual and emotional capacity to be a reliable witness. The police may seek records about a suspect's involvement in child protection conferences, hoping to find inculpatory statements. The prosecution may also wish to access statements by the carer about what happened. The defence will hope to find evidence relevant to the family and environment in which the child lived, the relationship between the suspect and the child, and the child's behaviour at the time of the alleged incidents, including any failure to complain of abuse. Therapeutic records may disclose inconsistent narratives by the child, or inappropriate questioning or pressure to induce disclosure.

For the past decade English courts have expressed concern at the burgeoning applications for production of social services records in particular, not least because these files almost invariably contain confidences the disclosure of which might imperil the trust established between the children and those who care for them.[91] However, empirical research for the Home Office suggests that these concerns are largely unfounded as both before and after the CPIA 1996, local authority social service and education departments only infrequently receive requests for voluntary disclosure or summonses in child abuse cases.[92]

There are three general approaches to third party disclosure in the jurisdictions we are evaluating:

- automatic immunity from disclosure of certain classes of documents or for certain relationships;
- automatic immunity from disclosure of certain types of communications between the record-keeper and the witness; or

---

[88] Crown Court (Advance Notice of Expert Evidence) Rules SI 1987 No 716. Non-compliance means that the expert opinion can only be adduced with leave of the court.

[89] C Tapper *Cross & Tapper on Evidence* (10th edn Butterworths, London 2004) 302.

[90] CPIA 1996 s 11.   [91] *R v Exeter Juvenile Court ex p H and H* (n 2) 246 (Simon Brown LJ).

[92] A Mackie and J Burrows *A Study of Requests for Disclosure of Evidence to Third Parties in Contested Trials* (Home Office Research, Development and Statistics Directorate, Research Findings No 134 2000).

- distinguishing disclosable from non-disclosable material using legal principles based upon the relevance of that specific evidence to the issues to be tried, and upon considerations of public policy, requiring a case-by-case analysis of the information sought.

1. Third party disclosure in English law

Disclosure by a reluctant third party is usually effected by an application by the prosecution or the defence for a summons *duces tecum*, which requires a representative of that party to attend court with the records in issue.[93]

(a) Disclosure to investigators and prosecutors of information possessed by the family court or a third party

It might be thought that given the frequent exhortations to inter-agency cooperation and joint investigations in *Working Together*,[94] as well as in other government guidelines and public inquiry reports into specific cases of child abuse, information can be readily pooled by the agencies involved.

On the contrary, until 2005 the Family Proceedings Rule 4.23(1)[95] forbade the disclosure of any document held by the court (other than a court order itself) to someone not involved in the child protection proceedings unless the family court gave permission. The prohibition had been restrictively interpreted by the Court of Appeal as applying only to documents actually filed with the court. Thus in *Re G (A Minor) (Social Worker: Disclosure)*[96] where the parents of a six-month-old baby had blamed one another for the serious injuries sustained by the child, the prosecution was forced into the position of dropping the proceedings, but the trial judge directed that the charge lie on file instead of ordering an acquittal. Three years later the local authority initiated interim care proceedings in respect of the newborn infant of the same parents. The parents were willing to discuss for the first time the circumstances of the brother's injuries, but only if they would not expose themselves to criminal proceedings if they made damaging admissions. The Court of Appeal held that a social worker could and indeed should disclose information obtained in the context of a child protection investigation to the police without a court order, as otherwise the joint investigation would be ineffective and each discipline would go its own way. The child protection case conference would be stymied, and the unsatisfactory arrangements widely in place before the Cleveland Inquiry might be reproduced.[97]

---

[93] Criminal Procedure (Attendance of Witnesses) Act 1965 s 2 as amended by the CPIA 1996, s 66. Where the proceedings are in magistrates' court, the summons will be issued under the Magistrates' Courts Act 1980 s 97, as amended by the CPIA 1996, s 47, Sch 1, para 8.

[94] Department of Health *Working Together to Safeguard Children* (1999) [3.57]–[3.64] emphasizes that the police and the local authority have mutual responsibilities to share evidence at child protection conferences if it is in the best interests of the child.

[95] Family Proceedings Rules 1991 (SI 1991/1247) Rule 4.23(1).

[96] *Re G (A Minor) (Social Worker: Disclosure)* [1996] 2 All ER 65 (CA).

[97] ibid 72–73 (Auld J dissenting); *Re W (Disclosure to Police)* [1998] 2 FLR 135 (CA).

In April 2005 the Family Proceedings Rules were amended by the Children Act 2004 to permit any party to family court proceedings to disclose information to a police officer serving in a child protection unit or paedophile unit of a police force, or for the purpose of a criminal investigation, or to a member of the CPS.[98] A protocol for disclosure to the police of local authority records was established in October 2003.[99] As soon as the police investigating a suspected crime believe relevant material may exist within social services or education files, they are to notify the local authority in writing, and designated disclosure officers appointed by each party will arrange to identify and review the material. The local authority cannot reveal to the police any relevant medical information without the consent of its author or a family court order.[100] The police disclosure officer is under a duty to identify any material which might undermine the prosecution case or might reasonably assist the defence case, which would fall within the disclosure provisions of the Criminal Procedure and Investigations Act 1996 (CPIA). The CPS is required to treat all disclosed material as sensitive, and will not disclose any of it to the defence unless by agreement with the local authority or by order of the court following a public interest immunity application.[101]

The 2005 Rules possibly have not brought the desired clarity for local authorities, police officers and the CPS. They draw distinctions between disclosure by a local authority to a police officer for child protection purposes and disclosure for an ongoing criminal investigation, which can pose difficulty where (as is often the case) one officer is performing both functions. In a decision in May 2006, Sumner J strove to resolve the problem by defining the police's child protection function as encompassing the investigation and prosecution of those who may be responsible for criminal offences to a child. Thus it was appropriate for social workers to give a police officer performing this dual function statements disclosed in a meeting of legal professionals for all parties by the parents of a four-week-old child about how he came by his multiple injuries, the father's statement withdrawing his confession to the police, as well as two medical reports including that the injuries were most likely non-accidental. Sumner J recalled that the case of Maria Colwell 30 years previously had tragically demonstrated the need for all agencies involved in child protection to house all of the relevant information.[102] Another distinction between disclosure of documents prepared for the family court proceedings (which requires the family court's permission), and divulging the information contained in them (which does not) may cause some confusion amongst child professionals.[103]

What of testimony in the child protection proceedings? Section 98 of the Children Act 1989 provides that no person shall be excused from giving evidence on any matter or answering a question on the ground that doing so might incriminate him

---

[98] Family Proceedings (Amendment No 4) Rules 2005 (SI 2005/1976) Rule 10.20A(3), discussed above Chapter 6 section D.

[99] CPS *A Protocol between the CPS Police and Local Authorities* (n 23).   [100] ibid [6.6].

[101] ibid [6.11]–[6.18].

[102] *Reading Borough Council v D, Chief Constable of Thames Valley Police* [2006] EWHC 1465, [2006] All ER (D) 211 [69]–[73]. Sumner J considered that the CPS is in the same position as police officers [89].

[103] ibid [69]–[71].

or his spouse of an offence; however, the witness is given so-called 'use immunity' in that any admission will not be admissible in evidence against that witness in a criminal proceedings other than for perjury. The inadmissible testimony nonetheless may provide the police with valuable leads to evidence which would be admissible in a criminal trial. In *Re EC*[104] a father, when testifying in care proceedings relating to a three-year-old child, admitted (after being warned under s 98) that he had thrown her baby sister onto the settee, causing her death. An earlier extensive police investigation had not resulted in charges against any of the five suspects present at the time. The police sought disclosure of the transcripts of the testimony of the father and other family members, as well as of medical witnesses. Wall J allowed the medical evidence to be disclosed to the police and CPS, but not the testimony from the family, holding that the public interest in encouraging frankness in child protection proceedings by preserving confidentiality outweighed the competing public interest in a full and proper investigation into the baby's death. The Court of Appeal reversed this decision, holding that the family court judge had jurisdiction to order disclosure to the police of material covered by s 98, the relevant factors in exercising his discretion being:

- the welfare and the interests of the child concerned and of other children generally;
- the maintenance of confidentiality in children's cases and the importance of encouraging frankness;
- the public interest in the administration of justice, as barriers should not be erected between one branch of judicature and another which would be inimical to the overall interests of justice;
- the public interest in convicting those who have been guilty of violent or sexual offences against children;
- the gravity of the alleged offence and the relevance of the evidence to it;
- the desirability of cooperation between the various agencies concerned with the welfare of children;
- in cases where s 98(2) applied, fairness to the person who had incriminated himself and to any others affected by the incriminating statement, and any danger of oppression; and
- any other material disclosure which had already taken place.[105]

Given the very grave allegation against the father, it was of prime importance that there should be a full and proper investigation of the killing. The police were entitled to all the material requested by them.[106]

Two years later the Court of Appeal took an even stronger line, holding that the police were *entitled*, without a court order, to request access to confidential information gathered by social workers in relation to a joint investigation of physical abuse conducted in accordance with *Working Together*, as both agencies are bound by the same

---

[104] *Re EC (Disclosure of Material)* [1996] 2 FLR 725 (CA).   [105] ibid 733.   [106] ibid 735.

obligation of confidentiality.[107] Furthermore, where a court disclosure order is necessary under Federal Court Rules (FCR) Rule 4.23, family court judges should hesitate before refusing to provide relevant and significant information to the police who are working with social services.[108] Notwithstanding this admonition, the police are not always successful in their application for disclosure of inculpatory statements given in care proceedings. Wall J has firmly stated that the Court of Appeal in reversing his own ruling in *Re EC* had not created a presumption in favour of disclosure.[109] He indicated that the court might refuse disclosure to the police in cases where there had been an acknowledgement of harm done by a parent, and the prospect of rehabilitation dependent on the gravity of the harm. Wall J also extended the use immunity under s 98 of the Children Act 1989 from oral testimony to statements or admissions made to expert witnesses, making those statements inadmissible in criminal proceedings, as otherwise parents would have little motivation to be frank.[110] He also warned lawyers representing parents that it is not acceptable practice to put pressure on experts to conduct their investigations on the basis of undertakings intended to protect the parents' position.[111] Nevertheless, in a case where two babies in the same family had died before their first birthday, Wall J directed that the expert's report filed in the causation phase of the care proceedings for the surviving son be disclosed to the police, because on the facts there was nothing to derogate from the general proposition that those responsible for the deaths of children should face a criminal investigation.[112]

The laudable objectives of *Working Together*'s dominant theme of interdisciplinary co-operation cannot conceal the clash of two systems which are constrained to take very different approaches to achieve their common goal of protecting the child. Social workers and health professionals are trained to cooperate with families in obtaining information with a view to securing the future welfare of the child, if possible within the birth family. The police are necessarily part of an adversarial process which family court judges are resistant to permit to intrude into child protection proceedings. In cases of physical abuse where the parents or carers refuse to identify the perpetrator, or accuse one another of being the culprit and there is no other evidence of identity, the police are understandably keen to obtain any evidence of admissions made to social services or health professionals to avoid a prosecution being stymied. As Elizabeth Lawson QC, a former Chair of the Family Law Bar Association, observed when sitting as a deputy High Court judge:

[T]here is no doubt in my mind that the impact of the reported authorities and the trend whereby disclosure is almost routinely ordered to the police, has greatly discouraged the frankness which is so necessary to the resolution of children's cases and which Parliament sought to protect. On the one hand, the courts have made full and frank disclosure in children's cases mandatory. On the other hand, the result for a parent of frankness, whether to the court or in

---

[107] *Re W (Disclosure to Police)* (n 97) 142–143 (notes of admissions by mother in the course of their seven interviews that she shook her baby who had sustained head injuries, ordered to be disclosed to police).
[108] ibid 145 (Butler-Sloss LJ).
[109] *Re AB (Care Proceedings: Disclosure of Medical Evidence to Police)* [2003] EWHC 2198, [2003] 1 FLR 579 (Fam Div Wall J) [65]–[67].   [110] ibid [57]–[58].
[111] ibid [93]–[101].   [112] ibid [67], [87], [114]–[122], [134].

the context of a discussion with a psychiatrist or a guardian ad litem, is that it is highly likely that the information will be disclosed to the prosecution authorities.

. . . In practice . . . it is those parents who make admissions who are prosecuted and those who deny all knowledge of how the injuries were caused [who] are not,[113] because where the child is too young to speak for himself the evidence to support a prosecution is often insufficient in the absence of an admission . . . Many of these parents will never have faced police questioning before. The fear that they will be prosecuted and sent to jail keeps many silent. They remain silent often for many months or clutch at the straws of alternative explanations for how the child came by his injuries. During those months the children's future is effectively put on hold until a court determines how the injuries occurred and who caused them, often to the detriment of that child.[114]

Moreover, the received wisdom in social services is that a denial of responsibility for a child's injuries increases the risk of future harm and is a barrier to the formulation of a child protection plan (other than removal of the child) and to the development of partnership with families to work toward rehabilitation.[115] Whether this position is valid or not—and we know that investigators can and do get it wrong—the result is that it is in the short- and long-term interests of the suspect and the family unit to acknowledge responsibility.

Notwithstanding these concerns, it is the Government's stated policy that the police should have access to all relevant evidence in the family law proceedings.[116]

Medical experts specializing in child protection have also expressed concern that the system of disclosure to criminal investigators operates against the interests of children by placing a greater value on the prosecution and conviction of offenders than on the welfare of victims of abuse and their siblings.[117]

Elizabeth Lawson QC proposed a disclosure test: could the material used in the care proceedings fairly be used against the parents in any criminal trial? The difficulty with this approach is that, as s 78 of the Police and Criminal Evidence Act 1984 stipulates, the fairness of admitting certain evidence, given the circumstances in which it was obtained, must be judged in the context of the criminal trial as a whole. Family court judges considering disclosure applications will rarely have the benefit of that perspective.

Wall J suggested that further thought be given to the relationship between the family courts and the police and the development of a protocol between the CPS and the family justice system governing mutual disclosure of information. The protocol would identify criteria for cases in which the CPS thinks prosecution is likely to be appropriate so that family lawyers would be able to advise their clients realistically

---

[113] This conclusion is confirmed in empirical research: C Cobley ' "Working Together?"—Admissions of Abuse in Child Protection Proceedings and Criminal Prosecutions' (2004) 16.2 Child and Family LQ 175.

[114] *Re M (Care Proceedings: Disclosure: Human Rights)* (n 22) (Elizabeth Lawson QC) 1324–1325. Wall J specifically disagreed with these observations in *Re AB* (n 109) [125].

[115] J Gumbleton and A Lusk 'Rehabilitation without Admission—A New Way Forward' [1999] Family Law 822.

[116] *Disclosure of Information in Family Proceedings Cases Involving Children* (n 4) 11, [5.5]–[5.6], accepting the submissions of ACPO and CPS, and rejecting the submissions of the Association of Lawyers for Children.

[117] *Re AB* (n 109) 590–591, describing the submissions of Professor David, a paediatrician.

about the likely attitude of the police and prosecutors to disclosure in a particular case.[118] As judicial disclosure decisions indicate, the difficulty will be that each case very much turns upon its own facts, so it would be difficult to develop more precise and detailed guidance than the factors already spelt out in *Re EC*.[119] The protocol which was developed in October 2003 is one way only: it applies to disclosure of information and family proceedings to the police.[120]

Another suggestion is that the Code for Crown Prosecutors expressly provide that an admission by the suspect in child protection proceedings should be a factor in favour of discontinuing any criminal proceedings,[121] presumably under the public interest test. However, it is difficult to see how much difference this would make. Empirical research has shown that under the public interest test the police already consider four factors: whether the child has suffered harm, whether the suspect is likely to harm this or another child in the future, whether the suspect was morally culpable, and whether a prosecution would worsen an already difficult family situation.[122] Prosecutors are already instructed to take into account the best interests of the child in deciding whether to lay or continue with criminal charges. All of the leading cases on disclosure have dealt with child homicide or grievous bodily harm, where the public interest in child protection is arguably the highest. Any such guidance cannot fetter the discretion of prosecutors under the Code for Crown Prosecutors. Therefore it is difficult to see what further assurances can be given to a carer in child protection proceedings that any disclosures of culpability will not be transmitted to the criminal investigators.

(b) Disclosure to the defence of information possessed by a third party

The significance of the rules governing third party disclosure for a fair trial—and the perception of the participants that the trial has been fair—must not be underestimated. The rules must mediate between the conflicting interests of the accused abuser and the complainant. On the one hand the defence can reasonably argue that it should be entitled to access evidence concerning the complainant in the hands of a third party which would be disclosable, and properly deployable in attacking credibility, if it were in the possession of the prosecution or could be ascertained by other means. The counter-argument is that the defence should not be permitted to invade the complainant's privacy by the proverbial fishing expedition, trawling through confidential records in the hope that some ammunition, however tenuous, might be found to attack his credibility. These issues take on a rather different complexion where

---

[118] ibid 611.

[119] The 2006 Crown Court protocol merely confirms current practice, that the holder of relevant material for the purposes of family proceedings must apply to the family court for leave to disclose information to the police or another third party: HM Court Service *Protocol* (n 73) [62].

[120] *Disclosure of Information in Family Proceedings Cases Involving Children* (n 4).

[121] C Cobley (n 113).

[122] C Keenan and L Maitland ' "There Ought to be a Law Against It": Police Evaluation of the Efficacy of Prosecution in a Case of Child Abuse' [1999] Child and Family LQ 397.

the complainant is a child who has little or no control over his mode of life and family circumstances,[123] who may be the victim of previous abuse, and who is likely to be puzzled and intimidated by cross-examination on matters extraneous to the incidents charged. The administrative burdens and expense imposed upon third parties should not be discounted. Underlying these disclosure issues is a conundrum: what evidence is logically probative of whether a witness is worthy of belief?

A third party has four possible avenues to resist disclosure:

• legal professional privilege attaches to the record;
• confidentiality attaches to the record;
• the 'mere credibility' rule; or
• public interest immunity attaches to the record.

Whilst the first two avenues can be dealt with quickly, the remaining two require further analysis.

(i) Legal professional privilege

We have seen that litigation privilege does not apply to evidence prepared for the purpose of child protection proceedings. Otherwise, if the document has been prepared for the dominant purpose of litigation, such as a tort claim by the complainant, or to obtain legal advice, legal professional privilege attaches to the record. Legal professional privilege is absolute in English law, and there is no implied exception for exculpatory evidence required by the defence to establish innocence in criminal law proceedings.[124]

(ii) Confidentiality

It is important to remember that in English law, unlike in some other common law jurisdictions, confidentiality itself is not a valid reason for non-disclosure of material which meets the criterion of relevance. However, confidentiality may be a very material consideration for an English judge to bear in mind when public interest immunity is claimed.[125] So something in addition to the simple assertion of confidentiality is required. Arguments requiring further exploration in the English courts include whether the necessary additional element may be added by the right to family life guaranteed by ECHR Article 8, and whether it can be claimed by someone other than the children who are directly the subject of the proceedings.[126]

---

[123] Lord Williams of Mostyn (Chair) *Childhood Matters: the Report of the National Commission of Inquiry into the Prevention of Child Abuse* (HMSO, London 1996) 125.

[124] *R v Derby Magistrates' Court ex p B* (n 14).

[125] *Alfred Crompton Amusement Machines Ltd v Customs & Excise Commissioners (No 2)* [1974] AC 405 (HL) 433; *Science Research Council v Nassé* [1980] AC 1028 (HL) 1067; *D v NSPCC* (n 15) 230.

[126] *Re B (Disclosure to Other Parties)* (n 27); cf *Re R (Care: Disclosure: Nature of Proceedings)* (n 45) 776.

(iii) The 'mere credibility' rule

In English criminal law, the threshold question for the court will be whether the documents sought meet the test of materiality stipulated by the Criminal Procedure (Attendance of Witnesses) Act 1965 s 2. Before 1996, the English courts had worked from the premise that where the liberty of the defendant is in issue and disclosure may be of assistance to him, the claim for disclosure by a third party will be strong.[127] However in 1996 the Court of Appeal set out a more stringent test of materiality than mere assistance to the defence, in *R v Reading Justices ex p Berkshire CC*:[128]

- To be material evidence, documents must not only be relevant to the issues arising in the criminal proceedings, but also be immediately admissible in evidence.

- Documents which are desired merely for the purpose of possible cross-examination on credibility are not admissible in evidence, and thus are not disclosable.

- The applicant seeking production must satisfy the court that the documents are 'likely to be material' in the sense indicated, 'likelihood' meaning a real possibility, although not necessarily a probability.

- It is not sufficient that the defence merely wants to find out whether or not the third party has such material documents. This procedure must not be used as a disguised attempt to obtain discovery.

These principles, which we have dubbed the 'mere credibility' rule, were subsequently approved by the House of Lords.[129] Third parties thus are no longer bound to disclose documents which might assist in the conduct of the defence case,[130] although they would be producible were they held by the prosecution.[131] The dilemma for defence solicitors and counsel is that they are at risk of a wasted costs order against them personally if the court concludes that their request for disclosure was improper, unreasonable, or negligent, when usually they will have little or no idea of what information is contained in the records and what might be inadmissible under the 'mere credibility' rule.[132] In some cases where disclosure is denied, the defence nonetheless might be able to obtain part of that information from other sources, for example, where a family member who knew of the complainant's history cooperates with the defence, in which case they are free to use that information in cross-examination, and so can operate perversely.[133]

---

[127] *R v K(DT) (Evidence)* [1993] 2 FLR 181 (CA).

[128] *R v Reading Justices ex p Berkshire CC* [1996] 1 Cr App R 239 (CA) 246.

[129] *R v Derby Magistrates' Court* (n 14).   [130] *Re S (Care Order: Criminal Proceedings)* (n 3).

[131] In *R v Azmy* (1996) 34 BMLR 45 (Manchester Crown Court), Mitchell J observed that for some years prior to the *Derby* case the courts had applied the same test to disclosure by third parties as to disclosure by the prosecution.

[132] *R v M (Wasted Costs Order)* [1996] 1 FLR 750 (QB); *R v H (L)* [1997] 1 Cr App R 176 (CA). Defence and prosecution are firmly enjoined from embarking on 'fishing expeditions' by HM Court Service *Protocol* (n 73) [59], and warned that the court will consider making a wasted costs order where the application 'is clearly unmeritorious and ill-conceived'. For examples see *Bristol Study* Cases 6A, 57B, 29B.

[133] As in case 29B of the *Bristol Study*. Some judges, concerned about the implications of the mere credibility rule, would give hints to defence counsel about the avenues they might need to pursue, based on information which they had seen on the file provided to the court [*Bristol Study* 51; HH Judge N Denison QC 'Disclosure' (1996) 36 Medical Science Law 283].

(iv) Public interest immunity claims

The concept of public interest immunity originated in considerations of national security, but it has now moved far beyond that boundary. Whilst there is no authoritative definition of public interest immunity, perhaps the best judicial definition is to be found in *D v NSPCC* where Lord Edmund-Davies described it as applying:

... where (i) a confidential relationship exists ... and (ii) disclosure would be in breach of some ethical or social value involving the public interest, the court has a discretion to uphold a refusal to disclose relevant evidence providing it considers that, on balance, the public interest would be better served by excluding such evidence.[134]

The Law Lords held that this public interest test was satisfied in the context of a civil negligence action in respect of the identity of an informer to the NSPCC who alleged that the plaintiff was abusing her baby, concluding that such informers should be granted the same protection as that given police informers in criminal trials.

In considering public interest immunity in the context of the disclosure of child protection records in criminal proceedings, the court must balance the importance of confidentiality in child protection proceedings against the public interest in seeing that the ends of justice are properly served; the family court should not seek to erect a barrier which would prejudice the operation of another branch of the judicature.[135]

As noted above, there is no longer an absolute immunity attaching to local authority records relating to the protection and welfare of a particular child.[136] Nevertheless, the Court of Appeal has held that local authorities have a positive duty to claim public interest immunity for any records in its possession concerning that child, even ordinary school records which are not directly related to child protection.[137] The rationale is that it is for the court, not the local authority, to balance the public interest in maintaining confidentiality of those documents against the public interest in seeing that justice is done, particularly in a criminal case involving the liberty of the subject. This is an important protection for the local authority as well as the defendant, in relieving the local authority from having to reconcile ethical conflicts created by their statutory duty to safeguard the welfare of children. Yet this seems to be contradicted by the October 2003 protocol between the CPS, police, and local authorities about the exchange of information in investigation and prosecution of child abuse cases. The protocol clearly states in several paragraphs that the local authority can consent to the disclosure of its own records by the CPS to the defence as a third party, in which case it is not necessary for CPS bring a public interest immunity application.[138] If the local authority voluntarily discloses information in its files directly to the defence, they

---

[134] *D v NSPCC* (n 15) 245.
[135] *Re D (Minors) (Wardship: Disclosure)* [1994] 1 FLR 346 (CA).
[136] *Re M (A Minor) (Disclosure of Material)* [1990] 2 FLR 36 (CA), discussed above section A.1.
[137] *R v Higgins* [1996] 1 FLR 137 (CA) 140.
[138] CPS *Protocol between the CPS Police and Local Authorities* (n 23) [4.3], [6.16]–[6.18].

must immediately notify the CPS and the police[139]—yet if the affected child is the defendant surely this constitutes a breach of confidence owed by the local authority to the child, and a court order should be required.

The potential conflict between the public interest immunity and 'mere credibility' rules is well illustrated by *R v Higgins*, where the accused was charged with indecently assaulting a visually impaired seven-year-old boy. The defence sought disclosure from the local authority of his statements of special educational needs, which included documents from the mother, the solicitor, teachers, psychologists, and the Royal National Institute for the Blind, annual review records from the same sources, and correspondence between the mother and the school and the mother and her solicitors. The Court of Appeal upheld the ruling of the trial judge that only three documents should be disclosed from these files, which suggested that the boy may have been backward in his intellectual development, that he had a propensity for mixing fact and fiction, and that he had a tendency to fantasize, even though the documents were seen as only at best marginally relevant.[140] In *Higgins*, the documents which were freed from public interest immunity clearly were only relevant to the credibility of the child complainant. Therefore, should not the 'mere credibility' rule in *Reading* have applied to prevent their disclosure?

(v) Two tests and two balancing acts?

The inconsistencies between the tests for public interest immunity and the 'mere credibility' rule were explored in the important and still unreported Court of Appeal decision in *R v Brushett* in 2000.[141] The case involved allegations of historic sexual abuse of 25 former pupils against the headmaster of a Welsh Community School responsible for looking after boys in care. The school records concerning the boys had been destroyed shortly after the school was closed down in 1980, and other records important to the defence had gone missing.[142] Before trial the defendant was denied access to documents in the social services files relating to the complainant and other witnesses on the basis of public interest immunity. It was significant to the eventual outcome of the appeal that the police had examined the social services files relating to 7 witnesses, and had also had access to information from files relating to 14 other witnesses on the understanding that public interest immunity attached to the documents, whereas no examination of social services files relating to the other witnesses had occurred. Therefore, it could be said that the former category of records had at one time been in the constructive possession of the prosecution. Nevertheless, the prosecution was not made a party to the applications for disclosure.

The Court of Appeal noted that the trial judge was faced with two lines of authority which are irreconcilable as each has a separate genesis: where the documents had been

---

[139] ibid [6.7]   [140] *R v Higgins* (n 137) 138–140.

[141] *R v Brushett* Case No 99/7712 21 Dec 2000; [2001] Crim LR 471 (CA).

[142] For an analysis of the unavailability of records as a basis to stay a prosecution as an abuse of process, see P Lewis Delayed *Prosecution for Childhood Sexual Abuse* (OUP, Oxford 2006) 57–60, 77–78.

seen by the police or prosecution, the issue is public interest immunity and is governed by *Keane*, whereas if the documents remained unseen and in the possession of a third party, then the more stringent 'mere credibility' materiality rule apparently applies.[143] The trial judge stated in the course of argument that if he found in the files information indicating that a complainant had previously made false allegations or that there was someone else indulging in similar activity with the child he would want to order that disclosed. The difficulty with that approach is that the 'mere credibility' rule would seem to preclude a disclosure order. The trial judge then concluded that while the 'mere credibility' rule was intended to discourage fishing expeditions and endless cross-examination as to credit on very peripheral matters, 'if circumstances arise where it would be unjust not to allow disclosure of certain other material, so a defendant would not receive a fair trial, in the sense that he could not establish his innocence where he might otherwise do so, then that material must be disclosed'.[144] The Court of Appeal commended this more flexible approach to the 'mere credibility' rule as being 'an eminently sensible and pragmatic approach'.[145] Moreover, this solution meant there was no breach of ECHR Article 6 because jurisprudence thereunder had recognized that legitimate restrictions may be placed upon the defendant's right to full disclosure in the public interest, provided that the restrictions are strictly necessary and that any difficulties for the defence are sufficiently counterbalanced by procedures by the judicial authorities.[146]

It is not entirely clear where *Brushett* has left the law. *Reading/Derby* had established that the test of materiality under the 'mere credibility' rule must be satisfied before public interest immunity falls to be considered. In *Brushett* the trial judge had identified that some of the documents did not meet the test of materiality and so were not disclosable under the 'mere credibility' rule, but then went on to hold that the public interest nonetheless required disclosure because they related to previous allegedly false allegations and sexual activity with others. This analysis apparently was applied to all the disputed documents regardless of whether or not the prosecution had previously had access to them.[147]

In effect, *Brushett* appears to have collapsed the distinction between the 'mere credibility' rule and public interest immunity where the overriding right of the defence to a fair trial demands disclosure. One factor in the issue of what disclosure is required for a fair trial is that there would be inequality of arms between the defence and prosecution where the prosecution knows of a significant piece of background information which the defence does not have.[148] While this must be right, the right of the defence to disclosure of evidence relevant to the credibility of the accuser should not turn upon whether the prosecution has or has not seen a document in the possession of a third party. The new focus on the essential issue of the entitlement of the defendant to a fair

---

[143] *R v Brushett* (n 141) 5–6.   [144] ibid 9–10.   [145] ibid 13–14.

[146] ibid 15, citing *Rowe v UK* (n 66), *Fitt v UK* (n 67) and *Jasper v UK* (2000) 30 EHRR 441 (ECtHR).

[147] The applications resulted in orders that some documents in the Crown's possession were disclosed and others were disclosed from the social services files.

[148] *R v Brushett* (n 141) 10 (*voir dire* ruling [5]).

trial is to be welcomed.[149] However, there has been a wide disparity of practice on the part of local authorities in the wake of *Brushett*,[150] sowing even greater confusion in all quarters about the disclosure rules.

Many barristers felt that the perversity[151] of the 'mere credibility' rule had been significantly mitigated by the *Attorney General's Guidelines on Disclosure* published on 20 November 2000.[152] Under that disclosure regime, when an investigator, disclosure officer, or prosecutor suspected that a non-government agency or other third party such as a social services department, hospital, doctor, school, or providers of forensics services has material or information which might be disclosable if it were in the possession of the prosecution, the prosecution would have to consider seeking access, and it would be important to do so if such material were likely to undermine the prosecution case or assist an identified defence. The prosecutor was given a 'margin of consideration' as to what steps he regards as appropriate in the particular case to secure disclosure of material or information he suspected was relevant, although he was required to act within the permissible limits afforded by the *Attorney General's Guidelines 2000*.[153] If the third party refused to allow access to the material or information without good reasons, the matter was not to be left, and the prosecutor or investigator should apply for a court order for production. When information came into the possession of the prosecution, they were required to consult with the other agency before it is disclosed to the defence, to ascertain whether a claim for public interest immunity should be advanced in court; otherwise it became producible under the CPIA 1996.

It had rightly been pointed out that there was a tension between the the 2000 *Guidelines* and the rules as to third party disclosure: the guidance advised prosecutors to apply for material relevant to the defence case, which would normally include any information affecting the credibility of a prosecution witness such as previous inconsistent statements—but under the 'mere credibility' rule such evidence was not disclosable even to the prosecution.[154]

The point remains unresolved in the November 2005 version of the *Attorney General's Guidelines*, which also make no reference to the 'mere credibility' rule.[155] The new edition made a positive change in requiring rather than merely exhorting investigators and prosecutors to seek out relevant evidence in the hands of third parties, and

---

[149] See *Re Z (Children) (Disclosure: Criminal Proceedings)* [2003] EWHC 61 (Fam Div Munby J) ordering that a witness statement in contact proceedings in the family court be disclosed to the defence in a murder trial to enable that witness to be cross-examined on any inconsistencies.

[150] A Perkins and E Tomlinson 'Disclosure of Social Services Documents into Criminal Proceedings' [2005] Fam LJ 806.

[151] For examples see *Bristol Study* Cases 6A, 57B, 29B. Some judges, concerned about the implications of the mere credibility rule, would give hints to defence counsel about the avenues they might need to pursue, based on information which they had seen on the file provided to the court [*Bristol Study* 51; Denison (n 133)].   [152] *Attorney General's Guidelines on Disclosure 2000* (November 2000).

[153] *R v Alibaji* [2004] EWCA Crim 681 [63].

[154] Rook and Ward (n 71) 620–621 (concerning the *Attorney General's Guidelines 2000*).

[155] *Attorney General's Guidelines on Disclosure 2005* (April 2005) [47]–[54].

the essentials of the procedures remained much the same.[156] However the Attorney General's preface emphasized that prosecutors should not abrogate their duties under the CPIA by making wholesale disclosure in order to avoid carrying out the disclosure exercise themselves, and again warned the defence of the consequences of pursuing the proverbial fishing expedition. The Attorney General expressed the hope that the courts would apply the legal regime under the CPIA 'rather than ordering disclosure because it is either easier or it would not do "any harm"', perhaps an oblique disapproval of the practice of many Crown Court judges to ignore the 'mere credibility' rule.

The point was driven home by the *Protocol for the Control and Management of Unused Material in the Crown Court* issued on 20 February 2006;[157] the accompanying outline note under the seal of the Court of Appeal states in [2.3] that the overarching principle is that material will fall to be disclosed 'if, and only if, it satisfies the statutory test for disclosure' ie that it is capable of undermining the prosecution case or assisting the defence case. Judges are instructed by the 2006 *Crown Court Protocol* to apply the 'mere credibility' rule to material in the hands of third parties, not the CPIA.[158] This seems to follow on from the denial in the Attorney General's 2005 *Guidelines* that material reviewed by investigators or prosecutors falls into their constructive possession.[159] However, *Brushett*'s distinction between documents seen by the police or prosecution, to which public interest immunity applies, and uninspected documents remaining in the possession of a third party, to which the 'mere credibility' rule applies, surely cannot be reversed by the *fiat* of the Attorney General.

Some barristers are concerned that prosecutors are heeding this injunction and taking a much stricter approach to the dual test of disclosure under the CPIA, and that this is a step backwards from the cooperative approach apparently commended in the 2000 *Guidelines*. This view is reinforced by the CPS policy on child witnesses published on 27 June 2006, which tells children that the CPS will apply the disclosure rules 'strictly to make sure that such information is only handed over when absolutely necessary, or when a court orders us to do so".[160]

It had been suggested that one possible way of circumventing the 'mere credibility' rule is where the documents might be classified as business records, so that they might be admissible under statutory exceptions to the hearsay rule.[161] This route has been relatively little explored but has been held to apply to social services records.[162] However, the new hearsay provisions do not furnish a test of *relevance*,

---

[156] ibid [47], the imperative nature of this expectation being helpfully reinforced and more explicitly stated by HM Court Service *Protocol* (n 73) [53].   [157] ibid [2.3].

[158] ibid [52], [60].   [159] *Attorney General's Guidelines on Disclosure 2005* (April 2005) [48].

[160] Crown Prosecution Service *Children and Young People: CPS Policy on Prosecuting Criminal Cases Involving Children and Young People as Victims and Witnesses* (27 June 2006) 13.

[161] CJA 2003 s 117.

[162] *Note: R v Higgins* (n 137), discussed in Rook and Ward (n 71) 616–617.

but only a test of *admissibility* of relevant evidence. The 'mere credibility' rule is not founded upon objections that the records are hearsay.[163] The 2006 *Crown Court Protocol* on disclosure in a poorly worded passage apparently advises judges that even if the evidence might be 'admissible' using the hearsay route of the CJA 2003 ss 114-20 applicable to business records, nevertheless the 'mere credibility' rule governs the issue.[164] Whatever the merits of the 'mere credibility' rule, this must be correct.

Some Crown Courts developed their own procedures for efficient review by the court of material in respect of which public interest immunity is claimed.[165] Whilst these protocols were commendable efforts to build communication links between local agencies, the variation in practices across the country could create difficulties for investigators and lawyers who had to work with several agencies operating under different protocols. Lord Justice Auld in his review of the criminal courts recommended that there be a single statutory protocol for third party disclosure, the specific mechanics of which could be guided by the local protocols.[166] In October 2003 the CPS published a model inter-agency protocol to provide a framework within which the CPS, police, and local authority social services and education departments can cooperate to share information on child protection investigations for the purpose of criminal prosecutions.[167] The national protocol is premised upon two principles:

- that social services and education departments of local authorities will always seek to act in the best interests of the children; and

- that the police and CPS are bound to protect the confidentiality of material held by local authorities and will not disclose any material to third parties without a court order or the consent of the local authority.

On the face of it, the 2003 model protocol seems to contradict cases from the Court of Appeal stating that the local authority *must* claim public interest immunity for any record it holds respecting a child involved in criminal proceedings in some way; paragraphs [6.16] to [6.18] of the model protocol refer to the local authority consenting to disclosure to the defence because it is required by the CPIA—which also is in apparent conflict with paragraphs [52] and [60] of the 2006 *Crown Court Protocol* requiring judges to apply the 'mere credibility' rule to records in the hands of third parties. It has been reported that many local authorities have refused to adopt the national protocol, anxious that it does not afford adequate recognition of their duty

---

[163] *R v Azmy* (n 131) (access to the complainant's counselling records denied notwithstanding that they qualified as business records).   [164] HM Court Service *Protocol in the Crown Court* (n 73) [60].
[165] HH Judge DAH Rodwell QC 'Applications for Third Party Material Where PII is Likely to be Claimed' [1998] Crim LR 332.   [166] Auld *Review of the Criminal Courts* (n 83) 474–476.
[167] CPS *A Protocol between the CPS Police and Local Authorities* (n 23) (developed by the CPS with the Association of Chief Police Officers, Local Government Association of England, and Association of Directors of Social Services and endorsed by the Home Office, Department for Education and Skills, and the National Assembly for Wales).

to safeguard the interests of the alleged victim and her family, in the absence of court scrutiny, and the legal basis for it has been questioned.[168]

The national Criminal Case Management Framework[169] promulgated in July 2005 may go some way towards uniformity of best practice and streamlining the process to ensure that third party disclosure is addressed early and at each stage of the process by the prosecution and defence teams so that it does not block case progression to trial. But before it can do this, the inconsistencies and ambiguities across this precarious raft of protocols and guidelines must be addressed.

In at least one case the Court of Appeal has expressed surprise that no one involved in the prosecution thought it necessary or desirable to seek social services records containing highly relevant and potentially damaging material for cross-examination of the child witness and her mother.[170] What seems clear is that there is a considerable risk that material which could be highly important to the defence can be intercepted by the perverse effects of the 'mere credibility' rule or public interest immunity. Given the courts' recognition that sexual offence cases are quintessentially a contest of credibility between the defendant and the complainant,[171] it is difficult to see how material in the hands of a local authority or other third party which might cast some doubt upon the complainant's credibility cannot be said to 'undermine the prosecution case' under the CPIA. In other words, it is arguable that the 'mere credibility' rule undermines the CPIA regime.

It is striking that the language of privacy rarely appears in the parties' or the criminal courts' analyses of the public interests at stake, notwithstanding that the complainant's right to a private life is expressly protected by ECHR Article 8 (subject to limitation for, *inter alia*, protection of the rights and freedoms of others).[172] Instead, the focus in the English and Welsh cases has been on the public interest in the record-keeper not being constrained by possible loss of confidentiality, and on the technicality of who holds the record, who has seen it, and the ways in which the information might be used at trial. The 2006 *Crown Court Protocol* on unused material reminds judges that victims do not waive the confidentiality of their medical records or the right to privacy under Article 8 by the mere fact of having made a complaint against the accused. This is a salutary reminder. The court is also warned that as a public authority it must ensure that any interference with the privacy rights of the child or others under Article 8 of the ECHR is in accordance with the law and necessary in pursuit of a legitimate public interest.[173]

---

[168] Perkins and Tomlinson (n 150). For a defence of the protocol by a local authority solicitor, see V Smith 'In Defence of the Prosecution Disclosure Protocol' [2006] Fam LJ 457.

[169] Department of Constitutional Affairs *The Criminal Case Management Framework* (2nd edn July 2005) [1.6] [2.4] [3.7] [4.3] [4.6] [15.6], [15.7] [16.13] [18.10] [20.14]-[20.15] [21.12] [21.13] [22.12] [23.11] [23.12].   [170] *R v M* Unreported, 5 November 1999 (No 98/03990/Y4) (CA) (Rose LJ).

[171] *R v Funderburk* [1990] 1 WLR 587 (CA).

[172] And to a degree by the Data Protection Act 1998 ch 29, although there are express exemptions in s 29 for the prevention or detection of crime and the apprehension or prosecution of offenders.

[173] HM Court Service *Protocol* (n 73) [57], [62].

Is this admonition sufficient protection? The right of the complainant to privacy is one of the dominant considerations in the third party disclosure rules in other common law jurisdictions, to which we now turn.

2. Third party disclosure in American law

We will first consider disclosure in American law, as Commonwealth jurisdictions have taken statutory and common law initiatives in the United States into account in devising their own disclosure procedures, especially for material possessed by third parties. Because of the multiplicity of American jurisdictions over criminal, family and child welfare, and tort law alike, we will focus our attention on issues directly relating to child protection and counselling records which are not in the possession of the prosecution.

(a) Access by an accused to child protection records

Under the Child Abuse Prevention and Treatment Act (CAPTA), in order to receive Federal funding States must preserve the confidentiality of all child abuse and neglect reports and records to protect the privacy rights of the child and of the child's parents or guardians, unless certain limited circumstances apply.[174] All 50 States and the District of Columbia have responded by enacting statutes that protect the confidentiality of their official records concerning child abuse.[175] Approximately 41 States and the District of Columbia have statutes authorizing the establishment of a statewide central registry of child maltreatment records to aid social services agencies in the investigation, treatment and prevention of child abuse cases, and to maintain statistical information for staffing and funding purposes.[176] A Federal privacy law (which generally pre-empts State law) exempts social services agencies involved in investigating child abuse, neglect or domestic violence from the statutory bar on disclosure of protected health information; agencies and professionals subject to State mandatory reporting laws are also exempt.[177]

The implications of these confidentiality laws for the constitutional rights of an accused were considered by the US Supreme Court in *Pennsylvania v Ritchie*.[178] The defendant was convicted of various sexual offences against his 13-year-old daughter. The defence subpoenaed the records of the Children and Youth Services (CYS) concerning the investigation of the immediate charges as well as earlier records compiled in a separate investigation instigated by a third party complaint that the defendant's children were being abused. Pennsylvania's non-disclosure law was subject to specified exceptions, one being that the agency could disclose reports to a court of competent jurisdiction pursuant to a court order. Ritchie, relying upon the confrontation and

---

[174] 42 USCA §5106a(b)(2)(A)(v) (West Supp 1998).

[175] *Pennsylvania v Ritchie* 480 US 39 (USSC 1987) 61 fn 17.

[176] US Department of Health and Human Services 'Disclosure of Confidential Records Statutes-at-a-Glance 2003' National Clearinghouse on Child Abuse and Neglect Information.

[177] Health Insurance Portability and Accountability Act 1996, as amended to 17 April 2003; US Department of Health and Human Services Office for Civil Rights Regulation Text 45 CFR Parts 160 and 164.   [178] *Pennsylvania v Ritchie* (n 175).

the compulsory process clauses of the Sixth Amendment, argued that the file might contain the names of favourable witnesses as well as other unspecified exculpatory evidence. Powell J writing for the majority held that a defendant's right to discover exculpatory evidence does not include the unsupervised authority to search through the State's files.[179] However:

> We find that Ritchie's interest (as well as that of the Commonwealth) in ensuring a fair trial can be protected fully by requiring that the CYS files be submitted only to the trial court for *in camera* review. Although this rule denies Ritchie the benefits of an 'advocate's eye', we note that the trial court's discretion is not unbounded. If a defendant is aware of specific information contained in the file (eg, the medical report), he is free to request it directly from the court, and argue in favor of its materiality. Moreover, the duty to disclose is ongoing; information that may be deemed immaterial upon original examination may become important as the proceedings progress, and the court would be obligated to release information material to the fairness of the trial.
>
> To allow full disclosure to defense counsel in this type of case would sacrifice unnecessarily the Commonwealth's compelling interest in protecting its child-abuse information. If the CYS records were made available to defendants, even through counsel, it could have a seriously adverse effect on Pennsylvania's efforts to uncover and treat abuse. Child abuse is one of the most difficult crimes to detect and prosecute, in large part because there often are no witnesses except the victim. A child's feelings of vulnerability and guilt and his or her unwillingness to come forward are particularly acute when the abuser is a parent. It therefore is essential that the child have a state-designated person to whom he may turn, and to do so with the assurance of confidentiality. Relatives and neighbors who suspect abuse also will be more willing to come forward if they know that their identities will be protected. Recognizing this, the Commonwealth—like all other States—has made a commendable effort to assure victims and witnesses that they may speak to the CYS counselors without fear of general disclosure. The Commonwealth's purpose would be frustrated if this confidential material had to be disclosed upon demand to a defendant charged with criminal child abuse, simply because a trial court may not recognize exculpatory evidence. Neither precedent nor common sense requires such a result.[180]

The Supreme Court expressly declined to consider whether the result would have been different if the statute had protected the child protection files from disclosure to anyone including law enforcement and judicial personnel.[181] Subsequent cases have held that where the statutory privilege is absolute, and the privilege holder refuses to permit the court to inspect the records privately, the witness's testimony must be stricken from the record.[182]

One lingering issue after *Pennsylvania v Ritchie* is the weight of the evidential burden on the applicant to justify the court's ordering production of the records for its private inspection. Trial courts cannot realistically expect defendants to articulate the precise nature of the confidential records without having prior access to

---

[179] ibid 59 [19].   [180] ibid 60–61 [20]–[21].   [181] ibid 58 fn 14.

[182] *State v d'Ambrosia* 548 A 2d 442 (Connecticut Supreme Ct 1989), *certiorari* denied 493 US 1063 (USSC 1990) 426; *People v Stanaway* 521 NW 2d 577 (Michigan Supreme Ct 1994), *certiorari* denied 115 S Ct 923 (USSC 1995) 577; *State v Esposito* 471 A 2d 949 (Connecticut Supreme Ct 1994) 949.

them.[183] In *Ritchie*, the defence had posited that the child protection files 'might' contain favourable information for its case, which would seem to be a minimal threshold.[184] State courts have stipulated more robust thresholds of materiality to the defence such as 'more than a mere possibility',[185] 'more than bare conjecture',[186] 'reasonable probability',[187] 'reasonable likelihood',[188] and 'reasonable ground to believe'.[189]

In considering whether the documents which have been inspected by the court should be released to the defence, the following factors are considered relevant:[190]

- the importance to the defence of the confidential or privileged information, such as impeachment by previous statements inconsistent with the testimony;[191]

- the strength of the State's interest in non-disclosure, such as deterring counselling or the embarrassment or humiliation of the child;[192]

- the terms of any applicable confidentiality statute, specifically: the policies served by it; the degree to which those policies might be frustrated by disclosure; and the defendant's need for discovery;[193]

- whether the statute confers an evidentiary privilege on the records, rather than merely labelling them as confidential;

- whether the defence has already had access to non-privileged material sufficient for its purposes;

- whether it is feasible to order partial or anonymized disclosure; and

- whether the prosecutor has already had access to the records.[194]

The appellate courts have been much occupied with defence complaints about the application of the thresholds for inspection and disclosure in specific cases, which appear to have been met with little success.

Finally, it should be noted that the same issues of access to child protection files arise in American courts where the defendant has been charged with making an unfounded report of child neglect.[195]

---

[183] *State v Gagné* 612A 2d 899 (New Hampshire Supreme Ct 1992).

[184] J Myers *Evidence in Child Abuse and Neglect Cases* (3rd edn John Wiley & Sons Inc, New York 1997) vol 1, 178–179.   [185] *State v Walther* 623 NW 2d 205 (Wisconsin App 2000).

[186] *State v Hoag* 749 A 2d 331 (New Hampshire Supreme Ct 2000).

[187] *State v Gagné* (n 183).

[188] *People v Arnold* 177 AD 2d 633 (New York App Div 1991); *Goldsmith v State* 651 A 2d 866 (Maryland CA 1995) 877.   [189] *State v Howard* 604 A 2d 1294 (Connecticut Supreme Ct 1992).

[190] Myers (n 184) vol 1, 183–188.

[191] *Commonwealth v O'Brien* 536 NE 2d 361 (Massachusetts App Ct 1989).

[192] *US v Antone* 981 F 2d 1059 (9th Cir 1992); *People v Foggy* 521 NE 2d 86 (Illinois Supreme Ct 1988), *certiorari* denied 486 US 1047 (USSC 1988).

[193] *Commonwealth v Fuller* 667 NE 2d 847 (Massachusetts Supreme Judicial Ct 1996).

[194] *People v Frost* 5 P 3d 317 (Colorado App 1999).

[195] *People v Berliner* 686 NYS 2d 673 (NY City Ct 1999); *Schaefer v State* 676 So 2d 947 (Alabama Crim App 1995).

(b) Privilege for confidential relationships

Federal Rule of Evidence 501 authorizes Federal courts to define new privileges by interpreting common-law principles 'in the light of reason and experience'.[196] This language echoes that of the US Supreme Court which encouraged the evolutionary development of evidential privileges.[197]

In *Jaffee v Redmond*,[198] the US Supreme Court recognized an unqualified class privilege for all communications between licensed psychiatrists and psychologists and their patients, on the basis that it is necessary for the mental health of Americans, which is 'a public good of transcendent importance'.[199] The Supreme Court noted that all 50 States and the District of Columbia had enacted into statute law some form of psychotherapist privilege, a consensus which indicated that 'reason and experience' support recognition of the privilege.[200] A different approach in federal cases would cut across the purposes of the State legislation enacted to foster these confidential communications.[201] The Court of Appeal and some States had created a qualified privilege which would not apply if in the interests of justice the evidentiary need for disclosure outweighed the patient's privacy interests. The majority rejected this approach on the basis that it would eviscerate the effectiveness of the privilege by making it impossible for participants to predict whether their confidential conversations would be protected[202]—the opposite conclusion to that reached by the Supreme Court of Canada in *M(A) v Ryan*, which we discuss below.[203] The majority also extended their newly minted common law blanket privilege to licensed social workers as their clients often include those who cannot afford the services of a psychiatrist and psychologist; the privilege applies only 'in the course of psychotherapy'.[204]

Statutory privileges applying to the physician–patient relationship are also common. Where the privilege attached to the relationship is not absolute, the courts have adopted the *Ritchie* procedure to balance the competing interests.[205] The Colorado

---

[196] Federal Rules of Evidence Rule 501, 28 USCA.

[197] *Hawkins v US* 258 US 74 (USSC 1958) 79; *Trammel v US* 445 US 40 (USSC 1980) 47.

[198] *Jaffee v Redmond* 518 US 1 (USSC 1996).   [199] ibid 11.

[200] ibid 12–13 and n 11 listing the State statutes. There is some divergence amongst the States concerning the types of therapy relationships protected and the exceptions recognized. A small number grant the privilege only to psychiatrists and psychologists, but most apply the protection more broadly to psychotherapy provided by a wide range of professionals. Compare New Zealand's restriction of class privilege to medical practitioners and clinical psychologists, below section C.5.

[201] *Jaffee v Redmond* (n 198) 11. Scalia J in dissent at 24 characterized this argument as 'a sort of inverse pre-emption: the truth-seeking functions of *federal* courts must be adjusted so as not to conflict with the policies of *the States*' (emphasis in original).   [202] ibid 17–18.

[203] *M(A) v Ryan* [1997] 1 SCR 157 (SCC) [35], referring to evidence used Scalia J's dissenting opinion in *Jaffee* to reinforce the opinion, discussed below section C.3(c).

[204] *Jaffee v Redmond* (n 198) 15–16. All but five of the States explicitly extend a testimonial privilege to licensed social workers: 16–17 n 17, 27.

[205] eg *State v Cressey* 628 A 2d 696 (New Hampshire Supreme Ct 1993) (psychologist in private practice); *State v Esposito* (n 182); *State v Cardall* 982 P 2d 79 (Utah Supreme Ct 1999); *State v Kohli* 672 A 2d 429 (Rhode Island Supreme Ct 1996); *State ex rel White v Gray* 2004 WL 1878198 (Missouri App W Dist 2004). The *Ritchie* procedure has also been used where the defence has applied for access to the diary of a sexual assault victim: *State v Enger* 539 NW 2d 259 (Minnesota App 1995).

legislation shows a useful compromise between the competing interests: whilst communications between a psychologist and a client in a professional context are privileged, there is an exception for any communication that is the basis of a report of abuse to the child protection authorities, pursuant to the psychologist's statutory duty to report suspicions of child abuse.[206]

There has been considerable academic pressure on the courts to create a parent–child privilege by analogy to spousal immunity, such that a parent could not be compelled to testify against a child, and vice versa.[207] While at least two States (Idaho and Minnesota) have created statutory privileges protecting confidential communications between minor children and parents,[208] these do not apply in child abuse litigation, just as spousal immunity is generally inapplicable in relation to assaults against minors. Massachusetts law prevents a minor child from testifying against a parent in a criminal proceeding, but this applies only where the victim was not a member of the parent's family and did not reside in the same household.[209] The courts have been generally reluctant to create a parent–child privilege, preferring to leave the policy decision to legislators.[210]

3. Third party disclosure in Canadian law

(a) Disclosure in child protection proceedings

Child protection and custody hearings in Canada are considered to be adversarial, and so they engage the parents' and the children's entitlements to security of the person under section 7 of the Canadian Charter of Rights and Freedoms. Therefore fairness requires that parents have an opportunity to present their cases effectively, as this is essential for determining the best interests of the child.[211] Fairness requires disclosure.[212]

The principles of disclosure in criminal proceedings were established by the Supreme Court of Canada in *R v Stinchcombe*.[213] The Crown has a legal duty to disclose all relevant information to the defence. The fruits of the investigation which are in its possession are not the property of the Crown for use in securing a conviction, but the property of the public to be used to ensure that justice is done. The obligation to disclose is subject to a discretion with respect to the withholding of information and to the timing and manner of disclosure. Crown counsel has a duty to

---

[206] *People v Kyle* Colo CA No 01CA122 (Colorado CA 29 July 2004), discussing Colorado Rev Stat 2003 §13-90-107(1)(g).

[207] See the articles cited in *In Re Grand Jury* 103 F 3d 1140 (3rd Cir 1997) *certiori* denied, 117 S Ct 2412 (1997) 1146 fn 12.   [208] Minnesota Stat Ann §595.02(1)(j); Idaho Cold §9-203(7).

[209] Massachusetts Gen L ch 233, §20 (1986 & Supp1996).   [210] *In Re Grand Jury* (n 207).

[211] *New Brunswick (Minister of Health and Community Services) v G(J)* [1999] 3 SCR 46 (SCC) [73]–[79].

[212] *K(SD) v Alberta (Director of Child Welfare)* (2002) 309 AR 219 (Alberta QB) [15]-[16]; R Vogl and N Bala 'Initial Involvement: Reporting Abuse and Protecting Children' in N Bala, MK Zapf, RJ Williams, R Vogl and JP Hornick (eds) *Canadian Child Welfare Law: Children, Families and the State* (2nd edn Thompson Educational Publishing Inc, Toronto 2004) 53–55.

[213] *R v Stinchcombe* [1991] 3 SCR 326 (SCC).

respect the rules of privilege and to protect the identity of informers. A discretion must also be exercised with respect to the relevance of information. The Crown's discretion is reviewable by the trial judge, who should be guided by the general principle that information should not be withheld if there is a reasonable possibility that this will impair the right of the accused to make full answer and defence.

These rules are relevant for present purposes because there are conflicting cases from the family courts as to whether the prosecution disclosure rules in *Stinchcombe* apply to child protection proceedings so as to lay an obligation of disclosure on child welfare agencies additional to that provided for by each provincial family law statute.[214] The statutory disclosure provisions generally recognize the need for confidentiality and balance it against the need of any parent or litigant to know the case they have to meet.[215] Some statutes prohibit disclosure of information obtained during a family conference or other alternate dispute resolution meeting unless this is necessary for the child's safety or the party holding the record has a statutory obligation to report that a child is or may be in need of protective intervention.[216]

The Canadian Charter of Rights nonetheless has given impetus to disclosure practices, such that most courts start from the position of full disclosure to the parents of all relevant information in the possession of child welfare agencies, subject to discretion, reviewable by the courts, not to disclose information which is irrelevant, which might disclose the identity of informers, or which might potentially harm a child's physical, mental or emotional health to such a degree as to outweigh the parents' entitlement to disclosure.[217] In Alberta, the duty to disclose obliges the Department of Child Welfare not only to produce documents in its possession, but also to obtain records from third parties, including the reports of psychologists retained by the Department, videotaped interviews with the child possessed by the police, and witness statements taken by police in any companion criminal investigation, even if this was not a joint investigation.[218] Disclosure of redacted investigation files is sometimes ordered.[219]

Reciprocal disclosure by the parents is usually required.[220] However this is subject to the parents' privacy rights, and so a child protection agency may not be entitled to

---

[214] *Stinchcombe* does not apply: *Anishinaabe Child and Family Services Inc v S(R)* (1993) 90 Man R (2d) 3 (Manitoba QB) [17]; for the contrary view see *Children's Aid Society for Sudbury & Manitoulin (Districts) v M(G)* (Ontario Prov Ct 17 January 1992); *Children's Aid Society of Peel (Region) v J(V)* [1994] WDFL 042 (Ontario Prov Ct).   [215] *Anishinaabe Child and Family Services Inc v S(R)* ibid [16].

[216] eg Child Youth and Family Services Act (Newfoundland & Labrador) s 57.

[217] *K(SD) v Alberta (Director of Child Welfare)* (n 212) [1] [39] [43].

[218] ibid [3] [54]–[68]. In Provinces which do not take the full disclosure principle as a starting point, a broad interpretation of the statutory obligation on child and family service agencies to provide particulars of the reasons for considering the child to be in need of protection, and all relevant information in the agency's possession, has generally been seen sufficient to protect the parents' rights to disclosure [*British Columbia (Superintendent of Family & Child Services) v H(J)* [1996] WDFL 225 (British Columbia Supreme Ct); *Anishinaabe Child and Family Services Inc v S(R)* (n 214) [16]; *Re Whitecap* (1979) 2 Sask R 429 (Saskatchewan UFC)]. See also Vogl and Bala (n 212) 54–55.

[219] *Re S(AL)* Burnaby F3957 12 December 1996 (British Columbia Prov Ct).

[220] *James v T* (5388/93, 5563/93, 4 February 1994) (Ontario Gen Div).

access to a parent's psychiatric or other medical files where it was in the child's best interests to have the mother continue with her treatment with a view to reuniting the family.[221]

(b) The prosecution's obligation to obtain relevant information possessed by third parties

Prosecution disclosure in Canadian criminal cases is embedded in the statutory and constitutional entitlement of the accused to make full answer and defence,[222] and is governed by the principles established by the Supreme Court of Canada in *R v Stinchcombe* outlined in the previous section.[223] The prosecution's duty to disclose applies only to information in its possession or control, but this is considered to extend to the police and other investigative arms of the state involved in an investigation, such as a social services agency.[224] *Stinchcombe* does not give *carte blanche* to the defence to access a complainant's social services records. In *R v Sanertanut*,[225] the accused was charged with sexual assault of a 16-year-old girl living with his parents as a foster child. She had been a ward of Social Services since early childhood. The defence sought access to the Department's records, contending that they were relevant to the complainant's competence to testify (the foster mother deposed that she was mentally slow and had problems with memory), her history of false allegations and recantations (a different person had been charged with sexual assault and she allegedly had retracted her complaint) and a history of previous sexual abuse which might have led her to misperceive the perpetrator of current abuse. The court ordered limited access to records relating to her testimonial competence, but dismissed the other applications as being merely fishing expeditions. Nothing suggested that she had a propensity to make false accusations of sexual assault.

(c) Privilege for confidential relationships in civil and criminal proceedings

Stinchcombe stipulated that the absolute withholding of information which is relevant to the defence can only be justified on the basis of the existence of a legal privilege which excludes the information from disclosure. This privilege is subject to judicial review, however, on the ground that it is not a reasonable limit on the right to make full answer and defence in a particular case. Therefore in Canadian constitutional and common law, unlike in English law,[226] there is no absolute privilege which can

---

[221] *Children's Aid Society of Oxford (County) v M(D)* [1993] WDFL 1630 (Ontario Gen Div); compare *Children's Aid Society v R(J)* (Doc Algoma 145/97 Feb 1998) (Ontario Prov Div) where the father's full medical records were ordered disclosed to the Children's Aid Society, the mother and the First Nations Band representative.

[222] Criminal Code of Canada s 650(3), Canadian Charter of Rights and Freedoms ss 7, 11(d).

[223] *R v Stinchcombe* (n 213).

[224] D Paciocco and L Steusser *The Law of Evidence* (3rd edn Essentials of Canadian Law Irwin Law' Toronto 2002) 211.   [225] *R v Sanertanut* [1995] NWTR 36 (Northwest Territories Supreme Ct).

[226] *R v Derby Magistrates' Court ex p B* (n 14) holding that legal professional privilege is absolute in adversarial proceedings was rejected by the Supreme Court of Canada in *Smith v Jones and Southam Inc* [1999] 1 SCR 455 (SCC).

block defence access to exculpatory evidence in criminal proceedings, but disclosure of material subject to solicitor–client privilege will be ordered only where it is 'absolutely necessary—a test just short of absolute prohibition'.[227] Another narrow exception to legal professional privilege, where public safety is at stake,[228] can also be relevant to child protection proceedings as well as criminal prosecutions.[229] Public interest immunity is also subject to the 'innocence at stake' exception.[230]

We have seen that in English law privilege from disclosure arises only in relation to lawyers and their clients, and that confidentiality per se is not a basis to refuse to disclose the information, but is treated as only one factor which might or might not trigger public interest immunity.[231] Canadian law has taken a much more expansive view, holding that the categories of privilege are not closed. Information will be protected from disclosure when the following tests, first propounded by Wigmore, are met in a particular case:[232]

- The communications must originate in a confidence that they will not be disclosed.
- This element of confidentiality must be essential for the full and satisfactory maintenance of relations between the parties.
- The relation must be one which in the opinion of the community ought to be sedulously fostered.
- The injury which would inure to the relation by the disclosure of the information must be greater than the benefit thereby gained for the correct disposal of litigation.[233]

Whilst the traditional categories of privilege are cast in absolute terms, a Canadian court in creating new privileges is enjoined not to accept the proposition that their price necessarily is occasional injustice. Even where the Wigmore criteria are satisfied, the court may order limited or even full disclosure of a particular class of documents where it is necessary to prevent an unjust result in a civil or criminal trial. This has been the case in relation to disclosure in criminal proceedings of social services files relating to complainants[234] and admissions made by the accused in family therapy sessions;[235] while the first three criteria were regarded as having been satisfied, the search for the truth in the prosecution of suspected child abuse prevailed over the need for confidentiality. For the same reason, the Ontario appellate courts have declined to

---

[227] *Goodis v Ontario (Ministry of Correctional Services)* 2006 SCC 31.

[228] *Smith v Jones and Southam Inc* (n 226).

[229] D Thompson 'Are There *Any* Rules of Evidence in Family Law?' (2003) 21 Can Fam LQ 245.

[230] *LLA v AB and the Queen* [1995] 4 SCR 536 (SCC) [51].

[231] *D v NSPCC* (n 15), discussed above section C.1(b)(iv).

[232] *R v Gruenke* [1991] 3 SCR 263 (SCC) [22].

[233] *Slavutych v Baker* [1976] 1 SCR 254 (SCC), adopting Wigmore's template for privilege; *LLA v AB* (n 230) [40].

[234] *R v Ryan* (1991) 69 CCC (3d) 226 (Nova Scotia CA) (trial judge erred in imposing a stay of proceedings on the basis that confidential Children's Aid Society files about the two complainants could not be disclosed and were crucial to the defence; trial judge should have used other protective devices to allay the concerns of the caseworkers over disclosure of their files, such as closing the court and imposing a publication ban).   [235] *R v S (RJ)* (1985) 19 CCC (3d) 115 (Ontario CA).

recognize a general privilege under the Wigmore criteria shielding Children's Aid Society records in protection proceedings, whilst acknowledging that this situation may change as the conditions of social legislation develop.[236]

In *LLA v AB*,[237] the Supreme Court of Canada was asked to create a class privilege over private records, and specifically those held by a sexual assault crisis centre. A class privilege entails a prima facie presumption that such communications are inadmissible and not subject to disclosure in criminal or civil proceedings, and the onus lies on a party seeking disclosure to show that an overriding interest commands disclosure. The relationship must be grounded in compelling policy reasons, and be inextricably linked with the justice system. In contrast, in a case-by-case privilege the communications are not privileged unless the party opposing disclosure can show that they should be, according to the fourfold utilitarian test of Wigmore described above.[238]

In *LLA v AB* the Supreme Court acknowledged the strong arguments of public policy militating in favour of protecting the confidentiality of counsellor–sexual assault complainant communications in criminal trials: otherwise victims might be deterred from seeking counselling and from reporting the crime, which would undermine the effectiveness of the criminal justice system. Moreover, records made in the course of counselling are both hearsay and inherently unreliable.[239] However, the Court found more powerful the countervailing public policies of the truth-finding process of the adversarial trial procedure, the possible relevance of some private records, the accused's right to make full answer and defence, and the difficulties of defining the categories of actors included in a class privilege.[240] The Court acknowledged that granting a case-by-case privilege may be appropriate in some circumstances. However, the development of such exceptions to the general evidentiary rule of admissibility and disclosure should not be encouraged, and in any event an ad hoc approach to privilege would not cure the deterrent effect which such production has on reporting and counselling.[241] A better solution was thought to lie in balancing the complainant's constitutional rights to privacy and equality with the accused's constitutional rights to a fair trial and a full answer and defence,[242] using the procedure in *O'Connor*,[243] which we describe below.

An order for partial privilege will more often be appropriate in civil cases, where the privacy interest is more compelling, than in criminal cases. In *M(A) v Ryan*[244] where a plaintiff claimed to have been sexually abused by her psychiatrist, the Supreme Court of Canada ruled that the records of her subsequent therapy with another psychiatrist should be the subject of limited disclosure in her tort action. Conditions were imposed relating to editing non-essential material and restrictions on the persons to have access,[245] to ensure the highest degree of confidentiality and the least damage to the protected relationship, whilst guarding against the injustice of cloaking the truth. The majority acknowledged that a test for privilege which permits the court

---

[236] *James v T* (n 220).   [237] *LLA v AB* (n 230).
[238] *R v Gruenke* (n 232) [22]; *LLA v AB* ibid [39]–[40].   [239] *LLA v AB* ibid [54].
[240] ibid [65]–[74].   [241] ibid [77].   [242] ibid [78]–[85].
[243] *R v O'Connor* [1995] 4 SCR 411 (SCC).
[244] *M(A) v Ryan* (n 203) (L'Heureux-Dubé J dissenting).
[245] The defendant psychiatrist was prohibited access, although his lawyers could review the records.

occasionally to reject an otherwise well-founded claim in favour of getting at the truth may not offer patients a guarantee that communications with their psychiatrists will never be disclosed.[246] Nevertheless, McLachlin J (as she then was) for the majority considered that the assurance that disclosure will be ordered only where clearly necessary, and then only to the extent necessary, would be likely to permit many to avail themselves of psychiatric counselling, when the prospect of certain disclosure might otherwise make them hesitate or decline.[247] Her Ladyship noted that of the 51 American jurisdictions which have enacted some form of psychotherapist privilege, none has adopted it in absolute form, which reinforced the majority's view that partial privilege can be effective.

Therefore, the protection afforded by the Canadian common law to confidential records is flexible and strongly fact-determinant. While there is no *a priori* presumption in favour of disclosure or preserving confidentiality, the language in *M(A) v Ryan* indicating that privilege may exist 'where the interest in protecting the privacy of the record is compelling and the threat to proper disposition of litigation either is not apparent or can be offset by partial or conditional discovery'[248] hints that the threat to the integrity of the verdict must be neutralized before confidentiality is permitted to prevail. The claimant may be found to have impliedly waived her right to confidentiality in her psychiatric records by putting her mental state in issue in the lawsuit, but nonetheless that will not be treated as necessarily authorizing unlimited and uncontrolled access to the medical record.[249]

(d) Procedures for disclosure of confidential records in criminal proceedings

The Canadian courts' flexible approach to conferring privilege on confidential documents is a necessary backdrop to our examination of their response to defence demands for access to such records in order to make full answer and defence.

In *R v O'Connor*,[250] the Supreme Court had to decide whether therapeutic records should be subject to a different disclosure regime than other kinds of information in the Crown's possession. In particular, the Court considered whether the Crown's disclosure obligations should be tempered by a balancing of the complainant's privacy interest in therapeutic records against the constitutional right of the accused to make full answer and defence. O'Connor was a Roman Catholic Bishop when he was charged with sexual offences against four complainants who had been pupils in a First Nations residential school where he was principal, some 30 years before. He applied for disclosure of the complainants' entire medical, counselling, and school records, but it was the therapy records that attracted the strongest privacy interest and so proved the most contentious. At the time disclosure was not addressed by statute and so the Supreme Court had to develop the applicable principles at common law. The Supreme Court's judgment was closely split on all three of the legal issues before it.

---

[246] The concern of the American Supreme Court which caused it to create an absolute privilege in *Jaffee v Redmond* (n 198).   [247] *M(A) v Ryan* (n 203) [35].

[248] ibid [36].   [249] *Glegg v Smith & Nephew Inc* 2005 SCC 31, [2005] 1 SCR 724.

[250] *R v O'Connor* (n 243).

The Supreme Court held that a class privilege should not be recognized for private records because it would apply to a wide range of records held by an indeterminate class of people; some of these records might be relevant, and so a class privilege would impede the truth-finding process of the adversarial criminal trial.[251] Therefore privilege had to be determined on a case-by-case basis, balancing the competing public interests. *O'Connor* prescribed the procedure for this exercise.

Some but not all of the documents had come into the possession of Crown counsel. The majority held that the prosecution's disclosure duties under *Stinchcombe* encompassed the therapeutic records in its possession, as the complainant no longer enjoyed an expectation of privacy in those records.[252] To resolve the issue of disclosure of records which were still in the hands of third parties, Lamer CJC and Sopinka J outlined a two-stage process, the first stage being the decision whether the court should order production for its inspection, and the second being the balancing of the competing interests in deciding whether to order production to the accused.

In the first stage, the onus was placed on the accused to establish whether the information in question is 'likely to be relevant'.[253] The purpose of the threshold was to prevent requests for production which were speculative, obstructive or time-consuming,[254] whilst not imposing too great a burden on the defence at this stage. Unlike in the Crown disclosure context under *Stinchcombe* where relevance is understood to mean 'may be useful to the defence', the threshold of likely relevance in relation to third parties required the presiding judge to be satisfied that there was 'a reasonable possibility that the information is logically probative to an issue at trial or the competence of a witness to testify'.[255] The shift in onus and a higher relevant threshold was justified because the information was not part of the Crown's 'case to meet', nor had it been given access to it, and because third parties were under no obligation to assist the defence.

In the second stage, the court after inspecting the document was to determine whether it should be produced to the accused, balancing the competing interests of the accused's rights against the complainant's rights to privacy and to equality without discrimination, using the following five factors:

- the extent to which the record was necessary for the accused to make full answer and defence;
- the probative value of the record;
- the nature and extent of the reasonable expectation of privacy vested in the record;
- whether the claim for production of the record was premised upon any discriminatory belief or bias (such as the twin myths associated with cross-examination of a complainant on her previous sexual experience);[256] and

---

[251] *LLA v AB* (n 243) [65]–[68].

[252] *R v O'Connor* (n 243) [7]–[9] (Lamer CJC and Sopinka J, Cory, Iacobucci and Major JJ concurring in the result). [253] ibid [19].

[254] ibid [24], [27]. [255] ibid [22].

[256] The twin myths being described in *R v Seaboyer* [1991] 2 SCR 577 (SCC), discussed below in Chapter 9 section D.3(b).

- the potential prejudice to the complainant's dignity, privacy or security of the person by production of the record.[257]

L'Heureux-Dubé, La Forest and Gonthier JJ dissented on the issue of third-party production, considering that there should be a higher threshold at stage one which would define 'likely relevance' as requiring 'cogent supporting evidence', and not just a bare unsupported assertion that a prior inconsistent statement might be revealed, or that the defence might discover allegations of sexual abuse by other people. The minority emphasized that the focus of therapy is vastly different from that of investigation or other processes undertaken for the purposes of a criminal trial. Whilst the latter are oriented toward ascertaining historical truth, therapy generally focuses on exploring the complainant's emotional and psychological responses to certain events after the alleged assault had taken place.[258] Similarly, the mere fact that a witness has a medical or psychiatric record could not be taken as indicative of the potential unreliability of the evidence.[259]

In the second stage, the minority stressed the importance of ascertaining that the records have significant probative value which is not substantially outweighed by the danger of prejudice to the proper administration of justice through discriminatory reasoning, or by the harm to the privacy rights of the witness or to the privileged relationship. They would have added two further factors to the balancing exercise: the extent to which production would frustrate society's interest in encouraging reporting of sexual offences, and its effect on the integrity of the trial process.[260]

In a companion appeal decided on the same day as *O'Connor*, *LLA v AB*,[261] the Supreme Court ruled that the third party holding the records (in that case, a sexual assault crisis centre) has standing to appeal an interlocutory disclosure ruling in a sexual assault criminal proceeding.

O'Connor's attempt to balance the accused's right to a fair trial against the complainant's rights to privacy and equality of treatment created difficulties from the outset, as those dealing with victims of alleged sexual assault were apprehensive that any record made would be used against their clients in court. In *R v Carosella*,[262] the complainant went to a sexual assault crisis centre for advice as to how to lay charges against her schoolteacher for abuse which had occurred 38 years earlier. The centre received government funding under an agreement which required it to develop a close liaison with justice agencies and to maintain the confidentiality and security of all material under the centre's control, which could not be disclosed except where required by law. In a lengthy interview with a social worker, the complainant was advised that the notes might be subject to a subpoena under *O'Connor*. The complainant agreed, and the centre's file was produced to the defence before trial. It was then discovered that the notes of the interview had been destroyed pursuant to the centre's policy of shredding files before they could be subpoenaed. The trial judge directed that the charges be stayed because the destruction of the notes had seriously

---

[257] *R v O'Connor* (n 243) [31].
[258] ibid [144] (L'Heureux-Dubé J, La Forest and Gonthier JJ concurring).   [259] ibid [143].
[260] ibid [145]–[146].   [261] *LLA v AB* (n 230).
[262] *R v Carosella* [1997] 1 SCR 80 (SCC).

prejudiced the accused by depriving him of the opportunity to cross-examine the complainant as to her previous statements about the alleged assault. The Supreme Court, dividing 5:4, upheld the trial judge's ruling as there was a reasonable possibility that the information in the destroyed notes could be logically probative as to the credibility of the complainant.[263] The minority held that, as a third party, the sexual assault centre had no obligation to the Crown, the accused or the courts to preserve evidence for prosecutions. While production of every relevant piece of evidence might be an ideal goal from the accused's point of view, it was inaccurate to elevate this objective to a right, non-performance of which would lead instantaneously to an unfair trial. It was not sufficient to speculate that there was potential for harm.[264]

Many thought that the *O'Connor* process did not work effectively, failing to give adequate protection to the privacy and equality rights of complainants in sexual assault cases.[265] Parliament responded with a new and comprehensive statutory regime for disclosure. Section 278.1 of the Criminal Code of Canada applies to any form of record that contains personal information for which there is a reasonable expectation of privacy, including 'medical, psychiatric, therapeutic, counselling, education, employment, child welfare, adoption and social service records, personal journals and diaries', and any record containing personal information which is protected from disclosure by any statute of Parliament or a provincial legislature.[266] It applies regardless of whether the documents have come into the possession of the prosecution, or even of the defence.[267] The statutory procedure applies to a broad category of sexual offences, including those related to prostitution. For other types of offences, the *O'Connor* common law rules still apply.

The statutory scheme sets up a multi-staged process. The defence must give notice of its disclosure application to the prosecution, the record holder, and the witness to whom the records relate, all of whom have standing in the process. The application must set out the basis upon which the record is likely to be relevant to an issue at trial or to the testimonial competence of a witness. The legislation deems certain arguments to be insufficient on their own to establish likely relevance; these include that the record sought:

- relates to medical or psychiatric treatment, therapy or counselling received by the complainant;
- relates to the incident which is the subject of the charges;
- may disclose a previous inconsistent statement of the complainant or witness;
- relates to the credibility of the complainant or witness;

---

[263] ibid [47] (Lamer CJC, Sopinka, Cory, Iacobucci and Major JJ).

[264] ibid [72] (La Forest, L'Heureux-Dubé, Gonthier and McLachlin JJ, dissenting).

[265] eg B Feldthusen 'Access to the Private Therapeutic Records of Sexual Assault Complainants' (1996) 75 Can Bar Rev 537; K Busby *Third Party Record Cases since R v O'Connor: a Preliminary Analysis for the Research and Statistic Section, Department of Justice Canada* (1998).

[266] All records in these categories are not automatically protected, but only those in which it is found as a question of fact that there was a reasonable expectation of privacy: *R v Mills* [1999] 3 SCR 668 (SCC); *R v Clifford (Robert)* (2003) 58 OR (3rd) 257 (Ontario CA).

[267] *R v Shearing* 2002 SCC 58, [2002] 3 SCR 33.

- relates to the reliability of the complainant's testimony, merely because she has received or is receiving psychiatric treatment, therapy or counselling;
- may reveal allegations of sexual abuse of the complainant by a person other than the accused;
- relates to the presence or absence of a recent complaint;
- relates to the complainant's sexual reputation; or
- was made close in time to the complaint or to the activity which is the subject matter of the charge.[268]

The proscribed arguments form part of a statutory scheme for criminal prosecutions in Canada which refuses to countenance attacks on complainants which are thought to arise from stereotypical views of their (lack of) credibility, including the prohibition of prosecution evidence of recent complaint[269] and cross-examination on previous sexual experience,[270] which we discuss later.[271]

The trial judge must then conduct an in camera hearing to determine whether to require production of the records to the court for review. The judge can order production only where it is considered to be necessary in the interests of justice (an additional criterion to the *O'Connor* test), having regard to the following factors:

- the extent to which the record is necessary for the accused to make a full answer and defence;
- the probative value of the record;
- the nature and extent of the reasonable expectation of privacy with respect to the record;
- whether production is based on a discriminatory belief or bias;
- the potential prejudice to the personal dignity and right to privacy of any person to whom the record relates;
- society's interest in encouraging reporting of sexual offences;
- society's interest in encouraging the obtaining of treatment by complainants of sexual offences; and
- the effect of the determination on the integrity of the trial process.[272]

While this appears to require the court to make factual findings in an evidential vacuum, experience showed that a sufficient basis to support production could be established through Crown disclosure, defence witnesses, cross-examination of Crown witnesses, and expert evidence as well as the nature of the records in question.[273]

If the trial judge orders the production of the record, she should examine them in the absence of the parties, and if necessary hold a hearing in camera.[274] The judge may order production of the record to the accused (on appropriate conditions) where it is necessary in the interests of justice, having regard to the salutary

---

[268] Criminal Code of Canada s 278.3(4).   [269] Criminal Code of Canada s 275.
[270] Criminal Code of Canada s 276.   [271] See below Chapter 9 sections C.4 and D.3(b).
[272] Criminal Code of Canada s 278.5.   [273] *R v Mills* (n 266) [124].
[274] Criminal Code of Canada s 278.6.

and deleterious effects of the determination on the accused's right to make a full answer and defence and on the complainant's or other witness's right to privacy and equality.[275]

It will be seen that the statutory disclosure scheme is considerably stricter than the *O'Connor* procedure. A constitutional challenge was mounted on this basis in *LC (the Complainant) and the Attorney General for Alberta v Mills*.[276] The accused was charged with sexual assault and unlawful sexual touching of an 11-year-old girl. Defence counsel had obtained partial disclosure of therapeutic records and notes relating to the child possessed by a counselling organization, but sought the disclosure of other records held by a psychiatrist and a child and adolescent services association. The trial judge ruled that the amendments to the Criminal Code of Canada were unconstitutional because they failed to protect the accused's right to make full answer and defence as set out in *O'Connor*. On an interlocutory appeal directly to the Supreme Court of Canada, the appeal was allowed.

The Supreme Court observed that just because Parliament had devised a procedure which differed significantly from the *O'Connor* regime did not mean that it was unconstitutional.[277] The factors enumerated were an attempt to reconcile fairness to the complainant with the right to the accused. Both sets of rights are informed by the equality rights at play in this context. Parliament was also to be understood as recognizing 'horizontal' equality concerns where women's inequality results from other individuals and groups rather than from the state. The list of proscribed assertions was intended to prevent speculative and unmeritorious requests for production on the basis of myths, stereotypes and generalized assumptions about sexual assault victims and classes of records, which could distort the search for truth.[278] With reference specifically to therapy records, the court found that the therapeutic relationship has important implications for the complainant's psychological integrity, and hence for her security of the person guaranteed by s 7 of the Canadian Charter of Rights. The possibility of disclosure can reduce complainants' willingness to report crime or deter them from seeking counselling.

The Supreme Court concluded that Parliament had the benefit of information not available to the Court when it penned *O'Connor*, and was able to evaluate how the *O'Connor* regime was operating. Parliament received many submissions that private records were routinely being produced to the court at the first stage, leading to the recurring violation of the privacy interests of complainant's witnesses.[279] Parliament was entitled to consider that a more restrictive disclosure regime was required, provided that it sufficiently protected the defence's constitutional interests.[280]

The Canadian experience is helpful in showing the development of a nuanced approach which explicitly acknowledges the need to balance the rights to privacy and equality of complainants against the accused's right to make full answer and

---

[275] Criminal Code of Canada s 278.7.   [276] *R v Mills* (n 266).

[277] For a similar stance respecting the right of Parliament to take a different view from the Supreme Court of Canada, see the discussion of the fate of the rape shield law below: Chapter 9 section D.3(b)(i).   [278] *R v Mills* (n 266) [89]–[91].

[279] ibid [125].   [280] ibid [55].

defence.[281] *O'Connor* and the legislation which supplanted it have successfully avoided the arbitrary and perverse results of the English 'mere credibility' rule whilst evading the thorns of public interest immunity, which tends to focus on the rights of the record-holder rather than on the rights of the person whom the records concern.[282] The Canadian experience also demonstrates not only how difficult it is to make determinations of relevance and admissibility on anything other than a case-by-case basis, but also how a detailed statutory framework can inform and enhance this analysis.

4. Third party disclosure in Australian law

(a) Pre-trial disclosure in criminal proceedings

Under the Australian common law, there is no right to discovery in criminal trials by either party,[283] although the prosecution has ethical obligations of disclosure,[284] and the court has discretion to order disclosure in particular cases where the defence request has a bona fide evidentiary purpose and non-disclosure could result in a miscarriage of justice.[285]

New South Wales has developed the most comprehensive and influential system for pre-trial disclosure. Disclosure by the prosecution of information in its possession is governed by a statutory regime which provides for a two-stage disclosure similar to the CPIA 1996 in England. However, the Criminal Procedure Amendment (Pre-Trial Disclosure) Act 2001 only relates to complex criminal trials.

The Australian solution to third party disclosure presents an interesting contrast to the Canadian approach, because it is narrowly focused on disclosure of records pertaining to sexual assault, whereas the Criminal Code of Canada has a wide and non-exclusive definition of records in which there is a reasonable expectation of privacy. There are three bases upon which material in the hands of the prosecution or third party can be withheld from the defence in a criminal trial, or from another party in civil proceedings, apart from legal professional privilege: a claim to public interest immunity; statutory protection of confidential communications; and sexual assault communication privilege.

---

[281] Although some feminist critics maintain that *Mills* and the cases applying it still provide only tenuous protection against vigorous pursuit of records by defence counsel bent on circumventing the statutory prohibition on cross-examination of the complainant on prior sexual experience: L Gotell 'The Ideal Victim, the Hysterical Complainant, and the Disclosure of Confidential Records: the Implications of the Charter for Sexual Assault Law' (2003) 40 Osgoode Hall LJ 251.

[282] The federal Department of Justice is considering giving the court power to make any order regarding disclosure materials to protect the privacy of any person affected by the proceedings (subject to the accused's right to full answer and defence), and the creation of an offence for the improper or collateral use of disclosed information which would violate any person's privacy [Justice Canada *Disclosure Reform: Consultation Paper* (Nov 2004) 18–21].   [283] *Maddison v Goldrick* [1976] 1 NSWLR 651 (New South Wales CA).

[284] *R v Lawless* (1979) 142 CLR 659 (Aus HC); *New South Wales Bar Code of Conduct* Rules 66 and 66A (Gazette No. 66 of 20 June 1997 558, 4564–4565); Director of Public Prosecution Guidelines.

[285] *Jamieson v The Queen* (1992) 60 A Crim R 68 (New South Wales CCA); *Alister v The Queen* (1984) 154 CLR 404 (Aus HC); *R v Saleam* (1989) 16 NSWLR 14 (New South Wales CCA).

(b) Public interest immunity

Claims to public interest immunity asserted before trial are governed by the common law, which is very similar to the English approach of balancing the competing public interests[286] which we have already discussed. The Uniform Evidence Act[287] applies to claims of public interest immunity advanced at trial and applies to both criminal and civil proceedings. It prevents the admission in evidence of information or documents that relate to 'matters of state', and so is narrower in scope than the English common law which, as we have seen, has become very elastic to encompass a wide range of confidential records maintained by bodies with public powers.

The common law doctrine of public interest immunity is considerably broader, and so can apply to communications in the course of a professional relationship of confidentiality.[288] However, greater clarity has been achieved through specific statutory provisions to which we now turn.

(c) Confidential communications

The Australian common law, like English caselaw, has never recognized confidentiality per se as a ground for non-disclosure.[289] However, privilege has been created by statute in some States for 'protected confidences'.

For example, the New South Wales Evidence Act 1995 confers on the court in criminal or civil proceedings the discretion to exclude a communication made in confidence in the course of a relationship where the confidant is acting in a professional capacity and is under an express or implied obligation not to disclose its contents.[290] The court is required to exclude the evidence where it is satisfied that it is likely that the evidence if admitted might cause harm, whether directly or indirectly, to the person who has made the protected confidence, and the nature and extent of the harm outweighs the desirability of the evidence being given. The court is to take into account a menu of factors: the probative value and importance of the evidence in the proceeding, the nature and gravity of the relevant offence or cause of action, the availability of any other evidence concerning the same matter, the likely effect of disclosing the protected confidence including the likelihood of harm, and the nature and extent of harm that would be caused to the protected confider, the means available to the court to limit the extent of the harm, such as an in camera hearing or publication ban.[291] For this purpose, 'harm' is very broadly defined as including actual physical

---

[286] *Sankey v Whitlam* (1978) 142 CLR 1 (Aus HC); *Alister v The Queen* (n 285).

[287] Uniform Evidence Act 1995 (Commonwealth of Australia) s 130(4), Evidence Act 1995 (New South Wales) s 130.

[288] *R v PML* (2000)160 FLR 263, affd (2001) 122 A Crim R 21 (South Australia Supreme Ct); *R v Liddy* (2001) SASR 401 (South Australia Supreme Ct).

[289] *R v Lowe* [1996] Vic Lexis 1330 (Victoria CA) 61–64 (incriminating information given to a psychotherapist in confidence admissible in the client's trial for murder of a six-year-old child).

[290] Evidence Act 1995 (New South Wales) Division 1A, Professional Confidential Relationship Privilege, ss 126A, 126B(1). The legislation also applies to 'protected identity information'. Equivalent provisions may be found in Victoria [Evidence Act 1958 (Victoria) ss 32B–32G] and South Australia [Evidence Act 1929 (South Australia) s 67D–67F]. There is no equivalent provision in the Uniform Evidence Act 1995 (Commonwealth of Australia).   [291] Evidence Act 1995 (New South Wales) s 126B(3).

bodily harm, financial loss, stress or shock, damage to reputation, or emotional or psychological harm such as shame, humiliation, and fear.[292] However, the discovery of documents has been held to be outside the ambit of the protection of the statutory privilege.[293]

The Queensland Law Reform Commission decided against recommending adoption of the New South Wales privilege model, because there could be reasonable grounds for a belief that therapy records could assist the defence, counselling might not be restricted to professional therapists (eg religious advisers or school counsellors), and extension of professional privilege should not be done on a piecemeal basis. Instead the Commission recommended development of a treatment protocol for therapists akin to the UK's *Memorandum of Good Practice* to avoid compromising the quality of the child's evidence, but (somewhat surprisingly) concluded that it should not provide for audio- or video-taping of therapy sessions.[294]

(d) Admissions and disclosures made in family mediation and therapy conferences

Admissions or disclosures made in the course of family therapy or statutory procedures such as family or child protection conferences enjoy a stronger form of privilege in most Australian States, in that the evidence is deemed inadmissible.[295] For example, the Commonwealth's Family Law Act 1975 provides that evidence of anything said or any admission made at a meeting or conference conducted by a family and child counsellor, or a court community or private mediator, is not admissible in any court or in any proceedings before a person authorized to hear evidence.[296] However, the

---

[292]   ibid s 126A(1).

[293]   *R v Young* [1999] NSWCCA 166, (1999) 46 NSWLR 681 (New South Wales CCA), discussed in Queensland Law Reform Commission *The Receipt of Evidence by Queensland Courts: the Evidence of Children* (Report No 55 Part 2 Dec 2000) 97–98.

[294]   *The Receipt of Evidence* ibid, Part 2 100–102.

[295]   Family Law Act 1975 (Commonwealth of Australia) s 19; Family Court Act 1997 (Western Australia) s 64; Community Welfare Act 1983 (Northern Territory) s 97 [statutory obligation of confidentiality of child protection records prevails over subpoenas issued by a party under the Family Law Act 1995 (Commonwealth of Australia), so that the manager of the Child and Family Protective Services unit was not obliged to produce records subpoenaed by a father accused of sexual abuse in guardianship proceedings: *Northern Territory of Australia v Gpao* [1999] HCA 8, 196 CLR 553 (Aus HC)]; Children and Young Persons Act 1989 (Victoria) s 82B (evidence arising from pre-hearing conferences inadmissible unless necessary to ensure the safety and well-being of the child); Children, Young Persons and Their Families Act 1997 (Tasmania) s 40 (evidence of anything said at a family group conference inadmissible except the record of the decision, with no inclusionary discretion); s 58 (personal information relating to alleged abuse of the child or at a family conference confidential unless disclosure is authorized or required by law); Child Protection Act 1999 (Queensland) ss 190–191 (government department may refuse to obey a subpoena by a party to a proceeding to produce records in relation to a child or a child's carer if its disclosure is likely to endanger a person's safety or psychological health, identification of the source of information is likely to prejudice the achievement of the Act's purpose, or it is a record of confidential therapeutic counselling with a child or a member of the child's family and its disclosure would prejudice the department's ability to provide counselling services; the court may order disclosure if the information is materially relevant to the proceeding and its disclosure is on balance the public interest) (enacted to reverse *Centacare Central Queensland v G* [1998] Fam CA 109 (Fam Ct of Aus) which had held that any admission made in family counselling sessions was not admissible in evidence in any court, and that the statutory confidentiality was not subject to the child welfare paramountcy principle); Children and Young People Act 1999 (Australian Capital Territory) s 405.   [296]   Family Law Act 1975 (Commonwealth of Australia) s 19N(2).

ban does not apply to an admission by an adult or disclosure by a child that a child has been abused or is at risk of abuse.[297] This exception applies unless in the opinion of the court there is sufficient evidence of the admission or disclosure available to the court from other sources.[298] The provision applies to any child under 18, and abuse is defined as an assault including a sexual assault, or sexual activity in which the child is used as a sexual object and there is an unequal power in the relationship with the other person involved.[299] Presumably this is designed to include child pornography.

The Commonwealth and Western Australia statutes have been restrictively interpreted such that 'in any court' referred only to a court dealing with family law matters, and not to criminal proceedings.[300] Therefore in a case where the accused was charged with sexual offences against young boys, the defence was entitled to subpoena records of statements made by an alleged victim during marriage counselling with Relationships Australia, to test the complainant's credibility in light of the delayed complaint. Admissibility fell to be determined under the doctrine of public interest immunity. The Western Australia Supreme Court held that in child welfare proceedings, the statutory guarantee of confidentiality of communications in the course of family counselling is to be preserved, notwithstanding that the child welfare legislation requires the admission of any relevant statement.[301]

(e) Sexual assault communication privilege

Six Australian jurisdictions have created a distinct statutory privilege for counsellors in sexual assault cases.[302] New South Wales was the first to do so,[303] in response to mounting concern over the use of subpoenas to obtain counsellors' notes which came to a head when a counsellor from the Canberra Rape Crisis Centre was imprisoned for contempt of court for refusing to hand over her records in December 1995. The legislation as originally drafted was interpreted as applying only at the trial, and not at the earlier pre-trial stage when a subpoena would be issued.[304] This ruling was reversed by statute in 1999[305] under the influence of the Canadian decision in *O'Connor*,[306] the rationale being that privacy once invaded cannot be regained and so must be protected from the outset.

---

[297] The Western Australian legislation does not contain this exception: Family Court Act 1997 (Western Australia) s 64.   [298] Family Law Act 1975 (Commonwealth of Australia) s 19N(3).
[299] ibid s 19N(4).
[300] *R v PML* (n 288); *Anglicare WA & Anor v Department of Family and Children's Services* [2000] Western Australia Supreme Ct 47.
[301] *Anglicare* (n 300) interpreting the Child Welfare Act 1947 (Western Australia) s 30(3), Family Law Act 1975 (Commonwealth of Australia) ss 19, 19N, and the Family Court Act 1997 (Western Australia) s 64.
[302] Evidence (Miscellaneous Provisions) Act 1991 (Australian Capital Territory) ss 56–67; Evidence Act 1958 (Victoria) ss 32B–32G; Evidence Act 1929 (South Australia) ss 67D–68; Evidence Act 2001 (Tasmania) s 127B; Evidence Act (Northern Territory) ss 56–56G. The specific provisions have very minor variations in the New South Wales model in the Criminal Procedure Act 1986 (New South Wales) s 126G.
[303] There is no equivalent provision in the Uniform Evidence Act 1995 (Australia).
[304] *R v Young* (n 293) interpreting Evident Amendment (Confidential Communications) Act 1997 (New South Wales) which inserted Division 1B in the Evidence Act 1995 (New South Wales).
[305] Criminal Procedure Amendment (Sexual Assault Communications Privilege) Act 1999 (New South Wales) ss 57–69.   [306] *R v O'Connor* (n 243), discussed above section C.3(d).

The New South Wales legislation sets up a rebuttable presumption of inadmissibility at trial[307] for a counselling communication made by, to or about an alleged victim of a sexual assault offence.[308] A counselling communication is a protected confidence if it relates to any harm[309] the person may have suffered, even if it was made before the incidents charged occurred (presumably to address ongoing abuse), or was not made in connection with alleged sexual assault. The communication does not lose the character of confidentiality if it is made in the presence of a third party such as a parent, carer or other supportive person who was present to facilitate communication or further the counselling process.

A counsellor is defined as being a person who has undertaken training or study or has experience that is relevant to the process of counselling persons who have suffered harm, and that person listens to and gives verbal or other support or encouragement, or advises, gives therapy to, or treats the other person, whether or not for fee or reward.[310] This expansive definition is the result of a strict judicial interpretation of the predecessor enactment which protected 'counselling, giving therapy to or treating the counselled person for any emotional or psychological condition'.[311] In *R v Norman Lee*[312] the Court of Appeal had ruled that the records of a supported living programme for young people living away from home which described discussions between the complainant and social workers about her sexual abuse by the accused schoolteacher were not privileged communications. The legislation was interpreted as applying only to the provision of expert advice and procedures by persons skilled by training or experience in the treatment of mental or emotional disease or trouble. The provision therefore did not include persons who merely sought to assist others suffering from an emotional or psychological condition, such as the social workers who referred her to doctors for treatment and facilitated family reconciliation.[313] The consequence of the ruling was that school counsellors, social workers and mental health workers working with sexual assault victims could be excluded from the ambit of the privilege.[314] The New South Wales legislature overcame *Norman Lee* by amendments defining counselling as including listening and giving verbal or other support or encouragement to the alleged victim, and providing that a person may be a counsellor even if that person lacks formal training.[315]

Another way of avoiding this problem of scope is to focus on the nature of the communication instead of the identity of the parties to it, by defining the counselling communication as one made in circumstances that give rise to a reasonable

---

[307] There is an absolute prohibition on the disclosure of a sexual assault communication in preliminary criminal proceedings: Criminal Procedure Act 1986 (New South Wales) s 297.

[308] Criminal Procedure Act 1986 (New South Wales) s 296(4). The definition encompasses all communications made in confidence between a counsellor and victim, a counsellor and a facilitator, and between counsellors [s 296(4)].

[309] 'Harm' is defined broadly by the Criminal Procedure Act 1986 (New South Wales) s 295(1), in the same terms as for confidential communications in the Evidence Act 1995 (New South Wales) s 126A(1) described above section C.4(c).   [310] Criminal Procedure Act 1986 (New South Wales) s 296(5).

[311] ibid s 148(4).   [312] *R v Norman Lee* [2000] NSWCCA 444 (New South Wales CCA).

[313] ibid [23].   [314] ibid [25]–[26].

[315] Criminal Procedure Amendment (Sexual Assault Communications Privilege) Act 1999 (New South Wales).

expectation or duty of confidentiality, as in the Australian Capital Territory[316] (just as the Criminal Code of Canada protects records in which there is a reasonable expectation of privacy). However, the problem could still arise in the Northern Territory,[317] Victoria,[318] Tasmania,[319] and South Australia[320] where the statutory definitions expressly or impliedly confine the privilege to professional counselling relationships.

The evidence or record must first be produced for inspection by the court. The court will order that it be made available to a party for inspection:

- if it has substantial probative value on its own or with other evidence;

- other evidence pertaining to the matters contained in the communication is not available; and

- the public interest in preserving the confidentiality of protected confidences and protecting the alleged victim[321] from harm[322] is substantially outweighed by the public interest in allowing inspection by the court.[323]

The court may give leave to a party to adduce the evidence at trial only if it is satisfied that the same three tests are met.[324] The alleged victim must be given notice of the application and has standing to make representations to the court.[325] It is noteworthy that the statutory requirement that the public interest in confidentiality be 'substantially outweighed' by the public interest in admitting the document as evidence is a more stringent test than that which applies to claims to public interest immunity or other confidential communications in Australian law.

These provisions do not generally apply to civil proceedings; however if the civil proceedings relate to 'substantially the same acts' which were in issue in the criminal proceedings, then evidence which would not be disclosable in a criminal trial retains that protected status.[326]

---

[316] Evidence (Miscellaneous Provisions) Act 1991 (Australian Capital Territory) Division 4.5(3).

[317] Evidence Act 1939 (Northern Territory) s 56 ('counsellor' defined as a person who is *treating* a victim for emotional, psychological or psychiatric condition).

[318] Evidence Act 1958 (Victoria) s 32B(1) (privilege confined to confidences to a registered medical practitioner or counsellor in the course of the relationship of counsellor and client).

[319] Evidence Act 2001 (Tasmania) s 127B(1) ('counsellor' defined as a person whose profession or work includes provision of psychiatric or psychological therapy to victims of sexual offences or who works for an organization that provides such therapy).

[320] Evidence Act 1929 (South Australia) s 67D (privilege confined to a counsellor or therapist whose profession or work includes providing psychiatric or psychological therapy to victims of trauma, including volunteers).

[321] Defined as the 'principal protected confider': Criminal Procedure Act 1986 (New South Wales) s 295(1).

[322] The court is required to take into account the likelihood, and nature or extent, of harm that would be caused to the alleged victim if the document is produced for inspection: Criminal Procedure Act 1986 (New South Wales) s 298(2).   [323] Criminal Procedure Act 1986 (New South Wales) s 298(1).

[324] ibid s 298 (3) (4) and (5).   [325] ibid s 299(3).

[326] Evidence Act 1995 (New South Wales) s 126H.

5. Third party disclosure in New Zealand law

(a) Prosecution and defence disclosure in criminal proceedings

Disclosure in criminal proceedings is governed by a complex amalgam of caselaw, statute law,[327] and ad hoc guidelines,[328] a situation which the New Zealand Law Commission has long regarded as being unacceptable.[329] The New Zealand Government has finally brought the Criminal Procedure Bill 2004 before Parliament, which will create a comprehensive disclosure code.[330] The disclosure requirements will apply to the prosecution, defence and third parties. However, in sharp contrast to the equivalent legislation in England and Wales, the defence will only have minimal disclosure obligations, pertaining to alibi and expert evidence, reflecting the position which the Ministry of Justice had urged on the Law Commission.[331] The key principle of the Bill is that the prosecution is required to disclose to the defence all relevant information, unless there is good reason to withhold it. Briefly, the legislation will set up a two-stage prosecution disclosure process: initial disclosure before a plea is entered of a summary of the facts, the maximum penalty for the offence, and any previous convictions of the defendant; and full and continuing disclosure thereafter.

At common law the prosecution is obliged to disclose the existence of any information in the hands of third parties of which it is aware,[332] leaving it to the defence to compel production of the evidence through the normal means of witness summonses and subpoenas. Under the current law as well as the proposals, there are three reasons why a party holding relevant records can refuse disclosure in civil and criminal proceedings: the public interest, class privilege, and confidentiality.

(b) The public interest and absolute class privilege

Apart from legal professional privilege protected by common law, current New Zealand law recognizes statutory class privileges for certain relationships, which are not subject to derogation by judicial discretion.

The Family Proceedings Act 1980 provides that no evidence shall be admissible in any court of any information, statement or admission disposed or made to a councillor exercising his functions under that Act, or in the course of a mediation

---

[327] Official Information Act 1982 (New Zealand), Crimes Act 1961 (New Zealand) s 344A.

[328] eg *Best Practice Guidelines for Disclosure in Criminal Cases in the High Court at Auckland* (1999); New Zealand Law Society *Guidelines for Law Practitioners under the Privacy Act 1993* <http://www.nz-lawsoc.org.nz/memprivact.asp> (last accessed 3 October 2006).

[329] New Zealand Law Commission *Criminal Procedure Part One: Disclosure and Committal* (Report No 14 1990) [64]–[66]; New Zealand Law Commission *Criminal Prosecution* (Report No 66 2000) [193]–[195]; New Zealand Law Commission *Juries in Criminal Trials* (Report No 69 2001).

[330] At the time of writing in October 2006 it has not yet been enacted.

[331] *Juries in Criminal Trials* (n 329) [325].

[332] Under the *Best Practice Guidelines* (n 328) [3.3] the Crown on request by the accused is to use its best endeavours to give the accused access to material which has never been in the possession of the police or the Crown, and a procedure is established for a court order requiring a third party to produce relevant material for the court's inspection and determination of admissibility.

conference.³³³ This privilege has been extended by judicial *fiat*, albeit on a discretionary basis, to information disclosed by or made to court-appointed psychologists under the Guardianship Act 1968 in relation to custody and access applications.³³⁴

Section 32 of the Evidence Amendment Act (No 2) 1980 (NZ) prohibits disclosure in civil proceedings of a 'protected communication' by a patient to a medical practitioner or clinical psychologist, being a communication necessary to enable the professional to examine, treat or act for the patient. This is an absolute privilege vested in the patient, whose consent is necessary before the professional can disclose the information to the court.³³⁵ The Law Commission has recommended that this privilege be repealed as they consider it better dealt with under the general judicial discretion to protect confidential communications.³³⁶

There is a parallel provision in s 33 of the same statute applicable in criminal proceedings, creating an absolute privilege for the defendant's protected communications to a medical practitioner or clinical psychologist which are necessary to enable them to examine, treat, or act for the defendant for drug dependency or any other condition or behaviour that manifests itself in criminal conduct, unless that examination was ordered by the court or other lawful authority.³³⁷ The Law Commission proposes giving this absolute privilege a wider scope to include all information acquired in confidence as a result of the examination or treatment of the condition, and to make it applicable in any criminal trial, not just the trial of the patient.³³⁸

Finally, s 31 of the 1980 Act provides that a minister of religion shall not disclose in any proceeding any confession made to him in his professional character³³⁹ without the consent of the person making the confession, unless the communication was made for a criminal purpose. This absolute privilege, which dates from 1885, is retained in the Law Commission's draft Evidence Code, and would be extended to any communication made in confidence to or by the minister for the purpose of obtaining religious or spiritual advice, benefit or comfort (but not for purely temporal purposes such as advice on control of a wayward child).³⁴⁰

Privilege and public interest immunity will be codified in relation to criminal proceedings under the Criminal Procedure Bill 2004. This sets up a closed list of 15 categories of information which the prosecutor may withhold in the public interest.

---

³³³ Family Proceedings Act 1980 (New Zealand) s 18.

³³⁴ *R v H* [2000] 2 NZLR 257 (New Zealand CA) [24]–[35], applying s 35 of the Evidence Amendment Act (No 2) 1980 (New Zealand) (accused father wished to rely upon the absence of any complaint of physical abuse to the psychologist by his daughter, as well as to cross-examine her about the relationship between the complainant and her parents).

³³⁵ Subject to specific exceptions relating testamentary capacity, life insurance or any communication made for any criminal purpose.   ³³⁶ *Juries in Criminal Trials* (n 329) Vol 2 Commentary [269].

³³⁷ Evidence Amendment Act (No 2) 1980 (NZ) s 33.

³³⁸ New Zealand Law Commission *Evidence* (Report 55 August 1999) Vol 2 Commentary [270]–[274], s 60 of the draft Evidence Code.

³³⁹ Therefore consulting a chaplain for emotional problems is not currently protected by s 31: *Re Leading Aircraftman F* [1998] 1 NZLR 714 (New Zealand Courts-Martial Appl Ct).

³⁴⁰ *Evidence* (n 338) Vol 2 Commentary [264]–[267], s 59 of the draft Evidence Code.

Those relevant for our purposes include where disclosure:

- is likely to prejudice the maintenance of the law, including the prevention, investigation and detection of offences;
- is likely to endanger the safety of any person;
- is material prepared by or for the prosecutor to assist the conduct of the hearing or trial;
- relates to information about undercover police officers;
- is likely to prejudice the security or defence of New Zealand or information entrusted to the government of New Zealand by other governments or international organizations on the basis of confidence;
- is likely to facilitate the commission of another offence;
- is information which could be withheld under any privilege applicable under the rules of evidence; or
- is relevant only because it reflects on the credibility of a witness who is not to be called by the prosecution but may be called by the defence.[341]

(c) Discretionary protection for confidentiality

In New Zealand as in England, public interest immunity appears to have become elided with confidentiality.[342] Under the Evidence Amendment Act (No 2) 1980 (NZ) s 35,[343] the court in any form of proceedings has discretion to excuse any witness from answering any questions or producing a new document if the public interest in having the evidence disclosed to the court is outweighed by the public interest in preserving the confidence. The court must first conclude that on the facts there was a special confidence, which may have arisen in the initial stages of a relationship, before making the public interest assessment.[344] In exercising its discretion, the court must have regard to:

- the likely significance of the evidence to the resolution of the issues in the proceeding;
- the nature of the confidence and other special relationship between the confinement and the witness; and
- the likely effect of the disclosure on a confidant or any other person.

This creates a 'contents privilege' based upon the nature of the disclosure and the specific relationship in question, in contrast to the absolute class privileges for medical practitioners, clinical psychologists and ministers of religion discussed

---

[341] Criminal Procedure Bill 2004 (NZ) Clause 31.

[342] See *R v Secord* [1992] 3 NZLR 571 (New Zealand CA) 572 and *M v L* [1999] 1 NZLR 747 (New Zealand CA) 752, relying upon *D v NSPCC* (n 15) 218.

[343] Enacted after the Torts and General Law Reform Committee considered the claims of various occupational and other groups to privilege and recommended deferment of a general judicial discretion: *R v Secord* ibid 572–573.   [344] *R v Lory (Ruling 8)* [1997] 1 NZLR 44 (New Zealand HC) 47–49.

earlier.[345] The New Zealand Court of Appeal has also recognized analogous protection for confidential information at common law, covering the discovery and inspection pre-trial stages of tort litigation.[346]

Even the fair trial rights guaranteed defendants by the New Zealand Bill of Rights do not give a criminal court jurisdiction to order a non-party to allow the defence access to material in its possession; all an applicant can do is to serve a subpoena or witness summons, and the trial judge will then be required to rule on any question of privilege or of confidence under s 35 which might arise.[347] Furthermore, the Court of Appeal in *R v Dobson*[348] cautioned that there can be no presumption in favour of disclosure of confidential material in criminal proceedings, and that the court in each case must weigh the competing interests carefully. If the outcome is to prejudice the conduct of the defence, then as a last resort a remedy can be given by way of stay or discharge of the prosecution.[349] This is a powerful message to the lower courts to take as a starting point for the balancing analysis the need to respect confidentiality. In *Dobson*, the defendant was charged with sexually assaulting four young boys aged 9 to 13; two of them had been previously physically abused and one had been under the care of a child psychiatrist. The defence motion for their medical and social welfare records was denied, as there was no realistic evidential basis for the defence theory that one of the boys had displaced responsibility for the abuse from the real perpetrator to someone else of less significance to him.

Section 35 has been frequently litigated in disclosure applications in both civil and criminal proceedings concerning children. It has been invoked to prevent disclosure in family law proceedings[350] and in criminal proceedings[351] of psychologists' and psychiatrists' reports prepared to advise the family court about a child's allegations of physical or sexual abuse or a party's capacity to parent a child. On the other hand, a report by a family court-appointed psychologist to whom the child had complained of sexual abuse by her grandfather was ordered by that court to be disclosed to the police to aid in their investigation, on the basis that the material was clearly relevant and disclosure would avoid the police having to instruct the same or another psychologist to interview the child.[352] Conversely, a psychiatric report ordered for sentencing purposes in unrelated criminal proceedings concerning the mother was withheld from counsel representing the child in custody proceedings, because it had been obtained compulsorily, and the relevant family legislation allowed the court to order a psychiatric or psychological examination only where the person concerned consented.[353]

Sexual abuse counsellors who do not come within the categories of medical practitioners and clinical psychologists accorded absolute privilege have been denied

---

[345] *M v L* (n 342) 758–764.   [346] ibid 750–751.

[347] *R v Dobson* (CA 25/95 1 June 1995) (New Zealand CA).   [348] ibid.

[349] ibid citing *R v Accused* (CA 357/94) (1994) 12 CRNZ 417 (New Zealand CA).

[350] *R v H* (n 334).

[351] *R v Ricardo John Moore* (CA 69/01 2 May 2001) (New Zealand CA) [23]–[26] (*obiter*).

[352] *V v G* [2001] NZFLR 1005 (New Zealand Fam Ct) (disclosure to the police of psychologist's report ordered by the Family Court).   [353] *S v Police* [1992] NZFLR 150 (New Zealand HC).

analogous class privilege in criminal[354] and tort[355] proceedings. The New Zealand Court of Appeal expressly declined to follow the US Supreme Court's creation of class privilege for psychotherapists in *Jaffee v Redmond*,[356] preferring the Canadian Supreme Court's case-by-case discretionary approach in *M(A) v Ryan*.[357]

The Law Commission's draft Evidence Code would extend the ambit of s 35 to permit the judge to direct that confidential information must not be disclosed by *any* witness, in civil as well as criminal proceedings. This would protect the information even if it had come into the hands of someone not bound by confidentiality, and even if the record-holder was willing to disclose it.[358] The menu of factors which the court would consider in exercising its discretion include:

- the extent of the harm that is likely to be caused by the disclosure;
- the nature of information and its importance to the proceeding;
- the nature of the proceeding;
- whether other means of obtaining the information are available;
- whether it is possible to prevent or restrict public disclosure;
- the sensitivity of the evidence; and
- society's interest in protecting the privacy of victims of sexual offences.

The last factor was added by the Law Commission as it was persuaded by the Canadian Supreme Court's policy reasoning for restricting disclosure of private records of sexual assault complainants in *O'Connor*[359] and the subsequent amendments to the Criminal Code of Canada discussed earlier.[360] The Law Commission was concerned to prevent speculative fishing expeditions in trials of sexual offences.[361]

In terms of procedure, the Law Commission had concluded that there was no need for their proposed statutory disclosure regime in criminal cases to deal specifically with third party disclosure issues,[362] but the Criminal Procedure Bill 2004 does address this area.[363] The procedure would permit the defendant to apply to the court for a hearing to determine whether information held by a non-party should be disclosed to the defence. If the court was satisfied that the defendant had established the existence and relevance of the information, a hearing would be granted at which the non-party would have standing as well as the prosecution. In determining whether the evidence was relevant and disclosure was necessary in the public interest, the judge would be required to take into account:

- the extent to which the information would assist the defendant to properly defend the charge;
- the probative value of the information;

---

[354] *R v Lory (Ruling 8)* (n 344) 47–49 (sexual abuse counsellor ordered to disclose confession to arson which killed six people). [355] *M v L* (n 342).

[356] *Jaffee v Redmond* (n 198). [357] *M(A) v Ryan* (n 203).

[358] New Zealand Law Commission *Evidence* (n 338) vol 2 Commentary [304].

[359] *R v O'Connor* (n 243) discussed above, section C.3(d). [360] See above, section C.3(d).

[361] *Evidence* (n 338) vol 2 Commentary [306]. [362] *Criminal Prosecution* (n 329) [219].

[363] Criminal Procedure Bill 2004 (New Zealand) clauses 39–44.

- the nature and extent of any reasonable expectation of privacy with respect to the information, including any expectation of a person to whom the information relates; and
- the effect of the determination on the fairness of the trial or hearing process.

The court would also have to consider whether the information should be withheld on any of the 15 categories of public interest grounds authorizing non-disclosure by the prosecutor described earlier.

We have seen that New Zealand has constructed a mixed system of disclosure of sensitive and private information. It is difficult to justify an absolute class privilege for information held by medical practitioners (including psychiatrists) and clinical psychologists, but not well-qualified sexual abuse counsellors who might be the only affordable recourse for victims.[364] The discretionary model in s 35, and the even more nuanced framework in the draft Evidence Code, openly address the competing claims to confidentiality and to a fair trial in criminal or civil proceedings, although the rulings can be difficult to predict. This however is the necessary price of a flexible system.

D. Access to Evidence: A Coherent System or Serendipity?

What is notable about the English courts' approach to third party disclosure is that the two primary bases for refusing disclosure, the 'mere credibility' rule and discretionary public interest immunity, afford only haphazard protection to the complainant's privacy interests. The Canadian, Australian, and American statutes which overtly balance the competing interests of privacy and due process for the person accused of abuse have the merit of a nuanced approach, particularly where there are guidelines identifying the factors in play. Furthermore, the Canadian and American approaches acknowledge that the privacy of the complainant will be invaded even where a judge privately inspects the documents, and therefore that the applicant must satisfy an evidentiary threshold before the holder of the confidential records is required to produce them for judicial inspection. It must also be acknowledged that judicial inspection in private poses legitimate concerns for the defence, as the judge may not be in the best position to know what is necessary to the defence.[365] Nevertheless, it presents the most viable compromise between complete disclosure or non-disclosure which would necessarily imperil one of the conflicting interests.[366]

---

[364] As argued by counsel for the plaintiffs in *M v L* (n 342) 755.

[365] *State v Ramos* 858 P 2d 94 (New Mexico CA 1993) 98–99; *Zaal v State* 602 A 2d 1247 (Maryland CA); *Commonwealth v Clancy* 524 NE 2d 395 (Massachusetts Supreme Judicial Ct 1988) 398–399.

[366] *US v Gambino* 741 F Supp 412 (US Dist Ct New York 1990) 414; *State v Cressey* (n 205).

1. A privilege for social services records?

The Association of Directors of Social Services has expressed concern that information relating to an individual should not be available to a criminal court simply
because she has been a child in care.[367] This is a valid point. Nevertheless, where
the alleged abuse is connected with the fact that the victim was in care, whether
because the abuse prompted the care proceedings or it was inflicted on a child already
in care, non-disclosure may result in a miscarriage of justice. What is clear is that
any information on social services records which has a bearing on the decision to
prosecute is very pertinent and must be disclosed to the defence. Apart from this
category, it is submitted that social services records should be disclosed in civil or
criminal proceedings only if the court is satisfied that their specific relevance to a fact
in issue has been clearly identified in a way which does not rely upon any stereotypical
reasoning.

2. A privilege for counselling records?

The arguments for an absolute privilege for communications with therapists are three-
fold. First, in a counselling relationship built on confidentiality, privacy, and trust
which enables a victim to explore issues concerning her sense of safety and self-
esteem, the knowledge that details of her conversations with the therapist might be
used against her in subsequent criminal proceedings can inhibit the counselling process and undermine its efficacy. It is argued that compared to this 'chilling effect',
the evidential benefit that would result from a denial of the privilege would be mod-
est, since patients will not make unprotected admissions against their interest,[368] and
'this unspoken "evidence" will therefore serve no greater truth-seeking function than
if it had been spoken and privileged'.[369] Second, allowing an accused and defence
counsel to have access to the victim's thoughts, feelings, insecurities and the recount-
ing of painful past experiences as revealed in counselling sessions may exacerbate
the trauma.[370] Third, the complainant's description of an abusive experience in the
course of a therapy session may not have the same attention to accuracy as it might
where she is making a formal complaint to the police or giving sworn testimony,
because the details of the experience are not so important in the therapeutic context
as is her response to it.[371]

Opponents of absolute privilege point out that the price of the benefits it purchases
must be occasional injustice, because it impedes the search for the truth.[372] The risk
of injustice may be particularly acute where the complainant's 'disclosures' may have

---

[367] J Plotnikoff and R Woolfson 'A Fair Balance'? Evaluation of the Operation of Disclosure Law (RDS
Occasional Paper No 76, Home Office 2001) 90.   [368] A questionable assumption.
[369] Jaffee v Redmond (n 198) 11–12.   [370] R v Young (n 293).
[371] LLA v AB (n 230) [54]–[62].
[372] Jaffee v Redmond (n 198) 18–19 (Scalia J, dissenting); LLA v AB (n 230) [65]–[69].

been instigated by dubious or improper psychotherapy techniques,[373] or the child has a history of serious emotional and behavioural problems which could affect the credibility of her testimony, or previous allegations have been proved to be false.[374]

We have seen that the Australian States have struggled to define satisfactorily the scope of counselling privilege, as definitions turning on qualifications or experience on the one hand, or the nature of the communication on the other, can be too restrictive or too vague. The New Zealand Court of Appeal refused to create a class privilege for counsellors for this reason.[375] Another difficulty arising from the Australian and American approach of protecting sexual assault communications is the privileging of counselling for one type of abusive experience. A person who has experienced childhood physical or emotional abuse or neglect by his family may be just as, or even more, traumatized as the victim of a one-off sexual assault.

The focus of the Criminal Code of Canada on the legitimate expectation of privacy attaching to the record or oral communication provides a better solution. It is submitted that England should develop a clear and detailed statutory procedure for the adjudication of disclosure issues in both criminal and civil cases, which mediates between the competing ECHR rights of the complainant or claimant in privacy and of the accused or defendant in civil proceedings in securing a fair trial. The 2006 *Crown Court Protocol* on disclosure, expressing the courts' obligation as a public authority to ensure that any interference with the child's privacy rights under Article 8 of the ECHR is in accordance with the law and necessary in pursuit of a legitimate public interest, is a salutary reminder of the competing interests, although in our submission the 'mere credibility' rule reinforced in the *Protocol* should be reconsidered.[376]

This suggestion raises the question as to whether the balancing test should differ in formulation or application between civil and criminal proceedings. In *M(A) v Ryan*, McLachlin J observed:

Just as justice requires that the accused in a criminal case be permitted to answer the Crown's case, so justice requires that a defendant in a civil suit be permitted to answer the plaintiff's case. In deciding whether he or she is entitled to production of confidential documents, this requirement must be balanced against the privacy interest of the complainant. This said, the interest in disclosure of a defendant in a civil suit may be less compelling than the parallel interest of an accused charged with a crime. The defendant in a civil suit stands to lose money and repute; the accused in a criminal proceeding stands to lose his or her very liberty. As a consequence, the balance between the interest in disclosure and the complainant's interest in privacy may be struck at a different level in the civil and criminal case; documents produced in a criminal case may not always be producible in a civil case, where the privacy interest of the complainant may more easily outweigh the defendant's interest in production.

On another view, it is arguable that the relevance of therapy records to the facts in issue takes on different complexions in criminal and civil proceedings. In tort litigation,

---

[373] E Loftus, J Paddock and T Guernsey 'Patient-Psychotherapist Privilege: Access to Clinical Records in the Tangled Web of Repressed Memory Litigation' (1996) 30 U of Richmond L Rev 109 110–111.
[374] *State v Boutwell* 558 A 2d 244 (Connecticut App 1989) 276–277; *State v Slimskey* 779 A 2d 723 (Connecticut Supreme Ct 2001); *State v McGill* 539 SE 2d 351 (North Carolina App 2000).
[375] *M v L* (n 342) 757–758.   [376] HM Court Service *Protocol* (n 73) [62].

the claimant is putting her state of mind directly in issue, because she is claiming compensation for the consequences of the alleged abuse, including the psychological trauma. In a criminal case, absent some evidence indicating that the complainant's memory traces have been contaminated by inappropriate therapy, the state of mind of the complainant is not in issue, at least in child abuse prosecutions where consent is no longer a defence. This suggests that there should be a higher threshold of relevance of therapy records for a criminal prosecution than in tort litigation before disclosure is ordered. Therefore targeting the relevance of the records should be the first, and arguably the foremost, consideration in any balancing test formulation.

8

The Child Witness

A. Testimonial Competence and Compellability

1. Testimonial competence and compellability in English law

(a) Criminal cases

The police officer and social worker video-interviewing a child must not only seek to elicit a complaint of a criminal offence against an identified perpetrator which can stand as examination-in-chief, itself a formidable task, but they must also obtain evidence demonstrating the competence of the child to give evidence in court.

Testimonial competence requires the capacity to observe past events (including interpretation), the capacity to recollect those events, and the capacity to communicate what is remembered.[1] The goal is not to ensure that the evidence is credible, but only that it meets the minimum threshold for being heard; the court's enquiry is into *capacity* to perceive, recollect, and communicate, not whether the witness *actually* perceived, recollects, and can communicate about the events in question.[2] The trial court therefore has a crucial role in filtering the witnesses whom the jury may hear. Psychologists[3] and law reform bodies have become increasingly sceptical of the utility of the competence test in enhancing the likelihood that the witness will ultimately give a truthful and accurate account.[4]

At common law, the competence of a witness to testify in court was welded to that witness's capacity to understand the nature and consequences of the oath to

---

[1] JW Strong *McCormick on Evidence* (4th edn West Pub Co, St Paul Minnesota 1992) vol 1, 242–248; J Wigmore *Evidence in Trials at Common Law* (1904, James H Chadbourne 1978 rev edn Little, Browne & Co, Boston) vol 2, 636–638.

[2] *R v Marquard* [1993] 4 SCR 223 (SCC) 236; *R v MAM* [2001] BCCA 6 (British Columbia CA) (Rowles J).

[3] N Bala, K Lee, R Lindsay and V Talwar 'A Legal & Psychological Critique of the Present Approach to the Assessment of the Competence of Child Witnesses' (2000) 38 Osgoode Hall LJ 409, 442–446.

[4] HH Judge Thomas Pigot QC (Chair) *Report of the Advisory Group on Video-Recorded Evidence* (HMSO, London 1989) (hereafter the *Pigot Report*) [5.11]; Ontario Law Reform Commission *Report on Child Witnesses* (1991) (hereafter Ontario LRC, *Child Witnesses*) 37; New Zealand Law Commission *The Evidence of Children and Other Vulnerable Witnesses: a Discussion Paper* (Preliminary Paper 26 October 1996) (hereafter NZLC, *Evidence of Children*) [25]–[36].

tell the truth. While the law did not automatically exclude a child of any age as a witness, many child witnesses failed the theological inquisition which was the necessary precursor to being declared capable of being sworn.[5] Under the Children and Young Persons Act (CYPA) 1933 (England) s 38,[6] the connection between testimonial competence and the oath was severed, and a child who did not understand the oath was permitted to give unsworn evidence if 'in the opinion of the court, he is possessed of sufficient intelligence to justify reception of the evidence, and understands the duty of speaking the truth'. A child who gives false unsworn testimony is liable to prosecution for the equivalent of perjury.[7] The unsworn testimony of a child was nonetheless devalued, as until 1988 as a matter of law a conviction could not be founded on the unsworn testimony of a child which was not corroborated by other material evidence.[8] Unsworn evidence from another child could not qualify as corroboration.[9] So it was still an advantage to the prosecution to have the court test the child's understanding of divine retribution for false testimony, to qualify for the oath. If the child could not pass this crucial test, often the case collapsed because there was no, or insufficient, other evidence for the prosecution to tender.[10]

In 1988 the legal distinction between the evidence of sworn and unsworn child witnesses was abolished,[11] so it became of little legal significance whether the child qualified as a competent witness by understanding the oath or by understanding the duty of speaking the truth. Nevertheless, the difficulty of the judicial task of exploring a child's notions of abstract concepts like 'truth' and 'duty' meant that young child witnesses still very rarely appeared in the criminal courts. In *Wallwork*[12] the Court of Appeal deprecated the calling of a witness aged five, stating that it was 'ridiculous' to suppose that any value could be attached to the evidence of such a young witness. This judicial policy was reiterated by the Court of Appeal in 1987 in *R v Wright and Ormerod*,[13] where it was stated that 'quite exceptional circumstances' would be required to justify receiving the evidence of a child of 'extremely tender years', such as age six, and that it would be 'a bold tribunal' which disregarded *Wallwork*. In practice, prosecutors did not tender children as witnesses unless they seemed to have the understanding normally to be expected of a child of about eight years.[14]

---

[5] *R v Brasier* (1779) 1 Leach 199, East P C 441; J Spencer and R Flin *The Evidence of Children: the Law and the Psychology* (2nd edn Blackstone Press, London 1993) 46–54.

[6] Originally enacted in the Criminal Amendment Act 1885 (England), but restricted at that time to certain sexual offences; after being gradually extended to other categories of offences, in 1933 children were permitted to give unsworn evidence in respect of all criminal offences.

[7] Criminal Justice Act 1988 (England) s 38 (CJA1988). However, the *doli incapax* doctrine would prevent any prosecution of a child under age ten; in *R v Norbury* (1992) 136 SJ LB 136 (full text available on Lexis), the Court of Appeal rejected a defence argument that immunity from prosecution for perjury justified finding a child under ten years incompetent.

[8] Section 38(1), repealed by the CJA 1988 s 34(1).   [9] *DPP v Hester* [1973] 1 AC 296 (HL).

[10] Spencer and Flin (n 5) 54–56.   [11] CJA 1988 s 33A.

[12] *R v Wallwork* (1958) 42 Cr App R 153 (CA) 160–161.

[13] *R v Wright and Ormerod* (1990) 90 Cr App R 91 (CA) 94–95.   [14] *Pigot Report*.

In 1989 the Advisory Group on Video-Recorded Evidence chaired by Judge Thomas Pigot QC reported to the Government on the way in which child witnesses testified in England and Wales.[15] The *Pigot Report* criticized the minimum age policy of prosecutors, noting that it contrasted sharply with Scotland, where despite a similar formal competence requirement, it was not unusual for children aged four to six to give evidence, and witnesses as young as three had testified.[16] Concern was widely expressed that the attitudes of English and Welsh courts resulted in de facto immunity being conferred on paedophiles who targeted very young children.[17] The Pigot Committee attempted to disrupt these entrenched judicial suspicions of young child witnesses, recommending that all children under the age of 14 give unsworn evidence, because 'if a child's account is available it should be heard'; juries should be left to weigh matters such as the demeanour, maturity, coherence and consistency of the child in deciding how much reliance to place on the testimony.[18] This recommendation was implemented in the CJA 1991.[19]

In 1990 Lord Lane CJ in *R v Z*[20] stressed that the disapproval expressed in earlier cases of tendering very young children as witnesses had been overtaken by a growing public perception that they can be just as reliable as their elders, when appropriate precautions are taken. The judiciary was admonished not to read into the 1933 statute a minimum age for receiving a child's unsworn evidence; competence had to be determined having regard to the nature and circumstances of the case and the child in question. Nevertheless, Lord Lane cautioned that 'it may be very rarely that a five-year-old will satisfy the requirements of s. 38(1)'.[21] Such *obiter dicta* are prone to misinterpretation, as *DPP v M* in 1996 illustrates; the Queen's Bench Division found it necessary to remind a judge that a child's evidence could not be automatically excluded by reason of her age alone.[22]

However, the abolition of the oath had left the competence conundrum fully exposed. How is a trial judge to ascertain whether a child is *capable* of giving reliable testimony, before relinquishing to the jury the final decision as to the reliability of that testimony? The competence test in the 1933 Act still bound together the intellectual capacity of a child to give a useful account, and that child's understanding of the duty to tell the truth; as John Spencer pointed out, the latter does not inexorably follow from the former in the case of very young children, yet should that mean the child is not heard at all?[23]

---

[15] The highly influential recommendations of the Pigot Committee are discussed in detail below section B.1(b)(i).   [16] *Pigot Report* [5.5].

[17] *Pigot Report* [5.7]–[5.12] reporting on the concerns of police witnesses; J Temkin 'Child Sexual Abuse and Criminal Justice: Part I' [1990] New LJ 352, 355.   [18] *Pigot Report* [5.12], [5.14].

[19] Amending the CJA 1988, s 33A(1). Nevertheless, as recently as 1996, at least one trial judge was still administering the oath to children under 14: see *R v Jackson* (CCA 19 November 1996) where, in an inversion of the traditional objection to reception of a child's testimony, the defendant claimed that his conviction was unsafe because one of the complainants, age 11, had given sworn evidence.

[20] *R v Z* [1990] 2 All ER 971 (CA).   [21] ibid 973.

[22] *DPP v M* [1997] 2 All ER 749 (QBD) The complainant was then age five, and was four years old at the time of the indecent assault.

[23] J Spencer 'Reforming the Competence Requirement' [1988] New LJ 147.

The Criminal Justice Act 1991 (England) (CJA 1991) in s 52(2) attempted to clarify the implications of the requirement that the evidence of all children under 14 be given unsworn, stating that 'accordingly the power of the court in any criminal proceedings to determine that a particular person is not competent to give evidence shall apply to children of tender years as it applies to other persons'.[24] This bland wording gave rise to a dangerous ambiguity, however: since the test of competence for an adult witness is not only his ability to give coherent evidence but also to understand the implications of the oath, it could be argued that Parliament had raised the competence standard above that required by the 1933 benchmark.[25] In *R v Hampshire* in 1994, the Court of Appeal concluded that an investigation of a child's competence in a *voir dire*[26] entailed inquiring whether the child knew the difference between truth and lies, and the importance of telling the truth.[27]

In 1994, Parliament attempted once again to provide clear direction to the courts, amending the Criminal Justice Act 1988 (England) (CJA 1988) s 33A(2A) to read: 'A child's evidence shall be received unless it appears to the court that the child is incapable of giving *intelligible* testimony.'[28] The test of competence was finally officially liberated from philosophical excursions into a child's understanding of abstruse concepts such as the truth, God, and a witness's duty to the court. The Court of Appeal gave a straightforward interpretation to that statutory test, stating that a child will be capable of giving intelligible testimony if she is able to understand questions and to answer them in a manner which is coherent and comprehensible.[29] Under the new, less rigorous, test of competence, it was no longer necessary to determine whether a child can distinguish between truth and lies, and the importance of speaking the truth.[30]

However, it was perhaps inevitable that the courts would find implicit in the 'intelligibility' test a requirement that the child at least demonstrate some appreciation of reality versus fiction. In *R v D and Others*[31] the Court of Appeal considered the 1991 wording, but with an eye to the 1994 amendment which had yet to be proclaimed. Reiterating that the plain object of the 1991 Act was to ensure that the evidence of a child would be received if that child could give a rational account of the events in question, and to simplify the court procedure in relation to children's evidence, the Court stated:

In our judgment, the test of the competence of a child witness under the provisions of s 52 is whether the child is able to understand the questions put to him or her, to communicate, and to give a coherent and comprehensible account of the matters in relation to which he or she is giving evidence. *Built into that concept must be an ability to distinguish between truth and fiction or between fact and fantasy.* If a child, by reason of extreme youth or for any other reason, is unable to distinguish between truth and fiction or between facts and fantasy, then

---

[24] CJA 1991 (England) s 52(2).

[25] A criticism made by Spencer and Flin (n 5) 62–63 and by DJ Birch 'Children's Evidence' [1992] Crim LR 262, which was accepted in *R v Hampshire* [1995] 2 All ER 1019 (CA) 1024–1025.

[26] A hearing conducted by trial judge in the absence of the jury in the course of a trial, to ascertain the admissibility of evidence.   [27] *R v Hampshire* (n 25).

[28] Criminal Justice and Public Order Act 1994 (England) Sch 9 s 33.   [29] *DPP v M* (n 22) 753.

[30] *R v Hampshire* (n 25).   [31] *R v D and Others* (CA 3 November 1995).

that child would be unable to give a coherent and comprehensible account of the matters in issue. In our view, the phraseology which we have adopted is more apt to a child witness under the legislation than an ability to distinguish between truth and lies, because (a) the abolition of the requirement of the child to take the oath and (b), perhaps, more importantly, lies by definition are an intentional or deliberate falsehood connoting an ability to tell the difference between lies and the truth. Once a child can give a comprehensible account and distinguish between fact and fiction, whether the child is telling the truth or not is a matter for the jury. (emphasis added)

The Court of Appeal concluded on this point by cautioning that 'save in the case of exceedingly young children, the competence of children to give evidence is likely to arise very rarely and in exceptional circumstances only'. Therefore, as with an adult, some evidential basis of incompetence beyond the age of the witness was required to overturn the presumption of competence.

Parliament tried once again to open the courtroom door to virtually all children capable of speech, however young, in the Youth Justice and Criminal Evidence Act 1999 (England) (YJCEA 1999). Section 53(1) sets up a general presumption of competence for all witnesses. A person of whatever age will not be competent if it appears to the court that he is not able to (a) understand questions put to him as a witness, and (b) give answers to them which can be understood.[32] The burden of proof lies upon the party calling the witness to show on the balance of probabilities in a *voir dire* that the witness can meet this minimal standard, with the support if necessary of Special Measures Directions.[33] A significant advance is a clear statement that expert evidence is admissible on the question of competence;[34] it is unlikely that this will be required in the case of children with normal mental and physical capacities for their age. The singling out of child witnesses as requiring their own test of competence has thus been abolished.

In most cases under both the CJA 1988 and the YJCEA 1999, a judge will assess a child witness's competence by watching the video recording in the context of a pre-trial application, to determine whether it is 'in the interests of justice' to exclude the video-recording from evidence.[35] After this initial ruling, however, the trial judge is required to keep the issue of competence under review, as competence relates to the whole of the child's evidence, and not just to part of it.[36] The issue of testimonial competence may need to be revisited during cross-examination if a child, especially a very young one, cannot give intelligible answers in cross-examination, particularly after a prolonged delay between the interview and trial.[37] It can also arise if the child claims not to know the difference between truth and lies, sometimes as a defensive mechanism when caught out on some inaccuracy or falsehood.[38] When this happens, the trial

---

[32] YJCEA 1999 (England) s 53(3).
[33] YJCEA 1999 (England) s 54(2),(3) and (4), discussed above Chapter 7 section B.2.
[34] YJCEA 1999 (England) s 54(5).
[35] CJA 1988 (England) s 32A(3)(c), and now YJCEA 1999 (England) ss 21(4)(b), 27(2); *R v Hampshire* (n 25); *R v MacPherson* [2005] EWCA Crim 365, [2006] All ER (D) 104.
[36] *R v Powell* [2006] EWCA Crim 03, [2006] All ER (D) 45.   [37] ibid 45.
[38] *Bristol Study* 63–64, case 27B.

judge should hold a *voir dire* in which the child will be examined in the absence of the jury.[39] The court must restrict itself to ascertaining the child's understanding of the questions and her ability to give understandable answers; questions of credibility and reliability go to the weight of the evidence, and should be considered, if appropriate, at the end of the prosecution case by way of a defence submission of 'no case to answer'.[40] Since the jury will already have seen the child's examination-in-chief in the videotape, if the child is ruled testimonially incompetent at this stage, there will likely be a mistrial.

The YJCEA 1999 preserves the threshold of 14 years for sworn testimony.[41] Witnesses over that age may be administered the oath if they have a sufficient appreciation of the solemnity of the occasion and the particular responsibility to tell the truth which is involved in taking an oath, there being a rebuttable presumption that they have a sufficient appreciation if they are capable of giving intelligible testimony.[42] If the opposing party satisfies an evidential burden to challenge the existence of that appreciation, the proponent of that witness must satisfy the court on the issue on a balance of probabilities.[43] Again, expert evidence is admissible on the question of whether the witness should be sworn.[44]

The apparent motivation behind requiring all child witnesses under 14 to give unsworn evidence, in attempting to spare them from an inquisition into their appreciation of the oath, is commendable, but jurors will not have to be particularly astute to notice that they have not been sworn to tell the truth, and may infer that their testimony is devalued by the criminal justice system. It is natural for jurors to want to be satisfied that the child can distinguish between truth and falsehood, and does understand the importance of telling the truth, given the implications for the accused.

Experimental research indicates that the ability of children to explain such abstract concepts as 'truth', 'lies' and 'promise' is not related to whether children actually tell the truth.[45] Furthermore, the studies show that truth-telling behaviour is not related to knowing that lying is 'bad'.[46] There is also empirical evidence that children who have been neglected or abused often show developmental delays due to the treatment they have suffered. Nevertheless, research shows that most maltreated children by age five have a basic understanding of the meaning and the immorality of lying.[47] Yet these are the children who are most likely to have difficulty demonstrating their understanding of the distinction between truth and lies, and their obligation to tell only the truth, particularly in a courtroom environment which inevitably will be intimidating. What the latest statutory definition accomplishes is to leave those issues as matters

---

[39] *R v Hayes* [1977] 1 WLR 234, [1977] 2 All ER 288 (CA).   [40] *R v MacPherson* (n 35).
[41] YJCEA 1999 (England) s 55(2)(a).   [42] ibid s 55(2)(b).   [43] ibid s 55(3) and (4).
[44] ibid s 55 (6).   [45] Bala, Lee, Lindsay and Talwar (n 3) 442–46.
[46] In the research sample of 130 children, 72 per cent of the liars said that it was bad to lie: ibid 444.
[47] T Lyon and K Saywitz 'Young Maltreated Children's Competence to Take the Oath' (1999) 3 *Applied Developmental Science* 16. An Australian research study found that 88 per cent of the sample of four-year-olds were able correctly to classify statements as truth and lies: K Bussey and E Grimbeek 'Children's Conceptions of Lying and Truth-Telling: Implications for Child Witnesses' (2000) 5 *Legal & Criminological Psychology* 187.

of weight for the jury to evaluate, rather than allowing them to intercept the child's testimony.

And so we have returned to the starting point of this discussion, that it is incumbent upon the police officer or social worker conducting the video interview to pose appropriate questions to the child in order to provide sufficient evidence to the court (and, in the first instance, the CPS) of the child's testimonial competence, should that become an issue, and otherwise to reinforce the reliability of the evidence which emerges in the interview. The guidance under the YJCEA 1999, *Achieving Best Evidence*, advises interviewers to explore with a witness who is very young, or has a learning disability, his understanding of the difference between truth and lies,[48] but later, in setting out how to do this, does not place such restrictions on the situations where the exercise would be appropriate, apparently recommending that it be carried out for all child witnesses who are video-interviewed, to preserve the evidential value of the interview.[49] Under the *Memorandum of Good Practice* which governed video interviews before the YJCEA 1999,[50] interviewers tended to ask questions which were obviously factually incorrect, such as misidentifying the colour of their shoes, but it was difficult for children (and possibly also jurors) to take such tests—and as a consequence perhaps also the interview—seriously. *Achieving Best Evidence* emphasizes that the examples chosen must really be lies, incorporating an intent to deceive another person rather than merely incorrect statements, which should serve to enhance considerably the value of the 'truth and lies' exercise.[51]

Perhaps the more difficult task will be to remind the child of the possible adverse consequences for another person of telling lies[52] without deterring full disclosure of events which the child is likely to realize could have those implications. The empirical psychological research discussed earlier has shown that while children as young as four years of age can understand that there is a moral difference between telling the truth and falsehood, an important determinant of the child's lying or truth-telling was the anticipated outcome of disclosure. The more the children in these studies anticipated getting into trouble for being honest, the less likely they were to be truthful.[53] Therefore the balance between admonition and reassurance by the interviewer may be critical to the reliability of the child's statements.

The Court of Appeal under the 1991 legislation commended the suggestion of the Pigot Committee that the trial judge, in the presence of the accused and the jury, give the child 'a softly worded and spoken reminder' of the importance of telling the truth

---

[48] Home Office et al *Achieving Best Evidence in Criminal Proceedings: Guidance for Vulnerable or Intimidated Witnesses, Including Children* (2001) [2.21] (hereafter *Achieving Best Evidence*).

[49] *Achieving Best Evidence* [2.102].   [50] Discussed above, Chapter 5 section G.2(c).

[51] *Achieving Best Evidence* [2.102]. This change was recommended by the *Bristol Study* 82. See also Scottish Executive *Guidance on Interviewing Child Witnesses in Scotland* (2003) [64]–[74].

[52] *Achieving Best Evidence* [2.102].

[53] K Bussey, K Lee and E Grimbeek 'Lies and Secrets: Implications for Children's Reporting of Sexual Abuse' in G Goodman and B Bottoms (eds) *Child Victims, Child Witnesses: Understanding and Improving Testimony* (Guildford Press, New York, London 1993) 151–153.

before cross-examination commences.[54] The Judicial Studies Board recommends that this practice continue under the YJCEA 1999.[55]

Finally, it should be noted that if a child satisfies the legal test of testimonial competence, she will then be compellable in the criminal proceedings on the same basis as any adult witness, and no prior leave of the court is required.[56] The prevailing judicial view is that children are citizens owing duties to society as a whole (including other children), which are appropriate to their years and understanding and are under the same duty as adults to testify in court; it is the criminal court rather than the family court which has jurisdiction in such matters.[57] In most such cases the child has been an eyewitness to domestic violence, and has been summoned by the defence. This raises the issue of s 44 of the Children Act 1989 which places an obligation on 'every court' in dealing with the child or young person who was brought before it' to have regard for the child's welfare. The magistrate is required to issue a witness summons if the child could give material evidence, regardless of any concerns about his welfare.[58] Any balancing of whether the harm to the defence is outweighed by the interests of the child should be performed by the trial judge when the moment arises to call the child as a witness.[59] The civil court's permission is required for the prosecution or the defence in criminal proceedings to interview a child who is a ward of the court (wardship now being very rare);[60] where it is a defence application, special provisions may be necessary to protect the child from trauma, such as having the Official Solicitor attend.[61] It is likely that an analogous procedure would be applied where the local authority has parental responsibility for a child who is a prospective witness.[62]

(b) Civil cases

Under the Children Act 1989, a child is technically compellable to testify in any proceedings involving an application for a care or supervision order, but only at the instance of the court rather than one of the parties.[63] The court may authorize a constable to bring the child before the court, and has jurisdiction to require

---

[54] *Pigot Report* [5.15]; *R v Hampshire* (n 25) 1029; although the Court of Appeal was clearly cognizant of the pending changes to the competence test in the Criminal Justice and Public Order Act 1994 (England), it appears that they still thought that this reminder was advisable.

[55] Judicial Studies Board Specimen Direction 22, *Evidence of Children*.

[56] Criminal Procedure (Attendance of Witnesses) Act 1965 (England) ss 2, 4; Magistrates Court Act 1980 (England) s 102(10); *Re K and others (Minors) (Wardship: Criminal Proceedings)* [1988] 1 All ER 214 (Fam Div) 221–22; *Re R and others (Minors) (Wardship: Criminal Proceedings)* [1991] 2 FLR 95 (CA) 198.

[57] *Re R and others* ibid 101 (Lord Donaldson).

[58] *R v Liverpool Magistrates Court ex p Pollock* [1997] COD 344 (QBD) (child aged seven); *Re F (Specific Issue: Child Interview)* [1995] 1 FLR 819 (CA) (twins aged 11); *R v Highbury Corner Magistrates' Court ex p D* [1997] 1 FLR 683 (QBD) (child aged nine).

[59] *R v Highbury Corner Magistrates' Court ex p D* ibid 685.   [60] Children Act 1989 s 100.

[61] *Practice Direction (Family Division)* [1988] 1 All ER 223, modified by [1988] 2 All ER 1015; *Re R and others* (n 56).

[62] Waite LJ drew on the analogy of wardship in *Re F (Specific Issue: Child Interview)* (n 58) 822 in upholding an order that the father's solicitor could interview the children notwithstanding the objections of the mother.

[63] Children Act 1989 (England) s 95; see also *R v B County Council ex p P* [1991] WLR 221 (CA) discussed below section B.4.

any person having information about the whereabouts of the child to disclose that the court.[64] Bainham points out that this may mean that children are required to attend when they do not wish to do so or may not be allowed to attend when they do.[65]

In principle, the older the child, the more likely it is that the application of a party for a witness summons will be granted; however in most cases involving a child aged 12 or younger, the court will have to rely upon hearsay to hear the child's story, with the potential consequence of weakening the case against the adult.[66] The special provisions respecting children's hearsay in civil cases will be discussed below.[67]

The Children Act 1989 imported the then current criminal definition of competence from the CYPA 1933, permitting the court to hear the child unsworn if the court is of the opinion that the child understands that is his duty to speak the truth and he has sufficient understanding to justify his evidence being heard.[68] This definition has not been amended as a consequence of the lowering of the threshold in the YJCEA 1999. It is important to note that the competence provisions of the Children Act 1989 apply to child witnesses in all civil proceedings and courts, not just to family law cases.[69]

2. Testimonial competence and compellability in Australian law

In all Australian jurisdictions a child who has been found to be incompetent to give sworn testimony may give unsworn evidence.[70] There is no unanimity however in delineating the circumstances in which children may be permitted to take the oath. The age thresholds under which investigation of the competence of a child witness is required vary from 12 years in South Australia and Western Australia to 14 years in Victoria and Tasmania.[71] The tests also vary; South Australia still uses the traditional common law definition requiring an understanding of the oath in terms of divine retribution,[72] whereas Tasmania, Queensland, and Western Australia have followed the modern English approach of determining competence on the basis of ability to distinguish between truth and falsehood and an acceptance of a higher obligation

---

[64] Children Act 1989 (England) s 95(5) and (6).

[65] A Bainham *Children: the Modern Law* (3rd edn Jordan Publishing Limited, Bristol 2005) 459.

[66] *Re P (Witness Summons)* [1997] 2 FLR 447 (CA).   [67] See section B.4.

[68] Children Act 1989 (England) s 96(2).

[69] *Re K and others (Minors)* (n 56) (prosecution witness); *Re R and others (Minors)* (n 56) (defence witness).

[70] Evidence Amendment (Children and Special Witnesses) Act 1995 (Tasmania) s 122C; Evidence Act 1929 (South Australia) s 12; Acts Amendment (Evidence of Children and Others) Act 1992 (Western Australia) s 106C; Oaths Act 1867 (Northern Territory) s 13; Evidence Act 1958 (Victoria) s 23; Evidence Act 1971 (Australian Capital Territory) s 64.

[71] Evidence Act 1929 (South Australia) s 12; Acts Amendment (Evidence of Children and Others) Act 1992 (Western Australia) s 106B; Evidence Act 1958 (Victoria) s 23; Evidence Amendment (Children and Special Witnesses) Act 1995 (Tasmania) s 122B.

[72] Australian Law Reform Commission and the Human Rights and Equal Opportunity Commission *Seen and Heard: Priority for Children and the Legal Process* (Report 84 1997) (hereafter Aus LRC, *Seen and Heard*) [14.60].

to tell the truth in court than in everyday life.[73] In Western Australia, intelligibility is the sole criterion to permit the child to testify unsworn,[74] and the Victorian Law Reform Commission has recommended that this be adopted for criminal trials in that State.[75] In Western Australia, when the whole of the child's evidence is video-recorded prior to trial,[76] the trial judge asks a few questions to ascertain whether the child can give an intelligible account of events, and that ruling cannot be displaced by cross-examination of the child, as it is for the jury to determine whether the child's answers were inaccurate or untruthful.[77]

Queensland, in the Evidence (Protection of Children) Amendment Act 2003, has made expert evidence admissible about the witness's ability to give an intelligible account, or to understand the obligations attendant upon taking the oath. Expert evidence is also admissible respecting a child under 12 years; an expert may testify about the witness's level of intelligence, including powers of reception, memory and expression, or any other relevant matter relevant to the issue of ability to give reliable evidence.[78]

The Commonwealth Evidence Act 1995 eliminates any special provisions for the competence of children, providing that every witness regardless of age is prima facie presumed to be competent to give sworn evidence in civil and criminal proceedings.[79] This presumption is rebutted if the person is incapable of understanding that he is under an obligation to give truthful evidence, in which case the court should ascertain whether the person meets the requirements for giving unsworn evidence, being an understanding of the difference between truth and lies, and an assurance that the person will not tell lies in the proceedings after being admonished by the court about the importance of telling the truth.[80] The court is permitted to 'inform itself as it thinks fit',[81] which is seen as a licence to admit expert evidence on the point, or to obtain the assistance of someone with whom the child has a rapport.[82]

An unusual feature of the federal statute is a saving provision that a person who is incapable of giving a rational reply to a question about a fact is not competent to give evidence about that fact, but nonetheless may be competent to give evidence about other facts.[83] Section 13(4) casts some light upon this otherwise rather puzzling provision, providing that a person is incompetent to testify about a fact if he is incapable of hearing or understanding, or of communicating a reply to, a question about the fact, and that incapacity cannot be overcome. The apparent intention is that a witness does not become incompetent due to a failure of communication with counsel or

---

[73] Evidence Amendment (Children and Special Witnesses) Act 1995 (Tasmania) s 122B; *Attorney-General's Reference No 2 of 1993* (1994) 4 Tas R 26 (Tasmania Ct Crim App); Acts Amendment (Evidence of Children and Others) Act 1992 (Western Australia) inserting s 106B in the Evidence Act 1906 (Western Australia); Evidence (Protection of Children) Amendment Act 2003 (Queensland) s 57, inserting s 9B in the Evidence Act 1977 (Queensland).   [74] Evidence Act 1906 (Western Australia) s 106C.

[75] Victorian Law Reform Commission *Sexual Offences: Final Report* (1 April 2004) Recommendations 132–138.   [76] Discussed below section B.3(b)(iii).

[77] *R v Stevenson* [2000] WASCA 301 (Western Australia SCA) [16], [36].

[78] Evidence (Protection of Children) Amendment Act 2003 (Queensland) s 57, inserting s 9C in the Evidence Act 1977 (Queensland).   [79] Evidence Act 1995 (Commonwealth of Australia) s 12.

[80] ibid s 13(1) and (2).   [81] ibid s 13(7).   [82] Aus LRC, *Seen and Heard* [14.64].

[83] Evidence Act 1995 (Commonwealth of Australia) s 13(3).

the court on a particular matter. The Australian Law Reform Commission considered that this is particularly valuable for child witnesses who may have differing language skills, abilities to make inferences, conclusions or estimates, or capacities to understand concepts such as time and spatial perspective.[84] The Australian Law Reform Commission recommended that all Australian States adopt this model;[85] New South Wales already has done so,[86] but Queensland chose not to do so in its 2003 reforms.

In Queensland, in child protection proceedings in the Childrens Court, a child aged 12 or over may testify, but only with leave of the court and only if the child agrees to testify and is represented by a lawyer. If the child gives evidence, he or she may be cross-examined only with the leave of the court.[87]

3. Testimonial competence and compellability in Canadian law

The Canada Evidence Act[88] which governs all criminal prosecutions in Canada was amended in 1987 to require the trial judge to conduct an inquiry into the testimonial competence of any proposed witness under 14 years, or whose mental capacity has been challenged. This provision placed the child witness in the same position as an adult whose competence has been challenged.[89] The court had to determine whether the person understands the nature of an oath or a solemn affirmation; and whether the person is able to communicate the evidence. In *R v Marquard*, the Supreme Court Canada by a majority held that the wording 'communicate the evidence' indicated more than mere verbal ability, and so the competence *voir dire* required the trial judge to explore whether the witness was capable of perceiving, remembering, and communicating events to the court. It was not however necessary to determine whether the child perceived and recollected the very events at issue in the trial.[90]

If the proposed witness passed the 'communication' test but not the 'nature of the oath' test, he could testify on promising to tell the truth. That promise was interpreted as implying not only an understanding of the difference between telling the truth and telling a lie, but also of the nature of a promise, requiring an understanding of the moral obligation to speak the truth 'in terms of everyday social conduct'.[91] This interpretation deviated from the recommendation of the report of the Committee on Sexual Offences against Children and Youth in 1984, which would have made every child who had a verbal capacity to reply to simply framed questions competent, leaving the cogency of that evidence to the jury.[92] The Law Reform Commission of Canada also considered that threshold tests of competence should be abolished

---

[84] Aus LRC, *Seen and Heard* [14.63].   [85] ibid Recommendation 98.
[86] Evidence Act 1995 (New South Wales) s 13.
[87] Child Protection Act 1999 (Queensland) s 112.
[88] Canada Evidence Act s 16.   [89] *R v Marquard* (n 2) 236.
[90] ibid, 236–237. L'Heureux-Dubé J (La Forest and Gonthier J concurring) considered that the standard was inconsistent with the trend to doing away with presumptions that child witnesses are unreliable.
[91] *R v Khan* [1990] 2 SCR 531 (SCC) 536; *R v Rockey* [1996] 3 SCR 829 (SCC) [25], [27]; *R v Ferguson* (1996) 112 CCC (3d) 342 (British Columbia CA) 362; *R v Farley* (1995) 99 CCC (3d) 76 (Ontario CA) 83.
[92] Badgley et al *Sexual Offences against Children: Report of the Committee on Sexual Offences against Children and Youth* (Ottawa: Supply and Services Canada 1984) (hereafter *Badgley Report*) 373.

because of the impossibility of stating and applying a consistent standard of mental capacity.[93]

These recommendations were finally adopted in July 2005, when Parliament amended the Canada Evidence Act[94] to set up a rebuttable presumption that every person under 14 years of age has the capacity to testify, defined as the ability to understand and respond to questions.[95] If a party satisfies the court that there is an issue as to the capacity of a child under 14, the court must conduct an inquiry to determine whether the proposed witness is able to understand and respond to questions.[96] All testimony from a witness under 14 must be given not under oath or by affirmation, but rather on a promise to tell the truth.[97] The amendments specifically prohibit any questioning of proposed witnesses under 14 regarding their understanding of the nature of the promise to tell the truth for the purpose of determining whether their evidence shall be received by the court.[98] The restriction of such questioning to the inquiry into capacity is presumably not intended to prevent the child being challenged as to her understanding of truth and lies in the course of cross-examination on her testimony.

In Canadian courts, the threshold issue of competence in the 1987 legislation was very important in practice, because if the child was ruled incompetent, the prosecution could apply to have her out-of-court statements ruled admissible, arguing that it was necessary to do so as the hearsay was the only means of hearing the child's story.[99] The Supreme Court of Canada in *R v Khan*[100] had stressed that trial judges in applying the statutory tests must not be swayed by the very young age of a complainant, as otherwise there would be danger that offences against such children could never be prosecuted. Nevertheless the prosecution often had to have recourse to the hearsay escape hatch.[101] This was never a wholly satisfactory solution, since the defence necessarily would be deprived of the opportunity to cross-examine the child. The 2005 amendments establishing the minimum possible threshold of competence could, paradoxically, provide a fairer trial for the Canadian defendant.

4. Testimonial competence and compellability in New Zealand law

Under New Zealand's Oaths and Affirmations Act 1957, a child under 12 may give unsworn evidence upon making a promise to tell the truth, provided that the court has ascertained that the child is sufficiently intelligent to be capable of giving a rational account, and that she understands the duty of speaking the truth, which entails an understanding of the difference between truth and lies, and an appreciation of the solemnity of the occasion.[102] However, the Court of Appeal has ruled that it would be 'a damaging misjudgment if the child witness were subjected to an emphatic test of general cognitive skills in the preliminary questioning on competence', and therefore

---

[93] Law Reform Commission of Canada *Report on Evidence* (1975) 88.
[94] Canada Evidence Act ss 16, 16.1, as amended by 53–54 Elizabeth II, 2004–2005 Bill C–2.
[95] ibid ss 16.1(1), 16.1(3).   [96] ibid ss 16.1(4), 16.1(5).   [97] ibid ss 16.1(2), 16.1(6).
[98] ibid s 16.1(7).   [99] Discussed below, section B.5.
[100] *R v Khan* (n 91) 539, interpreting the predecessor test.
[101] Discussed below, Chapter 9 section B.5.
[102] Oaths and Affirmations Act 1957 (New Zealand) s 13.

the trial judge should not embark on an interrogation seeking definition of words or concepts.[103] In practice, then, the child's ability to give a rational account of past events is not directly tested in New Zealand courts, which rely instead upon the interviewer to do this.[104] If the witness is over 12, she is presumed to be competent to take the oath unless her competence to do so is challenged, in which case the court must be satisfied that she realizes that taking an oath involves more than the ordinary social duty to tell the truth.[105] These requirements also apply to the videotaping of interviews with child complainant in sexual cases.[106]

The New Zealand Law Commission has proposed jettisoning all rules requiring that children under the age of 12 demonstrate their competence. In the Commission's view, an inquiry into a child's understanding of the nature of a promise does not assist in assessing reliability because there is no proved correlation between age, capacity to distinguish truth from falsehood, and honesty. As the promise to tell the truth cannot serve as a predictor of whether the witness will in fact give accurate evidence,[107] the promise itself becomes otiose.[108] The draft Evidence Code would abolish all threshold requirements of competence, so that no witness would be disbarred from giving evidence, regardless of age, mental incapacity or disorder.[109] If the witness was incoherent or otherwise was unhelpful, the court could use its general inherent discretion preserved by s 8 to exclude evidence where its negative effect outweighs its probative value. The Evidence Code would further require that a witness under 12 not be sworn or affirmed, or give a promise to tell the truth, but the trial judge would give a mandatory instruction of the importance of telling the truth and not telling lies.[110] These rules would apply in both criminal and civil proceedings.

5. Testimonial competence and compellability in Scottish law

In 2003 Scotland took the radical step of abolishing the competence test for all witnesses in all criminal and civil proceedings. The court is forbidden from taking any step prior to the witness giving evidence intended to establish whether the witness understands the nature of the duty to give truthful evidence or can distinguish between truth and lies.[111] There is no explicit discretion to disqualify a witness who has begun giving evidence which proves to be unintelligible, but the wording of the prohibition implies that the court retains inherent discretion to stop the testimony of such a witness.

---

[103] *R v Accused (CA 32/91)* [1991] 2 NZLR 649 (New Zealand CA) 653.

[104] *R v S* [1993] 2 NZLR 142 (New Zealand CA) 145, 151; *R v Accused (CA 449/91)* [1992] 2 N2LR 673 (New Zealand CA); NZLC, *Evidence of Children* [22]. [105] NZLC, *Evidence of Children* [18].

[106] Evidence (Videotaping of Child Complainants) Regulations 1990, SR 1990/164 (New Zealand).

[107] NZLC, *Evidence of Children* [27]–[33].

[108] New Zealand Law Commission *Evidence* (Report 55 August 1999) (hereafter NZLC, *Evidence*) Vol 1 [352]. This is a reversal of the provisional position taken by the Law Commission that the child should promise to tell the truth: NZLC, *Evidence of Children* [56]–[57].

[109] NZLC, *Evidence*, Vol 2, *Evidence Code* s 73 and commentary C294.

[110] ibid, Vol 2, *Evidence Code* s 78(2).

[111] Vulnerable Witnesses (Scotland) Act 2004.

6. Testimonial competence and compellability in American law

The American common law rules of evidence adopted the English common law in refusing to set a minimum precise age below which a child shall be deemed to be incompetent.[112] Most American States have adopted the approach of Federal Rule of Evidence 601 which sets up a rebuttable presumption that all witnesses, including children, are competent. There is therefore no minimum or baseline mental capacity requirement which witnesses must demonstrate before testifying.[113] This is elaborated in 18 USCA §3509(c), setting out the procedure for ascertaining whether the presumption is rebutted. The Rule applies only to children who have been a victim of physical or sexual abuse or exploitation, or have witnessed a crime committed against another. A competence examination regarding a child may be conducted only if the court determines that compelling reasons exist, based on evidence submitted by the opposing party; a child's age alone does not constitute a compelling reason. Evidence that the child has a level of mental functioning below her chronological age is also not a compelling reason if a child of that mental age would be competent.[114] The examination is to be conducted in the absence of the jury. The questions asked of the child must be appropriate to her age and developmental level and focus on determining her ability to understand and answer simple questions, which must not be related to the issues at trial. Any inconsistency in the child's story raises questions of credibility, not competence, which must be left to the trier of fact.[115] Psychological or psychiatric examinations to assess the child's competence may not be ordered unless 'compelling need' has been shown. The Rule is therefore strongly framed in favour of allowing the testimony of children, and the discretion of the trial judge must have been abused to permit appellate intervention.[116]

Questions as to whether the witness understands the need to be truthful are not treated as going to competence, but rather are required to satisfy Federal Rule of Evidence §603 which requires every witness to declare that the testimony will be truthful.[117] Some American States have gone further than the Federal Rule and have enacted rules that a child victim of abuse shall be considered a competent witness and must be allowed to testify without prior qualification in any judicial proceeding, leaving it to the trier of fact to determine the weight and credibility to be given to the testimony.[118] Notwithstanding the statutory presumption of competence, there is empirical evidence that challenges to child competence are not uncommon,[119] and

---

[112] *Wheeler v US* 159 US 523 (USSC 1895) 525.

[113] *US v Allen J* 127 F 3d 1292 (US CA 10th Cir 1997).   [114] ibid.

[115] *US v Bedoni* F 2d 782 (USCA 10th Cir 1990), *certiorari* denied 501 US 1253 (USSC 1991).

[116] *US v Allen* (n 113).   [117] *Wheeler v US* (n 112).

[118] Evidence (Videotaping of Child Complainants) Regulations 1990, SR 1990/164 (New Zealand); Connecticut General Statutes Ann §54–86H; Code Ann. §24-9.1, 24-9-5 (not limited to abuse offences; held constitutional in *Sims v State* 399 SE 2d 924 (Georgia Supreme Ct 1991)).

[119] GS Goodman, J Buckley, JA Quas and C Shapiro 'Innovations for Child Witnesses: a National Survey' (1999) 5 *Psychology, Public Policy and Law* 255 272.

indeed the admission of pre-trial recorded evidence is often based upon the finding by the trial judge that the child is not competent to testify at trial.[120]

7. Evaluation: should competence be incontestable?

The 2005 United Nations' Economic and Social Council's *Guidelines on Justice and Matters Involving Child Victims and Witnesses of Crime* advocate that:

age should not be a barrier to a child's right to participate fully in the justice process. Every child should be treated as a capable witness, subject to examination, and his or her testimony should not be presumed invalid or untrustworthy by reason of the child's age alone as long as his or her age and maturity allow the giving of intelligible and credible testimony, with or without communication aids and other assistance.[121]

We have seen that English law has stripped down the test of competence to this absolute minimum. This broadly conforms with the approach of other jurisdictions using the adversarial trial model. Provided the child is capable of answering questions, the trial judge can intercept the child's testimony only if the video interview raises such serious questions about the child's reliability that it is excluded from evidence 'in the interests of justice'.[122] Otherwise, any doubts which the court may entertain may be expressed only in directions to the jury.

By jettisoning any threshold requirements for the capacity of a witness, Scotland's approach is the most radical of any Commonwealth jurisdiction. However, in practical terms there is unlikely to be much difference between complete abolition of the rule subject to a residual discretion to bar witnesses who prove to be incoherent, as New Zealand proposes, and requiring a minimal standard of responsiveness to questions under the new English definition of competence. The approach of some American States of declaring that the competence of all child victims is incontestable evacuates the concept of competence of any meaning, and arguably goes too far in privileging complainants in one particular type of offence, child abuse, without a principled basis rooted in the reliability of that particular form of evidence. The new, minimalist, English definition of competence will mean that a witness who cannot attain that level of capacity could not possibly give any evidence of value to the court, even with the assistance of an intermediary or other Special Measures under the YJCEA 1999.[123] It is very unlikely that the police and the CPS would decide to tender such a witness. To that extent, the court's power to declare such witnesses incompetent should work as a prophylactic to forestall prosecutions which are bound to fail.

---

[120] Discussed above, Chapter 7 section B.2.

[121] United Nations Economic and Social Council *Guidelines on Justice in Matters Involving Child Victims and Witnesses of Crime* (Resolution 2005/20, E/2005/INF/2/Add. 1 July 2005) VI.18.

[122] YJCEA 1999 (England) ss 21(4)(b), 27(2).   [123] Discussed below, Sections B.2 and B.3(c).

B. Procedures for the Testimony of Child Witnesses[124]

> But justice, though due the accused, is due the accuser also. The concept of
> fairness must not be strained till it is narrowed to a filament. We are to keep the
> balance true.[125]

1. Tracing the influences on the current law

The integrity of the verdict in the adversarial trial model is dependent upon each
witness giving the best evidence of which he is capable, and having that evidence
thoroughly and fairly tested by the opposing party. Whilst this may be a trite observation to lawyers and judges engaged in the criminal justice system, until recently it
was not so obvious that the orthodox trial system itself must adapt to achieve that
objective for particular classes of witnesses, rather than forcing them to conform to
the system.

In the late 1980s, there was mounting criticism in England and in other common
law jurisdictions that the orthodox adversarial model for criminal trials was singularly
ineffective to try child abuse cases. Not only might its rigours damage the reliability
of the child's evidence, but it also could inflict further trauma on child participants.[126]
This was coupled with increasing awareness in many common law jurisdictions that
adult witnesses may also have difficulty contending with the rigours of the adversarial trial due to their intrinsic characteristics or their personal circumstances (such
as sexual assault, domestic abuse or intimidation). This led to major modifications
to criminal procedures for child witnesses in England and Wales and in all of our
comparator jurisdictions.[127]

The paradigm case for consideration of these reforms involves a child complainant
of sexual abuse with little, if indeed any, other direct evidence. However, it is also
important to remember that children are not just victims but also may be eyewitnesses respecting a wide range of offences, including those against other children or
other members of the family. Moreover, one must be cautious not to aggregate all child

---

[124] Some of the material in this section was previously published as LC Hoyano 'Variations on a Theme
by Pigot: Special Measures Directions for Child Witnesses' [2000] Crim LR 251, and LC Hoyano 'Striking
a Balance between the Rights of Defendants and Vulnerable Witnesses: Will Special Measures Directions
Contravene Guarantees of a Fair Trial?' [2001] Crim LR 927.

[125] *Snyder v Massachusetts* 291 US 97 (USSC 1934) 122 (Cardozo J).

[126] eg NSPCC *Child Abuse Trends in the England and Wales 1983–1987* (1989); Glanville Williams
'Child Witnesses' in P Smith (ed) *Essays in Honour of J. C. Smith* (Butterworths London 1987) 191–192;
Z Adler 'Prosecuting Child Sexual Abuse: a Challenge to the Status Quo' in M McGuire and J Pointing
(eds) *Victims of Crime: a New Deal?* (Open University Press, Milton Keynes 1988) Chapter 14.

[127] Scottish Executive Central Research Unit *Vulnerable and Intimidated Witnesses: Review of Provisions
in Other Jurisdictions* (2002); JE Myers 'A Decade of International Legal Reform regarding Child Abuse
Investigation and Litigation: Steps toward a Child Witness Code' (1996) 28 Pacific LJ 169; *Badgley Report*;
ALRC *Seen and Heard*; Law Reform Commission of Western Australia *Report on Evidence of Children and
Other Vulnerable Witnesses (Project No 87)* (April 1991); Law Reform Commissioner of Tasmania *Child
Witnesses* (Report No 62 1990); NZLC *Evidence of Children*; NZLC *Evidence*.

witnesses into a single category of vulnerability, from the naive five-year-old to the sexually experienced adolescent. This does not mean that the adolescent is less vulnerable. Anecdotal evidence from witness support officers suggests that young children have more family support, are more often believed by adults at the time of disclosure, and have greater access to formal support than some older children. Adolescents are often at risk of experiencing homelessness, drug and alcohol use and lack of family support, and are often exposed to more vehement and lengthy cross-examination than younger children.[128]

Most jurisdictions appear to consider this reform project to be ongoing, with the Canadian[129] and Scottish[130] Parliaments and the Idaho State Legislature[131] being the most recent to replace their measures for child witnesses devised in the 1980s and early 1990s with more radical reform.

(a) The international human rights context

Part of the impetus for continued enhancement of the rights of children in judicial proceedings has been supplied over the past two decades by the United Nations and the Council of Europe.[132]

As we noted earlier,[133] the Universal Declaration of Human Rights 1948 proclaims that childhood is entitled to special care and assistance.[134] The International Covenant on Civil and Political Rights, 1966 imposes obligations on the part of the child's family, society and the state to give children such measures of protection as are required by their status as minors.[135] These obligations have been reinforced and elaborated by the United Nations Convention on the Rights of the Child 1989, which requires States Parties to protect children from all forms of physical or mental violence, injury, neglect or exploitation including sexual abuse.[136] Article 3(1) requires that in all actions concerning children undertaken by courts of law or administrative authorities, the best interests of the child be a primary consideration. Under Article 12(2) legal systems must respect children's rights to be heard in any judicial and administrative proceedings affecting them. Only the United States and Somalia have not ratified the Convention on the Rights of the Child.

---

[128] A Whittam, H Ehrat and Office of the DPP for South Australia 'Child Witnesses in the Criminal Justice System—the Issue of Vulnerability' (Child Sexual Abuse: Justice Response or Alternative Resolution Conference (Australian Institute of Criminology) (May 2003)) 4–5.

[129] Bill C–2 An Act to Amend the Criminal Code (Protection of Children and Other Vulnerable Persons) and the Canada Evidence Act, passed by the House of Commons on 9 June 2005.

[130] Vulnerable Witnesses (Scotland) Act 2004 (amending the Criminal Procedure (Scotland) Act 1995) c 46.

[131] Uniform Child Witness Testimony by Alternative Methods Act (2003) Idaho Code §9–1801 to §9–1808.

[132] eg E Davies and F Seymour 'Child Witnesses in the Criminal Courts: Furthering New Zealand's Commitment to the United Nations Convention on the Rights of the Child' (1997) 4 *Psychiatry, Psychology and Law* 13. [133] See Chapter 4 section F.4.

[134] Universal Declaration of Human Rights, 1948 Articles 2, 25.

[135] United Nations International Covenant on Civil and Political Rights, 1966 Article 24.

[136] United Nations Convention on the Rights of the Child, 1989 Articles 19, 34 and 39.

The implementation of the Convention by States Parties is monitored by the Committee on the Rights of the Child, a body of independent experts that reports to the UN General Assembly through the Economic and Social Council. In 2002 the Committee criticized the UK for inadequate procedures and mechanisms to receive, monitor and investigate and prosecute instances of abuse, ill-treatment and neglect, and to ensure that the abused child is not victimized in legal proceedings.[137] The Council, building on groundwork laid by the Canadian-based International Bureau for Children's Rights, in July 2005 promulgated *Guidelines on Justice in Matters Involving Child Victims and Witnesses of Crime*, with the specific objective of providing children with special protection and support appropriate to their age, level of maturity, and unique needs, to prevent further hardship and trauma that might result from their participation in the criminal justice process.[138] Claiming to represent good practice based on the consensus of contemporary knowledge and relevant international and regional norms, standards and principles, the *Guidelines* state as a cardinal principle that children have the right to be protected from hardship during the justice process. This means that they have the right to measures which:

- ensure their privacy is protected as a matter of primary importance, including restricting disclosure of information which could lead to their identification, and measures to prevent undue exposure to the public by excluding them from the court room;
- provide professional support during the detection, investigation and prosecution process, and specifically to
  — support the child throughout his or her involvement in the justice process;
  — provide certainty about the process, with clear expectations as to how the child shall participate in the hearing and trial;
  — ensure that trials are expedited unless a delay is in the child's best interest;
  — use child-sensitive[139] procedures such as specially designed interview rooms, modified court environments and court sitting hours appropriate to the maturity of the child;
  — limit the number of interviews and reduce unnecessary contact with the justice process, for example through the use of video recording;
  — ensure the child is protected from being cross-examined by the alleged perpetrator himself;
  — ensure that the child is interviewed and examined in court out of sight of the alleged perpetrator;
  — ensure that the child is questioned in a child-sensitive manner, allowing for supervision by judges and measures to facilitate testimony and reduce potential

---

[137] *Concluding Observations of the Committee on the Rights of the Child: United Kingdom of Great Britain & Northern Ireland* (CRC/C/15/Add. 188 4 October 2002) [38(e)].

[138] *Guidelines on Justice in Matters Involving Child Victims and Witnesses of Crime* (n 121).

[139] Defined as 'an approach that balances the child's right to protection and that takes into account the child's individual needs and views' [*Guidelines on Justice in Matters Involving Child Victims and Witnesses of Crime* (n 121) Guideline IV(d)].

intimidation, for example by using testimonial aids or appointing psychological experts.[140]

Another influential human rights instrument for victims' rights is the European Convention on Human Rights (ECHR), Article 6 of which guarantees the right to a fair trial in criminal and civil proceedings. The European Court of Human Rights (ECtHR) has interpreted Article 6 as encompassing the interests of victims, which are a legitimate consideration in devising fair trial procedures.[141]

The Council of Europe Committee of Ministers in 1985 agreed to a recommendation that the needs of the victim should be taken into account to a greater degree throughout all stages of the criminal justice process, to enhance the victim's confidence in criminal justice and to encourage his cooperation, especially in his capacity as a witness.[142] To this end the Council recommended that whenever possible and appropriate, child victims should be questioned in the presence of their parents or guardians or other persons qualified to assist them. In 1997 this was bolstered by a further recommendation dealing with vulnerable witnesses to crime within the family,[143] advocating that criminal justice agencies strive to counter their traumatic effect on witnesses. This requires that video-recorded testimony from vulnerable witnesses be taken at the earliest possible stage of the criminal proceedings, and should not be repeated. Such examinations should be conducted by or in the presence of a judicial authority, with the defence having sufficient opportunity to challenge the testimony, but without face-to-face confrontation. The trial judge should closely supervise the examination of the witness, especially in cases concerning allegations of sexual offences. In 2006 the Council of Europe established a Committee of Experts on the Protection of Children against Sexual Exploitation and Abuse which will consider the promulgation of another international law instrument to deal with child-friendly procedures in court.

These international human rights instruments provide persuasive reasons, and at times legal obligations, for initiatives in common with law jurisdictions to mitigate the rigours of the adversarial trial process for child and other vulnerable witnesses. They acknowledge that children are not just 'people in the making'. They are rightsholders in their own right. They are not passive participants in society, nor should they be perceived as such in the criminal justice system. They are not just forensic problems.[144]

---

[140] ibid Guidelines X and XI.

[141] *Doorson v Netherlands* (1996) 22 EHRR 330 (ECtHR); Hoyano 'Striking a Balance (n 124), 954–956.

[142] Council of Europe *Recommendation No R (85) 11 of the Committee of Ministers to Member States on the Position of the Victim in the Framework of Criminal Law and Procedure* (adopted 28 June 1985) Guideline 8.

[143] Council of Europe *Recommendation No R(97)13 of the Committee of Ministers to Member States concerning Intimidation of Witnesses and the Rights of the Defence* (adopted 10 September 1997) Guidelines IV 23–29.

[144] M Rayner 'Management of Child Witnesses—Practical Solutions for Judges' (Local Court's Annual Conference 2003) 6, 7.

(b) The background to reform in England and Wales

The Westminster Parliament responded to criticism of the orthodox trial rules in 1988 and 1991 by implementing piecemeal reform for England and Wales which modified the statutory and common law rules governing children's testimony in criminal proceedings. The CJA 1988 s 34A(1) prohibited an accused from cross-examining a child witness in person.[145] Section 32 permitted child witnesses to give *viva voce* testimony at trial through closed-circuit television links from outside the courtroom. The Government deflected proposed amendments to the Bill to permit the court to receive testimony by children video-recorded before the trial[146] by establishing an advisory group chaired by HH Judge Thomas Pigot QC to consider the practical implications of the proposals.[147]

(i) The *Pigot Report*

The Pigot Committee's recommendations were premised on its finding that most children were adversely affected by giving evidence in the normal manner at trials involving serious offences.[148] The Committee established two guiding principles: first, that the involvement of child witnesses in the proceedings should be concluded as rapidly as is consonant with the interests of justice; and second, that children should give evidence in surroundings and circumstances which do not intimidate or overawe them.[149] These principles dictated a radical solution: children should be taken out of the formal criminal trial process altogether by videotaping their entire testimony before trial.[150]

(ii) The 1988 and 1991 Reforms

This proposal, 'full-Pigot' in common parlance, met with vigorous opposition. The Government opted for a diluted version in the CJA 1991 (amending the CJA 1988 and described hereafter as 'the 1988/1991 regime'). The principal features of this regime, colloquially known as 'half-Pigot', were as follows.

- A videotaped interview with a child witness, conducted by police officers (often together with social workers) was admissible at trial, subject to the trial judge's statutory discretion to exclude it if the interests of justice required that the recording ought not to be admitted.[151]

---

[145] This is a common provision in Commonwealth statutes for child witnesses; it has proved much more controversial for adult complainants in sexual offence trials [implemented by YJCEA 1999 (England) ss 34–39]. For summaries of existing legislation and reform proposals in Commonwealth jurisdictions, see New South Wales Law Reform Commission *Questioning of Complainants by Unrepresented Accused in Sexual Offence Trials* (June 2003) 16–21; Queensland Law Reform Commission *The Receipt of Evidence by Queensland Courts: the Evidence of Children* (Report No 55 Part 2 Dec 2000) (hereafter Queensland LRC *Evidence of Children*) 32–56].

[146] Glanville Williams 'Videotaping Children's Evidence' [1987] NLJ 108, 351 369.

[147] The proposals had first been presented to the Criminal Law Revision Committee in 1969: Williams 'Child Witnesses' (n 126) 193.   [148] *Pigot Report* (n 4).

[149] *Pigot Report* [2.14].   [150] *Pigot Report* [2.25]–[2.34].

[151] CJA 1988 (England) s 32A(3).

- There was no preliminary hearing for the taking of the child's evidence, as the *Pigot Report* had contemplated would be the normal course;[152] instead, the child was required to attend the formal trial for cross-examination.[153]

- The videotaped interview was expected to replace completely the usual examination-in-chief at trial, with supplementary questions by counsel permitted only where the prosecution had satisfied the trial judge that a matter was not 'dealt with adequately' in the child's recorded testimony.[154] The *Pigot Report* had contemplated that the interview would only *substantially* replace direct examination.[155]

- The videotaped interview was admissible only if the child was available to be cross-examined at trial,[156] which almost always took place many months after the interview.

- The child witness was not entitled as of right to use a video-link or screen when testifying at trial; instead, the prosecution had to seek leave of the court.[157]

- There was no statutory provision for an interlocutor through whom questions from counsel and the court could be relayed to the child, as a majority of the Pigot Committee had recommended.[158]

The Pigot Committee's proposals have delineated the parameters for the continuing campaign for further reform, not only in the UK but also in other jurisdictions.[159] A series of public inquiries in England and Wales into the investigation and prosecution of child abuse strongly endorsed the 'full-Pigot' recommendations.[160] In 1998 a government interdepartmental working party, following wide consultation, developed comprehensive recommendations for children and vulnerable adults appearing in the courts which broadly followed the 'full-Pigot' plan,[161] and which formed the basis of Part II of the YJCEA 1999.

---

[152] *Pigot Report* [2.25]–[2.29]   [153] CJA 1988 (England), s 32A(3)(a), s 32A(5)(a).
[154] CJA 1988 (England) s 32A(5), amended by the Criminal Justice and Public Order Act 1994 (England) s 50, and further amended by the Criminal Procedure and Investigations Act 1996 (England) s 62(2).   [155] *Pigot Report* [2.27], [2.31].
[156] CJA 1988 (England) s 32A(3)(a).   [157] CJA 1988 (England) s 32(1).
[158] *Pigot Report* [2.32]–[2.34].
[159] eg The Hon Justice JRT Wood *Royal Commission into the New South Wales Police Service: The Paedophile Inquiry* (August 1997), Vol V 1102–1107; LRC of Western Australia *Report on Evidence of Children*; Robyn Layton QC *Our Best Investment—A State Plan to Protect and Advance the Interests of Children* (South Australian Government 2003) [15.15]; LRC of Tasmania *Child Witnesses*; ALRC, *Seen and Heard* chapter 14. The New Zealand Law Commission had proposed implementation of pre-trial cross-examination along lines of 'full-Pigot' [NZLC *Evidence of Children* [200]], but retreated in the face of almost unanimous opposition from the defence Bar, preferring to wait to see more of the experience of other jurisdictions [NZLC *Evidence* Vol 1 *Reform of the Law* [459]–[460]].
[160] Lord Williams of Mostyn (Chair) *Childhood Matters: the Report of the National Commission of Inquiry into the Prevention of Child Abuse* (HMSO, London 1996)) [5.14], Royal College of Psychiatrists *The Evidence of Children* (January 1996); Sir William Utting *People Like Us: The Report of the Review of the Safeguards For Children living Away From Home* (HMSO, 1997) chapter 20; Richard Barker (Chair) Newcastle upon Tyne City Council *Abuse in Early Years: Report of the Independent Inquiry into Shieldfield Nursery and Related Events* (1998) 277–281.
[161] Home Office *Speaking Up for Justice: Report of the Interdepartmental Working Group on the Treatment of Vulnerable or Intimidated Witnesses in the Criminal Justice System* (June 1998) (hereafter *Speaking Up for Justice*).

Given the furore with which the *Pigot Report* was greeted in 1991, the passage through Parliament in 1999 of the legislation implementing a version of the 'full-Pigot' programme was remarkably smooth,[162] even though the Law Society renewed its strong opposition to many of the measures.[163] Indeed, the provisions pertaining to child witnesses were significantly strengthened at the Committee stage in the House of Commons to meet concerns from backbenchers from both sides of the House that the Bill did not sufficiently protect their interests.[164]

It is useful to identify the difficulties created by the 'half-Pigot' regime, as they have largely shaped the strengths and the weaknesses alike of the Special Measures introduced by the new regime.

(iii) Problems with 'Half-Pigot'

An empirical research study commissioned by the Home Office from a team at Bristol University (which included the authors of this book) was published in August 1999. The study was the first in Britain to evaluate the admissibility and sufficiency of evidence in child abuse prosecutions by tracking a sample of child abuse cases drawn from three Crown Prosecution Service areas and two Constabularies through the criminal justice system.[165] This research concluded that the 'half-Pigot' measures had bedded down fairly well in the areas studied.[166] However, it also identified several structural and procedural problems: the statutory framework was too complex to be applied properly by hard-pressed police officers and CPS personnel; the judicial discretion upon which the system was built created uncertainty as to how the child would give evidence which was often resolved only at trial; the rule prescribing the videotaped interview as examination-in-chief was too inflexible; the postponement of cross-examination until trial was deleterious to the child's credibility; and the system was widely perceived as failing very young witnesses.

Complexity of the statutory framework A complex set of statutory rules governed whether a child's videotaped interview could be tendered in evidence by the prosecution,[167] and whether the child could use a live video-link at trial.[168] The child witness must not have been the accused.[169] The child must have been under 14 years when the video recording was made and under 15 years of age at the time of trial if the offence being tried involved physical assault or cruelty to persons under 16.[170] If, however, the offence was sexual in nature and came within the ambit of one of the numerous

---

[162] The Official Opposition supported the thrust of the measures: *Hansard* HC Standing Committee E, 17 June 1999, 1:30 p.m., John Greenway MP.

[163] The Law Society lobbied MPs in opposing pre-trial cross-examination in particular: *Hansard*, Standing Committee E, 22 June 1999, 11:30 a.m., John Greenway MP.

[164] *Hansard*, HC Standing Committee E, 22 June 1999, 10:30 a.m., The Parliamentary Under-Secretary of State for the Home Department.

[165] G Davis, L Hoyano, C Keenan, L Maitland and R Morgan *An Assessment of the Admissibility and Sufficiency of Evidence in Child Abuse Prosecutions* (HMSO, London August 1999) [hereafter '*Bristol Study*'].

[166] *Bristol Study* xi.   [167] CJA 1988 (England) s 32A(1)(a).

[168] CJA 1988 (England) s 32(2).   [169] CJA 1988 (England) s 32A(2)(a).

[170] Under the Children and Young Persons Act 1933 s 1.

offences set out in five separate pieces of legislation,[171] then a videotaped interview was admissible if the child was under 17 when the video recording was made and under 18 at the time of trial. The discrepancies in protection for children testifying about violent and sexual offences originated with the Pigot Committee, but without much explanation.[172] It appeared to be based upon an assumption that older children do not have difficulty testifying about violence against them, but may still be reticent in describing sexual matters to a court.

The CPS Inspectorate observed that the complexity of the statutory triggers created difficulties for the police and Crown Prosecutors alike in identifying cases where they were applicable.[173] The *Bristol Study* noted a similar misunderstanding of the gateways to the videotaping provisions, particularly on the part of police officers not connected to a Child Protection Unit. This meant that written statements were taken from some alleged victims of sexual assault aged 15 to 17 who were entitled to be video-interviewed.[174] The *Bristol Study* recommended that all child witnesses under a stipulated age should have access to special procedures for their testimony, regardless of the nature of the offence charged.[175]

An additional complicating factor was that the measures for video examination-in-chief and live link applied only to proceedings in the Crown and Youth Courts, so that child witnesses in Magistrates' Courts had to testify in the normal way.[176] CPS prosecutors were encouraged by internal guidance to send cases involving child witnesses to the Crown Court to take advantage of the protective measures. However the CPS Inspectorate criticized this practice as distorting charging procedures; the nature of the evidence, not the characteristics of the witness involved, should determine the appropriate charge and court under the national mode of trial guidelines, even though this might cause some hardship for child witnesses.[177] Thus CPS lawyers were sent conflicting messages.

Discretion created uncertainty The prosecution could not confidently predict whether the court would permit a child witness to use the special procedures. Leave of the court had to be sought for admission of the video interview into evidence and use of the video-link for cross-examination. The legislation was bereft of concrete guidance for the court as to when leave should be denied; a nebulous 'interests of justice' test governed whether the video recording was to be excluded from evidence,[178] and there was no statutory criterion for use of the video-link.[179] Thus in practice (if not technically) the 'half-Pigot' regime was discretionary. Even more difficult to predict was whether leave would be granted to prosecuting counsel to ask supplementary questions to

---

[171] The Sexual Offences Act 1956, the Indecency with Children Act 1960, the Sexual Offences Act 1967, the Criminal Law Act 1977 s 54, or the Protection of Children Act 1978.

[172] *Pigot Report* [2.36].

[173] Crown Prosecution Service Inspectorate *The Inspectorate's Report on Cases Involving Child Witnesses* (Thematic Report 1/98 January 1998) [5.1]–[5.15].   [174] *Bristol Study* 19–20.

[175] *Bristol Study* 84.   [176] CJA 1988 (England) s 32(1A), 32A(1).

[177] CPS Inspectorate *Report on Cases Involving Child Witnesses* (n 173) [7.40]–[7.44].

[178] CJA 1988 (England) s 32A(3)(c).   [179] CJA 1988 (England) s 32(1)(b).

fill in lacunae in the videotaped interview, such applications being relatively rare.[180] Judicial discretion at several junctures in the process thus created uncertainty for the prosecution and anxiety for child witnesses.

There was no formal mechanism for ascertaining the child's expectations and wishes relating to the special procedures, and even where those wishes were known they might not be honoured, for reasons which might not be explained to the child and his carers. It was not uncommon for a child to arrive in court without any ruling having been made regarding the videotaped interview or the video-link because pre-trial hearings were often ineffectual for this purpose.[181] Postponement of rulings as to the mode by which a child would give evidence made it extremely difficult for child witness supporters to prepare that child for the court process with relevant information and assurance.

A system already creaking under these strains had additional burdens imposed on them in March 2001 by *R v Redbridge Youth Court*.[182] Latham LJ held that orders for the admission of video interviews and use of live link were appropriate only if there was 'a real risk' that otherwise it would be impossible to obtain any evidence from the child, or the quality of his evidence would be affected in that he could not give a full and proper account. Latham LJ said that the defence was unlikely to overcome the statutory presumption that the video interview be admitted if there was material before the court establishing that the child would be upset, intimidated or traumatized so as to affect the quality of his evidence or cause him to refuse to testify.[183] In effect this imposed a hitherto unsuspected evidential burden on the prosecution, as until this point the CPS was not routinely provided with such information by the police or the Witness Service.

The videotaped interview as examination-in-chief As indicated earlier, the 1988/1991 regime set up a presumption that the videotaped interview would constitute the child's examination-in-chief at trial, which could be displaced only if it were in the interests of justice to hear *viva voce* evidence-in-chief. 'Half Pigot' erected a procedural and legal structure that required those involved in the investigation and prosecution of child abuse to assume new professional roles and responsibilities. For crimes against children, the conventional bifurcation of the functions of investigator and prosecutor is blurred.[184] The 'half-Pigot' system demanded that the videotaped interview by police and social workers perform three functions, as:

- the initial step in the criminal investigation to ascertain whether an offence had been committed by an identified perpetrator;

---

[180] *Bristol Study* 60–61.

[181] *Bristol Study* 48–49. This was also noted by the CPS Inspectorate *Report on in Cases Involving Child Witnesses* (n 173) [8.61]–[8.64] and the NSPCC in 1995 [*Victims and Witnesses: Who Cares?* (Home Office Special Conference Unit, March, 1995) 9].

[182] *R (on the application of the DPP) v Redbridge Youth Court* [2001] EWHC Admin 209, [2001] 4 All ER 411 (QBD).   [183] ibid [15]–[16].

[184] *Bristol Study* 5.

- an inquiry into whether the child was in need of protection through civil proceedings; and
- the examination-in-chief of the child at trial.[185]

The *Bristol Study* concluded that these three purposes were extremely difficult to reconcile, and placed unrealistic demands upon interviewers.[186] In the space of about an hour, and usually in their first encounter with the child, interviewers were expected by the *Memorandum of Good Practice* to elicit a disclosure which established whether a specific criminal offence had been committed, the precise circumstances of that offence, and the identity of the alleged perpetrator. The interview was expected to yield a coherent, cogent, and chronological narrative which complied with the rules of evidence for examination-in-chief, rules which were quite alien to the interviewers' professional culture and in which they typically received inadequate training.[187] This starkly contrasted with the usual role of counsel at trial, who before embarking on direct examination of a witness will have developed a theory of their case, and will know how the testimony that witness can give fits into the broader evidential pattern.[188]

In child abuse cases, the keystone of the prosecution's case was regarded as being immutably fixed at the stage of the initial interview of the complainant.[189] Because of the restrictions on further interviews with the child imposed by the *Memorandum of Good Practice*[190] and the inflexible approach of the 1991 legislation to use of the videotaped evidence as the child's direct evidence, the prosecution normally could not improve its case beyond the initial stage of the investigation. If the interview produced an incoherent or rambling disclosure (as was often the case), contained significant breaches of the rules of evidence, or otherwise infringed the *Memorandum*, the prosecution had to decide whether to jettison the interview and proceed with live examination-in-chief at trial, or to abandon the prosecution altogether. The latter course was adopted if the CPS or prosecuting counsel concluded that the child was unlikely to produce better testimony in the court setting than in the more reassuring environment of the police interview suite.[191]

If the prosecution decided to proceed with a recording which was difficult to follow on first hearing and the jury requested that it be replayed in the course of their deliberations, the trial judge had the discretion to do so, provided that (a) it was replayed in open court with judge, counsel and defendant present; (b) the judge warned the jury against giving disproportionate weight to the child's examination-in-chief which they were hearing for the second time and that they should bear in mind the other evidence in the case; and (c) to assist in maintaining a fair balance, the

---

[185] C Keenan, G Davis, L Hoyano and L Maitland 'Interviewing Allegedly Abused Children with a View to Criminal Prosecution' [1999] Crim LR 863, 869.

[186] *Bristol Study* Summary of Key Findings ix.

[187] *Bristol Study* 26–27, 81–82. L Westcott 'Children, Hearsay, and the Courts: a Perspective from the United Kingdom' (1999) 5 *Psychology, Public Policy and Law* 282, 293, 295 reported concerns that the evidential constraints in investigative interviews were given priority over the child's needs.

[188] L Chapman *Review of South Australian Rape and Sexual Assault Law: Discussion Paper* (Government of South Australia, Adelaide 2006) [6].   [189] *Bristol Study* 60–61.

[190] Home Office et al *Memorandum of Good Practice on Video Recorded Interviews with Child Witnesses for Criminal Proceedings* (HMSO, London 1992) [1.11].   [191] *Bristol Study* Chapter IV.

judge reminded the jury of the cross-examination and re-examination of the child, regardless of whether the jury had requested this.[192]

Postponement of cross-examination until trial Notwithstanding the policy of the Lord Chancellor's Department that child abuse prosecutions be 'fast-tracked',[193] child abuse prosecutions routinely took longer to reach disposition than the national average for all types of offences.[194] Thus children continued to be caught up in the criminal justice system for prolonged periods, placing their welfare at risk, particularly if therapy was delayed pending the trial.

The interval between examination-in-chief and *viva voce* cross-examination could affect the integrity of the child's evidence. The accumulating stress for children who could not draw a line under painful experiences while awaiting the trial could make them less effective witnesses, particularly in cross-examination.[195] Juries might discount the credibility of what the child did remember, because of the effluxion of time.

Very young witnesses The 'half-Pigot' regime was also accused of failing to deal adequately with the problems posed by very young witnesses who seldom appeared in the criminal courts, notwithstanding repeated appellate warnings since 1990 that the judiciary should not impose a minimum age for receiving a child's unsworn evidence.[196] Nevertheless, the view that a prosecution could not proceed on the evidence of a child under five continued to predominate.[197]

This perception was reinforced by the controversy over the aborted prosecution of sexual abuse charges against two workers at the Shieldfield Day Nursery in Newcastle in 1994. An important factor in the ruling of Holland J that the children 'could not be available for cross-examination' on their videotaped evidence was the fact that at the earliest under the 'half-Pigot' system they would be subjected to cross-examination a year after their examination-in-chief, which itself was two years after the events in issue. By this time, when the child in the test application would be aged five, it was unlikely that she would be able to distinguish between what she could

---

[192] *R v Rawlins; R v Broadbent* [1995] Crim LR 335 (CA). Compare *R v O* [1996] 3 NZLR 295 (New Zealand CA) 298–299 holding that normally the trial judge should not replay the video, but had discretion to refresh the jury's memory by reading from the transcript.

[193] *Guidelines for Crown Court Listing* (Lord Chancellor's Department 1994); *Victim's Charter* (Home Office 1996); J Plotnikoff and R Woolfson *Prosecuting Child Abuse: an Evaluation of the Government's Speedy Progress Policy* (Blackstone Press London 1995) 44.

[194] The average time for the cases in the *Bristol Study* to be processed from receipt of the complaint to the first day of trial was 14 months, which was much slower than other cases in the same courts; ironically, the record of the Crown Court with a formal fast tracking system was worse than the Crown Court which did not [*Bristol Study* 51–53]. Joyce Plotnikoff and Richard Woolfson have made similar findings: *Prosecuting Child Abuse* ibid 25–27; J Plotnikoff and R Woolfson *In Their Own Words: the Experiences of 50 Young Witnesses in Criminal Proceedings* (NSPCC and Victim Support, London 2004) (hereafter Plotnikoff and Woolfson *In Their Own Words*) 10–11.   [195] *Bristol Study* 53–54.

[196] Discussed above, section A; *R v Z* (n 20); *DPP v M* (n 22).

[197] See the concerns voiced by MPs in the YJCEA 1999 (England) debates that the CPS was reluctant to prosecute any case involving children under five [*Hansard*, 15 April 1999, cols 442, 446].

and could not remember.[198] The wide publicity given to the finding of an inquiry commissioned by Newcastle City Council that the criminal justice system was unable to afford justice to very young victims, and instead was weighted in favour of the abusers avoiding responsibility for their crimes,[199] added to the pressure on the new Labour Government to implement 'full-Pigot'.

Apart from the difficulty of proving testimonial competence, a major factor influencing the reluctance by police and CPS lawyers to prosecute such cases is the widespread perception that a court appearance under the 'half-Pigot' regime was an arduous and painful ordeal for child witnesses, and that the experience was likely to be particularly harmful to very young children. Whilst cases where children were dealt with insensitively and subjected to aggressive cross-examination were the exception rather than the rule, they tended to assume disproportionate importance in the folklore of child abuse investigators and prosecutors.[200] Even so, a valid concern remained that the adversarial trial process was likely to be stressful for child witnesses which could in turn affect the quality of their testimony, even where they were treated with consideration by the trial judge and counsel and were shielded from the court room by the video-link or a screen.[201]

One measure of the success of the new regime for child witnesses under the YJCEA 1999 will be the extent to which it has addressed this array of problems.

2. Special Measures Directions under the Youth Justice and Criminal Evidence Act 1999

Diagrams 9, 10 and 11 map the labyrinth of Special Measures contemplated by Part II, Chapter I of the YJCEA 1999. Diagram 9 depicts the gateways to the Special Measures Directions (SMDs), and the basic procedure. Diagram 10 sets out the array of SMDs applicable to young witnesses. Diagram 11 does the same for adult witnesses, to illustrate that while the array of available protective measures is the same, judicial consideration of their use for child witnesses operates from a different platform. Our analysis addresses only the provisions as they apply to children. We will first trace our way through the labyrinth of new rules, and then analyse their effectiveness in dealing with the structural and procedural problems that afflicted the 'half-Pigot' system. We will not attempt to provide a comprehensive description of procedures for child witnesses in other jurisdictions using the adversarial trial model, because the 1999 reforms in England are in many senses the most radical. However, we will consider the approaches in other jurisdictions to the problems we identify as still lingering under the new English regime.

---

[198] *R v Christopher Lillie and Dawn Reed* ref no T931874 (QB 13 July 1994).

[199] *Abuse in Early Years* (n 160) vii, 277–281. The acquitted defendants successfully sued the authors of the Report and the Council for libel in relation to the Inquiry's findings that they did abuse very young children in the Shieldfield Nursery: *Lillie and Reed v Newcastle City Council, Richard Barker and others* [2000] EWHC 1600 (QB), discussed above, Chapter 4 section F.6.

[200] *Bristol Study* 30–31, 46, 61.   [201] *Bristol Study* 68.

Diagram 9. Gateways to and Procedures for Special Measures Directions

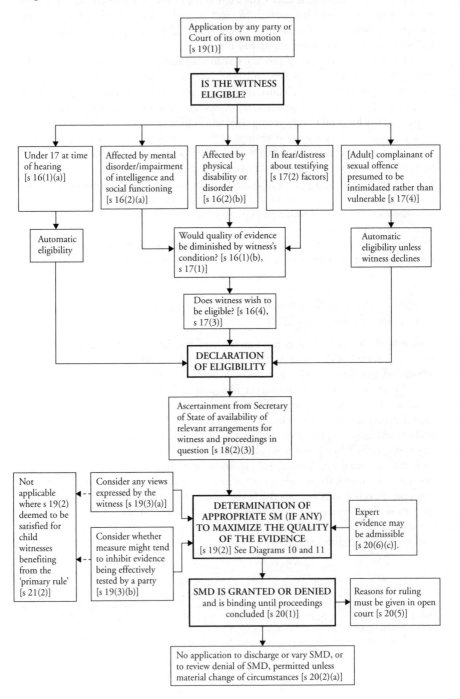

Diagram 10. Special Measures Directions for Young Witnesses

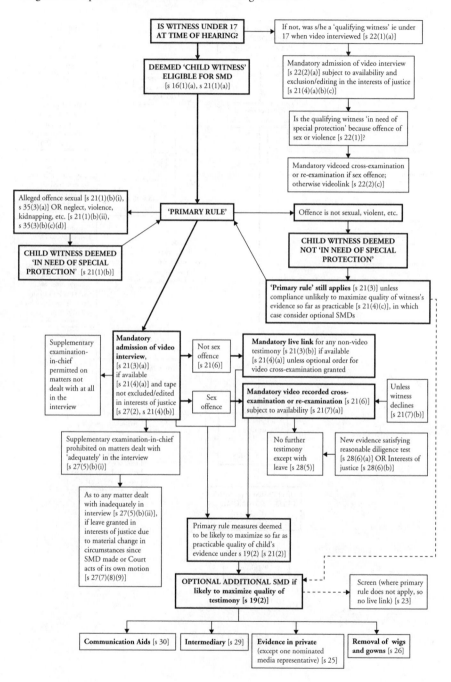

Diagram 11. Special Measures Directions for Adult Witnesses

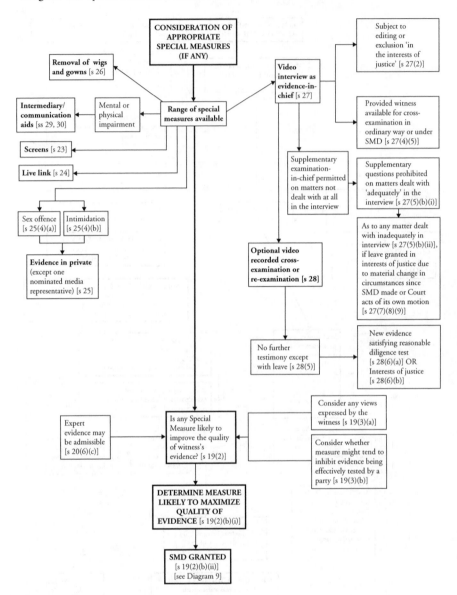

(a) Eligibility for Special Measures

(i) Gateways to the Special Measures

As Diagram 9 illustrates, the YJCEA 1999 s 16(1)(a) provides a single test of eligibility for Special Measures for child witnesses: that they must be under the age of 17 at the time of the hearing. Such children are irrebuttably deemed to be vulnerable, whereas for witnesses aged 17 and over the court must find that the quality of their evidence is likely to be diminished by reason of physical or mental disability or disorder, or fear or distress about testifying.[202] The single gateway for all witnesses under 17 is a welcome reform. It should be much more difficult for the defence to argue that adolescent witnesses are not entitled to any protective measures because of their (often negative) experiences of the world.

Nevertheless, problems endure in the identification of witnesses eligible for Special Measures, even for witnesses under 17. A recent empirical study found that whilst child victims of sexual offences were quite consistently appropriately identified by the police as being entitled to Special Measures, this was not the case for child witnesses to sexual offences against an adult, nor for children who were victims of or witnesses to violent offences.[203]

(ii) Child witnesses 'in need of special protection'

On the other side of the gate this simplicity is lost. The highly nuanced approach to the availability of particular Special Measures, dictated by the nature of the offence being tried and in some instances by the nature of the witness's vulnerability, yields an excessively complex framework. When the protections extended to child witnesses were strengthened as the Bill moved through Parliament, an already complex pattern became even more labyrinthine. The reader attempting to disentangle the numerous cross-references will empathize with the Opposition spokesman's complaint that the much-amended provisions for child witnesses resemble 'linguistic linguini' best digested in a darkened room with two aspirins.[204]

As Diagram 10 shows, a clear hierarchy of young witnesses does emerge. There are now three tiers of protection:

Class 1 Children deemed 'in need of special protection':
    Class 1A: sexual offences
    Class 1B: offences involving physical assault, neglect, kidnapping, false imprisonment or abduction under the Child Abduction Act 1984
Class 2 Children testifying in cases involving other offences.[205]

---

[202] YJCEA 1999 (England) ss 16, 17.

[203] M Burton, R Evans and A Sanders *Are Special Measures for Vulnerable and Intimidated Witnesses Working? Evidence from the Criminal Justice Agencies* (Home Office Online Report 01/06, London 2006) 32–33.

[204] John Greenway MP, HC Standing Committee E, *Hansard*, 22 June 1999, 10:45 a.m. debates.

[205] It has been argued that introducing the near-mandatory scheme for Class 1 may have the undesirable side effect of diminishing the importance of assistance for Class 2: D Cooper 'Pigot Unfulfilled:

No distinction is made between children who are alleged victims and those who are eyewitnesses to offences against others. The Special Measures still do not apply to child defendants.[206]

Children in all three classes theoretically have access to the full array of Special Measures offered by the legislation. However, the distinction between sexual offences and offences of physical violence is crucial in delineating the ambit of the court's discretion in prescribing which Special Measures should apply in a particular case.[207] In trials involving sex, or neglect, or violence where the child is deemed to be in need of special protection, there is a presumption that the video interview (edited if need be) will be admitted in evidence, unless it is excluded in the interests of justice. What happens next is determined by the nature of the offence. As Diagram 10 illustrates, the primary rule in s 21 *entitles* children alleged to be victims of or witnesses to sexual abuse to be cross-examined before trial on videotape unless they decline that measure, whereas for other offences the assumption is that the child witnesses will testify at trial through a live link unless the court considers that recorded cross-examination is more likely to maximize the quality of their testimony.

Moreover, the age/offence differential in the 1988/1991 statutory framework is perpetuated in relation to the prohibition on the defendant cross-examining a child in person.[208] A child under 17 is shielded from such cross-examination in a sexual abuse trial, but for offences of physical violence the ban applies only to children under 14.

The Government appeared to have concluded that it would be easier to defend mandatory measures under the Human Rights Act 1998 and the ECHR for sexual abuse cases than for other cases.[209] It is difficult to justify the distinctions drawn between child witnesses depending on categorization of the offences according to sexual contact, physical violence, and other offences. It is not self-evident that a child aged 15 will suffer trauma in testifying against or being cross-examined by her father in relation to sexual but not physical abuse, but all MPs debating the proposed primary rule accepted this assumption. The problems derived from the wide separation of examination-in-chief and cross-examination under the 'half-Pigot' system such as deterioration and contamination of memory, prolonged stress and postponed psychotherapy remain valid regardless of the nature of the offence, even if the degree of concern may vary according to the individual child. Nevertheless, this hierarchical conception of the seriousness of abuse permeates decision-making in the investigatory and prosecutorial phases as well as at the trial.[210]

Video-Recorded Cross-Examination under Section 28 of the Youth Justice And Criminal Evidence Act 1999' [2005] Crim LR 456, 461.

[206] YJCEA 1999 (England) s 19(1)(a), discussed further below section B.3(e).   [207] ibid s 21.

[208] ibid s 35(4).

[209] The Under-Secretary of State for the Home Department, HC Standing Committee E, *Hansard*, 22 June 1999 11:45 a.m. session.

[210] Although the formal guidance for police officers concerning whether a case should be prosecuted does not distinguish between types of abuse, child protection officers tend to view child sexual abuse as being more appropriate for prosecution than physical assault, on the basis that sexual offences almost always satisfy their informal criteria of actual harm to the child, dangerousness of the suspect, moral culpability

Some other jurisdictions are coming to discard such distinctions. On the recommendation of the Scottish Law Commission, the Vulnerable Witnesses (Scotland) Act 2004 does not draw any distinction between crimes of sexual and physical violence for any of its special measures for child witnesses.[211] In 2005 the Canadian Parliament stripped all distinctions based upon types of offence from the special procedures for child witnesses available under the Criminal Code of Canada.[212] The New Zealand Law Commission has also recommended erasing the current statutory distinction between physical and sexual cases[213] so as to give all child complainants parity of treatment in court.[214] In Australia the picture is more chequered, but the trend has also been to making special procedures available to all child witnesses regardless of the nature of the offence being tried.[215] Queensland and Western Australia have made their 'full-Pigot' regime mandatory for all offences of a sexual nature and offences of violence or neglect where there is a family relationship between the child and the defendant.[216]

(b) Optional Special Measures Directions

The pattern of protections becomes even more complex when the template of judicial powers is superimposed on these distinctions. The Pigot Committee had recommended that the court have no discretion in relation to the mode by which children would testify; the choice would lie with the prosecution and the children as to whether they would testify at the formal trial. The Government apparently concluded that it is necessary to preserve a substantial sphere of judicial discretion, at least in cases not involving sexual offences, in order to protect SMDs from challenge under Article 6 of the ECHR guarantee of a fair trial.

The web of cross-referenced sub-paragraphs in the YJCEA 1999 thus appears to be the product of two objectives: to herd the judiciary in a particular direction so as to counter sustained criticism of excessive ill-defined excuses to decline to use the special provisions in the 1988 Act; [217] and to preserve flexibility because it is impossible to predict every circumstance which might arise which could affect 'the interests of

---

and impact on the family, whereas physical abuse regarded as is often more explicable and so condonable. See the *Bristol Study* 17–19 (police views) and 31, 41–42 (CPS lawyers' views); C Keenan and L Maitland ' "There Ought to Be a Law Against It": Police Evaluation of the Efficacy of Prosecution in a Case of Child Abuse' [1999] Child and Family LQ 397.

[211] Vulnerable Witnesses (Scotland) Act 2004 s 271A; Scottish Law Commission, *Report on The Evidence of Children and Other Potentially Vulnerable Witnesses* (Scot Law Com No 125, 1990), [1.7], [4.55].

[212] Criminal Code of Canada ss 486 (closed court), 486.1 (support person), 486.2 (screens, testimony outside court room), 486.3 (bar on cross-examination by accused), 715.1 (video interview admissible).

[213] Evidence Act 1908 (NZ) s 23D.

[214] NZLC, *Evidence* Vol 1: *Reform of the Law,* ¶ 447 and vol 2: *Evidence Code and Commentary*, s 102 and ¶ C368.

[215] eg Queensland LRC, *Evidence of Children* 140–141, 153 recommending no distinction; Evidence (Children) Act 1997 (New South Wales) No 143 s 6.

[216] Evidence (Protection of Children) Amendment Act 2003 (Queensland); Evidence Act 1906 (Western Australia) s 106H, Schedule 7.

[217] Sir Robin Auld *Review of the Criminal Courts of England and Wales* [September 2001] [26].

justice'.[218] Both are laudable objectives, but it is inevitable that some points of friction between them will arise. The result, we shall see, is an unhappy compromise in some instances.

However, it is important to appreciate that judicial discretion in selecting Special Measures in a particular case will no longer be unconstrained. As Diagram 10 depicts, where the court is presented with a choice in physical abuse and other cases, child witnesses benefit from presumptions that the primary rule will apply such that:

- their videotaped interviews will be admissible unless editing or exclusion altogether is required 'in the interests of justice'; and
- they will give evidence by live link unless:
  — in physical abuse cases, the court opts for pre-trial video cross-examination;
  — in other cases where the child is not deemed 'in need of special protection', the court is satisfied that this will not 'maximise the quality of the child's evidence so far as is practicable'.

Adult witnesses deemed to be eligible for SMDs under ss 16 or 17 do not benefit from such presumptions.

If the primary rule does not apply to a child, or does apply but the witness may benefit from supplementary protections, the court must go on to consider optional additional SMDs:

- a screen if the child is to testify in the courtroom;
- removal of wigs and gowns by counsel and the judge;
- clearing the courtroom of spectators other than one nominated representative of the media;
- communication aids; and
- an intermediary.

In each instance the court must determine whether the measures would be likely to maximize so far as practicable the quality of the child's evidence, stating reasons for its opinion. Section 16(5) defines 'quality of a witness's evidence' to mean its 'completeness, coherence and accuracy', and further defines 'coherence' as referring to 'a witness's ability in giving evidence to give answers which address the questions put to the witness and can be understood both individually and collectively'. The court must consider 'all the circumstances of the case', including any views expressed by the witness, and whether the measure 'might tend to inhibit such evidence being effectively tested by a party to the proceedings'. Thus the criterion for invoking an optional Special Measure is sharply focused on enhancing the quality of the testimony. This reinforces rather than derogates from the precepts of the adversarial trial that the

---

[218] It is nonetheless unfortunate that the English legislation does not attempt to give any content to the nebulous phrase 'the interests of justice'. In the Australian Northern Territory legislation, a court is permitted to vary the statutory arrangements for vulnerable witnesses in the interests of justice, having regard to minimizing the harm and enhancing the effectiveness of the witness's evidence: Evidence Act (Northern Territory) s 21A(2B).

'best evidence' of which a witness is capable is in fact given and fairly tested before it is assessed by the trier of fact.

The new statutory framework is even more complex than the system it replaced, which hard-pressed police officers, social workers, CPS lawyers and victim support workers had found difficult to understand, administer and explain to prospective witnesses.[219] The provisions specifically relating to child witnesses are particularly impenetrable, and empirical studies which we discuss later[220] have shown that even with the best efforts of the drafters of the *Achieving Best Evidence* guidance, much confusion about the applicability of the legislation endures. The laudable objective of giving witnesses a measure of certainty and input, where the legislation requires that their views be sought and conveyed to the court, may be defeated by a failure to focus on the statutory provisions by the criminal justice agencies concerned, and inadequate training of their personnel dealing with vulnerable and intimidated witnesses.[221]

We turn now to consider a range of problems persisting under, and in some instances created by, the 1999 reform.

3. Problematic Special Measures

(a) The inflexible primary rule

(i) Mandatory admission of the video interview
A problem encountered early in the life of the legislation was the apparent requirement that under the primary rule the child had to give evidence in chief by video interview, and to use a live link for cross-examination, even if the child wished to give *viva voce* evidence in the courtroom.[222] Parliament's anxiety to strip the court of discretion to withhold such measures had the (perhaps unexpected) consequence of disempowering the child witness, which seems contrary to the ethos of the new regime. Research findings that the views of child witnesses were seldom sought or taken into account by the police and CPS[223] may be explicable by the primary rule. As the CPS Guidance for its prosecutors states, 'the mere fact that the child has expressed a preference to give evidence in open court with or without screens will not in itself be sufficient to avoid the deeming provisions of s 19. The legislation does not seek to give children a choice as to how they will give their evidence, it creates a new scheme by which their evidence will be heard'. The CPS guidance also stresses that there is no power for the court to refuse to apply the primary rule at a preliminary stage.[224]

---

[219] *Bristol Study* 84.   [220] See below, section B.4.
[221] Unfortunately this prediction seems to have come true, as of 2006: Burton, *et al* (n 203) *Evidence from the Criminal Justice Agencies*, discussed below, section B.4.   [222] For an example see ibid 54, 55.
[223] ibid 50; Plotnikoff and Woolfson *In Their Own Words* (n 194) 3, 16–18. In the latter study 32 of the 50 witnesses would have been subject to the primary rule.
[224] D Cooper and P Roberts *Special Measures for Vulnerable and Intimidated Witnesses: an Analysis of Crown Prosecution Service Monitoring Data* (Crown Prosecution Service, London June 2005) (hereafter Cooper and Roberts, *Analysis of CPS Monitoring Data*) 82 n 153, quoting Sheelagh Morton, *Part II The Youth Justice and Criminal Evidence Act 1999: Guidance—Children's Evidence* (unpublished guidance, CPS, 2003) [17], [12], [21]. Burton, Evans and Sanders are overly critical in stating that most participants in the criminal justice system, 'even judges', appear to believe that it is 'almost obligatory' to use video-recorded

In *R v Camberwell Green Youth Court ex p D*[225] Baroness Hale suggested that s 24(3) which permits variation of a live link order in the interests of justice may be invoked where the child is 'positively anxious to give evidence in the courtroom'. This is a helpful endorsement of an escape route already used by some prosecutors in sexual abuse trials where complainants wish to confront the defendant or to see the jury. A similar circumvention of the primary rule has been permitted by some judges to exclude the video interview 'in the interests of justice' under ss 27(2) and 21(4)(b) where the child wishes to tell her entire story in the courtroom.

In many instances it might not be advisable to take a video recording. Moreover, in some cases of prolonged abuse such as incest, several meetings might be required with the child by an officer from a child protection unit to elicit the complex evidence in a coherent and chronological narrative, which written statements rather than repeated video interviews might facilitate. Problems might also arise where it is suspected that the child has been a victim of abuse which has itself been video-recorded or photographed.[226] Another structural problem with s 21(6) is that in a case of sexual abuse the decision not to make a video recording, or to tender it in evidence, means that the child would lose the right to pre-trial cross-examination, when and if that Special Measure is implemented. This insistence on putting prosecutors in a straitjacket in presenting their cases carries over to the way in which that video interview is tendered in court.

(ii) Restrictions on supplementary examination-in-chief

As mentioned earlier, the *Pigot Report* had envisaged that the video interview would be shown to the child at the pre-trial hearing, and the child would be 'asked to confirm the account which it gives and to expand upon any aspects which the prosecution wishes to explore'.[227] Parliament in 1991 chose instead to impose an inflexible model on the prosecution, in effect requiring it to accept or reject the interview as constituting the evidence-in-chief of its primary witness.[228] This was tempered by an amendment in 1994 permitting supplementary questions in chief on any matter which in the opinion of the court had not been covered 'adequately' in the videotaped interview.[229]

In contrast, Canadian Crown prosecutors[230] have an unfettered choice as to how to use the videotaped interview as part of the child's examination-in-chief.[231] If the interview does not pose any evidential problems and fully discloses all the evidence that child has to offer, the prosecutor may elect to dispense with other direct examination

statements, 'no matter how disadvantageous to the witness' [Burton et al *Evidence from Criminal Justice Agencies* (n 203) 54]. That is what s 21(3)(a) requires for primary rule cases.

[225] *R v Camberwell Green Youth Court ex p D; R v Camberwell Green Youth Court ex p DPP (G, FC)* [2005] UKHL 4, [2005] 1 WLR 393 [35].

[226] *Achieving Best Evidence* [2.9] acknowledges this problem and encourages the taking of written statements if it is the best interests of the child.   [227] *Pigot Report* [2.31].

[228] Spencer and Flin reported in 1993 that trial judges were taking inconsistent positions on permitting supplementary questions in chief: Spencer and Flin *The Evidence of Children* (n 5) 182.

[229] Criminal Justice and Public Order Act 1994 (England) s 50.

[230] In Canada, it is the norm for barristers employed by the government department responsible for criminal justice both to decide whether a prosecution can proceed and to prosecute the case in all levels of court.   [231] *R v L(DO)* [1993] 4 SCR 419 (SCC) 449, 450.

altogether. More commonly it is used as an introduction to oral examination-in-chief, either partially to replace the child's narrative of the events, or simply as an historical record of how the disclosure was elicited (with the tangential benefit of demonstrating the child's consistency). This has several advantages.

- Interviewers have more freedom to act as investigators rather than attempting at the same time to perform the role of barristers. This gives them greater confidence that prosecuting counsel can fill in any gaps created by oversight or by interviewing errors which produce inadmissible evidence.

- Prosecutors can use the interview as evidence of how the disclosure emerged, and the child's emotional state, but can organize the evidence into a more coherent and chronological narrative for presentation through *viva voce* examination-in-chief, making it easier for the jury or magistrates to understand.

- The prosecutor can ease the child into the process of giving evidence prior to being challenged in cross-examination.

- Where examination-in-chief is given *viva voce*, objections to improper questions can and must be made immediately by opposing counsel. If an objection is upheld by the trial judge, examining counsel is often given the opportunity to rephrase the question. The English 1991/1994 system locking in the child's initial interview as examination-in-chief usually prevented such curative measures later at trial.

- The police, CPS, and counsel can make decisions about whether to proceed with a prosecution and can prepare for trial without having to predict whether the trial judge will grant leave to ask supplementary questions to bridge any evidential gaps in the case. This could result in more cases getting to court.

The New Zealand,[232] New South Wales,[233] Victoria,[234] Western Australia[235] and American[236] procedures similarly give prosecutors flexibility in the use of the recorded interview as examination-in-chief. In New Zealand the system has been so successful that the Court of Appeal has exercised its inherent jurisdiction to extend the admissibility of video interviews from sexual offences to physical abuse, relying upon the equivalent English legislation as identifying the incongruity of excluding victims of physical assault.[237]

Unfortunately, the YJCEA 1999 has arguably placed the prosecution in an even tighter straitjacket than heretofore by further restricting additional direct examination.

---

[232] Evidence Act 1908 (NZ) s 23D; *R v Lewis* [1991] 1 NZLR 409 (New Zealand CA) 411; *R v O* (n 192). The Department for Community Development & Western Australia Police Service Joint Response to Child Abuse *Video Recording of Children's Interviews* (August 2003) 10–12 reported that the New Zealand practice gives the prosecutor discretion as to how the videotaped interview was used as part of examination-in-chief, and recommended that Western Australia follow that model.

[233] Evidence (Children) Act 1997 (New South Wales) No 143 s 9(1).

[234] Evidence Act 1958 (Victoria) s 37B(2).

[235] Gail Archer, Principal Counsel, Legal Aid of Western Australia *Report on Fact-Finding Mission into the Videotaping of Children's Interviews* (March 2002) 22–24.

[236] National Center for Prosecution of Child Abuse *Investigation and Prosecution of Child Abuse* (3rd edn Sage Publications Inc, Thousand Oaks 2004) 442.

[237] *R v Moke and Lawrence* [1996] 1 NZLR 263 (New Zealand CA) 269, 271.

Supplementary questions can target only three classes of evidence: matters not dealt with at all in the video interview, matters dealt with adequately, and matters dealt with but inadequately. Section 27(5)(b) deals with these three classes in negative terms:

[T]he witness may not give evidence in chief otherwise than by means of the recording

(i) as to any matter which, in the opinion of the court, has been dealt with adequately in the witness's recorded testimony, or

(ii) without the permission of the court, as to any other matter which, in the opinion of the court, is dealt with in that testimony.

The prohibition in s 27(5)(b) would appear not to bite on the first class of questions, so by inference the prosecution can proceed with questions relating to wholly new matters without seeking leave of the court.[238]

However, in relation to a matter which has been dealt with in some degree in the interview, if the court considers that it has been dealt with inadequately, new strictures[239] have been placed upon the party tendering that evidence. Whereas under the 1994 amendment if the court concluded that the matter had not been dealt with adequately, that party (usually the prosecution) could then proceed as of right with supplementary questions, under the new regime the permission of the court must be sought. Section 27(7) requires that the court be satisfied that it is 'in the interests of justice' to grant permission, and further that if the court is not acting of its own motion but rather on application by a party to the proceedings, there must have been 'a material change of circumstances since the relevant time'. The 'relevant time' in turn is defined by s 27(8) as meaning—not (as one would expect) the date of the interview—but the time when the SMD was granted to admit the interview in evidence. This appears to mean that if something arises after the child's disclosure interview (which is not uncommon as police inquiries proceed) but before the prosecution applies to have the interview admitted under s 27, then the CPS will have to arrange for a further police interview with the child. The only alternative seems to be to ask the court to make a direction of its own motion to permit the supplementary questions under s 27(7)(b).[240]

This is a needlessly complicated process which could well delay the trial further. Why not simply allow the prosecution to run its case as it sees fit, as it is permitted to do with any other witness?[241] The concern that the child's testimony before the court be as brief as possible is laudable, but the preference of policy-makers that

---

[238] Under the 1994 amendment, the first class of 'matters not dealt with at all' appeared to have been treated as being subsumed under matters not dealt with 'adequately'; however, by necessary inference from the wording of YJCEA 1999 (England) s 27(5)(b) explicitly setting up the second and third classes, supplementary questions falling within the first class would appear to be unrestricted.

[239] This wording is a variation on an amendment introduced by the Criminal Procedure and Investigations Act 1996 s 62(2), which attracted criticism that it was likely to nullify the flexibility sought by the 1994 amendment [Roger Leng and Richard Taylor, *Blackstone's Guide to the Criminal Procedure & Investigations Act 1996* (Blackstone Press, London 1996), 115]. The revised 1999 wording raises the same objection, albeit on a somewhat different basis.

[240] A peculiar manoeuvre, but how else is the court to know that there is additional evidence available?

[241] Subject, of course, to compliance with the disclosure rules.

examination-in-chief be artificially truncated[242] such that the first question the child faces is from a hostile cross-examiner rather than from a sympathetic prosecutor, is perplexing. The Scottish Parliament departed from this inflexible model in the Vulnerable Witnesses (Scotland) Act 2004, making a previous statement of a vulnerable witness admissible as the whole or part of that witness's evidence-in-chief;[243] the witness is no longer required to adopt or otherwise speak to the statement in giving evidence in court.[244] It is submitted that the Westminster Parliament should follow the Scottish lead.

(iii) Mandatory use of the videolink

Another consequence of the rigid primary rule is to disregard the wishes of some child witnesses who prefer to testify from behind screens in court rather than through the live link, because then they may be shielded from the view of the defendant and spectators in the public gallery. When the videolink is used, the defendant can watch them testify on a monitor, but in the past they have not generally been visible to the public gallery. However, the Court Services' commendable desire to reduce the technological barriers to assessing a child's credibility by installing large plasma screens on the walls of the court room has only served to exacerbate the witness's perception that she is exposed to public gaze and, most critically, the defendant's scrutiny.[245] For this reason some commentators have urged that the defendant not be given access to a videolink monitor if this could inhibit the witness.[246] This would not require a statutory amendment, perhaps because of an inapposite cross-reference to the arrangements for screening a witness in the court room itself.[247]

However, it is submitted that the defendant has a right to see as well as hear the witnesses against him unless their identity must be concealed for their own physical safety.[248] If the demeanour of the witnesses is important to the trier of fact in weighing their evidence, then it is important to the defendant. The purpose of a screen, at least as originally conceived, was to prevent the witness from seeing the defendant, with the converse being merely a necessary consequence of its physical limitations;

---

[242] The justification of sparing the child a second narrative in chief has been aptly described as 'feeble but faintly plausible': Spencer and Flin (n 5) 182.

[243] Vulnerable Witnesses (Scotland) Act 2004 s 271M(2).

[244] Criminal Procedure (Scotland) Act 1995 s 260(2).

[245] Plotnikoff and Woolfson *In Their Own Words* (n 194) 7, 18–19.

[246] ibid 71; Cooper & Roberts *Analysis of CPS Monitoring Data* (n 224) 84.

[247] YJCEA 1999 (England) s 23(2). The common law authority for the use of a screen stipulated that the accused must be able to hear the witness: *R v Smellie* (1919) 14 Cr App R 128 (CA).

[248] On this basis the EComHR approved the use of screens for intimidated witnesses in Northern Ireland: *X v UK* (1992) 15 EHRR CD113 (App No 20657/92) (EComHR). The defendant is entitled to see a witness using CCTV or similar technology in Canada [An Act to Amend the Criminal Code (Protection of Children and Other Vulnerable Persons) and the Canada Evidence Act 53–54 Elizabeth II 2004–2005 s 486.2(7)]; New South Wales [Evidence (Children) Act 1997 (NSW), as amended 2001, 2003, 2004 s 23], in Western Australia [*Evidence of Children & Special Witnesses: Guidelines for the Use of Closed-Circuit Television, Videotapes, and Other Means for the Giving of Evidence, Approved by the Judges of the Supreme Court* April 1, 1996, revised May 1, 1998 (Supreme Court of Western Australia)] and in the United States, where the right of confrontation is usually interpreted as requiring that two-way CCTV be used [Federal Rules of Evidence 18 USCA §3509 (b)(D)].

however, even this can now be circumvented by allowing the defendant to use a TV monitor to watch the witness testifying from behind a screen.[249] The Court of Appeal has held that the default rule that the accused sees his accusers should only be denied in rare or exceptional circumstances.[250] Whilst this is a matter in the trial judge's discretion, depriving the defendant of his right to participate effectively in his defence merely because a witness does not want the defendant to see her could have important implications for the guarantee of a fair trial with equality of arms under ECHR Article 6.[251]

It is not only prosecution child witnesses for whom the inflexibility of the primary rule requiring that the live link be used has been problematic; it also has created serious difficulties in the Youth Courts where child defendants are denied access to special measures, which we discuss below.[252]

(b) Pre-trial cross-examination

The Home Secretary in Second Reading of the YJCE 1999 Bill had expressed the view that the power to order videotaped pre-trial cross-examination 'will be used sparingly and in special circumstances';[253] however, by the time the Bill emerged from Committee, pre-trial cross-examination was elevated to the norm for child sexual abuse cases, under the 'primary rule' in s 21(6).

The campaign for and against this central feature of 'full-Pigot' has been enveloped in rhetoric since 1989. It is useful therefore first to consider the potential advantages and drawbacks offered by pre-trial cross-examination, before considering how it has been implemented in other jurisdictions and whether it might work in England and Wales.

(i) The potential advantages of pre-trial videotaped testimony[254]

Improving the quality of the evidence

- While the memories of all witnesses about past events deteriorate with the passage of time, this particularly affects the quality of a child's evidence.[255] Where there is a

---

[249] As was done in *R v Taylor* [1995] Crim LR 253 (CA).

[250] ibid; *R v Watford Magistrates' Court ex p Lenman* [1993] Crim LR 388 (CA).

[251] *Van Mechelen v Netherlands* (1987) 25 EHRR 647 (ECtHR) [50]; *Hols v Netherlands* App No 25206/94 ruled inadmissible 19 October 1995 (EComHR) [7]; *Stanford v UK* [1994] ECHR 16757/90 (ECtHR) [26]. For further analysis see Hoyano 'Striking a Balance' (n 124) 963.

[252] See section B.3(f).   [253] *Hansard* HC 15 April 1999 Col 389.

[254] Some of these points are made in Aus LRC, *Seen and Heard* [14.41], [14.45]–[14.47]; Wood *The Paedophile Inquiry* (n 159) [15.64]–[15.83]; submissions to the Queensland LRC *Evidence of Children* 168–169; Victorian Law Reform Commission *Sexual Offences: Final Report* (1 April 2004) [5.58]; HH Judge Hal Jackson 'Child Witnesses in the Western Australian Criminal Courts' (2003) 27 Crim LJ 199; NCPCA *Investigation and Prosecution of Child Abuse* (n 236) 450–454, Figure VI.2; M Dixon ' "Out of the Mouths of Babes . . ."—A Review of the Operation of the Acts Amendment (Evidence of Children) Act 1992' (1995) 25 Western Australian L Rev 301, 314. Others were contributed by barristers interviewed for the *Bristol Study*.

[255] Delay was noted in interviews with children and parents as having very seriously weakened the quality of the testimony by K Murray *Live Television Link: an Evaluation of Its Use by Child Witnesses in Scottish Criminal Trials* (The Scottish Office Central Research Unit, Edinburgh 1995) [12.23].

considerable time gap between the videotape interview and the cross-examination, the cross-examiner may be able to exploit any lapses in memory that have occurred during that period. Deterioration of a child's memory may also damage the defence case by preventing an effective cross-examination, particularly where the witness is very young.[256] A pre-trial hearing captures all of the child's evidence whilst it is still comparatively fresh, and under less stressful conditions.

- Since the jury would see the child under cross-examination relatively shortly after the offence was reported, the jury's perceptions about the maturity of the child might be less distorted than if they see an older child whose appearance and cognitive development might have significantly altered in the time between charge and trial.

- If the judge and advocates are in the same informally arranged room as the child, as the Pigot Committee recommended,[257] the technological barriers to establishing a rapport with the witness and maintaining eye contact would be removed.

Facilitating pre-trial decisions and preparation by the prosecution and defence[258]

- From the prosecution's perspective, having all of the complainant's testimony video-taped before trial enables the decision to prosecute to be reassessed before trial. If the child retracts the complaint or makes damaging admissions on cross-examination, the prosecution has an early opportunity to withdraw (or downgrade) the charges, with consequent savings to the judicial system and to legal aid.[259] The prosecution is also better armed for any plea discussions with the defence, because the Crown's case no longer rests upon predictions of how its key witness will withstand cross-examination.

- From the defence's perspective, if the prosecution drops the charges, the defendant will be spared the stigma of a public trial for child abuse, and any time in custody will be reduced. If the child does well under cross-examination, then the defence lawyers will be able to advise their client at an earlier stage to be realistic about their prospects of conviction.

- The defence can better prepare for trial because it knows the content of the most crucial testimony in the case.[260]

- It will be less obvious to the jury that the child and the defendant were separated during the videotaping, and so less likely to give rise to prejudicial inferences such as might arise where the child uses live link for *viva voce* testimony.[261]

---

[256] Queensland LRC *Evidence of Children* 173. This factor rendered the video interview inadmissible in *R v Christopher Lillie and Dawn Reed* (n 198).   [257] *Pigot Report* 22–23.
[258] HH Judge Hal Jackson 'Child Witnesses in the Western Australian Criminal Courts' (n 254), 205.
[259] As in *Grindrod v R* [1999] WASCA 44 (Western Australia CA) (charges relating to one complainant dropped and two other charges relating to the remaining complainant withdrawn from the indictment).
[260] American prosecutors regard this as a significant disadvantage of videotaped testimony: NCPCA *Investigation and Prosecution of Child Abuse* (n 236) 450 Table VI-2.
[261] MH Graham 'Indicia of Reliability and Face to Face Confrontation: Emerging Issues in Child Sexual Abuse Prosecutions' (1985) 40 U of Miami L Rev 19, 93.

Facilitating the scheduling and conduct of the trial

- Court listing officers will be able to schedule child abuse cases without regard to the availability of the video-link room for the child witness. Courtrooms need only be equipped with a video player and television monitors.

- The urgency of scheduling child abuse cases might disappear if the children had already testified, relieving the pressures on the listing officers to find early fixed dates when all the participants and the technological equipment are available.[262]

- Any issues regarding the admissibility of portions of the child's evidence or conduct of the examination-in-chief or cross-examination can be resolved by judicial rulings at the end of the hearing; thus the flow of the child's evidence need not be interrupted by objections, and the jury will not have to wait whilst a *voir dire* is conducted during the trial, nor will there be any risk of evidence being heard by the jury which is subsequently ruled inadmissible.[263]

- Similarly any issues about the child's testimonial competence which may arise in the course of cross-examination might be dealt with without risking a mistrial.[264]

- Trials should be shorter, as it will not be necessary to adjourn frequently to wait for child witnesses to arrive in court, or to give them a break in the midst of testimony.

Minimizing 'system abuse' of child witnesses

- Additional stress for the child created by postponements of the trial or other delays can be avoided. The child is able to commence testifying at a specific date and time without having to wait for other cases to conclude or preliminary matters to be resolved.[265]

- The child at an early stage can put the events behind him or her and get on with life.[266]

---

[262] D Birch and R Powell *Meeting the Challenges of Pigot: Pre-trial Cross-Examination under s. 28 of the Youth Justice And Criminal Evidence Act 1999: a Briefing Paper for the Home Office* (Feb 2004) [134] argue that this point is at odds with the general interests of justice and the specific interests of the accused; however apart from the need to protect child witnesses there is no intrinsic reason to give child abuse cases priority in the queue over other very serious cases such as child homicide, especially if an accused is remanded in custody.

[263] Victorian Law Reform Commission *Sexual Offences: Final Report* (1 April 2004) [5.58].

[264] As was done in *R v Stevenson* (n 77) [2], [36], [49].

[265] Such delays still occur in English courts. Plotnikoff and Wolfson reported in 2004 that 28 of the 50 witnesses in their sample did not give evidence on the first trial date, and for 11 witnesses the case was rescheduled on 2 or 3 occasions [Plotnikoff and Woolfson *In Their Own Words* (n 194) 4, 33–34]. The Hamlyn study reported that in the study period between April and June 2003, 45% of VIWs in their sample had their trial dates rescheduled, and 33% were called to court on days when they did not give evidence at all [B Hamlyn, A Phelps, J Turtle and G Sattar *Are Special Measures Working? Evidence from Surveys of Vulnerable and Intimidated Witnesses* (Home Office Research, Development and Statistics Directorate, London June 2004) (hereafter Hamlyn et al *Surveys of VIWs*) 37, 44]. Delay in testifying is a chronic problem in most jurisdictions: Victorian Law Reform Commission *Sexual Offences: Final Report* (1 April 2004) [5.58]; Davies and Seymour (n 132) 16.

[266] Chronic problems of delay in getting to trial are discussed further below, section B.3(b)(v).

- Therapy, which the prosecution might prefer be postponed until after the child has been cross-examined,[267] might begin at an earlier stage.[268] It can engage directly with the incidents of abuse (which is proscribed by current CPS guidance)[269] without fear of contamination of testimony and so be more effective.[270] It will also obviate concerns about the defence seeking production of therapy records.[271]

- It will be easier to prevent the child and its carers coming into contact in the courthouse with the accused, or family or supporters of the accused.[272]

- If the case has to be tried again, whether because the first jury was unable to reach a verdict, or a re-trial was ordered on appeal for reasons unrelated to the child's testimony, the child's evidence can be presented at the second trial in the form of the same videotape, avoiding the emotional strain of going through the process again or being cross-examined on inconsistencies.[273]

(ii) The potential drawbacks of pre-trial videotaped testimony

- The solemnity of a jury trial helps bring home to child witnesses that what they say has crucial implications for the future of the defendant. This might be lost if the entire testimony of the child is taken in comfortable and reassuring surroundings.[274] Many prosecuting counsel believe that the video technology lacks the immediacy and persuasive impact of a child's live in-court testimony, making it more difficult to assess credibility. Pre-trial hearings can exacerbate this problem, as the jury might find it difficult to connect with proceedings unfolding entirely on television.[275]

---

[267] Although it is CPS policy that the best interests of the child regarding therapy should be determinative [Home Office, Crown Prosecution Service and Department of Health *Provision of Therapy for Child Witnesses Prior to a Criminal Trial: Practical Guidance* (2001)], there is some evidence that carers are still dissuaded from pursuing therapy because of police and CPS concerns that this could jeopardize the prosecution [Plotnikoff and Woolfson *In Their Own Words* 64–65, 69, 90 reporting that four children, including a six-year-old, were strongly discouraged from receiving pre-trial therapy.] The *Practical Guidance* [4.5] indirectly reinforces this view in advising that if there is a demonstrable need for the provision of therapy which possibly could prejudice the criminal proceedings, the CPS should consider abandoning the case in the interests of the child's well-being. Australian law reform bodies have received evidence to a similar effect: Queensland LRC *Evidence of Children* 92–93; ALRC *Seen and Heard* [14.53]–[14.54].

[268] Victorian LRC *Sexual Offences: Final Report* (1 April 2004) [5.58]; Queensland LRC *Evidence of Children* chapter 6.

[269] *Provision of Therapy for Child Witnesses* (n 267) [5.1]–[5.6], [6.11]–[6.13]. Plotnikoff and Woolfson *In Their Own Words* (n 194) 65 reported that two young witnesses did not find helpful pre-trial therapy which could not deal with the abuse, and others found that the length of the pre-trial delay meant post-trial counselling came too late to help them. The police are also concerned that restrictions in the *Guidance* do not allow for meaningful therapy (90).

[270] A Maxwell 'Pre-Trial Therapy for Child Complainant of Sexual Abuse in the Criminal Justice System: Forensic Implications' (Child Sexual Abuse: Justice Response or Alternative Resolution Conference 2003) 6; Queensland LRC *Evidence of Children* 94–95.　　　　　　　　　　[271] Discussed above, section C.

[272] Plotnikoff and Woolfson *In Their Own Words* (n 194) 20–21 reported that 9 of 50 young witnesses encountered the defendant in the courthouse, and 5 more spent time in public areas or saw supporters of the defendant.

[273] Evidence Act 1906 (Western Australia) s 106T(5)(b); Victorian LRC *Sexual Offences: Final Report* (1 April 2004) [5.58].

[274] This was expressed by the Queensland DPP to the Queensland LRC *Evidence of Children* 169, whilst recognizing there were countervailing advantages.

[275] NCPCA *Investigation and Prosecution of Child Abuse* (n 236) 450 Figure VI.2.

Even though at present they usually see only the child's image on the video link monitor, they do know that a crucial part of the child's testimony is being given 'live' in front of them.

- It might be unfair to require the defence to cross-examine the main prosecution witness before the formal trial has commenced so that the issues in the case are definitively identified.[276]

- The defence might have to show its hand to the prosecution prematurely, allowing the prosecution to trim its case at trial accordingly.[277]

- Defence lawyers are concerned that they cannot be ready to cross-examine the most important prosecution witness until shortly before the trial is scheduled, so the objective of shortening the time the child is in the criminal justice system will be defeated. This view rests upon two contentions:
  — The defence cannot begin to prepare its case until it has full disclosure of the prosecution case, which is often delayed and subject to dispute;[278] attempts to obtain third party disclosure, for example social services, school, and medical records, also delay preparation.
  — The defence case in child abuse prosecutions takes more time to mature than in other cases. It may take longer for defence witnesses to come forward, and for the defendant to confront the details of the case against him so as properly to instruct his lawyers.

- The defence might need to cross-examine the child again at trial, thereby exacerbating rather than minimizing the trauma to the child.

In weighing the relative merits of these points, the concern that the defence cannot be ready to cross-examine until shortly before the trial has considerable weight, in so far as possible procedural impediments are concerned. It is however difficult to give much credence to the argument that the defence cannot be ready to cross-examine until the trial has actually commenced, given that child complainants are usually the first prosecution witnesses of substance to be called. Arguably a videotaped interview is more revealing as to credibility than the usual written witness statements, enabling more effective preparation by the defence.

In considering the potential advantage which the prosecution might gain from early knowledge of the defence strategy gleaned through the cross-examination, it must be remembered that the accused's right to non-disclosure has already been greatly undercut in English law since the Criminal Procedures and Investigation Act 1996.

---

[276] As two barrister MPs contended during Second Reading of the YJCE Bill: *Hansard* Debates, 15 April 1999, Mr Hogg cols 418, 436–437; Mr Llwyd cols 417–419.

[277] Queensland LRC *Evidence of Children* 174–175; the Commission rejected this argument.

[278] Lord Justice Auld pointed out that there would need to be 'exceptionally vigorous pre-trial control of the case by the judge' to expedite disclosure to achieve the objective of scheduling the cross-examination shortly after the video interview: Sir Robin Auld *Review* (n 217) [125], [128].

There is some slender empirical support for the widespread belief in the legal professions in all our comparative jurisdictions[279] that the video technology distances the jury from the complainant, making it more difficult to assess credibility. For this reason the American National Center for Prosecution of Child Abuse recommends that videotaped pre-trial testimony be used 'only as a last resort'.[280] A Scottish study shortly after live television link was introduced reported that the evidence of children over live television link was significantly less detailed and complete than that given in the courtroom, with the young witnesses being somewhat less audible, less fluent, less effective and less credible.[281] It was suggested that a two-dimensional projection might appear false compared with the three-dimensional figure in the court: 'the child and the evidence transmitted from another place are cut off from the main theme of the story, imperfect and fragmented, so easy to render invisible'.[282] For this reason many British defence counsel prefer cross-examining through live link as the monitor can be switched off if the child becomes distressed.[283] Conversely, one American court claimed that a witness's testimony shown on a television monitor may be enhanced by 'status-conferral' as it bestows prestige and legitimizes the witness's status.[284] In England as in most jurisdictions using some form of video or live link testimony, trial judges routinely instruct the jury that this is a normal procedure to enable the witness to be more at ease when giving evidence, and must not in any way be considered by the jury as prejudicial to the accused.[285]

---

[279] G Davies, C Wilson, R Mitchell and J Milsom *Videotaping Children's Evidence: an Evaluation* (Home Office, London 1995) 8, 13; G Davies and H Westcott *Interviewing Child Witnesses under the Memorandum of Good Practice: a Research Review* (Police Research Series Paper 115, Police Policing and Reducing Crime Unit, Home Office Research, Development and Statistics Directorate, London 1999) 5; C Eastwood and W Patton *The Experiences of Child Complainants of Sexual Abuse in the Criminal Justice System* (Criminology Research Council, Canberra 2002) 94–96; BL Schwalb 'Child Abuse Trials and the Confrontation of Traumatized Witnesses: Defining "Confrontation" to Protect Both Children and Defendants' (1991) 26 Harvard Civil Rights-Civil Liberties L Rev 185 200–202; Goodman, Buckley, Quas and Shapiro (n 119), 261–263.   [280] NCPCA *Investigation and Prosecution of Child Abuse* (n 236) 451.

[281] Murray (n 255) [12.21]–[12.28]. Other empirical studies about the perceived impact of CCTV on juries yield mixed results. One Western Australian empirical study with actual jurors showed that most of them felt that the CCTV did not hinder their assessment of the child's credibility, and those that thought the opposite participated in trials where there were technical problems: C O'Grady *Child Witnesses and Jury Trials: an Evaluation of the Use of Closed Circuit Television and Removable Screens in Western Australia* (Ministry of Justice, Government of Western Australia, Perth Jan 1996). American research with mock jurors has come to the opposite conclusion: DF Ross, R Lindsay and DF Marsil 'The Impact of Hearsay Testimony on Conviction Rates in Trials of Child Sexual Abuse: Toward Balancing the Rights of Defendants and Child Witnesses' (1999) 5 *Psychology, Public Policy, and Law* 439, 442–443. See also from J Cashmore and ND Haas *The Use of Closed-Circuit Television for Child Witnesses in the ACT: A Report for the Australian Law Reform Commission and the Australian Capital Territorial Magistrates Court* (Sydney 1992); Burton et al *Evidence from the Criminal Justice Agencies* (n 203) 56–57.   [282] Murray ibid [12.27].

[283] As do defence lawyers in the US [J Montoya 'Lessons from *Akiki* and *Michaels* on Shielding Child Witnesses' (1995) 1 *Psychology, Public Policy, and Law* 340, 348] and in Queensland and New South Wales [Eastwood and Patton (n 279) 120–121].

[284] *Hochheiser v Superior Court* 161 Cal App 3d 777 (California CA 1984) 786.

[285] Judicial Studies Board Specimen Direction 22a: *Direction When Evidence is Given after Special Measures Direction*. Similar directions are made mandatory by New Zealand [Evidence Act 1908 s 23H] and by some Australian statutes [Evidence Act (Northern Territory) s 21A(3); Evidence Act 1958 (Victoria) s 37(4); New South Wales Evidence (Children) Act 19 ss 14, 25; Evidence (Protection of Children)

It is probably impossible to resolve the issue of the impact of the technology on English juries, since the Contempt of Court Act 1981 s 8 prohibits research using actual jurors. What is beyond dispute is that live link is the only means to enable many vulnerable witnesses to testify, and helps many to provide more complete and accurate evidence.[286] Some British judges believe that the new larger plasma screens installed in many courtrooms help jurors to observe and connect with the witnesses. In any event it is arguable that videotaped cross-examination would not exacerbate this problem, as most juries now see the child only through a television monitor for both the video interview and cross-examination. The only action they see unfolding directly before their eyes is counsel and the trial judge speaking to the child on video monitors.

Overall, the potential merits of pre-trial cross-examination for both the prosecution and the defence seemed decisively to outweigh the possible disadvantages, justifying the boldness of the reform. It remains to be seen whether pre-trial cross-examination can be made to work.

(iii) Could 'full-Pigot' work? Lessons from other jurisdictions
In 1988, the recommendation of the Pigot Committee that the entire evidence of a child witness be recorded at a pre-trial hearing was considered to be both radical and unprecedented. In the ensuing decade, however, a significant number of jurisdictions adhering to the adversarial trial model concluded that this was the way forward, and enacted legislation to implement it.

Western Australia Western Australia has become the model that other Australian jurisdictions are seeking to emulate.[287] In November 1997 the Australian Law Reform Commission and the Human Rights and Equal Opportunity Commission made joint recommendations respecting children's evidence under Federal and State law which would establish a uniform approach across the country, using the Western Australian version of 'full-Pigot'.[288]

The Western Australian statutory framework which came into operation in November 1992, and was revised slightly in 2000 and 2002, presents a comprehensive reform of the criminal trial process to accommodate the needs of child witnesses.[289] The legislation permits videotaped interviews to be used in lieu of examination-in-chief or to supplement questioning by prosecution counsel. However, as of 2002 in practice investigative interviews with child witnesses were not video-recorded; instead the police followed the same procedure as with adult complainants, taking written

Amendment Act 2003 (Queensland) s 21AW, Evidence (Miscellaneous Provisions) Act 1991 (Australian Capital Territory) ss 10, 46].

[286] J Cashmore 'Innovative Procedures for Child Witnesses' in H Westcott, G Davies and R Bull (eds) *Children's Testimony: a Handbook of Psychological Research and Forensic Practice* (John Wiley & Sons, Chichester 2002) 208; Eastwood and Patton (n 279) 96–97.

[287] Layton *Our Best Investment* (n 159) 15.15, 15.25–15.27 described Western Australia's 'Pigot system' as a 'best practice' model.   [288] Aus LRC, *Seen and Heard* [14.45]–[14.47], Recommendation 94.

[289] Acts Amendment (Evidence of Children and Others) Act 1992, No 36 of 1992 (Western Australia), amending the Evidence Act 1906, further amended by Acts Amendment (Evidence) Act 2000 (Western Australia) and Acts Amendment (Evidence) Act 2002 (Western Australia) No 27 of 2002. The system was put in place following recommendations from the Western Australia Child Sexual Abuse Task Force Report (Dec 1987) and LRC of Western Australia *Report on Evidence of Children* (n 127).

statements which are disclosed to the defence before the child's testimony.[290] Using videotaped interviews for testimonial purposes was not seen as a priority because having the whole of the child's evidence at a pre-trial hearing was seen, at least by the judiciary, as so successful,[291] and has the additional advantage of requiring the child to face testifying on only one occasion.[292]

The predominant practice is that prosecuting counsel leads the child's evidence in-chief at a videotaped pre-trial hearing, with the cross-examination and any re-direct examination usually immediately following. If a videotaped interview is admitted, it will be played at the pre-trial hearing, with any supplemental questions by the Crown prosecutor thereafter, followed by cross-examination and redirect examination.[293] Camera shots are taken to enable the jury to see the child's size and demeanour.[294] If necessary, more than one pre-trial hearing is held to receive the child's evidence. The trial judge has discretion over the manner in which pre-trial testimony is taken and may order editing of the videotape. The statute recognizes that some children may still be required to appear at trial for further questioning, but this has rarely been required.[295] The provisions are designed to create maximum flexibility, and are intended to be applied in the best interests of the child witness. This regime applies to children who are under the age of 18[296] on the date of the complaint, and in care proceedings under the Child Welfare Act 1947, or in criminal proceedings involving sexual offences and those causing physical harm.

In 1995 the Ministry of Justice conducted an empirical study of the use of the new procedures, including the use of CCTV at trial and pre-recorded evidence, in the first three years of operation. The report studied 75 jury trials, including interviews with the jurors, judges, counsel and the child witnesses. There was strong support across these sectors for the routine use of these procedures.[297] Access to jurors and child witnesses enabled the researchers to make detailed practical recommendations respecting the procedures, equipment and some aspects of the legislation, so as to make the child witnesses feel more comfortable, and to assist jurors in understanding and evaluating their testimony.[298]

---

[290] The primary reason seems to be that the inter-agency ethos for investigations has not yet caught on in Western Australia, so the police adhere to their normal investigative practices. Proposals for joint video interviewing have been under consideration [Archer *Report on Fact-Finding Mission* (n 235); *Video Recording of Children's Interviews* (n 232). They have been opposed by the Child Witness Service on the ground that the judiciary might then be less receptive to applications for full pre-trial recording of the child's evidence [information provided by Shannon Bellett, Co-ordinator, Child Witness Service, Court Service, Ministry of Justice, Perth, WA].

[291] Personal communication from Chief Justice David Malcolm, Supreme Court of Western Australia, 3 October 2003.   [292] Eastwood and Patton (n 279) 122.

[293] Archer *Report on Fact-Finding Mission* (n 235) 22. In 2003 the District Court judge overseeing the legislation said he had never known the video interview to be admitted as examination-in-chief: Jackson (n 254), 205–206.   [294] Jackson ibid, 206.

[295] Information provided to the Victorian Law Reform Commission *Sexual Offences: Final Report* (1 April 2004) [5.67].

[296] A 2002 amendment raised the maximum age from 16 and removed restrictions whereby the defendant had to be related to the child, live in the same household or at any time had regularly cared for the child [No. 27 of 2002 s 32].   [297] O'Grady (n 281).

[298] ibid iv, v.

Defence concerns when the system was first implemented led to most videotaping being done shortly before trial, which obviously can defeat the purpose of capturing the child's account before it deteriorates with time.[299] However, it is now the practice that prosecutors apply at the plea stage for an order for pre-trial videotaping. If the application is successful, the hearing is arranged for a date usually within eight weeks of the order. The child's involvement is completed five to six months earlier than if it were given at trial, and on average within seven months of the start of criminal proceedings.[300] The judicial *Guidelines* particularly endorse pre-trial hearings for cases involving very young children under ten on the basis that the child might have difficulty in giving evidence in another way,[301] and examples of this happening for children as young as five appear in the caselaw.[302] Other factors taken into consideration are whether it is likely that there will be a delay of more than six months before trial, and any special circumstances regarding the case of a child witness such as personal factors (for instance intellectual or physical handicap), family circumstances and any cultural factors which might make it more than usually difficult for the witness to talk in front of people.[303]

Whilst many prosecutors initially vigorously resisted the system, believing that the jury had to see the child face-to-face to assess credibility and that the impact of the child's testimony would be less compelling if viewed on a video screen, they now concede that experience and research has demonstrated that that view is 'entirely wrong'.[304] Prosecuting counsel who insist on putting children in the witness box have been chastised by the court.[305] The Chief Justice of Western Australia has said that the success of the system has been due to the level of skill developed by prosecutors participating in the video-recording of the evidence-in-chief, and by defence counsel in cross-examination.[306] It is important to note that defence counsel also support the pre-recording system as it assists them in preparing their case.[307]

In practice, court officials and counsel have found it easiest to use the CCTV facilities in the Supreme Court, although it was originally envisaged that the recording would be made in an informal 'round-table' format with all participants except the accused in the same room, as the Pigot Committee had recommended. The accepted procedure now is that the pre-trial recording is done with the same arrangements as if the evidence were being transmitted live to the courtroom.[308] The child is brought into a special witness room for filming (which is adjacent to a waiting room catering to

---

[299] ibid ii–iv.
[300] Information from the Ministry of Justice, Government of Western Australia.
[301] *Evidence of Children & Special Witnesses* (n 248) 16 (ii).
[302] eg *R v Stevenson* (n 77) (child aged five); *Grindrod v R* (n 259) (child aged six).
[303] *Evidence of Children & Special Witnesses* (n 248) 16 (iii) and (v).
[304] Archer *Report on Fact-Finding Mission* (n 235) 3.
[305] *Bourne v Elliss* [2001] WASCA 290 (Western Australia SCA) [7], [63].
[306] Personal communication from Chief Justice Malcolm 3 October 2003.
[307] D Carrick 'Child Witnesses' *The Law Report, Radio National* (20 May 2003), interviewing both prosecution and defence senior counsel and judges from Western Australia.
[308] O'Grady (n 281) 34–36.

children of all ages, with appropriate toys and models to assist them in understanding the court process and to alleviate stress).[309] Unlike in some other Australian States, Western Australian children have not been required to testify at committals since 1992.[310]

The success of the Western Australian variation of the 'full-Pigot' model appears to be largely attributable to the supporting structures set up to implement the new regime. A Child Witness Service was created in 1995 to promote the statutory measures, to coordinate their application in cases involving child witnesses, and to provide them with emotional and practical non-evidential court preparation and support.[311] Preparatory officers, senior social workers and psychologists prepare the children to testify, but strict guidelines require them not to discuss any of the child's evidence.[312] The Service assists defence as well as prosecution child witnesses.[313] The Service's dedicated comprehensive support has been instrumental in leaving child witnesses with a more positive view of their experiences in the criminal justice system.[314] From the outset the judiciary and the executive have collaborated to make the system work.[315] A Supreme Court judge chairs both an inter-agency reference group to support the Child Witness Service and a Committee of Justices which has developed detailed guidelines for the judiciary and counsel on the use of the special measure in trials.[316] These guidelines prescribe in detail the agenda for the hearing of applications for special measures, physical arrangements for pre-trial hearings, camera shots, procedures for dealing with objections to questions, explanation of the proceedings to the child by the trial judge, and editing and transcription of the videotapes. The *Guidelines* stress that the videotape of the hearing must be made with the jury in mind. They are kept under review and revised to reflect the courts' growing experience. It is clear that the judiciary strongly supports the 'full-Pigot' model.[317]

The Child Witness Service's figures show that in 2002 some 400 children (60% of all child witnesses) had their evidence pre-recorded; about 65% of them were complainants, mostly of sexual offences, and the other 35% were witnesses to crime and were called by either the prosecution or the defence.[318] Orders for pre-recorded testimony are given in almost all sexual offence cases involving child complainants.[319] An empirical study by Eastwood and Patton published in 2002 comparing experiences of child complainants in sexual assault trials in Western Australia, Queensland, and New South Wales, asked if they would ever report sexual abuse again following their

---

[309] Robyn Layton QC *Our Best Investment* (n 159) 15.25–15.26.
[310] Eastwood and Patton (n 279) 128.
[311] Jackson (n 254); *Evidence of Children & Special Witnesses* (n 301); S Bellett 'Child Witness Service: Meeting the Needs of Children—Innovative Practice' (Kids First Conference 1998).
[312] Robyn Layton QC *Our Best Investment* (n 159) 15.25–15.26.
[313] ibid 15.26.
[314] Eastwood and Patton (n 279) 129–130.
[315] Personal communication from Chief Justice Malcolm 3 October 2003.
[316] *Evidence of Children & Special Witnesses* (n 301).   [317] Jackson (n 254).
[318] Information provided to Robyn Layton QC *Our Best Investment* (n 159) 15.26.
[319] HH Judge A Kennedy, *Vulnerable Witnesses in Western Australia* (Paper Presented at the Annual Conference of the Judges of the District Court of Queensland, April 2000) 7, cited by Queensland LRC *Evidence of Children* 163 n 775.

experience in the criminal justice system; 64% of the Western Australian children in the study sample said they would, whereas in Queensland and New South Wales the positive responses were only 44% and 33% respectively.[320] The researchers concluded that the higher positive response in Western Australia was indicative of the more child-friendly routine provisions in that State, which they strongly endorsed as having changed the culture and attitudes of the criminal justice system towards child witnesses: '[t]he wide-ranging reforms in that State work well—and work for everybody'.[321]

Queensland Queensland had been the first Australian State to venture into 'full Pigot', in 1989.[322] The statute allowed the evidence of a 'special witness', including a child under the age of 12, to be videotaped under conditions specified by court order. The court was prohibited from making the order if it would 'unfairly prejudice . . . the person charged or the prosecution'. The DPP of Queensland used the provisions only rarely, due to two difficulties. First there was no provision for an early pre-trial hearing at which the conditions for the making of a videotape could be prescribed, causing delays of six months or more. Secondly, rules of court did not prescribe the conditions for the videotaped testimony, creating uncertainty and occasionally unsatisfactory arrangements; in some instances the child had been examined and cross-examined while alone in a room with the prosecutor or defence counsel.[323] Moreover, prosecutors were very reluctant to use CCTV, and many also refused to use screens, rendering the legislation 'virtually ineffective' and perpetuating a highly abusive system, according to an excoriating empirical report in 2002 by Eastwood and Patton.[324]

This led to the system being entirely revamped in the Evidence (Protection of Children) Amendment Act 2003. Although the Queensland Law Reform Commission had recommended the greatest possible degree of flexibility be built into the legislation,[325] the 2003 Act makes pre-trial recording of the evidence of children under 16 mandatory in criminal proceedings involving offences of a sexual nature, or offences of violence where there was a prescribed family or household or carer relationship between the child and the defendant.[326] Importantly, it does not apply to defence witnesses.[327]

In an apparent effort to thwart the recalcitrance of those within the criminal justice system which had caused the previous legislation to be stillborn, the 2003 legislation sets out its purposes as being (a) to preserve, to the greatest extent practicable, the integrity of an affected child's evidence; and (b) to require that a child's evidence be

---

[320] Eastwood and Patton (n 279) 43–45.   [321] ibid 130; see also 111, 112, 122, 127.

[322] The Criminal Code, Evidence Act and Other Acts Amendment Act 1989, No 17, amending Evidence Act 1977 (Queensland) s 21A.

[323] Information provided to the Western Australia Law Reform Commission by the Queensland Office of Director of Prosecutions [*Report on Evidence of Children and Other Vulnerable Witnesses* (Project No. 87, April, 1991) [4.38], Queensland LRC *Evidence of Children* 159–160].

[324] Eastwood and Patton (n 279) 111, 119–121.

[325] Queensland LRC *Evidence of Children* 173.

[326] Evidence (Protection of Children) Amendment Act 2003 (Queensland) ss 21AC, 21AF, 21AK.

[327] ibid s 21AI(2).

taken in an environment that limits, to the greatest extent practicable, the distress and trauma that might otherwise be experienced by the child when giving evidence. These purposes must be considered by the court if a party applies for exemption from the mandatory pre-recording provisions. The court must have 'good reason' to make the order, having regard to the child's wishes; the statute provides an example of such a reason, where the facilities are not available within a reasonable time and otherwise the case could be dealt with quickly.[328]

The 2003 Act stipulates the procedures for pre-recording testimony in considerable detail. The evidence is admissible in any rehearing or retrial of the criminal case, in another proceeding in relation to a charge arising from the same set of circumstances, and in any civil proceeding arising from the commission of the relevant offence.[329] The court may recall the child to give further testimony at trial, but only if this is required by the interest of justice and the judge is satisfied that it is not possible or practical to convene another preliminary hearing to take the further evidence.[330]

New South Wales In 2002 a Parliamentary standing committee recommended that New South Wales make pre-recording of children's entire evidence a statutory presumption, using the Western Australian model.[331] In 2003 the Government of New South Wales responded to the Eastwood and Patton report just discussed by establishing a pilot project for a specialist child sexual assault court, putting the pre-recording recommendation on hold. An empirical study by Cashmore and Trimboli in 2005 which compared cases in the specialist court with sampled child abuse prosecutions tried in the usual criminal courts concluded that there were no real benefits produced by the specialist courts, and that in terms of delays, technological problems and the treatment of children in court, there was little to distinguish the specialist courts from the general criminal courts.[332] Given the failure of the pilot project, the researchers recommended that New South Wales proceed with implementation of the Western Australian practice of pre-recording a child's entire testimony, as recommended by the Standing Committee in 2002.[333]

Northern Territory As of December 2005, the entire testimony of a child under 18 may be recorded before trial at a special hearing, at the election of the prosecution. The procedure applies to sexual offences and physical violence or neglect.[334] The Northern Territory has also introduced a statutory fast-tracking system for sexual offences requiring that trials must be commenced within three months of committal in the case of an indictable offence.[335]

---

[328] ibid s 21AO. [329] ibid s 21AM. [330] ibid s 21AN.

[331] Standing Committee on Law and Justice, Legislative Council, New South Wales Parliament *Report on Child Sexual Assault Prosecutions* (Report No 22 2002) [6.94]–[6.117], Recommendations 34–38.

[332] Apart from a remote witness suite located outside the courthouse: J Cashmore and L Trimboli *An Evaluation of the NSW Child Sexual Assault Specialist Jurisdiction Pilot* (New South Wales Bureau of Crime Statistics and Research, Sydney 2005) 64. [333] ibid 63–64.

[334] Evidence Act (Northern Territory) s 21B.

[335] Sexual Offences (Evidence and Procedure Act) (NT) s 3A. The preliminary investigation for indictable offences must begin within three months of the matter first being mentioned in court; trials for summary sexual offences must be commenced within three months of the matter first being mentioned in

Victoria In 2004 the Victorian Law Reform Commission published a comprehensive review of the law and procedures applicable to sexual offences. The LRC strongly advocated a statutory presumption in favour of video-recording children's evidence-in-chief and cross-examination before trial, which could be displaced only by the court being satisfied that the complainant knew of her rights and are wished to testify at trial by CCTV or in the courtroom.[336] In response to the Bar's concerns about ensuring that the defence could be ready to cross-examine and that the defendant's case could be fairly put to the child in a pre-trial hearing, the Victoria LRC considered that they could be resolved. It did not consider that fast-tracking a case was a better option, given the advantages of pre-recording.[337]

South Australia The South Australian government recently launched a major review of its rape and sexual assault law. The Cabinet has already committed itself to a package of ten special arrangements for vulnerable witnesses, the most unusual being the admission of out-of-court complaints by very young children or mentally disabled witnesses whilst dispensing that witness from being available to testify.[338] Proposals to adopt a system for pre-recording of a child's entire evidence on the Western Australian model were published for consultation in early 2006.[339] A specialist court operating a dual system of fast-tracking the entire trial for cases consisting mainly of a child's evidence (which would be recorded at trial in the event of a retrial or for use as similar fact evidence in other cases), or alternatively of pre-recording a child's evidence, has also been suggested.[340]

Scotland In 1990 the Scottish Law Commission recommended comprehensive reform of the procedures and rules of evidence governing the testimony of children and other vulnerable witnesses.[341] These proposals largely replicated those in the *Pigot Report*. In addition to the introduction of CCTV, screens, and the admission of children's previously videotaped statements,[342] the Commission recommended that as an alternative to in-court testimony the entire evidence of a child witness be videotaped in pre-trial proceedings.[343] In a curious inversion of the fate of the *Pigot Report*, the Westminster Parliament chose for Scotland to implement discretionary pre-trial videotaping of the child's entire testimony, but not to render admissible any earlier videotaped interviews with the child. The Prisoners and Criminal Proceedings (Scotland) Act 1993, ss 33 and 56 gave the court discretion to order that the entire evidence of a child witness under the age of 16 be video-recorded before a commissioner before the

court. The Evidence Act (Northern Territory) s 21D(2)(b) also provides that any proceedings in which a child as a witness should be resolved as quickly as possible. Queensland has the same provision: Evidence (Protection of Children) Amendment Act 2003 (Queensland).

[336] Victorian LRC *Sexual Offences: Final Report* (1 April 2004) recommendations 123–129.
[337] ibid [5.54]–[5.56], [5.66]–[5.69].   [338] Chapman (n 188) Appendix 1.
[339] ibid chapter 1.   [340] ibid [20]–[23], [38], Consultation Question 1.4.
[341] Scottish Law Commission, *Report on the Evidence of Children and Other Potentially Vulnerable Witnesses* (n 211).
[342] Recommendations 18–19, [4.45]–[4.66]. A written video- or audio-recorded statement would be admissible at trial provided that the witness indicated that he made the statement and its contents were true; leading questions or other forms of question which would be objectionable in court would not bar admissibility.   [343] Recommendation 10, [4.10]–[4.16].

trial. The Law Commission suggested that the pre-trial deposition should normally be taken as *near* to the date of trial as possible, to ensure that the defence is fully prepared.[344]

Although only a few consultees rejected the Law Commission's proposal, and Parliament extended the provisions for pre-trial testimony to vulnerable adult witnesses in 1997, no child witness gave evidence under these provisions in Scotland.[345] The failure of the legislation may be attributable to the fact that the Scottish legal system is deeply adversarial in nature, with two consequences: procurators fiscal, responsible for prosecuting criminal cases, are very reluctant to depart from the traditional mode of presenting a witness; and trial judges are vested with such broad discretion that they readily find a basis to decline to use procedures alien to them.[346]

The newly recreated Scottish Parliament re-enacted the provision for pre-trial evidence on commission in the Vulnerable Witnesses (Scotland) Act 2004 s 271I. The Scottish Executive considered that evidence on commission was so similar to the English Special Measure of video-recording cross-examination that separate provision would have no added benefits.[347] The Scottish *Guidance on the Questioning of Children in Court* urges practitioners to consider taking evidence on commission to enable a child to give evidence as soon as is reasonably practicable after the events.[348] The Scottish system of precognition can mean that young children may be interviewed before trial about the same events up to 30 times, by police, social workers and other civil child protection officers, doctors, the procurator fiscal or precognition officer, solicitors, and (the most startling feature to English lawyers) by agents for each accused in criminal cases, and by each party in family court proceedings.[349] The attendant risks of deterioration and contamination of the evidence and trauma to the child are well documented.[350] Given that one precept of the *Guidance* is that a child should be called as a witness to give evidence only when it is unavoidable in the interests of justice,[351] it may be that taking evidence on commission will become an accepted practical solution which will enable the child to exit from this prolonged ordeal at a much earlier date. However, as of June 2006 the Scottish Victims and Witnesses Unit had not heard of any case where evidence on commission has taken place, although

---

[344] Lord Advocate's Chambers *Report of the Lord Advocate's Working Party on Child Witness Support* (March 1999) 4.10–4.16.   [345] Plotnikoff and Woolfson *In Their Own Words* 26.

[346] We are indebted to Joyce Plotnikoff for this suggestion. This may also account for the low take-up rate in the use of CCTV at trial. In the first 27 months of operation of the live television link, applications were made to use it in respect of only 10% of all children cited to appear as prosecution witnesses in High Court proceedings [Murray (n 255) chapter 12]. By 1999 the usage rate for video-link had not substantially increased, and the use of special measures at trial remained unpredictable, making pre-trial preparation of child witnesses very difficult [*Report of the Lord Advocate's Working Party* ibid 11, 15, 26–27, 40–41, 51–52].

[347] Scottish Executive *Policy Memorandum to the Vulnerable Witnesses (Scotland) Bill* (SP 5) (2004) [40]–[42].   [348] Scottish Executive *Guidance on the Questioning of Children in Court* (2003) [12].

[349] Murray (n 255) [6.17].

[350] J Plotnikoff and R Woolfson *An Evaluation of Child Witness Support* (Scottish Executive Central Research Unit, Edinburgh 2001) 69–73; Murray ibid [6.17]–[6.19].

[351] *Guidance on the Questioning of Children in Court* (n 347) [4].

there might not have been sufficient time for cases to work through the system since implementation in November 2005.

The United States Under the American federal system, criminal prosecutions involving children as victims or eyewitnesses fall within State jurisdiction,[352] so there is a considerable variation across the 50 States in the procedural and substantive rules. Congress has also legislated special provisions for child witnesses in the Federal Rules of Evidence,[353] which, while little used in practice given the infrequency of federal prosecutions, nonetheless have provided a model for State legislatures. As of March 2002, Congress and 38 States had authorized the use of children's videotaped testimony at trial in lieu of live testimony.[354] Further, 27 States and Congress have entrenched 'fast-tracking' systems for criminal cases involving child witnesses or victims in legislation.[355]

Federal Rule of Evidence §3509[356] governing pre-trial cross-examination of child witnesses requires that the prosecutor or an attorney representing the child adduce evidence that the child is likely to be unable to testify in court in the physical presence of the defendant, jury, judge, and public. This inability may be caused by fear, or by conduct by the defendant or defence counsel which causes the child to be unable to continue testifying, or by a mental or other infirmity. Alternatively, expert testimony must establish that there is a substantial likelihood that the child would suffer emotional trauma from testifying in open court. If any of these grounds is established, the court must order that the child's depositions be taken and preserved by videotape. The trial judge must preside and rule on all questions as if at trial. The defendant is entitled to be present unless the court's finding of unavailability is based on evidence that the child is unable to testify in the defendant's physical presence. In that case two-way CCTV is to be used to enable the defendant and the child to see one another during the testimony, and the defendant must be provided with a means of private contemporaneous communication with his lawyer during the deposition. In the event that new evidence is discovered after the original videotaping and before or during trial, the court, if satisfied that good grounds have been established, may order an additional videotaped deposition, in which case the questioning must be restricted to the matters specified by the court as the basis for granting the order. The videotaped deposition will be used at trial only if the trial judge finds that the child continues to be unable to testify for one of the listed reasons.

The apparently stringent requirements for specific evidence of apprehended actual harm for a particular child witness and for an attenuated form of confrontation between the child and the accused have been dictated by constitutional constraints,

---

[352] Although there is limited federal jurisdiction in respect of some offences, such as those committed across State boundaries.   [353] US Code, 18 USCA §3509.

[354] NCPCA *Investigation and Prosecution of Child Abuse* (n 236) 452 Figure VI.2. For the configuration of the statutes see NW Perry and BD McAuliff 'The Use of Video Tape Child Testimony: Public Policy Implications' (1993) 7 Notre Dame J of Law, Ethics & Public Policy 387, 392–395.

[355] NCPCA ibid 256, Table IV.2.

[356] Federal Rules of Evidence 18 USCA §3509, effective 11 October 1996.

and in particular the right of confrontation under the Sixth Amendment to the American Constitution. The American trial system places particular emphasis upon the demeanour[357] of a complainant confronting an accused as an important indicator of credibility as 'it may confound and undo the false accuser, or reveal the child coached by a malevolent adult'.[358] It is assumed by jurors that a truthful child witness will display distress, but a child who has received witness preparation or has been interviewed several times or has matured whilst awaiting trial may well appear less anxious and emotional, and hence, paradoxically, less credible.[359]

The right of confrontation, if interpreted strictly, could bar all hearsay evidence and require a face-to-face encounter between a testifying witness and the accused. However, the US Supreme Court has generally given a fairly flexible interpretation to the right of confrontation to permit the orthodox adversarial trial to be adjusted for child witnesses. In the leading case of *Maryland v Craig*,[360] the Supreme Court approved State legislation governing the use of CCTV. A State's interest in the physical and psychological well-being of child abuse victims may be sufficiently important to outweigh, at least in some cases, a defendant's right to face his accusers in court. The finding of necessity must be case-specific.[361] The trial court must hear evidence and:

- determine whether the procedure is necessary to protect the particular child witness's welfare;

- find that the child would be traumatized, not by the courtroom generally, but by the defendant's presence (an evidential challenge in itself); and

- find that the emotional distress suffered by the child in the defendant's presence is more than *de minimis*. Without determining the minimum emotional trauma required for the use of a special procedure, the Maryland statute which required a determination that the child would suffer serious emotional distress such that he or she could not reasonably communicate sufficed to meet constitutional standards.

The necessity for a 'harm hearing' is a strong disincentive to prosecutors using innovative measures to protect the child whilst testifying.[362]

Another constitutional hurdle for the use of videotaped testimony of a child witness at trial which is related to the Confrontation Clause is that such evidence is hearsay.

---

[357] See Montoya (n 283), 347–348, 351–353 for a description of one such case where jurors told researchers that the children's lack of fear and distress indicated the defendant had not harmed them.

[358] *Coy v Iowa* 487 US 1012 (USSC 1988) 1020. The 8th Circuit US Court of Appeals recently held that confrontation between a child complainant and the defendant through a two-way CCTV system breached the Confrontation Clause because it did not have the 'same truth-inducing effect as an unmediated gaze across the court room' especially given the ubiquity of television [*US v Bordeaux* 400 F 3d 548 (US CA 8th Cir 2005) 554–556], but other courts continue to apply *Maryland v Craig* 497 US 836 (USSC 1990).

[359] PC Regan and SJ Baker 'The Impact of Child Witness Demeanour on Perceived Credibility and Trial Outcome in Sexual Abuse Cases' (1998) 13 *J of Family Violence* 187,188–189, 192–193.

[360] *Maryland v Craig* (n 358).

[361] Failure to require individualized findings of the needs of a particular child witness caused a statute authorizing the use of a screen to be ruled unconstitutional in *Coy v Iowa* (n 358).

[362] Goodman, Buckley, Quas and Shapiro (n 119), 273.

The US Supreme Court has found hearsay evidence admissible where the person making the hearsay statement is available to be cross-examined at trial.[363] The purpose of videotaping a child's testimony, however, is to obviate the necessity of the child appearing at the trial. In 1970 in *Ohio v Roberts*[364] the Supreme Court had established two general requirements for hearsay to be admissible: the prosecution had to show that the person making the hearsay statement was 'unavailable'; and the hearsay evidence bore adequate indicia of reliability. Relying upon *Roberts*, over 40 States enacted legislation protecting child witnesses from seeing the defendants in court by creating ways for their out-of-court statements to be adduced as evidence.[365] However, in 2004 in *Crawford v Washington* the Supreme Court reversed itself and overruled *Roberts'* reliability test, holding that the Confrontation Clause required that the defendant have had a prior opportunity to test 'testimonial' statements in the 'crucible of cross-examination'.[366]

Considering first the 'unavailability criterion', the refusal of the Supreme Court in *Maryland v Craig* to establish a requisite level of apprehended harm to the child witness to justify the use of CCTV has been viewed as endorsing statutory definitions of 'unavailability' which go beyond the usual reasons such as illness or refusal to testify, to include levels of emotional damage which usually amount to serious or significant harm.[367] The trauma of testifying in court suffices in several States, provided this is supported by expert psychological evidence.[368] Courts have held that the inability of a very young child to communicate to the jury suffices,[369] as does inability to testify through fear or incompetence.[370] The court must make a specific finding that the child witness is 'unavailable' in accordance with the relevant statutory definition before the videotaped deposition can be admitted at trial. However, the courts are given considerable latitude in determining whether a witness would suffer trauma sufficient to warrant excluding the defendant.[371]

---

[363] *California v Green* 399 US 149 (USSC 1970) 158–161 (1970), confirmed *Crawford v Washington* 541 US 36 (USSC 2004) 59; *García v Shriro* 2006 WL 988920 (US CA 9th Cir 2006) [1].

[364] *Ohio v Roberts* 448 US 56 (1980).

[365] E Thompson 'Child Sex Abuse Victims: How will Their Stories be Heard after *Crawford v Washington?*' (2004–2005) 27 Campbell L Rev 281 285–286.

[366] *Crawford v Washington* (n 363) 60–62. For a discussion of the implications of Crawford for hearsay, see below, Chapter 9 section B.8.

[367] eg in Indiana medical evidence must convince the court that testifying in the physical presence of the defendant would cause a child under 14 'to suffer serious emotional distress' such that the child 'cannot reasonably communicate': Indiana Code §35-37-4-6(2)(B)(i); National Centre for Prosecution of Child Abuse *Child Abuse and Neglect State Statutes Elements: Child Witness No 21 Admissibility of Videotaped Depositions or Testimony* (1999); *Perez v State* 536 So 2d 206 (Florida Supreme Ct 1988); Graham (n 261), 81–86.

[368] *People v Newbrough* 803 P 2d 155 (Colorado Supreme Ct 1990); *Virgin Islands v Riley* 754 F Supp 61 (Virgin Islands Dist Ct); *Thomas v People* 803 P 2d 144 (Colorado Supreme Ct 1990); *Altmeyer v State* 496 NE 2d 1328 (Indiana CA 1996).   [369] *Perez v State* (n 367).

[370] *People v Rocha* 547 NE 2d 1335 (Illinois App Ct 1989); *State v Chandler* 376 SE 2d 728 (North Carolina Supreme Ct 1989); *State v Robinson* 735 P 2d 801 (Arizona Supreme Ct 1987); *State v McCafferty* 356 NW 2d 159 (South Dakota Supreme Ct 1984).

[371] *State v Spigarolo* 556 A 2d 112 (Connecticut Supreme Ct 1989) *certiorari* denied 493 US 933 (USSC 1989).

Extrapolating from Supreme Court rulings respecting the admissibility of hearsay statements, at least 30 State appellate courts[372] relying upon *Ohio v Roberts* had found videotaped deposition statutes incorporating the following indicia of reliability to satisfy constitutional requirements for confrontation:

• the hearing is held under circumstances closely approximating those of a typical trial;
• the person making the statement is under oath;
• the defendant is represented by counsel;
• the defendant has every opportunity to cross-examine; and
• proceedings are conducted before a judicial tribunal equipped to provide an accurate record of the hearings.[373]

Since these indicia of reliability also meet the requirement of cross-examination reinstated by *Crawford*, statutes authorizing videotaped pre-trial testimony should continue to be constitutionally valid, as it is functionally equivalent to in-court testimony.[374] The Supreme Court has never had the opportunity to rule on such procedures.[375] Videotaped investigative interviews are being ruled inadmissible where the child is not available for cross-examination at trial on child welfare or competence grounds,[376] causing many convictions to be overturned, and many prosecutors to abandon cases involving young children.[377] The use of CCTV at trial approved by *Maryland v Craig*[378] has thus far withstood challenge under *Crawford*, although arguably the constitutionality of its derogation from an absolute right of confrontation has been undermined.[379]

---

[372] eg *State v Jarzbek* 527 A 2d 1245 (Connecticut Supreme Ct 1987, *certiorari* denied 484 US 1061 (USSC 1988)); *Kansas v Albert* 778 P 2d 386 (Kansas CA 1989); *State v Self* 564 NE 2d 446 (Ohio Supreme Ct 1990); *State v Curtis* 783 SW 2d 47 (Arkansas Supreme Ct 1990); *Brasher v State* 555 So 2d 184 (Alabama Ct of Crim App 1988). Three State appellate courts have found video-recording testimony provisions to be unconstitutional on the basis that their State constitutions require literal face-to-face confrontation: Illinois [*People v Bastien* 541 NE 2d 670 (Illinois Supreme Ct 1989)], Indiana [*Brady v State* 575 NE 2d 981 (Indiana Supreme Ct 1991)] and Massachusetts [*Commonwealth v Bergstrom* 524 NE 2d 366 (Massachusetts Supreme Judicial Ct 1988), but see *Commonwealth v Amirault* 677 NE 2d 652 (Massachusetts Supreme Judicial Ct 1997) holding that video-recorded depositions are constitutional if the defendant is physically present and the defence has an opportunity for cross-examination]. Many other State appellate courts with identical constitutional language have upheld statutes permitting video-recorded testimony: NCPCA *Investigation and Prosecution of Child Abuse* (n 236) 454.
[373] *California v Green* (n 363).
[374] *Blanton v State* 880 So 2d 798 (Florida App 2004); *Howard v State* 816 NE 2d 948 (Indiana App 2004) upholding its pre-*Crawford* ruling in *Guy v State* 755 NE 2d 248 (Indiana CA 2001); *Wisconsin v Kirschbaum* 535 NW 2d 462 (Wisconsin CA 1995); *Anaya v Husley* 2005 US Dist LEXIS 6104 (North Dakota CA 2005); V Vieth 'Keeping the Balance True: Admitting Child Hearsay in the Wake of *Crawford v Washington*' (2004) 16 Update (National Center for Prosecution of Child Abuse) 12.
[375] NCPCA *Investigation and Prosecution of Child Abuse* (n 236) 453.
[376] eg *People v Espinoza* 2004 WL 1560376 (California App 6 Dist 2004); *People v Sisavath* 13 Cal Rptr 3d 753 (California CA 2004); *Rangel v State* 2006 WL 1563058 (Texas CA 2006).
[377] Thompson (n 365), 290.   [378] *Maryland v Craig* (n 358).
[379] *State v Blanchette* 2006 Kan App LEXIS 480 (Kansas CA 2006); *State v Henriod* 131 P 3d 232 (Utah Supreme Court 2006) 16–19; A Phillips 'Out of Harm's Way: Hearings that are Safe from the Impact of *Crawford v. Washington*' (2005) 18 Update (National Center for Prosecution of Child Abuse) 8 (Part 1)

However, some courts are taking a generous view of what constitutes an opportunity to cross-examine under *Crawford*, and so if the State statute offers the defendant an opportunity to submit written interrogatories for a neutral interviewer to put to the child after the initial video interview, that might suffice to allow the interview to be admitted even if the defendant chose not to avail himself of that opportunity.[380] Moreover the constitutional guarantee is of an *opportunity* to cross-examine, and so has been fulfilled even if that cross-examination could not be effective in whatever way, and to whatever extent, the defence might wish, for example because the child was inarticulate or could not remember the event in question.[381]

It is possible that *Crawford* will mean a greater use of preliminary hearings to take videotaped testimony, although this escape route will not work if the child is eventually found incompetent to give evidence at trial. The American statutes permitting the admission at trial of pre-trial testimony where the defence has participated in some way in the questioning have been considered in a host of cases,[382] an indicator of quite widespread usage of this procedure—although, as mentioned earlier, the American Prosecutors Research Institute recommends that it be used only as a last resort because of the perceived disadvantages for the prosecution case when the jury does not see the child.[383] The appeals seem primarily to dwell upon the evidence of harm underpinning the trial court's finding that the child is unavailable to testify at trial, and so admitting the pre-trial testimony. The American Prosecutors Research Institute concludes that the use of videotaped testimony has been less controversial than the admissibility of videotaped interviews,[384] the very converse of the experience in most Commonwealth jurisdictions.

To summarize the results of our foray into other jurisdictions, pre-trial videotaped cross-examination has worked, and worked well, in many jurisdictions using England's adversarial trial model. Australia's trial system is closest to that used in England. Western Australia's very positive experience since 1992 with pre-recorded children's evidence has prompted all of the other Australian jurisdictions to implement their own versions or to contemplate doing so. In the United States, pre-trial depositions

---

and (Part 2) 9. For a contrary view see R Kinnally 'A Bad Case of Indigestion: Internalizing Changes to the Right of Confrontation' (2004) 89 Marquette L Rev 625, 640–641.

[380] *Rangel v State* (n 376) 6–8.

[381] *Delaware v Fensterer* 474 US 15 (USSC 1985) 20, applied in *US v Kappell* 2005 FED App 0333P (6th Cir Mich 2005); *Phillips v Kernan* 2006 US App LEXIS 2787 (North Carolina CA 4th Cir 2006); *US v Ricks* 2006 US App LEXIS 2787 (North Carolina 4th Cir 2006). For a contrary English judicial view that a child is not 'available' for cross-examination if it cannot be conducted effectively, see *R v Christopher Lillie and Dawn Reed* (n 198) [34], [57].

[382] eg *Strickland v State* 550 So 2d 1054 (Alabama Supreme Ct 1989); *State v Spigarolo* (n 371).

[383] NCPCA *Investigation and Prosecution of Child Abuse* (n 236) 451. Goodman confirmed that many prosecutors are reluctant to have to rely upon video recorded evidence, including interviews: Goodman, Buckley, Quas and Shapiro (n 119), 263, 267–2272; however, it should be noted that 66% of prosecutors in the survey said that videotaped depositions were not applicable in their experience. The most frequently cited reasons for not using video-recorded depositions were that the court did not give permission (59%), fear of a defence challenge or appeal (34%), concern about hurting the case (20%) and lack of money (13%). [384] NCPCA *Investigation and Prosecution of Child Abuse* (n 236) 451.

when the defendant had an opportunity to cross-examine have been used at trial in lieu of *viva voce* testimony since at least 1975;[385] indeed there are cases in admitting children's evidence from preliminary hearings instead of testimony at trial dating back to 1960.[386] In these jurisdictions, the practical problems are regarded as having been resolved without detriment to the defendant's rights.

(iv) Could pre-trial videotaped cross-examination work in England and Wales?

Section 28 of the YJCEA 1999 has never been brought into force, for reasons discussed in the next section. Here we discuss whether the framework constructed by section 28 for pre-trial cross-examination is workable. We think it could be, at least (and this is an important caveat) in so far as prosecution witnesses are concerned, as it avoids many of the pitfalls experienced initially by other jurisdictions. The assumption implicit in s 28(2) that the recording will take place before the judge presiding at the formal trial would ensure continuity of evidentiary rulings. The Home Office has developed detailed and practical guidelines for all involved in other Special Measures, and the judicial guidance in Western Australia provides an excellent model for pre-trial videotaped hearings. This would help overcome the problem experienced with the first Queensland initiative when prosecutors and courts were left to devise their own practical arrangements.

Most salutary perhaps are the statutory presumptions that child witnesses in abuse cases are eligible for pre-trial testimony under the primary rule, eliminating the need for specific evidence that the Special Measure is required in particular cases to avoid trauma, as in the United States, where the 'harm hearing' itself could, one suspects, be harmful to the child.[387]

Turning to the provisions of s 28, the stipulations that the recording be made in circumstances whereby the court and lawyers are able to see and hear the examination and can communicate with those present with the child, and that the accused can fully participate by observing the proceedings and communicating with his lawyer in effect replicate the current conditions under which cross-examination is conducted at the trial through the live link; the only difference of substance will be the timing.

Section 28(6) provides another example of the uneasy compromise between mandatory rules and preserving scope for judicial discretion. The provision attempts to

---

[385] Video-recorded pre-trial testimony to avoid the child having to testify at trial seems to have been first proposed in the United States in 1969 by D Libai 'The Protection of the Child Victim of a Sexual Offense in the Criminal Justice System' (1969) 15 Wayne L Rev 977, 1028–1032. Federal Rules of Evidence 28 USCA Rule 804(1)(B) was enacted in 1975. By 1985 such statutes had become commonplace: D Clark-Weintraub 'The Use of Videotaped Testimony of Victims in Cases Involving Child Sexual Abuse: a Constitutional Dilemma' (1985) 14 Hofstra L Rev 261, 263–271; K MacFarlane 'Diagnostic Evaluations and the Use of Videotapes in Child Sexual Abuse Cases' (1985) 40 U of Miami L Rev 135.

[386] *People v Terry* 180 Cal App 2d 48 (California Dist CA 1960).

[387] eg *Florida v Ford* 626 So 2d 1338 (Florida Supreme Ct 1993) (criterion of harm declared satisfied when a four-year-old eyewitness to the murder of her mother by her stepfather curled up in a foetal position and sucked her thumb when a defence psychiatrist questioned her in the presence of the trial judge and counsel to ascertain her ability to testify in open court). Compare *State v Vincent* 768 P 2d 150 (Arizona Supreme Ct 1989) (trial judge erred in finding that children aged six and eight would be traumatized if their testimony against their father in his trial for their mother's murder was not videotaped, in the absence of any evidence specific to those children).

counter the frequently expressed fear that pre-trial videotaped cross-examination will either subject a child to repeated cross-examination as the defence keeps returning for 'another bite at the cherry', or will prejudice the defence by compelling premature cross-examination of the prosecution's key witness. Its first solution in s 28(6)(a), permitting further cross-examination only where the applicant can show that it has become aware of fresh evidence that could not have been ascertained with reasonable diligence by the time of the first cross-examination, has worked satisfactorily in Western Australia and in prosecutions governed by the American Federal Rules of Court. However, the defence is then openly invited to apply for further cross-examination by s 29(6)(b), which empowers the court to permit it when 'for any other reason it is in the interests of justice'. The Government indicated in Parliament that this further ground was inserted to ensure that the pre-trial cross-examination provision would survive scrutiny under the ECHR Article 6,[388] but this was probably overly cautious as the European Commission on Human Rights has repeatedly ruled inadmissible complaints that Continental courts' imposition of restrictions on further cross-examination of prosecution witnesses contravened defendants' rights to a fair trial.[389] Given the understandable desire of the judiciary not to make a ruling which conceivably could prejudice the defence's right to a fair trial (particularly where a witness's response in cross-examination cannot be predicted), and the absence of a Crown right of appeal from any SMD, it would be a robust trial judge who will refuse any but the most specious applications for further cross-examination.

Paul Boateng MP, the Home Office Minister responsible for shepherding the legislation through the House of Commons, correctly said that successful implementation of the more innovative Special Measures would require a change in culture in the criminal justice system. A system of pre-trial recording of a complainant's evidence cannot work unless the defence has had full opportunity to prepare its case. This requires early and full disclosure by the police to the CPS, and the CPS to the defence, of the full prosecution case including, where appropriate, full transcripts of all interviews with the child, and any medical evidence. The defence must then make prompt decisions about whether to seek disclosure of information from third party sources. Strict judicial supervision would be required to ensure that all parties fulfil their obligations to enable the pre-trial hearing to proceed at an early date. It is apparent from the experience of other jurisdictions that everyone involved must be committed to the process for pre-trial hearings to be effective in eliciting quality evidence whilst curtailing the time during which child witnesses are engaged with the criminal justice system. The experience in Western Australia with pre-trial testimony is that the necessary cultural changes can be made within the criminal justice system when there is a common determination to do so.

---

[388] *Hansard*, Standing Committee E, 22 June 1999, Under-Secretary of State for the Home Department.
[389] eg *Finkensieper v Netherlands* unreported, Application No 19525/92, Report 17 May 1995 (EComHR); *Baegen v Netherlands* Unreported, Application No 16696/90, Report 20 Oct 1994 (EComHR) (rape victim); *Hols v Netherlands* (n 251); *Kremers v Netherlands* unreported, Application No. 25205/94, declaration of inadmissibility 19 October 1995 (EComHR) (the latter two cases involving victims of incest).

There are however three structural problems with s 28 which cannot be overcome by adjustments in the system. First, the provision is completely inflexible in presuming that in all sexual assault cases pre-trial cross-examination will be in the best interests of the child, whether the witness desires it or not. An additional problem arises where the child is an eyewitness to a sexual offence against another adult, and not a victim: the child's evidence would be taken before the victim had testified, contrary to normal procedures.[390] Only in Queensland is the pre-trial videotaping provision also made mandatory, for prosecution child witnesses in cases involving sexual offences or violence in the context of a prescribed family or carer relationship, and the court has jurisdiction to override this where appropriate.[391] In Western Australia and the Northern Territory, the procedure is at the election of the prosecution.[392] Under New Zealand's proposed Evidence Code, the prosecution is required to make an application for directions about how a child complainant will give evidence, and the court then has the discretion to order pre-trial recording of testimony.[393]

Second, the opening words of s 28 require that the videotaped interview be admissible as a precondition to pre-trial cross-examination. The restriction applies to all eligible witnesses, including children coming within the 'primary rule'. There does not appear to be any residual judicial discretion to order pre-trial testimony where the witness's circumstances have changed since the investigation began, or where the police's decision not to videotape an interview (in breach of *Achieving Best Evidence*) was ill-judged.[394] Policy-makers seem to have ruled out any possibility that the prosecution might opt for good reason for *viva voce* examination-in-chief (for instance because of poor interviewing techniques, or the preference of the witness), and that this could best be done in a video-recorded pre-trial hearing followed immediately by cross-examination, as is done in Western Australia.

Third, the mandatory application to defence child witnesses in effect means that the prosecution splits its case in chief, which cuts across one of the most fundamental principles of the English adversarial system, that the defence has to be put to its election to call evidence only when the prosecution has made out a case to answer. In no other jurisdiction using or contemplating pre-trial video-recorded testimony has it been made compulsory for defence witnesses; in some jurisdictions the measure is available only to complainants[395] or prosecution witnesses in general,[396] the choice

---

[390] A concern reported by Birch and Powell (n 262) [132].

[391] Evidence (Protection of Children) Amendment Act 2003 (Queensland), ss 21AC, 21AO.

[392] Evidence Act 1906 (Western Australia) s 106I; Evidence Act (Northern Territory) ss 21B(2), 21B(2).

[393] NZLC *Evidence* draft Evidence Code ss 102, 105(1)(a)(iii).

[394] In Plotnikoff and Woolfson's 2004 study, videotaped interviews were not tendered in evidence for 11 (22%) of the 50 child witnesses in the sample: Plotnikoff and Woolfson *In Their Own Words* 16. In their as yet unpublished 2006 study, a videotaped interview of evidence-in-chief had not been made for 39 (35%) of the 111 young people who gave evidence. In the Burton study published in 2006, little more than one-quarter of eligible children (sample size 116) were video-interviewed: Burton, Evans and Sanders (n 203) 40, 53.

[395] Evidence Act 1906 (Western Australia) s 106A defining 'affected child' as 'the child upon or in respect of whom it is alleged an offence was committed, attempted or proposed'.

[396] Evidence (Protection of Children) Act 2003 (Queensland) s 21AI(2); Federal Rules of Evidence 18 USCA §3509 applies only to a child under 18 who is a victim of or a witness to a crime.

being that of the prosecution, although some statutes provide for the court to act of its own motion.[397] In several States the application may be made by 'any party', not just the proponent of that witness, including a representative (such as an attorney or parent) of the child witness.[398] Requiring the defence to use special measures for its witnesses would almost inevitably be considered unconstitutional in America.

As these three problems could be remedied only by statutory amendment, they may have served to stymie the good intentions of the Home Office, which repeatedly delayed the launch of a pilot project to test s 28.[399]

(v) Is 'full-Pigot' still needed?

Concerns by the Bar about the practical implementation of s 28, apart from the three structural problems just identified, have turned on timing: it is argued that notwithstanding the *Attorney General's Guidelines on Disclosure*[400] the full disclosure which is obviously necessary before cross-examination can take place is typically a very lengthy and vexed process, particularly where records held by third parties are involved, and so it is usually completed only shortly before trial. Consequently there would be little point in having a separate pre-trial procedure to take the child's testimony.

A cross-current to this concern is the claim of various criminal justice agencies, in particular the CPS, that the fast-tracking of child abuse cases means that delay is no longer a crucial problem. This assertion relies upon a 2004 three-pronged Government initiative. The Lord Chief Justice, the Lord Chancellor, and the Attorney General launched the Criminal Case Management Programme to improve the efficiency and efficacy of the criminal justice system in processing cases with a view to increasing public confidence in the criminal justice system which has markedly waned in recent years. This has generated a 200 page *Criminal Case Management Framework*[401] to streamline the processing of cases and is the predecessor to a comprehensive criminal procedure code. Another limb of the initiative is the Effective Trial Management Programme, which together with the *No Witness No Justice* project referred to earlier aims to reduce 'cracked'[402] and ineffective trials by improving case preparation and progression, and victim and witness care. The third limb is a change in charging policy to make the CPS responsible for formulating the charges, in the expectation that this

---

[397] eg Mississippi Code Ann §13-1-407; Iowa Code §915.38(2).

[398] eg Indiana Code §35-37-4-8(d) (as amended in 2005); Connecticut Gen Stat Ann §54-86g (of the victim only); Iowa Code §915.38(2); Kentucky Rev Stat Ann §421.350; Mississippi Code Ann §13-1-407; Massachusetts Gen Laws Ann ch 278 §16D requires a motion by the proponent of the child witness or the court.

[399] *Speaking up for Justice* indicated that in the summer of 2000 the Home Office would consult on options for implementing s 28, with full implementation expected in the autumn of 2001; this was put back to a pilot project and national roll-out in 2003–2004 [Home Office Press Release 17/2002], and was postponed again to 2004–2005 for the pilot and implementation by 1 May 2005 [Home Office Circular 058/2005].   [400] Discussed above, section 2.

[401] Department of Constitutional Affairs *The Criminal Case Management Framework* (July 2005 2nd edn).   [402] Where the defence enters a late guilty plea.

will ensure that the charge is right for each offence from the start and that cases are constructed effectively from the outset.[403]

The claims that disclosure difficulties cause delay, and that cases already get to court as quickly as is feasible, are not contradictory but there are inconsistent elements to them. They were the catalyst for the Home Office to commission research from Nottingham University to consider whether the principles and objectives of the Pigot Committee were still valid in 2005, and to identify the major difficulties with implementing s 28. The report by Professor Di Birch and Rhonda Powell[404] concluded that *Pigot's* twin principles of expediting the exit of child witnesses from the criminal justice, system and taking their evidence in surroundings which would not intimidate them, have now been largely achieved, without the aid of s 28. The disclosure rules are now much more expansive and elaborate than in Judge Pigot's day, meaning that cross-examination cannot take place until very shortly before trial—or even at the start of the trial proper, before the jury is empanelled.[405] Conversely, they considered that his recommendations to expedite serious cases involving child witnesses had now in the main been implemented successfully,[406] and that anything which cut across fast-tracking would be counterproductive[407] (although it is not clear why s 28 would do this). Of the two evidential advantages secured by pre-recording, the 'necessity principle' of making crucial evidence available was a product of the inadequacies of the pre-*Pigot* trial, which can be mitigated by making trials more child-friendly, without pre-recording.[408] The 'reliability principle', improving the quality of evidence from child witnesses by obtaining it as early as possible, has largely been solved by widespread video interviewing, and whilst it would be equally advantageous for the child to deal with the defence case when his recollection of events is fresh, there would have to be some lapse of time between complaint and cross-examination to prepare the defence case.[409] Therefore Birch and Powell concluded that the pre-trial recording of the whole of a child's evidence was not the only way to meet the challenges identified by the *Pigot Report*.[410]

In considering their conclusion regarding the 'reliability principle', clearly there has to be a lapse of time between complaint (usually videotaped) and cross-examination. But there need not be a gap between examination-in-chief and cross-examination (and any re-examination), if the Western Australian practice is followed of having a one-shot hearing (with the addition of using, if the prosecutor so decides, the video interview as part of the child's direct evidence).

Birch and Powell recommended that the government should explore the possibility of using an informal, *Pigot*-style hearing involving examination-in-chief, cross-examination and re-examination. However, Birch and Powell contended that this hearing normally should take place *during the trial*.[411] The only advantage would seem to be to make the child witness more comfortable. One weakness of the Birch and

---

[403] Criminal Justice Act 2003 c 44 ss 29–30; Explanatory Notes [4].
[404] Birch and Powell *Meeting the Challenges of Pigot* (n 262).   [405] ibid [40], [105]–[106], [119].
[406] ibid [15]–[16], [107].   [407] ibid [133].   [408] ibid [22]–[23].
[409] ibid [24]–[26].   [410] ibid [22].   [411] ibid [148].

Powell report (which they prepared under great time pressure) was that it considered only the objectives of the Pigot committee in 1991. They did not address the ancillary advantages of the pre-trial hearing which we have canvassed above, in particular the advantages for the prosecution and defence of being able to make informed decisions about the charges and pleas, facilitating the scheduling and conduct of the trial, and minimizing system abuse for the child. Nor were they able to consider in any detail the practices of jurisdictions that have successfully implemented pre-trial videotaped testimony for child witnesses.

Moreover, whilst Birch and Powell accepted the official line that measures to expedite cases involving child witnesses have been (finally) effective, relying upon anecdotal evidence,[412] there is considerable empirical evidence to the contrary. The first edition of the *Framework* contained no reference to fast-tracking of child abuse cases,[413] and the second edition merely directs the user to consult other guidelines on the prioritization of cases involving child witnesses.[414] The difficulty for court officials is that there are so many directives about prioritizing cases for fixed trial dates. Plotnikoff and Woolfson in their 2004 study of child witnesses found that on average witnesses in Crown Court trials waited 11.6 months to be cross-examined at trial, those in the magistrates' courts waited 9.9 months, and those in the youth court waited 8.6 months. Of the 50 witnesses in the research sample, 14 waited for 12 months or more before the trial.[415] During this period, 35 children described themselves as very nervous or scared, 9 felt intimidated and 20 described symptoms of anxiety, depression, or insomnia, with 2 self-harming.[416] Plotnikoff and Woolfson concluded that delay in cases involving young witnesses remained as much of a problem in 2004 as it did in 1989 when the *Pigot Report* recommended pre-trial cross-examination.[417] Similar findings about delay and adjournments will be reported by Plotnikoff and Woolfson in their forthcoming evaluation of witness support in respect of 120 young witnesses who attended court in 2005.

Neither the CPS nor the Home Office has provided any statistical evidence to substantiate the claim that the fast-tracking system is working such that 'full-Pigot' is no longer necessary or even advisable. There were no fewer than four restatements of the child witness priority policy in 2005.[418] Despite these commitments, there is no national monitoring of such cases and therefore no national statistics about how long

---

[412] ibid [107]; they also cite in support an audience of about 80 judges at a Judicial Studies Board who were enthusiastic about the recent fast-tracking measures [133].

[413] Plotnikoff and Woolfson *In Their Own Words* 70.

[414] *The Criminal Case Management Framework* (n 401) [7].

[415] Plotnikoff and Woolfson *In Their Own Words* 2, 10–11.　　　[416] ibid 2, 11–14.

[417] ibid 70. For comparable figures in 1994 and 1995, see J Chandler and D Lait 'An Analysis of the Treatment of Children As Witnesses in the Crown Court' in *Children in Court* (Victim Support, London 1996) 97.

[418] Home Office *Witness Charter Consultation* (2005) Standard 13; Crown Prosecution Service *Children's Charter* (2005) [4.3]; Her Majesty's Courts Service *Every Witness Matters: Employee Handbook* (2005) 11; *The Criminal Case Management Framework* (n 401).

such cases take.[419] Although the Crown Court centres attempt to apply the policy, young witness cases are not systematically flagged as such on receipt[420] and courts did not monitor them separately. Local Criminal Justice Boards still do not routinely collect data about the time cases take to get to trial.[421]

The attack on the feasibility of pre-trial testimony is that disclosure problems cause delay. If disclosure is tackled in accordance with the *Criminal Case Management Framework*, then the pre-trial hearing could proceed without waiting for other witnesses to be available. There would be no need to force cases involving child witnesses to the front of the queue of cases awaiting fixed court dates.

Therefore the case that there is no longer any need for pre-trial videotaped hearings is not persuasive. However, s 28 in its present form would inevitably cause unnecessary problems for a pilot project, even if it were implemented only for prosecution witnesses. Because of the inflexibility of the primary rule and the restrictions on supplementary examination-in-chief, it should be amended only in the context of an overall statutory adjustment of Special Measures Directions, to which we return in section B.5, below.

(c) Intermediaries

The debate about the use of intermediaries has been both vigorous and polarized ever since the publication of the *Pigot Report* in 1991. Few lawyers would dispute the need for an intermediary to filter questions and explain answers for a witness with communication problems due to learning difficulties or physical impairment.[422] The issues about the merits of intermediaries which have concerned jurisdictions considering their use have related to

- whether they should be used for all child witnesses, including with communication capabilities typical for their age group;
- whether for such children they are to act merely as an amplifier of inaudible answers or also as 'explainer'; and

---

[419] Plotnikoff and Woolfson *In Their Own Words* 70 called for systematic monitoring and publication of relevant statistics. On 14 December 2004 the Deputy Chief Justice, Lord Justice Judge, wrote to all resident judges expressing concern that 'the average length of the process . . . is much longer than it should be'. He emphasized that addressing delay in Crown Court cases is the judiciary's responsibility.

[420] The Hamlyn report showed serious deficiencies in the identification of VIWs in all criminal justice agencies: Hamlyn, Phelps, Turtle and Sattar *Are Special Measures Working?* (n 265) chapter 4.

[421] Personal communication from Joyce Plotnikoff.

[422] The use of an intermediary in this limited capacity has already been approved at common law by the English Court of Appeal where only a social worker could understand a severely mentally handicapped adult's replies; the social worker was treated as being akin to a translator and therefore could give admissible evidence as to his impression and interpretation of what he understood the man to have said in his videotaped police interview [*R v Duffy* [1999] QB 919]. The social worker's 'transcript' of what the declarant said was treated as a translation of the videotaped police interview, which itself was admitted as hearsay under the CJA 1988 s 23(2)(a) as the man had died before trial; thus the problem of how to handle his testimony at trial did not arise.

- whether all questions by counsel or the court would have to be put through the intermediary, or whether they would intervene only on an 'as needed' basis.

The case for an interlocutor or intermediary for the pre-trial testimony of *all* children had been strongly argued in England first by Glanville Williams in 1987,[423] and ever since that time some child advocacy groups have contended that (at least) young children should never be directly questioned by counsel. Opponents, mostly advocates but also some Law Commissions,[424] have objected that intermediaries for children without communication disorders would introduce yet another interface between counsel and a witness testifying via video-link, might impair the quality of the child's evidence in direct and cross-examination, and might make the child less confident about her ability to tell the court what she has experienced or seen.

These issues were the only ones on which the members of the Pigot Committee diverged. However, the majority of the Pigot Committee had proposed that the judge should be able to use an 'interlocutor' only for examination of very young or very disturbed children, and only in very unusual circumstances where otherwise it would be 'absolutely impossible' for counsel to communicate successfully with the child. Implicitly this seemed to entail an explanatory function for the interlocutor. On the third question, the Pigot Committee anticipated that everyone with an interest would have to communicate with the child witness solely through the 'interlocutor' (most likely a child-care professional trusted by the child), who would be the sole person visible to the child. The Bar's representative, Ann Rafferty QC, dissented on the basis that the intervention of a specialist interlocutor would hinder rather than assist counsel in conducting the case. She contended that the difficulty should be overcome by allowing greater opportunities for counsel to establish a rapport with a child witness before the hearing took place.[425]

Section 29 of the YJCEA 1999 makes no attempt to prescribe minimum conditions for use of an intermediary, nor their qualifications. The Special Measure is available to all children under the age of 17, and to other witnesses with a physical or mental disability or disorder which could affect the quality of their evidence.

The experience of other jurisdictions with intermediary legislation shows that issues such as their qualifications, the circumstances in which one might be used, and the

---

[423] Williams 'Child Witnesses' (n 126) 193–195; Williams 'Videotaping Children's Evidence' (n 146), 351, 369 (commenting on the Bill which became the Criminal Justice Act 1988). In the United States the use of a 'child examiner' to assess the child's confidence to testify and, if need be, to relay questions from counsel and the court was first proposed in 1969: Libai (n 385), 1009–1012. See also GS Goodman and VS Helgeson 'Child Sexual Assault: Children's Memory and the Law' (1985) 40 U of Miami L Rev 181, 204. [424] Queensland LRC *Evidence of Children* 56–57.

[425] *Pigot Report* [2.32]–[2.34]. The feasibility of this alternative proposal has not been adequately tested because some prosecuting counsel still feel uncomfortable in speaking with child witnesses before they testify [*Bristol Study* 55] notwithstanding changes to the Bar Code of Conduct to facilitate this [*Bar Code of Conduct*, Articles 6.1.3–6.1.4, 6.2.1–6.2.2]. Unless the trial judge is present and approves, defence counsel are quite rightly concerned about the propriety of speaking informally to prosecution witnesses. In the United States defence counsel can seek a court order to permit them to have rapport-building sessions with child complainants, as it is in the defendant's interest that they appear untraumatized by the court room experience: Montoya (n 283), 349–351.

definition of their role, are not easy to resolve. Intermediaries have not become an established feature of adversarial trials in Australia,[426] New Zealand,[427] Canada, or the United States. They are used in the adversarial trial systems of Israel and South Africa, neither of which uses juries. In South Africa, where cross-examination of complainants in sexual assault cases is regarded as particularly aggressive,[428] the court has discretion to appoint an intermediary where any person under age 18 would be exposed to undue mental stress or suffering through testifying in court.[429] All questions must be directed through the intermediary, who may convey the general purport of any question to the witness. The child's answers are then interpreted from a child's developmental level to the legalese employed in courts. This means that the child does not give direct evidence and is not directly cross-examined.[430] There is a widespread view that the South African system is not working as effectively as it might in practice: many courts do not have intermediaries or will not allow children to use them, they lack accreditation and training, there is confusion as to their role in court, and defence lawyers are thought to be still given too much leeway in cross-examining children. Nonetheless there is strong support for the intermediary system, which is seen as being helpful for the vast majority of child witnesses.[431] In 1996 a constitutional challenge to the use of intermediaries, on the basis that it unduly undermined the effectiveness of the defence's right to cross-examination, was rejected.[432] Israel has used 'youth interrogators' since 1955, who have almost exclusive powers of pre-trial questioning of child victims, and who have the power to exclude children under 14 from the trial if their mental health might be jeopardized.[433]

In Western Australia, legislation enacted in 1992 permitting the use of a 'child communicator' to explain questions and to clarify the child's answers to the court still has not been implemented, as developing guidelines for the qualifications, training and role of intermediaries has proved to be an exceptionally difficult task, and there

---

[426] An intermediary system has been rejected by the Australian Law Reform Commission [ALRC, *Seen and Heard* [14.113]–[14.115]], and in New South Wales [New South Wales Attorney General's Department *Report of the Children's Evidence Task Force* (1995–96) [8.3.2.] and Queensland [Queensland LRC *Evidence of Children* ch 4 and Recommendation 4.1].

[427] Although there is statutory provision for intermediaries [Evidence Act 1908 (New Zealand) s 23E(4)], their role is restricted to putting questions to a witness, not to be phrasing them or interpreting the witness's answer. The New Zealand Law Commission's proposals in NZLC *The Evidence of Children* (n 4) to extend their use were strongly opposed by the New Zealand Law Society, High Court judges and the Courts' Committee and the Law Commission abandoned them NZLC *Evidence* Vol 2 [370]–[374].

[428] South African Law Commission *Sexual Offences: Process and Procedure* (Discussion Paper 102, Project 107 Dec 2002) Vol 3 [38.3.1]–[38.3.9]. One South African judge is quoted as saying 'cross-examination, intended as a scalpel to excise the tumour of untruth, has become a bludgeon with which justice is slowly clubbed to death' [38.3.1].

[429] Criminal Procedure Act 1977 (South Africa) s 170A (introduced in 1991).

[430] South African Law Commission *Sexual Offences: Process and Procedure* (n 428) Vol 3 [26.1.1].

[431] ibid Vol 3 [26.3.3], [26.3.20]–[26.3.26]; K Müller and K Hollely *Introducing the Child Witness* (Printrite, Port Elizabeth 2000) 16–17.

[432] *Klink v Regional Court Magistrate* (1996) 3 LRC 666 (Supreme Court (South Eastern Cape Local Division)), further described by Hoyano 'Striking a Balance' (n 124), 966–967.

[433] The Protection of Children Law of 1955 (Israel), described by Libai (n 385), 995–1001.

still is no recognized training course for child communicators.[434] There also does not seem to be any impetus for implementation of the measure in Western Australia, possibly because of the success of pre-trial recorded evidence for child witnesses.[435]

American courts have applied legislation authorizing 'interpreters' for witnesses in cases where very young children were unable to speak with sufficient distinctness or volume for the jury to hear them, or used idiosyncratic gestures and speech that the jury could not understand.[436] It is significant that the use of an interpreter has generally survived constitutional challenges on appeal only where the interpreter's role has been very narrowly defined and monitored by the trial judge. Where the child is inaudible due to timidity, the interpreter must be specifically instructed to repeat verbatim counsel's questions and the child's answers, without any interpolations.[437] Where the child's natural mode of communication is incomprehensible due to idiosyncrasies of pronunciation or gesture, an interpreter should be used only as and when each difficulty arises in the course of testimony, and then only to serve as a conduit to convey the child's specific communication to the jury. It is constitutionally impermissible for them to explain a question or answer.[438]

Under s 29(2) of the YJCEA 1999, the intermediary's role is not restricted to acting as a megaphone or conduit to translate idiosyncratic terms for the jury; rather, he is authorized to 'explain' the questions and answers 'so far as necessary to enable them to be understood' by the witness or questioner. This explanatory function makes it vital that the intermediary be competent, independent and impartial.

The Home Office has been wrestling with these issues for six years. Although the Interdepartmental Working Group was charged with implementing the measure in the Crown Court by autumn 2001,[439] as of mid-2006 the intermediary provision still has not come into force, and pathfinder pilots in six areas of England and Wales are still being evaluated. The Home Office has published numerous drafts of guidance. The difficulties the Home Office has been experiencing with implementation have caused Scotland[440] and Queensland[441] to decide not to include intermediaries in their packages of special measures for vulnerable witnesses for the time being. However, significant progress has been made: a National Register of approved intermediaries administered by the Intermediary Registration Board is now operational, and reports

---

[434] Evidence Act 1906 s 106F; Jackson (n 254) 203.

[435] Queensland LRC *Evidence of Children* 43.

[436] *US v Ricks* (n 381); see J Myers *Evidence in Child Abuse and Neglect Cases* (3rd edn John Wiley & Sons, Inc., New York 1997), vol 1, 224–232.

[437] *US v Romey* 32 MJ 180, 32 Fed. R Evid Serv 1315, *certiorari* denied 112 S Ct 337 (US Ct of Military Appeals, 1991).

[438] *In the Interest of RR, Jr* 6 ALR 4th 140 (New Jersey Sup Ct, 1979); Graham (n 261), 94. Mississippi allows the court to appoint an expert who has dealt with the child in a therapeutic setting concerning the offence to aid the court during the pre-trial testimony, but only on the stipulation of all parties [Mississippi Code Ann §13-1-407(5)].

[439] *Speaking up for Justice* (n 161) 9.

[440] Scottish Executive *Policy Memorandum* (n 347) [43]–[46].

[441] Queensland LRC *Evidence of Children* ch 4 and Recommendation 4.1.

from the judges and lawyers in the first 12 or so trials using intermediaries in the pathfinder areas are said to have been very positive.

The latest version of the *Intermediary Procedural Guidance Manual* dated October 2005,[442] together with guidance for police officers from Association of Chief Police Officers (ACPO),[443] provides a much clearer perspective on the role of the intermediary than the previous drafts. The *Manual* points out that intermediaries in England and Wales are working in an adversarial system which is different from that in Norway and some other countries where they are used, and so counsel may legitimately challenge the appointment of intermediaries, or question their methods, knowledge and the way in which they facilitate communication.[444] The intermediary must be impartial and neutral (and available to defence as well as prosecution witnesses), and ultimately his duties to the court are paramount.[445]

Criminal practitioners are exhorted to recognize that children do not have to display a 'disability' in order to qualify for an intermediary.[446] The initial Home Office guidance on eligibility had been confusing in that it indicated that an intermediary could be used only if the witness could otherwise not testify due to 'profound communication difficulties'.[447] This interpretation is contrary to the clear wording of s 29, and may have been adopted because of concerns from the criminal Bar that counsel would never be allowed to question a child witness directly. The new *Guidance* goes some way to clarify this. There must be an automatic initial assessment by the police of the nature of any child's vulnerability due to age, and consideration given to appropriate Special Measures.[448] The ACPO guidance points out that children do not need to have a disability or disorder to be eligible, and provides the following advice:

[A]s a general rule of thumb, an intermediary may be able to help improve the quality of evidence of any child who is unable to detect and cope with misunderstanding, particularly in the court context (i.e. if a child seems unlikely to be able to recognise a problematic question or tell the questioner that he or she has not understood, then assessment by an intermediary should be considered).[449]

The emphasis is on early and careful planning, and integrity and transparency in the way intermediaries are selected and used. The role of the intermediary in every step of the investigation and adjudicative processes is now carefully delineated, and here (unlike in the rest of the YJCEA 1999 Special Measures guidance) the differences for defence witnesses using an intermediary are addressed rather than sidestepped.[450] Crucially, the intermediary having made an initial assessment can

---

[442] *Intermediary Procedural Guidance Manual* (Home Office October 2005).

[443] Association of Chief Police Officers of England, Wales and Northern Ireland Victims and Witnesses Portfolio Group *When to Use an Intermediary: 2 Stage Test* (August 2005).

[444] *Intermediary Procedural Guidance Manual* (n 442) [2.3.5]–[2.3.6].   [445] ibid [2.3.1], [3.2.1].

[446] ibid [3.1.4].

[447] Home Office *Intermediaries—a Voice for Vulnerable Witnesses: Frequently Asked Questions* (2003) Question 1.   [448] *Intermediary Procedural Guidance Manual* (n 442) [3.1.4], [3.2.1].

[449] ACPO *et al When to Use an Intermediary: 2 Stage Test* (n 443) 2.

[450] *Intermediary Procedural Guidance Manual* (n 442) [3.4], [3.5.11]–[3.5.5], [3.7.7].

advise the police[451] whether the witness is able to give best evidence on her own if using other Special Measures.[452] Sensibly, a change in intermediary between the investigation and trial will now be 'exceptional' rather than required, as the initial draft guidance had stipulated, apparently in an overweening anxiety to avoid any allegations of partiality and contamination.[453]

Practical difficulties may nonetheless arise at the investigative stage, where the police must predict the likely responses of the defence and of the Court to the use of an intermediary for the investigative interview; the *Guidance* contemplates only retrospective confirmation of the appointment of the intermediary by the court at the Plea and Case Management Hearing.[454] If objections to the need for facilitated communication or to the choice of a particular intermediary[455] are upheld, it is likely that any video interview will be inadmissible and the witness will have to give *viva voce* evidence at the trial, or the case may even collapse on the basis that his testimony has become contaminated. If the charges are not dismissed, a challenge to any conviction under ECHR Article 6 may become available. Thus the decision to use an intermediary during the investigative stage is not free from risk, but that risk is significantly mitigated by the accreditation of trained intermediaries and the detailed record of their assessments before embarking upon the evidential phase of the investigation.

The parameters of the intermediary's explanatory function are necessarily drawn in rather general terms in the *Manual*, and include the following:[456]

- the reasons for and content of any explanation of a question to the witness shall also be given to the court;

- the witness's reply to a question shall be communicated as given, however irrelevant or illogical it appears; it is for the court to decide whether to seek clarification from the intermediary about the possible reasons for the response and whether to rephrase the question;

- the intermediary shall seek clarification from the court of any question he has not understood before putting it to the witness, such clarification being confined to matters of understanding in comprehension, not to any legal issues or purpose;

- the intermediary shall not hypothesize as to the intentions or motives of the witness, nor anticipate the intention of the questioner;

- the intermediary shall not alter the question or answer in the first instance, but will offer an alternative form of the question if required to facilitate understanding;

- the intermediary shall not alter the precise nature or thrust of questions put to the witness or the witness's answers for the purpose of shielding or protecting the witness;

---

[451] Or the defence solicitor, where a defence witness is involved.

[452] *Intermediary Procedural Guidance Manual* (n 442) [3.6.5].

[453] *Consultation Draft: Guidance for the Use of an Intermediary under s. 29 of the Youth Justice And Criminal Evidence Act 1999* (Home Office Justice and Victims Unit, May, 2001) [3.7.4]–[3.7.5].

[454] *Intermediary Procedural Guidance Manual* (n 442) [3.5.13], [3.10.1].   [455] ibid [3.10.3].

[456] ibid [3.11.3], Annex C Code of Practice.

- the intermediary shall not interrupt legal representatives unless there is an urgent need to seek clarification or to indicate that the witness has not understood something, nor may they unnecessarily impede or obstruct the pace and flow of court proceedings.

There is considerable evidence that lawyers and judges overestimate their present abilities to communicate with children in a judicial setting. Child witnesses tell a different story in numerous empirical studies.[457] Plotnikoff and Woolfson[458] reported that 42 of the 50 children in their research sample said they had problems with questioning, and 25 of them across all age groups from ages 7 to 16 had difficulty in understanding words or questions. Fifteen children followed the advice in the *NSPCC Young Witness Pack* (which was often reinforced by the judges, lawyers and supporters) and did tell the court that they did not understand. One can surmise that the evidential value of the answers of the 20 per cent who did not speak up might be significantly misleading. Another 2004 study reported that just 44 per cent of the child witnesses in their sample using Special Measures said the questions asked of them were always clear and straightforward, whereas 46 per cent said that some were but others were not. Whilst an impressive 87 per cent of all of the child and adult vulnerable witnesses in the sample felt they could ask for questions to be explained, the 13 per cent who said they did not feel able to do this[459] give cause for concern. In a Scottish empirical study children in interviews said that often they did not say all they wanted to in evidence, either because they were baffled by the questions or because the structure of the questioning prevented them.[460] Many children do not have the courage to speak up in the classroom to tell their teachers they do not understand something, and it must be all the more unrealistic to expect them to do so in the unfamiliar, formal and more stressful environment of a trial.

To say that the questions put to a child witness in court must be appropriate to the child's age and linguistic, cognitive and emotional development is to state the obvious, but nonetheless examples abound in every jurisdiction of judges and counsel confusing the witness (and themselves) with their lines of questioning. Here psychological studies of child development can provide invaluable guidance to those charged with effectively questioning children.[461] If counsel are properly trained, and are properly constrained by the court in the formulation of their questions and the

---

[457] In New South Wales and Queensland cross-examination can be particularly aggressive and hence confusing, notwithstanding statutory requirements that judges control questioning: Eastwood and Patton (n 279) 59–62, 74–88, 97–99, 122–128. The researchers reported a very different style of defence advocacy in Western Australia, where the culture and attitudes had changed, not just the legislation: 61–62, 121, 123, 125, 127.

[458] Plotnikoff and Woolfson, *In Their Own Words* 48–50, 73–74.

[459] Hamlyn *et al Surverys of VIWs* 55–56.   [460] Murray (n 255) [12.23].

[461] JP Schuman, N Bala and K Lee 'Developmentally Appropriate Questions for Child Witnesses' (1999) 25 Queen's LJ 251; J Myers 'The Child Witness: Techniques for Direct Examination, Cross-Examination and Impeachment' (1987) 18 Pacific LJ 801; J Myers, K Saywitz and G Goodman 'Psychological Research on Children as Witnesses: Implications for Forensic Interviewing and Courtroom Testimony' (1996) 28 Pac LJ 3; Cashmore and Trimboli (n 332) 46–56; E Davies and F Seymour 'Questioning of Complainants of Sexual Abuse: Analysis of Criminal Court Transcripts in New Zealand' (1998) 5 *Psychiatry, Psychology and Law* 47.

vigour of their cross-examination,[462] then the intervention of the intermediary is likely to be minimal.

It may well be that an intermediary can render the greatest service to the court and to the child by advising police interviewers, advocates and the trial judge how to make their questions and instructions intelligible to that particular child, intervening to provide that advice where necessary on an 'as needed' basis. In this way the child will know who is the questioner, and interference with the flow of examination will be minimized. We understand that this was the procedure adopted in the pathfinder pilot studies.

To return to the three issues laid out at the outset which have deterred experimentation with intermediaries in several other common law jurisdictions:

- Child witnesses whose communication capacities are typical for their age group are automatically eligible for an intermediary under s 29. However police guidance recommends that officers at an early stage of the investigation consider whether difficulties might be anticipated in communicating with the child, and consider involving an intermediary to conduct an initial assessment if there are any doubts on that score. This assessment might or might not result in the intermediary being involved in any interview.

- Whilst the intermediary does have the statutory authority to explain questions and answers, the parameters for doing so are carefully spelt out in the accompanying *Guidance* which implies that the intermediary's role during the child's testimony will be facilitative rather than strongly interventionist. The intermediary can perform a very valuable role before the trial in assisting both prosecuting and defence counsel to understand how best to communicate with that particular child. It is understood that this occurred in at least one of the trials in the pathfinder study.

- The *Manual* implies that counsel will only be entirely prevented from questioning a child or other vulnerable witness when the witness's communication difficulties are so profound that this becomes necessary. Otherwise counsel will normally be permitted to interact directly with the witness, with the intermediary intervening to advise counsel how a particular question might be reformulated.

Under these circumstances, then, intermediaries potentially have a valuable role to play in enabling children to participate fully in the trial, by ensuring their complete understanding of all that is said in the course of their evidence-in-chief (be it

---

[462] Judicial vigilance to ensure that advocates use language that is free of jargon and appropriate to the age of the child and to guard against over-rigorous cross-examination is counselled in the Judicial Studies Board Bench Book (2004) [4.4.3], quoted by Plotnikoff and Woolfson *In Their Own Words* 73. Queensland and the Northern Territory set out statutory principles for dealing with the child witness, which include that the child is to be treated with dignity, respect and compassion, and that the child should not be intimidated in cross-examination: Evidence (Protection of Children) Amendment Act 2003 (Queensland) s 57; Evidence Act (Northern Territory) s 21D, as amended in Dec 2005. These changes were introduced after an empirical study demonstrated that legislation to control cross-examination was not working: Eastwood and Patton (n 279) 126–128.

videotaped or *viva voce*) and cross-examination, and by ensuring understanding of the child's testimony on the part of all participants in the trial.

(d) Mandatory application to defence child witnesses

To a large degree defence witnesses are invisible to the criminal justice process until they are called to testify. In 2005 of the 387,794 referrals to the Witness Service, only about 2 per cent were defence witnesses, and they are not assisted by the Witness Care Units in each court district.[463] A particularly thorny trap created by the 1999 Act was the application of the mandatory provisions to child witnesses, especially children subject to the primary rule, called by the defence. In so far as the premise of Special Measures is to enable vulnerable witnesses to provide their best evidence, this decision was logical.

However, it was not at all practical: who is to video-interview defence witnesses? Police and social workers receive training under *Achieving Best Evidence*, but it is highly unlikely that defence counsel would wish to surrender their witnesses to interviewers who are often regarded by defendants as hostile to their interests, especially when the result would be examination-in-chief as part of the defence case. Where would the interviews be conducted, given the needs for technology, which is extremely unlikely to be available anywhere other than police stations, possibly making it awkward for defence witnesses to attend? When does that video interview have to be disclosed to the prosecution? What is there to prevent the prosecution from tailoring its evidence to that defence case if the video interview is required to be disclosed before trial? When is the mandatory pre-trial cross-examination by the prosecution to take place?

The Home Office's *Achieving Best Evidence* provides no practical guidance at all: it states merely that while some of the notes and recommendations are drafted with the particular needs and concerns of the prosecution in mind, they apply in general to all those involved in investigating, interviewing, safeguarding and examining child and other vulnerable witnesses.[464] Moreover, the FAQs on the Home Office website include a statement that defence witnesses 'will be able to apply' for Special Measures— which is actively misleading given that the mandatory primary rule also applies to defence child witnesses.

The Crown Court Rules for SMDs provides that any video-recording which the accused proposes to tender in evidence need not be sent to the prosecution until the close of the prosecution case at trial. This means that a defence application for admission of a video-recording may be made *ex parte*, before it has been disclosed to the prosecution.[465] This obviously is not a practical solution for mandatory 'full-Pigot' hearings.

---

[463] Victim Support *Annual Report and Accounts for the year ended 31 March 2005*, 7. Victim Support operates a Witness Service in every criminal court in England and Wales.

[464] *Achieving Best Evidence* (n 48) [1.10].

[465] The Crown Court (Special Measures Directions and Directions Prohibiting Cross-examination) Rules 2002 SI 2002 No 1688 (L.5) Rule 8(6) and (7).

None of the empirical studies commissioned by the Home Office into the effectiveness of Special Measures which we discuss below dealt with defence witnesses, so there is virtually no evidence of the treatment of defence witnesses in practice. Anecdotal evidence suggests that judges are allowing live link for defence witnesses if requested by the defence, but that otherwise the legislation is not being applied to them. The Queensland model which expressly exempts children who are witnesses for the defence from their 'full-Pigot' regime is a much more sensible approach.[466]

(e) *Exclusion of child defendants from Special Measures*

The YJCEA 1999 in ss 17(1) and 19(1)(a) expressly provides that defendants are not eligible for the Special Measures.[467] The Home Office and CPS have defended this stance on the bases that: the Code for Crown Prosecutors requires sufficient evidence before prosecuting; the burden and standard of proof on the Crown is high; there are already special procedures for interviewing vulnerable suspects; defendants are afforded considerable safeguards in the proceedings as a whole to ensure a fair trial such as the right to legal representation, to cross-examine, and the choice whether to give evidence[468] (unlike prosecution witnesses); the trial judge has an overriding duty to ensure a fair trial and has the power to stay proceedings as an abuse of process or to direct an acquittal.[469] It is also argued that many of the measures are designed to shield the witness from the defendant and so could not apply to her.

Curiously, none of these points persuaded the Scottish Parliament to withhold protective measures from defendants under the age of 16 in the Vulnerable Witnesses (Scotland) Act 2004; they are eligible for all special measures for their testimony except the use of a screen and video-recorded evidence before a commissioner.[470] In New South Wales all investigative interviews with a defendant under 16 must be video-recorded, and the child is entitled to have that interview constitute the whole or part of his examination-in-chief.[471] The court may also direct that a child defendant testify using CCTV, if it is satisfied that she might suffer mental or emotional harm if required to give evidence in the ordinary way or that the facts might be better ascertained if she used CCTV.[472] A child defendant like other child witnesses is also entitled to choose a supporter to be near her when she was giving evidence, who may act as an 'interpreter' to assist the child with any difficulty in giving evidence associated with a disability or to provide other support.[473] In the Northern Territory, all special

---

[466] Evidence (Protection of Children) Amendment Act 2003 (Queensland) s 21AI(2).

[467] This is also the case in Queensland: ibid defining 'affected child'.

[468] A right now fettered by the adverse inferences from failure to testify permitted by the Criminal Justice Act Public Order Act 1994 (England) s 35.

[469] As set out in *R v Camberwell Green Youth Court ex parte D* (n 225) and the Home Office website.

[470] Vulnerable Witnesses (Scotland) Act 2004 s 271F.

[471] Evidence (Children) Act 1997 (New South Wales), as amended 2001, 2003, 2004 ss 7–11.

[472] ibid s 19.   [473] ibid s 27(6).

measures for witnesses under 18 apart from video-recorded evidence[474] apply to child defendants.

There is a certain insouciance about the Home Office's explanations as to why child defendants do not need Special Measures. As we have seen, video interviews and 'full-Pigot' hearings are intended not only to shield the witness from the defendant, but also to capture the child's fresh account in circumstances which reduce to the greatest extent possible the intimidatory nature of the formal court proceedings. Testifying through the video-link might be helpful if a child defendant is potentially subject to intimidation by co-defendants or prosecution supporters in the public gallery, or apprehensive about testifying directly in front of the court. *S v Waltham Forest Youth Court*[475] exemplifies why such protection may be imperative in a given case. S, a 13-year-old girl with serious learning difficulties and described as a vulnerable child by an educational psychology service, was charged with two counts of robbery along with three other girls aged between 14 and 16. S wanted to testify in her own defence, but said she was too frightened to do so in the physical presence of her co-defendants because they had threatened her and her mother. When her counsel's application for her to use the live link was denied because she was deemed ineligible for an SMD, she chose not to testify. Moreover, there is no reason why vulnerable defendants should not benefit from communication aids or an intermediary, as they too might not be able to understand questions from counsel or the trial judge.

Lord Justice Auld in his comprehensive review of the court system in 2001 noted that there is 'a striking difference' between the care for children as witnesses in the YJCEA 1999 and 'a lack of any corresponding provision for them when they are accused of grave crimes in the Crown Court, a disparity that concerns many judges'.[476] Moreover there is evidence that the exclusion of child defendants from the Special Measures regime has distorted its application for other child witnesses. An empirical study commissioned by the Home Office has pointed out that the police and the CPS have withheld Special Measures from child witnesses where the defendant is also a child because of human rights concerns of parity of treatment. For this reason, and also because the discrimination is unfair, the authors urged that all the provisions available to vulnerable witnesses should be extended to vulnerable defendants.[477]

Article 6 affords accused children the right to participate effectively in their trial. The European Court held in *T & V v UK* that courtroom procedures in jury trials must be modified to make them less intimidating for child defendants.[478] In response the Lord Chief Justice issued a new Practice Direction[479] dealing with such procedural matters as removal of wigs and gowns, seating the child defendant with his family or others in a like relationship, and explanations of the trial process in child-appropriate

---

[474] Evidence Act (Northern Territory) s 21B (by necessary implication as only the prosecution can apply for pre-recorded evidence).

[475] *S v Waltham Forest Youth Court* [2004] EWHC 715 (Admin).

[476] Auld *Review of the Criminal Courts* (n 217) [126].

[477] Burton *et al Evidence from the Criminal Justice Agencies* (n 203) 69.

[478] *T & V v UK* (1999) 30 EHRR 121 (ECtHR).

[479] *Practice Direction: Trial of Children and Young Persons in the Crown Court* [2000] 2 All ER 285.

language. The 'overriding principle' in the 2004 version is that the trial process should not itself expose a young defendant to avoidable intimidation, humiliation, or distress, and that in high-profile cases the police must try to ensure that the young defendant is not exposed to intimidation, vilification, or abuse when attending court.[480] Neither Practice Direction says anything about the child's testimony; all that is said is that all possible steps should be taken to assist the young defendant to understand and participate in the proceedings, and that any discretionary procedural matter must be decided having regard to this principle.[481]

Article 6(3)(d) guarantees the accused the right to have defence witnesses examined '*under the same conditions as witnesses against him*'. Article 40(iv) of the United Nations Convention on the Rights of the Child 1989 contains a parallel guarantee.[482] While on a strict reading this might not apply to the defendant *qua* witness, the rights under the ECHR and the HRA 1999 are to be read generously using the canons of interpretation applicable to international human rights instruments, to fulfil their object of giving individuals 'the full measure of the fundamental rights and freedoms guaranteed'.[483] The principle of equality of treatment between prosecution and defence has evolved to reflect 'the increased sensitivity of the public to the fair administration of justice'.[484] The European Court has already suggested that equality of arms applies to the presentation of each party's *own* evidence, which must not place him at a substantial disadvantage vis-à-vis his opponent.[485]

A 2004 judgment from the ECtHR is forcing the UK government to reconsider its position on withholding Special Measures from child and other vulnerable defendants. In *SC v UK*,[486] an 11-year-old boy with severe learning difficulties and the cognitive abilities of a six- to eight-year-old was charged with attempted robbery of an elderly woman, to which he pleaded that he had acted under duress by a 14-year-old boy. Because of his criminal record his case was transferred to the Crown Court, where the court dismissed an application to stay the trial as an abuse of process because of the boy's low attention span and educational age. The boy was taken into care before the trial. After a one-day jury trial he was convicted. The boy testified in his own defence about the alleged duress, apparently in the normal manner. At his trial the boy was allowed to sit outside the dock with his social worker, who later stated that despite his efforts to explain the situation to SC, he did not comprehend the situation he was in. He also did not grasp that he risked a custodial sentence, and even after a detention sentence had been passed he thought he would be able to go home with

---

[480] Consolidated Criminal Practice Direction 2004 Part IV.39 Trial of Children and Young Persons.

[481] ibid s IV.39.16.

[482] The ECtHR has given considerable weight to the UN Convention in considering children's claims under the ECHR: *A v UK* (1998) FLR 959, 27 EHRR 611 (ECtHR) [22]; *Costello-Roberts v UK* [1993] ECHR 13134/87, 19 EHRR 112 (ECtHR) [27]; *V v UK* [1999] ECHR 24888/94 (ECtHR) [46].

[483] *Minister for Home Affairs v Fisher* [1979] 3 All ER 21 (PC); K Starmer *European Human Rights Law* (Legal Action Group, London 1999) [1.25]–[1.28].

[484] *Borgers v Belgium* (1981) 15 EHRR 92 (ECtHR) [24].

[485] *Dombo Beheer BV v Netherlands* (1993) 18 EHRR 213 (ECtHR) [32]–[33].

[486] *SC v UK* [2004] ECHR 263, [2005] FCR 347 (ECtHR).

his foster father.[487] The ECtHR held that the attribution of criminal responsibility to an 11-year-old child does not in itself give rise to a breach of the Convention, as long as he is able to participate effectively in the trial.[488] This means that he should be able to understand the general thrust of what is said in court, if necessary with the assistance of an interpreter, lawyer, social worker, or friend; this SC could not do.[489] Although efforts had been made to make the Crown Court more informal and less intimidating, where a defendant risks not being able to participate effectively because of his young age and limited intellectual capacity and it is decided that criminal proceedings should be instituted rather than some other form of intervention, it is essential that he be tried in a specialist tribunal which is able to give full consideration to and make proper allowance for the handicaps under which he labours, and adapt its procedure accordingly. Just because a child is found fit to stand trial does not mean that he is capable of participating effectively in his trial. Therefore the UK had breached SC's right to a fair trial.[490] The latest draft guidance for intermediaries indicates that it may be appropriate to consider use of an intermediary for defendants with communication needs in light of *SC v UK*, and suggests that defence solicitors should contact the Office for Criminal Justice Reform to discuss this.[491]

SC v UK was considered by the Divisional Court in 2005 where a 15-year-old with the IQ of an eight-year-old faced charges of robbery and attempted robbery in the youth court.[492] An application for a stay as an abuse of process was rejected because the child was being tried in a specialist court as required by *SC v UK*. The trial could be run keeping his level of cognitive functioning in mind, for example by using concise and simple language, being proactive in ensuring he had access to support, and ensuring that cross-examination was carefully controlled so that questions were short and clear and frustration was minimized.[493] One cannot help but think that Special Measures such as an intermediary might have helped this child defendant.

(f) The challenge to Special Measures Directions under the Human Rights Act 1998

The European Court has repeatedly upheld the principle, which is the bedrock of the English trial model, that Article 6 requires that all evidence be produced in the presence of the accused at a public hearing with a view to adversarial argument,[494] as an essential facet of the principle of equality of arms.[495] However, Article 6(3)(d) does not stipulate *when* or *how* a witness is to be available for examination by the defence, and so considerable leeway is afforded States Parties in establishing their criminal and civil procedures for the taking of evidence.

It was the stark disparity in protection between child defendants and child prosecution witnesses in the Youth Courts which triggered the first challenge to SMDs under the HRA 1998. Frequently all of the primary witnesses are children, but only

---

[487] ibid [33]. [488] ibid [27]. [489] ibid [29], [34]. [490] ibid [34]–[35].
[491] *Intermediary Procedural Guidance Manual* (n 442) [1.12].
[492] *R (on the Application of P) v West London Youth Court* [2005] EWHC 2583 (Admin), [2006] 1 All ER 477 (QB DC). [493] ibid [26].
[494] *Kostovski v Netherlands* (1989) 12 EHRR 434 (ECtHR) [41]; *Asch v Austria* [1991] ECHR 123 98/86 (ECtHR) [27]. [495] *Vidal v Belgium* [1992] ECHR 123251/86 (ECtHR) [33].

the child defendant is required to testify in court. Matters came to a head in a cluster of cases from the Youth Courts involving defendants all aged 16 or under and charged with robbery or assault. These gave rise to a question certified by the Divisional Court for the House of Lords: does s 21(5) of the YJCEA 1999 comply with ECHR Article 6 in so far as it prevents 'individualised consideration of the necessity for a special measures direction at the stage at which the direction is made'?

The question was targeted at the primary rule created by s 21(3) and (5). The primary rule had forced the Youth Courts into disarray. Of the six cases which generated the certified question, in two the district judges refused to give an SMD for a live link for prosecution witnesses, and in the third refused to admit the complainant's video interview. In another three cases, the justices ordered SMDs over the objections of the defence, on the basis of advice from their law clerks that they had no discretion. Rose LJ in consolidated appeals held that SMDs for prosecution witnesses do not breach Article 6.[496] On appeal to the House of Lords, counsel for the child defendants attacked the statutory rules on three bases. First, because the court's power to disapply the primary rule in the interests of justice granted under ss 20(2) and 24(3) can only be invoked after the SMD has been made, the absence of any judicial power to disapply the primary rule if there is a risk of injustice apparent at the outset breaches Article 6. Second, in an argument reminiscent of American authority, it was contended that Article 6(3)(d) confers on the defendant the right to confront his accusers directly; whilst the defence conceded that this right must yield in a given case if the prosecution shows that a child witness could not testify satisfactorily in the courtroom, s 21(5) excludes any individualized consideration of this nature. Third, the primary rule was attacked as creating an inequality of arms because ss 17(1) and 19(1)(a) expressly exclude child defendants from access to SMDs.

The House of Lords confirmed that SMDs, and in particular the primary rule, comply with Article 6 of the ECHR. On the first argument, while Parliament has prescribed that the norm for child witnesses 'in need of special protection' is that they give their evidence-in-chief by means of the video interview (if there is one), the court has discretion to exclude all or part of it in a preliminary hearing 'in the interests of justice' in 'all the circumstances of the case' under s 27(2). The absence of a comparable discretion to preclude cross-examination by live link is not surprising since the witness still can be seen and heard.[497] The statutory presumption that there is nothing intrinsically unfair in children giving their evidence in this way does not breach Article 6. The object of requiring a change in circumstances before a party can apply to discharge or vary an SMD is simply to avoid repeated attempts to revisit the issue. It would be irrational for the court to order an SMD and then immediately to vary or discharge it in the interests of justice.[498] The Law Lords concluded that the

---

[496] *R (on the application of D) v Camberwell Green Youth Court* [2003] EWHC 227, [2003] 2 Cr App R 16 (QB DC). In another case which was not under appeal, Eady J held that the court had no inherent jurisdiction to allow a defendant to give evidence by live link [*S v Waltham Forest Youth Court* (n 475) [86]].   [497] *R v Camberwell Green Youth Court ex p D* (n 225) [26].
[498] ibid [7], [33].

judge or magistrates trying the case are not prevented from taking whatever action is needed to secure a fair trial on the day.[499]

The second argument was also rejected, as there is no guaranteed right of face-to-face confrontation at English common law or under Article 6(3)(d) comparable to the American Sixth Amendment. The requirements of the ECHR are satisfied if the defence has an adequate and proper opportunity to challenge and question the witness,[500] either at the time the witness was making a statement or at some later stage of the proceedings.[501] Baroness Hale pointed out that the merit of the primary rule is that it can carry no implicit disparagement of the accused because it is the norm for all child witnesses.[502] It is however disappointing that Lord Rodger repeated the unverifiable criticism that SMDs can 'make it much easier for the dishonest witnesses to give their untruthful accounts in the most complete and coherent way of which they are capable', making the jury's task of assessing credibility even more difficult;[503] as Baroness Hale observed, the live link often makes witnesses visible at closer range than in many courtrooms,[504] which should make it easier to observe their demeanour.

Regarding the exclusion of child defendants from SMDs, the House of Lords held that a provision that is designed to allow truthful witnesses for both sides to give their evidence to the best of their ability cannot make a trial unfair simply because there is no corresponding provision designed to allow a truthful defendant to give his evidence to the best of his ability.[505] Baroness Hale trenchantly remarked that the fact that the accused may need assistance to give his best evidence cannot justify excluding the best evidence of others.[506] However the YJCEA 1999 does not affect any power of the court, in exercise of its inherent jurisdiction to ensure a fair trial, to make an order analogous to an SMD in a particular case in favour of a child defendant whose ability to give evidence satisfactorily might otherwise be impaired.[507]

It is submitted that, given the premise in s 19 that SMDs are likely to improve the quality of testimony from eligible vulnerable witnesses, it is not self-evident that a vulnerable defendant should not be equally entitled to special measures to facilitate her testimony. One may hope that the *dicta* of Lord Rodger and Baroness Hale will encourage the lower courts to take measures on a case-by-case basis to enable child defendants to give the best evidence of which they are capable in their own defence.

The firm and unanimous endorsement of SMDs for child and other vulnerable witnesses as being compatible in principle with Article 6 of the ECHR and consistent with the jurisprudence of the ECtHR had been predicted,[508] and should finally lay such arguments to rest. The House of Lords also quashed the argument that Article 6 requires the prosecution to prove in every case that the child's evidence would be adversely affected if she were required to testify in the normal way.[509] As we noted

---

[499] ibid [33], [45]–[46].   [500] ibid [12]–[15], [49]–[53].

[501] See also *Luca v Italy* (2003) 36 EHRR 46 (ECtHR).

[502] *R v Camberwell Green Youth Court* (n 225) [39].   [503] ibid [6].   [504] ibid [26].

[505] ibid [16], [57].   [506] ibid [63].

[507] ibid ([54]–[63] Baroness Hale, quoting from Hoyano 'Striking a Balance (n 124), 968), [17] (Lord Rodger, interpreting s 19(6)).   [508] Hoyano ibid.

[509] *R v Camberwell Green Youth Court ex parte D* (n 225) Hoyano (n 182) ibid.

earlier, the contention arose very late in the life of the 'half-Pigot' provisions in the CJA 1988 in *R (on the application of the DPP) v Redbridge Youth Court*.[510] It is a relief that the spectre of 'harm hearings' required by American constitutional law for every trial involving a child witness[511] raised by *Redbridge* has now been interred for all time.

We turn briefly to the compliance of other Special Measures with Article 6.[512] As the video interview as examination-in-chief has already been blessed by the House of Lords, it is very unlikely that pre-trial videotaped cross-examination will fall foul of Article 6. The Council of Europe recommended that vulnerable witnesses in intra-familial criminal proceedings should whenever possible be examined before a judicial authority at the earliest stage after the manner was reported, with their pre-trial evidence, including cross-examination, videotaped to avoid face-to-face confrontation and unnecessary repetitive examinations that might cause trauma.[513] Arguments that a fair trial requires direct confrontation with a child or vulnerable adult witness in a 'one shot' trial are likely be treated sceptically both in England and in Strasbourg. Videotaped cross-examination before trial in principle should comply with Article 6, as the proceedings will be controlled by the trial judge with full participation of the defence ensured as the defendant will be able to see and hear the examination and communicate with his legal representative.[514]

The use of intermediaries to act as an interface between counsel and the witness is not as alien a concept in inquisitorial systems as it is in the common law courts. Jurisprudence from the European Commission of Human Rights[515] suggests that requiring the defence to use an independent and disinterested intermediary to question a vulnerable witness may not contravene the right to examine prosecution witnesses guaranteed by Article 6(3)(d),[516] provided that the demeanour of the witnesses under questioning may be directly observed by the court. Similarly there should be no problems with the use of screens in court,[517] or closing the court to the public.[518]

The one circumstance contemplated by the YJCEA 1999 that may breach Article 6 is the possible denial of the right of cross-examination. Section 27(4) provides that if after an SMD has been granted it appears that the child will not be available for

---

[510] *R (on the application of the DPP) v Redbridge Youth Court*, discussed above, section B.1(b)(iii). This view had been reiterated under the YJCEA 1999 (England) in *R (on the application of H) v Thames Youth Court* [2002] EWHC 2046 [11].   [511] *Coy v Iowa* (n 358).

[512] For a detailed analysis see Hoyano 'Striking a Balance' (n 124).

[513] Council of Europe *Recommendation No. R(97)13* (n 143) [25], [27].

[514] YJCEA 1999 (England) s 28(2).

[515] *Baegen v Netherlands* (n 389); *Kremers v Netherlands* (n 389).

[516] This also suggests that the prohibition on cross-examination by the defendant in person of a 'protected witness' (defined as including a child witness or a witness who has given direct evidence by a video recording: YJCEA 1999 s 35) and of a complainant in proceedings for sexual offences [YJCEA 1999 s 34] in principle should not breach Article 6(3)(d). In *Croissant v Germany* [1992] ECHR 13611/88 [27], the ECtHR held that a statutory requirement that a defendant be assisted by counsel is not incompatible with Article 6(3)(c). Interestingly, the prohibition on cross-examination in person of a child witness, in place since 1991 [inserted in s 34A(1) of the CJA 1988], has never attracted the controversy stimulated by the 1999 proposal relating to adult sexual complainants.   [517] *X v UK* (n 248).

[518] *Hols v Netherlands* (n 251) [6]; *Riepan v Austria* [2000] ECHR 35115/97 (ECtHR).

cross-examination, and the parties have not agreed that there is no need for the witness to be available, the trial judge apparently is vested with the discretion to exclude the videotaped interview—not a duty, as under the CJA 1988 s 32A(3)(a). This appears to be an inclusionary discretion lying alongside the CJA 2003 s 116 admitting a hearsay statement if it is in the interests of justice where a witness is unavailable for the specified reasons of illness, death, fear, etc, which has already been held to comply with the HRA 1998.[519] The answer is not clear in the jurisprudence of the European Court, but the existence of strong independent corroborative evidence supporting the conviction is regarded as highly relevant.[520] The Supreme Court of Canada has permitted video interviews to be used in evidence when the child has refused to answer when questioned at trial.[521] It is possible that this situation could arise in an English court, and it will then fall to the trial judge to determine whether it is still possible for the defendant to have a fair trial.

4. Implementation of Special Measures Directions

The technological and training demands of the Special Measures have required that they be implemented in phased stages.[522] On 24 July 2002 six of the eight Special Measures were introduced in the Crown Court for child witnesses.[523] One of the exceptions, examination through an intermediary, has been piloted in 2006 in six Crown Court centres across England. The YJCEA 1999 s 28 providing for a mandatory video-recorded cross-examination and re-examination for children subject to the primary rule, has not been declared in force whilst the Home Office reviews the entire legislative framework, discussed further in the next section. In 2002 implementation in the Magistrates' and Youth Courts was initially restricted to the use of live links and video-recorded evidence-in-chief for child witnesses in need of special protection, but in 2004 was extended to screens, taking evidence in private and communication aids.[524]

The Home Office has commissioned three empirical studies to examine whether Special Measures Directions worked for vulnerable and intimidated witnesses ('VIWs' in the common parlance) over the initial period of implementation, considered from the perspective of the witnesses, the CPS and other criminal justice agencies.

---

[519] *R v Sellick* [2005] 2 Cr App R 15 (CA), citing *Luca v Italy* (n 501).

[520] Hoyano 'Striking a Balance' (n 124) 959–961, discussing *Finkensieper v Netherlands* (n 389); *Unterpertinger v Austria* (1991) 13 EHRR 175 (ECtHR) [31]–[32].

[521] *R v F(WJ)* [1999] 3 SCR 569 (SCC).

[522] The original schedule contemplated that all of the Special Measures would be available by autumn 2001 in the Crown Court and the Youth Court, with equipment to be installed in all magistrates' courts by spring 2003: *Speaking up for Justice* (n 161) 4–5, 9.

[523] The YJCEA 1999 (Commencement No 7) Order 2002 SI 2002 No.1739 (C 54); The Crown Court (Special Measures Directions and Directions Prohibiting Cross-examination) Rules 2002 SI 2002 No 1688 (L.5)

[524] The Magistrates' Courts (Special Measures Directions) Rules 2002 SI 2002 No 1687 (L4); Home Office Circular 58/2003, *The Implementation of 'Speaking up for Justice'*, Appendix 1, updated by Home Office Circulars 31/2004 and 38/2005.

The study conducted by Hamlyn, Phelps, Turtle and Sattar examined witness satisfaction, comparing national surveys of VIWs prior to the implementation of the new provisions (Phase 1), and after the new procedures had chance to bed down (Phase 2).[525] Child witnesses comprised 42 per cent of the second research sample; they tended to be more satisfied than adults with their experience of the criminal justice system (76 per cent satisfied overall compared to 64 per cent of witnesses aged 17 or over).[526] Because each of the six Special Measures was already available to child witnesses, either under the 1988/1991 statutory regime or through the inherent jurisdiction of the court, one might have expected little change in take-up, but this was not the case. The largest increases in the use of Special Measures were found in video-recorded evidence-in-chief (from 30 per cent to 42 per cent), video-link for giving evidence (almost doubling from 43 per cent to 83 per cent) and removal of wigs and gowns by council and judge (8 per cent to 15 per cent).[527] The support for videotaped examination-in-chief was very high with 91 per cent finding it helpful, the greatest benefits being not having to appear in court (43 per cent) and that it was easier to say things (22 per cent).[528] Child witnesses were much more confident that they were treated fairly and with respect (63 per cent compared with 55 per cent of adult witnesses).[529] Witnesses under 17 were also less likely than those in other age groups to say that they were upset with cross-examination by defence counsel, with only 35 per cent saying the experience had upset them 'a lot' compared to 48 per cent overall.[530] Child witnesses (32 per cent) were most upset by lawyers suggesting they were lying,[531] but this is unavoidable under the rules of the adversarial trial, as the defence must put its case to the complainant. It is noteworthy that video-recorded pre-trial cross-examination, had it been available, was also strongly supported (72 per cent), particularly amongst victims (77 per cent).[532] Interestingly, only four children (2 per cent) felt the need for an interpreter or intermediary.[533]

The fact that only 42 per cent of the children under 17 in the research sample were video-interviewed is perplexing given that this is now mandatory for children subject to the primary rule.[534] The 2006 companion study by Burton, Evans and Sanders evaluating the effectiveness of criminal justice agencies in implementing Special Measures was highly critical of the police and CPS. Prosecutors, counsel and judges shared the perception that police officers had little understanding of how Special Measures operate in practice.[535] The study concluded that CPS training had been 'minimal, and

---

[525] Hamlyn, Phelps, Turtle and Sattar (n 265). The Phase 1 survey took place between November 2000 and February 2001, and the Phase 2 survey took place between April and June 2003.

[526] ibid 95 Table 7.4.   [527] ibid xiii, 66, 70.   [528] ibid 66–67.   [529] ibid 101.

[530] ibid 53.

[531] ibid 54; Burton *et al Evidence from Criminal Justice Agencies* (n 203) 64; see also Plotnikoff and Woolfson *In Their Own Words* reporting that 23 out of 50 child witnesses were upset about being accused of lying by defence counsel. Australian researchers have reported the same finding: Eastwood and Patton (n 279) 59–62, 123; Cashmore and Trimboli (n 332) 49–50.

[532] Hamlyn et al *Surveys of VIWs* 67. This question appears to have been asked only in Phase 1.

[533] ibid 66.

[534] In Phase 2, 49 per cent of the sample of children and adults were witnesses for violence against the person cases, and 22 per cent for sexual offence cases [ibid 10].

[535] Burton *et al Evidence from Criminal Justice Agencies* (n 203) 42–43.

had minimal effect', even for supposedly specialist prosecutors, to the extent that one who was her area's designated 'VIW officer' did not understand what a VIW was.[536] The police were failing to identify children as being entitled to Special Measures who were victims of violent offences, or were eyewitnesses to sexual and violent offences against others (such as domestic violence), or were defence witnesses.[537] They also found it very surprising that the police decided to video-record only a minority of children, and concluded that the older the child, the less likely it was that a video interview would take place, perhaps because they were not perceived as vulnerable due to their physical appearance or life experiences.[538] This was the case even for younger children, when the defendant was also a child of a similar age to the victim witness, because of concerns about parity between the victim and defendant.[539]

CPS prosecutors themselves seemed to share these views, overlooking the mandatory nature of Special Measures for child witnesses in offences involving sex, violence or neglect; they sought orders for the video link in relatively few cases involving children.[540] This study endorsed to some extent our predictions about the practical difficulties that the complexity of the legislation created for hard-pressed police officers and prosecutors.[541] There was little agreement about whether the decision to make an application was the responsibility of the police or the CPS, and applications were cursorily prepared with inadequate background information.[542] Sharing of information between the police and the CPS and liaison was patchy and no strategy meetings had been held in any case in the sample.[543] The police and the CPS seemed unaware of their failure to correctly identify VIWs, in the absence of any adequate system for monitoring this.[544] Often witnesses were identified as being eligible only by the Witness Service. The CPS prosecutors rarely met VIWs, even when this could have helped the witness and the progress of the case.[545] When the CPS identified children as being vulnerable, they would arrange for the video link to be used at the trial, but would not refer them back to the police to be video-interviewed.[546] Applications for Special Measures were made at a late stage, in the case of screens routinely on the date the trial commenced.[547] Technical problems with video interviews could affect their intelligibility, but nonetheless these were regarded as the only option for presentation of children's examination-in-chief.[548] There was often a long gap between the video interview and the child's cross-examination in court.[549] The live link gave only a very partial view of the witness, making it difficult to observe the child's body language.[550]

It is significant, and dispiriting, that each of these problems was identified by the *Bristol Study* in respect of the 1988/1991 regime. Notwithstanding these problems, the police, CPS, judiciary, and Witness Service considered that the reforms had assisted VIWs significantly.[551]

---

[536] ibid 67, 68. The study noted that a national training programme for CPS staff had been undertaken after the research was completed.   [537] ibid 32–34.
[538] ibid 33.   [539] ibid 40, 52.   [540] ibid 52.
[541] Hoyano 'Variations on a Theme by Pigot' (n 124) 262–263; Burton *et al Evidence from Criminal Justice Agencies* (n 203) 55–56.   [542] Burton *et al* ibid 50, 51–52.
[543] ibid 68.   [544] ibid 37.   [545] ibid 43–44.   [546] ibid 33–34.
[547] ibid 52.   [548] ibid 54.   [549] ibid 48, 54; Plotnikoff and Woolfson *In Their Own Words*.
[550] Burton *et al Evidence from Criminal Justice Agencies* (n 203) 56.   [551] ibid 60–63.

The third empirical study by Cooper and Roberts completed in June 2005 analysed CPS monitoring data for a full calendar year between April 2003 and March 2004 from a database covering 76.5 per cent of CPS prosecutions across England and Wales.[552] Of the 6,064 witnesses identified by the CPS as vulnerable or intimidated, 74 per cent (4,508) were children—a marked contrast to the Hamlyn study showing that only 42 per cent of witnesses benefiting from the new regime were children.[553] Child abuse was involved in 1,615 cases, or 27 per cent of the overall sample.[554] Of the child witnesses considered for Special Measures, 59 per cent were alleged victims and 41 per cent were bystanders; the latter figure was interpreted as signalling a major advance over the 1988/1991 regime which, whilst not restricted to victims, was often interpreted as such by the police and CPS.[555] There was an almost equal gender split amongst child witnesses, in sharp contrast to strongly pro-female gender imbalance for adult witnesses.[556]

Cooper and Roberts reported that an application for at least one Special Measure was made in 87 per cent (3,930) of cases involving child witnesses.[557] Whilst this appears impressively high, it is important to remember that this means that in 578 cases children deemed eligible for Special Measures by statute did not receive them, for reasons that could not be gleaned from the CPS data. Bearing in mind that children testifying in cases involving sex, violence, kidnapping or neglect are designated as being in need of special protection and hence *entitled* to Special Measures, it is difficult to believe that 13 per cent of child witness cases over a 12-month period across the CPS involved other types of offences.

Of the 5,888 applications for Special Measures for children, 96 per cent were for live link, and 47 per cent were for video-recorded evidence-in-chief; applications for optional measures such as screens, a closed court, removal of wigs and gowns and communication aids were negligible.[558] This may reflect prosecutors' familiarity with the measures in use for more than a decade, or alternatively that the optional measures are not regarded as useful for child witnesses. However, it was not possible to ascertain the frequency with which video-recorded interviews are now routinely adduced in evidence under the primary rule.[559] Applications for live link or video-recorded examination-in-chief for children were refused by courts in only 1 per cent of cases, the highest rate of refusal being 6 per cent for screens. The researchers interpreted these data as confirming that the statutory presumptions applicable to child witnesses are being implemented faithfully, at least with regard to applications actually presented to the court.[560] One piece of CPS guidance was consistently breached, however: in

---

[552] The objective was to gather data for all CPS prosecutions in all 42 CPS Areas but the London Metropolitan and City Area and three provincial Areas produced implausibly low or nil returns: Cooper and Roberts, *Analysis of CPS Monitoring Data* (n 224) 1–2.

[553] This discrepancy might be attributable to a difference in methodology, as the Hamlyn researchers collected their samples from the Witness Service: Cooper and Roberts ibid 39–41, 169.

[554] ibid 53.   [555] ibid Table 2-B, 48–49.   [556] ibid *Data* 51.   [557] ibid 76, Table 3-B.
[558] ibid 80–81, Table 3-F, 110, Table 5-D.   [559] ibid 178.   [560] ibid 114, Table 5-H.

only 3 per cent of the sample did the CPS lawyer meet with the witness to discuss Special Measures before trial.[561] Such meetings have the potential to do much to make the witness less stressed about testifying and more satisfied with their experience of the criminal justice process.[562]

Significantly, the 3,694 cases involving child witnesses which proceeded to a final disposition (ie other than discontinuances, bind-overs and charges left on file) resulted in an overall conviction rate of 79 per cent, of which 57 per cent were guilty pleas.[563] In cases where a child witness was a victim the conviction rate held steady at 77 per cent of which 55 per cent were guilty pleas; the acquittal rate nonetheless remained higher than for adult vulnerable or intimidated victims.[564] Cases involving child victims for whom Special Measures orders were made resulted in convictions in 61 per cent of all of the child cases in the research sample (of which 39 per cent were guilty pleas), but in fact this is marginally less than the overall 64 per cent conviction rate for all of the cases involving children. However, the conviction rate after a trial was higher in cases involving Special Measures (22 per cent) than in the trial conviction rate for all child cases (18 per cent). Conversely, cases involving Special Measures resulted in a 23 per cent acquittal rate after trial,[565] which is less encouraging. It is difficult to identify precise causes underlying these figures, but it is highly likely that they reflect the specific evidence in each case.

These figures from 2003–2004 are comparable to a 1998 study by the CPS Inspectorate of 157 cases involving child witnesses tried under the 1988/1991 regime, which showed that guilty pleas in the Crown Court were substantially lower than the national average for all prosecutions (44.8 per cent and 70.1 per cent respectively). The conviction rate in the Crown Court for cases involving child witnesses was 63.2 per cent, 18 per cent lower than the national average.[566] This discrepancy may be an indication that evidentially weaker child abuse prosecutions are proceeding to trial, or are poorly prepared, or that juries still discount children's evidence unduly, or they are more cautious in such cases because of the stigma attached to convictions for child abuse; it is impossible to know.[567]

It should also be remembered that the phased implementation of the Special Measures at different rates in the Crown Court, the Magistrates' Court and Youth Courts has served to exacerbate the problems for criminal justice agencies created by the

[561] Home Office, Crown Prosecution Service and Association of Chiefs of Police *Early Special Measures Meetings between the Police and Crown Prosecution Service and Meetings between the Crown Prosecution Service and Vulnerable or Intimidated Witnesses: Practical Guidance* (2001) [43]–[63]; *Achieving Best Evidence* (n 48) [4.51]; Cooper & Roberts *Analysis of CPS Monitoring Data* (n 224) 4, 72–73, 175–176.

[562] In the Hamlyn study, 76 per cent of prosecution witnesses who had no contact with the prosecuting lawyer said they would like to have done so: Hamlyn *et al Surveys of VIWs* (n 265) 45.

[563] Cooper & Roberts *Analysis of CPS Monitoring Data* (n 224) 138, Table 5-N.

[564] ibid 140, Table 5-P.   [565] ibid 152, Table 5-Child.

[566] CPS Inspectorate *Report on in Cases Involving Child Witnesses* (n 173) [7.3]–[7.4].

[567] Cooper & Roberts *Analysis of CPS Monitoring Data* (n 224) 142–144, 157–164, 190–191.

labyrinthine complexity of the statutory provisions. This produced errors in identifying eligible witnesses and application rates,[568] and so affects the uptake statistics in the three empirical studies commissioned by the Home Office.

5. Pause for a rethink: the Home Office review

On 1 December 2004 Baroness Scotland, Minister of State for the Criminal Justice System and Law Reform, launched a Review of Child Evidence by the Office for Criminal Justice Reform, which was instigated by the Birch and Powell report on pre-trial cross examination.[569] The remit was to consider whether s 28 should be implemented, to review the performance of the Special Measures for child witnesses and other aspects of child evidence, and to consider measures for vulnerable defendants. The Minister indicated the review would be directed toward delivering the greater flexibility necessary to enable measures to be more tailored to the individual witness's needs.[570]

Publication of the Home Office's review of SMDs for child witnesses is overdue. Whilst its specific remit is to determine whether to implement s 28 providing for mandatory pre-trial videotaped cross-examination in primary rule cases, it is understood that one option under consideration is to permit greater flexibility to prosecutors in presenting a child's evidence, possibly by replacing the primary rule with statutory presumptions, as we have advocated here. The differences in protection of child witnesses dependent upon the class of offence should be removed, as well as the differential in age. In our view a child's firm wish to testify in the courtroom in the ordinary way, or with a screen, should be respected and should be overridden only in extraordinary circumstances. We also contend that whilst pre-trial video-recorded hearings for the whole of the child's testimony should not be mandatory, there are still cases in which it would be very useful, for example if a long delay to trial is anticipated for whatever reason, or if the child was very young or very distressed and in need of prompt and effective therapeutic intervention, or if a witness's welfare is at risk for some reason such as intimidation or a deteriorating illness. In short, pre-trial videotaping is advisable whenever there is a risk that 'no witness, no justice' might be the consequence of delay, and so we hope that that Special Measure will survive in some form.

6. Evaluation: can the adversarial trial provide justice for children?

The YJCEA 1999 has not given us 'full-Pigot' as originally conceived by the Pigot Committee, but rather a hybrid of mandatory and discretionary variations on their dominant theme, that the criminal justice system must be more cognizant of the special needs of child and vulnerable adult witnesses. The great merit of the YJCEA 1999 is the overt acknowledgement that the truth-seeking purpose of the criminal

---

[568] eg in 2003–2204 there were 130 applications for Special Measures on behalf of adult vulnerable and intimidated witnesses in the Magistrates' Courts and a further 71 applications in the Youth Court, when the only provision for them during the research period was in the Crown Court: Cooper & Roberts ibid 167, 180.

[569] Birch and Powell *Meeting the Challenges of Pigot* (n 262), discussed above, section 3(b)(v).

[570] *Hansard* House of Lords, 22 July 2004 Cols WS47-WS48.

trial can best be achieved by modifying the orthodox adversarial trial where its rigours impede that objective. The adversarial trial is no longer its own justification; it must adapt itself to the needs of the witnesses, and not vice versa. Fairness to witnesses can be accomplished without jeopardizing fairness to the accused. Contrary to the current rhetoric of British politicians about rebalancing the rights of victims and other witnesses *against* those of the accused,[571] protecting witnesses need not be at the expense of the defendant. It is not necessary to choose one over the other, as they are not in competition.[572]

Nevertheless it cannot be denied that it is impossible to make the criminal justice system stress-free for child witnesses; the very nature of abuse makes the experience of telling about it agonizing. Moira Rayner, a barrister and the founding Director of the Office of Children's Rights Commissioner for London, argues that the legal and procedural reforms to improve the quality of children's evidence 'mostly focus on the child as forensic object, but the strongest image is that of a piece of flotsam drawn along the floor of a formal, "procedurally fair" decision-making process that was not designed with their participation in mind'.[573] It must be possible to challenge children's testimony. The rules of advocacy legitimately require that defendants' version of events be put to them. But if the process inevitably will be stressful, it need not inevitably be abusive in and of itself.

There is cause for optimism that the chronically patchy provision of child witness support services in England and Wales[574] will be remedied by the Government initiative, *No Witness, No Justice*. By the end of 2005 Witness Care Units were set up in all 42 criminal justice areas in England and Wales staffed by the police and CPS with dedicated Witness Care Officers to provide a 'one-stop shop' for witnesses[575] to assess their needs and to provide ongoing practical and emotional support and information. The service is only available to prosecution witnesses, however, and there are few child witness support schemes which defence witnesses might be able to use. Whilst this initiative has the potential to be very beneficial, at present there is still no consistent provision of services to young witnesses even from these Units,[576] and policymakers would be wise to look at the operation of Western Australia's Child Witness Service

---

[571] eg Secretary of State for the Home Department, Lord Chancellor, Attorney General *Justice for All* (Cm 5563, July 2002) [0.22], [1.17]. [572] Jackson (n 254), 210.

[573] Rayner (n 144).

[574] Office for Criminal Justice Reform, Home Office *Inter-Agency Working Group on Witnesses: No Witness—No Justice: Towards a National Strategy for Witnesses*. (2003); Plotnikoff and Woolfson *In Their Own Words* (2004) 24–28 reported that while Witness Services are located in every court across the country, they are unable to provide the same level of service to young witnesses, and 14 of the 50 child witnesses in their sample had no contact before the trial date. Victim Support reported that in 2005–2006 they supported 28,189 young witnesses, comprising 8 per cent of the total number of witnesses supported. Hamlyn *et al Surveys of VIWs* (2004) 40–41 reported that only 6 per cent of VIWs recalled having contact with the Witness Service before going to court, and 11 per cent had no contact at any stage. On the importance of child witness support, see K Murray *Preparing Child Witnesses For Court: a Review of Literature and Research* (Scottish Office Home Department Central Research Unit, Edinburgh 1997).

[575] Avail Consulting Ltd for the CPS and ACPO *No Witness, No Justice (NWNJ) Pilot Evaluation Executive Summary* (29 October 2004). The National Witness Units were to be put in place nationwide by the end of 2005. [576] Personal communication from Joyce Plotnikoff June 2006.

which provides comprehensive services to children in the criminal justice system, as best practice which Witness Care Units should emulate.

The impact of the Special Measures in the YJCEA 1999 has been most notable for adult vulnerable and intimidated witnesses rather than child witnesses. This is not a sign of failure, because six of the eight Special Measures implemented thus far were already available to child witnesses either under the statutory 1988/1991 regime or, in respect of screens[577] and communication aids,[578] through the common law developed by trial courts exercising their inherent jurisdiction to control procedures in a particular case. The YJCEA 1999 put all of these measures on a statutory footing which, combined with the accompanying Guidance *Achieving Best Evidence*, should be conducive to more consistent practice in all of the criminal justice agencies.

We have seen that in many respects—routine joint investigative interviews, presumptive admission of videotaped interviews as examination-in-chief, use of live link or screens for testimony at trial—English Special Measures are well ahead of their Australian, Canadian, and American counterparts. However, the absence of 'full-Pigot'-style pre-trial testimony is a serious gap in the Special Measures available to child witnesses. Significantly, almost three-quarters of witnesses in the first phase of the Hamlyn study thought it would have been helpful to have been cross-examined on videotape before the trial,[579] an indication that, contrary to the official views of the CPS and the Home Office, expedited trials have not satisfied all of the needs of VIWs for an expedited exit from the criminal justice system. The experience abroad shows that videotaped testimony is both workable and can be highly advantageous, especially where young children are concerned, and English policy-makers could learn much from the Western Australian system.

It is impossible to know how SMDs have affected the outcome of child abuse cases, not least because there is no comparable database of outcomes in child abuse prosecutions before the YJCEA 1999 was implemented.[580] We have seen that the conviction rate in cases involving child witnesses stubbornly remains about 18 per cent below the national conviction rate for all prosecutions. We should not however conclude that because Special Measures have not yielded a harvest of increased convictions, they have failed child witnesses. What has not been capable of measurement thus far is the number of cases which proceeded only because an SMD was granted. The Hamlyn study reported that 33 per cent of witnesses in their sample said they would not have been willing or able to testify in the absence of a Special Measure, a figure rising to 44 per cent for sex offence victims, and

---

[577] *R v Smellie* (n 247); *Re X, Y, Z* (1990) 91 Cr App R 36 (CA).

[578] Hamlyn *et al Surveys of VIWs* (n 265) 69 reported that very occasionally communication aids were used to assist vulnerable witnesses in the first phase of their research before the statutory measure was implemented; there was no significant increase in uptake in the second phase.

[579] ibid 80; while the finding was reported in phase 1 of the study, the researchers seemed to extrapolate this finding to the witnesses in phase 2: xv.

[580] Cooper and Roberts *Analysis of CPS Monitoring Data* (n 224) 106–107.

those who testified without Special Measures wished that they had been afforded them.[581]

The Special Measures implemented thus far have not solved—nor perhaps could they solve—all of the problems with the predecessor 'half-Pigot' system identified at the beginning of this chapter. As we have seen, the Government built several serious traps for itself in the highly prescriptive legislation: the rigidity of the primary rule which can thwart children's preferences as to how they will give evidence; the mandatory application of the primary rule to child witnesses called by the defence; and the denial of Special Measures to child defendants. The Government should not be hesitant about embarking on further legislative reform, and soon.

Above all it is important to appreciate that changes in systems do not guarantee sensitive and fair treatment; human beings working within systems do. To quote again Moira Rayner:

Judges and magistrates work daily in a system that has only recently sought to adapt its end-of-the-line to improve the quality of children's evidence, to achieve that system's objectives, not what the child expects . . . Children should not seem to be 'special' witnesses any more than any other witness deprived of the confidence to speak. A child witness is now what the judges and lawyers focusing upon him once were. We have all had the experience. The way technology is used, questions are framed and answers understood depend [*sic*] on an understanding of the child's perspective. It is not reasonable to expect a child to turn their worldview into something we recognise. We need to walk around in their skin, and understand theirs. Anyone involved in an investigation in our justice system should do so from a values basis: that the child is entitled to be treated with respect for what she or he is now, not what he or she will become, as a participant in a process that started long before the child got near a court.[582]

---

[581] Hamlyn et al *Surveys of VIWs* (n 265) 78–79, Table 6.2, 112, 113.
[582] Rayner (n 144) 3.

9

Testing the Credibility of the Child Complainant

Child sexual abuse is widely regarded in all common law jurisdictions as being singularly difficult to prosecute because the case rests primarily or even entirely upon the shoulders of a single witness of fact, a child. The inevitably difficult task of evaluating a witness's credibility is exacerbated where she is young, awkward in expressing herself, and without the vocabulary to describe her experiences. As we noted earlier,[1] until very recently common law jurisdictions regarded children's evidence as inherently suspect, on the theory that children are more prone than adults to fantasize and to fabricate stories. In this chapter we examine several evidential doctrines which are used to test a witness's credibility. While they are not expressly devised for child witnesses, they take on a unique significance when used in that context.

---

[1] Discussed above, Chapter 6.

A. Corroboration Warnings

1. Corroboration warnings in English law

The suspicion of children's testimony was typically evinced in the common law by two rules of evidence: first, a statutory requirement that a conviction could not be founded on the unsworn testimony of a child which was not corroborated by other material evidence,[2] which could not be supplied by the unsworn evidence from another child;[3] and second, mandatory warnings to the jury about the dangers of convicting on the unsupported evidence of a child.

Common law doctrine holds that a conviction based on the evidence of a single witness is normally presumed to be safe and satisfactory. However, for certain categories of witnesses and offences, the trial judge was required to warn the jury that it would be dangerous to convict on the basis of the evidence of a single witness, without independent corroboration. Victims of child abuse were subjected to a double burden of suspicion, because the common law required that the warning be administered in all cases of alleged sexual offences and for all child witnesses.

The warning in respect of child witnesses was considered warranted by an assumption that children are more susceptible to the influence of third persons, and may allow their imagination to run away with them.[4] The justification for warning about the unreliability of the testimony of complainants of sexual assault was explained by Lord Justice Salmon in *R v Henry*:

What the judge has to do is to use clear and simple language that will without any doubt convey to the jury that in cases of alleged sexual offences it is really dangerous to convict on the evidence of the woman or girl alone. This is dangerous because human experience has shown that in these courts girls and women do sometimes tell an entirely false story which is very easy to fabricate but extremely difficult to refute. Such stories are fabricated for all sorts of reasons which I need not now enumerate, and sometimes for no reason at all.[5]

The purported reasons for the inherent unreliability of complaints of sexual assault were enumerated, and accepted without question, by the Criminal Law Revision Committee in its 11th Report: 'the complainant may have made a false accusation owing to sexual neurosis, jealousy, fantasy, spite or a girl's refusal to admit that she consented to an act of which she is now ashamed'.[6]

The conventional direction took the following form:

Experience has shown that people who say that sexual offences have been committed against them sometimes, for a variety of reasons, tell lies. Such false allegations are easy to make and

---

[2] First enacted in the Criminal Amendment Act 1885 (England) s 4, and re-enacted in s 38(1), repealed by the Criminal Justice Act 1988 (England) s 34(1). The complainant's distressed condition could constitute corroboration, showing the thinness of the materiality requirement in some cases: *R v Redpath* (1962) 49 Cr App R 319 (CA).   [3] *DPP v Hester* [1973] 1 AC 296 (HL).

[4] *R v Dossi* (1918) 13 Cr App R 158 (CA) 169.

[5] *R v Henry* (1969) 53 Cr App R 150 (CA), 153, accepted in *Kelleher v The Queen* (1974) 131 CLR 534 (Aus HC) 543, 553, 559.

[6] Criminal Law Revision Committee *Eleventh Report (1972) Evidence (General)* (Cmnd 4991) [186].

frequently very difficult to challenge, even by an entirely innocent person. So it is dangerous to convict on the evidence of the complainant alone unless it is corroborated, that is, independently confirmed, by other evidence.[7]

Deane J of the Australian High Court forcefully criticized this wording as inappropriate, noting that its first limb (the ease with which the allegation is made) is belied by the distress and even humiliation to which a complainant in a sexual case is commonly subjected, particularly where an assault within the family unit is involved; and the second limb (the difficulty of rebutting it) runs the risk of diverting the jury's attention from the proper working of the onus of proof.[8] Nevertheless, it was reversible error for an English trial judge to express any misgivings about the assumptions underpinning the direction.[9]

The determination of whether evidence could constitute corroboration[10] became entangled in extreme technicality,[11] making the decision whether to prosecute a case very difficult as the police and CPS would have to predict, for example, whether a young child would be found competent to take the oath, so that her testimony might be capable of corroborating that of other complainants. The consequence of the mandatory corroboration warning was that the police and (since 1985) the CPS were extremely reluctant to prosecute any case of child abuse which relied primarily or entirely upon the testimony of child witnesses.

The Criminal Justice Act 1988 (CJA 1988) s 34 abolished both the corroboration requirement for any conviction founded upon the unsworn evidence of a child, and the obligatory warning to the jury about the dangers of convicting the accused on the uncorroborated evidence of a child, 'where such a warning is required by reason only that the evidence is the evidence of a child'.[12]

These reforms left intact the mandatory warning for all cases of child sexual abuse. The only concession was to provide that the unsworn evidence of a child admitted under the Children and Young Persons Act 1933, s 38 could corroborate the evidence (sworn or unsworn) given by any other person.[13] In 1994, the recommendations of the Pigot Committee[14] and the Law Commission[15] were finally implemented, and the remaining mandatory warnings in respect of complainants of sexual offences (and accomplices) were abolished.[16] However, the trial judge still has residual discretion to administer a corroboration warning where she considers it warranted. The relevant considerations in exercising this discretion have become known as the *Makanjuola* guidelines:[17] the circumstances of the case; the issues raised; the content and quality

---

[7] *R v Chambers*, The Times, 6 May 1993 (CA).

[8] *Longman v The Queen* (1989) 168 CLR 79 (Aus HC) 94.   [9] *R v Chambers* (n 7).

[10] The requirements for what qualifies as corroborative evidence were propounded in *R v Baskerville* [1916] 2 KB 658 (HL) 667: (a) independent evidence which (b) implicates the accused by confirming in some material particular that: (i) the crime has been committed, and (ii) the crime was committed by the accused.   [11] eg *R v Izard* (1992) 157 JP 58 (CA).

[12] CJA 1988 (England) s 34(2).   [13] CJA 1988 (England) s 34(3).

[14] HH Judge Thomas Pigot QC (Chair) *Report of the Advisory Group on Video-Recorded Evidence* (HMSO, London 1989) (hereafter *Pigot Report* [5.25]–[5.31].

[15] Law Commission of England and Wales *Corroboration of Evidence in Criminal Trials* (Law Com 202 Cmnd 1620 1991) [2.20]–[2.23].   [16] Criminal Justice and Public Order Act 1994 (England) s 32.

[17] *R v Makanjuola, R v Easton* [1995] 3 All ER 730 (CA) 732–733.

of the witness's evidence; and, most significantly, whether there is an evidential basis for suggesting that the testimony of the witness might be unreliable which goes beyond her status as a complainant of a sexual offence, and beyond mere suggestion by cross-examining counsel. Examples given by Lord Taylor CJ where a strong warning might be advisable included where the witness is shown to have lied, to have made previous false complaints, or to bear the defendant some grudge. If the witness is shown to be unreliable, the trial judge may merely counsel caution. Any warning that is given need not follow the 'whole florid regime' prescribed by the common law; the Court of Appeal warned that attempts to reimpose the straitjacket of the old corroboration rules were strongly to be deprecated.[18] The Court indicated that it will not interfere with the exercise of the trial judge's discretion in deciding whether to give a warning, and its strength and terms, unless it is unreasonable in the *Wednesbury*[19] sense. Since the Crown does not have a right of appeal from alleged errors in the trial judge's directions to the jury, in practice this means that only refusals to give corroboration warnings are susceptible to appeal.[20]

One example where the Court of Appeal held that the trial judge had acted unreasonably in not considering giving a corroboration warning (although defence counsel had not sought it) is *R v Walker*,[21] where the child retracted her complaints of rape against her stepfather, and then withdrew her retraction, claiming that she was coerced into making it. The Judicial Studies Board has recommended that juries be told to take particular care with the evidence of a very young child, quite independently of the rules as to corroboration.[22]

Most other common law jurisdictions have also abolished the mandatory corroboration warning in respect of child witnesses and sexual offences.

2. Corroboration warnings in Australian law

Most Australian jurisdictions have enacted reforms such that a child's sworn or unsworn evidence need not be corroborated before a person can be convicted of an offence.[23] However, in South Australia the requirement lingers in respect of unsworn evidence,[24] making it very difficult to prosecute any case involving a child under the age of seven.[25]

---

[18] ibid 733.

[19] That is, that the decision was so unreasonable that no reasonable authority (or court) could ever have come to it: *Associated Provincial Picture Houses Ltd v Wednesbury Corp* [1948] 1 KB 223 (CA) 230.

[20] eg *R v L* [1999] Crim LR 489 (CA). J Hartshorne 'Corroboration and Care Warnings after *Makanjuola*' 2 Int'l J of Evidence & Proof 1, 9 notes that the consequence is that the corroboration warning has become a question of 'luck of the judge' rather than legal principle.

[21] *R v Walker* [1996] Crim LR 742 (CA).

[22] Judicial Studies Board Specimen Direction 22 *Evidence of Children* [3].

[23] Evidence Act 1995 (Commonwealth of Australia) s 164; Evidence Act 1958 (Victoria) s 23(2A); Evidence Act 1939 (Northern Territory) s 9C; Evidence Act 1899 (Qld) s 632; Evidence Act 1906 (Western Australia) s 106D; Evidence Act 2001 (Tasmania) s 164(1).

[24] Evidence Act 1929 (South Australia) s 12(A).

[25] Australian Law Reform Commission and the Human Rights and Equal Opportunity Commission *Seen and Heard: Priority for Children and the Legal Process* (Report 84 1997) (hereafter Aus LRC, *Seen and Heard)* n 173.

At common law the warning about the need for corroboration in cases of sexual offences against children based upon their testimony reached 'almost the reverence of a rule of law'.[26] All Australian States have removed the mandatory corroboration warning,[27] albeit in varying terminology which has given rise to interpretive difficulties.[28] The Australian High Court has interpreted such legislation as eliminating the requirement to warn of the general danger of acting on the uncorroborated evidence of alleged victims of sexual offences as a class, but not as preventing a warning where necessary to avoid a 'perceptible risk of a miscarriage of justice' in the circumstances of the case other than (albeit in conjunction with) the sexual character of the issues.[29]

Western Australia, Queensland, Tasmania, the Northern Territory, and Victoria all have legislation prohibiting judicial commentary suggesting that children are an unreliable class of witness.[30] In construing the Western Australia legislation, the High Court of Australia in *Longman v The Queen* stated that, in exercising discretion to comment on the evidence, judges should not convey a message to the jury that complainants of sexual offences, including children, are generally unreliable and untrustworthy as a class of witnesses. Rather, judges should encourage the jury to make their own evaluation of the evidence of the witness 'in light of common human experience'.[31]

Nevertheless, strong judicial warnings concerning the evidence of children continue to be standard practice in many Australian courts,[32] perhaps because failure to give a warning where an appellate court deems appropriate constitutes reversible error.[33] *Longman* itself indicated that delayed complaint calls for judicial comment, and delayed prosecution prejudicing the defence requires a clear warning of the dangers of convicting on uncorroborated evidence.[34]

Federal and New South Wales legislation permit judges to warn juries about evidence which 'may be unreliable', and indeed make it mandatory where one party requests that the jury be cautioned about accepting it.[35] The New South Wales Evidence Act goes further in permitting a trial judge in any case involving a child

---

[26] *Kelleher v The Queen* (n 5) 553 (Gibbs J) quoting *Hargan v The King* (1919) 27 CLR 13 (Aus HC) 24 (Isaacs J).

[27] Aus LRC, *Seen and Heard* [14.67]; Evidence Act 1995 (Commonwealth of Australia) s 164; Crimes Act 1900 (New South Wales) ss 164, 165A and 165B; Criminal Code Act 1899 (Queensland) s 632; Evidence Act 1929 (South Australia) s 12A [removed for sworn testimony only]; Evidence Act 2001 (Tasmania) s 164(4); Crimes Act 1958 (Victoria) s 62(3); Evidence Act 1906 (Western Australia) s 50.

[28] *R v Peter James Robinson* (1997) CA No 314 1997 (Queensland CA); *R v Pahiya* (1988) 49 SASR 272 (South Australia Supreme Ct).   [29] *Longman v The Queen* (n 8) 89.

[30] Criminal Code Act 1899 (Queensland) s 632; Evidence Act 1929 (South Australia) s 12a; Criminal Code (Tasmania) s 122D; Evidence Act 1939 (Northern Territory) s 9C; Evidence Act 1906 (Western Australia) s 106D; Evidence Act 1958 (Victoria) s 23(2A) (see also Crimes Act 1958 (Victoria) s 61 forbidding warnings about complainants in sexual cases being unreliable as a class).

[31] *Longman v The Queen* (n 8) 87.

[32] Aus LRC, *Seen and Heard* [14.70]. The South Australian Supreme Court described this as a 'rule of practice', apparently virtually mandatory in the case of an child of immature age, in that case a witness aged 13: *R v B and D* (1993) 66 A Crim R 192 (South Australia Supreme Ct) [13]–[14].

[33] *Longman v The Queen* (n 8).

[34] ibid 91 (Deane J disagreeing on this point 96–97); *Doggett v The Queen* [2001] HCA 46, 208 CLR 343 (Aus HC) 355–356.

[35] Evidence Act 1995 (Commonwealth of Australia) s 165; Evidence Act 1995 (New South Wales) s 165.

witness to 'warn or inform' the jury that the evidence of the particular child may be unreliable because of the child's age.[36] When a New South Wales judge decides to comment on a child's testimony, the warning must take the form that 'in all cases of serious crime it is customary for judges to stress that where there is only one witness asserting the commission of the crime, the evidence of that witness must be scrutinised with great care',[37] which the Australian Law Reform Commission has commended for its neutrality.[38] A good example where a corroboration warning was seen as appropriate by the Court of Appeal of Victoria is *R v NRC*,[39] where the court considered that the defence had been prevented from effectively cross-examining the alleged victim on inconsistencies in her videotaped statement by the child's age (five), and the contaminating influence of improper interviewing techniques in no less than 40 interviews.

3. Corroboration warnings in Canadian law

In 1975, the Canadian Parliament abrogated the requirement for corroboration for rape and forbade the trial judge from instructing the jury that it is unsafe to find the accused guilty in the absence of corroboration.[40] The statutory requirements for corroboration of a child's unsworn evidence by some other material evidence were repealed in 1987.[41] In 1992 the Supreme Court of Canada cautioned the lower courts against introducing through the back door a corroboration requirement by relying upon outmoded stereotypes about the inherent unreliability of children's testimony and so insisting on confirmatory evidence.[42] Instead, children's testimony must be judged with common sense, without demanding the same exacting standard of precision and detail as that expected of adults.[43] Abolition of the statutory mandatory corroboration warning in respect of child witnesses followed in 1993.[44] Trial judges are still free to administer cautions about the frailties of a particular child's testimony and to advise the jury to seek confirmatory evidence;[45] where there is conflicting evidence, the failure of a trial judge to give this warning in clear and sharp terms may constitute reversible error.[46] Nevertheless, intervention by an appellate court on this ground seems to be relatively rare.[47]

---

[36] Evidence Act 1995 (New South Wales) s 165B.

[37] *R v Murray* (1987) 39 A Crim R 315 (New South Wales CCA) 322.

[38] Aus LRC, *Seen and Heard*, recommendation 100.

[39] *R v NRC* [1999] 3 VR 537 (Victoria CA), [33]–[37].

[40] Criminal Law Amendment Act 1975 (Canada) s 8, now applicable to all sexual offences: Criminal Code of Canada s 274.

[41] An Act to Amend the Criminal Code of Canada and the Canada Evidence Act, SC 1987 c 24 s 15, repealing Criminal Code of Canada s 586, Canada Evidence Act s 16(2), Young Offenders Act s 61(2).

[42] *R v W(R)* [1992] 2 SCR 122 (SCC).   [43] ibid [26]; *R v B(G)* [1990] 2 SCR 30 (SCC) 54–55.

[44] Criminal Code of Canada s 659.

[45] *R v Marquard* [1993] 4 SCR 223; *R v E(AW)* [1993] 3 SCR 155.

[46] *R v McKenzie* (1996) 141 Sask R 221 (Saskatchewan CA).

[47] *R v Wismayer* (1997) 115 CCC (3d) 18 (Ontario CA); *R v K(V)* (1991) 68 CCC (3d) 18 (BC CA); *R v Stymiest* (1993) 79 CCC (3d) 408 (British Columbia CA).

4. Corroboration warnings in New Zealand law

A mandatory corroboration warning was abolished for all sexual cases in 1985,[48] but the legislation made it clear that comment on the absence of corroboration was not prohibited by stipulating that there was no particular form of words required should the judge decide to comment. The New Zealand Court of Appeal had held in 1968 that a formal corroboration warning was not mandatory as a matter of law or practice in all non-sexual cases featuring a child witness, while noting that it was almost invariable custom to advise juries to scrutinize with special care the evidence of young children.[49] The Court of Appeal in 1989 took judicial notice of recent psychological studies challenging assumptions about the unreliability of child witnesses, but nonetheless stated:

... we think ordinary human experience indicates that with younger children particularly, it still remains prudent for a Judge to give such advice to a jury and that this will be appropriate in all cases, whether sexual or not. However, this is essentially a counsel of prudence, not an inflexible rule, and in appropriate cases the trial Judge will make his own assessment and determine whether such a warning should be given.[50]

The Court of Appeal appears generally to give short shrift to complaints by defendants about the absence of corroboration warnings in respect of child witnesses.[51]

5. Corroboration warnings in American law

American jurisdictions do not seem to have made as heavy weather of corroboration as their counterparts in the Commonwealth. At common law, corroboration of the testimony of a complainant of a sex offence was not required.[52] In the 1970s and 1980s, most American courts and legislators, like their Commonwealth counterparts, moved to eliminate blanket corroboration requirements in respect of sexual offences. Now corroboration is generally required on a case-by-case basis to underpin a conviction only where the evidence of the complainant, whether child or adult, is inconsistent, contradicts admitted facts, or otherwise is clearly weak.[53] Even recantation may not be sufficient to create a 'cloud of doubt' so as to trigger a corroboration requirement, if on the entire record the child's inconsistencies are explicable.[54]

---

[48] Evidence Amendment Act (No 2) 1980 (New Zealand) s 3, inserting 23AB into the Evidence Act 1908 (New Zealand). [49] *R v Parker* [1968] NZLR 325 (New Zealand CA).
[50] *R v Accused (CA 298/88)* [1989] 2 NZLR 698 (New Zealand CA).
[51] eg *AG v B* [1992] 2 NZLR 351 (New Zealand HC); *R v Accused (CA 160/92)* [1993] 1 NZLR 385 (New Zealand CA).
[52] J Myers, *Evidence in Child Abuse and Neglect Cases* Vol 2, (3rd edn John Wiley & Sons, Inc., New York 1997) 66–67 §6.22; V Gulbis 'Modern Status of Rule regarding Necessity for Corroboration of Victim's Testimony in Prosecution for Sexual Offense' (1984 updated to October 2006) 31 American L Rev 4th 120.
[53] eg *State v Carver* 380 NW 2d 821 (Minnesota Ct App 1986); *State v Howell* 839 P 2d 87 (Montana Supreme Ct 1992); *Pennycuff v State* 727 NE 2d 723 (Indiana App 2000); *People v McLoud* 737 NYS 2d 216 (New York App Div 2002). [54] *State v Griggs* 999 SW 2d 235 (Missouri App 1998).

Nevertheless, corroboration warnings *per se* do not feature in these cases, probably because it is considered improper for American trial courts to review or comment on the weight of the evidence,[55] instead confining their directions to boilerplate instructions on the law. Instead, appellate cases concern whether the trial judge in sexual assault cases should have administered a 'cautionary instruction' advising the jury to examine the complainant's testimony with care because of the nature of the crime. Such directions often mimic the familiar 'easy to make/difficult to refute' formula.[56] In 1975 in *People v Rincon-Pineda*,[57] the California Supreme Court critically reviewed the genesis of the direction in the 17th century writings of Sir Matthew Hale, at a time when the rights of the defence were 'barely nascent'. The court took judicial notice of empirical evidence of low conviction rates for rape, and concluded that the mandatory instruction was 'a rule without a reason' since 'it does not in fact appear that the accused perpetrators of sex offenses in general and rape in particular are subject to capricious conviction by inflamed tribunals of justice'.[58] Therefore in California the instruction should no longer to be given mandatory application, nor should any discretionary direction deploy such outmoded wording. Instead, juries should be simply told: 'Testimony which you believe given by one witness is sufficient for the proof of any fact. However, before finding any fact to be proved solely by the testimony of such a single witness, you should carefully review all of the testimony upon which proof of such fact depends.' Notwithstanding the force of the criticism in *Rincon-Pineda*, in some States the cautionary direction remains mandatory, including for child complainants.[59] American prosecutors are advised to request the trial judge to instruct the jury in all cases that the uncorroborated testimony of a child is sufficient to convict the defendant if believed beyond a reasonable doubt, lest the jury, uninstructed, think otherwise.[60]

6. Evaluation: law and practice in conflict?

Corroboration is one of several areas in respect of child abuse where law reform has not necessarily penetrated practice. In interviews for the *Bristol Study*, some Child Protection Unit officers maintained that they were forbidden by statute from laying charges of child sexual abuse based solely upon the uncorroborated evidence of a child.[61] The *Bristol Study* found that some judges in cases in the research sample continue to administer corroboration warnings almost routinely in respect of child

---

[55] *State v Settle* 531 P 2d 151 (Arizona Supreme Ct 1975).

[56] K Jarnezis 'Propriety of, or Prejudicial Effect of Omitting or of Giving Instruction to Jury, in Prosecution for Rape or Other Sexual Offence, as to Ease of Making or Difficulty out of Defending against Such a Charge' (1979 updated to October 2006) 92 American LR 3d 866.

[57] *People v Rincon-Pineda* 538 P 2d 247 (California Supreme Ct 1975), overruling *People v Putnam* 129 P 2d 367 (California Supreme Ct 1942).   [58] *People v Rincon-Pineda* ibid 882.

[59] K Jarnezis (n 56).

[60] *Investigation and Prosecution of Child Abuse* (3rd edn National Center for Prosecution of Child Abuse, American Prosecutors Research Institute Sage Publications, Thousand Oaks, 2004) 437.

[61] Some authors in the field have shared this misconception, eg J LaFontaine *Child Sexual Abuse* (Polity Press, Cambridge 1990) 50, 219.

witnesses, with little attempt to seek a substantial evidential basis for so doing.[62] Without a Crown right of appeal,[63] this practice by some judges cannot be effectively challenged, and it influences the thinking of police officers and CPS lawyers, making them wary of prosecuting cases that rest entirely on the credibility of the child complainant.[64] The Australian Law Reform Commission also identified lingering judicial resistance to the abolition of corroboration warnings, even in those jurisdictions where warnings are expressly prohibited, and recorded concern that the warnings might be motivated by individual judges' prejudices and assumptions regarding the capacity of children to give reliable evidence.[65] The Commission recommended that judges in all Australian jurisdictions be prohibited from suggesting that children are an unreliable class of witness, and that a warning be permitted only where a party can show exceptional circumstances affecting the reliability of that particular child's evidence.[66]

In English courts, it is still common for defence counsel to submit to the jury that it is easy for a child to fabricate an allegation of sexual assault, and difficult for the defendant to refute it, along the lines of the now obsolete jury direction. The latter observation may initially have some intuitive force, but the burden of proof in criminal cases is expected to serve as a sufficient bulwark against wrongful convictions in sexual as in other types of offences involving a contest of credibility, such as fraud or narcotics offences, and the steep decline in the conviction rate for rape in English courts to 5.6 per cent[67] suggests that defendants are not unduly hampered in meeting allegations. At bottom the 'ease of fabrication' assertion amounts to a claim that complainants of sexual offences are presumptively entitled to less credence than those who testify as the alleged victims of other crimes.[68] It is even more difficult to square the 'easy to make' assertion with the distress and even psychological trauma which, it is now widely accepted, is a frequent consequence of the child's encounter with the criminal justice system, and which is often evident even in the comfort of the police interview suite. Because English criminal trial procedures always require the prosecution to address the jury first,[69] prosecuting counsel cannot counterbalance such a submission, rather than by anticipating it in her own speech.

The mythology which continues to envelop the evidence of children, particularly in relation to sexual acts, cannot detract from the simple and obvious fact that an allegation which is not corroborated is weaker than one which is. It is of critical

---

[62] Thus in Case 6A the trial judge directed the jury to seek corroboration because of the 11-year-old complainant's 'age and disabilities and behaviour', although there was no evidence of any mental disability which could affect the child's capacity to give accurate testimony other than a rudimentary arithmetic and spelling test which defence counsel took her through in cross-examination [*Bristol Study* 67].

[63] The CJA 2003 confers the right of appeal on the prosecution only from a ruling which terminates the trial short of a jury verdict.   [64] *Bristol Study* 66–7.

[65] Aus LRC, *Seen and Heard* [14.71].   [66] ibid [14.67]–[14.73], recommendation 100.

[67] L Kelly, J Lovett, L Regan *A Gap or a Chasm? Attrition in Reported Rape Cases* (Home Office Research Study 293, Feb 2005) ix, Figure 3.6, Appendix 1. The conviction rate for cases actually prosecuted in 2002 was 21% for adults, and 23% for children under 16: Figure 3.2.

[68] *People v Rincon-Pineda* (n 57) 877.

[69] Unlike in Canada, where the defence must make closing submissions first if the defence has called evidence [Criminal Code of Canada s 651].

importance therefore that investigators and prosecutors continue to search for cor-roboration. Evidence of opportunity should not be automatically discounted. The child's statement should be scrutinized for circumstantial details which can be con-firmed by other witnesses, such as timing and the environment in which the incidents were claimed to have taken place. In the absence of independent evidence, prosecutors can usefully emphasize the absence of any motivation to fabricate, lack of exaggera-tion and sophistication in the account, and persistence in an allegation throughout the often painful aftermath of disclosure (including any major disruption to the child's life), to reinforce a complainant's credibility.

B. Hearsay Evidence

Campaigners for law reform of child abuse prosecutions often identify hearsay as being the paradigm example of probative evidence which could bolster a child's credibility but which is routinely withheld from the trier of fact. Hearsay evidence is probably the single most difficult evidential concept for those involved in the criminal justice system to understand and apply. This is not surprising, because, as Lord Reid acknowledged, it is 'difficult to make any general statement about the law of hearsay which is entirely accurate', and 'in many cases there was no justification either in principle or logic' for the boundaries of the exceptions.[70] In this section, we begin by considering the common law doctrine of hearsay. We analyse the significant reforms of the English doctrine brought about by the Criminal Justice Act 2003 (CJA 2003), and compare them with bold reforms in other jurisdictions put in place not only by legislators but also, in the case of Canada, by the judiciary. We conclude that creating specific statutory exceptions to the hearsay rule for children's out-of-court statements about sexual or physical abuse is not justified, because such statements are not inherently more trustworthy than the statements of adults.

1. The common law hearsay rule defined

The rule against hearsay developed by the common law may be concisely formulated as follows: an assertion other than one made by a person while giving oral evidence in the proceedings is inadmissible as evidence of the truth of any fact asserted.[71] The doctrine is an adjunct of the 'principle of orality' cherished by the adversarial trial system, that all evidence must be tendered through witnesses giving *viva voce* evidence from their personal knowledge, before the trier of fact, in a 'one-shot' hearing.

An 'assertion' onto which the rule bites may be written, oral, or by conduct, as long as it is intended to communicate something. The hearsay doctrine applies both to statements by persons who become witnesses, and those who never appear at the

---

[70] *Myers v DPP* [1965] AC 1001 (HL) 1019, 1021.
[71] *R v Sharp* [1988] 1 WLR 7 (HL). For a comprehensive study of the hearsay rule, see A Choo *Hearsay and Confrontation in Criminal Trials* (Clarendon Press, Oxford 1996).

formal trial; both are often referred to in this context as 'declarants'. The common law doctrine encompasses a subsidiary rule that the previous assertions of a person who does testify are inadmissible as evidence of the facts stated (sometimes described as the 'rule against self-corroboration' or the 'rule against prior consistent statements'), as this is seen as impermissibly bolstering the credibility of that witness, as well as being superfluous. Where the declarant does not testify, the common law considers hearsay evidence to be dangerous primarily because of the absence of cross-examination to test its credibility and reliability. It is thought that without cross-examination, it is difficult to test the sincerity, as well as the powers of accurate observation, recall and narration, of both the original declarant and the witness relaying the evidence. These perceived hazards of course vary in degree according to the type of evidence and the capacities of the particular declarant and witness.

The hearsay ban applies to all parties to the proceedings. This was memorably illustrated by *R v Sparks*:[72] a statement by a three-year-old victim of a sexual assault to her mother identifying her assailant as a 'coloured boy' was ruled inadmissible when tendered on behalf of a white defendant.

An out-of-court statement may evade the hearsay ban if the party tendering the statement can identify a relevant purpose other than relying upon its contents as the truth. Evidence tendered for this limited purpose is often termed 'original evidence'. A statement is not hearsay if it is tendered:

(1) to establish the fact that the statement itself was made, which may be relevant to facts in issue such as:

　(a) the state of mind of the declarant sometime in the past,[73] such as a child's statement that he feared retribution to explain his delayed disclosure;

　(b) the state of mind of the person to whom the statement was made,[74] such as a threat to a child that the family will be broken up if she complains of abuse;

　(c) establishing a motive for the offence charged, for example a child's intention to complain to the authorities of sexual abuse, as a motive for killing the child;[75]

　(d) the credibility of the declarant, where inferences may be drawn from the demonstrable falsity of the contents of the statement, such as a concocted alibi of a suspect,[76] or where his lies may be probative as circumstantial evidence of a consciousness of guilt;[77]

(2) to rebut an accusation of 'recent fabrication', that is, concoction of a story after the alleged event, by tendering a previous statement made by the same witness consistent with her testimony;

---

[72] *R v Sparks* [1964] AC 964 (PC).
[73] *Ratten v The Queen* [1972] AC 378 (PC); compare *R v Newport* [1998] Crim LR 581.
[74] *Subramaniam v Public Prosecutor* [1956] 1 WLR 965 (PC).
[75] *Howse v The Queen* [2005] UKPC 30 (PC on appeal from New Zealand CA) [21], [38].
[76] *R v Mawaz Khan* [1967] 1 AC 454 (HL).
[77] *R v Lucas* (1981) 732 Cr App R 159 (CA); *R v Goodway* [1993] 4 All ER 894 (CA); *R v Harron* [1996] Crim LR 581 (CA).

(3) to prove that the complainant made a 'recent complaint' about a sexual assault so as to establish the alleged victim's consistency in telling her story (which we consider separately below);[78]

(4) to refresh the memory of a witness whilst testifying, from a note made contemporaneously with the event (such as a doctor's or police officer's notes);

(5) to prove a negative[79] (for example, to show that there is not a relevant entry in a record, so the prosecution might tender hospital records to prove that parents did not seek medical attention for an injured child as they claimed); or

(6) where the information is recorded by mechanical means without the intervention of the human mind (for example, a security camera recording a child abduction, or a database of child pornography showing that the defendant had accessed the web page).[80]

Therefore, the key to admissibility of out-of-court statements is to identify the objective for which it is tendered. If the court can be persuaded that the statement is relevant for non-hearsay purposes, then it is admitted in evidence and the trier of fact must be directed to use it only for that purpose (although of course there is no way of ensuring that the jurors restrict themselves as instructed, and do not rely upon it as truth).

The hearsay rule is qualified by an immensely complicated web of common law and statutory exceptions. Diagrams 12 and 13 depict those exceptions where the out-of-court statement is made by a non-witness and by a witness respectively.

These exceptions were developed on a piecemeal basis without any clearly artic-ulated overarching principle. However, evidence scholars have attempted to apply *post hoc* rationalizations identifying circumstantial guarantees of trustworthiness: the necessity of calling hearsay as the only evidence available, and its reliability. We shall only give an overview of the exceptions of particular relevance to child abuse cases, to explain the constraints under which investigators, decision-makers and advo-cates have operated in common law systems, and to set the stage for discussion of statutory and judicial reform. It is essential to bear in mind in this discussion that to qualify as a true exception, the statement must be tendered 'testimonially', that is, reliance is placed on the truth of what is stated; otherwise, the hearsay rule is not engaged at all. The two primary common law exceptions of particu-lar interest in the context of child abuse cases are admissions against interest and *res gestae*.

Admissions against interest are statements by persons which are contrary to their self-interest, the most frequent example being an inculpatory statement by a suspect. An alleged victim's retraction of a complaint might become admissible as evidence of the falsity of the original allegation under this exception. The most commonly cited rationale for admissibility is that a person will not make an admission against

---

[78] Section C. The common law recent complaint doctrine applied to sexual offences only, but this was made applicable to all offences by the Criminal Justice Act 2003 (England) (hereafter CJA 2003) s 120(7).

[79] *R v Shone* (1983) 76 Cr App R 72 (CA).

[80] *R (on the application of O'Shea) v Coventry Magistrates Court* [2004] EWHC 905 (DC).

Diagram 12. The Admissibility of Out-of-Court Statements Made by a Non-Witness Before the Criminal Justice Act 2003

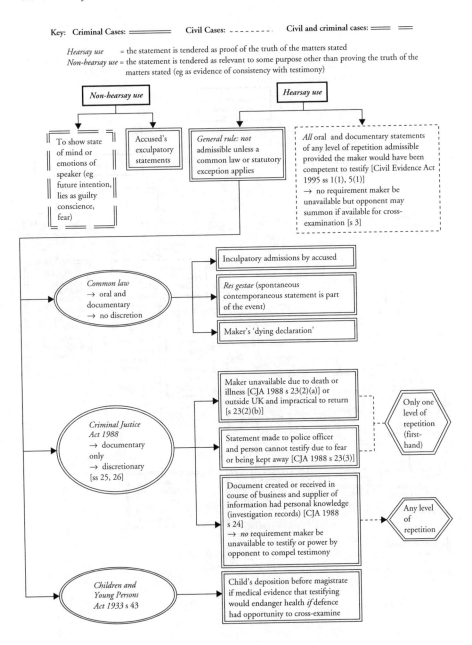

Key: Criminal Cases: ═══════ Civil Cases: ─ ─ ─ ─ ─ · Civil and criminal cases: ══ ══

Hearsay use = the statement is tendered as proof of the truth of the matters stated
Non-hearsay use = the statement is tendered as relevant to some purpose other than proving the truth of the matters stated (eg as evidence of consistency with testimony)

Non-hearsay use

To show state of mind or emotions of speaker (eg future intention, lies as guilty conscience, fear)

Accused's exculpatory statements

Hearsay use

General rule: not admissible unless a common law or statutory exception applies

All oral and documentary statements of any level of repetition admissible provided the maker would have been competent to testify [Civil Evidence Act 1995 ss 1(1), 5(1)]
→ no requirement maker be unavailable but opponent may summon if available for cross-examination [s 3]

Common law
→ oral and documentary
→ no discretion

Inculpatory admissions by accused

Res gestae (spontaneous contemporaneous statement is part of the event)

Maker's 'dying declaration'

Criminal Justice Act 1988
→ documentary only
→ discretionary [ss 25, 26]

Maker unavailable due to death or illness [CJA 1988 s 23(2)(a)] or outside UK and impractical to return [s 23(2)(b)]

Statement made to police officer and person cannot testify due to fear or being kept away [CJA 1988 s 23(3)]

Only one level of repetition (first-hand)

Document created or received in course of business and supplier of information had personal knowledge (investigation records) [CJA 1988 s 24]
→ *no* requirement maker be unavailable to testify or power by opponent to compel testimony

Any level of repetition

Children and Young Persons Act 1933 s 43

Child's deposition before magistrate if medical evidence that testifying would endanger health *if* defence had opportunity to cross-examine

Diagram 13. The Admissibility of Out-of-Court Statements Made by a Witness Before the Criminal Justice Act 2003 Reforms

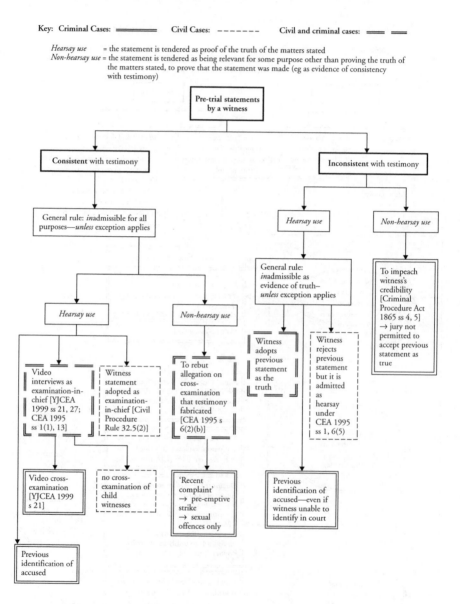

Key: Criminal Cases: ════════   Civil Cases: ───────   Civil and criminal cases: ══ ══

Hearsay use   = the statement is tendered as proof of the truth of the matters stated
Non-hearsay use = the statement is tendered as being relevant for some purpose other than proving the truth of the matters stated, to prove that the statement was made (eg as evidence of consistency with testimony)

his own interests unless it is true; it does not lie in that person's mouth to complain of the unreliability of his own statements.[81] This rationale has been greatly undermined in recent years as the courts have acknowledged that an innocent suspect may be induced to confess for multifarious reasons.[82] Child protection officers are familiar with complainants retracting allegations of sexual assault, because they have been pressured to do so, or they do not want to face the ordeal of an adversarial trial. Another rationale for this exception is that the customary frailties of hearsay are not present, as a party can hardly object that he had no opportunity to cross-examine himself or that he is only worthy of credence when speaking under sanction of an oath.[83]

Res gestae applies to statements made in the course of an event which have explanatory force.[84] In *Teper*,[85] Lord Normand pointed out that *res gestae* rests on two propositions: human utterance is both a fact and a means of communication; and human action may be so interwoven with words that the significance of the action cannot be understood without the correlative words, and the dissociation of the words from the action would impede the discovery of truth. The basic thesis is that *res gestae* admits declarations which form part of the fact or act, that is, statements which either accompany and explain a fact in issue, or are relevant to a fact in issue. The statements thus must form part of the story (hence the Latin tag) and not be a mere narration of past facts. While this topic is bedevilled by classification issues and convoluted caselaw, it is generally accepted that there are four classes of statements which may be admissible under the *res gestae* doctrine.

(a) Spontaneous statements or excited utterances

Statements made in the heat of the moment are at the core of the *res gestae* doctrine. The modern test for this category is that hearsay evidence may be admitted if the statement is made in such conditions of approximate but not exact contemporaneity, and of involvement or pressure, as to exclude the possibility of concoction or distortion to the advantage of the maker or the disadvantage of the accused.[86] The circumstantial guarantee of trustworthiness is thought to be supplied by the requirement that the event must be so unusual or startling or dramatic as to dominate the thoughts of the person making the statement and to give him no real opportunity for reasoned reflection (that is, concoction); this means that the event must still be 'operative'.[87] Any concerns about accuracy in the reporting of the words spoken should be treated as a matter of weight rather

---

[81] *R v Dipietro* (1994) 13 Alta LR (2d) 1 (Alberta CA).

[82] See, eg R Pattenden 'Should Confessions be Corroborated?' (1991) 107 LQR 317; JUSTICE *Unreliable Evidence? Confessions and the Safety of Convictions* (London 1994).

[83] E Morgan *Basic Problems of Evidence* (Joint Committee on Continuing Legal Education of the American Law Institute and the American Bar Association, Philadelphia 1963) 265–266; E Morgan 'Hearsay Dangers and the Application of the Hearsay Concept' (1948) 62 Harvard L Rev 177.

[84] While there was some confusion in the past as to whether *res gestae* encompassed both hearsay and original evidence [eg Gooderson [1957] CLJ 56], the prevailing view is that *res gestae* is firmly ensconced as an exception to the hearsay rule [*Ratten v The Queen* (n 73); *R v Andrews* [1987] AC 281 (HL)].

[85] *Teper v The Queen* [1952] AC 480 (PC)   [86] *Ratten v The Queen* (n 73).

[87] *R v Andrews* (n 84).

than admissibility.[88] It is debatable whether spontaneity and contemporaneity provide sufficient guarantees of reliability. *Res gestae* is grounded upon a dubious hypothesis that the declarant is both capable of accurately observing startling events as they unfold, which is empirically suspect,[89] and not sufficiently quick-witted to be tempted to invent a narrative. Another difficulty arises in identifying when an event begins and ends, as it is necessary to identify whether the statement was part of the event, in which case it may be admissible, or whether it is merely a narrative of the event, in which case it is not *res gestae*. Trial judges have been driven to devise a fictitious 'continuing transaction' to expand the timeframe of the event to encompass the words they wish to admit; each case will turn on its own facts.

Notwithstanding its suspect foundations, this form of the *res gestae* doctrine is of considerable utility to prosecutors, especially where the victim is deceased, incompetent, or otherwise unable to testify, or a witness cannot be identified or located. However, there is no precondition that the witness not be available, although admission may render the trial unfair under ECHR Article 6.[90] A young child's statement describing the person who inflicted physical injuries on him might be admissible provided the statement was made sufficiently close to the event to be deemed still to dominate the child's mind. Before the reforms introduced by the CJA 2003 prosecutors sometimes attempted to tender complaints of sexual assault as *res gestae*, to bootstrap the statement to a higher evidential plane than the common law 'recent complaint' doctrine[91] could achieve. However, the 'excited utterances' route to admissibility is not apposite where a very young child does not understand what has occurred, such as fondling or indecent exposure, and so may not be very perturbed by it, or she delays disclosure, or reports only when prompted by questions; such circumstances negate the spontaneity and emotional disturbance which purports to make the utterances reliable.[92] This problem has tempted courts in Canada and the United States to attenuate the requirements for the exception, to admit statements which they may regard as reliable for other reasons, such as the naïveté of the report.[93]

(b)   Statements accompanying and explaining relevant acts
Thus a child might be allowed to recount the explanation which an abuser gave in giving the child a gift, for example to induce secrecy.

(c)   Statements about contemporaneous physical sensations of the declarant

---

[88] *Ratten v The Queen* (n 73).

[89] Psychological empirical studies have shown that whereas powers of observation tend to be heightened by states of moderate excitement, they can be impaired by great excitement [E Loftus *Eyewitness Testimony* (Harvard University Press, Cambridge, Mass 1979) 31–36, 156; M Stone *Proof of Fact in Criminal Trials* (W Green & Son Ltd, Edinburgh 1984) 35–36, 55–61; D Greer 'Anything but the Truth? The Reliability of Testimony in Criminal Trials' (1971) 11 *British J of Criminology* 131, 133–134, 144–145; A Ashworth and R Pattenden 'Reliability, Hearsay Evidence and the Criminal Trial' (1986) 102 LQR 292].

[90] *Attorney General's Reference (No 1 of 2003)* [2003] EWCA Crim 1286, [2003] 2 Cr App R 29 [17]–[22].   [91] Discussed below, section C.

[92] M Misener 'Children's Hearsay Evidence in Child Sexual Abuse Prosecutions: a Proposal for Reform' (1991) 33(4) Criminal LQ 364, 366–367.   [93] Discussed below, sections B.5(a) and B.8(b).

(d) *Statements about the contemporaneous state of mind of the declarant*

These two exceptions for subjective sensations may be conveniently considered together. The assignment of statements as to mental or physical states to the *res gestae* is debatable. The cases are not easy to reconcile.[94] There often is no obvious contemporaneous 'event' which can be identified as connected to the statement, and the declarant certainly has the opportunity to concoct the assertion beforehand. Whatever their classification, such statements are admissible at common law as evidence of the existence of such a state, because a person's statements are the best and sometimes the only means of demonstrating this fact.[95] Therefore a child's statement to an examining doctor about her physical sensations arising from her injuries will be admissible under this exception, but not her statement as to who inflicted them.[96] A person overhearing a child's cries of pain could testify about what she heard, as evidence that the child was being assaulted at that time. This device has also, controversially, been extended by some courts to admit a statement of intention of future action to support an inference that that intention was carried out;[97] such as a child's statement to a friend that she intended to walk home by a particular route as circumstantial evidence that she carried out that intention, if she never arrived home.

2. The impetus for hearsay reform

All common law jurisdictions in recent years have acknowledged a degree of discomfort with the hearsay rule; while frequently such concerns have been felt most acutely in the specific context of child abuse cases, reform has sometimes been initiated on a much broader front. Reform has tended to take the following forms:

- creation of special hearsay exceptions for out-of-court statements by children to third parties;
- tinkering with the rules applicable to hearsay statements generally; or
- replacing the exclusionary rule with a reconfigured admissibility rule.

We consider videotaped interviews and pre-trial testimony separately; while most jurisdictions would regard videotaped evidence as technically hearsay,[98] because of their form the trier of fact hears directly what the witness has to say, and so the dangers

---

[94] Law Commission *Evidence in Criminal Proceedings: Hearsay and Related Topics* (Consultation Paper No 138, 1995) [3.38]–[3.49].

[95] C Tapper *Cross & Tapper on Evidence* (10th edn Butterworths, London 2004) 600.

[96] Unless the identification of the abuser may be relevant to a present emotion such as fear of continued contact with that person, which is relevant to a fact in issue.

[97] *Walton v The Queen* (1989) 166 CLR 283 (Aus HC) [criticized by C Tapper '*Hillman* Rediscovered and *Lord St Leonards* Resurrected' (1990) 106 LQR 441]; *R v Starr* 2000 SCC 40, [2000] 2 SCR 144; *Mutual Life Insurance Co v Hillman* 145 US 284 (USSC 1892). See also Tapper *Cross & Tapper* (n 95) 600–605.

[98] eg Queensland Law Reform Commission *The Receipt of Evidence by Queensland Courts: the Evidence of Children* (Report No 55 Part 2 Dec 2000) 126. It is arguable that videotaped testimony is not subject to the hearsay ban because it is directly presented rather than being channelled through another human mind, so the only concern is whether the declarant can be cross-examined.

attendant upon hearsay (of misunderstanding, concoction, or erroneous repetition) are absent.

3. Hearsay reform in English criminal cases

In *Myers v DPP*, the Law Lords famously allocated the task of further reform of the common law hearsay rules to Parliament, on the basis that a wholesale revision was required because 'a policy of make do and mend is no longer adequate'.[99] The consequence was to forestall any further attempts by the English judiciary to modify and modernize the rules they themselves had created. By 1992, at least one Law Lord became restive at Parliament's ad hoc approach to hearsay reform, and urged his colleagues to embark on the project themselves,[100] but again the majority felt constrained to inaction by *Myers*.[101] In 1994 the Law Commission was finally instructed by the Home Secretary to conduct the long-sought comprehensive review, and their report was published in 1997.[102]

The CJA 2003[103] made sweeping changes to the hearsay doctrine.[104] All of the common law rules governing the admissibility of hearsay evidence appear to have been abolished, except for those expressly preserved in s 118(1). The statutory reform applies only to statements submitted as evidence of any matter stated therein, and therefore does not bite on statements used as original evidence, explained earlier. A 'statement' is defined as any representation of fact or opinion made by a person by whatever means, including a sketch, photofit or other pictorial form;[105] therefore, as at common law, human input is required to constitute hearsay, and so mechanically recorded data, such as automated computer records showing that the defendant accessed child pornography on the internet or contacted a child's mobile telephone, are admissible without reference to the CJA 2003.

A 'matter' in a statement is classified as hearsay only if the purpose of the maker appears to have been to cause another person to believe it, or to cause another person to act, or a machine to operate, on the basis that the matter is as stated.[106] This definition is opaque until it is appreciated that its purpose is to abolish the common law rule applying to so-called 'implied assertions', where a statement is tendered, not to prove the truth of any facts expressly narrated by the words or conduct, but rather to prove some other inference which could be drawn from them. The House of Lords in 1992 in *Kearley* had held that implied assertions were nevertheless

---

[99] *Myers v DPP* (n 70) 1021–1022.

[100] *R v Kearley* [1992] 2 AC 228 (HL) 237 (Lord Griffiths).

[101] ibid, 251 (Lord Bridge of Harwich), 258 (Lord Ackner), 278 (Lord Oliver of Aylmerton), 287 (Lord Browne-Wilkinson).

[102] *Evidence in Criminal Proceedings: Hearsay and Related Topics* (n 94) hereafter Law Com No 245, Hearsay.

[103] The hearsay provisions of the statute came into force on 4 April 2005 [The Criminal Justice Act 2003 (Commencement No.8 and Transitional and Saving Provisions) Order 2005 Sch1 s 6].

[104] Although at least one commentator is disappointed with their breadth: D Birch 'The Criminal Justice Act 2003: Hearsay: Same Old Story, Same Old Song?' [2004] Crim LR 557.

[105] CJA 2003 (England) s 115(2).   [106] ibid s 115(3).

caught by the hearsay ban because the declarant was not present in court.[107] This was so even where the declarant was neither expressly nor intentionally asserting anything at all by his behaviour. Therefore, at common law a telephone call inquiring about the availability of child prostitutes could not be tendered to prove that child prostitutes were available through that telephone number, nor even to establish an inference that the caller believed this to be the case, because according to *Kearley* this belief was irrelevant to the guilt of the registered owner of that number. The statutory definition therefore removes implied assertions from the realm of hearsay.[108]

Diagrams 14 and 15 map the new provisions for the admission of statements where the makers do not appear as witnesses at the trial, and where they do testify. The following discussion expands on the diagrams in the areas most germane to child abuse prosecutions.

(a) The admissibility of out-of-court statements by a non-witness

As depicted in Diagram 14, the most radical reforms are the expansion of the statutory exceptions to encompass oral hearsay, and to admit multiple levels of hearsay, in criminal proceedings.[109] There are now four routes to admission of a statement where the maker is not called as a witness at the trial.

(i) The preserved common law exceptions

For our present purposes, the most significant of the exceptions preserved by s 118(1) is *res gestae*. Three species of the doctrine are expressly recognized: where the declarant (who may be unidentified)[110] is emotionally overpowered by an event; where the statement accompanies and explains an act; and a statement of physical sensations or mental state. The common enterprise exception applies where several persons are involved in the commission of the offence, so that a statement made by one party becomes admissible against an accomplice. This is of particular value in child abuse prosecutions where it is alleged that the defendant conspired with others to commit the offence charged, for example to operate a paedophile ring, traffic in child prostitutes, or create child pornography. Where multiple hearsay is involved, a statement admissible under the common law exceptions must still pass through the filter of s 121, discussed below.

---

[107] *R v Kearley* (n 100); for the opposite interpretation see *R v Edwards* (1994) 19 OR (3d) 239 (Ontario CA).

[108] Although some dispute this, contending that the common law continues to apply to implicit statements outside the catchment area of the statutory definitions of 'statement' and 'matter' in ss 114 and 115; since the CJA 2003 (England), contrary to the recommendation of the Law Commission [Law Com No 245, *Hearsay* draft Bill s 1(2)], does not expressly abolish the common law hearsay doctrine, this would mean that *Kearley* could live on: see Tapper *Cross & Tapper on Evidence* (n 95) 636 n27 (who does not necessarily agree with the argument).

[109] Under the CJA 1988 (England) ss 23 and 26, statements from unavailable witnesses had to be in writing, and only one level of hearsay was permitted.

[110] Unlike the 'unavailable declarant' exception: CJA 2003 (England) s 116(1)(b).

(ii) Unavailable witnesses

The 1988 legislation purported to limit the statutory exception for unavailable witnesses to 'first-hand hearsay', that is, where the declarant had direct knowledge of the facts stated, and direct oral testimony by that person would have been admissible.[111] However, the CJA 2003 exception appears to apply to multiple hearsay, since it requires that the original maker of the statement could have given admissible oral evidence of its subject matter, and s 121 gives the court discretion to admit multiple hearsay. Unlike the common law exceptions, the unavailable declarant must be identified 'to the court's satisfaction'.[112] The five categories of unavailability in s 116(2) parallel those under the CJA 1988. The party tendering the statement must prove that its maker:

(a) is dead;
(b) is unfit to testify due to his bodily or mental condition;
(c) is absent from the UK, and it is not reasonably practicable to return for the trial;
(d) cannot be found after all reasonably practicable steps have been taken; or
(e) through fear does not give oral evidence.

The party tendering the statement must also prove that its maker had the 'required capability' when the statement was made, meaning that she was 'capable of understanding questions and giving understandable answers about the matter',[113] essentially replicating the test for competence to testify.[114] This minimal test is unlikely to create a significant difficulty in child abuse prosecutions. It should be noted that there is no parallel mental capacity requirement for the *res gestae* and the other preserved common law exceptions, nor for the reconfigured recent complaint doctrine discussed later.[115]

The witness claiming to be intimidated and so seeking refuge from a subpoena in s 116(2)(e) is likely to be the most problematic condition. This avenue might be used, for example, by a mother refusing to testify against a violent partner about his abuse of their baby. Two definitional issues which had arisen under the CJA 1988 s 23 are clarified, if not entirely resolved. Firstly, 'fear' is stipulated to be widely construed, to include fear of harm to another as well as to the maker, and fear of financial loss;[116] the cause of the apprehended financial loss, and its extent, remain unspecified. Beyond this, the provision does not specify the source or basis of the fear. Caselaw under s 23 of the 1988 Act had held that the fear alleged by the reluctant witness need not be connected with the crime itself or anything occurring in its aftermath,[117] nor need it be fear of the accused.[118] No inquiry into the precise reason for the fear was necessary,[119] and so the fear need not be based on reasonable grounds.[120] This generous approach

---

[111] CJA 1988 s 23. Although the shoulder note in the Act indicated that the exception applied to first-hand hearsay, it was arguable that multiple hearsay could be admitted where a common law exception to the exclusionary rule applied: P Roberts and A Zuckerman *Criminal Evidence* (OUP, Oxford 2004) 629–630.   [112] CJA 2003 (England) s 116(1)(b).
[113] ibid s 123. This was unclear under CJA 1988 (England) s 23: *R v D* [2002] EWCA Crim 990, [2003] QB 90 (CA) [35].   [114] Discussed above Chapter 8 section A.1(a).
[115] CJA 2003 (England) s 120(7), discussed in section C.   [116] ibid s 116(3).
[117] *R v Martin* [1996] Crim LR 589 (CA).   [118] *R v Rutherford* [1998] Crim LR 490 (CA).
[119] *R v Martin* (n 117).   [120] *Acton Justices ex p McMullen* (1991) 92 Cr App R 98 (CA).

Diagram 14. The Admissibility of Out-of-Court Hearsay Statements Made by a *Non*-Witness Under the Criminal Justice Act 2003

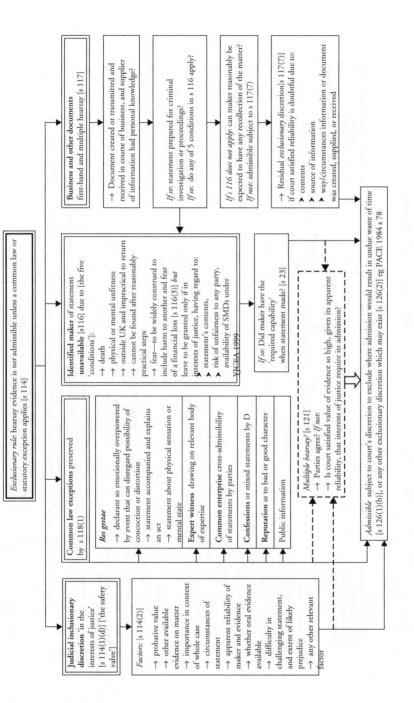

Exclusionary rule: hearsay evidence is *not* admissible unless a common law or statutory exception applies [s 114]

Judicial inclusionary discretion 'in the interests of justice' [s 114(1)(d)] ['the safety valve']

Factors: [s 114(2)]
→ probative value
→ other available evidence on matter
→ importance in context of whole case
→ circumstances of statement
→ apparent reliability of maker and evidence
→ whether oral evidence available
→ difficulty in challenging statement, and extent of likely prejudice
→ any other relevant factor

Common law exceptions preserved by s 118(1)

Res gestae
→ declarant so emotionally overpowered by event that can disregard possibility of concoction or distortion
→ statement accompanied and explains an act
→ statement about physical sensation or mental state

Expert witness drawing on relevant body of expertise

Common enterprise cross-admissibility of statements by parties

Confessions or mixed statements by D

Reputation as to bad or good character

Public information

Identified maker of statement unavailable [s116] due to [the five 'conditions']:
→ death
→ physical or mental unfitness
→ outside UK and impractical to return
→ cannot be found after reasonably practical steps
→ fear—to be widely construed to include harm to another and fear of a financial loss [s 116(3)] *but* leave to be granted only if in interests of justice, having regard to:
  ▸ statement's contents,
  ▸ risk of unfairness to any party,
  ▸ availability of SMDs under YJCEA 1999

If so: Did maker have the 'required capability' when statement made? [s 23]

Business and other documents first-hand and multiple hearsay [s 117]

→ Document created or transmitted and received in course of business, and supplier of information had personal knowledge?

If so: statement prepared for criminal investigation or proceedings?
If so: do any of 5 conditions in s 116 apply?

If s 116 does not apply: can maker reasonably be expected to have any recollection of the matter?
If not: admissible subject to s 117(7)

→ Residual *exclusionary* discretion [s 117(7)] if court satisfied reliability is doubtful due to:
  ▸ contents
  ▸ source of information
  ▸ way/circumstances information or document was created, supplied, or received

Multiple hearsay? [s 121]
→ Parties agree? *If not:*
→ Is court satisfied value of evidence so high, given its apparent reliability, that interests of justice require its admission?

Admissible subject to court's discretion to exclude where admission would result in undue waste of time [s 126(1)(b)], or any other exclusionary discretion which may exist [s 126(2)] eg PACE 1984 s 78

Diagram 15. The Admissibility of Out-of-Court Hearsay Statements Made by a *Witness* under the Criminal Justice Act 2003

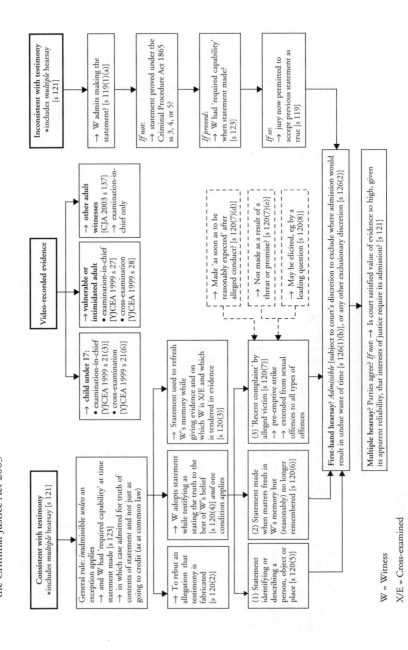

W = Witness

X/E = Cross-examined

is likely to be continued, given the statutory admonition to the courts to construe this exception widely.

The second clarification is that the statement may be admitted to supplement the testimony of a witness who 'freezes' in the witness box,[121] or who professes not to be able to remember very obvious points (such as a victim claiming to be unable to recall his assailants after identifying them in his witness statement).[122] It is highly improbable however that s 116(2) could be used for witnesses who simply fear the adversarial trial process, although it may be very difficult to discern this distinction in a given case.

Possibly due to concern that it will be too easy for a reluctant witness to speak only through the safe medium of a written statement, a prerequisite for admission of the statement under the 'fear' condition is that the trial judge grants leave, whereas admission under the four other conditions is automatic once the ground has been established through evidence. Section 116(4) requires the court to conclude that it is in the interests of justice to admit the statement, having regard to its contents, any risk that its admission or exclusion will result in unfairness to any party to the proceedings (in particular any difficulty in challenging the statement), and the availability of a Special Measures Direction under the Youth Justice and Criminal Evidence Act 1999,[123] as well as any other relevant circumstances. The Court of Appeal has admonished prosecutors to take 'very great care in every case' of allegedly frightened witnesses, and to pay attention to the letter and spirit of the ECHR's guarantee of a fair trial to the accused, which will likely be breached if the hearsay statement provides the sole or determinative evidence against him.[124]

How is the foundation for the statutory excuses to be laid without contravening the hearsay rule? The procedure will probably be the same as that used under the 1988 Act. The trial judge will hold a *voir dire* to receive the evidence explaining the witness's absence.[125] If it is the prosecution who is tendering the hearsay statement, the reasons for the witness's absence must be established beyond reasonable doubt, suspicion not sufficing;[126] if the statement is submitted by the defence, the standard of proof is on a balance of probabilities.[127] The evidence of 'fear' must itself be admissible. In practical terms, under the 1988 Act this meant that police officers could testify that the absent witness had spoken directly to them about her fear, as evidence of her state of mind, but officers could not testify as to explanations from third parties.[128] Since s 121 of the 2003 Act permits multiple hearsay for *res gestae*, it may be that more distant chains of hearsay to explain the unavailability of the maker of the statement will be allowed; commentators have taken different positions,[129] but early indications

---

[121] ibid 105 (Watkins LJ).   [122] *R v Waters* [1997] Crim LR 823 (CA).

[123] Discussed above, Chapter 8 section B.2.

[124] *R v Kenneth Arnold* [2004] EWCA Crim 1293 [30], citing *Luca v Italy* (2003) 36 EHRR 46 (ECtHR).   [125] *R v Jennings and Miles* [1995] Crim LR 810 (CA).

[126] *R v James* [1995] Crim LR 812 (CA).   [127] *R v Mattey* [1995] 2 Cr App R 409 (CA).

[128] *Neill v North Antrim Magistrates' Court* [1992] 4 All ER 846 (HL).

[129] Colin Tapper contends that s 116(1)(a) requires that the evidence be admissible without the assistance of a hearsay exception, ie be first-hand hearsay [Tapper *Cross and Tapper on Evidence* (n 95) 636], whereas Roberts and Zuckerman state that the absence condition may be proved by evidence which is itself hearsay, provided that such evidence is independently admissible under a common law or statutory exception to

suggest that the Court of Appeal will not be perturbed by multiple hearsay if the record of the statement is reliable and it is unlikely that the statement could be challenged effectively on cross-examination.[130]

(iii) Business documents

The reliability of business documents is supposed to be assured by two preconditions stipulated by s 117: the document must have been prepared or received[131] in the course of a trade, business, profession or other occupation or as the holder of a paid or unpaid office, and the information must have been supplied by a person who had, or might reasonably be supposed to have had, personal knowledge of the matters concerned. Unlike ordinary documents, business documents are automatically admissible regardless of how many layers of hearsay underpinned the information they contain, provided that each link in the supply chain was formed in the course of business.[132] There is no general requirement that the supplier of the information be unavailable to testify. A major and inexplicable gap in the new legislation, as with its predecessor, is that the opposing party (usually the defence) cannot insist that an available maker or source of the business information be produced for cross-examination; there is little point in the defence issuing a subpoena to that witness because then they cannot cross-examine him or ask leading questions (although that predicament may set up an issue under the ECHR Article 6).[133] The only basis for a ruling that the document is inadmissible is the exercise of judicial exclusionary discretion under s 117(6) and (7), but that discretion is now limited to situations where the court is satisfied that the reliability of the document is doubtful, whereas under the 1988 Act the criterion was the open-textured 'interests of justice'.[134] In contrast, in civil proceedings the opposing party is entitled to cross-examine an available maker of a hearsay document, although that party now bears the onus of locating and summoning that witness.[135]

While documents such as witness statements, interview notes or tapes prepared specifically for the criminal investigation or proceedings are technically business documents, they sensibly receive different statutory treatment. They can be produced without cross-examination only if the witness is unavailable under the conditions in s 116 (death, illness, fear etc), or if the witness cannot reasonably be expected to have any recollection of the matters in the statement due to the lapse of time since he made it.[136] This latter route to admitting hearsay evidence is mystifying; it appears to be

---

the exclusionary rule [Roberts and Zuckerman (n 111) 628–630]. The Law Commission had recommended that cumulative use of hearsay exceptions to explain the unavailability of a witness under s 116 should be permitted only through a business document, and not through a double use of s 116 or a preserved common law exception, but their draft multiple hearsay provision reflecting this recommendation was not carried over to the CJA 2003 (England) s 121 [Law Com No 245 *Hearsay* [8.18]–[8.26], Recommendation 7, draft Bill s 10(2)].

[130] *R v Xhabri* [2005] EWCA Crim 3135, [2006] 1 Cr App R 26 (complainant contacted two people who in turn contacted the police, but could not later be located).

[131] A more dubious 'guarantee' of reliability.   [132] CJA 2003 (England) s 117(2)(c), s 121(1)(a).

[133] *Attorney General's Reference (No 1 of 2003)* (n 90) [22].   [134] CJA 1988 (England) s 25.

[135] Civil Evidence Act 1995 (England) s 3.   [136] CJA 2003 (England) s 117(5).

a vestigial remnant of a ground of unavailability which had applied to all business documents under the preceding legislation.[137] Just why the frailties of human memory should come into play only at the relatively late stage of a criminal investigation is difficult to fathom. It is likely that s 116, like its predecessor, will be used primarily by prosecutors to admit witness statements taken in the course of the investigation under s 9 of the CJA 1967.[138] It should be noted however that 'document' is defined very broadly in the 2003 Act, to encompass 'anything in which information of any description is recorded',[139] and so could include videotaped interviews of a child or other vulnerable witness subsequently unable to testify through fear or physical or mental illness.[140]

(iv) Judicial inclusionary discretion

While to this point the CJA 2003 has largely tinkered with the admissibility rules erected by the CJA 1988, it is innovative in creating what the Law Commission dubbed a 'safety valve', to allow the trial court to admit a hearsay statement by a non-witness when it is 'in the interests of justice'.[141] Of the list of factors which the court is required to consider,[142] most are directed to the reliability and cogency of the statement and to any difficulty by the opposing party in challenging it. The factor which may be problematic to apply is s 114(2)(c), being the importance of the matter or evidence in the context of the case as a whole. No guidance is given by the legislators as to how the 'importance' factor is to be applied: there is a risk that if the evidence cannot be found elsewhere,[143] the greater the importance of the hearsay evidence to the case, and so the greater the temptation to admit it.[144] But the greater the importance of the evidence, the greater the potential prejudice to the opposing party of admitting it without being tested in cross-examination of its maker.

While multiple hearsay is automatically admissible for business documents, s 121 imposes an additional condition for its admission under the other gateways:[145] either all of the parties to the proceedings must agree, or the court must be 'satisfied that the value of the evidence in question, taking into account how reliable the statements

---

[137] Police and Criminal Evidence Act 1984 s 68(2)(a)(iii).

[138] Also noteworthy is the Criminal Procedure and Investigations Act 1996 s 68 and Sch 2, which renders a statement and depositions admitted at committal procedures admissible at trial, subject to the right of an opposing party to object, which the court has discretion to override. For criticism, see Law Com No 245, *Hearsay* [4.46]–[4.50].   [139] CJA 2003 (England), s 134(1).

[140] As in *R v D* (n 113); *Attorney General's Reference No 69 of 2001 (John Archibald)* [2002] EWCA Crim 858 [18]–[31] (where complainant of sexual assault suffering from dementia became incompetent after her police video interview which was admitted under CJA 1988 s 23).

[141] CJA 2003 (England) s 114(1)(d).

[142] ibid s 114(2).   [143] A mandatory consideration under ibid s 114(2)(b).

[144] Similar difficulties arose in Canadian courts in applying the 'necessity' criterion: see below, section B.5(a).

[145] Admittedly it is odd to have the inclusionary 'safety valve' qualified by the exclusionary discretion for multiple hearsay, both being predicated on the demands of the interests of justice, but that is what s 114(1)(d) and s 121 appear to require.

appear to be, is so high that the interests of justice require the later statement to be admissible for that purpose'.

(v) Exclusionary discretion?

A significant difference between the common law exceptions and the statutory exceptions under the CJA 1988 was that the statutory regime was constructed upon a judicial discretion to exclude otherwise admissible hearsay if it was not in the interests of justice to do so.[146] At common law, if the out-of-court statement could be fitted within a hearsay exception or could be made relevant to a non-hearsay purpose, the court had to receive the evidence regardless of any concerns about its reliability or of any resulting unfairness to the opposing party.[147] The CJA 2003 departs radically from its statutory predecessor in that the only exclusionary discretion applicable to all categories of hearsay by non-witnesses, conferred by s 126(1), is restricted, somewhat perplexingly and clumsily, to the situation where the court is satisfied that the case for excluding the statement (taking account of the danger that to admit it would result in undue waste of time) 'substantially outweighs' the case for admitting it, taking account of the value of the evidence. By a late amendment to the Bill, the 'interests of justice' argument may now be heard, but only to support a submission that multiple hearsay evidence be admitted—not excluded—under the common law exceptions preserved by s 118, the unavailable maker under s 116, or the judicial inclusionary discretion conferred by s 114, on the basis of the reliability, and hence high value, of the statement. Counsel wishing to object to first-hand hearsay evidence on the basis of unfairness (instead of waste of time) must have recourse to s 78 of the Police and Criminal Evidence Act 1984.[148]

Significantly, there is no statutory prohibition of a conviction founded entirely upon hearsay. Instead, s 125 allows the court to direct an acquittal or to declare a mistrial at any time after the close of the prosecution case, where the case against the defendant is based wholly or partly on the hearsay statement, and that evidence is 'so unconvincing' that, considering its importance to the case against the defendant, his conviction would be unsafe. The sequence is somewhat perplexing: the court may have no choice but to admit the evidence, regardless of doubts as to its reliability,[149] but then must wait until the prosecution has concluded its case in order to direct an acquittal. Nevertheless this provision is likely to prove sufficient to deflect a challenge to the hearsay provisions under the fair trial guarantees in Article 6(1) of the ECHR.[150]

---

[146] CJA 1988 s 25(1).   [147] *Attorney General's Reference (No 1 of 2003)* (n 90).

[148] Expressly preserved by CJA 2003 (England) s 126(2)(a). Section 126(2)(b) preserves 'any other power of the court to exclude evidence at its discretion', but as there is no common law power to exclude otherwise admissible evidence, it is not clear to what this paragraph pertains.

[149] Under ibid s 116 (unavailable maker) or s 118 (common law exceptions), which unlike business documents do not have their own inbuilt exclusionary discretionary mechanism.

[150] In *R v Xhabri* (n 130) [42]–[45] the inclusionary discretion in s 114 was found not to breach Article 6, as it is available for defence as well as prosecution evidence, and in that case the original declarant of the first-hand and second-hand hearsay statements, the complainant, was available for cross-examination.

How can an opponent demonstrate that hearsay which has been admitted is 'so unconvincing' that the case should be halted? The 2003 Act purports to ameliorate the harshness of admitting evidence without cross-examination through artificial mechanisms, whereby counsel may seek to impugn the credibility of a witness who never crosses the threshold of the courtroom by leading any evidence which could have been used in cross-examination, such as any prior or subsequent inconsistent statement.[151] If however defence counsel does so, evidence of the accused's prior convictions or other misconduct may be admitted, on the basis that he has cast an imputation upon a prosecution witness.[152] The statutory framework is such that it is unlikely that defence counsel could persuade a trial judge that the penalty attendant on mounting such an attack created by the hearsay provisions would warrant excluding the hearsay altogether. The court is also in a predicament, because it must judge the credibility of a witness it has never seen, based on attacks on her credibility to which she cannot respond.

(b) The admissibility of hearsay statements by a witness

As depicted in Diagram 15, the CJA 2003 provides the first systematic treatment of out-of-court statements by someone who does testify in court. At common law, a previous statement which was consistent or inconsistent with the witness's testimony at trial could be used by the trier of fact only to assess the credibility of that testimony; the statement could not be used as evidence of the truth of what it narrated. In other words, the statements could not be used for a hearsay purpose. The new statutory regime makes the statement admissible as an exception to the hearsay ban; it will be open to the trier of fact to decide that the previous statements, and not the in-court testimony, represent the truth. Furthermore, the previous statements may encompass multiple levels of hearsay.

Previous statements consistent with the witness's testimony were barred from evidence by the common law as being superfluous 'oath-helping'. Section 120 lays out the circumstances recognized by the common law as permitting the previous consistent statement to be put to the witness, but now converts them to proof of what actually happened, and not merely to buttress the creditworthiness of the witness. The most significant substantive change in the context of child abuse prosecutions is to the recent complaint doctrine, which we address in detail below.[153]

Previous inconsistent statements are commonly, and entirely properly, put to child witnesses in cross-examination, in an attempt to impeach their credibility. Whereas previously the jury would be directed to ignore the previous statement except to the extent that it undermined the child's in-court testimony, now the jury will be told that they are free to accept the previous statements as being true. This can be a trap for the unwary cross-examiner. For example, the child may have stated in her video-recorded evidence that the sexual assault took place in the bedroom, but testified in court that it occurred in the kitchen. The cross-examiner's position is that the assault never

---

[151] CJA 2003 (England) s 124, which replicates the approach of CJA 1998 Sch 2, s 1.
[152] CJA 2003 (England) s 101(1)(g).   [153] See section C.

occurred at all, but by putting the previous inconsistent statement to the witness, he now runs the risk that that statement becomes evidence against his client. Section 119 also opens up the possibility that an inconsistent witness statement might also now be tendered by the prosecution if a complainant retracts her complaint in the course of her testimony, or otherwise does not come up to proof, as has occurred in Canadian criminal courts.[154]

Finally, it should be noted that in English criminal law, there were no common law exceptions specifically designed to admit statements by children to third parties. Statutory exceptions for children are currently restricted to depositions under oath taken before a justice of the peace from a child complainant whose life or health would be seriously endangered by testifying in court,[155] and to the provisions for admission of videotaped interviews as examination-in-chief,[156] and videotaped testimony under cross-examination which we considered earlier.[157]

4. Hearsay reform in English civil cases

The strict rules of evidence, including hearsay, have not been applied to wardship proceedings for decades.[158] Section 97 of the Children Act 1989 extended this policy to all proceedings concerning the upbringing, maintenance or welfare of a child under that Act and the Child Support Act 1991, through The Children (Admissibility of Hearsay Evidence) Order 1993,[159] which makes a statement made by a child in such proceedings admissible notwithstanding any rule of law relating to hearsay. It is common to present a child's story and views through welfare reports and reports of guardians *ad litem*.

Hearsay is often admitted in custody and access proceedings in the Family Division without objection, particularly in cases of alleged child sexual abuse. Where objection is taken, however, the issue of whether to summon the child to attend is a thorny one. In the leading case, *R v B County Council ex p P*,[160] a girl aged 17 made allegations of serious sexual abuse against her stepfather in care proceedings involving her and three other children. Criminal proceedings had been dismissed after the prosecution offered no evidence. The local authority decided not to call the child to testify because of the likely harmful effect on her, instead relying upon her written statement to the police and her oral statement to a child psychiatrist which were admissible under The Children (Admissibility of Hearsay Evidence) Order. The stepfather, strenuously denying the allegations, applied for a witness summons, but wanted another party to call the

---

[154] *R v U(FJ)* [1995] 3 SCR 764 (SCC), discussed below, section B.5.

[155] Children and Young Persons Act 1933 (England) ss 42, 43.

[156] CJA 1988 (England) s 32A, replaced by Special Measures Directions under the YJCEA 1999 (England) s 27, discussed above, Chapter 8 section B.3(a).

[157] Introduced by the YJCEA 1999 (England) s 28, but not yet in force.

[158] *Official Solicitor v K (Infants)* [1965] AC 201 (HL).

[159] The Children (Admissibility of Hearsay Evidence) Order 1993 (SI 1993 No 621) Rule 2, extending and replacing Orders made in 1990 (SI 1990 621 No 143) and 1991 (SI 1991 No 1115), enacted pursuant to the Children Act 1989 s 96(3).

[160] *R v B County Council ex p P* [1991] 1 WLR 221 (CA). See also *Re P (Witness Summons)* [1997] 2 FLR 447 (HC).

child as their witness so that he could put to her that she was a 'consummate liar' in cross-examination. Had he summoned her himself, he would not have been permitted to ask leading questions nor to challenge her credibility. The Court of Appeal upheld the magistrate's refusal to issue the summons, on the basis that while the child as a party to the care proceedings was technically compellable to testify, the court's duty was to the child. Butler-Sloss LJ observed that the philosophy behind the Children Act 1989 would be thwarted if the abuser was able to require the attendance of the child in court.[161] The Court endorsed the warning of Neill LJ before the first Hearsay Order took effect in 1990 that 'hearsay evidence is admissible as a matter of law, but this evidence and the use to which it is put has to be handled with the greatest care and in such a way that, unless the interests of the child make it necessary, the rules of natural justice and the rights of the parents are fully and properly observed'.[162] Nicholls LJ (as he then was), emphasizing that the child was 17, expressed 'grave disquiet' about the consequences of having the care application turn upon hearsay, however:

In the normal course of events I would have thought that fairness and the best interests of all these minors marched hand-in-hand in requiring the veracity of J.'s statements and of her stepfather's vehement denials to be probed by at least *some* questioning of J. As it is, I am concerned there is a real danger that, in deciding where the future of the three younger children lies, great weight may be attached to J.'s statements without her stepfather or his counsel ever having had any opportunity at any stage so much as to ask her one question on any aspect of what she has said . . . It ought to be possible to investigate such serious allegations or statements or disclosures, however they are to be described, in a more satisfactory manner than will now be possible, when the stipendiary magistrate will hear evidence from the stepfather and read J.'s statements, coupled with an expression of view on her credibility by the psychiatrist who has interviewed her.[163]

The Civil Evidence Act 1995 abolished the hearsay ban for all civil cases. Section 1(1) makes admissible all hearsay, whether recorded or oral and whatever the level. The only restriction on admissibility is that the maker of the statement (who by necessary implication must be identified) must have been competent at the time the statement was made.[164] This very occasionally could have implications for out-of-court statements by very young children who might still be incompetent even under the low threshold in ss 53 to 54 of the YJCEA 1999. However, no such limitation appears in the Children (Admissibility of Hearsay Evidence) Order 1993 applicable to family proceedings.[165] Where hearsay evidence is adduced pursuant to this Order, the source of the information must be declared or a good reason given for not doing so.[166]

The classic hearsay concerns such as contemporaneity, multiple levels of hearsay, and motives by the maker to conceal or misrepresent, are matters going to the weight of the evidence rather than its admissibility.[167] The court will need to assess the evidential value of the child's hearsay statement having regard to the child's age, the child's

---

[161] *R v B County Council ex p P* ibid 228.　　[162] ibid 227.　　[163] ibid 231.
[164] Civil Evidence Act 1995 s 5(1).　　[165] Enacted pursuant to the Children Act 1989 s 96(3).
[166] *Practice Direction of 31 January 1995 (Case Management)* [1995] 1 FLR 456 (President of the Family Division) [3].　　[167] Civil Evidence Act 1995 (England) s 4.

previous behaviour including any tendency to lie or fantasize, and the circumstances in which the statement was made.[168] Where sexual abuse is alleged, the court is particularly concerned about relying solely on an uncorroborated and untested allegation by the child.[169]

5. Hearsay reform in Canadian law

The Supreme Court of Canada took a different approach than the Law Lords[170] to reform of the hearsay role, reasoning that if the judiciary have created problems in the common law of evidence, then it cannot abdicate responsibility to solve them.[171] Beginning in 1990 in the specific context of child abuse criminal prosecutions, the Supreme Court has proceeded to reconfigure completely the hearsay rule from an exclusionary to an inclusionary doctrine applicable to all criminal and civil cases where the common law still governs.

(a) Hearsay in Canadian criminal courts

The Canadian hearsay revolution began with *R v Khan*.[172] The defendant was a physician who was charged with sexually assaulting his patient, aged three-and-a-half. After the child had been alone with the doctor, her mother noticed that she was picking at a wet spot on her sleeve. About 15 minutes after leaving Dr Khan's office, the mother asked her daughter what he had been talking to her about, and the child volunteered: 'he said "open your mouth". And do you know what? He put his birdie in my mouth, shook it and peed in my mouth'. The police tested the child's garment and found a mixture of semen and saliva. The trial judge held that the child was not competent to give unsworn evidence, and also refused to admit the mother's evidence as to the child's statement because it was not contemporaneous with the event, and so did not constitute part of the *res gestae*. The Supreme Court of Canada held that the trial judge had imposed too exacting a standard of testimonial competence.[173] The Ontario Court of Appeal had held that the statement should have been admitted as part of the spontaneous declaration class of *res gestae*, relaxing the requirement of contemporaneity, a stratagem familiar to English lawyers. McLachlin J (as she then was), writing for a unanimous court rejected this escape route, holding that the gap of 15 minutes prevented the statement from being contemporaneous, nor was it made under pressure or emotional intensity.[174]

Instead, the Supreme Court seized the opportunity to re-examine the hearsay rule itself. Noting that the traditional absolute rule had only the merit of certainty to commend it, McLachlin J identified a judicial trend in several jurisdictions to a more flexible approach to meet new needs in the law, 'rooted in the principle and the policy

---

[168] A Bainham *Children: the Modern Law* (2nd edn Family Law, Bristol 1998) 462.
[169] *R v B County Council ex p P* (n 160); *Re W (Minors) (Wardship: Evidence)* [1990] FLR 286(A).
[170] In *Myers v DPP* (n 70); *R v Kearley* (n 100).
[171] *Ares v Venner* (n 171); *R v Khan* [1990] 2 SCR 531 (SCC); *R v B(KG)* [1993] 1 SCR 740 (SCC).
[172] *R v Khan* ibid.   [173] ibid 540 discussed in Chapter 8 A.3.   [174] ibid 540.

underlying the hearsay rule rather than the strictures of traditional exceptions'.[175] The principles underpinning the doctrine and its exceptions could be subsumed into two: *necessity*, as there is no other way of obtaining the evidence; and *reliability*, through circumstantial guarantees of trustworthiness. The *res gestae* exception upon which the Crown had tried to rely in the case at Bar did not satisfy these principles, because the child's spontaneous declaration would have been admissible even if the child had been able to testify, there was no requirement that the reliability of her statement be first established, and there was no opportunity for the trial judge to impose conditions upon its admission in evidence because of the rule's absolute 'in-or-out' character.[176]

McLachlin J considered that the evidence of a child of tender years may bear its own special stamp of reliability, because young children 'are generally not adept at reasoned reflection or at fabricating tales of sexual perversion. They, manifestly, are unlikely to use their reflective powers to concoct a deliberate untruth, and particularly one about a sexual act which in all probability is beyond their ken.'[177] Accordingly, the hearsay rule must be reconfigured to be determined by two questions:

The first question should be whether reception of the hearsay statement is necessary. Necessity for these purposes must be interpreted as 'reasonably necessary'.[178] The inadmissibility of the child's evidence might be one basis for a finding of necessity. But sound evidence based on psychological assessments that testimony in court might be traumatic for the child or harm the child might also serve. There may be other examples of circumstances which could establish the requirement of necessity.

The next question should be whether the evidence is reliable. Many considerations such as timing, demeanour, the personality of the child, the intelligence and understanding of the child, and the absence of any reason to expect fabrication in the statement may be relevant on the issue of reliability. I would not wish to draw up a strict list of considerations for reliability, nor to suggest that certain categories of evidence (for example the evidence of young children on sexual encounters) should be always regarded as reliable. The matters relevant to reliability will vary with the child and with the circumstances, and are best left to the trial judge.

In determining the admissibility of the evidence, the judge must have regard to the need to safeguard the interests of the accused. In most cases a right of cross-examination, . . . would not be available. . . . Where trauma to the child is at issue, there would be little point in sparing the child the need to testify in chief, only to have him or her grilled in cross-examination. While there may be cases where, as a condition of admission, the trial judge thinks it possible and fair in all the circumstances to permit cross-examination of the child as the condition of the reception of a hearsay statement, in most cases the concerns of the accused as to credibility will remain to be addressed by submissions as to the weight to be accorded to the evidence, and submissions as to the quality of any corroborating evidence.

---

[175] ibid 540, citing *Ares v Venner* (n 171) (making hospital records admissible without calling the staff who made the notes) as the breakthrough in Canadian law. [176] ibid 543–544.

[177] ibid 542, quoting with approval Robbins JA in the court below [(1988) 42 CCC (3d) 197, 210].

[178] In *R v Smith* [1992] 2 SCR 915 (SCC) 933 Lamer CJC clarified that 'necessity' does not mean 'necessary to the prosecution case', as this would produce the illogical result that uncorroborated hearsay evidence would be admissible, but could become inadmissible if corroborated. This could be an important point for English courts in construing the 'importance in the context of the whole case' factor in the exercise of inclusionary discretion under the CJA 2003 (England) s 114(2).

McLachlin J cautioned that this did not make out-of-court statements by children generally admissible; in particular the requirement of necessity would probably mean that in most cases children would still be called to give *viva voce* evidence. In the case at Bar, the mother's statement should have been received. It was necessary, the child having been ruled (albeit incorrectly) incompetent to testify. It was also reliable. The child had no motive to falsify her story, which emerged naturally and without prompting. Moreover, the fact that she could not be expected to have knowledge of such sexual acts imbued her statement with its own peculiar stamp of reliability. Finally, her statement was corroborated by real evidence, the semen on her sleeve.[179] The Supreme Court did not however impose any precondition of corroboration, unlike many American states, as we will see below.[180]

Uncertainty as to whether *Khan* had any wider implications beyond child abuse prosecutions[181] was soon dispelled by the Supreme Court in *R v Smith*:[182]

The decision of this Court in *Khan* should be understood as the triumph of a principled analysis over a set of ossified judicially created categories.... [T]he approach that excludes hearsay evidence, even when highly probative, out of the fear that the trier of fact will not understand how to deal with such evidence, is no longer appropriate. ... [H]earsay evidence of statements made by persons who are not available to give evidence at trial ought generally to be admissible, where the circumstances under which the statements were made satisfy the criteria of necessity and reliability set out in *Khan*, and subject to the residual discretion of the trial judge to exclude the evidence when its probative value is slight and undue prejudice might result to the accused. Properly cautioned by the trial judge, juries are perfectly capable of determining what weight ought to be attached to such evidence, and of drawing reasonable inferences therefrom.[183]

Smith therefore confirmed a general inclusionary rule to hearsay evidence applicable to all witnesses in the criminal courts in Canada.[184] To the extent that the various hearsay exceptions might conflict with the requirements of a principled analysis, it is the principled analysis that should prevail. The new hearsay doctrine is 'a two-way street' and it is possible for a statement which would be automatically admitted under the traditional hearsay exceptions to be excluded on grounds of lack of necessity or unreliability, although this is likely to be rare.[185] However, important questions remained to be decided.

In the context of child abuse prosecutions, the most difficult criterion to interpret has been the 'necessity' test in relation to children's out-of-court statements. *R v Rockey*[186] dealt with this issue where the child was unavailable to testify. The accused was charged with anal penetration of a two-and-a-half-year-old boy whom he had been

---

[179] *R v Khan* (n 171) 546–547, 548.

[180] An omission deplored by some commentators: Misener (n 92) 377–378; D Rowsell 'Necessity and Reliability: What is the Impact of *Khan* on the Admissibility of Hearsay in Canada?' (1991) 49 (2) U of Toronto Faculty of L Rev 294, 299.   [181] Rowsell ibid.

[182] *R v Smith* (n 178) 932.   [183] ibid 930, 937.

[184] Confirmed again in *R v Finta* [1994] 1 SCR 701 (SCC).

[185] *R v Starr* (n 97) [211]–[214]. However, the three-way split in the Court failed to resolve the analytical sequence in relation to the traditional common law exceptions and the new principled approach which a trial court should apply.   [186] *R v Rockey* [1996] 3 SCR 829 (SCC).

looking after. The child's behaviour had changed markedly in the months following the incident, exhibiting fear of social encounters with men, and engaging in inappropriate sexual behaviour with other children. At trial, expert evidence that the child would be traumatized by being called as a witness was uncontradicted. The Crown tendered seven hearsay statements he made about the incident, to his parents, a play therapist and a paediatrician, from two days after the alleged event to the date of trial. Reliability of the statements was not in issue. The Supreme Court held that necessity on the *Khan* test may be satisfied:

- if the child is incompetent to testify;[187]
- if the child is unable to testify;
- if the child is (physically) unavailable to testify; or
- if the trial judge is satisfied, based on expert evidence of psychological assessments, that testimony in court might traumatize or otherwise harm the child.[188]

The child here was found to be incompetent as it was unrealistic to think that the child could have communicated as evidence in any useful sense. In any event the necessity test on the ground of trauma was satisfied by the expert evidence; the court was not required to wait for proof of actual harm to the child.[189] While mere discomfort would be insufficient to establish necessity, a prediction of any degree of trauma would suffice.[190]

What if the child does testify? In *Rockey*, in *obiter*, Sopinka J suggested that the out-of-court statements might nonetheless be reasonably necessary in order to put a full and frank account of the child's version of the relevant events before the jury.[191] This might mean that where the child's testimony was incomplete, the hearsay statements could be used to complete the Crown's case. This arose for consideration in *R v R(D)*,[192] where the courts had to deal with three young siblings who undoubtedly had been severely damaged physically and psychologically by prolonged sexual abuse, the only live issue at trial being the identity of the perpetrator. A relative of their foster carers had pleaded guilty to sexually assaulting the children, after the trial of their own parents and stepfather. One of the five-year-old twins when testifying could not recall one incident where she returned from an unsupervised visit with her father; when her foster mother questioned her about blood on her underpants, she said that her father had digitally penetrated her. The majority held that her statements were not

---

[187] As in *R v P(J)* [1993] 1 SCR 469 (SCC), affirming (1992) 74 CCC (3d) 276 (Quebec CA) admitting hearsay statements by an incompetent toddler.

[188] *R v Rockey* (n 186) [28]. However, in *R v R(M)* [2004] JQ No 9288 (Quebec CA) where a four-year-old made six statements about ongoing abuse at a nursery, the first spontaneous and the others essentially repeating the first, it was not necessary to have a psychologist testify about the trauma and harm likely to result if she gave *viva voce* evidence, to satisfy the necessity criterion.

[189] Unlike in many American jurisdictions, where evidence of actual trauma may be required: see above Chapter 8 section 3(b)(iii). [190] *R v Rockey* (n 186) [28].

[191] ibid [20].

[192] *R v R(D)* [1996] 2 SCR 291 (SCC). For the subsequent success of a malicious prosecution action brought by 11 other adults charged with offences against these children, who eventually recanted their allegations, see *Kvello, Klassen and Sharp et al v Miazga, Dueck and Bunko-Ruys et al* [2003] SKQB 559, 234 DLR (4th) 612 (Saskatchewan QB) discussed above Chapter 4 section F.2(b).

sufficiently reliable to be admitted because the girl's young brother had admitted to having sexual contact with both his sisters on that visit, and there was evidence that the children liked to cover up the sexual activity amongst themselves. A hearsay statement should not be admitted when it is equally consistent with other hypotheses.[193] This conclusion seems to require the court to examine the content of the statement in the context of other evidence in the *voir dire*, rather than confining itself to the source and circumstances of the hearsay in determining its 'admissibility reliability'. L'Heureux-Dubé J dissented on the basis that the trial judge in the *voir dire* merely had to determine a threshold of admissibility, rather than ultimate probative value, and so the statement should have been left to the jury.[194]

What if the child testifies, but her evidence is inconsistent with the out-of-court statements? The necessity and reliability criteria of *Khan* and *Smith* were applied by the Supreme Court of Canada in *R v B(KG)*[195] in 1993 to videotaped statements by eyewitnesses identifying the accused as the victim's killer, when they resiled from their statements at trial. The Court overruled its previous decisions which had held that past inconsistent statements are admissible only to impeach the witnesses' credibility, as 'original evidence',[196] which is the English common law position. Instead the Supreme Court ruled that they are admissible as proof of the truth. To arrive at this conclusion, the Court had to clarify its definition of 'necessity', holding that the unavailability of the witness is not an indispensable condition; rather, necessity must be given 'a flexible definition capable of encompassing diverse situations', including where a witness recants.[197]

This then opened the door to the Supreme Court's conclusion in *R v U(F)*[198] that a Canadian court could receive and accept a child's allegations of incest against her father in her police interview,[199] notwithstanding her recantation of her complaints at trial.[200] Admission of the previous statement was necessary 'because evidence of the same quality cannot be obtained at trial'[201]—an odd way to describe contradictory evidence from a competent witness. Cross-examination of the recanting witness at trial was 'an almost perfect substitute for contemporaneous cross-examination'.[202] The accused's inculpatory admissions in his video-recorded interview reinforced the reliability of the child's initial disclosures. A similar result will now be possible in English criminal courts under s 119 of the CJA 2003, which permits previous inconsistent statements to be admitted as evidence of any matters stated if the witness admits making the statement.

Finally, what if the child does testify at trial but refuses to answer any questions about the alleged assault, and refuses to adopt the videotaped interview with the police (which is a statutory precondition in Canada to the admissibility of the videotape)?[203] This occurred in *R v F(WJ)*[204] with a child aged five at the time of the alleged assaults

---

[193] *R v R(D)* ibid [32]–[35].   [194] ibid [68]–[71].   [195] *R v B(KG)* (n 171).
[196] *Deacon v The King* [1947] SCR 531 (SCC) 537–538.   [197] *R v B(KG)* (n 171) 796–799.
[198] *R v U(FJ)* (n 154).
[199] The initial police interview was not recorded because the tape recorder malfunctioned, but the Supreme Court permitted the police officer's summary from his notes to be admitted as substantive evidence.
[200] *R v U(FJ)* (n 154) [30], [32].   [201] ibid [35].   [202] ibid [36]–[37].
[203] Criminal Code of Canada s 175.1.
[204] *R v F(WJ)* [1999] 3 SCR 569 [also reported *sub nom R v Folino*] (SCC).

and aged six years and eight months at trial. The trial judge held that the Crown had failed to offer any evidence as to why the witness had stopped testifying, and refused to infer that hearsay evidence was now necessary. The Crown presented no further evidence and the accused was acquitted.[205] McLachlin J (as she then was), writing for the majority, noted that the child exhibited great difficulty in giving verbal responses during the preliminary inquiry into competence, and concluded that it was self-evident from the circumstances that direct evidence would be unavailable with reasonable efforts, making it unnecessary to seek extrinsic evidence of reasonable necessity.[206] Her Ladyship explained the context for the 'child-sensitivity policies' emerging in Canadian law, as follows:

The law, through the efforts of Parliament and the courts, now recognizes that children may encounter greater problems in giving their evidence than adults. The difficulty begins with understanding the oath or the obligation imposed by a promise to tell the truth. But it does not stop there. The entire court process may be alien and frightening to children, no matter how well briefed. The child finds him- or herself in a strange world, surrounded by stern and imposing adult strangers, demanding on pain of perhaps incompletely understood consequences that the child reveal what he or she knows. Sexual assault cases bring yet another anxiety. The child is asked to reveal to these imposing and intimidating strangers the most private details of what was done to him or her. From infancy, the child may have been trained not to discuss such things with strangers. He or she has acquired a sense of privacy, and perhaps a sense of shame and guilt about such matters. The child finds him- or herself conflicted. Many children, despite these problems, prove equal to the task. But it is not surprising that a few find themselves unable to respond in any meaningful way. The policy of the law in recent decades points to seeking to understand and recognize these difficulties. When we do, it becomes apparent that a child's inability to answer questions about upsetting and highly personal events some time in the past may well establish reasonable necessity in Wigmore's sense of unavailability. Instead of treating the child witness more harshly than the adult, as those who insist on special evidence of necessity suggest, we should be seeking to understand the child's special situation.[207]

Therefore, while fear or disinclination to testify, without more, does not constitute necessity, evidence as to the reason why the child fails to give evidence in court is not essential.[208] A new trial was ordered.

The minority of three Supreme Court Justices would have upheld the trial judge's approach on the basis that a finding of necessity is not a mere formality whenever a witness is uncommunicative for some unknown reason. Without knowing why a witness is refusing to testify, the court cannot know whether that witness is genuinely unavailable so as to satisfy the necessity test. It is submitted that the minority's position is to be preferred. Hearsay is usually very much inferior to oral evidence. *R v F(WJ)* illustrates how far the admission of hearsay evidence can undermine the traditional precepts of the adversarial trial, resulting in convictions based upon untested evidence.

---

[205] It will be recalled that in Canada the prosecution may appeal from an acquittal (discussed above, Chapter 1 section B.1). [206] *R v F(WJ)* (n 204) [39]–[41].
[207] ibid [43]. [208] ibid [44]–[45].

The role of corroboration in determining the reliability criterion of crucial hearsay evidence in Canadian law remains unclear,[209] sowing confusion in the lower courts.[210] Some appellate courts have taken a narrow view, looking only at the circumstances surrounding the making of the statement,[211] whereas others have looked to extrinsic confirmatory evidence,[212] as indeed did *Khan*.[213]

(b) Hearsay in Canadian civil courts

Logically there is no reason for the common law hearsay rules applicable to civil proceedings not to adopt the flexibility of the criminal courts, and so it has proved.[214] Indeed, the hearsay statement of the complainant in *Khan* was admitted in the disciplinary proceedings for professional misconduct against Dr Khan, applying the Supreme Court's criteria.[215] The Ontario Court of Appeal held that the fact that the child, by then aged eight, did testify before the disciplinary tribunal served to enhance the reliability of the hearsay statement because she was cross-examined, but this did not displace the necessity of admitting the hearsay statement. The following factors were considered relevant to the determination of necessity:

- the age of the child at the time of the alleged event and at the time of testimony;
- the manner in which the child testifies including the extent to which it is necessary to resort to leading questions to elicit answers;
- the child's demeanour when testifying;
- the substance of the child's testimony, particularly the coherence and completeness of the child's description of the events in question;
- any professed inability by the child to recall all or part of the relevant events;
- any evidence of matters occurring between the event and the time of the child's testimony which may reflect on the child's ability at provide an independent and accurate account of the events; and
- any expert evidence relevant to the child's ability at the time of testimony to comprehend, recall or narrate the events in issue.

---

[209] *R v Starr* (n 97) held that a hearsay statement about the deceased's future intentions was inadmissible even though its reliability was corroborated by extrinsic evidence, but in *R v R(D)* (n 192) extrinsic evidence was used to show that a hearsay statement was unreliable.

[210] The situation has been described as 'verging on doctrinal incoherence': B Archibald 'The Canadian Hearsay Revolution: Is Half a Loaf Better Than No Loaf at All?' (1999) 25 Queen's LJ 1, 61–62.

[211] *R v C(B) and G(K)* (1993) 12 OR (3d) (Ontario CA); *R v Conway and Husband* (1997) 36 OR (3d) 579 (Ontario CA).

[212] *R v Big Eagle* (1997) 163 Sask R 73 (Saskatchewan CA); *R v Pearson* (1994) 36 CR (4th) 343 (British Columbia CA); *Winnipeg Child and Family Services v LL* [1994] 6 WWR 458 (Manitoba CA); *R v F(RG)* [1997] 6 WWR 273 (Alberta CA); *R v W(LT)* (1995) 131 Sask R 47 (Saskatchewan CA); *R v Dubois* (1997) 118 CCC (3d) 544 (Quebec CA).

[213] In relation to the physical evidence of semen and saliva on the child's sleeve.

[214] G Renaud 'Hearsay after *R v Khan* and *R v Smith*' (1995) 17 Advocates' Quarterly 30.

[215] *Re Khan and College of Physicians and Surgeons of Ontario* (1992) 94 DLR (4th) 193 (Ontario CA).

Unlike English family courts, Canadian courts in child protection and custody proceedings do not treat hearsay statements by children as automatically admissible,[216] nor do they assume that the children cannot or should not be called to testify.[217] Most Canadian family courts flexibly apply the threshold criteria of necessity and reliability to the admission of children's hearsay in civil protection and private proceedings where child abuse is alleged.[218]

6. Hearsay reform in Australian law

(a) Hearsay in Australian criminal courts

In criminal proceedings, Australian law reformers at the State level have tended to adopt the approach of treating out-of-court statements by children as warranting specific statutory exemption from the hearsay rule.[219] In Western Australia, the 1992 reforms of children's evidence included abrogation of the hearsay rule, giving the trial judge discretion to admit any relevant pre-trial statement to another person by a child complainant under 16, whether the statement is recorded in writing or electronically, or not recorded at all.[220] Thus any oral statement by the child to an adult, for example, would be admissible even if it did not meet the common law criteria for recent complaint, although this consequence tended to be overlooked in appeals regarding the recent complaint doctrine in the early years immediately following the amending legislation.[221] Tasmania has similar legislation, but limited to statements recorded in writing or electronically or by other means, again conditional upon the child's availability for cross-examination.[222] South Australia has also unshackled young children's complaints of sexual assault from the requirements of the 'recent complaint' doctrine, making all complaints regardless of form admissible on a discretionary basis.[223]

---

[216] *Millar v Millar* (1994) 148 AR 225 (Alberta QB).

[217] eg *JPG v Superintendent of Family and Child Services (BC)* (1993) 25 BCAC 116 (BC CA) 120; *Child and Family Services of Winnipeg West v G(NJ)* [1990] MJ No 633 (Manitoba QB).

[218] D Thompson 'Are There *Any* Rules of Evidence in Family Law?' (2003) 21 Can Fam LQ 245, 295–296.

[219] The Commonwealth of Australia's Evidence Act 1995, which applies to Federal cases and to the Australian Capital Territory, takes a fairly conventional approach to hearsay, codifying the common law definitions of hearsay and original evidence and the exceptions, and adopting the standard statutory exceptions for business documents, etc. [ss 59–75]. The New South Wales Evidence Act 1995 follows the Federal model.

[220] Acts Amendment (Evidence of Children and Others) Act 1992 (Western Australia), s 106H amending the Evidence Act 1906 (Western Australia), which implemented the recommendation of the Law Reform Commission of Western Australia [*Report on Evidence of Children and Other Vulnerable Witnesses* (April 1991) [3.29]–[3.33]. The age limit is defined by Sch 7 s 1(b) as being determined as of the date of complaint, or on the date of indictment in the case of prosecutions under s 579 of the Criminal Code.

[221] M Dixon ' "Out Of the Mouth of Babes . . ."'—a review of the operation of the Acts Amendment (Evidence of Children) Act 1992' (1995) 25 Western Australia Law Review 301, 315.

[222] Evidence Amendment (Children and Special Witnesses) Act 1995 (Tasmania No 37 of 1995) s 122F.

[223] Evidence Act 1929 (South Australia) s 34ca; see the discussion of recent complaint below, section C. 'Young child' is defined as meaning a child of or under the age of 12 years [s 4].

In Queensland, repeal of the hearsay rule has been less bold, making documentary evidence of statements by children under 12 years made shortly after the occurrence, or to investigators at any time, admissible in any type of proceedings as evidence of the facts disclosed in the statement.[224] The child must be available for cross-examination, as must be the person recording the statement. While 'document' is broadly defined as including any sound record or any record of information whatever,[225] the requirement that there be a record of the statement makes the provision of limited value in relation to initial reports of abuse which typically are oral, unless of course the person to whom the complaint is made takes notes. The court retains residual discretion to exclude the hearsay evidence if it is considered to be 'inexpedient in the interests of justice' to admit it.[226] The Queensland Court of Criminal Appeal has held that a statement should not be automatically excluded where the child cannot remember the incident. The child may be required to testify that the statement was actually made; the fact that the child cannot be effectively cross-examined on the statement would go to weight rather than admissibility.[227] However, in another case it was suggested that the extent to which the child's statement could be adequately tested in cross-examination should be a factor in the trial court's exercise of its exclusionary discretion, in considering whether the evidence would have a prejudicial effect disproportionate to its probative value.[228] The Queensland Law Reform Commission recommended in 2000 that the existing legislation be amended: to apply to all children under 16 and to 'special witnesses'[229] aged 16 or 17; to remove the requirement of near-contemporaneity with the event when the statement is not made to an investigator, because it filtered out reports of historic abuse; and to give the court specific discretion to exclude an out-of-court statement which otherwise complies with the statutory requirements, for example because of delayed disclosure.[230] The Queensland Law Reform Commission declined to limit the range of material currently admissible to video-recorded statements. The child would still have to be available for cross-examination at trial, but would not be required to have a present recollection of the matters in the statement as a precondition of admissibility.

The Australian Law Reform and the Human Rights and Equal Opportunity Commission in its 1997 Report *Seen and Heard* expressed concern that because patterns of disclosure among child victims of abuse often include disclosure of small pieces of information over periods of time, the doctrine of recent complaint and other exceptions to the hearsay ban are not sufficient to get all relevant previous statements by children into evidence to prove the facts in issue at a trial.[231] The Commissions

---

[224] Evidence Act 1977 (Queensland) s 93A.　　　[225] ibid s 3.　　　[226] ibid ss 98, 130.

[227] *R v Cowie ex p Attorney-General* [1994] 1 Qd R 326 (Queensland CA), applying Evidence Act 1977 (Queensland) s 93A(3).

[228] *R v Far* [1996] 2 Qd R 49 (Queensland CA), 54–55 (Fitzgerald P), the *obiter dictum* not being confirmed by the rest of the Court.

[229] Currently defined as including a person who if required to give evidence in the normal way would be likely to suffer severe emotional trauma, or be disadvantaged as a witness because of cultural differences or intimidation: Evidence Act 1977 (Queensland) s 21A(1)(b).

[230] Queensland LRC *The Receipt of Evidence* (n 98) 149–156, Recommendation 8.1.

[231] Aus LRC, *Seen and Heard* (n 25) [14.79].

recommended that all Australian jurisdictions create an additional exception to the hearsay rule restricted to the statements of children relating to alleged child abuse, where admission of the hearsay statement is necessary and the statement is reasonably reliable. An important additional caveat, however, would be that no person could be convicted of an offence based solely on the evidence of one hearsay statement admitted under this statutory exception. However, it apparently was envisaged that the corroboration requirement would be rather loosely applied, with other statements by the same child, or medical evidence or expert psychological evidence, sufficing.[232]

(b) Hearsay in Australian civil courts

Care and protection proceedings in all Australian States and Territories are not bound by the rules of evidence.[233] If children are not directly involved in family law proceedings (whether as witnesses or parties) the rule against hearsay is relaxed.[234] Children are commonly heard in family law litigation through expert witnesses, court counsellors' reports or though a child's representative appointed for that purpose. The Family Law Act 1975 also suspends the rule against hearsay in relation to children's evidence in proceedings in the federal Family Court, established in 1976.[235]

Abandoning the rules of evidence can have deleterious consequences for the quality of the information presented to the court, however; as the Victoria Children's Court submitted to the Australian Law Reform Commission, 'it is not unusual to see words attributed to very young children which are well beyond the child's vocabulary. This practice can only detract from the probative value of the child's words and affect the credit of the evidence being given.'[236] This concern prompted the Australian Law Reform Commission to recommend that the national care and protection standards should stipulate that direct evidence by a witness should be preferred, except when the declarant is the subject child, in which case the child's hearsay statements should as far as possible be presented in the child's own words.[237]

7. Hearsay reform in New Zealand law

New Zealand's evidence legislation was amended in 1980 to introduce comprehensive provisions governing hearsay. Documentary first-hand hearsay evidence is rendered admissible in both criminal and civil cases if the maker of the statement had personal knowledge of the matters dealt with the statement and is unavailable to give

---

[232] Aus LRC, *Seen and Heard* [14.82], Recommendation 102.

[233] eg Children (Care and Protection) Act 1987 (New South Wales) s 70(3); Children and Young Persons Act 1989 (Victoria) s 82(1)(d); s 5(1); Community Welfare Act 1983 (Northern Territory) s 39(2).

[234] The Evidence Act applies to the Family Court wherever the Family Law Act 1975 is silent on evidentiary matters: Evidence Act s 8(1). The Family Law Act 1975 s 69ZT suspends the operation of the hearsay rule in relation to proceedings under Pt VII of the Act which deals specifically with matters relating to children. The court may give whatever weight to hearsay evidence it thinks fit: ss 69ZT, 69ZV(3).

[235] For further discussion of the current Australian statutory framework, see Aus LRC, *Seen and Heard* ch 16.   [236] ibid [17.59].

[237] ibid Recommendation 171.

evidence.[238] Oral hearsay is also admissible in criminal[239] and civil[240] proceedings if the same criteria are satisfied, but in criminal cases the statement must qualify for admission as a statement in the course of duty, or under other customary common law exceptions.[241]

In determining the weight to be attached to an admissible hearsay statement, the court is required to have regard to all the circumstances from which any inference could reasonably be drawn about its accuracy, and in particular the timing of the statement in relation to the occurrence described and any motive by the maker to conceal or misrepresent any fact or opinion.[242] The trial judge has discretion to reject any otherwise admissible statement if its probative value is outweighed by its prejudicial effect, or if for any other reason the court is satisfied it is not necessary or expedient in the interests of justice to admit the statement.[243] Of particular importance in this assessment will be the existence of corroborative evidence for the main allegations in the statement, and whether there are issues about the reliability of the statement which cross-examination could have profitably explored.[244] Unusually, the New Zealand Court of Appeal has jurisdiction to substitute its own discretion for that of the trial judge,[245] and interlocutory appeals from pre-trial admissibility rulings may be brought.[246] A previous statement by a testifying witness, whether consistent or inconsistent, may be admitted only if the court is of the view that the statement's probative value outweighs that witness's *viva voce* evidence.[247]

The New Zealand Law Commission has drafted a comprehensive Evidence Code which would liberalize rather than abolish the hearsay rule for both criminal and civil cases, adopting the Canadian criteria of necessity and reliability.[248] The hearsay provisions would apply only to non-witnesses, witnesses being defined as persons who give evidence and can be cross-examined.[249] Necessity is predicated upon the unavailability of the maker of the statement on the grounds of death, absence from New Zealand, unfitness to be a witness due to age or physical or mental condition, or non-compellability.[250] It is unclear whether the testimonial incompetence of a very young child, as in the Canadian case of *Khan*,[251] would constitute unfitness due to age so as to satisfy the necessity criterion. An additional ground of unavailability for civil cases only is undue delay or expense if the maker is required to be a witness.[252]

---

[238] Evidence Amendment Act (No 2) 1980 (New Zealand) s 3(1)(a).   [239] ibid s 7.

[240] ibid s 7.   [241] Codified in Evidence Amendment Act (No 2) 1980 (New Zealand) ss 9–14.

[242] ibid s 17.   [243] ibid s 18.

[244] *R v L* [1994] 2 NZLR 54 (New Zealand CA); *R v J* [1988] 1 NZLR 20 (New Zealand CA).

[245] Evidence Amendment Act (No 2) 1980 (New Zealand) s 19. The more conventional approach is to require an error of law on the part of the trial court before an appellate court could override its exercise of discretion.   [246] Crimes Act 1961 (New Zealand) s 379A.

[247] Evidence Amendment Act (No 2) 1980 (New Zealand) s 4.

[248] NZLC *Evidence* (Report No 55) vol 1 [52], [63]–[64].

[249] ibid vol 2 Draft Evidence Code s 4. Previous statements by witnesses are subject to a different set of rules [s 37]. Implied assertions are excluded from operation of the rule [vol 2, [C22]].

[250] ibid vol 2 Draft *Evidence Code* s 16(2).

[251] *R v Khan* (n 171) discussed above, section B.5(a).

[252] NZLC *Evidence* (n 248) Draft Evidence Code s 18.

The reliability test is the same for both civil and criminal proceedings: the circumstances must provide a 'reasonable assurance' that the statement is reliable,[253] having regard to the nature and contents of the statement, the circumstances in which it was made, and anything relating to the truthfulness or accuracy of the observation of the maker.[254] Multiple layers of hearsay is a factor in considering the reliability of the statement. Judicial warnings about hearsay evidence are not mandatory, but the Code would require the trial judge to consider whether they would be appropriate.[255] There are no special provisions for statements by children, presumably because they would be encompassed by the new flexible rules.

8. Hearsay reform in American law

(a) The constitutional dimension to the hearsay rule

The use of hearsay testimony in child abuse cases has been described as representing perhaps the most dramatic shift in the American legal system in the past 300 years.[256] Reference has already been made in the context of the admissibility of videotaped testimony[257] to the Confrontation Clause in the American Constitution, and also in many State constitutions, which provides that 'in all criminal prosecutions, the accused shall enjoy the right to be confronted with the witnesses against him...' The right of confrontation, if interpreted strictly, could bar all hearsay evidence. However, as noted earlier, the US Supreme Court historically gave a fairly flexible interpretation to the right of confrontation. The Supreme Court has found hearsay evidence admissible where the person making the hearsay statement is available to be cross-examined at trial.[258] Where the declarant is not available, the Supreme Court in *Ohio v Roberts*[259] in 1980 established two general requirements for hearsay to be admissible:

- the prosecution had to show that the person making the hearsay statement was 'unavailable'; and
- the hearsay evidence had to bear adequate indicia of reliability, being satisfied if the statement fell within a 'firmly rooted hearsay exception', or bore 'particularised guarantees of trustworthiness'.[260]

However, in 2004 the US Supreme Court reversed *Ohio v Roberts*, in *Crawford v Washington*,[261] holding that where testimonial statements are in issue, the only indicium of reliability sufficient to satisfy constitutional demands is confrontation, ie testing in the 'crucible of cross-examination', whereas the 'unpardonable vice'[262]

---

[253] ibid Draft Evidence Code s 18 (civil), 19 (criminal). [254] ibid Draft Evidence Code s 16(1).
[255] ibid vol 1 [70], Draft Evidence Code s 108(2)(a).
[256] DF Ross, AR Warren and LS McGough 'Foreword: Hearsay Testimony in Trials Involving Child Witnesses' (1999) 5 *Psychology, Public Policy and Law* 251, 252.
[257] Chapter 8 Section B.3(b)(iii). [258] *California v Green* 399 US 149 (USSC 1970) 158–161.
[259] *Ohio v Roberts* 448 US 56 (USSC 1980). [260] ibid 66.
[261] *Crawford v Washington* 541 US 36 (USSC 2004) (Rehnquist CJ and O'Connor J dissenting).
[262] ibid 63.

of the *Roberts* test admitted statements of *ex parte* testimony upon a mere reliability finding.[263] *Roberts'* framework was criticized as unpredictable because whether a statement was deemed reliable depended on which factors a judge considered and how much weight he accorded each of them.[264] The majority accepted that where 'non-testimonial hearsay'[265] is at issue, the States have constitutional flexibility in the development of hearsay law. However, where 'testimonial evidence' is at issue, then the 6th Amendment demands what the common law required: the unavailability of the maker of the statement, and a prior opportunity for cross-examination.[266]

Crawford has thrown American hearsay law into disarray, generating a plethora of seemingly irreconcilable cases. *Roberts* had been relied upon in *Idaho v Wright*[267] in which the US Supreme Court had ruled that child hearsay statements admitted under residual exceptions to the hearsay rule could withstand challenge under the Confrontation Clause if the witness was unavailable and there were particularized guarantees of trustworthiness shown from the totality of the circumstances surrounding the making of the statement.[268] This uncertainty as to the implications of *Crawford v Washington* for children's statements[269] must be borne in mind in the following discussion of American common law and statutory reform of hearsay.

(b) American hearsay reform at common law

The common law hearsay exception most frequently invoked in child abuse proceedings is the American equivalent of *res gestae*, 'excited utterances' or spontaneous declarations. In the context of sexual offences against children, the rule is sometimes described as the 'tender years' exception; the hearsay statement is admissible as proof that a sexual assault has occurred, even in the absence of corroborating evidence.[270] There are three requirements:

• there must be an event or condition which startles or excites the child;
• the statement must be made while the child is under the stress of excitement caused by the event or condition; and
• the statement must relate to the startling event.[271]

---

[263] ibid 60–62.   [264] ibid 37.

[265] Much difficulty has arisen in relation to what constitutes 'testimonial statements'; the Supreme Court only gave some examples of a 'core class of testimonial statements,' including affidavits, depositions, and previous testimony not subject to cross examination [*Crawford v Washington* ibid 52]. See *US v Peneaux* 432 F 3d 888 (US CA 8th Cir 2005) holding that a child's statement to a medical examiner at a Child Advocacy Center alleging sexual and physical abuse was not testimonial and hence was admissible hearsay; W Bough 'Why the Sky Didn't Fall: Using Judicial Creativity to Circumvent *Crawford v Washington*' (2004–2005) 38 Loyola of Los Angeles L Rev 1835.   [266] *Crawford v Washington* (n 261) 68.

[267] *Idaho v Wright* 497 US 805 (USSC 1990).

[268] *Idaho v Wright* had been strongly criticized for being too narrow in its application to child hearsay, by preventing juries from considering the reliability of statements in the context of the entire case, and not just the circumstances of the making of the statement: J Myers, A Redlich, G Goodman and L Prizmich 'Jurors' Perceptions of Hearsay in Child Sexual Abuse Cases' (1999) 5 *Psychology, Public Policy, and Law* 388.

[269] E Thompson 'Child Sex Abuse Victims: How will Their Stories be Heard after *Crawford v Washington*?' (2004–2005) 27 Campbell L Rev 281.   [270] Myers (n 52) vol 2, 218.

[271] *NCPCA Investigation and Prosecution of Child Abuse* (n 60) 354; Myers ibid vol 2, 215–240 §7.33. The rule as it applies to witnesses in general is codified in Federal Rule of Evidence 803(2).

American courts have liberalized the requirements in the case of very young children who are victimized by sexual assault, particularly in relation to the lapse of time, on the theory that the danger of fabrication is more remote.[272] The child need not be testimonially competent for the statement to be admitted. In *White v Illinois*, involving a sexual assault on a four-year-old girl, the US Supreme Court held that excited utterances may be admitted without the prosecution having to show that the child is unavailable or will testify later, because such statements have substantial probative value and their reliability could not be recaptured by later court testimony, and so the considerations underpinning the Confrontation Clause do not obtain.[273] However, the Supreme Court in *Crawford v Washington* specifically referred to *White v Illinois*, and questioned whether the child's statements admitted in that case would survive the Court's new confrontation clause analysis.[274]

(c) American hearsay reform by statute

Notwithstanding this liberalized view of the timeliness requirement, State legislators have been concerned that too many statements from children have not fit into common law hearsay exceptions.[275] By March 2002, 34 State legislatures had created special hearsay exceptions for criminal child abuse cases.[276] Many of these so-called 'tender years' statutes also apply to civil proceedings. We will discuss here only those statutory models which are not dependent upon the child being available to testify at the trial proper,[277] and which do not require that the out-of-court statement be in the form of videotaped evidence, which we have considered earlier.[278]

The Alabama statute[279] is an example of a highly particularized list of factors to satisfy the unavailability and reliability criteria. The hearsay provisions apply to any victim or witness under 12 years of age at the time of the proceeding, where the crimes being tried involve sexual or physical abuse or exploitation. The statement

---

[272] *US v DeNoyer* 811 F 2d 436 (8th Cir 1987) 438; *State v Wagner* 508 NE 2d 164 (Ohio App 1986) 166; *Commonwealth v Bailey* 510 A 2d 367 (Pennsylvania Superior Ct 1986) 368; *State v Logue* 372 NW 2d 152 (South Dakota SC 1985) 159; *State v Doe* 719 P 2d 554 (Washington CA 1986).

[273] *White v Illinois* 502 US 346 (USSC 1992) 356–357. The Supreme Court reached the same conclusion in relation to statements made by a patient seeking medical diagnosis or treatment.

[274] *Crawford v Washington* (n 261) fn 8.

[275] M McGrath and C Clemens 'The Child Victim as a Witness in Sexual Abuse Cases' (1985) 46 Montana L Rev 229.

[276] For an overview of the typical provisions see LS McGough 'Hearing and Believing Hearsay' (1999) 5 *Psychology, Public Policy, and Law* 485.

[277] Only three States make availability of the child to testify at trial an absolute precondition for the admission of an out-of-court statement: Georgia: Ga Code Ann §24-3-16; Texas Code Crim P Ann §38.072; and Vermont R Evid 804a. Indiana requires that the child has been available for face-to-face cross-examination when the statement was made: Indiana Code §35-37-4-6 (due to an explicit constitutional requirement for 'face-to-face' confrontation: *Pierce v State* 677 NE 2d 39 (Indiana 1997)), and Maine requires that a judge has been present: Maine Rev Stat Ann tit 15 §1205.

[278] Discussed above Chapter 8 section B.3(b)(iii).

[279] Alabama Code §15-25-31 to 33 (1985, amended 1994).

must concern a material element of the offence charged. The child must be unavailable due to:

- the child's death;
- the child's intentional removal from the jurisdiction by the defendant or someone acting for him;
- the child's total failure of memory;
- the child's physical or mental disability;
- the child's testimonial incompetence (including an inability to communicate because of fear); or
- a substantial likelihood that the child will suffer severe emotional trauma by testifying.

The finding of unavailability must be supported by expert testimony.[280] The court is directed to consider the following factors in determining the trustworthiness of the statement:

- the child's personal knowledge;
- the child's age and maturity;
- certainty that the statement was in fact made, including the credibility of the person testifying about the statement;
- any apparent motive the child may have to falsify or distort the event, including bias, corruption or coercion;
- timing of the statement;
- whether more than one person heard the statement;
- whether the child was suffering from pain or distress when making the statement;
- the nature and duration of the alleged abuse;
- whether the statement represents a graphic account beyond the child's knowledge and experience;
- whether the statement has a 'ring of veracity', has an internal consistency or coherence, and uses terminology appropriate to the child's age;
- whether the statement is spontaneous or directly responsive to questions; and
- whether the statement is suggestive due to improperly leading questions.

It is not necessary for all these reliability factors to be satisfied. For example, in a case involving a three-year-old girl the Alabama appellate court held that the trial court did not abuse its discretion by allowing testimony regarding her statements, notwithstanding the defence's argument that 3 of the 13 enumerated factors pointed in favour of disallowing them; the trial judge could still base his decision on any one of 10 remaining factors, plus any factor not enumerated, in order to show particularized guarantees of trustworthiness.[281] This legislation was found to pass constitutional muster;[282] indeed, until *Crawford v Washington*[283] only in Arizona has a child hearsay statute been found unconstitutional under either the federal or State Constitution.[284]

---

[280] Expert evidence is also required by the Indiana Code §35-37-4-6.
[281] *Fortner v State* 582 So 2d 581 (Alabama Cr App 1990).   [282] ibid.
[283] *Crawford v Washington* (n 261).   [284] *State v Robinson* 735 P 2d 801 (Arizona 1987).

Other models provide narrower bases of unavailability, such as a requirement that there be a finding of fact that testifying might result in severe emotional or mental harm to the child.[285] Most statutes shore up the reliability criterion by an additional requirement that the statement must be corroborated in relation to the acts they describe if the child is unavailable to testify at trial.[286] Several States restrict the hearsay provisions to sexual offences.[287]

In Federal charges of child abuse, prosecutors often rely upon Federal Rule of Evidence 807, which is a residual hearsay exception making a statement admissible where it is not specifically covered by other provisions but has equivalent circumstantial guarantees of trustworthiness, if the court determines that:

- the statement is offered as evidence of a material fact;
- the statement is more probative on the point for which it is offered than any other evidence which the proponent can procure through reasonable efforts; and
- the general purposes of these rules and the interests of justice will best be served by admission of the statement into evidence.[288]

The provision is also used for tort litigation under Federal law.[289] The US Supreme Court held in *Tome v US*[290] that a child's previous consistent statement describing the offence is admissible to rebut a charge of recent fabrication or improper motive only if the prosecution can prove that the statement was made before the alleged motive arose. This ruling has been criticized as excluding many relevant and reliable out-of-court statements made by child victims, when they often make poor witnesses in court.[291] The ruling is logical in its own terms, but does create almost insuperable difficulties for the prosecution in pinpointing a time at which arose the alleged motive—such as parental conflict or a child's unhappiness at home—when cause and effect are likely to be so entangled evidentially. Thus far Congress has not followed the example of State legislators to create a specific 'tender years' hearsay exception in the Federal Rules of Evidence, possibly because so few prosecutions of child abuse are mounted in federal courts.[292]

---

[285] Florida Stat Ann ch 90.803(23); Pennsylvania Cons Stat Ann §5985.1.

[286] Alaska Stat §12.40.110; Arizona Rev Stat. §13-1416; Colorado Rev. Stat §13-25-129, §18-3-411; §18-3-411; Florida Stat Ann ch 90.803(23); Idaho Code §19-3024; 725 Illinois Comp Stat Ann §5/115-10; Maryland Ann Code art 27 §775 (corroboration only required as to opportunity to commit the offence); Minnesota Stat Ann §595.02(3); Mississippi Code Ann §13-1-407 and Mississippi R Evid 80325(25); New Jersey R Evid 803c(27); North Dakota R Evid 803(24); Ohio R Evid 807; Oklahoma Stat Ann tit 12 §2803.1; Oregon Rev Stat § 40.460(18b); South Dakota Codified Laws §19-16-38; Washington Rev Code Ann § 9A.44.120.

[287] Alaska, Arkansas [Arkansas R Evid 803(25)], California (child's hearsay statement admissible only in order to admit the accused's confession), Colorado, Maine [Maine Rev Stat Ann tit 15 §1205], Massachusetts [Massachusetts Gen Laws ch 233 § 81], Michigan [Michigan R Evid 803A], Mississippi, New Jersey, Nevada [Nevada Rev Stat §51.35], North Dakota, Utah, and Vermont [Vermont R Evid 804a].

[288] Formerly Federal Rule of Evidence 803(24).

[289] *Doe v US* 976 F 2d 1071, (7th Cir 1993) *certiorari* denied 510 US 812.

[290] *Tome v US* 513 US 150 (USSC 1995).

[291] D Lathi 'Sex Abuse, Accusations of Lies, and Videotaped Testimony: a Proposal for a Federal Hearsay Exception in Child Sexual Abuse Cases' (1997) 68 U of Colorado L Rev 507, 508.

[292] *Tome v US* (n 290) was tried in a Federal court because the offence alleged occurred on an Indian reservation, which is governed by Federal law.

The implications of *Crawford v Washington* for child abuse cases remain unclear at present. Some State hearsay statutory provisions for children have been found unconstitutional where the child was not an available witness for the trial; the public policy in favour of limiting a child victim's exposure to a potentially traumatizing courtroom experience did not suffice to overcome the constitutional objections.[293]

Crawford applies only to criminal prosecutions, and therefore will not affect civil child protection proceedings to which the constitutional guarantee of confrontation does not apply.[294] It is unclear whether it applies to firmly rooted hearsay exceptions, although the majority's criticism of the excited utterances exception implies that it does.[295] The majority unfortunately declined to give a comprehensive definition to 'testimonial evidence' which triggers the right of confrontation, but held that it applies at a minimum to previous testimony, depositions, confessions and police interrogations,[296] where the statement was made under circumstances which would lead an objective witness reasonably to believe that the statement would be available for use in a later trial.[297] In June 2006 the Supreme Court clarified that statements to police will be regarded as non-testimonial if made in an ongoing emergency requesting assistance, but will be treated as testimonial once the circumstances objectively indicate the emergency is over.[298] Therefore, a child's statement made to a social worker or police officer would seem to fall within the forbidden category, although prosecutors are developing arguments that interdisciplinary interviews by child protection teams or by medical examiners are not primarily for the purpose of criminal litigation, but to determine whether the child is at risk and needs medical or other care.[299] The American Prosecutors Research Institute is advising interviewers not to canvass 'truth and lies' with a child because this is indicative of a testimonial statement.[300] Rather oddly to Commonwealth lawyers, *Crawford* incorporates into the test of what is 'testimonial' a statement which would lead an objective witness reasonably to believe that the

[293] eg *Snowdon v State* 867 A 2d 314 (Maryland CA 2005) 89–90; *State v Carothers* 692 NW 2d 544 (South Dakota Supreme Ct 2005); *TP v State* 2004 Ala Crim App LEXIS 236 (Alabama Crim App 2004).

[294] A Phillips 'Out of Harm's Way: Hearings that are Safe from the Impact of *Crawford v. Washington*' (2005) 18 Update (National Center for Prosecution of Child Abuse) 8 (Part 1) and 9 (Part 2).

[295] However, an hysterical four-year-old child's complaints immediately following the alleged incident were held to be excited utterances and not subject to *Crawford* in *State v Doe* 103 P 3d 967 (Idaho CA 2004).   [296] *Crawford v Washington* (n 261) 68.

[297] ibid 54.

[298] *Davis v Washington, Hammon v Indiana* 05-5224, 05-5705 (19 June 2006) (USSC).

[299] V Vieth 'Keeping the Balance True: Admitting Child Hearsay in the Wake of *Crawford v Washington*' (2004) 16 Update (National Center for Prosecution of Child Abuse) 12. The strategy was successful in *Bobadilla v Minnesota* 709 NW 2d 243 (Minnesota Supreme C 2006) where a forensic interview of a three-year-old complainant of buggery was admitted when he was found incompetent to testify, because the interview had been conducted under the mandatory reporting laws for multiple purposes, only one of which was with an eye toward a criminal trial. See also *People v Vigil* 2006 Colo LEXIS 65, (Colorado Supreme C 2006) reversing 104 P 3d 258 (statements by a seven-year-old child to a doctor on a child protection team). There are however contrary cases holding investigatory interviews inadmissible under *Crawford*: *State v Henderson* 129 P 2d 646 (Kansas CA 2006); *Rangel v State* 2006 WL 1563058 (Texas CA 2006); *Contreras v State* 2005 Fla App LEXIS 1443 (Florida Dist Ct App 4th Dist 2005).

[300] A Phillips *Cases Interpreting Crawford -v- Washington* (National Center for Prosecution of Child Abuse, American Prosecutor's Research Institute, Alexandria Virginia 2006) 89.

statement would be available for use at a later trial,[301] which some courts have softened in the context of child abuse into what a reasonable child of that age would understand about the purpose of the investigation and court process.[302] Moreover, it is important to appreciate that *Crawford* will not apply to a child's previous statements if the child is available for cross-examination at trial or at a pre-trial hearing, and so it will have its greatest impact where the child is found incompetent or too traumatized to testify.[303]

9. Evaluation: special admissibility rules for child hearsay?

American empirical research shows that juries are much more reluctant to convict a defendant of sexual abuse where they do not hear the child tell the story, so that the prosecution's case rests upon hearsay.[304] This suggests that prosecutors should not rush to call hearsay witnesses if there is any other way of getting that evidence before the jury.

The US Supreme Court in *Tome v US* warned that while courts must be sensitive to the difficulties attendant upon the prosecution of alleged child abusers, especially since the child is often the prosecution's only eyewitness, they should not alter the evidentiary rules merely because litigants might prefer different rules in a particular class of cases.[305] This caution is particularly apposite in relation to hearsay. In the absence of compelling empirical evidence that children's out-of-court statements about sexual or physical abuse are inherently more trustworthy than the statements of adults, it is submitted that creating a special statutory exception for children cannot be justified by the paucity of other evidence. The risk of miscarriages of justice is too great.

The Canadian approach of admitting hearsay evidence where it is reliable and necessary has the appeal of being strongly oriented towards the assessment of the circumstances of the individual case. Professor Thompson has distilled from the Canadian criminal and civil child abuse cases the following factors which are typically considered by trial judges in evaluating a child hearsay statement under the reliability criterion of admissibility:[306]

(1) circumstances surrounding the statement:
- spontaneity,
- use of leading questions or prompting,
- timing or recency of the statement
(2) the adult in-court reporter
- objectivity or bias
- note-taking or recording
- presence of custody or access dispute
- appropriate preparation for an interview with the child

---

[301] *Crawford v Washington* (n 261) 51–52.

[302] *People v Vigil* (n 299) (seven-year-old); *State v Brigman* 2006 NC App LEXIS 1071 (North Carolina CA 2006) (children aged two and five).   [303] Discussed earlier, Chapter 8 section B.3(b)(iii).

[304] DF Ross, R Lindsay and DF Marsil 'The Impact of Hearsay Testimony on Conviction Rates in Trials of Child Sexual Abuse: Toward Balancing the Rights of Defendants and Child Witnesses' (1999) 5 *Psychology, Public Policy, and Law* 439.   [305] *Tome v US* (n 290) 166.

[306] Thompson (n 218) 295–296.

(3) the child
- no reason to fabricate
- age of child
- intelligence and maturity
- details of demeanour

(4) the contents of the statement
- spontaneous reproduction
- sufficient detail
- coherence
- the conscious notion of sexual acts
- consistency over time

(5) child behaviours accompanying the statement
- initial denial
- recantation
- sexual behaviours
- gestures

(6) relationship of the statement to other reliable evidence
- corroboration by real or physical evidence
- consistency with other testimony.

The Canadian hearsay revolution replacing rigid formulaic rules with flexibility strongly focusing on the facts of specific cases has much to commend it. That said, the state of the current caselaw in Canada makes it possible for an accused to be convicted on the basis of a child's hearsay statement which the defence has not had any opportunity to challenge directly in a meaningful way, and which has not been corroborated in any way. This raises fundamental questions about the continued viability of the values incarnated in the adversarial trial. Canadian courts, like their American counterparts before *Crawford v Washington*, seem to have accepted without much discussion that the 'necessity' or 'unavailability' criterion meets any constitutional objection based upon the absence of the opportunity to cross-examine.[307]

Imposing a separate requirement of corroboration where the child has not been available for cross-examination, as have the majority of American States with specific child hearsay exceptions, has initial appeal. However, it does reopen questions foreclosed by statutory reforms in the 1980s and 1990s abolishing the requirement of external corroboration of children's allegations, implying their assumed inherent unreliability as truth-tellers. The appeal courts would doubtless be invited to canvass anew technical issues as to what constitutes corroboration on the facts of each case. An additional difficulty is that a ruling on the admissibility of the hearsay evidence usually must be made early in the prosecution's case, when other potentially corroborative evidence has not yet been tendered. It has been argued that the farther afield the court goes in seeking confirmatory evidence, the greater the dangers of a 'bootstrap' approach

---

[307] The issue was directly addressed in *R v Collins* (1997) 118 CCC (3d) 514 (British Columbia CA), where the complainant died before trial.

whereby the admissibility of hearsay risks being determined, not on the statement's own merits, but by prejudgment of the strength of the other evidence available.[308]

It has been suggested that the Canadian hearsay revolution has been driven by a judicial perception that the credibility of the justice system rests upon its effectiveness as a crime control mechanism, reflecting a victim-oriented set of assumptions about the legitimacy of claims by classes of declarants.[309] This criticism is perhaps exaggerated, given the Canadian Supreme Court's doctrinal emphasis on the intrinsic issues affecting hearsay. However, 'rebalancing the system in favour of victims, witnesses and communities' is the proudly proclaimed rationale for the current English statutory reform of the rules of evidence.[310] The broad power created by the CJA 2003 to admit hearsay evidence of any level and of any form, where it is 'in the interests of justice',[311] and the narrowly framed discretion to exclude otherwise admissible hearsay because it would result in an 'undue waste of time' outweighing its probative value,[312] will create considerable unpredictability for those involved in child abuse prosecutions, making pre-trial decisions by the CPS and counsel (even) more difficult. Because the power to admit hearsay is cast as exercisable where 'the court is satisfied' it should do so,[313] and the power of exclusion is cast as discretion,[314] appellate courts may be reluctant to interfere with the trial judge's rulings, imposing a *Wednesbury* standard of irrationality as a threshold test.

That said, the CJA 2003 does open the door to the admission of a child's out-of-court statements where they are made in circumstances indicative of reliability, such as statements to professionals describing the offences which are properly recorded to eliminate any doubt as to how the statement was elicited and what the child actually said. Such strong guarantees of reliability do not feature in the reform to the doctrine of recent complaint, to which we now turn.

C. 'Recent' and Delayed Complaint

1. Recent complaint in English criminal cases

(a) The common law doctrine

The so-called 'recent complaint' doctrine is an example of an admissible out-of-court statement which at common law was unique to prosecutions for sexual offences. A complaint by the alleged victim shortly after the offence is admissible as evidence-in-chief for the prosecution. The doctrine imbues the timing of the complaint with evidential significance as being relevant to the alleged victim's credibility as a witness.

For the statement to be admissible, the prosecution must call the witnesses to whom she made the complaint; the evidence of the complainant that she complained will not

---

[308] Archibald (n 210) 37.   [309] ibid 32–33.
[310] See the Government's White Paper which preceded the Criminal Justice Bill 2003: *Justice for All* (Cmnd 5563 July 2002).   [311] CJA 2003 (England) s 114.
[312] ibid s 126.   [313] ibid ss 114(1)(d), 121.   [314] ibid s 117(7).

suffice.[315] Where the common law rule still prevails the jury must be instructed that the complaint is not evidence of the truth of the allegations because it is not independent of the complainant, so it can be used only to show that the complainant's conduct was consistent with her testimony.[316] The common law doctrine thus is an exception to the general ban on previous consistent statements discussed earlier,[317] and is a principle of freestanding admissibility on the basis that it is 'original' rather than hearsay evidence, because it is not admitted for proof of the truth of what was actually said in the complaint.[318] The evidence is admissible only to bolster the complainant's credibility, to rebut an anticipated attack by the defence alleging fabrication of the complaint. Nowhere else in the law governing out-of-court statements is such a pre-emptive attack countenanced.[319]

The justification accepted by modern English courts for limiting the admissibility of recent complaint at common law to sexual offences was that in these cases more hinged on the credibility of the participants than in most other areas, because sexual activity tends to take place in private and is usually kept secret, thus restricting the amount of other evidence which is likely to be available.[320] In the 13th century the rule was recorded by Bracton as being rooted in a presumption that a violated woman would immediately raise the 'hue and cry'.[321] Conversely any delay in complaining must be explicable by women's tendency to fantasize about sexual encounters and to make false allegations about them.[322] The same assumptions are still applied to young children.[323] The doctrine has been decried on the basis that it was founded on stereotypical and sexist assumptions which no longer prevail[324] (if they ever did),[325] and remains an indefensible anomaly. However, modern defenders of the rule point out that admissibility no longer depends on the gender of the victim,[326] and ascribe its probative value to common sense, on the basis that it is more likely than not that a victim of unwanted sexual advances will take an early opportunity to complain to a third party, particularly someone in a position of authority or of trust.[327]

---

[315] *White v The Queen* [1999] AC 210 (PC).

[316] *US v White Horse* 177 F Supp 2d 973 (US DC, South Dakota, 2001). See the Judicial Studies Board model direction recited in *R v Islam* [1999] 1 Cr App R 22 (CA) [1998] Crim LR 575.

[317] Discussed above section B.1 and Diagrams 13 and 15.

[318] Explained above sections B.1 and B.3(b).   [319] Noted by Buxton LJ in *R v Islam* (n 316).

[320] ibid citing with approval C Tapper (ed) *Cross on Evidence* (7th edn Butterworths, London 1990) 284.

[321] Raising the 'hue and cry' was a precondition to prosecuting the offence: Bracton, *De Legibus Angliae,* Lib. iii fol. 147 (ca 1250); *R v Lillyman* [1896] 2 QB 167 (C of Crown Cases Reserved); *R v Osborne* [1905] 1 KB 551 (CCR) 559. In 1898 the rule was described as 'a perverted survival' of the 'hue and cry' requirement by Holmes J in *Commonwealth v Cleary* [1898] 172 Mass 175 (Massachusetts Supreme Judicial Ct 1898) (cited with approval by Buxton LJ in *R v Islam* (n 316)).

[322] These assumptions were identified and accepted without question in *R v Osborne* ibid 558–561.

[323] eg *R v Osborne* ibid (the recent complaint doctrine applies even for offences to which a child cannot consent in law); *R v B* [1997] Crim LR 220 (CA) [victim aged ten]; *R v French* (unreported, 18 July 1997, CA) [victim aged eight].   [324] *R v Islam* (n 316) (Buxton LJ).

[325] See the withering attack on these assumptions by Thomas J in *R v H* [1997] 1 NZLR 673 (New Zealand CA) 686–689; *R v Batte* (2000) 145 CCC (3d) 498 (Ontario CA) [142]–[154].

[326] *R v Camellari* [1922] 2 KB 122 (CA).

[327] eg *R v Churchill* [1999] Crim LR 664 (CA); DJ Birch also defended the doctrine as 'rational' in her commentary and urged that it be extended to other offences depending on the complainant's veracity.

Yet retrospective empirical studies consistently show that only one-third of adults who suffered child sexual abuse revealed the abuse to anyone during childhood.[328] We shall revisit this issue after canvassing the scope of the modern doctrine.

The technical criteria prescribed by the English common law for admission of a complaint were:[329]

(1) the offence charged must be sexual in nature, although consent need not be in issue;[330]

(2) the statement must be spontaneous, and not elicited by questions of a leading or suggestive character (although a statement elicited by cross-questioning may still be admissible);[331]

(3) the complaint must have been made at the first reasonable opportunity after the offence was committed;

(4) the complaint must also have been made within a reasonable period following the alleged offence;[332] and

(5) the statement must amount to a complaint of sexual assault.[333]

If the criteria are not satisfied so as to permit the statement to become part of the prosecution's case, it may still become admissible following cross-examination of the complainant specifically alleging recent fabrication,[334] at least where a complaint is made before the alleged motivation for fabrication arose.[335] This rule of admissibility, conditional upon a previous defence attack on credibility, is thus distinct from the freestanding admissibility of the recent complaint doctrine.

The admissibility criteria have become so attenuated by caselaw that the term 'recent complaint' may be a misnomer. The alleged victim need not have intended to communicate the 'complaint' to a third party at all,[336] and indeed a written statement need not have been communicated at all at the time it was prepared.[337] What

---

[328] K London, M Bruch, S Ceci and D Shuman 'Disclosure of Child Sexual Abuse: What Does the Research Tell Us about the Ways That Children Tell?' (2006) 11 *Psychology, Public Policy, and Law* 194, 198–201, 203.   [329] *R v Lillyman* (n 321); *R v Osborne* (n 321) 561.

[330] *R v Churchill* (n 327); *R v Wannell* (1923) 17 Cr App R 53 (CA).

[331] The jury should however be directed to take into account the fact that the statement was elicited by cross-questioning in considering its weight, particularly where a young and arguably suggestible child is concerned [*R v NK* [1999] Crim LR 980 (CA)].

[332] *R v Birks* [2003] EWCA Crim 3091, [2003] Crim LR 401.

[333] Even where counts of physical abuse are jointly tried with sexual assault, prompt complaints of the physical abuse are not admissible: *R v Greenwood* [1993] Crim LR 770 (CA).

[334] Cross-examination on prior written consistent statements does not suffice: *R v Beattie* (1999) 89 Cr App R 302 (CA) 306–307.

[335] *R v Tyndale* [1999] Crim LR 320 (CA). The American rule is the same: *Tome v US* (n 290) construing Federal Rule of Evidence 801(d)(1)(B).

[336] *R v B* (n 323) (a ten-year-old passed the wrong note to her schoolmate, but nonetheless it was held to constitute a complaint).

[337] *R v Peter M* (9 August 2000 CA) (letter written after the complainant saw a ChildLine advertisement one year after the alleged abuse stopped, was hidden by her in a cupboard instead of being sent to ChildLine as she had originally intended, ruled to constitute a complaint; the complainant did not approach the police until ten years later).

apparently remains crucial to admissibility is that the statement on its face must be capable of being characterized as a complaint rather than merely a self-corroborating narrative[338]— a distinction which might be regarded as artificial and difficult to apply. The Court of Appeal in *Valentine* held that 'first reasonable opportunity' to make a complaint should now be liberally construed to take into account the character of the complainant, the relationship between the complainant and the person to whom the complaint was made, and the persons to whom she might have complained but did not do so.[339] Delays of several days or even a week no longer necessarily disqualify a complaint.

The statement which is tendered in evidence need not be the first complaint, provided that the subsequent complaint was made as speedily as reasonably could be expected.[340] The prosecution should not however lead evidence of a series of complaints, as this could mislead the jury as to their evidential value.[341] This concern is justified, because even experienced lawyers and judges have misunderstood its evidential purpose.[342] Technically the complaint cannot provide corroboration for the commission of the offence by the accused.[343] Rather, the complaint merely shores up the credibility of the complainant as a witness, although it has been pointed out that in the ordinary sense of the word a complaint is corroborative in that it supports or strengthens other evidence,[344] making its misuse by the jury even more likely.

This necessary link with credibility as a witness means that the doctrine is not available to the prosecution where the victim will not testify, or is incompetent to do so,[345] or fails to come up to proof.[346] Its limitations have led some jurisdictions to create special hearsay exceptions to admit complaints by children who do not testify, which we considered above.[347]

Because one justification for admission of what otherwise would be a hearsay statement is to prove consistency, evidence of what the complainant said as well as the fact that he/she made a complaint is now admissible,[348] as well as evidence of the complainant's demeanour, such as distress, at the time of a complaint or shortly thereafter.[349] This may also be relevant as tending to negative consent.[350] This expanded role for recent complaint has led the Court of Appeal to suggest that the statement

---

[338] ibid [20].   [339] *R v Valentine* [1996] 2 Cr App R 213 (CA) 223.

[340] ibid 224; *R v Lee* (1912) 7 Cr App R 31 (CA) 33; *R v Wilbourne* (1917) 12 Cr App R 820 (CA).

[341] *R v Valentine* 224.

[342] Including experienced CPS prosecutors interviewed for the *Bristol Study*. For examples of mangled jury directions on this point see *R v Jarvis* [1991] Crim LR 374 (CA); *R v Churchill* (n 327).

[343] *R v Lillyman* (n 321) 170; *R v Redpath* (n 2) 320; *R v Spencer, R v Smails* [1987] 1 AC 128 (HL); *R v Willoughby* (1988) 88 Cr App R 91 (CA).

[344] Sir John Smith in his commentary on *R v Islam* (n 316) 576.

[345] *R v Wallwork* (1958) 42 Cr App R 153 (CA) 161–162 (five-year-old child too frightened to testify against her father); (child aged three considered too young to testify; defence application to adduce recent complaint describing someone other than the accused as the abductor and assailant denied).

[346] *R v Wright and Ormerod* (1990) 90 Cr App R 91 (CA) 96 (testimony of witness aged six inconsistent with complaint).   [347] Discussed above, section B.8.

[348] *R v Lillyman* (n 321); *R v S* [2004] EWCA Crim 1320, [2004] 3 All ER 689 698 [23].

[349] *R v Lynch* [1993] Crim LR 868 (CA); *R v Nigel Anthony Keast* [1998] Crim LR 748 (CA).

[350] *R v Lillyman* (n 321); *R v Wallwork* (n 345) 161; *White v The Queen* (n 315).

has greater evidential value than simply to rebut an allegation of recent fabrication, for which purpose proof that the statement was made should suffice.[351] If there are discrepancies between the events described by the recent complaint witness and the complainant in their testimony, such as where a child describes indecent assault to her friend, but not penetrative sexual acts, is the foundation of admissibility destroyed?[352] The test is whether the complaint evidence is sufficiently consistent that it could, depending on the view taken by the jury of the evidence, support or enhance the credibility of the complainant. It will generally not be necessary that the complaint disclose the ingredients of the offence provided some unlawful sexual conduct is described, as victims often cannot bring themselves to disclose at that time the full extent of the conduct alleged.[353]

The English courts have claimed a 'greater understanding' of the plight of victims of sexual offences, male or female, and in particular of their need for time before they can bring themselves to tell what has been done to them,[354] but they have not seen fit to challenge the common law doctrine itself, instead merely stretching it to accommodate the facts of what they deem to be deserving cases.

(b) Application of the recent complaint doctrine to young complainants

The recent complaint doctrine can be viewed as helping victims of sexual assaults by bolstering their credibility. However, its flip side is that the credibility of victims is still vulnerable to attack for any delay in making the complaint, however minor, because delay in complaining is viewed as being logically inconsistent with their story of assault, raising the inference that they are lying.[355] Even young children are put on the defensive to explain their actions following the alleged attack. In *Wright and Ormerod*, the Court of Appeal observed that a five-year-old girl who had disappeared and was later found in the flat of two men in a distressed and intoxicated state 'did not avail herself' of two opportunities on the same day to complain of sexual misconduct, telling her mother 24 hours later; the Court expressed 'serious misgiving' as to whether the complaint was sufficiently recent.[356] In *R v B*,[357] the Court of Appeal took judicial notice of the typical reasons why child victims of sexual abuse perpetrated by a close family member often delay disclosure, sometimes for many years:

- the offences occur when the children are immature and uncertain of their position, and even uncertain of the criminality of the conduct against them;
- they may have been told that no one will believe them if they complain;
- they may blame themselves for what has happened;

---

[351] *R v Islam* (n 316).   [352] As occurred in *R v S* (n 348).

[353] ibid [28]–[31], citing with approval *R v Braye-Jones* [1996] Qd R 295 (Queensland CCA) 297–300, *R v Nazif* [1987] 2 NZLR 122 (New Zealand CA).   [354] *R v Valentine* (n 339) 224.

[355] *R v Osborne* (n 321) 559, 560, adopting Sir Matthew Hale's *Pleas of the Crown* (1678) Vol i, 633. Wigmore also accepts this inference: J Wigmore *Evidence in Trials at Common Law* (1904 James H Chadbourne 1978 rev edn Little, Brown & Co, Boston) [1135].

[356] *R v Wright and Ormerod* (n 346) 93, 97.

[357] *R v B* [1996] Crim LR 406 (CA). See also *R v Peter M* (n 333), noting that a 'hallmark' of intra-family abuse cases were requests for secrecy, gifts bestowed when resistance was shown, and the fear that telling anyone would lead to the family splitting up.

- they may be reticent about speaking to third parties, particularly prosecuting authorities, about sexual matters;
- they may fear break-up of the family or distress to innocent members of the family; or
- their abuser may have in some way corrupted them or put them in fear.[358]

These observations in *R v B* were however made in the context of a defence application for a stay of proceedings for abuse of process due to a complainant's 22-year delay in disclosing the alleged abuse rather than the evidence at a trial. Where delayed complaint is argued by the defence to have undermined a complainant's credibility when testifying, the prosecution must have some evidential foundation for explaining the delay. The Court of Appeal ruled in *Greenwood*[359] that the prosecution may explain the complete absence of a complaint to a person in whom the victim would normally be expected to confide such as the child's mother.[360] This requires the prosecution to ask the child for an explanation in examination-in-chief (in practical terms, during the video interview, when the interviewers will be anxious not to make the child defensive) or to subpoena the mother to state the reason, which may not be feasible. Any explanation of the delay offered by the child to third parties would be inadmissible hearsay at common law, and is likely to continue to be inadmissible under the CJA 2003 chapter 2.[361]

A requirement which is even more problematic for child abuse prosecutions, and which emerged only in 2003, is that the complaint must not only have been made at the first reasonable opportunity, but also within a reasonable time of the alleged offence. In *R v Birks*,[362] the complainant alleged that sexual abuse began when she was five or six, and ended when she was six or seven years old. However, she did not tell anyone until she watched a television programme about child abuse with her mother, some time between 2 and 12 months following the last incident. A prosecution was brought only when the complainant was 19. Counsel were agreed that there was no other case of recent complaint involving a complaint delayed by more than one week from the date of the alleged incident. The Court of Appeal expressed sympathy with the position of prosecuting counsel that modern awareness of the difficulties of very young children in speaking about sexual abuse should allow a more elastic interpretation of the requirement of timeliness, to weeks or

---

[358] For a similar, but more detailed, list of reasons for delayed complaints by child incest victims, see *KM v HM* [1992] 3 SCR 3 (SCC) 26–32.   [359] *R v Greenwood* (n 333).

[360] For an example of highly probative, albeit highly prejudicial, evidence tendered to explain the absence of complaint, see *R v M(T) and others* [2000] 1 WLR 421 (CA) 425, 426, a case of multi-generational abuse where the prosecution was permitted to lead background evidence of the culture of sexual abuse into which the defendant had been inducted as a young boy, including being taught to abuse two of his sisters, to explain why he was confident that another ten-year-old sister would not seek out the protection of her parents when he raped her.

[361] Such a statement would not normally fall within any of the principal categories of admissibility set out in ss 116–120, so the court would have to exercise its residual discretion conferred by s 114(1)(d) to admit the evidence if it is satisfied that it is 'in the interests of justice' to do so.

[362] *R v Birks* (n 332).

even years, but considered that it was unable to do so given the current state of the law.

Interviewers already face a difficult task in breaking through the secrecy in which the abuser has enveloped a victim. As Roland Summit, a clinical psychologist, has explained:

Virtually no child is prepared for the possibility of molestation by a trusted adult; that possibility is a well-kept secret even among adults. The child is, therefore, entirely dependent on the intruder for whatever reality is assigned to the experience. Of all the inadequate, illogical, self-serving, or self-protective explanations provided by the adult, the only consistent and meaningful impression gained by the child is one of danger and fearful outcome based on secrecy. . . . However gentle or menacing the intimidation may be, the secrecy makes it clear to the child that this is something bad and dangerous. The secrecy is both the source of fear and the promise of safety: 'Everything will be all right if you just don't tell'.[363]

Australian experimental psychologists have shown that a significant proportion of children aged three and five could be coerced or otherwise induced into keeping the transgressions of an adult secret.[364]

The *Bristol Study* found that the police and CPS consider a prompt complaint of sexual abuse as valuable evidence buttressing the child's credibility, which may tip the balance in favour of prosecution.[365] Conversely, child complainants were attacked in cross-examination for delaying complaint, even as briefly as one hour.[366] The doctrine is likely to continue to provide fuel for frequent appeals in child abuse cases on the issues of recency, and the adequacy of the trial judge's direction to the jury.[367] Thus the doctrine is likely to continue to have a robust influence on child abuse prosecutions in England and Wales.

It should be noted that the doctrine of recent complaint intersects with several other issues: disclosure of everything said about the incident by the complainant to third parties such as family and friends, the police, social workers, sexual assault crisis centres, and therapists;[368] disclosure of any previous allegations of sexual assault;[369] and the admissibility of expert evidence as to the reasons for delayed disclosure of sexual abuse by children.[370]

---

[363] R Summit' The Child Sexual Abuse Accommodation Syndrome' (1983) 7 *Child Abuse & Neglect* 177, 181.

[364] K Bussey, K Lee and E Grimbeek 'Lies and Secrets: Implications for Children's Reporting of Sexual Abuse' in G Goodman and B Bottoms (eds) *Child Victims, Child Witnesses: Understanding and Improving Testimony* (Guildford, Press New York, London 1993), 157–162 report that across all types of appeals for secrecy (bribes, threats, trickery and concern), 30% of the children refused to disclose the adult's transgression; 79% of the three-year-olds broke their promise, compared to 61% of the five-year-olds; and disclosure rates were lowest for both the three-year-olds (64%) and five-year-olds (50%) in the threat condition. The secret-keeping rate greatly increased when the transgressor was a parent (48 of 49 children kept their promise not to tell). Disclosure rates were also strongly influenced by whether the transgressor was present when the child was questioned in his presence: 31% of three-year-olds disclosed compared to 25% of five-year-olds; in his absence, 63% and 69% respectively.

[365] *Bristol Study* 36.   [366] *Bristol Study* 65 (case vignette 38A).

[367] eg *R v J* [1998] Crim LR 579 (CA); *R v Guelbert* [2001] EWCA Crim 1604; *R v Croad* [2001] EWCA 644.   [368] Discussed above, Chapter 7 section C.

[369] Discussed below, section D.3(a)(ii).   [370] Discussed below, Chapter 11 section C.

(c) Statutory reform

Courts in almost all common law jurisdictions have expressed at least some measure of discomfort with the assumptions underpinning the inference that the timing of disclosure is relevant to the alleged victim's credibility. Several approaches have been assayed:

- modifying the criteria to reflect the particular circumstances of the case;
- abolishing the doctrine so that the complaint can no longer be tendered as part of the prosecution's case;
- special explanatory directions to the jury to place the complaint, or its absence, in context and to attempt to dispel stereotypical assumptions; or
- abolishing the hearsay rule generally or in relation to children.

The Criminal Law Revision Committee in 1972 recommended that the rule be abrogated in England and Wales,[371] but no action was taken on the proposal. The Law Commission in 1997 took a contrary view, recommending that the recent complaint doctrine be extended to all offences, and that the complaint be admissible as proof of the truth of the subject matter of the complaint.[372] The fact that the complainant had been helped to articulate the statement, such as by leading questions, should go to weight rather than admissibility. The Law Commission was satisfied by the recent liberalization in *Valentine* of the recency requirement and felt that there was no need to change the existing requirement as to how soon a complainant 'can be expected to make a complaint'.[373]

The Law Commission's recommendation was incorporated as s 120(7) in the CJA 2003. The recent complaint rule is elevated to a statutory exception to the hearsay ban, making the contents of the statement admissible as proof of the facts stated, rather than merely going to credibility of the complainant.[374]

Section 120(7)(d) requires that the statement be made 'as soon as could reasonably be expected after the alleged conduct'. In *R v Birks*,[375] the Court of Appeal expressed concerns about this wording, then still in Bill form, pointing out that it lends itself to the argument, on the one hand, that 'as soon as' is strong wording requiring a necessarily early complaint, and on the other, a broader test 'in light of an entirely new legislative beginning', allowing complaints delayed even longer than a year, depending upon the circumstances. Notwithstanding this judicial warning about ambiguity, the wording in the Bill was not changed by Parliament.

The statement must have been made not as a result of a threat or promise, although it is irrelevant if the complaint was elicited in some other way, such as by a leading question.[376] Importantly, the statement cannot be adduced until after the witness gives

---

[371] Criminal Law Revision Committee, *11th Report* (n 6) [232].

[372] Law Commission *Evidence in Criminal Proceedings: Hearsay* (n 94) [10.8]–[10.10], [10.22]–[10.26], [10.38], [10.53]–[10.61].   [373] ibid [10.58].

[374] *R v Xhabri* (n 130) [35]–[36] (contemporary complaints by sex-trafficked Latvian aged 17, including double hearsay report to police, that she was being held captive admitted as proof she was being held against her will).   [375] *R v Birks* (n 332).

[376] CJA 2003 (England) s 120(8).

oral evidence in connection with its subject matter.[377] This requirement means that recent complaint is of no assistance to the prosecution where the complainant has been ruled incompetent to testify at trial.[378] Furthermore, although a child complainant might have matured enough by the trial to be testimonially competent, the statement will still be inadmissible if she 'did not have the required capability' at the time when the statement was made,[379] meaning that she was incapable of understanding questions put to her about the matters stated, and of giving answers to such questions which can be understood.[380]

The requirement that the complainant testify before the statement can be admitted suggests that the doctrine in its statutory form is still intended to bolster the credibility of the complainant, even though the complaint can now be used as proof of guilt. However, the prosecution need not, it seems, await an attack by the defence on the complainant in cross-examination alleging fabrication[381] before the evidence becomes relevant to a fact in issue, which is now transformed from the complainant's credibility as a witness into whether the assault occurred, and by whom. It is likely that the common law cases will still be considered relevant in determining whether the statement complies with the statutory criteria.

Crucially, like the common law, the legislation does not challenge the expectation of how the 'reasonable victim' *should* react to a sexual assault.

2. Recent complaint in English civil cases

Until 1995, the doctrine of recent complaint did not figure prominently in the Family Division, because children rarely appeared as witnesses there, so their testimonial credibility was not placed in issue. Since the hearsay ban was abolished in its entirety in all of the civil courts by the Civil Evidence Act 1995,[382] out-of-court statements by allegedly abused children are admissible for their truth in any event, so there is no need to rely upon a recent complaint for its limited purpose as evidence of consistency.

3. Recent complaint in American law

The American common law doctrine, known as 'fresh complaint' evidence, survives relatively unmodified in most States and in Federal prosecutions,[383] albeit often with

---

[377] However, the statement could still be used under CJA 2003 (England) s 116 if a competent complainant is unavailable on one of the enumerated grounds (death, mental or bodily unfitness, absent from the UK, disappearance, or intimidation).

[378] As in *R v Sparks* (n 72) and *R v Khan* (n 171), discussed above sections B.1 and B.5(a).

[379] CJA 2003 (England) s 123(1), replicating the competence test in the YJCEA 1999 (England) s 53.

[380] CJA 2003 (England) s 123(3). A *voir dire* to determine the issue of capability must be held if the issue was raised; evidence is admissible from experts and from the person to whom the statement is made. The burden of proof is on the person seeking to adduce the statement, and the standard of proof is the balance of probabilities (ibid s 123(4)).

[381] ibid s 120(2) makes evidence of a previous consistent statement admissible as proof of the matters stated therein to rebut an attack suggesting recent fabrication of the witness's oral evidence.

[382] Discussed above, section B.4.

[383] Federal Rules of Evidence R 801(d)(1)(B); *Tome v US* (n 290) USSC.

relaxed requirements where sexual abuse of young children is alleged. Such cases are considered to be a factually distinct branch of the general doctrine,[384] requiring that allowances be made for timeliness,[385] and questions to elicit the statements from children.[386] In considering whether a child's complaint is sufficiently 'fresh' to be admissible, the court may consider the child's age, lack of knowledge of sexual matters, embarrassment, confusion and fear, relationship with the alleged offender and whether he was in a position of trust or supervision with the child, any threats or coercion to induce silence, and the length of time the child was out of the abusive setting before complaining.[387] Delay in reporting in a particular case may be explained and justified to the jury. Unlike English common law, in some States the statement can serve as corroboration even though it is not tendered as hearsay, ie as proof that the offence was committed.

In *People v Brown*,[388] the California Supreme Court abandoned the fresh complaint rule itself because of its outmoded premises, but revived it under a different guise, to permit the fact of the disclosure and its circumstances, but not its details, to be tendered for non-hearsay purposes, to avert false conclusions by the jury as to the victim's behaviour. For this limited purpose, the timing of the complaint and the way it was elicited becomes irrelevant. It is noteworthy however that the California Supreme Court considered that it was merely assimilating sexual offences with the general principles of evidence governing other offences such as robbery, where evidence of the victim's response to the alleged offence is admissible. This would not be the case under English common law as it would be considered to be self-corroboration through a previous consistent statement, and hence superfluous to that witness's direct evidence.

4. Recent complaint in Canadian law

In 1983, the Canadian Parliament expressly 'abrogated' the rules relating to evidence of recent complaint in sexual offences,[389] after the Supreme Court of Canada had expressed disquiet about the doctrine's assumption that the 'true' victim of a sexual offence normally will complain at the first reasonable opportunity, and therefore that the silence of an alleged victim has 'special probative value' undermining his or her credibility.[390]

---

[384] *Commonwealth v Feury* 632 NE 2d 1230 (Massachusetts Supreme Judicial Ct 1994); *Commonwealth v Amirault* 535 NE 2d 193 (Massachusetts Supreme Ct 1989).

[385] *Commonwealth v Allen* 665 NE 2d 105 (Massachusetts AC 1996). Sometimes the rule is attenuated on a fairly restricted basis as where the child does not comprehend the offensiveness of the contact, or the perpetrator is in a position of trust, as in *Commonwealth v Snoke* 580 A 2d 295 (Pennsylvania Supreme Ct 1990).   [386] See Myers *Evidence in Child Abuse and Neglect Cases* (n 52) Vol. 2, 240–264.

[387] See the authorities cited in *Commonwealth v Feury* (n 384).

[388] *People v Brown* 883 P 2d 949 (California Supreme Ct 1994).

[389] Criminal Code of Canada s 275.

[390] *Timm v The Queen* [1981] 2 SCR 315 (SCC); see also *R v W(R)* (n 42). A task force reporting to the Uniform Law Conference of Canada in 1982 had also argued that in contemporary society there is no logical connection between the genuineness of the complaint and the promptness with which it is made [*Report of the Federal/Provincial Task Force on Uniform Rules of Evidence* (1982) 301].

The consequences of the statutory abrogation are twofold: trial judges are no longer required to instruct juries that failure to complain at the first reasonable opportunity entitles them to infer that the complainant is not truthful;[391] and the Crown can no longer lead as part of its case evidence of the complainant's prompt complaint to prove her consistency in making the allegation. The prosecution during its case in chief can still prove that a complaint was made, as part of the 'narrative' of how the case reached trial, but, unlike the English recent complaint doctrine, details of that complaint are inadmissible at this stage, unless the statement falls within the common law *res gestae* hearsay exception for statements accompanying and explaining an event.[392]

To qualify a child's statement as part of the 'narrative', the prosecution must show that the statement advances the story from offence to prosecution, or explains why so little was done to terminate the abuse or bring the perpetrator to justice. This part of the narrative provides chronological cohesion and eliminates gaps which would divert the juror's mind from the central issue.[393] These statements may support the central allegation in the sense of creating a logical framework for its presentation, but the jury must be warned not to use it as confirmation of the truthfulness of the child's testimony. For this reason the content of the complaint is not relevant unless the defence decides to explore it,[394] to exploit any delay as evidence that the complainant fabricated the allegation,[395] or any inconsistency between the earlier description and his testimony at trial. The allegation of fabrication may be implicit in the cross-examination.[396] If the defence opens this door, the Crown can lead rebuttal evidence of the details of that complaint, in accordance with the general evidentiary rules governing previous statements of a witness, but the jury must be directed that in this context the complaint is relevant only for the non-hearsay purpose of establishing consistency of the story.[397]

While the basis for the admissibility of 'narrative' evidence can be defined fairly clearly, the question of the use to which the jury can put this evidence becomes mired in difficulty. In several cases appellate courts have suggested that the jury can use the complainant's conduct disclosed by the narrative to test the credibility of her testimony, and that the defence must be permitted to explore this.[398] The Ontario Court of Appeal concluded, perhaps optimistically, that leaving it to the trier of fact

---

[391] *R v Ay* (1994) 93 CCC (3d) 456 (British Columbia CA) 470, noting that in practical terms the negative inference had attained the persuasive quality of a rebuttable presumption.

[392] Explained above, sections 1 and B.3(a)(i).

[393] *R v B(O)* (1995) 103 CCC (3d) 531 (Nova Scotia CA). If the narrative sufficiently explains the reasons for a child's delay in disclosing abuse, expert evidence to provide the jury with further contextual information may not be necessary [*R v C(G)* (1997) 8 CR (5th) 21 (Ontario Gen Div)].

[394] *R v F(JE)* (1993) 85 CCC (3d) 457 (Ontario CA) 472–476; *R v George* (1985) 23 CCC (3d) 42 (British Columbia CA) 45; *R v H(LM)* (1994) 39 BCAC 241 (British Columbia CA), appeal dismissed [1994] 3 SCR 758 (SCC). For criticism of this restriction, see *R v B(DC)* (1994) 70 WWR 727 (Manitoba CA).   [395] *R v Heinrich (John)* (1996) 108 CCC (3d) 97 (Ontario CA).

[396] *R v Simpson (O'Connor)* (1995) 100 CCC (3d) 285 (Ontario CA) 293.

[397] *R v Llorenz* (2000) 145 CCC (3d) 535 (Ontario CA) [34]; *R v K(A) and K(N)* (1999) 176 DLR (4th) 665 (Ontario CA); *R v F(DS)* (1999) 43 OR (3d) 609 (Ontario CA); *R v Bradford* (2002) 158 OAC 140 (Ontario CA).

[398] *R v F(JE)* (n 394) 476; *R v Ay* (n 391) 469; *R v Ross* [1996] OJ No 1361 (Ontario Gen Div); *R v M(PS)* (1992) 77 CCC (3d) 402 (Ontario CA); *R v Heinrich (John)* (n 395).

to determine what to make of any explanation for delay would avoid rather than promote stereotypical responses.[399] To guard against this, the Alberta Court of Appeal held that where there is no evidence of prompt complaint the trial judge should warn the jury that as a matter of law one cannot say that a victim of sexual assault will always complain at the first opportunity; conversely, abrogation of the recent complaint doctrine does not mean that a jury can never draw an adverse inference from delayed complaint, as this would introduce a new stereotype. Rather, the jury must decide whether this complainant acted after the alleged incident in a way that is consistent with her story, having regard to her state of mind, age and level of maturity, sense of confidence and composure, and her relationship with the alleged abuser.[400]

Faith in the efficacy of directions to the jury to avoid stereotypical assumptions caused a narrow majority on the Supreme Court of Canada in *R v D(D)*[401] to terminate the practice of admitting expert evidence on the reasons for delayed disclosure of child sexual abuse. Major J held that the following direction was adequate to convey to the jury the 'simple irrefutable proposition' that the timing of the disclosure signifies nothing in diagnosing child sexual abuse:[402]

[T]here is no inviolable rule on how people who are the victims of trauma like a sexual assault will behave. Some will make an immediate complaint, some will delay in disclosing the abuse, while some will never disclose the abuse. Reasons for delay are many and at least include embarrassment, fear, guilt, or a lack of understanding and knowledge. In assessing the credibility of a complainant, the timing of the complaint is simply one circumstance to consider in the factual mosaic of a particular case. A delay in disclosure, standing alone, will never give rise to an adverse inference against the credibility of the complainant.[403]

5. Recent complaint in New Zealand law

New Zealand also inherited the common law doctrine of recent complaint,[404] but the courts in the 1980s and 1990s moved away from the orthodox doctrine, providing greater leeway in particular for complaints from children.[405] Judges stressed the need to consider the dynamics of family relationships and the possibility that a child in a relationship of dependency may have a natural unwillingness to disclose matters of intimacy.[406] Reporting delays of three years have not prevented complaints of intra-familial child sexual abuse from being deemed 'recent'; multiple complaints have also been admitted in evidence.[407] Complaints from young

---

[399] *R v Heinrich (John)* ibid.

[400] *R v Mountain* (1996) 110 CCC (3d) 179 (Alberta CA).

[401] *R v D(D)* [2000] 2 SCR 275 (SCC) (Iacobucci, Major, Binnie and Arbour JJ; McLachlin CJC, L'Heureux-Dubé and Gonthier JJ, dissenting).   [402] ibid [66], [59].

[403] ibid [65].

[404] *R v Nazif* (n 353). The 1980 hearsay amendments specifically preserved the common law governing the admissibility of complaint evidence [Evidence Amendment Act (No 2) 1980 (New Zealand) s 20(3)(c)].

[405] *R v M* [1994] 3 NZLR 641 (New Zealand CA).

[406] *R v Accused* (1997) 15 CRNZ 26 (New Zealand CA).

[407] *R v Emile Tuagalu* [2001] NZCA 235 (New Zealand CA).

children elicited by leading questions have also been admitted.[408] Recent complaint evidence can be given even though the alleged victim does not herself testify about making the complaint, or even denies it altogether.[409] As in England, the jury must be warned that the statement cannot be treated as corroboration of the complainant's testimony.[410]

In 1985, the New Zealand Parliament attempted to mitigate the 'flip side' of the doctrine by providing that whenever in any trial for a sexual offence evidence is given or any question asked or comment made tending to suggest an absence of, or a delayed, complaint, 'the Judge may tell the jury that there may be good reasons why the victim of such an offence may refrain from or delay in making such a complaint'.[411] The New Zealand Court of Appeal has held that the provision did not affect the requirement that to be admissible the complaint must be made at the first reasonable opportunity.[412] However, it apparently resulted in fewer overt attacks on complainants by the defence for delaying or refraining from disclosure.[413]

Judicial warnings have not quelled criticism of the doctrine, however. In *R v H*, Thomas J mounted an excoriating attack on the current rule, describing it as 'not so much dysfunctional as unconscionable',[414] and noting that the explanation of delayed complaint authorized by statute is in tension with the subsisting admissibility requirement of prompt complaint, the premise of which is that delayed complaints are more likely to be false:

On the one hand Parliament has stipulated that there may be good reasons why the victim of a sexual offence may refrain from or delay in making a complaint while, on the other, the Courts continue to apply a rule founded on the notion that the victim's credibility can only be bolstered if she did in fact complain within a reasonable time. Good reasons for delaying or refraining from making a complaint will be of no avail in obtaining the admission of evidence which could demonstrate, as much as evidence of an early complaint, the consistency of her conduct with her testimony. …Judges should feel awkward applying a rule which, in effect, has this meaning: evidence of a complaint is only admissible if the complaint is made at the first reasonable opportunity, notwithstanding that there may be good reasons why the complaint was not made at that time![415]

Thomas J argued that while it would be logical to abandon the doctrine altogether, abolition would leave the complainant exposed to prejudice and scepticism without the opportunity to redress her credibility by demonstrating that her prior conduct was in fact consistent with her testimony; therefore the rule should be re-formulated to remove the requirement of proximity in time to the offence, and permit evidence of subsequent complaints. However, the other two judges on the panel declined to follow this lead. They held that there is no evidentiary value in a delayed complaint, and that an exception to the general ban on evidence of previous consistent statements which already favoured victims of sexual offences should not be extended without careful

---

[408] *R v Duncan* [1992] 1 NZLR 528 (New Zealand CA).
[409] The denial is regarded as going to weight rather than to admissibility: *R v Walker* [2000] NZCA 121 (New Zealand CA).   [410] *R v T* [1998] 2 NZLR 257 (New Zealand CA) 268.
[411] Evidence Act 1908 (New Zealand) s 23A-C.   [412] *R v M* (n 405).
[413] *R v H* (n 325) 692 (Thomas J).   [414] ibid 693 (CA).   [415] ibid 690 (CA).

consideration for the implications for the general law of evidence, which the New Zealand Law Commission would be best placed to conduct.[416]

The Law Commission's proposals would treat recent complaint in the same way as a previous consistent statement of any witness. Thus the pre-emptive strike would be abolished, the complaint becoming admissible if the credibility of the witness has been challenged, and then only to the extent necessary to meet that challenge. An alternative ground for admission which breaks with the common law is where the statement provides 'information' which that witness is unable to recall.[417] If defence counsel improperly challenges the complainant's credibility for the first time in closing submissions, the Code would allow further evidence to be called such as evidence of the complaint.[418] Once admitted, as with the English reform, the statement could be used to prove the truth of the contents of the statement as well as to support the truthfulness and accuracy of the complainant. There would be no need for inquiry into the timing of the complaint; this would go to weight rather than admissibility.[419] Nevertheless the Law Commission would preserve the existing judicial direction to juries that there may be good reasons for the victim of a sexual offence to delay complaint or fail to complain,[420] but this would be coupled with a warning to scrutinize the way that young children been questioned.[421]

6. Recent complaint in Australian law

Australian courts also adopted the restrictions on the recent complaint doctrine imposed by the English common law, including its limited evidential use by the jury.[422] The High Court of Australia has said however that the historical assumptions underpinning the recent complaint doctrine do not apply to cases of child sexual assault by a person who has the child's trust and confidence.[423] This has not meant however that the doctrine is not applied to child abuse cases, and the complaint may still be ruled inadmissible on the basis of delay in the particular circumstances, such as where the child is in a supportive and secure family environment.[424]

Only the Australian Capital Territory has followed the Canadian lead in abrogating the doctrine.[425] This initiative was criticized by one trial judge as 'well-meaning but futile', as the presumption that delayed complaint made it incredible 'has long since ceased to exist save as a fantasy in the mind of some ill-advised advocates', the result

---

[416] ibid 680, Eichelbaum CJ and Heron J.
[417] NZLC *Evidence* (n 248) Vol 1 [143] n 30, draft Evidence Code s 98(3)(b).
[418] ibid [143]–[144], draft Evidence Code s 37.   [419] ibid [144], volume 2 [C168].
[420] ibid [143]–[144], draft Evidence Code s 113.   [421] ibid [488]–[493].
[422] *Kilby v R* (1973) 129 CLR 460 (Aus HC); *Breen v The Queen* (1976) 180 CLR 233 (Aus HC); *R v Ugle* (1989) 167 CLR 647 (Aus HC); *M v The Queen* (1994) 181 CLR 487 (Aus HC); *Crofts v The Queen* (1996) 186 CLR 427 (Aus HC); *Jones v The Queen* [1998] HCA 23, (1997) 149 ALR 598 (Aus HC); *Suresh v The Queen* (1998) 153 ALR 145 (Aus HC); *Papakosmas v The Queen* (1999) 196 CLR 297 (Aus HC).   [423] *M v The Queen* ibid 515 (Gaudron J).
[424] *Suresh v The Queen* (n 422) [50]–[52] (HC). In *R v LTP* [2004] NSWCCA 109 (New South Wales CCA) Howie J queried how any inference can be legitimately drawn about the veracity of a young child from a delayed complaint.
[425] Evidence Act 1971 (Australian Capital Territory) (as amended in 1985), s 76C1(1).

being to disadvantage sexual assault victims by leaving them open to attack by the defence.[426] Higgins J interpreted the legislation as barring evidence of the complaint where that was tendered to prove credibility, but exploited the statutory exception for a complaint 'otherwise admissible under any other rule of law practice'[427] to admit the statement under the statutory hearsay exception[428] as proof that a sexual act had taken place, to which the complainant had not consented.[429] As it will be almost inconceivable for a sexual offence to be prosecuted where one or both of these issues are not contested, it would seem that very little content is left to the statutory abolition of the recent complaint doctrine.

South Australia has discarded all of the limiting rules of the common law as it applies to children aged 12 and under, providing that the court may in its discretion admit evidence of the nature and contents of a complaint of a sexual offence if the court is of the opinion that the evidence has sufficient probative value to justify its admission given the nature and circumstances of the complaint.[430] What evidential purpose the complaint may serve is unclear, as the court may admit it only if the alleged victim has been called or is available to be called as a witness, implying that it is to be treated as going to the child's credibility as a witness.[431]

Queensland in its 2003 statutory reform relating to child witnesses[432] has opted to retain the restriction of the doctrine to sexual offences, but has deleted any time constraints, making all complaints made prior to a formal statement to the police admissible regardless of when they were made. In a jury trial, the judge is prohibited from warning or suggesting in any way to the jury that the law regards the complainant's evidence to be more reliable or less reliable only because of the length of time before the complaint was made; apart from this, the judge may make any comment about the complainant's evidence which is appropriate in the interests of justice. The court retains its residual discretion to exclude the complaint where its admission would be unfair to the defendant.

Victoria, New South Wales, Western Australia, and Tasmania have opted for judicial directions rather than altering the doctrine itself, requiring the trial judge to warn the jury that delay in complaining does not necessarily indicate that the allegation is false, and that there may be good reasons why a victim of a sexual assault may hesitate in complaining about it.[433] Mandatory warning provisions have not however altered the admissibility criteria of the common law. Furthermore, they have been interpreted in *Crofts* as still requiring the trial judge to give a 'balancing direction' to the jury that delayed complaint may affect the credibility of the complainant's account, as the legislation was not intended 'to "sterilise" complainants from critical comment' where

[426] *R v Kirkman* [2000] ACTSC 2 (unreported ruling on *voir dire*, 3 Feb 2000) (Australian Capital Territory Supreme Ct) [17]. [427] Evidence Act 1971 (n 425) s 76C1(2).
[428] Evidence Act 1995 s 66. [429] *R v Kirkman* (n 426) [58]–[61].
[430] Evidence Act, 1929 (South Australia), as amended, s 34ca(1), s 4. [431] ibid, s 34ca(2).
[432] Evidence (Protection of Children) Amendment Act 2003, No. 55 of 2003 (Qld) s 40, inserting s 4A into the Criminal Law (Sexual Offences) Act 1978. Notwithstanding the title of the amending Act, statutory reform of recent complaint is not limited to child complainants.
[433] Crimes Act 1958 (Victoria) s 61; Crimes Act 1900 (New South Wales) s 405B(2); Evidence Act 1906 (WA) s 36BD; Criminal Code Act 1924 (Tasmania) s 371A.

the particular facts of the case make it appropriate.[434] Worryingly, a delayed complaint also means that the trial judge is required to give a '*Longman* warning'[435] to the jury that it is dangerous to convict on the uncorroborated evidence of the child, even in States where mandatory corroboration warnings have been abolished by statute.[436] *Longman* has been interpreted as creating an irrebuttable presumption of fact that the accused has been prejudiced by the complainant's delay in making a complaint.[437] Gaudron and Gummow JJ of the High Court of Australia have expressed concern that a 'good reason for delay' direction may lead the jury to conclude that a previous consistent complaint, however late, enhances the credibility of an alleged victim, and so it necessarily would follow that if a previous complaint was wrongly admitted as being recent, and the case turns on the credibility of the child, a new trial must be ordered.[438] The combined warnings have been criticized as complex, confusing and sometimes even contradictory, and as reinstating false stereotypes 'by the backdoor'.[439]

As in England, fact-based appeals based on the fulfilment of the recent complaint criteria frequently come before the Australian State courts,[440] and the Australian High Court considered the doctrine no fewer than five times in the 1990s. Apart from proposed statutory modifications to the *Longman* and *Crofts* warnings,[441] reform initiatives in Australia have tended to focus on creating specific statutory exceptions for hearsay in relation to children, or more generally, which would subsume the doctrine of recent complaint, whilst making the statement evidence of the truth of the complaint.[442] We have discussed the merits of such sweeping reform of the hearsay rule for children's out-of-court statements earlier.[443]

7. Recent complaint in South African law

In South Africa, sexual offences are tried without a jury, but this has not erased concern about stereotypical inferences from the timing of a complaint. The South African Law

---

[434] *Crofts v The Queen* (n 422) [48]; *Reynolds v The Queen* [1998] WASCA 217 (Western Australia CA) (trial judge erred in omitting the word 'necessarily', stating that the delayed complaint was not evidence that the offences had not occurred; retrial ordered). [435] *Longman v The Queen* (n 8).
[436] *Crofts v The Queen* (n 422) [48]–[50]; *Robinson v The Queen* [1999] HCA 42; *R v Jolly* [1998] VICSC 56 (Victoria Supreme Ct). For a summary of the composite directions required by appellate cases, see *R v BWT* (2002) 54 NSWLR 241 (New South Wales CCA). [437] *R v BWT* ibid [13]–[15].
[438] *Suresh v The Queen* (n 422) [5]–[6].
[439] Tasmania Law Reform Institute *Warnings in Sexual Offences Cases Relating to Delay in Complaint* (Issues Paper No 8 2005) [2.1.1]–[2.1.22].
[440] *Eastough v The Queen* [1998] WASCA 53 (Western Australia CA); *R v Singleton* [1997] SADC 3619 (South Australia Dist Ct).
[441] The Victorian Law Reform Commission *Sexual Offences: Law and Procedure, Final Report* (2004) [7.122]–[7.132] would require the trial judge first to be satisfied that there was evidence of specific forensic disadvantage due to a substantial delay in reporting, and that the delay affected the complainant's credibility. The Tasmania Law Reform Institute *Warnings in Sexual Offences* (n 439) [3.1.12] proposes precluding the trial judge from suggesting that lack of recent complaint reflected on the complainant's credibility except in exceptional circumstances, where it could be shown on the balance of probabilities that the delay could be ascribed to fabrication or there was another genuine and identifiable connection to her credibility.
[442] *Papakosmas v The Queen* (n 422) interpreting the New South Wales Evidence Act 1995 s 66 setting up exceptions to the hearsay rule as permitting a recent complaint to be admitted as evidence that the rape occurred. [443] See above, Chapter 7 section C.4.

Commission has noted that the courts have given some recognition to the invalidity of the assumption that 'no earlier report means there was nothing to report', but nonetheless considers that more far-reaching reform is required. The Law Commission has recommended that previous consistent statements by complainants be admissible only if made at the first reasonable opportunity, but that legislation should state clearly that a negative inference as to credibility may not be drawn solely from the absence of or delay in making a complaint. It was thought that this compromise was necessary to preserve the presiding officer's broad discretion in evaluating the evidence.[444]

8. Evaluation: a useful albeit illegitimate doctrine?

Reform of the recent complaint doctrine presents a conundrum.[445] The fact that a complaint was made and its timing in itself is not evidence that the offence occurred. The chain of reasoning which purports to make a prompt complaint probative of the credibility of the alleged victim was set out (with approval) by McGechan J of the New Zealand Court of Appeal:

When a complainant states she (or he) was sexually abused at some point in the past, and asks the listener to believe it, a natural human reaction is to ask, 'well, has she ever said that before to anyone?' If the allegation comes as something new and novel, it may be less readily believed. If, on the other hand, she can point to something said to like effect previously, and preferably close to the alleged offence itself, her word may well be accepted more readily. It is not then, after all, 'a new story'.[446]

Defenders of the doctrine maintain that, however flawed its foundations, it helps protect victims of sexual offences by bolstering their credibility where often no other evidence supports them.[447] The California Supreme Court argued that the doctrine disabuses jurors of misconceptions about the behaviour of victims by preventing them from assuming that no report was made and hence inferring that no crime occurred, and contended that the need for 'fresh report' evidence has not declined.[448] However, this stance ultimately endorses rather than dismantles those misconceptions. In its operation the doctrine protects victims only to the extent that they conform to a particular fallacious stereotype about how a victim of sexual assault *should* respond and behave.

The doctrine's assumption that the complainant is not quick-witted enough to fabricate a false complaint shortly after the alleged incident is clearly untenable.[449]

---

[444] South African Law Commission *Sexual Offences: Process and Procedure* (Discussion Paper 102, Project 107 December 2002) Executive Summary: 'Admissibility of previous consistent statements'; draft Sexual Offences Act, s 17.　　　　　　　　　　　　[445] See the discussion in the *Bristol Study* at 64–66.

[446] *R v Duncan* (n 408).　　　[447] *R v H* (n 325) 692, (Thomas J).

[448] *People v Brown* (n 388) 958; *Battle v US* 630A 2d 211 (US DC 1993) 217; *Commonwealth v Licata* 591 NE 2d 672 (Massachusetts Supreme Judicial Ct 1992); *State v Hill* 578 A 2d 370 (New Jersey Supreme Ct 1990). This view is endorsed by Myers (n 52) Vol. 2, 243–245. A nationwide survey of American prosecutors reported that the defence challenges a child's credibility on the basis of delayed report always (29%) or frequently (54%) [GS Goodman, J Buckley, JA Quas and C Shapiro 'Innovations for Child Witnesses: a National Survey' (1999) 5 *Psychology, Public Policy, and Law* 255, 275].

[449] As was recognized in *R v Islam* (n 316).

All that the recent complaint proves is the complainant's consistency, whether that be in telling a false or a true story. It thus does not have any intrinsic probative value, unless and until the defence attacks the complainant by alleging that the story was concocted after the time when the complaint was made.

Even setting those reservations aside, a child's complaint affects her credibility only when set in the context of all of the surrounding circumstances, including the child's age and maturity, past exposure to sexual matters, relationship with the alleged perpetrator, family circumstances, and availability of support from others whom the child can trust. Thomas JA of the Queensland Court of Appeal has argued that the circumstances of first emergence of the complaint, regardless of its timing, may enable the story to be seen in a different light; for example, the identity of the person chosen by the complainant may give an insight into the complainant's motivation (if the complainant might have been trying to gain attention), or permit the inference that the complainant became locked into the complaint once further steps were taken; conversely, in a family with a dominant father, and an apparently selfish or financially dependent mother, it might be easy to accept that a molested child saw no point in sharing her misery with her mother.[450]

The Canadian approach has the merit of abolishing the *automatic* inference that delayed complaint indicates that the allegation is false, leaving the credibility of the complainant to be assessed in all the circumstances. However, it must be difficult for jurors to preclude from this assessment reasoning founded on misconceptions, unless they are given specific guidance on how to analyse credibility. The fact that under the Canadian rule the complaint can be adduced only in cross-examination of the complainant, or in redirect examination by the prosecution following an allegation of recent concoction, may mean that it is less likely that the complainant's credibility will be artificially enhanced by a 'reasons for delay' direction.[451]

Creating a special hearsay exception for statements by child witnesses is also difficult to justify; as we have argued in the foregoing section, statements by children as a class are unlikely to be intrinsically *more* reliable than those of adults in similar circumstances. The approach taken by the CJA 2003 (England) has the merit of treating previous statements by sexual assault complainants on the same basis as those by all other alleged victims of crime, although it is difficult to see how making the previous complaint admissible for its truth will add anything of value to the totality of information to be considered by the trier of fact.

Perhaps the least unsatisfactory solution is a mandatory statutory warning by the trial judge in any case where the timing of a complaint becomes an issue, that the jury should not automatically infer that it supports or undermines the truthfulness of the complaint without considering all the circumstances, coupled with an explanation as to why children might delay disclosure. However, it is difficult to ignore the ineradicable contradiction between requiring such instructions in a case of delay, whilst

---

[450] *R v Schneider* [1998] QCA 303 (Queensland CA) [11].
[451] As was the Australian High Court's concern in *Suresh v The Queen* (n 422) [5]–[6].

condoning the subsistence of a recent complaint admissibility rule predicated on the probative value of prompt disclosure. Preserving a rule of evidence because of lingering prejudice is unappealing if the evidence itself has no inherent value and distorts the process of proof in favour of or against either the alleged victim or the accused.

D. Character Evidence Pertaining to the Complainant

1. Evidence of bad character in English criminal cases

(a) Admissibility at common law

The character of witnesses other than the defendant is likely to arise in cross-examination with a view to impugning their credibility by demonstrating, for example, that they have criminal convictions. Until the CJA 2003, the rules for attacking the credibility of non-defendants were largely governed by the common law. Briefly, the common law (which still applies to civil proceedings) conferred a general licence on cross-examining counsel to attack the credibility of a witness of fact—including the complainant—through her prior convictions or other misconduct, bias, corruption or lack of veracity, subject only to three limitations.[452]

First, the evidence has to be shown to be relevant to the credibility of the witness. The common law assumes that a witness's character is indivisible, and so any previous misconduct is regarded as reflecting negatively on her character, and hence her credibility as a witness; the same notion of the indivisibility of character applies to the defendant who testifies.[453]

Second, the 'collateral issue' or 'finality' rule means that counsel generally cannot adduce evidence to contradict a witness's denial of the discreditable allegation said to undermine her credibility, the rationale being that chasing issues of credibility to this extent would only serve to derail the trial from the factual issues at hand. The test as to whether a matter is 'collateral' is usually framed in terms of whether this is a matter which that party would have been entitled to prove in chief,[454] and so is not dependent for its relevance upon contradicting the witness's denial in cross-examination.[455] The Court of Appeal has noted that the test is circular, but its utility 'may lie in the fact that the answer is an instinctive one based on the prosecutor's and the court's sense of fair play rather than any philosophic or analytic process'.[456] There are some clearly

---

[452] Tapper *Cross & Tapper on Evidence* (n 95) 381–388; Roberts and Zuckerman (n 111) 254–269.

[453] Discussed below Chapter 10 section C.

[454] An echo of the 'mere credibility' rule applicable to third party disclosure, discussed above Chapter 7 section C.1(b)(iii).

[455] *AG v Hitchcock* (1847) 1 Exch 91, 154 ER 38, 42. This test was endorsed by the Supreme Court of Canada in *R v R(D)* (n 192), holding that the defence should be entitled to lead evidence on the contamination of the memories of child witnesses through improper interview techniques, as their credibility was at the heart of the case. For the varied formulations of the finality rule, see D Paciocco 'Using the Collateral Facts Rule with Discretion' (2002) 46 Crim LQ 160.

[456] *R v Funderburk* [1990] 1 WLR 587 (CA) 598.

delineated exceptions to the finality rule, the most notable being that counsel can lead evidence to rebut a denial of previous convictions,[457] a previous inconsistent statement pertaining to the evidence in the proceedings,[458] and a denial of bias.

R v Cargill[459] provides a graphic example of how rigorous the finality rule can be. The defendant was charged with unlawful sexual intercourse with a child, whom his counsel alleged in cross-examination was a prostitute. He was not allowed to rebut her denial, even though she had claimed to be a virgin in her direct evidence, since legally she could not have consented to the sexual act and therefore the allegation went only to her credibility. The difficulty, of course, is that with sexual offences the prosecution's case often relies entirely on the credibility of the complainant. This, it is said, reduces the distinction between questions going to the issue arising from the indictment and questions going merely to credibility to a vanishing point.[460] Thus in *R v Funderburk*, again involving a charge of unlawful sexual intercourse, the 13-year-old complainant implied in her testimony that she was a virgin when the first of ten alleged incidents of abuse occurred. The defence applied for leave to cross-examine her as to whether she had had sexual intercourse with two men before the first alleged incident, and if she denied it, to call a rebuttal witness who would say that the complainant had told her about these previous experiences. The trial judge denied the applications, on the basis that the question of her virginity was irrelevant to the offence charged. The Court of Appeal ruled that the defence should have been permitted to cross-examine her on this issue (whilst noting that the trial judge was rightly concerned as to 'the ordeal of this child'),[461] and if necessary to call the rebuttal evidence, because it could have explained her detailed account of the varied sexual acts which she described as having experienced with the defendant, as 'detail often adds verisimilitude'.[462] We address the admissibility of the complainant's previous sexual experience in more depth below.[463]

The third limitation, which continues to be valid in both criminal and civil proceedings, is that the trial judge as part of her inherent jurisdiction to control the proceedings is required to prevent questioning of an unduly offensive or oppressive nature.[464] Counsel must test the evidence of each witness, but are under a corresponding ethical duty not to make statements or to ask questions 'which are merely scandalous or intended or calculated only to vilify, insult or annoy either a witness or some other person'.[465] However, in line with the common law, the Bar Code of Conduct expressly recognizes that counsel may ethically test a witness's credibility by reference to misconduct, provided the allegation appears to be supported by reasonable grounds.[466]

---

[457] Under the Criminal Procedure Act 1865 s 6. If the conviction is classified as being 'spent' under the Rehabilitation of Offenders Act 1974, leave of the court is first required: *Practice Direction (Crime: Spent Convictions)* [1975] 1 WLR 1065.   [458] Criminal Procedure Act 1865 ss 3, 4.

[459] *R v Cargill* (1913) 8 Cr App R 224 (CA).   [460] *R v Funderburk* (n 456) 597.

[461] ibid 593.   [462] ibid 597.   [463] See below, section 3.

[464] *Wong Kam-Ming v R* [1980] AC 247 (PC) (Lord Edmund-Davies). For a similar declaration in civil cases, see *Mechanical and General Interventions Co Ltd v Austin* [1935] AC 346 (HL) 359–360.

[465] *Code of Conduct of the Bar of England and Wales* (8th edn London 2004) Rule 708(g).

[466] ibid Rule 708(j).

Trial judges understandably have often been reluctant to intervene in an aggressive cross-examination on behalf of the defence, to ensure that the accused has had full opportunity to contest the prosecution's case. Child witnesses have been attacked for misdemeanours which can appear very trivial to adult eyes. In one case in the *Bristol Study*, the defence conceded that an 11-year-old girl with some learning difficulties had been sexually abused, but disputed her identification of her uncle as the abuser. She was cross-examined about a lie she allegedly had told about having done her homework, and whether she had taken £5 from her mother's handbag without permission.[467]

(b) Statutory reform

In *Speaking Up for Justice*, a Government Working Group expressed concerns that witnesses feel intimidated by cross-examination by defence counsel, particularly when the manner of questioning is perceived to be aggressive.[468] However, most defence counsel interviewed for the *Bristol Study* considered it to be counter-productive to be antagonistic with child witnesses in child abuse cases, for fear of alienating the jury.[469] Nevertheless, it will be a rare sexual abuse prosecution where the defence case is not driven to allege that the child complainant is lying.

The result of the widespread perception that criminal trials routinely victimize ordinary witnesses is s 100 of the CJA 2003. As Diagram 16 illustrates, the new legislation abolishes the common law licence to attack ordinary witnesses, instead instituting a general prohibition on admitting evidence of their bad character evidence.[470] This is subject to three exceptions, where the bad character evidence:

(1) is 'important explanatory evidence',[471] the parallel gateway for background evidence which discloses the defendant's bad character;[472]

(2) has 'substantial probative value' in relation to a matter in issue and which is of substantial importance in the context of the whole case,[473] (there being no analogous threshold pertaining to evidence against defendants);[474] or

(3) is agreed by all parties[475] to be admissible.[476]

---

[467] Unpublished data for Case 6A, *Bristol Study*.

[468] Home Office *Speaking Up for Justice: Report of the Interdepartmental Working Group on the Treatment of Vulnerable or Intimidated Witnesses in the Criminal Justice System* (June 1998) 55–56 and Recommendations 43–44. See also J Plotnikoff and R Woolfson *In Their Own Words: the Experiences of 50 Young Witnesses in Criminal Proceedings* Victim Support and NSPCC (2004), reporting that 19 of the 50 children interviewed felt that the defence lawyers were 'not polite', describing their questioning with adjectives such as 'aggressive', 'rude', 'scary' and 'pushy'. [469] *Bristol Study* 61.

[470] CJA 2003 s 100(1). [471] ibid s 100(1)(a).

[472] ibid s 101(1)(c) and s 102, discussed below, Chapter 10, section D.

[473] ibid s 100(1)(b). [474] *R v Weir* [2005] EWCA Crim 2866, [2006] 2 All ER 570 [36].

[475] Of course the ordinary witness is not treated as a 'party' in a criminal trial and so his interests can only be asserted by the counsel calling him as a witness. [476] CJA 2003 s 100(1)(c).

Diagram 16. Evidence of the Bad Character of Witnesses other than the Defendent [CJA 2003 Part 11, Ch 1]

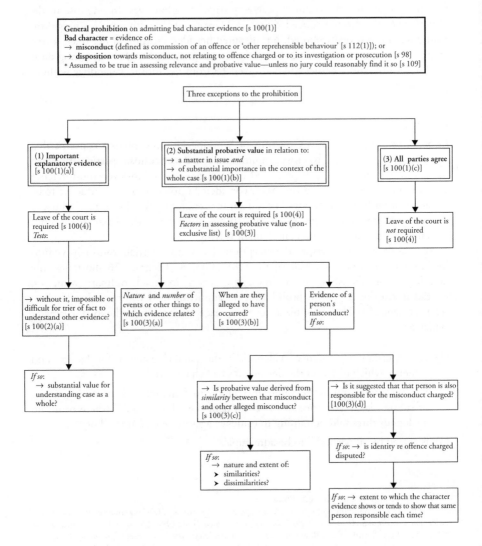

Unless the parties have agreed, leave of the court is required to adduce evidence of an ordinary witness's bad character.[477] This inclusionary power is in sharp contrast to evidence of the defendant's bad character under the CJA 2003, where judicial exclusionary discretion is limited to only two of the seven gateways (where the evidence is relevant to an important issue between the defendant and prosecution, or where the defendant attacks another person's character).[478]

Thus the asymmetry which the common law had constructed, allowing open season on ordinary witnesses whilst shielding the defendant from such attacks (subject to forfeiture) has been reversed. It will be quite difficult to challenge ordinary witnesses about their record of misconduct, with the cross-examiner first having to clear a high hurdle proving that the answer will have significant probative value for an important issue in the case.[479] For the defendant, in stark contrast, it will be assumed that his other misconduct is relevant, as his propensity to commit an offence of the same type charged, or to be untruthful, will be deemed to be an important issue between the defendant and the prosecution. This is a curious and highly significant inversion of the common law model.

2. Evidence of bad character in English civil cases

As indicated earlier, the common law rules described above still apply to bad character evidence in civil proceedings.[480] In cases in the family courts, the character of the person making allegations of abuse against someone responsible for caring for the child, such as a parent embroiled in custody proceedings, will clearly be relevant. Evidence of so-called 'parental alienation syndrome' may be adduced, to attack both the credibility of the accusing parent as a witness and her fitness to be a custodial parent. Also relevant will be any misconduct by any other person who may come into contact with that child, such as a parent's new partner. In this context, the past discreditable conduct is used for its predictive qualities, in contrast to the criminal cases where the trier of fact is asked to extrapolate from that evidence to draw inferences about whether a past event (abuse), about which that witness has testified, actually occurred.

In tort cases, the courts take a rather lenient view of cross-examination on other misconduct, provided that its relevance can be established, and subject to the trial judge's discretion to disallow improper questioning. It has been held that a question is proper only if the answer could seriously impair the witness's credibility, the matter

---

[477] It should be noted that the prosecution has a statutory obligation to disclose any convictions of prosecution witnesses [Criminal Procedure and Investigations Act 1996 s 3]. It is unclear whether under the CJA 2003 the prosecution will still be obliged to inform the jury of these convictions before calling that witness, as is the current practice [*R v Taylor; R v Goodman* [1999] 2 Cr App R 163 (CA)], but it is likely that this will be so, with the evidence being admitted by agreement under CJA 2003 s 100(1)(c).

[478] See Diagram 19 discussed below in Chapter 10 section D.1.

[479] Tapper points out that this higher relevance requirement should permit rebuttal of any denial: *Cross & Tapper on Evidence* (n 95) 389–390.

[480] Criminal Procedure Act 1865 s 6 governs proof of a conviction in both criminal and civil cases if the witness denies it, and impliedly authorizes that line of questioning.

is not too remote in time, and the imputation is not substantially disproportionate to the importance of that witness's testimony to the case.[481] In civil proceedings there is also greater latitude to rebut denials where that witness's credibility is central to the case.[482] In civil proceedings, evidence suggesting that the abuse was caused by a third party rather than by the defendant would appear to be admissible once its relevance is made out.[483]

3. Special protection for complainants in sexual assault cases: restrictions on cross-examination on previous sexual experience

In sexual assault cases, the defence may attempt to use a complainant's previous sexual experience to impeach her credibility. Before statutory intervention, the common law regarded such cross-examination as relevant. This stance was predicated on a stereotypical link between chastity and veracity which has long been discredited. The Supreme Court of Canada,[484] followed by the House of Lords,[485] identified 'twin myths' which permeated the common law's approach to such cross-examination: the object was to show that by reason of such sexual behaviour on other occasions, the complainant (a) was more likely to have consented to the sexual conduct at issue in the trial, or (b) in any event was less worthy of belief. Both courts found that restricting such questioning is a legitimate aim for legislators, because the rule of law is impaired if the criminal justice system does not protect essential witnesses from unnecessary humiliation or distress by irrelevant (or only marginally relevant) questioning.[486]

Beginning in the 1970s, all common law jurisdictions have enacted legislation to restrict cross-examination on past sexual history, often called 'rape shield' statutes (although most apply to all sexual offences). The Westminster Parliament has made two attempts to regulate such questioning, both of which have generated scathing criticism from all sides of the debate.[487] The primary thrust of such legislation, in England and Wales as well as in other common law jurisdictions, has been to forestall the use of past sexual experience to buttress the defence of consent.[488] The campaign for further statutory reform took place against a backdrop of a steady decline in

---

[481] *Hobbs v Tinling & Co Ltd* [1929] 2 KB 1 (CA).

[482] Tapper *Cross & Tapper on Evidence* (n 95) 382–395.   [483] ibid 395.

[484] *R v Seaboyer* [1991] 2 SCR 577 (SCC) 630 (McLachlin J). The Criminal Code of Canada s 276(1) specifically prohibits the twin inferences from evidence of the complainant's other sexual activity.

[485] *R v A (No 2)* [2001] UKHL 25, [2002] 1 AC 45 [76] (Lord Hope), [123] (Lord Clyde), [147]–[149] (Lord Hutton).   [486] ibid [92]–[95]; *R v Seaboyer* (n 484) [52].

[487] For a representative sample, see L Ellison 'Cross-Examination in Rape Trials' [1998] Crim LR 605; D Birch 'Rethinking Sexual History Evidence: Proposals for Fairer Trials' [2002] Crim LR 531; J Temkin 'Sexual History Evidence—Beware the Backlash' [2003] Crim LR 217; D Birch 'Untangling Sexual History Evidence: a Rejoinder to Professor Temkin' [2003] Crim LR 370.

[488] For contrasting views on the relevance of sexual history to consent, see A McColgan 'Common Law and the Relevance of Sexual History Evidence' (1996) 16 Oxford J Legal Studies 275 and M Redmayne 'Myths, Relationships and Coincidences: the New Problems of Sexual History' (2003) 7 International J of Evidence & Proof 75.

the conviction rates[489] for rape, which fell from 32 per cent of reported cases in 1977 to an all-time low of 5.57 per cent in 2002, in the face of a steady rise in reporting rates.[490] Whilst the conviction rate for rape of children under 16 is significantly higher, it still shows a dramatic drop from 40 per cent of prosecuted cases in 1999 to 23 per cent in 2002.[491]

The relevance of sexual history to child abuse cases in English law is much more limited now than it was since the Sexual Offences Act 2003 has removed the anomaly whereby consent was a defence to rape even where the complainant was legally incapable of giving consent.[492] The usual practice of the Crown Prosecution Service had been to charge rape alone in cases involving adolescents, notwithstanding that the defence's allegation of consent necessarily meant that the defendant had committed the offences of unlawful sexual intercourse and indecent assault, to which consent was not a defence. Thus the first of the twin myths, likelihood of consent, is no longer an issue in child abuse prosecutions. The abolition of consent as a defence to sexual offences against children should also mean that the defence can no longer bring out in evidence that the child complainant is involved in prostitution. Nevertheless a child's previous sexual experience, regardless of whether it is non-consensual in fact or in law, continues to be relevant in ways which can be subtly different from adult complainants, and so it is necessary that we thread our way through the legislation governing cross-examination on previous sexual experience.

In a child abuse prosecution, the applicability of so-called 'rape shield' legislation may become an issue in respect of four areas of evidence:

- previous allegations of sexual abuse made against third parties;
- an alleged motive to fabricate the allegations against the defendant;
- previous abuse to explain physical indicators of sexual abuse; and
- previous abuse or other sources of sexual knowledge to explain a child's precocious knowledge or sexualization.

We will consider each in turn, examining primarily cases involving children. It is important to bear in mind in the course of this discussion that the admissibility of evidence under these heads assumes that such evidence is available to the prosecution and hence to the defence. Here the rules governing pre-trial disclosure by the prosecution or third parties bite sharply.[493]

---

[489] Which include guilty pleas.

[490] Kelly, Lovett, Regan (n 67), Appendix 1. The attrition rate is even greater, because official statistics exclude reports treated as 'no crime' very early in the investigation. See also J Harris, S Grace *A Question of Evidence? Investigating and Prosecuting Rape in the 1990s* (Home Office Research Study 196 1999); PN Rumney 'False Allegations of Rape' (2006) 65(1) Camb LJ 128, 131–133. The declining conviction rate may be influenced by the increasing numbers of reports by women who have known their assailants, which do not fit the stereotype of stranger rape with violence.

[491] Kelly, Lovett, Regan ibid 26, Figure 3.2.

[492] Sexual Offences Act 2003 ss 5 (child under 13), 9 (child under 16) discussed above Chapter 3 section E.

[493] Discussed above, Chapter 7 section C.1(b).

(a) Previous sexual experience in child abuse prosecutions in England and Wales

(i) The statutory framework

Before the Youth Justice and Criminal Evidence Act 1999 (England) (hereafter the YJCEA 1999 (England)) was enacted, the permissible boundaries of such cross-examination were governed by s 2 of the Sexual Offences (Amendment) Act 1976, which provided that in trials of a 'rape offence' no evidence could be adduced and no question in cross-examination could be asked at the trial about any sexual experience of a complainant with a person other than that defendant, without leave of the court. The judge could give leave 'if and only if he is satisfied that it would be unfair to that defendant to refuse to allow the evidence to be adduced or the question to be asked'. The test thus went directly to the implications of the statutory prohibition on the fairness of the trial. The Court of Appeal interpreted the legislation as requiring that the defence identify the fact in issue to which the evidence was argued to be relevant beyond a simple attack on credibility.[494] This provided the basis for extending the protection of s 2 to sexual offences other than rape, and to offences against children where consent was legally irrelevant.[495] Some trial judges were prepared to allow the defence to explore an adolescent complainant's previous sexual activity on the basis that it was relevant to consent, which they considered should never be barred under s 2.[496] The *Bristol Study* found that in trials in the research sample children were cross-examined on previous sexual experience which was non-consensual either in fact or in law, often with only tenuous relevance to the facts in issue in the trial.[497]

There was vigorous academic and political debate as to how effective s 2 of the 1976 Act was in protecting complainants from irrelevant questioning. *Speaking Up for Justice* considered the issue against the background of a high attrition rate in rape cases, and concluded that there was 'overwhelming evidence' that the legislation was not working, and that a frequent defence ploy was to besmirch the complainant's character in a way which did not relate to the issue of consent.[498] Many judges and advocates vehemently contested this conclusion.[499] Nevertheless the Government accepted the Report's recommendation that the legislation should prescribe circumstances in which sexual history evidence could be admitted, although it did not

---

[494] *R v Viola* [1982] 1 WLR 1138 (CA) 1142–1143.   [495] *R v Funderburk* (n 456).

[496] *Bristol Study* (n 467). This stance that sexual history evidence going to consent was never barred by s 2 is supported by *R v Viola* (n 494). Paul Boateng, then a Home Office minister, took the position that s 41 would overturn *Viola* [House of Commons Committee Stage, Standing Committee E, *Hansard*, 24 June 1999, quoted by D Birch and R Leng *Blackstone's Guide to the Youth Justice & Criminal Evidence Act 1999* (Blackstone Press Ltd, London 2000) 93].

[497] *Bristol Study* ibid 61–63 and Appendix C, cases 6A, 29B, 38A and 43A.

[498] *Speaking Up for Justice* (n 468) [9.62], [9.64].

[499] See Lord Bingham, then the Lord Chief Justice, in the second reading of the Bill, House of Lords, *Hansard* 15 December 1998 Vol. 327, col 1272, quoted by Birch and Leng (n 496) 104; N Kibble *Judicial Perspectives on Section 41 of the Youth Justice and Criminal Evidence Act 1999* 15–23 (June 2004, summary published as 'Judicial Perspectives on the Operation of s. 41 and the Relevance and Admissibility of Prior Sexual History Evidence: Four Scenarios' [2005] Crim LR 190, 263). See also Baroness Mallalieu QC, *Hansard* HL Deb vol 598 Col 16 (8 March 1999) stating that 'the days of insensitive judicial comment and the permitting of unjustified cross-examination, which was irrelevant, insulting and gratuitously intrusive, are, in my personal experience, ones which relate to a bygone age.'

accept its preference for the Scottish model which incorporated a residual inclusionary discretion.[500]

Parliament's second attempt to regulate the area produced Chapter III of Part II[501] of the YJCEA 1999, which took a radically different approach from the 1976 Act. Diagram 17 maps the new provisions, which suffer from the convoluted drafting which infects that statute.[502] There are several features of the new regime which are pertinent to our discussion.

- Subsection 41(4) forbids evidence if it appears to the court to be reasonable to assume that the purpose (or main purpose) for which it would be adduced or asked would be to establish or elicit material for impugning credibility of the complainant as a witness. The subsection thus seeks to prevent questions or evidence to impugn credibility which otherwise the court would have viewed as relevant.[503] While Lord Steyn in *R v A (No 2)* described the methodology adopted by the statute as 'legislative overkill',[504] Lord Hope concluded that the proportionality test for compliance with the ECHR Article 6(1) was satisfied, because where the object is to impugn credibility, no inferences can be drawn from sexual behaviour on other occasions.[505] While the situation is necessarily rather different when young children are involved, the prohibition in s 41(4) has been held to be proportionate and consistent with the ECHR, because investigation of the implications of their other complaints for their credibility inevitably leads to scrutiny of their sexual behaviour.[506]

- Subsections 41(3) and (5) establish a closed list of relevant evidential targets for which the evidence *might* properly be adduced. The only gateways which are not predetermined in terms of the substance of the evidence are those which apply where the target does not relate to consent. In other words, Parliament has definitively prescribed the situations where other sexual behaviour is relevant to consent, regardless of the other evidence in the trial. Subsection 41(5) is triggered by the way in which the prosecution has put its case. So s 41(3)(a) is the only gateway through which the defence may seek entry by the way it formulates its case. Thus the primary focus of the prohibition of sexual behaviour evidence remains factual consent which, as indicated earlier, is no longer directly relevant to prosecutions of offences against children under 16.

- The House of Lords in *R v A (No 2)* held that the courts must interpret the 'similarity/coincidence' gateway in s 41(3)(c) sufficiently broadly (by subordinating the 'niceties' of the statutory language of 'similarity' and 'coincidence')[507] to ensure that evidence is admitted where it is 'so relevant to consent that to exclude it would

---

[500] *Speaking Up for Justice* (n 468) Recommendation 63.

[501] Which came into force on 4 December 2000.

[502] We are indebted to HH Peter Rook QC and Neil Kibble, University of Wales, Aberystwyth for their very helpful comments on Diagram 17.

[503] *R v Martin* [2004] EWCA Crim 916, [2004] 2 Cr App R 22 [18]; *R v Floyd Charles Darnell* [2003] EWCA Crim 176 [39].   [504] *R v A (No 2)* (n 485) [43].

[505] ibid [91]–[95].   [506] *Dennis Andrew Etches v R* [2004] EWCA Crim 1313 [11]–[13].

[507] *R v A (No 2)* (n 485) [45] (Lord Steyn).

Diagram 17. The Admissibility of Defence Evidence of the Complainant's Previous Sexual Experience under the YJCEA 1999

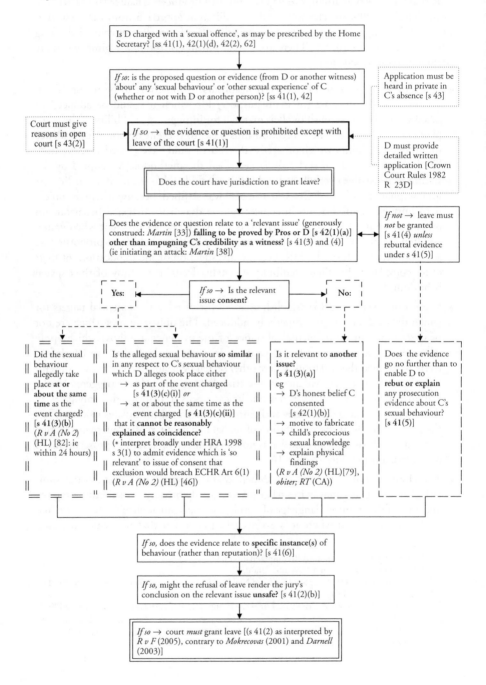

endanger the fairness of the trial' under the ECHR Art 6(1).[508] This conclusion could be buttressed if necessary[509] by s 3(1) of the Human Rights Act 1998 which requires that 'so far as it is possible to do so, primary legislation. . .must be read and given effect to in a way which is compatible with the Convention rights'. Whilst that case was specifically directed to the admission of evidence of a previous consensual sexual relationship between the adult complainant and the defendant, the Law Lords had rejected any elastic interpretation of the temporal requirements of s 41(3)(b).[510]

- Relevance to another identified issue under s 41(3)(a) seems sufficiently open-textured to allow the normal principles of interpretation to operate without recourse to the HRA 1998 s 3(1). Thus far the lower courts have not found it necessary to invoke s 3(1), instead claiming that the normal canons of purposive and contextual statutory interpretation have yielded the desired results.[511]

- The Court of Appeal initially stressed that the decision of the trial judge to grant leave under s 41(2) is discretionary,[512] but in 2005 in *R v F* concluded that a trial judge has no general discretion to exclude or limit the evidence of sexual behaviour which is related to a relevant issue in the case; it must be allowed to pass through the applicable gateway, s 41(4) being the only additional filter.[513] As Diagram 17 illustrates, given that the trial judge must first have made a finding that the refusal of leave might render the jury's conclusion on the relevant issue unsafe under s 41(2)(b), it would seem odd for a trial judge, having decided that that condition was satisfied, to decline to grant leave. On the other hand, s 2 of the 1976 Act had provided that the judge 'shall' grant leave if and only if he is satisfied that it would be unfair to that defendant to refuse to allow the evidence. One must assume that the choice of different, permissive, language was deliberate. Perhaps what is intended by the earlier decisions of the Court of Appeal is that the trial judge must evaluate the risk of the jury being misled, either by the evidence or by the absence of the evidence, and if the risk is seen as high, or the evidence has only marginal relevance, the judge may disallow the evidence. Such an interpretation could be supported by reference to Lord Hope's concern in *R v A (No 2)* that a balance must be struck between the probative value of the evidence of sexual behaviour and its potential prejudice in diverting the jury from the real issue,[514] language reminiscent of the problems created by propensity evidence relating to the accused.[515] As Lord Steyn observed in *R v A (No 2)*, the concept of a fair trial requires the court to take account of 'the familiar triangulation of interests

---

[508] ibid [46] (Lord Steyn).
[509] Lord Hope did not consider it necessary to invoke HRA 1998 subs 3(1) because of the dearth of information about the evidence of similarity which A might be able to show at trial: ibid [106].
[510] ibid [12] (Lord Slynn), [40] (Lord Steyn), [156] (Lord Hutton).
[511] *Dennis Andrew Etches v R* (n 506) [11]-M.[13]; *R v RD* [2002] EWCA Crim 2893 [39]–[41]; *R v Martin* (n 503) [33]–[38].
[512] *R v Mokrecovas* [2001] EWCA Crim 1644, [2002] 1 Cr App R 20 [11]; *R v Floyd Charles Darnell* (n 503) [35].   [513] *R v F* [2005] EWCA Crim 493, [2005] 2 Cr App R 13 (CA).
[514] *R v A (No 2)* (n 485) [55], adopting *R v Seaboyer* (n 484) 634.
[515] Discussed below, Chapter 10 sections B.4 and D.

of the accused, the victim and society', and in this context proportionality has a role to play.[516]

- It is unclear whether *R v A (No 2)* created a general *inclusionary* power to admit evidence which does not fit through any of the gateways,[517] nor whether it is an inclusionary counterweight to the final exclusionary hurdle of s 41(2)(b), that without the evidence the jury's conclusion might be unsafe. Lord Hope considered that any form of inclusionary discretion was not possible under the statutory model.[518] Even if His Lordship's view is strictly correct, the judiciary applying s 41 in the courtroom are of the view that *R v A (No 2)* restored a measure of judicial discretion without which the legislation was unworkable.[519]

- The prohibition on evidence of 'sexual behaviour' applies only to the defence[520] (as did s 2 of the 1976 Act). The prosecution without seeking leave of the court can adduce evidence of the complainant's sexual experience, for example to support a contention that the defendant had targeted a particular child for abuse knowing that he had previously been a victim of other abusers. However, the Court of Appeal has suggested that the trial judge should exercise his discretion to exclude evidence under the Police and Criminal Evidence Act s 78 if the use of previous sexual experience evidence by the prosecution would render the trial unfair to the defence.[521]

- The gateway in s 41(5) can be opened only by the prosecution; therefore the defence can no longer attempt to pre-empt apprehended inferences by the jury, for example that the incident charged was the child's first sexual encounter.[522] Further, the rebuttal evidence must directly address and contradict the complainant's specific assertion.[523] The trial judge has no discretion to refuse to admit or to limit relevant rebuttal evidence.[524]

- The statutory prohibition applies not just to the cross-examination of the complainant, but also to any evidence elicited by the defence from any witness, including

---

[516] *R v A (No 2)* (n 485) [38].

[517] So that on the flowchart there would be an 'inclusionary discretion' box alongside the box 'does the court have jurisdiction to grant leave?'. We are indebted to Neil Kibble for this point.

[518] *R v A (No 2)* (n 485) [109] (Lord Hope).

[519] Kibble (n 499) 31–32. The empirical study, commissioned by the Criminal Bar Association, was based on interviews with over 50 judges from the Circuit Court and High Court, Court of Appeal and House of Lords, as well as some advocates.

[520] Birch 'Rethinking Sexual History Evidence' (n 487), 534 argues that this contravenes the due process principle of equality of arms in the ECHR Article 6(3)(d).

[521] *R v Naveed Soroya* [2006] EWCA Crim 1884 [28] (*obiter*).

[522] J Temkin 'Sexual History Evidence: the Ravishment of Section 2' [1993] Crim LR 3, 4. For an example of this strategy see *R v SMS* [1992] Crim LR 310, quashing a conviction where the trial judge had not allowed cross-examination of the 14-year-old complainant as to whether she had had sexual intercourse with anyone else, as the defence suggested it would be difficult for the jury to believe that she would consent to her first act of intercourse with someone who had one hand and a false eye.

[523] *R v Minhas and Haq* [2003] EWCA Crim 135 (defence properly not permitted to cross-examine 13-year-old about her history of sexually transmitted disease to rebut her assertions in cross-examination that she would never have done anything like sleeping with the 36-year-old defendant or taking drugs).

[524] *R v F* (n 513).

from the defendant himself when testifying. If the defendant unexpectedly blurts an allegation about the complainant's sexual reputation or behaviour on other occasions, this could result in a mistrial.

- The application may be made to the trial judge in a preparatory hearing[525] and the defendant may appeal an adverse ruling to the Court of Appeal and House of Lords before the trial commences.[526] While this interlocutory procedure means that trials can be run more efficiently, it also has disadvantages because the courts do not know how the factual context for the disputed evidence will unfold in live testimony. Often the prosecution at this stage will not know whether a complainant would respond to the question with a denial or an admission, which can become an important issue in terms of the defence's right to lead rebuttal evidence.

- Section 41 applies only to defence evidence relating to the complainant's 'sexual behaviour', which is further defined by s 42(1)(c) as including 'other sexual experience' whether or not it involved the accused or any other person (and so could apply to solitary sexual activity). Where very young children are involved, the fact that they might not understand their experiences as sexual is irrelevant.[527] Therefore an important issue will be whether the proposed evidence of conduct constitutes 'sexual behaviour', which may in turn depend upon the specific factual context— again raising problems for interlocutory applications and appeals. If defence counsel contends that the question is not directed at the complainant's sexual behaviour, she still has a professional obligation to apply for a ruling that s 41 is *not* triggered.[528]

- Finally, it is unclear whether the defence now must also satisfy the requirements for cross-examining a witness on bad character under the CJA 2003 s 100 as well as the YJCEA 1999 s 41, if the alleged previous sexual experience was discreditable to the complainant.

We turn now to the four categories of sexual experience evidence of particular relevance to child abuse prosecutions.

(ii) Previous or subsequent allegations of sexual abuse made against third parties

To place this issue in context, it is important to acknowledge a fact which may seem obvious to professionals working in child protection: sexually abused children often are at great risk of revictimization at the hands of other offenders.[529] There are several reasons:[530]

- the betrayal of trust where family members or respected adults exploit children can leave them unable to make reasonable judgements about others, and so they are vulnerable to further manipulation;

- the inability to resist sexual assaults can leave a child resigned to being a powerless victim;

---

[525] Criminal Procedure and Investigations Act 1996 ss 29, 31.
[526] ibid ss 35, 36.   [527] *Dennis Andrew Etches v R* (n 506) [4]–[6].
[528] *R v MH; R v RT* [2001] EWCA Crim 1877, [2002] 1 Cr App R 22 [41].
[529] The Michigan Court of Appeals took judicial notice of this in *People v Morse* 586 NW 2d 555 (Michigan CA 1998) 559.   [530] NCPCA *Investigation and Prosecution of Child Abuse* (n 60) 260.

- sexual abuse can make children feel valueless, and the loss of self-esteem can lead to self-harming and other destructive behaviour such as promiscuity, prostitution and involvement in drugs, increasing their vulnerability to victimization;
- potential offenders who suspect or know of a child's previous experiences of abuse may find the child's vulnerability particularly attractive and enticing.[531]

The defence strategy[532] in seeking the admission of evidence of allegations against others may be:

- to show the complainant's propensity to make false allegations about sexual matters;
- to support the theory that the complainant has confused perpetrators and has wrongly attributed the abuse to the defendant; or
- to show that the complainant is familiar with mechanisms for reporting abuse (for example through 'keep safe' training),[533] to rebut an explanation for delayed complaint.

These contentions can raise several difficult issues arising from two questions which the trial court must address:

- Can the defence put the other allegation to the complainant in cross-examination?
- If the initial question about another allegation of other sexual experience may be asked, does the 'collateral issue' or 'finality' rule apply, so that the defence is barred from pursuing a complainant's denial in further cross-examination and from calling evidence to rebut that denial?

We will start with the threshold question, whether the defence will be permitted to ask any question of the complainant about an allegation against someone else. The first two issues here pertain to the definition of 'sexual behaviour' or 'other sexual experience'. First of all, do the statutory restrictions on evidence of previous sexual experience apply where it is non-consensual, whether in fact or in law? The English courts (unlike their Canadian counterparts) have generally not drawn any distinction between consensual and non-consensual sexual experience, regarding both as constituting 'sexual behaviour' and so coming within the scope of the statutory restrictions in principle. Therefore the child complainant is in principle afforded the protection of s 41 in relation to previous sexual abuse.

Secondly, do the statutory restrictions on evidence of 'sexual behaviour' apply where the defence claims that the other allegations were false? The answer is (perhaps surprisingly) complex. Prior to the 1999 Act, the English courts admitted such evidence, on the basis that it was relevant to the complainant's testimonial credibility in relation to the charge, and was not an attempt to discredit her generally through her sexual history per se.[534] However, this form of relevance appears to be what is forbidden

---

[531] See *Bristol Study* 99–100 Case 38A for an example of how this argument can be deployed in the trial.

[532] S Chapman 'Section 276 of the Criminal Code and the Admissibility of "Sexual Activity" Evidence' (1999) 25 Queen's LJ 121, 145–146.   [533] *Bristol Study* (n 467) 39.

[534] eg *R v Todd* No 96/7540/W4, 21 March 1997 (CA).

by s 41(3), as its thrust is to impugn the complainant's credibility. Lord Williams of Mostyn, the Government spokesperson in the House of Lords during the passage of the Bill, stated that evidence about previous false complaints would not be excluded by s 41 because such evidence is about untruthful conduct on prior occasions, and that there is a very clear difference.[535] Unfortunately, seven years after the Act was passed, the claimed clarity is still lacking.

In conjoined appeals in 2001, the Court of Appeal considered the meaning of 'about sexual behaviour'.[536] In each case the defendant denied that the incidents charged had ever occurred. In *R v RT*, the defendant was charged with two counts of indecent assault and one count of rape of his niece over a four-year period. The trial judge would not permit the defence to cross-examine her on her failure to mention the alleged incidents when she was asked by police on two occasions (when she was aged 8 and 11) whether she had been abused, when they were investigating alleged sexual abuse of her brothers. Counsel intended to put to her that either the incidents had never happened or she was confused about which adult had done what to her over the course of her very troubled childhood. In the second case, *R v MH*, the defendant was charged with indecent assault of his stepdaughter when she was aged 14. He wished to establish that she had lied on four occasions in the past about sexual matters, and also about a supposed abortion induced by her mother with a knitting needle, maltreatment by her mother, and her own involvement in drugs and with a gang. The strategy was to establish that she had a propensity to lie. In each case the trial judge had ruled that the questions were about the complainant's sexual behaviour and that since their purpose would be to impugn her credibility, they were inadmissible under s 41(4). The Court of Appeal ruled that in both cases the questions were relevant in the 'normal, non-statutory sense of that term', so that s 41 on its face did not apply.[537] Keene LJ accepted that the purpose of the questions was to 'establish or elicit material for impugning the credibility of the complainant as a witness', which was expressly deemed not to be relevant by s 41(4).[538] However,

it seems to this Court that normally questions or evidence about false statements in the past by a complainant about sexual assaults or such questions or evidence about a failure to complain about the alleged assault which are the subject matter of the charge, while complaining about other sexual assaults, are not ones 'about' any sexual behaviour of the complainant. They relate not to her sexual behaviour but to her statements in the past or to her failure to complain.[539]

RT and *MH* might have established a clear rule that such evidence is about lies and not about the subject matter of lies, were it not for an apparently conflicting decision of the Court of Appeal some three weeks earlier by a different panel, to which the subsequent case did not refer. In *R v Mokrecovas*[540] the defence wished to put to the 17-year-old complainant that she had had consensual sexual intercourse with the accused's brother earlier the same night, and that she was lying in denying this incident and in making the rape allegation against the accused. Lord Woolf CJ ruled that the

---

[535] *Hansard* 8 March 1999 column 34, quoted by Keene LJ in *R v MH; R v RT* (n 528) [35].
[536] *R v MH; R v RT* ibid.   [537] ibid [25].   [538] ibid [36].   [539] ibid [33].
[540] *R v Mokrecovas* (n 512).

proposed questions about the supposed lies would be 'about sexual behaviour' and so would breach the bar on the use of such evidence to impugn the complainant's credibility.[541] Counsel were warned about using s 41(3)(a) 'to ride a coach and horses through the desirable policy reflected in s 41(4) of the Act. It would elicit material by the back door to impugn the credibility of the complainant as a witness.'[542] However, as we will discuss in the next section, another solution was found to the defence's predicament in *Mokrecovas*.

It is significant that the premise in the cases analysed thus far was that the previous complaints were false. What if the defence does not take that position? In *R v Alan David C and Julie B*,[543] decided 18 months after the cases just discussed, the parents of twins were jointly charged with sexual abuse after they complained to their foster parents. In their video interviews the twins, by then aged seven, made complaints of sexual abuse against other persons as well as their parents. These other complaints were edited out. The defence wanted the video interviews played in their entirety, as well as the evidence of the complaints to the foster parents. The defence's position was that the incidents charged had never occurred. Medical evidence that the girl's hymen was abnormal and consistent with a history of vaginal penetration was excluded by the trial judge for reasons which did not appear in the record. It appears that the defence strategy was not to suggest that her abuse had been inflicted by third parties, but rather that the twins' full interviews would disclose strikingly similar features about the other complaints as well as inconsistencies, and that the 'sanitized' videotape might have improperly affected the jury's verdict. The trial judge had concluded that questions about the children's failure to complain earlier and about inconsistencies in their allegations against their parents were authorized by *RT* and *MH*, but would not permit questions about the abuse allegedly inflicted by third parties. In dismissing the appeal, Mance LJ interpreted *RT* and *MH* as indicating that

... absent any basis for suggesting that such complaints were false, such questioning is 'about [the] sexual behaviour of the complainant'. The rationale, as we see it, must be that, if evidence is adduced about complaints which cannot properly be challenged as false, then the intention must be to elicit that other sexual behaviour or experience, the subject of such complaints, and so to deploy it in one way or another to the complainant's discredit, eg by arguing that it has been wrongly transposed and attributed to the present defendant in the complainant's account. On that basis, the judge would have been right to consider that the extent to which it was permissible was a matter for his discretion.[544]

Under this interpretation, therefore, the issue whether s 41 is triggered by complaints against third parties is determined by the truth or falsity of those complaints, not by their substance. Yet can it really be said that telling lies about sex does not constitute 'sexual behaviour', but telling the truth about sex does?

Moreover, according to *RT* and *MH* silence about sexual abuse inflicted by the defendant when disclosing abuse by others is not 'sexual behaviour' because it is not

---

[541] ibid [15]–[19].　　　[542] ibid [20].
[543] *R v Alan David C and Julie B* [2003] EWCA Crim 29.　　　[544] ibid [27].

necessary to investigate whether those complaints were true or false.[545] The distinction is critical because *Alan David C and Julie B* held that if s 41 does not apply, the trial judge has no general discretion to restrict cross-examination on that area.[546]

The third issue arising from the question whether the defence should be permitted to put the question at all is the evidential threshold for the defence's assertion that a previous allegation was false. *RT* and *MH* placed an important caveat on the licence to cross-examine on complaints against others: the defence must have 'a proper evidential basis' for asserting that any such previous statement was (a) made and (b) untrue, failing which the questions are considered to be 'about sexual behaviour' and prohibited.[547] It is unclear whether this imposes a higher standard than had been the case under s 2 of the 1976 Act, where defence counsel were required to have supporting grounds for the attack but they did not have to possess admissible evidence to prove the correctness of their assertion.[548]

Can an inference of falsity be drawn from the allegations themselves? In *Dennis Andrew Etches*,[549] the accused was convicted of four specimen counts of indecent assault against his two daughters, who were aged six and four at the time of the video interviews. Some 15 months later they were interviewed again as a result of complaints they subsequently made to their foster parents. The older sister alleged sexual abuse similar to that against her father, but that it was committed by her mother, two aunts and an uncle and cousin. She also alleged physical abuse against an aunt and two other persons. The younger girl made no further allegations of sexual abuse, but complained of physical abuse by several people. No one was charged as a consequence of these further disclosures. The difficulty facing counsel defending the father was that because none of the later allegations had been further investigated, there was no evidence that they were untrue. On appeal, he argued that their extensive nature made them simply implausible, and so he should have been allowed to put the allegations to the girls and to explore their truth or falsity with them. The Court of Appeal in dismissing the appeal held that if the children had asserted that their subsequent complaints had been true, then the court would have been faced with the dilemma of either letting those allegations of criminal conduct by named third parties stand unanswered, or descending into factual inquiries with no obvious limit and wholly collateral to the issue in the case.[550]

S (Paul F), Bond and Cook[551] is another example of subsequent allegations undermining credibility. It was common ground that the children, aged 13 and 11 at the time of trial, had been subjected to prolonged and severe sexual abuse, the issue being by whom. In their pre-trial interviews, the children identified five abusers, and the eldest confirmed that she had disclosed all her complaints. After the trial, however,

---

[545] *R v MH; R v RT* (n 528) [34].   [546] *R v Alan David C and Julie B* (n 543) [32].

[547] *R v MH; R v RT* (n 528) [41]; see also *R v Alan David C and Julie B* (n 543), [27]; *R v TW* [2004] EWCA Crim 3103; *R v Abdelrahman* [2005] EWCA Crim 1367. The Court of Appeal has held that counsel cannot seek to satisfy this requirement by asking the complainant if the previous allegation was true: *R v Lee Archer* [2003] EWCA Crim 2072 (CA) [14]; *R v Stephan H* [2003] EWCA Crim 2367 (CA) [30]–[31].   [548] *R v C* [1996] Crim LR 37 (CA); *R v Howes* [1996] 2 Cr App R 490 (CA).

[549] *Dennis Andrew Etches v R* (n 506).   [550] ibid [9]–[10].

[551] *R v S (Paul F), Bond and Cook* [2003] EWCA Crim 3435.

she made further allegations against a total of 18 people, and for the first time impli-cated her mother. The Court of Appeal, in allowing the appeals on a referral from the Criminal Cases Review Commission, stated that they were 'in a thoroughly unsatis-factory state of mind' as they had no doubt that the children had been the victims of widespread abuse within what was highly likely to have been a paedophile ring. However, had the additional complaints been made before trial the defendants would have had more material for cross-examination to press their case of mistaken identity, and to make positive suggestions of confabulation.[552] No reference was made to the permissibility of such cross-examination under s 41.

Should an inference of falsity be drawn from evidence that the complainant did not cooperate with the police investigating the allegation? Here much will depend upon the circumstances;[553] for example falsity might not be a plausible inference if the complaint had been made by a third party, without the child's consent.

It is of great importance that an inference of falsity not be drawn from the mere fact that the police chose not to proceed with the prosecution against the third party. As the *Bristol Study* showed, there is a myriad of reasons why the police or the Crown Prosecution Service may decide to take no further action which do not relate to the credibility of the complainant.[554] This was recognized in *R v PB*,[555] where the eight-year-old child made it clear at the outset that she wanted to speak about sexual matters involving two men, and the video interview dealt first with the other man, DR. The police file showed that their recommendation for no further action against DR was based upon the insufficiency of evidence arising from the absence of opportunity to commit the crime and lack of corroboration, as well as the child's refusal to talk about the alleged incident, insisting on only describing it in writing. Mance LJ pointed out that at best the defence could only elicit from the child the fact that no charge had been pursued, but not the reasons:

Such reasons constitute in reality no more than the views of a third party which might be right or wrong. They have no evidential weight and to explore them or indeed question whether the police believed the counts made by the claimant [*sic*] against DR, which we are told they did in this case, would not be admissible.[556]

One odd feature of the *PB* case was that the medical evidence indicated that the child had been subjected to digital but not penile penetration, which would be consistent with the allegation against PB but not (allegedly) against the man who had not been charged. Counsel for PB regarded this as indicating that she was lying about DR. To this argument, the Court of Appeal replied:

It seems to us therefore very far from accurate to suggest that the medical evidence under-mined the accuracy of the claimant's [*sic*] account or. . .meant that it could not possibly be true. The medical evidence suggested that this may not have been penile penetration but we doubt whether this at the time eight-year-old complainant is to be taken as necessarily suggesting that there had been. What she was saying was that, as she put it, horrid sexual

---

[552] ibid [67]–[69].   [553] *R v V* [2006] EWCA Crim 1901, [2006] All ER (D) 404 [28].
[554] *Bristol Study* chapter IV 'The Decision to Prosecute'.   [555] *R v PB* [2001] EWCA Crim 3042.
[556] ibid [21].

things have happened to her in the vaginal area and on the medical evidence so it appears that they had.[557]

This case demonstrates how strained the arguments can become where the permissibility of questions turns on such distinctions.

An important ancillary issue is whether, if the question is permitted and the complainant denies either having made the previous allegations or that they were false, the defence can further cross-examine her, or tender evidence contradicting her denial. As explained earlier, the finality or collateral issue rule prevents a cross-examiner from adducing evidence, whether in further cross-examination or by calling other witnesses, where a witness denies an allegation which is not directly germane to the specific issues being tried, and so goes only to that witness's general creditworthiness.[558] The rule is justified on the basis that it keeps the trial tightly focused on the specific issues being tried, without distracting the jury with extraneous matters. The application of the finality rule is notoriously difficult, particularly in sexual assault cases which typically involve a credibility contest.[559] However, the difficulty in discerning the difference between questions going to a specific fact in issue and those going to general credibility may be exaggerated; how can it be said that complaints against someone else can go to the issue being tried, unless those allegations are somehow connected with the incidents on the indictment? For example, in the leading case of *Funderburk*[560] the connection was made by the 13-year-old complainant herself when she claimed to be a virgin at the time of the assault charged, and hence the evidence went to the specific credibility of her story.

This interpretation of the finality rule is supported by two inadequately reported cases before the 1999 Act, where the Court of Appeal applied the rule to thwart the defence's attempts to call as witnesses men who would say that the complainant had made false allegations against them. The Court was concerned that allowing the defendant to pursue the issue of which version of events was correct would mean that the prosecution might wish to call further rebuttal evidence, and so would require the jury to embark on an extremely difficult and complex task.[561] The defence thus will normally be bound by the complainant's denial that the previous allegation was false.[562] However, where the defence claimed that the complainant had previously admitted that another rape allegation was false, the defence should have been permitted to pursue the point in cross-examination, because that question was really about her complaint rather than about having had sexual intercourse.[563]

In contrast, where the complainant denied making the previous rape allegation at all, the Court of Appeal was prepared to countenance an exception to the finality rule, at least where the defendant claimed that the assault charged never took place.[564]

---

[557] ibid [9].   [558] *R v Funderburk* (n 456); Criminal Procedure Act 1865 ss 4, 5.

[559] *R v Funderburk* ibid 598; *Palmer v The Queen* (1998) 193 CLR 1 (Aus HC) [51]–[52] (McHugh J, dissenting).   [560] *R v Funderburk* ibid.

[561] *R v S (Snook)* [1992] Crim LR 307 (CA); *R v Todd* (n 534).

[562] *R v S (Snook)* (ibid); *R v MH; R v RT* (n 528) [40].

[563] *R v David Cox* (1986) 84 Cr App R 132 (CA) 136–137.

[564] *R v Nagrecha* [1997] 2 Cr App R 401 (CA).

The boundaries of this mooted exception remain ill-defined. In *PB*, Mance LJ indicated that its scope is defined pragmatically, apparently turning on how easily the falsity could be demonstrated, for example by proving that the alleged perpetrator of the other assault was abroad at the relevant time. When defence counsel for PB claimed that she could elicit evidence of falsity simply by adducing the medical report, or by cross-examining the child's mother or the police as to why there was no prosecution, the Court retorted:

> ... the defence cannot pick and choose and put in those bits which suit it. Either the complainant's answers are final or the issue of the truth or falseness of the other complaint is appropriate to be determined and in that case it must be properly and fully determined. There is no halfway house on such a situation.[565]

In *R v Alan David C and Julie B*, Mance LJ made no reference to this supposed exception, flatly stating that if the twins had denied making the complaints, or had repeated or endorsed them, the defendants would not have been able to adduce material they might actually possess tending to prove that the children were lying.[566] In 2004, Buxton LJ stated that it is a matter of discretion rather than a rule whether the denial can be pursued, which should be 'very sparingly exercised', because the threat posed to the objectives of s 41 by investigation of other complaints remains very real.[567]

The Court of Appeal in *RT* and *MH* noted that even if the finality rule is applied by the trial judge, the damage to the complainant's reputation may already be done, and the deterrent effect on other potential complainants and sexual cases would continue to operate.[568] This is why the Court insisted that the defence have a proper evidential basis for asserting that the complaint was false. Thus the operation of the finality rule can disadvantage the prosecution's case as well as the defence because the matter is left dangling.

(iii) Motive to fabricate the allegations against the defendant

Lord Hope in *obiter dicta* in *R v A (No 2)* considered that the issue of a motive to concoct a complaint should pass through the gateway in s 41(3)(a) as being relevant to an issue other than consent.[569] However, a motive to fabricate strictly speaking does not 'fall to be proved' by the prosecution or defence[570] and so would seem not to qualify as a 'relevant issue' under s 42(1)(a), the consequence being that it would be prohibited under s 41(1). In any event, it is difficult to understand how a question suggesting a bias against the defendant or a motive to fabricate could be anything other than an attempt to impugn the complainant's credibility as a witness,

---

[565] *R v PB* (n 555) [15].

[566] *R v Alan David C and Julie B* (n 543) [32]. See also *R v EF* [2002] EWCA Crim 1773, holding that the defence could not call a witness to contradict a 13-year-old complainant's denial of having told alleged lies to a friend boasting of sexual experience, where the defence was that she had made a false accusation of indecent assault against the defendant to deflect theft allegations.

[567] *Dennis Andrew Etches v R* (n 506) [8].   [568] *R v MH; R v RT* (n 528) [40].

[569] *R v A (No 2)* (n 485) [78]–[79].

[570] P Rook and R Ward *Rook & Ward on Sexual Offences Law and Practice* (3rd edn Sweet & Maxwell, London 2004) 555 [18.44]; Birch 'Untangling Sexual History Evidence' (n 487), 380.

and so one might think that it would be barred under s 41(4) before the gateway of s 41(3)(a) is even approached.[571] It is submitted that the only way of reconciling this apparent contradiction is to interpret the prohibition on credibility evidence in s 41(4) as relating only to the second impermissible *general* inference—that merely by virtue of the complainant's previous sexual behaviour she is less worthy of belief. This would then permit the defendant to enter the gateway in s 41(3)(a) on the basis of a specific, relevant and permissible inference of spiteful concoction of the allegation being tried.[572] Otherwise, the trier of fact would be deprived of the essential thrust of the defence case.[573]

Mokrecovas provides the best example of how s 41 can be applied in this context. It will be recalled that the 17-year-old complainant alleged that she had been raped during a night spent in the flat of the accused's brother, and the defence wished to put to her that she had had two consensual sessions of sexual activity with the brother as well as with himself that night. The defence argued that this evidence should be allowed through the gateway of s 41(3)(a) as it explained her reasons for falsely alleging rape, to provide an excuse to her parents for her absence from home all night and her intoxication, and so to allay their suspicions that she had been guilty of sexual behaviour of which they would disapprove.[574] The Court of Appeal held that the question whether sexual intercourse took place added nothing to the foundations for the alleged motive to lie. All of the points on which the defence wished to rely could be made without reference to her sexual behaviour with the brother. Therefore stripping the sexual contact from the questions going to motive would not result in any relevant issue not being explored, whilst avoiding unnecessarily invading the complainant's privacy and humiliating her. The application therefore failed to clear the final hurdle of s 41(2)(b).[575]

The facts of *Mokrecovas* presented a convenient escape route for the court, permitting it to 'sanitize' the motive by air-brushing out its sexual context.[576] However the parties' competing claims to fairness will unavoidably collide in the 'relevant to another issue' gateway where the complainant's alleged motive to lie is inextricably tied to sexual behaviour, for example to explain away her pregnancy or sexually transmitted disease. In such a case, it is difficult to conceive of the ingenious argument necessary to maintain that the question is not 'about sexual behaviour' intended to impugn her credibility as a witness, and so trapped in the filter of s 41(4), unless the restrictive scope of that filter urged above is adopted. In *Martin*, the Court of Appeal construed the prohibition as applying only to questions sole or main purpose of which is to attack the complainant's credibility. Therefore where the defendant

---

[571] Potter LJ expressed some perplexity on this point in *R v Floyd Charles Darnell* (n 503) [41]–[42].

[572] This interpretation is arguably implicit in *R v A (No 2)* (n 485) [76], [78], [79] (Lord Hope, citing with approval the distinction drawn by McLachlin J in *R v Seaboyer* (n 484) 613–615), and [138] (Lord Clyde). [573] *Rook & Ward* (n 570) 556 [18.48].

[574] *R v Mokrecovas* (n 512) [15]. [575] ibid [16]–[18].

[576] For another example see *R v R* [2004] EWCA Crim 1964 [12]–[21], where the defendant's allegations of promiscuity against his stepdaughter as a motive to concoct allegations were excised from his police interview, and replaced by a statement that their arguments related to her behaviour and male company she was keeping.

claimed that the allegations were motivated by him scorning her sexual advances after she had performed oral sex on him, one purpose of the questions was to reinforce the defendant's credibility, and so they were not intercepted by the blanket exclusion in s 41(4).[577] It is submitted that this is a less satisfactory solution, because the cross-examiner's purpose in putting virtually any challenging question to the complainant will be to strengthen the defendant's version of events, subverting the purpose of the prohibition altogether.

A 1998 decision under the 1976 Act, *R v Elahee*,[578] shows how slippery this approach is. It was held that the defence should have been allowed to cross-examine the 13-year-old complainant on a previous single act of consensual intercourse with her boyfriend a year earlier, to strengthen the plausibility of the 43-year-old defendant's story that she had approached him at a takeaway restaurant and made sexual advances which he rejected. Yet the evidential inference invited is so tenuous as to be indiscernible. If instead, as submitted above, the prohibition is interpreted as being directed only to the second of the twin myths, the general link between chastity and veracity, then the evidence in *Martin* would be admitted as it directly related to a contemporaneous event supporting the inference of a specific motive to fabricate, but the evidence in *Elahee* would be excluded as being intended to besmirch the child's credibility through her previous sexual behaviour.[579]

Neil Kibble's empirical study of judicial approaches to s 41[580] included a hypothetical scenario where a 14-year-old girl complained that her stepfather had raped and assaulted her. The defendant complained that the allegation was malicious as he had caught her having sexual intercourse with her boyfriend in the house, ordered him to leave immediately, and forbade her to see him again. The complainant admitted to police that this incident had occurred but maintained that she had not invented the accusation. The defence wished to cross-examine the complainant about her sexual intercourse with the boy and to call him to give evidence. Kibble reports that almost without exception the judges interviewed thought that the questioning should be allowed under s 41(2)(b), as this went to the heart of his defence of spiteful fabrication; thus they would circumvent s 41(4) by narrowly interpreting it. Some judges would have limited cross-examination to avoid the details of the sexual intercourse being explored, but all but one judge felt that the sexual context was necessary for the jury to appreciate the seriousness of the row. Whether leave should be given to call the boyfriend would depend upon what the complainant said in cross-examination.[581]

The caselaw as well as Kibble's study shows that a flexible, even result-oriented, interpretation of the prohibition in s 41(4) is driven by judicial pragmatism allied to a powerful intuition as to what evidence will ensure the defendant a fair trial.

It is common practice for prosecuting counsel to ask the defendant in cross-examination whether he can offer any explanation why the complainant should

---

[577] *R v Martin* (n 503) [37]–[38]. *R v F* (n 513) confirmed the position that evidence of a motive to fabricate, whilst in one sense involving a direct attack on the complainant's credibility, should not be intercepted by s 41(4).　　　　　　[578] *R v Elahee* [1999] Crim LR 399 (CA).

[579] Especially as the jury had been informed that the defendant was not responsible for her ruptured hymen.　　　[580] Kibble (n 499).　　　[581] ibid Scenario 1, 56–76.

make allegations against him, and then to comment to the jury on the absence of such explanation.[582] This practice has been disapproved of by some Canadian[583] and Australian[584] courts on the basis that it subtly diminishes or reverses the onus of proof, and wrongly suggests that a complainant who is not deliberately lying must be correct and that a complainant without an obvious motive to lie must be sincere. However, the English Court of Appeal[585] has preferred the position of the New Zealand Court of Appeal[586] that such questions are permissible, because if a positive response is made, this would tend to undermine the complainant's credibility. The fact that a negative answer is anticipated by prosecuting counsel should not determine the admissibility of the question. The question must be confined to eliciting any facts known to the accused, and not invite him to speculate about possible motives, and the jury must be instructed as to its limited evidential use.[587] It is submitted that this must be right: if the complainant can be cross-examined on an alleged motive to concoct the complaint, then fairness requires that the defendant be cross-examined on the same point.

(iv) Previous abuse to explain medical findings of sexual abuse
Explanatory evidence regarding medical findings and precocious sexualization was also listed by Lord Hope as examples of issues which the defence should be able to enter through the s 41(3)(a) gateway.[588] Both issues often arise in a given case. It is both logical and entirely appropriate that the defence be able to challenge evidence of physical findings on which the prosecution relies to prove the *actus reus* of a sexual offence, on the basis that it is explicable by other activity.[589]

(v) Previous abuse or other sources to explain the child's precocious knowledge or sexualization
Evidence of previous abuse, or of previous exposure to sexual matters, may become relevant to forestall an inference by the trier of fact that the child could not describe the defendant's act unless it had actually occurred (sometimes called the 'sexual innocence inference').[590] The defence's argument is that this previous sexual experience demonstrates that the child possessed the capacity to fabricate a charge against the defendant, or alternatively has innocently transposed a sexual offence committed by a third party to the defendant.

For evidence of precocious sexual awareness to be admissible through the 'relevant to another issue' gateway, the defendant must clearly link it to a source other than

---

[582] *Rook & Ward* (n 570) 445 [15.17].

[583] *R v Kusk* (1999) 132 CCC (3d) 559 (Alberta CA); *R v Vandenberghe* (1995) 96 CCC (3d) 371 (Ontario CA); *R v Batte* (n 325) [115]–[126].

[584] *Palmer v The Queen* (n 559) [7]–[10], (McHugh J dissenting).

[585] *R v B* [2003] EWCA Crim 951, [2003] 1 WLR 2809.   [586] *R v T* (n 410).

[587] *R v B* (n 585) [29], [40]–[42].   [588] *R v A (No 2)* (n 485) [78]–[79].

[589] See *R v Barnes* [1994] Crim LR 691 (CA), ordering a retrial where the defence was not permitted to cross-examine the child about her sexual experience of other men and about the vibrator found in her bedroom, which could have caused the rupture of her hymen.

[590] C Fishman 'Consent, Credibility and the Constitution: Evidence Relating to a Sex Offense of Complainant's Past Sexual Behavior' (1995) 44 Cath U LR 709, 806.

his interaction with the child, and that must explain the type of sexual activity which she alleges. Thus in *R v RD*, where a child alleged that she had been sexually abused between the ages of six and nine by a neighbour who rubbed her genital area, the allegation that the child had engaged in similar contact with a fellow pupil at school during this period was irrelevant, particularly as it did not explain the source of the allegation of gross indecency.[591]

In contrast, in the Scottish case of *Love v HM Advocate*,[592] a conviction for sodomizing a boy between the ages of 10 and 14 was quashed when the defence was not allowed to cross-examine him on a sexual relationship he allegedly had with a social worker which began at age 12, and which could explain both the medical findings and his detailed narrative of the sexual acts allegedly committed by the accused. The House of Lords in *R v A (No 2)* regarded this case as a paradigm example of how sexual behaviour could be relevant to another issue under s 41(3)(a).[593]

One difficulty defence counsel will have to deal with under the English legislation is that under s 41(6) the question must relate to specific instances of behaviour. Arguably the provision is intended to prohibit evidence of sexual reputation,[594] but in *R v White* Laws LJ held that s 41(6) has 'intellectual coherence' only if it requires that there be something about the circumstances of the specified episode which has potential probative force.[595] It is unlikely that the defence in the circumstances we are considering here could identify specific instances of abuse by others.[596]

Kibble's empirical study of judicial perspectives on s 41 included a hypothetical scenario which directly addressed these issues. It concerned charges of indecent assault and rape of a girl aged 11. The defence wished to cross-examine her on another alleged sexual relationship to provide alternative explanations of both her detailed and explicit descriptions of sexual matters and the injuries consistent with penile penetration of her vagina. While initially many of the judges interviewed considered that the defence was indulging in a fishing expedition, the great majority would have permitted very limited and tightly controlled questioning as to whether she had had sexual intercourse with anyone else, disregarding s 41(6) if necessary. Many considered that the issue of sexual awareness was much less probative than the cause of the medical findings, particularly given sex education in schools.[597]

To sum up, we have seen that the English legislation controlling evidence of previous sexual experience lacks coherence in the specific context of child sexual abuse

---

[591] *R v RD* (n 511) [39], [41].

[592] *Love v HM Advocate* [1999] SCCR 783, [2000] JC 1 (Scottish High Court of Judiciary on Appeal).

[593] *R v A (No 2)* (n 485) [79] (Lord Hope), [129] (Lord Clyde).

[594] Kibble (n 499) 117–118.

[595] *R v White* [2004] EWCA Crim 946 [16] (where the prohibited evidence was that the complainant was a prostitute).

[596] *R v R* (n 576) [9] (friend of the12-year-old complainant told police three years after a rape trial that she had been having sex with her boyfriend, contrary to the complainant's denial in her initial police interview of any sexual contact with anyone else; had it not been for the doubt which this cast upon the objective medical evidence of recent forcible intercourse, the friend's evidence would have been excluded by YJCEA 1999 (England) s 41).

[597] Kibble (n 499) Scenario 4, 117–125. We are indebted to Mr Kibble for sharing with us his unpublished data on this issue.

prosecutions. The treatment of previous complaints of sexual abuse is particularly problematic. Some, but not all,[598] judges have sought to draw a distinction between true allegations, which are about sexual behaviour and hence subject to s 41, and complaints which are claimed to be false, which are not about sexual behaviour and so are unshielded by the legislation.[599] There is also confusion about the applicability of the collateral issue rule to curtail further cross-examination and rebuttal evidence: some decisions state that the restricting rule should apply if the complainant denies that the other allegation was false,[600] but not if she denies making the allegation at all;[601] but again there is no consistency in maintaining this distinction.[602] We turn now to consider how these difficulties with evidence of previous sexual experience are handled in child abuse prosecutions in other common law jurisdictions.

(b) Previous sexual experience in child abuse prosecutions in Canadian law

(i) The statutory framework

Canadian parliamentarians have made three legislated attempts to restrict cross-examination of complainants of sexual assault on their sexual history, in a saga which has influenced British policymakers and legislators[603] and the judiciary.[604]

In 1976, s 142 of the Criminal Code of Canada was enacted which provided for an *in camera* hearing where the trial judge had to determine whether the weight of the sexual history evidence was such that to exclude it would prevent a just determination of a fact in issue, including the credibility of the complainant. Paradoxically, this provision was interpreted by the Supreme Court of Canada as actually fortifying the relevance of previous sexual experience evidence by elevating credibility to the status of a material issue; the narrowed scope of permitted cross-examination was regarded as having been traded off against the judicial abolition of the collateral issue or finality rule to allow the defence to contradict a complainant's denial of particular sexual activity.[605] What is more, the complainant was regarded as having become a compellable witness in the *voir dire*.[606]

In 1982, Parliament responded to concerns that the judiciary had thwarted the intention of the 1976 amendment[607] by creating a new model in s 276 of the Criminal Code of Canada. This established a blanket prohibition of any evidence on behalf of the accused concerning the sexual activity of the complainant with any person other than the accused. There were three exceptions: to rebut prosecution evidence; evidence seeking to incriminate another person as guilty of the offences; and evidence related to the incident charged and relevant to the accused's belief in the complainant's consent.

---

[598] *R v Mokrecovas* (n 512).
[599] *R v MH; R v RT* (n 528); *R v Alan David C and Julie B* (n 543).
[600] *R v S (Snook)* (n 561); *R v Todd* (n 534). [601] *R v PB* (n 555).
[602] *R v Alan David C and Julie B* (n 543); *Dennis Andrew Etches v R* (n 506).
[603] eg *Hansard* HL Deb Vol 598 Cols 19–20 (Lord Thomas of Gosford), Cols 21–23 (Lord Lester of Herne Hill QC) (8 March 1999).
[604] *R v A (No 2)* (n 485) [33] (Lord Steyn), [77], [100]–[101] (Lord Hope), [149] (Lord Hutton).
[605] *R v Forsythe* [1980] 2 SCR 268 (SCC). [606] ibid [16].
[607] C Boyle 'Section 142 of the Criminal Code: a Trojan Horse?' (1981) 23 Crim LQ 253, 258–259.

The legislation was interpreted as having reinstated the finality rule which, as noted above, had been treated as abrogated in relation to the specific topic of sexual history.[608]

The 1982 provision was struck down by a majority of the Supreme Court of Canada in *R v Seaboyer*[609] on the basis that it breached the accused's constitutional rights not to be deprived of security of the person except in accordance with the principles of fundamental justice guaranteed by s 7, and the right to a fair trial guaranteed by s 11(d), of the Canadian Charter of Rights and Freedoms. Justice Beverly McLachlin for the majority considered that s 276 had the laudable purpose of abolishing outmoded sexist use of sexual conduct evidence which might unduly prejudice the trier of fact against the complainant. However, it overshot the mark by failing to recognize that relevance cannot be determined in a vacuum; the provision was unconstitutional as it excluded evidence which in the appropriate factual context could be relevant to the defence, such as evidence to explain physical findings, to show a bias against the defendant or a motive to fabricate, or to support the defence of honest belief in consent. The Supreme Court however upheld the constitutionality of s 277 which excluded evidence of sexual reputation for the purpose of challenging or supporting the credibility of the complainant.

The majority in *Seaboyer* concluded that striking down the 'rape shield' law did not revive the previous common law rules. The 'fishing expeditions' which had occurred in the past were not permitted. The recasting of the notion of prejudice as interference with the search for the truth—notwithstanding that it might assist the accused—was hailed as a major shift in philosophy.[610] *Seaboyer* provided detailed guidance to trial judges setting out the parameters of a constitutional shield for consensual sexual conduct on other occasions[611] which were largely adopted by Parliament in 1992. The new version of s 276 rescinded the mandatory model in favour of guided judicial discretion. Evidence of the complainant's other sexual activity with persons other than the accused is not admissible to support an inference that the complainant is more likely to have consented to the sexual activity charged, or is less worthy of belief—a codification of the debunking of the 'twin myths'.[612] However, such evidence may be admitted where the trial judge determined in a *voir dire* held *in camera*[613] that the evidence:

(a) is of specific instances of 'sexual activity'; and
(b) is relevant to an issue at trial; and
(c) has significant probative value that is not substantially outweighed by the danger of prejudice to the proper administration of justice.[614]

The adverb 'substantially' serves to protect the accused by raising the standard for the judge to exclude evidence once the accused has shown it to have 'significant' probative

---

[608] *R v Meddoui* [1991] 3 SCR 320 (SCC) 320–321; *R v W (BA)* [1992] 3 SCR 811 (SCC), reversing (1991) 59 OAC 325 (Ontario CA).   [609] *R v Seaboyer* (n 484).

[610] C Boyle and M MacCrimmon '*R v. Seaboyer*: a Lost Cause' 1991 7 CR (4th) 225, 227.

[611] *R v Seaboyer* (n 484) [106].   [612] Criminal Code of Canada s 276(1).

[613] ibid ss 276.1, 276.2. The accused must file an affidavit setting out the particulars of the proposed evidence and its relevance to an issue at trial, on which he may be cross-examined by the Crown. The complainant is no longer a compellable witness at the *voir dire*: s 276.2(2).   [614] ibid s 276(2).

value. In a sense, both sides of the equation are heightened in this test, which serves to direct judges to the serious ramifications of the use of evidence of previous sexual activity for all parties in these cases.[615] The trial judge is specifically required by s 276 to consider factors such as:

(a) the interests of justice, including the accused's right to full answer and defence;
(b) society's interest in encouraging the reporting of sexual assault offences;
(c) whether there is a reasonable prospect that the evidence will assist in arriving at a just determination in the case;
(d) the need to remove from the fact-finding process any discriminatory belief or bias;
(e) the risk that the evidence might unduly arouse sentiments of prejudice, sympathy, or hostility in the jury;
(f) the potential prejudice to the complainant's personal dignity and right of privacy;[616]
(g) the right of the complainant and of every individual to personal security and the full protection and benefit of the law; and
(h) any other factor the court considers relevant.

The constitutionality of the revised version was upheld by the Supreme Court of Canada in *R v Darrach*[617] due to its flexibility. Section 276 did not create a blanket exclusion of relevant evidence; it limits the exclusion of evidence to that used to invoke the 'twin myths'. The phrase 'by reason of the sexual nature of the activity' in s 276 is a clarification by Parliament that it is inferences from the sexual nature of the activity, as opposed to inferences from other potentially relevant features of the activity, that are prohibited. If evidence of sexual activity is proffered for its non-sexual features, such as to show a pattern of conduct or a past inconsistent statement, it may be permitted.[618] Section 276 was designed by Parliament to filter out not only irrelevant information but also relevant information that is more prejudicial to the administration of justice than it is probative.[619] An accused has never had a right to adduce irrelevant evidence. Nor does he have the right to adduce misleading evidence to support illegitimate inferences. Therefore, s 276 does not infringe the accused's right to make full answer and defence.[620]

In *R v A (No 2)*, counsel for the Home Secretary argued that s 41 of the YJCEA 1999 was modelled upon the revised Canadian model[621] and consequently that it did not offend ECHR Article 6. However, this assertion is patently incorrect, as Lord Steyn pointed out.[622]

Lord Hope's examples in *R v A (No 2)* of purposes for which sexual experience evidence could be relevant to issues other than consent[623] were derived from McLachlin J's list of probative defence evidence which was barred by the unconstitutional version

---

[615] *R v Darrach* [2000] 2 SCR 443 (SCC) [40] (Gonthier J).
[616] Criminal Code of Canada s 276(3).　　[617] *R v Darrach* (n 615).　　[618] ibid [30]–[31].
[619] ibid [43].　　[620] ibid [37].
[621] As indeed had the Home Office Minister Lord Williams of Mostyn in the debates on the Bill: *Hansard* HL Deb Vol 598 Col 32 (8 March 1999).
[622] *R v A (No 2)* (n 485) [33].　　[623] ibid [79] (Lord Hope).

of s 276. We will explore the approach of Canadian courts to the four categories of sexual history evidence identified earlier as being relevant in child abuse prosecutions.

(ii) Previous or subsequent allegations of sexual abuse against third parties in Canadian law

Reverting to our threshold question, can the defence put other allegations of sexual abuse to the complainant in cross-examination? Significantly, the guidelines set out by the majority in *Seaboyer* were stated to be applicable to *consensual* sexual conduct on other occasions.[624] However, this restriction does not appear explicitly in the re-enacted s 276. This raised the crucial issue of whether the 'rape shield' law protects child complainants from being cross-examined on previous allegations of abuse, whether true or false. Several trial and appellate courts ruled that it does not, interpreting the phrase 'engaged in sexual activity' as implying only consensual sexual behaviour, protecting the right to keep confidential a chosen lifestyle.[625] The view that s 276 was not triggered did not mean however that the evidence of non-consensual sexual activity was automatically admitted at the behest of the defence; instead, these courts scrutinized the evidence by reference to the common law rules set out in *Seaboyer* requiring that the prejudice to the proper administration of justice must substantially outweigh the probative value of the evidence to warrant exclusion.[626] They also closely circumscribed the scope of the questioning allowed, and required directions to the jury on the limited permissible inferences therefrom.[627] These decisions overlooked the ruling of the Supreme Court of Canada in *R v Crosby* that a complainant's previous statement to the police describing unwanted sexual touching by another man on the same night as the incident charged should have been excluded under s 276, so implicitly accepting that the 'rape shield' applies to non-consensual sexual contact.[628]

The issue was finally settled in 2000 in *R v Darrach*, where Gonthier J for a unanimous court held that s 276 applies to non-consensual as well as consensual sexual activity.[629] The rationale for this extension was that it can equally defeat the purposes of the prohibition by distorting the trial process when it is used to evoke stereotypes, for example that victims of assault must have deserved it, or are unreliable witnesses. It also could deter people from reporting assault by humiliating them in court.[630]

---

[624] *R v Seaboyer* (n 484) [106].

[625] *R v Vanderest* (1994) 91 CCC (3d) 5 (British Columbia Supreme Ct); *R v B(O)* (n 393) [61]; *R v C(RC)* (1996) 107 CCC (3d) 362 (Nova Scotia CA) [15]; *R v Sebastian* (1996) 22 OTC 397 (Ontario Gen Div); *R v H(DT)* (1995) 137 Nfld & PEIR 77 (Prince Edward Island Supreme Ct TD) [9]–[12]; *R v M(H)* (1999) 177 Sask R 189 (Saskatchewan CA) [14]–[15]; *R v Doherty* [2000] WL 1437045 (Ontario SCJ); *R v Blundon* (1993) 84 CCC (3d) 249 (Newfoundland CA) [11].   [626] *R v B(O)* ibid [63].

[627] *R v Vanderest* (n 625) (questions limited to why complainant did not accuse the defendant of rape when she gave a statement to police about seven other men); *R v Fiqia* (1993) 87 CCC (3d) 377 (Alberta CA) leave to appeal refused (1994) 176 NR 160n (SCC) (questions limited to the sexual activity which had led the complainant to consult the defendant psychologist, to explain the 'therapeutic' nature of his own sexual acts with his patient).

[628] *R v Crosby* [1995] 2 SCR 912 (SCC), applied in *R v M(A) (No 3)* [1998] BCJ No 1915 (British Columbia Supreme Ct) [14]–[17].

[629] *R v Darrach* (n 615) [33]. Admissibility of evidence of non-consensual sexual activity is also to be determined by the procedures stipulated in s 276.   [630] ibid [33].

Darrach thus implicitly authorized trial judges to look beyond the two inferences stipulated as being illegitimate in s 276 to consider other myths typically associated with non-consensual sexual activity, such as that a single victim is unlikely to suffer sexual assault by more than one perpetrator, or that persons who allege multiple sexual assaults are crying 'wolf'.[631]

The second issue is whether the statutory restrictions on evidence of 'sexual activity' apply where the defence claims that the allegations are false. As in English law, there is no clear answer here. In *R v Gauthier*, the British Columbia Court of Appeal held that the redrafted s 276 does not apply to admittedly fabricated claims of consensual sexual encounters, because these are not activities in which the complainant has ever engaged.[632] This seems to be borne out by the emphasis placed by Gonthier J in *Darrach* on the narrow confines of the revised prohibition to two specific illegitimate inferences from the 'sexual nature' of the activity,[633] which apparently could expose the complainant to at least an initial question to elicit other allegedly false statements about other sexual experiences.[634] Nevertheless, appellate courts have encouraged trial judges to take a robust approach to evidence of another allegation. They have considerable latitude to rule that it is irrelevant to credibility so as to prevent even an initial question,[635] unless the defence can show that this is one of 'those relatively rare cases where the complainant may be fraudulent, cruelly mischievous or maliciously mendacious'.[636] Alternatively, trial judges can apply the finality rule to curtail further contradiction by the defence, governed by their view of the degree of relevance of the evidence to its prejudicial value.[637] Thus in *R v W (BA)* the accused was convicted of sexually abusing his two stepdaughters. The trial judge had dismissed the defence application to put to one of them that she had lied in a statement she had given to the police about being sexually assaulted by the accused's son and his friends, on the basis that any lie in the statement would be irrelevant to her complaints. The Supreme Court of Canada held that in the absence of an indication that the complainant's evidence on collateral matters might be false, the claim for its relevance was tenuous, whereas its prejudice and its potential to mislead jurors was significant.[638] This conclusion exposes judicial uncertainty about the proper role for the finality rule, in that even the initial question was barred.[639]

The ruling in *W (BA)* has been interpreted by lower courts as requiring the defence to lay the groundwork for relevance before cross-examination will be permitted, whether under the common law or statutory version of the prohibition.[640] The Ontario Court of Appeal has held that the defence must be in a position to establish that

---

[631] *R v Porter* 2001 WL 451836 (Ontario SCJ) [3]. Some courts have maintained a restrictive interpretation of the bar in s 276, however: *R v Anstey* (2002) 209 Nfld & PEIR 264 (Newfoundland CA) [17]–[35]; *R v A(S)* 2002 WL 37422 (Ontario CJ) [9]–[10].

[632] *R v Gauthier* (1995) 100 CCC (3d) 563 (British Columbia CA) [17].

[633] *R v Darrach* (n 615) [32]–[33].   [634] *R v Anstey* (n 631) [23]–[26].

[635] *R v Blundon* (n 625) [12]; Chapman (n 532), 145–160; *R v Gervais* (1990) 58 CCC (3d) 141 (Quebec CA); *R v K(K)* (2002) 224 Nfld & PEIR 302 (Newfoundland Supreme Ct TD) [30].

[636] *R v Osolin* [1993] 4 SCR 595 (SCC) 672.   [637] *R v W(BA)* (n 608).   [638] ibid.

[639] Paciocco (n 455) 174.   [640] *R v Blundon* (n 625); *R v Gervais* (n 635) [21].

the complainant has recanted her earlier accusations[641] or that they are 'demonstrably false'.[642] An acquittal of the other person whom the child had accused may not suffice,[643] even where the trial judge strongly criticized the child's credibility.[644] Expert opinion developing a theory that the complainant may have transferred blame from the perpetrator to the defendant may be admissible in principle,[645] but does not justify exploring the other alleged abuse unless it is grounded in the factual evidence at trial,[646] such as a striking similarity in the details of the allegations.[647] This robust common law position is very significant given the lingering uncertainty as to whether defendants proposing to cross-examine a complainant on an allegedly false complaint against a third party must bring themselves within s 276.[648]

ARB v The Queen[649] shows how difficult it can be to distinguish collateral and specific attacks on a complainant's credibility. The accused was convicted of various counts of sexual assaults against his adopted daughter over a 13-year period. The defence had called evidence from other family members living in the same small house stating that they had no knowledge of the alleged abuse. The complainant had given police a statement that two of her brothers and their friends also had abused her, which she attributed to their having seen the accused molest her and their belief that they could do so also. Defence counsel wished to cross-examine the complainant on those other allegations in order to widen the credibility battleground and, in anticipation of her maintaining her accusations, to call the other family members and friends to deny them. The defence contended that this was not a collateral issue because the allegations against her father were part of a sweeping allegation of concurrent familial abuse and her credibility had to be evaluated in that context. Three levels of court ruled that this evidence would be irrelevant. The majority of the Ontario Court of Appeal considered that the defence strategy was an attempt to pit the complainant against her whole family so that instead of a straightforward case of parental incest, it would require the jury to consider four or five criminal cases. The accused hoped that by discrediting at least one of her allegations of sexual abuse, a reasonable doubt might be raised in the charges against her father; this was inimical to the spirit of the principle underlying s 276, as well as the collateral issue rule.[650] Muldaver JA dissented on the basis that the Crown was allowed to leave the jury with a false impression that since only the father had assaulted the child, it was possible that her

---

[641] As in *R v H(DT)* (n 625) [19].

[642] *R v Riley* (1992) 11 OR (3d) 151 (Ontario CA), leave to appeal to SCC refused [1998] SCCA No 567.   [643] ibid [9].

[644] *R v R(P)* (1998) 132 CCC (3d) 72 (Quebec CA) [33]–[37] (permitting the acquittal to be put to the complainant, but applying the collateral issue rule to curtail cross-examination).

[645] *R v Bell (No 1)* (1997) 115 CCC (3d) 107 (Northwest Territories CA).

[646] *R v Blundon* (n 635) [13]–[22]; *R v Bell (No 2)* (1998) 126 CCC (3d) 94 [42]–[44], [48]–[54] (Northwest Territories CA); *R v C(HJ)* (1993) 87 CCC (3d) 66 (Manitoba CA) [8]–[11]; *R v M(D)* (2000) 37 CR (5th) 80 (Ontario Supreme Ct) [20]–[27]; *R v S(DJ)* (1998) 105 BCAC 185 (British Columbia CA) [15]–[16].   [647] *R v C(HJ)* ibid; *R v Anstey* (n 631).

[648] eg *R v Gauthier* (n 632) 569–570; *R v Porter* (n 631) [10]; *R v K(K)* (2002) 224 Nfld & PEIR 302 (Newfoundland Supreme Ct TD) [21]–[28], [41]–[43]; *R v Anstey* ibid.

[649] *ARB v The Queen* (1998) 41 OR (3d) 361 (Ontario CA), appeal dismissed [2000] 1 SCR 781 (SCC).   [650] ibid [9]–[17] (Finlayson JA, Abella JA concurring).

story was true notwithstanding the cramped living quarters and lack of privacy within the family. He argued that the multiple nature of the allegations constituted a specific rather than a general attack on her credibility going to the heart of the defence, that the complainant's version of events was so highly improbable that she should not be believed.[651] The Supreme Court of Canada accepted the majority's view that the evidence was irrelevant.[652]

Thus three approaches to the problem of cross-examining complainants on allegations against third parties can be discerned in the Canadian decisions: applying s 276; applying the trial judge's inherent discretion at common law to exclude relevant evidence where its potential prejudice outweighs its probative value; and permitting an initial question but applying the finality rule to curtail any further cross-examination on the point. Although this approach may lack analytical clarity, its pragmatism has generally not led to indefensible conclusions, and in particular to undue constraints upon the defence.

(iii) Motive to fabricate the allegations against the defendant in Canadian law

A motive to fabricate allegations was one of the instances given by McLachlin J in *Seaboyer* where probative evidence could be excluded by the rigid framework of s 276 as originally formulated.[653] The common law *Seaboyer* guidelines requiring that probative value substantially outweigh the danger of prejudice to the proper administration of justice should determine admissibility.[654] Thus childish boasts of sexual experience to impress friends cannot reasonably give rise to an inference that a complainant maintained a false allegation of sexual assault in perjured testimony at a criminal trial, as the motivations could be entirely dissimilar.[655]

(iv) Previous abuse to explain medical findings of sexual abuse or the child's premature sexualization in Canadian law

In *Seaboyer*, Madame Justice McLachlin stated:

In the case of young complainants, where there may be a tendency to believe their story on the ground that the details of their account must have come from the alleged encounter, evidence of past sexual activity may be relevant to show other activity which provides an explanation to the complainant's knowledge.[656]

Where the prosecution relies upon the child's detailed knowledge of sexual activity as proof that the accused committed the assaults she describes, the defence must be allowed to call rebuttal evidence suggesting that she acquired it from being victimized by another person, even if she and the person named deny the allegations.[657] If the

---

[651] ibid [35]–[39], [47] (Moldaver JA, dissenting).

[652] Compare *R v Vanderest* (n 625) [55]–[64] holding that the defence should have been allowed to adduce evidence that the complainant had also alleged abuse by her brother, her uncle and two neighbours, to avoid leaving the jury with the impression that her father was solely responsible for her lost virginity at an early age, and her troubled life of drug addiction and failed marriages. The Court of Appeal specifically noted that the evidence could not be admitted to show a pattern of false allegations, in the absence of proof of falsity.   [653] *R v Seaboyer* (n 484) [106].

[654] *R v Gauthier* (n 632) [20].   [655] ibid [23]–[25].   [656] *R v Seaboyer* (n 484) [57].

[657] *R v M(A) (No 3)* (n 628) (holding that s 276 does apply to such rebuttal evidence).

complainant links the disclosure of the offence charged with previous abuse, that may open the door to the defence exploring the source of his sexual knowledge.[658]

The defendant is also entitled to rebut evidence that someone else caused a physical 'consequence' ascribed by the Crown to the alleged sexual contact,[659] such as a sexually transmitted disease.[660]

The Canadian legislation like its English counterpart prohibits only defence evidence, and therefore the prosecution can lead evidence about the complainant's previous lack of sexual experience,[661] even though this may have the result of bolstering the complainant's credibility by engendering sympathy through the converse of the stereotypical myths. This however will open the door to rebuttal from the defence.[662]

(c) *Previous sexual experience in child abuse prosecutions in American law*

(i) The statutory framework

Statutory restrictions on evidence of sexual behaviour and reputation in sexual offence prosecutions exist in all 50 American States and the District of Columbia,[663] as well as in Federal Rule of Evidence 412.[664] The provisions vary widely in their detail. Haxton[665] identifies four statutory models: 'special scrutiny' of the probative value and prejudicial effect of the sexual conduct evidence, without any categorical exclusions; 'pure exceptions', providing an absolute prohibition with a few exceptions, minimizing judicial discretion;[666] 'scrutinised exceptions', a hybrid of the first two categories, with listed exceptions which the court must subject to special scrutiny before applying them (often referred to as the 'Michigan model'); and 'mixed by issue', whereby the approach varies depending upon the issue (consent, credibility etc).

Most State courts have extended the protection of the legislation to child victims by interpreting sexual conduct as including previous sexual victimization,[667] the rationale being that a child no less than an adult should be protected from 'having her

---

[658] *R v Slocum* 2003 WL 38816 (Ontario Supreme Ct) [8]–[10].

[659] *R v Seaboyer* (n 484) [106].

[660] eg *R v P(TE)* (1993) 32 BCAC 124 (British Columbia CA) [24].

[661] *R v Brothers (Robert James)* (1995) 40 CR (4th) 250 (Alberta CA).

[662] *R v T(R)* (2001) 205 Nfld & PEIR 352 (Newfoundland Supreme Ct TD) [17].

[663] A summary and full text of all American rape shield statutes has been compiled by the American Prosecutors Research Institute: <http://www.ndaa-apri.org/pdf/ncpa_statute_rape_shield_laws_june_06.pdf> (updated to 28 June 2006).

[664] Federal Rule of Evidence 412 applies to civil as well as criminal proceedings, but in civil cases, not only must the evidence fit within one of the specific exceptions, but its probative value must substantially outweigh the danger of harm to any victim and unfair prejudice to any party. Reputation evidence is admissible only if the victim places it in issue.

[665] D Haxton 'Comment: Rape Shield Statutes: Constitutional Despite Unconstitutional Exclusions of Evidence' [1985] Wisconsin LR 1219, 1221–1231. See also H Galvin 'Shielding Rape Victims in the State and Federal Courts: a Proposal for the Second Decade' (1986) 70 Minnesota LR 763.

[666] Michigan Penal Code Act 328 of 1931 s 750.520j.

[667] *State v Wright* 776 P 2d 1294 (Oregon Ct App 1989) 1297–1298; *State v Muyingo* 15 P 3d 83 (Oregon Ct App 2000) 225; *Commonwealth v Johnson* 566 A 2d 1197 (Pennsylvania Superior Ct 1989); *State v Oliver* 760 P 2d 1071 (Arizona Supreme Ct 1988) 1075–1076; *State v Kulmac* 644 A 2d 887 (Connecticut Supreme Ct 1994); *People v Aldrich* 849 P 2d 821 (Colorado CA 1992); K Steinmetz 'Note: *State v. Oliver*: Children with a Past: The Admissibility of the Victim's Prior Sexual Experience in Child Molestation Cases' (1989) 31 Arizona LR 677.

prior sexual history paraded in public and from having unfair inferences drawn there-from'.[668] Exceptions for the categories we have been discussing are typically recognized by statute or caselaw.[669] Often statutes include an undefined exception where exclu-sion of the evidence would breach the defendant's constitutional rights,[670] but the constitutional caveat would seem to apply in any event. The constitutionality issue is a fact-dependent analysis,[671] in which the court must first determine the relevance of the proposed evidence to the defence, and whether its probative value outweighs its prejudicial effect,[672] the latter pertaining to the likely trauma to the child if the evidence cannot be elicited from another source (such as a criminal conviction of the earlier abuser), and the degree to which its admission would invade the child's privacy.[673]

(ii) Previous or subsequent allegations of sexual abuse against third parties in American law

Eight jurisdictions expressly provide for the admissibility of a history of false allega-tions of sexual assaults,[674] and the courts in many other States have often found a way to admit such evidence, although the Federal Courts have ruled that such evidence is barred by Rule 412.[675] Some State courts have adopted the same approach as the English Court of Appeal[676] in holding that evidence of previous allegations to impeach credibility is not 'sexual conduct' and hence it is not prohibited by the rape shield law.[677] An Oregon court has gone so far as to say that evidence of previous false rape charges is admissible not just to impeach credibility but as independent evidence that the offence charged did not occur.[678] The defence must lay an evidential foundation for the falsity of the previous allegations,[679] a mere denial by the person previously

---

[668] *Commonwealth v Appenzeller* 565 A 2d 170 (Pennsylvania Superior Ct 1989) 172.

[669] NCPCA *Investigation and Prosecution of Child Abuse* (n 60) 262–266.

[670] eg Federal Rules of Evidence Rule 412(b)(C). Twelve other jurisdictions' statutes have express exceptions to the prohibition where required to protect the defendant's constitutional rights: Connecticut, District of Columbia, Hawaii, Illinois, Iowa, Maine, New Hampshire, North Dakota, Oregon, Tennessee, Texas, and Utah. For further discussion see Haxton (n 665); Myers (n 52) Vol 2 §6.35.

[671] *Michigan v Lucas* 500 US 145 (USSC 1991) 151, 153; *Lajoie v Thompson* 217 F 3d 663 (US CA 9th Cir 2000) 668–669; *People v Arenda* 330 NW 2d 814 (Michigan Supreme Ct 1982).

[672] *State v Budis* 593 A 2d 784 (New Jersey Supreme Ct 1991) applying *Crane v Kentucky* 476 US 683 (USSC 1986) 689–690.   [673] *State v Budis* ibid 790–791.

[674] Arizona, Colorado, Idaho, Minnesota, North Carolina, Oklahoma, Vermont, and Wisconsin.

[675] *US v White Buffalo* 84 F 3d 1052 (US CA 8th Cir 1996); *US v Withorn* 54 Fed R Evid Serv 255 (USCA 8th Cir 2000) [7]–[8]; *US v Bartlett* 856 F 2d 1071 (US CA 8th Cir 1988) 1088–1089.

[676] In *R v MH; R v RT* (n 528), discussed above section D.3.

[677] *Clinebell v Commonwealth* 368 SE 2d 263 (Virginia Supreme Ct 1988); *Smith v State* 377 SE 2d 158 (Georgia Supreme Ct 1989) *certiorari* denied 493 US 825 (USSC); *People v Mikula* 269 NW 2d 195 (Michigan App 1978) 198–199; *State v Baron* 292 SE 2d 741 (North Carolina CA 1982) 743–744; *Cairns v Commonwealth* 40 Va App 271 (Virginia CA 2003) (permitting the defendant to lead evidence of journals kept by a 14-year-old complainant to show that she had boasted of other sexual encounters but made no reference to the defendant).

[678] *State v Nab* 421 P 2d 388 (Oregon Supreme Ct 1966) 390–391; *People v Hurlbert* 333 P 2d 82 (California CA 1958) 86.

[679] eg *State v Kobow* 466 NW 2d 747 (Minnesota CA 1991); *People v Passenger* 572 NYS 2d 972 (New York App Div 1991).

accused being insufficient.[680] In some States a standard of proof of 'reasonable probability of falsity' is imposed;[681] in contrast, in Rhode Island the defendant's inability to
prove that the accusations were in fact false or withdrawn does not make the evidence
irrelevant.[682]

(iii) Motive to fabricate the allegations against the defendant in American law

Five American jurisdictions expressly permit evidence of other sexual conduct to
support the claim that the complainant has a motive in accusing the defendant.[683] A
statutory exception is probably not necessary, as in criminal proceedings the defendant
has a broad constitutional right to cross-examine prosecution witnesses regarding bias
or ulterior motive.[684] Generally the right to cross-examine as to bias trumps rape shield
legislation where the motive necessarily depends upon previous sexual conduct, such
as to explain a pregnancy.[685] Evidence that a previous abuse allegation had led to a
change in the child's home environment which she desired may support a defence
argument that a similar motive existed on this occasion as well, provided that there is
an evidential basis for the inference of a motive to lie.[686] American courts have been
known to 'sanitize' evidence as to bias to strip out the sexual conduct if what remains is
sufficient to impeach the credibility of the witness,[687] as the English Court of Appeal
did in *R v Mokrecovas*.[688]

(iv) Previous abuse to explain medical findings of sexual abuse in American law

Thirty American jurisdictions as well as the Federal Rule of Evidence 412 expressly
permit evidence of specific instances of sexual behaviour offered to prove that a
person other than the accused was the source of semen, injury or other physical evidence such as a sexually transmitted disease or pregnancy.[689] Again statutory intervention is probably otiose, since as in all common law systems it is
well settled that the defence is entitled to rebut evidence of the child's physical condition upon which the prosecution relies as proof of sexual abuse by the

---

[680] *Richardson v Commonwealth* 590 SE 2d 618 (Virginia CA 2004).

[681] *Shelton v State* 395 SE 2d 618 (Georgia Ct App 1990); *Clinebell v Commonwealth* (n 677); *State v
Barber* 766 P 2d 1288 (Kansas App 1989) 1290.

[682] *State v Oliveira* 576 A 2d 111 (Rhode Island Supreme Ct 1990).

[683] Arizona, Maryland, Oregon, Texas, and Virginia.   [684] Myers (n 52) Vol 2 §6.43.

[685] *People v Gray* 568 NE 2d 219 (Illinois App 1991) 224–225; *State v DeLawder* 344 A 2d
446 (Maryland Ct Special App 1975) 454; *State v Jalo* 557 P 2d 1359 (Oregon App 1976) 1362
(10-year-old complainant's alleged motive was to forestall the defendant from disclosing to her parents
her sexual activities with adolescents).

[686] *Commonwealth v Wall* 586 A 2d 1203 (Pennsylvania Superior Ct 1992) 160–164 (desire to escape
her new carer's severe discipline).

[687] *Kelly v State* 452 NE 2d 907 (Indiana Supreme Ct 1983) 909–910; *Commonwealth v Elder* 452 NE
2d 1104 (Massachusetts Supreme Judicial Ct 1983).

[688] *R v Mokrecovas* (n 512), discussed above, section D.3 (a) (ii) and (iii).

[689] Arizona, Colorado, Connecticut, District of Columbia, Florida, Hawaii, Idaho, Indiana, Iowa, Ken-
tucky, Louisiana, Maine, Maryland, Massachusetts, Michigan, Minnesota, Missouri, Montana, Nebraska,
New Jersey, New York, North Dakota, Ohio, Oklahoma, South Carolina, Tennessee, Utah, Vermont,
Virginia, and Wisconsin.

accused.[690] Strict application of the notice rules to preclude such evidence may be unconstitutional.[691]

(v) Previous abuse or other sources to explain the child's precocious knowledge or sexualization in American law

No State has an express statutory exception for evidence that a third party was responsible for the child's premature sexualization, but courts generally allow such evidence.[692] This may be so even where the prosecution does not expressly rely upon the complainant's sexual naïveté, as the jury may draw the inference;[693] the prosecutor may be able to foreclose that avenue for evidence of previous abuse by stipulating (ie making a formal admission) that children of the complainant's age usually possess enough sexual knowledge to fabricate the events.[694]

When evidence is offered to show a child's knowledge of sexual acts, its relevance also depends on whether the past abuse closely resembles the acts in question, as these are more likely to affect the child's ability to describe them.[695] A graphic description of abuse which is very similar to a previous complaint may satisfy the relevance test.[696] To be capable of rebutting the prosecution's case, the past sexual conduct must account for how the child could provide all of the testimony's sexual detail without having suffered the defendant's alleged conduct.[697] A sophisticated knowledge of sexual terminology must be shown to be unusual for the child's age before it triggers a defence right to provide an alternative explanation for its source.[698] Other factors which courts have considered relevant are evidence suggesting the complainant had a motive to fabricate a charge against the defendant,[699] or has indulged in sexual fantasies.[700] Generally the

---

[690] eg *Tague v Richards* 3 F 3d 1133 (US CA 7th Cir 1993); *People v Mikula* (n 677); *State v Douglas* 797 SW 2d 532 (Missouri Ct App 1990); *US v Azure* 845 F 2d 1503 (US CA 8th Cir 1988) (prosecution evidence of a forcible injury does not render admissible evidence of 10-year-old child's previous consensual acts of intercourse with a boy aged 13).

[691] *Lajoie v Thompson* (n 671) 671–673; *State v Pulizzano* 456 NW 2d 325 (Wisconsin Supreme Ct 1990) 335.

[692] See the cases cited in Myers (n 52) Vol 2, 114 fn 604; TB Marcketti 'Rape Shield Laws: Do They Shield the Children?' (1993) 78 Iowa LR 751, 760–764; *Lajoie v Thompson* ibid 65. See however *People v Kyle* Colo CA No 01CA122 (Colorado CA 29 July 2004) ruling that the statutory exception to admit 'any similar evidence of sexual intercourse' permits only evidence to explain the source or origin of physical evidence, and not to explain the origin of the victim's detailed sexual knowledge.

[693] *State v Jaques* 558 A 2d 706 (Maine Supreme Judicial Ct 1989); *State v Budis* (n 672); *State v Howard* 426 A 2d 457 (New Hampshire Supreme Ct 1981) 462; *Lajoie v Thompson* ibid; *State v Pulizzano* (n 691) 335; *State v Carver* (n 53) 843–844. For a contrary view, see *People v Arenda* (n 671) 818; *State v Wright* (n 667) 1298–1299; *Commonwealth v Appenzeller* (n 668) 172.   [694] Fishman (n 590) 807–809.

[695] *State v Padilla* 329 NW 2d 263 (Wisconsin Ct App 1982) 271.

[696] Marcketti (n 692) 772–773.   [697] *People v Morse* (n 529) 559.

[698] *US v Torres* 937 F 2d 1469, 1474 (USCA 9th Cir 1991), *certiorari* denied 502 US 1037 (USSC 1992); *Lajoie v Thompson* (n 671) 676–677 (Ferguson J, dissenting); *State v Rolon* 777 A 2d 604 (Connecticut Supreme Ct 2001) (child's grandfather had been convicted for sexually abusing her between the ages of eight months and five years); *State v John W Brisco* 852 A 2d 746 (Connecticut App Ct) (inference is not available for child aged 14 at time of abuse).

[699] *Commonwealth v Wall* (n 686); *People v Arenda* (n 671) 814.

[700] *State v Howard* (n 693) 462; Marcketti (n 692) 759.

courts require an evidential foundation, or at least a plausible case,[701] for a defence argument that the child has confused the defendant with a third party perpetrator, before they will permit evidence of previous abuse to be adduced for this purpose.[702] In weighing the probative value of the evidence against its potential prejudicial effect, the court will consider whether the latter can be minimized by the defence calling evidence from another source, to avoid traumatizing the child.[703]

To conclude, American courts have had to tread a careful path between the defendant's constitutional rights to cross-examine prosecution witnesses under the Sixth Amendment, and the constitutionally legitimate[704] concerns of legislators to protect complainants in sexual assault cases from humiliation and invasion of their privacy. Significantly, judicial discussion of the prejudicial effect of previous sexual experience evidence usually focuses on the complainant's interests, rather than on the distortion which stereotypes and prejudice may introduce into the jury's reasoning process, which has been the primary concern of Canadian and English courts. While extending the protection of rape shield statutes to child witnesses, they have generally recognized that evidence of previous sexual experience can be peculiarly relevant in child molestation cases, and have found ways to ensure that this evidence comes before the jury; however, there is some truth in Galvin's observation that often a just result in a given case came about in spite of, rather than as a result of, the applicable statutes.[705]

(d) Previous sexual experience in child abuse prosecutions in Australian law

(i) The statutory framework in Australian law

All Australian jurisdictions have enacted rape shield laws.[706] The statutes have all been interpreted as applying to sexual offences against children,[707] and do not apply in civil proceedings. Apart from this they do not follow a common pattern or use common terminology, although there are recurring elements. In all States save Western Australia,[708] the legislation regulates the admission of evidence of sexual history by any party, not just by the defence.

All jurisdictions prohibit evidence of sexual reputation, some absolutely[709] and some provisionally.[710] In respect of previous sexual activity, leave of the court is required, and

---

[701] *State v Rolon* (n 698) 621.   [702] Fishman (n 694) 809–810.

[703] ibid 808–809; *State v Rolon* (n 698) 624.

[704] *Michigan v Lucas* (n 671) 146; *Branzburg v Hayes* 408 US 665 (USSC 1972); *People v Arenda* (n 671) 817.   [705] Galvin (n 665), 824, 826–827.

[706] For a useful overview, see J Gans and A Palmer *Australian Principles of Evidence* (2nd edn Cavendish, Sydney 2004) chapter 13.

[707] *HG v The Queen* [1999] HCA 2, 160 ALR 554 (Aus HC) [28]–[32], [147].

[708] Evidence Act 1906 (Western Australia) s 41.

[709] Criminal Procedure Act 1986 (New South Wales) s 293(2); Evidence (Miscellaneous Provisions) Act 1991 (Australian Capital Territory) s 50; Criminal Law (Sexual Offences) Act 1978 (Queensland) s 4(1); Evidence Act 1958 (Victoria) s 37A Rule (1). Western Australia also absolutely prohibits evidence of the complainant's 'sexual disposition': Evidence Act 1906 (Western Australia) s 36BA, which nonetheless has been interpreted as being subject to an implied exclusion for evidence which can properly be adduced for another purpose but incidentally tends to show the complainant's sexual disposition [*Bull v The Queen* (2000) 201 CLR 443 (Aus HC) 473–475].

[710] Crimes Act 1914 (Commonwealth of Australia) s 15YB; Sexual Offences (Evidence and Procedure) Act (Northern Territory) s 4(1)(a); Evidence Act 1929 (South Australia) s 34I(2)(a).

all jurisdictions except New South Wales impose a heightened threshold of relevance, usually expressed in the form of 'substantially relevant to facts in issue'.[711]

New South Wales, South Australia, Tasmania and Western Australia all require the trial judge to balance the probative value of the evidence against any distress, humiliation or embarrassment which the complainant might suffer,[712] rather than against the distorting effect of the rape myths which have concerned the Canadian and English courts. Mahoney JA has caustically remarked that this statutory model 'places distress above imprisonment', in that if the probative value and distress weigh equally, then the evidence is excluded notwithstanding that it may establish the innocence of the accused.[713] In contrast, Queensland's law expressly states that the purpose of the prohibition is to ensure that the complainant is not regarded as less worthy of belief as a witness only because the complainant has engaged in sexual activity (the second of the rape myths)—unless because of special circumstances the court considers that the evidence would be likely to materially impair confidence (impliedly properly) in the reliability of the complainant's evidence.[714] The New South Wales Law Reform Commission recommended that their State's legislation be substantially reformed so as expressly to identify the twin myths as the forbidden reasoning, with any distress, humiliation or embarrassment which the complainant might suffer being downgraded to one of six factors in evaluating whether the evidence has significant probative value which substantially outweighs the danger of prejudice to the proper administration of justice.[715] However, to date those recommendations have not been implemented by the New South Wales Parliament.

The Commonwealth of Australia's legislation is of particular interest, because it applies only to sexual offence proceedings involving child witnesses (other than child defendants).[716] Evidence of a child's sexual reputation is admissible with leave of the court only if the evidence is substantially relevant to facts in issue in the proceedings, and must not be treated as relevant to the child's credibility.[717] Evidence of a child's

---

[711] Crimes Act 1914 (Commonwealth of Australia) s 15YC(2)(a); Evidence (Miscellaneous Provisions) Act 1991 (Australian Capital Territory) s 53(3). However, the Act stipulates that the 'substantial relevant' test is an alternative ground for granting leave because the evidence of sexual activities 'is a proper matter for cross-examination about credit', as does the Criminal Law (Sexual Offences) Act 1978 (Queensland) s 4(3); Sexual Offences (Evidence and Procedure) Act (Northern Territory) s 4(1); Evidence Act 1929 (South Australia) s 34I(2)(a) ('of substantial probative value' and an added requirement that its admission is required in the interests of justice); Evidence Act 2001 (Tasmania) s 194M(2)(a) ('direct and substantial relevance to a fact or matter in issue').

[712] Criminal Procedure Act 1986 (New South Wales) s 293(4); Evidence Act 1929 (South Australia) s 34I(2); Evidence Act 2001 (Tasmania) s 194M(2)(b) and (4) (which requires the court to consider the witness's age and number and nature of the likely questions in assessing the amount of distress, humiliation or embarrassment which may be suffered); Evidence Act 1906 (Western Australia) s 36BC(2)(b).

[713] *R v Morgan* (1993) 67 A Crim R 526 (New South Wales CCA) 535.

[714] Criminal Law (Sexual Offences) Act 1978 (Queensland) s 4(5). This proviso also appears in the Evidence (Miscellaneous Provisions) Act 1991 (Australian Capital Territory) s 53(3); Criminal Procedure Act 1986 (New South Wales) s 293(2)(b); Sexual Offences (Evidence and Procedure) Act (Northern Territory) s 4(2)(b); Evidence Act 1929 (South Australia) s 34I(2)(b); Evidence Act 1958 (Victoria) s 37A Rule (4)(b).

[715] New South Wales Law Reform Commission *Reform of Section 409B* (Report No 87 1998) Recommendation 2.   [716] Crimes Act 1914 (Commonwealth of Australia) ss 15YB, 15YC.

[717] ibid s 15YB.

experience of sexual activities is admissible only with leave of the court, or if the evidence is of sexual activities with the defendant.[718] There are two bases for granting leave: the evidence is substantially relevant to facts in issue other than inferences it may raise as to the child's general disposition; or it relates to the credibility of the child witness in cross-examination and has 'substantial probative value'. The court is required to include in its consideration of probative value whether the evidence tends to prove that the witness knowingly or recklessly made a false representation when under an obligation to tell the truth, and the period elapsed since the acts or events to which the evidence relates.

New South Wales adopted a closed list of highly specific exceptions to the general prohibition which minimizes judicial discretion,[719] emulating the Michigan model. New South Wales is also unique amongst Australian jurisdictions in applying the rape shield to any evidence which discloses or implies that the complainant has *or lacks* sexual experience, or did or did not take part in any sexual activity.

The New South Wales model has been singled out for judicial criticism on the basis that its operation has excluded highly probative evidence, the two most significant problems identified relating to child abuse prosecutions being where the accused denied that the alleged abuse occurred or where the evidence which was excluded related to sexual experience or activity, or lack of it. The appeal court has asserted jurisdiction to quash a conviction when the provision had been properly applied, if the reviewing court considers that a miscarriage of justice had resulted from exclusion of what might be exculpatory evidence.[720] The Australian High Court in refusing leave to appeal in the same case called for a review of the provision by legislators in light of the experience with its operation.[721] In response, the New South Wales Law Reform Commission undertook a comprehensive review of the provision in 1998,[722] but its recommendation of a guided discretion model along the lines of the Canadian post-*Seaboyer* legislation[723] has not been implemented.

We turn now to the four categories of evidence pertaining to sexual history most likely to arise in child abuse prosecutions. We will focus on cases interpreting the New South Wales legislation, as it is most similar in form to the 'closed categories' model in YJCEA 1999 (England) s 41.

(ii) Previous or subsequent allegations of sexual abuse against third parties in Australian law

The New South Wales Law Reform Commission identified the impact of the rape shield law on this category as being one of the two most problematic issues, because it prevents the defence from bringing information before the jury which might cause them to doubt the complainant's version of events, so causing injustice.[724]

---

[718] ibid s 15YC.   [719] Criminal Procedure Act 1986 (New South Wales) s 293(4).

[720] *R v PJE* (CCA 60216/95, 9 October 1995) (New South Wales CCA) 4–5 (Cole CJ), 7–8 (Grove J) leave to appeal refused No 5154/95 (Aus HC, 9 Sept 1996). The Court of Appeal allowed the defendant's appeal from a trial judge who stayed a prosecution because exculpatory evidence would be excluded by the rape shield law.   [721] ibid.

[722] *Reform of Section 409B* (n 715).   [723] ibid [6.114].   [724] ibid [4.8], [4.16]–[4.20].

Evidence that the child has a general propensity to lie or make false allegations has been ruled inadmissible in at least two cases.[725] In *R v M*,[726] the appellant was convicted of several sexual offences against three young girls, the oldest of whom was T, aged ten. Defence counsel sought to lead evidence from other witnesses and to cross-examine her about allegations that during or shortly after the period when the alleged offences had been committed, she had alleged that male members of her own family were having sexual intercourse with her. He deployed the same argument which we have seen has met with some success in some English[727] and Canadian[728] courts, that the rape shield did not intercept such evidence because it was not about her sexual experience but about her sexual fantasies. The Court of Criminal Appeal ruled that as the proscription was directed not only to sexual experience but to lack of sexual experience, it applied, for the evidence would have disclosed or implied that she had not participated in the sexual activity which was the subject of the alleged lies. It was therefore immaterial that the forensic purpose of the proposed evidence was for another objective, to show that she was unreliable as a witness because she had previously made false allegations.[729] The Court also refused to read into the legislation an implied exception for false accusations of sexual misconduct, as this was not consonant with Parliament's objective, as recorded in *Hansard*, to enact a blanket ban with narrow exceptions and no inclusionary judicial discretion.[730]

(iii) Motive to fabricate the allegations against the defendant in Australian law

The New South Wales legislation contains an express exception for evidence that the allegation was first made following the realization or discovery of the presence of pregnancy or disease in the complainant,[731] the implicit basis for the exception being that this gives rise to an inference of a motive to fabricate an allegation.

Apart from this rather odd provision, it would seem that evidence of previous sexual activity, or lack thereof, is not admissible to prove an improper motive. This is borne out by *HG v The Queen*,[732] where the High Court had to consider the admissibility of a psychologist's report opining that the ten-year-old complainant had transposed earlier sexual abuse by her mentally ill father (since deceased) when she was three (for which there was no evidence other than his opinion) to her stepfather, the defendant, in resentment at his discipline. The Court concluded that the New South Wales legislation did not apply to the conclusion that the child had not been abused by the stepfather, but it did properly bar the conclusion of earlier possible abuse by her father. The Court found the report to be inadmissible, because the opinion without

---

[725] The New South Wales Law Reform Commission cites *R v Bernthaler* No 60394/93, 17 December 1993 (New South Wales CCA) and *R v McIlvanie* No 93/11/14 95, Shillington DCJ, 30 August 1994 (New South Wales DC).   [726] *R v M* (1993) 67 A Crim R 549 (New South Wales CCA).

[727] *R v MH; R v RT* (n 528), discussed above, section D.3(a)(ii).

[728] *R v Gauthier* (n 632) discussed above, section D.3(b)(ii).   [729] *R v M* (n 726) 554–555.

[730] ibid 555–558.   [731] Criminal Procedure Act 1986 (New South Wales) s 293(4)(e).

[732] *HZ v The Queen* (n 707).

the central thesis of transference from earlier abuse would have been misleading, and the stepfather's conviction was upheld.[733]

(iv) Previous abuse to explain medical findings of sexual abuse

The New South Wales legislation includes an express exception for evidence relevant to whether the 'presence of semen, pregnancy, disease or injury is attributable to the sexual intercourse alleged to have been had by the accused person'.[734] The reference to sexual intercourse makes the provision inapplicable to other forms of child sexual abuse.

The provision has apparently been interpreted narrowly. In the unreported case of *R v Morris*,[735] in the course of the investigation of an alleged rape the medical examiner found the child to have a ruptured hymen. Counsel informed the court that the complainant had had sexual intercourse with a third party at age six which could account for the rupture, but it was concluded that this historical evidence was barred by the rape shield law. To permit the medical evidence to be given without the history would be unfairly prejudicial to the accused, so it was decided not to call the medical examiner as a witness. The jury asked two questions: about any medical examination of the complainant after the assault was reported, and about the child's testimony that this was not the first time she had seen an erection. The trial judge concluded that the jury's questions, which he considered to be sensible and obvious, could not be answered by adducing further evidence without infringing the statutory ban or causing unfair prejudice to the accused, and further that he could give no jury direction which would enable the accused to have a fair trial. He therefore discharged the jury.

The prohibition of evidence of sexual abuse of a child by someone other than the accused was identified by the New South Wales Law Reform Commission as one of the two major problems with the legislation.[736] Nevertheless, the Government has not moved to amend it.

(v) Previous abuse or other sources to explain the child's precocious knowledge or sexualization in Australian law

As mentioned earlier, in New South Wales the closed list of exceptions includes evidence which rebuts any disclosure or implication in the prosecution evidence that the complainant had sexual experience or—more relevant for child abuse prosecutions—a lack of sexual experience. This was recently considered in *R v Rahme*[737] where the defendant was charged with a number of offences connected with coercing a 15-year-old girl into prostitution at his family-owned brothel in Sydney. The trial judge ruled that evidence from a witness that the child had worked as a prostitute in Newcastle

---

[733] Gleeson CJ also concluded, it is submitted correctly, that the witness's opinion was inadmissible in any event as it was based upon speculation and a process of reasoning which went well beyond his qualifications as a psychologist: ibid [36]–[45].

[734] Criminal Procedure Act 1986 (New South Wales) s 293(4)(c)(ii).

[735] *R v Morris* (70005/89, Wood J, 18 October 1990) (New South Wales Supreme Ct), described in detail in *R v PJE* (n 720) 28–29.　　　[736] *Reform of Section 409B* (n 715) [4.10]–[4.15], [6.75].

[737] *R v Charbel Rahme* [2004] NSWCCA 233 New South Wales CCA 233.

before coming to Sydney, to raise funds to travel to the US to visit her boyfriend, was not admissible as rebuttal evidence to any implication in the Crown's case. However, the Court of Criminal Appeal held that the complainant had put herself forward, as had the Crown, as an emotionally vulnerable young runaway from home who had been skilfully seduced into a relationship in which he corrupted her with drug abuse; therefore the defence should have been allowed to cross-examine her about her alleged previous experience as a prostitute, as its potential probative value outweighed any distress, humiliation, or embarrassment that the complainant might suffer as a result of its admission.[738]

The New South Wales experience illustrates how fallible legislative predictions of relevance may be, and consequently how a 'closed categories' rape shield model can intercept evidence of clear relevance to the defence. It is useful however in highlighting that logically sexual behaviour should encompass a witness's claims about previous sexual experience, or lack thereof, whether they be true or false, and therefore that some restrictions on such questions are advisable.

(e) Previous sexual experience in child abuse prosecutions in New Zealand law

(i) The statutory framework in New Zealand law

In 1977 the New Zealand Parliament enacted its own version of rape shield legislation, which was re-enacted in 1985 to apply it to 'any case of a sexual nature'.[739] Section 23A of the Evidence Act 1908 follows a discretionary model. It prohibits any evidence or question relating directly or indirectly to the sexual experience of the complainant with any person other than the accused, and the reputation of the complainant in sexual matters, without leave of the trial judge. The court must be satisfied that the evidence is of such direct relevance to facts in issue in the proceeding, or to the issue of the appropriate sentence, that to exclude it would be contrary to the interests of justice. There is a further caveat, that the direct relevance test cannot be satisfied by reason only of any inference as to the complainant's general disposition or propensity in sexual matters.[740]

The New Zealand Court of Appeal has observed that the provision is more stringent than its 1976 English counterpart, and that the phrase 'the interests of justice' is wider than (but certainly includes) fairness to the defendant (the corresponding proviso in the English 1976 rape shield provision).[741] While the legislation has considerably circumscribed the common law rights of the defendant,[742] inevitably trial judges have to strive to strike a just balance between protecting the complainant from

---

[738] ibid [63]–[64] (Sully J), [193]–[194] (James J). The Court of Criminal Appeal also ruled that the evidence was also admissible under another exception, for evidence of sexual experience at or about the time of the commission of the alleged offence, and pertaining to events forming part of a connecting set of circumstances in which the alleged offence was committed [Criminal Procedure Act 1986 (New South Wales) s 293(4)(a)].

[739] New Zealand Law Commission *Character and Credibility* (Preliminary Paper 27) (Feb 1997) 104.

[740] Evidence Act 1908 (New Zealand) s 23A(2) and (3).

[741] *R v McClintock* [1986] 2 NZLR 99 (New Zealand CA) 14–15.

[742] *R v Bills* [1981] 1 NZLR 760 (New Zealand CA) 764–765.

undue harassment and unduly hampering the defence.[743] The New Zealand Law Commission considers that the courts had generally achieved this objective.[744] This may be because the Court of Appeal has interpreted the legislation as requiring the proposed evidence to have a strong degree of direct relevance, and has cautioned the lower courts that many questions going only to credit should be excluded because they have only indirect relevance to facts in issue.[745] Previous sexual acts with third parties must be so closely connected with the alleged rape either in time or place or by other circumstances that they acquire direct relevance.[746] For example, where a stepfather was alleged to have raped his 18-year-old stepdaughter, evidence that she had had consensual intercourse with boys from the age of 15 was irrelevant to the charges.[747]

(ii) Previous or subsequent allegations of sexual abuse against third parties in New Zealand law

The issue which has troubled the courts elsewhere about whether previous complaints constitute evidence of sexual experience or behaviour has not been problematic in New Zealand. Leave of the court is required by the rape shield legislation before any such question is put to the complainant. The Court of Appeal considers that the legislation is framed widely enough to intercept questions about previous allegations of abuse,[748] including allegedly false complaints, notwithstanding that this is not the primary aim, which is to preclude a character-blackening exercise often with little direct relevance. In *R v Duncan* McGechen J observed:

> It can be very relevant, particularly in child abuse cases, to explore the possibility of fabrication to gain attention or through malice, or transferred attribution from actual offender to present accused. Habitual or false previous complaints can be an indicator. There can be occasions when questioning along these lines, far from being a character-blackening exercise of little relevance, is well justified in the overall interests of justice. In such situations, Courts will not be unduly reticent over granting leave for examinations which are beyond mere fishing expeditions.[749]

Therefore admitting evidence that the 12-year-old complainant had written letters making similar allegations against a male boarder, and had told her mother that she had been sexually abused when much younger, would in principle be in the interests of justice.[750]

Does a defendant in New Zealand have to lay an evidential foundation for an allegation that the other complaint was fabricated? This is unclear. In *R v Accused (CA*

---

[743] *R v McClintock* (n 741) 15–16.

[744] New Zealand Law Commission *Evidence Law: Expert Evidence And Opinion Evidence*, (Preliminary Paper 18 Dec 1991) 105 [324].

[745] *R v McClintock* (n 741) 103; *R v Daniels* [1986] 2 NZLR 106 (New Zealand CA) 115.

[746] *R v McClintock* ibid 104.

[747] *R v NSM* [1997] DCR 711 (New Zealand DC). However, the trial judge went on to rule that evidence that the complainant had been a prostitute since age 16 should be admitted, as the evidence against the defendant was 'very compelling'—an unconvincing rationale.

[748] *R v Accused (CA 92/92)* [1993] 1 NZLR 553 (New Zealand CA).

[749] *R v Duncan* (n 408) 535.   [750] ibid 535.

92/92),[751] it emerged in the child's police interview that another named person had indecently assaulted her in very similar circumstances a few months earlier. On an interlocutory appeal, the Crown noted that there was no suggestion that the complainant habitually made false assertions of sexual offending nor was there anything raising a suspicion of concoction of the other complaint. The Court of Appeal held that although the case was close to the borderline, this was not a fishing expedition because of the remarkable similarity in the complaints. Eichelbaum CJ stated that in a credibility contest, any matter bearing on the complainant's credibility in a significant way, at any rate when closely connected with the complaint against the accused, is difficult to dismiss as remote or trivial,[752] thereby appearing to move New Zealand law closer to the position of the English Court of Appeal in *Funderburk*.[753] However, the trial judge had erred in making leave conditional upon the defence eliciting evidence of the falsity of the other complaint, as the jurisdiction to do so might not exist, and in any event the usual rules should govern once the evidence was adduced.[754] If the child denied that the other allegation was false, the collateral issue rule would curtail cross-examination and any attempt to rebut that denial, to avoid the trial expanding into an investigation of an unrelated incident.[755] It is submitted that this is incorrect; further evidence of alleged falsity of another complaint to rebut a denial is quite different from the threshold test of direct relevance to the offence charged. In this case the substantial similarity of the two allegations (that a family friend put his hand under the child's nightwear while they were watching television when other members of the household were engaged elsewhere) might be sufficient to raise a suspicion of falsity, so as to warrant an initial question in cross-examination, but that should not be regarded as licensing unsupported allegations of falsity where such an obvious link is absent.

The New Zealand Law Commission considered that evidence of fabrication by the complainant based on an earlier false complaint should not be excluded, because such evidence is of such direct relevance to the facts in issue that to exclude it would be contrary to the interests of justice.[756] It did not however address the question of what if anything is required of the defence by way of proof of falsity.

(iii) Motive to fabricate the allegations against the defendant in New Zealand law
New Zealand courts also do not make heavy weather of the admissibility of evidence suggesting a motive. In *R v Rust*[757] evidence that the defendant had attempted to break up an ongoing sexual relationship with a third party, which the 14-year-old complainant admitted, was admissible in support of the defence theory that she had a motive for fabricating the rape allegation.[758]

---

[751] *R v Accused* (n 748).   [752] ibid 556
[753] *R v Funderburk* (n 456), discussed above, sections D.1(a), D.3(a)(ii).
[754] *R v Accused* (n 748) 557.   [755] ibid 557–558.
[756] *Character and Credibility* (n 739) 112 [352].
[757] *R v Rust* CA 572/95 (New Zealand CA, 12 September 1996) discussed in *R v NSM* (n 747).
[758] ibid 5.

(iv) Previous abuse to explain medical findings of sexual abuse

The New Zealand courts have considered that medical evidence of previous or sub-sequent sexual activity meets the statutory test of direct relevance to a fact in issue,[759] although if this seems entirely speculative it appears that cross-examining counsel must be in a position to impute the offending to some other named perpetrator.[760] The New Zealand Law Commission has criticized a few cases where there was a sufficient gap in time between the previous sexual activity and event charged to raise doubts as to its direct relevance.[761]

(v) Previous abuse or other sources to explain the child's precocious knowledge or sexualization in New Zealand law

The admissibility of explanatory evidence regarding precocious sexual knowledge or sexualization has not figured in the reported cases considering the rape shield law. Possibly this dearth of authority is attributable to s 23G of the Evidence Act 1908 which makes opinion evidence admissible as to whether a child's behaviour is consistent or inconsistent with sexual abuse,[762] which presupposes that evidence has been led as to the child's behaviour. In a 2004 case, *R v Aymes*,[763] extensive evidence was led from a mother about her daughter's highly sexualized behaviour between the age of three and eight (and hence starting in a period before she had contact with the accused) with a view to establishing the factual basis for an expert's opinion under the Evidence Act 1908 s 23G(2)(c) that her more aggressive and intrusive behaviour was consistent with (but not diagnostic of) sexual abuse. No issue was taken regarding the admissibility of the evidence under the rape shield law.

The New Zealand Law Commission has regarded the discretionary rape shield legislation as generally working well, and, unlike the New South Wales Law Reform Commission, has not identified any particular difficulties in relation to prosecuting child abuse. Its recommended changes for the new Evidence Code would extend the shield to the complainant's sexual experience with the defendant and would replace the qualified prohibition on evidence relating directly or indirectly to the complainant's reputation in sexual matters with an absolute prohibition if tendered for the purpose of relevance to credibility or consent.[764] The Law Commission considered that the latter recommendation would not preclude evidence of a complainant's reputation for making false allegations of sexual assault, as this would not relate to a reputa-tion in sexual matters.[765] This reasoning would introduce into New Zealand law the dubious distinction between sexual behaviour and lies about sexual behaviour which we criticized earlier,[766] the result being that allegedly false complaints would not be intercepted by the reformed rape shield law, whereas under the existing legislation

---

[759] *R v Phillips* (1989) 5 CRNZ 405 (New Zealand HC) (presence of semen in the complainant's vagina). [760] *R v S* [1998] 3 NZLR 392 (New Zealand CA) 395.
[761] *Character and Credibility* (n 739) 105 [327]. [762] Analysed below, Chapter 10 section C.7.
[763] *R v Aymes* (CA123/04, 16 December 2004) (New Zealand CA).
[764] *Evidence* (n 248) Vol 2 Evidence Code and Commentary, draft Evidence Code s 46.
[765] ibid Vol 2 Evidence Code and Commentary, 124 commentary C212.
[766] In our discussion of *R v Mokrecovas* (n 512) above Chapter 8 section D.3(a).

leave of the court would be required.[767] The Law Commission did not identify this as being the consequence of its proposed reform.

4. Evaluation: the credibility conundrum

Commentators have identified two fundamental flaws in rigid rape shield provisions. The first is that they misidentify the evil to be addressed as being evidence of sexual activity, when in fact the harm lies in using this for misleading and irrelevant purposes. The second is that they adopt a 'pigeonhole' approach, predicting relevance by a series of rules or categories, which cannot possibly anticipate all factual circumstances which can arise in sexual assault trials.[768] The New South Wales Court of Appeal has observed that the 'wisdom of so Draconic a restriction upon judicial discretion and of so bold an assumption of perfect prescience may be questioned.'[769]

The YJCEA 1999 (England) s 41 exemplifies both defects. Subsection 41(4) intercepts *all* evidence of sexual behaviour, the (main) purpose of which is to impugn the credibility of the complainant, before the gateways of permissible uses are even approached. The premise of s 41(4) is that all evidential uses of other sexual behaviour to assess credibility are illegitimate. But, as McLachlin J pointed out in *Seaboyer*, this is so only to the extent that the evidence is deployed to invoke the twin myths reasoning.[770] The new version of the rape shield law in the Criminal Code of Canada expressly recognizes this.

The YJCEA 1999 then erects four quite narrow gateways for the defence to squeeze through. True, s 41(3)(a) appears to be potentially quite wide in that it permits sexual behaviour evidence to be admitted if relevant to an issue other than consent, but the critical precondition is that the defence's objective must not be to attack the credibility of the complainant. In sexual assault cases where there is no physical evidence, the credibility of the accused and the accuser is necessarily the central issue, a factor which is a key determinant of police and CPS decisions not to proceed with a prosecution.[771] Credibility cannot be bleached out of any of the evidence in the case. We have seen that the consequence is a tortured analysis of relevance to 'other issues' when it is obvious that an attack on credibility must be the ultimate objective of the defence. This is demonstrated by the peculiar lines of argument invoked where the defence wishes to raise a motive to fabricate under s 41(3)(a) when the motive necessarily involves sexual behaviour. This is reminiscent of the long-derided common law approach to hearsay, whereby admission was dependent upon the ingenuity of counsel in fitting it within a permissible but inflexible category, when everyone in court knew it was very likely that the jury would use it as they saw fit in their deliberations in disregard of the 'limited use' instructions of the trial judge.

---

[767] *R v Accused (CA 92/92)* (n 748); *R v Duncan* (n 408).

[768] Galvin (n 665) 814; D Doherty ' "Sparing" the Complainant Spoils the "Trial" ' (1984) 40 CR (3d) 55 57; *R v Seaboyer* (n 484) [52]–[67]. [769] *R v M* (n 726) 558 (Allen J).

[770] *R v Seaboyer* (n 484) [96]. [771] Kelly, Lovett, Regan (n 67) 46–53, 58.

Turning to the specific issues relating to the previous sexual experience of adolescents and younger children, we have seen that much difficulty arises in relation to whether children can and should be provided the protection of the rape shield laws developed to address twin myths strongly imbued with fallacious reasoning about consent and the credibility of sexually active women.[772] Evidence of previous sexual abuse and of previous allegations of abuse does not rely for its relevance on the old common law inferences.[773] Nevertheless, the risks of trauma to the victim in reliving past events not directly germane to current charges, and confusion for both the complainant and the jury, may be even greater where children are concerned.[774]

However, courts also need to be cognizant of the particular myths attendant upon child witnesses, especially in sexual abuse cases. As recently as 1984 a leading commentator on the law of evidence, now a Justice of the High Court of Australia, asserted that children are prone to live in a make-believe world, so that they magnify incidents which happen to them or invent them completely. He went on to claim that:

... children sometimes behave in a way evil beyond their years. They may consent to sexual offences against themselves and then deny consent. They may completely invent sexual offences. Some children know that the adult world regards such matters in a serious and peculiar way, and they enjoy investigating this mystery or revenging themselves by making false accusations.[775]

Thus the risk of distorted reasoning from myths about younger children may take a different form than that conventionally addressed by 'rape shield' legislation. This makes s 41 singularly inapposite for child abuse cases. It is arguable that the application of the 'rape shield' can result in wrongful convictions in child abuse prosecutions because it forces the prosecution to construct what is essentially a distorted picture of the environment in which the child was placed at the material time. Moreover, whilst the 'relevance to another issue' gateway in s 41 has been widened by the English appellate courts to allow the defence to explore previous sexual abuse to explain medical findings and precocious sexualization, the requirement that the evidence relate to specific instances of behaviour in s 41(6) can place the defence in an impossible position.

We have seen that a previous allegation of abuse is the most difficult area in all common law jurisdictions. Such evidence takes on relevance to general testimonial

---

[772] L Kelly, J Temkin and S Griffiths *Section 41: an Evaluation of New Legislation Limiting Sexual History Evidence in Rape Trials* (Home Office Online Report 20/06, London 2006) vi, 74, argue that sexual history evidence regarding children raises concerns that, irrespective of the exploitative nature of the past events, children are more often represented as sexually active than sexually vulnerable, and that prosecutors have no strategy of presenting an alternative account, with the result that cases are discontinued.

[773] NSWLRC *Reform of Section 409B* (n 715) [6.14]. However, an empirical study found that CPS prosecutors apply invoke twin myth reasoning to cases involving child complainants: there is only one authentic response to sexual violation (ruling out children who did not show distress), and only those with unblemished reputations automatically qualify as victims, ruling out those who made past allegations: Kelly et al *Section 41*, ibid 33.

[774] *State v Oliver* (n 667) 1075–1076; *People v Arenda* (n 671), 818 (Mitchigan Supreme Ct. 1982).

[775] J Heydon *Evidence: Cases and Materials* (2nd edn Butterworths, London 1984).

credibility only if there is a sufficient basis from which the trier of fact can conclude that the allegation was false. The setting of the threshold for allowing the jury to hear the evidence is critical. Empirical research suggests that false allegation rates are no higher for rape than for other crimes, contrary to the perceptions of police officers and the media.[776] There is good reason for caution.

Previous allegations raise an issue of general importance: is YJCEA 1999 s 41 subject to the elevated admissibility barriers for bad character of witnesses other than the defendant in s 100 of the Criminal Justice Act 2003? Neither provision refers to the other. On one view it is not, because s 41(4) prohibits the use of sexual behaviour evidence for the purpose of impugning the complainant's credibility as a witness, and that is the usual target for bad character evidence. On the other hand, that prohibition is subject to the defence's right to rebut prosecution evidence under s 41(5) which makes the bad character evidence relevant.

Thus far the Court of Appeal has given little guidance about how other allegedly false complaints of abuse should be handled. Whilst confirming that s 41 does not apply to lies about sexual behaviour, in *R v V* in 2006 a panel observed that cross-examination about an allegedly false sexual allegation may require a ruling in relation to s 41 as well as leave under s 100, and that in many cases s 41 'will be the more formidable obstacle to overcome'.[777] Unfortunately the Court did not identify the circumstances where orders under both provisions are required, and in practice when the previous sexual experience might also constitute 'reprehensible behaviour', prudent defence counsel are applying for leave to cross-examine under both provisions. It is submitted that the admissibility of previous or subsequent allegedly false complaints of abuse by the complainant, and a motive to concoct the complaint, should be determined not by the inapposite rape shield provisions of s 41, but rather by the safeguards in s 100 of the CJA 2003 (England).[778] The requirements that the evidence of another complaint be 'important explanatory evidence' or have 'substantial probative value' in relation to an issue of 'substantial importance' to the proceedings[779] might well result in the defendant having to show that the allegation was *demonstrably* false, rather than merely arguably false, before being allowed to put the question. If the question meets that high threshold of probative value, then in our submission the finality rule should not apply to any denial by the complainant, and the defence should be permitted to cross-examine further and to adduce rebuttal evidence, thereby evading altogether the notorious credit/issue trap in *Funderburk*.[780]

Even if the previous allegation cannot be proved as false, previous victimization is not necessarily irrelevant, as it may take on significance in respect of the child's specific credibility in her description of the assaults charged and how she responded to them.

---

[776] The most recent Home Office study estimates that only 3% of reports in the research sample were possible or probable false allegations: Kelly et al (n 67) *A Gap or a Chasm?* 47–53. Rumney (n 490), 142 points out that the empirical studies deploy different methodological parameters, particularly how an allegation is judged to be false, which makes verification and comparison difficult.

[777] *R v V* (n 553) [25] (the panel comprising Sir Igor Judge P and Crane and Dobbs JJ).

[778] Birch 'Untangling Sexual History Evidence' (n 487) 383.

[779] CJA 2003 (England) ss 100(1)(a) and 100(1)(b), as depicted in Diagram 16.

[780] *R v Funderburk* (n 456).

As we noted earlier, a child who has previously been abused by others is likely to feel a sense of fatalism and learned helplessness. It is submitted that English courts should follow the American practice[781] of requiring an evidential foundation for any defence arguments that the child has deliberately or innocently confused the defendant with a previous perpetrator before evidence of previous abuse is admitted for this purpose.

Evidence explaining physical signs of abuse as being attributable to another cause is of obvious, and great, relevance. Evidence indicative of precocious knowledge or premature sexualization is more ambiguous. As one American appellate court has observed,[782] in a society inundated with sexual information, evidence of past sexual experience is less probative in cases involving older children as they are likely to have learned about sexuality from many sources. Conversely, the possibility of prejudice increases as a child matures, as the evidence may divert the jury's attention from the behaviour of the defendant to that of the complainant. The evidence may mislead a jury to conclude that a person who assaults a more sexually experienced child is not culpable, especially if the child initiated the encounter.[783] Nevertheless, if the proffered defence evidence of previous abuse or access to other sources of sexual knowledge is capable of rebutting any inference of sexualization by the defendant, then its probative value is legitimately powerful, and it should be admitted.[784]

The problems with s 41 are fundamental. *R v A (No 2)* notwithstanding, these problems are not amenable to cure by generous judicial interpretation. The Canadian position post-*Seaboyer* (notwithstanding its drawbacks) presents a more nuanced, flexible, and arguably more honest solution to the dilemma of protecting both the complainant and the accused, and ultimately the integrity of the trial. The sensible solution is to develop a flexible previous sexual experience doctrine requiring that the court address directly the probative force of the sexual experience evidence for the defence case, and weigh it against its potential prejudice by sidetracking the jury into collateral issues or leading them into invoking stereotypical and mythological reasoning.

An analyst of this area of English evidence law is likely to concur with the lament of Lord Woolf CJ that s 41 is 'by no means easy to interpret and apply'.[785] This uncertainty exacerbates the difficulties for the police, the CPS and those supporting child complainants in forecasting how their credibility may be attacked on the basis of sexual matters which have arisen previously or subsequently to the allegation charged.[786] It still remains the case that the more turbulent the child's background and environment, the more likely it is that the child's credibility will be attacked on the basis of her previous negative experiences of the world.

---

[781] Discussed above section D.3(c)(ii).   [782] *State v Budis* (n 672).   [783] ibid 791.

[784] Galvin (n 665), 865–867; J Myers 'The Child Witness: Techniques for Direct Examination, Cross-Examination and Impeachment' (1987) 18 Pacific LJ 801, 905–907.

[785] *R v Mokrecovas* (n 512) [6].

[786] Kelly et al *Section 41*(n 772) vii, 33, 35, 36 reported that in cases involving minors, a guilty plea to a lesser offence was offered and accepted in a greater proportion of cases where sexual history material was present (87%), than where it was not (69%). Previous allegations played a part in CPS decisions to discontinue. However, guilty pleas and verdicts were higher where sexual history material was found on CPS files (69%) than where it was absent (53%).

10

Testing the Credibility of the Alleged Abuser

A. Evidential Uses of Character Evidence

Lay observers of a trial of an alleged child abuser in a common law courtroom might well be perplexed when evidence of his paedophilia emerges only at the sentencing stage. This is because all common law jurisdictions adopt the premise in criminal and tort cases that the defendant is on trial for what he allegedly did, not for who he is. Consequently, the common law purports to prohibit evidence of (a) the defendant's misconduct on occasions which do not relate to the offence charged, or (b) his disposition or propensity to behave in a particular way, or (c) his bad character traits. Viscount Sankey LC in *Maxwell v DPP* described this principle as 'one of the most deeply rooted and jealously guarded principles of our common law'.[1] Yet it is not self-evident that a fair trial necessarily demands this. Legal systems on the European Continent espouse the principle of 'free proof' in criminal trials, and so adjudicators throughout the trial are exposed to information about the accused's criminal record, character and past life and are free to use it in deciding guilt.[2]

---

[1] *Maxwell v DPP* [1935] AC 309 (HL) 475; for similar rhetoric see *Michelson v US* 335 US 469 (USSC 1948) 489 (Rutledge J, dissenting).

[2] M Damaška 'Symposium on the Admission of Prior Offense Evidence in Sexual Assault Cases: Propensity Evidence in Continental Legal Systems' (1994) 70 Chicago-Kent LR 55 56–60. The criminal record cannot however be used to discredit the accused's testimony.

Notwithstanding the common law's general bar on admissibility, character evidence may come into play in criminal and civil trials in all the jurisdictions we examine at several junctures, and in a range of contexts. In so far as the defendant is concerned, his previous conduct and reputation may be argued to be relevant and hence admissible:

- as direct, albeit circumstantial, proof of *guilt*, forming part of the prosecution's or claimant's case in chief:
  — as evidence *intrinsic* to the offence charged, to establish the background or factual context in which the offence charged is alleged to have occurred, such as a child being groomed by an alleged paedophile;
  — as evidence *extraneous* to the specific offence charged, to establish that the defendant had a propensity to commit sexual or physical abuse of children (which is often referred to by the misnomer[3] 'similar fact evidence'), and hence provides the basis for an inference of guilt respecting the events charged; or
- as indirect proof of guilt or innocence, as evidence pertaining to the *credibility* of the defendant's denials respecting the events charged:
  — as part of the defence case in chief to establish that the defendant has a good reputation as to character, and hence he does not have the disposition to abuse children as charged, and his denials should be believed;
  — in cross-examination of the defendant, to rebut his claim to good character;
  — in cross-examination of the defendant, where the defence has made imputations against the character of the alleged victim or prosecution witnesses.

Thus the common law rules draw a distinction between the admissibility of the defendant's other misconduct as evidence of guilt, and as evidence that the defendant is lying in denying guilt. This is sometimes called the 'issue/credit' divide. The distinction has been collapsed in English law by the Criminal Justice Act 2003 (CJA 2003), which has abrogated the common law rules[4] and has substituted radical statutory rules in both substance and procedure. We will first examine the common law rules which the CJA 2003 replaced as these have strongly influenced the law in other Commonwealth and American jurisdictions, which we will also consider as a prelude to examining the most recent reforms by the Westminster Parliament. We will also explore the approaches of these other jurisdictions to the relevance of bad character to the defendant's creditworthiness. For the purposes of this comparative discussion, then, it is convenient to preserve the categories of evidence of other misconduct disclosing propensity as part of the prosecution case (hereafter 'propensity evidence') and bearing on testimonial credibility (hereafter 'credibility evidence').

We shall discover that the propensity character evidence doctrines in all of the common law jurisdictions we examine have largely evolved in the context of sexual and physical assaults against children. They also have a common foundation in their

---

[3] In that most jurisdictions have retreated from a strict requirement of similarity, and that the term 'fact' assumes that the allegations of other misconduct have been proved.

[4] Although the common law will continue to govern good character and background evidence, and jury directions as to probative value and prejudicial effect: P Roberts and A Zuckerman *Criminal Evidence* (OUP, Oxford 2004) 502.

admissibility tests: a balancing of the potential probative value of the evidence against its apprehended prejudicial effect on the jury. This test is predicated upon the assumption that both elements can be measured with some accuracy by a trial judge, and moreover that the exercise can be conducted before that evidence is heard and tested in cross-examination, and indeed often at an early point in the trial before the prosecution has adduced the rest of its case. Appellate courts throughout the common law world have struggled to identify both the ways in which such evidence 'properly' can be used to establish guilt, and the degree of relevance required as a threshold to admissibility. As the starting premise of the common law rules of evidence is that mere relevance suffices for admissibility, weighing potential evidence in this way is a relatively unusual gatekeeping role for trial judges. Legislatures in all of the jurisdictions we examine except Canada have intervened to lower the admissibility threshold for propensity evidence, on the ground that the common law rules were withholding from juries too much highly relevant evidence. We consider empirical evidence suggesting that the judges who created the similar fact evidence rule at common law were probably justified in concerns about the moral prejudice associated with propensity reasoning, and that the moral panics about paedophiles in the community have enhanced the risk of a conviction being based upon who the defendant is, and not on proof of what he allegedly did. We conclude that it would be both unwise and unnecessary for English law to follow many American jurisdictions in adopting special rules for other misconduct evidence in child sexual abuse cases. We also have grave misgivings about the statutory reform in the CJA 2003, which elevates the chain of reasoning from propensity, forbidden by the seminal cases, to deemed relevance to an important issue between defence and prosecution, and hence is presumptively admissible.

We will also explore the other route to admission of other misconduct evidence, where the reasoning is from propensity to commit a criminal offence or other misconduct to propensity to lie under oath (although even the latter requirement that the accused must have taken the witness stand has disappeared under the CJA 2003). We conclude that the hazards of convictions based on 'bad man reasoning' rather than proof of the charge beyond reasonable doubt are as strong here as with propensity evidence, especially where the alleged previous misconduct relates to moral misconduct.

B. The Defendant's Other Misconduct as Direct Proof of Guilt: Reasoning from Propensity in Criminal Cases

1. The procedural context

Propensity evidence is often described as 'previous misconduct evidence' or 'uncharged acts/offences'. However, these terms can be misleading, because frequently the admissibility issues arise where several charges are jointly charged against the one defendant, or several defendants are charged on the same indictment, which the prosecution proposes to try at the same time. The prosecution's concern may be to provide a fuller picture of the accused's actions and motivation, or to protect vulnerable witnesses from the ordeal of testifying on more than one occasion. These charges may relate to the same victim or different victims, or to two or more defendants. One issue will be whether the evidence pertaining to one charge is admissible in relation to another charge (known as 'cross-admissibility'), on the basis that it demonstrates a pattern of behaviour by the defendant or defendants. This is why we have chosen to describe propensity evidence as '*other* misconduct evidence' when discussing the different channels to admissibility. We will analyse the difficulties posed by joinder and severance of counts when we consider the approach of each jurisdiction to other misconduct evidence.

2. Balancing probative value and potential prejudicial effect

Other misconduct evidence when tendered in the prosecution case is circumstantial evidence. Courtroom battles over its admissibility turn on identifying and weighing the inferences to which that evidence can give rise. What are these inferences intended to prove? By what process of reasoning do they prove it? How strong is the proof they provide? When is the effect of these inferences judged to be so unfair as to be excluded on the grounds of policy and the presumption of innocence?[5]

The chain of evidential inferences from other misconduct evidence which is generally prohibited at common law is that

(1) the defendant committed specific discreditable acts[6] in the past;
(2) therefore the defendant has a propensity or disposition for committing such acts;
(3) therefore the defendant acted in conformity with that disposition or propensity and committed the offences charged.

This sequence of double inferences is often referred to as 'the forbidden chain of reasoning',[7] and will be labeled 'propensity reasoning' in the discussion which follows.

Jurists have differed as to whether other misconduct evidence—assuming that it can be proved to the stipulated standard[8] to be true—is generally barred because it does not satisfy the universal precondition of admissibility, being relevance, or because it is relevant but its use would be unfair. Initially, the House of Lords was adamant that evidence of other occurrences which merely tends to deepen suspicion does not

---

[5] *R v Handy* 2002 SCC 56, [2002] 2 SCR 908 [27].

[6] Whilst the seminal case of *Makin v A-G for New South Wales* [1894] AC 57 (PC) 65 refers to 'criminal acts', all jurisdictions to be discussed have expanded this to any acts of a discreditable nature: *R v Ball* [1911] AC 47 (HL) (incestuous behaviour before it was criminalized); *R v Robertson* [1997] 1 SCR 918 (SCC) 941.   [7] *DPP v Boardman* [1975] AC 421 (HL) 453 (Lord Hailsham).

[8] In American [*US v Huddleston* 485 US 681 (USSC 1988)], Canadian [*R v Arp* [1998] 3 SCR 339 (SCC)], and New Zealand law [*R v Accused (CA 8/96)* (1996) 13 CRNZ 677 (New Zealand CA) 678–679], the standard of proof of the previous act is a balance of probabilities. In Australia, the standard of proof is beyond reasonable doubt: *R v Liddy* (2001) SASR 401 (South Australia Supreme Ct). The House of Lords has not directly considered this issue, but given that past acquittals are now admissible [*R v Z (Prior Acquittal)* [2000] 2 AC 483 (HL)] by implication the standard must be less than beyond reasonable doubt.

go to prove guilt.[9] Lord Hailsham observed in the leading case of *DPP v Boardman*: '[w]hen there is nothing to connect the accused with the particular crime except bad character or similar crimes, the probative value of the evidence is nil'.[10] However, he suggested that the evidence can *become* relevant when serving as corroboration of other evidence pointing to guilt, thus implying that it can act as a 'makeweight' for the prosecution. For Lord Simon of Glaisdale in *DPP v Kilbourne*, other misconduct evidence is inadmissible 'not because it is irrelevant, but because its logically probative significance is considered to be grossly outweighed by its prejudice to the accused, so that a fair trial is endangered if it is admitted'.[11]

The Supreme Court of Canada initially considered that evidence merely showing disposition has no real probative value,[12] but later accepted that it could be relevant.[13] The Ontario Court of Appeal has said that as a matter of 'logic and human experience', the fact that the defendant has previously sexually assaulted a child is relevant to the decision whether he has done so on the charged occasion.[14] The American courts also take the view that such evidence is highly relevant in any case, and that therein lies the difficulty.[15] The very fact that the common law courts authorize the use of propensity evidence in circumstances they regard as exceptional demonstrates that the law regards it as capable of being relevant.

The claim for the probative value of other misconduct can be tested only by reference to empirical psychological data and recidivism statistics, and here there is considerable controversy both as to the reliability of the data and the viability of their interpretation. Psychological research lends some support to the inference of guilt from propensity, suggesting that character, meaning a relatively stable set of behavioural traits, or 'characteristics', can have some predictive validity in relation to behaviour on a particular occasion.[16] Hence it should satisfy the minimal threshold of admissibility as it is relevant in that it could rationally affect the assessment of the probability of the existence of a fact in issue in the proceeding.

Bare relevance does not however measure cogency, in the sense of the strength of the predictive inference. Theories as to the indivisibility of a person's character have not been borne out by empirical studies, which have failed to find that behaviour is *straightforwardly* consistent or predictable across varying situations.[17] The most recent

---

[9] *Harris v DPP* [1952] AC 694 (HL) 708 (Viscount Simon); *Thompson v The King* [1918] AC 221 (HL) 232 (Lord Sumner).   [10] *DPP v Boardman* (n 7) 452.

[11] *DPP v Kilbourne* [1973] AC 729 (HL) 757.

[12] *Cloutier v The Queen* [1979] 2 SCR 709 (SCC) 709 (Pratt J).

[13] *Morris v The Queen* [1983] 2 SCR 190 (SCC) 203; *R v Arp* (n 8) [39] (Cory J, specifically disagreeing with Lord Hailsham's dictum in *Boardman*, above n 7).

[14] *R v B(L)* (1997) 35 OR (3d) 35 (Ontario CA) [18]–[19].

[15] *Michelson v US* (n 1) 475–476; J Myers *Evidence in Child Abuse and Neglect Cases* (3rd edn John Wiley & Sons, Inc, New York 1997) (hereafter *Myers Evidence in Child Abuse Cases*) 419–420.

[16] T Reed 'Reading Gaol Revisited: Admission of Uncharged Misconduct Evidence in Sex Offender Cases' (1993) 21 Am J Crim L 127, 154–155 contends that the recidivism rate for exhibitionists, paedophiles and adolescent child abusers in America, including estimated undetected recidivism, may be as high as 50 per cent.

[17] For useful summaries of the psychological research, see Law Commission of England and Wales *Evidence in Criminal Proceedings: Previous Misconduct of a Defendant* (Consultation Paper No 141 1996) Part VI and J Aluise 'Evidence of Prior Sexual Misconduct in Sexual Assault and Child Molestation

school of empirical psychology holds that behaviour is a function of the interaction between subjective disposition and objective circumstance; in other words, people tend to behave consistently in similar situations, but not according to broad character generalizations across diverse situations.[18] Even if an individual has a specific character trait, its existence cannot be inferred with confidence from a single observation of a person's character, nor will it necessarily assist in predicting an instance of conduct in isolation.[19] As Justice Binnie of the Supreme Court of Canada has tartly observed, people are not robotic.[20] Conversely, however, the greater the similarities between instances, and the more instances that are known, the safer it will be to infer that the same behaviour will be repeated.[21] Therefore, there seems to be a broad consensus among psychologists to support the common sense inference that past behaviour can be probative of the issue whether a defendant is likely to have acted in the way alleged by the prosecution or claimant.

There is a common perception that previous sexual misconduct, especially in relation to children, has particularly powerful probative value. The analysis accompanying the special propensity admissibility rules for sexual offences and child molestation in the US Congress claimed that previous sexual misconduct indicates that the child sex offender has the 'unusual combination of aggressive and sexual impulses that motivates the commission of such crimes, and a lack of effective inhibitions against acting on such impulses' placing him in 'a small class of depraved criminals'; what is more, the evidence of past sex crimes is probative 'on account of the inherent improbability that a person will innocently or inadvertently engage in similar, potentially criminal conduct on a number of different occasions'.[22] The same idea that a multiplicity of allegations refutes coincidence underpins the recently created rule in English common law that previous allegations which had resulted in acquittals may also be tendered as similar fact evidence—even though, obviously, those allegations have not been proved to the criminal standard to be true.[23] These conclusions are strongly disputed by some analysts of the psychological data, in particular the assertion that previous instances of sexual misconduct against other victims are more probative than, for example, previous similar conduct in a homicide, physical assault, or burglary trial.[24]

The question whether it is possible for propensity evidence to be used fairly in the adversarial trial setting is even more tricky. In a sense, all evidence which tends to prove the prosecution's case is prejudicial to the defendant. So the source of the prejudice must be found elsewhere than in its relevance. There is of course the premise of the penal system that rehabilitation of offenders is possible, suggesting that it is

---

Proceedings: Did Congress Err in Passing Federal Rules of Evidence 413, 414, and 415?' (1998) 14 J of Law & Policy 153, 167–173.

[18] M Cammack 'Using the Doctrine of Chances to Prove Actus Reus in Child Abuse and Acquaintance Rape: *People v Ewoldt* Reconsidered' (1996) 29 UC Davis LR 355, 405.

[19] *Evidence in Criminal Proceedings: Previous Misconduct of a Defendant* (n 17) [6.16]–[6.21].

[20] *R v Handy* (n 5) [35].

[21] *Evidence in Criminal Proceedings: Previous Misconduct of a Defendant* (n 17) [6.28].

[22] Analysis Statement accompanying the Violent Crime Control and Law Enforcement Act of 1994, 137 Cong. Rec. S3214 (daily ed March 13, 1991) page S3240–S3241. The latter proposition is often described by Americans as the 'doctrine of chances'. [23] *R v Z (Prior Acquittal)* (n 8).

[24] Aluise (n 17) 172.

unfair to use a defendant's past convictions against him again to prove his guilt on another charge. If propensity evidence were routinely admitted, it might encourage the police simply to 'round up the usual suspects' instead of making a proper unblinkered investigation of each particular case.[25] There is also the process value of fairness, in not requiring the defendant to fight the prosecution case on such a wide front.[26]

However, the focus of prejudice in the context of other misconduct evidence has generally been on its impact on the jury's deliberations. A useful definition of 'unfair' prejudice is 'an undue tendency to suggest decision on an improper basis, commonly, though not necessarily, an emotional one'.[27]

Whilst labels vary, academic commentators conventionally classify the perceived potential unfairness to the defendant as taking two forms.[28]

(1) *Reasoning prejudice*:[29] it is feared that jurors will wrongly interpret the propensity evidence by according it greater weight than is warranted. This argument assumes that the probative value of evidence can be calibrated quite precisely by an entirely rational trier of fact. Reasoning prejudice may occur in three ways.

(a) The jury may extrapolate from limited information about one outstanding 'good' or 'bad' quality to make a generalized judgement about that person's personality which may be invalid (sometimes called the 'halo effect').[30] So, for example, a mother's numbed response to the sudden death of her infant may be interpreted as callousness, and raise suspicions that the death was unnatural.[31]

(b) If the validity of the evidence of the extraneous misconduct is not admitted by the defendant, the jurors will have to decide whether they accept that it has been proved by the prosecution to the stipulated standard,[32] before they can then consider whether it is relevant to the offences on which they must return a verdict. This creates the risk that the trial becomes a battleground for extraneous uncharged allegations, wasting court time and distracting the jury from the task at hand. It may also be difficult for the defendant to contest the other misconduct evidence, for example if it is so vague that cross-examination could not be meaningful, but the jury might not appreciate this.[33]

---

[25] *R v Handy* (n 5) [38].
[26] ibid [25] (defendant on trial for one incident but admission of similar fact evidence meant he was confronted with eight different incidents involving someone else, of which seven were not the subject of any charge).
[27] Advisory Committee on Evidence Rules to the US Congress *Note on Federal Rule of Evidence 403*.
[28] Roberts and Zuckerman (n 4) 505–511; RC Park 'Character at the Crossroads' [1998] Hastings LJ 717.
[29] Also described by some academics as 'disposition prejudice' or 'inferential error prejudice': Park ibid, 720–721; P Mirfield 'Similar Fact Evidence of Child Sexual Abuse in English, United States, and Florida Law: a Comparative Study' (1996) 6 *J of Transnational Law and Policy* 7. The three forms of reasoning prejudice were acknowledged by Sopinka J in *R v D(LE)* [1989] 2 SCR 111 (SCC) 127–128. For a contrary view disputing the existence of undue prejudice, see M Bugaric and K Amarasekara 'The Prejudice against Similar Fact Evidence' (2001) 5 *Int J of Evidence Proof* 71.
[30] *Evidence in Criminal Proceedings: Previous Misconduct of a Defendant* (n 17) [6.19]–[6.20]; Aluise (n 17), 187.
[31] As the prosecution alleged in *R v Cannings (Angela)* [2004] EWCA Crim 01, [2004] 1 All ER 725 [42], [157].   [32] See n 8, above.
[33] *R v BFB* [2003] SASC 411, 87 SASR 278 (South Australia CA) 282.

(c) Related to the second form of reasoning prejudice, the jury may be drawn into a logical fallacy whereby, having satisfied themselves of guilt on the extraneous misconduct, they conclude that the defendant must be guilty of the offence charged, without analysing the evidence directly pertaining to that charge. In effect, the prosecution thereby proves a fact in issue by a chain of reasoning which assumes the truth of that fact.[34] This risk is particularly acute where several separate incidents are charged and tried together, resulting in a 'bootstrapping', or even circular,[35] exercise in analysis of the evidence on each count.[36] Regardless of whether the propensity evidence relates to incidents which are charged in the same indictment, the jury may assume that the defendant would succumb to that propensity whenever the opportunity arose, and ignore the possibility that someone else of like disposition may have committed the offence charged.[37] The result may be to replace the presumption of innocence with a presumption of guilt.[38]

(2) *Moral prejudice*:[39] it is feared that the jury will convict, not because they are convinced beyond all reasonable doubt that the defendant is guilty of the offences charged, but rather because he is a bad person deserving of punishment and a threat to society. The defendant would be convicted because of who he is, and not because of what he has done.

There is some empirical evidence to support the moral prejudice argument. Because the Contempt of Court Act 1981 makes research involving actual jurors illegal, the methodology adopted in the few English studies is avowedly problematic, as mock jurors were asked to evaluate evidence which they had not heard tested in court, and to make decisions which they knew had no implications for a defendant. In research for the Law Commission in 1995, Sally Lloyd-Bostock of the Centre for Socio-Legal Studies at Oxford University sought to ascertain the effect on mock juries of knowing that the defendant had a previous conviction.[40] Her finding that a similar previous conviction consistently produced significantly more guilty verdicts replicated the findings of a study conducted between 1968 and 1973 at the London School of Economics,[41] as well as Canadian[42] and American[43] studies. Significantly for the present discussion, one specific objective of the Oxford research was to ascertain whether a previous conviction for child sexual abuse creates undue prejudice where the defendant is charged with a different type of offence. Lloyd-Bostock reported:

[I]t was clear that a previous conviction for indecently assaulting a child had a very marked and consistent negative effect on perceptions of the defendant, producing the highest rate of guilty

---

[34] *Perry v The Queen* (1982–83) 150 CLR 580 (Aus HC) 612.
[35] ibid 594–595; *Evidence in Criminal Proceedings: Previous Misconduct of a Defendant* (n 17) [7.9].
[36] Mirfield labels this 'accumulation prejudice': (n 29) 15.
[37] *Pfennig v The Queen* (1995) 182 CLR 461 (Aus HC) 488.
[38] *Perry v The Queen* (n 34) 594.   [39] Or 'nullification prejudice': Park (n 28), 745.
[40] S Lloyd-Bostock 'The Effect on Juries of Hearing about the Defendant's Previous Criminal Record: a Simulation Study' [2000] Crim LR 734.
[41] W Cornish and A Sealy 'Juries and the Rules of Evidence' [1973] Crim LR 208; A Sealy and W Cornish 'Jurors and Their Verdicts' (1973) 36 MLR 496. The study is summarized in Appendix C of the *Evidence in Criminal Proceedings: Previous Misconduct of a Defendant* (n 17).
[42] V Hans and A Doob 'Section 12 of the Canada Evidence Act and the Deliberations of Simulated Juries' (1975–76) 18 Crim LQ 235.   [43] See the studies cited by S Lloyd-Bostock (n 40).

verdicts both before and after deliberation. Thus, after deliberation, 25 per cent of verdicts were 'guilty' where there was a previous conviction for indecently assaulting a child. . . . Rates were 16.7 per cent or lower for all other offences. The negative effect of a conviction for indecently assaulting a child was repeated in analyses of all the scales measuring impressions of the defendant. . . . [His] testimony was least believed, and he was perceived as most likely to commit the kind of crime he was on trial for (which in no case was indecent assault on a child), least trustworthy, most deserving of punishment, most likely to have committed crimes he has got away with, and most definitely not given a job where he would look after children; as well as most likely to tell lies in courts. . . . [A] previous conviction for indecently assaulting a child again produces a consistent and for some offences statistically significant increase in ratings of likelihood that he would commit *dissimilar* offences.[44]

This finding of the markedly higher prejudicial effect of a past conviction for child sexual abuse replicated an American simulation study which also found that participants said they would most regret a mistaken acquittal, as compared with a wrongful conviction, where the charge was child sexual abuse.[45] Other American studies involving actual jurors consistently reveal juror disgust with defendants accused of sexual misconduct.[46] In a study in Ontario of 25 actual criminal trials involving charges of child sexual abuse, 849 prospective jurors, having heard the charges, were asked whether they could set aside any preconceived biases, prejudices or partiality and render a fair and impartial verdict. An average of 36 per cent said under oath that they could not. Where the record indicated their reasons, for many the issue was not mere abhorrence of sex abuse but rather attitudes and beliefs bearing upon the presumption of innocence.[47]

Generic bias is not limited to sexual offences against children. In a 1984 empirical study of a prominent jury trial in an Ontario rural county, 50 per cent of residents, and 60 per cent of prospective jurors challenged for cause, indicated that they would hold a mother accused of killing her 14-month-old son criminally responsible even if the evidence indicated that the co-accused father was the killer, on the basis that any mother has strict responsibility for her child's welfare.[48] Ultimately the lay triers of bias found that only 38 per cent of the people summoned for jury service were impartial in the case.[49]

The Oxford study concluded that 'very thin information about a previous conviction (merely the name of the offence) is evidently sufficient to evoke quite a rich stereotype, so that a similar recent conviction, especially for child sexual abuse, is

---

[44] ibid 748–749.

[45] D Grant *From Prior Record to Current Verdict: How Character Affects the Jurors' Decisions* (University of California at Irvine 1996), discussed by S Lloyd-Bostock ibid, 738. This is sometimes called the 'regret matrix': New Zealand Law Commission *Character and Credibility* (Preliminary Paper 27 February 1997) 16, [51].   [46] Aluise (n 17), 190–193.

[47] N Vidmar 'Generic Prejudice and the Presumption of Guilt in Sex Abuse Trials' 21 (1997) *Law and Human Behavior* 4, 18. The range in the 25 trials was from 11% to 49%. One hidden motivation may have been the desire to avoid jury duty in any type of case.

[48] N Vidmar and J Melnitzer 'Juror Prejudice: an Empirical Study of a Challenge for Cause' (1986) 22 Osgoode Hall LJ 487, 503.

[49] ibid 487, 505. In Canada, when a prospective juror has been challenged for cause, the issue of bias is determined not by the trial judge but by the two jurors last selected: Criminal Code of Canada s 638.

potentially damaging for no reason that the law permits'.[50] This conclusion is disputed by Redmayne, who argues that recidivism statistics demonstrate that recent same-crime previous convictions have considerable probative value, and that the 'presumption' of the Law Commission and most commentators that previous convictions are more prejudicial than probative is based on a lack of understanding of offending patterns.[51] However, recidivism data must be treated with caution because they have not been compiled in order to test the viability of evidential rules. Furthermore, data based on re-arrest or charge rates are vulnerable both to false positives (innocent persons known to have a record may be arrested on the basis of 'round up the usual suspects', and possibly charged, then released or acquitted), and to false negatives (subsequent offences are undetected).[52] The studies do not employ a consistent methodology as to what counts as re-offending; for example, one study reporting an alarming recidivism rate of 42 per cent for child molesters counted all re-convictions for violence, even without a sexual element.[53] No clear picture emerges from the welter of American recidivism studies on sex offenders.[54] The only thing that can be stated with confidence is that the strength of each element of the probative value/prejudicial effect equation of other misconduct evidence is entirely context-driven.

3. Models for controlling the admissibility of propensity evidence

Jurisdictions using the adversarial mode of trial have tended to adopt versions of two basic models for the admissibility of evidence of a defendant's other misconduct:

(a) the '*other purposes*' model, whereby if the prosecutor can identify another purpose for which the evidence is relevant (such as opportunity, plan, motive, absence of mistake or accident), it can be admitted with a direction to the jury forbidding them from using that evidence simply to infer guilt from propensity;

(b) the '*propensity reasoning*' model, which with varying degrees of forthrightness recognizes an exception to the prohibition on admitting other misconduct evidence to prove guilt, with three approaches discernible from the caselaw:

    (i) the '*crime-specific*' approach, whereby propensity evidence is deemed to be relevant and admissible because it is considered always to have unusually high probative value in that class of crime (usually sexual offences, particularly those against children);

    (ii) the '*guided balancing*' approach, whereby trial judges in considering evidence of a previous act which is prima facie relevant to a fact in issue are given

---

[50] S Lloyd-Bostock (n 40). The Law Commission commissioned a parallel study involving 222 lay magistrates, which found that their decisions were also likely to be affected by information about previous convictions, although they were not affected to the same extent as the mock jurors by knowledge of an unrelated conviction for indecent assault on the child: Law Commission of England & Wales *Evidence of Bad Character in Criminal Proceedings* (Law Com 273, Cm 5257 October 2001), Appendix A.

[51] M Redmayne 'The Relevance of Bad Character' [2000] CLJ 684, 700, 713–714.

[52] Park (n 28), 769–771.

[53] R Hanson and others 'Long-Term Recidivism of Child Molesters' (1993) 61 *J Consulting & Clinical Psychol* 646, analysed by Aluise (n 17) 179–181.   [54] Aluise (ibid) 173–184.

a menu of factors such as similarity, proximity in time, frequency, and the strength of proof of that act[55] to consider in weighing its probative value against its potential prejudicial effect; and

(iii) the *'unguided balancing'* approach, whereby trial judges are required to balance probative value against prejudicial effect without specific statutory or appellate guidance.[56]

Diagram 18 maps some of the variations on these models as a general guide in our exploration of the approaches adopted by common law jurisdictions.

4. Propensity or 'similar fact evidence' in English criminal law before the Criminal Justice Act 2003

(a) The 'other purposes' model constructed

The seminal case developing the common law approach to propensity evidence in the Commonwealth is the notorious 1895 Privy Council case of *Makin v A-G for New South Wales.*[57] The defendant husband and wife were charged with the murder of an infant left in their care. They alleged that the child had died of natural causes. The prosecution tendered evidence of the discovery of the bodies of 12 other babies in the gardens of several houses occupied by the defendants. These infants, like the baby who was the subject of the charges, had been entrusted to the defendants by their parents upon assurances that the defendants would adopt the children, in return for payment of a sum which would have been wholly inadequate to provide more than short-term care. In short, the defendants were operating a 'baby farm'. This evidence, the prosecution claimed, helped establish the *actus reus* of the murder. Commentators have often pointed out that the relevance of the evidence involved statistical improbability reasoning—that so many infants had died of natural causes whilst in the defendants' care—rather than true propensity reasoning. In a celebrated, but ultimately ambiguous, *dictum*, Herschell LC stated:

It is undoubtedly not competent for the prosecution to adduce evidence tending to shew that the accused has been guilty of criminal acts other than those covered by the indictment, for the purpose of leading to the conclusion that the accused is a person likely from his criminal conduct or character to have committed the offence for which he is being tried. On the other hand, the mere fact that the evidence adduced tends to shew the commission of other crimes does not render it inadmissible if it be relevant to an issue before the jury, and it may be so relevant if it bears upon the question whether the acts alleged to constitute the crime charged in the indictment were designed or accidental, or to rebut a defence which would otherwise be open to the accused. The statement of these general principles is easy, but it is obvious that it may often be very difficult to draw the line and to decide whether a particular piece of evidence is on the one side or the other.[58]

The Privy Council found that the evidence was relevant and admissible.

---

[55] Practically speaking, this is only in issue where the alleged past act did not result in a criminal conviction.

[56] A modification of Park's 'structured balancing' and 'open balancing' for the third and fourth models: Park (n 28), 775–758.   [57] *Makin v A-G for New South Wales* (n 6).

[58] ibid 65.

Other Misconduct Evidence to Guilt

PV = probative value relating to the permitted purpose
PE = prejudicial effect

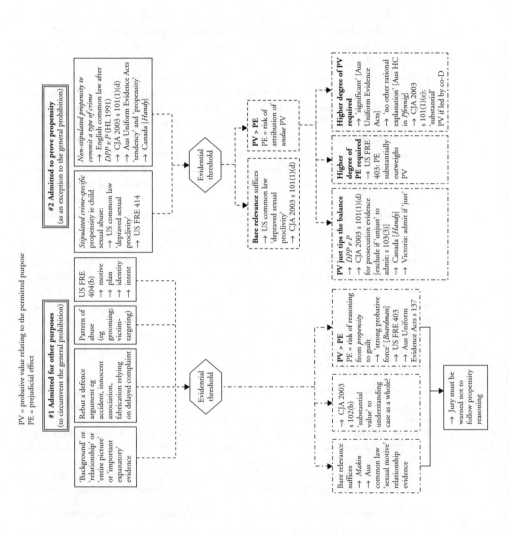

Makin established a dichotomy which has been judicially described as 'an uneasy mixture of logic, common sense and expediency':[59] it is reasoning from (bad) disposition which is forbidden; if however the prosecution can establish another purpose for which the evidence is relevant, and that purpose falls within an established category of exception, then it is admissible. Under the first limb, the exclusionary rule bites only on evidence that is (a) otherwise relevant, (b) is relevant only through the forbidden chain of reasoning from propensity to guilt, and (c) is discreditable to the accused. One of the most difficult problems of logic created by Lord Herschell's dual principles is their interplay. If the second limb admits all evidence 'relevant to an issue before the jury', does that not effectively deprive the exclusionary principle of all meaning, since irrelevant evidence is inadmissible in any event? Furthermore, the relevance of the other misconduct evidence in the famous cases of *Straffen*[60] (three child murders) and *Thompson*[61] (possession of child pornography and powder puffs to facilitate seduction of young boys) could really only be explained on the basis of reasoning from propensity to commit crimes against children. Note also that the emphasis was on the *type* of relevance, not the *degree* of relevance,[62] and that the Privy Council did not refer to the effect, prejudicial or otherwise, of such evidence on the jury.

'Prejudicial effect' entered the lexicon of the English similar fact evidence rule in 1974, in *DPP v Boardman*,[63] again in the context of offences against children. The appellant was the headmaster of a school which largely catered for boys up to age 19 from foreign countries. He was charged with two counts of incitement and buggery with two pupils aged 16 and 17. There was no suggestion that the complainants had collaborated in concocting a story. Each described the defendant coming into the dormitory late at night and inviting him to his sitting room, where he induced the boy to play the active part in buggery, which the courts in the case considered to be an unusual role for a homosexual paedophile. All levels of court hearing the case ruled that the evidence of the two complainants was cross-admissible. Lord Hailsham explained the first limb of *Makin* as follows:

> When there is some evidence connecting the accused with the crime, in the eyes of most people, guilt of similar offences in the past might well be considered to have probative value. ...Nonetheless, in the absence of a statutory provision to the contrary, the evidence is to be excluded under the first rule in *Makin* ...because its prejudicial effect may be more powerful than its probative effect, and thus endanger a fair trial because it tends to undermine the integrity of the presumption of innocence and the burden of proof. In other words, it is a rule of English law which has its roots in policy, and by which, in Lord du Parcq's phrase in *Noor Mohamed v The King* [1949] A.C. 182, 194, logicians would not be bound.[64]

Lord Hailsham then reiterated the operation of the second limb of *Makin*:

> It is perhaps helpful to remind oneself that what is *not* to be admitted is a chain of reasoning and not necessarily a state of facts. If the inadmissible chain of reasoning is the *only* purpose

---

[59] *R v Brooks* (1991) 92 Cr App R 36 (CA) 39.   [60] *R v Straffen* [1952] 2 QB 911 (CA).

[61] *Thompson v The King* (n 9).

[62] *R v B(CR)* [1990] 1 SCR 717 (SCC) [46] (McLachlin J); L Hoffmann 'Similar Facts after *Boardman*' (1975) 91 LQR 193, 200.   [63] *DPP v Boardman* (n 7).

[64] ibid 451.

for which the evidence is adduced as a matter of law, the evidence itself is not admissible. If there is some other relevant, probative purpose than for the forbidden type of reasoning, the evidence is admitted, but should be made subject to a warning from the judge that the jury must eschew the forbidden reasoning. The judge also has a discretion, not as a matter of law but as a matter of good practice, to exclude evidence whose prejudicial effect, though the evidence be technically admissible on the decided cases, may be so great in the particular circumstances as to outweigh its probative value to the extent that a verdict of guilty might be considered unsafe or unsatisfactory if ensuing. ...In all these cases it is for the judge to ensure as a matter of law in the first place, and as a matter of discretion where the matter is free, that a properly instructed jury, applying their minds to the facts, can come to the conclusion that they are satisfied so that they are sure that to treat the matter as pure coincidence by reason of the 'nexus,' 'pattern,' 'system,' 'striking resemblances' or whatever phrase is used is 'an affront to common sense' [*Reg. v. Kilbourne* [1973] A.C. 729, per Lord Simon of Glaisdale, at p. 759]. In this the ordinary rules of logic and common sense prevail... (emphasis in original).[65]

By adjusting the focus to the probative value of the other misconduct evidence *Boardman* naturally raised the question as to the degree of relevance required. Perhaps one of the most pernicious interpretations of the second limb of *Makin* was the assumption that bare relevance to an issue before the jury was sufficient to render the similar fact evidence admissible. *Boardman* placed the requisite weight of the evidence on a much higher scale: what is required is a 'strong degree of probative force',[66] being 'such a close striking similarity or such an underlying unity'[67] so as to trigger the probability reasoning which it would be an affront to common sense to prohibit.

(i) One approved purpose: 'background' evidence

One of the most potent examples of the 'other purposes' route to admission is so-called 'background evidence',[68] which is intrinsic to the case and constitutes direct evidence pertaining to the offence charged. It is admitted because the account pertaining to the charges would be incomplete or incoherent if the jury was required to view events and the participants in total isolation from their history:

This evidence may disclose a course of events leading up to the first charged incident, which enables the jury to understand that the incident did not, as it were, 'come out of the blue'. The evidence will also sometimes explain how the victim might have come to submit to the acts the subject of the first charge. Without the evidence, it would probably seem incredible to the jury that the victim would have submitted to what would seem an isolated act, and likewise it might seem incredible to the jury that the accused would suddenly have committed the first crime charged. The evidence of uncharged acts may also disclose a series of incidents that make it believable or understandable that the victim might not have complained about the incidents charged until much later in the piece, if at all. They may show a pattern of behaviour under which the accused has achieved the submission of the victim. The evidence may establish a pattern of guilt on the part of the child, that could also explain the submission and silence of the child.[69]

---

[65] ibid 453–454.　　[66] ibid 444 (Lord Wilberforce).　　[67] ibid 441 (Lord Morris).

[68] Known to American lawyers as the 'entire picture doctrine' [eg *State v Kristich* 359 P 2d 1106 (Oregon SC 1961)], discussed below section B.5(a), and to Australian lawyers as 'relationship evidence' [*Pfennig v The Queen* (n 37)], discussed below section B.6(a). For an analysis of the prejudicial effect of background evidence, see P Lewis *Delayed Prosecution for Childhood Sexual Abuse* (OUP, Oxford 2006) 183–186.

[69] *R v Nieterink* [1999] SASC 560, 76 SASR 56 (South Australia Supreme Ct) 65 (Doyle CJ).

A history of domestic violence and oppression may be necessary in order to understand why a complainant did not report abuse earlier or did not leave the abusive environment, or why the defendant 'snapped' and attacked her abuser.[70] Such evidence is admissible without being required to satisfy the propensity evidence rules, and notwithstanding that the whole account may involve including evidence of an offence with which the defendant is not charged.[71]

A graphic example is provided by *R v M(T) and others*,[72] which concerned systemic sexual abuse across three generations of the same family. The prosecution's case was that the defendant had been groomed into the family web of abuse. It was permitted to adduce evidence that the defendant had been encouraged by his father from a young age to act as a spectator when his two sisters were raped and buggered, and was later forced to take part. This provided necessary background to the Crown's contention that M(T) at age 16 started abusing his youngest sister, secure in the knowledge that he was not the only abuser and that she could not complain to her parents.

While the Court of Appeal has been vigilant that background evidence is not used as a vehicle for smuggling in otherwise inadmissible evidence for less than adequate reasons,[73] the distinction between propensity and background evidence may be difficult to discern in a particular case.[74] Thus in cases where a child has died and where accident or identity is in issue, evidence may be admitted of previous suspicious injuries or of earlier incidents of bad temper exhibited by the defendant in responding to the child, as background evidence of motive and attitude;[75] however, evidence of the defendant's violence against inanimate objects has been viewed as extremely prejudicial and going only to propensity for violence, and so inadmissible.[76]

(b) The 'other purposes' model dismantled

The five speeches in *Boardman* did not yield a clear principle. Lords Hailsham and Salmon were firm that the chain of reasoning from propensity to guilt was still forbidden.[77] However, the other three Law Lords appeared to accept that a jury could properly infer guilt from evidence of disposition where the high and specific relevance of that evidence warranted such an inference.[78] Notwithstanding this ambiguity, the lower courts continued to adhere to what Mirfield derided as the 'slot machine' or 'laundry list' approach[79] whereby the admissibility of other misconduct evidence was entirely dependent upon the prosecution strategy in targeting a purpose other than direct reasoning from propensity.

The central issue in *DPP v P*[80] was whether 'striking similarities' were essential to admissibility, as *Boardman* had appeared to require. The defendant in that case was

---

[70] *R v Diana Butler* [1999] Crim LR 835 (CA); *R v Underwood* [1999] Crim LR 227 (CA); *R v F(DS)* (1999) 169 DLR (4th) 639 (Ontario CA).　　[71] *R v Pettman* (unreported) 2 May 1985 (CA).
[72] *R v M(T) and others* [2000] 1 WLR 421 (CA).
[73] *R v Dolan* [2002] EWCA Crim 1859 [23].　　[74] Roberts and Zuckerman (n 4) 528–531.
[75] *R v Fulcher* [1995] 2 Cr App R 251 (CA).　　[76] *R v Dolan* (n 73) [23], [27].
[77] *DPP v Boardman* (n 7) 453 (Lord Hailsham), 462 (Lord Salmon).
[78] ibid 439–441 (Lord Morris), 457–458 (Lord Cross); 442–444 (Lord Wilberforce). See also McLachlin J in *R v B(CR)* (n 62) [49].　　[79] Mirfield (n 29), 10.
[80] *DPP v P* [1991] 2 AC 443 (HL).

convicted on four counts of rape and four counts of incest in respect of each of his two daughters. Lord Mackay of Clashfern LC said:

When a question of the kind raised in this case arises …the judge must first decide whether there is material upon which the jury would be entitled to conclude that the evidence of one victim, about what occurred to that victim, is so related to the evidence given by another victim, about what happened to that other victim, that the evidence of the first victim provides strong enough support for the evidence of the second victim to make it just to admit it notwithstanding the prejudicial effect of admitting the evidence. This relationship, from which support is derived, may take many forms and while these forms may include 'striking similarity' in the manner in which the crime is committed, consisting of unusual characteristics in its execution the necessary relationship is by no means confined to such circumstances. Relationships in time and circumstances other than these may well be important relationships in this connection. Where the identity of the perpetrator is in issue, and evidence of this kind is important in that connection, obviously something in the nature of what has been called in the course of the argument a signature or other special feature will be necessary. To transpose this requirement to other situations where the question is whether a crime has been committed, rather than who did commit it, is to impose an unnecessary and improper restriction upon the application of the principle.[81]

Boardman had also stimulated a lively academic debate as to the structure of the similar fact rule it propounded: was it a narrow and absolute prohibition of a chain of reasoning directly from propensity, or was it a broad prohibition with specific exceptions permitting reasoning from propensity? This in turn raised questions about the role of judicial discretion to exclude probative propensity evidence on the basis of apprehended prejudicial effect.[82] *DPP v P* scythed through the analytical tangle by propounding a single test of admissibility based overtly on the underlying policy considerations:

[T]he essential feature of evidence which is to be admitted is that its probative force in support of the allegation that an accused person committed a crime is sufficiently great to make it just to admit the evidence, notwithstanding that it is prejudicial to the accused in tending to show that he was guilty of another crime. Such probative force may be derived from striking similarities in the evidence about the manner in which the crime was committed … But restricting the circumstances in which there is sufficient probative force to overcome prejudice of evidence relating to another crime to cases in which there is some striking similarity between them is to restrict the operation of the principle in a way which gives too much effect to a particular manner of stating it, and is not justified in principle. Once the principle is recognised, that what has to be assessed is the probative force of the evidence in question, the infinite variety of circumstances in which the question arises, demonstrates that there is no single manner in

---

[81] ibid 462.

[82] Hoffmann (n 62); T Allan 'Similar Fact Evidence and Disposition: Law, Discretion and Admissibility' (1985) 48 MLR 253; P Mirfield 'Similar Facts—*Makin* out?' (1987) 46 CLJ 83. A similar debate occurred in the US: J Stone 'The Role of Exclusion of Similar Fact Evidence: England' (1933) 46 Harvard LR 954 and J Stone 'The Role of Exclusion of Similar Fact Evidence: America' (1938) 51 Harvard LR 988; D De La Paz 'Sacrificing the Whole Truth: Florida's Deteriorating Admissibility of Similar Fact Evidence in Cases of Child Sexual Abuse' (1999) 15 *New York Law School J of Human Rights* 449.

which this can be achieved. Whether the evidence has sufficient probative value to outweigh its prejudicial effect must in each case be a question of degree.[83]

Gone is the 'strong probative force' language of *Boardman*, apparently replaced by a diluted[84] test which can be satisfied merely by tipping the balance in favour of probative value. The House of Lords thus definitively abandoned the 'other purposes' model in favour of the 'unguided balancing' variation of the propensity reasoning model. This had the beneficial effect of rendering obsolete these doctrinal disputes which had engendered confusion in the lower courts. Nevertheless, the decision was criticized as opening 'the dyke holding back the seas of prejudice'.[85]

For similar fact evidence to be admitted in cases of child sexual abuse, then, it was no longer necessary for the prosecution to look for evidence beyond what Lord Lane CJ described as the 'paederast's or the incestuous father's stock in trade' before one victim's evidence could be properly admitted upon the trial of another.[86] However, the Court of Appeal held in a subsequent case involving indecent assaults against two adolescent girls that it is still necessary to invoke some identifiable common feature constituting a significant connection, focusing on the similarity of the allegations rather than the events described, such as the engineering of the opportunity, nature of the interference, nature of the assault or breach of trust.[87]

Even the *obiter dictum* in *DPP v P* that striking similarity or a 'signature' may be required where identity is in issue has fallen by the wayside in subsequent cases.[88] The House of Lords controversially has expanded the scope of the evidence which can be tendered by the prosecution by holding that a previous acquittal of another offence might also be relevant and admissible under the propensity reasoning model, rejecting the objection that this would constitute a collateral attack on the previous verdict.[89]

(c) Probative value, collusion and unconscious contamination

The probative value of other narratives of abuse lies in the improbability that two liars could concoct similar but false stories independently of one another.[90] However, the risk of collusion between complainants in sexual abuse cases, whether deliberate or innocent, is real. How does it affect the admissibility of propensity evidence under the new probative value/prejudicial effect regime?

In *DPP v P*, the House assumed that there had been no collusion in ruling that the evidence of the young children in the family should be cross-admissible. This assumption was tested in the House of Lords in 1995 in *R v H*.[91] The defendant was charged in 1992 with sexual offences alleged to have been committed against his

---

[83] *DPP v P* (n 80) 460–461.　　　[84] *R v John Allen Venn* [2003] EWCA 236 [43] (Potter LJ).

[85] C Tapper 'The Probative Force of Similar Fact Evidence' (1991) 108 LQR 26, 30.

[86] *DPP v P* (n 80) 461 (quoted by Lord Mackay of Clashfern).

[87] *R v John Allen Venn* (n 84) [35]–[36].　　　[88] *R v John W* [1998] 2 Cr App R 289 (CA).

[89] *R v Z (Prior Acquittal)* (n 8), qualifying *Sambasivum v Public Prosecutor, Federation of Malaya* [1950] AC 458 (PC) 479.

[90] *DPP v Boardman* (n 7) 461 (Lord Cross); *R v Hoch* [1988] 165 CLR 292 (Aus HC) 295–296.

[91] *R v H* [1995] 2 AC 596 (HL).

adopted daughter, S, and stepdaughter, C, between 1987 and 1989, starting when they were 9 and 14 respectively. The allegations were first made to the police after S, then aged 14, spoke to the defendant's wife; C initially told S that nothing had happened to her but she then reported an indecent assault. At trial, it was common ground that there was a risk that the girls had collaborated and concocted a false story against their father. The defence on appeal submitted that where there is a real risk of contamination, similar fact evidence is not logically probative, and should be neither admissible nor corroborative.

Lord Mackay LC for a unanimous panel ruled that where the defence applies to exclude evidence on the basis of actual or unconscious collusion, the trial judge should approach the question of admissibility on the basis that the similar facts alleged are true, and then apply the probative value/prejudicial effect balancing test. In a very exceptional case the trial judge might have to hold a *voir dire* to hear the evidence on a preliminary basis. The default rule is that it is for the jury to decide whether they are satisfied that the evidence can be relied upon as free from collusion.[92] If the evidence is admitted and it then emerges in the trial proper that no reasonable jury could accept the evidence as free from collusion, the judge should direct the jury that it cannot be relied upon for any purpose adverse to the defence. Lord Mustill pointed out that if the defence argument that the prosecution must first rule out the possibility of collusion was accepted, complainants in every case would be subjected to the ordeal of a 'first inquisition' in a *voir dire*, only to have to undergo it again in the presence of the jury if their evidence is, 'against all the odds', admitted. His Lordship went on:

> ... the possibility of innocent infection is one amongst many factors which the jury will have to take into account; but to treat it as a unique 'threshold issue' loads the scales unfairly against the prosecution, and hence against the interests of those who cannot protect themselves. The risk to an innocent defendant of false inferences drawn from multiple allegations must never be underestimated, but some proportion is essential.[93]

Although *R v H* can be viewed as a straightforward application of the fundamental principle that matters of a witness's credibility are for the jury, its logic is arguably flawed. Since the probative value of other misconduct evidence depends upon the improbability of two witnesses *independently* making similar false allegations, to direct the trial judge to assume that the allegations are true in weighing its probative value for the purposes of admissibility makes the entire filtering exercise meaningless.[94] For this reason, the Supreme Court of Canada[95] and the Australian High Court[96] do not follow the House of Lords' approach to collusion.

---

[92] ibid 617. The jury must also be warned about the possibility of innocent contamination: *R v Alan V* [2003] EWCA Crim 3641 [27].   [93] ibid 617.

[94] C Tapper 'Similar Fact Evidence, Memorandum 64' (Submitted to the Home Affairs Select Committee of the House of Commons, Westminster: The Conduct of Investigations into Past Cases of Abuse in Children's Homes 2002) [7]–[11]; P Lewis 'Similar Facts and Similar Allegations in Delayed Criminal Prosecutions of Childhood Sexual Abuse' [2004] Crim LR 39, 41–43.

[95] *R v Handy* (n 5) [112], discussed below, section B.8.

[96] *R v Hoch* (n 90) discussed below, section B.6(d).

(d) Propensity evidence in child physical abuse and homicide

Whilst propensity evidence has acquired the highest profile for child sexual abuse, the recent English cases involving allegations of Munchhausen's syndrome by proxy where successive deaths of young infants have occurred in the same family have shown that it can be as powerful, and potentially as hazardous, in the context of physical abuse and suspicious deaths. Most significant in this context is the criminal trial of Angela Cannings which we discuss in detail in Chapter 11 concerning expert evidence.[97] Although the charges pertained to the death of her second and third children, the Court of Appeal had ordered that evidence of all three deaths, as well as each Acute Life-threatening Event (ALTE) suffered by the babies, would be cross-admissible in relation to each count. On appeal from the subsequent guilty verdicts, the Court of Appeal (differently constituted) defended this ruling on the basis that:

there could be no denying that the death of three apparently healthy babies in infancy while in the sole care of their mother was, and remains, very rare, rightly giving rise to suspicion and concern and requiring the most exigent investigation. Given the overwhelming consensus of medical evidence, it would indeed have been an affront to common sense to treat the deaths of the three children and the ALTEs as isolated incidents, completely compartmentalised from each other. All of the available relevant evidence had to be examined as a whole.[98]

However, Judge LJ for a unanimous court stressed the importance when dealing with the similar fact evidence of identifying the correct starting point for its analysis: they rejected the approach that 'lightning does not strike three times in the same place'[99] as a hidden trap, in favour of taking as the starting point that the deaths were natural:

If, for example, at post mortem it was positively established that Matthew's [the third baby's] death had resulted from natural causes, the situation reverted to precisely where it stood before he died. The concerns which would have arisen as a result of his death—as the third in the sequence—would have been dissipated. There would have been a positive innocent explanation for the death, which would no longer be a SIDS,[100] and might help to confirm that the earlier deaths were indeed natural deaths. Equally, if there were unequivocal evidence that one of these deaths, or even one of the ALTEs, had resulted from deliberate infliction of harm by the appellant, that would be likely to throw considerable light on the question whether the other deaths, or ALTEs, resulted from natural or unnatural causes. If, after full investigation, the deaths, or ALTEs, continued to be unexplained, and there was nothing to demonstrate that one or other incident had resulted from the deliberate infliction of harm, so far as the criminal process was concerned, the deaths continued properly to be regarded as SIDS, or more accurately, could not properly be treated as resulting from unlawful violence.[101]

Judge LJ concluded that 'whether there are one, two or even three deaths, the exclusion of currently known natural classes of infant death does not establish that the death or deaths resulted from deliberate infliction of harm'.[102] It is important to note, however, that had the jury been instructed to take this starting point, and had it still returned

---

[97] Discussed below, Chapter 11 section B.　　[98] *R v Cannings (Angela)* (n 31) [12].
[99] ibid [11].
[100] Sudden Infant Death Syndrome, or more colloquially 'cot death' or 'crib death'.
[101] *R v Cannings (Angela)* (n 31) [12].　　[102] ibid [13].

a guilty verdict, it would have been impregnable, at least on the issue of the similar fact evidence, regardless of whether they complied with that direction.

(e) *Joinder and severance of counts*

The issue of whether charges relating to different events can be tried in the same trial is determined under Rule 9 of the Indictment Rules 1971,[103] which provides that charges for any offence may be joined on the same indictment 'if those charges are founded on the same facts, or form or are part of a series of offences of the same or a similar character'. This threshold test is determined on the basis of the evidence the prosecution proposes to call. In *Ludlow v Metropolitan Police Commissioner*[104] the House of Lords interpreted 'same or similar character' as meaning that there must be a nexus between the offences, requiring a similarity both in law and in the facts constituting the offences; merely a slight similarity suffices for the latter, and there is a presumption that such charges will be tried together.[105] Two charges may constitute a series.[106]

In cases of alleged child sexual abuse, the events to which the charges relate may be widely separated in time, whether because the alleged abuser has waited for each child within a family to mature to a particular age, or, in the case of extra-familial abuse, because the pattern of allegations made to the police do not establish a historical continuum. In *R v O'Brien*,[107] the headmaster of a preparatory school was charged on the same indictment with sexually assaulting boys aged 11 to 12 in his care, two in the 1970s and two in the 1990s. The issue was whether these widely separated counts constituted a 'series'. The Court of Appeal held that the longer the gap, the clearer must be the nexus establishing the relationship between the events. Given the fact that over 850 former pupils had been contacted by the police, and 600 had been individually interviewed, but only these 4 made complaints, an historical continuum between the 1970s and 1990s could not be made out, and the counts should be severed for the retrial.[108] In contrast, allegations against a scoutmaster of indecent assaults against four boys between 1989 and 2002 were held to be properly joined because the gaps in time were not as long, and there were similarities in the boys' accounts of genital fondling in their tents on expeditions.[109] If the testimony of each complainant is viewed as capable of corroborating the other's, such as similar grooming techniques, that can constitute a sufficient nexus to form a series, notwithstanding a gap of several years.[110]

Rule 5(3) confers on the trial judge a residual discretion to sever counts satisfying the threshold nexus test, if the accused may be 'prejudiced or embarrassed in his defence' by a single trial, or if for any other reason separate trials are desirable. In *Ludlow*, the Law Lords held that there is no duty on the trial judge to direct separate

---

[103] Indictments Act 1915, Indictment Rules 1971 Rule 9.

[104] *Ludlow v Metropolitan Police Commissioner* [1971] AC 29 (HL).   [105] ibid 41.

[106] ibid; *R v Kray* [1970] 1 QB 125 (CA) 130.   [107] *R v O'Brien* [2000] Crim LR 863 (CA).

[108] ibid [44], [49]–[50].

[109] *Attorney General's Reference (No 33 of 2003) sub nom R v David Scrivener* [2004] EWCA Crim 2093 (CA).   [110] *R v Paul Baird* (1992) 97 Cr App R 308 (CA) 317.

trials unless there is some special feature of the case which would make a joint trial of the separate counts prejudicial or embarrassing to the accused and additionally, separate trials are required in the interests of justice.[111]

What if the trial judge has ruled that the counts are not cross-admissible? The cases are clear that this does not necessarily mean that the sets of alleged offences could not constitute a series.[112] However, in *Boardman*[113] two of the Law Lords stated that in a case where sexual assault allegations are made by more than one child and the counts are not cross-admissible, normally the trial judge should invoke the discretionary power to sever the counts, on the basis that the jury should not be expected to perform the 'mental gymnastics' of segregating the evidence on one count from their consideration of the evidence on another count.[114] Lord Cross cautioned that so long as there is a similar fact evidence rule, 'the courts ought to strive to give effect to it loyally and not, while paying lipservice to it, in effect let in the inadmissible evidence by trying all the charges together.'[115]

In practice the Court of Appeal has refused to interfere with the decision of a trial judge not to order a severance where there was no cross-admissibility, even where the evidence was arguably very prejudicial.[116] However, for a time the Court of Appeal appeared to apply a different rule in cases of child sexual abuse and readily severed counts, although there were apparently conflicting *dicta*.[117] In 1996 in *Christou*, the House of Lords ruled that there is no special category for sex offences. To make one would fetter the statutory discretion under Rule 5(3), and there would be inescapable difficulties in determining to which cases of sexual offences the fetter should apply. For example if it were limited to sexual abuse of children, then the court would have to grapple with age limits and whether it applied to adults complaining of childhood abuse.[118] The Lord Chief Justice held that:

> . . . the essential criterion is the achievement of a fair resolution of the issues. That requires fairness to the accused but also to the prosecution and those involved in it. Some, but by no means an exhaustive list, of the factors which may need to be considered are:— how discrete or inter-related are the facts giving rise to the counts; the impact of ordering two or more trials on the defendant and his family, on the victims and their families, on press publicity; and importantly, whether directions the judge can give to the jury will suffice to secure a fair trial if the counts are tried together. In regard to that last factor, jury trials are conducted on the basis that the judge's directions of law are to be applied faithfully.[119]

---

[111] *Ludlow v Metropolitan Police Commissioner* (n 104) 41.

[112] *R v Paul Baird* (n 110) 314.   [113] *DPP v Boardman* (n 7).

[114] ibid 459 (Lord Cross), 442 (Lord Wilberforce). *R v D(CR)* [2003] EWCA Crim 2424, [2005] Crim LR 163 is an example where convictions for sexual abuse of two stepdaughters were quashed because the trial judge had not directed the jury to perform these 'mental gymnastics'.

[115] *DPP v Boardman* (n 7) 421, citing *R v Sims* [1946] KB 531 (CA) 536.

[116] *Evidence in Criminal Proceedings: Previous Misconduct of a Defendant* (n 17) [2.97].

[117] *R v Brooks* (n 59) (no justification for joining incest counts relating to accused's three daughters once the trial judge had ruled similar fact evidence was not involved); *R v Paul Baird* (n 110) (sexual counts against two boys who did not know one another, separated by nine years, were properly joined due to a similar grooming pattern).   [118] *R v Christou* [1997] AC 117 (HL) 128–129.

[119] ibid 129.

However, where the defendants are not alleged to have participated in each other's offending in relation to the same children, and one has a previous conviction for incest, the counts should be severed and tried separately.[120]

Two reports for the Government in 1997 and 1998 concluded that severance of counts was in fact being ordered too frequently in child sexual abuse cases,[121] and the issue remains under consideration by the Home Office and the Lord Chancellor's Department.[122]

(f) Propensity evidence and institutional abuse

The issue of collusion is particularly acute in relation to historic complaints of abuse in an institutional setting.[123] Campaigners for those accused of systematic physical and sexual abuse in children's residential homes in England and Wales have argued that the police investigating such complaints have 'trawled'[124] for former residents who have been enticed to make false allegations by the prospect of recovering substantial compensation through the tort system and the Criminal Injuries Compensation Scheme.

The all-party Home Affairs Select Committee of the House of Commons concluded in 2002 that a new genre of miscarriages of justice has arisen from the 'over-enthusiastic pursuit' of allegations of child abuse.[125] The Select Committee recommended that the law of similar fact evidence be reformed to require 'striking similarity' in historical child abuse cases before multi-count and multi-complainant cases could be tried together, with a presumption that counts where the evidence is not cross-admissible should be severed.[126] In stark contrast, Sir William Utting in his report on safeguards for children living away from home recommended that counts on an indictment be severed only if requested by the prosecution. His rationale was that if the defence successfully undermines the credibility of a key witness in the first case to be tried, the other cases might not proceed, allowing 'those who are guilty to go free'.[127] Given that it is the CPS which decides in the first instance which counts appear together on an indictment, it is rather odd to recommend that only the CPS have standing to apply for severance.

The Government in its reply strongly criticized as unsubstantiated the Select Committee's assumptions that a large number of miscarriages of justice had occurred, and

---

[120] *R v Bratley* [2004] EWCA Crim 1254 [39], [43].

[121] Sir William Utting *People Like Us: The Report of the Review of the Safeguards For Children Living Away From Home* (HMSO, 1997) Chapter 20; Home Office *Speaking Up for Justice: Report of the Interdepartmental Working Group on the Treatment of Vulnerable or Intimidated Witnesses in the Criminal Justice System* (June 1998) hereafter *Speaking up for Justice* [9.19]–[9.24] and Recommendation 56.

[122] Home Office *Action for Justice: Implementing the Speaking Up for Justice report on vulnerable or intimidated witnesses in the criminal justice system in England and Wales* (March 1999), response to Recommendation 56.   [123] Lewis *Delayed Prosecution for Childhood Sexual Abuse* (n 68) 186–192.

[124] The Government and the Association of Chief Police Officers prefer the less pejorative term 'dip sampling': *Report of the House of Commons Home Affairs Committee: The Conduct of Investigations into Past Cases of Abuse in Children's Homes* (Fourth Report of Session 2001–2002, HC 836-I 31 October 2002) [25].   [125] ibid [2].

[126] ibid [93]–[97].   [127] Sir William Utting *People Like Us* (n 121) 193, [20.22].

that civil compensation claims have driven false allegations to prosecuting authorities.[128] It rejected the Committee's recommendations, arguing that the *Boardman* rule had excluded too much evidence which could assist the jury in assessing the cogency of a witness's account. In the Government's view, a presumption in favour of severance would not add anything to the current rules which are centred on fairness. No special evidential rules should be developed for historical child abuse cases.[129] In our submission this must be right. There would be an obvious difficulty of defining what constitutes 'historical' cases, given the common phenomenon of delayed complaint in sexual abuse cases. The issues surrounding allegedly stale evidence and multiple allegations are not unique to child sexual abuse; devising specially high (or low) evidential thresholds for one class of offences requires powerful justification which, thus far at least, has not been forthcoming.

(g) *Propensity to comply with the law: good character evidence*

Paradoxically, English jurors are invited to reason directly from a lack of known propensity to innocence by the so-called 'good character direction' to which a defendant is entitled if there is no evidence of previous convictions or uncharged misconduct,[130] or the convictions are spent.[131] The asymmetry in treatment is highlighted where one defendant has no previous convictions, and so benefits from the good character direction, whereas his co-defendant with a criminal past does not,[132] which may cause the jury to draw inferences which may be erroneous. Propensity evidence may be introduced for the sake of a co-defendant's defence,[133] in which case the Crown may also benefit from that evidence, which might not have been admitted at the behest of the prosecution.

Our review of the English common law governing propensity evidence has shown that *DPP v P* and subsequent cases significantly diluted[134] the constraints on the common law similar fact evidence doctrine, raising the question why further reform was thought necessary. The Law Commission in 1996 contended that there were still gaps left by *Boardman* and *DPP v P*,[135] but these gaps could be (and to some extent were[136]) filled in by subsequent cases directly raising those points. The Law Commission was correct in stating that the caselaw was still not clear on the essential point: when is it just to admit evidence of bad character in the prosecution case?[137] While this issue of principle had not greatly troubled the pragmatic common law courts, the open texture of the unstructured balancing exercise and the greater latitude

---

[128] *The Conduct of Investigations into Past Cases of Abuse in Children's Homes: the Government Reply to the Fourth Report from the Home Affairs Select Committee Session 2001–2002 HC 836* Cm 5799, April 2003 [10]–[13], [68].   [129] ibid [55]–[58].

[130] *R v Vye; Wise; Stevenson* (1993) 97 Cr App R 134 (CA); *R v Aziz* [1996] 1 AC 41 (HL); Judicial Studies Board *Crown Court Bench Book* (2004) Ch III Evidence Direction 23.

[131] *Speaking Up for Justice*; Judicial Studies Board *Crown Court Bench Book* (2004) Ch III Evidence, Direction 23, note 3.   [132] *R v Aziz* (n 130).

[133] *Lowery v The Queen* [1974] AC 85 (PC); *R v Randall* [2003] UKHL 69, [2004] 1 WLR 56.

[134] *R v John Allen Venn* (n 84) [43].

[135] *Evidence in Criminal Proceedings: Previous Misconduct of a Defendant* (n 17) 168, [10.21].

[136] eg whether a 'signature' is required in identity cases: *R v John W* (n 88) (no), and whether judges have any residual discretion after the rule in *DPP v P* had been applied: *R v John Allen Venn* (n 84) (no).

[137] *Evidence in Criminal Proceedings: Previous Misconduct of a Defendant* (n 17) 168, [10.21].

it gave to trial judges in assessing whether a combination of features, not striking in themselves, amounted to a sufficient connection,[138] still made it very difficult for those involved in investigating, prosecuting and defending a case to predict whether the other misconduct evidence would be admissible.

5. Propensity evidence in American criminal law

One American appellate court has observed that 'the history of evidentiary rules regarding a criminal defendant's sexual propensity is ambiguous at best, particularly with regard to sexual abuse of children'.[139] The fundamental common law rule excluding propensity evidence in both criminal and civil proceedings is expressed in the United States Federal Evidence Rule 404(a): 'evidence of a person's character or trait of character is not admissible for the purpose of proving action in conformity therewith on a particular occasion'. There are specific exceptions for evidence considered directly to implicate the defendant in the crime. All of these exceptions are qualified in Federal law (in Rule 403) and usually also in State law by a residual judicial discretion to exclude relevant evidence if its probative value is substantially outweighed by the danger of unfair prejudice, confusion of the issues, or misleading the jury, or by considerations of undue delay, waste of time, or needless presentation of cumulative evidence.[140] In cases of concurrent rather than past allegations, the American Federal courts work from the starting point that prejudice is likely to result, so that counts in general will be severed.[141]

(a) The 'other purposes' model in American law

Federal Evidence Rule 404(b) allows the admission of evidence against a criminal defendant of the commission of past crimes, wrongs, or acts for a broad range of specified purposes, including proof of motive, opportunity, intent, preparation, plan, knowledge, identity, or absence of mistake or accident.[142] This rule replicates the common law '*Molineux* rule' dating back to 1901,[143] and also is reflected in the evidential rules of most States.[144] It is comparable to the 'other purposes' rule prevailing in English common law under *Makin* and *Boardman* discussed earlier: provided that the misconduct can be targeted at some evidential purpose other than inviting the jury to reason from propensity, it is admissible.[145]

In cases of physical abuse and homicide, the list of approved evidential purposes includes negating accidental injury through proof of similar assaults in similar

    [138] *R v John Allen Venn* (n 84) [43].
    [139] *US v Castillo* 140 F 3d 874 (US CA 10th Cir 1998) 881.
    [140] Federal Rule of Evidence Rule 403, 28 USCA.
    [141] Federal Rule of Evidence Rule 8(a); P Mirfield 'Similar Fact Evidence (n 29), 40.
    [142] For extended analyses of the application of Rule 404(b) to child physical and sexual abuse, see *Investigation and Prosecution of Child Abuse* (3rd edn National Center for Prosecution of Child Abuse, American Prosecutors Research Institute Sage Publications, Thousand Oaks 2004) 269–272; Myers *Evidence in Child Abuse Cases* vol 2, 459–503.
    [143] *People v Molineux* 61 NE 286 (New York CA 1901).
    [144] NCPCA *Investigation and Prosecution of Child Abuse* (n 142) 268.
    [145] *Estelle v McGuire* 502 US 62 (USSC 1991) 483; *Getz v State* 538 A 2d 726 (Delaware Supreme Ct 1988); *State v Edward Charles L* 398 SE 2d 123 (West Virginia Supreme CA 1990) 129.

circumstances on the victim ('battered child syndrome')[146] and other children,[147] proof that the defendant had the requisite state of mind for the offence,[148] the identity of the assailant,[149] and the instrument used.[150] Prosecutors are advised to comb the medical records for any claim by the defendant that the injuries were accidentally caused, which could then open the door to admitting evidence of the previous incidents to rebut that claim.[151] American law has also developed a distinct 'doctrine of chances', described by Wigmore as the mind applying 'this rough and instinctive process of reasoning, namely, that an unusual and abnormal element might perhaps be present in one instance, but that the oftener similar instances occur with similar results, the less likely is the abnormal element likely to be the true explanation of them'.[152] This can be particularly cogent to rebut defence claims of accidental injury,[153] although English lawyers would recognize the potential fallacy of such reasoning exposed by the English Court of Appeal in *R v Angela Cannings* discussed earlier.[154]

Evidence of previous uncharged sexual assaults on the same victim is admitted in most States[155] to prove the defendant's motivation, intent and opportunity, provided that the trial court finds that its probative value outweighs its prejudicial effect.[156] Prosecutors are advised to argue that such evidence is relevant in that it provides the jury with a comprehensive framework within which to evaluate the charged offences, and to understand any escalation of the sexual abuse. It is also thought useful to explain away any inconsistencies in the victim's account of the charged incidents, difficulty in recalling and differentiating incidents, and delays in complaint,[157] and so is reminiscent of the English 'background evidence' doctrine. Its use to prove intent and motive appears to be invoked more boldly than the English 'other purposes' doctrine, particularly in child sexual abuse cases,[158] and can come perilously close to direct reasoning from propensity, founded as it is on the assumption that possessing criminal intent on one occasion increases the likelihood that the same intent exists on other, similar occasions.[159]

---

[146] *People v Jackson* 18 Cal App 3d 504 (California CA 1971) 507.

[147] Even where the defendant does not allege the injuries were accidentally caused: *Estelle v McGuire* (n 145) 480–481; *State v Ostlund* 416 NW 2d 755 (Minnesota CA 1987); *State v Holland* 346 NW 2d 302 (South Dakota Supreme Ct 1984); *State v Donahue* 549 A 2d 121 (Pennsylvania Supreme Ct 1988).

[148] Against the same child: *People v Harris* 580 NE 2d 185 (Illinois App Ct 1991); against other children: *People v Summers* 559 NE 2d 1133 (Illinois App Ct 1990); *State v Coffey* 389 SE 2d 48 (North Carolina Supreme Ct 1990).

[149] Even where the person committing the previous assaults is not proved to be the defendant: *Estelle v McGuire* (n 145) 480; *Rivera v State* 561 So 2d 536 (Florida Supreme Ct 1990); *State v Hudgins* 810 SW 2d 664 (Missouri CA 1991).   [150] *State v Coffey* (n 148); *State v Hudgins* ibid.

[151] NCPCA *Investigation and Prosecution of Child Abuse* (n 142) 272.

[152] J Wigmore *Wigmore on Evidence* (Tillers rev edn 1983) § 301.   [153] Cammack (n 18).

[154] Discussed above, section B.4(d).

[155] New York is a notable exception: *People v Lewis* 506 NE 2d 915 (New York CA 1987).

[156] *State v Tecca* 714 P 2d 136 (Montana Supreme Ct 1986).

[157] *Investigation and Prosecution of Child Abuse* (n 142) 268.

[158] eg D Bryden and R Park ' "Other Crimes" Evidence in Sex Offense Cases' (1994) 78 Minnesota LR 529, 543.   [159] Myers *Evidence in Child Abuse Cases* 454–478.

Where Rule 404(b) is used to admit evidence of sexual abuse of other children, on the pretext that this establishes motive, the distinction vanishes altogether. In *Elliott*, where the defendant was charged with raping his nine-year-old stepdaughter, the Wyoming Supreme Court approved the admission of evidence of uncharged sexual assaults by him on the victim's sister three years earlier as proof of motive, the reasoning being that 'one who is a paraphiliac, whose preference or addiction for unusual sexual practices occurs in the form of pedophilia, could well be recognized as having a motive to commit the acts complained of by the victim'.[160] In weighing the probative value of the evidence of other misconduct, the court will evaluate such matters as the similarity between the current charged offences and the other acts, their proximity in time, the surrounding circumstances, and the tendency of the other acts to establish a common plan.[161] The caselaw suggests that these constraints are at times leniently applied.[162]

(b) Propensity evidence to prove guilt in American law

Using their common law powers, the courts in more than 20 American jurisdictions have created a limited exception to the bar on propensity evidence, to prove that the defendant had a 'lustful disposition towards children' or a 'depraved sexual instinct', opening the evidential inference that he probably acted in conformity with that propensity on the occasion charged.[163] This crime-specific model permits propensity reasoning for homosexual and paedophilic conduct, a device rejected by the House of Lords in *Boardman*.[164] While in some jurisdictions the exception is limited to previous acts with the complainant,[165] in others it is not so restricted.

Generally the acts are required to be with victims of the same gender, and occurring near in time to the acts charged, to show a continuing 'emotional propensity for sexual aberration'.[166] An exact replication between the charged acts and the uncharged acts is not required. In the leading case of *Lopez*,[167] the Arizona appellate court identified 'numerous' similarities between the uncharged and charged acts which justified admission at trial: in each case, the defendant made sexual advances to an adolescent male between the ages of 14 and 16, making promises to procure a woman or girl to have sex with the boy; the victim had been offered or had actually obtained employment

---

[160] *Elliott v State* 600 P 2d 1044 (Wyoming Supreme Ct 1979) 1048–1049.

[161] Federal Rule of Evidence Rule 404(4), 28 USCA; *George v State* 813 SW 2d 792, supplementary opinion 818 SW 2d 951 (Arkansas Supreme Ct 1991) 797 (conviction of daycare operator two months previously for sexual assault of another two and a half-year-old girl admissible to prove 'depraved sexual intent').

[162] eg *State v Moore* 819 P 2d 1143 (Idaho Supreme Ct 1991) (evidence of the defendant sexually abusing his children admissible in trial for abuse of his grand-daughter, to show a plan to exploit and abuse them); *State v Jendras* 576 NE 2d 229 (Illinois Ct App 1991) (teacher's sexual assault against boys 15 years earlier by enticing them to use his pool and sauna admissible to show ongoing plan); *State v Crane* 799 P 2d 1380 (Arizona Ct App 1990) (previous acts of vaginal intercourse with underage girls, albeit of different ages, admitted).   [163] Reed (n 16), 168–169.

[164] *DPP v Boardman* (n 7) 441 (Lord Morris).

[165] eg Oregon *State v McKay* 787 P2d 465 (Oregon Supreme Ct 1990); *State v Pace* 212 P2d 755 (Oregon Supreme Ct 1949); *State v Kristich* (n 68).

[166] eg *State v McFarlin* 110 Ariz 225, 517 P2d 87 (Arizona Supreme Ct 1973); *State v Lachterman* 812 SW 2d 759 (Missouri CA) *certiorari* denied 112 S Ct 1666 (1992).

[167] *State v Lopez* 822 P 2d 465 (Arizona CA 1991).

with the defendant; and two of the other boys suffered a sexual assault while under the defendant's supervision. The defendant had argued that the emotional propensity exception offended the equal protection guarantees of the United States and Arizona Constitutions because evidence of other similar crimes is admitted against those charged with sexual offences but not those accused of other types of crime. The court held that the exception was rational because 'the usually secret nature of the crime and the resultant problem of proof by the prosecution justified an additional, carefully circumscribed exception to the general prohibition of other crime evidence at trial'.[168]

Most controversial are Federal Rules of Evidence introduced in 1994 permitting evidence of other misconduct in sexual misconduct[169] and 'child molestation'[170] prosecutions. The new rules for sex offence cases authorize admission and consideration of evidence of an uncharged offence for its bearing 'on any matter to which it is relevant'. This includes the defendant's propensity to commit sexual assault or child molestation offences, and assessment of the probability or improbability that the defendant has been falsely or mistakenly accused of such an offence. The provision applies to any prosecution in Federal courts of an offence against a child under 14 under Federal or State law involving sexual contact or gratification. Such crime-specific admissibility rules can create anomalies: for example, if the defendant is charged with rape followed by murder of a child, his previous convictions for sexual offences would be admissible under Federal Rule 414, but not his record for homicide offences.[171] The prosection is required to provide the defendant 15 days' notice of its intention to offer evidence under this Rule. This apparently radical initiative was justified by its sponsor in Congress as follows:

The proposed reform is critical to the protection of the public from rapists and child molesters, and is justified by the distinctive characteristics of the cases it will affect. In child molestation cases . . . a history of similar acts tends to be exceptionally probative because it shows an unusual disposition of the defendant—a sexual or sadosexual interest in children—that simply does not exist in ordinary people. Moreover, such cases require reliance on child victims whose credibility can readily be attacked in the absence of substantial corroboration. In such cases, there is a compelling public interest in admitting all significant evidence that will illumine the credibility of the charge and any denial by the defence.[172]

No time limit is imposed on the uncharged offences for which evidence may be admitted. The presumption is in favour of admission. The underlying 'strong legislative judgment'[173] is that the other misconduct evidence is typically relevant, and that 'in general, the probative value of such evidence is strong, and is not outweighed by any overriding risk of prejudice'.[174] Therefore the courts have been slow to exercise

---

[168] ibid 471.

[169] Federal Rule of Evidence 413, 28 USCA.   [170] Federal Rule of Evidence 414, 28 USCA.

[171] Park (n 28), 757.

[172] S Molinari 'Concerning the Prior Crimes Evidence Rules for Sexual Assault and Child Molestation Cases' (Congressional Record H8991-92, Aug 21, 1994)

[173] *US v LeCompte* 131 F 3d 767 (US CA 8th Cir 1997) 769.

[174] Analysis Statement accompanying the Violent Crime Control and Law Enforcement Act of 1994, 137 Congressional Record S3214 (daily ed March 13, 1991) S3240–S3241.

their discretion to exclude it,[175] notwithstanding that it may be inflammatory.[176] Like its common law analogue, Federal Rule 414 has been upheld as constitutional under the Due Process Clause largely because of that residual exclusionary discretion under Federal Rule 403.[177] Prosecutors have been cautioned that Federal Rule 414 does not entitle them to introduce whatever evidence they wish, of no matter how minimally relevant and potentially devastating to the defendant.[178]

Notwithstanding the initial fierce controversy,[179] American Federal courts have frequently applied Rule 414, and the overwhelming majority of appellate decisions have upheld the trial judge's decision to admit the propensity evidence.[180] Previous incidents 10 to 27 years earlier have been admitted where there has been sufficient similarity in *modus operandi*,[181] or intra-familial abuse continued into later generations with gaps whilst the victims matured[182] or the defendant was incarcerated for part of the time, making continued offending impossible.[183] The previous misconduct need not have involved actual child abuse provided it showed paedophilic tendencies.[184] Several States have enacted similar legislation.[185] The courts in other State jurisdictions stretch the Federal Rule 404(b) 'other purposes' list, especially 'motive' and 'intent',

---

[175] *US v LeCompte* (n 173); *US v Meacham* 115 F 3d 1488 (Utah CA 1997); *US v Castillo* (n 139) 883.

[176] *US v LeMay* 260 F 3d 1018, *certiorari* denied 534 US 1166 (US CA 9th Cir 2001).

[177] ibid; *Doe by Glanzer v Glanzer* 232 F 3d 1258 (USCA 9th Cir 2000); *US v Castillo* (n 139); *US v Mound* 149 F 3d 799, rehearing denied 157 F 3d 1153, *certiorari* denied 525 US 1089 (US CA 8th Cir, 1998). [178] *US v LeMay* (n 176) 1022.

[179] The proposals were strenuously opposed by the Judicial Conference Committee on Rules of Practice and Procedure and the Advisory Committee on Evidence Rules on the basis that they were unnecessary and would make trials more complex [United States Code Annotated Rule 413]. They also spawned a flurry of academic debate, eg in opposition: Aluise (n 17); and in support: A Kyl 'The Propriety of Propensity: the Effects and Operation of New Federal Rules of Evidence 413 and 414' (1995) 37 Arizona LR 659; D Collins 'Character Evidence and Sex Crimes in Alabama: Moving Toward the Adoption of New Federal Rules 413, 414 & 415' (2000) 51 Alabama LR 1651; D Karp 'Evidence of Propensity and Probability in Sex Offense Cases and Other Cases (Symposium on the Admission of Prior Offense Evidence in Sexual Assault Cases)' (1994) 70 Chicago-Kent LR 15.

[180] For a digest of the cases, see R Davis 'Admissibility, in Prosecution for Sexual Offense, of Evidence of Similar Offenses' 77 American LR 2d 841 (updated to 2006).

[181] eg *People v Waples* 79 Cal App 4th 1389 (California 4th Dist 2000); *Kirkland v State* 440 SE 2d 542 (Georgia CA 1994); *State v Dykes* 867 So 2d 908 (Louisiana CA 2d Cir 2004).

[182] *Snow v State* 445 SE 2d 353 (Georgia App 1994); *Commonwealth v Smith* 635 A 2d 1086 (Pennsylvania Superior Ct 1993). [183] *Harden v State* 438 SE 2d 136 (Georgia App 1993).

[184] *Touchton v State* 437 SE 2d 370 (Georgia CA 1993) (evidence of a guilty plea to receiving and sending child pornography admissible in proving sexual battery of step-grand-daughter aged 13). Compare *Burris v State* 420 SE 2d 582 (Georgia App 1992) where the prosecution was permitted to lead evidence that the defendant possessed sexually explicit materials and sexual devices, even though they did not concern children, as evidence of his bent of mind and lustful disposition.

[185] eg *People v Harris* (n 148); *People v Summers* (n 148); Missouri Ann Stat §566.025; Indiana Code Ann §35-30 7-4-15. In Texas the legislature acted in 1995 [Texas Code of Criminal Procedure Article 38.37 §2] to reinstate a long-standing common law exception for previous sexual abuse of the same child by one standing in a parental relationship [*Battles v State* 140 SW 783 (Texas CCA 1911)] which had been eliminated by the Texas Court of Criminal Appeals in 1992 on the basis that it had been superseded by the adoption of the 'other purposes' model in Federal Rule 404(b) [*Vernon v State* 841 SW 2d 407 (Texas Crim App 1992) 410–411]. For the same reason the Indiana Supreme Court abolished the common law exception in 1993 [*Lannan v State* 600 NE 2d 1334 (Indiana Supreme Ct 1992)].

thereby reducing the exclusionary rule to vanishing point, or resort to the 'lustful disposition' exception discussed earlier.[186]

Thus the American treatment of propensity evidence exemplified in the Federal Rules of Evidence has incorporated three of the approaches identified earlier:[187] the 'other purposes' model in Rule 404(b) and the propensity reasoning model using the 'crime-specific' approach in Rule 414 for child molestation offences, subject to the safeguard of a 'guided balancing' exclusionary discretion in Rule 403. It is significant that the appellate courts considering the constitutionality of the statutory 'crime-specific' approach have stressed that judges using common law powers have routinely allowed propensity evidence for sexual misconduct and child molestation cases under Rule 404(b) whilst disallowing it in other criminal prosecutions.[188] So it is arguable that legislation creating special admissibility rules targeting child sexual abuse may not make that much difference in practice.

6. Propensity evidence in Australian criminal law

Like English law, the Australian doctrine governing the admissibility of other misconduct evidence has evolved to a considerable extent in the context of offences against children. The Australian High Court has successively adopted the 'other purposes' test of *Makin*,[189] the 'striking similarity' and 'underlying unity' tests in *Boardman*,[190] and the probative value/prejudicial effect test in *DPP v P*.[191] Analysis of the Australian position is complicated by the labels used to describe other misconduct evidence. The High Court has divided propensity evidence into three subcategories: similar fact evidence, relationship (or background) evidence, and identity evidence.[192] Nevertheless the lower courts have continued to regard relationship evidence as separate from propensity evidence, on the basis that the former establishes the context against which the evidence of the complainant and the accused fall to be evaluated, whereas the latter is adduced to prove the commission of the offence charged.[193] It is not always clear how the evidence has been categorized by the court.[194]

(a) Admissibility of propensity evidence in Australian common law

In the leading case of *Pfennig*, the majority opinion in approving the unguided balancing test of *DPP v P* deviated somewhat from the 'tip the balance' approach of the House of Lords by focusing on the nature and degree of relevance: the propensity

---

[186] eg California Evidence Code §1108(b); Alaska Rule of Evidence 404(4)(b); Missouri Ann Stat §566.025; Indiana Code Ann §35—30 7-4-15.   [187] Above section B.3 and Diagram 18.
[188] *US v LeMay* (n 176).   [189] *Markby v The Queen* (1978) 140 CLR 108 (Aus HC).
[190] *Perry v The Queen* (n 34); *R v Hoch* (n 90).   [191] *Pfennig v The Queen* (n 37).   [192] ibid.
[193] Queensland Law Reform Commission *The Receipt of Evidence by Queensland Courts: the Evidence of Children* (Report No 55 Part 2) 324, 344–345; (hereafter Queensland LRC *Evidence of Children*); *R v AH* (1997) 42 NSWLR 702 (New South Wales CCA) 708. See also *R v Best* [1998] 4 VR 603 (Victoria CA) 611 (Callaway JA expressing relief that the Victoria courts need not take a position in that controversy).
[194] As illustrated in *Gipp v The Queen* (1998) 194 CLR 106 (Aus HC) where the four written judgments each characterized the history of uncharged sexual abuse differently.

evidence must have a specific connection with the commission of the offence charged which gives a high degree of cogency, or strong probative force,[195] to the prosecution case. Often that can be found only where there is striking similarity, underlying unity or a signature pattern common to the incidents disclosed by the totality of the evidence, but this is not necessary in all cases.[196] *Pfennig* thus established for the first time in Australian law that other misconduct evidence which is *dissimilar* can be admitted in its own right, permitting the trier of fact to reason directly from propensity.[197]

Pfennig stressed that the trial judge in balancing probative value against prejudicial effect must recognize that propensity evidence is circumstantial evidence only, so it should not be admitted unless there is no reasonable view or explanation of that evidence consistent with the innocence of the accused, as otherwise its probative value cannot transcend its prejudicial effect.[198] Prejudice operates when neither logic nor experience necessarily requires the answer that the evidence points to the guilt of the accused.[199] This is a much more stringent test than that approved by the House of Lords in *DPP v P*, which the majority justified as necessary to prevent the balancing exercise being one of discretion rather than of principle.[200] As Kirby J stated in his dissent, the 'no rational explanation' test dictates a result without any balancing open to the trial judge, even in cases where the risk of prejudice is very small.[201] The *Pfennig* test applies regardless of whether the other misconduct evidence is disputed by the defence, or proved by a previous conviction.[202] In Pfennig's trial for abduction and murder of a ten-year-old boy whose body was never recovered, his later conviction for the abduction and rape of a young boy was admissible to prove the *actus reus* that the missing boy had been abducted and killed. Unlike in England,[203] previous acquittals on similar charges are not admissible as similar fact evidence under Australian common law.[204]

(b) Admissibility of other misconduct evidence under Australian statutes

The comprehensive codification of the rules of evidence in the Uniform Evidence Acts adopted by the Commonwealth of Australia,[205] New South Wales and Tasmania, and currently under consideration in Western Australia,[206] provides the clarity which can be difficult to glean from the Australian High Court's multiple opinions in each

---

[195] The term preferred in *Sutton v R* (1984) 152 CLR 528 (Aus HC) 533.

[196] *Pfennig v The Queen* (n 37) 488.

[197] *R v Darren Douglas Ellis* 60764/01, 2003 NSWCCA 319 (New South Wales CCA) [77]. The Australian Law Reform Commission had debated at length whether propensity reasoning was absolutely prohibited at common law in Australia: Australian Law Reform Commission *Evidence* (Interim Report No 26 1985) vol 2, [400]–[402]; Australian Law Reform Commission *Evidence* (Report No 38 1987) [176].

[198] *Pfennig v The Queen* (n 37) 488; see also *Perry v The Queen* (n 34) 594–595, 598–599.

[199] *Sutton v R* (n 195) 564.   [200] *Pfennig v The Queen* (n 37).   [201] ibid 516.

[202] ibid 482.   [203] *R v Z (Prior Acquittal)* (n 8) discussed above, section B.2.

[204] *Kemp v The King* [1951] HCA 39; (1951) 83 CLR 341 (Aus HC); *R v Colby* [1999] NSWCCA 261 (New South Wales CCA).

[205] Which applies to the trial of all federal offences as well as criminal trials conducted in the Australian Capital Territory.

[206] As recommended by Western Australian Law Reform Commission *Review of the Civil and Criminal Justice System* (Report No 92 1999) Recommendation 221.

case. The rather muddled common law concepts of propensity evidence have been transmuted into two categories. '*Tendency evidence*' is defined as evidence of 'the character, reputation or conduct of a person, or a tendency the person has or had to act in a particular way or to have a particular state of mind'.[207] '*Coincidence evidence*' is defined as 'evidence that two or more events occurred' which is tendered 'to prove that, because of the improbability of the events occurring coincidentally, a person did a particular act or had a particular state of mind'.[208] The events will not be considered as related for the purpose of the coincidence definition unless they are 'substantially and relevantly similar' and the circumstances in which they occurred are substantially similar.[209]

The model of the Uniform Evidence Acts is useful in targeting the other misconduct evidence at two conceptually distinct chains of reasoning:[210] the use of disposition to act in a particular way or have a particular state of mind, to prove the *actus reus* or *mens rea* of the offence charged; and the (im)probability reasoning[211] which underpins the common law similar fact evidence doctrine. They use a version of the 'unguided balancing' model for propensity evidence, in that the degree of relevance is stipulated but without specific guidance as to the way that is to be evaluated.

Evidence of tendency or coincidence which meets the general test of relevance is barred, unless the party adducing it has provided reasonable notice in writing to the other parties, and the court concludes that the evidence has 'significant probative value'.[212] 'Significant' has been judicially interpreted as meaning 'important', something more than mere relevance but less than a substantial degree of relevance.[213] There is an additional admissibility hurdle where the tendency or coincidence evidence is tendered by the prosecution as part of its case:[214] it cannot be used against the defendant unless its probative value 'substantially outweighs any prejudicial effect it may have on the defendant.'[215] This requirement does not apply however where the prosecution adduces the evidence in rebuttal of tendency or coincidence evidence led by the defence.[216]

R v Lockyer shows how tendency evidence might be used by the defence, in the familiar 'unidentified perpetrator' situation involving physical violence.[217] The accused was charged with murdering his baby. He wished to lead evidence suggesting that the child's mother had previously injured that child and a sibling, with a view to raising a reasonable possibility that the mother (who was not charged) was the killer. The trial judge held that it was open to the court to exclude tendency evidence submitted

---

[207] Evidence Act 1995 (Commonwealth of Australia) s 97(1); *R v Lockyer* (1996) 89 A Crim R 457 (New South Wales Supreme Ct Crim Div).

[208] Evidence Act 1995 (Commonwealth of Australia) s 98(1).   [209] ibid s 98(2).

[210] Although both might properly be deployed in relation to a single piece of evidence.

[211] *R v Hoch* (n 90) 295–296.

[212] Evidence Act 1995 (Commonwealth of Australia) ss 97(1), 98(1).

[213] *R v Lockyer* (n 207) 459, approved in *R v Martin* [2000] NWSCA 332 (New South Wales CA) [67].

[214] Evidence Act 1995 (Commonwealth of Australia) ss 101(3), 101(4).   [215] ibid s 101(2).

[216] ibid s 97(2)(b).

[217] Discussed above, Chapter 3 section C.8. For a Canadian analogue, see *McMillan v The Queen* (1975) 23 CCC (2d) 160 (Ontario CA), affirmed [1977] 2 SCR 824 (SCC).

by the defence if persuaded that its probative value was substantially outweighed by the danger that it would be unfairly prejudicial to the Crown's case.[218] Such prejudice is not established by the mere fact that the evidence has only slight probative value or that it might reduce the effect of the Crown case, but only if there was a danger that the trier of fact would use the evidence on a basis logically unconnected with the issues in the case.[219] Here, the tendency evidence was probative in the way the defence proposed to use it, and such unfair prejudice to the Crown did not arise.

Initially the New South Wales courts imported the 'no other rational view' test decreed by *Pfennig* into the statutory balancing tests for both tendency and coincidence evidence,[220] but it would seem that this weighted the scales against the prosecution to a much greater degree than the drafters intended. A five-judge panel of the New South Wales Court of Criminal Appeal ruled in *Ellis* in 2003 that the statutory threshold must be applied, rather than the more exigent test of *Pfennig*.[221] The Uniform Evidence Acts had relabelled the common law doctrines and provided precise and comprehensive definitions, thereby signalling an intention to state the principles comprehensively and afresh.[222] *Pfennig*'s 'no rational explanation' test focuses on only one element of the balancing formula, and so the trial judge might fail to give adequate consideration to the actual prejudice in the specific case which the probative value of the evidence must, under the statute, substantially outweigh.[223] Although the five judges in *Ellis* were unanimous in holding that the statutory test must prevail, two of them were clearly uneasy about its relatively low threshold, stating that the balancing exercise should be guided by the recognition that such evidence is likely to be highly prejudicial, and that the test for admissibility remains one of 'very considerable stringency'.[224]

If the evidence is not used for the purpose of directly proving guilt through tendency or coincidence, but is admissible for other purposes, then the statutory rules do not apply and the evidence will be admissible, subject to the various exclusionary discretions conferred by the Uniform Evidence Acts.[225] The trial judge must take the initiative to warn the jury not to use it as an element in the chain of proof of guilt, notwithstanding that the warning might serve to highlight evidence prejudicial to the accused.[226]

---

[218] *R v Lockyer* (n 207) 459–460, interpreting Evidence Act 1995 (Commonwealth of Australia) s 135 as replicating the common law exclusionary discretion confirmed by *R v Christie* [1914] AC 545 (HL) 599, 564.   [219] *R v Lockyer* (n 207) 460.

[220] *R v Lock* (1997) 91 A Crim R 356, 363 (New South Wales Supreme Ct Crim Div); *R v AH* (n 193) 709.   [221] *R v Darren Douglas Ellis* (n 197) [83]–[90].

[222] ibid [75]–[77].   [223] ibid [94]–[95].

[224] ibid [104]–[105] (Hidden and Buddin JJ). This view was explicitly rejected by Spigelman CJ, Sully and O'Keefe JJ concurring, [99].

[225] Queensland LRC *Evidence of Children* 341. Evidence Act 1995 (Commonwealth of Australia) s 135 confers general discretion to exclude evidence which might be unfairly prejudicial to a party, or misleading or confusing, or result in undue waste of time. Section 136 permits the court to limit the use of the evidence if there is a danger that a particular use might be unfairly prejudicial to a party or be misleading or confusing. Section 137 permits the court to refuse to admit prosecution evidence if its probative value is outweighed by the danger of unfair prejudice to the defendant.

[226] *BRS v The Queen* (1997) 191 CLR 275 (Aus HC) 302, 305–310, 326–332.

Some of the jurisdictions which have not adopted the Uniform Evidence Acts have also been unhappy with the effect of *Pfennig*. The 'no rational explanation' test was reversed by statute in Victoria, which devised its own general test for the admissibility of propensity evidence: the court must conclude that in all the circumstances it is 'just' to admit it notwithstanding any prejudicial effect it may have on the accused. The possibility of a reasonable explanation consistent with innocence is a matter for weight rather than admissibility.[227] Victoria's statutory test has been interpreted as applying to all disclosures of other offences or other discreditable conduct, whatever the purpose for which the evidence is tendered, including as background evidence.[228] Although Callaway JA in *R v Best* stated that this statutory test reverts to the English test in *DPP v P*,[229] Lord Mackay had directly tied the conclusion that it is 'just' to admit the propensity evidence to its 'probative force',[230] whereas the Victoria model does not even specify the counterweight to prejudice. Justice may also relate to process values, so for example it may be just to admit other misconduct evidence if that means that a vulnerable witness would have to testify only once instead of in successive trials.[231] Callaway JA suggested that while the legislation had adopted a flexible criterion of admissibility similar to that proposed by McHugh J in his dissent in *Pfennig*,[232] it nonetheless would make little difference to the reception of similar fact evidence; it should still be treated with great caution, and the jury must still be given the classic common law direction about the forbidden chain of reasoning from propensity to guilt, even where concurrent charges are cross-admissible.[233] Under this interpretation the Victoria legislation has done little to change the common law or practice in criminal trials.[234]

In Queensland, the Court of Appeal has also diluted *Pfennig* in two ways. It has held that it is the evidence as a whole which must be reasonably capable of excluding all innocent hypotheses, not merely the propensity evidence.[235] Secondly, it has interpreted *Pfennig* as requiring the trial court in conducting the balancing exercise to assess the probative value of the evidence without evaluating its reliability by examining inconsistencies in the statements.[236] Only the Northern Territory,[237] South Australia[238] and Western Australia[239] continue to apply *Pfennig* in full measure, and

---

[227] Crimes Act 1958 (Victoria) s 398A, inserted by the Crimes (Amendment) Act 1997 (Victoria) s 14.
[228] *R v Best* (n 193) 607.   [229] ibid 607, 608.   [230] *DPP v P* (n 80) 460.
[231] Thus in *R v Camilleri* [2001] VSCA 14, 119 A Crim R 106 (Victoria CA) 124, in a trial for the rape and murder of two schoolgirls, the trial judge took into account fairness to the accused, the prosecution and 'wider society' in admitting the evidence of a woman who had been abducted and raped three weeks earlier by him.   [232] *Pfennig v The Queen* (n 37) 528–530.
[233] *R v Best* (n 193) 612, 616.
[234] A view confirmed in *R v Tektonopoulos* [1999] 2 VR 412 (Victoria CA) 416. In *R v Mitchell* [2000] VSCA 54, 112 A Crim R 315 (Victoria CA) 317 [8] Tadgell JA confirmed that s 398A makes it no longer appropriate to look for striking similarity in determining whether it is just to admit the evidence.
[235] *R v O'Keefe* [2000] 1 Qd R 564 (Queensland CA) 564–566, 571, 573–574.
[236] *R v Graham Lenard Noyes* [2003] QCA 564 (Queensland CA) [32].
[237] *Melbourne v The Queen* [1999] HCA 32, 198 CLRI (Aus HC) on appeal from Northern Territory Supreme Ct).   [238] *R v Nieterink* (n 69).
[239] *Stickland v The Queen* [2002] WASCA 339 (Western Australia CCA).

Western Australia is actively considering adopting the approach to the propensity evidence of the uniform evidence model.[240]

(c) 'Relationship evidence' in Australian law

A lingering problem arising from *Pfennig*'s categorization of relationship (or background) evidence as a subspecies of propensity evidence is whether it is subject to the 'no rational explanation' test. There are conflicting cases on this question.[241] The predominant view appears to be that it does not, on the basis that *Pfennig* dealt with the special dangers inherent in propensity reasoning, which are not thought to arise with relationship evidence.[242] This may be optimistic; in cases of alleged ongoing sexual abuse the trial judge is required to explain that such evidence is relevant to show the existence of a 'guilty sexual passion' or relationship, but that it must not be used to establish the accused's predilection to commit the offences charged, or that he committed them.[243] If the distinction is difficult to discern where the indictment contains counts of specific acts of abuse,[244] it is all the more so where the accused is charged with maintaining a sexual relationship with a child who is under his care, an offence devised by several Australian States[245] in response to general community concern about child sexual abuse. The relationship must be proved by sexual acts on at least three occasions, but the evidence need not disclose the dates or exact circumstances of those occasions. This creates the danger that generalized evidence to establish the relationship, which is difficult to disprove, will be used by the jury as propensity evidence to convict on other specific charges.[246] As the Uniform Evidence Acts do not make any reference to relationship evidence, the prevailing judicial view is that it is not subject to the tendency evidence rule, and so is subject only to the relevance test and the residual exclusionary discretion under s 137.[247] The Victoria Court of Appeal has confirmed that relationship evidence is subject to the 'justice' statutory test in s 398A discussed in the previous section.[248]

---

[240] Department of Justice, Government of Western Australia *Joinder of Sexual Offences: Final Report* (August 2003) 7. [241] Queensland LRC *Evidence of Children* 334–337.

[242] *Conway v The Queen* (2000) 98 FCR 204 (Aus Fed Ct Full Ct) 233; *KRM v The Queen* [2001] HCA 11, 206 CLR 221 (Aus HC) 229–230 (McHugh J); *B v The Queen* (1992) 175 CLR 599 (Aus HC) 602, 608, 610–611; *R v Nieterink* (n 69) 64, 66; *R v Beserick* (1993) 30 NSWLR 510 (CCA) 519–520.

[243] *R v LSS* [2000] 1 Qd R 546 (Qld CA) 547, 555; *R v Vonarx* [1999] 3 VR 618 (Victoria CA); *R v AH* (n 193) 708; *B v The Queen* ibid; *KRM v The Queen* ibid 230–233 (McHugh J) (*obiter*).

[244] In *R v Knuth* No 64 of 1998, 23 June 1998 (Queensland CA) 22–23 Lee J suggested that the distinction between background evidence of a sexual relationship and propensity evidence is artificial, as both relate to sexual desire.

[245] eg Crimes Act 1958 (Victoria) s 47A(1); Criminal Code Act 1899 (Queensland) s 229B(1).

[246] *KBT v The Queen* (1997) 191 CLR 417 (Aus HC) 431–433 (Kirby J); *KRM v The Queen* (n 242) 248–250 (Kirby J).

[247] *R v AH* (n 193) 708; *Conway v The Queen* (n 242) 234; *R v Lock* (n 220) 364, 365.

[248] *R v GAE* (2000) 109 A Crim R 419 (Victoria CA) 425–426, 437; *R v Loguancio* (2000) 110 A Crim R 406 (Victoria CA) 414.

(d) The risk of collusion and unconscious influence in Australian law

The logical consequence of the 'no rational explanation' test in *Pfennig* is that since propensity evidence holds probative value only if it raises the objective improbability of some event having occurred other than as the prosecution alleges, it loses its probative value where the allegations may reasonably be explained by collusion, because there is then another rational view of the evidence. Thus in *Hoch*, where a schoolteacher was alleged by two brothers and their friend to have committed very similar sexual assaults, and there was evidence that one complainant had antipathy towards the accused even before the alleged events, the evidence of each boy was not cross-admissible and the High Court of Australia ruled that the counts should have been severed.[249] If necessary the trial judge must hold a *voir dire* to exclude the possibility of concoction.[250]

Hoch has been much criticized. The Queensland Court of Appeal expressed concern that the mere possibility of collusion gave rise to 'dire consequences' both evidentially and in the framing of indictments.[251] The Australian Law Reform Commission noted that as *Hoch* held that the *possibility* of joint concoction arises simply from a 'sufficient relationship between the victims', this necessarily arises when the child victims are siblings or friends and are abused by a relative, family friend or teacher.[252] Motive and opportunity (which the High Court also required[253]) can often readily be hypothesized in such situations. Notwithstanding these criticisms, the *Hoch* approach has been applied in the Uniform Evidence Acts jurisdictions, on the basis that the risk of collusion deprives the evidence of significant probative value, regardless of its substantial and relevant similarity. However, in New South Wales Mason P interpreted *Hoch* as requiring that the 'possibility of collusion' be a reasonable possibility or real chance of collusion as distinct from a speculative or conjectural one.[254]

The Western Australian Criminal Court of Appeal has similarly striven to mitigate the strictness of *Hoch* by emphasizing that the possibility of concoction must be understood as a reasonable rather than a fanciful possibility, based upon some factual foundation.[255] In Queensland, the rule has been reversed by statute, so that where the probative value of similar fact evidence outweighs its potentially prejudicial effect, it must not be ruled inadmissible on the ground that it may be the result of collusion or suggestion, the weight of that evidence being a question for the jury.[256] In effect this adopts the House of Lords' approach to the determination of collusion in *R v H*.[257] The Western Australian Law Reform Commission has recommended reform on the same basis,[258] and it appears that the Western Australian Government is prepared to do so.[259]

---

[249] *R v Hoch* (n 90) 296, 302.

[250] *BRS v The Queen* (n 226) 300–301.   [251] *R v S* [2001] QCA 501 (Queensland CA) [32].

[252] Australian Law Reform Commission and the Human Rights and Equal Opportunity Commission *Seen and Heard: Priority for Children and the Legal Process* (Report 84 1997) [14.87].

[253] *R v Hoch* (n 90) 297.   [254] *R v Colby* (n 204) [107], [111].

[255] *Hamilton v The Queen* Library No 970082 4 March 1997 (Western Australia CCA) 10.

[256] Evidence Act 1977 (Queensland) s 132A, inserted by Criminal Law Amendment Act 1997 (Queensland) s 122 Sch 2.   [257] *R v H* (n 91), discussed above, section B.4(c).

[258] Western Australian LRC *Review of the Civil and Criminal Justice System* (n 206) Recommendation 272.   [259] *Joinder of Sexual Offences: Final Report* (n 240) 7, 23.

Victoria has accomplished the same result indirectly by requiring that the possibility of a reasonable explanation consistent with innocence (of which collusion is an obvious candidate) be left to the jury.[260] Even where there is a strong possibility of collusion or any other basis of unreliability, as where the principal of a Christian Brothers' primary school was charged with 18 counts of sexual offences relating to five former pupils, and a previous trial of charges relating to five other pupils had received widespread media coverage, this cannot be taken into account in the prejudice side of the equation. The balancing of justice against prejudice must proceed on the basis that the evidence will be accepted as true.[261] The jury must then be directed that they must be satisfied beyond reasonable doubt that no factor such as collusion or unconscious influence was operating before they can use disputed propensity evidence as part of their reasoning.[262]

The question of whether there is a risk of collusion amongst complainants has a direct bearing on the procedural issue of whether multiple counts of sexual assault should be tried together, to which we now turn.

(e) Joinder and severance of charges in Australian law

The Australian High Court in *De Jesus*, and confirmed in *Hoch*, took the position that in sexual offence cases separate trials should be ordered whenever the evidence relating to each count does not satisfy the similar fact evidence rules, due to the perceived risk of impermissible prejudice to the accused.[263] This is contrary to the House of Lords' flexible position in *Christou* discussed earlier.[264] The rule in *De Jesus* can make cases involving multiple counts and multiple complainants extraordinarily complex.[265]

The Australian Law Reform Commission and the Human Rights Commission jointly recommended in 1997 that the rules in *De Jesus* and *Hoch* be revisited because their combined effect was to cause hardship to child victim witnesses by forcing them to testify 'numerous times', first about what happened to them and then what they witnessed happening to other children. The Commissions were concerned that these rules mean that when the complainant's credibility is attacked, evidence that would support the witness is disallowed and the jury is kept in ignorance of the fact that there are multiple allegations of abuse against the accused.[266]

Some Australian States have heeded this call. The rule in *De Jesus* has been removed by statute in Victoria: a specific statutory exception to the general power to sever

---

[260] Crimes Act 1958 (Victoria) s 398A(4). In *R v Best* (n 193) 610, Callaway JA noted that this provision could only apply to explanations like collusion and unconscious influence which affect the truth of the propensity evidence and so ought to be adduced, and not to explanations like coincidence, as this would make the judge's task impossible in the case of similar fact evidence.   [261] *R v Best* ibid 607.

[262] ibid 616.

[263] *De Jesus v The Queen* (1986) 68 ALR 1 (Aus HC); *R v Hoch* (n 90) 294, 298.

[264] *R v Christou* (n 118) 128–129, discussed above, section B.4(e).

[265] eg *R v B* [1989] 2 Qd R 343 (Queensland CCA), where the accused was charged with 19 counts against his 3 daughters, only 8 of which were ultimately tried together due to complex rulings on cross-admissibility, such that the 3 sisters were required to give evidence at two trials. Had the facts been slightly different sisters would be required to testify at three trials: Queensland LRC *Evidence of Children* 385–387.

[266] Aus LRC *Seen and Heard* (n 252) [14.87]–[14.89] and Recommendation 103.

counts which would prejudice or embarrass the defence is created for sexual offences which are presumed to be triable together. The presumption cannot be rebutted merely because the evidence on one count is inadmissible on another count.[267] The explanatory memorandum to the Bill expressly stated that this was intended to align Victorian law with the House of Lords' approach in *Christou*.[268] The Victorian Court of Appeal has interpreted the legislation conservatively,[269] emphasizing that there will be an unacceptable risk of prejudice in cases of offences 'of an unnatural character or offences that arouse the strong emotions or excite revulsion',[270] which typically involve sexual offences against young children.[271] Some commentators believe that the intended impact of the reform has been substantially reduced by its lukewarm reception by the Victorian judiciary.[272] The Western Australia Law Reform Commission has recommended reform of the *De Jesus* presumption[273] along similar lines to Victoria's changes, but with a proviso that the trial judge could decline to sever the counts if she was of the view that prejudice could be overcome by an appropriate jury direction.[274] The State Government is currently examining this position.[275]

In Queensland, the Court of Appeal has cautioned trial courts that *De Jesus* did not set up an absolute rule requiring severance of all sexual offences involving multiple complainants; the ultimate touchstone is the prejudicial effect of evidence which would not otherwise be heard by the jury, and the capacity of the court to counter such prejudice.[276] A 1997 statutory amendment provides that the court in considering whether to sever sexual counts must not have regard to the possibility that propensity evidence which passes through the probative value/prejudicial effect filter may be the result of collusion or suggestion.[277] The Queensland Law Reform Commission has recommended against further special legislated rules for joinder of child sexual abuse charges, concluding that the statutory stipulation that the issue of collusion be left to the jury has meant that evidence of real probative value on different counts is likely to be cross-admissible, permitting a single trial. The Commission was not satisfied that in trials of sexual charges involving

---

[267] Crimes (Amendment) Act 1997 (Victoria) amending Crimes Act 1958 (Victoria) ss 372, 372(3AA), 372(3AB). [268] Cited by Callaway JA in *R v TJB* [1998] 4 VR 621 (Victoria CA).

[269] *R v TJB* ibid. A somewhat more robust approach was taken in *R v KRA* [1999] 2 VR 708 (Victoria CA). [270] *R v TJB* ibid 630–631.

[271] *R v KRA* (n 269) 716.

[272] Department of Justice, Government of Western Australia *Joinder of Sexual Offences: Final Report* (August 2003) 5.

[273] Western Australian LRC *Review of the Civil and Criminal Justice System* (n 206) Recommendation 271.

[274] *Stickland v The Queen* (n 239) [8], [117], [127], ruling that some of the dissimilar counts should have been severed in the trial of a Scout leader on 63 counts of abusing 9 Boy Scouts.

[275] The Department of Justice, Government of Western Australia *Joinder of Sexual Offences: Final Report* (August 2003) has recommended that this proposal not be adopted.

[276] *R v S* (n 251) [34]. Nevertheless the court ruled that charges relating to the accused's two stepdaughters should have been severed once the trial judge had ruled that the evidence was not cross-admissible as similar fact evidence ([41]).

[277] Criminal Code Act 1899 (Queensland) s 597A (1AA), inserted by the Criminal Law Amendment Act 1997 (Queensland).

children, which are peculiarly likely to arouse prejudice, a limiting direction could protect the accused by ensuring that the jury does not consider evidence which was not admitted on that charge. The Commissioners also concluded, as had the House of Lords in *Christou*, that it would be difficult to formulate a rational basis on which to determine which types of proceedings should be subject to a special non-severance rule.[278]

Australia thus presents a variety of solutions to the conundrum of propensity evidence. The Australian High Court has set particularly high benchmarks for the admission of such evidence and the trial of multiple counts, to which legislators have responded with a clear message that the rules must be more lenient. Whilst the leading cases have involved sexual or violent offences against children, judges and legislators alike have generally resisted the temptation of their American counterparts to craft special rules for these categories of offences, and so arguably have adopted more principled, if divergent, approaches.

7. Propensity evidence in New Zealand criminal law

(a) Admissibility of propensity evidence in New Zealand common law

The New Zealand Court of Appeal moved relatively early to the unguided balancing model, discarding the labels of 'similar fact' or 'striking similarity';[279] indeed the House of Lords regarded the New Zealand appellate jurisprudence as a harbinger of the correct approach which it adopted in *DPP v P*.[280] The New Zealand appellate court has specifically disapproved of the Australian High Court's 'no rational explanation' approach in *Pfennig* as being too strict, adding that it is 'difficult to imagine that there could ever be a case where similar fact evidence of itself could conclusively prove the accused's guilt.'[281] However, the Court of Appeal has found it necessary to chide Crown counsel for too frequently resorting to propensity evidence under *DPP v P* without clearly identifying a specific factual link between the propensity evidence and the direct evidence of the crime in question.[282]

New Zealand trial judges are expected to approach the probative value/prejudicial effect inquiry in three stages, considering (a) whether the facts in question are similar to the facts alleged in the indictment, (b) what probative value those similar facts have on the case, bearing in mind that the standard of proof for their existence is on the balance of probabilities, and (c) whether the probative value is so slight that the prejudicial effect makes it unfair for the evidence to be admitted.[283] It is not sufficient for the prosecution simply to state that the evidence is relevant to the credibility of

---

[278] Queensland LRC *Evidence of Children* 398–402 and Recommendation 17.1.

[279] *R v Accused (CA 208/87)* [1988] 1 NZLR 573 (New Zealand CA); *R v Huijser* [1988] 1 NZLR 577 (New Zealand CA); *R v Narain (No 2)* [1988] 1 NZLR 593 (New Zealand CA).

[280] *DPP v P* (n 80) 462. The New Zealand Court of Appeal subsequently endorsed *DPP v P* as accurately reflecting New Zealand law: *Crime Appeal (CA 202/91)* 13 Aug 1991 (New Zealand CA); *R v Accused (CA 247/91)* [1992] 2 NZLR 187 (New Zealand CA).

[281] *R v Fissenden (CA 227/94)* 28 March 1995 (New Zealand CA).

[282] *R v M* [1999] 1 NZLR 315 (CA) 15; *R v O* [1999] 1 NZLR 347 (New Zealand CA).

[283] *R v Accused (CA 8/96)* (n 8) 678–679.

the complainant, without identifying in what respect it is so relevant, and why. It is not legitimate for the Crown to postulate a theoretical defence and argue that the evidence is admissible to meet it, nor to contend that the evidence gives an insight into his behaviour. 'If it were, evidence of almost any prior offending would qualify and would permit general character blackening'.[284]

Also as in England,[285] but contrary to the position in Canada[286] and Australia,[287] previous acquittals of similar charges have also been held to be potentially relevant and admissible in New Zealand courts, the onus being upon the defence to identify a particular feature of unfairness or abuse of process which would justify exclusion, even though this might effectively require the accused to give evidence.[288] The Court of Appeal rejected the position taken in some Canadian cases that a verdict of not guilty is the equivalent of a declaration of innocence, on the basis that it 'risks elevating perceived theory over the realities of criminal practice'.[289]

(b) Background evidence in New Zealand law

The New Zealand courts have tended to elide background evidence[290] into the similar fact doctrine, applying the probative value/prejudicial effect test generally to all other misconduct evidence. Thus in *R v Meynell*, where a stepfather was charged with the murder of a 16-month-old child, two previous acts of violence towards the child shortly before his death, to which the defendant had pleaded guilty before the murder trial, were admitted as being probative of his hostile attitude towards the child, and that he and not the mother was responsible for the fatal assault.[291] In contrast, in *R v Howes*, where the accused was charged with the murders of his two stepdaughters aged 11 and 12, the prosecution should not have been allowed to tender evidence of their numerous complaints to their friends of sexual abuse as hearsay evidence that the abuse had occurred and hence of his motive in wishing to silence them, because the youngest girl had retracted her complaints and their unreliability made them more prejudicial than probative.[292]

(c) Proposals for statutory reform of the New Zealand doctrine

The New Zealand Law Commission concluded that New Zealand's approach to propensity evidence is reasonably close to that taken by the English courts.[293] In its preliminary paper the Commission suggested however that the imprecise nature of the unguided balancing model frequently created litigation at the appellate level.[294]

---

[284] *R v M* (n 282) 19–20.   [285] *R v Z (Prior Acquittal)* (n 8).

[286] *Grdic v The Queen* [1985] 1 SCR 810 (SCC) 825; *R v Arp* (n 8) [76]–[78].

[287] *Kemp v The King* (n 204); *R v Colby* (n 204).

[288] *R v Degnan* [2001] 1 NZLR 280 (New Zealand CA) (indecent assaults on young men invited by the defendant to spend the night at his home).   [289] ibid [34].

[290] New Zealand courts describe background evidence as *res gestae* evidence, a very attenuated form of the doctrine.   [291] *R v Meynell* [2004] 1 NZLR 507 (New Zealand CA).

[292] *R v Howes* [2003] 3 NZLR 767 (New Zealand CA). The fact that the complaints were made was properly admissible as original evidence of the defendant's motive, but the prosecution sought to strengthen their case by relying upon the truth of the allegations.

[293] New Zealand Law Commission *Character and Credibility* (n 45) 82.   [294] ibid 82.

However, in its final report the Commission held that the common law similar fact evidence doctrine operated well and provided the desired consistency and flexibility.[295] The proposed Evidence Code would codify these principles,[296] but would substitute a guided balancing model. In assessing the probative value of propensity evidence, the trial judge would be required to identify the nature of the issue in dispute to which the propensity evidence is said to be relevant, and then to assess its probative value by comparing the tendered evidence with the offences charged, by reference to, among other things,

- the frequency of the occurrences;
- their connection in time;
- the extent of their similarity;
- the number of persons making similar allegations against the defendant, and whether these allegations might be the result of collusion or suggestibility; and
- the extent to which the acts or omissions are unusual.

The probative value must 'clearly outweigh' the risk that the evidence might have an unfairly prejudicial effect on the defendant. The Law Commission admitted to having considerably more difficulty in defining guidelines for assessing prejudicial effect,[297] but concluded that it would be helpful to codify the way in which prejudicial effect could occur, as including:

- whether the evidence is likely to unfairly predispose the fact finder against the defendant; and
- whether the fact finder will tend to give disproportionate weight in reaching a verdict to evidence of other acts or omissions.[298]

In assessing prejudicial effect, the Commission suggested that the trial judge would be likely to consider whether these risks could be mitigated by an appropriate direction to the jury. [299]

8. Propensity evidence under Canadian criminal law

Canadian courts readily imported the English rule that general propensity evidence must be subject to a strong presumption of inadmissibility,[300] but have recognized an exception where other misconduct evidence exceptionally has such high probative value that 'it displaces the heavy prejudice which will inevitably inure to the accused where evidence of immoral or illegal acts is presented to the jury'.[301] The Supreme Court of Canada openly acknowledged that when similar fact evidence is admitted the chain of reasoning from propensity to guilt is inevitably being deployed,[302] well before

---

[295] New Zealand Law Commission *Evidence* (Report 55 August 1999) Vol 1, 50.
[296] ibid Vol 2, 120–123, Draft Evidence Code s 45.   [297] *Character and Credibility* (n 45) 85.
[298] New Zealand Law Commission *Evidence* (n 295) Vol 2, 122, s 45(3) and s 45(4).
[299] ibid Vol 2, 123, C206.   [300] *R v Handy* (n 5) [37], [55].
[301] *R v B(CR)* (n 62) [23], [56] (McLachlin J).
[302] *Cloutier v The Queen* (n 12) 735; *Morris v The Queen* (n 13) 201–202; *R v Handy* (n 5) [51]–[67]; R Delisle 'Similar Facts: Let's Be Realistic' (2000) 30 CR (5th) 309.

their English counterpart had done so. As Binnie J observed, 'propensity evidence by any other name is still propensity evidence'.[303] Indeed, Canadian courts now recognize that propensity reasoning is usually inevitable, given the nature of the evidence and the reason for its admission.[304]

A majority of the Canadian Supreme Court led by McLachlin J appeared to reject the 'other purposes' model in 1997 in *R v B(CR)*,[305] opting for 'a sliding scale' of admissibility based on the degree of relevance;[306] in effect this is a single-step unguided balancing model of probative value against prejudicial effect,[307] terminology already familiar to Canadian courts in a wider context of the law of evidence.[308] The conceptual clarity of *R v B(CR)* was undermined by subsequent decisions of the Supreme Court which sought to distinguish between evidence which *solely* shows the accused's disposition to commit that type of crime, and evidence where the context vests it with greater probative value. This was suggestive of a reversion to the arguably more restrictive[309] 'other purposes' model, whilst incorporating the unguided balancing test in a two-step analysis, and the need for a limited use instruction to the jury.[310] This approach led to an expanded concept of background or narrative evidence under the pretext of providing necessary context to the incidents which are the subject of the charge, including sexual motive; however, unlike the English common law, this route to admitting previous misconduct evidence was subject to unguided balancing of probative value against prejudicial effect.[311]

The confusion[312] created by these apparently conflicting pronouncements was finally resolved in 2002 with *R v Handy*, in a judgment remarkable for its incisiveness and clarity.[313] Binnie J, writing for a unanimous bench of all nine Supreme Court Justices, confirmed that *R v B(CR)* states Canadian law, and firmly adhered to the single step test:

In *any* case, the strength of the similar fact evidence must be such as to outweigh 'reasoning prejudice' and 'moral prejudice'. The inferences sought to be drawn must accord with common sense, intuitive notions of probability and the unlikelihood of coincidence. Although an element

---

[303] *R v Handy* ibid [59].

[304] ibid [67], approving *R v B(L)* (n 14) [45] (Charron JA).

[305] *R v B(CR)* (n 62) [57] (McLachlin J), relying upon *R v Guay* [1979] 1 SCR 18 (SCC) 32. Sopinka J disputed this interpretation in his dissent in *R v B(CR)* ibid [10]–[17].

[306] *R v B(CR)* ibid [58] (McLachlin J).

[307] *Sweitzer v The Queen* [1982] 1 SCR 949 (SCC) 953.

[308] *R v Wray* [1971] SCR 272 [54]; *R v Seaboyer* [1991] 2 SCR 577 (SCC) 609.

[309] L Hanson '*R v B(FF)* Re-Visited: Possibilities for Admitting Similar Fact Evidence Via Relevance to Other Matters in Issue' (1994) 20 Queen's LJ 139.

[310] *R v C(MH)* [1991] 1 SCR 763 (SCC) [18] (McLachlin J for a unanimous court); *R v B(FF)* [1993] 1 SCR 697 (SCC) 731 (Iacobucci J in a court divided 3:2); *R v Arp* (n 8) [80] model direction number (5), (Cory J for a unanimous court). The reversion to a form of the 'other purposes' model was applauded as safeguarding the interests of the accused by L Stuesser 'Similar Fact Evidence in Sexual Offence Cases' (1996–1997) 39 Crim LQ 160, 178.

[311] *R v B(FF)* ibid (evidence of complainant's siblings of sexual and physical abuse to rebut innocent association and to explain failure to complain for over 30 years); *R v Litchfield* [1993] 4 SCR 33 (SCC); L Hanson (n 309) 148–161.

[312] Which the Ontario Court of Appeal had sought to dispel in *R v B(L)* (n 14) [49].

[313] For a contrary view, see M Redmayne 'Similar Facts, Similar Obfuscation: *R v Handy*' (2002) 6 *Int J of Evidence and Proof* 243.

of 'moral prejudice' may be introduced, it must be concluded by the trial judge on a balance of probabilities that the probative value of the sound inferences exceeds any prejudice likely to be created. ...Canadian case law recognizes that as the 'similar facts' become more focussed and specific to circumstances similar to the charge (i.e., more situation specific), the probative value of propensity, thus circumscribed, becomes more cogent. ...Ultimately the policy premise of the general exclusionary rule (prejudice exceeds probative value) ceases to be true.[314] (emphasis in original)

Therefore, while identification of the specific live issue in the case defines the precise target for which the evidence is offered and so calibrates its particular probative value in relation to its prejudicial effect, that analysis does not change the inherent nature of propensity evidence which must be recognized for what it is, to keep its 'potentially poisonous nature' front and centre before the court.[315]

The Supreme Court in *Handy* appeared to appreciate the difficulties posed for trial judges by the unguided balancing model ordained in its earlier decisions. The Court had already rejected the 'striking similarity' touchstone of admissibility[316] for cases where identity is not at issue.[317] Where it is, the inference that the accused is the person who committed the crime is made possible only if the high degree of similarity between the acts renders the likelihood of coincidence objectively improbable.[318] In *Handy*, the Court provided non-prescriptive guidance as to the evaluation of the probative value of the proffered propensity evidence in relation to issues other than identity. The principal driver of probative value is the degree of connectedness or nexus between the propensity evidence and the offences alleged. However, there should be no stipulated degree of similarity, as the nature of the connecting factors will depend upon the specific inference at which the evidence is targeted, be that identity, commission of the *actus reus*, or establishing the requisite *mens rea*.[319] Trial judges should consider the cogency of the proffered propensity evidence in relation to the identified relevant inference having regard to connecting factors such as:[320]

- proximity in time of the similar acts [as a time gap opens up a greater possibility of character reform or 'maturing out' personality change];[321]
- extent of similarity in detail to the charged conduct;
- number of occurrences of the similar acts;
- similarities of circumstances; and
- any distinctive features.

---

[314] *R v Handy* (n 5) [42], [48].   [315] ibid [58]–[61], [69]–[75].
[316] *R v Robertson* (n 6) 943 (Wilson J).   [317] *R v B(CR)* (n 62) [43]–[48].
[318] *R v Arp* (n 8) [43]–[44]. This test applies regardless of whether the alleged similar acts are definitively attributed to the accused, or are the subject of a multi-count indictment [59]. An acquittal at a previous trial cannot be used as evidence of similar acts in Canadian law: *Grdic v The Queen* (n 286) 825; *R v Cullen* (1989) 52 CCC (3d) 459 (Ontario CA) [5]. However, on multi-count indictments the jury may nonetheless use the evidence relating to one count on which they have decided to acquit as evidence on another count: *R v Arp* ibid [76]–[78]. For criticism see L Stuesser 'Admitting Acquittals as Similar Fact Evidence' (2000) 45 Crim LQ 488; R Mahoney 'Acquittals as Similar Fact Evidence: Another View' (2003) 47 Crim LQ 265.   [319] *R v Handy* (n 5) [76]–[80].
[320] ibid [81]–[82].   [321] ibid [122].

Countervailing factors in assessing prejudice include:[322]

- inflammatory nature of the similar acts, including whether they are more serious then the offence charged;[323]
- whether the prosecution can prove its point with less prejudicial evidence;
- potential distraction of the trier of fact from its proper focus on the facts charged; and
- the potential for undue time consumption.

For example, where there is a situation-specific propensity to abuse sexually children to whom a defendant stands in a parental relationship,[324] the observed pattern of propensity operating in a closely defined and circumscribed context justified reception of the evidence.[325]

In *R v Shearing*,[326] which was argued at the same time as *Handy*, the probative value/prejudicial effect template was applied to an exceptionally inflammatory situation because of the combination of sex and religion.[327] The accused was the spiritual leader of a cult which believe that enlightenment is reached through ascension by steps of consciousness. He preached that sexual experience was a way to progress to higher levels of awareness. He claimed that he, as the cult leader, could be instrumental in enabling young girls to reach higher levels of spiritual contact and in fending off the invasion of their bodies by disembodied minds. He was charged with 20 counts of sexual offences against 11 complainants, 9 of them being his disciples, and 2 of them being unbelievers who were the daughters of his housekeeper who lived with him. The defence in respect of the disciples was consent, and in respect of the sisters that there was never any sexual contact. The Supreme Court of Canada upheld the trial judge's ruling that the evidence on all the counts was cross-admissible. The cogency of the similar fact evidence rested on the validity of the double inference that firstly, the accused had a situation-specific propensity to groom adolescent girls for sexual gratification by exploiting the cult's beliefs and its domestic arrangements, and secondly, that he proceeded in that way with each complainant. Similarity and unity of the incidents involving the sisters and the others lay in the accused's *modus operandi*, his abuse of power in a closed domestic and 'spiritual' system under his authority, and the theme of quack spiritualism. Trial judges should not take an excessively mechanical approach as dissimilarities can always be exaggerated at microscopic levels of detail.[328] These incidents overlapped and were to some extent concurrent. This proximity in time made the evidence more cogent. The incidents were also spread over many years, demonstrating, if believed, a degree of extended consistency in behaviour. Similar fact evidence supported a finding of situation-specific behaviour and it was thus open to the jury to draw the double inference.[329] The risk of moral prejudice was significant, given the sheer cumulative number of alleged incidents, and as the juxtaposition of the disciples' and the non-disciples' complaints which afforded reciprocal aggravation as well as mutual insight.[330] However, the fact that the jury had acquitted the defendant

---

[322] ibid [83].   [323] ibid [140], [152].
[324] As in *R v B(CR)* (n 62) [74]–[75]; *R v B(L)* (n 14) [42]–[49].   [325] *R v Handy* (n 5) [90]–[91].
[326] *R v Shearing* 2002 SCC 58, [2002] 3 SCR 33.   [327] ibid [36], [66].   [328] ibid [60].
[329] ibid [31]–[63].   [330] ibid [63].

in respect of four of the disciples showed that they must have heeded the warning not to reason from general disposition.[331]

(a) The standard of proof on the voir dire in Canadian law

Controversially, the Supreme Court of Canada had held in *R v Arp* that where identity is in issue, the trial judge need only be satisfied that it is *likely* that the same person committed both acts to conclude that the probative value outweighs the prejudicial effect.[332] This standard of proof was assumed to apply generally to all propensity evidence in *Handy*.[333] Thus the trier of fact need be satisfied only on the balance of probabilities that coincidence is unlikely before applying the other misconduct evidence to each count.[334] In other words, two allegations can support each other to the point of constituting proof beyond a reasonable doubt, even where a reasonable doubt might exist in relation to each in isolation. This chain of reasoning has been described as the 'pooling' or 'cumulative' approach.[335] The Supreme Court of Canada specifically rejected the Australia High Court's stipulation in *R v Pfennig*[336] that propensity evidence should be admitted only if it is virtually conclusive of guilt, on the basis that this does not sit well with the balancing model, and takes the trial judge's gatekeeper function too far into the domain of the ultimate trier of fact.[337]

(b) Collusion and unconscious contamination in Canadian law

On the vexed issue of collusion, after some initial prevarication,[338] the Supreme Court of Canada held in *R v Handy*[339] that the trial judge's role as gatekeeper in assessing the weight as well as reliability of other misconduct evidence includes intercepting evidence tainted by collusion, and so to that extent disagreed with the House of Lords' insistence in *R v H* on leaving all issues of collusion to the jury.[340] If the evidence of collusion amounts to no more than opportunity to collude, the issue usually is best left to the jury.[341] Where there is some evidence of actual collusion, or at least an 'air of reality' to the allegations of collusion,[342] the Crown is required to satisfy the trial judge on a balance of probabilities that the other misconduct evidence was not tainted with collusion. This is because collusion destroys the premise upon which the cogency of that evidence is based, being the improbability of coincidence. If the Crown discharges this burden, it would then be for the jury to make the ultimate determination of its worth.[343]

---

[331] ibid [67].   [332] *R v Arp* (n 8) [48].   [333] *R v Handy* (n 5) [42].
[334] *R v Arp* (n 8) [66].   [335] ibid [65], [75].
[336] *Pfennig v The Queen* (n 37), discussed above section B.6(a).
[337] *R v Handy* (n 62) [93]–[97].
[338] *R v B(CR)* (n 62) [29] (Sopinka J, dissenting, suggesting that the Crown must negative collusion to the criminal standard); *R v Burke* [1996] 1 SCR 474 (SCC) [37]–[41] (Sopinka J, *obiter*).
[339] *R v Handy* (n 5).   [340] ibid [104]–[106]; *R v H* (n 91), discussed above, section B.4(c).
[341] As in *R v Shearing* (n 326), where there was evidence of some communication amongst the eleven complainants, but defence suggestions of collaboration were speculative.
[342] As in *R v Handy* (n 5), where there was consultation between the complainant and the defendant's ex-wife prior to the alleged offence about the prospect of financial profit from the Criminal Injuries Compensation Board.   [343] ibid [110]–[113].

(c) Joinder and severance of counts in Canadian law

Judges at first instance determine applications for severance of counts by the single statutory criterion of the 'interests of justice'.[344] This language has been read to impose a burden upon the defendant to prove on a balance of probabilities that the interests of justice require severance, so the issue is distinct from similar fact evidence where the prosecution bears the burden.[345] As in England, severance is not required merely because the evidence on the multiple counts has been ruled not to be cross-admissible.[346]

Applications may be brought even in the course of the trial, but then the application should rest on some prejudice which has arisen in the trial and was not apparent at the beginning, the defence bearing a heavy burden.[347] The factors that a trial judge should consider include:

(1) the factual and legal nexus between the counts;
(2) general prejudice to the accused;
(3) the undue complexity of the evidence;
(4) whether the accused wishes to testify on some counts, but not others;
(5) the possibility of inconsistent verdicts; and
(6) the desire to avoid a multiplicity of proceedings.[348]

In *R v Litchfield*[349] the Supreme Court of Canada indicated that 'an appellate court should not interfere with the issuing judge's exercise of discretion unless it is shown that the issuing judge acted injudiciously or the ruling resulted in an injustice'. Adjudicative fairness in sexual assault cases permits the court to take into account the interests of the complainant and the Crown in considering a defence application for severance.[350] In *Litchfield*, the Supreme Court emphasized that it is important in individual cases that courts not create unnecessary barriers to considering all the circumstances surrounding conduct which is alleged to constitute a sexual assault.[351] The Supreme Court sent a strong message that multiple counts involving the same complainant should not be severed:

The order denies the reality of how the complainants experienced the conduct which they have alleged constituted sexual assaults. Each aspect of one complainant's contact with the respondent interlocks with all the other aspects to form the larger context within which that complainant felt that the respondent's actions were inappropriate.[352]

We will evaluate the problems presented by propensity evidence for child abuse trials at the end of this chapter. It is important however to bear in mind the extraordinary intellectual effort expended by the judiciary in all common law jurisdictions on

---

[344] Criminal Code of Canada s 591.   [345] *R v Arp* (n 8) [52].
[346] ibid [51] citing *DPP v Boardman* (n 7).
[347] *R v Cuthbert (Delmain Aiken)* (1996) 106 CCC (3d) 28 (Ontario CA), appeal dismissed [1997] 1 SCR 8 (SCC); *R v Cross* (1996) 112 CCC (3d) 410 (Quebec CA), leave to appeal refused 215 NR 160n (SCC).   [348] *R v Cuthbert* ibid [9].
[349] *R v Litchfield* (n 311) [35].   [350] *R v L(DO)* [1993] 4 SCR 419 (SCC) ibid [38].
[351] *R v Litchfield* (n 311) [13].   [352] ibid [39] (Iacobucci J).

determining thresholds of probative value to admit other misconduct evidence as part of the prosecution case. This stands in startling contrast to the rules for the admission of other misconduct evidence during the defence case to which we now turn. Here it has been taken as a given that such evidence is always relevant to the credibility of the accused *as a witness*, and hence is admissible without the application of any threshold tests of value or prejudice associated with such evidence.

C. The Defendant's Previous Misconduct as Credibility Evidence in Criminal Cases

In this context we are addressing credibility in the sense of truthfulness, rather than reliability or accuracy. The chain of reasoning in this context is arguably even more dubious than that deployed with propensity evidence:

(1) the defendant has committed criminal offences in the past;
(2) this criminal history is relevant to the defendant's credibility as a witness;
(3) therefore the defendant is lying on oath in denying the current charges.

In short, a propensity to commit a crime is transmuted into a propensity to lie under oath. English common law does not restrict this chain of reasoning to previous offences for perjury or dishonesty. The blanket connection between criminal behaviour and truthfulness under oath is not substantiated by psychological research.[353] The hazards of reasoning directly from propensity to guilt, rather than from other misconduct to credibility to guilt, are as strong here as where the evidence is adduced as part of the prosecution case, especially where the previous convictions are similar to the offence charged.

The English, Canadian, Australian, New Zealand and American rules regarding credibility evidence, as in propensity evidence, operate on another assumption which is possibly also fallacious:[354] that juries will both understand and obey a direction from the trial judge limiting the use of the evidence. This was the model direction recommended by the Judicial Studies Board for Crown Court judges in England and Wales before the radical reform wrought by the CJA 2003:

You must not assume that the defendant is guilty or that he is not telling the truth because he has been convicted on a previous occasion. This conviction is not relevant at all to the likelihood of his having committed the offence. It is relevant only as to whether you can believe

---

[353] Law Commission of England and Wales *Evidence in Criminal Proceedings: Previous Misconduct of a Defendant* (n 17) 104–105.

[354] American and Canadian empirical studies suggest that jurors often disregard such directions: K Pickel 'Inducing Jurors to Disregard Inadmissible Evidence: a Legal Explanation Does Not Help' (1995) 9 *Law & Human Behavior* 407; R Wissler and M Saks 'On the Inefficacy of Limiting Instructions: When Jurors Use Prior Conviction Evidence to Decide on Guilt' (1995) 9 *Law & Human Behavior* 37; Hans and Doob (n 42), 240, 247, 251–252. The fallacy was accepted by Kirby J in *BRS v The Queen* (n 226) 322–323, citing Schaefer and Hanson, 'Similar Fact Evidence and Limited Use Instructions: an Empirical Investigation' (1990) 14 Crim LJ 157, and by Randall J in *State v Schwab* 409 NW 2d 876 (Minnesota CA 1987) 882.

him. It is for you to decide the extent to which, if at all, his previous conviction helps you about that.[355]

As with a 'good character' direction relating to propensity, an asymmetry arises from the entitlement of a defendant without previous convictions to a direction that his denial of having committed the offence is for this reason more likely to be true.[356]

When defendants became competent to testify in their own defence towards the end of the 19th century, legislators in jurisdictions using the adversarial mode of trial were faced with a dilemma: how to ensure effective cross-examination by the prosecution to test their testimonial credibility, whilst preventing the triers of fact from reasoning from propensity. Legislators generally adopted one of two models for dealing with this problem: either defendants are treated much like other witnesses, and therefore are subject to cross-examination on previous misconduct; or defendants who elect to testify enjoy special protection against disclosure of their past misdeeds, which they may forfeit through the way their defence has been conducted in the particular case. We will briefly consider each model.

1. The first model: defendants lose their shield by choosing to testify

Under Canadian[357] and American[358] law, the defendant by choosing to testify is deemed to have put his credibility as a witness in issue, which the prosecutor can exploit by cross-examining him about past convictions and other previous discreditable acts (if the latter are thought to reflect adversely on the defendant's credibility). This rule can cause perverse side-effects,[359] as the defendant may have a credible story to tell, but might be deterred from testifying because his criminal record inevitably will be disclosed.[360] In Canada, it is customary for defence counsel to elicit previous convictions from their clients in examination-in-chief, hoping to minimize their impact on the jury.[361]

The due process implications of this rule were explored by the Supreme Court of Canada in *R v Corbett*, where the accused on a murder charge claimed that he was deprived of his right to a fair trial[362] because, notwithstanding the judicial direction to the contrary, the trier of fact would be incapable of restricting the use of the evidence

---

[355] Judicial Studies Board *Crown Court Bench Book* (n 130), chapter III Evidence, Direction 18.

[356] *R v Vye; Wise; Stevenson* (n 130); *Crown Court Bench Book* ibid Ch III Direction 23. This Direction remains valid under the CJA 2003 (England).

[357] eg Canada Evidence Act s 12(1). All Canadian provinces except Quebec have legislated in similar terms for summary conviction offences within their jurisdiction. As a matter of practice, cross-examination is limited to identification of the crime, the substance and effect of the indictment, the place of conviction and the penalty imposed.

[358] *Wigmore on Evidence* (n 152) vol 3A §925, §980A, §985–988; vol 1A §55–60; *Reagan v US* 157 US 301 (USSC 1895) 304–305; *US v Lollar* 606 F2d 587 (US CA 5th Cir 1979) 588.

[359] Park (n 28) 756.

[360] However, in Canada, if the accused adduces evidence of his good character, the prosecution is entitled to rebut this with evidence of previous convictions (but not of other misconduct): Criminal Code of Canada s 666; *Morris v The Queen* (n 13).

[361] Such evidence is admissible under the Canada Evidence Act s 12: *R v St Pierre* (1974) 3 OR (2d) 642 (Ontario CA).   [362] Guaranteed by s 11(d) of the Canadian Charter of Rights and Freedoms.

of his previous murder conviction to the issue of his credibility.[363] Dickson CJC held that the jury could be trusted to abide by the limited use direction, and that to exclude the evidence would have given the jury an imbalanced view of his credibility when compared with that of prosecution witnesses with convictions.

Notwithstanding this avowal of trust in juries, in both Canada and the United States, the severity of the rule has been mitigated by judicial discretion to exclude evidence of past convictions where the evidence is seen as more prejudicial than probative and so would undermine the right to a fair trial. In Canada, the trial judge is expected to consider the nature of the previous conviction, its similarity to the offence charged, its remoteness in time, and the nature of the defence, including whether it consisted of a deliberate attack upon the credibility of Crown witnesses.[364] In a prosecution for sexual assault, suggesting that the complainant's account is not true is not regarded as creating the potential for the imbalance between the defendant and other witnesses posited in *Corbett*, and so may warrant exclusion.[365] It is also open to a trial judge to 'sanitize' the accused's record by editing it to limit its prejudicial effect, for example by describing a conviction for sexual assault of children as merely an assault,[366] or editing out some convictions thought to be particularly prejudicial.[367]

In most American jurisdictions, the trial judge can prevent the use of past convictions[368] and other misconduct[369] as impeachment evidence where the jury is likely to use the evidence improperly to reason from propensity notwithstanding the limited use direction, one factor being similarity between the convictions and the offence charged.[370] Nevertheless, in several cases previous convictions for child sexual abuse have been admitted as having legitimate impeachment value notwithstanding their similarity to the offences charged,[371] where the natural inference for the jury would be a propensity to abuse children.[372] In contrast, where the sexual abuse did not result in convictions, courts have refused to permit cross-examination on the basis that the evidence was not sufficiently probative of truthfulness.[373]

---

[363] *R v Corbett* [1988] 1 SCR 670 (SCC).   [364] ibid 740–744.

[365] *R v Batte* (2000) 145 CCC (3d) 498 (Ontario CA) [47].   [366] ibid [51].

[367] *R v T(DB)* (1994) 89 CCC (3d) 466 (Ontario CA).

[368] eg Federal Rule of Evidence 609(a)(1) which provides that evidence that an accused has been convicted of a crime punishable by more than one year's imprisonment shall be admitted if the court determines that the probative value of admitting this evidence outweighs its prejudicial effect to the accused. However, the balancing provision does not apply where the conviction is one of dishonesty or involves a false statement.

[369] eg Fed R Evid 608, Fed R Evid 403. Under Rule 608(b), specific instances of misconduct other than convictions may not be proved by extrinsic evidence. They may, however, be explored in cross-examination of the witness in the discretion of the court, if considered probative of truthfulness or untruthfulness.

[370] Bryden and Park (n 158), 535.

[371] *State v Schwab* (n 354); *People v Hall* 453 NE 2d 1327 (Illinois App Ct 1983), *certiorari* denied 467 US 1228 (USSC 1984); *Jackson v State* 447 NW 2d 430 (Minnesota CA 1989).

[372] Bryden and Park (n 158), 535.

[373] *State v Scott* 347 SE 2d 414 (North Carolina Supreme Ct 1986) 415, 417–418; *Summerlin v State* 643 SW 2d 582 (Arkansas CA 1982) 583–585; Bryden and Park (n 158) 535–538.

2. The second model: defendants retain their shield, subject to forfeiture

Until the CJA 2003 (England), cross-examination of English defendants was governed by the Criminal Evidence Act 1898, which permitted questions about previous convictions or bad character if and only if:

- the evidence was already admissible as part of the prosecution case (eg as similar fact evidence); or

- they put their own character in issue by offering evidence of good character, either personally or through witnesses as to their reputation; or

- they attacked prosecution witnesses, or a deceased victim, by 'casting imputations' on their credibility (regardless of whether the attack is necessary, merited, or independently proved through convictions, and notwithstanding any similar attacks by the prosecution on defence witnesses); or

- by offering evidence against a co-defendant.

The legislation was very poorly drafted, and resulted in tortuous judicial interpretation making abstruse and subtle distinctions.

Before the CJA 2003, a defendant standing trial in England and Wales could circumvent the impeachment of credibility rule by choosing not to testify.[374] Under legislation enacted in 1994, this decision acquired an additional penalty, because the jury is invited to 'draw such inferences as appear proper from his failure to give evidence', unless the court concludes that the accused's physical or mental condition makes it undesirable for him to give evidence.[375]

The dilemma created for defence counsel by the 1898 Act was alleviated somewhat by judicially created discretion to restore the shield to defendants. In *Selvey*[376] the Law Lords acknowledged that cases must occur in which it would be unjust to admit evidence of a character greatly prejudicial to the accused, even though there might be some tenuous grounds for holding it technically admissible.[377] The principles approved by the House of Lords in *Selvey* required trial judges to weigh the prejudicial effect of the questions against the damage done by the attack on the prosecution's witnesses, and to exercise their discretion so as to secure a trial fair both to the defence and the prosecution. However, similarity between the criminal record and the charges did not of itself require exclusion, even if the convictions have the incidental effect of suggesting a tendency to commit that sort of offence.[378] In *Britzman*,[379] the Court of Appeal established guidelines for the exercise of discretion where the conduct of the defence necessarily involved an allegation that

---

[374] *R v Butterwasser* [1948] 1 KB 4 (CA).

[375] Criminal Justice and Public Order Act 1994 (England) s 35. In *R v Cowan* [1996] QB 373 (CA) the Court of Appeal rejected the argument that the availability of the adverse inference effectively forced the accused to testify, and to face the possible disclosure of his prior record.

[376] *Selvey v DPP* [1970] AC 304 (HL)

[377] Summarized by Ackner LJ in *R v Burke* (1985) 82 Cr App R 151 (CA) 161.

[378] *R v McLeod* [1994] 1 WLR 1500 (CA) 1511.

[379] *R v Britzman* [1993] 1 WLR 350 (CA) 355.

a prosecution witness had concocted evidence. Discretion was to be invoked if the defendant merely denied an act, however emphatically or offensively denied. Cross-examination was only to be allowed if the judge was sure that there was no possibility of mistake, misunderstanding or confusion on the part of the defendant, and that the jury would inevitably have to decide whether the prosecution witness had fabricated evidence. This of course is the dominant issue in most child sexual abuse trials.

Like the Canadian courts, English judges also developed a special rule for rape cases, whereby a defendant who alleged consent on the part of the victim was not regarded as having cast imputations on the character of the complainant, on the rationale that it was unjust to put the defendant at risk of losing his shield by merely denying one of the ingredients of the offence.[380] This was significant in child abuse cases before the Sexual Offences Act 2003, when the defendant could plead consent as a complete defence to a rape charge even where the complainant was below the legal age of consent.

Notwithstanding all the difficulties created by the Criminal Evidence Act 1898, New Zealand[381] and several Australian States adopted that model. Prompted by the Australian Law Reform Commission's concern[382] about the divergence of interpretation and practice amongst States and the implications of a High Court ruling that an accused who contests the prosecution case is always at risk of being cross-examined on past misconduct,[383] the Australian Uniform Evidence Acts take a more restrictive position. Evidence relevant only to credibility is admissible only if it has 'substantial probative value', and it cannot be elicited in cross-examination without leave of the court. Leave can only be granted to rebut evidence of the defendant's good character, or in response to a defence attack on the credibility of a prosecution witness, if it is suggested that the witness has a tendency to be untruthful.[384]

The New Zealand Law Commission originally proposed merely to codify the existing rules derived from the English law,[385] but in its final report moved to a more restricted basis of admissibility. Evidence about the defendant's truthfulness would be admissible at the instance of the prosecution or the defence only if the defendant has either offered evidence of her own truthfulness or challenged the truthfulness of a prosecution witness, the court has given leave, and the evidence would be substantially helpful in assessing her truthfulness.[386]

---

[380] *Selvey v DPP* (n 376).
[381] Evidence Act 1908 (New Zealand) s 5(4). *R v Clark* [1953] NZLR 823 (New Zealand CA) held that New Zealand courts should exercise exclusionary discretion in accordance with the English caselaw under the Criminal Evidence Act 1898.   [382] Aus LRC *Evidence* (n 197) Ch 14.
[383] *R v Phillips* (1968) 60 ALJR 76 (Aus HC).
[384] Evidence Act 1995 (Commonwealth of Australia) ss 102, 103. The Australian Law Reform Commission is undertaking a review of several provisions of the Uniform Evidence Acts, including the coincidence and credibility rules, and was expected to report in 2005.
[385] NZLC *Character and Credibility* (n 45) 9.
[386] NZLC *Evidence* (n 295) Vol 1 45–47 and Vol 2, Draft Evidence Code ss 39–40.

D. Radical Reform: Expanded Admissibility of Propensity and Credibility Evidence Under the Criminal Justice Act 2003

The UK Government in its 2002 White Paper *Justice for All* declared that its 'single clear priority' was to 'rebalance the criminal justice system in favour of the victim and the community'. The Government committed itself to convict more of the guilty by ensuring that the case focuses on 'the relevant issues', and to overhaul the rules of evidence to ensure that magistrates, judges and juries 'are able to hear the widest range of material, including relevant previous convictions' that fairly bears on defendants' guilt or innocence.[387] The need for systematic reform to codify and render coherent the character evidence rules is beyond dispute,[388] but the 'seesaw' metaphor validates the widespread misconception that the criminal justice system is about balancing the defendant's rights *against* society's interests in suppressing and punishing crime— instead of recognizing that one is a necessary support for and reinforcement of the other. The Home Secretary's solution for the rules of evidence was to redefine what is meant by 'fair' and 'relevant', and the product is the CJA 2003.

1. The new statutory model

The CJA 2003 makes radical changes to the admissibility of propensity and credibility evidence:

- all of the common law rules governing the admissibility of character evidence in criminal proceedings have been abolished [s 99];
- the bad character provisions of the Criminal Evidence Act 1898[389] protecting the defendant when testifying have been repealed;
- the distinction between similar fact evidence as part of the prosecution's case, and the admissibility of previous misconduct going to credibility if the defendant testifies, which the Law Commission wished maintained, has been erased; and
- the new admissibility rules apply regardless of whether the defendant testifies.

Diagram 19 maps the new provisions governing the admissibility of evidence of the character of the defendant.

It will be immediately apparent that the legislation takes a general *inclusionary* approach subject to a limited residual judicial discretion to exclude the evidence. This

---

[387] Secretary of State for the Home Department, Lord Chancellor, Attorney General *Justice for All* (Cm 5563, July 2002) Executive Summary Part 1 and 68.

[388] Law Commission *Evidence of Bad Character* (n 50) Summary [18] described the bad character rules as 'a haphazard mixture of statute and common law rules which produce inconsistent and unpredictable results, distort the trial process in crucial respects, make tactical considerations paramount and inhibit the defence in presenting its true case to the fact-finders whilst often exposing witnesses to gratuitous and humiliating exposure of long-forgotten misconduct.'

[389] Criminal Evidence Act 1898 (England) s 1(1)(e) and (f), renumbered as s 1(3) by the Youth Justice and Criminal Evidence Act 1999 (England) Sch 4 para. 1(7).

Diagram 19. Evidence of the Bad Character of the Defendant [CJA 2003 Part 11, Ch 1]

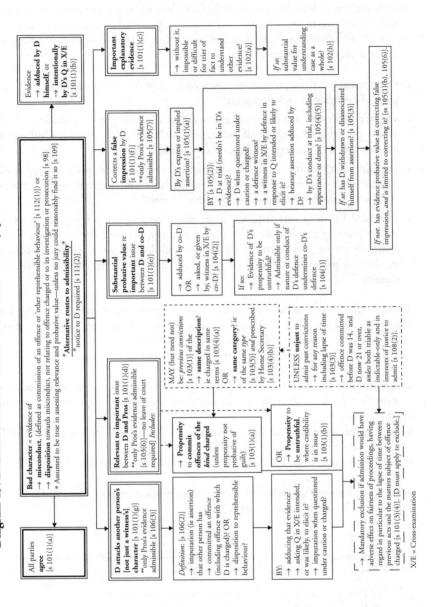

represents a fundamental shift in approach not just from the common law's exclusionary rule with exceptions, but also from the Law Commission's firm recommendation of a guided balancing model which would have been premised upon a general exclusionary rule[390] with clearly delineated exceptions, subject to the following four safeguards directed at prejudicial effect:[391]

- a requirement that the prosecution apply for leave of the court to adduce a particular piece of evidence in each category;[392]
- a higher dual evidential threshold applicable to all of the gateways to admissibility, in that the evidence must be of 'substantial probative value' and be of 'substantial importance in the context of the case as a whole';[393]
- a requirement that the court consider and balance the risk of prejudice against its probative value, including whether other evidence could be given on the matter to avoid adducing the bad character evidence;[394] and
- a detailed list of factors required to be considered in balancing probative value against prejudicial effect, focusing on the number, nature and time of the events, and their nature and extent of similarities and dissimilarities where the basis of its claimed probative value is to prove an element of the charged offence or identity.[395]

There would also have been a strictly drawn inclusionary discretion.[396] The Law Commission's draft bill had also maintained the clear distinction between evidence going to a matter in issue and evidence going to credibility.

In contrast, the model created by the CJA 2003 in Part 11 Chapter 1:

- takes an inclusionary approach[397] where the notice provisions replace the requirement for a prosecution application, so that the burden is on the defendant to apply for exclusion;
- contains no evidential threshold of probative value beyond mere relevance for the most crucial category, propensity evidence;
- the previous one-stage test which balanced probative value and prejudicial effect is made obsolete;[398] and
- the court has only exclusionary rather than inclusionary discretion, which tightly constrains its room for manoeuvre.[399]

---

[390] *Evidence of Bad Character* (n 50) [6.65].

[391] For detailed comparison of the Law Commission's recommendations and the CJA 2003 (England), see C Tapper 'The Criminal Justice Act 2003 (3): Evidence of Bad Character' [2004] Crim LR 533, 541–545.   [392] *Evidence of Bad character* (n 50) [8.13].

[393] ibid Draft Bill clause 8.   [394] ibid [8.13] and Draft Bill clause 8(2).

[395] ibid Draft Bill clause 5(2).   [396] ibid Draft Bill clause 17.

[397] *R v Weir* [2005] EWCA Crim 2866, [2006] 2 All ER 570 [36].   [398] ibid [36].

[399] All of the Lord Justices in the Court of Appeal Criminal Division expressed a preference for inclusionary rather than exclusionary discretion: The Lord Chief Justice *Second Reading of the Criminal Justice Bill: Background Notes to Speech by the Rt Hon the Lord Woolf of Barnes* (House of Lords Library memorandum HMF 2003/1315 16 June 2003) 5 [16].

Returning to Diagram 18 depicting the different approaches to propensity evidence taken by common law jurisdictions, we can see that the CJA 2003 requires English judges to apply a model with minimalist thresholds for admissibility.

As Diagram 19 shows, there are now seven alternative gateways to the admission of evidence of bad character, defined by section 98 as being evidence of misconduct or a disposition towards misconduct.[400] 'Misconduct' is later defined as commission of an offence (which is straightforward) or 'other reprehensible behaviour' (which is not).[401] The misconduct must not relate to the offence charged or to its investigation or prosecution; if it does relate to background or motive, then there is no need to manoeuvre the evidence through a gateway as it will be automatically admissible.[402]

Although many of the gateways mimic those familiar to the law which has been superseded, as indicated above their operation will be significantly different. Moreover, the Court of Appeal has interpreted the legislation as permitting evidence of bad character, once admitted through one gateway, to be used for any purpose for which it is relevant in the case. Thus where the evidence is admitted through the gateway for an attack on another person's character, it can be treated as relevant not only to credibility but also to propensity to commit offences of the kind with which the defendant has been charged.[403]

Most significant for our present discussion is the elevation of the 'forbidden chain of reasoning' to a primary ground of both admissibility in the prosecution's case[404] and utility for the trier of fact in deciding guilt.[405] In other words, a disposition to misconduct, expressly described as propensity evidence—whether to commit offences of the kind charged or to be untruthful—is explicitly *presumed to be relevant to an important matter* in issue between the defendant and the prosecution,[406] unless that particular propensity makes it no more likely that he is guilty of the offence.[407] As the Lord Chief Justice and the other appellate judges from the Criminal Division stated in a Parliamentary memorandum criticizing the Bill, '[e]vidence that would previously have been considered neither admissible nor relevant will apparently be treated as both admissible and relevant'.[408]

Propensity to commit offences of the kind charged may (but need not) be proved by previous convictions of the 'same description', ie they would be charged on an

---

[400] Thereby preserving the admissibility of misconduct for which the defendant has not been charged, or has been acquitted: *R v Z (Prior Acquittal)* (n 8). Tapper argues that when this is combined with the statutory assumption of truth, this creates a presumption of guilt in respect of the charge which resulted in an acquittal [C Tapper 'The Criminal Justice Act 2003' (n 391) 547–548].

[401] CJA 2003 (England) s 112(1). See R Munday 'What Constitutes "Reprehensible Behaviour" under the Bad Character Provisions of the Criminal Justice Act 2003?' [2005] Crim LR 24.

[402] Although the distinction may be difficult to establish in a particular case: *R v Edwards and Rowlands* [2005] EWCA Crim 3244.

[403] *R v Highton, Van-Nguyen, Carp* [2005] EWCA Crim 1985; [2005] 1 WLR 3472.

[404] CJA 2003 (England) s 103(6).   [405] ibid s 103(1)(a).   [406] ibid s 101(1)(d).

[407] ibid s 103(1)(a). Colin Tapper argues that minimal ingenuity by the prosecution can readily evade this proviso: 'The Criminal Justice Act 2003' (n 391) 543.

[408] *Background Notes to Speech by the Rt Hon the Lord Woolf of Barnes* (n 399) 4 [13].

indictment in the same terms,[409] or of the 'same category' as the charged offence. The 'same category' is clumsily defined as being offences of the 'same type',[410] as prescribed by the Secretary of State.[411] As expected, the first Order made by the Secretary of State under the Act defined all sexual offences against children under the age of 16 as constituting a single category for the purposes of the propensity to misconduct gateway.[412] There is no bar to using spent convictions, but the court is given discretion to exclude the evidence for, amongst other reasons, lapse of time.[413]

What is more, an alleged propensity to be untruthful is also deemed to be an important issue between the defence and prosecution, even where the defendant does not testify, provided that the defendant's credibility is in issue[414]—and it will be a rare case where it is not, especially in a contested prosecution for offences against children. Nor does the defendant have to attack a prosecution witness's character or lay claim to his own good character before his credibility is put in issue,[415] as was the case under the Criminal Evidence Act 1898.

Furthermore, the evidential threshold for propensity to misconduct or propensity to be untruthful is set at the absolute minimum: mere relevance to a matter in issue suffices. This stands in stark contrast to character evidence relating to other witnesses, which must have substantial probative value in relation to a matter in issue and be of substantial importance in the context of the whole case before it can be admitted.[416] The Law Commission had regarded it as a key principle that bad character evidence in respect of all participants in the trial should be subject to the same 'enhanced relevance' test: that it must be of 'substantial value for determination of the case.[417] This asymmetry in treatment caused great concern when the Bill was examined by the Select Committee on Home Affairs,[418] but is now a key feature of the new statutory regime.

The only protection from disclosure of propensity evidence available to a defendant is the shield of judicial discretion, which may feature in an odd series of ways:

- for previous convictions for the same type of offence:
  — if it is 'unjust' to admit them for any reason, including the length of time since the conviction;[419] or
  — if the offence was committed before the defendant was 14 and he is now 21 or over, unless both offences are triable only on indictment and the court is satisfied that the interests of justice require the evidence to be admitted;[420]

---

[409] CJA 2003 (England) s 103(4)(a).   [410] ibid s 103(5).   [411] ibid s 103(4)(b).

[412] The Criminal Justice Act 2003 (Categories of Offences) Order 2004, SI 2004 No 3346, Part 2.

[413] CJA 2003 (England) s 103(3).   [414] ibid s 103(1)(a).   [415] ibid s 101(1)(g).

[416] ibid s 100(1)(a); discussed above Chapter 9 section D.1 and Diagram 16.

[417] *Evidence of Bad Character* (n 50) 2–3 [1.8].

[418] *Second Report of the Select Committee on Home Affairs on the Criminal Justice Act 2003, Part 11 Chapter 1: Evidence of Bad Character* (4 December 2002) [122].

[419] CJA 2003 (England) s 103(3). The trial judge should if necessary encourage a defence application whenever by reference to the ECHR Art 6 it appears that the admission of the evidence would have such an adverse effect on the fairness of the proceedings that it should be excluded: *R v Weir* (n 397) [38].

[420] CJA 2003 (England) s 108(2).

- for propensity to misconduct or to untruthfulness, or where the defence has attacked another person's character, the defendant can apply for a ruling to exclude the bad character evidence due to the adverse effect it would have on the fairness of the proceedings,[421] the length of time between the past misconduct and that charged being a mandatory consideration.[422]

It is likely that the judiciary in applying the nebulous tests of 'justice' and 'fairness' in the absence of any other meaningful guidance from the legislators will have recourse to the familiar formula of balancing probative value against prejudicial effect which is notable by its absence from the Act.[423] Indeed, Lord Phillips of Worth Matravers in an *obiter dictum* has asserted that sections 101–106 of the CJA 2003 'preserve . . . by rules of some complexity, the requirement that the similar fact evidence should have an enhanced probative value'.[424]

Oddly, the other two gateways for evidence of a defendant's disposition towards misconduct which are likely to be directly pertinent to child abuse prosecutions have explicit, and much higher, evidential thresholds:

- where the evidence is an important issue between the defendant and a co-defendant, for example which of two carers had physically or sexually abused a very young victim or other children; in this case the evidence must have 'substantial probative value' in relation to that important issue;[425] and

- where it is 'important explanatory evidence' without which it would be impossible or difficult for the trier of fact to understand other evidence, and it has 'substantial value' to understanding the case as a whole[426]—in effect, a codification of the common law concept of background evidence.

The court is instructed to assume that the evidence is true in determining its relevance or probative value,[427] thereby replicating the controversial approach of *R v H*.[428] However, the trial judge is spared this fiction if she concludes from the material before the court, including any *viva voce* evidence, that no court or jury could reasonably find it to be true.[429] Furthermore, if it should emerge in the course of the trial that the bad character evidence which has been admitted is contaminated, and that this would render any conviction unsafe, the court must direct the jury to acquit, or order a retrial.[430]

---

[421] ibid s 101(3). The language is clearly reminiscent of the general exclusionary discretion in section 78 of the Police and Criminal Evidence Act. [422] ibid s 101(4).

[423] Notwithstanding the Lord Chief Justice's call for it to be expressly included: *Background Notes to Speech by the Rt Hon the Lord Woolf of Barnes* (n 399) 5–6 [17].

[424] *O'Brien v Chief Constable of South Wales Police* [2005] UKHL 26, [2005] 2 All ER 931 [33].

[425] CJA 2003 (England) s 101(1)(e). [426] ibid s 101(1)(c). [427] ibid s 109(1).

[428] *R v H* (n 91), discussed above section B.4(c). [429] CJA 2003 (England) s 109(2).

[430] ibid s 107; *R v C* [2006] EWCA Crim 1079 (contamination of one child complainant's evidence through discussions with the mother should have raised the inescapable inference of contamination of the sibling's testimony and so the jury should have been discharged).

2. Joinder and severance

The formal procedural rules governing joinder and severance have not been altered by the CJA 2003. However, practice in relation to cross-admissibility of the evidence on different counts will be changed somewhat. Under s 112(2), where a defendant is charged with two or more offences in the same criminal proceedings, the provisions on bad character are to be applied as if each offence were charged in separate proceedings. Therefore, it appears that cross-admissibility of other misconduct evidence will be determined on the basis of whether the evidence on Count 1 is 'relevant to an important issue' between the defendant and the prosecution on Count 2 (which we have seen is deemed to include propensity to commit offences of the kind charged)[431] or whether it is 'important explanatory evidence'.[432] It is possible that under the new regime cross-admissibility rulings in child abuse cases will become more frequent.

3. The new statutory model: judicial interpretation

The Lord Chief Justice and all the Lord Justices of the Court of Appeal Criminal Division deposited a memorandum in the Parliamentary library strongly opposing the bad character proposals in the Bill, warning:

The provisions as a whole are extremely confusing and will prove very difficult to interpret. They will result in lengthy arguments in court, more appeals and more scope for technical errors on the part of the trial judge that could give rise to convictions being overturned.[433]

This distaste may be a harbinger of an inclination by the appellate judiciary to treat the new provisions with circumspection. The Court of Appeal has already castigated the bad character provisions as being 'perplexing legislation' using 'obfuscatory language', which was implemented prematurely before judicial training could be completed.[434] The Court has told the prosecutors not to tender propensity evidence routinely, simply because the defendant has previous convictions.[435] It has also warned against the risk of 'satellite litigation'.

In *R v Hanson*,[436] the court provided trial judges with the following analytical template for bad character evidence under the new regime:

- Does the history of conviction(s) establish a propensity to commit offences of the kind charged?
  - There is no minimum number of events necessary to demonstrate such a propensity; a single previous conviction may suffice where it shows a tendency

---

[431] CJA 2003 (England) s 103(1)(a).   [432] ibid s 101(1)(c).
[433] *Background Notes to Speech by the Rt Hon the Lord Woolf of Barnes* (n 399) 4 [13].
[434] *R v David Benjamin Bradley* [2005] EWCA Crim 20 [38]–[39].
[435] *R v Hanson; R v Gilmour; R v P* [2005] EWCA Crim 824, [2005] 2 Cr App R 21 [4]. Rose LJ cautioned against routine prosecution application to adduce such evidence; however, no such application is required under the Act, only notice to the defendant being required under s 111(2).
[436] ibid [7].

to unusual behaviour, such as child sexual abuse, or where its circumstances demonstrate probative force in relation to the offence charged.[437]

- Does that propensity make it more likely that the defendant committed the offence charged?

- Is it unjust to rely upon the conviction(s) of the same description or category; and, in any event, will the proceedings be unfair if they are admitted?

  — The exclusionary power under s 101(3) is mandatory ('must not admit' is stronger than the comparable provision in the Police and Criminal Evidence Act 1984 s 78, 'may refuse to allow').[438] Nevertheless, the Court of Appeal will be very slow to interfere with a trial judge's ruling unless it is clearly wrong or so unreasonable that no rational tribunal could have reached that conclusion.[439] (In this context, note that the CJA 2003 ss 62 and 63 now give the prosecution the right to appeal against evidential rulings that significantly weaken the prosecution case.)

  — Old convictions with no special feature shared with the offence charged are likely seriously to affect the fairness of proceedings adversely unless, despite their age, it can properly be said that they show a continuing propensity to commit that type of offence.[440]

  — As to propensity for untruthfulness, previous convictions, whether for offences of dishonesty or otherwise, are only likely to be capable of showing such propensity where truthfulness was an issue, and either there was a plea of not guilty and the defendant gave an account which the jury must have disbelieved, or the way in which the offence was committed shows a propensity for untruthfulness, for example by the making of false representations.[441]

  — The caselaw developed under the Criminal Evidence Act 1898 will continue to apply in assessing whether an attack has been made on another person's character, to the extent that it is consistent with the new provision[442] (the innovation being that the defendant does not need to have testified to forfeit her shield).

Once the evidence becomes admissible by passing through any of the seven gateways in s 101, it then may be used by the jury for any purpose for which bad character evidence is relevant in the particular case.[443] There will be a very close relationship between the prerequisites of fairness in use of the evidence in s 101(3) and relevance. Moreover, trial judges should also apply the exclusionary discretion in s 78 of the Police and Criminal Evidence Act 1984 as a 'sensible precaution' to ensure compliance with ECHR Article 6 and the Human Rights Act 1998 s 3.[444]

---

[437] ibid [8]. [438] ibid [10]. [439] ibid [15]–[16]. [440] ibid [11].
[441] ibid [13]. [442] ibid [14]. [443] *R v Highton, Van-Nguyen, Carp* (n 403) [9]–[10].
[444] ibid [12]–[14].

Finally, the Court of Appeal in *Hanson* provided the framework for a model jury direction[445] concerning the use of propensity evidence, to be developed by the Judicial Studies Board.

- The jury must be warned clearly against placing undue reliance on previous convictions, and concluding that the defendant is guilty or untruthful merely because of his past convictions.

- It is for the jury to decide whether the convictions in fact show a propensity, taking into account what the defendant has said about his previous convictions.

- The jury must be told that although the convictions may show a propensity, this does not mean he has committed this offence or been untruthful in this case.

- Although they are entitled to take propensity into account, it is only one relevant factor, and they must assess the significance in the light of all the other evidence in the case.[446]

Rose LJ warned that evidence of bad character cannot be used simply to bolster a weak case, or to prejudice the minds of the jury against the defendant; however it is difficult to see what evidentiary value the bad character evidence will have if it is not to serve as a makeweight for the prosecution case.

E. Propensity and Credibility Evidence in Civil Cases

All common law jurisdictions take a much more relaxed view of propensity and credibility evidence in civil cases than they do in criminal cases.

We have seen that the strict rules of evidence do not apply in the English family courts, relevance being the only filter. Where the issue being tried is whether the child is suffering or is likely to suffer significant harm which is attributable to the care given or likely to be given to the child,[447] the character of, and previous misconduct by, a carer or someone else with access to the child is clearly of great relevance and probative value. Other common law jurisdictions take much the same position, the rationale being that the best interests of the child at present and in the future must be the paramount consideration.[448]

In English civil courts trying allegations of breach of civil law obligations, the leading authority from the Court of Appeal, *Mood Music*, made similar fact evidence admissible if it was logically relevant to determining the matter in issue, provided that it was not oppressive or unfair and that the other side has had fair notice and is able to

---

[445] Departure from the *Hanson* guidelines will not result in a conviction being quashed, so long as the trial judge has clearly warned the jury not to place undue reliance on previous convictions: *R v Edwards; R v Fysh; R v Duggan; R v Chohan* [2005] EWCA Crim 1813.

[446] *R v Hanson, Gilmour* etc (n 435) [18]. [447] Children Act 1989 s 31(2).

[448] US: Myers *Evidence in Child Abuse Cases* Vol 2, 425–428; Canada: *Re R(AS)* (1998) 218 AR 276 (Alberta Prov Ct); *S(B) v British Columbia (Director of Child, Family & Community Service)* (1998) 160 DLR (4th) 264 (British Columbia CA); D Thompson 'Are There *Any* Rules of Evidence in Family Law?' (2003) 21 Canadian Fam LQ 245, 253–254.

deal with it.[449] Thus the familiar formula of balancing probative value and prejudicial effect is deployed, but as the trier of fact is usually a judge sitting without a jury, practically speaking it is impossible to argue reasoning prejudice or moral prejudice, so the opponent tends to be thrown back on procedural fairness arguments.

In 2005 in *O'Brien v Chief Constable of South Wales Police*,[450] the Law Lords had their first opportunity since 1881[451] to consider the admissibility of similar fact evidence in civil cases, in the context of the principles of recent civil procedure reforms giving case management judges and trial judges the discretion to deal with evidence in a way that is proportionate to what is involved in the case, and in an expeditious and fair manner.[452] Lord Bingham held that there are two stages to the admissibility inquiry.[453] The first question is whether the evidence is logically probative in making the fact in issue more or less probable and so legally admissible. The second question is whether the evidence should actually be admitted, bearing in mind that 'justice requires not only that the right answer be given but also that it be achieved by a trial process which is fair to all parties'.[454] The court should consider the risk of distorting the trial and distracting the attention of the decision-maker by focusing on collateral issues (especially where trial is by jury), and the burden which admission would place upon the resisting party, including cost and stress, the potential prejudice to witnesses called upon to recall matters long thought to be closed, the loss of documentation, and the fading of recollections.[455] The probative value versus prejudicial effect formula familiar to criminal courts is also necessary in civil proceedings; Lord Bingham said that unless the former outweighs the latter 'by a considerable margin', the evidence is likely to be excluded.[456] Thus the principle in *Mood Music* has been approved,[457] and arguably strengthened.

In English tort cases, therefore, the admissibility of evidence that the defendant abused other children is likely to be affected by the same considerations as those applying in criminal cases. However, it must be remembered that in all the leading tort cases involving child abuse allegations before the CJA 2003, such similar fact evidence was ruled to be properly admitted.[458] Thus it is unlikely that much will change in tort actions for child abuse as a consequence of *O'Brien*.

The principle in *Mood Music* has been frequently applied by Canadian courts trying tort and fiduciary cases involving child sexual and physical abuse, particularly in an institutional setting.[459] The mode of analysis in *Handy*, particularly in respect of the

---

[449] *Mood Music Publishing Co Ltd v De Wolfe Ltd* [1976] 1 All ER 763 (CA) 766.

[450] *O'Brien v Chief Constable of South Wales Police* (n 424).

[451] *Metropolitan Asylum District Managers v Hill* (1881) 6 App Cas 193, [1881–5] All ER 536 (HL).

[452] Civil Practice Rules 1998 (Eng) S1 1998/313, Rules 1.2, 1.4, 32.1; *O'Brien v Chief Constable of South Wales Police* (n 424) [54]. [453] *O'Brien* ibid [4]–[5].

[454] ibid [6]. [455] ibid [6]. [456] ibid [6]. [457] ibid [72], [76].

[458] eg *C v D and SBA* [2006] EWHC 166, [2006] All ER (D) 329 (QB) (similar fact allegations made against the same monk by other pupils at an Abbey school admitted).

[459] *B(V) v Cairns and Watch Tower Society* (2003) 65 OR (3d) 343 (Ontario Supreme Ct) [30]–[33] (evidence as to how Jehovah's Witnesses habitually covered up child sexual abuse ruled inadmissible as irrelevant, oppressive and unfair); *M(C) v AG of Canada* (2004) 130 ACWS (3d) 1227 (Saskatchewan QB) [62]–[67] (similar fact evidence admitted to rebut defendant's assertion that he confined his sexual activity to boys and so could not have assaulted the female plaintiff; plaintiffs' evidence in separate actions

possibility of collusion or unconscious contamination as an element of probative value, has been applied in the civil context.[460] The same position is taken in New Zealand common law.[461] Under the draft New Zealand Evidence Code, a party could offer evidence in civil proceedings about a person's truthfulness only if the evidence is 'substantially helpful' in assessing that person's truthfulness.[462] Propensity evidence would be tendered in civil proceedings without any special statutory controls.[463]

Under the Australian Uniform Evidence Acts, the tendency and coincidence rules apply in civil proceedings as they do in criminal trials, but without the constraint that the probative value of the evidence must substantially outweigh any prejudicial effect.[464] Witnesses may be cross-examined about other misconduct evidence where it has 'substantial probative value', two factors being whether the witness has made a false representation whilst under an obligation to tell the truth, and the time that has elapsed.[465] This is a significant departure[466] from Australian common law which had tended to admit similar fact evidence in civil cases whenever it was seen as being relevant to a fact in issue.[467]

F. Evaluation: An Irresolvable Conflict of Incommensurable Concepts?

Other misconduct evidence exposes the tensions in the criminal adversarial trial process between concepts of relevance, probative value, and prejudicial effect. The common law constructed complex exclusionary rules betraying a distrust of the jury as fact-finder whilst at the same time reposing great confidence in the assumption that juries both understand and will apply complex directions from the trial judge as to how to use that evidence. As one English barrister has observed, in the Crown Court the ruling on admissibility is as close as a judge comes to single-handedly deciding the outcome of a case.[468] To the extent that other misconduct evidence is used to shore up the prosecution case, it exposes the fundamental difficulties of fact-finding on

---

tried concurrently ruled cross-admissible); *A(M) and A(T) v Attorney General of Canada* [2001] SKQB 504, 212 Sask R 241 (Saskatchewan QB) [63]–[66] (evidence of other victims admissible to establish defendant's pattern of abusive physical and sexual behaviour in a First Nations residential school); J Sopinka, SN Lederman and AW Bryant *The Law of Evidence in Canada* (2nd edn Butterworths, Toronto 1999) 594–596.

[460] *G(JRL) v Tyhurst* (2003) 226 DLR (4th) 447 (British Columbia CA) (similar fact evidence admitted in action for breach of fiduciary duty by psychiatrist by 'treating' young female patients with a physically and emotionally abusive master/slave contract); *BG v British Columbia* [2003] BCSC 1890 (British Columbia Supreme Ct) [121]–[149] (in action against the Provincial Crown for damages arising from alleged sexual abuse of boys at a provincial training school, similar fact evidence was not admitted because of the extensive contact amongst the witnesses in prison, contamination through media reports, and financial motivation in their own tort actions.)   [461] *Cook v Evatt* [1992] 1 NZLR 673 (New Zealand HC).

[462] NZLC *Evidence* (n 295) Vol 2 Draft Evidence Code s 39(1).

[463] ibid Vol 2 Draft Evidence Code s 42(1).

[464] eg Evidence Act 1995 (Commonwealth of Australia) ss 94–101.   [465] eg ibid s 103.

[466] *Jacara Pty Ltd v Perpetual Trustees Wa Ltd* (2000) 180 ALR 569 (Aus Federal Ct).

[467] *Sheldon v Sun Alliance Australia Ltd* (1989) 53 SASR 97 (Aus Federal Ct) 145.

[468] G Durston 'Similar Fact Evidence: A Guide for the Perplexed in the Light of Recent Cases' (1996) 160 *Justice of the Peace J & Local Government Law* 359, cited with approval in *R v Handy* (n 5) [138].

incomplete forensic evidence. As Lord Justice Auld stated in his review of the criminal justice system, '. . . it is a poor prosecution case that needs to rely on a man's previous convictions in order to convict him. If the case is strong, why bother? If the case is weak, it is unfair.'[469] As cases such as *Makin*[470] and *Rosemary West*[471] illustrate, cross-admissibility of such allegations raises the spectre of a conviction based on statistics rather than proof.

The propensity character evidence doctrines in all common law jurisdictions have a common foundation, albeit sometimes differently expressed: to be admissible, the probative value of the evidence must outweigh its potential prejudicial effect. As noted at the beginning of this discussion, this balancing concept proceeds from the dubious premise that both probative value and prejudicial effect can be measured with at least some precision by a rational adjudicator of the admissibility question—and often without having heard *viva voce* evidence. Nevertheless, there is both common sense and logic in the notion that the higher the probative value of the evidence, the less the risk that the trier of fact will find the accused guilty, not on the strength of the evidence marshalled against him in relation to the charged events, but on the strength of his bad character.[472] However, there is a clear risk of circularity in defining what evidence properly relates to the charged events, and specifically how it does so.

We have seen that legislators in virtually all common law jurisdictions[473] have intervened to lower the admissibility thresholds to allow juries to hear propensity evidence, on the basis that this evidence is highly relevant to their deliberations. It is regrettable that the significance of similarity as the threshold to admissibility has been downgraded in English law, first by *DPP v P*, and then by the CJA 2003 s 101(1). If the probative value of other misconduct evidence rests upon 'such an underlying unity between the [accusations] as to make coincidence an affront to common sense',[474] then evidence of significantly dissimilar offences must correspondingly be much lower, yet this might not be taken on board by a jury distracted by moral prejudice. True, this could be taken into account by the trial judge in exercising her exclusionary discretion.[475] However, it is arguable that the risk of the jury sideslipping into moral prejudice is decreased where the evidence is so similar as to channel their deliberations into an examination of the probabilities of coincidence.

---

[469] Sir Robin Auld *Review of the Criminal Courts of England and Wales* (September 2001) [114].

[470] *Makin v A-G for New South Wales* (n 6).

[471] Rosemary West was convicted of the murders of ten young girls whose bodies were found buried in several properties occupied by the West family. Her husband committed suicide before trial having retracted his confessions and identified his wife as the perpetrator. Similar fact evidence by four of the witnesses testifying about their own abduction, physical and sexual torture by both spouses, and about Rosemary's bisexual proclivities, featured prominently in the trial to inculpate her in the murders [*R v Rosemary West* [1996] 2 Cr App R 374 (CA)].

[472] *R v B(L)* (n 14) [50]. Binnie J however argues that the two weighing pans on the scales of justice may rise and fall together, so that prejudice does not necessarily recede as probative value advances: *R v Handy* (n 5) [149].   [473] Canada being the notable exception.

[474] *DPP v Kilbourne* (n 11) 759 (Lord Simon).   [475] CJA 2003 (England) s 103(3), s 108(2).

1. The probative value of propensity evidence in child sexual abuse cases: a special rule?

What is no coincidence is that in most common law jurisdictions the leading common law cases delineating the admissibility of propensity evidence were concerned with the physical and sexual abuse of children. It is clear that the sharp edge of the propensity evidence rules is felt when past sexual misconduct with children is concerned. Spencer and Flin have vigorously argued that evidence that the defendant lusts after children has exceptionally high probative value, without which the jury will be given a false picture and may assume that his sex drive is 'normal' and so he is unlikely to have committed the offence.[476] In contrast, the House of Commons Home Affairs Select Committee has urged that English law revert to the 'striking similarity' test for child sexual abuse cases because of the greater prejudice such cases tend to engender.[477] Whilst some American jurisdictions have developed specific rules admitting propensity evidence in relation to sexual crimes, and the Australian common law rules have come close to this with their 'sexual motive' application of relationship evidence, both the English[478] and the Canadian[479] courts have rejected any special approach to sexual offences.

A record of other misconduct, particularly relating to child sexual abuse, can be seen as having heightened relevance and hence probative value, because such behaviour is viewed by society as being so repugnant and such an aberration that the fact that the defendant overcame such powerful moral and social inhibitions in the past may logically give rise to the inference that he did so on the occasion charged. Arguably, the probative value of similar fact evidence in the specific context of sex offences against children lies not in the external similarities between the acts charged and the alleged previous misconduct, but in the accused's state of mind or feelings.[480] However, where the other misconduct evidence involves the same child, its use under the pretext of background evidence to establish a guilty sexual passion or motive[481] does not enhance the probative value of the evidence of *mens rea* pertaining to the offence charged, and is only likely to confuse the jury.[482]

Stacking up the evidence of sexual misconduct in this way can be highly prejudicial. It may induce in the minds of the jury 'sentiments of revulsion and condemnation which might well deflect them from the rational, dispassionate analysis upon which the

---

[476] J Spencer and R Flin *The Evidence of Children: the Law and the Psychology* (2nd edn Blackstone Press, London 1993) 227–228. L Hanson 'Sexual Assault and the Similar Fact Rule' (1993) 27 U of British Columbia L Rev 51 71–75 argues that for this reason restrictions on similar fact evidence have a disproportionate impact on child and family sexual assault.

[477] *The Conduct of Investigations into Past Cases of Abuse in Children's Homes* (n 124) [96].

[478] *DPP v Kilbourne* (n 11) 751 (Lord Reid); *DPP v Boardman* (n 7) 443 (Lord Wilberforce).

[479] *R v B(CR)* (n 62) [2] (Sopinka J, dissenting on another point).

[480] As argued by DG Sturgess QC, Queensland Director of Public Prosecutions *Report of an Inquiry into Sexual Offences Involving Children and Related Matters* (Nov 1985) [7.134], [7.155], in urging the creation of specific admissibility provisions for similar fact evidence in cases of incest and sexual offences against children.   [481] As in *R v Beserick* (n 242) 515–519.

[482] *R v Nieterink* (n 69) 65–66 (Doyle CJ, suggesting that relationship evidence should be subject to the exclusionary rule). See also *R v Merz* (1999) 46 OR (3d) 161 (Ontario CA) [59].

criminal process should rest.'[483] Furthermore, the claim that previous sexual contact with children is so remarkable that it should be routinely admissible is dissonant with the tendentious assertion that paedophilia is endemic, at least in Western societies.[484] Thus evidence of previous sexual abuse may have exaggerated probative value such that to admit it would have a disproportionately prejudicial effect on the reasoning of the trier of fact.[485] The Queensland Law Commission decided that there was no rational basis on which to devise a purpose-built rule for the admissibility of propensity evidence in offences against children,[486] as has the Supreme Court of Canada.[487]

The prospect of a juror being infected by moral prejudice or 'bad person' reasoning might even be heightened by the prominence of political discourse about controlling (or failing to control) risks of abuse through sexual offender registration and surveillance schemes, and through public campaigns by parents demanding 'the right to know' whether a released sex offender is living within their communities.

Some courts have suggested that admitting propensity evidence is justifiable in child sexual abuse cases because of the paucity of independent evidence to support the child's credibility typical of such cases.[488] In *R v Handy* Mr Justice Binnie of the Supreme Court of Canada acknowledged but refused to succumb to the temptation to create special rules for cases with child witnesses:

The 'common sense' condemnation of exclusion of what may be seen as highly relevant evidence has prompted much judicial agonizing, particularly in cases of alleged sexual abuse of children and adolescents, whose word was sometimes unfairly discounted when opposed to that of ostensibly upstanding adults. The denial of the adult, misleadingly persuasive on first impression, would melt under the history of so many prior incidents as to defy innocent explanation. That said, there is no special rule for sexual abuse cases. In *any* case, the strength of the similar fact evidence must be such as to outweigh 'reasoning prejudice' and 'moral prejudice'.[489]

It is submitted that this must be right. Credibility is an issue which pervades most trials and, as Binnie J pointed out, anything that blackens the character of an accused may as a by-product enhance the credibility of the complainant.[490] The fact that evidence may be seen as helpful or even necessary to buttress the prosecution's case does not inevitably mean that it serves more to illuminate than inflame. As Bryden and Park point out, the youth of the alleged victim magnifies the need for some 'other evidence', but also magnifies the danger that admission of that evidence will divert

---

[483] *R v D(LE)* (n 29) 399 per McLachlin JA (as she then was), dissenting, appeal allowed [1989] 2 SCR 111 (SCC).

[484] *Lannan v State* (n 185) 1337, noting that accusations of child abuse no longer appear improbable as a rule, which undercuts the justification for the American 'depraved sexual instinct' exception at a time when the need to prosecute is greater.

[485] A concern acknowledged by the Queensland LRC *Evidence of Children* 362.

[486] ibid 373–377.   [487] *R v Handy* (n 5) [42].

[488] eg *Heuring v State* 513 So 2d 122 (Florida Supreme Ct 1987) holding that other misconduct evidence should always be admissible in intrafamilial sexual abuse cases to corroborate the testimony of the complainant, discussed by P Mirfield 'Similar Fact Evidence of Child Sexual Abuse (n 29), 28–31.

[489] *R v Handy* (n 5) (emphasis in original) [42].   [490] ibid [115]–[116].

the jury's attention from weaknesses in the prosecution case.[491] It is unprincipled to deem evidence admissible merely because it is corroborative.[492] However, there is a real risk that English law will sideslip into special rules for child sexual abuse cases, given that sexual offences against persons under 16 have been ordered by the Home Secretary to constitute the first category where propensity to commit offences of the kind charged is deemed to be relevant to an important issue between the defence and prosecution under the CJA 2003.[493]

2. Propensity evidence in child physical abuse and homicide

We saw that a form of the American 'doctrine of chances' was deployed by the prosecution in the Angela Cannings criminal trial, and how the adjudicators—both judge and jury—could slip into a logical fallacy if they reasoned from the premise that so many sudden deaths must be explicable only by deliberate wrongdoing.[494]

The cases of Angela Cannings, Sally Clark and Trupti Patel also raised a further alternative to those of crimes and coincidence: that multiple infant deaths might have a genetic link. In short, in cases of alleged physical abuse, fabricated illness and infanticide—as in the paradigmatic case of *Makin*—the 'doctrine of chances' has probative power only to the extent that the events fall within the ambit of validated medical knowledge. This however is an argument not for exclusion of evidence of physical harm suffered by other children in the family, as here if nowhere else this context is vital, for example if there is evidence that the parents were given an apnoea alarm because of concerns that an infant might have breathing difficulties. Rather, it is an argument for the paramount importance of a clear explanation of the analytical structure which the trier of fact must follow in first being satisfied beyond reasonable doubt that one death or injury was deliberately inflicted before applying that evidence to the indicated charge.

3. Collusion and contamination

Serial offending against several victims within the same social unit or environment, such as a family, youth club, church, school or residential care facilities, is common paedophilic behaviour. The more remarkably similar the stories of several alleged victims, the more potentially probative the propensity evidence, but also the more it could be argued that this is suggestive of collusion and concoction, creating a 'Catch-22' situation.[495]

It is submitted that the approach of the Supreme Court of Canada in *R v Handy* should be preferred over that of the Law Lords in *R v H* which was replicated in the

---

[491] Bryden and Park (n 158) 582.

[492] *R v B(CR)* (n 62) 752 (Sopinka J, dissenting, Lamer J concurring).

[493] CJA 2003 (England) s 103(4)(a), The Criminal Justice Act 2003 (Categories of Offences) Order 2004, SI 2004 No 3346 Part 2.   [494] *R v Cannings (Angela)* (n 31), discussed above section B.4(d).

[495] *Stickland v The Queen* (n 239) [19] (Malcolm CJ); Sir William Utting *People Like Us* (n 121) [20.22].

CJA 2003 s 109.[496] The Canadian solution to the dilemma permits the trial judge, in assessing the improbability of coincidence and hence the probative value of the propensity evidence, to take account of any *actual* evidence indicating that there is 'an air of reality' to the defence's allegation of collusion. Requiring the prosecution then to rebut collusion on a balance of probabilities before the evidence is admitted would seem to be the best available compromise between the logical flaw of the English courts' approach of disregarding the possibility of collusion and remitting all matters of credibility to the jury, and the Australian common law approach of requiring the prosecution to negative the possibility of collusion to set up the 'no rational explanation' premise of admissibility.[497]

4. Joinder of counts in a single trial

It is intriguing that some jurisdictions take the position that all indictments charging multiple sexual offences against children should be severed,[498] whilst others have created special exceptions to the severance rules to require that such charges be tried together.[499] The argument for the former position is the exceptional prejudice which a child sexual abuse prosecution attracts, and for the latter the exceptional probative value of multiple complaints in cases of credibility contests where corroboration is more valuable. It is submitted that neither generality is sustainable.

The reasons for the drive for more consolidation of counts of child sexual abuse into the same indictment are typically clustered under three main points: the efficiency and reduced costs to the criminal justice system of a single trial; avoidance of hardship to child witnesses who might have to face the ordeal of testifying more than once; and giving the full picture to the jury. The first argument wilts before the onslaught of the paramount importance of ensuring a fair trial for the accused. The second argument is powerful, but furnishes another reason to adopt a regime of videotaping the complete testimony of vulnerable witnesses before the trial.[500] The third argument has considerable persuasive force, but all common law jurisdictions have avenues to admit background or relationship evidence in some form, so that the jury can more fully evaluate such credibility issues as the submission of the child victim to the abuse, or delayed complaint. What is troubling is the willingness of some American and Australian States to admit evidence of 'guilty sexual passion' towards the complainant under the pretext of background evidence, when it is indistinguishable from the forbidden chain of reasoning from propensity to guilt, and is tantamount to otiose oath-helping of the prosecution's main witness.

Other misconduct evidence can be a two-edged sword for the prosecution, particularly when offences alleged by several complainants are joined on the same indictment.

---

[496] For a defence of the English common law and statutory approach, see Roberts and Zuckerman (n 4) 534–538; for criticisms, see Lewis (n 68) 187–191. [497] *R v Hoch* (n 90) 300–301.
[498] Such as the Australian High Court in *R v Hoch* ibid.
[499] As in Victoria: Crimes (Amendment) Act 1997 (Victoria) amending Crimes Act 1958 (Victoria) s 372, s 372(3AA), 372(3AB). [500] Queensland LRC *Evidence of Children* 401.

Joinder may actually assist the defence by offering the cross-examiner a broader target, because if any of the complainants is discredited, for example through imputations of fabrication motivated by a desire for compensation or retaliation, this can undermine the credibility of the others' testimony as well.[501] Indeed, the English Court of Appeal has held that where the defence alleges collusion, that is all the more reason not to sever the counts, as the defence itself provides a link between the complaints which would not otherwise have existed (if they have been ruled not to be cross-admissible).[502] The Queensland Court of Appeal has pointed out that it may be oppressive to subject an accused to multiple successive trials.[503] Other advantages of a single trial to the accused include the possibility of concurrent rather than consecutive sentences.[504] Furthermore, unlike cases where the propensity evidence is not before the court as charges, the defence is not taken by surprise, nor is it limited in its response to each allegation by the collateral issue rule.[505]

If one focuses instead on the potential for reasoning prejudice, it is likely that the English courts are overly sanguine in their confidence that where the prosecution has been denied a cross-admissibility ruling, limited use instructions will serve to construct leak-proof compartments encapsulating the evidence pertaining to each count.[506] Other Commonwealth and American courts are more sceptical.[507] As Calloway J of the Victorian Court of Appeal has pointed out, 'a blind and unquestioning faith in the efficacy of judicial warnings would lead to the conclusion that severance should never be ordered on account of prejudice, because any prejudice at all could be overcome by judicial instruction'.[508] A statutory starting point of severance requiring separate trials for all sexual counts which are not cross-admissible may be defensible, provided that it is not structured as rigidly as the Australian High Court's doctrine in *De Jesus* and *Hoch*. It is submitted that a flexible means of joinder in the context of a particular case is the only defensible means of securing a fair trial for both the accused and the alleged victim.

To conclude our extended exploration of character evidence: perhaps we are deluding ourselves in thinking that evidence can be quantifiably and comparatively evaluated for its probative value and prejudicial effect. Perhaps English common law gave what is in essence a value judgement a quasi-rational veneer which it did not deserve. Toohey J of the Australian High Court has astutely observed that prejudicial effect and probative value are incommensurables, with no standard of comparison since probative value goes to proof of an issue, and prejudicial effect to the fairness of

---

[501] D Birch and C Taylor ' "People like Us"? Responding to Allegations of Past Abuse in Care' [2003] Crim LR 823, 841–842. See *R v Williams-Rigby and Lawson* [2003] EWCA Crim 693 where fresh evidence which discredited one complainant rendered convictions respecting other complainants unsafe.

[502] *R v Stephen Cullip* Lawtel LTL 18/2/2000 (CA, 18 Feb 2000).   [503] *R v S* (n 251) [25].

[504] Western Australian LRC *Review of the Civil and Criminal Justice System* (n 206) 217.

[505] *R v Shearing* (n 326) [70].

[506] In the campaign to acquit the so-called Bridgewater Four who had been convicted of the murder of 13-year-old Carl Bridgewater, the jury foreman braved possible criminal prosecution under the Contempt of Court Act 1981 s 8 in stating publicly that the jury had disregarded a direction not to use a purported confession by one accused against the other three.

[507] eg *De Jesus v The Queen* (n 263) 4–5 (Gibbs CJ), 12 (Brennan J), 16 (Dawson J); *Michelson v US* (n 1) 485.   [508] *R v TJB* (n 268) 629.

the trial.[509] Nevertheless, the formula does have the merit of being strongly embedded in the factual matrix of a particular case, be it criminal or civil, and of focusing the court's attention on the probable *effect* of the evidence on the deliberations of the trier of fact.

Unfortunately the formula has been abandoned[510] by the CJA 2003 Part 11, Chapter 1 in favour of the *deemed* relevance of other misconduct evidence to propensity to commit offences of the kind charged, and propensity to be untruthful where credibility is in issue. The focus of admissibility is on probative value without the explicit mediation of prejudicial effect. The accused's interests are protected only to the extent that the court can intercept evidence of past convictions if it would have an adverse impact on the fairness of the proceedings to admit them. Since injustice must arise wherever there is unfairly prejudicial evidence, it is likely that the English courts will not be able to abandon the legacy of *DPP v P*. As Lord Hailsham said in *Boardman*, the 'rules of logic and common sense are not susceptible of exact codification when applied to the actual facts of life in its infinite variety'.[511]

---

[509] *Pfennig v The Queen* (n 37) 528 (Toohey J), cited with approval in *R v Handy* (n 5) [148].

[510] Although the *obiter dictum* of Lord Phillips in *O'Brien v Chief Constable of South Wales Police* (n 424) [33] discussed earlier may imply that appellate courts may strive to resuscitate the formula under the CJA 2003 (England) ss 101–106 for defendants, as it already does for other witnesses under s 100.

[511] *DPP v Boardman* (n 7) 452.

11

The Admissibility of Expert Evidence

A. General Principles

'Opinion' in the law of evidence means any inference from observed facts.[1] Lay witnesses can testify only to facts directly observed by them; what those facts mean for the issues in the case are inferences to be drawn by the trier of fact. However, in some matters the trier of fact requires specialized knowledge or skill in order to draw valid inferences; the assistance which an expert witness can provide about those inferences is commonly called opinion evidence. The distinction between factual and opinion evidence can sometimes be difficult to discern. A paediatrician is giving evidence of fact in describing bruises observed on a child's body, even though expertise may be required in making those observations, but is giving an opinion in stating that the bruises are consistent with a particular type of instrument being used, and that they were not accidentally caused.[2]

In this chapter we consider how expert evidence is deployed in the criminal and family courts by parties seeking to prove or disprove that a child has been sexually or physically abused or neglected, or unlawfully killed. Until recently medical evidence relating to physical signs of abuse and neglect was not on the public radar in England and Wales, partly because parents involved in child protection proceedings in the family courts were not permitted to publicize their cases under threat of contempt of court.[3] However some widely publicized miscarriages of justice where mothers were wrongfully convicted of killing their children have thrust the forensic work of paediatricians into the spotlight. We will also be considering an area of expert testimony to which the family courts in England have been receptive but the criminal courts hostile: psychological evidence pertaining to the behaviour of victims and perpetrators.

1. The legal questions

Concerns about the admissibility of expert evidence in common law jurisdictions are formulated as two questions of law:[4]

- whether the scientific foundations for the opinion have been validated, such that the evidence is sufficiently reliable to warrant placing it before the jury (in essence, a risk analysis); and

- whether the opinion would assist lay triers of fact in determining the facts in issue in the case,[5] (a utility test which in essence is an estimation of what lies within the ordinary experience and competence of typical jurors).

In respect of both questions courts have set different admissibility thresholds for the probative value of the proffered expertise. Some courts may tolerate a significant degree of controversy about the scientific validity of the area of expertise, whilst others

---

[1] C Tapper *Cross & Tapper on Evidence* (10th edn Butterworths, London 2004) 556.
[2] D Burrows 'Opinion Evidence' [2000] Fam Law 121.   [3] Discussed above Chapter 7 section A.
[4] For a detailed analysis of the admissibility criteria, see M M Redmayne *Expert Evidence and Criminal Justice* (OUP, Oxford 2001) chapters 5, 6.   [5] *R v Mohan* [1994] 2 SCR 9 (SCC) [25]–[29].

require widespread acceptance; similarly, some jurisdictions insist that the evidence must be necessary for the jury to adjudicate properly, whilst others will admit it if it would merely be helpful to the jury.

The two legal questions are connected; embedded in the utility test is the criterion that the body of claimed expertise must be sufficiently reliable to provide the necessary assistance to the trier of fact.[6] While reliability of the particular area is only infrequently addressed overtly as a factor in the English courts,[7] it is a major threshold factor in American[8] and Canadian courts.[9]

The utility or necessity test reflects judicial concerns that the value of the expert evidence may be overestimated by the trier of fact and so distort the fact-finding process, reducing the jury to acting as a referee in a contest of experts.[10] This is the best justification for the now enfeebled common law 'ultimate issue' rule, that an expert cannot opine on the very issue before the trier of fact. In the words of Sopinka J of the Canadian Supreme Court, 'dressed up in scientific language which the jury does not easily understand and submitted through a witness of impressive antecedents, this evidence is apt to be accepted by the jury as being virtually infallible and as having more weight than it deserves'.[11] The Supreme Court of Canada has institutionalized this concern by requiring that the expert evidence be subjected to what is in effect a risk/benefit analysis, ie it must have such probative value that this overbears its potential prejudicial effect on the efficiency and integrity of the trial.[12]

The procedure typical of jurisdictions using adversarial trial models is that the trial judge must make a ruling in a *voir dire* on both the necessity of opinion evidence and whether the witness is suitably qualified through study or experience to provide that specialized assistance, before the expert can commence giving an opinion in examination-in-chief before the trier of fact. The proposed expert witness can be called to be examined and cross-examined on both of these points in the *voir dire*. The factual basis upon which the expert opinion is based must be proved by admissible evidence, either through the expert witness's own observations, or through lay witnesses. The trial judge thus has an important 'gatekeeper function'.[13]

2. Expert qualifications

In the diagnosis of child abuse, the English family courts tend to value the experience of professionals working with children who may have been abused above an academic study of signs and symptoms.[14] As Judge Hall stated in *Cleveland CC v C*, 'the diagnosis

---

[6] *R v Silverlock* [1894] 2 QB 766 (QBD) 771.

[7] See the discussion in the next section about the controversial Munchhausen's syndrome by proxy. See also *R v Robb* (1991) 93 Cr App R 161 (CA); *R v Guilfoyle (No 2)* [2001] 2 Cr App R 57; *R v Dallagher* [2002] EWCA Crim 1903 (CA); *R v Hassana Francis* (CA 8 November 2000).

[8] See the discussion of *Frye v US* 293 F 1013 (USDC Circ 1923) and *Daubert v Merrell Dow Pharmaceuticals Inc* 113 S Ct 2786 (USSC 1993) below section C.6.

[9] *R v Mohan* (n 5) 25; *R v M(B)* (1998) 42 OR (2d) 1 (Ontario CA) [82].

[10] *R v Mohan* (n 5) 24.   [11] ibid 21.

[12] ibid; A Mewitt 'Character as a Fact in Issue in Criminal Cases' (1984–85) 27 Criminal LQ 29, 33.

[13] *R v J-LJ* 2000 SCC 51, [2000] 2 SCR 600 [28]–[29].

[14] *Cleveland County Council v C* [1988] FCR 607 (DC, Hall J) 612.

of child sexual abuse is not, as I understand it an academic study. Detailed knowledge appears to reside principally amongst those who have had long experience of its practice.' Nevertheless experience, however extensive, must usually be combined with the appropriate academic qualifications. For example in *Re N (Child Abuse: Evidence)*[15] the court found that a *guardian ad litem*, trained as a psychiatric social worker with considerable experience of working with a renowned child psychiatrist,[16] needed to have clinical experience beyond social work 'as or akin to a child psychologist or child psychiatrist' in order to give opinion evidence.[17] The court must also decide whether a particular qualification is relevant to the evidence that an expert will give in the case. In *Rochdale BC v A and Others*,[18] which concerned the alleged satanic abuse of children, the court concluded that a qualification and experience in child psychology rather than just in clinical psychology was required where the opinion was based upon the interpretation of a child's video interview. In this instance the court also rejected the evidence of the clinical psychologist because her experience was predominantly confined to adults and she had never worked with children who had allegedly suffered satanic or ritual abuse.[19]

The family courts may use the relative experience of experts whose opinions conflict on the specific issue to help them chose between conflicting evidence. In *Manchester CC v B*,[20] the experts were divided on whether haemorrhaging around a baby's brain had been caused by an episode of shaking or by minor impact when the baby's head was accidentally knocked on a door-jamb. Bracewell J preferred the evidence of the consultant espousing the abuse explanation as he had had extensive experience of shaking injuries in babies, whereas the defence expert's particular specialist intervention was not usually required with this type of injury.

It is extremely important that the family courts not become lax in the admission of opinion evidence. A major concern in Canada has been the extent to which social workers employed by the child protection agency involved in the proceedings should be permitted to express opinions about the central issues; many courts have been resistant to this practice due to the lack of independence of the witness.[21]

B. Expert Evidence Relating to Physical Signs of Abuse or Neglect

Medical evidence regarding the presence or absence of physical signs of sexual or physical abuse or neglect is commonplace in both criminal and civil courts in England

---

[15] *Re: N (a Minor) (Child Abuse: Evidence)* [1997] 1 WLR 153 (CA).
[16] Dr Bentovim, a child psychiatrist working at Great Ormond Street Hospital for Children, who developed the first diagnostic interviews for children in cases of suspected abuse.
[17] *Re: N (a Minor)* (n 15) 223.
[18] *Rochdale BC v A and Others* [1991] 2 FLR 192 (Fam Div, Douglas Brown J).   [19] ibid 216.
[20] *Manchester County Council v B* [1996] 1 FLR 324 (Fam Div, Bracewell J) 330–331.
[21] *Catholic Children's Aid Society, Hamilton Wentworth (Regional Municipality) v S (JC)* [1986] OJ No 1866 (Ontario Family Ct); *Children's Aid Society of the Niagara Region v M(D)* [2002] OJ No 1421 (Ontario Supreme Ct of Justice); N Bala and A Saunders 'Understanding the Family Context: Why the Law of Expert Evidence is Different in Family Law Cases' (2002) 20 Canadian Fam LQ 277.

and Wales. One point which child protection authorities and prosecutors should not overlook is that it is permissible for an expert witness to explain to a trier of fact that the absence of physical signs, for example of vaginal or anal penetration, does not mean that the abusive act alleged did not occur; a negative finding does make a child's history of critical importance to a conclusion as to whether abuse has occurred.[22]

The controversies here as to what opinion an expert witness may reliably express generally lie in the medical rather than the legal realm.[23] The diagnosis of phenomena such as Sudden Infant Death Syndrome (SIDS), Shaken Baby Syndrome and the repeatedly discredited Temporary Brittle Bone Syndrome[24] continue to be highly problematic for medical professionals and hence for the courts in both criminal and civil proceedings.

Very recently a storm of controversy has arisen over expert findings of Munch-hausen's syndrome by proxy (MSBP), also known as factitious or fabricated illness by proxy. MSBP was first identified by Professor Sir Roy Meadow in 1977.[25] The term describes a psychiatric condition in which the perpetrator, typically the mother, either fabricates or deliberately induces illness in a child in her care, in order to attract attention to herself. Paediatricians agree that MSBP exists, but it is very rare. The most notorious English case is that of Beverly Allitt, a hospital nurse who was convicted of murdering four children and the attempted murder of nine other child patients in 1993; she is currently serving 13 life sentences.

Covert video surveillance in hospital wards can provide the best evidence of active inducement of illness by carers interfering with medical tests, disconnecting

---

[22] For a detailed discussion, see J Myers 'Expert Testimony in Child Sexual Abuse Litigation' (1989) 68(1) Nebraska L Rev 1, 37–49.

[23] This is not to say that issues of the reliability of particular physical findings do not come before the courts; see, for example, *R v Dieffenbaugh* (1993) 80 CCC (3d) 97 (British Columbia CA), where evidence of 'anal gaping response' was excluded on appeal because there was no scientific information concerning what proportion of the general population will exhibit this response absent a sexual assault, as there had never been a control study. Amongst the plethora of resources available to legal practitioners: R Reece (ed) *Child Abuse: Medical Diagnosis and Management* (Lea & Febiger, Philadelphia 1994); A Heger, SJ Emans and D Muram *Evaluation of the Sexually Abused Child: a Medical Textbook and Photographic Atlas* (2nd edn OUP, Oxford 2000); J Myers *Evidence in Child Abuse and Neglect Cases* (3rd edn John Wiley & Sons, New York 1997) chapters 4, 5.

[24] The evidence of the chief expositor of Temporary Brittle Bone Syndrome, Dr Colin Paterson, was rejected in *Re AB (Child Abuse: Expert Witness)* [1995] 1 FLR 181 (CA) 194–199, because he ignored evidence which contradicted his views. His conduct as an expert witness was again strongly criticized in J Brophy 'Keepers at the "Gate": Effective Case Management in the Use of Experts in Care Proceedings' (1999) 12(5) *Practitioner's Child Law Bulletin* 55, 108. Nevertheless, his evidence continued to be tendered in the family courts: C Williams 'A Controversial Expert Witness' [2000] Fam Law 175. Dr Paterson was struck off by the General Medical Council for 'blatant disregard' of judicial criticisms of his evidence, and providing misleading and inadequately researched evidence to the Courts in *Re X (Non-Accidental Injury: Expert* Evidence [2001] 2 FLR 90 (Fam Div, Singer J) and in a later criminal case in Arizona, thereby potentially exposing vulnerable children to further risk (decision of the Professional Conduct Committee of 6 April 2004 (text available at <http://www.gmc-uk.org/>)). Margaret Hodge, the Children's Minister, wrote to local authorities suggesting that they review care cases in which Dr Paterson gave evidence, where (by his own estimate) 60 to 70 children were returned to their parents (*The Guardian* 8 Nov 2004).

[25] Sir Roy Meadow 'Munchausen Syndrome by Proxy: The Hinterland of Child Abuse' (1977) 2 *Lancet* 343.

monitors, injecting or forcing the children to consume noxious substances or excessive sodium, and attempting to suffocate them or induce apnoea with their hands, clingfilm, or pillows.[26] Nevertheless surreptitious surveillance has sparked controversy in both England[27] and America, not least because a 'successful' video recording means that the child has been subjected to harm, or at least the risk of injury.[28] American legal academics have also raised violation of privacy interests with human rights implications,[29] but such arguments are unlikely to be given weight in English courts, at least when applied to surveillance in National Health Service hospitals.

In the absence of direct positive evidence such as covert video surveillance, it can be extremely difficult to differentiate between SIDS (popularly known as cot death or crib death) and non-accidental death.[30] Because MSBP in particular is often a diagnosis of exclusion where sudden and unexpected deaths of infants are concerned, in criminal and family court cases the court is asked to draw inferences of deliberate harm from the absence of other causes. Professor Meadow developed an aphorism which had a powerful effect on juries: 'one sudden infant death [in the same nuclear family] is a tragedy, two is suspicious, three is murder unless proven otherwise'.[31] In three high-profile cases in England in 2003, this approach was brought into disrepute. Sally Clark was freed after serving three years in prison having been convicted of murdering her two children on the basis of discredited evidence from Professor Meadow. Nevertheless, in the murder trial a few weeks later of Trupti Patel, accused of smothering her three babies, the prosecution again relied upon testimony of Professor Meadow; the

---

[26] In a controversial study conducted between June 1986 and December 1994, covert video surveillance in hospital wards claimed to have detected parents suffocating, poisoning, and inflicting fractures and other emotional and physical abuse in 30 of 39 suspected cases: DP Southall, MW Banks, AF Falkov and MP Samuels 'Covert Video Recordings of Life-threatening Child Abuse: Lessons for Child Protection' (1997) 100 *Pediatrics* 735. The 39 patients undergoing surveillance had 41 siblings, 12 of whom had previously died suddenly and unexpectedly. Eleven of the deaths had been classified as sudden infant death syndrome but after the surveillance study, four parents admitted to suffocating eight of these siblings. One additional sibling who had died suddenly with *rotavirus gastroenteritis* was reinvestigated after video surveillance of her sister revealed poisoning, and death was found to be caused by deliberate salt poisoning. Other signs of abuse were documented in the medical, social, and police records of an additional 15 of the siblings. For examples of similar American cases, see B Yorker 'Covert Video Surveillance of Munchausen Syndrome by Proxy: the Exigent Circumstances Exception' [1995] *Health Matrix: Journal of Law-Medicine* 325, 328–329. For considerations in using covert video surveillance as an investigative tool, see National Center for Prosecution of Child Abuse *Investigation and Prosecution of Child Abuse* (3rd edn Sage Publications Inc, Thousand Oaks 2004), 164–167, 400–401.

[27] Professor David Southall's diagnosis of MSBP in several cases involving the use of covert video surveillance has been a subject of a complaint to the General Medical Council. Professor Southall was suspended from child protection work for three years for his intervention in the Sally Clark case.

[28] M Flannery 'First, Do No Harm: the Use of Covert Video Surveillance to Detect Munchausen Syndrome by Proxy—an Unethical Means of "Preventing" Child Abuse' (1997–1998) 32 *U of Michigan J L Reform* 105, 106–107, 119, 144–150.

[29] ibid 153–157; T Thomas 'Covert Video Surveillance' (1994) 144 NLJ 966.

[30] See the diagnostic guidelines of the American Academy of Paediatrics' Committee on Child Abuse and Neglect 'Distinguishing Sudden Infant Death Syndrome From Child Abuse Fatalities' (2001) 107 *Pediatrics* 437.

[31] Sir Roy Meadow *ABC of Child Abuse* (3rd edn BMJ Pub Group, London 1997) 29.

jury acquitted. Angela Cannings, jailed for the murder of her two sons,[32] was released by the Court of Appeal in December 2003.

In *Clark*, the second appeal succeeded primarily because the Home Office forensic pathologist who conducted the autopsies of both infants had failed to disclose microbacterial tests indicating that the second boy had a streptococcal infection in the spinal cord, conduct which the Court of Appeal described as falling 'a very long way short of standards to be expected of someone in his position upon whose evidence the court was inevitably going to be so dependent'.[33] The court also castigated the testimony of Professor Meadow that the odds of two cot deaths from natural causes in the same family were 1 in 73 million, which was founded on a basic arithmetical error:[34]

Putting the evidence of 1 in 73 million before the jury with its related statistic that it was the equivalent of a single occurrence of two such deaths in the same family once a century was tantamount to saying that without consideration of the rest of the evidence one could be just about sure that this was a case of murder.[35]

Furthermore, even the base statistic relied upon by Professor Meadow that the chance of a non-smoking family with a wage-earner suffering a cot death was 1 in 8,543 was not suggested by the empirical research study from whence it came as enabling diagnosis of an unnatural death in a particular case,[36] nor could it do anything to prove whether the case before the court was one of those rare instances.[37] A further concern was that statistical evidence of this type encouraged jurors to consider the counts together as a package, to that if they concluded one child's death was not due to SIDS, then logically the other death statistically was extremely unlikely to be caused by SIDS, whereas they were required to return separate verdicts on each count.[38] As we discussed earlier, this chain of reasoning is a fundamental risk with similar fact evidence.[39]

In *Cannings*, Judge LJ noted:

... the flawed evidence he [Professor Sir Roy Meadow] gave at Sally Clark's trial serves to undermine his high reputation and authority as a witness in the forensic process. It also ... demonstrates not only that in this particular field which we summarise as 'cot deaths', even the most distinguished expert can be wrong, but also provides a salutary warning against the possible dangers of an over-dogmatic expert approach.[40]

[32] The prosecution dropped charges of killing her first child and attempting to kill her surviving daughter. However, in an interlocutory appeal the Court of Appeal had held that the fact of three infant deaths in the same family provided admissible evidence relevant to each count: *R v Cannings (Angela)* [2004] EWCA Crim 01, [2004] 1 All ER 725 [12], discussed above, Chapter 10, section B.4(d).

[33] *R v Clark (Sally)* [2003] EWCA Crim 1020, [2003] 2 FCR 447 [164]. Sally Clark and her husband Stephen have sued the pathologist for misfeasance in public office: *The Guardian* 19 September 2005, 12.

[34] ibid [94]–[110].   [35] ibid [175].

[36] ibid [100], commenting on the report of a government-funded multidisciplinary research team, the Confidential Inquiry into Sudden Death in Infancy, to which Professor Meadow had written the preface.

[37] ibid [174].   [38] ibid [173].   [39] Discussed above Chapter 10 section B.4(d).

[40] *R v Cannings (Angela)* (n 32) [17].

The Court of Appeal's trenchant conclusions are worthy of quotation at length, as they have had an enormous impact on the scrutiny of expert evidence in cases of alleged physical abuse and death of children:

We recognise that the occurrence of three sudden and unexpected infant deaths in the same family is very rare . . . and therefore demands an investigation into their causes. Nevertheless the fact that such deaths have occurred does not identify, let alone prescribe, the deliberate infliction of harm as the cause of death. Throughout the process great care must be taken not to allow the rarity of these sad events, standing on their own, to be subsumed into an assumption or virtual assumption that the dead infants were deliberately killed, or consciously or unconsciously to regard the inability of the defendant to produce some convincing explanation for these deaths as providing a measure of support for the Prosecution's case. If on examination of all the evidence every possible known cause has been excluded, the cause remains unknown.

The trial, and this appeal, have proceeded in a most unusual context. Experts in many fields will acknowledge the possibility that later research may undermine the accepted wisdom of today. 'Never say never' is a phrase which we have heard in many different contexts from expert witnesses. That does not normally provide a basis for rejecting the expert evidence, or indeed for conjuring up fanciful doubts about the possible impact of later research. With unexplained infant deaths, however, . . . in many important respects we are still at the frontiers of knowledge. Necessarily, further research is needed, and fortunately, . . . it is continuing. All this suggests that, for the time being, where a full investigation into two or more sudden unexplained infant deaths in the same family is followed by a serious disagreement between reputable experts about the cause of death, and a body of such expert opinion concludes that natural causes, whether explained or unexplained, cannot be excluded as a reasonable (and not a fanciful) possibility, the prosecution of a parent or parents for murder should not be started, or continued, unless there is additional cogent evidence, extraneous to the expert evidence, . . . which tends to support the conclusion that the infant, or where there is more than one death, one of the infants, was deliberately harmed. In cases like the present, if the outcome of the trial depends exclusively or almost exclusively on a serious disagreement between distinguished and reputable experts, it will often be unwise, and therefore unsafe, to proceed.

In expressing ourselves in this way we recognise that justice may not be done in a small number of cases where in truth a mother has deliberately killed her baby without leaving any identifiable evidence of the crime. That is an undesirable result, which however avoids a worse one. If murder cannot be proved, the conviction cannot be safe. In a criminal case, it is simply not enough to be able to establish even a high probability of guilt. Unless we are sure of guilt the dreadful possibility always remains that a mother, already brutally scarred by the unexplained death or deaths of her babies, may find herself in prison for life for killing them when she should not be there at all. In our community, and in any civilised community, that is abhorrent.[41]

These trenchant remarks caused the Attorney General immediately to initiate a review of 298 completed and pending criminal cases where the prosecution had alleged that a parent had killed a child under two years of age.[42] Of these cases, he concluded that 28 convictions gave cause for concern, and invited the defendants to appeal directly to the Court of Appeal or to go through the Criminal Cases Review Commission.[43]

---

[41] *R v Cannings (Angela)* (n 32) [177]–[179].

[42] *Hansard* HL Deb vol 656 col 908 (20 Jan 2004).

[43] Statement of the Attorney General in the House of Lords 21 December 2004, *Hansard* HL Deb Vol 667 cols 1657–1659 (21 Dec 2004).

However, at the time of writing only two of these cases had resulted in murder verdicts being quashed.[44]

In *Patel* and *Cannings*, the parents' extended families had suffered cot deaths and acute life-threatening events with statistically unusual frequency; researchers at Manchester University and elsewhere are pursuing the possibility of a genetic link.[45] Researchers are also exploring the possibility that cisapride, commonly prescribed for digestive problems, and which was withdrawn in the UK and the US in 2001 after it was linked to 136 infant deaths worldwide caused by breathing difficulties and interruption to heart rhythm, might have resulted in misdiagnoses of MSBP.[46]

The sequelae of the *Sally Clark* and *Angela Cannings* cases demonstrate the irreparable harm which ill-founded or ill-expressed, and superficially compelling, expert evidence can inflict, when due regard is not paid to the limits, gaps, and weaknesses in current scientific knowledge. In response, the Royal College of Pathologists and the Royal College of Paediatrics and Child Health established a Working Group chaired by Baroness Helena Kennedy QC to develop the agency protocol for care investigation in all cases of sudden unexpected death in infancy. Their report made some trenchant criticisms about the role of the expert witness:

Those who give medical evidence to courts have a duty to ensure that the foundation of that evidence is sound. Unfortunately, doctors are occasionally drawn into error because they base their testimony on medical belief rather than scientific evidence. There is also the temptation, particularly in the very adversarial arena of the criminal courts, to be pushed into certainties where there are none. Barristers for the Crown hate the words 'I do not know', whereas the defence lawyer loves them. In criminal cases where guilt must be based on the high standard of proof 'beyond reasonable doubt', an expert's reservation may be the rock upon which a prosecution founders. However, the expert witness should constantly remind himself or herself that they are independent and are not there to win for a side. This can be very difficult because just as lawyers and judges can experience case hardening, so can doctors. Those regularly involved with child abuse can find it hard to be dispassionate and indeed sometimes become hawkish.[47] A doctor can be convinced, based on his or her experience, that the defendant is guilty but unless there is compelling evidence supported scientifically, he or she should not express that view in criminal proceedings.[48]

---

[44] *R v Donna Anthony* [2005] EWCA Crim 952; and Lorraine Harris (the only verdict to be quashed in the conjoined appeals in *R v Harris, R v Rock, R v Cherry, R v Faulder* [2005] EWCA Crim 1980, [2006] 1 Cr App R 5).

[45] J Sweeney and B Law, 'Gene Find Casts Doubt on Double "Cot Death" Murders', *The Observer* 15 July 2001.

[46] J Doward, 'Child Abuse Probe Uncovers Deadly Role of Axed Drug', *The Observer*, 1 February 2004.

[47] Although the Working Party did not refer to this, this observation is supported by the General Medical Council's suspension of Professor David Southall from child protection work for three years when he insisted, in the face of all the medical evidence, that Sally Clark's husband had killed all three of their babies, an opinion which he formed after watching a Channel 4 documentary and in which he persisted in the GMC hearing. The High Court imposed stricter conditions on his suspension: *Council for the Regulation of Healthcare Professionals v Southall* [2005] EWHC 579 (QBD (Admin)).

[48] Baroness Helena Kennedy QC, Chair *Sudden Unexpected Death in Infancy: a Multi-Agency Protocol for Care and Investigation (the Report of the Working Group Convened by The Royal College of Pathologists and The Royal College of Paediatrics and Child Health)* (Sept 2004) 4.

The Working Group further noted that doctors are insufficiently trained in the differences between the issues and differing burdens of proof in the family courts and the criminal courts. They also sometimes failed to appreciate that there is a difference between the role and expectations of professional witnesses of fact and expert witnesses. They recommended that paediatricians involved in the acute management of patients should not be expected to give expert testimony in cases involving those patients. The choice of an expert should take into account that a paediatrician whose expertise is child abuse will have a very different perspective from one whose expertise is in sudden infant deaths, the majority of which are a result of natural causes.[49]

It was also recommended that the trial judge should ensure that the expert should have recent clinical experience, peer-reviewed research, and not roam outside of his or her expertise or push a theory from the far end of the medical spectrum.[50] In criminal proceedings the trial judge at the Plea and Direction Hearing should also order a pre-trial meeting of experts to establish areas of conflict and to set them out in writing for the court. All test results must be disclosed, even if the expert considers them irrelevant, because it is when experts start to make such judgements that serious miscarriages of justice can take place.[51] Judges are also cautioned to be alert to the risks that can arise when a cosiness develops in the courtroom because the same witnesses appear time and time again.[52] This can be a problem in the family courts, where the credentials of the expert are often assumed to be acceptable because she has been qualified to give opinion evidence before.

It is important however to recognize that *Cannings* does not apply to all infant deaths on which there is conflicting expert opinion. In *R v Kai-Whitewind*[53] the Court of Appeal has restricted the rule in *Cannings* to cases that depend on inferences based on coincidence, or the unlikelihood of two or more infant deaths in the same family, or one death where another child had suffered unexplained apparent life-threatening events.[54] It does not apply to a single death nor where a conviction would not be based entirely on conflicting expert opinion because there is additional cogent evidence.[55]

At the same time as the Attorney General's announcement of the review of criminal convictions, the Solicitor General also announced a parallel review of some 5,000 care orders issued by the family court as a result of an expert diagnosis of MSBP; she noted that in these cases where care orders were determined to have wrongfully been issued, additional considerations would have to be brought to bear, since in many cases the children had been adopted by other families. In January 2004 the President of the Family Division issued administrative directions to ensure that family cases arising as a result of *Cannings* were transferred to the High Court. Arguably miscarriages of justice based on misdiagnoses of MSBP are more likely to be made in family court cases, where the best interests of the child are of paramount importance, the standard of proof that the child is at risk is only on the balance of probabilities, and the evidence

---

[49] ibid 5–6.   [50] ibid 8.   [51] ibid 6–7.   [52] ibid 7–8.
[53] *R v Kai-Whitewind* [2005] EWCA Crim 1092.
[54] ibid [82].   [55] *R v R (Mark)* [2005] EWCA Crim 2257.

is not tested as rigorously as it would be in the more adversarial arena of the criminal courts. In two cases the European Court of Human Rights has held that precipitously granted care orders arising from assumptions that the child was at risk of MSBP had unjustifiably breached the parents' right to family life under Article 8 and the right to a fair trial under Article 6(1).[56]

However, the impact of the criminal cases of *Cannings*, *Clark* and *Patel* on civil care proceedings must not be overestimated.[57] The Civil Division of the Court of Appeal has held that *Cannings* does not require a local authority to refrain from taking care proceedings, nor to discontinue them, in any case where there is a substantial disagreement among the medical experts, as the family courts have the benefit of evidence on a much wider canvas about the family, and the consequences of a false positive finding may not be as dire as care orders can be revisited.[58]

C. Expert Evidence Relating to Psychological Signs of Abuse or Neglect

We turn now to an area of even greater, and more widespread, controversy. Law reform in common law jurisdictions over the past two decades has been predicated on the view that the evidence of children is not inherently unreliable, and so the assessment of the credibility of child witnesses may safely be left to juries without special precautionary rules such as corroboration. This conclusion in turn has raised the question whether triers of fact may be assisted in their task by expert opinion from psychiatrists and clinical psychologists specializing in child abuse. In several other common law jurisdictions the criminal courts have been more receptive than have the English courts to expert testimony in principle, within limits.

A remarkable divergence of approach between civil and criminal proceedings occurs in English courts in relation to psychiatric evidence concerning behavioural symptoms of abuse exhibited by the complainant and the child's mental state. Such evidence is commonly heard in the family courts. The criminal courts in contrast take the firm position that such evidence is not admissible—at least where it is the prosecution which wishes to tender it.

The common law exclusionary rule rests on two foundations: first, it would usurp the function of the jury in evaluating the credibility of witnesses to reach a conclusion on the issues being tried; and second, expert evidence is admissible only respecting matters which are not within the common experience of laypersons, and jurors do not require expert assistance in assessing complaints of child abuse. As civil and criminal proceedings often proceed in parallel, it is important to consider first what types of evidence child psychologists could provide to courts, and then the reasons advanced for permitting such evidence supporting or negating the occurrence of sexual abuse

---

[56] *P, C and S v UK* [2002] 2 FLR 631, [2002] 3 FCR 1, [2002] Fam Law 811; *Venema v Netherlands* [2003] 1 FLR 552, [2003] 1 FCR 153 (ECtHR).

[57] C Keenan 'The Impact of *Cannings* on Civil Child Protection Cases' (2005) 27 J Soc Wel & Fam L 173.   [58] *Re LU (a Child) and LB (a Child)* [2004] EWCA Civ 567 [23]–[30].

to be heard in custody, care, or related family proceedings, but not in the criminal court, in relation to the same child.

Psychological testimony may be tendered by the prosecution (or child protection authority) or by the defence for two distinct evidential purposes:

- to prove that abuse has or has not occurred (described as 'diagnostic' or 'substantive' or 'predicting back' evidence); or
- to support or undermine the complainant's evidence by identifying behavioural patterns characteristic of child victims (described as 'rehabilitative' or 'counter-intuitive' or 'social framework' evidence).

The first category, here called 'diagnostic evidence', permits the expert to express an opinion about the child witness in the case before the court. It may take two forms: a strong form, of directly expressed opinion that the child has or has not been abused; and a weaker form, of an opinion that the behaviour exhibited by the complainant is consistent or inconsistent with that typical of child abuse victims. The second form tends to attract less controversy than the first, although one American court has wryly observed that the phrase 'consistent with' is the 'customary cautious professional jargon' for causation.[59] It has also been astutely noted that the 'consistent with' terminology which is frequently deployed by physicians in relation to physical as well as behavioural findings is merely an observation that at least some abused children exhibit the condition, without giving any indication as to the frequency with which the condition occurs in abused versus non-abused child populations, and hence the relevance of the point to diagnosing abuse.[60]

The second category, here called 'rehabilitative' evidence, is directed to dispelling common misconceptions about the behaviour 'expected' of victims of sexual abuse, which could subvert the truth-seeking function of the trial process.[61] The objective is to place evidence about the child's response to the alleged abuse in context where the child's credibility is in issue (as it almost invariably is). The expert cannot, however, comment on the conduct or testimony of the child witness in the case. 'Consistent with' terminology may be more helpful in rebuttal than for diagnosis in evidence in chief, in showing that a defence attack does not demonstrate that abuse did not occur, because at least some abused children exhibit (or do not exhibit) the symptom.[62]

There are two primary types of psychological evidence which might be offered: analysis of the behavioural characteristics exhibited by abuse victims and by the complainant, and analysis of the complainant's actual disclosure using techniques such as 'Statement Validity Analysis'.

---

[59] *US v DeNoyer* 811 F 2d 346 (US CA 8th Cir 1987) 483 n 3.

[60] TD Lyon and JJ Koehler 'The Relevance Ratio: Evaluating the Probative Value of Expert Testimony in Child Sexual Abuse Cases' (1996) 82 Cornell L Rev 43, 51–54.

[61] *R v Marquard* [1993] 4 SCR 223 [70] (L'Heureux-Dubé J).

[62] Lyon and Koehler (n 60), 54–58. The safest course for admission of rehabilitative evidence may be based upon a double negative: that (for example) delayed complaint is 'not inconsistent' with abuse having occurred: R Roe 'Expert Testimony in Child Sexual Abuse Cases' (1985–6) 40 University of Miami L Rev 97, 108.

1. Psychological behaviour as diagnostic evidence[63]

The utility of psychological evidence to prove sexual abuse has occurred rests upon the premise that child victims exhibit predictable behavioural characteristics which can be accurately profiled. Four important points emerge from the literature:[64]

- There is no behaviour or symptom observed in all or a majority of sexually abused children, nor is there a single constellation of psychological symptoms or behavioural indicators which can validate that sexual abuse has occurred; there is thus no sexual abuse analogue to 'battered child syndrome'[65] which can substantiate that injuries are not accidental.[66]

- Similarly, the use of 'syndrome evidence' such as 'Child Sexual Abuse Syndrome', 'Child Sexual Abuse Accommodation Syndrome', 'Post-traumatic Stress Disorder', 'the Traumagenic Dynamics Model'[67] or other theoretical models to detect or diagnose abuse is deeply suspect.

- Up to one-third of sexual abuse victims demonstrate no outward behavioural manifestations—at least at the time of assessment.[68]

- Nevertheless, the presence in a child of certain behaviours and symptoms can provide some evidence which may justify a clinical opinion that a child has been sexually abused.[69] Some behaviours such as fear, sleep disturbance, bed-wetting and depression are commonly observed in abused children, but also are often experienced by non-abused children, and so in isolation cannot establish that the child has been abused, indicating merely that the child may have suffered some traumatic event.[70] Other behaviours which are infrequently seen in non-abused children, such as sexualized activities which are more aggressive or more imitative of adult sexual behaviour than children of that age usually demonstrate, are good markers of sexual abuse provided alternative explanations for the child's knowledge are ruled out,[71]

---

[63] Myers 'Expert Testimony in Child Sexual Abuse Litigation' (n 22), 51–65 reviews the clinical studies; Myers *Evidence In Child Abuse Cases* Vol 1 [5.28]–[5.56]; SJ Ceci and H Hembrooke (eds) *Expert Witnesses in Child Abuse Cases: What Can and Should be Said in Court* (American Psychological Association, Washington DC 1998).   [64] Myers, *Evidence in Child Abuse Cases*, Vol 1 [5.28].

[65] C Kempe, F Silverman, B Steele, W Droegemueller and H Silver 'The Battered-Child Syndrome' (1984) 181 *J of American Medical Association* 17.

[66] CB Fisher and KA Whiting, 'How Valid are Child Sexual Abuse Allegations?' in SJ Ceci and H Hembrooke (eds) *Expert Witnesses in Child Abuse Cases* (n 63) 159, 162; L Berliner and J Conte 'Sexual Abuse Evaluations: Conceptual and Empirical Obstacles' (1993) 17 *Child Abuse and Neglect* 111, 116; Myers 'Expert Testimony in Child Sexual Abuse Litigation' (n 22), 67.

[67] Helpfully described by Fisher and Whiting, ibid 159, 162–168.

[68] K Kendall-Hackett, LM Williams, D Finkelhor 'Impact of Sexual Abuse on Children: a Review and Synthesis of Recent Empirical Studies' (1993) 113 *Psychological Bulletin* 164, 168–170. Some of the studies reviewed showed a rate of asymptomatic assessment as high as 36% and 49%.

[69] Myers 'Expert Testimony in Child Sexual Abuse Litigation' (n 22), 61–65.

[70] *State v Cressey* 628 A 2d 696 (New Hampshire Supreme Ct 1993); ibid 64.

[71] Myers (n 22) 59–61.

particularly if this central core of sexual behaviours is accompanied by non-sexual behaviours commonly observed in sexually abused children, and there is medical evidence of sexual abuse.

The probative value of evidence of specific behaviours can be measured by a ratio comparing the frequency with which the behaviour appears in abused and non-abused children.[72] It is the ratio which is critical, as infrequently encountered signs may nonetheless have considerable relevance if they are virtually non-existent in non-abused children.[73] There is a potential methodological problem in validating the abuse versus non-abuse status of the children involved in the studies, which necessarily is based upon fallible, and largely intuitive, clinical judgement.[74] Further, potential biases can taint case-control research. 'Exposure suspicion bias' occurs when an awareness of the child's symptoms (eg sexualized behaviour) increases the intensity of the search for and recognition of a putative cause (sexual abuse). Conversely, 'diagnostic suspicion bias' occurs when the awareness of the child's exposure to a putative cause (sexual abuse) increases the intensity of the search for and recognition of symptoms (sexualized behaviour).[75] In the therapeutic and forensic settings alike, over-emphasis on the presence or absence of certain behaviours can result in false positive and false negative conclusions.[76] Fisher and Whiting wisely warn that a diagnostic assessment of a child's psychological well-being should not be confused with the evidence of an abuser's behaviour.[77]

Notwithstanding these reservations, such evidence may provide another perspective to jurors in understanding and evaluating the prosecution narrative of alleged abuse. Myers concludes that while much more needs to be learnt, recent studies are beginning to lay the empirical foundation for the conclusion that the presence of sexual behaviours that are seldom observed in non-abused children provide evidence of sexual abuse.[78] However, some American and Canadian courts have expressed scepticism about the reliability and validity of diagnoses of sexual abuse based on behavioural characteristics of the child, pointing to the divergence of opinion amongst experts in behavioural science.[79] The rapidly evolving research in this field means that caution is warranted in analysing judicial pronouncements on the probative value of such evidence.

---

[72] Lyon and Koehler, (n 60) 46–54.

[73] TD Lyon and JJ Koehler, 'Where Researchers Fear to Tread: Interpretive Differences among Testifying Expert in Child Sexual Abuse Cases' in SJ Ceci and H Hembrooke, *Expert Witnesses in Child Abuse Cases* (n 63) 249, 252–253.

[74] P Ornstein and BN Gordon, 'The Psychologist as Expert Witness: a Comment' in SJ Ceci and H Hembrooke, *Expert Witnesses in Child Abuse Cases* (n 63) 237, 239; Berliner and Conte (n 66), 113.

[75] Lyon and Koehler (n 73) 249, 257, citing DL Sackett, 'Bias in Analytic Research' (1979) 32 *Journal of Chronic Disease* 51.   [76] ibid 249, 252–253.

[77] Fisher and Whiting (n 66) 177.

[78] Myers, *Evidence in Child Abuse Cases*, Vol 1, 522; Lyon and Koehler 'Where Researchers Fear to Tread (n 73) 251.

[79] *Re Gina D* 645 A 2d 61 (New Hampshire Supreme Ct 1994)); *R v RM* (1995) 29 NR 241 (SCC) [80]; *R v RAD* (1993) 80 CCC (3d) 97 (British Columbia CA) 107.

2. Psychological behaviour as 'rehabilitative' evidence

Although the line may be fine, the distinction between a description of behaviour presented as proving child abuse has occurred, and as indirectly supporting a child's credibility by explaining that such conduct is not inconsistent with the allegation, is crucial from a legal perspective.[80] Courts and behavioural scientists often have difficulty in identifying this line.[81] This is demonstrated by the use of 'child sexual abuse accommodation syndrome' (CSAAS), first identified by Dr Roland Summit as describing a constellation of behavioural features common in children subjected to continuing sexual abuse: (1) secrecy, (2) helplessness, (3) entrapment and accommodation, (4) delayed, conflicting, and unconvincing disclosure, and (5) retraction or recantation.[82] These characteristics were intended by their originator as a summary of clinical observations for therapeutic purposes which assumed the presence of abuse, and not as a diagnostic tool establishing that abuse has occurred, but were soon transmuted into 'scientific' diagnostic indicators by others,[83] prompting attacks on the empirical basis for the diagnostic response behaviour of secrecy, and especially denial and recantation.[84] The 'Child Sexual Abuse Syndrome' deployed by the prosecution in the infamous *Michaels* case in New Jersey where nursery care workers were convicted of systematic sexual abuse of very young children in their care[85] was also devised as a therapeutic protocol but suffered the same distortion in the forensic process.[86]

These misconceptions have caused some American and Canadian courts to become suspicious of the ability of mental health professionals to diagnose sexual abuse, considering that their diagnoses rely upon subjective assessment of a vague symptomatology with unquantifiable results which cannot be tested effectively in cross-examination.[87] Some judges are also sceptical of the capacity of jurors to distinguish between the diagnostic and rehabilitative purposes of such evidence.[88]

---

[80] *R v Llorenz* (2000) 145 CCC (3d) 535 (Ontario CA); *R v Gagné* [1996] Carswell Qué 787 (Quebec CA) [15].

[81] See the criticism of the misapplication of CSAAS by mental health professionals and lawyers in *New Jersey v JQ* 617 A 2d 1196 (New Jersey Supreme Ct 1993).

[82] R Summit 'The Child Sexual Abuse Accommodation Syndrome' (1983) 7 *Child Abuse & Neglect* 177.

[83] R Summit 'Abuse of The Child Sexual Abuse Accommodation Syndrome' (1992) 1 *J of Child Sexual Abuse* 153. Post-traumatic stress disorder has similarly been misapplied as a diagnostic tool: *R v C(G)* (1997) 8 CR (5th) 21 (Ontario Gen Div) 44.

[84] K London, M Bruch, S Ceci and D Shuman 'Disclosure of Child Sexual Abuse: What Does the Research Tell Us about the Ways That Children Tell?' (2006) 11 *Psychology, Public Policy and Law* 194, 217–220.

[85] Analysed in detail in SJ Ceci and M Bruck *Jeopardy in the Courtroom: a Scientific Analysis of Children's Testimony* (American Psychological Association, Washington DC 1995).

[86] S Sgroi *Handbook of Clinical Intervention in Child Sexual Abuse* (Lexington Books, Lexington MA 1982).

[87] *Hellstrom v Commonwealth* 825 SW 2d 612 (Kentucky Supreme Ct 1992); *New Jersey v JQ* (n 81).

[88] *R v K(A) and K(N)* (1999) 176 DLR (4th) 665 (Ontario CA) [124]–[136]. In *R v Norman* (1993) 87 CCC (3d) 153 (Ontario CA), a trial judge sitting without a jury made the same mistake, treating the psychiatric testimony as corroborating the validity of the memories alleged to have been recovered through the counselling process.

Nevertheless, evidence of the spectrum of behaviours often exhibited by child abuse victims, drawing upon the patterns identified by such clinical child abuse experts, can serve to educate the jury in evaluating defence attempts to use a child's troubled personality to discredit her testimony, by explaining how the apparent indicia of unreliability may be the product of the offence rather than the source of false allegations.[89] According to Dr Summit, 'the CSAAS is used appropriately in court testimony, not to prove a child was molested, but to rebut the myths which prejudice endorsement of delayed or inconsistent disclosure.'[90] There is an obvious non sequitur in the proposition that since the child denies that the event occurred, it must have occurred,[91] particularly if the complainant has persisted in the retraction. The same logical difficulty does not arise if retraction is used, not as diagnostic evidence, but instead to respond to impeachment of a complainant who has recanted and then reinstituted a complaint; here, 'superficially bizarre behaviour by its emotional antecedents'[92] can be explained by evidence that victims of familial abuse are often ambivalent about pursuing the complaint as they are beset by family pressure and by feelings of guilt, personal responsibility, and grief for loss of the abuser's emotional warmth.[93] The expert must be extremely careful in the rebuttal phase of testimony not to stray into the territory of diagnosing abuse from that pattern of behaviour, so that evidence considered unreliable in evidence in chief is let in through the back door of rehabilitative opinion evidence.[94]

3. Expert analysis of the child's disclosure

'Statement Validity Analysis', also known as 'Criteria-Based Content Analysis', has been routinely used in German courts for about 50 years, and also in Scandinavia, to assess the validity of a child's disclosure of abuse.[95] A forensic psychologist, usually appointed by the court, is given access to the case file and has a right to examine the child outside the courtroom using 'psychodiagnostic' methods. The analysis is highly structured, focusing on the individual characteristics of the child witness, the possible motives for the witness to make a false accusation, and the content of the statement itself.

---

[89] *R v C(G)* (n 83) 47–48, citing with approval D Paciocco, '*R v Wakabayashi:* the Relevance of Expert Evidence of Psychological Characteristics of Sexual Abuse on the Credibility of Child Witnesses' (1996) 2 *Sexual Offences Law Reporter* 153, 154,155. See *R v Llorenz* (n 80) [36], [66]–[70] for a discussion (in a split Court) of the relevance of behavioural evidence where the defence attacks the complainant's credibility on the basis of aberrant behaviour following the alleged incidents.

[90] R Summit 'Abuse of the Child Sexual Abuse Accommodation Syndrome' (n 83) 153, 160.

[91] A Cohen 'The Unreliability of Expert Testimony on the Typical Characteristics of Sexual Abuse Victims' (1985) 74 Georgetown LJ 429, 446.

[92] Cohen misunderstood the rehabilitative use of the evidence, and thus his criticism of this case is misconceived (ibid 444–447).

[93] J Myers 'Expert Testimony in Child Sexual Abuse Litigation' (n 22), 87 n 370, quoting D Jones and M McQuiston, *Interviewing the Sexually Abused Child* (Royal College of Psychiatrists 1988) 8.

[94] LS McGough, 'The Impact of *Daubert*: a Legal Commentary' in SJ Ceci and H Hembrooke (eds) *Expert Witnesses in Child Abuse Cases* (n 63) 265, 274–275.

[95] M Steller and T Boychuk 'Children as Witnesses in Sexual Abuse Cases: Investigative Interview and Assessment Techniques' in H Dent and R Flin (eds) *Children As Witnesses* (Wiley, Chichester 1992).

A leading exponent of the technique in common law legal systems is a Canadian forensic psychologist, Dr JC Yuille, whose 'Step-Wise' technique for investigative interviewing[96] has been adopted in England in the *Memorandum of Good Practice* and now in the new guidance under the Youth Justice and Criminal Evidence Act 1999, *Achieving Best Evidence,* as well as the United States.[97] As the technique has been adapted for common law courts, there are typically two phases to the analysis.[98] The Criteria-Based Content Analysis examines the statement for 19 specific indicators of veracity such as logical consistency, quantity of details, superficial details, embedding the event in contexts such as daily events, unusual details, and accurately reported sexual details which are misunderstood by the child.[99] There are five criteria which usually should be present in a credible statement:

1. The allegation should be of a coherent event.
2. It should be described in a spontaneous fashion.
3. It should have the quantity and quality of detail one would expect for this particular child.
4. Depending on how long ago the event occurred, the allegation should have a context, a sense of time and space.
5. It should include descriptions of the interactions between the child and the perpetrator.

The remaining 14 criteria do not have to be present but can reinforce the credibility of the allegations.[100]

The second step is an assessment of all the other aspects of the evidence in the case, employing a Validity Checklist which includes an evaluation of the complainant's demeanour during each interview, the adequacy of the interview, the motives for disclosure, and any other forensic evidence in the case. The objective is to ascertain whether the allegation has the features of a real memory, that is, a memory of a personally experienced event, and so may be seen as particularly useful in cases of allegations of historic child abuse by adult complainants. The evaluation leads to one of three conclusions: that the allegation is credible; that it is not credible; or that it is indeterminate. Yuille maintains that the word 'credible' is not synonymous with 'truthful', nor is a finding of 'non-credibility' synonymous with a lie. It is possible to conclude that an allegation is credible when in fact it is not true, but in his view few people would have the ability to maintain an invented story in the face of a competent

---

[96] J Yuille 'The Systematic Assessment of Children's Testimony' (1988) 29(3) *Canadian Psychology* 247.

[97] J Gallett and M Finn 'Corroboration of Child Sexual Abuse Allegations with Behavioral Evidence' (2002) 25 Am Jur Proof of Facts 3d 189 §19 (updated to July 2006).

[98] Described in detail in *R v H(SC)* [1995] 5 WWR 427 (British Columbia Supreme Ct) and in *R v H(RJ)* [2000] Carswell BC 1515 (British Columbia Supreme Ct) [101]–[115].

[99] Günter Köhnken 'The Evaluation of Statement Credibility: Social Judgment and Expert Diagnostic Approaches' in JR Spencer, G Nicholson, RH Flin and R Bull, (eds) *Children's Evidence in Legal Proceedings: an International Perspective,* (Cambridge U Law Faculty 1989) 39–51; Günter Köhnken 'Statement Validity Analysis' (conference paper presented at *Children's Evidence in the Courts* (University of Southampton Faculty of Law London 16 December 1997).   [100] *R v H(RJ)* (n 98).

investigative interview. Nor does a finding that the allegation lacks credibility mean that it is not true; alternative explanations are that the complainant is unable or unwilling to provide the required details.

Thus far, English[101] and Canadian[102] courts have not been receptive to this type of evidence. American courts have also been reticent in admitting Statement Validity Analysis as part of the prosecution's or claimant's case in chief, allowing it only to rebut a specific attack on the complainant's statement as not being an account of real events.[103] Some American and English commentators are doubtful about the utility of the technique.[104]

The primary stumbling block for an adversarial criminal justice system is that the analysis expresses a direct opinion of the child's credibility ('oath-helping'), however much the expert disclaims this message,[105] whereas psychological evidence, where it is admissible, must be based on factors independent of the child's accounts of abuse.[106] It is important to note that child abuse cases in Germany and Scandinavia are tried without juries, and so it is likely that the courts in those jurisdictions are not so concerned about expertise mesmerizing the trier of fact. Some Canadian courts have also expressed doubt about whether the reliability of the technique has been scientifically validated.[107]

A weaker form of disclosure analysis which has met with a more favourable reception in common law courts considers the impact upon the reliability of disclosure of improper interviewing techniques, such as leading questions, an oppressive environment, use of anatomical props, and repeated interviewing. Typically tendered by the defence, the expert may claim that improper interviewing techniques can both produce inaccurate statements from children and also cause them to incorporate suggested information into their memory of the event. Cross-examination of the child may not be effective to disclose this contamination because the child genuinely believes the version that has been constructed in the course of the interviews.

---

[101] *G v DPP* [1997] 2 All ER 755 (QBD).

[102] Ruled inadmissible: *R v Jmieff* (1994) 94 CCC (3d) 157 (British Columbia CA); *R v H(SC)* (n 98); *R v C (Roy H)* 87 OAC 366 (Ontario CA); *R v Llorenz* (n 80); *R v Gagné* (n 80) [16], [20], [27] (but no reversible error because the trial judge, sitting alone, formed his own opinion on credibility). One trial judge, sitting without a jury, recently accepted SVA evidence as prosecution evidence in chief—and as deploying an analytical formula familiar to judicial fact-finders—in a case involving historic allegations of familial abuse of three daughters, and of spontaneously and independently 'recovered memories' following dissociative amnesia, Dr Yuille's expert testimony primarily relating to the latter: *R v H(RJ)* (n 98) [153].

[103] *Vasquez v State* 975 SW 2d 415 (Texas CA 1998), applying *Schutz v State* 957 SW 2d 52 (Texas Crim App 1997); *Mensch v Pollard* 99 Wash App 1005 (Washington CA 2000). In *State v Clark Martin Smith* 971 P 2d 1247 (Montana Supreme Ct 1998), the defence was not permitted to lead an expert in Statement Validity Analysis because there had been no attempt to impugn the complainant's credibility as she was not cross-examined.

[104] See articles cited by Myers, *Evidence in Child Abuse Cases*, Vol 1 & 1.34, n 477; Fisher and Whiting 'How Valid are Child Sexual Abuse Allegations?' (n 66),175–176; PN Rumney 'False Allegations of Rape' (2006) 65(1) CLJ 128, 151–155.

[105] *R v Jmieff* (n 102); *R v C (Roy H)* (n 102); *R v Llorenz* (n 80). There appears to be no similar impediment however to admissibility of Statement Validity Analysis in family court proceedings: *T(J) v T(M)* [1996] Carswell Ontario 3522 (Ontario Gen Div).   [106] *Re Gina D* (n 79).

[107] *R v Jmieff* (n 102); *R v Gagné* (n 80) [27].

Here again the evidence may be tendered in one of two forms: a generalized commentary on the contaminating effects of improper interviewing as background information for the trier of fact to use in evaluating defence allegations that the child was suggestible, or a particularized analysis of the interviewing techniques in the case itself, correlating the research findings with the specific questions and answers to ana-lyse the reliability of the child's statement. The research base for such 'suggestibility' evidence was initiated by Stephen Ceci and Maggie Bruck,[108] and continues to attract controversy.[109] This form of evidence was first admitted in a notorious nursery abuse 'scandal' in New Jersey in 1993, *State v Michaels*, and we shall see that it has been accepted in English civil courts.

4. The admissibility of expert psychological evidence in English civil courts

The Family Division has been increasingly receptive to expert evidence which, directly or indirectly, supports or undermines the reliability of the child's story. However, the Civil Division of the Court of Appeal, concerned that a party against whom a finding of child abuse has been made might feel he has been tried by the experts and not by the judge,[110] has attempted in several cases to delineate the boundary between permissible and impermissible expert opinion. In *Re S and B (Minors) (Child Abuse: Evidence)*,[111] a psychiatric social worker was permitted to give her opinion about the psychiatric state of an adult who claimed she had been sexually abused by her brother as a child, and to comment on her propensity to fantasize or invent. She could also support these opinions by expressing her view that the witness's account of her previous history was apparently credible. What she could not do was directly to express an opinion that she was telling the truth and not telling malicious lies. Butler-Sloss LJ has explained the distinction as being that an expert may advise the judge, but may not tell the judge what her decision ought to be. The question for the judge is whether she believes the complainant, not whether the judge believes those who believe her.[112]

Expert witnesses might feel with some justification that this distinction in *Re S and B* offered little practical guidance as to how their opinions should be framed. Further assistance was offered by Ward LJ in *Re N (a Minor) (Sexual Abuse: Video Evidence)*[113] as to the proper role for an expert commenting on video interviews with children. It is for the judge to decide the weight and credibility of the recording; this requires the judge to consider whether the disclosure was elicited in response to

---

[108] Particularly in the groundbreaking book, *Jeopardy In The Courtroom* (n 85); SJ Ceci and M Bruck 'Suggestibility of the Child Witness: a Historical Review and Synthesis' 113 *Psychological Bulletin* 403.

[109] eg B Holmgren 'Should Expert Testimony on Children's Suggestibility be Admissible?' 10(3) Update (monthly newsletter of the National Center for Prosecution of Child Abuse, American Prosecutors Research Institute) 1. For less partisan accounts of the research, see J Myers, K Saywitz and G Goodman 'Psychological Research on Children as Witnesses: Implications for Forensic Interviewing and Courtroom Testimony' (1996) 28 Pac LJ 3; R Flin and J Spencer 'Annotation: Children As Witnesses—Legal and Psychological Perspectives' 36 *J Child Psychol Psychiat* No 2 171, 180–182.

[110] *Re FS (Child Abuse: Evidence)* [1996] 2 FLR 158 (CA).

[111] *Re S and B (Minors) (Child Abuse: Evidence* [1990] 2 FLR 489 (CA) 498, 499.

[112] *Re FS* (n 110).

[113] *Re N (a Minor) (Sexual Abuse: Video Evidence)* [1996] 4 All ER 225 (CA) 231–233.

leading questions or pressure, to assess the internal consistency and inconsistency of the story, and to look for any inherent improbabilities in what the child relates. The judge must determine whether, stripped of embellishments of fancy or exaggeration, there remains nonetheless a hard core of truth.

The expert may explain and interpret the video for the court, discussing the nuances of emotion and behaviour, the gestures and body movements, the use or non-use of language and its imagery, the vocal inflections and intonations, the pace and pressure of the interview, the child's intellectual and verbal abilities, or lack of them, and any signs or the absence of signs of fantasizing. (Note that here the expert is being permitted to comment on demeanour of a witness, which is normally regarded as being reserved to the trier of fact.) Ward LJ cautioned that the expert ordinarily should not indicate his or her belief in the truth of what the child is saying, because this usurps the judge's function. The expert's advice should be couched in terms that a particular fact is consistent or inconsistent with sexual abuse, and that it renders the child's evidence capable or incapable of being accepted by the judge as true. However, a medical witness may be accorded greater latitude, because a diagnosis of sexual abuse, absent obvious physical injury, often must rest upon the clinician's view as to the veracity of the child. Ward LJ commented: 'One cannot, however, expect the subtleties of the law of evidence to be understood by the child psychiatrist and the child psychologist. Experience shows that the subtleties are not always understood by the legal practitioners.' The ultimate safeguard, therefore, must be the judges who must ensure that the decision as to whether child witnesses are telling the truth is theirs.[114]

Three months later, in *Re M and R (Minors) (Sexual Abuse: Expert Evidence)*[115] another panel of the Court of Appeal Civil Division finally conceded that the distinctions drawn in previous cases were too subtle and 'impossibly fine' to be understood properly. The court noted that the earlier rulings of the Court of Appeal had not considered the abolition of the 'ultimate issue rule' by the Civil Evidence Act 1972 s 3, which had prohibited expert witnesses from opining on the final question the court had to decide. Butler-Sloss LJ held that an expert can express an opinion on the accuracy or truthfulness of child complainants, provided the expert is qualified to do so, and it is for the judge to accord that expert opinion its proper weight, and to make the ultimate decision as to whether the child is to be believed. Thus the decision of a trial judge that, contrary to the psychiatric evidence offered by all sides, children have not been abused, will not be impugned by the Court of Appeal if the judge has considered all the evidence, correctly interpreted the law and given reasons.[116]

It is important to recall that civil actions involving child abuse are not limited to the family courts, but also include tort proceedings. Here also there is no difficulty with the admissibility of expert evidence, possibly because such cases are also typically tried by a judge without a jury. Christopher Lillie and Dawn Reed worked in a local

---

[114] ibid 233.

[115] *Re M and R (Minors) (Sexual Abuse: Expert Evidence)* [1996] 4 All ER 239 (CA).

[116] ibid 249–255. For criticism of this approach, see M Hayes 'Reconciling Protection for Children with Justice for Parents' (1997) 17(1) LS 1.

authority nursery in Newcastle, and were acquitted[117] of charges of systematic sexual abuse of very young children in their charge. They sued in defamation the authors of an investigatory report commissioned by the local authority, who concluded they had committed the offences. The primary defence was justification, ie that the allegations were true. Expert testimony by paediatricians and behavioural psychologists was tendered by all parties respecting the diagnostic inferences to be drawn from the physical examinations and 'disclosure interviews' of the children.[118] Professor Bruck's devastating critique of the contaminating interviewing techniques provided a crucial foundation for the trial judge's robust finding[119] that no sexual or physical abuse whatever had occurred at the nursery—although the children had been subjected to an abusive investigation.

5. The admissibility of expert psychological evidence in English criminal courts

The absence of the seasoned judicial mind as the trier of fact is probably the primary reason why the criminal courts have been very reluctant to countenance expert evidence commenting on a witness' reliability, although, paradoxically, the avowed reason for the ban is the consummate ability of the lay juror to make such judgements without expert assistance.

In the leading case of *Turner*,[120] the Court of Appeal Criminal Division held that psychiatric evidence about the state of mind or reliability of a witness is inadmissible, absent evidence that that witness is 'mentally disordered'. In a famous *dictum* Lawton LJ observed: 'Jurors do not need psychiatrists to tell them how ordinary folk who are not suffering from any mental illness are likely to react to the stresses and strains of life . . . The same reasoning applies to . . . admissibility on the issue of credibility.'[121] A very generous view of the capacity of juries to understand, unassisted, any mental state short of 'abnormality', prevailed until relatively recently, when in *Raghip*[122] and in *Ward*,[123] the Court of Appeal accepted that psychological evidence could be adduced by the defence to show that a defendant's confession was unreliable, even if the defendant was not suffering from a condition which could properly described as mental illness.[124]

---

[117] The trial judge, Holland J, ordered an acquittal after ruling in a *voir dire* that the video interviews of six sample witnesses were inadmissible: *R v Christopher Lillie and Dawn Reed* ref no T931874 (QB 13 July 1994), discussed above Chapter 8 section A.1(a).

[118] *Lillie and Reed v Newcastle City Council, Barker and others* [2002] EWHC 1600 (QB) [77]–[148], discussed above Chapter 4 section F.5(c).

[119] The defamation action was tried by Eady J, sitting without a jury.

[120] *R v Turner* [1975] QB 834 (CA) 841, confirming *R v Chard* (1971) 56 Cr App R 268 (CA).

[121] The same reasoning was invoked in *R v Weightman* (1991) 92 Cr App R 291 (CA) to justify excluding evidence of the defendant's histrionic personality disorder to explain why she had allegedly lied in confessing to killing her two-year-old daughter, and in *R v Guilfoyle (No 2)* (n 7) to exclude evidence as to the allegedly suicidal state of mind of the deceased. Mike Redmayne argues that 'the credibility taboo' is not supported by *Turner*: (n 4) 161–164, but *Turner*'s reputation as having established this proposition remains robust.   [122] *R v Raghip* The Times, 9 December 1991.

[123] *R v Ward (Judith Theresa)* (1993) 96 Cr App R 1 (CA).

[124] Lord Hobhouse has warned that caution is required in admitting psychological evidence as to the credibility of defendants' statements, asserting that 'the suggestibility of some persons is well within the

However, in *Robinson*[125] the Court of Appeal restricted the potential application of this emerging principle in child abuse prosecutions. The alleged rape victim was aged 15 but was illiterate and had a mental age of 7 or 8. She nonetheless was found competent to testify after a *voir dire* where expert evidence was accepted from an educational psychologist who had tested her long before the alleged offences. Lord Taylor CJ held that the prosecution could not call that educational psychologist as part of their case in chief to tell the jury her opinion that the girl was incapable of adopting suggestions from others, notwithstanding that the defence had suggested in cross-examining her mother and the interviewing police officer that she was suggestible. While such prosecution evidence might be admissible to rebut a defence expert witness impugning the child's reliability, or where there was a clear and specific attack by the defence in cross-examination, the prosecution could not seek to bolster her credibility by a pre-emptive move.

Such evidence is also not admissible when tendered by the defence to attack the credibility of the prosecution witness; in *G v DPP*[126] the Court of Appeal ruled that the defence could not tender an expert who had applied Statement Validity Analysis and 'Thematic Emergence of Anomaly' to the complainant's videotaped interviews, as the reliability of the interviews is a matter for the magistrates or the trial judge.

In *R v D and Others*,[127] the Criminal Division attempted to explain the different approaches taken by the civil and criminal courts to expert evidence in determining whether a child had been abused. After a trial lasting seven months, the six appellants had been convicted of operating a paedophile ring in South Wales which committed very serious sexual offences against eleven children, some of them from the appellants' families. Ten of the children had testified at trial, the eleventh being only aged three when physical evidence of buggery was detected.

The defence had tendered a psychologist and a psychiatrist with extensive clinical experience in child abuse to criticize the manner in which the investigation and inquiries by the police and local council were carried out, including breaches of the Cleveland Guidelines for interviewing children and the *Memorandum of Good Practice*; they also proposed to critique the children's evidence, and to opine on their reliability and truthfulness. One such opinion was that one boy's allegations had to be treated with very great caution, because he was a compulsive and skilled liar, a manipulator, and desperate for attention and approval. He had been exposed to a faulty investigative process which took no account of these difficulties or of his need to gain sympathy because of an insecure foster placement. The Crown accepted that expert evidence about interviewing and investigative practices was admissible, but its objections to the admissibility of opinions as to the value of the evidence of the children were upheld by the trial judge. The defence argued on appeal that the criminal courts should adopt the practice of the Family Division judges to receive such evidence, provided the witness does not say that the child is telling the truth or lying, and pointed out that both experts had testified and their opinions had been accepted in the parallel care

experience of the ordinary members of juries': *R v Pendleton* [2001] UKHL 66, [2002] 1 Cr App R 34 [45]–[46] (apparently speaking for himself only).   [125] *R v Robinson* (1994) 98 Cr App R 370.
[126] *G v DPP* (n 101).   [127] *R v D and Others* (CA 3 November 1995).

proceedings. Swinton Thomas LJ began an extensive analysis of the civil and criminal cases by noting:

The dividing line between an expression of opinion as to the reliability of a child witness and the truthfulness of the witness is a very narrow one. It is, nonetheless, an important one, particularly in a criminal trial in which the ultimate decisions rest with the jury and not with the Judge. If such evidence is admitted in a criminal trial, it would be well nigh impossible to draw the distinction. A witness expressing strong views on the reliability of the child would be likely, at the very least, to give the jury the impression that the witness did not consider that the child was telling the truth.

The Court of Appeal concluded that the trial judge had correctly disallowed the evidence:

We conclude that the law is clear that psychiatric or psychological evidence . . . is admissible to show that the witness or an accused is suffering from some abnormality of mind or mental disability or deficiency which would not be capable of assessment by a jury without expert assistance, and that evidence is material and relevant to an issue which arises in the case. None of the children in this case were said to be suffering from any such abnormality.[128] Their only disability as witnesses, if it be such, is that they were children and that was a fact within the knowledge of the jury.

It is fundamental that experts must not usurp the function of the jury in a criminal trial. Save in particular circumstances, it is the task of the jury to make judgments on the questions of reliability and truthfulness. Particular circumstances arise when there are characteristics of a medical nature in the makeup of the witness, such as mental illness, which would not be apparent to the jury or the effect of which would not be known to the jury without expert assistance. Those circumstances do not arise in the case of ordinary children who are not suffering from any abnormality. It may well be open to the parties in a particular case to call general expert evidence in relation to the Cleveland Guidelines and, for example, to tell the Judge or a jury that over-interviewing as a matter of generality has been shown by expert research to have a much more adverse effect on children than on adults but the witness cannot express an opinion whether a particular child witness is a reliable or truthful witness. That is precisely the province of the jury in a criminal case, or the judge when considering the admissibility of evidence under s. 78 of the Police and Criminal Evidence Act.

The gulf between the reception of expert evidence in parallel civil and criminal proceedings thus remains wide.[129]

---

[128] Although the gross abuse which they were found to have suffered from an early age must have seriously damaged them psychologically.

[129] It is possible that the width of the gulf can be overstated: in *R v Archibald*, where the adult complainant, the defendants and the eyewitnesses were all substantially mentally impaired (indeed by trial the complainant was rendered incompetent by Huntington's Chorea), expert evidence was admitted without objection on the effects of the complainant's disease on memory and therefore the reliability of accounts given immediately after the event and then later. The psychologist was permitted to testify that she was incapable of telling or sustaining a deliberate untruth; however it was also explained that one aspect of the disease is the propensity to confabulate events where true memory fails. The jury also heard expert evidence about another brain-damaged witness, explaining that his problem was language and speech processing but that his perception and recall of events would be unaffected. So the evidence was ostensibly directed to reliability rather than credibility per se. The jury also heard expert testimony about the intellectual limitations

6. The admissibility of expert psychological evidence in American courts

American courts were the first in the common law world to admit evidence of typical patterns of human behaviour in relation to the credibility of witnesses, although from the outset such evidence in child abuse cases has provoked controversy.[130] By this time Federal Rule of Evidence 702, which provides a model for State legislatures, had abandoned the 'outside common knowledge' necessity test in favour of one of helpfulness to the trier of fact in understanding the evidence or determining a fact in issue. Since behavioural science is regarded as 'novel scientific evidence', trial judges must investigate the reliability of the proposed evidence to ascertain whether it may safely be placed before lay triers of fact.

Until 1993 this assessment was determined by the degree to which the general theory, procedures and techniques relied upon by the proposed expert witness had gained general acceptance within the relevant scientific community, commonly described as the *Frye* test.[131] This conservative test meant that the courts might be deprived of expertise until it had received the blessing of a majority of scientists, even though it might validly challenge the prevailing consensus. In contrast, the English Court of Appeal has held that a witness may give opinion evidence reflecting a minority view in the relevant profession, as his defence of that position can be tested before the jury.[132] In 1993, in the landmark case of *Daubert v Merrell Dow Pharmaceuticals Inc,*[133] the US Supreme Court moved away from *Frye's* deference to the judgement of the scientific community. The Court ruled that it had been supplanted by Federal Rule of Evidence 702 which was interpreted as requiring judges to ascertain themselves whether the expert's underlying reasoning or methodology is scientifically valid and can be properly applied to the facts in issue. The Supreme Court branded as 'overly pessimistic' the argument that abandonment of 'general acceptance' as the exclusive requirement for admission would result in a 'free-for-all' in which 'befuddled juries are confounded by absurd and irrational pseudoscientific assertions', because vigorous cross-examination, the presentation of contrary evidence, and careful instruction on the burden of proof are the traditional and appropriate means in the adversarial system of dealing with shaky but admissible evidence.[134]

Since *Daubert*, American trial courts apply a non-exclusive[135] checklist to the admissibility of novel expert evidence in criminal and civil cases, regardless of whether they

of the accused, on the basis of which the trial judge instructed the jury not to draw adverse inferences from his failure to give evidence or to clarify the inconsistencies in his police interview [*R v Archibald* Reading Crown Court Ref No 200007367Y1*1; appeal on other grounds dismissed [2002] EWCA Crim 858].

[130] Cohen, (n 71).   [131] *Frye v US* (n 8).

[132] *R v Robb* (n 7). This position is consistent with the standard of care applied by English courts in professional malpractice tort cases, according to which the defendant is not negligent if she acts in accordance with a reasonable, albeit minority, body of opinion within her profession: *Bolam v Friern Hospital Management Committee* [1958] 1 WLR 582 (CA); *Bolitho v City & Hackney Health Authority* [1998] AC 232 (HL).   [133] *Daubert v Merrell Dow Pharmaceuticals Inc* (n 8).

[134] ibid 2798.

[135] *Tyus v Urban Search Management* 102 F 3d 256 (US CA 7th Cir 1996) (noting that the factors applied by the Supreme Court in *Daubert* do not neatly apply to sociology).

are formally governed by the Federal Rules of Evidence:

- whether the scientific technique can be tested, so that its reliability can be challenged in some objective sense;
- whether the technique or theory has been subjected to peer review and publication;
- the known or potential rate of error when the theory or technique is applied;
- the existence and maintenance of standards and controls; and
- whether the scientific theory or method has attracted widespread acceptance within the relevant scientific community.

Effective 1 December 2000, Congress modified the language of Rule 702 by adding a three-part test making expert testimony admissible if:

(1) the testimony is based upon sufficient facts or data (intended to be a quantitative rather than qualitative analysis);[136]
(2) the testimony is the product of reliable principles and methods; and
(3) the witness has applied the principles and methods reliably to the facts of the case.

The effect of the amendment is twofold: all experts from all disciplines, whether 'hard' or 'soft' science, are now clearly included;[137] and the role of the trial judge as a 'gatekeeper' in assessing the reliability of the testimony is strengthened. The proponent of the testimony must demonstrate on a preponderance of evidence that the opinion is properly grounded in an accepted body of learning or experience in the expert's field, and is well reasoned and not speculative.[138] The emphasis is on the reliability of the methodology used rather than of the conclusion, and therefore the changed Rule is not intended to eliminate conflicts between experts being explored before the jury.[139]

The *Daubert* test, as it is known, is more receptive than *Frye* to new developments in experimental science, although reliance upon Popperian falsifiability as the litmus test of scientific validity raises problems for behavioural psychology, commonly regarded as an inexact and young science.[140] American prosecutors in child abuse cases see the sharper focus on reliability of the 2000 amendment to Rule 702 as potentially useful in requiring defence experts tendered to discuss the memory and suggestibility of child witnesses to be held to the same standard of scrutiny as paediatricians and

---

[136] *Notes of Advisory Committee on Rules to Federal Rule of Evidence 702*; the Committee did not indicate how 'sufficiency' is to be measured. For an attempt at a rigorous definition of relevance that courts may use to evaluate the probative value of proffered scientific testimony, using probability theory, see Lyon and Koehler 'The Relevance Ratio' (n 60).

[137] Codifying *Kumho Tire Co v Carmichael* 526 US 137 (USSC 1999) 1178.

[138] *Notes of Advisory Committee on Rules to Federal Rule of Evidence 702*.

[139] *In Re Paoli RR Yard PCB Litigation* 35 F 3d 717 (US CA 3d Cir 1994) 744; *Ruiz-Troche v Pepsi Cola* 161 F 3d 77 (US CA 1st Cir 1998) 85.

[140] DL Faigman 'The Evidentiary Status of Social Science under Daubert: Is it "Scientific," "Technical," or "Other" Knowledge?' (1995) 1 *Psychology, Public Policy, and Law* 960; M Kovera and E Borgida 'Expert Scientific Testimony on Child Witnesses in the Age of *Daubert*' in SJ Ceci and H Hembrooke (eds) *Expert Witnesses in Child Abuse Cases* (n 63) 185.

pathologists.[141] Nevertheless, in reviewing the American jurisprudence it is important to bear in mind that much of it was decided applying the more restrictive *Frye* test of scientific community acceptance.

There is a strong consensus amongst American criminal courts that an expert witness cannot directly comment on the veracity of a child witness.[142] Thus the defence cannot tender an expert to describe 'lying child syndrome'.[143] This is also the predominant view in civil cases, often supported by invocation of the due process constitutional guarantee.[144]

Judicial views diverge where opinion evidence is tendered as diagnostic evidence to prove that sexual abuse has or has not occurred. While some courts permit experts to opine directly that a child has been sexually abused,[145] the majority view appears to be that such evidence, if tendered in the strong sense described earlier, is inadmissible, either because the expert is telling the jury to believe the child, or because there is no clear scientific nexus between behavioural patterns and the conclusion that abuse is the cause.[146] Some courts consider that an opinion that a child was sexually abused does not stray into the forbidden zone of commentary on the veracity of the child's disclosure, provided the expert takes factors other than the child's statement into account.[147] Some States will permit expert opinion framed in the weaker sense, that the child's symptoms are 'consistent with' those seen in abused children,[148] but others regard the 'consistency' formulation as a subterfuge to conceal an impermissible conclusion that the conduct proves the assault.[149]

In contrast to the division of judicial views respecting diagnostic expert evidence, American criminal courts are almost unanimous in permitting expert opinions to be tendered for the second purpose, to rehabilitate a child witness's credibility. They have concluded that there is sufficient 'specialised knowledge' as to the typical behaviour of sexually abused children and their families to permit conclusions to be drawn by

---

[141] D Brown 'The New 702: How it Affects the Use of Experts' 14 Update (monthly newsletter of the National Center for Prosecution of Child Abuse, American Prosecutors Research Institute) No 3. See also Holmgren (n 109) arguing that defence opinion evidence by Ceci and Bruck, admitted in *State v Michaels* 642 A 2d 1372 (New Jersey Supreme Ct 1993) that improper interviewing techniques can produce inaccurate statements and cause children to incorporate suggestive information into their memory, did not comply with the *Daubert* criteria.

[142] Emphatically stated in *State v Milbradt* 756 P 2d 620 (Oregon Supreme Ct 1988), 624; *State v Lindsey* 720 P 2d 73 (Arizona Supreme Ct 1986) 76; *US v Binder* 769 F 2d 595 (US CA 9th Cir 1985) 601; *State v Sargent* 813 A 2d 402 (New Hampshire Supreme Ct 2002) 408. Hawaii was the notable exception: *State v Kim* 645 P 2d 1330 (Hawaii Supreme Ct 1982), but the Supreme Court has now reversed its position and overruled *Kim*: *State v Batangan* 799 P 2d 48 (Hawaii Supreme Ct 1990).

[143] *Jennette v State* 398 SE 2d 734 (Georgia CA 1990).

[144] See cases cited in Gallett and Finn (n 97).

[145] eg *Townsend v State* 734 P 2d 705 (Nevada Supreme Ct 1987).

[146] *People v Bledsoe* 189 Cal Rptr 726 (California Supreme Ct 1984); *People v Bowker* 249 Cal Rptr 886 (California CA 1988); *US v Harrison* 31 MJ 330 (Court-Martial App 1990); Myers 'Expert Testimony in Child Sexual Abuse Litigation' (n 22), 65–66.

[147] eg *State v Rimmasch* 775 P 2d 388 (Utah Supreme Ct 1989) 392.

[148] *State v Kallin* 877 P 2d 138 (Utah Supreme Ct 1994); *State v Jensen* 432 NW 2d 913 (Wisconsin Supreme Ct 1987); *US v Harrison* (n 146).   [149] *State v Cressey* (n 70).

experts as to such behavioural patterns.[150] Only Kentucky,[151] Pennsylvania[152] and Tennessee[153] take a different view. Experts are permitted to describe CSAAS if the evidence is targeted to a specific myth or misconception suggested by the evidence, such as delayed or retracted complaints. Thus expert witnesses may explain why some sexually abused children delay disclosure, recant, give inconsistent accounts, make piecemeal disclosures, display disruptive behaviour, run away from home, or conversely wish to return to their abuser, or appear 'emotionally flat' following the assault.[154] The jury should be instructed that CSAAS is not designed to determine whether the complainant's claim of abuse is true but rather describes the coping process frequently identified in victims, and so is useful to fact-finders solely for the purpose of showing that the child's reactions are not inconsistent with having been molested.[155] Many courts limit the experts' testimony to discussing a class of victims generally, without reference to the child witness in the case,[156] allowing the jury to draw any inferences linking the general information to the factual evidence they have heard about that child.[157]

The defence may also tender experts to comment on the interviewing techniques employed by investigators; they are permitted to comment on the general effect of bias and suggestion by the interviewers upon the reliability of children's accounts, and to identify specific problematic features of the interviews with the child witness in the case, but usually without opining on the effect of the improper techniques on the children's memory.[158] Where the factual evidence warrants, some courts permit psychologists to testify that the child's memory has been tainted by suggestive influences during the investigation such as actions by social services personnel and investigators to remove the child from home.[159] Such evidence is regarded as necessary because cross-examination of the child can be ineffectual if the child sincerely takes his or her recollections to be grounded in facts, and does not remember the improper interview procedures which may have suggested them.[160]

In civil child abuse cases, behavioural evidence is widely admitted.

---

[150] *US v Snipes* 18 MJ 172 (Court-Martial App 1984) 179.

[151] *Newkirk v Commonwealth* 937 SW 2d 690 (Kentucky Supreme Ct 1994); M McCarthy 'Admissibility of Expert Testimony on Child Sexual Abuse Accommodation Syndrome in Kentucky' [1992–93] 81 Kentucky LJ 728; DL Steele 'Expert Testimony: Seeking an Appropriate Admissibility Standard for Behavioural Science in Child Sexual Abuse Prosecutions' (1999) 48 Duke LJ 932.

[152] *Commonwealth v Garcia* 588 A 2d 951 (Pennsylvania Superior Ct 1991), overruled to the extent that prosecution expert evidence as to the absence of physical signs of sexual assault as being consistent with the allegation is now admissible, confirmed *Commonwealth v Minerd* 753 A 2d 225 (Pennsylvania Supreme Ct 2000); LR Askowitz 'Restricting the Admissibility of Expert Testimony in Child Sexual Abuse Prosecutions: Pennsylvania Takes it to the Extreme' (1992) 47 U of Miami L Rev 201.

[153] *State v Nicholson* 2000 WL 122244 (Tennessee Crim App 2000).

[154] Myers *Evidence In Child Abuse Cases* Vol 1 [5.49].

[155] *People v Bowker* (n 146); *New Jersey v JQ* (n 81).

[156] *US v Antone* 981 F 2d 1059 (US CA 9th Cir 1992); *People v Grey* 187 Cal App 3d 213 (California CA 1986).　　　　　　　　　　　　　　　　　　　　[157] *People v Bowker* (n 146).

[158] *State v Sargent* (n 142) 576–577.

[159] *US v Rouse* 1997 WL 169279 (US CA 8th Cir 1997).

[160] *State v Kirschbaum* 535 NW 2d 462 (Wisconsin CA 1996); *US v Rouse* ibid; Ceci and Bruck, *Jeopardy In The Courtroom* (n 85).

7. The admissibility of expert psychological evidence in Canadian courts

In Canada the 'ultimate issue' rule has been judicially abolished, removing the first objection to expert testimony.[161] In 1994 *R v Mohan* established admissibility tests for expert evidence which largely parallel the *Daubert* test, requiring that novel scientific evidence be subjected to special scrutiny to determine whether it meets a basic threshold of reliability, and whether it is necessary, in the sense that the trier of fact will be unable to come to a satisfactory conclusion without the assistance of the expert. The necessity test should not be judged by too strict a standard; absolute necessity is not required.[162]

The Canadian Supreme Court has concluded that acknowledging the fact-finding competence of modern jurors does not mean that they should be deprived of assistance in interpreting human behaviour, particularly where behavioural characteristics run counter to intuitive notions of what constitutes 'normal' human responses in certain situations,[163] as is often the case with systematically abused children.[164] Expert evidence can help to unmask misplaced assumptions about human behaviour which can drive the trier of fact to draw incorrect inferences from the evidence.[165] Canadian courts, like their American counterparts, think it possible to maintain a distinction between ensuring that a jury's evaluation of a child's credibility is properly informed, and telling a jury whether to believe a particular child witness. The jury must be carefully instructed as to its function and duty in making the final decision without being unduly influenced by the expertise of the witness.[166]

Canadian courts are alive to concerns that behavioural evidence may be a 'soft science' based on standards that cannot be objectively validated,[167] but generally they rely upon the adversarial process to expose deficiencies in expertise and methodological and interpretive differences between experts, for the trier of fact to weigh.[168] The trial judge retains discretion to exclude expert evidence, like any other form of evidence, where its prejudicial effect outweighs its probative value, assessed on a case-by-case basis; this power has served to screen behavioural psychological evidence that is strictly admissible but of tenuous probative value or relevance to the specific case.[169]

---

[161] *R v Burns* [1994] 1 SCR 656 (SCC) 666.

[162] *R v Mohan* (n 5); DM Paciocco 'Coping with Expert Evidence about Human Behaviour' (1999) 25 Queen's LJ 305, 321–328.   [163] *R v Lavalée* [1990] 1 SCR 852; *R v Burns* (n 161).

[164] A Mewett 'Credibility and Consistency' (1991) 33 Crim LQ 385, 386.

[165] *R v Marquard* (n 61) (L'Heureux-Dubé J).

[166] *R v Mohan* (n 5); Mewett (n 164) 385, 386; Paciocco 'Coping with Expert Evidence (n 162), 309.

[167] *R v RM* (n 79); *R v McIntosh* 117 CCC (3d) 385 (Ontario CA) 102; Paciocco ibid.

[168] *R v Béland* [1987] 2 SCR 398 (SCC); Mewett (n 164) 385; *R v M(B)* (1998) 42 OR (2d) 1 (Ontario CA) [79].

[169] eg *R v M(W)* (1997) 115 CCC (3d) 233 (British Columbia CA), upholding the trial judge's exclusion of defence expert evidence concerning operation of the complainant's memory, where the evidence was unspecific and the expert had not interviewed her. See also *R v C(G)* (n 83); *R v K(A) and K(N)* (n 88); *R v Villamar* [1996] Ontario OJ 2742 (Ontario Gen Div) appeal dismissed [1999] OJ 1923 (Ontario CA); *R v Dieffenbaugh* (n 23) 108, excluding expert evidence of 'anal gaping' as evidence of sexual assault on a 17-month-old child where the scientific reliability of the diagnosis was dubious and its prejudicial value was 'overwhelming'.

In Canada, expert evidence may be tendered by the prosecution either as part of the prosecution's case to prove the substantive allegation of abuse, or to rehabilitate the complainant's credibility.[170] The defence may tender expert evidence to counter the prosecution case in either respect,[171] and benefits from a relaxed standard of 'necessity'.[172]

In the first category, there is some authority that expert observations as to the psychological and physical conditions and behaviour which frequently result from child sexual abuse are admissible to assist the trier of fact as to whether an assault has occurred.[173] Indeed, expert evidence is mandatory if the Crown relies upon descriptions of the complainant's emotional condition by lay witnesses as direct evidence that she had been sexually abused, if there is no other evidence to connect the emotional condition described to the offence charged.[174]

It is now much more common for expert evidence to be tendered for the second purpose, to counter 'ordinary inferences' about the response of young victims to abuse.[175] Such 'social framework evidence' is defended as necessary in child abuse cases 'not because the subject is not a matter of common knowledge but rather because what is "known" about it is simply wrong'.[176] Experts may explain: why victims may initially deny abuse, make inconsistent disclosures, or recant their original complaints,[177] particularly if they are not supported by the non-abusing parent;[178] why they may wish to protect parental abusers or the family unit; and why association between abused and abuser may continue after the abuse.[179] Experts may also comment on children's capacity to remember, how victims' memory might improve in a protected environment, and the means by which their memory may become corrupted.[180] The defence can lead expert evidence to challenge the effect of interviewing techniques on children's memories.[181] Psychiatrists may testify about the reliability of a therapeutically induced memory recall process.[182] Such evidence is justified as putting the witness's testimony in its 'proper context' and assisting the jury to determine whether there is an explanation for what might otherwise be regarded as conduct inconsistent with that of a truthful witness.

In both criminal and tort cases, Canadian courts insist that expert testimony must not cross the line between elucidating human behaviour and assessing the veracity

---

[170] *R v RM* (n 79) affirming the reasoning of the Quebec CA.   [171] eg *R v M(B)* (n 9).

[172] *R v Bell (No 1)* (1997) 115 CCC (3d) 107 (Northwest Territories CA) 118; *R v M(B)* ibid [88]–[89].

[173] *R v B(G)* [1990] 2 SCR 30 (SCC); *R v R(S)* (1992) 73 CCC (3d) 225 (Ontario CA) 230–231.

[174] *R v F(JE)* (1993) 85 CCC (3d) 457 (Ontario CA) 478.

[175] *R v C(R)* (1993) 85 CCC (3d) 522 (British Columbia CA); *R v K(A) and K(N)* (n 88), [106]–[114].

[176] J Norris and M Edwards 'Myths, Hidden Facts and Common Sense: Expert Opinion Evidence and the Assessment of Credibility' (1995) 38 Crim LQ 73, 83.

[177] *R v B(G)* (n 173); *R v Markovitch* (1994) 91 CCC (3d) 51 (British Columbia CA); *R v P(C)* (1992) 74 CCC (3d) 481(British Columbia CA) 486; *R v F(JE)* (n 174) 471–472; *R v Jmieff* (n 102); *R v Talbot* C 35019 17 Jan 2002 (Ontario CA) [33]–[42].

[178] *R v P (Clary)* (1992) 15 CR (4th) 121 (Ontario Gen Div).

[179] *R v C(RA)* (1990) 57 CCC (3d) 522 (British Columbia CA); *R v J(RH)* (1994) 86 CCC (3d) 354 (British Columbia CA), leave to appeal to SCC denied (1994) 29 CR (4th) 35; *R v Meyn (Andreas Alexander)* 2003 BCCA 401, (2003) 176 CCC (3d) 505 (British Columbia CA).

[180] *R v R(D)* [1996] 2 SCR 291 (SCC) [36]–[40]; *R v C(RA)* ibid.   [181] *R v R(D)* ibid.

[182] *R v K(A) and K(N)* (n 58) (expert testimony adduced by both the Crown and defence).

of a child.[183] Thus an expert in child behaviour can explain why children may lie to hospital staff about the cause of their injuries, but cannot comment on which of the child's accounts is true.[184] Nor is it permissible for an expert witness to state that false accusations of sexual abuse are rare.[185] While Canadian courts openly acknowledge that such evidence has its hazards, they believe that these can be overcome by ensuring that the expert is properly qualified, keeping the scope of the testimony properly constrained to avoid undue emphasis,[186] and by directions to the jury not to become mesmerized by her qualifications and that they alone must decide whether the complainant is telling the truth.[187]

Recently, the Supreme Court of Canada curbed the impetus to tendering behavioural opinion evidence in child abuse prosecutions. In *R v D(D)*[188] the Court split four to three on whether expert evidence was properly admitted as rehabilitative evidence after defence counsel had attempted to impeach the ten-year-old complainant in cross-examination on a delay of two and a half years in disclosing sexual assaults alleged to have occurred when she was five or six. The majority were clearly concerned by the time and expense consumed by the proliferation of expert testimony 'of questionable value'.[189] Major J held that the opinion evidence failed to meet the necessity requirement of *Mohan,* because the timing of the disclosure, standing alone, signifies nothing in diagnosing cases of child sexual abuse; this fact was not unique or scientifically puzzling, but rather was the proper subject for a simple jury direction to dispel the risk of stereotypical reasoning.[190] Because the proposition was 'simple and irrefutable', there was no need for it to be tested by cross-examination.[191]

The minority, led by McLachlin CJC, objected to an appellate Court laying down broad rules that categories of expert evidence are always admissible or inadmissible, contending that the necessity criterion of *Mohan* should not be adumbrated with sub-rules relating to the type of science at issue; instead, trial judges should be left to determine necessity in each individual case. The number of decided cases on the issue indicated that there was still a significant need perceived by the lower courts for explanation of children's reactions to abuse, as it may be outside the knowledge and experience of ordinary people. Jurors need to know that there is no 'normal' child response, and that the timing of the complaint does not help to diagnose whether it is true or fabricated. The fact that the child herself gave some explanation for the delay did not mean that the psychologist's evidence as to the factors behind delay—fear of reprisal, lack of understanding, fear of disrupting the family, the nature of the child's relationship with the abuser, and the nature of the abuse—was inadmissible and unnecessary. Here, the defence had asked the jury to infer from the delayed disclosure that it was fabricated, and a warning would

---

[183] Mewett 'Credibility and Consistency' (n 164), 386, cited with approval by McLachlin J (as she then was) in *R v Marquard* (n 61) [40]–[54].   [184] *R v Marquard* ibid [53].

[185] *R v Quesnel (Paul Albert)* (Ontario CA 16 Dec 1994).

[186] *R v K(A) and K(N)* (n 98) [115]–[116], [119].   [187] *R v J(RH)* (n 179).

[188] *R v D(D)* 2000 SCC 43, [2000] 2 SCR 275.   [189] ibid [56].

[190] ibid [58]–[59].

[191] ibid [64]. The majority position is criticized by D Thompson 'Are There *Any* Rules of Evidence in Family Law?' (2003) 21 Can Fam LQ 245, 276–279.

not have been a complete substitute for the psychologist's evidence to rebut that inference. The minority were also apprehensive about the majority's revival of the dubious assumptions about jurors' understanding of 'normal' and 'abnormal' human behaviour.[192]

While the broader *dicta* of the majority in *R v D(D)* might be taken as casting doubt on the utility of behavioural psychology in child abuse prosecutions, the impact of the case has been limited thus far. In *R v Talbot*, the Ontario Court of Appeal held that *D(D)* applied only to expert testimony restricted to delayed disclosure, and that expert evidence on the patterns of disclosure, including inconsistencies and retractions as well as delay, remained admissible.[193] The British Columbia Court of Appeal has interpreted *D(D)* as merely requiring that the necessity of expert evidence about the behaviour of sexual assault victims turns on the specific features of the case,[194] and has admitted rehabilitative evidence as to why children repeatedly molested over a protracted period may continue to associate with their abusers.[195] These cases suggest that the views of the minority in *D(D)* may yet prevail.

8. The admissibility of expert psychological evidence in New Zealand courts

In 1987 the New Zealand Court of Appeal held that a child psychologist could not testify about tests administered to ascertain the ability of a mentally handicapped child aged 12 to give an accurate account of her experiences, and whether her emotional response was indicative of abuse. Two judges on the panel suggested that child psychology had not yet advanced to the point where diagnoses of sexual abuse could be sufficiently reliable to allow the jury to hear them.[196] In another judgment in 1989, the Court of Appeal ruled that the Crown could not call expert evidence that the complainant's behaviour such as self-harm was consistent with the behavioural patterns displayed by sexually abused children generally, to rebut a defence allegation that the complainant had fabricated allegations of sexual abuse by her father to conceal her misconduct at school.[197]

The New Zealand Parliament responded to these decisions in 1989 by amending the Evidence Act 1908 to permit expert evidence respecting circumscribed topics. In cases concerning child sexual assault, s 23(G)(2) permits expert opinion by psychiatrists and psychologists experienced in the professional treatment of sexually abused children respecting:

(a) the intellectual attainment, mental capability and emotional maturity of the complainant;

(b) the general development level of children of the same age group as the complainant; and

---

[192] ibid [21]–[32].   [193] *R v Talbot* (n 177) [39]–[42].
[194] *R v Tayebi* (2001) 161 CCC (3d) 197 (British Columbia CA).
[195] *R v Meyn (Andreas Alexander)* (n 179).   [196] *R v B* [1987] 1 NZLR 362 (New Zealand CA).
[197] *R v Accused (CA 174/88)* [1989] 1 NZLR 714 (New Zealand CA).

(c) whether any evidence given during the proceedings regarding the complainant's behaviour is consistent or inconsistent with the behaviour of sexually abused children of the same age group as the complainant.

In forming an opinion respecting the first point, the expert may rely on examination of the complainant before giving evidence, or on observation of the complainant testifying, whether directly or on videotape,[198] but may also consult other relevant material such as interviews and investigations, provided that the opinion is limited to evidence eventually tendered in court.[199] The trial judge is also entitled to call for and receive reports from qualified persons to advise on the effect on a child complainant of giving evidence in person in the ordinary way, or by alternative modes prescribed in the statute.[200]

New Zealand law therefore permits expert evidence for both diagnostic (in the weaker sense described at the beginning of this chapter) and 'rehabilitative' purposes, provided that it is tailored to come within the strict parameters of the legislation.[201] The Court of Appeal in a succession of cases has interpreted those parameters as follows:

- Before expert evidence can be given, there must be admissible evidence of such behaviours; the cogency of that evidence in terms of time, place and circumstance to an issue in the trial must be clearly demonstrated, such that its probative value exceeds its prejudicial effect.[202]

- Expert evidence is not required where the behaviours to be commented on are within what one would assume to be the ordinary collective knowledge of the jury.[203] However, some behaviours might be beyond the normal competence of jurors, and so expert opinion might be beneficial, such as where the behaviour may seem counterintuitive.[204] Thus expert evidence about the effects of post-traumatic stress disorder contemporaneous with the alleged abuse may be permissible to explain why the child did not complain or remained in an abusive relationship.[205]

- Where the prosecution intends to rely upon evidence of sexual behaviour to bolster its case, it is likely that expert evidence under s 23G(2)(c) will be required.[206]

- An expert is not permitted to comment even indirectly[207] on the credibility of the witnesses who describe the behaviour of the complainant, as that is a matter for the

---

[198] Evidence Act 1908 s 23(G)(2)(a)(i) and (ii). The videotape may be admissible for the purpose of evaluating behaviour even where the child is considered too young to testify: *R v KMP* [1996] DCR 380 (New Zealand Dist Ct).

[199] *R v Aymes* (CA123/04, 16 December 2004) (New Zealand CA) [124]–[127].

[200] Evidence Act 1908 (New Zealand) s 23(D)(3).

[201] *R v S* (New Zealand CA 244/91 20 December 1991) (New Zealand CA, Hardie Boys J); *R v S* [1995] 3 NZLR 674 (New Zealand CA); *R v B* [2003] 2 NZLR 777 (CA) [25].

[202] *R v Aymes* (n 199) citing *R v G* (CA 414/03, 26 October 2004) (New Zealand CA) [37], [39].

[203] *R v Walker* (CA 417/03, 15 June 2004) (New Zealand CA) [26], cited in *R v Aymes* ibid [111].

[204] *R v Aymes* ibid [112].

[205] *R v B* (n 201) [20]–[21], [27]; *R v Guthrie* 15 CRNZ 67 (New Zealand CA).

[206] *R v Aymes* (n 199) [112].   [207] *R v B* (n 201) [25].

jury; nor is the expert permitted to give an opinion as to whether the complainant has in fact been sexually abused, or the likelihood of abuse having occurred.[208]

- *A fortiori* the expert cannot comment directly or indirectly on the credibility of the complainant's evidence.[209]

- The expert can identify and discuss the evidence (including the accused's explanations)[210] considered significant as being consistent or inconsistent with abuse having occurred, but cannot take into account the child's allegations as part of this 'behaviour'.[211] The expert must articulate how consistent the behaviour is, and also if it is consistent with other factors such as another possible trauma in the child's life, the proper use of statistics being important in measuring consistency and hence probative value.[212]

- The witness can express an opinion on the internal and external consistency of the child's own evidence in evaluating her intellectual attainment, mental capability and emotional maturity under s 23(G)(2)(a).

Counsel must ensure that expert witnesses keep within those narrow limits,[213] which may be difficult to accomplish in the flow of oral testimony. The trial judge should also explain to the jury the difference between an opinion as to consistency of behaviour and a conclusion as to whether the child has been sexually abused— a distinction which, the Court of Appeal wryly noted, the caselaw suggests is not even well understood by the experts or by prosecuting counsel—and that it is for the jury to decide if the behaviours described in evidence upon which the opinion relies happened, and if any abuse they conclude occurred was perpetrated by the accused.[214]

Notwithstanding the repeated warnings of the Court of Appeal about the need to comply strictly with s 23G, it is not a comprehensive code as to what may be addressed by psychiatrists or psychologists in court.[215] One law court recently held that the provision is no impediment to a psychiatrist or psychologist explaining the principles and techniques which should be observed by interviewers in interviewing young children.[216]

The New Zealand Law Commission's draft Evidence Code would introduce a generally applicable threshold test that expert testimony must be 'substantially helpful' to the jury in understanding other evidence or ascertaining any material fact, replacing the 'common knowledge of jurors' test.[217] This test is intended to function as an additional safeguard beyond the qualifications test, focusing on the reliability and value of the proposed evidence in considering whether the validity of the underlying

---

[208] *R v W* [1995] 1 NZLR 548 (New Zealand CA); *R v S* [1995] (n 201) 676, 680; *R v B* (n 201) [25]–[26].   [209] *R v Baillie* (CA418/02, CA, 10 March 2003) (New Zealand CA).
[210] *R v Tait* [1992] 2 NZLR 666 (New Zealand CA) 669.   [211] *R v S* [1995] (n 201) 677.
[212] *R v Aymes* (n 199) [113], [135].   [213] *R v Tait* (n 210); *R v B* (n 201) [25]–[27].
[214] *R v Aymes* (n 199) [142]–[148].   [215] ibid [104].
[216] *The Queen v M* [2002] NZ FLR 91 (New Zealand HC) [3], [9]–[20].
[217] New Zealand Law Commission *Evidence* (Report 55 August 1999), Draft Evidence Code s 23(1), Vol 1 [75]–[77]; K Belt 'Psychological Syndrome Evidence' unpublished research paper for the New Zealand Law Commission, September 1997.

scientific theory is established.[218] Thus it could filter and focus evidence relating to psychological syndromes which is viewed as warranting careful treatment.[219]

The general 'substantial helpfulness' provision would subsume the current s 23G(2)(a) and (b) which allow expert evidence of the general development level of the complainant compared to other children of the same age group. Concern that the substantial helpfulness test might inadvertently abolish s 23G(2)(c) and so preclude experts from commenting on the consistency of the complainant's behaviour with that of sexually abused children of the same age group, has prompted the Law Commission to propose that the substance of the existing provision be explicitly re-enacted.[220]

The purpose for which such behavioural evidence could be tendered by the prosecution remains somewhat unclear. The Law Commission declares that it is not diagnostic evidence, but rather 'educative', to impart specialized knowledge the jury may not otherwise know, to help them understand and evaluate the evidence of and about the complainant.[221] The effect of counterintuitive evidence would be to recalibrate a complainant's credibility from a debit balance, because of jury misapprehension, back to a zero or neutral balance, not to prove or disprove that the complainant has been sexually abused.[222] However, the Law Commission then goes on to state that evidence of behaviour consistent with sexual abuse can be circumstantial evidence which can combine with other evidence to prove beyond reasonable doubt that abuse has occurred—which one would think means it is deployed for a diagnostic (in the weaker sense) rather than merely an educative purpose.[223] The Code would extend the existing provision to apply where the complainant has become an adult (age 17) by the time of the proceeding, and where a child complainant is not a witness.[224] The Law Commission withdrew its recommendation for court-appointed experts in both civil and criminal proceedings because of opposition from the legal profession, although non-legal professionals were reported as strongly supporting it.[225]

The draft Evidence Code would impose an express legal duty on an expert witness giving behavioural evidence about child abuse to give a fair and balanced explanation of the conclusions by reference to research and experience. The Law Commission explains that its effect would be to ensure that a fuller picture is given, so that if the expert concludes that the complainant's behaviour is consistent with abuse, she must also

---

[218] NZLC Report No 55, *Evidence* Vol 2 commentary [C99].

[219] Belt (n 217); New Zealand Law Commission *Evidence Law: Expert Evidence And Opinion Evidence,* (Preliminary Paper 18 December 1991)18–21.

[220] NZLC *Evidence* (n 217), Draft Evidence Code s 24, Vol 1 [81]–[84]. The Law Commission thus reversed its proposal to repeal s 23G: New Zealand Law Commission *The Evidence of Children and Other Vulnerable Witnesses: a Discussion Paper* (Preliminary Paper 26 October 1996) [67].

[221] *Evidence* ibid Draft Evidence Code commentary Vol 2 [C110].

[222] ibid Draft Evidence Code commentary Vol 2 [C111].

[223] ibid Draft Evidence Code commentary Vol 2 [C112].

[224] ibid Vol 2 Draft Evidence Code s 24(1) and (2). Similar provisions would not be re-enacted for adults with an intellectual disability, who are presently included in s 23(G)(2)(c), because the Law Commission found no research indicating that they react to sexual abuse any differently from other adults ibid Vol 1, [82 note 25]. [225] ibid Vol 1 [84].

indicate whether it might also be consistent with the child having had other traumatic experiences. One would think that this provision is superfluous in an adversarial system as other possible explanations should be susceptible to cross-examination.[226]

The New Zealand special expert evidence provisions in child abuse prosecutions have not been free of controversy,[227] in particular s 23(G)(2)(c) governing 'consistency' opinions, and have often proved difficult to apply in the context of an adversarial criminal trial.

9. The admissibility of expert psychological evidence in Australian courts

The Commonwealth's Evidence Act 1995 has abolished the 'common knowledge' and the 'ultimate issue' rules derived from English common law,[228] as has the New South Wales Evidence Act 1995.[229] Theoretically this might have cleared the way for expert evidence about the ways in which children may respond to abuse, but both statutes prohibit evidence to bolster credibility, and have narrower provisions than the common law governing the rehabilitation of witnesses whose credibility has been attacked.

Several State appellate courts have rejected expert evidence pertaining to the typical behaviour of child victims of sexual abuse on the orthodox bases that juries do not require the assistance of child psychologists in evaluating the behaviour of alleged victims of sexual abuse, and that such evidence lacks scientific rigour.[230] However, in *Farrell v The Queen*[231] the High Court of Australia opened the door to expert evidence about the psychological and physical conditions which may lead to a certain behaviour relevant to credibility, provided it is tendered to attack or rehabilitate a witness's credibility, rather than merely to reinforce it in chief.[232] *Farrell* has encouraged the admission of expert evidence on the distorting effects of repeated interviewing and of breach of interviewing protocols on the accuracy of a child's recall of events.[233]

The Australian Law Reform Commission and the Human Rights and Equal Opportunity Commission have advocated relaxation of the strictures on expert evidence where 'a child's behaviour on the witness stand or during the investigation process

---

[226] Possibly the proposed provision is intended to forestall sweeping conclusions by expert witnesses based on generalized references to research which can be difficult to challenge in cross-examination, as was deplored in *R v Tait* (n 210).

[227] Campaigners in support of Peter Ellis, the convicted defendant in the Christchurch Civic Creche case, have targeted s 23G as a major factor in the alleged miscarriage of justice: R Mahoney 'Review of Evidence' [2000] New Zealand L Rev 101; L Hood *A City Possessed: the Christchurch Civic Creche Case—Child Abuse, Gender Politics and the Law* (Longacre Press, Dunedin 2001) 105–107, 445–446; Anonymous 'Editorial: the Ellis Case' [Feb 2002] New Zealand LJ 1.

[228] Evidence Act 1995 (Commonwealth of Australia) s 80.

[229] Evidence Act 1995 (New South Wales), s 80.

[230] *R v F* (1995) 83 A Crim R 502 (New South Wales CCA); *C v R* (1993) 60 SASR 467 (South Australia Supreme Ct) [17]–[20]; *R v J* (1994) 75 A Crim R 522 (Victoria CA); *Ingles v R* (1992 No. CCA 82/1921) (Tasmania Supreme Ct).   [231] *Farrell v The Queen* (1998) 194 CLR 286 (Aus HC).

[232] ibid 292, 300, 322.   [233] *R v NRC* [1999] 3 VR 537 (Victoria CA) [41]–[44].

may be contrary to a jury's expectations of an "abused" child's behaviour'.[234] They considered that expert testimony may be necessary to explain a child victim's behaviour or demeanour in court, fearing that a child's particularly flat and disconnected attitude while testifying about traumatic experiences might be misinterpreted by a judge or jury as indicating that the event could not have happened. The Commissions recommended that all Australian jurisdictions enact legislation to make expert evidence admissible to explain why general assumptions about the behaviour of a child witness or a certain line of cross-examination might not reflect adversely on a particular child witness's credibility. Their recommendation that expert testimony be admissible to comment on the child's demeanour whilst testifying appears to go well beyond the boundaries of permissible opinion evidence in other common law jurisdictions.

The Queensland Law Reform Commission has concluded that the 'common knowledge' rule perpetuates misunderstandings about the testimony of child witnesses, but has defended the 'ultimate issue' rule, particularly as it pertains to bolstering credibility of witnesses before the court.[235] However, legislation should provide that expert evidence be admissible about the psychological state of a child witness once the child's credibility has been impugned on the basis of his conduct.[236] Expert evidence would also be admissible as to the factors which can affect a young child's reliability, such as age and cognitive development, susceptibility to suggestion, and lapse of time.[237] The extent to which the expert would be permitted to relate the opinion to the individual child witness is unclear from the recommendations.[238] The Queensland Law Commission, like the New Zealand Law Commission,[239] recommended against permitting court-appointed experts in criminal proceedings, as being incompatible with the adversarial trial model.[240] The proposals pertaining to expert evidence do not appear to have been adopted by the government, as they were not included in the Evidence (Protection of Children) Amendment Act 2003.[241]

It is noteworthy that when Tasmania adopted the Uniform Evidence Act in 2001, it inserted a specific provision permitting a person who has specialized knowledge of child behaviour, including the impact of sexual abuse on children, to testify as to child development and behaviour both generally and specifically if a child has had a sexual or similar offence committed against her.[242]

The Government of South Australia is considering a recommendation to adopt the New Zealand model, which would be extended to make admissible expert evidence

---

[234] *Seen and Heard: Priority for Children and the Legal Process* (1996 Commonwealth of Australia) [14.74]–[14.77] and Recommendation 101.

[235] Queensland Law Reform Commission *The Receipt of Evidence by Queensland Courts: The Evidence of Children* (Report No 55 December 2000) Part 2, 316.   [236] ibid Part 2, 316–317.

[237] ibid Part 2, 318.

[238] ibid Part 2, Recommendations 15.2, 15.4. The recommendations would also make expert testimony admissible on the issues of testimonial competence and eligibility to be declared a 'special witness' for videotaped pre-trial testimony under the Evidence Act 1977 (Queensland) s 21A, and for other special protective measures whilst giving evidence at trial [Recommendations 15.3, 15.5, 15.6].

[239] NZLC *Expert Evidence And Opinion Evidence* (n 218) [92].

[240] Queensland LRC *Evidence of Children* (n 235) Part 2, 319–320.

[241] Evidence (Protection of Children) Amendment Act 2003, (Queensland).

[242] Evidence Act 2001 (Tasmania) s 79A.

to explain a child witness's particular disability, the characteristics of the disability and the likely physical responses of the child to the court environment and process.[243]

10. The admissibility of expert psychological evidence in Scottish courts

Scotland is the latest jurisdiction to reconsider its stance on the admissibility of psychological evidence, after expert evidence explaining why children might make a staged disclosure was ruled inadmissible in *Grimmond v HMA*.[244] The Vulnerable Witnesses (Scotland) Act 2004 permits the admission in sexual offences cases of expert psychological or psychiatric evidence relating to 'any subsequent behaviour or statement of the complainer' for the purpose of rebutting any inference adverse to the complainer's credibility or reliability as a witness which might otherwise be drawn from the behaviour or statement.[245]

11. Evaluation of behavioural science and the child witness

There is a broad consensus amongst Canadian, American and New Zealand courts that:

- while it is impermissible for an expert to express a direct opinion as to whether a child witness is telling the truth, it is possible for experts to educate the jury about patterns of responses to child abuse without infringing this rule;[246] and

- 'rehabilitative' evidence is scientifically valid and should be admitted for limited purposes which should be explained to the jury.

Significantly, in these jurisdictions, expert witnesses are tendered by the defence as often as by the prosecution, suggesting an equality of arms on this battleground.

While knowledge of the dynamics of child sexual abuse has developed greatly over the past two decades, the caution of English criminal courts about accepting inferences from human behaviour as diagnostic tools is understandable. Diagnostic evidence remains contentious, and many courts are sceptical about the strength of the scientific research currently underpinning such evidence. A fundamental difficulty is that empirical research on the accuracy of allegations of traumatic child sexual abuse is necessarily severely constrained; as the New Zealand Court of Appeal has pointed out, its very definition precludes anything in the nature of clinical trials, and the ascertainment of accuracy is seldom capable of finite assessment.[247] While

---

[243] Robyn Layton QC *Our Best Investment—A State Plan to Protect and Advance the Interests of Children* (South Australia Government 2003) 15.17.

[244] Cited in the Policy Memorandum accompanying the Vulnerable Witnesses (Scotland) Bill [52].

[245] Vulnerable Witnesses (Scotland) Act 2004 s 5, inserting s 275C into the Criminal Procedure (Scotland) Act 1995.

[246] Some defence counsel are sceptical as to whether juries will appreciate the distinction: Norris and Edwards (n 176), 89–90; see also *R v Olscamp* (1994) 35 CR (4th) 37 (Ontario Gen Div).

[247] *R v Peter Hugh McGregor Ellis* (New Zealand CA 120/98, 14 October 1999) [31] (the notorious Christchurch Crêche case). Berliner and Conte (n 66), 113–115 demonstrate the problem of finite assessment in a critical survey of 'determinative' diagnostic models in vogue as of 1993.

expert evidence as to the potential effect of interviewing techniques on the accuracy of disclosure can be valuable in assisting the jury to evaluate a child's evidence, inferences drawn from behaviour are more problematic and are potentially circular—'children whom I believed had been abused exhibited this behaviour, therefore this child has been abused'. Thus empirical research is not immune from the inevitable fallibility of judgement in the judicial process: that what is really being measured is the degree to which the child is convincing rather than truthful.[248]

While these reservations must be acknowledged, they do not entail that psychological evidence should remain alien to the criminal judicial process. As Fisher and Whiting point out,

The overzealous forensic use of clinically relevant, but diagnostically unsubstantiated, techniques for assessing symptoms of child sexual abuse and the corresponding attempts to discount all psychological data as irrelevant to judicial decisions are threatening the perceived credibility of psychologists as expert witnesses and violating the welfare and rights of both victimised children and innocent defendants.[249]

In 1967 Lord Parker CJ noted that juries and justices 'need all the help they can get' when it comes to evaluating the impact of something on the minds of children of different ages.[250] American empirical research in the early 1990s[251] found that the typical juror was not familiar with the dynamics associated with child sexual abuse, and in particular was misinformed about the reliability of child sexual abuse reports and typical victim responses, in specific areas where there was consensus amongst child abuse experts. Over half of the jurors in the sample believed that children are easily manipulated into giving false reports and that most children are physically damaged by sexual abuse, so there should be accompanying physical evidence. Slightly more than one-third believed that sexual abuse allegations often proved to be false and that the typical reaction of a 'true' victim would include resistance, crying for help, or escape, rather than a reluctance to report.[252] A significant number also tended to adhere to the 'dirty old man' stereotype of the typical abuser, and were unfamiliar with the fact that most sexual assaults occur within the home and are perpetrated by someone known to the child.[253] The researchers concluded that expert rehabilitation testimony regarding recantation, delayed reporting, inconsistencies and reluctance to report could be particularly useful to educate jurors who are typically misinformed on these topics.[254] It must be recognized however that the issue of child sexual abuse has become a much higher profile issue in the public consciousness in the past decade, and so judicial directions, and persuasive submissions by prosecutors,[255] may do much to

---

[248] Berliner and Conte ibid 111, 119.   [249] Fisher and Whiting (n 66).
[250] *DPP v A and BC Chewing Gum Ltd* [1968] 1 QB 159 (QBD) 164–165.
[251] S Morison and E Greene 'Juror and Expert Knowledge of Child Sexual Abuse' 16 (1992) *Child Abuse & Neglect* 595.   [252] ibid 607–609.
[253] ibid 595, 608.   [254] ibid 609.
[255] J Bulkley 'The Prosecution's Use of Social Science Expert Testimony in Child Sexual Abuse Cases: National Trends and Recommendations' (1992) 1(2) *J Child Sexual Abuse* 73 argues that better prosecutorial skills in rehabilitating child witnesses and other lay witnesses through redirect examination about the child's behaviour can do much to replace expert testimony.

dispel any lingering myths, at least where they may be reinforced in the jury room by more informed jurors.

Australian, New Zealand and Canadian judges have given a salutary warning that courts must ensure that the objectionable orthodoxy that the evidence of complainants of sexual assault is intrinsically unreliable is not replaced by a new and equally objectionable orthodoxy that the credibility of complainants is unchallengeable.[256] Caution is required to ensure that the process is not transformed into 'trial by expert', detached from the testimony of factual witnesses.[257] Care must also be taken to avoid another, paradoxical, stereotype, that would demand that children be traumatized by their experiences in order to be believed. The challenge, it has been rightly observed, is to find methods of addressing the conceptions antithetical to the rendering of a true verdict, without at the same time compromising the fairness of the trial.[258]

It would probably be unwise, at least at this stage of behavioural research, to permit a psychologist to testify before a criminal jury about the results of a Statement Validity Analysis or Criterion Based Content Analysis, because this would amount in effect to a child abuse expert telling the jury whether to believe the child. Nevertheless, this and similar analytical techniques could be very useful for the investigators and prosecutors in evaluating a child's videotaped interview to determine whether there is sufficient evidence to proceed with a prosecution, in a more structured and nuanced way than at present.[259] The Home Affairs Select Committee of the House of Commons has recommended that Statement Validity Analysis be researched and piloted as a tool for evaluating the credibility of witness testimony in complex historical child abuse cases.[260] Both prosecuting and defence counsel could also benefit from training in the technique as they could then highlight in closing submissions to the jury specific factors in the child's evidence to consider in evaluating her honesty and reliability.[261]

There are signs (largely in *obiter dicta*) that the Court of Appeal Criminal Division is relaxing its antipathy towards psychological evidence as a class of expertise. The court has implied that it is awaiting a test case where the human psychology expert identifies criteria by reference to which the court can test the quality of the opinion, there is a database from which to make comparisons between the witness and others, and there is a substantial body of academic writing approving the methodology used.[262]

---

[256] *R v George Frederick Thorne* (1995 Vic Lexis 1064) (Victoria CCA); *R v B* [1987] (n 196) 370 (Somers J); *R v K(V)* (1991) 68 CCC (3d) 18 (British Columbia CA) 35 (Wood JA); *R v L(Z)* (2000) 144 CCC (3d) 444 (British Columbia CA). The extreme to which counterintuitive contention can go is illustrated by one diagnostic psychological model outlined in 1986, one indicator of a 'true' case being delayed and conflicted disclosure, often with retraction, while conversely a 'false' allegation was characterized by easy and apparently spontaneous disclosure [A Green 'True and False Allegations of Sexual Abuse in Child Custody Disputes' 25 *J American Academy of Child Psychiatry* 449].

[257] *R v C(G)* (n 83) 37.   [258] Norris and Edwards (n 176), 75.

[259] *Bristol Study*, 32–35. This approach is recommended for American prosecutors: *R v Strudwick and Merry* [1994] 99 Cr App R 326 (CA); NCPCA *Investigation and Prosecution of Child Abuse* (n 26) Vol 1, 88–93.

[260] House of Commons Home Affairs Committee *The Conduct of Investigations into Past Cases of Abuse in Children's Homes* (Fourth Report of Session 2001–02 2002) [48]–[50].

[261] As suggested by Trafford J in ruling Statement Validity Analysis inadmissible as having little probative value in *R v Villamar* (n 169).   [262] *R v Guilfoyle (No 2)* (n 7) [25].

In other words, the expert witness must furnish the court with the necessary scientific criteria for testing the accuracy of the conclusions, so as to enable the judge or jury to form their own independent judgment by the application of those criteria to the facts proved in evidence. The Court of Appeal in the context of expert interpretations of real evidence has expressly drawn an analogy between the current English approach and *Daubert's* interpretation of Federal Rule of Evidence 702.[263]

This is an entirely reasonable position, but the family courts' experience in routinely admitting psychological evidence pertaining to child abuse suggests that this test has already been satisfied. Family court judges are deemed capable of evaluating the professional qualifications and experience of individual specialists tendered as expert witnesses. It is no longer assumed that all such testimony is either unreliable or unhelpful to triers of fact. Defendants will not be called upon to counter an opinion given 'by a quack, a charlatan or an enthusiastic amateur' just because the witness is a psychologist or psychiatrist.[264]

It is anomalous that trial judges presiding at criminal trials are now permitted to have the benefit of expert evidence in determining whether a vulnerable prospective witness is capable of giving intelligible evidence[265] and is entitled to Special Measures Directions[266] under the YJCEA 1999, but those experts are not permitted to testify in the same trial before the jury which has to evaluate the reliability of that witness. English jurors are currently entrusted with the task of deciding whether to accept conflicting expert testimony respecting difficult areas of forensic science, such as pathology and DNA evidence. Until such time as empirical research may be permitted into the ways British jurors absorb and analyse the evidence and judges' directions,[267] we will not know how effective the adversarial process is in testing the reliability of such evidence.[268] Nevertheless, it is appropriate now to revisit the perception that jurors cannot be assisted by, or are incapable of dealing appropriately with, expert evidence relating to human behaviour.

---

[263] *R v Dallagher* (n 7) [29].

[264] To use the caustic phrase of Bingham LJ (as he then was) in *R v Robb* (n 7) 166.

[265] YJCEA 1999 (England) s 54(5) discussed above Chapter 8 section A.1(a).

[266] YJCEA 1999 (England) s 20(6)(c). See also the Crown Court (Special Measures Directions and Directions Prohibiting Cross-examination) Rules 2002 SI 2002/1688 Rule 9.

[267] The Contempt of Court Act 1981 (England) s 8 currently requires that jurors' deliberations remain absolutely confidential, thereby prohibiting academic research into how actual juries work in England and Wales. The Government has consulted on whether to repeal or amend s 8: Department of Constitutional Affairs *Jury Research and Impropriety: A consultation paper to assess options for allowing research into jury deliberations and to consider investigations into alleged juror impropriety* (CP 04/05 21 January 2005). It has concluded that the legislation should not be amended unless it becomes apparent that specific and detailed research cannot be conducted using shadow juries [Department of Constitutional Affairs *Jury Research and Impropriety: Response to Consultation CP 04/05* (8 November 2005) [1]–[4]].

[268] American research challenging the effectiveness of cross-examination in testing the reliability of opinion evidence [see the empirical studies cited by M Kovera and E Borgida 'Expert Scientific Testimony on Child Witnesses in the Age of *Daubert*' in SJ Ceci and H Hembrooke (eds) *Expert Witnesses in Child Abuse Cases: What Can and Should be Said in Court* 185, 204–208] is not readily transplantable to the English criminal justice system because American judges only deliver boilerplate instructions on the law without reference to the evidence, whereas English jurors have the benefit of the trial judge's assistance in identifying and analysing the evidential issues and applicable legal principles.

12. Behavioural psychology and the defendant: offender profiling

In the 1980s and 1990s, forensic psychologists began to develop inductive models whereby the characteristics of offenders could be inferred from the nature of the crimes they committed,[269] in an attempt to replace the police culture of anecdote and intuition, which is often the basis of criminal investigations, with empirically invalidated principles of criminal behaviour.[270] Such empirical research can be very useful in disrupting false stereotypes which can influence the decisions of police officers and courts alike. Empirical research involving convicted child sex offenders, conducted in a forensic instead of therapeutic context, has contradicted the commonly held view of the child molester as an older man whose criminal activity is restricted to sexual deviance, primarily or even exclusively in relation to children, and whose offences typically escalate from relatively minor abuse.[271] The implications of such profiling for investigatory and sentencing practices are significant.

(a) Offender profiling as prosecution evidence

There is now a strong empirical case that there is no psychological *test* that reliably detects persons who have sexually molested children or who may do so, and hence there is no profile of a typical child abuser.[272] Consequently, expert evidence that an accused fits a general or case-specific psychological profile expected of the perpetrator remains inadmissible as proof of the guilt of the accused in virtually all common law jurisdictions. In England, following the controversial prosecution and directed acquittal of Colin Stagg,[273] the then Lord Chief Justice Lord Taylor indicated extra-judicially that while psychological profiling could be a useful investigatory tool, it should never be admissible in court as evidence of guilt because the material merely created suspicion founded upon conjecture, inviting assumptions without a proper basis.[274] This position has now been confirmed (in *obiter dicta*) by the Court of Appeal, in refusing to admit evidence of a 'psychological autopsy' of the deceased in a murder case with a view to showing that she was suicidal:

[I]f evidence of this kind were admissible in relation to the deceased, there could be no difference in principle in relation to evidence psychologically profiling a defendant. In our judgment, the roads of enquiry thus opened up would be unending and of little or no help to a jury. The use

---

[269] The methodology of offender profiling is described by D Canter and D Young 'Beyond "Offender Profiling": the Need for Investigative Psychology' in D Carson and R Bull (eds) *Handbook of Psychology in Legal Contexts* (2nd edn Wiley, Chichester 2003); D Canter and R Heritage 'A Multivariate Model of Sexual Offence Behaviour: Developments in "Offender Profiling"' (1990) 1(2) *Journal of Forensic Psychiatry* 185.

[270] D Canter and S Kirby 'Prior Convictions of Child Molesters' (1995) 35(1) *Science & Justice* 73, 74.   [271] ibid 73, 74.

[272] Myers *Evidence in Child Abuse Cases* Vol 1 [5.54].

[273] Ognall J, in an unreported ruling in *R v Stagg* (Colin) on 14 September 1994, excluded prosecution evidence from an undercover police officer who, acting under the direction of a psychological profiler, set out to entrap Stagg into engaging in violent sexual fantasies, the prosecution intention being to show that he fit the 'psychological profile' of the murderer of Rachel Nickell on Wimbledon Common in 1992.

[274] Speech to the British Academy of Forensic Science, London, 2 November 1994, reported in *The Guardian*, 3 November 1994.

of psychological profiling as an aid to police investigation is one thing, but its use as a means of proof in court is another... The present academic status of psychological autopsies is not, in our judgment, such as to permit them to be admitted as a basis for expert opinion before a jury.[275]

In American law, such prosecution evidence is likely to run foul of the bar on character evidence 'for the purpose of proving action in conformity therewith on a particular occasion' under Federal Rule of Evidence 404(a).[276] Some American courts have held that expert evidence about the 'grooming' process used by paedophiles is unduly prejudicial because it implies guilt based on the characteristics of known offenders—at least when tendered by the prosecution as part of its case in chief, rather than in rebuttal to defence evidence that the defendant's conduct is inconsistent with paedophilia.[277] The California Supreme Court has, however, held that the prosecution may offer expert testimony that there is no profile of a 'typical' child molester, and that abusers are found in all walks of life, to counter jurors' false stereotype of the 'dirty old man'.[278]

In Canada, such prosecution evidence would have to be established as relevant for some other purpose than to show disposition to commit the crime charged.[279] The Supreme Court has accepted that 'psychical as well as physical characteristics may be relevant to identify the perpetrator of the crime',[280] but in *R v Mohan*[281] held that the personality trait must be sufficiently distinctive and operate virtually as a badge or mark identifying the perpetrator. The fact that the accused is a member of an abnormal group, with some members who have the unusual behavioural characteristics shown to have been possessed by the perpetrator, is not regarded as sufficient. However, the Supreme Court left open the possibility that such evidence could be admissible at the behest of the Crown if it could be shown that all members of the group have the distinctive unusual characteristics, subject to the trial judge's duty to exclude it if its prejudicial effect outweighs its probative value.[282]

(b) Offender profiling as defence evidence

Notwithstanding the general bar on offender profiling as prosecution evidence, there have been attempts by defence counsel to adduce it as exculpatory rather than inculpatory evidence, to show that the accused does not fit the psychological profile of a child abuser. Under American[283] and Canadian[284] rules of evidence, the defence is

---

[275] *R v Guilfoyle (No 2)* (n 7) [25] citing with approval *R v Valley* 26 CCC (3rd) 207 (Ontario CA), 237 holding that this psychiatric or psychological evidence was inadmissible in a murder trial to show that the deceased had sado-masochistic tendencies because it was conjectural.

[276] *US v Gillespie* 852 F 2d 475 (US CA 9th Cir 1988) 789–790.

[277] *State v Braham* 841 P 2d 785 (Washington CA 1992).

[278] *People v McAlpin* 812 P 2d 563 (California Supreme Ct 1991) 570–571.

[279] *R v Morin* [1988] 2 SCR 345 (SCC); *R v Mohan* (n 5).

[280] *R v J-LJ* (n 13) [32], quoting with approval Martin JA in *McMillan v The Queen* (1975) 23 CCC (2d) 160 (Ontario CA), affirmed [1977] 2 SCR 824 (SCC) 173.   [281] *R v Mohan* (n 5).

[282] ibid 26, citing *R v Morin* (n 279) 371.

[283] *State v Miller* 709 P 2d 350 (Utah Supreme Ct 1985); *People v Stoll* 783 P 2d 698 (California Supreme Ct 1989).   [284] *R v Mohan* (n 5) 26.

not bound by the prohibition on character evidence to show disposition or propensity, and so in principle may adduce evidence of a pertinent character trait to negative guilt. Nevertheless, most American courts which have considered such testimony have excluded it, precisely because there is no generally accepted profile of a 'typical' sex offender.[285]

The Supreme Court of Canada dealt with the issue in *R v Mohan*, where a paediatrician charged with sexual assault on four of his female patients aged 13 to 16 attempted to lead evidence from a psychiatrist that the perpetrator of each of the offences alleged would be part of one of three groups with distinct and unusual psychosexual profiles, and that if one person committed all four then he would be a sexual psychopath. He would then testify that Dr Mohan did not have the characteristics attributable to any of the three groups in which most sex offenders fall. The Supreme Court, in confirming the ruling of the trial judge excluding the evidence, clarified its position on the so-called 'abnormal group exception' in which the caselaw had been floundering.[286] To be admissible, the proponent of the expert evidence must satisfy the trial judge that, as a matter of law, either the perpetrator of the crime or the accused has distinctive behavioural characteristics such that comparison of one with the other will be of material assistance in determining innocence or guilt. This test necessarily entails that the scientific community have developed a standard profile for the offender who commits this type of crime, so that the profile is capable of being a reliable indicator of membership in a distinctive group.[287] In *Mohan*, there was no material before the court to support a finding that the profile of a paedophile or psychopath has been standardized to the extent that it could be said that it matched the supposed profile of the offender depicted in the charges. The expert's group profiles were not seen as sufficiently reliable to be considered helpful.[288]

Recently the issue has been reignited in American and Canadian courts with a test protocol called the Abel Assessment for Sexual Interest (AASI), which its developer claims can objectively and reliably differentiate between abusers and non-abusers.[289] The subject answers a 389-item questionnaire about his sexual behaviour, and then views 160 suggestive slides and reports the time spent viewing and his arousal response to each slide. Three scores result from predictive logistic regression equations purporting to indicate the probability of the subject being an abuser of pre-adolescent girls or

---

[285] See the conflicting cases cited by Myers *Evidence in Child Abuse Cases* Vol 1 587 n 933, and by G Sarno 'Admissibility of Expert Testimony as to Criminal Defendant's Propensity toward Sexual Deviation' (2004) 42 American LR 4th 937. Wisconsin admits expert evidence that the defendant did not suffer from a sexual disorder typical of a child abuser, subject to weighing its probative value against prejudicial effect: *State v Richard AP* 589 NW 2d 674 (Wisconsin CA 1998); *State v Davis* 645 NW 2d 913 (Wisconsin CA 2002).

[286] First mooted in *R v Lupien* [1970] SCR 263 (SCC); *McMillan v The Queen* (n 280); Mewitt (n 12), 35–36; R Pattenden 'Conflicting Approaches to Psychiatric Evidence in Criminal Trials: England, Canada and Australia' [1986] Crim LR 92.   [287] *R v Mohan* (n 5) 37.

[288] ibid 38.

[289] GG Abel, A Jordan, CG Hand, CL Holland and A Phipps 'Classification Models of Child Molesters Utilising the Abel Assessment for Sexual Interest' (2001) 25(5) *Child Abuse and Neglect* 703.

boys under 14, or of him lying when denying an allegation.[290] The evidence has been ruled inadmissible in South Dakota[291] and Texas[292] on the basis that it does not meet the reliability criteria of *Daubert*. In *US v White Horse*, the error rate for false negative results, where 24 per cent of admitted paedophiles were inaccurately classified as non-paedophiles, was found to be too high to assist the jury in deciding whether the accused sexually assaulted his son.[293] Both courts held that in rating the likelihood the subject was telling the truth and level of cognitive distortion (measuring whether a person is changing his thinking to justify being sexually involved with children), the evidence was an impermissible comment on the accused's credibility, and so was inadmissible, on the same basis as polygraph tests.[294] Probability values could not determine guilt or innocence.[295]

In Canada, the Supreme Court rejected expert evidence deploying a similar methodology in *R v J-LJ*,[296] where the accused was charged with a series of sexual assaults, including anal intercourse, on two boys aged three and five of whom he had custody. The defence tendered the evidence of a psychiatrist to establish that in all probability a serious sexual deviant had inflicted the abuse alleged, and that no such extreme deviant personality traits were disclosed by the accused in various tests including penile plethysmography. The expert conceded that he could not identify a single set of behavioural characteristics shared by every adult male paedophile, and so the *Mohan* challenge of a 'standard profile' was not met. The trial judge had excluded the expert evidence because it purported to show only lack of general disposition to commit such offences, and was not saved by the 'distinctive group' exception recognized in *Mohan*, but the Quebec Court of Appeal had reversed the conviction on the basis that his evidence of the accused's behavioural profile was nonetheless useful.

In restoring the conviction, the Supreme Court held that penile plethysmography failed the special scrutiny demanded for novel science.[297] The psychiatrist was a pioneer in Canada in trying to use something originally devised as a therapeutic tool for known sexual deviants as a forensic tool to identify deviancy, and he declined to provide the court with the psychological data which formed the basis of his opinion; the trier of fact was being asked to make an act of faith rather than of informed judgment.[298] The 'distinctive group' exception sought to be applied in *R v J-LJ* required the personality profile of the perpetrator group to identify truly distinctive psychological elements that would in all probability be present and operating in the perpetrator at the time of the offence.[299] This profile must be 'standard' to ensure that it is not put together on an

---

[290] J Peters 'Using the *Abel Assessment for Sexual Interest* to Infer Lack of Culpability in a Criminal Case' 14(12) Update (monthly newsletter of the National Center for Prosecution of Child Abuse, American Prosecutors Research Institute).

[291] *US v White Horse* 177 F Supp 2d 973 (US DC, South Dakota, 2001).

[292] *In the matter of JG* 1998 WL 271053 (Texas CA 1998).   [293] *US v White Horse* (n 291) [10]

[294] ibid [12]; *In the matter of JG* (n 292) 3. The Supreme Court of Canada ruled that polygraph tests are inadmissible for the same reason, in *R v Béland and Phillips* [1987] 2 SCR 398.

[295] *US v White Horse* (n 291) [15].   [296] *R v J-LJ* (n 13).

[297] Penile plethysmography was rejected in North Carolina for the same reason: *State v Spencer* 459 SE 2d 812, review denied 462 SE 2d 524 (North Carolina App Ct 1995).

[298] *R v J-LJ* (n 13) [56]–[60].   [299] ibid [38], [40].

ad hoc basis for the purpose of the particular case.[300] Beyond that, the question whether the 'profile' is sufficient depends on the expert's ability to identify and describe with workable precision what exactly distinguishes the distinctive or deviant perpetrator from other people, and on what basis the accused can be excluded. Here, the expert did not satisfy the trial judge that the underlying principles of methodology of the tests administered to the accused were reliable and applicable. Even passing over the doubts that *only* a paedophile would be capable of the offence, the error rate for false negatives of 52.5 per cent in the tests administered made them useless for the purposes of exclusion, and so the risk that the profile evidence would distort the fact-finding process was very real.[301]

North American courts have therefore clearly set out the benchmarks which offender profiling must achieve before it can be tendered on behalf of the defence or the prosecution. In these courts, the issue must be regarded as not being closed, but forensic psychology will have to become more accepted as a scientific discipline, and its empirical parameters and methodology more clearly established, before it will be accepted as a tool to prove or disprove identity of a perpetrator.

Thus far the English courts have not taken as methodical an approach to psychological profiling. The orthodox position has been that expert psychiatric and psychological evidence is not admissible to show the accused's state of mind as direct evidence of guilt or innocence,[302] unless it is contended that the accused is abnormal in the sense of suffering from insanity or diminished responsibility, which the trier of fact cannot assess without expert assistance.[303] In the controversial case of *Lowery v The Queen*,[304] the Privy Council allowed King to tender a psychiatrist in evidence against his co-accused, Lowery, showing that King was psychologically less likely than Lowery to have committed the sadistic murder of a young girl, as Lowery had the more aggressive personality. The case appears to stand alone in the British courts in permitting evidence of a psychological profile to be admitted.[305] The House of Lords recently approved *Lowery*, at least in so far that it held that where two accused are jointly charged with a crime, and each blames the other for its commission, one accused can rely on the criminal propensity of the other, as evidenced by his previous convictions;[306] while no comment was made about the psychological evidence in *Lowery*, the door may now be open a crack to such evidence in the English courts.

The reliability of offender psychological profiling, in the present state of empirical research, would seem to be too tenuous to warrant its admission in the criminal courts, whether at the instance of the defence or the prosecution. It is suggested that this territory should not be chosen by English advocates as a battleground on which to test the continuing viability of the 'credibility taboo'[307] symbolized by *Turner*.[308]

---

[300] ibid [44].   [301] ibid [51], [55].

[302] Psychological evidence to challenge the admissibility or reliability of a confession under the Police and Criminal Evidence Act 1984 ss 76 and 78 has been admissible since *R v Raghip* (n 122), and *R v Ward (Judith Theresa)* (n 123).   [303] *R v Chard* (n 120); *R v Turner* (n 120).

[304] *Lowery v The Queen* [1974] AC 85 (PC).

[305] See the analysis of Tapper *Cross & Tapper on Evidence* (n 1), 372–373.

[306] *R v Randall* [2003] UKHL 69, [2004] 1 WLR 56.

[307] To use the phrase coined by Redmayne (n 4) 171.   [308] *R v Turner* (n 120).

D. Evaluation: Is Expert Evidence Superfluous, Dangerous or Probative?

It has become fashionable to decry the work of expert witnesses as unnecessarily impeding the efficient disposition of cases in both the civil and criminal courts. There can be no doubt that the profligate appointment of experts can lead to unnecessary expense and delay of cases, but these concerns are best dealt with through procedural rules rather than admissibility rules.[309] Similarly, complaints about overly adversarial experts who become advocates for the parties instructing them are best handled in the courtroom through exposure to cross-examination and judicial control,[310] and by professional governing bodies. These are not reasons to keep useful expert testimony out of the courtroom altogether. It is essential however that the defence have equal access to qualified and experienced experts compared with the prosecution,[311] and that the prosecution remain alert to the possibility of unreliable forensic evidence and faulty expert testimony in its own case.[312] Similarly, in child protection proceedings it is crucial that the parents have the same level of access to qualified experts as local authorities to protect their rights under Articles 6 and 8 of the ECHR.[313]

It must be remembered that scientific knowledge is fluid, and consequently that rigid rules on admissibility of a particular category of expert evidence may persist long past their 'sell-by date'. A strong case can be made that this is what has occurred in English criminal law with *Turner*, as behavioural science has repeatedly demonstrated the fallacy of the 'normal/abnormal' distinction drawn in that case. Furthermore, the factual evidence in a particular case may render expert opinion more or less relevant and cogent, making a case-specific examination of the admissibility issues desirable.[314]

---

[309] See for example *Re CB and JB* [1998] 2 FLR 2 (CA), where 13 medical and psychiatric experts were retained to ascertain which parent had shaken the child, and where there was no disagreement of substance amongst the 7 medical experts. Such problems should be alleviated, if not eliminated altogether, by the Civil Procedure Rules 1998 (SI 1998/3131) which permits the court to require experts for all parties to meet before trial to agree common ground and identify points in issue [Rule 35.12] and may direct the appointment of joint experts [Rule 35.7]. Concerns have been expressed however that jointly instructed experts in the family courts may lead to less rigorous scrutiny of the evidence by counsel and the court: J Brophy, P Bates, L Brown, S Cohen, P Radcliffe and C Wale *Expert Evidence in Child Protection Litigation: Where Do We Go from Here?* (Stationery Office, London 1999); Lord Chancellor's Department *The Guardian ad Litem and the Use of Experts Following the Children Act 1989, Research Series 3/99* (1999)108.

[310] The Civil Procedure Rules 1998 (SI 1998/3131) Rule 35.3 reinforces the common law principle that expert witnesses are servants of the court required to provide unbiased and objective evidence. See also the judicial guidelines issued by Cazalet J for child abuse cases in *Re J (Child Abuse: Expert Evidence)* [1991] FCR 192 (CA).

[311] In the United States, defendants have a constitutional right to expert assistance [*R v Ake* 470 US 68 (USSC 1985)], although some argue that in practice that right has been eroded [PC Giannelli '*Ake v. Oklahoma*: the Right to Expert Assistance in a Post-*Daubert*, Post-DNA World' (2004) 89 Cornell L Rev 1305].

[312] Department of Justice Canada *FPT Heads of Prosecutions Committee Report of the Working Group on the Prevention of Miscarriages of Justice* (September 2004) ch 9.

[313] *Re W (A Child) (Non-Accidental Injury: Expert Evidence)* [2005] EWCA Civ 1247, [2005] All ER (D) 370 [37]–[40]. This is not a new problem; four inter-related research studies conducted between 1992 and 1996 reported that many parents received poor-quality legal representation and often did not have access to the same experts as the professional parties: Brophy *et al* (n 309).   [314] *R v C(G)* (n 83) 35.

Child sexual abuse in particular has been plagued by myths, stereotypes and fashionable views which render such cases, and child complainants in particular, prone to be the target (and sometimes the beneficiary) of sweeping assumptions and generalizations, both within and outside courtrooms. Expert evidence affords the adversarial trial system a forum in which to expose and test such assumptions, an opportunity which should not be dismissed lightly on the basis of the 'common sense' of jurors. The diminishing conviction rate in rape cases which are prosecuted to trial, which for adults has dropped from 28 per cent in 1998 to 21 per cent in 2002, and for complainants under 16 from 40 per cent in 1999 to 23 per cent in 2002,[315] has motivated the Office for Criminal Justice Reform to issue a consultation paper which includes proposals for the admissibility of behavioural psychology expert evidence 'to dispel myths and stereotypes concerning how the victim should behave, and help a judge and jury understand the normal and varied reactions of such victims'. The objective is to 'level the playing field' between the prosecution and defence by providing an alternative explanation to the defence's assertions.[316] One flaw in the proposals is that psychological expert evidence would be available only for rape cases, when we consider that it should be available for any sexual offence against children.

The attack on expert evidence in relation to child deaths continues.[317] In June 2005 the Court of Appeal heard four consolidated appeals turning on conflicting expert evidence about the indicia of 'Shaken Baby Syndrome', or Non-Accidental Head Injury, and concluded that the 'triad' of intracranial injuries consisting of encephalopathy or swelling of the brain, subdural haemorrhages, and retinal haemorrhages can no longer be considered as an infallible tool for diagnostic purposes.[318] In some rarer cases a comparatively minor fall may generate serious injuries.[319] Nor is there any scientific method of correlating the amount of force used and the severity of the damage caused,[320] which is critical in determining whether any criminal intent to injure the child is established, and in distinguishing murder from manslaughter.[321] The Crown accepted that a verdict of murder was unlikely ever to be justified on the basis of the 'triad' standing alone.[322]

In the same month, Dr Alan Roy Williams, the pathologist who performed the autopsies on the two sons of Sally Clark, was found guilty of serious professional misconduct by the General Medical Council. The findings included that he conducted the autopsies incompetently, gave incompetent and self-contradictory evidence in the Clark trial and failed to use his best endeavours to express fair, accurate and objective expert opinions.[323] On 15 July 2005 the General Medical Council struck

---

[315] L Kelly, J Lovett, L Regan *A Gap or a Chasm? Attrition in Reported Rape Cases* (Home Office Research Study 293, Feb 2005) 26, Table 3.2.

[316] Office for Criminal Justice Reform *Convicting Rapists and Protecting Victims—Justice for Victims of Rape: a Consultation Paper* (Spring 2006) ch 4.   [317] *R v Kai-Whitewind* (n 53) [83]–[85].

[318] *R v Harris, R v Rock, R v Cherry, R v Faulder* (n 44) [69], [152]

[319] ibid [257].   [320] ibid [76], [148].   [321] ibid [184].   [322] ibid [183].

[323] *General Medical Council v Alan Roy Williams* 3 June 2005 (General Medical Council Fitness to Practice Panel).

off Professor Sir Roy Meadow from the Medical Register for serious professional misconduct, in relation to the misleading statistical evidence he gave in *Clark*. The High Court reversed the GMC's finding of serious professional misconduct; Collins J ruled that a witness's immunity from civil action should be extended to immunity from disciplinary proceedings, where the expert witness has given his testimony honestly and in good faith.[324] On 26 October 2006 the Court of Appeal partially allowed the GMC's appeal, holding that it would be wrong in principle for the court to cut across or impliedly to limit the powers of a statutory regulatory body to evaluate the fitness to practise of a professional who had testified in a trial. The doctrine of witness immunity from civil proceedings should not be extended in either absolute or conditional form to encompass disciplinary, regulatory and fitness to practise proceedings, the purpose of which was to protect the public in the future.[325] Nor should there be any special category of immunity for paediatricians testifying in sensitive and sometimes high-profile cases in the criminal courts and in the family justice system.[326] Rather, the threat of such proceedings is in the public interest because it helps to deter those who might be tempted to give partisan evidence and not to discharge their obligation to assist the court by giving conscientious and objective evidence, thereby helping to preserve the integrity of the trial process and public confidence both in the trial process and the standards of the professions from which expert witnesses come.[327] The Court of Appeal further held, by a majority, that Professor Meadow was guilty of some professional misconduct in putting forward a theory of the improbability of recurrence of unexplained and seemingly natural infant deaths founded on a 'fundamental fallacy' that the recurrence of a second sudden infant death in the same family could be calculated by simply squaring the figure applicable to the first such death. He could properly be criticized for not disclosing his lack of expertise in the use of statistics or calculations of probability, but he did not intend to mislead the trial court, and he had honestly believed in the validity of his evidence when he gave it, and so his incompetence or negligence did not reach such a high degree as to justify a finding of serious professional misconduct.[328]

Controversies over the probity of expert testimony are not limited to England. In 2005 the Government of Ontario announced a review of forty child homicide cases when it was discovered that a paediatric forensic pathologist, Dr Charles Smith, had conducted incompetent autopsies and had failed to disclose, and even lost, vital evidence.[329]

Whereas hitherto practitioners in the field of child protection have been accustomed to high-profile controversies surrounding their diagnoses of sexual abuse, public

---

[324] *Meadow v General Medical Council* [2006] EWHC 146 (Admin), [2006] All ER (D) 229 (QBD).
[325] *Meadow v General Medical Council* [2006] EWCA Civ 3090 [2006] All ER (D) 315 [32], [45], [50]–[58].   [326] ibid [62]–[64].
[327] ibid [46].
[328] ibid, [201]–[207], [210]–[211], [216]–[221] (Auld LJ) [251]–[281] (Thorpe LJ); [71]–[83] (Clarke MR dissenting).
[329] Office of the Chief Coroner of the Government of Ontario *Results of Audit into Tissue Samples Arising from Homicide and Criminally Suspicious Autopsies Performed at the Hospital for Sick Children* (2005).

confidence has now been severely shaken in paediatricians' ability to diagnose with confidence the causes of an unexpected infant death. Paediatricians have claimed that they are being made the scapegoats in hindsight of a flawed judicial process,[330] causing many to refuse to do child protection work. This was one of the avowed reasons for the judgment of the High Court reversing the General Medical Council's finding of serious professional misconduct in the Meadow case.[331] Yet, as the General Medical Council stated in Dr Williams' disciplinary hearing in relation to the *Clark* case, high standards are neither an option nor an 'ivory tower' mirage, but the obligation of expert witnesses, because a fair trial hinges on their evidence.[332] Fortunately the Court of Appeal has now reinforced this message in *Meadow*.[333]

The Court of Appeal in the consolidated appeals relating to 'shaken baby syndrome' reminded experts of their obligations to the court:

• Expert evidence presented to the court should be seen to be the independent product of the expert uninfluenced as to form or content by the exigencies of litigation.

• An expert witness should provide independent assistance to the court by way of objective unbiased opinion in relation to matters within his expertise. An expert witness in the High Court should never assume the role of advocate.

• An expert witness should state the facts or assumptions on which his opinion is based. He should not omit to consider material facts which detract from his concluded opinions.

• Developments in scientific thinking should not be kept from the court, simply because they remain at the stage of a hypothesis. It is of the first importance that the true status of the expert's evidence, and the degree to which it is controversial, is frankly indicated to the court. All material used must be placed before the court and available to other expert witnesses, including material which contradicts the hypothesis.[334]

• An expert should make it clear when a particular question or issue falls outside his expertise.

• If an expert's opinion is not properly researched because he considers that insufficient data are available, then this must be stated with an indication that the opinion is no more than a provisional one.

---

[330] R Horton 'Editorial: In the Defence of Roy Meadow' (July 2005) 366 *The Lancet* 3. For Sally Clark's rebuttal to *The Lancet* editorial, see <http://www.sallyclark.org.uk/Lancet050701.html> (last accessed 31 October 2006).

[331] *Meadow v General Medical Council* (n 324) [6]–[7]. The Court of Appeal urged the GMC and other bodies regulating expert witnesses to address this problem and to revise its rules so as to reduce 'to an absolute minimum the risk of expert witnesses being vexed by unmeritorious complaints' to them: *Meadow v General Medical Council* (n 325) [66]–[67].

[332] *General Medical Council v Alan Roy Williams* (n 323) [19].

[333] *Meadow v General Medical Council* (n 324) [66], [204], [207].

[334] Quoting Wall J in *Re AB (Child Abuse: Expert Witness)* (n 24) 192.

- If, after exchange of reports, an expert witness changes his view on material matters, such change of view should be communicated to the other side without delay, and when appropriate to the court.[335]

Medical practitioners should not be deterred from taking on child protection work by being required to adhere to these high standards of competence and ethics in formulating their opinions.

---

[335] *R v Harris, R v Rock, R v Cherry, R v Faulder* (n 44) [270]–[273].

PART V

CHILD ABUSE LAW AND POLICY: EVALUATION

12

Themes and Future Directions

The numerous controversies about the response of agencies to allegations of child abuse,[1] as well as campaigns to reform the treatment of child witnesses in criminal trials,[2] provided the impetus for legal reform in England and Wales for both criminal and civil proceedings in the late 1980s and 1990s. These legal initiatives were ad hoc responses to specific problems, and not part of a coherent and integrated programme of reform across the criminal and civil systems. The changes required professionals across the child protection spectrum to assume unfamiliar roles, and to surrender their accustomed control to other agencies, in a way alien to their own professional culture. This led social workers and medical professionals to question child protection procedures which give primacy to the evidential requirements of the criminal and family courts, rather than therapeutic concerns. Furthermore, this background of crisis created a highly sensitized, and even defensive, environment for what is in any event forensically challenging and emotionally taxing work. Unfortunately the crisis about child abuse never died down. We now have layer upon layer of law and procedure which tries to regulate the social and legal response to child abuse.

A. Where the Law is Now

In family law the reforms have been piecemeal and often case-led. The British courts have been increasingly influenced by jurisprudence stemming from the European Convention on Human Rights (ECHR), especially Article 8 (respect for family life)

---

[1] Chapter 2 section A, Chapter 3 section A, Chapter 5 section A.　　[2] Chapter 8 section B.

and Article 6 (the right to a fair trial) with respect to the responsibilities of the local authority in relation to the care of children. However, awareness by the judiciary in England and Wales, and in all of our comparator jurisdictions, of the pressures and limited resources available to those working in child protection, also underlies many of the judgments on the provision of services to children in both family courts and civil courts adjudicating negligence claims.

In criminal law there has been a new Sexual Offences Act 2003[3] and some reform of the defence of reasonable chastisement[4] as well as the law relating to child homicide when the identity of the perpetrator is unclear.[5] Of the reforms, the Sexual Offences Act 2003 remains the most substantial; the other reforms merely tinker with the fatal and non-fatal offences against children, in response to campaigns about those particular issues. The wider questions, in relation to a 'lack of fit' between the nature and reality of child death and injury and the offences currently available to prosecutors to charge alleged perpetrators, remain to be answered in England and Wales, although jurisdictions in Canada and the United States are in the process of resolving them.[6] In contrast, the drafters of the Sexual Offences Act 2003 tried to redress the numerous problems caused by the inability of the previous law to reflect the nature of sexual assault as it is now understood; however the Act is a maze of unwieldy provisions, which mirror equally complicated reforms in other jurisdictions.

In tort law, the approach of the English appellate courts in shielding child protection investigators and social services from any form of negligence liability was shown to be no longer defensible by jurisprudence from the European Court of Human Rights and the highest courts in the Commonwealth, as the Law Lords acknowledged in 2005. The House of Lords, following the lead of the Supreme Court of Canada, has also rewritten the doctrine of vicarious liability to hold those with a legal connection with the abuser, such as an employer, strictly liable for his intentional torts against children, in circumstances which in English law (unlike in Canada) remain unnecessarily vaguely defined. This change alone has created massive tort liability in other jurisdictions for institutions such as churches, schools and residential child care facilities, with claims now beginning to move through the English and Welsh courts. With English tort law in the area of child protection in this state of flux, the developments in other common law jurisdictions have become all the more relevant for counsel and for the judiciary.

In the law of evidence, the judiciary and practitioners are continually struggling to adapt to the hectic pace of reform dictated by successive Home Secretaries to 'rebalance the criminal justice system in favour of the victim' (and implicitly against the accused), a seesaw metaphor which is deeply regrettable. The extensive, but still not comprehensive, reform of the law pertaining to vulnerable witnesses in the Youth Justice and Criminal Evidence Act (YJCEA) 1999 is still in the process of implementation, and recent empirical studies show that there is a long way to go to ensure that practice reflects the aspirations of the Act. When fully

---

[3] Chapter 3 section E. [4] Chapter 3 section D.4. [5] Chapter 3 section C.8.
[6] Chapter 3 section C.

implemented, the vulnerable witness regime has the potential to demonstrate that fairness to witnesses can be accomplished without jeopardizing fairness to the accused. Unfortunately the same cannot be said about the sweeping reforms to the law governing character evidence and hearsay in the Criminal Justice Act 2003, which do not reflect the Law Commission's well-balanced recommendations in a series of reports.

B. Points of Mismatch Between Legal Systems

We have identified many points at which the criminal and family systems of justice are incompatible. The laudable objectives of *Working Together*'s dominant theme of interdisciplinary cooperation cannot conceal the clash of two systems; which are constrained to take very different approaches to achieve their common goal of protecting the child. Social workers and health professionals are trained to cooperate with families in obtaining information with a view to securing the future welfare of the child, if possible within the birth family. The police are necessarily part of an adversarial process, which family court judges insist should not intrude into child protection proceedings.

Whilst the Government's position has been firm that there should be full disclosure of evidence in family proceedings to the police, this will necessarily inhibit parents' participation in child protection conferences, where candour may be critical to their being permitted to continue to care for their children.[7] Moreover, the House of Lords has determined that the principle of full disclosure in child protection proceedings trumps the usual legal litigation privilege which attaches to expert reports commissioned on behalf of the parents, even if their legal team decide not to use that evidence. This contradicts the position in criminal and other adversarial civil proceedings where litigation privilege is absolute and cannot be abrogated even where the privileged material might assist the defence of a person accused of murder. If the child protection case proceeds before the criminal trial then any evidence created in that context will not be privileged in the criminal trial; conversely if the expert is instructed by the criminal solicitor, then it will remain privileged in the child protection proceedings.

The rules of third party disclosure are also incoherent, as local authorities are mired in guidance which fails to clarify which tests to apply when: public interest immunity, the 'mere credibility' rule of disclosure, and the rights of a defendant to a fair trial under the ECHR Article 6. Significantly, the privacy interests of the child in confidential records are rarely acknowledged, unlike in Canada and Australia.

English law takes a paradoxical approach in relation to expert evidence about the behaviour of abused children: a juror in a criminal trial is assumed to be omnicompetent in relation to children who are not 'abnormal', whereas a seasoned family court judge is thought to be in need of that expert assistance in the determination of whether

---

[7] Chapter 7 sections A and C and Chapter 5 section H.1.

a child has been or is at risk of being abused. As a consequence negative stereotypes about how a 'real' victim would respond to abuse go uncorrected in the criminal courts.

Any decision about the extent to which one legal system should take account of the law in another should be consciously made and with a clear view of the implications and overall effect of that decision. For example we would contend that the decision to highlight the importance of the welfare of the child as a priority in the policies of the Crown Prosecution Service (CPS) on prosecuting child abuse was ill-conceived; because the implications of acknowledging the context and priorities of the family law system in guidance relating to the criminal law were not thought through.[8] The CPS policy states that if a crime against a child is serious and the evidence is strong enough they will 'nearly always prosecute' although they will 'think about the effect on the child of going to court'[9]—making promises of witness support which too often it cannot deliver.[10] While it is hoped by all involved in a prosecution that a child will not be damaged by the process of giving evidence during the trial of the person who allegedly abused them, the goal of prosecution is to punish offenders and label them as dangerous, so as to protect other children in the future. If the decision whether to prosecute were made on the same basis as all family law decisions, the welfare of the particular child complainant, few prosecutions would take place, as it is rarely in the best interests of the child who has already been abused to go through the criminal justice process.

We would also argue that the development of the law may also be damaged when the priorities of one system bleed into another legal system without a conscious decision to that effect. For example, in family law, considerations about the effects on adults of a finding that they have abused a child, has led to a special interpretation of the standard of proof in child abuse cases. The 'cogent evidence' test requires that the more serious an allegation, the less likely it is that the event occurred, and hence the stronger should be the evidence before the court concludes that the allegation is established in the balance of probability. Yet seriousness is arguably defined in terms of the seriousness to an adult of a court finding that he has committed that type of abuse, rather than the seriousness to a child of suffering that type of abuse.[11] Moreover, this test fits ill with the level of present knowledge about the prevalence in society of child sexual abuse.

C. Legal Doctrines Which Condone Stereotypes

Some evidence which remains admissible in criminal prosecutions is based upon lingering prejudice against child witnesses and alleged victims of sexual assault. The common law's deeply ingrained suspicion of children as witnesses still makes an

---

[8] Crown Prosecution Service *Children and Young People: CPS Policy on Prosecuting Criminal Cases Involving Children and Young People as Victims and Witnesses* (27 June 2006) 6.   [9] ibid 8.
[10] Chapter 8, section B.4.
[11] Chapter 2, section E.1 (c); see also termination of parental rights in the USA, Chapter 2 section E.2.

appearance in criminal courts; some trial judges use almost any pretext to warn the jury of the dangers of convicting on the uncorroborated evidence of a child—even in circumstances where it is difficult to conceive how corroborative evidence could be available.[12] One doctrine, recent complaint, paradoxically artificially bolsters the credibility of the complainant,[13] but more frequently evidence is deployed to denigrate the child inappropriately, such as delayed and initially incomplete disclosure, ambivalence about remaining with the abuser, and vacillation about pursuing the complaint.

Defence counsel in England still frequently tell juries that allegations of sexual assault are easy to make and difficult to refute. At bottom the 'ease of fabrication' assertion amounts to a claim that complainants of sexual offences are presumptively entitled to less credence than those who testify as the alleged victims of other crimes. It is even more difficult to square the 'easy to make' assertion with the distress and even psychological trauma which, it is now widely accepted, is a frequent consequence of the child's encounter with the criminal justice system. The low conviction rate suggests that the 'difficulty of refutation' contention is not generally valid either. As prosecuting counsel always address juries first in England and Wales, it is very difficult for them to counter such submissions inviting stereotypical responses by the triers of fact.

The law of evidence seldom candidly addresses this conundrum: what evidence is logically probative of whether a child witness is worthy of belief? When and how are previous allegations of abuse against others relevant? Is previous consensual sexual behaviour relevant, even if the child was legally incapable of consenting? If an adolescent had consensual sexual experiences, does that mean that she cannot be vulnerable to exploitation by an adult? The 'rape shield' law under YJCEA 1999 (England) s 41 is singularly inapposite for children, because it is directed at refuting myths grounded upon fallacious reasoning about consent and the credibility of sexually active women. Moreover its sheer complexity means it is very difficult to interpret and apply.[14] This uncertainty exacerbates the difficulties for the police, the CPS and those supporting child complainants in forecasting how their credibility might be attacked. It still remains the case that the more turbulent the child's background and environment, the more likely it is that her credibility will be attacked on the basis of her previous negative experiences of the world.

To what extent, if at all, is demeanour indicative of credibility? Empirical studies in the United States show that many jurors expect abused children to be very distressed when testifying, but witness support programmes may have the perverse effect of calming them to the extent that they are not believed.[15] Not all children are traumatized by misbehaviour which they may not really understand, such as indecent assault or exposure to sexual acts. Prosecutors in all jurisdictions using the adversarial mode of trial prefer to have the child in the witness box in the courtroom, so that if she starts to sob the jury will get the full impact of her distress, whereas the defence often prefer

---

[12] Chapter 9 section A.   [13] Chapter 9 section C.   [14] Chapter 9 section D.3.
[15] Chapter 8 section B.

using the live link because then the monitors in the courtroom can be shut off if the child breaks down.

It must also be recognized that there are myths about abusers as well. Sex offenders are assumed by the public to be innately evil and incapable of rehabilitation, whilst 'ordinary' violence against children is thought to be explicable by misjudgement or overreaction to trying behaviour. American courts and legislators have created special propensity admissibility rules for evidence showing 'depraved sexual instinct' or 'lustful disposition towards children'. Special admissibility rules for child sex abusers were rejected by the House of Lords in *Boardman*, as they have been rejected by the Supreme Court of Canada and the Queensland Law Commission, because they lacked a rational foundation.[16] But we would contend they have been institutionalized through the Criminal Justice Act 2003, in deeming propensity to commit a sexual offence against a person under 16 to be an important issue between the prosecution and defence.[17] We described in Chapter 10 how the Criminal Justice Act 2003 has completely inverted the common law, so that it is now easier to attack the credibility of the defendant on the basis of past misconduct than to make a parallel attack on the credibility of any prosecution witness. As the Supreme Court of Canada has acknowledged, propensity evidence of this form is 'potentially poisonous',[18] and this is borne out by empirical studies in England,[19] yet English law has now abandoned the common law formula of weighing its probative value against its potential prejudicial effect on the deliberations of the trier of fact.[20] The deemed relevance of evidence of a propensity to sexually abuse children may now make it easier for the prosecution to stack up charges on the same indictment, raising the possibility that the defendant will be convicted on the basis of the number of allegations and not on the proof of each one beyond reasonable doubt.

English law also assumes an indivisibility of character in relation to the credibility of both the child and the defendant as witnesses, which is also suspect.[21] It is still permissible to deploy the chain of reasoning that (1) the child has misbehaved in some way on a previous occasion; (2) therefore the child is not worthy of belief; (3) therefore the child must be lying about the abuse. Alleged lies about sexual behaviour have been deemed not to relate to sexual behaviour itself, and therefore fall outside the stringent statutory rules prohibiting cross-examination as to previous sexual experience.[22] The relationship of the previous sexual behaviour rules and the requirements of enhanced probative value required for a character attack on a prosecution witness under s 100 of the Criminal Justice Act 2003 remain unclear. The permissible chain of reasoning respecting the defendant's credibility is as tenuous: (1) the defendant committed a criminal offence previously (2) therefore the defendant has a propensity to break the law (3) therefore the defendant is committing perjury in denying the offence.[23]

---

[16] Chapter 10 section F.2. [17] Chapter 10 section D.
[18] *R v Handy* 2002 SCC 56, [2002] 2 SCR 908 [58], [138], [141], Chapter 10 section B.8.
[19] Chapter 10 section B.2. [20] Chapter 10 section F. [21] Chapter 10 sections B.2 and C.
[22] Chapter 9 section D.3(a). [23] Chapter 10 section C.

D. Points of Mismatch Between Black Letter Law and Practice

Despite the seemingly inexhaustible faith of the public and politicians in legal change to produce social results, it is debatable whether legal change alone can significantly alter social attitudes, for example in encouraging child abuse to be reported[24] or in reducing the level of chastisement of children which is physically damaging,[25] without a significant programme of social education. This is because there remains such a wide variation in the behaviour that is acceptable towards children across Britain's multicultural society, that it is unlikely that the law alone can create a shared understanding of what child abuse is, particularly because legal definitions tend to be context-specific and relate to a particular type of legal intervention.

However, although law cannot on its own effect change in social attitudes, its own principles should not reinforce false stereotypes about the nature of child abuse which linger in society. For example, one starting premise of the criminal law in England and Wales and Australia in relation to caregivers is that failing to act to protect a child is necessarily less deliberate and hence less culpable, than acting to harm a child. This is not borne out, even on the facts of the cases which appear before the courts in these jurisdictions.[26] There should be an acceptance in English law, as there is in Canadian law, of the reality that an omission to act by a caregiver can be as deliberate and as harmful in some cases.[27]

Prosecuting practice is heavily biased towards pursuing cases of sexual assault, however minor; whereas police and prosecutors are much less inclined to prosecute physical assault, because that is seen as more 'forgivable', and the defence of reasonable chastisement makes it difficult to predict success.[28] Similarly several rules of criminal procedure perpetuate this perceived hierarchy of harm, and are based on a false premise that testifying in a case about physical violence is essentially less damaging to children than sexual abuse. For example, a child can be cross-examined by the accused in person in offences of physical and emotional abuse and neglect, but in the trial of sex offences the trial judge must appoint counsel to cross-examine the child if the accused insists on representing himself.[29] The primary rule under Special Measures Directions also operates differently if the case is about sex rather than violence.[30]

E. Negative Effects of the Law on Practice

Law can improve practice in child abuse cases. Decision-making can be made more rigorous if it has to be justified to the court. In contrast when the courts are sidestepped by child protection professionals, as they have been in the United States in relation to emergency protection powers, this can lead to widespread arbitrary removal

---

[24] Chapter 5 sections D and E.3.   [25] Chapter 3 section D.4.
[26] Chapter 3 sections C.2 (b) (i) and C.6.   [27] Chapter 3 section C.5.
[28] Chapter 5 section I.3.   [29] Chapter 8 section B.2.   [30] ibid.

of children from their homes.[31] However the courts can only safeguard children from the acknowledged dangers of arbitrary state action if they are rigorous themselves in applying the law and in insisting on sufficient and credible evidence before making an order. Court orders have been rightly challenged when they have been made on the sole evidence of the word of practitioners who have actually had very little evidence for the conclusions that they have reached,[32] and this now is more likely to trigger a tort action.[33]

In return the demands that the law places on practitioners must be realistic; otherwise they may be simply ignored, or only the letter rather than the spirit of the law be observed. For example legislators only exacerbated the problems in the investigation of child abuse in States across the USA by creating a mandatory duty to investigate allegations of child abuse within a certain time frame. State child protection agencies were already widely viewed as being in crisis with a poorly trained and beleaguered workforce. The law only led to a dangerous practice of closing the child's file once the time limit for a response had expired, irrespective of whether an investigation had been undertaken, so that statutory time limits were fulfilled.[34] This in turn engendered tort liability to a child for failing to investigate the case properly, or at all.[35]

The law must also not become so excessively detailed and impenetrable that it becomes impossible for those working in the field to understand and use it. Where this is the case, law and procedure will simply be ignored or only half-understood and mis-applied. It is now well recorded that some social workers have denied the existence of a raft of child protection procedures because they found them overwhelming.[36] There is also a danger of over-complication in legislation. For example the Sexual Offences Act 2003 (England) created a great number of new sexual offences against children. The acknowledged reason for this was an attempt to ensure that there was a crime to fit every kind of sexual abuse of a child. However the legislators ran the risk that prosecutors would only use a small range of offences because they could not in practice become familiar with them all and comfortable in their use—a problem which had already occurred with implementation of the previous sexual offences legislation.[37]

Similarly if the courts are placed in the position of watchdog it must be possible for them fulfil that role. For example there has been considerable debate in England about whether it is possible for the courts to supervise the implementation of the care plan for a particular child by the local authority following a care order. There have been several legal challenges following a local authority's failure to do so. However the experience of the United States demonstrates that it is an almost impossible role to fulfil effectively because of the number of cases which the court would need to review. In the United States the process of review of the implentation of orders by the courts has become a 'rubber stamping' exercise where hard-pressed courts have had to accept the word of social workers that the case is progressing effectively rather than

---

[31] Chapter 5 section F.3.   [32] Chapter 5 section E.2.   [33] Chapter 4 section F.
[34] Chapter 5 section E.3.   [35] Chapter 4 section F.2.   [36] Chapter 5 section A.
[37] Chapter 3 section E.1.

making a real judgment in the light of the evidence.[38] However, this then lays social services open to a tort action for failing to manage the child's care plan, blighting a child's future prospects.[39]

Law cannot make up a shortfall in resources and expertise on the ground by simply providing the 'stick' in the form of legislation which requires practitioners to act in a certain way. Firstly, if there are insufficient resources to enable the child protection system to function effectively, then there is often also no money to police the law and ensure that those who do not adhere to it are brought to account. The cost of enforcing mandatory reporting laws has reduced them to the status of an empty threat in the jurisdictions we have studied.[40] Secondly, even if the sanction is enforceable, it has often led to a situation in which child protection agencies take money reserved for some children, in order to fulfil their legal obligations to another group. In England this has happened in relation to the provision of services to children. The local authority has a discretion to provide services to children 'in need' under the Children Act 1989 s 17, but an obligation to fulfil the terms of a court order requires them to provide services to children suffering or likely to suffer significant harm. This has meant that the pot of child protection money has historically been used to fulfil their legal obligations, rather than their discretionary ones, even though this undermines one of the central tenets of the Children Act 1989 that if possible crisis in children's cases should be avoided by the provision of services at an early stage.[41] Tort liability for negligent exercise of child protection powers of investigation similarly diverts resources from the local authority's other commitments (unless it carries liability insurance); however it can and should have the indirect effect of reallocation of resources and better training to deflect future tort liability. To this extent, it may make those responsible for allocating funds pause and think about priorities.

For lawyers the question of what the law may do in relation to child abuse has been further complicated by the increasing acknowledgement that the wrong response to child abuse by policy-makers and state actors can itself be enormously damaging to the child, the child's family and the organizations involved. The acceptance of the concept of system abuse is largely an acceptance that the state, like everyone else involved in child protection, may get the answer wrong in determining what behaviour is damaging to children, and how best to respond to it. A significant number of the more recent child abuse scandals have been about the 'inappropriate response' of professionals to an allegation of child abuse, rather than about the fact that a child could have been abused at all. But magnified perceptions of 'system abuse'—and specifically perceptions of the damage which the criminal justice system can inflict on a child victim—directly affect the decisions of social workers and police child protection officers. One atypical case of a ruthless cross-examination of a child witness can quickly enter the folklore in child protection professional circles and distort perceptions of the criminal justice system.

---

[38] Chapter 2 section F.   [39] Chapter 4 section F.3(c).
[40] Chapter 5 sections D.3, D.4 and D.6.   [41] Chapter 2 section D.1 (b).

F. Future Directions

We are acutely aware that it is easier to criticize than to reform. We believe we have made a case for simplifying and rationalizing the law across family and criminal courts. One area which desperately needs comprehensive reform is the rules of evidence. Recent changes to character evidence and hearsay in criminal law have only served to exacerbate the problems of complexity and to create yet more anomalies.[42] The labyrinthine provisions governing child witnesses cannot be properly and consistently applied by hard-pressed practitioners, especially non-lawyers responsible for generating the testimony of such witnesses.[43] A comprehensive Code of Evidence which addresses civil as well as criminal proceedings would force legislators to make positive determinations as to whether the admissibility rules for a specific form of evidence should differ between criminal and civil proceedings, and so would be conducive to coherence across systems. The Uniform Evidence Acts in Australia and the Evidence Code currently before the New Zealand Parliament provide excellent models of such systems. In 2001 the British Government announced its intention to develop such an Evidence Code for England and Wales in its White Paper *Justice for All*, but nothing has emerged into the public light in furtherance of that objective. We suggest that it should be as a matter of urgency. Only then can the full landscape of child protection law be seen and be rationalized.

---

[42] As pointed out by Sir Robin Auld *Review of the Criminal Courts of England and Wales* (September 2001) [26], above, Chapter 9 sections B.3 and D, Chapter 10.   [43] Chapter 8, section B.

Bibliography

REPORTS AND GUIDANCE[1]

United Kingdom

Association of Chief Police Officers of England, Wales and Northern Ireland, Victims and Witnesses Portfolio Group *When to Use an Intermediary: 2 Stage Test* (August 2005)

Attorney General's Guideline, on Disclosure 2000 (November 2000)

Attorney General's Guideline, on Disclosure 2005 (April 2005)

Sir Robin Auld *Review of the Criminal Courts of England and Wales* (September 2001)

Richard Barker (Chair) Newcastle upon Tyne City Council *Abuse in Early Years: Report of the Independent Inquiry into Shieldfield Nursery and Related Events* (1998)

Sir Michael Bichard, Chair *Bichard Inquiry Report* (HC 653 June 2004)

L Blom Cooper (Chair) *A Child in Mind: Protection of Children in a Responsible Society: Report of the Commission of Inquiry into the Circumstances Surrounding the Death of Kimberley Carlile* (London Borough of Greenwich 1987)

M Brandon and others, *Safeguarding Children with the Children Act 1989* (HM Stationery Office, London 1999)

British Medical Association *Doctors' Responsibilities in Child Protection Cases: Guidance from the Ethics Department* (BMA, London 2004)

British Psychological Society *Recovered Memories: the Report of the Working Party of the British Psychological Society* (1995)

Dame Elizabeth Butler-Sloss *Report of the Inquiry into Child Abuse in Cleveland 1987* (Cm 412)

Central Council for Education and Training in Social Work and the Department of Health Expert Group *Quality Standards for Residential Care* (1992)

Chief Secretary to the Treasury *Every Child Matters* (HM Stationery Office, London Green Paper 2003 Cm 5680)

Childline *Child Abuse* (Childline London Information Sheet 2)

Children Act Advisory Committee *CAAC Annual Report 1992/93* (Department of Health, London 1993)

DJ Christie and SR Moody *The Work of Precognition Agents in Criminal Cases* (Crime and Criminal Justice Research Findings No 32, Scottish Executive Central Research Unit Edinburgh 1999)

Churches Child Protection Advisory Service *Guidance to Churches Model Procedures* (CCPAS 2003)

H Cleaver and P Freeman *Parental Perspectives in Cases of Suspected Child Abuse* (HMSO, London 1995)

The Right Hon Lord Clyde *Report into the Inquiry into the Removal of Children from Orkney in February, 1991* (HMSO, 1992)

Committee on the Rights of the Child *Concluding Observations: United Kingdom* February 1995 [35] in 'Joint Committee on Human Rights United Kingdom Parliament Nineteenth Report

---

[1] For ease of reference, reports and official responses to them, consultation papers and ensuing reports, and different editions of various government guidance and protocols, are listed together rather than being in strict alphabetical order.

Part 4 [152]' <http://www.publications.parliament.uk/pa/jt200304/jtselect/jtrights/161/ 16107.htm> (last accessed 26 October 2004)

Committee on the Rights of the Child *Concluding Observations: United Kingdom of Great Britain & Northern Ireland* (CRC/C/15/Add. 188 4 October 2002)

HM Courts Service *Every Witness Matters: Employee Handbook* (2005)

HM Courts Service *A Protocol for Control and Management of Unused Material in the Crown Court* (20 February 2006)

Criminal Law Revision Committee *Eleventh Report (1972) Evidence (General)* (Cmnd 4991)

Crown Prosecution Service *Children and Young People: CPS Policy on Prosecuting Criminal Cases Involving Children and Young People as Victims and Witnesses* (27 June 2006)

Crown Prosecution Service *Children's Charter* (2005)

Crown Prosecution Service *Code for Crown Prosecutors* (2004)

Crown Prosecution Service and Association of Chief Police Officers *No Witness, No Justice (NWNJ) Pilot Evaluation Executive Summary 29 October 2004 (for the Crown Prosecution Service and Association of Chief Police Officers)* (29 October 2004)

Crown Prosecution Service *Prosecutors' Manual, Child Abuse and Child Witnesses: Guidance: Evidential Considerations: Disclosure of Material in Possession of Social Services* (London)

Crown Prosecution Service *A Protocol between the Crown Prosecution Service Police and Local Authorities in the Exchange of Information in the Investigation and Prosecution of Child Abuse Cases* (October 2003)

Crown Prosecution Service Inspectorate *Report on Cases Involving Child Witnesses* (Thematic Report 1/98 January 1998)

Dartington Research Unit *Place of Safety Orders* (University of Bristol, Dartington Research Unit, Bristol 1984)

G Davies and H Westcott *Interviewing Child Witnesses under the Memorandum of Good Practice: a Research Review* (Police Research Series Paper 115 Police Policing and Reducing Crime Unit, Home Office Research, Development and Statistics Directorate, London, 1999)

Department of Constitutional Affairs *Confidence and Confidentiality: Improving Transparency and Privacy in Family Courts* (Cm 6886 July 2006)

Department of Constitutional Affairs *The Criminal Case Management Framework* (July 2005 2nd edn)

Department of Constitutional Affairs *Disclosure of Information in Family Proceedings Cases Involving Children: a Consultation Paper* (CP 37/04 16 December 2004)

Department of Constitutional Affairs *Disclosure of Information in Family Proceedings Cases Involving Children: Response to the Public Consultation* (Cm 6623 July 2005)

Department of Constitutional Affairs *Jury Research and Impropriety. A Consultation paper to assess opinion for allowing research into jury deliberations and to consider investigations into alleged juror impropriety* (CP 04/05 21 January 2005)

Department of Constitutional Affairs *Jury Research and Impropriety: Response to Consultation CP 04/05* (8 November 2005)

Department for Education and Skills Circular 10/95—*Protecting Children from Abuse: The Role of the Education Service NUT Education the Law and You* (2003)

Department for Education and Skills *Children in Need in England; Results of a Survey of Activity and Expenditure as Reported by local Authority Social Services' Children and Families Teams for a Survey week in February 2003: Local Authority Tables and Further National Analysis* (National Statistics Volume Issue Number 01-2004) *and February 2005* (National Statistics Volume Issue Number vweb 02–2006)

Department for Education and Skills 'Statistics of education: referrals, assessments and children and young people on child protection registers: year ending 31 March 2005' (2006)

<http://www.dfes.gov.uk/rsgateway/DB/VOL/v000632vol01–2006textvI.pdf> (accessed 6 October 2006)

Department of Health *The Challenge of Partnership in Child Protection: Practice Guide* (Social Services Inspectorate HMSO, London 1995)

Department of Health *Child Protection: Messages from Research* (Studies in Child Protection HMSO, London 1995)

Department of Health *The Children Act 1989 Guidance and Regulations* Volume 1—*Court Orders; Regulations* Volume 2: *Family Support* Volume 4: *Residential Care* (HMSO, London 1991)

Department of Health *Framework for the Assessment of Children in Need and their Families* (The Stationery Office London 2000)

Department of Health *Government to clarify law on parental discipline (Press Release)* (Department of Health London, 7 November 1997)

Department of Health *Guidance on Permissible Forms of Control in Children's Residential Care* (Department of Health, London 1993)

Department of Health, Home Office, Department of Education and Skills *Keeping Children Safe: the Government's Response to the Victoria Climbié Inquiry and the Joint Inspectors' Report Safeguarding Children* (Department of Health, London 2003)

Department of Health, Home Office, Department for Education and Skills, Department for Culture, Media and Sport, Office of the Deputy Prime Minister and the Lord Chancellor's Department *What To Do If You Suspect That a Child is Being Abused* (Children's Services Guidance, London 2003)

Department of Health and Social Security *Review of Child Care Law* (HMSO, London 1985)

Department of Health and Social Security, Home Office, Lord Chancellor's Department, Department of Education and Science, Welsh Office and Scottish Office *The Law on Child Care and Family Services* (HMSO, London 1987)

Department of Health and Social Security *The Report of the Committee of Inquiry into the Care and Supervision Provided in Relation to Maria Colwell* (HMSO, London 1974)

Department of Health and Social Security *Review of Child Care Law* (HMSO, London 1985)

M Eagle 'Reply to Parliamentary Question from Department of Education and Skills' (31 October 2005) <http://www.publications.parliament.uk/pa/cm200506/cmhansrd/cm051031/text/51031w39.htm> (3 July 2006)

HM Government *Care Matters: Transforming the Lives of Children and Young People in Care 2006* <http://www.everychildmatters.gov.uk/_files/Green9020Paper.pdf> (accessed 11 October 2006)

HM Government *Common Assessment Framework for Children and Young People: Practitioners Guide* (2006)

HM Government *Every Child Matters* <http://www.everychildmatters.gov.uk>

HM Government *Information Sharing: Practitioners' Guide to Integrated Working to Improve Outcomes for Children and Young People* (HM Stationery Office, London 2006)

HM Government *Statutory Guidance on Making Arrangements to Safeguard and Promote the Welfare of Children under s 11 Children Act 2004* (HM Stationery Office, London 2005)

C Hallett and E Birchall *Co-ordination and Child Protection* (HMSO, Scotland 1992)

J Harris, S Grace *A Question of Evidence? Investigating and Prosecuting Rape in the 1990s* (Home Office Research Study 196 1999)

J Holton and L Bonnerjea *The Child The Court and The Video: A Study of the Memorandum of Good Practice on Video Interviewing of Child Witnesses* (Social Services Inspectorate, London 1994)

Home Affairs Select Committee, House of Commons, *Second Report on the Criminal Justice Act 2003, Part 11 Chapter 1: Evidence of Bad Character* (4 December 2002)

Home Affairs Select Committee, House of Commons *The Conduct of Investigations into Past Cases of Abuse in Children's Homes* (Fourth Report of Session 2001–2002, HC 836-I 31 October 2002)

The Conduct of Investigations into Past Cases of Abuse in Children's Homes: the Government Reply to the Fourth Report from the Home Affairs Select Committee Session 2001–2002 HC 836 Cm 5799, April 2003

Home Office, Lord Chancellor's Department, Crown Prosecution Service, Department of Health, the National Assembly for Wales *Achieving Best Evidence in Criminal Proceedings: Guidance for Vulnerable or Intimidated Witnesses, Including Children* (2001)

Home Office *Children and Families Safer from Sexual Crime* (Home Office Communications Directorate, London 2004)

Home Office, Crown Prosecution Service and Association of Chiefs of Police *Early Special Measures Meetings between the Police and Crown Prosecution Service and Meetings between the Crown Prosecution Service and Vulnerable or Intimidated Witnesses: Practical Guidance* (2001)

Home Office, Lord Chancellor, Attorney General *Justice for All* (CM 5563, July 2002)

Home Office *Intermediaries—a Voice for Vulnerable Witnesses: Frequently Asked Questions* (2003)

Home Office *Intermediary Procedural Guidance Manual* (Home Office October 2005)

Home Office and Department of Health *Memorandum of Good Practice on Video Recorded Interviews with Child Witnesses for Criminal Proceedings* (HMSO, London 1992)

Home Office *Protecting Children, Supporting Parents: A Consultation Document on the Physical Punishment of Children* (Home Office, London 1999)

Home Office *Protecting the Public: Strengthening Protection Against Sexual Offenders and Reforming the Law on Sexual Offences* (HM Stationery Office, London 2002)

Home Office, Crown Prosecution Service and Department of Health *Provision of Therapy for Child Witnesses Prior to a Criminal Trial: Practical Guidance* (2001)

Home Office *Setting the Boundaries—Reforming the Law on Sexual Offences* (Home Office, London 2000)

Home Office *Speaking Up for Justice: Report of the Interdepartmental Working Group on the Treatment of Vulnerable or Intimidated Witnesses in the Criminal Justice System* (June 1998)

Home Office *Action for Justice: Implementing the Speaking Up for Justice Report on Vulnerable or Intimidated Witnesses in the Criminal Justice System in England and Wales* (March 1999 and November 1999)

Home Office *Victim's Charter* (1996)

Home Office *Witness Charter Consultation* (2005)

B Hughes, H Parker and B Gallagher *Policing Child Sexual Abuse: The View from Police Practitioners* (Home Office, Police Research Group, London 1996)

Independent Police Complaints Commission *Independent Investigation into the Police Response to the Report of the Abduction of Child A from Her Home in Rumney on 2 January 2006* (26 July 2006)

HM Inspectorate of Constabulary *Child Protection—Thematic Report* (Home Office, London 1999)

HM Inspectorate of Constabulary *Keeping Safe, Staying Safe: Report of the Thematic Inspection of the Investigation and Prevention of Child Abuse* (HM Inspectorate of Constabulary 2005)

Institute for the Study of Children, Families and Social Issues, Birkbeck, University of London, *Implementing Sure Start Local Programmes: An In-Depth Study* (January 2005) <http://www.surestart.gov.uk/_doc/P0001450.pdf>

Joint Chief Inspectors *Safeguarding Children: The Second Joint Chief Inspectors Report on Arrangements to Safeguard Children* (HM Stationery Office, London 2005)

L Kelly, J Lovett, L Regan *A Gap or a Chasm? Attrition in Reported Rape Cases* (Home Office Research Study 293, February 2005)

L Kelly, J Temkin and S Griffiths *Section 41: an Evaluation of New Legislation Limiting Sexual History Evidence in Rape Trials* (Home Office Online Report 20/06, London 2006)

Baroness Helena Kennedy QC, Chair *Sudden Unexpected Death in Infancy: a Multi-Agency Protocol for Care and Investigation (the Report of the Working Group Convened by The Royal College of Pathologists and The Royal College of Paediatrics and Child Health)* (September 2004)

A Kirkwood *The Leicestershire Inquiry—The Report of the Inquiry into Aspects of the Management of Children's Homes in Leicestershire between 1973 and 1986* (Leicestershire County Council 1993)

Law Commission of England & Wales *Aggravated, Exemplary and Restitutionary Damages* (Law Com 247 1997)

Law Commission of England & Wales *Children: Their Non-Accidental Death or Serious Injury (Criminal Trials)* (Law Com 282 2004)

Law Commission of England & Wales *Corroboration of Evidence in Criminal Trials* (Law Com 202 Cmnd 1620 1991)

Law Commission of England & Wales *Domestic Violence and Occupation of the Family Home* (Law Com 207 1992)

Law Commission of England & Wales *Evidence of Bad Character in Criminal Proceedings* (Law Com 273, Cm 5257 October 2001)

Law Commission of England & Wales *Evidence in Criminal Proceedings: Previous Misconduct of a Defendant* (Consultation Paper No 141) (1996)

Law Commission of England & Wales *Evidence in Criminal Proceedings: Hearsay and Related Topics* (Consultation Paper No 138, 1995)

Law Commission of England & Wales *Evidence in Criminal Proceedings: Hearsay and Related Topics* (Law Com 245 Cm 3670 1997)

Law Commission *Legislating the Criminal Code: Involuntary Manslaughter* (Law Com 237 1996)

Law Commission of England & Wales *Limitation of Actions* (Law Com 270, 9 July 2001)

Law Commission *A New Homicide Act for England and Wales? A Consultation Paper No 177* (Law Commission, London 2005)

Law Commission of England and Wales *Murder, Manslaughter and Infanticide* (Law Com 304 HC 30, 2006)

Law Commission of England & Wales *Partial Defences to Murder Consultation Paper* (HM Stationery Office, London 2003 LC No 173)

Law Commission of England & Wales *Partial Defences to Murder Final Report* (HM Stationery Office, London 2004)

A Levy and B Khan *The Pindown Experience and the Protection of Children* (Staffordshire County Council 1991)

Lord Advocate's Chambers *Report of the Lord Advocate's Working Party on Child Witness Support* (March 1999)

Lord Chancellor's Department *Guidelines for Crown Court Listing* (1994)

Lord Chancellor's Department *The Guardian ad Litem and the Use of Experts Following the Children Act 1989*, Research Series 3/99 (1999)

Lord Chancellor's Department *Judicial Statistics 1999* (HM Stationery Office, London 2000)

Lord Laming (Chair) *Victoria Climbié Inquiry* (Cm 5730, 2003)

Liberty *Sexual Offences Bill: Liberty Response* (Press Release 29 January 2003)

B Lindley and M Richards *Protocol on Advice and Advocacy for Parents* (Centre for Family Research Cambridge 2002)

London Borough of Brent *A Child in Trust: The Report of the Panel of Inquiry into the Circumstances Surrounding the Death of Jasmine Beckford* (London Borough of Brent 1985)

London Borough of Lambeth *Whose Child?: The Report of the Public Inquiry into the Death of Tyra Henry* (London Borough of Lambeth 1987)

The Lord Chief Justice *Second Reading of the Criminal Justice Bill: Background Notes to Speech by the Rt Hon the Lord Woolf of Barnes* (House of Lords Library memorandum HMF 2003/1315 16 June 2003)

A Mackie and J Burrows *A Study of Requests for Disclosure of Evidence to Third Parties in Contested Trials* (Home Office Research, Development and Statistics Directorate, Research Findings No 134 2000)

M MacLeod *Child Protection—Everybody's Business* (ChildLine/Community Care, London 1997)

G McDonald and A Winkley *What Works in Child Protection* (Barnardos, London 2000)

Fiona McTaggart (Home Office Minister) 'Review of Murder Draft Terms of Reference' <http://www.lawcom.gov.uk/murder.htm> (31 July 2006)

NSPCC *Child Abuse Trends in the England and Wales 1983–1987* (1989)

NSPCC (P Cawson, C Wattam, S Brooker and G Kelly) *Child Maltreatment in the United Kingdom* (NSPCC, London 2000)

NSPCC (B Stone) *Child Neglect: Practitioners' Perspectives* (NSPCC, Policy Practice Research Series London 1998)

NSPCC (B Essam, Chair) *Review of Legislation Relating to Children in Family Proceedings* (NSPCC, London 2003)

NSPCC *Sexual Offences Act Media Briefing* (NSPCC, London 30 April 2004)

NSPCC *Not Naughty but Normal: Protecting Your Baby and Toddler* (NSPCC, London 2003)

NSPCC *Victims and Witnesses: Who cares?* (Home Office Special Conference Unit, March 1999)

National Evaluation of Sure Start Programmes (NESS) *Implementing Sure Start Programme: an In-Depth Study* (2005) <http://www.swestart.gov.uk/_obc/P0001450.pdf> (accessed on 9 October 2006)

Newham Area Child Protection Committee *Ainlee [Walker] Born 24.06.1999 died 07.01.2000 Chapter 8 Review* (December 2002)

Norfolk Health Authority *Summary Report of the Independent Health Review of the Health Services Treatment of Lauren Wright* (March 2002)

Office for Criminal Justice Reform *Convicting Rapists and Protecting Victims—Justice for Victims of Rape: a Consultation Paper* (Spring 2006)

Office for Criminal Justice Reform, Home Office *Inter-Agency Working Group on Witnesses: No Witness—No Justice: Towards a National Strategy for Witnesses.* (2003)

Office of Law Reform *Physical punishment in the home: thinking about the issues, looking at the evidence* (OLR, Belfast 2001)

J Packman *Decision Making on Admissions of Children to Local Authority Care* (unpublished)

HH Judge Thomas Pigot QC (Chair) *Report of the Advisory Group on Video-Recorded Evidence* (HMSO, London 1989)

J Plotnikoff and R Woolfson *'A Fair Balance'? Evaluation of the Operation of Disclosure Law* (RDS Occasional Paper No 76, Home Office 2001)

J Plotnikoff and R Woolfson *The Pace of Child Abuse Prosecutions: a Follow-Up Study of the Government's Speed Progress Policy for the Department of Health* (August 1995)

Quality Protects website <http://www.dfes.gov.uk/Qualityprotects/info/publications> (last accessed 4 October 2006)

Royal College of Paediatrics and Child Health *Responsibilities of Doctors in Child Protection Cases with Regard to Confidentiality* (RCPCH, London 2004)

Royal College of Psychiatrists *The Evidence of Children* (January 1996)

Royal College of Physicians *Physical Signs of Sexual Abuse in Children* (RCP, London 1991)

Royal College of Physicians *Physical Signs of Sexual Abuse in Children* (RCP, London 1997)

Scottish Executive *Guidance on Interviewing Child Witnesses in Scotland* (2003)

Scottish Executive *Guidance on the Questioning of Children in Court* (2003)

Scottish Executive *Policy Memorandum to the Vulnerable Witnesses (Scotland) Bill (SP 5)* (2004)

Scottish Executive Central Research Unit *Vulnerable and Intimidated Witnesses: Review of Provisions in Other Jurisdictions* (2002)

Scottish Law Commission *Report on the Evidence of Children and Other Potentially Vulnerable Witnesses* (Scot Law Com No 125 14 February 1990)

Social Services Select Committee, House of Commons *Second Report (Session 1983–1984) Children in Care* (HMSO London 1984)

Social Services Inspectorate *Modern Social Services—A Commitment to Reform—The 11th Annual report of the Chief Inspector of Social Services 2001-2002* (Department of Health, London 2002)

J Thoburn, A Lewis and D Shemmings *Partnership and Paternalism? Family Involvement in the Child Protection Process* (HMSO, London 1995)

J Timms and J Thoburn *Your Shout! A Survey of the Views of 706 Children and Young People in Public Care* (NSPCC, London 2003)

University of East Anglia and National Children's Bureau *Realising Children's Trust Arrangements: National Evaluation of Children's Trusts—Phase 1 Report* (2005)

Sir William Utting *People Like Us—The Report of the Review of the Safeguards For Children living Away From Home* (HMSO, 1997)

Victim Support *Annual Report and Accounts for the year ended 31 March 2005*

Lord Justice Wall 'A Report to the President of the Family Division on the publication by the Women's Aid Federation of England entitled 'Twenty-Nine Child Homicides: Lessons Still to be Learnt on Domestic Violence and Child Protection' with Particular Reference to the Five Cases in Which There was Judicial Involvement' (The Judiciary of England and Wales 2006) <http://www.judiciary.gov.uk/docs/report_childhomicides.pdf> (4 July 2006)

Sir Ronald Waterhouse, Chair *Lost in Care: Report of the Tribunal of Inquiry into the Abuse of Children in Care in the Former County Council Areas of Gwynedd and Clwyd since 1974* (HM Stationery Office, London 2000)

C Wattam and C Woodward 'And Do I Abuse My Children? No!—Learning About Prevention From People Who Have Experienced Child Abuse' in *Childhood Matters: The Report of the National Commission of Inquiry into the Prevention of Child Abuse* (Vol 2 Background Papers HMSO London 1996)

C Wattam 'Kids on Film' *Community Care* (7 October 1993)

P Wheeler and M McDonagh *A Report into the Police Investigation of Shaken Baby Murders and Assaults in the UK* (Home Office, London 2002)

Lord Williams of Mostyn (Chair) *Childhood Matters: the Report of the National Commission of Inquiry into the Prevention of Child Abuse* (HMSO, London 1996)

G Williams and J McCreadie *Ty Maur Community Home Inquiry* (Cwmbran Gwent County Council 1992)

***Working Together* Guidance**

Department of Health and Social Security and the Welsh Office *Working Together—Draft* (HMSO, London 1986)

Department of Health and Social Security *Working Together: A Guide to Arrangements for Inter-agency Cooperation for the Protection of Children from Abuse* (HMSO, London 1988)

Department of Health, Home Office, Department of Education and Science and the Welsh Office *Working Together—Under the Children Act 1989* (HMSO, London 1991)

Department of Health, Home Office and the Department of Education and Employment *Working Together to Safeguard Children* (HM Stationery Office, London 1999)

HM Government *Working Together to Safeguard Children: a Guide to Inter-Agency Working to Safeguard and Promote the Welfare of Children* (HM Stationery Office, London 2006)

Australia

Gail Archer, Principal Counsel, Legal Aid of Western Australia *Report on Fact-Finding Mission into the Videotaping of Children's Interviews* (March 2002)

Australian Catholic Bishops Conference *Pastoral Statement on Child Protection and Child Sexual Abuse* (1993)

Australian Law Reform Commission *Evidence* (Interim Report No 26 1985)

Australian Law Reform Commission *Evidence* (Report No 38 1987)

Australian Law Reform Commission *The Judicial Power of the Commonwealth: a Review of the Judiciary Act 1903 and Related Legislation, Part 25 Liability of the Commonwealth at Common Law and in Equity* (ALRC Report 92 2001)

Australian Law Reform Commission and the Human Rights and Equal Opportunity Commission *Seen and Heard: Priority for Children and the Legal Process* (Report 84 1997)

Australian Law Reform Commission *Speaking For Ourselves: Children and the Legal Process* (1996 Commonwealth of Australia)

Brown and others *Child Abuse in the Family Court* (Australian Institute of Criminology, Canberra 1998)

J Cashmore and ND Haas *The Use of Closed-Circuit Television for Child Witnesses in the ACT: A Report for the Australian Law Reform Commission and the Australian Capital Territorial Magistrates Court* (Sydney 1992)

J Cashmore and L Trimboli *An Evaluation of the NSW Child Sexual Assault Specialist Jurisdiction Pilot* (New South Wales Bureau of Crime Statistics and Research, Sydney 2005)

Child Protection and Juvenile Justice Branch *Case and Care Planning Practice Guidance for Child Protection Practitioners* (Victoria 2004)

Department for Community Development and Western Australia Police Service Joint Response to Child Abuse *Video Recording of Children's Interviews* (August 2003)

Department of Human Services, Victoria *An Integrated Strategy for Child Protection and Placement Services* (Community Care Division 2002)

Department of Justice, Government of Western Australia *Joinder of Sexual Offences: Final Report* (August 2003)

C Eastwood and W Patton *The Experiences of Child Complainants of Sexual Abuse in the Criminal Justice System* (Criminology Research Council, Canberra 2002)

Evidence of Children and Special Witnesses: Guidelines for the Use of Closed-Circuit Television, Videotapes, and Other Means for the Giving of Evidence, Approved by the Judges of the Supreme Court April 1, 1996, revised May 1, 1998 (Supreme Court of Western Australia)

Family Law Council *Family Law and Child Protection Final Report* (Commonwealth of Australia, Melbourne 2002)

Leneen Forde, Chairperson *Report of the Commission of Inquiry into Abuse of Children in Queensland Institutions* (1999)

Human Rights and Equal Opportunity Commission of Australia *Bringing Them Home: Report of the National Inquiry into the Separation of Aboriginal and Torres Strait Islander Children from Their Families* (Sydney 1997)

Robyn Layton QC *Our Best Investment—A State Plan to Protect and Advance the Interests of Children* (South Australia Government 2003)

Law Reform Commissioner of Tasmania *Child Witnesses* (Report No 62 1990)

Law Reform Commission of Western Australia *Report on Evidence of Children and Other Vulnerable Witnesses (Project No. 87)* (April 1991)

Western Australian Law Reform Commission *Review of the Civil and Criminal Justice System* (Report No 92 1999)

New South Wales Attorney General's Department *Report of the Children's Evidence Task Force* (1995–96)

New South Wales Law Reform Commission *Questioning of Complainants by Unrepresented Accused in Sexual Offence Trials* (June 2003)

New South Wales Law Reform Commission *Reform of Section 409B* (Report No. 87 1998)

New South Wales Parliament Standing Committee on Law and Justice, Legislative Council, *Report on Child Sexual Assault Prosecutions* (Report No 22 2002)

Office for Children *Protection Children: The Next Steps* (Melbourne 2005)

C O'Grady *Child Witnesses and Jury Trials: an Evaluation of the Use of Closed Circuit Television and Removable Screens in Western Australia* (Ministry of Justice, Government of Western Australia, Perth Jan 1996)

Queensland Law Reform Commission *The Receipt of Evidence by Queensland Courts: the Evidence of Children* (Report No 55 Part 1 June 2000, Part 2 December 2000)

Senate of Australia, Community Affairs References Committee *Forgotten Australians: a Report on Australians Who Experienced Institutional or Out-of-Home Care as Children* (August 2004)

Senate of Australia, Community Affairs References Committee *Protecting Vulnerable Children: a National Challenge; Second Report on Inquiry into Children in Institutional or Out-Of-Home Care* (March 2005)

State Government of Victoria *White Paper: Every Child, Every Chance*

DG Sturgess QC, Queensland Director of Public Prosecutions *Report of an Inquiry into Sexual Offences Involving Children and Related Matters* (November 1985)

Tasmania Law Reform Institute *Warnings in Sexual Offences Cases Relating to Delay in Complaint* (Issues Paper No 8 2005)

Uniting Church in Australia *Procedures For Use When Complaints of Sexual Abuse are Made against Ministers* (1994)

Victoria Parliament Crime Prevention Committee *Combating Child Sexual Assault: an Integrated Model: First Report upon the Inquiry into Sexual Offences against Children and Adults* (1995)

Victorian Law Commission *Defences to Homicide: Final Report* (Victorian Law Commission, Melbourne 2004)

Victorian Law Reform Commission *Sexual Offences: Final Report* (1 April 2004)

Victorian Law Reform Commission *Sexual Offences: Law and Procedure, Final Report* (2004)

The Hon Justice JRT Wood *Royal Commission into the New South Wales Police Service: The Paedophile Inquiry* (August 1997)

Canada

Agreement in Principle between Canada, The Assembly of First Nations, The General Synod of the Anglican Church of Canada, the Presbyterian Chruch in Canada, the United Church of Canada and Roman Catholic Entities <http://www.irsr-rqpi.gc.ca/english/pdf/AIP–English.pdf> (accessed 20 November 2005)

Badgley et al *Sexual Offences against Children: Report of the Committee on Sexual Offences against Children and Youth* (Ottawa: Supply and Services Canada 1984)

K Busby *Third Party Record Cases since R v O'Connor: a Preliminary Analysis for the Research and Statistic Section, Department of Justice Canada* (1998)

Chief Coroner of the Government of Ontario *Results of Audit into Tissue Samples Arising from Homicide and Criminally Suspicious Autopsies Performed at the Hospital for Sick Children* (2005)

Child and Family Services *Child Welfare in Canada 2000—the Role of Provincial and Territorial Authorities in the Provision of Child Protection Services: Practice Standards in Child Protection* (2000)

Department of Justice *Allegations of Child Abuse in the Context of Parental Separation: A Discussion Paper* (Department of Justice Canada 2001)

Department of Justice Canada *FPT Heads of Prosecutions Committee Report of the Working Group on the Prevention of Miscarriages of Justice* (September 2004)

C Farris-Manning and M Zandstra *Children in Care in Canada—A Summary of Current Issues and Trends with Recommendations for Future Research* (Child Welfare League of Canada, Ottawa 2004)

Federal/Provincial Task Force on Uniform Rules of Evidence *Report* (1982)

Federal/Provincial/Territorial Working Group on Child and Family Services Information *Child Welfare in Canada—The Role of Provincial and Territorial Authorities in the Provision of Child Protection Services* (CFS information, Quebec 2002)

Judge T Gove (Commissioner) *Matthew's Story: The Inquiry into Child Protection in British Columbia* (Vancouver British Columbia 1995)

Hon Ted Hughes OC, QC *BC Children and Youth Review: an Independent Review of BC's Child Protection System* (7 April 2006)

Justice Canada *Disclosure Reform: Consultation Paper* (November 2004)

The Hon Fred Kaufman CM, QC *Searching for Justice: an Independent Review of Nova Scotia's Response to Reports of Institutional Abuse* (Government of Nova Scotia 2002)

King and others *Child Protection in Ontario Past, Present and Future* (University of Western Ontario, London CA 2003)

Law Reform Commission of Canada *Report on Evidence* (1975)

Canadian Law Reform Commission *Sexual Offences Working Paper No 22* (Law Reform Commission Canada, Ottawa 1978)

Law Commission of Canada *Minister's Reference on Institutional Child Abuse* (Discussion Paper 1998)

Law Commission of Canada (R Bessner) *About Us: Part I Inventory of Different Institutions at which Children in Canada have been Physically, Sexually, and Psychologically Abused; Part II Redress for Abusive Acts in Government-Funded and Government-Operated Institutions for Children* (Research Paper 1998)

Law Commission of Canada (G M Shea) *Institutional Child Abuse in Canada: Civil Cases* (October 1999)

Law Commission of Canada (G M Shea) *Institutional Child Abuse in Canada: Criminal Cases* (October 1999)

Law Commission of Canada (A Bowlus, K McKenna, T Day and D Wright) *The Economic Costs and Consequences of Child Abuse in Canada* (March 2003)

Law Commission of Canada (DA Wolfe, PG Jaffe, JL Jetté and SE Poisson) *Child Abuse in Community Institutions and Organisations: Improving Public and Professional Understanding* (2002)

Law Commission of Canada (S Alter) *Institutional Child Abuse: Apologising for Serious Wrongdoing: Social, Psychological and Legal Considerations* (1999)

Law Commission of Canada (M Gannage) *An International Perspective: a Review and Analysis of Approaches to Addressing Past Institutional or Systemic Abuse in Selected Countries [Argentina, South Africa and Australia]* (1998)

Law Commission of Canada (Rhonda Claes and Deborah Clifton) *Needs and Expectations for Redress of Victims of Abuse at Native Residential Schools* (Research Paper 1998)

Law Commission of Canada (Institute for Human Resource Development) *Review of the Needs of Victims of Institutional Abuse* (1998)

Law Commission of Canada *Restoring Dignity: Responding to Child Abuse in Canadian Institutions* (2000)

Law Reform Commission of Canada *Report on Evidence* (1975)

Ontario Law Reform Commission *Report on Child Witnesses* (1991)

Ontario Ministry of the Attorney General *Protecting Our Students: a Review to Identify and Prevent Sexual Misconduct in Ontario Schools* (2000)

Royal Commission on Aboriginal Peoples, Canada *Report of the Royal Commission on Aboriginal Peoples: Vol 1: Looking Forward, Looking Back* (1996)

Hon Stuart G Stratton, former Chief Justice of New Brunswick, for the Nova Scotia Department of Justice *Report of an Independent Investigation in Respect of Incidents and Allegations of Sexual and Other Physical Abuse at Five Nova Scotia Residential Institutions* (1995)

Council of Europe

Council of Europe *Recommendation No. R(97)13 of the Committee of Ministers to Member States concerning Intimidation of Witnesses and the Rights of the Defence* (adopted 10 September 1997)

Council of Europe *Recommendation No R (85)11 of the Committee of Ministers to Member States on the Position of the Victim in the Framework of Criminal Law and Procedure* (adopted 28 June 1985)

Republic of Ireland

Commission to Inquire into Child Abuse (Hon Mr Justice Sean Ryan, Chair) *Identifying Institutions and Persons under the Commission to Inquire into Child Abuse Act 2000: a Position Paper*

Irish Law Reform Commission *Consultation Paper on the Law of Limitation of Actions Arising from Non-Sexual Abuse of Children* (LRC CP 16-2000, [2000] IELRC 2)

Judge Francis Murphy *Report of the Ferns Inquiry* (25 October 2005)

New Zealand

Best Practice Guidelines for Disclosure in Criminal Cases in the High Court at Auckland (1999)

Judge M Brown, *Care and Protection is about Adult Behaviour: the Ministerial Review of the Department of Child, Youth and Family Services Report to the Minister of Social Services and Employment Hon Steve Maharey* (2000)

Commissioner for Children *Final Report on the Investigation into the Death of James Whakaruru* (Wellington 2000)

Department of Child Youth and Family Services *Annual Report 2003* (CYFS, Wellington 2004)

Department of the Child, Youth and Family Services *The Child, Youth and Family Care and Protection Handbook* (1996 and 1997)

Department of Child Youth and Family Services *First Principles Baseline Review* (Ministry of Social Development, CYFS and the Treasury, Wellington 2003)

J Hancock *Case Summaries: Parental Corporal Punishment of Children in New Zealand: Report for UN Committee on the Rights of the Child* (Action for the Child, Aotearoa 2003)

Judge K Mason *Report of the Ministerial Review Team to the Minister of Social Welfare Hon Jenny Shipley* (Auckland 1992)

New Zealand Law Commission *Criminal Procedure Part One: Disclosure and Committal* (Report No 14 1990)

New Zealand Law Commission *Criminal Prosecution* (Report No 66 2000)

New Zealand Law Commission *Character and Credibility (*Preliminary Paper 27) (Feb 1997)

New Zealand Law Commission *The Evidence of Children and Other Vulnerable Witnesses: a Discussion Paper* (Preliminary Paper 26 October 1996)

New Zealand Law Commission *Evidence Law: Expert Evidence And Opinion Evidence* (Preliminary Paper 18 December 1991)

New Zealand Law Commission *Evidence* (Report 55 August 1999)

New Zealand Law Commission *Juries in Criminal Trials* (Report No. 69 2001)

New Zealand Law Society *Guidelines for Law Practitioners under the Privacy Act 1993* [<http://www.nz-lawsoc.org.nz/memprivact.asp>]

New Zealand Minister of Justice *Comments on the Investigation and Interviewing of Children in the Ellis Case, Appendix A to Sir Thomas Eichelbaum, The Peter Ellis Case: Report of the Ministerial Inquiry* (2001)

New Zealand Office for the Commissioner for Children (G Maxwell, L Barthauer and R Julian) *The Role of Primary Health Care Providers in Identifying and Referring Child Victims of Family Violence* (Wellington 2000)

Te-Ata-Tu *Report of the Ministerial Advisory Committee on a Maori Perspective for the Department of Social Welfare* (Wellington 1986)

South Africa

South African Law Commission *Sexual Offences: Process and Procedure* (Discussion Paper 102, Project 107 December 2002)

United Nations

United Nations Economic and Social Council *Guidelines on Justice in Matters Involving Child Victims and Witnesses of Crime* (Resolution 2005/20, E/2005/INF/2/Add.1 July 2005)

Committee on the Rights of the Child *Concluding Observations of the Committee on the Rights of the Child: United Kingdom of Great Britain and Northern Ireland* (CRC/C/15/Add.188 4 October 2002)

United States

Advisory Committee on Evidence Rules to the US Congress, *Note on Federal Rule of Evidence 403*

Advisory Committee on Evidence Rules to the US Congress, *Note on Federal Rule of Evidence 702*

S Badeau and S Geserich *A Child's Journey Through the Child Welfare System* (Evidence to the Pew Commission on Children in Foster Care 2003)

Richard Gelles, Director, University of Rhode Island's Family Violence Research Program 'Improving the Well-Being of Abused and Neglected Children: Statement at the Hearing Before the Senate Committee on Labor and Human Resources' (104th Cong 16 1996) <http://www.hhs.gov/asl/testify/t961120a.html> (28 September 2004)

National Center for Prosecution of Child Abuse *Child Abuse and Neglect State Statutes Elements: Child Witness No 21 Admissibility of Videotaped Depositions or Testimony* (1999)

National Clearinghouse on Child Abuse and Neglect Information *Gateways to Information: Protecting Children and Strengthening Families: Central Registries/Reporting Records: Establishment and Maintenance* (2003)

National Clearinghouse on Child Abuse and Neglect Information *Gateways to Information: Protecting Children and Strengthening Families: Mandatory Reporters of Child Abuse and Neglect* (2003)

National Study of Social Services to Children and their Families SREP NO 336 96th Cong 2nd Sess 3 (1980)

Office of the Executive Secretary of the Supreme Court of Virginia *Child Dependency Report* (November 2002) <http://www.courts.state.va.us/publications/child_dependency_mediation_report.pdf>

Sub-Committee on Human Resources of the Committee on Ways and Mean, House of Representatives, 106th Congress, *Promoting Adoption and Other Prominent Placements: Hearing Testimony July 20 1999* (serial number 106-309) <http://www.liftingtheveil.org/106-39.pdf>

United States Department of Justice *Child Victimizers: Violent Offenders and Their Victims* (March 1996)

United States General Accounting Office 'Child Welfare: States' Progress in Implementing Family Preservation and Support Services' (Washington DC 1997) (GAO/HEHS–97–34) <http://www.gao.gov/archive/1997/he97034.pdf> (17 September 2004)

US Department of Health And Human Services 'Disclosure of Confidential Records Statutes-at-a-Glance 2003' National Clearinghouse on Child Abuse and Neglect Information

OTHER SOURCES

SL Abbott 'Liability of the State and Its Employees for the Negligent Investigation of Child Abuse Reports' (1993) 10 Alaska L Rev 401

GG Abel, A Jordan, CG Hand, CL Holland and A Phipps 'Classification Models of Child Molesters Utilising the Abel Assessment for Sexual Interest' (2001) 25(5) Child Abuse and Neglect 703

GG Abel 'Self-Reported Sex Crimes of Non-Incarcerated Paraphiliacs' (1987) 2 J of Interpersonal Violence 3

M Adcock 'Significant Harm: Implications for the Exercise of Statutory Responsibilities' in M Adcock, R White and A Hollows (eds) *Significant Harm* (Significant Publications, Croydon 1991)

JM Adler 'Relying upon the Reasonableness of Strangers: Some Observations about the Current State of Common Law Affirmative Duties to Aid or Protect Others' [1991] Wisconsin L Rev 867

Z Adler 'Prosecuting Child Sexual Abuse: a Challenge to the Status Quo' in M McGuire and J Pointing (eds) *Victims of Crime: a New Deal?* (Open University Press, Milton Keynes 1988)

T Allan 'Similar Fact Evidence and Disposition: Law, Discretion and Admissibility' (1985) 48 MLR 253

H Allen *Justice Unbalanced: Gender Psychiatry and Judicial Decisions* (Open University Press, Milton Keynes 1987)

M Allen (ed) *Elliott and Woods Cases and Materials on Criminal Law* (8th edn Sweet & Maxwell London 2001)

JR Allinson 'Limitation of Actions in Child Abuse Cases' [April 1996] J of Personal Injury Litigation 19

P Alston, S Parker and J Seymore (eds) *Children Rights and the Law* (OUP Oxford 1991)

J Aluise 'Evidence of Prior Sexual Misconduct in Sexual Assault and Child Molestation Proceedings: Did Congress Err in Passing Federal Rules of Evidence 413, 414, and 415?' (1998) 14 J of Law & Policy 153

American Academy of Paediatrics' Committee on Child Abuse and Neglect 'Distinguishing Sudden Infant Death Syndrome From Child Abuse Fatalities' (2001) 107 Pediatrics 437

American Law Institute *Restatement (Second) of Torts*

American Law Institute *Restatement (Third) of Torts* (Proposed Final Draft April 2005) 'Damages'

Anonymous 'Editorial: the Ellis Case' [February 2002] New Zealand LJ 1

Archbold (Sweet & Maxwell London 2002)

B Archibald 'The Canadian Hearsay Revolution: Is Half a Loaf Better Than No Loaf at All?' (1999) 25 Queen's LJ 1

A Ashworth 'The Doctrine of Provocation' (1976) 35 CLJ 292

A Ashworth *Principles of Criminal Law* (5th edn OUP, Oxford 2006) (2nd edn OUP, Oxford 1995)

A Ashworth 'Criminal Justice Act 2003: Part 2 Criminal Justice Reform—Principles, Human Rights and Public Protection' (2004) Crim LR 516

A Ashworth and R Pattenden 'Reliability, Hearsay Evidence and the Criminal Trial' (1986) 102 LQR 292

LR Askowitz 'Restricting the Admissibility of Expert Testimony in Child Sexual Abuse Prosecutions: Pennsylvania Takes it to the Extreme' (1992) 47 U of Miami L Rev 201

B Atkin and G McLay 'Suing Child Welfare Agencies—a Comparative View from New Zealand' (2001) 13 Child and Family LQ 287

Avail Consulting Ltd for the CPS and ACPO *No Witness, No Justice (NWNJ) Pilot Evaluation* (29 October 2004)

L Baca, P Jendrucko and D Scott 'Silent Screams'—One Law Enforcement Agency's Response to Improving the Management of Child Abuse Reporting and Investigations' (2002) 22 J Juvenile L 29

R Bagshaw 'Children Through Tort' in J Fionda (ed) *Legal Concepts of Childhood* (Hart, Oxford 2001)

M Bailey 'The Failure of Physicians to Report Child Abuse' (1982) 40 U of Toronto Faculty L Rev 49

S Bailey 'Public Authority Liability in Negligence: the Continued Search for Coherence' (2006) 26 Legal Studies 155

S Bailey and M Bowman 'Public Authority Negligence Revisited' (2000) 59(1) Cambridge LJ 85

V Bailey and S McCabe 'Reforming the Law of Incest' [1979] Crim LR 749

R Bailey-Harris and J Dewar 'Variations on a Theme—Child Law Reform in Australia' (1997) 9(2) Child and Family LQ 149

R Bailey-Harris and M Harris 'The Immunity of Local Authorities in Child Protection Functions—Is the Door Now Ajar?' (1998) 10(3) Child and Family LQ 227

A Bainham 'The Children Act 1989: The State and the Family' (1990) 20 Family L 231

A Bainham *Children: the Modern Law* (3rd edn Jordan Publishing Limited, Bristol 2005)

A Bainham and B Brookes-Gordon 'Reforming the Law on Sexual Offences' in B Brookes-Gordon, L Gelsthorpe, M Johnson and A Bainham (eds) *Sexuality Repositioned: Diversity and the Law* (Hart, Oxford 2004)

N Bala 'Child Witnesses in the Canadian Criminal Courts' (1999) 5 Psychology Public Policy & Law 323

N Bala 'Reforming Ontario's Child and Family Services Act: Is the Pendulum Swinging Back Too Far?' (1999-2000) 17 Canadian Fam LQ 121

N Bala 'Response to the Department of Justice Consultation Paper on Child Witnesses and the Criminal Justice System' (2000) <http://www.qsilver.queensu.ca/law/witness/witness.htm> (10 August 2004)

N Bala, K Lee, R Lindsay and V Talwar 'A Legal & Psychological Critique of the Present Approach to the Assessment of the Competence of Child Witnesses' (2000) 38 Osgoode Hall LJ 409

N Bala 'Tort Remedies and the Family Law Practitioner' (1998) 16 Canadian Fam LQ 423

N Bala and A Saunders 'Understanding the Family Context: Why the Law of Expert Evidence is Different in Family Law Cases' (2002) 20 Canadian Fam LQ 277

N Bala, MK Zapf, RJ Williams, R Vogl and JP Hornick (eds) *Canadian Child Welfare Law: Children, Families and the State* (2nd edn Thompson Educational Publishing, Toronto 2004)

Bar Council of England and Wales *Code of Conduct of the Bar of England and Wales* (8th edn London 2004)

E Bartholet *Nobody's Children: Abuse and Neglect, Foster Drift, and the Adoption Alternative* (Beacon Press, Boston 1999)

C Barton and G Douglas *Law and Parenthood* (Butterworths, London 1995)

M Bell 'Working in Partnership in Child Protection: The Conflicts' (1999) 29 British J of Social Work 437

R Bell 'Sexual Abuse and Institutions: Insurance Issues' (1996) 6 Canadian Insurance LR 53

S Bellett 'Child Witness Service: Meeting the Needs of Children—Innovative Practice' (Kids First Conference 1998)

K Belt 'Psychological Syndrome Evidence' unpublished research paper for the New Zealand Law Commission, September 1997

M Bennett, C Blackstock and R de la Ronde *A Literature Review and Annotated Bibliography Focussing on Aspects of Aboriginal Child Welfare in Canada* (2nd edn First Nations Child and Family Caring Society of Canada 2005)

L Berliner and J Conte 'Sexual Abuse Evaluations: Conceptual and Empirical Obstacles' (1993) 17 Child Abuse and Neglect 111

M Bernstein, H Bernstein and LM Kirwin *Child Protection Law in Canada* (Thompson Canada Ltd)

MM Bernstein, C Regehr and K Kanani 'Liability for Child Welfare Workers: Weighing the Risks' in N Bala, M Zapf, R Williams, R Vogl and J Hornick (eds) *Canadian Child Welfare Law: Children, Families and the State* (Thompson Educational Publishing Inc Toronto 2004)

D Berridge and I Brodie 'Residential Child Care in England and Wales—The Inquiries and After' in M Hill and M Algate (eds) *Child Welfare Services* (Jessica Kingsley, London 1996)

D Besharov 'Child Abuse and Neglect Reporting and Investigation: Policy Guidelines for Decision Making' in M Robin (ed) *Assessing Child Maltreatment Reports: The Problem of False Allegations* (Haworth Press, New York 1991)

D Besharov 'Gaining Control Over Child Abuse Reports: Public Agencies Must Address Both Under and Over Reporting' [1990] Public Welfare 34

D Besharov 'The Legal Aspects of Reporting Known and Suspected Child Abuse and Neglect' (1977) 23 Villanova L Rev 458

R Best 'Emergency removal of children for their care and protection' (2003) AJFL LEXIS 14

N Biehal, J Clayden, M Stein and J Wade 'Moving On: Young People and Leaving Care Schemes' in Department of Health (ed) *Caring for Children Away from Home—Messages from Research* (John Wiley, Chichester 1999)

D Birch 'A Better Deal for Vulnerable Witnesses' [2000] Crim LR 223

DJ Birch 'Children's Evidence' [1992] Crim LR 262

D Birch 'The Criminal Justice Act 2003: Hearsay: Same Old Story, Same Old Song?' [2004] Crim LR 557

D Birch Note on *R v Stevens* [1995] Crim LR 651

D Birch 'Rethinking Sexual History Evidence: Proposals for Fairer Trials' [2002] Crim LR 531

D Birch 'Untangling Sexual History Evidence: a Rejoinder to Professor Temkin' [2003] Crim LR 370

D Birch and R Leng *Blackstone's Guide to the Youth Justice and Criminal Evidence Act 1999* (Blackstone Press Ltd, London 2000)

D Birch and R Powell *Meeting the Challenges of Pigot: Pre-Trial Cross Examination under s 28 of the Youth Justice And Criminal Evidence Act 1999—a Briefing Paper for the Home Office* (Nottingham University February 2004)

D Birch and C Taylor, ' "People like Us"? Responding to Allegations of Past Abuse in Care' [2003] Crim LR 823

DA Bjorkland 'Crossing *DeShaney*: Can the Gap be Closed between Child Abuse in the Home and the State's Duty to Protect?' (1990) 75 Iowa L Rev 791

D Blenner Hassett '*KLW* and Warrantless Child Apprehensions: Sanctioning Gross Intrusions into Private Spheres' (2004) 67 Saskatchewan L Rev 161

KM Blum '*DeShaney*: Custody, Creation of Danger, and Culpability' (1994) 27 Loyola of Los Angeles L Rev 435

D Bonner, H Fenwick and S Harris-Short 'Judicial Approaches to The Human Rights Act' (2003) 52(3) Int Comp LQ 549

B Bookwalter 'Throwing The Bath Water Out With The Baby: Wrongful Exclusion of Expert Testimony on Neonaticide Syndrome' (1998) 78 Boston U L Rev 1185

W Bough 'Why the Sky Didn't Fall: Using Judicial Creativity to Circumvent *Crawford v Washington*' (2004–2005) 38 Loyola of Los Angeles L Rev 1835

C Boyle 'Section 142 of the Criminal Code: a Trojan Horse?' (1981) 23 Crim LQ 253

C Boyle and M MacCrimmon '*R v. Seaboyer*: a Lost Cause' (1991) 7 CR (4th) 225

Bracton, *De Legibus Angliae* (ca 1250) liber iii

S Bradley 'Child Law Update' [2005] New LJ 591

S Brandon, J Boakes, D Glaser and R Green 'Recovered Memories of Child Sexual Abuse: Implications for Clinical Practice' (1998) 172 British J of Psychiatry 296

S Brooks 'A Family Systems Paradigm For Legal Decision Making Affecting Child Custody' (1996) 6 Cornell L Rev 1

J Brophy 'Keepers at the "Gate": Effective Case Management in the Use of Experts in Care Proceedings' (1999) 12(5) Practitioner's Child Law Bulletin 55

J Brophy, P Bates, L Brown, S Cohen, P Radcliffe and C Wale *Expert Evidence in Child Protection Litigation: Where Do We Go from Here?* (HM Stationery Office, London 1999)

D Brown 'The New 702: How it Affects the Use of Experts' 14 Update (monthly newsletter of the National Center for Prosecution of Child Abuse, American Prosecutors Research Institute) No 3

K Brown Olson 'Child Protection in the 21st Century: Lessons Learned from a Child Protection Mediation Program: If at First You Succeed and then You Don't' (2003) 41 Fam Ct Rev 480

A Brusca 'Postpartum Psychosis: A Way Out For Murderous Moms' (1990) 18 Hofstra L R 1133

D Bryden and R Park ' "Other Crimes" Evidence in Sex Offense Cases' (1994) 78 Minnesota L Rev 529

SJ Buck 'Church, Liability for Clergy Sexual Abuse: Have Time and Events Overthrown *Swanson v Roman Catholic Bishop of Portland*?' (2005) 57 Maine L Rev 259

M Bugaric and K Amarasekara 'The Prejudice against Similar Fact Evidence' (2001) 5 Int J of Evidence and Proof 71

J Bulkley 'The Prosecution's Use of Social Science Expert Testimony in Child Sexual Abuse Cases: National Trends and Recommendations' (1992) 1(2) J Child Sexual Abuse 73

L Burnside and D Bond 'Making a Difference Mentoring Programmes in Child Welfare Agencies' (2002) 1(1) Envision: the Manitoba Journal of Child Welfare 50

D Burrows *Evidence in Family Proceedings* (Family Law, Bristol 1999)

D Burrows 'Opinion Evidence' [2000] Fam Law 121

M Burton, R Evans and A Sanders *Are Special Measures for Vulnerable and Intimidated Witnesses Working? Evidence from the Criminal Justice Agencies* (Home Office Online Report 01/06 London 2006)

D Buss ' "How the UN Stole Childhood": The Christian Right and the International Rights of the Child' in J Bridgeman and D Monk (eds) *Feminist Perspectives on Child Law* (Cavendish, London 2000), 271

K Bussey and E Grimbeek 'Children's Conceptions of Lying and Truth-Telling: Implications for Child Witnesses' (2000) 5 Legal & Criminological Psychology 187

K Bussey, K Lee and E Grimbeek 'Lies and Secrets: Implications for Children's Reporting of Sexual Abuse' in G Goodman and B Bottoms (eds) *Child Victims, Child Witnesses: Understanding and Improving Testimony* (Guildford Press, New York, London 1993)

K Bussman *Evaluation of the German Prohibition on Violence Against Children* (European Society of Criminology, Toledo 2002)

A Buti 'Unfinished Business: the Australian Stolen Generations' (2000) 7 Murdoch U Electronic J of Law

Dame Elizabeth Butler-Sloss 'The Protocol for Judicial Case Management in Public Law Children Act Cases' [2003] 2 FLR 719

M Cammack 'Using the Doctrine of Chances to Prove Actus Reus in Child Abuse and Acquaintance Rape: *People v Ewoldt* Reconsidered' (1996) 29 U of California Davis LR 355

B Campbell *Unofficial Secrets* (Virago Press, London 1988)

T Campbell 'Psychology and the Law: Interviewing Children: Taking Notes or Relying on Memory is Not Good Enough' (2002) 81 Michigan Bar J 32

D Canter and R Heritage 'A Multivariate Model of Sexual Offence Behaviour: Developments in "Offender Profiling" ' (1990) 1(2) Journal of Forensic Psychiatry 185

D Canter and S Kirby 'Prior Convictions of Child Molesters' (1995) 35(1) Science & Justice 73

D Canter and D Young 'Beyond "Offender Profiling": the Need for Investigative Psychology' in D Carson and R Bull (eds) *Handbook of Psychology in Legal Contexts* (2nd edn Wiley, Chichester 2003)

M Caplan QC and S Parkinson 'Testing the PII Template' [2004] New LJ 238

Card 'Sexual Relations with Minors' [1975] Crim LR 370

C Carpenter 'On Statutory Rape, Strict Liability and the Public Welfare Offense Model' (2003) 53 Am U LR 313

D Carrick 'Child Witnesses' *The Law Report, Radio National* (20 May 2003)

D Carson and R Bull (eds) *Handbook of Psychology in Legal Contexts* (2nd edn Wiley Chichester 2003)

PB Carter QC 'Forbidden Reasoning Permissible: Similar Fact Evidence a Decade after *Boardman*' (1985) 48 MLR 28

J Cashmore 'Innovative Procedures for Child Witnesses' in H Westcott, G Davies and R Bull (eds) *Children's Testimony: a Handbook of Psychological Research and Forensic Practice* (Wiley Chichester 2002)

SJ Ceci and M Bruck *Jeopardy In The Courtroom: a Scientific Analysis of Children's Testimony* (American Psychological Association, Washington DC 1995)

SJ Ceci and M Bruck 'Suggestibility of the Child Witness: a Historical Review and Synthesis' 113 Psychological Bulletin 403

SJ Ceci and H Hembrooke (eds) *Expert Witnesses in Child Abuse Cases: What Can and Should be Said in Court* (American Psychological Association, Washington DC 1998)

SJ Ceci, DF Ross and MP Toglia (eds) *Children's Eyewitness Memory* (Springer-Verlag New York 1987)

SJ Ceci, DF Ross and MP Toglia 'Age Differences in Suggestibility: Narrowing the Uncertainties' in SJ Ceci, DF Ross and MP Toglia (eds) *Children's Eyewitness Memory* (Springer-Verlag New York 1987)

L Challis (ed) *Joint Approaches to Social Policy—Rationality and Practice* (Cambridge University Press, Cambridge 1988)

J Chandler and D Lait 'An Analysis of the Treatment of Children as Witnesses in the Crown Court' in *Children in Court* (Victim Support, London 1996)

L Chapman *Review of South Australian Rape and Sexual Assault Law: Discussion Paper* (Government of South Australia, Adelaide 2006)

S Chapman 'Section 276 of the Criminal Code and the Admissibility of "Sexual Activity" Evidence' (1999) 25 Queen's LJ 121

Childline <http://www.childline.org.uk/howcommonischildabuse.asp> (31 July 2006)

Children are Unbeatable Alliance <http://www.childrenareunbeatable.org.uk>

P Chill 'Burden of Proof Begone: The Pernicious Effect of Emergency Removal in Child Protective Proceedings' (2004) 42 Fam Ct Rev 540

R Chisholm 'The Paramount Consideration: Children's Interests in Family Law' (2002) 16 Australian J Family Law 9

A Choo *Hearsay and Confrontation in Criminal Trials* (Clarendon Press, Oxford 1996)

H Clark *The Law of Domestic Relations in the United States* (West Publishing 1988)

D Clark-Weintraub 'The Use of Videotaped Testimony of Victims in Cases Involving Child Sexual Abuse: a Constitutional Dilemma' (1985) 14 Hofstra L Rev 261

Clarke, Hall and Morrison's Law Relating to Children and Young Persons (10th edn Butterworths, London 1985, updated to July 2004)

M Coady and C Coady 'There Ought to be a Law Against It: Reflections on Child Abuse, Morality and Law' in P Alston, S Parker and J Seymore (eds) *Children Rights and the Law* (OUP, Oxford 1991)

C Cobley 'Criminal Prosecutions When Children Die or are Seriously Injured' (2003) Fam Law 899

C Cobley 'The Legislative Framework' in A Matravers (ed) *Managing Sex Offenders in the Community: Managing and Reducing the Risks* (Willan Publishing, Devon 2003)

C Cobley ' "Working Together?"—Admissions of Abuse in Child Protection Proceedings and Criminal Prosecutions' (2004) 16.2 Child and Family LQ 175

C Cobley, T Sanders and P Wheeler 'Prosecuting Cases of Suspected "Shaken Baby Syndrome"—A Review of Current Issues' [2003] Crim LR 93

A Cohen 'The Unreliability of Expert Testimony on the Typical Characteristics of Sexual Abuse Victims' (1985) 74 Georgetown LJ 429

C Cole and E Loftus 'The Memory of Children' in SJ Ceci, M Toglia and DF Ross (eds) *Children's Eyewitness Memory* (Springer-Verlag New York 1987)

SA Collier 'Note, Reporting Child Abuse: When Moral Obligations Fail' (1983) 15 Pacific LJ 189

D Collins 'Character Evidence and Sex Crimes in Alabama: Moving Toward the Adoption of New Federal Rules 413, 414 & 415' (2000) 51 Alabama LR 1651

M Connell 'The Postpartum Psychosis Defense and Feminism: More or Less Justice for Women?' (2002) 53 Case Western Reserve L Rev 143

K Connerton 'The Resurgence of the Marital Rape Exemption: The Victimization of Teens by Their Statutory Rapists' (1997) 61 Albany L Rev 237

MA Conway (ed) *Recovered Memories and False Memories* (OUP Oxford 1997)

D Cooper 'Pigot Unfulfilled: Video-Recorded Cross-Examination under Section 28 of the Youth Justice and Criminal Evidence Act 1999' [2005] Crim LR 456

D Cooper and P Roberts *Special Measures for Vulnerable and Intimidated Witnesses: an Analysis of Crown Prosecution Service Monitoring Data* (Crown Prosecution Service, London June 2005)

B Corby, M Millar and L Young 'Parental Participation in Child Protection Work: Rethinking the Rhetoric' (1996) 26 British J of Social Work 475

W Cornish and A Sealy 'Juries and the Rules of Evidence' [1973] Crim LR 208

25 *Corpus Juris Secundum* ¶122

A Cossins and R Pilkington 'Balancing the Scales: the Case for the Inadmissibility of Counselling Records in Sexual Assault Trials' (1996) 19 U of New South Wales LJ 222

J Courts 'Standards of Proof in the Divorce Court' (1951) 14 MLR 411

P Craig *Administrative Law* (5th edn Sweet & Maxwell, London 2003)

P Craig and D Fairgrieve '*Barrett*, Negligence and Discretionary Powers' [1999] Public Law 626

S Creighton and N Russell *Voices from Childhood* (NSPCC, London 1995)

W Crenshaw and others 'Mental Health Providers and Child Sexual Abuse: A Multivariate analysis of the Decision to Report' (1993) 2 J Child Sexual Abuse 19

S Cretney *Family Law* (4th edn Sweet & Maxwell, London 2000)

CA Crosby-Currie and ND Reppucci 'The Missing Child in Child Protection: the Constitutional Context of Child Maltreatment from *Meyer* to *DeShaney*' (1999) 21 Law & Policy 129

W Crossley 'Defining Reasonable Efforts: Demystifying the State's Burden Under Federal Child Protection Legislation' (2003) 12 BU Pub Int LJ 259

B Dalley *Family Matters—Child Welfare in Twentieth Century New Zealand* (Auckland University Press, Auckland 1998)

M Damaška 'Symposium on the Admission of Prior Offense Evidence in Sexual Assault Cases: Propensity Evidence in Continental Legal Systems' (1994) 70 Chicago-Kent LR 55

S Davidson 'When is Parental Discipline Child Abuse?— The Vagueness of Child Abuse Laws' (1995) 34 U of Louisville J of Fam L 403

C Davies 'Developing Interests in Child Care Outcome Measurement: A Central Government Perspective' (1998) 12 Children and Society 155

E Davies and F Seymour 'Child Witnesses in the Criminal Courts: Furthering New Zealand's Commitment to the United Nations Convention on the Rights of the Child' (1997) 4 Psychiatry, Psychology and Law 13

E Davies and F Seymour 'Questioning of Complainants of Sexual Abuse: Analysis of Criminal Court Transcripts in New Zealand' (1998) 5 Psychiatry, Psychology and Law 47

G Davies, C Wilson, R Mitchell and J Milsom *Videotaping Children's Evidence: an Evaluation* (Home Office, London 1995)

G Davis, L Hoyano, C Keenan, L Maitland and R Morgan *An Assessment of the Admissibility and Sufficiency of Evidence in Child Abuse Prosecutions* (HMSO, London August 1999)

R Davis 'Admissibility, in Prosecution for Sexual Offense, of Evidence of Similar Offenses' 77 American LR 2d 841 (updated to 2006)

H Davison 'A Model Child Protection Legal Reform Instrument: The Convention on the Rights of the Child and its Consistency with United States Law' (1998) 5 Georgetown J Fighting Poverty 185

S Deakin, A Johnston and B Markesinis *Markesinis & Deakin's Tort Law* (5th edn OUP, Oxford 2003)

D De La Paz 'Sacrificing the Whole Truth: Florida's Deteriorating Admissibility of Similar Fact Evidence in Cases of Child Sexual Abuse' (1999) 15 New York Law School J of Human Rights 449

RJ Delisle 'Similar Facts: Let's Be Realistic' (2000) 30 CR (5th) 309

RJ Delisle 'Previous Statements of the Complainant as Narrative' 39 CR (4th) 89

HH Judge N Denison QC 'Disclosure' (1996) 36 Medical Science Law 283

I Dennis *The Law of Evidence* (3rd edn Sweet & Maxwell, London 2007)

H Dent and R Flin (eds) *Children as Witnesses* (Wiley, Chichester 1992)

N Des Rosiers 'Childhood Sexual Assault—Will There Be a Meaningful Remedy?: *Gray v Reeves*' (1992) 10 Canadian Cases on the Law of Tort 86

N Des Rosiers, B Feldthusen and O Hankivsky 'Legal Compensation for Sexual Violence: Therapeutic Consequences and Consequences for the Judicial System' (1998) 4 Psychology, Public Policy and Law 433

N Des Rosiers and L Langevin *L'Indemnisation de la Violence Sexuelle et Conjugale devant les Instances Civiles* (Yvon Blais Cowansville, Quebec 1998)

Sir Patrick Devlin *Trial by Jury* (Stevens & Sons, London 1956)

J Dickens 'Assessment and Control of Social Work: An Analysis of Reasons for the Non-Use of the Child Assessment Order' (1993) 2 JSWL 88

R Dingwall, JM Eekelaar and T Murray 'Childhood as a Social Problem: A Survey of the History of Legal Regulation' (1984) 11(2) J of Law and Society 207

M Dixon ' "Out of the Mouths of Babes . . ."—A Review of the Operation of the Acts Amendment (Evidence of Children) Act 1992' (1995) 25 Western Australian L Rev 301

SA Dobbin, SI Gatowski and M Springate 'Child Abuse and Neglect: A Summary of State Statutes' (1997) 48 Juvenile and Family Ct J 43

V Dobson and B Sales 'The Science of Infanticide and Mental Illness' (2000) 6 Psychology Public Policy and Law 1098

D Doherty ' "Sparing" the Complainant "Spoils" the Trial' (1984) 40 CR (3d) 55

M Doolan 'The Family Group Conference Ten Years On' <http://www.iirp.org/library/vt/vt_doolan.html> (10 August 2004)

G Douglas and C Willmore 'Diagnostic Interviews as Evidence in Cases of Child Sexual Abuse' (1987) 17 Fam Law 151

BM Douthett 'The Death of Constitutional Duty: the Court Reacts to the Expansion of Section 1983 Liability in *DeShaney v Winnebago County Department of Social Services*' (1991) 52 Ohio State LJ 643

Hon John Doyle and J Redwood 'The Common Law Liability of Public Authorities: the Interface between Public and Private Law' [1999] Tort L Rev 30

J Duane 'The New Federal Rules of Evidence on Prior Acts of Accused Sex Offenders: a Poorly Drafted Version of a Very Bad Idea' (1994) 157 Federal Rules Decisions 95

J Dunne and M Hendrick 'The Parental Alienation Syndrome: An Analysis of Sixteen Selected Cases' (1994) 21 J of Divorce and Remarriage 21–38

J Durrant 'Legal Reform and Attitudes Toward Physical Punishment in Sweden' (2003) Int J of CR 147

G Durston 'Similar Fact Evidence: A Guide for the Perplexed in the Light of Recent Cases' (1996) 160 Justice of the Peace J and Local Government Law 359

J Dwyer 'Parents' Religion and Children's Welfare: Debunking the Doctrine of Parents' Rights' (1994) 82 California L Rev 1371

TA Eaton and ML Wells 'Governmental Inaction as a Constitutional Tort: *DeShaney* and Its Aftermath' (1991) 66 Washington L Rev 107

S Edwards 'Current Developments' (2001) 23 J Social Welfare and Family Law 227

J Eekelaar 'Investigation under the Children Act 1989' [1990] Fam Law 486

L Ellison 'Cross-Examination in Rape Trials' [1998] Crim LR 605

R Ereison 'The Division of Expert Knowledge in Policing and Security' (1994) 45(2) *British Journal of Sociology* 149

DL Faigman 'The Evidentiary Status of Social Science under *Daubert*: Is it "Scientific," "Technical," or "Other" Knowledge?' (1995) 1 Psychology, Public Policy and Law 960

D Fairgrieve 'Pushing Back the Boundaries of Public Authorities Liability' in Duncan Fairgrieve, Mads Andenas and J Bell (eds) *Tort Liability of Public Authorities in Comparative Perspective* (British Institute of International and Comparative Law London 2002)

D Fairgrieve *State Liability in Tort: a Comparative Law Study* (OUP Oxford 2003)

D Fairgrieve, M Andenas and J Bell *Tort Liability of Public Authorities in Comparative Perspective* (British Institute of International and Comparative Law, London 2002)

'Family Law—The Protocol For Judicial Case Management in Public Law Children Act Cases' (2003) 10(7) Magistrates CP 7

S Farley 'Neonaticide: When the Bough Breaks and the Cradle Falls' (2004) 52 Buffalo LR 597

E Farmer and M Owen *Child Protection Practice: Private Risks and Public Remedies* (HMSO, London 1995)

C Fazio and J Comito 'Rethinking The Tough Sentencing of Teenage Neonaticide Offenders In The United States' (1999) 67 Fordham L Rev 3109

B Fehlberg and F Kelly 'Jurisdictional Overlaps Between the Family Division of the Children's Court of Victoria and the Family Court of Australia' (2000) AJFL LEXIS 13

D Feldman 'The "Scarlet Letter Laws" of the 1990s: A Response to Critics' (1997) 60 Albany L Rev 1081

B Feldthusen 'Access to the Private Therapeutic Records of Sexual Assault Complainants' (1996) 75 Canadian Bar Rev 537

B Feldthusen 'The Canadian Experiment with the Civil Action for Sexual Battery' in N Mulaney (ed) *Torts in the Nineties* (LBC Information Services, Sydney 1997)

B Feldthusen 'The Civil Action for Sexual Battery: Therapeutic Jurisprudence?' (1993) 25 Ottawa L Rev 203

B Feldthusen 'Damage Quantification in Civil Actions for Sexual Battery' (1994) 44 U of Toronto LJ 133

H Ferguson 'Cleveland in History: the Abused Child and Child Protection 1800–1914' in R Cooter (ed) *In the Name of the Child—Health and Welfare 1880–1940* (Routledge, London 1992)

J Finn 'Culpable Non-Intervention: Reconsidering the Basis for Party Liability by Omission' (1994) 18 Crim LR 90

CV Fisher and KA Whiting 'How Valid are Child Sexual Abuse Allegations?' in S Ceci and H Hembrooke (eds) *Expert Witnesses and Child Abuse Cases: What Can and Should Be Said in Court* (American Psychological Association, Washington DC 1998)

RP Fisher and MR McCauley 'Improving Eyewitness Testimony with the Cognitive Interview' in MS Zaragoza, JR Graham, GC Hall, R Hirschman and YS Ben-Porath (eds) *Memory and Testimony in a Child Witness* (Sage Publications, Thousand Oaks 1994)

C Fishman 'Consent, Credibility and the Constitution: Evidence Relating to a Sex Offense of Complainant's Past Sexual Behavior' (1995) 44 Catholic U L Rev 709

E Fishwick 'Child Protection Inadequate in Australia' (1993) 2 Human Rights Defender

MR Flaherty 'Tort Liability of Public Authority for Failure to Remove Parentally Abused or Neglected Children from Parents' Custody' 60 American LR 4th 942

M Flannery 'First, Do No Harm: the Use of Covert Video Surveillance to Detect Munchausen Syndrome by Proxy—an Unethical Means of "Preventing" Child Abuse' (1997–1998) 32 U of Michigan J L Reform 105

R Flannigan 'Fiduciary Regulation of Sexual Exploitation' (2000) 79 Canadian Bar Rev 308

R Flin and J Spencer 'Annotation: Children As Witnesses—Legal and Psychological Perspectives' 36 J Child Psychol. Psychiat No 2 171

DS Florig 'Insurance Coverage for Sexual Abuse or Molestation' (1995) 30 Tort Trial and Insurance Practice LJ 699

R Ford 'Minister Defends Parents' Right to Smack Children' *The Guardian* 8 November 1997

J Fortin *Children's Rights and the Developing Law* (1st edn Butterworths, London 1998)

J Fortin 'The HRA's Impact on Litigation Involving Children and Their Families' (1999) 11(3) Child and Family LQ 237

S Fournier and E Crey *Stolen from our Embrace: the Abduction of First Nations Children and the Restoration of Aboriginal Communities* (Douglas and McIntyre Ltd, Vancouver 1997)

L Fox 'Two Value Positions in Recent Child Care Law and Practice' (1982) Vol 12 (3) British J of Social Work 265

L Fox-Harding *Perspectives in Child Care Policy* (Longman, London 1991; 2nd edn London 1997)

MA Franklin and M Ploeger 'Of Rescue and Report: Should Tort Law Impose a Duty to Help Endangered Persons or Abused Children?' (1999–2000) 40 Santa Clara L Rev 991

MDA Freeman 'Care after 1991' in D Freestone (ed) *Children and the Law* (Hull University Press Hull, 1990)

M Freeman 'Children are Unbeatable' (1999) 11 Children and Society 130

M Freeman 'The End of the Century of the Child?' (2000) 53 *Current Legal Problems* 505

M Freeman 'Child Protection in the 21st Century: Privatization of Child Protective Services: Getting the Lion Back in the Cage?' (2003) 41 Fam Ct Rev 449

M Freeman *The Moral Status of Children—Essays on the Rights of the Child* (Martinus Nijhoff Publishers, The Hague 1997)

M Frias-Armenta and B Sales 'Discretion in the Enforcement of Child Protection Laws in Mexico' 34 California Western L Rev 203

T Fundudis 'Young Children's Memory: How Good is It? How Much Do We Know about It?' (1997) 2 Child Psychology and Psychiatry Review 150

J Gallett and M Finn 'Corroboration of Child Sexual Abuse Allegations with Behavioural Evidence' (2002) 25 Am Jur Proof of Facts 3d 189 (updated to July 2006)

H Galvin 'Shielding Rape Victims in the State and Federal Courts: a Proposal for the Second Decade' (1986) 70 Minnesota L Rev 763

J Gans and A Palmer *Australian Principles of Evidence* (2nd edn Cavendish, Sydney 2004)

K Garcia 'Battered Women and Battered Children: Admissibility of Evidence of Battering and Its Effects to Determine The Mens Rea of a Battered Woman Facing Criminal Charges for Failing to Protect a Child From Abuse' (2003) 24 J Juvenile L 101

R Gardener *The Parental Alienation Syndrome and the Differentiation between Fabricated and Genuine Sexual Abuse* (Creative Therapeutics, Cresskill NJ 1987)

R Gardener *The Parental Alienation Syndrome* (1992)

R Gardener *Protocols for the Sex-Abuse Evaluation* (Creative Therapeutics, Cresskill NJ 1995)

R Gardener *Psychotherapy With Sex-Abuse Victims: True, False, and Hysterical* (Creative Therapeutics, Cresskill NJ 1996)

R Gardener 'Recent trends in divorce and custody litigation' 29 (2) Academy Forum 3-7

R Gardener *Sex Abuse Hysteria: Salem Witch Trials Revisited* (Creative Therapeutics, Cresskill NJ 1991)

R Gardener *Testifying in Court: A Guide for Mental Health Professionals* (1996)

R Gardener *True and False Accusations of Child Sex Abuse* (Creative Therapeutics, Cresskill NJ 1992)

R Gardener *Sex Abuse Trauma? or Trauma From Other Sources?* (2002)

C Gearty 'Revisiting Section 3 of the Human Rights Act' (2003) 119 LQR 551

R Gelles *The Book of David: How Preserving Families Can Cost Lives* 143 Cong Rec H2012–06, H2022 (daily ed April 30 1997)

District Judge Gerlis 'The Family Homes and Domestic Violence Bill—Undermining the Undertaking' [1994] Fam Law 700

PC Giannelli '*Ake v. Oklahoma*: the Right to Expert Assistance in a Post-*Daubert*, Post-DNA World' (2004) 89 Cornell L Rev 1305

J Gibbons, S Conroy and C Bell *Operating the Child Protection System* (HMSO, London 1995)

K Gieve 'Where Do Families Stand After the Cleveland Inquiry?' in P Riches (ed) *Responses to Cleveland—Improving Services for Child Sexual Abuse* (National Children's Bureau, London 1989)

P Giliker 'Rough Justice in an Unjust World' (2002) 65 Modern L Rev 269

A Gillespie 'Indecent Images, Grooming and the Law' [2006] Crim LR 412

D Glaser 'Evaluating the Evidence of a Child—The Video-Taped Interview and Beyond' (1989) 19 Fam Law 487

P Glazebrook 'Which of You Did It?' [2003] Crim LR 541

DH Gleaves, SM Smith, LD Butler, and D Spiegel 'False and Recovered Memories in the Laboratory and Clinic: a Review of Experimental and Clinical Evidence' (2004) VII N1 Clinical Psychology: Science and Practice

HM Goldberg 'Liability for Government Actions: a Comparative Study of English and American Law' in Duncan Fairgrieve and Sarah Green (eds) *Child Abuse Tort Claims against Public Bodies: a Comparative Law View* (Ashgate, Aldershot 2004)

HM Goldberg 'Tort Liability for Federal Government Actions in United States: an Overview' in Duncan Fairgrieve, Mads Andenas and J Bell (eds) *Tort Liability of Public Authorities in Comparative Perspective* (British Institute of International and Comparative Law London 2002)

J Goldstein, A Freud and A Solnit *Beyond the Best Interests of the Child* (Collier Macmillan London 1973)

L Goldthorpe 'Every Child Matters: A Legal Perspective' (2004) 13 Child Abuse Rev 115

GS Goodman 'Child Sexual and Physical Abuse: Children's Testimony' in S Ceci, M Toglia and DF Ross (eds) *Children's Eyewitness Memory* (Springer-Verlag, New York 1987)

GS Goodman and B Bottoms (eds) *Child Victims, Child Witnesses: Understanding and Improving Testimony* (Guildford Press New York, London 1993)

GS Goodman 'Children's Testimony in Historical Perspective' (1984) 40 J of Social Issues 9

GS Goodman, J Buckley, JA Quas and C Shapiro 'Innovations for Child Witnesses: a National Survey' (1999) 5 Psychology, Public Policy, and Law 255

GS Goodman and VS Helgeson 'Child Sexual Assault: Children's Memory and the Law' (1985) 40 U of Miami L Rev 181

J Gordley 'Tort Law in the Aristotelian Tradition' in DG Owen (ed) *Philosophical Foundations of Tort Law* (Clarendon Press, Oxford 1995)

R Gordon 'Drifting Through Byzantium: The Promise and Failure of the Adoption and Safe Families Act of 1997' (1999) 83 Minnesota L Rev 637

L Gotell 'The Ideal Victim, the Hysterical Complainant, and the Disclosure of Confidential Records: the Implications of the Charter for Sexual Assault Law' (2003) 40 Osgoode Hall LJ 251

TL Gowen and RJ Kohlman 'Professional Liability for Failure to Report Child Abuse' 38 Am Jur Trials 1 (updated to June 2006)

EK Grace and SM Vella *Civil Liability for Sexual Abuse and Violence in Canada* (Butterworths, Toronto and Vancouver 2000)

EK Grace and SM Vella 'Vesting Mothers with Power They Do Not Have: the Non-Offending Parent in Civil Sexual Assault Cases: *J.(L.A.) v J.(H) and J.(J.)*' (1994) 7 Canadian J of Women and the Law 184

L Graham 'The Past Never Vanishes: A Contextual Critique of the Existing Indian Family Doctrine' 23 American Indian L Rev 1

MH Graham 'Indicia of Reliability and Face to Face Confrontation: Emerging Issues in Child Sexual Abuse Prosecutions' (1985) 40 U of Miami L Rev 19

D Grant *From Prior Record to Current Verdict: How Character Affects Jurors' Decisions* (University of California at Irvine 1996)

A Green 'True and False Allegations of Sexual Abuse in Child Custody Disputes' (1988) 25 J American Academy of Child Psychiatry 449

D Greer 'Anything but the Truth? The Reliability of Testimony in Criminal Trials' (1971) 11 British J of Criminology 131

E Griew 'The Future of Diminished Responsibility' [1988] Crim LR 75

S Grover 'Nowhere to Turn: the Supreme Court of Canada's Denial of a Constitutionally-Based Governmental Fiduciary Duty to Children in Foster Care' (2004) 12 International J of Children's Rights 105

GH Gudjonsson 'Accusations by Adults of Child Sexual Abuse: a Survey of the Members of the British False Memory Society (BFMS)' (1997) 11(1) Applied Cognitive Psychology 3

M Guggenheim 'Somebody's Children: Sustaining the Family's Place in Child Welfare Policy' (2000) 113 Harv L Rev 1716

V Gulbis 'Modern Status of Rule Regarding Necessity for Corroboration of Victim's Testimony in Prosecution for Sexual Offense' (1984 updated to October 2006) 31 American LR 4th 120

E-A Gumbel QC 'Child Abuse Compensation Claims: a Practitioner's Perspective' in D Fairgrieve and S Green (eds) *Child Abuse Tort Claims against Public Bodies: a Comparative Law View* (Ashgate, London 2004)

E-A Gumbel QC, M Johnson and R Scorer *Child Abuse Compensation Claims* (The Law Society, London 2002)

J Gumbleton and A Lusk 'Rehabilitation without Admission—A New Way Forward' [1999] Family Law 822

MI Hall 'After Waterhouse: Vicarious Liability and the Tort of Institutional Abuse' (2000) 22(2) Journal of Social Welfare and Family Law 159

MI Hall 'Responsibility without Fault: *Bazley v Curry*' (2000) 79 Canadian Bar Rev 474

MI Hall 'Duty, Causation and Third-Party Perpetrators: the Bonnie Mooney Case' (2005) 50 McGill LJ 597

MI Hall 'Institutional Tort Feasors: Systemic Negligence in the Class Action' (2006) 14 Tort LJ 135

B Hamlyn, A Phelps, J Turtle and G Sattar *Are Special Measures Working? Evidence from Surveys of Vulnerable and Intimidated Witnesses* (Home Office Research, Development and Statistics Directorate, London June 2004)

V Hans and A Doob 'Section 12 of the Canada Evidence Act and the Deliberations of Simulated Juries' (1975–76) 18 Crim LQ 235

L Hanson 'Sexual Assault and the Similar Fact Rule' (1993) 27 U of British Columbia L Rev 51

L Hanson '*R v B(FF)* Re-Visited: Possibilities for Admitting Similar Fact Evidence Via Relevance to Other Matters in Issue' (1994) 20 Queen's LJ 139

R Hanson, R Karl, R Steffy and R Gauthier 'Long-Term Recidivism of Child Molesters' (1993) 61 J Consulting & Clinical Psychol 646

FV Harper and PM Kime 'The Duty to Control the Conduct of Another' (1934) 43 Yale LJ 886

M Harries and M Clare *Mandatory Reporting of Child Abuse Evidence and Options Report by the Discipline of Social Work and Social Policy for the Western Australia Child Protection Council* (University of Western Australia 2002)

S Harris-Short 'Family law and the Human Rights Act 1998: judicial restraint or revolution?' (2005) 17(3) Child and Family LQ 329

S Harris-Short 'Putting The Child at the Heart of Adoption?—*Re B (Adoption: Natural Parent)*' (2003) 14(3) Child and Family LQ 325

J Hartshorne 'Corroboration and Care Warnings after *Makanjuola*' 2 Int'l J of Evidence & Proof 1

J Harwin and M Owen 'Research—The Implementation Of Care Plans and its Relationship to Children's Welfare' (2003) 15(1) Child and Family LQ 71

D Haxton 'Comment: Rape Shield Statutes: Constitutional Despite Unconstitutional Exclusions of Evidence' [1985] Wisconsin LR 1219

J Hayes and M Hayes 'Child Protection in the Court of Appeal' [2002] Fam Law 817

M Hayes 'Case Commentary—*Re O and N; Re B*—Uncertain Evidence and Risk-Taking In Child Protection Cases' (2004) 16(1) Child and Family LQ 63

M Hayes 'Criminal Trials where the Child is the Victim: Extra Protection for Children or a Missed Opportunity?' (2005) 17 (3) Child and Family LQ 307

M Hayes 'The Proper Role of Courts in Child Care Cases' [1996] Child and Family LQ 201

M Hayes 'Protecting Children in England and New Zealand' (1999) 7 Canterbury LR 297

M Hayes 'Reconciling Protection for Children with Justice for Parents' (1997) 17(1) Legal Studies 1

R Heaton 'Anything Goes' (2001) 10(2) Nottingham LJ 50

A Heger, SJ Emans and D Muram *Evaluation of the Sexually Abused Child: a Medical Textbook and Photographic Atlas* (2nd edn OUP, Oxford 2000)

H Hendrick *Child Welfare England 1872–1989* (Routledge, London 1994)

D Herring 'New Perspectives on Child Protection The Adoption and Safe Families Act—Hope and its Subversion' (2000) 34(3) Fam LQ 329

J Herring *Family Law* (Longman Pearson Education Ltd, Harlow 2001)

J Herring *Criminal Law: Text Cases and Materials* (OUP Oxford 2004)

RFV Heuston and R Buckley *Salmond and Heuston on the Law of Torts* (21st edn Sweet & Maxwell, London 1996)

J Heydon *Evidence: Cases and Materials* (2nd edn Butterworths, London 1984)

K Hirosawa 'Are Parents Acting in the Best Interests of their Children when they make Medical Decisions based on their Religious Beliefs?' (2006) 44 Fam Ct Rev 316

M Hirst 'Assault, Battery and Indirect Violence' [1999] Crim LR 557

C Hobbs, C Hanks and J Wynne *Child Abuse and Neglect: a Clinician's Handbook* (Churchill Livingstone 1999)

L Hoffmann 'Similar Facts after *Boardman*' (1975) 91 LQR 193

Lord Hoffmann 'Human Rights and the House of Lords' (1999) 62 MLR 159

B Hogan 'The Killing Ground: 1964–73' [1974] Crim LR 387

GD Hollister 'Parent-Child Immunity: a Doctrine in Search of Justification' (1982) 50 Fordham L Rev 493

B Holmgren 'Should Expert Testimony on Children's Suggestibility be Admissible?' 10(3) Update (monthly newsletter of the National Center for Prosecution of Child Abuse, American Prosecutors Research Institute) 1

T Honoré 'Are Omissions Less Culpable?' in P Cane and J Stapleton (eds) *Essays for Patrick Atiyah* (Clarendon Press, Oxford 1991)

L Hood *A City Possessed: the Christchurch Civic Crêche Case—Child Abuse, Gender Politics and the Law* (Longacre Press, Dunedin 2001)

K Hort 'Is Twenty-Two Months Beyond the Best Interest of the Child? ASFA's Guidelines For The Termination of Parental Rights' 28 Fordham Urb LJ 1879

R Horton 'Editorial: in the Defence of Roy Meadow' (July 2005) 366 Lancet 3

H Howard 'Care Plans and Cash Restraints' (1998) 12(5) Public Child Law Bulletin 1

H Howard 'Conspiracy to Cause Delay' (1998) 11(1) Public Child Law Bulletin 1

D Howe 'Child Abuse and the Bureaucratisation of Social Work' (1992) 40(3) Sociological Rev 491

J Howells *Remember Maria* (Butterworths, London 1974)

LC Hoyano 'The Flight to the Fiduciary Haven' in P Birks (ed) *Privacy and Loyalty* (Clarendon Press, Oxford 1997)

LC Hoyano 'Misconceptions about "Wrongful Conception"' (2002) 65 MLR 883

LC Hoyano 'Policing Flawed Police Investigations: Unravelling the Blanket' (1999) 62 MLR 912

LCH Hoyano 'The "Prudent Parent": the Elusive Standard of Care' (1984) 18 U of British Columbia L Rev 1

LC Hoyano 'Striking a Balance between the Rights of Defendants and Vulnerable Witnesses: Will Special Measures Directions Contravene Guarantees of a Fair Trial?' [2001] Crim LR 927

LC Hoyano 'Variations on a Theme by Pigot: Special Measures Directions for Child Witnesses' [2000] Crim LR 251

'Human Rights Act 1998' (2000) XIII(9) Practitioners' Guide to Child Law Newsletter 109

J Hunt, A McLeod and C Thomas *The Last Resort—Child Protection, the Courts and the 1989 Children Act* (HM Stationery Office, London 1999)

D Jack *Sexual Offences Bill will Create Culture of Fear and Confusion* (Brook Advisory Service Press Release 17 September 2003)

HH Judge Hal Jackson 'Child Witnesses in the Western Australian Criminal Courts' (2003) 27 Crim LJ 199

M Jacobs 'Criminal Law: Requiring Battered Women Die: Murder Liability For Mothers Under Failure To Protect Statute' (1998) 88 J Crim L & Criminology 579

K Jarnezis 'Propriety of, or Prejudicial Effect of Omitting or of Giving Instruction to Jury, in Prosecution for Rape or Other Sexual Offence, as to Ease of Making or Difficulty out of Defending against Such a Charge' (1979) (updated) 92 American LR 3d 866

S Jenkins *Are Children Protected In The Family Court? A Perspective From Western Australia* (Child Sexual Abuse: Justice Response or Alternative Resolution Conference convened by the Australian Institute of Criminology and held in Adelaide, 1–2 May 2003)

S Jenkins 'Child Welfare as a Class System' in AL Schorr (ed) *Children and Decent People* (George Allen and Unwin, London 1975)

CE Johnson 'A Cry for Help: an Argument for Abrogation of the Parent–Child Tort Immunity Doctrine in Child Abuse and Incest Cases' (1993) 21 Florida State U L Rev 617

J Jones 'Kentucky Tort Liability For Failure To Report Family Violence' (1999) 26 North Kentucky L Rev 43

Judicial Studies Board Specimen Direction 22, *Evidence of Children*

Judicial Studies Board Specimen Direction 22a *When Evidence is Given after Special Measures Direction*

Judicial Studies Board *Crown Court Bench Book* (2004, updated to October 2006)

JUSTICE *Unreliable Evidence? Confessions and the Safety of Convictions* (London 1994)

A Kabat 'Scarlet Letter Sex Offender Databases and Community Notification: Sacrificing Personal Privacy for a Symbol's Sake' (1998) 35 American Crim L Rev 333

K Kanani, C Regehr and M Bernstein 'Liability Considerations in Child Welfare: Lessons from Canada' (2002) 26 Child Abuse & Neglect 1039

D Karp 'Evidence of Propensity and Probability in Sex Offense Cases and other Cases' (1994) 70 Chicago-Kent LR 15

S Katz 'When Parents Fail' in T Taylor 'The Cultural Defense and its Irrelevancy in Child Protection Law' (1997) 17 BC Third World 331

A Kavanagh 'The Elusive Divide between Interpretation and Legislation under the Human Rights Act 1998' (2004) 24(2) OJLS 259

A Keane *The Modern Law of Evidence* (6th edn LexisNexis UK, London 2005)

MK Kearney 'Breaking the Silence: Tort Liability for Failing to Protect Children from Abuse' (1994) 42 Buffalo L Rev 405

C Keenan *The Development and Implementation of Procedures for the Investigation of Allegations of Child Sexual Abuse* (University of Shelfield , PhD Thesis, 1995)

C Keenan 'The Impact of *Cannings* on Civil Child Protection Cases' (2005) 27 J Social Welfare and Fam L 173

C Keenan, G Davis, L Hoyano and L Maitland 'Interviewing Allegedly Abused Children with a View to Criminal Prosecution' [1999] Crim LR 863

C Keenan and L Maitland ' "There Ought to Be a Law Against It": Police Evaluation of the Efficacy of Prosecution in a Case of Child Abuse' [1999] Child and Family LQ 397

C Keenan 'The Use of Folk Law in Child Protection Practice' (2002) 32 Fam Law 838

C Kelly 'The Legacy of Too Little, Too Late: The Inconsistent Treatment of Postpartum Psychosis as a Defense to Infanticide' (2002) 19 J Contemporary Health Law & Policy 247

C Kempe, F Silverman, B Steele, W Droegemueller and H Silver 'The Battered-Child Syndrome' (1984) 181 J of American Medical Association 17

K Kendall-Hackett, LM Williams and D Finkelhor 'Impact of Sexual Abuse on Children: a Review and Synthesis of Recent Empirical Studies' 113 Psychological Bulletin 164

N Kibble *Judicial Perspectives on Section 41 of the Youth Justice and Criminal Evidence Act 1999* (June 2004, summary published as 'Judicial Perspectives on the Operation of s. 41 and the Relevance and Admissibility of Prior Sexual History Evidence: Four Scenarios' [2005] Crim LR 190, 263)

MA King and JC Yuille 'Suggestibility and the Child Witness' in SJ Ceci, MP Toglia and DF Ross (eds) *Children's Eyewitness Memory* (Spring-Verlag New York 1987)

R Kinnally 'A Bad Case of Indigestion: Internalizing Changes to the Right of Confrontation' (2004) 89 Marquette L Rev 625

S Kneebone *Tort Liability of Public Authorities* (LBC Information Services, Sydney 1998)

G Köhnken 'The Evaluation of Statement Credibility: Social Judgment and Expert Diagnostic Approaches' in J Spencer, G Nicholson, R Flin and R Bull (eds) *Children's Evidence in Legal Proceedings: an International Perspective* (Cambridge University Law Faculty, Cambridge 1989)

G Köhnken 'Statement Validity Analysis' (paper presented at *Children's Evidence in the Courts* (University of Southampton Faculty of Law, London 16 December 1997))

M Kovera and E Borgida 'Expert Scientific Testimony on Child Witnesses in the Age of *Daubert*' in S Ceci and H Hembrooke (eds) *Expert Witnesses in Child Abuse Cases: What Can and Should be Said in Court* (American Psychological Association, Washington DC 1998)

CA Kubitschek 'Social Worker Malpractice for Failure to Protect Foster Children' (2005) 41 Am Jur Trials 1

HHJ Patricia Kvill 'Concluding Thoughts from the Bench: the Failed Promises' in N Bala, MK Zapf, RJ Williams, R Vogl and JP Hornick (eds) *Canadian Child Welfare Law: Children, Families and the State* (2nd edn Thompson Educational Publishing, Inc, Toronto 2004)

A Kyl 'The Propriety of Propensity: the Effects and Operation of New Federal Rules of Evidence 413 and 414' (1995) 37 Arizona LR 659

J LaFontaine *Child Sexual Abuse* (Polity Press, Cambridge 1990)

ME Lamb, KK Sternberg and PW Esplin 'Conducting Investigative Interviews of Alleged Sexual Abuse Victims' (1998) 22 Child Abuse and Neglect 813

Lord Laming 'Speech' (8 June 2004) <http://www.victoria-climbié-inquiry.org.uk/keydocuments/lordstate.htm> (accessed 30 June 2006)

P Lamond 'The Impact of Mandatory Reporting Legislation on Reporting Behaviour' (1989) 13 Child Abuse and Neglect 471

R Lansdowne 'Infanticide: Psychiatrists in the Plea Bargaining Process' (1990) 16 Monash U L Rev 41

D Lathi 'Sex Abuse, Accusations of Lies, and Videotaped Testimony: a Proposal for a Federal Hearsay Exception in Child Sexual Abuse Cases' (1997) 68 U of Colorado L Rev 507

R Lavery 'The Child Assessment Order—a Reassessment' [1996] Child and Family LQ 41

MC Lear 'Just Perfect for Pedophiles? Charitable Organisations that Work with Children and Their Duty to Screen Volunteers' (1997) 76 Texas L Rev 143

E Leberg *Understanding Child Molesters: Taking Charge* (Sage Publications Thousand Oaks CA 1997)

M Leichtman and S Ceci 'The Effects of Stereotypes and Stands on Preschoolers' Reports' (2005) 31 *Developmental Psychology* 568

M Leippe, A Manion and A Romanczyk 'Discernibility or Discrimination?: Understanding Jurors' Reactions to Accurate and Inaccurate Child and Adult Eyewitnesses' in G Goodman and B Bottoms (eds) *Child Victims, Child Witnesses: Understanding and Improving Testimony* (Guildford Press New York, London 1993)

R Leng and R Taylor *Blackstone's Guide to the Criminal Procedure and Investigations Act 1996* (Blackstone Press, London 1996)

N Levitt 'The Kindness of Strangers: Interdisciplinary Foundations of a Duty to Act' (2001) 40 Washburn L J 463

Allan Levy QC 'Inquiries into Child Abuse: How Valuable are They?' Fifth Australasian Conference on Child Abuse and Neglect, Melbourne 18 October 1995

Allan Levy QC 'The Human Rights Act 1998: the Implications for Children' (2000) 6 Child Care in Practice 288

Allan Levy QC 'Do Children Have Human Rights?' [2002] Fam Law 204

P Lewis 'Similar Facts and Similar Allegations in Delayed Criminal Prosecutions of Childhood Sexual Abuse' [2004] Crim LR 39

P Lewis *Delayed Prosecution for Childhood Sexual Abuse* (OUP, Oxford 2006)

D Libai 'The Protection of the Child Victim of a Sexual Offense in the Criminal Justice System' (1969) 15 Wayne L Rev 977

A Linden 'Reconsidering Tort Law As Ombudsman' in F Steel and S Rodgers-Magnet (eds) *Issues in Tort Law* (Carswell, Toronto 1983)

B Lindley and M Richards *'Working Together* 2000—How Will Parents Fare Under the New Child Protection Process?' [2000] Child and Family LQ 213

B Lindley and M Richards *Protocol on Advice and Advocacy for Parents* (Centre for Family Research, Cambridge 2002)

S Lloyd-Bostock 'The Effect on Juries of Hearing about the Defendant's Previous Criminal Record: a Simulation Study' [2000] Crim LR 734

E Loftus *Eyewitness Testimony* (Harvard University Press Cambridge, Mass 1979)

E Loftus and K Ketcham *The Myth of Repressed Memory* (St Martin's Press, New York 1994)

EF Loftus 'The Reality of Repressed Memories' (1993) 48 American Psychologist 518

EF Loftus 'Repressed Memory Accusations: Devastated Families and Devastated Patients' (1997) 11 Applied Cognitive Psychology 25

E Loftus, J Paddock and T Guernsey 'Patient–Psychotherapist Privilege: Access to Clinical Records in the Tangled Web of Repressed Memory Litigation' (1996) 30 Y of Richmond LR 109

K London, M Bruch, S Ceci and D Shuman 'Disclosure of Child Sexual Abuse: What Does the Research Tell Us about the Ways That Children Tell?' (2006) 11 Psychology, Public Policy and Law 194

N Lowe and G Douglas *Bromley's Family Law* (Butterworth's, London 1999)

CE Luus and GL Wells 'The Perceived Credibility of Child Witnesses' in H Dent and R Flin (eds) *Children As Witnesses* (Wiley, Chichester 1992)

J Lynch 'A Matter of Trust: Institutional Employer Liability for Acts of Child Abuse by Employees' (1992) 33 William and Mary L Rev 1295

C Lyon 'What Happened to the Child's "Right" to Refuse?—*South Glamorgan CC v W and B*' (1994) 6(2) JCL 84

C Lyon *Loving Smack or Lawful Assault? A Contradiction in Human Rights and Law* (IPPR, London 2000)

TD Lyon and J Koehler 'The Relevance Ratio: Evaluating the Probative Value of Expert Testimony in Child Sexual Abuse Cases' (1996) 82 Cornell L Rev 43

TD Lyon and J Koehler 'Where Researchers Fear to Tread: Interpretive Differences among Testifying Expert in Child Sexual Abuse Cases' in S Ceci and HH Hembrooke (eds) *Expert Witnesses in Child Abuse Cases: What Can and Should Be Said in Court* (American Psychological Association, Washington DC 1998)

TD Lyon and K Saywitz 'Young Maltreated Children's Competence to Take the Oath' (1999) 3 Applied Developmental Science 16

TD Lyon 'The New Wave in Children's Suggestibility Research: a Critique' (1999) 84 Cornell L Rev 1005

J Macfarlane 'Neonaticide and the "Ethos of Maternity": Traditional Criminal Law Defenses and the Novel Syndrome' (1998) Cardozo Women's L J 175

K MacFarlane 'Diagnostic Evaluations and the Use of Videotapes in Child Sexual Abuse Cases' (1985) 40 U of Miami L Rev 135

Lord Mackay of Clashfern 'Perceptions of the Children Bill and Beyond' [1989] 139 NLJ 505

Lord Mackay of Clashfern 'The View Across the Tweed' (1988) Denning LJ 89

Lord Mackay of Clashfern 'Joseph Jackson Memorial Lecture' (1989) 139 NLJ 505

R Mackay 'The Consequences of Killing Very Young Children' [1993] Crim LR 21

R Mahoney 'Review of Evidence' [2000] New Zealand L Rev 101

R Mahoney 'Acquittals as Similar Fact Evidence: Another View' (2003) 47 Crim LQ 265

TB Marcketti 'Rape Shield Laws: do they shield the children?' (1993) 78 Iowa L Rev 751

B Markesinis, J-B Auby, C Waltjen and S Deakin *Tortious Liability of Statutory Bodies: a Comparative and Economic Analysis of Five English Cases* (Hart, Oxford 1999)

M Marsh (Latest Developments) <http://www.childrenareunbeatable.org.uk/> (accessed 4 December 2004)

P Marsh 'Partnership, Child Protection and Family Group Conferences—the New Zealand Children, Young Persons and their Families Act 1989' (1994) 6(3) J of Child Law 109

P Marsh and G Crow *Family Group Conferences in Child Welfare* (Blackwell Science 1998)

LH Martin 'Caseworker Liability for the Negligent Handling of Child Abuse Reports' (1991) 60 U of Cincinnati L Rev 191

J Masson 'The Impact of the Adoption and Children Act 2000—Part 2—The Provision of Services for Children and Families' (2003) 33 Fam LJ 644

J Masson, M Winn-Oakley and C McGovern *Working in the Dark—Executive Summary* (University of Warwick)

J Masson, M Winn-Oakley and K Pick *Emergency Protection Orders—Court Orders for Child Protection Crises* (Warwick University 2004)

R Masterman 'Taking the Strasbourg Jurisprudence into Account: Developing a "Municipal Law of Human Rights" under the Human Rights Act' (2005) Int Comp LQ 907

A Maxwell 'Pre-Trial Therapy for Child Complainant of Sexual Abuse in the Criminal Justice System: Forensic Implications' (Child Sexual Abuse: Justice Response or Alternative Resolution Conference 2003)

A McAlinden 'Sex Offender Registration: Some Observations on Megan's Law and the Sex Offenders Act 1997' (1999) 1(1) Crime Prevention and Community Safety 43

A McAlinden 'Managing Risk: From Regulation to the Reintegration of Sexual Offenders' (2006) 6 Criminology and Criminal Justice 197

NJ McBride 'Vicarious Liability in England and Australia' [2003] Cambridge LJ 255

NJ McBride and R Bagshaw *Tort Law* (2nd edn Pearson Longman, Harlow 2005)

M McCarthy 'Admissibility of Expert Testimony on Child Sexual Abuse Accommodation Syndrome in Kentucky' [1992–93] 81 Kentucky LJ 728

A McColgan 'Common Law and the Relevance of Sexual History Evidence' (1996) 16 Oxford J Legal Studies 275

A McColgan 'General Defences' in D Nicholson and L Bibbings (eds) *Feminist Perspectives on Criminal Law* (Cavendish Publishing, London 2000)

WE McCurdy 'Torts Between Persons in Domestic Relation' (1930) 43 Harvard L Rev 1030

J McEwan 'Where the Prosecution Witness is a Child: The Memorandum of Good Practice' (1993) 5 J CL 16

L McFarlane and P Bocji 'Cyberstalking: Defining the Invasion of Cyberspace' (2003) 72 Forensic Update 18

L McGough 'Children as Victims and Witnesses in the Criminal Trial Process: Good Enough for Government Work: The Constitutional Duty to Preserve Forensic Interviews of Child Victims' (2002) 65 Law and Contemporary Problems 179

LS McGough 'For the Record: Videotaping Investigative Interviews' (1995) 1 Psychology, Public Policy and Law 370

LS McGough 'Hearing and Believing Hearsay' (1999) 5 Psychology, Public Policy, and Law 485

L McGough 'The Impact of *Daubert*: a Legal Commentary' in S Ceci and H Hembrooke (eds) *Expert Witnesses in Child Abuse Cases: What Can and Should Be Said in Court* (American Psychological Association, Washington, DC 1998)

M McGrath and C Clemens 'The Child Victim as a Witness in Sexual Abuse Cases' (1985) 46 Montana L Rev 229

C McIvor 'Expelling the Myth of the Parental Duty to Rescue' (2000) 12 Child and Family LQ 229

C McIvor *Third Party Liability in Tort* (Hart, Oxford 2006)

G McLay 'Antipodean Perspectives on Child Welfare Tort Claims against Public Authorities' in D Fairgrieve and S Green (eds) *Child Abuse Tort Claims against Public Bodies: a Comparative Law View* (Ashgate, Aldershot 2004)

J McLeod and T Daley McLeod *Child Custody Law and Practice* (Thompson Canada, Westlaw 2004)

Sir Roy Meadow 'Munchausen Syndrome by Proxy: The Hinterland of Child Abuse' (1977) 2 The Lancet 343

Sir Roy Meadow *ABC of Child Abuse* (3rd edn BMJ Pub Group, London 1997)

J Meier 'Domestic Violence, Child Custody, And Child Protection: Understanding Judicial Resistance and Imagining the Solutions' (2003) 11 Am U J Gender Society Policy and Law 657

A Memon and M Young 'Desperately Seeking Evidence: the Recovered Memory Debate' (1997) 2(2) Legal and Criminal Logical Psychology 131

A Mewitt 'Character as a Fact in Issue in Criminal Cases' (1984–85) 27 Criminal LQ 29

A Mewett 'Credibility and Consistency' (1991) 33 Crim LQ 385

J Meyers 'A Theory of Vicarious Liability' (2005) 43 Alberta L Rev 1

BA Micheels 'Is Justice Served? The Development of Tort Liability against the Passive Parent in Incest Cases' (1997) 41 St Louis U LJ 809

B Midson 'Child Homicide in New Zealand: Charges, Convictions and Sentencing' in C Breen (ed) *Children's Needs, Rights and Welfare—Developing Strategies for the Whole Child in the 21st Century* (Thompson Dunmore Press, Victoria 2004)

John Stuart Mill *On Liberty* (1859)

M Miller 'Revisiting Poor Joshua: State-Created Danger Theory in the Foster Care Context' (2000) 11 Hastings Women's LJ 243

S Millham, R Bullock and M Haak *Lost in Care: The Problems of Maintaining Links between Children in Care and their Families* (Gower, Aldershot 1986)

P Mirfield 'Similar Facts—*Makin* out?' (1987) 46 CLJ 83

P Mirfield 'Similar Fact Evidence of Child Sexual Abuse in English, United States, and Florida Law: a Comparative Study' (1996) 6 J of Transnational Law and Policy 7

M Misener 'Children's Hearsay Evidence in Child Sexual Abuse Prosecutions: a Proposal for Reform' (1991) 33(4) Criminal LQ 364

C Mitra 'Judicial Discourse in Father–Daughter Incest Appeal Cases' (1987) 15(2) IJ of Sociology of Law 121

S Molinari 'Concerning the Prior Crimes Evidence Rules for Sexual Assault and Child Molestation Cases' (Congressional Record H8991-92, Aug 21,1994)

J Montoya 'Lessons from *Akiki* and *Michaels* on Shielding Child Witnesses' (1995) 1 Psychology, Public Policy, and Law 340

E Morgan 'Hearsay Dangers and the Application of the Hearsay Concept' (1948) 62 Harvard L Rev 177

E Morgan *Basic Problems of Evidence* (Joint Committee on Continuing Legal Education of the American Law Institute and the American Bar Association, Philadelphia 1963)

S Morison and E Greene 'Juror and Expert Knowledge of Child Sexual Abuse' 16 (1992) Child Abuse & Neglect 595

J Morris *Still Missing? Vol 2 Disabled Children and the Children Act* (Who Cares? Trust, London 1998)

J Morton 'Videotaping Children's Evidence—A Reply' (1987) 137 New LJ 216

J Mosher 'Challenging Limitation Periods: Civil Claims by Adult Survivors of Incest' (1994) 44 U Toronto LJ 169

R Mosteller 'Child Abuse Reporting Laws and Attorney–Client Confidences: the Reality and the Spectre of Client as Informant' (1992) 42 Duke LJ 203

RA Mowbray *The Development of Positive Obligations under the European Convention on Human Rights by the European Court Of Human Rights* (Hart, Oxford 2004)

K Müller and K Hollely *Introducing the Child Witness* (Printrite, Port Elizabeth 2000)

Sir James Munby 'Access to and Reporting of Family Proceedings' [2005] Fam Law 1

Sir James Munby 'Making Sure that the Child is Heard' [2004] Fam Law 34

R Munday 'What Constitutes "Reprehensible Behaviour" under the Bad Character Provisions of the Criminal Justice Act 2003?' [2005] Crim LR 24

E Munro 'Improving Social Workers' Knowledge Base in Child Protection Work' (1998) 28 British J of Social Work 89

C Murphy 'Legal Images of Motherhood: Conflicting Definitions From Welfare "Reform", Family, and Criminal Laws' (1998) 83 Cornell L Rev 688

K Murray *Live Television Link: an Evaluation of Its Use by Child Witnesses in Scottish Criminal Trials* (The Scottish Office Central Research Unit, Edinburgh 1995)

K Murray *Preparing Child Witnesses for Court: a Review of Literature and Research,* (Scottish Office Home Department Central Research Unit, Edinburgh 1997)

J Myers 'The Child Witness: Techniques for Direct Examination, Cross-Examination and Impeachment' (1987) 18 Pacific LJ 801

J Myers *Legal Issues in Child Abuse and Neglect* (Sage Publications, Newbury Park 1992)

J Myers 'A Decade of International Legal Reform regarding Child Abuse Investigation and Litigation: Steps toward a Child Witness Code' (1996) 28 Pacific LJ 169

J Myers *Evidence in Child Abuse and Neglect Cases* (3rd edn John Wiley & Sons, Inc, New York 1997) 2 vols

J Myers 'Expert Testimony in Child Sexual Abuse Litigation' (1989) 68(1) Nebraska L Rev 1

J Myers 'New Era of Skepticism regarding Children's Credibility: Suggestibility of Child Witnesses—the Social Science Amicus Brief in *The State of New Jersey v Margaret Kelly Michaels*' (1905) 1 Psychology, Public Policy, and Law 387

J Myers, A Redlich, G Goodman and L Prizmich 'Jurors' Perceptions of Hearsay in Child Sexual Abuse Cases' (1999) 5 Psychology, Public Policy and Law 388

J Myers, K Saywitz and G Goodman 'Psychological Research on Children As Witnesses: Implications for Forensic Interviewing and Courtroom Testimony' (1996) 28 Pacific LJ 3

J Myers 'Taint Hearings for Child Witnesses? A Step in the Wrong Direction' (1994) 46 Baylor L Rev 873

National Center for Prosecution of Child Abuse *Investigation and Prosecution of Child Abuse* (3rd edn Sage Publications Inc, Thousand Oaks 2004)

J Neeb and S Harper *Civil Action for Childhood Sexual Abuse* (Butterworths Canada Ltd, Toronto 1994)

J Neyers 'A Theory of Vicarious Liability' (2005) 43 Alberta L Rev 1

New South Wales Bar Council *Code of Conduct* (Gazette No. 66 of 20 June 1997)

New South Wales Bar Council *The New South Wales Barristers' Rules* (Consolidated April 2001)

D Nicholson 'What the Law Giveth It Also Taketh Away: Female Specific Defences to Criminal Liability' in D Nicholson and L Bibbings (eds) *Feminist Perspectives on Criminal Law* (Cavendish Publishing, London 2000)

AL Nilsen 'Speaking out against Passive Parent Child Abuse: the Time Has Come to Hold Parents Liable for Failing to Protect Their Children' (2000) 37 Houston L Rev 261

J Norris and M Edwards 'Myths, Hidden Facts and Common Sense: Expert Opinion Evidence and the Assessment of Credibility' (1995) 38 Crim LQ 73

M Oberman 'Understanding Infanticide in Context: Mothers Who Kill, 1870–1930 and Today' J Crim L and Criminology 707

P O'Connor 'Squaring the Circle: How Canada is Dealing with the Legacy of its Indian Residential Schools Experiment' [2000] Australian J of Human Rights 9

M O'Hara 'Post-partum "Blues", Depression, and Psychosis: A Review' (1987) 7 J Psychosomatic Obstetrics and Gynaecology 205

L Oren 'The State's Failure to Protect Children and Substantive Due Process: *Deshaney* in Context' (1990) 68 North Carolina L Rev 659

D Ormerod 'Sexual Assault: Whether Touching of Complainant's Clothing Without Bringing Pressure Against Complainant's Body "Touching" for Purposes of Sexual Assault' [2005] Crim LR 735

D Ormerod *Smith & Hogan Criminal Law* (10th edn Butterworths London 2002)

P Ornstein and B Gordon 'The Psychologist as Expert Witness: a Comment' in S Ceci and H Hembrooke (eds) *Expert Witnesses in Child Abuse Cases: What Can and Should Be Said in Court* (American Psychological Association, Washington, DC 1998)

S Ost 'Getting to Grips with Sexual Grooming? The New Offence under the Sexual Offences Act 2003' (2004) 26 J of Social Welfare and Family L 147

DM Paciocco 'Coping with Expert Evidence about Human Behaviour' (1999) 25 Queen's LJ 305

D Paciocco and L Steusser *The Law of Evidence* (3rd edn Essentials of Canadian Law Irwin Law, Toronto 2002)

D Paciocco '*R v Wakabayashi*: The Relevance of Expert Evidence of Psychological Characteristics of Sexual Abuse on the Credibility of Child Witnesses' (1996) 2 Sexual Offences L Reporter 153

D Paciocco 'Using the Collateral Facts Rule with Discretion' (2002) 46 Crim LQ 160

E J Paddock and T Guernsey 'Patient-Psychotherapist Privilege: Access to Clinical Records in the Tangled Web of Repressed Memory Litigation' (1996) 30 U of Richmond L Rev 109

E Palmer 'Courts, Resources and the HRA: Reading Section 17 of the Children Act 1989 Compatibly with Article 8 ECHR' [2003] 3 European Human Rights L Rev 308

RC Park 'Character at the Crossroads' [1998] Hastings LJ 717

P Parkinson 'Child Protection Law in Australia' in M Freeman (ed) *Overcoming Child Abuse: A Window on a World Problem* (Ashgate, Dartmouth 2000)

P Parkinson 'Child Protection, Permanency Planning and Children's Right to Family Life' (2003) 17 Int J of Law Policy and the Family 147

P Parkinson *Children and Young Persons (Care and Protection) Act 1998 (An Overview)* (Faculty of Law University of Sydney 2000)

P Parkinson 'Keeping in Contact: the Role of Family Relationship Centres in Australia' (2006) 18(2) Child and Family LQ 157

N Parton *Governing the Family—Child Care, Child Protection and the State* (Macmillan, Basingstoke 1991)

N Parton 'From Maria Colwell to Victoria Climbié: Reflections on Public Inquiries into Child Abuse a Generation Apart' [2004] 13 Child Abuse Rev 80

N Parton *The Politics of Child Abuse* (Macmillan, London 1985)

N Parton, D Thorpe and C Wattam *Child Protection—Risk and the Moral Order* (Macmillan, Basingstoke 1997)

R Pattenden 'Conflicting Approaches to Psychiatric Evidence in Criminal Trials: England, Canada and Australia' [1986] Crim LR 92

R Pattenden 'The Risk of Non-Persuasion in Civil Trials: The Case Against a Floating Standard of Proof' [1988] Civ JQ 220

R Pattenden 'Should Confessions be Corroborated?' (1991) 107 LQR 317

KC Pearson 'Cooperate or We'll Take Your Child: The Parents' Fictional Voluntary Separation Decision and a Proposal for Change' (1998) 65 Tennessee L Rev 835

M Pendergrast *Victims of Memory: Incest Accusations and Shattered Lives* (HarperCollins London 1996)

A Perkins and E Tomlinson 'Disclosure of Social Services Documents into Criminal Proceedings' [2005] Fam LJ 806

CM Perman 'Diagnosing the Truth: Determining Physician Liability in Cases Involving Munchausen Syndrome by Proxy' (1990) 54 J of Urban and Contemporary Law 267

A Perry 'Safety First? Contact and Family Violence in New Zealand: an evaluation of the presumption against unsupervised contact' (2006) 18(1) Child and Family LQ 1

NW Perry and BD McAuliff 'The Use of Video Tape Child Testimony: Public Policy Implications' (1993) 7 Notre Dame J of Law, Ethics and Public Policy 387

J Peters 'Using the *Abel Assessment for Sexual Interest* to Infer Lack of Culpability in a Criminal Case' 14(12) Update (monthly newsletter of the National Center for Prosecution of Child Abuse, American Prosecutors Research Institute)

A Phillips *Cases Interpreting Crawford -v- Washington* (National Center for Prosecution of Child Abuse, American Prosecutor's Research Institute, Alexandria Virginia 2006)

A Phillips 'Out of Harm's Way: Hearings that are Safe from the Impact of *Crawford v. Washington*' (2005) 18 Update (National Center for Prosecution of Child Abuse) 8 (Part 1) and 9 (Part 2)

A Phillips 'Reasonable Efforts' (2004) 1(2) American Prosecutors Research Institute (Child Protection) Newsletter 1–2

G Phillipson '(Mis)-Reading Section 3 of the Human Rights Act' (2003) 119 LQR 183

C Phipps 'Children, Adults, Sex and the Criminal Law' (1997) 22 Seaton Hall J 1

C Phipps 'Responding to Child Homicide: A Statutory Proposal' (1999) 89 J Crim L & Criminology 535

K Pickel 'Inducing Jurors to Disregard Inadmissible Evidence: a Legal Explanation Does Not Help' (1995) 9 Law & Human Behaviour 407

J Plotnikoff and R Woolfson *An Evaluation of Child Witness Support* (Scottish Executive Central Research Unit, Edinburgh 2001)

J Plotnikoff and R Woolfson *In Their Own Words: the Experiences of 50 Young Witnesses in Criminal Proceedings* (NSPCC and Victim Support London 2004)

J Plotnikoff and R Woolfson *Prosecuting Child Abuse: an Evaluation of the Government's Speedy Progress Policy* (Blackstone Press, London 1995)

J Plotnikoff and R Woolfson *Report of the Lord Advocate's Working Party on Child Witness Support Part 2: Research Report* (Lord Advocate's Chambers Edinburgh March 1999)

DA Pollard 'Banning Corporal Punishment: A Constitutional Analysis' (2002) 52 American U L Rev 447

L Radford 'Peace at Home—Safety and Parental Contact Arrangements for children in the Context of Domestic Violence' in C Breen (ed) *Children's Needs, Rights and Welfare: Developing Strategies for the 21st Century* (Thompson Dunmore Press, Victoria 2004)

S Ramsey 'The United States Child Protective System—a Triangle of Tensions' [2001] Child and Family LQ 25

S Raymond 'Where are the Reasonable Efforts to Enforce the Reasonable Efforts Requirement?: Monitoring State Compliance Under the Adoption Assistance and Child Welfare Act of 1980' (1999) 77 Texas L Rev 1235

M Rayner 'Management of Child Witnesses—Practical Solutions for Judges' (Local Court's Annual Conference 2003)

M Rayner 'The State of Children's Rights in Australia' in B Franklin (ed) *The New Handbook of Children's Rights—Comparative Policy and Practice* (Routledge, London 2002)

M Redmayne *Expert Evidence and Criminal Justice* (OUP, Oxford 2001)

M Redmayne 'Myths, Relationships and Coincidences: the New Problems of Sexual History' (2003) 7 International J of Evidence & Proof 75

M Redmayne 'The Relevance of Bad Character' [2000] CLJ 684

M Redmayne 'Similar Facts, Similar Obfuscation: *R v Handy*' (2002) 6 Int J of Evidence and Proof 243

R Reece (ed) *Child Abuse: Medical Diagnosis and Management* (Lea & Febiger, Philadelphia 1994)

T Reed 'Reading Gaol Revisited: Admission of Uncharged Misconduct Evidence in Sex Offender Cases' (1993) 21 Am J Crim L 127

PC Regan and SJ Baker 'The Impact of Child Witness Demeanour on Perceived Credibility and Trial Outcome in Sexual Abuse Cases' (1998) 13 J of Family Violence 187

A Reiniger and others 'Mandated Training of Professionals: A Means for Improving Reporting of Suspected Child Abuse' (1995) 24 Child Abuse & Neglect 63

G Renaud 'Hearsay after *R v Khan* and *R v Smith*' (1995) 17 Advocates' Quarterly 30

W Renke 'The Mandatory Reporting of Child Abuse under the Child Welfare Act' (1999) 7 Health LJ 91

P Resnick 'Child Murder by Parents: A Psychiatric Review of Fillicide' (1969) 126 American J Psychiatry 325

P Resnick 'Murder of the Newborn: A Psychiatric Review of Neonaticide' (1970) 126 American J Psychiatry 1414

O Reynolds 'Tortious Battery: Is "I didn't Mean any Harm" Relevant?' (1984) 37 Oklahoma L Rev 717

H Roades 'Posing as Reform: The Case of the Family Law Reform Act' (2000) 14 Australian J Family Law 9

D Roberts 'Access to Justice: Poverty, Race, and New Directions In Child Welfare Policy' (1999) 1 Washington U J of Law & Policy 63

P Roberts and A Zuckerman *Criminal Evidence* (OUP, Oxford 2004)

HH Judge DAH Rodwell QC 'Applications for Third Party Material where PII is likely to be Claimed' [1998] Crim LR 332

R Roe 'Expert Testimony in Child Sexual Abuse Cases' (1985) 40 University of Miami L Rev 97

P Rook and R Ward *Rook & Ward on Sexual Offences Law and Practice* (3rd edn Sweet & Maxwell, London 2004)

C Ross 'The Tyranny of Time: Vulnerable Children, "Bad" Mothers, and Statutory Deadlines in Parental Termination Proceedings' (2004) 11 Virginia J Soc Policy and L 176

DF Ross, R Lindsay and DF Marsil 'The Impact of Hearsay Testimony on Conviction Rates in Trials of Child Sexual Abuse: Toward Balancing the Rights of Defendants and Child Witnesses' (1999) 5 Psychology, Public Policy, and Law 439

DF Ross, AR Warren and LS McGough 'Foreword: Hearsay Testimony in Trials Involving Child Witnesses' (1999) 5 Psychology, Public Policy and Law 251

D Rowsell 'Necessity and Reliability: What is the Impact of *Khan* on the Admissibility of Hearsay in Canada?' (1991) 49 (2) U of Toronto Faculty of L Rev 294

PN Rumney 'False Allegations of Rape' (2006) 65(1) CLJ 128

SA Dobbin, SI Gatowski and M Springate 'Child Abuse and Neglect: A Summary of State Statutes' (1997) 48 Juvenile and Fam Ct J 43

I Sagatun and L Edwards *Child Abuse and the Legal System* (Nelson-Hall Publishers, Chicago 1995)

CB Sailor 'Qualified Immunity for Child Abuse Investigators: Balancing the Concerns of Protecting Our Children from Abuse and the Integrity of the Family' (1991) 29 J of Family L 659

A Sampson *Acts of Abuse: Sexual Offenders and the Criminal Justice System* (Routledge, London 1994)

D Sanders 'Towards Creating a Policy of Permanence for America's Disposable Children: The Evolution of Federal Funding Statutes for Foster Care from 1961 to Present' (2003) 17 International Journal of the Law, Policy and the Family 211

G Sarno 'Admissibility of Expert Testimony as to Criminal Defendant's Propensity toward Sexual Deviation' (2004) 42 American LR 4th 937

Hilary Saunders 'Twenty-nine Child Homicides: lessons still to be learnt on domestic violence and child protection' (Women's Aid Federation of England London 2004) <http://www.womensaid.org.uk/page.asp?section=00010001000900005000500090004> (4 July 2006)

Schaefer and Hanson 'Similar Fact Evidence and Limited Use Instructions: an Empirical Investigation' (1990) 14 Crim LJ 157

JP Schuman, N Bala and K Lee 'Developmentally Appropriate Questions for Child Witnesses' (1999) 25 Queen's LJ 251

BL Schwalb 'Child Abuse Trials and the Confrontation of Traumatized Witnesses: Defining "Confrontation" to Protect Both Children and Defendants' (1991) 26 Harvard Civil Rights-Civil Liberties L Rev 185

R Schweitzer, L Buckley, P Harnett and NJ Loxton 'Predictors of failure by medical practitioners to report suspected child abuse in Queensland, Australia' (2006) 30 Australian Health Review 298

R Scorer 'Paying for the Sins of the Fathers' 8 July 2005 New LJ 1029

A Sealy and W Cornish 'Jurors and Their Verdicts' (1973) 36 MLR 496

S Sgroi *Handbook of Clinical Intervention in Child Sexual Abuse* (Lexington Books, Lexington MA 1982)

S Shargy '*CD (A Child By Her Litigation Friend VD) v Isle of Anglesey County Council*— Comment' (2004) 154 NLJ 1321

J Sheldon '50,000 Children are Waiting: Permanency, Planning and Termination of Parental Rights under the Adoption Assistance and Child Welfare Act of 1980' (1997) 17 B C Third World 211

MA Shields 'Liability of Church or Religious Organization for Negligent Hiring, Retention or Supervision of Priest, Minister, or Other Clergy Based on Sexual Misconduct' (2005) 101 American LR 5th 1

A Simester and G Sullivan 'Burden of Proof' <http://www.hartpub.co.uk/updates/crimlaw/crimlaw_burden05.htm>

A Simester and G Sullivan *Criminal Law—Theory and Doctrine* (2nd edn Hart Oxford 2003)

A Sinden 'In Search of Affirmative Duties toward Children under a Post-*DeShaney* Constitution' (1990) 139 U of Pennsylvania L Rev 227

P Skidmore 'Telling Tales—Media Power, Ideology and the Reporting of Child Sexual Abuse in Britian' Papers given to European Group for the Study of Social Control and Deviance Annual Conference (September 1994)

DL Skoler 'A Constitutional Right to Safe Foster Care?—Time for the Supreme Court to Pay Its IOU' (1991) 18 Pepperdine L Rev 353

C Smart *Feminism and the Power of Law* (Routledge, London 1989)

C Smart 'A History of Ambivalence and Conflict in the Discursive Construction of the "Child Victim" of Sexual Abuse' (1999) Social and Legal Studies 391

G Smith 'Good Practice or Yet Another Hurdle: Video Recording Children's Statements' (1993) 5(1) J of Child L 21

R Smith ' "Hands-Off Parenting?"—Towards A Reform of the Defence of Reasonable Chastisement in the UK' (2004) 16(3) Child and Fam LQ 261

V Smith 'In Defence of the Prosecution Disclosure Protocol' [2006] Fam LJ 457

SA Soehnel 'Governmental Tort Liability for Social Service Agency's Negligence in Placement, or Supervision after Placement, of Children' 90 American LR 3d 1214 (updated 2006)

J Sopinka, S Lederman and A Bryant *The Law of Evidence in Canada* (2nd edn Butterworths, Toronto 1999)

DD Southall, M Plunkett, M Banks, A Falkov and M Samuels 'Covert Video Recordings of Life-threatening Child Abuse: Lessons for Child Protection' (1997) 100 Pediatrics 735

J Spencer *Evidence of Bad Character* (Hart Oxford 2006)

J Spencer 'Reforming the Competency Requirement' [1988] New LJ 147

J Spencer 'The Sexual Offences Act: The Child and Family Offences' [2004] Crim LR 347

J Spencer and R Flin *The Evidence of Children: the Law and the Psychology* (2nd edn Blackstone Press, London 1993)

J Spencer G Nicholson R Flin and R Bull (eds) *Children's Evidence in Legal Proceedings: an International Perspective* (Cambridge University Law Faculty Cambridge 1989)

J Stapleton 'Civil Prosecutions Part 1: Double Jeopardy and Abuse of Process' (1999) 7 Torts LJ 244

J Stapleton 'Civil Prosecutions Part 2: Civil Claims for Killing and Rape' (2000) 8 Torts LJ 15

J Stapleton 'The Golden Thread at the Heart of Tort Law: the Protection of the Vulnerable' (2003) 24 Australian Bar Rev 135

K Starmer *European Human Rights Law* (Legal Action Group, London 1999)

DL Steele 'Expert Testimony: Seeking an Appropriate Admissibility Standard for Behavioural Science in Child Sexual Abuse Prosecutions' (1999) 48 Duke LJ 932

K Steinmetz 'Note: *State v. Oliver*: Children with a Past: The Admissibility of the Victim's Prior Sexual Experience in Child Molestation Cases' (1989) 31 Arizona LR 677

M Steller and T Boychuk 'Children As Witnesses in Sexual Abuse Cases: Investigative Interview and Assessment Techniques' in H Dent and R Flin (eds) *Children as Witnesses* (Wiley, Chichester 1992)

DJ Stewart and AE Knott 'Australian School Authorities' Liability (Without Fault) for Sexual Abuse of Students by Employees' (2003) 170 Education LJ 4

J Stone 'The Role of Exclusion of Similar Fact Evidence: England' (1933) 46 Harvard LR 954

J Stone 'The Role of Exclusion of Similar Fact Evidence: America' (1938) 51 Harvard LR 988

M Stone *Proof of Fact in Criminal Trials* (W Green & Son Ltd, Edinburgh 1984)

D Strange M Garry and R Sutherland 'Drawing Out Children's False Memories' (2003) 17 Applied Cognitive Psychology 607

JW Strong *McCormick on Evidence* (4th edn West Pub Co, St Paul Minnesota 1992)

L Stuesser 'Similar Fact Evidence in Sexual Offence Cases' (1996–1997) 39 Crim LQ 160

L Stuesser 'Admitting Acquittals as Similar Fact Evidence' (2000) 45 Crim LQ 488

R Sullivan 'Trespass to the Person in Canada: a Defence of the Traditional Approach' (1987) 19 Ottawa L Rev 533

R Summit 'Abuse of the Child Sexual Abuse Accommodation Syndrome' (1992) 1 J of Child Sexual Abuse 153

R Summit 'The Child Sexual Abuse Accommodation Syndrome' (1983) 7 Child Abuse & Neglect 177

R-A Surma 'A Comparative Study of the English and German Judicial Approach to the Liability of Public Bodies in Negligence' in D Fairgrieve, M Andenas and J Bell (eds) *Tort Liability of Public Authorities in Comparative Perspective* (British Institute of International and Comparative Law London 2002)

PA Swain 'Social Workers and Professional Competence—a Last Goodbye to the Clapham Omnibus?' (1995) 4 Torts LJ 24

J Sweeney 'In the Shadows of Justice' *The Guardian* (London 19 June 2006) 1–2

C Tapper 'The Criminal Justice Act 2003 (3): Evidence of Bad Character' [2004] Crim LR 533

C Tapper *Cross & Tapper on Evidence* (10th edn Butterworths, London 2004)

C Tapper 'Evidential Privilege in Cases Involving Children' (1997) 9 Child and Family LQ 1

C Tapper '*Hillman* Rediscovered and *Lord St Leonards* Resurrected' (1990) 106 LQR 441

C Tapper 'The Probative Force of Similar Fact Evidence' (1991) 108 LQR 26

C Tapper 'Similar Fact Evidence, Memorandum 64' (Submitted to the Home Affairs Select Committee of the House of Commons, Westminster: The Conduct of Investigations into past Cases of Abuse in Children's Homes 2002)

T Taylor 'The Cultural Defense and its Irrelevancy in Child Protection Law' (1997) 17 B C Third World L Journal 331

J Temkin 'Child Sexual Abuse and Criminal Justice: Part I' [1990] New LJ 352

J Temkin 'Do we need the Crime of Incest?' (1991) Current Legal Problems 185

J Temkin *Rape and the Legal Process* (2nd edn OUP Oxford 2002)

J Temkin 'Sexual History Evidence—Beware the Backlash' [2003] Crim LR 217

J Temkin 'Sexual History Evidence: the Ravishment of Section 2' [1993] Crim LR 3

J Temkin and A Ashworth 'The Sexual Offences Act 2003: (1) Rape, Sexual Assaults and the Problems of Consent' [2004] Crim LR 328

T Thomas 'Covert Video Surveillance' (1994) 144 NLJ 966

T Thomas *Sex Crime: Sex Offending and Society* (Willan Publishing, Devon 2000)

T Thomas and B Hebenton 'Tracking Sex Offenders' (1996) 35(2) *Howard Journal* 97

D Thompson 'Are There *Any* Rules of Evidence in Family Law?' (2003) 21 Canadian Fam LQ 245

D Thompson 'The Cheshire Cat, or Just His Smile? Evidence Law in Child Protection' (2003) 21 Canadian Fam LQ 319

D Thompson 'Taking Children *and* Facts Seriously: Evidence Law in Child Protection Proceedings—Part 1' (1988) 7 Canadian J Fam L 11

E Thompson 'Child Sex Abuse Victims: How will Their Stories be Heard after *Crawford v Washington*?' (2004–2005) 27 Campbell L Rev 281

D Thorpe *Evaluating Child Protection* (OUP, Buckingham 1994)

R Tobin 'Civil Actions for Sexual Abuse in New Zealand' (1997) 5 Tort L Rev 190

S Todd 'Liability in Tort of Public Bodies' in N Mullany and A Linden (eds) *Torts Tomorrow—a Tribute to John Fleming* (LBC Information Services, North Ryde 1998)

S Todd 'Twenty Years of Professional Negligence in New Zealand' (2005) 21(4) PN 257

A Torrinson *Current Issues in Child Protection Policy and Practice* (National Child Protection Clearing House Australian Institute of Family Studies 2004)

B Townsend 'Defending the "Indefensible": A Primer to Defending Allegations of Child Abuse' (1998) 45 Air Force Law Rev 261

M Trepiccione 'At the Crossroads of Law and Social Science: is Charging a Battered Mother with Failure to Protect Her Child an Acceptable Solution When Her Child Witnesses Domestic Violence?' (2001) 69 Fordham L Rev 1487

C Trost 'Chilling Child Abuse Reporting: Rethinking the CAPTA Amendments' (1998) Vanderbilt LR 183

J Varendonck 'Les témoignages d'enfants dans un procès retentissant' (1911) 11 Archives de Psychologie 129

R Vernier 'Parental Rights and the Best Interests of the Child: Implications of the Adoption and Safe Families Act of 1997 on Domestic Violence Victims' Rights' (2000) 8 American U J Gender SPL 517

N Vidmar 'Generic Prejudice and the Presumption of Guilt in Sex Abuse Trials' (1997) 21 Law and Human Behavior 4

N Vidmar and J Melnitzer 'Juror Prejudice: an Empirical Study of a Challenge for Cause' (1986) 22 Osgoode Hall LJ 487

V Vieth 'Keeping the Balance True: Admitting Child Hearsay in the Wake of *Crawford v Washington*' (2004) 16 Update (National Center for Prosecution of Child Abuse) 12

P Vines '*New South Wales v Lepore; Samin v Queensland; Rich v Queensland*: Schools' Responsibility for Teachers' Sexual Assault: Non-Delegable Duty and Vicarious Liability' [2003] 27 Melbourne U LRev 612

R Vogl and N Bala 'Initial Involvement: Reporting Abuse and Protecting Children' in N Bala, MK Zapf, RJ Williams, R Vogl and JP Hornick (eds) *Canadian Child Welfare Law: Children, Families and the State* (2nd edn Thompson Educational Publishing, Inc, Toronto 2004)

M Wald 'State Intervention on Behalf of "Neglected" Children: A Search for Realistic Standards' (1975) 27 Stanford J Child Sexual Abuse 19

E Walsh 'Centres Forwards' (2006) 32 Fam Law 150

B Walter *In Need of Protection: Children and Youth in Alberta* (Children's Advocate, Edmonton 1993)

J Wangmann 'Liability for Institutional Child Sexual Assault: Where Does *Lepore* Leave Australia?' (2004) 28 Melbourne U L Rev 169

A Warren and L McGough 'Research on Children's Suggestibility: Implications for the Investigative Interview' in B Bottoms and G Goodman (eds) *International Perspectives on Child Abuse and Children's Testimony* (Sage, London 1996)

C Wattam, N Parton and D Thorpe *Child Protection Risk and the Moral Order* (Macmillan, Basingstoke 1997)

C Wattam '*Kids on Film*' Community Care (7 October 1993)

D Webb, J Adams, M Heneghan, B Atkin and J Caldwell *Family Law in New Zealand* (8th edn Butterworths, Wellington 1997)

D Webb, B Atkin, J Caldwell, J Adams, M Heneghan, D Clarkson, D Partridge and P Treadwell *Butterworths Family Law in New Zealand* (12th edn Butterworth's, Wellington 2006)

E Weinrib 'Understanding Tort Law' (1989) 23 Valparaiso L Rev 485

A Wells 'Section 37 Directions: Are They Working' (1994) 6(4) Journal of Child Law 181–186

D West 'Sexual Molesters' in N Walker (ed) *Dangerous People* (Blackstone Press, London 1996)

HL Westcott 'Children, Hearsay, and the Courts: a Perspective from the United Kingdom' (1999) 5 Psychology, Public Policy and Law 282

I Weyland 'The Response of Civil Courts to Allegations of Child Sexual Abuse' (1989) 19 Fam Law 240

D Wheeler 'Publicity in Children Proceedings' [17 Dec 2004] New LJ 1886

G Whipple 'The Psychology of Testimony' (1911) 8 Psychology Bulletin 307

P White 'You May Never See Your Child Again: Adjusting the Batterer's Visitation Rights to Protect Children From Future Abuse' (2005) 13 American U J Gender Society Policy & Law 327

R White, P Carr and N Lowe *The Children Act in Practice* (Butterworths, London 1995)

A Whittam, H Ehrat and Office of the DPP for South Australia 'Child Witnesses in the Criminal Justice System—the Issue of Vulnerability' (Child Sexual Abuse: Justice Response or Alternative Resolution Conference (Australian Institute of Criminology) (May 2003))

J Wigmore *Evidence in Trials at Common Law* (1904, James H. Chadbourne 1978 rev edn Little, Browne & Co, Boston; Tillers rev edn 1983)

A Wilcyzinski *Child Homicide* (OUP, Oxford 1997)

A Wilcyzinski and A Morris 'Parents Who Kill Their Children' [1993] Crim LR 31

P Wilhelm 'Permanency at What Cost? Five Years of Imprudence Under the Adoption and Safe Families Act of 1997' (2002) 16 ND J L Ethics and Public Policy 617

Glanville Williams 'Child Witnesses' in P Smith (ed) *Essays in Honour of J. C. Smith* (Butterworths London 1987)

Glanville Williams *Criminal Law: the General Part* (2nd edn Stevens, London 1961)

Glanville Williams 'Videotaping Children's Evidence' [1987] New LJ 108, 351

Glanville Williams 'Which of You Did It?' (1989) 52 MLR 170

C Williams 'A Controversial Expert Witness' [2000] Fam Law 175

G Williams and J McCreadie *Ty Maur Community Home Inquiry* (Gwent County Council Cwmbran 1992)

L Wimberley 'The Perspective from Victims of Child Abuse Laws' in J Myers (ed) *The Backlash: Child Protection under Fire* (Sage Publications, Thousand Oaks, California 1994)

R Wissler and M Saks 'On the Inefficacy of Limiting Instructions: When Jurors Use Prior Conviction Evidence to Decide on Guilt' (1995) 9 Law & Human Behaviour 37

Justice J Wood 'Child Witnesses—Best Practice For Courts' A paper presented at The Australian Institute of Judicial Administration: District Court of New South Wales, Parramatta, Friday 30 July 2004' <http://www.lawlink.nsw.gov.au/sc% 5Csc.nsf/pages/wood_30072004> (6 October 2006)

J Wright 'Child Abuse Claims against Public Authorities under the Human Rights Act 1998' in D Fairgrieve and S Green (eds) *Child Abuse Tort Claims against Public Bodies: a Comparative Law View* (Ashgate, London 2004)

J Wright *Tort Law & Human Rights* (OUP, Oxford 2001)

S Yeo 'Am I My Child's Keeper? Parental Liability in Negligence' (1998) 12 Australian J of Family Law 150

B Yorker 'Covert Video Surveillance of Munchausen Syndrome by Proxy: the Exigent Circumstances Exception' [1995] Health Matrix: Journal of Law-Medicine 325

J Yuille 'The Systematic Assessment of Children's Testimony' (1988) 29(3) Canadian Psychology 247

L Zedner *Women, Crime and Custody in Victorian England* (OUP, Oxford 1991)

H Zeitlin 'Investigation of the Sexually Abused Child' (1987) The Lancet 842

G Zellman 'Child Abuse Reporting and Failure to Report Among Mandated Reporters: Prevalence, Incidence and Reasons' (1990) 5 Interpersonal Violence 3

Index